ISRAEL
A PERSONAL
HISTORY

David Ben-Gurion

ISRAEL

A PERSONAL HISTORY

FUNK & WAGNALLS, INC., NEW YORK
SABRA BOOKS, NEW YORK, TEL AVIV
DISTRIBUTED BY THOMAS Y. CROWELL COMPANY

The publishers wish to acknowledge their gratitude to the following:

Haim Israeli of the Ministry of Defense, Israel;
The Librarian and the Personnel of the Photographic Archives at the Government Press Office,
    Tel Aviv;
The Personnel at the Archives of Bemachanch, Army Newspaper, Tel Aviv;
The Personnel at the Military Archives, Givatayim;
The Zionist Archives and Library, New York, for many of the photographs in this book.

Translated by Nechemia Meyers and Uzy Nystar.
Maps by Nurit Shraga, adapted by Miklos Pinther.

Composed by Keter, Inc. Jerusalem
Printed in the United States of America
L. C. Card 73–162585
1 2 3 4 5 6 7 8 9 10

Table of Contents

INTRODUCTION
The Unique Character and Mission of the State of Israel

CHAPTER ONE: THE REBIRTH OF A NATION
After Centuries of Pioneering, a State is Established

CHAPTER TWO: DANGERS FROM WITHIN AND WITHOUT
From the Establishment of the State to the First Truce

CHAPTER THREE: BETWEEN CAMPAIGNS
War Renewed, Israeli Victories, and Second Truce

CHAPTER FOUR: LINKS IN A CHAIN

Maps and Illustrations

MAPS

PHOTOGRAPHS

Following pages 260 and 544

A CHRONOLOGY OF ISRAEL'S HISTORY

LANDMARKS OF 4,000 YEARS

I. BIBLICAL PERIOD
(Before the Common Era)

1st half of second millennium
  The Patriarchs: Abraham, Isaac and Jacob
13th century Exodus from Egypt
12th to 11th centuries
  Israelite return to the Promised Land
Judges: Deborah, Gideon, Samson; King Saul

c.	1000	David makes Jerusalem the capital
c.	960	Solomon builds the Temple
c.	930	Kingdom divided into Judah and Israel
721		Conquest of Israel by Assyrians
586		Conquest of Judah by Babylonians; sacking of Jerusalem and destruction of First Temple
538–515		First return from Babylon; rebuilding of Temple

II. SECOND TEMPLE PERIOD

457–424	Second return to Zion; Ezra and Nehemiah
333	Conquest by Alexander the Great
323–168	Greek rule
168	Revolt of the Maccabees (Hasmonaeans)
63	Beginning of Roman rule
37	End of Hasmonaean dynasty

(Common Era)

66	Jewish revolt against Rome
70	Destruction of Second Temple
73	Last stand of rebels at Masada

III. ALIEN SUZERAINTY

132–135		Bar-Kochba's rising against Rome
c.	200	Completion of Mishnah (codification of Jewish Law)
395–636		Byzantine rule
c.	400	Completion of Jerusalem Talmud
c.	500	Completion of Babylonian Talmud
614		Persian invasion, supported by local Jews
636		Beginning of Arab rule
1072		Seljuk conquest
1099		Crusaders take Jerusalem and massacre its Jews
1141		Yehuda Halevi's journey to Palestine
1267		Nachmanides revives Jewish community of Jerusalem
1291		End of Crusader rule; Mamluk conquest
1517		Ottoman conquest
1565		Publication of Caro's *Shulhan Aruch*, written in Safad
1799		Napoleonic expedition

IV. RETURN TO ZION

1870	Agricultural school founded in Mikve Israel
1878	Petah Tikva, first pioneering village, founded
1882	Pinsker's *Autoemancipation;* First Aliya begins
1895	Theodor Herzl's *Judenstaat* published
1897	First Zionist Congress in Basle
1904–1914	Second Aliya; start of labor movement
1909	Tel Aviv, first all-Jewish city, founded; Degania, first kvutza (collective village) founded
1917	Balfour Declaration; cornerstone of Hebrew University laid
1917–18	British Army, with Jewish contingents, liberates the Holy Land from the Turks
1920	Third Aliya begins; Histadrut (labor federation) founded
1921	Nahalal, first moshav (cooperative village) founded

V. BRITISH MANDATORY PERIOD

1922	British Mandate over Palestine confirmed by League of Nations; Britain excludes Trans-Jordan from Jewish National Home
1925	Hebrew University opened on Mount Scopus
	Peel Commission proposes partition, one part as Jewish State
1939	British White Paper limits Jewish immigration and land purchase
1941	Zionist Movement calls for Jewish State
1944	Jewish Brigade Group organized in Allied Forces
1946	Anglo-American Committee favors admission of 100,000 displaced persons
1947	
29 Nov.	United Nations General Assembly adopts partition plan, providing for establishment of Jewish State

VI. INDEPENDENT ISRAEL REBORN

1948	
14 May	Proclamation of State
15 May	British withdraw; invasion of Israel by Arab armies
1949	
25 Jan.	Elections to First Knesset
16 Feb.	Dr. Chaim Weizmann elected President
24 Feb.	Armistice agreement with Egypt
10 Mar.	First regular Government, under David Ben-Gurion
11 May	Israel admitted to United Nations
20 July	Armistice agreement with Syria (last to be signed)
12 Sept.	Compulsory Education Law passed
2 Nov.	Inauguration of Weizmann Institute of Science
20 Nov.	Jewish population reaches first million
1950	
5 July	Law of Return confirms right of every Jew to dwell in Israel
Sept.	Airlift of 45,000 Jews from Yemen completed
29 Nov.	500,000th immigrant since 1948
1951	
July	Airlift of 110,000 Jews from Iraq
14 Aug.	Twenty-third Zionist Congress opens in Jerusalem
1952	

| 9 | Nov. | Death of President Weizmann |
| 8 | Dec. | Itzhak Ben-Zvi elected President |

1953
| 7 | Dec. | Ben-Gurion retires to Sde Boker in the Negev |

1954
| 26 | Jan. | Moshe Sharett becomes Prime Minister |
| 2 | June | Hebrew University dedicates new campus at Givat Ram in Jerusalem |

1955
21	Feb.	Ben-Gurion rejoins Cabinet as Minister of Defense
24	May	Lachish regional development plan inaugurated
19	July	Yarkon-Negev pipeline, to water 25,000 acres, opened
22	Sept.	Oil struck at Heletz, in Negev
27	Sept.	Egyptian-Czech arms deal announced
3	Nov.	Ben-Gurion again becomes Prime Minister

1956
| 29 | Oct. | Israel, in self-protection, clears Egyptian guerrilla bases and troop concentrations in Sinai; occupies Gaza Strip |

1957
| 8 | Mar. | Israel completes evacuation of Sinai and Gaza Strip; UN peace-keeping forces installed |
| 31 | Oct. | Arid Zone Research Institute opens in Beersheba |

1958
| 16 | Jan. | Opening of Beersheba-Eilat highway |

1960
| 23 | May | Arrest of Adolf Eichmann announced |

1961
| 30 | July | Millionth newcomer since re-establishment of State |
| 8 | Dec. | Israel becomes full member of GATT |

1962
9	Feb.	New Economic Policy, based on rate of IL3 per dollar
31	May	Eichmann executed
30	June	United States Operations Mission, no longer necessary in view of Israel's progress, wound up
27	Sept.	US agrees to supply Israel with Hawk ground-to-air missiles
30	Oct.	Ben-Zvi re-elected for third presidential term

1963
23	Apr.	Death of President Ben-Zvi
21	May	Schneur Zalman Shazar elected as third President
26	June	Levi Eshkol takes office as Prime Minister

1964
| 5 | Jan. | Pope Paul VI on pilgrimage to Holy Sites in Israel |
| 4 | June | Trade agreement between Israel and European Common Market |

1965
26	Apr.	Herut-Liberal electoral bloc formed
11	May	Israel Museum in Jerusalem inaugurated
12	May	Israel and West Germany agree to establish diplomatic relations
20	May	Agreement on Mapai-Ahdut Haavoda alignment

1966
| 12 | May | Economic agreement between Israel and West Germany |
| 30 | Aug. | New Knesset building opened in Jerusalem |

1	Dec.	Military Government in border areas abolished
10	Dec.	Shmuel Yosef Agnon receives Nobel Prize for Literature

1967

15	May	Nasser moves massive armored forces into Sinai
19	May	UN Emergency Force in Sinai and Gaza Strip withdraws at Nasser's demand
23	May	Nasser declares Tiran Straits closed to Israeli shipping and cargoes; announces readiness for all-out war
30	May	Hussein of Jordan signs anti-Israel pact with Egypt
4	June	Iraq signs anti-Israel pact with Egypt
5–10	June	The Six-Day War
29	June	Jerusalem, Israel's capital, reunified
22	Nov.	UN Security Council resolution calls for permanent peace settlement in the Middle East

1968

1	Apr.	World Jewish Economic Conference opens in Jerusalem
8	Sept.	Egypt mounts heavy artillery barrage across Suez Canal
8	Oct.	Foreign Minister Abba Eban presents nine-point peace plan to UN General Assembly
26	Dec.	Arab terrorists attack El Al plane in Athens

1969

20	Jan.	Israel Labor Party and Mapam form alliance
18	Feb.	Arab terrorists attack El Al plane in Zurich
26	Feb.	Death of Prime Minister Levi Eshkol
March		Egyptians shell Israeli positions on Suez Canal
17	Mar.	Golda Meir installed as Israel's fourth Prime Minister
21–22	Aug.	Fire at el-Aqsa Mosque speedily extinguished; Israeli Police arrest arsonist
29	Aug.	Arab terrorists hijack TWA plane; two Israeli passengers detained by Syria
28	Oct.	Elections to the Seventh Knesset
27	Nov.	Arab terrorists bomb El Al office in Athens
15	Dec.	Second National Unity Cabinet installed

1970

10	Feb.	Arab terrorists attack El Al passengers at Munich
9	Apr.	Maiden flight of *Arava*, first Israel-made aircraft
29	Apr.	Israel discloses operational flights by Soviet pilots over Suez
22	May	Arab terrorists kill 8 children and 4 adults in school bus ambush
4	Aug.	Israel accepts US peace initiative
7	Aug.	Standstill cease-fire comes into force in Suez Canal Zone
8	Aug.	Egypt violates cease-fire by advancing missile sites
6	Sept.	Three airliners hijacked by Arab terrorists; attempt to hijack El Al plane foiled; Israel suspends participation in Jarring peace talks pending redress of breaches of standstill agreement
28	Dec.	Israel decides to return to Jarring talks

DAVID BEN-GURION: A SHORT BIOGRAPHICAL NOTE

BORN: October 16, 1886, in Plonsk, Russian Poland.

EDUCATION: Traditional religious schools; private tuition in languages and general studies; Istanbul University (Faculty of Law); a lifetime of independent studies.

Active in Zionist Labor Movement (Poalei Zion) from early youth; settled in Israel in 1906; exiled by the Turkish administration in 1915; founded the Hehalutz (Pioneer) Organization in the United States; in World War I, helped to raise the Jewish Legion and served in its ranks.

Among the founders of the Histadrut (General Federation of Jewish Labor in Israel) and its Secretary-General (1921–1935); one of the founders of Mapai (Israel Labor Party) in 1930, and founder of Rafi (Israel Labor List) in 1965; elected to the Jewish Agency Executive, 1933, and its Chairman, 1935–1938.

Following the United Nations Partition Resolution of November 29, 1947, elected Chairman of the National Administration and in charge of security and defense; announced the establishment of the independent State of Israel, May 14, 1948.

Prime Minister and Minister of Defense in the Provisional Government (1948) and all following Cabinets until December 7, 1953, when he tendered his resignation and settled at Sde Boker in the Negev. Rejoined the Government as Minister of Defense, February 21, 1955; Prime Minister and Minister of Defense, November 3, 1955–June 16, 1963; Member of the first five Knessets for Mapai, the Sixth Knesset for Rafi, the Seventh Knesset on the State List; resigned his seat in May, 1970.

Visited most countries of Europe, and traveled extensively in the North and South American continents on Zionist and Israel State missions, also in Africa. Has conducted formal and informal correspondence and exchange of views on a wide range of philosophical, political, religious and social subjects with the foremost personalities of our time.

In recognition of his cultural leadership and achievements, he was awarded the Bublick Prize by the Hebrew University, 1949; the Bialik Prize by the Tel Aviv Municipality, 1952, and other literary prizes; honorary doctorates by the Jewish Theological Seminary of America, 1952; the Hebrew University, 1955; Brandeis University, 1960; the Technion, 1962, the University of Tel Aviv, 1970 and the Henrietta Szold Award by the Hadassah Women's Zionist Organization of America, 1958, for "distinguished humanitarian service."

Married to Paula Munweiss, 1916; one son and two daughters. Mrs. Ben-Gurion died in 1964.

Member of Kibbutz Sde Boker and founder of the Negev College at Sde Boker.

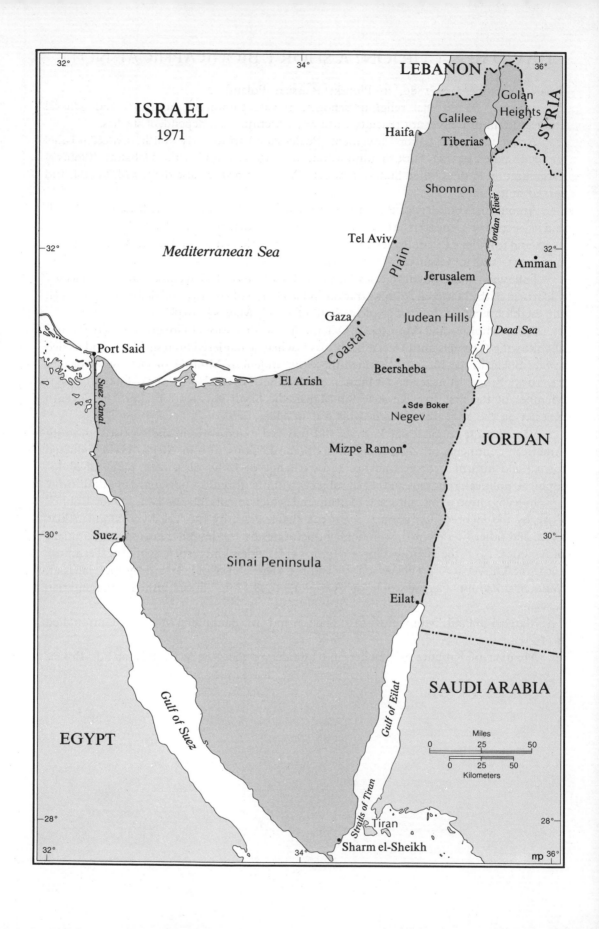

INTRODUCTION

The Unique Character and Mission
of the State of Israel

F ROM THE moment of their appearance on the stage of history the Jewish people have been more than a political entity. Without grasping their unique spiritual and moral character and historic mission, it is impossible to understand the history of the Jewish nation, the ability to maintain its integrity in every era and every place, both as a more or less independent nation in its own land and as wanderers in exile. We must take into account that uniqueness, preserved by stubborn struggle not only in the physical, economic, political, and military areas, but in the spiritual, moral, and ideological spheres. The Jewish people have always been engaged in this struggle, even as they are today and probably will be to the end of time.

One hard physical fact has had many consequences in the past and in the present. It is that we were always a small people. "For ye were the fewest of all peoples," said Moses (Deuteronomy 7:7); therefore he demanded that they behave as a chosen people, maintaining their spiritual ascendancy. Undoubtedly it is our destiny to remain a small people, and we will survive only through our spiritual vitality.

In ancient times our neighbors were Egypt and Babylon. Both of them surpassed Israel, not only in population, wealth, military power, and territory, but also in some intellectual and scientific achievements. The picture of Egypt painted in Genesis and Exodus is incomplete and therefore distorted. Five thousand years ago Egypt had reached a high cultural level. It had laid the foundations of science in arithmetic, engineering, chemistry, and medicine, and had developed a rich and varied literature in religion, science, and history.

Babylon even surpassed Egypt in the quality of its poetry and prose. The story of Gilgamesh, translated into Hebrew by Saul Tchernikovsky, is a great epic. Also surviving are hymns and historic records. Babylon explored the disciplines of medicine and engineering and advanced far beyond other ancient nations in law. For generations the Babylonian tongue was the language of international diplomacy in all the Biblical lands that today are called the Middle East. The Jewish defense against these two giant neighbors was more than political and military; it was especially cultural and spiritual. The primary task of the Prophets was to counteract neighboring influences that might dilute the Israelites' religious and moral concepts and social customs.

The Jewish culture was not the only ancient civilization to be exposed to the dual pressures from Egypt and Babylon. Nothing now remains of the others, however: they vanished without a trace. The Israelites struggled and triumphed, however, finally returning to this precious region where they first appeared four thousand years ago. But now everything is changed. The ethnic, political, and cultural pattern of the area has been totally transformed. There has been an absolute break in the evolutionary process. The languages, cultures, traditions—even the names—of the ancients have almost disappeared from the face of the earth. Only the Israelites, although torn physically from their native soil two thousand years ago, continue along the linguistic, cultural, and spiritual path of their forefathers as if there had been no interruption, no break in the course of Jewish history.

The Jewish people today certainly are not identical with those of the First and Second Temples. The entire world has changed and the Jews with it. In ancient times, for instance, our role in science was insignificant, but from Spinoza onward the scientific approach has had a profound impact upon our people. For the past three centuries we have been perhaps disproportionately important partners in the march of scientific progress.

Neither the material and spiritual nor the political and cultural changes in the thousands of years of our existence, however, have destroyed or even shaken the marvelous vitality that has preserved the Jews through all the twists and turns of history. They have failed to undermine our unique national character, as they did to so many of the ancient peoples among whom we lived. A secret resource safeguards our existence and our uniqueness. This is our Bible, which has given us the strength to remain steadfast in the face of hostile forces and influences that have threatened our national and spiritual integrity.

Obviously not all Jews possess this historic resource. Over the generations many have been swept away: individual Jews, whole tribes and communities. But the core of the Jewish people remained inviolate. Inspired by an inner vision, the Israelites as a whole struggled and triumphed.

Even the Greek culture, for all its richness, was unable to assimilate the Jewish nation, as it had absorbed so many other cultures in the East. Essentially, the conflict between the Hasmoneans (Maccabees) and the Greeks was a cultural contest. One of the most dramatic confrontations in human history, it pitted two creative peoples who, perhaps more than any others, helped to shape mankind. The Israelites learned a great deal from the Greeks. A rich and varied Hellenistic-Jewish literature evolved in history, poetry, commentary, and philosophy. But the Jewish individuality survived.

The most difficult and prolonged threat to Jewish survival was the development of Christianity. The cultures of Egypt and Babylon, and later of Greece and Rome, were foreign to Judaism. But Christianity grew out of Judaism. Jesus probably differed little from many other Jews of his generation. The new religion was given an anti-Jewish emphasis by Saul, who was the son of a Roman citizen, though in childhood he had been a pupil of Rabbi Gamliel (head of the Sanhedrin or "Supreme Court") in Jerusalem. In the beginning Saul (later called Paul) was a fanatic opponent of the Christian sect that developed in Jerusalem. But after he "saw the light" on the road to Damascus, he gave Christianity a new direction. He sought to uproot Jewish law and commandments, and to eliminate Judaism as a national entity striving to achieve the Messianic vision of the Prophets. Saul was perhaps the greatest Jewish assimilationist. From a Messianic vision that prophesied redemption for both the Jewish nation and the world, he based Christianity on faith in a divine redemption brought by a Messiah who supposedly had already come.

Christianity arrived when Jewish independence had been undermined and then destroyed by the Romans, who sought to rule the world. The hopeless struggle of the Jews against their Roman oppressors from the days of Yohanan of Galilee and Eliezer Ben Shimon of Jerusalem to the time of Shimon Bar Kochba (Koziba) and Rabbi Akiva ended in defeat and the loss of independence. The Christian sect of the Jews did not participate in this national struggle. Paul called upon his disciples to submit to civil authority. In his Epistle to the Romans he said: "Let every soul be subject unto the higher powers. For there is no power but of God: the powers that be are ordained of God."

Nor did Christianity, which in the fourth century became the dominant religion, forgive Jewish persistence. For generations the Jews were persecuted in the name of a religion of love. Our people refused to surrender, despite the fact that for centuries they stood alone in their spiritual resistance.

About five hundred years after Bar Kochba's defeat the Land of Israel was overrun by the Arabs. The invaders were armed with military force and the new doctrine of Mohammed. This religion did not originate in Israel, though it was strongly influenced by Judaism and was closer to Judaism than to Christianity in its monotheistic principles. The conquests of Mohammed and his disciples were swifter and more remarkable than those of the Christians. Islam spread across the tribes of the Arabian Peninsula in the seventh century, and shortly afterward swept through Asia and North Africa. Arabic became the language of the Aramaic and Assyrian peoples and those of North Africa. The entire Middle East and North Africa accepted the religion of Mohammed, willingly or under force, except the Jews: they stood against, and survived, the Moslem tide.

Another great inundation that threatened the national integrity and spiritual independence of the Jewish people was the spirit of the French Revolution at the end of the eighteenth century and the Russian Revolution at the beginning of the twentieth century. The French uprising, with its vision of liberty, equality, and fraternity, affected all of Europe. It gave the initial impetus to the social liberation of the Jews and their acquisition of equal rights in Western Europe. Implicit, however, in this revolution was the demand that Jews jettison their heritage, and many Western European Jews welcomed this. A wave of assimilation seemed likely to engulf the entire Jewish people. The Jewish historian Dubnov wrote: "It seems that this ancient race, which had stood firm in the face of the storms of history the whole world over, could not hold out against the blizzard of the nineteenth century, but succumbed and disavowed its being, and lowered itself to the level of a religious sect, whose parts are incorporated in the bodies of other nations."★ But Israel's historic will to live survived this fresh assault.

The emancipation of the Jews led not to assimilation but to a new expression of their national uniqueness and Messianic longings. The faith that Israel would return to its land and regain its independence took new form. No longer was the vision a mystic dream. A pioneering course of action became possible: emigration to the Land of Israel to build a fruitful Jewish nation through Jewish labor and creativity. The ancient Hebrew tongue

★ Dubnov, Simon, *History of an Eternal People*, Hebrew edition (Tel Aviv: Dvir, 1952), p. 537.

once again became a living language with a secular literature. The emancipation, a gift of external revolutionary forces, became self-emancipation—a movement to free the Jews from the shackles of exile and dependence on others. The first foundations were laid for the renewal of national independence by emigration to the original Homeland and creation there of agriculture, crafts, industry, transport, and literature, as well as self-government and self-defense. Thus the groundwork was laid for the new Jewish state in the historic Land of Israel.

This renewed belief of the Jews in their own ability, after hundreds of years of exile, is one of the greatest wonders in their wondrous history. For centuries they had submitted to their fate as exiles dependent on the good will of others. Passively, they had waited for miracles and the Messiah. Over the years they had almost lost faith in their own power and capabilities. The renewed confidence in the Jewish individual and the Jewish people, in their capacity to be creative and to defend themselves, drew inspiration from three sources: the restored influence of the Bible because of the literature of the Haskala (Enlightenment); the nineteenth-century revolutions in European countries where a great majority of the Jews were concentrated; and direct creative contact with the soil of the Homeland. The literature of the nineteenth-century Haskala restored the Bible to all its glory for Jewish youth. Young Jews felt the awareness of nationhood. The Love of Zion was rekindled in their hearts. Then followed the pioneering immigration of the latter third of the nineteenth century. This movement confirmed the creativity and strength of the Jewish people, and demonstrated their determination to take their fate into their own hands.

In the social and national revolutions of Europe the best sons of the Jewish people became aware of every man's value to a people struggling for freedom. These upheavals showed what could be accomplished by the courage of the repressed and the enslaved, and fanned the flames of liberation in the hearts of tens of thousands. They demonstrated the strength of men who worked the land toward realization of the ancient dream of salvation: a return to labor and to the soil of the Homeland.

The pioneering immigration that followed foreshadowed and embodied a faith in the power of man and the creative will of the Jewish people. Daring, self-confident Jews rooted themselves once more in the soil of Israel. Hebrew villages were established on desolate tracts, on swamps and sands, on deserted and barren hillsides. The language of the Prophets, thought stilled forever, was heard again in the fields of Judea and Galilee from the mouths of little children. A new era in the Jews' history and their land began as the immigrants grasped their destiny and defended themselves successfully when they were attacked.

The Russian Revolution was not contained within the borders of the nation where it began. It confronted the Jewish people with an ideological challenge and an historical ordeal as grave as any they had survived earlier. The Russian Revolution proclaimed equality to all the peoples and tribes of the Czarist Empire. The Soviet Union, ruled by a dictatorship of the heads of the Communist Party, formally planned a federation of nations, each with equal rights, each with its own national territory, each autonomous within its ancestral boundaries. Later an area in the Birobijan region, in eastern Siberia, was even allocated to the Jews, but very few of them were attracted to it; the area was both distant and foreign to the Jewish people and their history.

Millions of Jews remained scattered throughout European and Asiatic Russia, where they were denied their right to learn Hebrew, their historic tongue; later the language spoken in Eastern Europe, Yiddish, was also proscribed. National silence was imposed on the Jews. Against their will they were cut off from their Homeland. Although their culture was more venerable than that of any other people in Russia, the Jews were deprived of their historic heritage. Jewish schools were closed. Hebrew literature was forbidden. Millions of Jews, comprising the largest Jewish community at that time, who stood in the forefront of Jewish creativity, saw their national heritage strangled.

No such heavy blow had been struck since the struggle between Bar Kochba and Hadrian in ancient Roman times. All the measures available to a dictatorship were employed to uproot Judaism and forcibly to assimilate millions of Jews. Yet all these pressures, physical and psychological, could not destroy Russian Jewry. Even after the Bolsheviks gained power, the Russian Jews gave the Land of Israel some of its best sons. The accomplishments of Russian youth in Israel show what resources lie hidden within Russian Jewry. We should not give up hope that the Jews of Russia will eventually be able to contribute to the national revival of the Jewish people in their ancient Homeland.

With the establishment of the State of Israel, the victories of its army, and successes scored in settlement and cultural growth over the past twenty years, the prolonged struggle of the Jewish people might appear to have reached a successful conclusion. But this is a dangerous illusion. We have not completed the work of reconstruction. The ingathering of the exiles has hardly begun. Our neighbors have yet to accept our existence. Their dream of destroying Israel persists, despite the fact that they have been defeated every time they tried to interfere with our work, from the establishment of the State on May 14, 1948, until this very day.

The Jews of Israel will never be able to compete in physical power with neighbors who do not accept their rights to exist. But for thousands of years the Jews have survived because of their moral qualities. While populating the land and making it fruitful, while creating economic and cultural enterprises, they will survive only if they maintain their moral, spiritual, and intellectual standards. These have been the secret of their existence for four thousand years. With these advantages they will endure and win friends among the enlightened peoples of the world who will share their vision of national and international redemption—the vision that has been in the hearts of the Jewish people from the beginning and found its expression in the Book of Books, a beacon to the nations of the world.

After thousands of years of wanderings and sufferings all over the world, the Jews have begun a national renaissance in their Homeland. They will not relinquish their profound historic belief in a fusing of national redemption with the redemption of all mankind. Their national movement will not be shorn of its universal implications. In the State of Israel there is no distinction between the Jew and the human being. The moral values of our Prophets—truth and justice, human fraternity and compassion—are based on our belief that man was created in the image of God; not a white man or a black man or a yellow man, but man in the image of the father of all men. This concept is eternal, all-encompassing, having neither beginning nor end, neither body nor form. The story of the creation of man in the image of God is the foundation of the belief in the fraternity and equality of all peoples, revealed by the Prophets of Israel to all mankind.

Jews have always rejected the *supremacy* of the body and of physical strength, but this does not ignore the value of physical power. We would be refuting Jewish history from the time of Moses and Joshua to the days of the Israel Defense Forces if we dismissed the value of physical prowess. Rejection of all force would be a denial of the world in which we live, a denial of life itself. This has always been foreign to the Jewish spirit and one of the basic differences between the doctrines of Judaism and Christianity. From the Prophets to Einstein, Jewish genius never accepted the duality of matter and spirit, a doctrine propounded by some of the greatest thinkers from the Greeks and the Persians to Descartes and his followers. Jewish intuition, both religious and scientific, has always emphasized the unity of creation and experience.

Although the greatest Jewish Prophets, scholars, and sages have always stressed the spiritual mission of the Jewish people, they have never disparaged the body or its needs. One of the sages of the Mishna, Rabbi Eliezer Ben Azariya, expressed this attitude in simple but profound terms: "If there be no flour, there can be no learning; if there is no learning, there will be no flour." Emphasis on the supremacy of the spirit does not disregard the importance of military might, but this might depends first and foremost on the spirit. The Israel Defense Forces are aware of this truth and as a result they have triumphed whenever they have been forced into battle. *Only if we mobilize all our moral strength and intellectual resources* will we be able to overcome the enormous obstacles that confront us as we strive to fulfill our national destiny.

The seeds of nationhood were sown in the fields of Mikve Israel, Petah Tikva, Rishon LeZion, Rosh Pina, Zikhron Yakov, Gedera, and the settlements that came after them. The first immigrants endured the trials and tribulations that always confront pioneers. They fought the forces of nature, the perils of the desert, hostile neighbors, malaria, the lack of water; the difficulties of putting down roots in a land that is both loved and desolate; of unifying tribes from distant corners of the earth and creating a renewed national entity.

We must make similar and even greater efforts now if we are finally to achieve the peace and tranquillity we seek.

ISRAEL
A PERSONAL
HISTORY

I

THE REBIRTH OF A NATION

After Centuries of Pioneering, a State Is Established

Section 1. The Storms of the Twentieth Century

HUMAN history has been completely transformed in the twentieth century. Events have occurred that never occurred before. The laws of nature have not been altered, but basic changes have taken place in the patterns of history and in relations between peoples. The conditions of human life have been transformed, and with them the abilities of man, his spiritual and political world, his social, cultural, and economic existence. Developments once inconceivable, both good and evil, can today strike us and others.

Though Jewish history is unique, it does not exist in a vacuum. It is part of overall human history, subject to the same vicissitudes; just as the character of mankind has changed, so has that of the Jews. This century has seen wars that have spread across the face of the earth and affected, directly or indirectly, the entire human race. This is a phenomenon unique to the twentieth century. Totalitarian regimes have arisen that are without parallel among all the tyrannies of history. Some still exist, are expanding, and may grow still larger. The world has never seen such despotic regimes and such mass slaughter as in Stalin's Russia and in Hitler's Germany.

At the same time, mankind has never enjoyed such rapid social and economic advance; and high standards of living, once available only to privileged individuals or groups, are commonplace today for masses of people in villages and cities. Modern transportation and communication have reduced the distances between countries, continents, and peoples. Any event anywhere, however distant, has immediate repercussions around the globe.

Only a generation or two ago the dense forests of Africa held cannibals, whose existence was unknown even in other parts of that continent. But today, when a leader in the Congo is assassinated, the entire world is shocked, not so much because of the murder itself, but because of the international political implications. Rivalry between individuals and tribes in an African country, a conflict between North and South Vietnam or North and South Korea, endangers all mankind, for all nations are interdependent. Whatever happens to a people, large or small, free or enslaved, affects everyone. No people any longer lives an independent existence.

We are witnessing the spectacle of the greatest revolutionary liberation movement in history. Continents, peoples, and tribes subject to the rule of foreign oppressors for decades or even centuries are gaining their independence. Two hundred years ago, almost all the nations on five continents in the Old and New Worlds—Asia, Africa, the Americas, and Australia—were colonies of one of the European countries: Russia, Britain, France, Spain, Portugal, Turkey, Holland, or Belgium. In Europe there were countries and peoples under the rule of stronger neighbors: these included the Baltic States, some of the Slavic peoples in the Hapsburg Empire, the Balkan peoples under Turkish rule, and the Irish.

The American continent was the first to throw off the yoke of foreign rule. The United States of America was established after the Revolutionary War. At first there were only thirteen British colonies, but in time the United States spread across the continent from the Atlantic to the Pacific, and to distant islands of both oceans. Until the First World War this great power cut itself off from the rest of the world; since then its power and influence have been felt in almost every corner of the globe. The emancipation that started in the thirteen English colonies spread to the other countries of North and South America and to the islands in the Atlantic Ocean.

At the beginning of the twentieth century most of the peoples of Asia and almost all of the peoples of Africa were ruled by European imperialism. During the First World War several European nations won their independence, including Finland, Poland, the Baltic States (to be swallowed up later by the Stalinist empire), the non-Germanic peoples of the Austro-Hungarian Empire, Ireland. In Asia the Chinese giant gained independence, and by the last quarter of the twentieth century may become the most powerful (and perhaps the most developed) country in the world.

After the Second World War the British Empire in Asia came to an end. India, Pakistan, Burma, and Ceylon gained their freedom. A few years later the French Empire in Indochina fell to pieces: Vietnam, Cambodia, and Laos became sovereign nations. Indonesia, which had been under Dutch rule and which had fallen into Japanese hands during World War Two, gained its independence four years after the end of the war. The same was true in Malaysia.

The spirit of liberation reached the peoples of black Africa, who had been under European rule for centuries. After the Second World War, they gained their independence one by one. Completion of this process is only a matter of time. Portugal still administers a few colonies in Africa, and not all the peoples of South Africa, where blacks and non-whites are several times more numerous than the ruling whites, have attained freedom, but this condition surely will not endure for very long.

Only the Russian Empire, now called the Soviet Union, has grown larger since the end of the Second World War. It controls its Christian neighbors in the West (Eastern Europe) and even more peoples in the East (Moslems for the most part, together with a few Buddhists). In theory it is a federation. Indeed, according to its constitution, each state of the union is free to leave it, but this is a constitution that exists only on paper. Real power, essentially unlimited, is concentrated in the hands of the rulers in Moscow.

The United Nations Organization, established in 1945, was chartered with forty-six members; by now it includes one hundred and twenty-six states. The United Nations Charter is a wonderful document, stressing fraternity and peace. So far however, it has remained little more than a scrap of paper.

The first Article of the United Nations Charter obligates all its members:

1. To maintain international peace and security, and to that end: to take effective collective measures for the prevention and removal of threats to the peace, and for the suppression of acts of aggression or other breaches of the peace, and to bring about by peaceful means, and in conformity with the principles of justice and international law, adjustment or settlement of international disputes or situations which might lead to a breach of the peace;
2. To develop friendly relations among nations based on respect for the principle of equal rights and self-determination of peoples, and to take other appropriate measures to strengthen universal peace;
3. To achieve international cooperation in solving international problems of an economic, social, cultural, or humanitarian character.

Article 2 of the Charter obligates the UN and its members, "in pursuance of the purposes stated in Article 1," to "act in accordance with the following principles:"

1. The Organization is based on the principle of the sovereign equality of all its Members.
2 All Members shall settle their international disputes by peaceful means in such a manner that international peace and security, and justice, are not endangered.
3. All Members shall refrain in their international relations from the threat or use of force against the territorial integrity or political independence of any state, or in any other manner inconsistent with the purposes of the United Nations.

Of all Israel's neighbors that accepted the obligations enumerated in the United Nations Charter, Egypt has been the most blatant in its violations of international law, the principles of the United Nations, and the Armistice Agreement with Israel signed on February 24, 1949.

In the war against Hitler the two great world powers, Russia and America, were united. Their joint resources, with those of other allies, crushed Nazi Germany and its allies, and then established the United Nations Organization with its charter of peace. But shortly after the Second World War the Cold War began. Soviet Russia was not content simply to destroy the Nazi enemy: she also sought to absorb the lands she had saved from the Nazis and to impose communist regimes on them. America, for her part, wanted to safeguard the freedom of her allies. Russia succeeded, thanks to her use of military force, in imposing communist regimes on Czechoslovakia, Poland, Rumania, East Germany, and the Baltic and Balkan States. Through the agency of the Marshall Plan, America rehabilitated the countries of Western Europe, which had been pauperized by the war, and these nations were able to maintain their democratic regimes. The conflict between the two giant powers grew sharper during the period of Stalin's rule, and it was primarily responsible for frustrating the aims of the United Nations Charter: peace and human fraternity.

The liberation of the peoples of Asia and Africa emphasizes a problem no less painful than that of colonialism. I refer to the growing gap between the rich, developed, and culturally advanced nations of Europe, North America, and Japan on the one hand, and the poor, backward, and educationally deprived countries of Asia, Africa, and to some extent Latin America on the other. This is the greatest international problem of our era; it sharpens the Cold War, since both sides in that war are struggling to win over the young and poor nations. Particularly in Africa many of the new states are inhabited by populations without a clear national identity. Some tribes lack even a common language or a unifying national tradition. The countries are only names on a map, and were given their present shapes by the colonial regimes that formerly ruled them. We have seen the estab-lishment of this new type of sovereign entity, never before known in human history. Such entities are growing in number and exerting an increasing influence on the inter-national scene, without reference to the ideals of the United Nations.

The Cold War and the large number of new states that owe no allegiance to the ideals of the United Nations Charter have almost deprived the UN of its meaning and the name of its significance. The member nations are not united, and the principles embodied in the Charter do not obligate them. Decisions of the General Assembly adopted by a two-thirds majority and decisions of the Security Council, which according to the Charter are binding on all members, are not carried out. This became clear to the State of Israel on the day it was born.

When the General Assembly voted by more than a two-thirds majority to establish the State of Israel, a decision supported by both Russia and the United States, the Arab states used force to prevent its implementation from the moment that British rule ended. Indeed, several hours after our Declaration of Independence and the establishment of the Jewish State, Arab armies invaded the country in order to destroy it and the people living within its borders. But not one nation lifted a finger to defend the United Nations' decision. Without the Israel Defense Forces the State of Israel would have been wiped from the map and its citizens slaughtered. The invaders were not even ordered to withdraw by the United Nations General Assembly or the Security Council.

To cite another instance: *The Security Council twice decided that the Suez Canal and the Gulf of Aqaba would be open to all countries.* The rulers of Egypt closed both the canal and the gulf to Israeli shipping without a single state so much as protesting this act.

Hostile blocs have been organized within the United Nations. With the increase in members there has been a parallel increase in the number of such blocs. The controversies stem not from differing interpretations of the Charter, which theoretically binds all members, but are concerned with local or regional interests, sometimes even with per-sonal conflicts. They involve attempts to gain control of individual countries and the creation of spheres of influence. There are also rivalries rooted in ideological differences, national clashes, and racial prejudices.

Though the name of the UN is not yet justified, a supreme human authority is de-veloping that attempts to safeguard world peace and end strife between peoples. This authority is not yet consistent, nor is it in any sense objective. To a considerable extent it is capricious and subjective: the weak tend to be discriminated against. The United Nations' authority depends in no small measure on sporadic combinations of forces that band together in particular circumstances. Nonetheless, the mere existence of the United Nations proves the need for international unity. We should not deny completely the organization's role in strengthening world peace.

The great changes in our generation are not confined to political modifications in the world map and shifts in international affairs. The extraordinary achievements of applied science in this century have resulted in a revolution in our concept of nature as depicted by pure science. Undoubtedly this revolution will continue even more rapidly in the days ahead. Science has brought mankind to the threshold of a new era: one of peace and prosperity—or of death and destruction.

Technology based on the discoveries of pure science has given contemporary man the means to control the forces of nature. This has immeasurably increased wealth, health, productivity, the speed of transportation and communications. It may even permit the conquest of the universe. Science can improve life to an extent never before dreamed. At the same time it can bring disaster, perhaps the complete destruction of mankind, in a fashion unimaginable fifty years ago.

A progressive change has taken place in the status of scientists and technologists in relation to social, political, and international life. Science today is integral to every facet of human endeavor, affecting the economy, health, and security. Pure science and practical affairs are bound together. The conquests of science enrich everyday life and are influenced by it. The importance of scientists is greater today than ever before, and so are the social and moral responsibilities of scientists.

In ancient Greece, the birthplace of scientific thought and philosophy, a great chasm existed between the thinkers and the philosophers on the one hand and the workers on the other. (Archimedes of Syracuse was an exception.) Plato, the greatest thinker, showed an aristocratic scorn for the workers, even if they were freemen. Theory, contemplation, and philosophy were worlds away from everyday life. The opposite holds true today.

Scientific research and its achievements are no longer abstract intellectual interests, of concern solely to a few philosophers and researchers. They are now central factors in daily life. Along with the work of other members of society, with the growing role of machines, science is a prerequisite to the advancement of a civilized people. Workers in fields, factories, and mines, in the air and on the sea, in construction and in industry must understand the processes of nature and the scientific foundations of their own work. Today an enlightened worker can contribute in considerable measure to the understanding of a researcher and to the improvement of his methods, just as the discoveries of the researcher can improve the performance of the worker. The discovery of scientific principles is an end in itself and a means to an end—the enhancement of man's control over nature for the spiritual, social, and moral progress of the individual, the nation, and the human race.

Certain scientists, those who received most of their education in the last quarter of the nineteenth century or the beginning of the twentieth, are disturbed by the direction of contemporary science. They fear that science is degenerating, becoming divided into fragments, so that one scientist no longer understands another. At the same time, philosophy is divesting itself of real significance. We may reach a point, they argue, at which the expert will know everything about nothing and the philosopher will know nothing about everything. These fears are not unjustified. The development of science has brought us many blessings. The specialization process has opened new opportunities for delving deeply into the microscopic details of the secrets of nature. But the necessary and valuable specialization calls for a broad substratum of general knowledge and understanding, available to all scientists, indeed to all mankind.

To the extent that we increase knowledge for the workingman, we will increase his enjoyment of his work and make him more productive. The more the entire people come to know the fundamentals of science, the more scientific research will develop. The very fact that science has become a decisive factor in health, security, and the economy makes it imperative that the bond between the scientist and the workingman be strengthened, to give every individual a basic understanding of science.

For all its importance, science in itself is neither good nor evil. Science permits man to understand and control his world outside (and perhaps his inner world as well), but it cannot tell him how to choose his path in life. Apart perhaps from the search for truth—which is a prerequisite of science and also an exalted moral ideal—the values of individual, social, and international morality are not derived from science or demonstrable by it. The achievements of science can be a blessing, but they can also cause illimitable havoc and destruction. The tree of knowledge of good and evil does not grow in the soil of science. Science strives to lay bare the secrets of nature, and with its aid man can find out *how* to do things, but not *what* to do.

Without scientists, however, there is no science. The scientist is not a thinking machine. He is a personality, with a high degree of moral responsibility. Science is not responsible for the crisis for which pessimists today blame it. If a hydrogen bomb is produced capable of destroying the civilized world, that is not the fault of science. It is the fault of international policy that is not founded on the moral principles of peace, freedom, justice, and brotherhood taught by Israel's Prophets. The duty of scientists—but not theirs alone—is to prevent a divorce between their conquests of science and moral values. Scientific achievement rests on human wisdom, while moral values reflect the demands of the human conscience, which is the divine part of man.

No one has yet discovered the secret of the human mind. Within continually expanding limits, the mind can grasp the structure of the cosmos and all that is in it. Nor has anyone unraveled the riddle of conscience, which makes a man capable of giving his life for ideals more precious to him than life itself. But both exist. The scientist will not perform his function or be fit for his task, nor will his work benefit mankind, if he merely intensifies the power of science and extends the scope of pure knowledge. He must also endeavor to foster moral values as the basis for the relations between men and states. Just as every man must be taught the fundamentals of science, so the tree of knowledge of good and evil must be planted in the soul of every man.

We should be sinning against truth if we were to say that the greatness of ancient Greece was confined to the spheres of wisdom and beauty. In the work of Plato, Aristotle, and Plotinus we find profound aspirations for the good and the just. We should be no less guilty if we were to say that the greatness of ancient Judaism lay only in the religious and ethical tidings of its Prophets: the books of the Bible are full of sublime beauty and great wisdom.

But the Prophets of Israel understood the supreme secret of being, of which there is none higher and which has no beginning and no end. Isaiah proclaimed this secret in brief and penetrating sentences: "I am the Lord and there is none else, beside Me there is no God . . . . For there is none beside Me. I am the Lord and there is none else; I form the light and create darkness; I make peace, and create evil. I am the Lord, that doeth all these things" (Isaiah 45:5–7).

And to an anguished Job, crying in torment: "I will speak in the bitterness of my soul: I will say to God: Do not condemn me; make me know wherefore Thou contendest with me. Is it good unto Thee that Thou shouldst oppress?" (Job 10:12). God answers out of the whirlwind: "Where wast thou when I laid the foundations of the earth? Declare, if thou hast the understanding . . . . Wilt thou even make void My judgment? Wilt thou condemn Me, that thou mayest be justified?" (Job 38:4; 40:1). And Job submissively acknowledges: "I know that Thou canst do everything, and that no purpose can be withholden from Thee" (Job 42:1).

The Prophets of Israel and their disciples had neither need nor desire to investigate the workings of nature and its amazing phenomena. They knew the supreme and ultimate reply and were content with it: "I am the Lord, that doeth all these things."

But when the spirit of research and questioning was renewed during the past three centuries, Jews of genius, from Baruch Spinoza to Albert Einstein, played their part in the progress of science in all branches, though their Jewish identity was masked. Spinoza used Latin and was regarded as a citizen of Holland; Einstein, Paul Ehrlich, and Gustav Hertz* were natives of Germany and counted among its scientists; Sigmund Freud was born in Austria and wrote in German. In Karl Marx's childhood his father abandoned Judaism, and Marx wrote with scorn and hostility of the Jewish people to which he belonged; J. Robert Oppenheimer and Edward Teller were deemed American men of science. Only in Israel have Jewish scientists and scholars emerged from their anonymity —another of the unique manifestations of our people's renaissance in its own land.

The four basic changes that have occurred in the life of the Jewish people in the last hundred years are worth mentioning.

Until the seventeenth century the Jews were mainly an Oriental people, if Moorish Spain is included among the countries of the East. Beginning with the eighteenth century the situation changed: the proportion of Jews living in Europe grew constantly larger. By the end of the eighteenth century there were 2.5 million Jews in the world, of whom a million lived in North Africa and the Middle East (including Turkey), while another 1.5 million lived in Europe. Of the latter, a million resided in Russia, Poland, and Galicia, while the rest lived in Central and Western Europe.

A constant growth, in absolute numbers and in percentages, continued in the European Jewish population. The natural increase of Oriental Jews was very low because of their high rate of infant mortality. Jews living in Europe increased more rapidly, thanks to improved health standards and economic conditions. By 1880 the percentage of Jews living in Europe reached its peak. There were then some 7,750,000 Jews in the world; 6,858,000 (88.5 percent) resided in Europe, 620,000 (8 percent) in Asia and Africa, and 250,000 elsewhere.**

The absolute number of Jews in Europe continued to rise even after 1880, and by 1935 there were some 9.7 million Jews residing on that continent. But by that time they constituted only 58.2 percent of world Jewry because, in the interval, new Jewish communities had grown up overseas. The 1880s saw the beginning of mass Jewish emigration from Europe, particularly from Eastern Europe. As a result two new centers of Jewish population evolved. One was in the United States, where a large Jewish community with considerable economic and political strength developed. The second, much smaller in numbers but more important because of its quality and its influence on the fate of Jewry, was the new community in the Land of Israel.

Between 1881 and 1914, 3 million Jews left Eastern Europe. From 1914 until the Second World War a million more departed. Until 1930 the Jews migrated mainly to North America: in the fifty years between 1880 and 1930 almost 3 million Jewish migrants entered the United States. At the beginning of the nineteenth century American Jewry numbered only a few thousand, and by the middle of the century no more than fifty thousand. By the end of the nineteenth century there were more than a million Jews in

* Ehrlich, Nobel Prize-winner in 1908, found a cure for syphilis; Hertz was awarded the Nobel Prize in physics in 1925.—EDITORS

** Arthur Ruppin. *The Jewish Struggle for Survival*, p. 30.

the United States, and by 1939 4.8 million. Jewish communities developed in other parts of the American continents as well, the largest of them in Argentina and in Canada. Jewish migration also reached South Africa, and between 1850 and 1935 the number of Jews in that country grew from five hundred to one hundred thousand.

Despite this mass migration, Europe still contained the majority of Jews up until the Second World War—almost 10 million. And until the Second World War, European Jewry was the nucleus, the source of strength, and the determining influence in world Jewry.

Until the nineteenth century almost all the Jews in the world, whether they lived in Europe or in the East, were orthodox. The general adherence to Jewish laws and religious customs served as a bond uniting all Diaspora Jews.★ In their hearts the Jews retained a feeling of their uniqueness and of their historical mission, though this expressed itself in the religious sphere rather than in terms of modern nationalism. The traditional education that every Jew sought to impart to his sons—though not to his daughters—gave the Jews, consciously or otherwise, a sense of unity and historical continuity, as well as a faith in ultimate salvation. And though Hebrew was not a spoken tongue, it lived in the hearts of the people because it was the language of prayer, poetry, and religious literature, and served as the medium of communication among the Jews of various countries. The religious holidays, rich in national memories, served as a substitute for communal life in the Homeland. There were only a few thousand Jews in the Land of Israel, but every Jew carried the Land of Israel in his soul. Indeed, the land of his fathers was closer to his heart than the land in which he had been born and lived.

In the wake of the emancipation and the spread of the Haskala (Enlightenment) movement in the nineteenth century, adherence to traditional forms of faith and law was shaken, first in Western Europe and later in Eastern Europe. The upper strata of Jews started to use the languages of the secular rulers and began to imitate the dress, customs, and education of the Gentiles. Assimilationism developed rapidly in the West, although it was impeded by continuing anti-Semitism.

In Eastern Europe Jewish nationalism took over the love of the Hebrew tongue and the longing for Zion from the religious heritage, which meantime had lost much of its appeal. A religious literature had continually developed through the ages in Hebrew except for the Aramaic Talmud. Now a secular Hebrew literature began. Stories were written in Hebrew and Hebrew poetry began to flourish again. Scientific texts appeared in Hebrew. Hebrew newspapers were established, reporting the day-to-day affairs of Jews and Gentiles alike.

Jewish studies in the modern sense developed in Germany, thanks to men like Leopold Zunz (1794–1886), Abraham G. Geiger (1810–1874), Merritt Steinschneider (1816–1901), Heinrich Graetz (1817–1891), and others. But the Jews of Eastern Europe maintained their spiritual hegemony in Jewish life. I speak here mainly of the Jews of Russia, which also encompassed Poland, Latvia, Lithuania, and Estonia, as well as Bukhara in the East. A special form of Jewish life was maintained in those countries. The great majority of Jews spoke Yiddish, a German-Jewish dialect. There were great centers of religious learning as well as a new literature in Hebrew and Yiddish. Finally, in the 1880s, the Hibbat Zion (Lovers of Zion) movement and the Hehalutz (pioneering) movement arose.

★ Diaspora—in Hebrew: *Galut*—is a generic name for all countries outside of Israel.—EDITORS

Hibbat Zion in Russia decided to promote the settlement of the Land of Israel. From the First Zionist Congress in 1897 the Russian Jewish community became the bastion of the Zionist movement. It provided dozens, hundreds, and finally thousands of settlers to revitalize the Land of Israel.

This Jewish community was struck a mortal blow by the 1917 Revolution, which came at almost the same time as the Balfour Declaration. Though they promised national autonomy within a Soviet federation to all the peoples of Russia, the communists denied national rights to the scattered Jewish communities. While Lenin lived, the Habimah Hebrew Theatre was allowed to exist and was even given state support. The Hehalutz organization was accorded legal status. But with the rise of Stalin the situation worsened and this Jewish community was cut off from world Jewry. Hebrew and Jewish education were prohibited, the Zionist movement was outlawed as a counter-revolutionary organization, and obstacles were placed in the path of Jews who wished to leave Russia for the Land of Israel.

A still more terrible blow was struck at European Jewry by the Nazis, who sought to carry out "the final solution"—the complete annihilation of the Jewish people, down to the last man, woman, and child—in Eastern and Western Europe. Six million Jews, two-thirds of European Jewry, were murdered by the Nazi Germans in the Second World War. The mass migration of European Jews that had begun in the 1880s proved in large measure providential. The murderers and their allies did not reach the Jews of North and South America, or of Africa, Asia, and Australia. Miraculously, they also failed to reach the Jews of the Land of Israel, though Hitler's armies were almost at its southern gates.

In the last ten years of the first half of the twentieth century, we reached the pinnacle of tragedy in the history of the Jews: the Holocaust. We also reached the pinnacle of salvation: the birth of the State of Israel.

Section 2. The Pioneers

Lovers of Zion and the Rise of Zionism

A s so often happens with events and undertakings that renew and transform the destiny of peoples, the beginnings of revolutionary movements are buried unseen in the dark bosom of history.

The State of Israel was established on May 14, 1948. But that is merely the date when it was proclaimed. Scores of years of pioneering work and creation preceded it: the heroic building of Jewish villages and towns; the revival of a language and a culture; the development of agriculture, industry, and communications on land, at sea, and in the air; revelation of a will and a striving toward national independence; the organization of an armed Jewish defense force.

The First Zionist Congress met in Basle, Switzerland, in August 1897 and set out to marshal the masses of Jewry for political activity that would bring about a "secure refuge" in the Land of Israel. Even that month and year are not the commencement.

The Zionist Congress was preceded by the Kattowitz Conference of November 6, 1884, headed by Dr. Leo Pinsker. We lack a full written record of this conference, called on the one hundredth birthday of Sir Moses Montefiore, just as we lack a full record of the Zionist Congresses. But we do have the speech of Dr. Leo Pinsker, one of the most important in the history of the Zionist movement, which exists in its German original:

On the occasion of the one hundredth birthday of Sir Moses Montefiore, a man with outstanding achievements to his credit, we have assembled from various countries in order to perpetuate his name by establishing an institution that will be appropriate to our times, benefit the Jewish people, and be worthy of Montefiore.

Please permit me to present my views in a few words.

The situation of the Jews in the countries where they are concentrated, and their severe suffering as a result of that situation, have led me to the conclusion that it can be improved only by charting an entirely new course for our people.

There can be no denying the fact that during their two thousand years of exile, the Jews have been alienated from agriculture, often through no fault of their own. We should also pay heed to another fact, which explains perhaps more than any other the stilted development of their spiritual and material life, and caused them to lose prestige in the eyes of others.

The Jews have long since become the prototype of a merchant people. But what is considered quite acceptable in the case of others is not so considered when it comes to Jews. Other peoples live in their own countries and must work their own land. They are productive in the most direct sense of that term. There is also indirect production through trade, the professions, science, and art. These other activities are certainly worthy ones, even if they are not essential nor highly visible. The development of the spiritual and material resources of other peoples is, therefore, more or less normal: with them trade and the professions are legitimate vocations within the overall framework of society. The same thing, unfortunately, cannot be said of the Jews. They were removed, against their will, from agriculture and over the years have lost their feeling for it. The activities of the Jews have thus appeared to be unduly one-sided, and sometimes even harmful to their physical development.

In the past, when communications were poorly developed and most people lived in villages, the Jews served as a connecting link in the same way as the railway and the telegraph do today. They lived mainly in the cities and devoted themselves chiefly to commerce. Now the situation is different. As the urban population has grown denser and modern trade has developed, the Jews have become even more concentrated in the cities and, as a result, have come into greater conflict with others, causing dangerous disturbances and anti-Semitism.

The commercial activities of the Jews have been considered unjustified in the eyes of unfriendly nations, and frequently used against them. This indicates that we should take the masses of our people, rotting away in small-scale trade and crafts, and return them to the ancient, honorable, and natural calling of our forefathers, namely, agriculture. The land loves to be exploited and is grateful for it much more than are human beings, who exploit each other, but do not wish to be exploited in return, particularly if the exploiter is a Jew. We have already reached the point at which our very existence is considered an act of exploitation.

We must, therefore, carefully analyze contemporary developments, however hard they are to comprehend, learning to adjust ourselves to prevailing economic conditions. This task clearly becomes imperative if we take into consideration the social and economic revolution of recent years. It is still to be seen whether, justifiably or otherwise, war will be declared on capitalism, with an ensuing life-and-death struggle. But one thing is certain:

the Jews are bound to be the victims, perhaps the only ones, of this struggle, as they have been in its earliest stages.

As we find ourselves in danger of strangulation, we must seek air to breathe and an opportunity to exist. Until now we have served as a link between men. Now we must return to the soil, which blesses the hands that work it and judges people not according to their background, but their diligence. Just as we were once able to transform ourselves from farmers to merchants, so we should now go back to the plough.

We can depend to a greater extent on the energy and adaptability of our people than on the negative force of anti-Semitism; the Jews will understand the importance of the transformation and have the strength to set about the difficult and unusual task of bringing it about. Jews, known for their ability to think, will quickly realize that the goal cannot be achieved by hasty and unplanned action. A people cannot be transformed just by declaring that a transformation is necessary. Moreover, we will be deceiving ourselves if we expect to see the fruits of our labor in our own generation. But what are a few generations to an eternal people? We will soon enough develop sufficient energy and wisdom to make the change. Fortunately, our task is made easier by the fact that Jews have already begun to sense the need for a transformation.

Henceforth our slogan will be settlement. Work has already begun. With the aid of Russian Jews, who have an undeservedly bad reputation, settlements have been established, within the short space of two years, that demonstrate what our people are capable of and justify our most fervent hopes. It is regrettable that our longings for the Holy Land have been greeted so antagonistically in various quarters. Montefiore himself has always shown great love and devotion to the Land.

Those assembled here have the great privilege of placing the holy task under the banner of a man who, during the hundred years of his life, has earned the gratitude of his people for his constant efforts on their behalf.

By establishing an organization in Montefiore's name which will aid tillers of the soil, particularly those in the Land of Israel, we will be paying him tribute in an appropriate and permanent manner, as well as blazing a new path that will lead our people to happiness and honorable labor.

Theodor Herzl's *Jewish State* made a powerful impression upon Jewish opinion in Europe and in America. But it had been anticipated by Dr. Leo Pinsker's brochure "Auto-Emancipation." Herzl confessed that had he read that first, he would not have written his own book. Yet both works, milestones though they were, had their precursor in Moses Hess's *Rome and Jerusalem*. Hess, a German Jew, friend and pupil of Karl Marx, for the first time put forward the concept of a Jewish State *in the Land of Israel*, which neither Pinsker nor Herzl did.

And long before Herzl or Pinsker or Hess, stirrings of redemption were visible in effort after effort of national reestablishment in the ancestral Homeland of the Jewish people. Those three great visionaries of Jewish revival did no more than give voice to the yearnings that pulsed in every Jewish heart in every generation. Immigration to the Land of Israel preceded the Zionist and Lovers of Zion movements and the State of Israel. and this immigration helped bring about the establishment of the Third Commonwealth.

Immigration to Palestine Before the Zionist Movement

When we speak today of the First, Second, and Third Aliya,* we use misleading terms. These waves of immigration were preceded by the immigration of Yemenite Jews, Sephardi Jews, and Ashkenazi Jews, both Hassidim and Perushim.** The earlier settlers built the "old" Yishuv.***

The Aliya from Yemen was the most wondrous yet painful of all Aliyot. The first we hear of it is in a letter of Rabbi Obadiah Bartenura to his brother, written in Jerusalem in 1489: "And in these days, there came hither Jews from the land of Yemen, and they told us that there are in that land today great and numerous communities of Israel." Yehya ben-Saadiah el-Zahari, one of the great poets of Yemen, visited Israel before 1568. Author of *The Book of Morals,* an elegant collection of verse modeled on the style of Yehuda Alharizi [Spanish-Hebrew poet, 1170–1235], he describes Safad with a Jewish community of fourteen thousand souls and eighteen yeshivot (academies). With fervid emotion he speaks of visits to Jerusalem and Tiberias, where he found "scholars of Holy Writ and the Mishna."

Emissaries from the Land of Israel, of whom the first was the Safad printer Rabbi Abraham, son of Isaac Ashkenazi, helped to tighten the links between the Jews of Yemen and of Israel. Rabbi Abraham visited Yemen in 1579, and while there engaged in the sale of books.

About 1730 the emissary was Rabbi Yehuda, son of Amram Divan. In 1735 Rabbi Jacob Bonshiniver of Hebron also took Hebrew books with him for distribution. An important immigrant from Yemen in those days was Rabbi Shalom Sharabi, of Sharab, who became the preeminent eighteenth-century Cabbalist of Jerusalem. Rabbi Baruch, son of Samuel, went from Safad to Yemen in 1833–1834. Born in Pinsk, in Russia, this "envoy of the Ten Tribes" left a vivid mark. Quitting Safad in 1830, he voyaged through Damascus, Aleppo, Kurdistan, Mosul, Baghdad, Basra, Bushire, and Muscat. From there he sailed to Aden, then went on to Sanaa, capital of Yemen, which he reached after two years and nine months of travel. In vain he sought to enter the wilderness of Haidan, to seek the Ten Tribes, and had to return to Sanaa, where he was put to death by the Imam in 1834.

---

* Aliya: a wave of immigration; plural: Aliyot.

** Sephardi Jews are those of Spain and their descendants, wherever resident. After their expulsion from Spain in 1492 Sephardi Jews settled along the North African coast, in Egypt, Syria, the Balkans, and the Turkish Empire. They differ in some synagogue rites and in their pronunciation of Hebrew from the Ashkenazi Jews, those of the rest of Europe (excluding the Sephardi communities), wherever resident. Hassidim (Pietists) belong to a religious movement founded in Eastern Europe by Israel Baal Shem Tov in the mid-seventeenth century; following terrible persecutions and massacres in Poland and southeastern Europe at that time, the unlearned Jewish masses were attracted to the Hassidic doctrine of worshipping God through joy and emotion, rather than study and intellect, as practiced by their opponents, the Mitnagdim, mainly in the Jewish centers of the Baltic region. Today no animosity prevails between the two denominations. Perushim (literally: to separate from) were Mitnagdim who established communities in Palestine in opposition to Hassidic groups already there.—EDITORS

*** *Yishuv* (literally: settlement) means the entire Jewish community in Palestine.

At Suez in 1836 the missionary Joseph Wolff met two emigrants from Sanaa—Shalom, son of Zachariah, and his brother, Baruch, who had come by ship from Jedda. Wolff writes: "Their garments were torn and threadbare. I asked them: 'Do you intend to return to Yemen?' They answered: 'Heaven forbid that we forsake the Holy City once it is our merit privilege to enter it. There we shall remain until our dying day.'"

The most important envoy in the nineteenth century was Jacob Saphir. In 1822, aged ten, he came to Israel from Oshmiano in the District of Vilna, Poland. His parents were among the disciples of the famed Gaon of Vilna. In 1858 he departed for the lands of the East as envoy of the Jerusalem congregation of Perushim. For four years and nine months he traversed Egypt, the shores of the Red Sea, Yemen, India, the Pacific islands, and Australia. Yemen attracted him strongly, for he too hoped to find there vestiges of the Ten Tribes. Indeed, he "discovered" the Yemenite Jews, for he brought word of them to all places where Jews dwelt, and in his book, *Even Saphir*, he described their annals and status, their ways and customs, their literature and vocations.

After the Turkish conquest in 1872 communication between Yemen and the Land of Israel was eased. From 1882, the year of the Russian "Bilu" Aliya, to 1884, Yemenite Jews arrived in Palestine in great numbers. By mid-1884 there were four hundred Yemenite immigrants in Jerusalem. I. D. Frumkin, editor of *Havazelet*, who helped these people to find housing in the village of Siloach, describes some of their hardships:

> They had set their hearts on relinquishing a land whose inhabitants trampled underfoot every freedom and every right of man. The Jew there might cry aloud his wrath, but there was none to listen, and all his honor was stripped from him. This group resolved to settle in the Holy Land. They sold their homes and land for a song, and made their arduous way for days, even weeks, through the desert, climbing mountains, fording gorges, women and children on camel and donkeyback, men on foot, until they came to the port of Hodeida and were taken by ship to Jaffa. From there, at last, to Jerusalem, with all the buffetings of travel and destitution, with nothing but the breath in their bodies.

At the outset privation and indigence were their lot; a few even lived in caves outside Jerusalem. But gradually they found their place, notably with the help of Frumkin and his society, Aid for the Needy. During the Feast of Hanukah in 1885 the first Yemenite families entered homes built with their own hands in Siloach. They organized and began to preach to brethren still in Yemen, printing prayerbooks for them in the familiar liturgy and sending emissaries. Newcomers arrived almost every year; most joined the congregation in Jerusalem, a handful settled in Jaffa.

In 1907 an overwhelming urge to return to Zion came upon the Jews of northern Yemen in the districts of Haidan and Saada. In one great caravan two hundred and twenty people set off. These were villagers, experienced farm laborers, and they went to work in the settlements of Judea—Rehovot, Rishon LeZion, and Petah Tikva. In retrospect they were in fact a part of the Second Aliya, which unfurled the flag of labor in Palestine.★

Samuel Yavnieli, an envoy of the Second Aliya, went to Yemen in 1910 with the help of the Palestine office headed by Dr. Arthur Ruppin. Leaving Jaffa at the end of 1910, Yavnieli stayed in Yemen until mid-1911. To its Jews he brought tidings of a national resurgence through Jewish labor and agricultural settlement. From then on the flow of Aliya from Yemen, merging with the main stream of the labor movement in Palestine,

★ Abraham Yaari, *Letters of the Land of Israel*, pp. 524–525.

began to swell. Abraham Tabib, the guiding figure, was present in Petah Tikva in 1919 when the workers of Palestine united and their Socialist-Zionist Union, Ahdut Avoda, was born. In 1921 he sent a letter of encouragement to his people in Yemen, recounting the growth of the Yishuv in the previous forty years and what had happened to those Yemenites who had become part of it since the Turkish seizure of Sanaa.

Tabib speaks of the work of the Yemenites in Israel and is full of praise for the "young generation of Yemenites in towns and settlements who do any work beneficial to the Yishuv. They toil, in Rehovot, Rishon LeZion and Petah Tikva, in Zikhron Yacov and Hadera, in Yavniel and Kinneret. There is no calling in which Yemenites are not found—builders, plasterers, stonecutters, carpenters, mechanics, blacksmiths, welders, tinsmiths, silversmiths and goldsmiths, tailors and cobblers, saddlers, weavers, butchers, and businessmen, everything except doctors and pharmacists."

When the State of Israel was established, the entire Jewish community in Yemen was rescued from a degrading exile and borne to independent Israel by planes—"on eagles' wings."

Since the dawn of an organized Hibbat Zion movement, and the Zionist movement after it, we have been accustomed to sneer at "the old Yishuv," which flourished in Israel before terms like "Hibbat Zion" and "Zionism" gained currency. This is indefensible arrogance. It disregards utterly the historic feelings of a people and its proud chronicles. "The old Yishuv" was the result of Aliyot of Yemenite, Sephardi, and Ashkenazi Jews hundreds of years before these terms were invented. Individual immigrants and whole groups were impelled by ideals and Messianic promptings to suffer tribulations far worse and perils more formidable than subsequent Aliyot endured.

In the Middle Ages and in the centuries preceding the last quarter of the nineteenth century the journey to Israel meant torments that no one of our generation can imagine; Jewish existence in Israel was in constant jeopardy and under ceaseless pressures. The times called for courage and an extraordinarily high sense of dedication from any that came to live here. Those generations, pioneers of "the old Yishuv" with all its faults, before the "Genesis" of the four following generations, deserve our respect and admiration, even if we are distant from their modes of thought and life. With body and soul they forged an unbreakable link between people and land. They contributed significantly to the eventual reestablishment of a state. Let us never forget it!

Nonetheless, there are fresh starts in history. Although the Land of Israel attracted Jews in every generation, the momentous innovation of our recent past was the decision to achieve redemption through land and labor. We should not otherwise have come to sovereign independence. The earlier Aliyot gravitated chiefly to the four holy cities: Jerusalem, Safad, Tiberias, and Hebron. There were enclaves of Jewish farming when the Turks overran the Land in the reign of Sultan Selim (1516) and even earlier, such as Ma'on near Tiberias, Kfar Hakok, Peki'in, Kfar Yasif, Kfar Alma, Kfar Hanania, Kfar Julis (now largely inhabited by the Druzes), and Kfar Kana. These remnants failed to attract the newcomers.

Even the attempt of Don Joseph Nasi, authorized in the second half of the sixteenth century by Sultan Suleiman the Magnificent, to resettle Tiberias and its environs, was short-lived. Don Joseph was the scion of a noble and wealthy Sephardi family that settled in Turkey after the expulsion of the Jews from Spain. Though he had enemies at the court in Istanbul, including ambassadors of European states, he won the Sultan's friendship and trust and was granted a charter for Tiberias and a number of neighboring villages. Don Joseph sent an agent, Joseph ibn Ardit (or Ardito), to wall the town and settle Jews in it for the purpose of developing agriculture, fishing, and industry. The Arab sheikhs and village mukhtars in the vicinity resented the encroachment and spread a story among their people that on the day Jewish Tiberias arose Islam would fall.

Don Joseph's plans did not even gain the good will of Jews driven from Spain or of the Italian refugees who reached Israel at that time. After Don Joseph's death in 1579 the Arabs wrecked all his works and only a few Jews remained in Tiberias. The failure of this first attempt at Jewish resettlement on a "governmental" basis can be ascribed partly to the mentality of the Jews in Israel and the Diaspora. Obsessed by the mystic notion of a supernatural redemption, they could not grasp the idea of deliverance by their own efforts.

The important urban community in Safad, engaged in handicrafts and industry and deep in Cabbalistic introspection, began to go downhill at the end of the sixteenth and the beginning of the seventeenth century. "After the glorious era of Safad, which lasted nearly three generations, the rivulet of Aliya that had entered the Land of Israel from Turkey, North Africa, and Eastern Europe was checked. Upheavals in the heartland of Turkey led to serious economic depression: business, crafts, and agriculture no longer held a primary place; public security was undermined; Turkey ceased to be a lodestar for exile Jewry."*

A severe crisis also afflicted the Jews of Jerusalem. Moslem masters laid burdensome taxes upon them. In 1586 they were robbed of their only synagogue, one built by the great Nahmanides. The great majority fled to Hebron, Tiberias, and Gaza. Shabtai Zvi (the false messiah) arrived in Jerusalem in 1663 and preached abstinence and fasting.** Only at the beginning of the eighteenth century, in 1700–1701, did several hundred Jews from Poland, led by Rabbi Yehuda the Hassid and Rabbi Chaim Malach, enter Jerusalem.

In Galilee conditions also improved during the regime of Sheikh Daher in Safad and Tiberias. He invited Rabbi Chaim Aboulafia of Smyrna in 1742 "to come and inherit the land of his ancestors." (The grandfather of Rabbi Chaim was Rabbi of Tiberias in the previous century.) Rabbi Chaim revived a Tiberias that had been bereft of Jews for seventy years, renewing the tradition of Don Joseph Nasi in settling Jews in the villages and establishing an agricultural community in nearby Shfaram.

In 1777 Hassidic disciples of the Baal Shem Tov settled in Israel, under the banner of Rabbi Menahem Mendel Vitebisker and Rabbi Abraham Klisker and Rabbi Israel of Politzk. A small community of Jews lived then in Jerusalem, fifty souls all told. But because they were Perushim, not Hassidim, the followers of Rabbi Vitebisker settled in Safad and Tiberias. The Jerusalem community, however, grew with the arrival of disciples of the Vilna Gaon under Rabbi Menaham Mandil and Rabbi Israel from Shelow in 1805.

When the power of Sheikh Daher in Galilee was broken, his successors began again to harass the Jews of Safad, Tiberias, and the Galilean villages. The Druze rising of 1834 brought further catastrophe to the Jews of Safad and Galilee. To this was added the cruelty

* Ben-Zvi, *The Land of Israel and Its Settlements During the Turkish Regime*, pp. 205–206.

** Shabtai Zvi (1626–1676), native of Smyrna, Turkey, is the most prominent of the many Jewish false messiahs in modern times. He proclaimed himself the messiah in 1655. His following in Europe grew rapidly, and in 1666 he led the believers to the Holy Land and got as far as Constantinople, where he was arrested and forced to convert to Islam. — EDITORS of nature: an earthquake in Safad and its neighborhood in 1837 brought grave damage to Jews and Arabs, and sent many of the Jews of Safad and Tiberias in flight to Jerusalem and Hebron.

In 1840 the entire Jewish world was shocked by the "blood libel" of Damascus.* To the defense of his people came the most eminent public figure of British Jewry, Sir Moses Montefiore, a man of Italian origin. Together with Adolfe Cremieux of France and others, he succeeded in wiping out that hideous indictment so thoroughly that the Ottoman government by edict forbade its revival. In 1856 Sir Moses acquired the first Jewish orange grove in Israel, near Jaffa, with a view to shifting Jews to agricultural vocations. This was the first modern attempt to make Jews farmers again. More effective, significant, and enduring was the work of Karl Netter, an Alsatian Jew. With Cremieux and others he propounded the idea of the global unity of the Jewish people. The result was the founding in 1860 of the Alliance Israelite Universelle. The organization set itself two principal aims: worldwide activity toward equality of rights for Jews and their moral advancement, and practical help to all that suffered for their Jewishness. Netter was selected secretary of the Alliance, which soon received appeals for help from such tortured lands of the Diaspora as Iran, Russia, and Rumania.

In 1868 the Alliance sent Netter to study the condition of Jews in Israel and means of improving it. In his report he said: "The hungry ask for bread to eat, a garment to don, but with the wages of their labor and not as charity. All the time I was in Jerusalem, not one single person of sound health asked for an outright gift. The many who knocked each day upon my door only wanted some work to do." Netter thereupon recommended the founding of an agricultural school. "I present to you," he wrote, "a plan for a new institution where you can educate the next generation in farming. Thus you will construct a refuge for our many brethren who, today or tomorrow, must flee from their dwelling places because their Gentile neighbors hate them. Little by little, you will resettle the Holy Land, to which the eyes of all Israel are ever lifted up, if farming truly expands there and our brethren come as settlers in their multitudes from the Diaspora. Then we will see the New Jerusalem with our own eyes."

On December 3, 1868, the Alliance, under the presidency of Cremieux, accepted Netter's recommendation and charged him to carry out the plan. Netter went to Istanbul at once and succeeded in procuring from the Sultan a firman granting the Alliance a ninety-nine-year leasehold on 2600 *dunams* (650 acres) near Jaffa for an agricultural school. In 1870 he built the institution, called Mikve Israel, and for the next four years was himself both principal and instructor. He returned three times: in 1877, in 1881, and 1882, on which visit he took ill and died on October 2; he was buried in Mikve Israel. Netter was fortunate to witness the beginnings of the new agricultural settlement, in Petah Tikva and Rishon LeZion. His high hopes for Jewish farming were disappointed, but his love for Israel never faltered. During his last sojourn, when he found Bilu** settlers working in Mikve, he was filled with affection and admiration for them.

The outstanding merits of these two distinguished figures in the Jewry of Western Europe, Montefiore and Netter, should never be underestimated. They ushered in Jewish

---

* The charge that Jews murdered Christians to use their blood in Passover rites. The falsehood persisted into the early twentieth century: for instance, the notorious Beilis case in Russia.—EDITORS

** Bilu: the first pioneer movement from Russia in 1880's. The name is an abbreviation of four Hebrew words: "O House of Jacob, come, and let us go!" (Isaiah 2:5).—EDITORS

agriculture in the nineteenth century. But in truth they were only helping others. The historic turning point, destined to end in the reestablishment of the State, was the dedication of Jews to life upon the land on their own pioneering initiative. Not settling someone else to farm, but making agriculture a way of life *for themselves*—that was the most important, revolutionary, and constructive change ever wrought in Israel. Among the founding fathers of Jewish agriculture the laurel wreath by right belongs to those who founded Petah Tikva, Rishon LeZion, Zikhron Yacov, Rosh Pina, and Gedera, and to those who followed them, year after year, until the proclamation of the State.

Jerusalem and Safad Jews Interested in Agricultural Settlement ★ *Establishment of Petah Tikva and Gei-Oni*

The honor was Jerusalem's. One of its sons was first of the first: Joel Moses Salomon, third generation in the land, grandson of Abraham Shlomo Zalman Zoref (murdered by Arabs in 1851), who came to Israel in 1811 and was a pioneer of the Ashkenazi community in that city. Zoref's son Mordekhai aspired to farming. In his letter to Montefiore on that philanthropist's visit to Jerusalem in 1839, these words appear: "When I gave heed and saw that the land was pleasing, and its merchandise of merit, I said: the Holy Land is abundant in sustenance if its soil be worked by vigorous hands, and so I have ventured to plough the earth alone." Undoubtedly this letter was one of the forces behind Montefiore's idea of bringing the Jews of Israel back to the soil. Mordekhai did not live to fulfill his ambition, but his own son Joel did.

Joel, born in 1838, a founder of Petah Tikva, was in his youth an innovator, in the positive sense of that word. Together with six companions, including Joseph Rivlin and Joshua Yellin, father of David, he left the walls of Old Jerusalem and established the suburb of Nahlat Shiva. In 1863 he also founded a Jerusalem journal, *The Lebanon*, a monthly that did not last long; the last issue appeared in 1864. Thirteen years later Joel produced a periodical called *Judah and Jerusalem*. For more than a year he preached to the Jews of Jerusalem: "Go out and work the land!" His wish was realized in the end with the aid of two Hungarian Jews, David Guttmann and Joshua Stampfer. Yehiel Michael Pines could say: "Petah Tikva was founded thanks to three things—the idea, which was Joel Moses Salomon's, the cash, which was David Meir Guttmann's, the energy, which was Joshua Stamfer's. That was the triple thread."

Joshua, youngest of the three, was born in 1852 in a Hungarian village where his father was a dayan, or judge, in the Jewish religious court. Joshua's first lessons were in a cheder, a traditional Jewish school, and next in a secular high school, for among Hungarian Jews Torah and piety then went hand in hand. After high school Joshua entered the Berlin yeshiva of Rabbi Azriel Hildesheimer. His father looked with disfavor upon the resultant sophistication and stopped his allowance. The young man, not wishing to return home, went to stay in a village with his uncle Eliezer Raab, who was also to be among the first farmers of Petah Tikva. Raab corresponded with Rabbi Zvi Kalisher and Rabbi Eliahu Gutmaher, the founders of Hibbat Zion. When his uncle let him read these letters, they fired Joshua with passion for the return of Zion.

The first elections of the Hungarian Parliament also moved him deeply, as he heard rousing patriotic songs sung by the Hungarians. A burning zeal to help in the restoration of his people so consumed him that he resolved to go to the Land of Israel. In 1869, thrusting maps of Israel, Europe, and Asia into his pockets, he marched through Serbia and Bulgaria to Salonica. There a rabbi gave the young pilgrim a ticket on a ship bound for Smyrna. From Smyrna Joshua marched on again, until, after the long travail, he came first to Beirut and then to Safad. Though Safad was the home of sages of the Cabbala, he would not stay there and trudged on to Jerusalem. His "going up" to the land took four months and six days to accomplish.

Joshua studied for a while in a yeshiva again, but the situation in Jerusalem was not to his liking. What he longed for was to farm in the Holy Land. As soon as he came to know Joel Salomon and David Guttmann, each his senior by many years, the plan materialized to establish a Jewish farming village in Israel.

Guttmann was the wealthy one. Also a Hungarian, born in 1827, he had come to Israel in 1876 with a large sum of money. The heads of the Hungarian congregation wanted to attract him, as an Orthodox Jew, but he too dreamed of an Israel resurrected by the ploughshare. That dream seized some forty-five others in Jerusalem, including Joshua Yellin,★ Joseph Rivlin, and Benjamin Salant. This trio in 1872 had already decided to buy land near Jericho and call it Petah Tikva—the Gate of Hope. Because they were foreign nationals, nothing came of it. They tried also to buy the lands of Duran, which today is Rehovot, but failed again.

After a further year of searching, Joel and his friends were told of land on the Yarkon River, part of the village of Muleibis, which Tayan, a Christian effendi of Jaffa, was willing to sell; another Christian merchant of Jaffa, Kassar, also had land for disposal there. With Zorah Barnet and a few others the trio went out to look at the land. They surveyed the Tayan area and came upon the ruined fortress of Antipatris, where they found springs emptying into the river. In the village they were shocked to see fellahin stricken by malaria. Joel stayed on a day or two to ascertain the cause of the disease. He was told that the river was neglected by the government. Nearby lay carcasses of sheep and cattle abandoned by the shepherds. Pestilential swamps had formed, with swarms of anopheles mosquitoes. The worst by far was Tayan's property along the Yarkon, while Kassar's bordered the village of Yehudiyeh (the Jehud of the Book of Joshua 19, 45).

Joel reported back to his group, which invited a Greek doctor named Mazarakis to look into local health conditions. The medical finding was that the area was bereft of inhabitants because the air was poisoned by marshy vapors and was unfit for man or beast.

The friends were dumfounded at first, but on reflection Joel's bold counsel was, "In spite of it all!" Joshua echoed, "We shall try." Guttmann was heartened to consent. They decided, for the time being, to take Kassar's land, away from the swamps, 3375 dunams (850 acres), for 21,500 francs. Guttmann furnished most of the capital, but Joel and Joshua, Jacob Blumenthal, Michael Leib Katz, Eliezer Raab, David Ragner, Nathan Griengart, and Zorah Barnet each contributed a little. The contract was signed in 1878

★ Even before then Yellin had bought a plot in the village of Motza near Jerusalem (the Motza of the Book of Joshua), but not to settle on. He rented it to an Arab peasant and later built a hotel on it which he rented to a Christian. See his *Memoirs of a Jerusalemite*, p. 56.

in the presence of the Austrian consul (in Turkish times foreign consuls wielded wide powers thanks to their status under the Capitulations). And they named the place Petah Tikva.

Stamfer's diary describes how in 1878 Raab and his son Judah, Guttmann, Joel, and he left Jerusalem to start work at Petah Tikva. "The first chores were done collectively, with twelve yoke of oxen, five horses, and a few donkeys." They dug a well and after a laborious start eventually struck water some twenty meters down, in 1879. The first buildings were put up without an official permit. The permit had to be obtained from the Mutessarif, or Governor, of Jerusalem, and he was against the project. At that distance from a town, however, the settlers trusted that their construction work would not become known to the authorities.

When Ragner, also a Hungarian and skilled in agronomy, arrived, he taught the settlers how to use European ploughs instead of the primitive Arab tool. As Eliezer Trufa recounts:

> Many of the new settlers expressed a wish to go down to the riverbank and establish themselves there, not on the hill of the first ones. They declined to heed the founders' warnings. They were sure that the river would irrigate their gardens and vineyards, that they could fish in it, and that every inch of soil would be as rich as could be. They were not to be dissuaded. They built three stone houses, as well as six earthen houses and huts. They sowed vegetables, irrigating from the river; they even drank the river water. Within a few months the spot was looking most attractive, deep in a verdant and refreshing greenery, and the haul of fish was large and constant.
>
> Then came the summer of 1880. Malaria began to take its toll. Every house had its victim. Finally the winter arrived with angry and torrential rains that lashed the earth. The swollen river overflowed its banks; the place was inundated and waterlogged. The flood swept away the farmsteads; the earthen houses collapsed like decks of cards. The occupants were incommunicado, the flood and the mud kept them indoors. After four days the deluge subsided. Men from up the hill at Petah Tikva came and rescued them all, save for an old man who had died.
>
> Opinions then were divided. Some of the unfortunates said "Let us go back to Jerusalem. Why should we perish in this morass?" Others stoutly protested, "No, let us die here!" But when the storm subsided and they realized that their dwellings were on the brink of disintegration, they fled for their lives to Jerusalem. Only a very few crossed to the hill; most of what had been set up on the banks of the Yarkon the heavens washed away, and Arab robbers completed the job. No evidence remained of all that toil.
>
> In 1882 the founders took heed of the settlement once more. Again Raab was their envoy. The houses were roofless, the home of jackals, wild boars, and hyenas. Returning in great distress, he begged his friends to go back and restore the ruins. Yehiel Michael Pines came to their help On his advice Abraham Koppelman was despatched to the Diaspora to sell parcels of land.*

Koppelman was a Jew from Slonim, a timber merchant, and a Lover of Zion since childhood. In 1880 he bought a parcel of land in Petah Tikva, and at the end of the year came out to stay. Charged now with persuading affluent co-religionists to come and own land in Israel, he succeeded in organizing a small group from various East European towns, chiefly Bialystok, to buy plots in Petah Tikva and ultimately to settle there.

* Eliezer Trufa, *The Beginning: Seventy Years of Petah Tikva*, 1948, p. 28.

Petah Tikva gained a new lease on life when pioneering immigration from Russia was resumed in 1882–1883, and especially again with a contingent from Bialystok. These were the protagonists of the principle of self-labor enshrined in the first article of the Rules of the Brotherhood and Labor Society, which they founded. The article proclaims: "Labor must be with our own hands and not otherwise. As long as the owners are themselves capable of doing any task, they have no right to hire laborers to do it. Women and children, if free from kitchen and classroom and strong enough to work or do guard duty, must help us. In the spirit of this canon, every individual must look after his horse and his cows and lodge with them, and put them out to graze." In practice this fine principle was not observed for very long, but we should not deny its virtue as a vision.

The three founders of Petah Tikva are gone: Guttmann died in 1984, Stampfer in 1908, Salomon in 1913.

About that time Safad Jews endeavored to buy 2400 dunams (600 acres) of the Jaouneh land, calling the place Gei-Oni—"Vale of Strength." There is little exact information: Moses Smilansky says:

> One day a wonderful person called Simon came to the Galilee, and rode round Mount Canaan on a donkey or a mule. Enchanted by the natural beauty, by the sacred murmur of ancient memories that every crag seemed to whisper, by every valley and every hilltop, he wrote a pamphlet entitled *Simon's Travels*, overflowing with ardent love for the Holy Land and its soil, praying for its cultivation by Jewish hands.
>
> His words had a tremendous effect on a certain Jew, Friedmann, who was a buyer of citrons. One day Friedmann traveled to the Mountains of Naphtali to rent a grove from an Arab, passing through Jaouneh on the way, and when he saw the village, its loveliness won his heart. So he bought a portion of their land from the Arabs, paying a medjidieh for every dunam, and conceived a plan to establish a Jewish settlement on it. Unhappily, it all came to nothing, for he could find no response anywhere He sent letters to the Diaspora and presented the plan to prominent Jews, but his was a voice crying in the wilderness. In holy Safad, however, a number of Jews, conspicuously Eliezer Rokah, embarked upon a project of agricultural settlement and, with their own means, acquired parcels of land in Jaouneh. Some actually built abode huts and settled down to farm. But they succeeded even less than the villagers. Rokah went abroad to awaken the sympathy of Jewish philanthropists and secure backing for the pioneers. But his efforts were unavailing, the Diaspora did not respond. Little by little, the Jaouneh pioneers disbanded.

Russian Bilu Organization ★ *The Work of Y. M. Pines*

In the last quarter of the nineteenth century the center of Diaspora Jewry was Czarist Russia. The emancipation of the French Revolution produced opposing trends in European Jewry—assimilationism and nationalism. Assimilationism made headway among the Jews in the West, nationalism among the Jews in the East, but the geographical division was not absolute. Assimilationists made their appearance in Russian Jewry, while proponents of the national revival were not wanting in the West.

The greatest of the latter was Moses Hess, preaching a Jewish State in the Land of Israel, something not even the great leaders who followed—Pinsker and Herzl—were to do. They certainly envisaged a Jewish State as the only solution to the Jewish question, but not necessarily in Israel. In the West three great men of action arose: Moses Montefiore in England, Karl Netter and Baron Edmond de Rothschild in France. Montefiore and Netter, as I have said earlier, tried to divert the Jews to Palestine to agriculture. Rothschild was responsible for a far-flung enterprise of settlement and rightly earned the title "Father of the Yishuv." The pioneering immigration that laid the foundations of the State, however, was mainly East European, with Jews of Russia in the vanguard.

The first pioneering organization was Bilu, formed at the beginning of the 1880s. As with most such groups an external factor was present: the anti-Jewish pogroms in 1881 after the assassination of Alexander II. Pious Jews put their trust in God and hoped for His help. Among the less pious, the affluent and rich were not gravely harmed. Scarcely anybody asked what the future held for Jewry and its free development, and even those few were divided. One group, styling itself Cosmopolitans, favored emigration to America, the land of freedom and equality. A minority was for a return to the Homeland.

There was a stirring call from Israel, written in 1881 by Israel Dov Frumkin and entitled "A Voice from the City," published in *The Book of Covenant and Memory* by the Society of the Founders of the Yishuv. That body had taken the place of an earlier one formed at Petah Tikva in 1879, with the motto:

> And I will bring again the captivity to my people of Israel, and they shall build the waste cities, and inhabit them; and they shall plant vineyards, and drink the wine thereof; they shall also make gardens, and eat the fruit of them.
>
> And I will plant them upon their land, and they shall no more be pulled up out of their land which I have given them, saith the Lord thy God (Amos 9:14, 15).

Israel Belkind, one of the first of the Bilu, writes:

> My attitude to Israel was not conditioned by anything external. I read the Bible over and over again in childhood. The books of Abraham Mapu, *Love of Zion* and *Samaria's Guilt*, were powerful influences. When I was nineteen and entered high school, I devoured historical volumes. The annals of the great moved me powerfully, men who had done tremendous things for their people in their generation. And so my resolution took form, to devote my life to the revival of my people in its land.
>
> But this was in the seventies, and the eyes of all the enlightened in Russian Jewry were turned anxiously toward the "main arena," the ferment of "emancipation" as such in all of Russia. Jewish pupils in the high school were embroiled in secret cells and pored over forbidden books. To talk with them of my ambition and my people would have been dangerous. I had only one school friend, a Pole, and I would open my heart freely to him. Together we shared secrets about our futures, and one secret was our resolve, when we grew up, to work, each of us, for the good of his people and his country, he in Poland, I in Israel.

Menahem Mendel Ussischkin in his *Yehiel Tchlenov* (1937) writes:

> It happened in Moscow in 1881. I was eighteen, in the top class of high school. In a house in "Dirty Alley" lived two Jewish families cheek by jowl—the Tchlenovs and the Ussischkins, and their sons, Yehiel and I, naturally got to know each other and became very good friends. We had barely finished our talks and arguments on general issues when the pogroms of 1881–1882 broke out and our national movement, Hibbat Zion, was born. Almost at that precise moment we both joined it. The first meeting we went to was in January 1882. It was attended by Jewish students from Moscow, one or two girls included. On the agenda was the question of emigration from Russia, where to, Israel or America?

Which should be chosen for the founding of an independent Jewish State? It was all clandestine; we had to keep out of the way of the police. Discussion was stormy and went on for four or five hours; we spoke Russian, of course.

When we left the hall, the two of us were already enthusiastic Lovers of Zion, and resolutely bent on forming a body of young people who would settle in Israel. Within three months we had twenty-five members; the inaugural meeting took place during Passover, 1882, in a hovel on the outskirts of the city, and lasted nearly a week, night and day, and again, of course, in secret. The main dispute was not over practical questions, how to collect the means for the journey, to buy land, and so forth. No, what principally occupied our minds was the kind of government the future Jewish State should have. On that point our membership broke into three different camps, with three different aims. One demanded a monarchial regime, with absolute powers vested in the sovereign; I was its protagonist. A second was for a free republic with a President elected every seven years; Hessin led it. The third, with Tchlenov as its spokesman, wanted a constitutional monarchy.

Of these three only Hessin joined the First Aliya. Ussischkin came after the Bolshevik Revolution, although he had paid earlier visits, and Tchlenov, by then a leader of the Zionist Organization, died in Europe.

When the first Biluists went to work in Mikve Israel, the pioneer aura of its beginnings had already vanished from an institution its founders had planned as the Jewish "agricultural nursery" of Israel. Its principal was Samuel Hirsch, who was entirely antipathetic to that basic notion. Yehiel Michael Pines writes of him and in allusion to Biluists working at Mikve: "It was not by chance that Solomon in his wisdom said, For these things the earth is disquieted. For a servant when he reigneth; and a fool when he is filled with meat, and so on. Hirsch has a servile soul. With heavy-footed arrogance he will stamp on all the immigrants under his control. In his eyes they are a feckless lot, a gang of itinerants who keep on knocking at the doors." (He was referring to members of the Bilu.)

On August 12, 1882, Hessin and his friends first went to work in Mikve. His diary for August 21 says:

> Nine days ago I went to work for the first time. We rise at five in the morning, with the sun; work begins at six. We drink no tea; we just make our beds, grab a hunk of loaf that weighs about one and a half pounds, and off we go. Though few of us can stomach food so early, yet by the time—it is only twenty minutes away—we get to our destination, only a quarter of the ration is uneaten.
>
> Our group arranged with Hirsch to work eight hours a day, from six to ten in the morning and from two-fifteen to six-thirty in the afternoon. We take up our mattocks, we fill our jarra with water (a jarra is a big earthenware vessel that holds about as much as a bucket), and, escorted by the overseer, one of the older pupils, off we go to the garden. We strip off outer garments, roll up our sleeves and commence digging about three decimeters deep, pulling out weeds and roots.
>
> This is a tough school we have to go through. Light work such as arranging seedbeds, planting, harvesting, irrigation, and the like is never given to us. They only send us to hoe and hoe and hoe. The overseer is exacting; he allows us not a moment's pause, for those are his orders. Hirsch is doing it willfully, to drive the "spirit of folly" out of our hearts and force us to quit. He simply cannot understand how Russian Jews (of whom their French brethren have the worst possible opinion), and intelligent ones at that, will be able to do simple work.
>
> Once Hirsch jokingly suggested we clean out the toilets. We did not shirk even from that. We did the disgusting chore a whole day.

On August 30, 1882 Karl Netter arrived. "P" argued stoutly that, as the Alliance is not in favor of settlement, we must regard him as an adversary. We thought differently. For the moment he was our only hope. At Mikve there was an official called Assowetzki, an immigrant from Brody whom Netter had appointed to teach. Next day Assowetzki told us Netter had talked with him at length and asked a lot of questions about us; whether we work well, how long, how many of us there are. Netter, he said, would be coming next day to see our work for himself, so we had better do our best, for we might hope for great things from him. The German vine grower told us that Netter questioned him too, in detail, about us and our work. The German had spoken well of us and asked us, if Netter wanted to know whether we were taught by him, to answer yes. About nine o'clock we heard a cry, "Netter!" All of us, as one man, swung our mattocks. Certainly, our work that day was outstanding. Netter was accompanied by staff members—Hirsch was in Paris. Greeting us, he asked kindly of "S," the first in line: "How is the work going, how have you settled down? Work, gentlemen! Don't despair! I would be very happy myself if I had the energy to farm in the Holy Land, land of our forefathers, but my years forbid it!"

[September 22:] Ill-luck dogs us. We had begun to hope we should get a rent-free house this winter and a rise in wages, but suddenly all our castles in the air evaporated. Ten days ago we heard Netter was slightly indisposed. Two days afterward we were told to stop work on the foundations, and that was the end of them. Netter had a chronic illness, but refused to see a doctor, and on Monday, September 20, he died.* The funeral was yesterday afternoon. Tarbushed and sandaled Sephardi Jews sat on the ground. Representatives of foreign governments and all the notables of Jaffa came. The pallbearers kept changing, and we too took our turn beneath the bier of the man on whom our hopes had been pinned. At the southern boundary of Mikve, among the vineyards, a deep grave was dug in the sand and the coffin was lowered into it. A dignified old man advanced to the edge—it was the American Minister,**—and in moving words he catalogued the virtues of Netter, a man devoted to his country, a father and brother to all Jews, a friend of all humankind; throughout his lifetime, he said, Netter dreamt of restoring Israel's people by manual labor and especially by agriculture, and that had been his object in founding Mikve.

We found a new friend—Yehiel Michael Pines. At its meeting in 1877 the committee of the Montefiore Foundation appointed Pines as its Director in Jerusalem. The two Lovers of Zion papers, David Gordon's *Hamagid* and Yehiel Brill's *The Lebanon* (which was first published in Jerusalem in conjunction with Joel Moses Salomon and afterward transferred by Brill to Mayence), greeted the appointment with fervor. They called Pines "a man in a thousand, in whom faith and knowledge go hand in hand with love and peace; great are his achievements in the realms of theory and practice alike."

Pines had come to the Land of Israel two months after the founding of Petah Tikva. The best elements among the Orthodox Jews of Jerusalem at that time were waking to the idea of settlement, with Joel Moses Salomon in the forefront. But the local zealots, led by the Rabbanit of Brisk (wife of Rabbi Joshua Leib Diskin, whom that contentious woman had already driven from appointments in Sheklov, Lomza, and Brisk to Jerusalem), declared war on Pines and excommunicated him. The act aroused a storm in the Diaspora and triggered a violent controversy in the press. The poet I. L. Gordon wrote a forceful article in a *Hamelitz*, ending: "Shall the Lord sell Jerusalem for a woman, and the hope of His people that dwells in Zion?" And at least one rabbi in Jerusalem bravely came forth

* Hessin used the old Russian calendar: the Gregorian date is October 2, 1882.
** Actually it was the American consul.

to defend Pines: Rabbi Salant affirmed that ever since his arrival, Pines had associated with God-fearing men of wisdom and understanding, great scholars. Meanwhile Pines immediately proceeded to examine the conditions for settlement.

He was a practical, shrewd man, but he was also a visionary, ready to consider the boldest of ideas. He writes: "There has never been a great idea that was not a dream at first; yet in the end it is realized if we are not over-cautious." In 1882, with Eliezer Ben Yehuda, he founded the Rebirth of Israel Society to revive "the real Israel and lift it out of its degradation, fortify its spirit and renew its original glory." To avert Turkish suspicions, they cautiously added: "and all in utter loyalty to the government." A central provision of the organization's rules was this:

> Members living in Israel shall speak Hebrew to one another within the Society and in its hall, nor shall they be ashamed to speak it in the market and the street. And they shall take heed to teach it to their sons and daughters and their whole household. The Society will strive to purify and enrich Hebrew, and make it the language of instruction in the schools.

In a letter to Rashi Fein, the two men explain that in the printed rules they could not say all that was in their hearts:

> Lest the evil eye be upon it, so we made it a rule not to be garrulous but only to whisper to those who are with us, of whose sincerity we can be sure. Our aim is to reestablish the people of Israel in the land where they grew up, from their day of birth to the dreadful day the overwhelming might of Rome destroyed us. The Society believes, wholly and without reserve, that only upon this soil, soaked with the blood of thousands of our finest sons, can our nation exist. It can, if we multiply our numbers until we are a majority. And it is not beyond our ability, once we sincerely devote ourselves to this goal, for the land is still derelict and uninhabited, no longer settled as it was when we were its inhabitants.

After Netter's death, the Biluists had almost despaired of ever founding a settlement. But Pines came to them and said: "Rebirth does not depend only on farming. Trade and industry also count, and you must not give up hope. Here is my suggestion: some of you should stay and work in Mikve and Rishon, until there is a chance for you to settle on your own land; others should go to Jerusalem to learn a trade." This approach is reflected in the minutes of the Rebirth of Israel, organized by Pines and Ben Yehuda:

> Our people will not survive on the soil alone, nor will they survive without it. The first thing is to give back trade and industry the prestige they once enjoyed among Jews; it has ebbed dismally in the millennia of our dispersion. The Society resolves to support bright young men, of both secular and religious schooling, who choose to learn a trade, or acquire any practical skill.

Nine Biluists agreed and went to Jerusalem—Samson Belkind, Zeev Dubnov, Jacob Shertok (father of Moshe and Yehuda Sharett), David Yudelevitz, Ozer Dov Lifshitz, Jacob Mohilenski, Hillel Mintz, Deborah Sirota, and Nahman Rozovski. Belkind and Dubnov were apprenticed to Markel the carpenter; Shertok and Rozovski to Yehiel Hirsch the engraver; Yudelevitz to a German Templar, Gottlieb Dea, a knife-grinder, Mintz to Hirsh Ellenhorn, a blacksmith in Mazkeret Moshe; Lifshitz entered the Alliance's Nissim Behar school. Deborah helped to look after her companions' domestic needs— midday meal, mending linen, the laundry, and so forth. Ben Yehuda cast Mohilenski

in the role of a rabbi. "It is essential," he observed, "to prepare a proper political representation, for this country as well as overseas. Our spokesman today is the Haham Bashi,
and how poor a national figure he cuts! Our Chief Rabbis are ineffectual. We must bring
up a truly great rabbi, great in Torah, in wisdom, in worldly knowledge and political
discernment, in short, a great Jew whom rabbinical dignity will truly become, within
the land and beyond."

Mohilenski, a very gifted yeshiva student in his time, undertook the part. Without
a murmur he took off his workaday dress, grew sidecurls, and entered the seminary of
Rabbi Isaac Leib Diskin, all to the exalted end of bearing aloft the banner of Israel's rebirth. This Jerusalem group of Biluists called itself "Shau," an acrostic of the Hebrew
words "Return of smith and graver." Its purpose was to bring crafts and manufacturing
in the Holy Land within the reach of skilled workers who would advance the national
aim. *Hamelitz* wrote in 1883 "On every product of the group *Shau-Jerusalem* will
be stamped."

After the founding of Rishon in 1882 Hirsch agreed to transfer the Biluists there.
In 1885, with the aid of Pines, Gedera was founded, the "colony" of the Biluists.

Goal of Immigration as One Biluist Saw it ★ Foundation of Rishon LeZion

The "thunders," the "gales from the South"—names for the anti-Jewish outbreaks
in Russia in the 1880's—were admittedly a major impetus for the Aliya movements that
developed then in Russia and Rumania. These led to the foundation of the first settlements
after Petah Tikva: Rishon, Zikhron, Rosh Pina, Yesod Hamaala, Ekron, Gedera, and
others.

Unquestionably, pogroms and overt anti-Semitism were a powerful and perhaps
the main cause of Jewish migration down the centuries, but they never set the direction
of those wanderings; least of all did they send the exiled and the expelled to Aliya and
agriculture in the Land of Israel. Those who went knew how insecure and economically
unstable Israel was. Its standard of living was below that of any European country where
Jews lived. The land was in a virtual state of anarchy. The Turkish government cared
for little else but collecting taxes; it had neither the will nor the power to establish law
and order. The vocations Jews followed in Europe were unsuitable for primitive, neglected,
and derelict Israel. At that time the entire free and liberal world, and particularly the
United States, was wide open to Jewish immigrants.

Without a Messianic, emotional, and ideological impetus, without the vision of
restoration and redemption, without a yearning for the ancestral land and the dream
of a Jewish State, there was no earthly reason why even oppressed and underprivileged
Jews, second-class citizens in Europe, should wander off to Israel of all places. At that
juncture, indeed, Israel was a land that Christians and to some extent Jews left, not entered.
So when masses of Jews began to migrate in the eighties, most of them went to the United
States.

Aliya to Israel, starting to flow after the "thunders" at the beginning of the eighties,
was set in motion by a Messianic magnetism. The movement had put aside its mystic
exterior, and taken on a rational and pioneering quality, one that called for the most

exacting devotion and did not flinch from difficulty or defeat. The immigrants were seized by an immortal vision of redemption, which became the principal motivation of their lives. The vision was clearly, comprehensively, yet succinctly defined by Zeev Dubnov, who had come with the Biluists on September 21, 1882, and gone to work at Mikve Israel. Writing to his brother, the historian, in November 1882, he said:

> Do you think the purpose of my coming here is to solve my own problems? And that if I do, I attain my object, and if not, I am to be pitied? No! My ultimate purpose, and the purpose of so many others, is magnificent, far-reaching, and sublime, but not unattainable. It is to seize the Land of Israel in the course of time and give the Jews back the national independence they were robbed of two thousand years ago. Do not laugh! This is not a daydream.
>
> The means of achieving that end are three: agricultural and artisan settlements; all kinds of workshops and factories; and the constant expansion of both. In short, a sustained effort to bring the Land and all its economy into Jewish ownership. Besides that, we must train our youth and the next generation to use firearms (in wild and uncontrolled Turkey you can do anything!), and then—but here I dream—the glorious day will dawn that Isaiah foretold in his sermons of comfort, and, armed if need be, with a clarion call, we shall proclaim ourselves lords of our ancient Land. It doesn't matter if this day comes only in fifty years, or afterward. You must agree that it is a grand and sublime vision.

In all that was written by Lovers of Zion and Zionists it would be hard to find as penetrating, as compact, yet as exhaustive a definition of the vision of revival as this, privately propounded by a young pioneer eighty years ago. Fewer than a quarter of one percent of world Jewry lived in Israel at the time. The only settlement, then four years old, was still neglected by its founders because of the malarial infection and the stench of the swamps. Zeev's letter encompasses every aspiration and act that, sixty-six years later, almost identically in the manner it describes, led to the reestablishment of the State of Israel. It was this great vision that guided the pioneers and urged on that previous band of brothers, who were born in the Land itself, like Joel Moses Salomon and his friends, or who had come from the exile of Russia and Rumania.

In 1882, 3340 dunams (825 acres) of land was purchased for a new settlement at Ein Hakoré (the Arabic Ayun-Kara) from the brothers Mustapha and Musa al-Dajani. The purchaser was Chaim Amzalek, the British Vice-Consul, acting on behalf of the first ten founders. They were: Zeev Abramovitz of St. Petersburg; Levi Eisenband and Shraga Feivel Heissman of Nikolayev; Judah Leib Hankin, Reuven Yudelevitz, the brothers Zalman David and Zvi Levontin of Kremenchuk; Zvi Feinberg of Simferopol; and the brothers Aaron Mordekhai and Jacob Peretz Freiman of Warsaw. The transaction followed several abortive attempts to buy land elsewhere. In accordance with a previous decision, the place was called Rishon LeZion.

A rich, childless Jew, Zvi Levontin, himself took 1650 dunams and agreed to apportion 360 dunams of it among six poor families, who would pay for it in installments over five years, the proceeds going to build a synagogue in Rishon in his name. The first seventeen settlers consisted of the ten founders plus Isaiah Horovitz, Noah Botoshinski, Eliezer Shalit, Naftali Hillel, Moshe Cohen, Mendel Rozenofski, and Isaac Garberg. Only Hankin had any experience in farming. Hankin, who once traveled around the German villages in Russia and rented land there, brought along three graduates of Mikve—Wolf Leib Grinstein, Saul Hilsner, and Judah Raab.

In the *Jubilee Book* A. M. Freiman observes that "the rules were drawn up on the partnership (commune) pattern; the land was not to be divided, but farmed collectively." Z. D. Levontin, in his *Land of Our Forefathers*, writes that "under the rules I drew up, the land had to be worked in common, every member contributing to the communal exchequer a sum adjusted to the area he owned, and, if he did a communal job, getting a franc and a half a day for his pains." These rules did not last very long.

Newcomers in the first year were Isaac Leib Toporovski of Yekaterinoslav, Moshe Cohen of Poltava, and Benjamin Fein, a Ukrainian brought up in Odessa.

"The site was a bleak wilderness. There was not a hut, not a tree, not a human being, nothing but endless sand dunes and thorn bushes. Everywhere jackals abounded, their mournful howling making the desert night hideous." This appears in *Rishon LeZion 1882–1941*, and was written by David Yudelevitz (who later called himself "Yodeh-Lev-Ish"). There was no water. The spring that gave the place its former name had silted up, and crawled with worms, insects, and leeches. Water was brought from Mikve, but the path was hazardous. Neighboring German farmers advised digging a well on a hillock. The settlers reached a depth of twenty-five meters, but still found no water.

Menashe Merovitch, who came in 1882, speaks of the early days:

> Physical suffering, sleeping on the ground amidst all kinds of snakes and creeping things, a scarcity of water, of decent lodgings and food and, in the end, the rains—all seriously depressed the settlers. No one ventured to set about to build a house or to bring out his family, from uncertainty as to whether the settlement would survive. Garberg was the first to risk living in a tent with his wife and daughter, and the Heissmans followed suit. It needed only one believer to hearten the rest, and that was Hankin, the first to build a house.

The Turkish government forbade such building, but the protection of the British Vice-Consul in Jaffa saved the day. The land was registered in his name, and thanks to that and the good offices of Joseph Krieger, chief interpreter to the Mutessarif of Jerusalem, the obstacle was removed.

Meanwhile the settlers abandoned the dry borehole on the hill. On lower ground they sent a second shaft, only to strike rock forty-six meters down. For twelve days they drilled through the rock, then suddenly felt the drill plunge into a veritable ocean. Water! The cry went up in Yiddish, Russian, even Arabic, and the settlers came running to the well from every direction. They jumped, they danced, they hugged one another, they wept like babies. The air rang and resounded with an exploding clamor: "Hurrah, hurrah, water!!"

Barely a fortnight after its foundation Joseph Feinberg was sent overseas to get help for Rishon. Austria and Germany produced nothing. In Paris he talked with Rabbi Zadok Cohen and Michael Erlanger, who arranged for him to see Baron de Rothschild in September 1882. As Levontin tells it:

> Feinberg won the heart of the great philanthropist. The Baron granted an initial subsidy of 30,000 francs and promised more should the need arise, provided ten to fifteen new families were taken in, that Rishon would ask no one else for aid, and would keep his support secret. He also undertook to install an artesian well and sent out a horticulturist to sow, plant, and guide the men who were not yet used to farming. He made Hirsch of Mikve Israel manager of his enterprises in the Yishuv. The great philanthropist gives to the Yishuv not as an act of charity, but *as a great Jew who wishes to build up the Land of his forefathers* through a widespread development of Jewish settlement.

Here are words going to the very heart of a momentous and historic truth. Roth-schild, rightly called the Father of the Yishuv, was not merely a munificent philanthropist, although he gave more to the Yishuv than any other Jew, perhaps more than all Jewry put together up to the reestablishment of the State. No, Israel and its agriculture were not for him simply an object of benevolence. This French scion of the Rothschilds, financial giants of contemporary Europe, was spurred by the vision of his people restored to their ancestral Homeland. Till his dying day that vision guided him.

He was neither the first nor the only man to have such a vision, but he was the first and only one to carry through patiently such a great enterprise, using his immense wealth and showing unwearying dedication. There was no public preaching, no seeking of sup-port from strangers. The start was humble; the end was vast. From helping one or two embryo settlements, he advanced to the founding of new ones. He bought land up and down the country, west and east of the Jordan, as part of a far-sighted political strategy, a plan of almost royal proportions. Plainly and from the outset, he defined his ultimate aim. On his first visit to the Land of Israel in 1887, he attested his belief that "we shall yet live to see the Ingathering of the Exiles and all Israel shall dwell securely in its Land."

Rothschild understood what many early settlers failed to understand or forgot: namely, the overwhelming importance of Jewish labor. Ahead of many prominent Zion-ists, he demanded Hebrew education and speech. He opposed the efforts of some settlers to make French culture dominant. As fallible as any mortal, the Baron was not immune to blunders. His greatest mistake was to grant undue power to his officials who some-times tried to turn farmers into slaves. The sturdier ones resisted violently, and there were many "revolts" against the management.

Rumanian Jews Establish Rosh Pina and Zikhron Yacov

The Rumanian Jews were in much the same plight as their Russian brethren, and the Aliya movement that started in Russia at the beginning of the eighties did not pass them by. In 1879 Lawrence Oliphant, who will be remembered as the author of *The Land of Gilead*, which proposed Jewish settlement in Trans-Jordan visited Rumania. This arrival caused a tremendous flutter among the Jews. He also visited Istanbul, attempting unsuccess-fully to win the Turkish government over to his plan. But his links with the Rumanian Jews were enduring: they called him the Second Cyrus and the Delivering Angel.

In 1880 Eliezer Rokah arrived from the Land of Israel and traveled from town to town, appealing to Jews to go to Israel and earn their living there on the land. In Yassy, Rumania, he founded a weekly, *Israel*, to propagate the idea. With Dr. Karpel Lipa, a veteran Lover of Zion who lived in Yassy, Rokah set up the first society for the settle-ment of Israel. A similar society was formed in Bucharest; its president was the local rabbi, Isaac Shor, and its object was to collect money to buy land in Israel and to settle poor but robust Jews on it. Subsequently, well-to-do Jews also came together in Bucharest to buy land in Israel, determined to farm it themselves. The same thing happened in other places.

A conference of all the Hibbat Zion societies in Rumania was held on December 30, 1881, in the hall of the Jewish school of Focsani; fifty-one delegates, representing thirty-two societies, attended the conference. Rabbi Moses Aaron Goldring defined its purposes: to enable Jews exhausted by suffering to go to Zion and labor in its fields and vineyards; to free Jewry from the taunt of Gentiles who said "the sons of Israel are weaklings, all they are good for is making money"; to restore the people's dignity, and reawaken in the heart of the Children of Israel the sanctity that had been weakened by the privation and persecution suffered by the Jews over thousands of years.

The impetus for action came from the Hovevei Zion Society in Moinesti. What Yavnieli says in *The Period of Hibbat Zion* about Russian Aliya is also true of the Rumanian Aliya: "This was the first Zionist Aliya, that is, one which Zionists brought about but did not take part in. They contented themselves with calling for Aliya, they did not lead the immigrants, or journey with them from Russia to the Land of Israel, partaking of their material and spiritual experiences."

In Istanbul, Moses David Shaub, a Rumanian Jew and a founder of Rosh Pina, met with Moses Joseph Rosenzweig, who was born in Safad and later was secretary of Rosh Pina. Rosenzweig gave him a letter to his fellow townsman, Saul Zifris, a young man well versed in the Land and its ways. Sailing on a Russian ship, Shaub reached Beirut in a fortnight. Another Jew was on board, an old man also on his way back to Safad. In Beirut the two hired mules from Arabs for the four-day journey to Safad. As they forded the Kasimiya, the older Jew pointed out the border of Palestine. Shaub dismounted to kiss the earth and, weeping with joy, pronounced the blessing, "Thou has kept us alive till this day." In Safad no hotel, paved road, or bed was to be found. Shaub slept the first night at his uncle's house, on a stony "mattress," for the luxury of wooden or iron bedsteads was unknown in the town.

In Rumania a Safad Jew had told him that Jews had bought land at Jaouneh and called it Gei-Oni. He went to see it and found three rough Arab-type fellah dwellings: two of them were occupied by two poor Jewish brothers and their families who did not farm; in the other was an Arab who tilled part of the land. Shaub surveyed the village and its three springs; the place appealed to him very much. He wrote to his society, but the mails were irregular, there was no telegraph office, and it was more than two months before a reply came.

In the interval the Hibbat Zion Center set up at the Focsani Conference dispatched three representatives of its own—Alter Klepper of Galatz, Salomon Brill, a soil analyst, and Abraham Ezra Friedman, also of Safad, who could speak Arabic. Independently, the Moinesti society sent out David Buchshtater to help Shaub. The search for land continued for over eight months, as negotiations back and forth with Moinesti were protracted. Finally the decision was made to buy the Jaouneh lands. True, the village was not linked by road to the coastal towns of Haifa and Jaffa, but the excellent air and the pure springs turned the balance.

Now Shaub discovered that the resources of most of the immigrants were inadequate and that some were practically penniless. He recommended that at least for the first year the land be worked in common. Each person, rich or poor, would hand over all he had to an appointed treasurer, while a committee would deal with building houses, assigning tasks, and providing family sustenance. Whatever his means, each would share in the field work and be paid for it; the area would be divided equally. Six dissenting householders got their money back and departed. Everybody else agreed and a committee of six was elected: Mordekhai Motel Katz, chairman and treasurer; Shaub, secretary; and

Enoch Hanih Bergman, David Buchshtater, Israel Goldenberg, Daniel Bendel, members. The Sephardi Rabbi Jacob Hai was made honorary president and his brother Isaac Morde-khai an honorary member; both were very helpful in the purchase of the land.

One of the rules was this: "Each person must do whatever work the committee assigns him: disobedience is punishable if a majority of the committee so decrees. At six A.M. (European time) or noon (Turkish time) every person shall go out to his work and stay at it until the corresponding hour of evening, with a midday break of two hours." In his memoirs Shaub confesses that this collective social regime soon broke down, "for the idea has not yet taken hold and those who know the history of the Yishuv will be familiar with many of the other factors that caused it to fail."

The farmers went out to plough for the first time on the second day of the Hebrew month of Tevet 1883. The first rains were late, so they chose that second day to mark the birth of the settlement.

The venturesomeness of the men of Moinesti had its repercussions in Rumania; two hundred and twenty-eight immigrants from Galatz soon embarked for Israel on a ship of the Austrian Lloyd Line. But the Turkish ban on Jewish immigration was still enforced, and the passengers were forbidden to disembark. They cruised about for three months, changing from ship to ship, shuttling from Haifa to Jaffa, to Alexandria, to Beirut. But at long last, by dint of guile or bribes, and intercession in Haifa and Jaffa, all got ashore. Most of the Moinesti people gathered in Safad, ready to found a settlement on the land already bought at Jaouneh. A few families stayed in Haifa, intending to buy land in the neighborhood. They had many offers of all kinds, but the land that attracted them, whose very name won their hearts, was in Samaria. Even before they saw it, they loved it.

Haifa, in 1882, was no more than a village. Its center was a market place and a dimly lit street of shops. There was no harbor, no breakwater. Ships anchored far out in the bay. Between Haifa and the German colony were derelict fields through which a dirt track passed. After the immigrants had gone through hell in the hostel of Abraham Yossel Morgenstern, they moved to rented rooms in the Khan Zahlan, an inn of unplastered masonry; there were no beds, they just slept on the bare tiled floor.

In the same November of 1882, these families in Haifa had a crucial offer of the land the Arabs called Zamarin, in Samaria. In Arabic Zamarin means a beautiful spring, but its origin is undoubtedly Samaria, and for a number of years the place was called Shomron in the Hebrew and Yiddish press. The immigrants were represented in the negotiations by a Bacau Jew who had settled in Haifa several years before—Samuel Igner, nicknamed Watchmaker from his trade, and he undertook the assignment without fee.

The land stretched over the crest of a hill in the Carmel range. Much was scrub and little of it arable; an area in the plain below at Tantura belonged to the same owner, M. Germain, French Consul in Haifa. Besides Zamarin village, the land up for sale included Darkuma on the western hillside, with two mud-clay huts on the top, and beyond that Zamarin it-self, with about ten similar huts, already in ruins. The whole came to 5000 dunams, of which barely a fifth was fit for field crops. Haifa was only 8 hours away by wagon or horseback, a very special virtue in the eyes of the immigrants. So they decided to send two men to inspect the property: Moses Gorland and Mordekhai Kleister, who rode out one day with an Arab guide and came back the next.

The group assembled in a room of the Khan: there was utter silence, rapt attention. "What shall we say, what shall we tell you?" Kleister dramatically wound up his report, "There are thousands of olive trees on the site, I saw them myself." "And I saw a tree flowing with honey," Gorland added. You could hear our hearts thumping: so it was foul slander what people had said of the Land, that it was derelict and barren. Moses spoke the truth and his Torah is true: "A land flowing with milk and honey." This will be your inheritance, and no other. Quickly a bargain was struck on the purchase price, with the extra bit at Tantura—47,000 francs, besides 5000 francs for expenses.

Particulars were cabled to the Central Committee in Galatz: it approved and the money was remitted. In a very few days the transaction was completed, and the deeds of sale were registered in the name of the Chairman of the Committee, Isaac Loebl.*

One settler, Yerachmiel Halperin, wrote in his diary:

On Monday, December 6, 1882, we went up to the colony of Shomron and settled in four Arab houses. We found the soil too rock-strewn to plough, and had first to gather up all the stones and clear the land for tilling. We tried our best to discover the tree Gorland solemnly vowed he had seen with his own eyes, a tree dripping honey. Unhappily, we never did, nor were we lucky enough to track down Kleister's thousands of olive trees. We found only a few wild ones in the wood.

Isaac Goldstein recounts:

On the first day of Hanukah, a few of us went out to our land with an Arab guide. The sight of a forbidding cliff dismayed us: a steep narrow track wound between the thorns and crags. Sitting down in our weariness, we munched the crusts we had brought. Suddenly a snake wriggled into our midst. It was soon followed by scorpions, rats, and all manner of crawling and creeping things. We were frightened and discouraged.

And here is Batia Leibman's story:

Men, women, and children crowded together into a wagon and set off. There were no highways then and the journey took the entire day. At nightfall we were at the foothills of Samaria. We did not speak the language, and so, though dying of thirst, could not ask for water from passers-by. We were blanketed in darkness. Our oxen would go no further. Two of our menfolk began to slash the thick thorn bushes with hatchets, urging the beasts ahead, and we women, babes in our arms, followed. We ran that grim gauntlet for hours, a murky pall and a deathly stillness all about us. Only the howling of jackals broke the silence. Thanks to our livestock, we safely made the hilltop, to be welcomed joyfully by comrades who had made the perilous ascent before us. They sat round a fire and we sat beside them, to warm our frozen limbs and relieve our thirst and hunger.

The settlers soon realized that things were not as bad as they seemed at first. In the spring of 1883 Meir Hirsh Haifler writes to a friend:

We have been working now for three weeks and, thank God, already see the results of our labors; the wheat is sprouting finger-high. When you come here and see the mountain facing you, you may be alarmed, but once you climb it your heart is gladdened by a vista of pleasant fields, and bracing air, healthful and wholesome—there is nothing to equal it. Our drinking water is far better than Haifa's, sweet where that is salty. What do we lack? We have lots of trees, plenty of stones to build houses with and timber for every purpose. We have already ploughed several fields to sow potatoes, and next week are going to lay out a vegetable plot in Tantura.

* Arieh Samsonov, *Zikhron Yacov, a Chapter of History, 1882–1940*, pp. 56–58.

Major Goldsmid, who visited the place in its first year, wrote in the London *Jewish Chronicle:* "I was greatly taken by the settlement of Samaria where I stopped two days. Many parts of it, at the outset thought unlikely to do well, are yielding wheat and barley and all kinds of oil-seeds. There is a good track to Haifa, where the women and children are living until the sixty new houses are built."

At the end of 1883, Rothschild also took Zamarin under his wing, and two years later his agent suggested it be renamed Zikhron Yacov, after the Baron's father. Naturally, the farmers agreed.

Striking Roots in a New Settlement in Upper Galilee

A group dedicated to the creation of a village in the Land of Israel was established in 1883 by Jews of Mazritz, Poland, and Brisk, Lithuania. The moving spirit of the Field and Vineyard Society was Baruch Meir Rosenblum. In 1883 Leib Rubin was sent to the Land of Israel with 1000 rubles ($500) to purchase land for the society. He visited the four existing settlements (Petah Tikva, Rishon LeZion, Zikhron Yacov, and Rosh Pina). Rosh Pina particularly appealed to him. He wanted to buy land in the vicinity, but the farmers there told him that they intended to buy that land and suggested that the members of his society settle in Rosh Pina.

Since he had been sent to establish a new settlement, he widened his search to the area of the Huleh. He spent five months fruitlessly looking for a suitable plot. Meanwhile the members of the society in Mazritz had heard that Fischel Salomon was about to leave for the Land of Israel, and so they authorized him to join Leib Rubin in the search for land. That same year a plot of 2500 dunams (625 acres) was acquired for 5000 rubles. The people in Mazritz were informed and came to the country after the holidays. They were Shabtai Klarman, Joseph Gadulter, Chaim Minshensky, Avraham Feldman, Yehezkel Zamir, Meir Zonblum, and Zeev Becker. They were joined by two others, one a member of the Mizrahi family of Safad, and the other an immigrant from the United States, Leib Leibovski. They called the place Yesod Hamaala.

Differences of opinion developed between the two emissaries. Rubin thought they should not begin work in the village until they received official authorization from the Turkish authorities, while Fischel insisted that they begin work immediately, since the required permits would be received eventually. Rubin refused to yield. When his approach was rejected, he left for Russia, never to return to the Land of Israel. None of the seven immigrants had any previous agricultural experience, but Salomon obtained a visa for a young agricultural expert named Israel Ashkenazi, who came to the country together with Salomon's family. On his arrival the work began. The settlers planted citron, pomegranate, olive, and fig trees. A well was dug and water discovered quite near the surface.

The residents of nearby Safad warned the settlers that their plot was not favorably located. The Huleh swamp was nearby, and the children of the Bedouin in the area suffered from malaria. But the settlers would not listen; they regarded the warnings as slander. The newcomers had no homes. They settled in a large old barn that they called Beit Haotzar. It was twenty-five meters by ten. The building was not in good condition, but when they tried to repair it, they were pestered by government officials. Only after the usual bribes had been given were they left alone. The same structure housed the men and their work animals. The women and children remained in Safad. Enormous man-eating fleas infested the building, but to sleep outside was impossible because of the cold and rain. Finally, the fleas drove the men out of the building. They put up straw huts for themselves, leaving the animals inside.

Israel Ashkenazi, the only agricultural expert in the settlement, wrote:

> One Friday all the men went to Safad and only Mendel Feldman and myself remained to take care of the oxen. As usual, we took off our clothes and went into one of the sheds to tie up the oxen. At that moment one of them ran away. We chased after it for three kilometers before we were able to catch it and bring it back. We returned to the settlement cut up and bleeding, as we had pursued the animal through fields of shoulder-high thorn bushes. When we got back, after darkness, we found that all the other oxen had run away. Fortunately I recalled something I had learned in Russian villages. I put my ear to the ground and listened. Sure enough, I heard the oxen in the distance and was able to find them and bring them back.

The first long-awaited harvest finally began at Yesod Hamaala. The settlers had brought scythes with them from Russia, but they were without handles. Moreover, the villagers discovered that no handles were to be found in Safad. Ashkenazi took several of the more enterprising men with him to the other side of the Huleh, where there was a tree that could provide wood for scythe handles. They cut the wood and, with great difficulty, carried it home. Ashkenazi fashioned the handles and then went to Safad, where, after wandering up and down innumerable alleyways, he finally obtained the necessary iron rings for the handles. Thus the scythes were ready for the harvest. Ashkenazi returned to Yesod Hamaala and taught the men the art of harvesting. On Saturday night, they left for the fields, where they lived the entire week in a tent, returning to Safad for the Sabbath.

For two years the families endured the "Beit Haotzar" and the straw huts; still there was no building permit. Ashkenazi went to see what kind of dwellings were inhabited by the Bedouin living in the Huleh plain. He discovered that they lived in huts made of reeds and papyrus, both readily available in the Huleh. He watched long enough to learn how to build such huts himself.

The next morning he rose at dawn and walked to the Huleh. He cut down reeds, grasses, and papyrus, and tied them in bundles. While he was at work, Fischel Salomon arrived from Safad. "What are you doing?" he asked. After Israel had explained, Salomon suggested that they work together. Ashkenazi agreed. They decided to build a reed hut for every settler. Obtaining a boat from a Safad Jew, they loaded it up and, with great difficulty, took the cargo through the swamp to the village. But they also needed trees for supports. Some distance away, on the eastern side of the Jordan, there was a grove with high trees. Though the path to the grove was dangerous because Bedouin robbers operated in the vicinity, the villagers crossed the Jordan, cut down a number of trees, loaded them on their backs, and returned to the settlement. There they put up the new huts. A government official came by and started to interfere. He pointed out that the settlers had no license to build the huts. A bribe silenced his protests, however, and the work was successfully completed. The settlers finally had a place in which to rest and sleep.

During their first years, the villagers lived in terrible conditions. Their requests for help to the Hovevei Zion Society in Russia went unanswered. Their attempt to attain legal title to the land was unsuccessful.

When Rothschild came to Rosh Pina on May 1, 1887, the farmers from Yesod Hamaala asked for his help. Rothschild ordered their request to be written up and put in his briefcase, so that he could study it on his return to Paris.

Rothschild's intention was to go on horseback to Damascus, crossing the Jordan River on his way. He was accompanied by Ben-Mishol, his representative in Rosh Pina, Dr. Bleiden, the Rosh Pina doctor, and the doctor's wife. On his way to the Bnot Yacov Bridge, he saw the expanses of Huleh. "This is a magnificent place," the Baron said to Ben-Mishol. "On the right I can see the Kinneret, and on the left I can see the Huleh. Listen, this plain must be purchased in its entirety, just as it is." And when he saw the huts of the settlers of Yesod Hamaala, he asked: "Who lives there?" "That is a settlement of Jewish pioneers called Yesod Hamaala," Dr. Bleiden said. "They are Jews from Poland who settled there three years ago, and until this very day they live in those wretched huts." The Baron made a wide sweep with his hand. "This entire plain must belong to them," he declared. He turned to Ben-Mishol and told him to take care of the Yesod Hamaala settlers.

Assistance arrived promptly. In a letter of June 20, 1880, to Dr. Pinsker, head of the Hovevei Zion, Ben-Mishol announced that he had already succeeded in obtaining legal title to the Yesod Hamaala lands for the settlers, and that he would help them get farm animals and agricultural implements. In addition, he had received part of the money needed to build houses for them, and was certain that he would get the rest from the Baron.

The Yesod Hamaala settlers began to plant citrus and almond groves, other fruit trees, and vineyards. The project was directed by Yehoshua Assowetzki, a representative of Baron de Rothschild. One of the Baron's other representatives, Bachor El-Hadif, became so enchanted with the place that he sold his lands in Petah Tikva and Jaffa and invested all his money in Yesod Hamaala. This was also done by another one of the Baron's agents, Warhaftig (Amitai), who remained in Yesod Hamaala the rest of his life.

The suffering undergone in the early years had fostered cooperation among the settlers. "It was our custom," one of them said, "that when Farmer A finished work before Farmer B, Farmer A would go over to help Farmer B." This same relationship existed between the Jewish settlers and their Arab neighbors. In normal circumstances, the Arabs reciprocated. "When one farmer needed something, another would hasten to supply it. When one did not feel well enough to go out to plough, another would quickly plough his neighbor's field." In the same way, the farmers supplied animals and seeds to the nearby Arabs. "When the people at Yesod Hamaala obtained harvesters, they also helped to harvest the fields of the Arabs, and did it for nothing." This generous assistance helped reduce Arab attacks on the village.

One of the Yesod Hamaala elders, Shimon Bar-Gadolter, told his son Alter on his deathbed: "Please promise me that you will always do your best to help Ali Mahmud al-Auma and Saliman Abu-Ali, who gave us supplies when we were in difficult straits. Moreover, when they felt we were ashamed to receive their help, they would sneak by and throw food into our tents so that we would have something to eat."

The Huleh swamp served to spread malaria among the settlers at Yesod Hamaala. At first, the disease was little known. As time passed, it claimed more and more victims, particularly among the children. There was no doctor in the village. After the Baron transferred the management of the settlements he was helping to the JCA (The Alliance), its director, Emile Meyerson, came to the settlers and suggested that they abandon the village. He told them:

> The most difficult problem is the health situation. At first, the Baron thought that the planting of eucalyptus trees would help reduce the malaria. But a careful investigation showed that this was not the case. The very large swamp to the north of your village extends over an area of tens of thousands of dunams, and cannot be compared to the deadly swamps at Hadera. Here there is no hope of changing the situation, and therefore it is my sincere suggestion that you accept the JCA proposal and abandon the village. Some of you will be able to settle in other villages in this country. As for the rest, those who want compensation will receive it; and those who want to remain in farming will be sent, at JCA expense, to Argentina, where they will be given excellent conditions.

When the Baron's representative had finished speaking, a deathly silence reigned in the room. The villagers were as white as ghosts. Suddenly, Fischel Salomon turned to the agent and declared:

> My dear Mr. Meyerson, we came here before the great philanthropist, and did so in response to God's command. The Baron has given us much assistance, and in so doing fulfilled his sacred duty to his people and his land. If he wants to continue helping us, he should by all means do so; if he doesn't want to, so be it. But we will not be moved—not by the JCA, nor by the Baron, but only by God himself, who brought us here. No human being will move us from this place.

Again there was a heavy silence in the room. Finally Meyerson asked: "What do the rest of you think?" Moshe Amitai (Warhaftig), Michael David Grinker, and David Eisenberg immediately rose and said: "Our comrade, Mr. Salomon, has already given you our answer."

Meyerson announced that he would send them the official JCA decision. After a few days the settlers received notification that the JCA had decided to eliminate several of the groves, particularly the citrus grove where hired workers were employed. The workers were given severance pay. Three of those who did not want to leave (Aharon Orenstein, Mordekhai Stern, and Yehuda Barazani) remained as farmers on their own plots of land. The other JCA assistance to the settlers—such as health services, guards, a midwife, a ritual slaughterer, etc.—was continued, and indeed the field crops branch was even enlarged. A year later Fischel Salomon told one of the farmers: "When Meyerson made his statement at the meeting, we were afraid that we would be taken away by force. But remembering the face, and particularly the shining eyes, of our brother, Baron de Rothschild, I was not worried. I thought to myself that such a person would not destroy with his own hands what he had built up with so much love and devotion."

The situation continued as it was until the First World War. Then the Turks turned over the Huleh, which was government land, to the prominent Turkish Sursik family.

The Huleh concession was purchased by the Jewish National Fund in 1935. After the establishment of the State of Israel, the Huleh swamp was drained. As a result, the entire area from the edge of the Kinneret to Israel's northern border became the most fertile section of the country.

The Question of Jewish Labor in the First Settlements

Bitter and frequent were the birth pangs of farm settlement in Israel. Plagues of nature, the desolation of the terrain, Arab enmity, corrupt Turkish administrators, antagonism from the zealots of the "old Yishuv" in Jerusalem, the agricultural ignorance of all but a few settlers, the unsatisfactory representatives of Rothschild—all this, and much else, almost ruined daring pioneering undertakings. No one today can even begin to comprehend the grand sweep of purpose, the vision, the dedication, demanded of those pathfinders. They arrived with the fixed aim of altering their whole way of life in the Land of Israel, of remaking the laws of nature, of creating everything anew. Many fell by the wayside, many returned to the lands of exile. But it was their bold pioneering initiative that opened a new chapter in Jewish history.

They did not aspire just to be landowners. No. They meant to *work the land* as well as own it. The idea of Jewish labor was not conceived by the Second Aliya, which only began in 1904, twenty-two years after the Bilu. The men who settled in Petah Tikva, Rishon, Zikhron, Rosh Pina, and preeminently the Biluists, were resolved to live by their own toil and sweat. The ideal had two facets—land and labor. A recurring motif was "to work the soil and defend it." Many immigrants, penniless on arrival, kept themselves entirely, at all events to begin with, by working in the settlements as hired help. Biluists became craftsmen and factory hands in Jerusalem, as we have seen; Zeev Dubnov and others like him were far-sighted enough to realize that trade and industry must be fostered as well as agriculture. They even envisaged military service. The idea of cooperation and of the commune was not foreign to them, though early attempts to put it into practice failed.

But soon the single concept of working the soil split into two: soil on the one hand and work on the other. More and more labor was hired in the settlements, especially as plantations expanded. Rothschild's emphasis on the importance of Jewish labor, his desire that the farmers employ Jews, did not prevent the number of Arab laborers from constantly expanding. They were cheaper, more docile, more experienced. The controversy over Jewish labor, the foundation stone of resettlement and reconstruction, was fiercer than the conflict over Jewish farming. Rokah to Lilienblum in 1887:

> This year many of our young brethren came to the Holy Land, talented men with a background in both sacred and secular learning, and all they wanted, for the moment, was to work the beloved soil as day laborers. They formed a Workers' Society, planning that its committee should keep looking for jobs, so that, if possible, no member would be unemployed; any members out of work would get a little assistance. All would live as a unit and cook and eat together, and so save a great deal. Everybody knows that they did not come to the Holy Land simply to subsist, but out of a spirit of idealism.★

Rehovot, founded in 1890 and needing no subsidy from the Baron, became the center of Jewish labor. A. Z. Levin Epstein, the guiding spirit, describes the prevailing attitudes toward Jewish and Arab workers.

★ *Notes on the History of Hibbat Zion*, Part II, pp. 132–133.

In the Baron's settlements—and there were virtually no others then—the labor force was numerous. Not only the Baron's managers but the farmers too needed and used hired labor, for dependent as they were upon the Baron, they had to keep their costs down and employed cheap Arab labor to that end. The agents, who built and planted on their own account, would also take on a few Jews, that being the Baron's wish. They could not understand that the Baron genuinely aspired to carry out a grandiose plan to rebuild Israel for Jews, by Jews, and with Jewish labor. But if the Baron deliberately wanted Jews to work, they said, let his wish be "slightly" obeyed! . . .

But we members of "Haven and Home," who founded Rehovot, because among other reasons we wanted to show the Baron how to build a *Jewish* settlement, decided to employ as many Jews as we could. First of all, I invited all who were on the lookout for jobs elsewhere to come and work with us. They were even willing to sleep out of doors, under the stars, so long as they could work in Rehovot. And so they did. They were content, far more than you can imagine, to be among people who valued their labor and devotion. By the summer of 1891 as many as five hundred Jews were working in Rehovot every day, and in that season alone almost five thousand passed through. Some did not stay at all, some stayed only a few days, but on any given day there were always five hundred there.*

As the stream of Aliya swelled, the hired hands in Rehovot and many Yishuv leaders made an attempt to unite all Jewish workers into a body called "Land and Labor." Among its founders were Meir Dizengoff and Aaron Eisenberg. The preamble to the rules gives clear and cogent expression to certain ideas which afterward guided the Second Aliya and its successors:

A. Some of the first settlers came here with funds, some empty-handed, but all came to work. It makes no difference that their early efforts, as was natural and unavoidable, did not go well.

B. Last year produced something novel for the Yishuv. Men of means abroad began to buy land here and develop it, not, however, by their own exertions, but by the investment of money. This has converted the Yishuv into a species of merchandise. Sweat and toil link creation with creator in a bond that cannot be snapped without danger to life itself. But the bond between money and merchandise is a loose knot that can be easily undone. These men of property will never enable us to attain the ultimate end of increasing the number of Jewish farmers on the soil of the Holy Land.

C. Without Jewish workers the settlements cannot exist; Arab workers cannot be depended upon. Jewish workers are the lifeblood of the Yishuv. They will protect it from decay and dissolution.

But these fine ideals did not strike roots in the Yishuv, either among the farmers or, surprisingly, among many workers who boycotted Jewish labor on becoming farmers in their own right.

When Rothschild visited Israel in 1899, he pleaded with the farmers to employ Jews in their vineyards: "Each man should help his brother: remember you were once poor yourself; do not forget your brethren and give work only to others." But they would not listen. In 1900, on the transfer of his "subsidized" villages—only Rehovot fell outside that category—to the Jewish Colonization Association, there were 532 workers' families all told. For that year, we have the very first census of Jewish workers in the

---

* *Memoirs*, pp. 152–162.

settlements taken by an official of the Workers' Federation that preceded the Second Aliya, A. Komaroff of Nes Ziona. In the twelve settlements he found 473 workers: Zikhron 161, 81 of them in the wine cellars, where for reasons of *kashrut** the exclusive employment of Jews was mandatory; Rishon 103, 80 of them also in the wine cellars; Petah Tikva 52; Rosh Pina 40; Ekron 25; Rehovot 22; Hadera 20; Nes Ziona 16; Yesod Hamaala 14; Metulla 12; Mahanayim 4; and Mishmar Hayarden 4.

A. S. Hirshberg speaks of a visit to Israel in 1901:

> The attitude of the settlers toward the Jewish workers does the former little credit. Almost all prefer the Arabs for jobs a Jew could easily do, because the Jewish worker is rather brusque toward his Jewish employer. Besides, the Jewish farmer can hardly impose on a fellow Jew menial tasks outside the province of his "agricultural" duty. At first, the settlers were forced to use Jews for some work, such as pruning and grafting, for which special skills were necessary. But the Arabs gradually learned these skills as well and the Jews were ousted again.

In 1912 Ahad Ha'am, the most lucid and penetrating intellect of Hibbat Zion, came to Israel for the third time and studied conditions in the settlements as they had evolved over thirty years. The resulting essay he called "The Sum-Total":

> ... not of exact numbers of specific sets, but of my deepest impressions, formed in the sixty days I was steeped in the atmosphere of our national effort, living it and thinking only of it: ten days in Basle, for the Tenth Zionist Congress, and the next fifty days in the Land of Israel.
>
> Naturally, one's heart exults to behold the great progress in most of the settlements. This is all well and good so long as you regard the Yishuv as something to love for its own sake. But when you remember the political objective, the first paragraph of the Basle program, your optimism seeps away, and everything seems cold, bleak, and discouraging. For how does all this contribute to the establishment of a safe refuge? An upper class of farmers such as these, dependent on alien labor, cannot do so.
>
> A State is founded on its rural proletariat, laborers and farmers, earning a bare livelihood by their own toil, on their own small holdings or on estates of the upper class. No rural proletariat yet exists in Israel, and it is difficult for us to foresee how it will emerge, even if settlements proliferate in every corner of the Land. It is common knowledge that most of the work in our settlements is done by fellahin from surrounding Arab villages, some on daily wages, others employed on a permanent basis and living in the settlement itself with their wives and children. All these are working together with us to make a "safe refuge"! If the number of settlements is to rise, it will be because capitalists will establish more "rich" villages of the present type. Settlements for peasant farmers can only be established by public institutions and in very restricted numbers, negligible compared with the necessity to create a rural proletariat who will till the Land and conquer it with its labor.
>
> We must therefore resign ourselves to the idea that the agrarian community of Israel, even if it be expanded in the course of time to its very limit, will always be an "upper class" element, a cultured minority, strong only in intellect and capital. The rural proletariat, the majority, will still be lacking. This radically alters the quality and purpose of Zionism.**

---

* Ritual preparation of kosher food, in this case wine. —EDITORS
** *Collected Works of Ahad Ha'am*, pp. 421–425.

Ahad Ha'am was right in assuming that without Jewish labor to tackle every task, simple or difficult, there could be no Jewish State, or, as they termed it in Zionist Congress jargon, no "safe refuge." But what he did not grasp was that this assumption also ran counter to his own concept of spiritual Zionism. How could there be "a national spiritual center for Jewry, a center of learning and wisdom, of language and literature, of physical effort and purity of soul, a true microcosm of the people of Israel as it ought to be," as he defined his own beliefs? How could there be such a center in the "upper-class" Yishuv of a cultured minority that relied on the labor of a working-class majority belonging to another race? How could a settlement be "marked by the stamp of Jewry and enveloped in the nation's aura" if alien hands did its work, if most of its workers were non-Jews? What content, what virtue, moral or cultural, national or human, could there be in an upper class of farmers who live on the labor of strangers? Is that minority not doomed to moral and cultural decay, perhaps also to physical and political extinction?

"Insofar as one is capable of predicting events in the light of contemporary reality, one is bound to conclude that practical work in Israel is not likely to bring about redemption," Ahad Ha'am writes in a supplement to "The Sum-Total." "If, nevertheless, we see that this kind of work has such a powerful appeal, this only proves that it is, in fact, connected with some other goal to which, wittingly or not, people are attracted. That goal is not a safe refuge for the people of Israel, but a permanent center for Israel's spirit."★

If events had followed the course that Ahad Ha'am had predicted, there would have been neither a Jewish State nor a spiritual center. Luckily, Ahad Ha'am was wrong. And that was not his only mistake. The great philosopher of Hibbat Zion was a shrewd observer, but imagination and vision were not among his virtues. He did not perceive a people's capacity to respond to historic needs which can turn any current reality upside down.

Even the people who saw the birth of Petah Tikva were largely skeptical of the need for or the possibility of modifying current reality. They never considered that Jewish agriculture could become permanent. But Joel Moses Salomon of Jerusalem, Joshua Stampfer, Eliezer Raab, and David Guttmann of Hungary—men of vision and resolution —saw beyond current reality and founded Petah Tikva. Troubles bedeviled them; they retreated for a time, but went back and carried on. The Biluists were men of the same breed. Netter's matter-of-fact analysis, which also was based on current reality, did not deter them. They, too, saw beyond it. To their far-sightedness Zeev Dubnov whom I have already quoted, gave classic form in a letter to his brother Simon, and the facts of the next sixty-six years confirm it entirely and in every detail.

In those first years of the twentieth century what did the pioneers of the Second Aliya, bearing the banner of labor in their hands, find in the Land of Israel?

There were no Zionist funds. The Jewish National Fund had yet to begin work and no one dreamt of labor colonization. The ideas of self-labor and national ownership of the soil had still to gain currency, even among the workers themselves. All twenty-five settlements stood for unadulterated private enterprise, for private property and hired labor, though most of their capital came not from individual colonists but from Jewry in general or from Jews who gave magnificently for the common good, as did Baron de Rothschild, and though the hired labor was virtually all non-Jewish.

★ *Ibid.*, p. 429.

The following passage gives a brief but comprehensive survey of how things were at the onset of the Second Aliya:

> The Jewish settlements have swallowed up 90 million francs, and almost the whole of this gigantic sum, except for cash left with the managers, has filled Arab pockets. Part of it, the payment for land and building materials, was of course bound to feed other people's incomes—we had not come here to grab. But the lion's share went to enrich others, not by force but voluntarily. It is not overstating the case to say that 45 million francs passed to Arabs in wages alone! Today we have about a thousand farmers, and each furnishes a livelihood for an average of three Arab families, so that Arabs are getting close on a million francs year after year from us for their work. Out of all this colossal sum nothing comes back to us, for the Arab has no need to buy from the urban Jew and everything he gets in the settlement he takes home. Every Jewish farmer added to our number means sustenance and livelihood for three extra Arab families. . . . *Let Israel clearly know that Jewish landlords will never restore the land to Israel unless there be Jewish workers.*

No member of the Second Aliya wrote this, but a veteran of the Yishuv, himself a farmer, an early settler in Rehovot—Moshe Smilansky.

The men of the First Aliya, founders of Mikve Israel, Petah Tikva, Rishon, Rosh Pina, Zikhron, Yesod Hamaala, Gedera, Rehovot, Hadera, and Metulla, differed widely in education, in values, and in cultural background from most of the men in the Second Aliya. More than once, confronting each other in hostile camps, they clashed. But deep down in their hearts, they were one and the same; the selfsame revolutionaries and men of action. Men whom no reality can subjugate, no difficulty daunt. Their spirit is alive and responsive to great ideas and the challenge of the future.

Section 3. The Balfour Declaration and the Birth of the State

Pure Political Zionism and Zionism through Immigration and Settlement

ON NOVEMBER 2, 1917, the day on which the Balfour Declaration was promulgated, I was in American exile with my friend Yitzhak Ben-Zvi. In 1915 we had been expelled "forever" from the Ottoman Empire, which included the Land of Israel, by order of Turkish dictator Kemal Pasha. I had never previously been in England. All I knew about the Jews of that country was what I had learned from Jewish history. The most famous and distinguished Jew of the nineteenth century, Moses Montefiore, had been knighted by Queen Victoria. Benjamin Disraeli, one of the greatest nineteenth-century British statesmen, was a Jew who, though baptized as a child, always remained proud of his Jewish heritage. And I knew that Britain was a free and democratic country, where the Jews were not persecuted as they were in the land of my birth, Russian Poland.

A few days after the publication of the Balfour Declaration, which made an enormous impression on the Jews of America, I published an article on the Declaration in *Der Yiddische Kempfer*, the Labor Zionist weekly in the United States. The article, which appeared on November 14, 1917, stated, *inter alia:*

England has not given us back the Land of Israel. It is at this very moment, when we feel joy at the great victory, that we must make it very clear: *England cannot give us back the Land of Israel.* This is not because the country is not, or not yet, under her control. Even after England exercises sovereignty over the entire Land of Israel, from Beersheba to Dan, it will not become ours simply because that is her desire, not even if all the other countries of the world agree as well. *A land can be won by a people only through their own efforts and creativity, their building and settlement.*

England has done a great deal: she has recognized our existence as a political entity and our right to the country. *The Jewish people must now transform this recognition into a living reality,* by investing their strength, spirit, energy, and capital in building a National Home and achieving full national salvation.

My article was not well received by the majority of American Zionists. At the time, they regarded the Balfour Declaration not as the beginning, but as almost the culmination of Zionism. The American Zionist movement, headed by Louis D. Brandeis—who was both a Supreme Court Justice and a close friend of President Woodrow Wilson— had already been expanding before the Declaration. Its leaders thought that I had belittled the importance of the victory. In my introduction to a second article, published on November 26, 1917, I expressed my concern about how the Zionist program was being carried out in the following words:

We have taken a giant step forward, quickly traversing a long and difficult road that we thought would require much more time and many more sacrifices. Zionist realization is now on the agenda. *It is the great responsibility that we now face.*

We must bring back the people of Israel to the Land of Israel. History will not wait. A non-Jewish Land of Israel waited for 1800 years for Jews. A Land of Israel promised to the Jewish people cannot wait over eighteen years for Jews. We must create a Jewish majority in the Land of Israel in the next twenty years. That is the central issue in this new historical situation.

In the third article, published at the beginning of January 1918, I wrote:

From a political viewpoint, we have been granted our national desire. The declaration issued by the English will soon be ratified by other peoples. We are still confronted by crucial challenges, but not in that sphere. The Zionist task vis-à-vis the outside world has, in a very basic sense, been completed. The question of the link between the people of Israel and the Land of Israel, and the question of revitalizing the ancient Jewish Homeland, has been placed on the world's agenda and will never be removed until the problem is solved to the benefit of the Jewish people, as historical justice demands.

Zionism now has a second task, which is *more important, more serious, and more difficult:* putting Zionist realization on the agenda of every individual Jew; *connecting the creation of a Homeland with the fate of the Jewish masses.*

Zionism must now look inward, focusing on the Jewish people. Every material and spiritual resource must now be devoted to the urgent and demanding task of *building* a Homeland.

Looking back, fifty years after the publication of the Balfour Declaration, I must say regretfully that the Zionist leadership of that period, which was undoubtedly a great period in the history of the Jewish people, did not pay proper attention to the main, internal task.

Dr. Chaim Weizmann, through whose political efforts and personal magnetism the Balfour Declaration was obtained, had opposed the official Zionist leadership since the days of Herzl. As a member of the Democratic faction, together with Leo Motzkin and others, and in contrast to Herzl, he demanded practical work in the Land of Israel under all conditions, with or without the approval of the authorities. Herzl initially believed that he would be able to obtain a charter for settlement in the Land of Israel from the Turks, and always opposed infiltration—that is, settlement in violation of Ottoman laws, which prohibited Jewish immigration and permitted visits for only three months. These laws also forbade the purchase of land by non-Turkish Jews. The members of Hovevei Zion ignored these edicts. Emigration to the Land of Israel continued; land was purchased and settled.

The person who did most to foster settlement, as pointed out earlier, was Edmond de Rothschild, justifiably called "the Father of the Yishuv." In contrast, the Zionist Organization did nothing in Israel during the period of Herzl's life. When it despaired of receiving a charter from the Turks, it turned to England, which offered them El Arish and then Uganda. Jews living in Russia opposed the Uganda proposal. Theirs was the most important center of Jewry at that time and the area of greatest Jewish suffering. Only seven years after the First Zionist Congress, Herzl, still a young man, died in 1904 of a broken heart.

Dr. Weizmann had not yet assumed a central role in the Zionist movement. He was constantly aware of the need for labor and settlement, with or without Turkish permission, and was one of the few Zionist leaders who saw the necessity, during the Turkish regime of 1907–1908, of visiting Israel. Although Weizmann was a follower of Ahad Ha'am, and until Hitler's rise to power in 1933 did not see the importance of immigration, he appreciated the value of practical work, particularly of agricultural settlement, alongside the political activity that reached its acme with the Balfour Declaration.

The official Zionist leadership was in Berlin during the First World War. But because the men there were unable to maintain contact with Jewish leaders in Eastern and Western Europe and in the United States, the real center of direction moved to England, where the finest leaders of British Jewry gathered around Weizmann. These included Harry Sacher, Dr. Moses Gaster, Israel Sieff, Joseph Cohen, and Simon Marks. Weizmann made a great impression on Balfour, mainly because Balfour saw him as a Jewish Jew. As an intellectual he was deeply impressed by Weizmann's profound Jewishness. The fact that Weizmann was a distinguished chemist also contributed significantly to obtaining the Balfour Declaration. England's decision, however, was influenced in large, perhaps decisive measure, by international factors: her desire to win the sympathy of American Jewry and that of Russian Jewry after the Bolshevik Revolution.

The Berlin Zionist Executive, elected at the last prewar Zionist Congress in 1913, lost almost all significance when Weizmann became the actual leader of the movement. He aided Vladimir Jabotinsky* importantly in obtaining the agreement of the British government to draft young Jewish citizens of Russia for the Jewish Legion to fight in the Land of Israel. But in the decisive days of the Balfour Declaration, which engendered

* Vladimir Jabotinsky (1880–1940): Zionist leader who in World War One persuaded Britain to recruit Jews to fight on the Palestine front. The resulting force was called the Jewish Legion.—EDITORS

waves of enthusiasm among the Jewish masses, the need of Aliya was almost completely disregarded. The largest Aliya to come in the wake of the Balfour Declaration was, in fact, that of the Jewish Legion from the United States which numbered more than four thousand men. Not all of these Americans remained in Israel after the war, partly because of the apathetic attitude of the Zionist Executive, concentrated then in the Zionist Commission, which went to Israel in 1918. The commission did not offer any assistance to the American volunteers who wished to remain in the Land of Israel.

Even the arrival of a British High Commissioner, Sir Herbert Samuel, himself a Jew, who was received by the Yishuv as a second Babylonian Nehemiah, did not greatly alter the situation. In 1919, a year before he arrived, some eighteen hundred Jews came to the country. In Samuel's first four years the annual immigration numbered scarcely more than eight thousand. Weizmann emphasized agricultural settlement rather than immigration as the most important aspect of Zionist work; he did a great deal for settlement, even after 1931, when the Congress failed to elect him president of the Zionist Organization. More than anyone except Baron Edmond de Rothschild, Weizmann was responsible for the expansion of agricultural settlements, and particularly the labor settlements, in the pre-State period.

Relations with the Mandatory Government Until the End of World War Two

There was a considerable confusion at the time about the borders of the Land of Israel. Even many Zionists thought that Trans-Jordan was not part of Israel. After the San Remo Conference, in April 1920, had ratified the British Mandate over Palestine, in order that a National Home for the Jewish people be established there, the International Union of Labor Zionists presented a memorandum to the British Labour Party. It was prepared by me and signed by Shlomo Kaplansky and myself; we were representatives of the Union in London. It dealt with two matters: the meaning of the term "National Home," and the borders of the Land of Israel. I wrote:

> The British Declaration of November 1917, which was approved by the French government, automatically superseded the border arrangements of 1916, set forth in the Sykes-Picot Treaty. The Balfour Declaration and subsequent international agreements make it clear that the border question must be settled in only one way: the creation of a single economic and political unit within the framework of a Jewish Commonwealth. The basic prerequisite to mass settlement is a just and proper solution to the question of the borders in the North and East.
>
> The Land of Israel is not a large country. It will encompass, within proper borders, 33,000 miles of territory, providing room for hundreds of thousands of suffering Jews. If we are to prepare to absorb most of these Jews within a short period of time, the dimensions of the country cannot be diminished in an arbitrary manner. It is necessary that the water sources, upon which the future of the Land depends, should not be outside the borders of the future Jewish Homeland. The fields of Hauran, which rightfully belong to the country, should not be taken away. For this reason we have always demanded that the Land of Israel

include the southern banks of the Litani River, the headwaters of the Jordan, and the Hauran Region from the El Adja spring south of Damascus. *All of the rivers run from east to west or from north to south.* [Emphasis in the original.] This explains the importance of the Upper Galilee and the Hauran for the entire country. The most important rivers of the Land of Israel are the Jordan, the Litani, and the Yarmuk. The Land needs this water. Moreover, the development of industry depends on water power for the generation of electricity.

The Peace Treaty with Turkey gave Great Britain the Mandate of the Land of Israel, but not in order that it become a British colony. The League of Nations is to retain control until the Jewish Commonwealth can stand on its own feet.*

Of the three parties of the British Parliament, the Labour Party was the friendliest to the Zionist cause and the most faithful to the Balfour Declaration. The heads of the party—Ramsay MacDonald, Arthur Henderson, George Lansbury, and others—were loyal supporters of the Zionist idea. It is extremely strange, therefore, that the most serious and painful attack on the Zionist enterprise took place in 1930 during the second Labour government, headed by the same MacDonald who had published enthusiastic articles praising Zionism after his visit to the Land of Israel in 1922. The Colonial Secretary in the MacDonald government was Sidney Webb, who became Lord Passfield after his elevation to the House of Lords.

After the riots at the Western Wall in Jerusalem in 1929 a number of committees were sent to investigate what had happened. Although the Jews were the only victims of the riots, they were charged with responsibility for them. In 1930 Lord Passfield published a White Paper intended to abrogate the Balfour Declaration and to prevent Jewish immigration. In protest Dr. Weizmann resigned from the presidency of the Zionist Organization.

Perhaps the strangest aspect of this whole affair was that Ernest Bevin caused the White Paper to be withdrawn. Bevin was not himself a member of Parliament, but his union had fifteen representatives in the House of Commons. The Labour Party did not have a Parliamentary majority and was not even the largest party. The Tories enjoyed that distinction. Labour ruled thanks only to the support of the Liberals. A fine young Mapai leader, Dov Hos, who got along very well with Englishmen and had established particularly friendly ties with Bevin, was sent to London to discuss the White Paper with him. Hos was extremely successful. He and Bevin called each other "brother," and when Brother Bevin heard the details of the White Paper, which in fact closed the country to Jewish immigration, he told Hos that he would order "his boys" to vote against the government if the White Paper were not dropped. Bevin in fact went to MacDonald and warned him of what would happen if there were no change in the White Paper policy. MacDonald immediately appointed a new Cabinet committee headed by Arthur Henderson, a loyal friend of the Zionist movement and a more sincere man than MacDonald. Henderson "interpreted" Passfield's White Paper in a way that turned it upside down. The government approved this interpretation in what is called the MacDonald Letter.

Published shortly before the 1931 Zionist Congress, the letter was credited to Weizmann, but he was nevertheless forced to leave the presidency because of an interview he had given to the Jewish Telegraphic Agency in which he had said that there was

* David Ben-Gurion, *From Class to People*, pp. 73–76.

no need for a Jewish majority in the Land of Israel. At this Congress Weizmann asked Professor Louis B. Namier, a British Zionist leader, and myself, to meet in London with Prime Minister MacDonald to clarify the government's policy toward Zionism. When we met MacDonald at Chequers, the British Prime Minister's summer home, he promised that he would soon appoint a new High Commissioner, though he mentioned no name, who would be faithful to the Balfour Declaration. When I raised the question of Jewish settlement in Trans-Jordan, MacDonald replied that the Balfour Declaration and the Mandate did not contemplate the Jews' receiving only the western half of the country. The Arabs had already received a number of countries (Hejaz, Iraq, Syria) after the war; the Jews had only the Land of Israel. I returned to Basle and informed Weizmann of MacDonald's promise. An anti-Weizmann majority, however, had already developed at the Congress, and so Nahum Sokolow was chosen president of the Zionist Organization.

MacDonald's promise regarding a High Commissioner faithful to the Balfour Declaration was fulfilled: in 1931 General Sir Arthur Wauchope was appointed to the post.

Chaim Arlosoroff had been elected to the Zionist Executive in 1931 and appointed head of the Political Department in Jerusalem. For some reason he lost faith in the existing regime in the country and in the High Commissioner. In a letter to Dr. Weizmann he argued that there was no hope of carrying out a Zionist program without a Jewish dictatorship during the transition period. The letter was published only after Arlosoroff's death. Perhaps the small-scale immigration during the first years of General Wauchope's term of office was the cause of Arlosoroff's despair.

A radical change took place in the Zionist movement in 1933. After its success in the elections to the Eighteenth Zionist Congress the Labor faction took the reins of leadership. At the Congress Eliezer Kaplan, Moshe Shertok [Sharett]* and David Ben-Gurion were elected as Labor representatives to the Zionist Executive, along with Yitzhak Gruenbaum, representing the Progressive Zionists, and Dr. Arthur Ruppin on behalf of the German Zionists. The Mizrahi and right-wing General Zionists refused to participate in a coalition with a Labor majority. Nahum Sokolow was again chosen president, but he took little interest in the work of the Executive, devoting himself mainly to literature and to preparing a Hebrew dictionary. Kaplan took over as treasurer and Sharett as head of the Political Department. The Labor portfolio was entrusted to Gruenbaum, and Dr. Ruppin continued to head the Settlement Department.

I did not accept any post, but agreed to participate in the work of the Political Department, since I saw immigration as the central issue facing Zionism. At the second session of the fourth Histadrut Convention, which met after the Eighteenth Zionist Congress, I defined the tasks of the Zionist Executive as follows:

> At this difficult and dangerous time, the movement has assumed a heavier responsibility than ever before, the responsibility for the future of Zionism. The tragedy that has struck the Jews of Germany has not struck them alone. Hitler's regime endangers Jews everywhere. Hitler attacks the Jews of the entire world because he regards them as the bearers of the ideals of justice, peace, and freedom, and therefore as an obstacle to his plan to make the

* Most Israeli leaders eventually changed their "exile names" to a Hebrew equivalent, or adopted entirely new Hebrew names. Thus Shertok would become Sharett, Golda Myerson would become Golda Meir, etc. Throughout the book the author usually indicates the future names, and in some cases the original name, in brackets. — EDITORS

German race rulers of the world. Hitler's Germany is not threatening the Jewish people alone. It cannot exist for very long without embarking upon a war of revenge against France, Poland, and Czechoslovakia and other neighboring countries where Germans live, or against vast Soviet Russia. Germany will not go to war today because she is not prepared. However, she is preparing. I don't want to be a prophet, but it does appear that the danger of war today is as great as it was in 1914. And if war breaks out again, it will cause greater havoc than the last one.

The Jewish people are not important enough in the world to prevent a war, or even to limit its impact. But there is one corner of the world where they are a very important factor, if not yet the decisive one. It is on this corner of the world that our future as a people will depend. What will be our strength and importance here when disaster strikes the world? Who knows, this terrible day may be only four or five years away (if not less). *In the meantime, we must double our numbers*, for the size of the Yishuv on the day of decision may well determine its future.

That is one of the reasons the question of immigration is the most important one facing us. We now have a perfect right to demand that the government make a drastic change in its immigration policy. That is not only because there is a greater need, but also because the absorptive capacity of the country has grown. In 1931, 4000 immigrants arrived. In 1932, the number rose to 10,000. This year, 1933, will conclude with an immigration of about 30,000. The growth in immigration certainly does not match the growth in the country's absorptive capacity, for, despite the settlement of a large number of tourists (who are not included in the aforementioned figures), there is still a severe labor shortage. During recent months all our efforts, both here and in London, have been directed toward guaranteeing a legal immigration consistent with the country's full absorptive capacity.

Considering the gravity of the immigration question, I must emphasize that not only the Mandatory government must change its attitude; we must change as well. The key to the future of the country is not only in the hands of the Government. It is not only political policy that determines immigration. In addition to the political key, *there is also an economic key, which is in our hands*. Our creativity will help determine the scope of immigration.*

Immediately after the Eighteenth Zionist Congress, I traveled to London to discuss immigration policy with the British government. I turned at first to Dr. Weizmann, who, while a private person at the time, was as interested in Zionist affairs as he had been during his tenure as president of the Zionist Organization. Hitler's rise to power had changed Weizmann's attitude toward immigration. At my request he invited the Colonial Secretary, Conlif-Lister, to discuss with me the possibilities of increasing immigration. Conlif-Lister showed great interest and good will. He promised to take up the matter with the High Commissioner in Palestine, General Wauchope.

Moshe Sharett and I had found Wauchope sympathetic. Between 1933 and the end of 1935, there was a considerable increase in immigration. It rose from 30,377 in 1933 to 42,259 in 1934 and to 61,854 in 1935. These numbers do not include the tourists who settled in the country. Those were the years of greatest immigration during the British Mandate. The German-Jewish influx, which brought to the country knowhow, ability, capital, and enterprise, was an important factor in the development of industry and settlement. Only in 1925, the last year of Sir Herbert Samuel's term of office, did immigration

---

* *Ibid.*, pp. 474–477.

reach the figure of 34,389. In 1935 the Zionist Executive also succeeded in purchasing the Huleh concession, which had belonged to Arab effendis.

As the man responsible for Zionist immigration policy I could not ignore the Arab problem. After my election to the Executive, I began discussion with Arab leaders in the country [Israel] as well as with representatives of Syria, Lebanon, Egypt, and Saudi Arabia. I sought to work out a program satisfactory to the Zionist movement and to Arab nationalism. I had discussed the matter beforehand with General Wauchope, a devoted friend of the Zionist enterprise at the time. I asked him whether the British government would support a Jewish-Arab agreement if I were able to bring it about. General Wauchope told me frankly that he was not authorized to speak on behalf of the British government, but that insofar as he was acquainted with its attitudes, he was certain that it would support any such agreement.

Though I was at odds with the late Dr. Judah L. Magnes* on political questions, he was of great assistance to me in arranging the meetings with Arab leaders—Musa Alami, Uni Abed el-Hadi, and Antonious. The talks continued for more than two years, in this country, in neighboring countries, and in Geneva, which was the headquarters of the Palestinian-Syrian Committee headed by Shekib Arsalan and Ikhan Bey el-Jabri. Though the discussions took place in an atmosphere of cordiality and mutual respect, they did not reach any practical conclusions.

In 1935 Mussolini's Italy attacked Ethiopia, which was a member of the League of Nations. Emperor Haile Selassie turned to the League for assistance. Led by France and England, the League seemed ready to impose sanctions on the Italian aggressor, but nothing was actually done. The primitive Ethiopian Army was unable to stand up against the Italians, who were armed with modern weapons. On May 5, 1936, the Italians entered Addis Ababa and the King of Italy was proclaimed Emperor of Ethiopia.

This event was the cause, directly and indirectly, of the riots that erupted in Jaffa on April 19, 1936. They were then spread through the country by agents of the Mufti, aided by Mussolini and Hitler. The riots, and the international powers behind them, Italy and Germany, caused the British government—of which Neville Chamberlain was Prime Minister and Malcolm MacDonald was Colonial Secretary—to abrogate the Balfour Declaration and renounce the obligations it had assumed under the terms of the Mandate. The British aimed to make the Land of Israel an Arab state under their control.

At the Nineteenth Zionist Congress in 1935 Dr. Weizmann was again elected president of the Zionist Organization. At this Congress a broad coalition was established, including representatives of two new parties: the Mizrahi and the General Zionists B; Rabbi Yehuda Leib Fishman [Maimon] of the Mizrahi and Dr. Emil Shmorak of the General Zionists B joined the Executive. When negotiations were resumed, the enlarged Executive was represented by Dr. Chaim Weizmann, Professor Zelig Brodetsky, and myself. The British Government was represented by Malcolm MacDonald; his deputy Lord Plymouth; the permanent Under-Secretary of the Colonial Office, Cosmo Parkinson; General Wauchope; and director of the Government Immigration Department in Jerusalem, Eric Mills. Despite the friendly atmosphere, there were no practical results.

* Judah L. Magnes (1877–1948): Early American Zionist; first president of Hebrew University, Jerusalem; advocated a binational (Jewish-Arab) Palestine. — EDITORS

A month later, on November 25, 1935, a united Arab delegation presented the High Commissioner with three main demands: (1) The establishment of an elected national government; (2) the complete stoppage of Jewish immigration; (3) a ban on the sale of land to Jews. The High Commissioner transmitted these demands to the British government. Meanwhile, James P. L. Thomas had replaced Malcolm MacDonald as Colonial Secretary. The Arab memorandum caused us concern, for it was clearly influenced by the Ethiopian-Italian dispute and the developing ties between the Mufti on the one hand, and Hitler and Mussolini on the other.

On April 19, 1936, riots broke out against the Jews of Jaffa; sixteen were murdered in one day. Shortly thereafter the Arab High Command declared a general strike, affecting not only workers but trade and transport. The Arabs demanded that all stores be closed, all work stopped, and all transport halted until their three demands were accepted. The demand for an elected government, if met, would have turned the Land of Israel into an Arab state. The riots grew in intensity. Arab terror spread to all corners of the country.

The Jaffa port was almost completely dependent on Jewish trade and immigration, although no Jew was allowed to work there. When it was closed, the Jewish Agency Executive demanded that the High Commissioner do one of two things: open the Jaffa port or permit the Jews to open a port in Tel Aviv. After a few days the High Commissioner announced that he did not want to open the Jaffa port by force, which would have caused bloodshed, and agreed that the Jews be allowed to develop a port in Tel Aviv. Work at the Haifa port did not cease, since there were already some Jewish workers there and their numbers increased because of the Arab strike.

At the beginning of 1936 Sir Arthur Wauchope was reappointed for another five-year term. On May 18, 1936, the Colonial Secretary, Thomas, announced to the House of Commons that a Royal Commission would be appointed to investigate the causes of the riots in Palestine, and would hear testimony from both Jews and Arabs. Thomas was soon replaced by Ormsby-Gore, the only pro-Zionist Colonial Secretary. But the Prime Minister at the time was the weak Stanley Baldwin. The Arab strike did not cause any damage to the Jewish economy. On the contrary, the number of Jewish workers in the villages grew from five to six thousand in 1936 to twelve thousand at the end of the year. The number of Jewish port workers, of whom there were only a few hundred previously, rose to two thousand. Jewish agricultural production grew, and the Yishuv defended itself with courage, wisdom, and restraint. Innocent Arabs were not harmed, despite the provocations of the Arab rioters. Not one Jewish settlement was abandoned; instead, new ones were established.

The damage caused to the Arab economy, however, was tremendous, so that there was increasing pressure on the Arab High Command to end the strike. The committee was ready to do so, even without acceptance of its three conditions, if the Mandatory Government would at least stop Jewish immigration while the Royal Commission, due soon, was in the country. This demand was unacceptable to the British. Finally, supposedly because of the intervention of the Arab kings, the strike was called off on October 11, 1936.

The Royal Commission, headed by Lord Peel, arrived on November 11, 1936, and Dr. Weizmann appeared before it on November 25. He gave what was perhaps his best Zionist speech. He spoke of the six million Jews in Europe whose existence and future depended on emigration to Israel and the establishment of a Jewish State. Not only did the six million want and need a Jewish State, they also had the desire and the ability, economic and cultural, to establish and develop it. The speech made an enormous impression on the Royal Commission and undoubtedly influenced its decision to propose the establishment of a Jewish State in a part, albeit a small part, of the Land of Israel.

The Royal Commission's report was published on July 7, 1937. The first section contained a brief survey of the history of the country and of the Jewish people, the continuing historical connection between the country and the Jewish people. It cited the problems of the Jews in the Diaspora, the settlement work of the Jews, the eternal values that the Jewish people had created in the Land of Israel for all mankind, and their determination to revive their ancient Homeland. The report contained the best description of Jewish settlement ever to appear.

The Royal Commission also pointed out that the Arab community had received its fair share of benefits from Jewish immigration and settlement, and that the obligations to the Arabs, as laid down in the Mandate, had therefore been fulfilled. The Arab economy, the Royal Commission said, had not suffered in any way because of the National Home.

The Royal Commission's report revealed for the first time the principal intention of the Balfour Declaration. "We were permitted to examine the documents," the report said, "and it is clear to us that by the words 'establishment of a National Home in Palestine,' H. M. Government recognized that in the course of time a Jewish State was likely to be established, but it was not in their power to say when it would happen." They quoted the statement made by President Wilson on March 3, 1919: "It is clear to me that the Allies, in complete agreement with our government and people, have decided on the establishment of a Jewish Commonwealth in Palestine." They pointed out that Emir Feisal, who represented the Arabs at the Peace Conference, had agreed to the Balfour Declaration and to a program of cooperation between the Arab states and Palestine.

Nevertheless, the Royal Commission reached the conclusion that the Mandate was unworkable. It proposed that Palestine west of the Jordan be divided into two unequal parts, with a Jewish state in the smaller part (the north and west), and an Arab state, united with Trans-Jordan, in the south and east.

The British government published a White Paper, together with the report of the Royal Commission, in which it announced that it had considered the Commission's recommendations and in general had agreed with them. The British press also expressed general agreement. Nevertheless, Lloyd George—who had been Prime Minister when Balfour as Foreign Secretary had sent the Declaration to Lord Rothschild—vehemently attacked the White Paper in an article entitled "The Scandalous Report." He said it was a gross violation of the promises given to the Jewish people. In July the Royal Commission's report was debated in both Houses of Parliament. During the debates criticism was leveled against three aspects of the report: the small amount of territory allocated to the Jewish state, the removal of New Jerusalem from the Jewish state, and the inclusion of the Negev in the Arab state. In the wake of this criticism the British government withdrew its approval of the report. Instead, it decided to turn the matter over for discussion to the League of Nations and to present new proposals to Parliament.

My talks with members of the Royal Commission led me to conclude that there was no possibility that the British government would faithfully carry out the terms of the Mandate. This meant that the return of the Jews to their land and the development of an independent Jewish economy thereafter depended solely on the establishment of a Jewish State, not in the days of the Messiah or in the distant future, but very soon. This Jewish State was only a means to an end, not an end in itself. It was, perhaps, the only means of reaching the final goal of national redemption. At a meeting of the Histadrut Labor Council on February 7,1937, I explained:

> The most vital issue before us now is immigration. The scope of immigration will determine everything else—including the very existence of the Yishuv and the achievement of the "final goal." Just as a Jewish majority does not in itself fulfill Zionist aspirations, so a Jewish State is not everything. If we were to be offered a Jewish State on both sides of the Jordan, on condition that not more than a million and a half Jews would enter it—even if this million and a half were enough to give us a majority on both sides of the Jordan—we would have to reject the proposal out of our dedication to Jewish needs.
>
> This is not to say that Zionism means the concentration of all 17 million Jews in the Land of Israel. I am not certain that all 17 million would want to come, or that the country could hold them. But a real Zionist program must be based on saving all of the Jews who desire to find salvation in the Land of Israel—neither more nor less than that. A Jewish State of a million and a half Jews, which had neither the right nor the desire to bring in more, would be a distortion of Zionism. We want a Jewish majority and a state because they are prerequisites for the fulfillment of Zionism. They are not an end, but only a means to an end. We need a majority and a state so that we can assume the enormously difficult task of gathering in the exiles, and so that we can decide by ourselves about large-scale immigration and settlement, which will be possible only when we have the apparatus of government at our disposal.
>
> The realization of Zionism means more than just a Jewish State. Zionism is the complete and absolute solution to the Jewish problem, and this was the burden of my remarks to the Royal Commission. The scope of immigration during the next few years will determine the fate of Zionism and of the country. It is not only a question of how many Jews we will manage to save in the near future from degradation and death in the lands of exile. The real issue is how firm a foundation we will create in this country for our future activities. The initial impetus for the April 1939 riots came from the war between Italy and Ethiopia. Who knows what would have happened to the Yishuv had these riots—promoted by outside elements—both communist and fascist, with the aid of the Arab kings and of Arab bands in Syria and Iraq—broken out not in 1936, when the Yishuv already numbered 400,000, but five or six years earlier. Who knows how they would have ended in that case? Who knows what their military and political results would have been?
>
> Moreover, we are not yet cognizant of all the dangers facing us. The war in Ethiopia was, after all, only a short and distant episode. There is no way of knowing what will happen in another few years. The threat of another World War, and an attendant holocaust, hangs over our heads. We cannot prevent this terrible catastrophe, but our fate on Judgment Day —if it comes—will depend on the strength that we have accumulated in this country. Immigration during the next few years will determine our entire future. Therefore, we are now concentrating on the political sphere, where the immigration question will be decided.*

* David Ben-Gurion, *The Struggle*, Vol. A: *A Vision That Can Be Fulfilled*, pp. 52–55.

On April 10, 1937, three months after the publication of the Peel Commission Report, I explained to the Central Committee of Mapai, the Israel Labor Party, how immigration and settlement were endangered by that commission and by English public opinion. I put forward a plan for a Jewish State in the part of the country comprising the Galilee, the coastal plain, the Negev, and the shore of the Dead Sea, up to and including Jerusalem. Some members said my plan was unrealistic because the English would never agree to it. I replied:

> What I have suggested is not a guaranteed solution, but a possible one. While the English will obviously not ignore Arab objections, they cannot easily ignore Jewish demands either. In the face of a sharpening conflict between the two peoples, what might they do?
>
> Let us consider several possibilities:
>
> 1. Maintaining the status quo. One of the members told me that he would not agree to a State based on the status quo of 1935. Let us assume for a moment that this approach is correct from a Jewish viewpoint. But what about the English viewpoint? If the status quo means more revolts, more shooting, the dispatch of more troops and a constant conflict between Jews and Arabs—it could hardly constitute an ideal solution for the English.
>
> 2. A second solution that might be acceptable to England would be based on a drastic reduction in immigration. One of the members told me that this would be preferable to a State in part of the country, which would mean losing half of it. I do not agree. The Land of Israel without Jews is not the Land of Israel. We should consider, as an alternative to such a disaster, the possibility of solving the problem by establishing a Jewish State in a reasonably large part of the country.
>
> It is said that partition would be unacceptable to the English, and is therefore politically unrealistic. This assumption is not based on fact. Partition as a solution has been accepted by a good many Englishmen, because it was first put forward by one of them (Stafford Cripps). Several British statesmen support the idea of two states in the Land of Israel. Britain must find a way out of her dispute with Jews and Arabs alike. She will not find it by maintaining the status quo. Moreover, she wants to rid herself of this conflict once and for all. Jewish independence is not against British interests. It can certainly be argued that a division of the country would serve British interests better than a constant conflict with the Jews and Arabs alike.
>
> I don't see partition unacceptable from a British viewpoint. However, is it acceptable to the Jews? What are they likely to say? If we had a government in alliance with the English which also enjoyed full control over immigration, could enact its own laws, and had enough territory under its control, we would bring in and settle two or three million Jews. *The Jewish Agency could not do this; a State could.* A Jewish government could carry out a planned settlement program involving hundreds of thousands of people. Those who fear that Jews would not come to the Land of Israel after it had been partitioned do not know the Jewish people.
>
> Some argue that the Arabs would not accept such a solution, that they would revolt. In this context it should be borne in mind that, had it been up to the Arabs to decide, there would have been no mandate. We should not underestimate Arab opposition, but we should not overestimate it either. Every Arab revolt in this country has always, paradoxically, brought new advances to the Jews. This recent revolt has brought us a Jewish port, and may bring us even greater political advantages.*

* *Ibid.,* pp. 217–221.

At the Zionist Congress in Zurich in August 1937 the American Zionists and some Israeli Zionists opposed the Royal Commission's partition plan. The majority of delegates decided that the proposals were unacceptable, but called on the Executive to discuss plans for the establishment of a Jewish State with the British government. If a new plan was put forward, a Congress would be called to decide upon it. Only a small minority at the Congress, members of the left-wing Hashomer Hatzair movement, rejected every proposal for a Jewish State, even one encompassing the entire Land of Israel.* They demanded a binational state.

Meanwhile, the British government sent a new commission, headed by Sir John Woodhead. The partition plan proposed by the Woodhead Commission was a slap in the face to the Arabs. It called for the abolition of the Mandate but left Britain in control of the country.

The international situation worsened. France and Britain abandoned Austria and Czechoslovakia to Hitler, and a new World War loomed.

The British adopted the plan recommended by the Woodhead Commission as an alternative should the partition proposal be unacceptable. It called for a reduction in Jewish immigration to twelve thousand a year, a figure the commission felt was in line with the country's absorptive capacity.

Everyone realized that immigration had to continue, even without government permission. The first attempt to bring in immigrants without certificates was carried out in 1927, when the government reduced the number of immigration certificates to practically zero. (In 1927, 3034 immigrants arrived with government permission; in 1928, 2171; in 1929, 5247; and in 1930, 4944.) With the assistance of the French government, which had a mandate over Syria and Lebanon, a training farm was established in Syria not far from the border of this country. That farm served as a jumping-off point for immigrants, who usually crossed the border with the assistance of members of Kfar Giladi, a Jewish settlement near the Lebanese-Syrian border. In 1933 the first illegal immigrant ship arrived. It was a small Greek vessel, the *Velos*, authorized to carry 150 passengers. But the train from Warsaw had brought 350 pioneers to Athens, and all of them crowded onto the boat. When the *Velos* neared the shores of this country, the immigrants were taken by small boats to Jewish villages along the coast.

In 1938, when the government instituted restrictions on immigration, in accordance with the Woodhead Commission's alternative plan, illegal immigration began on a much larger basis. Groups of 300, 800, and even 1400 arrived. The governments of the countries of departure were helpful. Altogether, 115,000 illegal immigrants were brought in, 105,000 of them by Aliya Bet [which organized illegal immigration into Palestine], the rest by the Revisionists and private agencies.

---

* Political parties in Zionism and Israel: The dominant party is Mapai, of which Ben-Gurion is a leader, a Zionist Labor Party, socialist-centrist in ideology. Other parties have included: Mapam, left-wing Marxist socialist (evolved from the radical Hashomer Hatzair movement); Agudat Israel, extreme Orthodox religious party; Poalei Agudat Israel, more labor- and farmer-oriented than Agudat Israel, from which it derives; General Zionists, a free enterprise party, later known as General Zionists B; Progressives, liberal wing of General Zionists, has also been known as General Zionists A; Herut, right-wing ideologically, was formed out of Irgun Zvai Leumi, principal dissident underground movement, which was itself an offshoot of the militant Revisionist Zionist Party; Ahdut Haavodah, a leftist socialist party but non-doctrinaire; Mizrahi, a religious party; Hapoel Hamizrahi, a religious labor party; Communist Party of Israel.—EDITORS

In 1939, following the rejection by both Jews and Arabs of the Woodhead Commission proposals, the British government invited representatives of Iraq, Jordan, Egypt, and the Arabs of Palestine, together with the Jewish Agency and representatives of British and American Jewry, to discuss the future of the country. The Arabs refused to meet face to face with the Jews. Two separate meetings were arranged at St. James's Palace under the chairmanship of Prime Minister Neville Chamberlain, and with the participation of Lord Halifax, the Foreign Secretary, Malcolm MacDonald, the Colonial Secretary, and their assistants. Dr. Weizmann and I met beforehand with Malcolm MacDonald, who in earlier years had displayed a great deal of sympathy for Zionism. We asked him whether the purpose of the London meeting was to condemn the Jews to being an eternal minority. If this was the case, there was no point in our participating in the gathering, we said. MacDonald assured us that the government had no such intention and that there was no basis for our suspicions.

On March 15, 1939, after a number of meetings between the Jews and the British (as well as between the Arabs and the British), MacDonald presented a final formulation of British policy. Its main provisions called for: (1) the establishment of an independent Palestinian government that would be neither Jewish nor Arab; (2) the creation of a National Assembly of the Palestinian people to frame a constitution for an independent state; (3) during the following five years, ten thousand Jews were to be allowed to immigrate each year; in addition, twenty-five thousand Jewish refugees were to be admitted if the country's absorptive capacity proved sufficient, but further Jewish immigration would be permitted only with Arab agreement; (4) the High Commissioner would be given permission to limit the sale of land during the transition period; three areas would be designated: one where land could be freely sold, a second, where sales were restricted, and a third, where land sales were forbidden. This plan was also presented to the Arabs.

The Jewish delegation announced that it saw no value in continued discussions. The Arabs also rejected the government's proposal.

On May 17, 1939, the Chamberlain government published a White Paper that in effect abrogated the Balfour Declaration and the obligations assumed by Britain under the Mandate. It stated that only seventy-five thousand Jewish immigrants would be allowed to enter the country during the following five years; that Jews would be able to purchase land only within an area encompassing 5 percent of the country; and finally that, after an interval of ten years, a Palestinian State would be established.

The House of Commons approved the White Paper on May 23, 1939. It was supported by the Conservative majority and strongly opposed by the Labour Party and the Liberals, as well as by a few Conservative leaders, notably Winston Churchill and Leopold Amery.

The Zionist Executive in Jerusalem published the following statement: "The pioneers of the Land of Israel, who for three generations have shown their ability to revitalize a barren land, will display their courage in defending immigration, the National Home, and the freedom of the Jewish people."

The Twenty-first Zionist Congress met in Geneva in August 1939. Dr. Weizmann declared:

> During the three years of Arab terror, which began in April 1936, the Yishuv has established fifty new settlements, built a Jewish port overnight, organized large-scale defense,

and achieved a greater measure of economic independence. The Jews will stand united in defense of their rights in the Land of Israel, rights based on international agreements and the eternal link between the people and their Homeland.

In the beginning of September, a few days after the Zionist Congress, the Second World War broke out with Hitler's attack on Poland. As chairman of the Zionist Executive, I declared: "We will fight with the British against Hitler as if there were no White Paper; we will fight the White Paper as if there were no war."

The executive called on the younger generation to join the armed forces. About 130,000 men and women of military age volunteered. Arab leaders in Israel and several heads of Arab states, particularly Iraq and Egypt, supported Hitler. Nevertheless, all of the efforts made to establish a Jewish military unit were unsuccessful because of the British government's opposition. Not until September 1944 did Prime Minister Churchill, acting on his own, approve the creation of a Jewish Brigade organized in this country. The Brigade fought together with the other Allied units in Italy and contributed to the defeat of Mussolini's armies.

America's entrance into the war left no room for doubt that after the war the United States rather than England would call the tune. In my capacity as chairman of the Executive in Jerusalem, I traveled to the United States in 1940 and 1942 to enlist the support of American Jewry in the struggle to cancel out the White Paper and establish a Jewish State after the war.

All of the Zionist organizations and parties met in May 1942 for the first conference of the US Zionist movement. It was held at the Biltmore Hotel in New York and the plan it adopted was afterward known as the Biltmore Program. It stated:

> The new world order that will follow victory cannot be established on foundations of peace, justice and equality unless the problem of Jewish homelessness is finally solved. The Conference urges:
>   1. That the gates of Palestine be opened to Jewish immigration;
>   2. That the Jewish Agency be vested with control of immigration into Palestine and with the necessary authority for up-building the country, including the development of its unoccupied and uncultivated lands;
>   3. That Palestine be established as a Jewish Commonwealth integrated into the structure of the new democratic world.

This Biltmore Program was adopted unanimously, with only the delegate of Hashomer Hatzair abstaining; it was presented to the Zionist General Council at its meeting in Jerusalem on October 15, 1942. After a bitter debate, in which the representatives of Hashomer Hatzair were particularly active, it was approved by a large majority and became the official platform of the World Zionist Movement.

Relations with the Mandatory Government and British Leaders

On May 7, 1945, a few days before the conclusion of the war in Europe, I met with Col. Oliver Stanley, who had been appointed Colonial Secretary in 1943. While he was neither pro- nor anti-Zionist, he was a decent and straightforward person. I understood from him that the British government would not continue with the Mandate much longer. The British were unable to decide between the demands of the Arabs and the Jews. They knew that the United States and the Soviet Union supported Jewish demands and the establishment of a Jewish State, a fact which was not publicly known at the time, but they did not want to enter into conflict with the Arab peoples and therefore would soon abandon the Mandate.

Two days after this discussion the war in Europe ended. I wrote in my diary that day: "Rejoice not, O Israel, unto exultation, like the peoples" (Hosea 9:1). I knew what had happened to us in the Second World War. The six million Jews of Europe, who Dr. Weizmann had told the Royal Commission needed a Jewish State and were capable of building it, were no longer among the living. But there were still masses of Jews who needed a State. Moreover, when the British left the country, we would have to face the Arab armies. Therefore we had to concentrate on preparing ourselves to confront that danger, which meant, first and foremost, the acquisition of all types of weapons.

A few days later I met with the French Foreign Minister, Georges Bidault, in Paris. He had read the speeches made at the Biltmore Conference and all the other material that had appeared in French. He knew that I regarded she establishment of a Jewish State as an absolute necessity for our people and asked me whether it would be established without a Jewish majority. He knew that America and Russia were in favor of such a State. I told him: If the gates of the Land of Israel are opened, we will soon be a majority. He asked whether the Arab governments would permit the creation of a Jewish State. I replied that we had always been outnumbered and yet survived—we would survive again.

I returned to London. After a conversation with Colonel Stanley, it was clear to me that we had no one but ourselves to depend on. Though I knew that even Stalin favored a Jewish State, I realized that he would not fight our battles and that we would stand alone, facing the Arab armies, as soon as the English left. We would not be up against the Arabs of Palestine, but the Arab States. The Hagana,* operating as an underground movement, could neither purchase heavy weapons nor train its members in their use. We must therefore buy heavy weapons in good time and lay the foundations for an industry capable of producing them. Clearly, with the end of the war the United States would dismantle a large part of its arms industry. An effort must be made to obtain our necessary machinery from that source. On May 15 I left London for the United States.

In New York I met with Henry Montor, director of the United Jewish Appeal, who was well acquainted with American Jewry. He gave me a list of several dozen Jews who could be depended upon. I met with my friend Rudolf Sonnenborn in New York and told him that I wanted to use his home to discuss a very important matter with a number of Jews. He readily agreed. The next day Montor gave me a list of seventeen men: Harold Goldberg of Minneapolis, Sam Sher and Jacques Torczyner of New York, Sam Sachs of Toronto, Julius Flegelman of Los Angeles, S. Bros of Miami, Philip Lown of Lewiston, Eli Cohen of Lynn, Ezra Shapiro of Cleveland, Albert Schiff of Columbus,

* Hagana (literally, Defense): Palestine's volunteer military organization, before the creation of the State of Israel, later absorbed by the regular Israel Defense Forces; although operating underground, it was not a dissident formation. The dissident military undergrounds were Etzel and the smaller Lehi group, both right-wing.—EDITORS

Alex Lowenthal and Charles Rosenbloom of Pittsburgh, William Sylk of Philadelphia, Adolph Hamburger of Baltimore, Robert Travis of Atlanta, Max Livingston of New York, and Sonnenborn himself.

I told Montor to invite them to Sonnenborn's home on Friday, July 1, 1945, at 9:30 A.M. All arrived on time. Also present at the meeting were Eliezer Kaplan, treasurer of the Jewish Agency in Jerusalem, Meyer Weisgal, Reuven Zaslani [Shiloah], and Montor.

I told the participants that I felt that Britain would be leaving the Land of Israel in a year or two and that the neighboring Arab states would then send in their armies to conquer the country and destroy the Jews living there. Though we were few in number —only some 550,000—I was certain that we would be able to repel the Arab armies if only we had the necessary weapons. Before the war the Hagana had secretly purchased weapons in Belgium and Poland. But in shattered and chaotic postwar Europe there was no certainty that these sources would remain open. Moreover, what we had purchased then was suitable only for combat with Arab bands, not with regular Arab armies, most of them equipped by the British. A Jewish arms industry in the Land of Israel must be established in good time. America was already dismantling most of her military industry, though the war with Japan had not yet ended. This process would undoubtedly be speeded up after the defeat of Japan.

The necessary machinery, I said, could now be purchased cheaply. Even so, hundreds of thousands of dollars were needed. I asked the men in the room if they were willing to supply the funds required for the purchase of the machinery. They asked questions about the situation in the country, the strength of the Hagana, our relations with the British. The meeting lasted until 5:30 P.M. During the lunch break Kaplan and Zaslani also took part in a discussion of economic and political questions. All those present enthusiastically promised to give their full support, and I cabled to Chaim Slavin, head of the Hagana's underground arms industry, to come immediately to New York. He arrived and met with Yacov Dori, who was already in New York to handle the purchases.

The machinery was bought and sent to Israel. Those were the two worst years of our relations with the Mandatory Government. The increasing terrorist activities of the dissident organizations, Etzel and Lehi, and the beginning of a revolt by the entire Hagana, led to searches for arms in settlements and cities. But all the heavy machinery arrived safely at its destination even before the British left. They did not imagine that it was being brought in for military purposes and thus did not seize a single machine. But we were unable to establish a heavy arms industry until the British left.

I returned to London on the *Queen Elizabeth* on July 26, 1945. We had already heard on board ship about the election results in England. For the first time the British Labour Party had received an absolute majority. This news aroused great hopes in the Jewish world, particularly the Zionist movement.

The British Labour Party had opposed the White Paper in 1939. At its December 1944 conference it had adopted a resolution calling for the establishment of a Jewish State in all of Palestine, adding a demand never made by the Zionist movement: the transfer of all the Arabs of Palestine to the Arab countries. The new British Prime Minister was Clement Attlee, while Ernest Bevin, who had helped bring about the abrogation of the Passfield White Paper in 1931, became Foreign Secretary.

In August 1945 a Zionist Conference was called in London. This was the first Jewish conference after the Second World War, during which six million Jews had been murdered by the Nazis and their collaborators in the conquered areas. Nevertheless, the mood at the conference was buoyant, thanks to the Labour Party victory. I felt it necessary to throw some cold water on the enthusiasm and stated:

> The assumption that a party in power will fulfill the pledges it made while in opposition is a highly dubious one. We have no reason to be certain that a party reaching power will demand from itself what it previously demanded from others. In England, and perhaps in other countries as well, power does not reside solely in the hands of elected politicians. There is also a permanent Civil Service. Governments come and governments go, but most of the Civil Service remains. This is true of England as a whole, and particularly in regard to matters affecting the British Empire. The great majority of the members of the Colonial Civil Service are anti-Zionist, as they have been since the time of the Balfour Declaration, and they will remain in office. Let us not underestimate their influence on the Labour government.

Soon enough we were confronted with a reality far graver than that against which I had warned. On November 13, 1945, Moshe Sharett and I were invited to call on the new Colonial Secretary, George Hall. He presented us with a statement that Ernest Bevin was to make in the House of Commons. It declared: "There is no room for compromise between the conflicting viewpoints of the Jews and Arabs. It is therefore necessary to place Palestine under the control of an international authority." In other words, British rule would continue, but without a Mandate and the obligations assumed under its terms. Bevin did not abrogate the White Paper. He tried to convene the Jews and Arabs in London again, but he was unwilling to reach an agreement with either side. On February 18, 1947, he announced in Parliament that the British government would accept the demands of neither the Jews nor the Arabs, and would therefore turn the whole problem over to the United Nations.

The Twenty-second Zionist Congress, the first to be held after the Second World War, met in Basle in December 1946. Differences of opinion developed between the president of the Zionist Organization, Dr. Weizmann, and myself as chairman of the Zionist Executive in regard to relations with the British. I believed that Zionist diplomatic efforts now must be centered on the United States rather than on England. Dr. Weizmann was not reelected to the Presidency.

Military Power of Neighboring Countries ★ Preparations To Meet This Threat ★ United Nations Inherits Palestine Problem

The Zionist Congress in Basle adopted the following resolution:

> Only the establishment of a Jewish State will fulfill the original aim of the mandate. The Congress opposes any form of trusteeship to replace the mandate. It calls on the United Nations Organization and all its member states to support the demand of the Jewish people for the establishment of their own State in the Land of Israel, and their acceptance into the family of nations.

Until that Congress I had not accepted any portfolio in the Executive, because I regarded the promotion of immigration as the central task of the Zionist movement and all members of the Executive dealt with immigration. With the end of the war and the Labour Party's assumption of power under the leadership of Clement Attlee and Ernest Bevin, England's role in the Land of Israel was clearly coming to an end. The final struggle would be between the Jews and the Arabs, with military force determining the outcome.

I devoted most of my speeches at the Twenty-second Congress to attacking the Morrison Plan, which called for dividing the Land of Israel into four areas: the Negev, the Jerusalem district, the Jewish district (including the existing Jewish settlements), and the Arab district (encompassing the rest of the country). Power would be retained by a British High Commissioner, the Jews and the Arabs dealing with internal matters in their areas. Immigration into the Jewish district was to be decided by the central authority, namely, the High Commissioner.

Only in the Political Committee of the Congress, whose minutes were not made public, could I dwell on security matters, which I felt would determine the fate of the Yishuv and the Jewish people. At the meeting of this committee on December 18, 1946, I said:

> The major problem now is security. As you are aware, this is not a new problem in our country, but it has now been posed under new and entirely different circumstances from those we have faced during the past seventy years, from the days of Petah Tikva. Formerly it was a vital issue for the small and developing Yishuv, which had to defend itself and ensure its physical security. But until recently, it was only a question of resisting the Arabs of the country, who lacked, as we did, the tools of government, and who from time to time would attack individual Jewish settlements or the entire Jewish community.
>
> Now we are in a completely different situation. The country is surrounded by independent Arab states. And from a political, cultural, or economic viewpoint, it makes no difference that their independence is purely fictitious. As far as our security is concerned, they are independent states. They have the right to purchase and produce arms, to establish and train armies. . . . Attacks by the Arabs of Palestine on the Yishuv do not endanger it. But we may be confronted by the armies of the neighboring Arab states sent to attack and destroy us. We must prepare for that possibility by exploiting our technical and financial capacities to the fullest. . . . It is the duty of the Yishuv, the Zionist movement, and the Jewish people to take cognizance of the security problem in all its scope, gravity, and immediacy, and to recognize the dangers that face us. Perhaps the confrontation will not come today or tomorrow—the Arab states are not yet ready—but we are entering into a period of violent change and we must not ignore the dangers that await us. We must prepare immediately and to the maximum possible extent. As far as I am concerned, this is the most important task facing Zionism today.*

At the Congress I was given, in my capacity as chairman of the Executive, a special portfolio: Defense. I considered it my responsibility to make a very thorough investigation of the Hagana's capacity, equipment, and training, as well as to see to what extent it was capable of meeting the grave tests that awaited it. My investigation continued for several months, from March 27 to November 8, 1946. The Hagana's budget in 1946 was PL670,000; in 1947 it was PL770,000 (the Palestinian pound was worth $5). Of that sum,

* David Ben-Gurion, *The Struggle*, Vol. 5, pp. 135–136.

in 1946, the Hagana spent PL200,000 on its arms industry, PL120,000 on the Palmah,*
PL10,000 on intelligence, PL40,000 on training, and PL12,000 on assistance to prisoners
and legal aid. In 1947 it spent PL310,000 on its arms industry, PL130,000 on intelligence
and field units, PL60,000 on regional bodies, PL7,000 on the Gadna Youth Battalions**
and information, PL80,000 on administration, and PL12,000 on compensation.

The Hagana's National Command was composed equally of representatives of the
Histadrut and of the Citizens' Union (in practice, the Tel Aviv Municipality and the
Farmers' Association). It was directed by the head of the National Command, appointed
by the chairman of the Executive as his representative. The head of the National Command
at that period was Moshe Kleinbaum [Sneh] from the General Zionists A Party. The National Command did not exert effective control over the Hagana in that there was considerable distrust between its two policymaking components. Hagana branches generally
acted on their own initiative.

I met with the National Command as a whole and with each member individually.
I visited various settlements, talked with local, district, and regional officers, as well as
with rank-and-file Hagana members. Few of the commanders had had any military
experience. For some reason no attempt had been made to attract to the Hagana men who
had served in the Jewish Brigade and in the Artillery Unit.

Most Hagana commanders thought in terms of regional defense. There was scarcely
anyone who considered the possibility of a full-scale military conflict. I checked the weapons that were at the Hagana's disposal in April 1947 and found the following: 10,073
rifles, of which 8720 were in the possession of the local settlement units, 336 with the
Central Command, 656 with the Palmah, and 361 with the field units; 190 submachine
guns, of which 785 were in the settlements, 424 with the field units, 130 with the Palmah,
and 561 with the Central Command; 186 Bren guns, of which 31 were in the settlements, 35 with the field units, 5 with the Palmah, and 115 with the Central Command;
444 machine guns, of which 338 were in the settlements, 37 in the field units, 33 with
Palmah, and 46 with Central Command. The heavy equipment consisted of 672 2-inch
mortars and 96 3-inch mortars. There was obviously not a single artillery piece or a heavy
machine gun, no antitank weapons, no antiaircraft guns, no armored cars, and not the
least evidence of an air force or a navy. There weren't even any facilities for land transport.

The meager supply of weapons at the disposal of the Hagana had been obtained by
brave and daring acts. Their transport from abroad had demanded an extraordinary degree of devotion and organizational skill. The Hagana's own arms industry, which had
begun production before the First World War, manufactured only primitive weapons
in secret and in dangerous circumstances.

Just a few of the Hagana's commanders had had any military experience, and even
fewer had had really good military training. A few had served in the Russian Army and
in the Allied Jewish units of the First and Second World Wars.

---

* Palmah: an elitist paid military unit of Palestine's Jewish community, established in 1941 to face
the threat of German invasion; leftist but not ideologically doctrinaire, its members initially combined military duties with agricultural work. — EDITORS

** Gadna Youth Battalions: youth groups that worked on the soil and were trained in quasi-military
duties. — EDITORS

I tried to clarify at the time—in April–June 1947—the strength of the armies in the neighboring Arab states. The largest country was, of course, Egypt, with a population of 19 million. Until the Second World War, Egypt had an army of only thirteen thousand men. With the outbreak of the war the army was enlarged to twenty-two thousand men. At the end of 1946 it numbered twenty-five thousand and in 1947 thirty-five thousand or, according to other sources, forty-five thousand. More than 80 percent of the men who reported for mobilization were rejected for health reasons.

In 1939 the military budget was raised from 3 million Egyptian pounds to 5 million. In 1942–43 it reached nearly 7 million and in 1946–47 8.4 million (8 percent of the overall budget). The weapons supplied by the British included tanks and planes. A British military delegation trained the army. The Egyptian Air Force numbered 4030. These included 200 flying officers and 20 flight sergeants; the rest were ground crew and civilian employees. The Air Force had 177 planes, divided into 10 wings, of which 8 were combat wings. The Egyptian Navy had 2 transport ships and 4 motorboats for coast guard duty. There was no local military industry.

Syria gained her independence at the end of the Second World War, thanks to the British. At the end of 1945 there were 3500 men in the Syrian gendarmerie, including 113 officers and 785 warrant officers. This force was divided into 6 units. The Syrian Army consisted of 7 regiments with 500 men each. In addition, there were garrisons of 500 men each in Damascus and Aleppo, a motorized desert regiment of 600 men, a camel corps of 1100 men, 8 Circassian cavalry units with a total of 1000 men, and six Druze cavalry units with 900 men. Equipment consisted of rifles, machine guns, submachine guns, light armored cars, and three batteries of artillery.

The 1947 defense budget totaled 26.5 million Syrian pounds (37 million pounds sterling) out of a total national budget of 120 million pounds. The army was trained by the English. The Syrians had purchased 9 training planes in 1946 and were about to open a pilots' training school.

Lebanon had 3 regiments of gendarmerie, with a total of 2000 men. Its army consisted of 3500 men, 105 of them officers. It was divided into 4 infantry regiments, an artillery company, a motorized company, a cavalry unit, an engineering company, and several auxiliary units. In 1947 L£10 million (approximately 1.1 million English pounds) were allocated to the army out of a total national budget of L£50 million.

The Iraqi Army had been founded in 1921 and compulsory conscription was introduced in 1936. In 1937–1938 it comprised 18,000 soldiers and about 850 officers. At the beginning of the Second World War, according to one source, it had 31,000 men: 28 infantry regiments (each with 800 men), 3 cavalry regiments, 9 batteries of heavy artillery (each with 4 guns and 80 gunners), 6 light batteries, and a mechanized battery. According to another source, there were 2 infantry divisions (with 4 brigades in each) in Iraq on the eve of the Rashid Ali revolt, as well as a regiment of artillery and a brigade of cavalry. After the revolt the British dispersed, purged, and reorganized the army. By the beginning of 1945 its strength was estimated at 2000 officers and 35,000 infantrymen. The Iraqi military budget in 1946–1947 was 6,533,700 dinars (1 dinar equalled one pound sterling). Of this, 5,042,000 dinars were allocated to the ground forces, 490,000 dinars were spent on general equipment, and 225,000 dinars went to the air force. Iraq had a number of air wings and bountiful quantities of ammunition. It also possessed schools for artillery, infantry, cavalry, communications, and transport.

Trans-Jordan's principal military force was the Arab Legion, founded by the English in 1922. In 1938 the Legion numbered 1500 men, and by 1947 15 to 18,000. Its budget was £7.5 million a year. The Legion possessed 50 artillery pieces and 400 tanks, a number of armored cars (40 of them very modern), submachine guns, and rifles. In addition, there was a Frontier Force, under British command, which by 1947 totaled 15,000 men.

The Saudi Arabian Army was not important. It had 10 to 12,000 men in tribal militias and 25,000 men (according to another source only 5000) in infantry units.

Thus the total strength of all the Arab armies was as follows:

Egypt	army	35,000
Syria	army	8,000
	gendarmerie	3,500
Lebanon	army	3,605
	gendarmerie	2,000
Iraq	army	25,000 (or 35,000)
Trans-Jordan	Arab Legion	18,000
	desert camel corps	6,000
	Frontier Force	15,000
Saudi Arabia	army	25,000 (or 5,000)
	tribal militia	12,000
	Total	153,405 (or 142,000)

The best-trained unit was the Arab Legion.

Some of the heads of the Hagana expressed dissatisfaction at the emphasis I placed on the dangers facing us from the Arab armies. After the publication of the White Paper in 1939 they felt that our principal struggle was a political one against the Mandatory Government, which had not lived up to its international obligations. Some of them, headed by Moshe Sneh, interpreted my emphasis on the Arab armies as a deliberate attempt to play down the "imperialist" danger represented by the British.

On June 18, 1947, I published the following statement on the past and future of the Hagana:

> When Hashomer, the first Jewish military force, was established by the Yishuv forty years ago, its principal task was the defense of *lives and property* in the Jewish villages against Arab *thieves and marauders*. This task was carried out by trained watchmen, organized on a national basis, and subject to strict discipline. They were trained to use rifles and were expert horsemen. They taught their Arab neighbors to respect Jewish courage and strength, and at the same time developed friendly relations with them, insofar as possible.
>
> After the First World War, Hashomer was disbanded and the Hagana established. Its task was the *defense of Jewish settlements* against Arab attacks, not by individuals but by bands incited and organized by a *central Arab political body*. In the early years of the Mandate, the British recognized, in part, that the Jews had a right to defend themselves. But the Hagana was not a legal body and did not depend on the Mandatory Government for anything. There

were, however, legal defense units, consisting of regular and supernumerary police organized by the government.

Unlike Hashomer, the Hagana was based not on professional watchmen, but on *volunteers* who trained intermittently and were subject to less strict discipline than was the case in Hashomer. The Hagana groups acted as local defense forces when necessary, rather than as units subordinate to a central authority.

As Arab terror increased in intensity, the Hagana steadily developed into a more centralized body, with a National Command responsible for the coordination of defense needs on a countrywide basis. But its authority remained limited and ineffective even after the abolition of independent local bodies during the last ten years.

The first fully mobilized units were established during the period of the riots before the Second World War. They were called the Field Forces. In 1941 a special striking force was established. This group, the Palmah, trained in the settlements and supported itself by doing agricultural work there.

During the Second World War the Hagana was faced with a new, almost contradictory task: cooperation with the British Army against the common Nazi enemy, not only by the establishment of Jewish military units, but also by the participation of Hagana units in various operations, some in the neighboring countries.

With the end of the Second World War and the continuation of the White Paper, the Hagana turned its attention once again to the main political front, where a struggle was in progress against the attempt to impose an anti-Zionist regime in the spheres of immigration, settlement, and political organization.

The political front remains important. The White Paper government is adopting ever more extreme anti-Zionist and anti-Jewish policies. However, now there is a new front— *the Arab front*. We face not only the attacks from the local Arab rioters, but also *the hostility of the rulers of the Arab States* and, therefore, we must prepare quickly and diligently to meet this threat.

The two fronts—the British and the Arab—are intertwined. The anti-Zionist policies of the Mandatory Government serve to stoke the fires of Arab hostility. Arab aggression grows, thanks to the encouragement and the support—moral, political, and material (in the form of military equipment and training)—it receives from the British Government.

But it is vitally necessary that we *distinguish between the two fronts*. The struggle against the White Paper policy is basically a *political rather than a military one*. Even the military operations that are necessary from time to time in the course of the political struggle serve primarily to support it. In this context, defense is merely one of the challenges facing us. Only a concerted effort by the Yishuv and the entire Jewish people in the fields of construction, settlement, illegal immigration, and international policies will ensure our victory.

Arab aggression is a different matter. There, the Hagana is the most important, indeed the decisive, factor. An armed attack by the Arabs can only be stopped by Jewish military might. The Hagana will be neglecting its basic responsibility, and endangering the very survival of the Yishuv and of the Zionist enterprise, if it does not turn its attention to this matter.

There are over 110,000 soldiers in Egypt, Iraq, Lebanon, Syria, and Trans-Jordan with various degrees of training and equipment. The best military force in terms of training and equipment is the Trans-Jordanian Army, which is maintained financially by the British and is under British command.

Our most crucial task now is to prepare the Hagana to meet this challenge, to defend successfully not only Jewish settlements and the Yishuv as a whole, but in time of need to defend the entire Land of Israel and our whole national future.

In February 1947 Ernest Bevin turned over the Palestine problem to the United Nations. The General Assembly began to discuss it in May 1947. Andrei Gromyko, the Soviet delegate to the United Nations, surprised the General Assembly and the world by demanding, in his first appearance before the Assembly, the establishment of a Jewish State in Palestine: "It would be unjust to ignore the desire of the Jews for an independent state of their own, or to deny them to right to realize that goal. This would be unjustifiable, particularly in view of what the Jews suffered during the Second World War."

The United Nations General Assembly established a special committee to investigate the Palestine problem. The committee included representatives of the five political and geographic blocs at the UN, except for Britain and the Arabs. The committee came to Palestine in June 1947 and published its conclusions in September of the same year. It stated: (1) the British Mandate should be concluded at the earliest possible date; (2) independence should be granted to Palestine at the earliest possible date; (3) the transition period should be as short as possible; (4) the United Nations Organization should be responsible for the country during the transition period. On other questions the committee was divided. The minority was in favor of a federal state, with a small Jewish and a large Arab area. The majority wanted to divide the country into a Jewish State and an Arab State linked in an economic union, with Jerusalem remaining as a separate entity under international control.

The Zionist General Council, meeting in Zurich, expressed its support for the recommendations of the majority and said that the Jewish people would adopt their final attitude after the conclusion of the UN General Assembly debate. This decision was opposed by three parties: Ahdut Haavoda, Hashomer Hatzair, and the Revisionists.

The United Nations debate on the committee's recommendations lasted for two months. Finally, on November 29, 1947, the General Assembly decided by more than a two-thirds majority to accept the recommendations for partition. Thirty-three countries voted for the resolution, including the Soviet Union and the United States, while thirteen voted against it, including six Arab states: Egypt, Syria, Lebanon, Iraq, Saudi Arabia, and Yemen. Also opposing the resolution were four non-Arab Moslem states: Afghanistan, Pakistan, Iran, and Turkey. The other three countries opposing the resolution were India, Greece, and Cuba. Ten members abstained, among them Great Britain. The British government stated that it would not implement the General Assembly decisions unless they were accepted by both the Jews and the Arabs. This announcement served to stiffen Arab resistance. The Arab states announced that they would use force to prevent the establishment of a Jewish State.

From 1939 to 1947 there were scarcely any Arab attacks on the Yishuv. The Arabs had learned a lesson from the 1936–1939 riots, when the terror campaign and the general strike had hurt them more than us. Arab losses in the riots were several times as large as ours. Our position in the country was not weakened, but actually strengthened. New settlements were established and Jewish police units enlarged. The Arabs learned to respect our strength and determination. For more than eight years there had been peace and quiet in the country.

There was also complacency in our own ranks. Meanwhile, however, the peace and quiet ended. Security became more important than ever before. The Mufti returned, not as a refugee, but as the spokesman of the Arabs in Palestine. At his command, the Arabs, including the Arab communists, boycotted the UN committee.

There was a second change. Under the guidance of the British Foreign Office, an Arab League was established. Its main purpose was to combat Zionism.

And there was a third change. Not only did the White Paper policy continue under the Attlee-Bevin government, but the British also mobilized the Arab and Moslem worlds against Zionism, particularly the Moslems of India.

With Bevin's decision to transfer the Palestine problem to the United Nations the country was on the brink of a political decision. As the date of decision grew closer it became clear that we might be facing the entire Arab world, including the armies of the Arab states, which would have as their aim the *destruction of the Yishuv*.

At a meeting of the Mapai Council in Tel Aviv in mid-August 1947 I posed cruel questions:

> Can we be certain of the continued existence of the Yishuv? I do not refer to its eco-nomic existence, but to its very physical existence, and I refer not only to the lives of the 600,000 Jews living here. In order to make my meaning clear, I would like to ask a second, no less brutal, question. If the Yishuv were, God forbid, destroyed—and it should be re-membered that six million Jews were destroyed—would the Jewish people be capable of creating another one? Could the remnants of European Jewry, the Jews scattered in the Oriental countries, and the Jewish community of the United States bring forth the pio-neering and creative forces, imbued with the vision and determination necessary to rebuild this enterprise—and would our Arab neighbors allow them to rebuild it?
>
> Is there a danger to the survival of the Yishuv? With this brutal question in the air, it would be a grave, perhaps fatal, error to refuse to take a clear-eyed view of the situation and *prepare to meet it with all our strength*.
>
> We will be facing the Arabs and this means *not Arab bands but Arab armies*. These armies are not the finest in the world, but they are armies with military equipment, machine guns, artillery, and in some cases bombers and fighters as well.
>
> I do not want to frighten you, but we would be making a grave mistake if we did not take a realistic view of the hard and bitter realities. It is not only a question of our own survival, but the survival of the entire Jewish people, of the enterprise of salvation and de-liverance, of the hope and future of all the remnants of the Jews in the world.
>
> We must ask ourselves: Can we meet the threat?
>
> We are few, but we have considerable advantages, moral and intellectual, which are of prime importance when it comes to a showdown. But we will be able to exploit these advantages only if we are prepared to meet any eventuality, or any danger, swiftly and with all our strength and energy. We must regard defense preparations as the central issue, *the task on which everything else depends*. During the next two years this task must be central to all our activities, internal and external. It must determine the structure of the Zionist and local budgets, as well as our *internal organization*.
>
> We have one body, the Hagana, in which there are no differences of ideology or party, class or community, where there is neither right nor left, neither workers nor bourgeoisie. That unity makes Hagana uniquely important. The Hagana can accomplish a great deal; let us prepare it in good time for the momentous tasks that it faces.
>
> I do not know what recommendations the United Nations committee will put for-ward, or what the UN General Assembly will decide. But I do know *two things* which the world community cannot ignore. First, the Jewish community in this country is unlike other Jewish communities, for it is a community which is also a *nation*, with all the charac-teristics of an independent nation rooted in its Homeland. Secondly, the Jews of the Dias-pora are longing to come to Israel. There are masses of Jews for whom Aliya is literally a

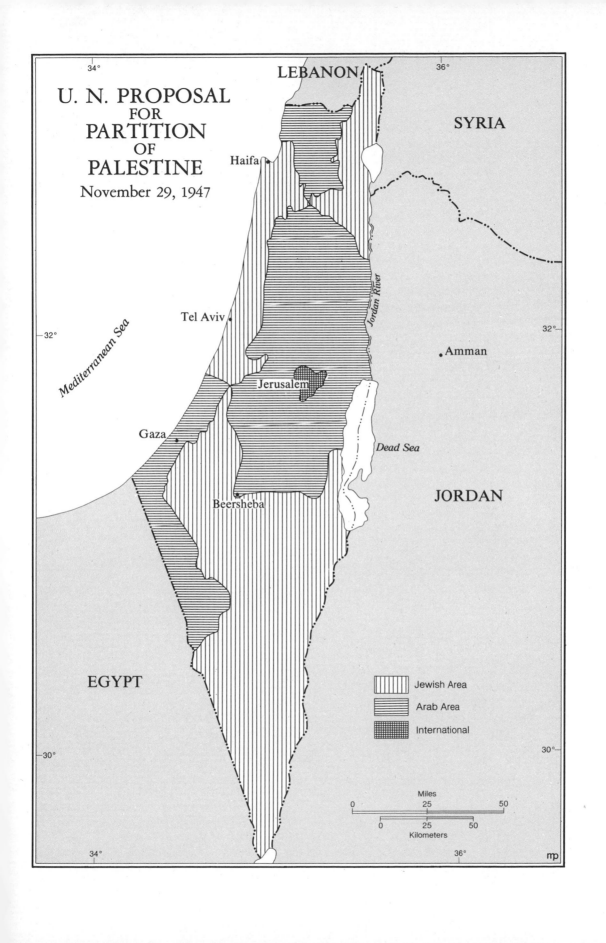

U. N. PROPOSAL
FOR
PARTITION
OF
PALESTINE

November 29, 1947

LEBANON

SYRIA

Haifa

Mediterranean Sea

Tel Aviv

Jordan River

Amman

Jerusalem

Gaza

Dead Sea

Beersheba

JORDAN

EGYPT

Jewish Area

Arab Area

International

Miles
0   25   50

0   25   50
Kilometers

mp

life-and-death question. And it is inconceivable that the world should fail to understand
that there is a Jewish nation here that will not be ruled by either the English or the Arabs.
It is inconceivable that the world should fail to understand that there are Jews who will
not let anything prevent them from coming to this country. These facts must be made
absolutely clear.

Finally, our first concern at this juncture must be defense; everything depends on it.
Today, in my view, this is the entire doctrine of Zionism.

I believed it was especially urgent to obtain heavy arms: tanks, halftracks, artillery,
and heavy mortars for our ground forces, fighter planes for the establishment of an air
force, torpedo boats, submarines, and other vessels for a navy.

The first large sum that I received from the Zionist Executive—large, that is, in
relation to what had previously been given—was $3 million. It was allocated in August
1946 at a meeting of the Executive in Paris. By 1947 $3 million seemed an extremely
small amount. I would like to make special mention of the good will and understanding
shown by the treasurer of the Zionist Executive, Eliezer Kaplan, who readily responded
to all my financial requests and dug up large sums for the purchase of more heavy equipment in addition to that obtained by Slavin in the United States. Slavin purchased modern
machinery for our arms industry. But we could not use these machines until the British
left the country.

Altogether we purchased 24 airplanes, 59 vessels of various types, 40 tanks, 144 halftracks, 416 artillery pieces, 24 heavy mortars, 158 heavy machine guns, 1417 medium
machine guns, 6034 light machine guns, 52,391 rifles, 523 submachine guns, 1755 pistols.
We were only able to bring in a small part of this equipment before the establishment of
the State. This included 20 airplanes (purchased from the British Army in this country),
52 halftracks, 26 artillery pieces, a heavy machine gun, 54 medium machine guns, 464
light machine guns, 6240 rifles, 417 submachine guns, and 500 pistols. It was with these
weapons, the weapons that the Hagana had retained from its underground period, and
those produced locally that we had to meet the attack of the Arab armies immediately
after the establishment of the State.

UN Resolution for Jewish State Touches Off Arab Invasions ★ Ben-Gurion Pleads for Single Supreme Authority

The Arab riots began the day after the UN General Assembly passed its November 29
resolution. The Arab High Committee called for a three-day strike. On December 2
an Arab mob burned the Jewish commercial center in Jerusalem while the British police
prevented members of the Hagana from coming to the assistance of their brethren. Two
weeks after the General Assembly resolution the Arab League, meeting in Cairo, decided
to send soldiers to the country in the guise of volunteers. The British did not lift a finger
to stop this military invasion. They also refused to cooperate with the UN committee
charged with supervising implementation of the Assembly resolution. At the same time,
the Arabs living in the districts destined to become part of the Jewish State began to flee
to the Arab states on the orders of the Arab High Committee.

The Arab attacks, in which bands from the neighboring states played a major part, increased. As I explained to Mapai's Central Committee on January 8, 1948:

> These are not riots. They are a real war, with three objectives. The first is to destroy the Jewish community, for the Arabs know that there can never be an Arab regime in this country as long as there is a Jewish community able to defend itself. The second is to prevent the establishment of a Jewish State, even in part of the country. It is a war designed to prevent the implementation of the November 29 resolution. Such resolutions have been thwarted before. Finally, if the first two goals are not achieved—if the Jewish community is not destroyed and a State is indeed established—the attacks will be aimed at reducing the dimensions of the Jewish State, in the Negev, Galilee, perhaps also in Haifa and other places.
>
> Though this is a war against a United Nations resolution, the burden of fighting falls on us, and us alone. In two cities, Jaffa and Haifa, we have so far had the upper hand. This is not only because of our military strength, but also because of the belt of Jewish settlements around these cities. According to reliable reports, fifteen to twenty thousand Arabs have already fled from Haifa, and many more are preparing to leave. On April 10, when the Hagana defeated the Arab bands in Haifa, it promised the Arabs of the city full rights, on one condition—that they turn over their arms. The local Arab committee agreed. But the Arab High Committee from its headquarters in Cairo ordered the Arabs to leave because within two weeks the Arab armies were to enter the country and throw the Jews into the sea. In the end, nearly 60,000 Arabs left Haifa, and only 4,000 Arabs, who refused to heed the orders of the Arab High Committee, remained behind. The same thing occurred in Tiberias, Safad, Beit Sha'an, and finally Jaffa as well. Only in Jaffa did some 3,000 Arabs remain in defiance of the orders of their leaders. In all the other towns every last Arab left, though the Hagana told them that they could remain as citizens with equal rights in the Jewish State that was destined to be established when the British forces withdrew on May 15.

The British High Commissioner promised the Zionist Executive that he would safeguard freedom of movement to Jerusalem. But although he still had some one hundred thousand British troops in the country, the road was closed by the Arabs. At the end of March 1948 I ordered the Hagana High Command to mobilize our forces in order to open the road to Jerusalem. The High Command decided to call up four hundred men, the largest number ever gathered at one time, for an offensive action. This force did not seem to me adequate. I demanded that at least fifteen hundred men be called up, since the Arabs were also aware of the value of Jerusalem. If they could liquidate the hundred thousand Jews of Jerusalem, by hunger or by bullets, they might be striking a death blow against the Yishuv. Members of the High Command argued that the situation was critical on all fronts and that the Hagana's defensive strength could not be reduced. I telegraphed immediately, on the evening of March 31, summoning all commanders to Tel Aviv.

When I explained the special importance of Jerusalem, each agreed to allocate half his forces to Operation Nahshon (the name given to the April 1948 operation to open the road to Jerusalem). Only the commanders in the Galilee, who were under heavy pressure, were allowed to keep their forces intact. That same night we received the first shipment of weapons from Czechoslovakia. They were sent immediately from the port to the fifteen hundred men entrusted with the task of opening up the road to Jerusalem. One of the Arab commanders, Abdul el-Kadar el-Husseini, fell in that campaign at the Kastel. The road to Jerusalem was opened. The British Army did not interfere on that occasion. But the road to Jerusalem did not remain open for very long. So we decided to open up a secret "Burma Road" to Jerusalem. Quietly, a pipeline was laid along this road from Rosh Ha'ayin to Jerusalem, for we were not certain that the existing pipeline through Arab settlements would remain intact.

The Zionist General Council met at the beginning of April 1948, mainly to approve the decision made at the beginning of March by the Zionist Executive and the National Council to establish a Provisional Government and Parliament, even before the British departed. The first of these institutions, with thirteen members, would become the Provisional Government on the departure of the British, until such time as elections could be held. The other, with thirty-seven members, would become a Provisional Parliament pending elections. The Provisional Parliament would contain representatives of all the parties in the Yishuv: the Labor parties, the General Zionists, the Mizrahi, the Revisionists, the Communists (who became avid supporters of a Jewish State after Gromyko's speech in the UN General Assembly in May 1947), the Sephardim, and the Agudat Israel.

I surveyed the situation on April 6, 1948, in a speech to the Zionist General Council. I said:

> Over 900 Jews have been killed in the four months since the Arab attacks began on November 30, the day after the UN General Assembly decided on the establishment of a Jewish State in part of the country. The Jews of the Old City of Jerusalem have been under siege for several months. Jewish Jerusalem as a whole is almost completely cut off from the rest of the country and is under constant threat of starvation. Almost all of the roads in the country are dangerous; no Jew can travel without risking his life. Thousands of foreign Arabs, many of them soldiers or officers in the armies of the neighboring states, have already invaded the country, and more are coming in all the time. They have arrived mainly from Syria, Iraq, Trans-Jordan, and, to a much lesser extent, from Egypt. The Arab Legion is encamped in this country, with the approval of the Mandatory Government. The Legion is supposedly the army of Trans-Jordan, but it is maintained by the British. It is the best disciplined, best equipped, and best trained of all the Arab military formations.
>
> Government in this country is breaking down, but the British are still trying, on the eve of their departure, to hinder the Yishuv's efforts to defend itself. Despite the UN resolution, the British refused to withdraw from the port of Tel Aviv on the first of February, although their policemen and troops have already left the Tel Aviv area. British warships still patrol day and night off the shores of Tel Aviv. The Mandatory Government maintains a de facto naval blockade of the country, directed against the Jews, at a time when the land frontiers to the east, north, and south can be crossed with impunity by the Arabs, including Arab bands and armies.
>
> On May 15, when the Mandatory regime is formally ended, the country will be open to full-scale attack by Arab forces. The ratio between the Jews in this country and the Arabs here and in the neighboring states, without taking North Africa into consideration, is about 1 to 40. Moreover, the Arabs have the tools of government at their disposal. Six Arab States are members of the UN, while a seventh, Trans-Jordan, is an ally of England, and is receiving a large proportion of its weapons from the departing British forces. The Jews under attack lack both a government and international recognition, at a time when they are faced by seven independent Arab states: Lebanon, Syria, Trans-Jordan, Iraq, Egypt, Saudi Arabia, and Yemen. The Arab states have more or less trained armies. Some have air forces. Egypt also has a navy. This is, in brief, the situation—one that confronts us with a more fateful problem than any we have faced in over 1800 years.
>
> The question is not whether or not we should defend ourselves or surrender—no such alternative exists. All we must consider is *how to fight in order to win*, and thus ensure our people freedom, a national future, and international status.
>
> At the last meeting of the Zionist General Council in August 1947 I unsuccessfully attempted to make the Zionist movement aware of the fact that security was the most vital

problem facing us. The Zionist movement was apparently not ready to accept such an evaluation. Now there is no need to convince the Zionist movement, and certainly not the Yishuv, that we face a grave situation fraught with many dangers. Yet even now I am not certain that the Zionist movement, or even the Yishuv, has drawn all the relevant conclusions.

Military force alone will not ensure our victory. In this era, war is not fought only by armies. Moreover, our struggle is even more difficult than others. For a war has been declared not only against the Jewish Army but against the entire Yishuv. No distinction can be drawn between the front lines and the home front. All of us—important and unimportant, men and women, old and young—are at the front, whether we like it or not. War has already been declared on us, though we do not yet enjoy the status of a sovereign state or have a recognized government. It is not difficult to blockade our sea coast, just as we are being blockaded along our land frontiers. An army in itself—even a much larger army than the one we have been able to establish—will not be able to stand up to the challenge *if we do not mobilize all our material and moral resources*. Military men themselves realize that moral strength is two-thirds of military strength.

There is one question that concerns all of us. Will we be able to survive at all? There is no obvious answer to this question. For myself, I am certain that we can meet the challenge, though I will not try to prove my contention as one proves a mathematical theory. If we were to turn to strategic and economic experts, men who did not know the *soul* of the Yishuv, and were to tell them that the Jewish community numbers 650,000 people, and also give them the breakdown of men and women in particular age groups, as well as the Yishuv's agricultural, industrial, military, and financial resources, and, at the same time, we were to point out that there is an Arab population of 1.1 million in this country, and another 30 million Arabs in the surrounding countries, that the Arab countries devote millions to military expenditures and have artillery, planes, and ships, in addition to the weapons they receive from England, and that they can easily attack the Yishuv—if we were to list all these things, I suspect that the experts would shake their heads and say that there was no hope for the Yishuv.

When the attack began four months ago, after the November 29 resolution, the Yishuv had no army, it had only *local* defense forces which for seventy years had been defending their own localities as the need arose. The men in these units were not well-trained soldiers. They were not even up to the standards of Hashomer, the organization which existed forty years before, because they were not professional military men. They were people who went about their daily affairs, devoting only a few hours a week to military training. Aside from these units, there was only one small brigade, with several thousand partially mobilized members. Even they devoted half of their time to working, and only half to military training. But at least this unit was always ready to answer a call for help and its operations were not limited to a particular locality. I speak of the Palmah. Another formation, also established on a voluntary basis, was being organized. Its members were trained for operations on a countrywide basis, but even with these units, the Field Forces, training was a spare time affair.

It was in this situation that the attacks began on November 30, 1947, and have continued ever since. The cities, the roads, and the agricultural settlements all over the country have been under fire. However, during these four months the enemy has not penetrated a single one of our settlements, some of which are thinly populated. Not one settlement has been destroyed or abandoned. At the same time, our defense units have penetrated many Arab localities in the Galilee, Samaria, Judea, and the Negev. Many have been abandoned by the Arab residents. A bitter struggle is now going on for control of Jerusalem. But the western, Jewish part of Jerusalem has never been so homogeneously Jewish as it is today. There is a large section of Jerusalem, which is similar in many ways to Tel Aviv. It is 100 percent Jewish. Jerusalem contains not only areas of contiguous Jewish settlement, but also Jewish islands in Arab districts—Romema, Kerem eh Sula, Sheikh Badar have been abandoned. But no Jewish neighborhood in an Arab district has been abandoned, even where such a neighborhood has been under twenty-four-hour-a-day attack for the last two months. A third of the Arab population has also fled from Haifa [this statement was made three weeks before the mass flight of Arabs from Haifa, Tiberias, Safad, Beit Sha'an, and Jaffa]. The Jews have not fled from any city. This gives us reason for faith in the future, but it does not justify us in drawing far-reaching conclusions. We should not assume that the danger has been passed. We must realize that the Arab potential has not yet been fully tested.

But manpower is only one factor in the struggle. Equipment is no less important and most important of all is *moral and intellectual stamina. This factor will ensure our victory.* While we should not underestimate the importance of quantity, it is not quantity that will be decisive. In terms of numbers we are weak. *Our principal advantage is in the qualitative sphere.* We will emerge victorious only if we exploit that advantage to the full.

Five things are required if we are to meet the challenge and emerge victorious:

A. We must mobilize all our manpower for military and economic tasks in the most rational possible manner, with security considerations being given priority.

B. We must prepare to produce or purchase the equipment we need on land, on the sea, and in the air, in accordance with the preparations that have been and are being made.

C. We must establish procedures to deal with finances, industry, agriculture, exports and imports, the distribution of foodstuffs and raw materials, etc., in order to strengthen our military forces without undermining our economy.

D. Most important of all, we must establish a single central body which will have authority over defense, industry, agriculture, finances, and government. This body will receive the full support of the Zionist movement and the Jewish people in the Diaspora.

E. We must not be satisfied simply to defend ourselves. We must attack at the right time all along the front, and not only within the boundaries of the Jewish State or the Land of Israel. We must attack the enemy wherever we can find him.

The specific task of this meeting of the Zionist General Council is, in my opinion, to authorize the carrying out of the fourth task—*establishment of a single, supreme authority in the Yishuv,* for without such an authority, we cannot survive. The Jewish Agency cannot turn over its responsibility to some other body without a clear directive from the Zionist General Council, and *without a new central authority, there can be no security.*

After extensive discussion, and as a result of outside pressures and fears that a vacuum would remain with the abolition of the Mandate, it was decided to establish two new institutions: a Provisional State Council, with 36 or 37 members, and a Provisional Government, with 13 members.

We have a great many bodies operating in the sphere of defense, and all of them have a record of notable achievements. If I were going to write a history book, I would give credit to the Jewish Agency Executive in Jerusalem, the Executive of the National Committee, as well as to the National Command and the Security Committee for their contributions to the defense of the Yishuv. I would not overlook the activities of the Mobilization Appeal and the Emergency Committee—all served the cause of security.

But this is no time to be writing history. We are facing life-and-death struggle and our only concern must be to emerge victorious. In view of this vital necessity, these many worthy institutions must be replaced by one institution which will control all resources and see to it that defense is given first priority. The military struggle that has been forced upon us, and which will reach its full dimensions on next May 15, necessitates the establishment of a single authority in the Yishuv, one which will enjoy the full support of the World Zionist Movement.*

Actually, there were other bodies that dealt with security matters in addition to the ones I mentioned. Every local authority, and particularly the Tel Aviv Municipality, was concerned with defense, which was by tradition a local matter. There were independent entities even within the Hagana itself. The Palmah had its own staff, which mobilized and trained men and, in some instances, acted on its own initiative. The National Command was not homogeneous—as I have mentioned, it was made up in equal parts of representatives of the Histadrut and the Citizens' Union, and even the two parts were not cut of one cloth. The Histadrut was composed of various political parties. Its representatives in the National Command were, in fact, representatives of parties, particularly of Mapai and Mapam. Mapam was the party of the Kibbutz Artzi and the Kibbutz Hameuhad—Ahdut Haavoda, which united before the establishment of the State. The representatives of the Citizens' Union were also a diverse group. Finally, there were the two dissident organizations, Etzel and Lehi, which did not recognize national authority, though they sometimes cooperated with the Hagana. In the fragmented Yishuv there were cases when sectional interests were put above the interests of the community as a whole. The government of the country was foreign and sometimes hostile; in internal Jewish matters every group could act as it saw fit.

On the Eve of the Proclamation of the Jewish State ★ Provisional Government Formed ★ Hagana Victories ★ Declaration of Independence Drafted

After a debate that lasted some ten days the Zionist General Council, by a majority of forty to eighteen (the minority was composed of ten representatives of Mapam and eight of the Revisionists), adopted the following resolution:

> In accordance with the decision of the World Zionist Organization and with the approval of Jews everywhere we resolve that with the termination of the British Mandate and the end of foreign rule, the Jewish people will establish an independent regime in their Homeland.

On the basis of this decision, two supreme governing bodies were established, the thirty-seven-member Provisional State Council and the thirteen-member National Administration [executive branch]. The latter, with the termination of the Mandate, would become the Provisional Government of the Jewish State. The Zionist General Council's most important decision was to concentrate all security matters, mobilization, civil defense, and the direction of the war in the hands of one body, the National Administration, which would be accountable to the Provisional State Council. The Zionist Executive retained responsibility for settlement, immigration, Zionist information and propaganda,

---

* *Israel Goes to War—the Four-Month Struggle and Its Lessons*, pp. 81–93.

education in the Diaspora, He'halutz (pioneering youth) affairs, the development of Jerusalem, and fund-raising.

The Zionist General Council's decision had no legal standing vis-à-vis the outside world, since the Mandatory Government was still in power. But as far as the Yishuv was concerned, the Council decision paved the way for the Declaration of Independence on May 14, 1948. Supreme authority in defense matters, at least in theory, had until then rested with the Zionist Executive. Since the Twenty-second Zionist Congress, held in Basle in December 1946, David Ben-Gurion, the chairman of the Executive, had headed the Defense Department.

However, the Executive's control of defense was far from complete. The dissident organizations recognized neither the National Committee nor the Zionist Executive. Even the Hagana's National Command, which was supposed to be responsible to the head of the Executive's Defense Department, operated independently to a large extent, and not always on the basis of unanimous decisions. The National Command, theoretically under the jurisdiction of the National Committee of the Yishuv, had two masters. Half the members of the National Command were nominated by and responsive to the Citizens' Union; the other half were nominated by and responsive to the Histadrut. But the Histadrut half was not united, for Mapam members controlled the Palmah (it was the Kibbutz M'uhad which indeed established, fostered, and ruled the Palmah), and did not always accept orders from the Histadrut Executive. The National Administration was to take over from all the other bodies.

At a meeting of the Zionist Executive on April 11, 1948, which took place during the sessions of the Zionist General Council, the decision was reached to allocate ten of the thirteen seats in the National Administration in the following manner: four to Mapai, two to the General Zionists, two to Mizrahi and Hapoel Hamizrahi, and two to Mapam. There were four candidates for the remaining three seats: the Sephardim, the Aliya Hadasha Party (later called the Progressives), Agudat Israel, and the Citizens' Union. At a meeting of the Zionist Executive, one seat each was allocated to the Aliya Hadasha, the Sephardim, and Agudat Israel. The parties nominated the following men: Mapai—Ben-Gurion, Eliezer Kaplan, David Remez, and Moshe Shertok [Sharett]; the General Zionists— Peretz Bernstein and Gruenbaum; Mapam—Mordekhai Bentov and Aharon Zisling; Mizrahi and Hapoel Hamizrahi—Rabbi Y. L. Fishman [Maimon] and Moshe Shapira; Aliya Hadasha—Felix Rosenblueth [Rosen]; Sephardim—Behor Shitreet; and Agudat Israel—Rabbi Yitzhak Meir Levin.

The Provisional State Council was composed of the following members: Daniel Auster, Yitzhak Ben-Zvi, Eliyahu Berlin, Rabbi Wolf Gold, Meir Grabovsky [Argov], Dr. Abraham Granovsky [Granot], Eliyahu Dobkin, Meir Wilner, Herzl Vardi, Zerah Warhaftig, Rachel Cohen, Kalman Kahana, Sa'adia Kobashi, Meir David Levinstein, Zvi Luria, Golda Myerson [Meir], Nahum Nir, Zvi Segal, David Pinkas, Moshe Kolodny [Kol], Dr. Abraham Katznelson [Nisan], Berl Repetur, Mordekhai Shattner, and Ben-Zion Goldberg.

Thus a number of parties not represented in the National Administration did have members in the Provisional State Council. These were the Revisionists, the Communists, the Yemenites, Poalei Agudat Israel, and WIZO (Women's International Zionist Organization). Mapai had ten representatives, the General Zionists six; Mizrahi and Hapoel Hamizrahi five; Mapam five; Agudat Israel and Poalei Agudat Israel three; Aliya Hadasha one; the Yemenites one; and the Sephardim one.

The Zionist General Council decided that representatives of Arabs recognizing the Jewish State would be asked to join the Provisional State Council, but no such Arabs were found until after the War of Independence.

We learn from the memoirs of President Harry S. Truman, who contributed greatly to the establishment of the State and also recognized it immediately after the Declaration of Independence on May 14, 1948, that the State Department and the Pentagon were not exactly enthusiastic over the idea of a Jewish State. Two members of the American delegation to the United Nations, Eleanor Roosevelt and Gen. John H. Hildring, were favorably disposed to our cause, but the delegation as a whole was indifferent, and the State Department was unfriendly. On March 20, 1948, Senator Warren B. Austin, the American Ambassador to the UN, said that his government would propose the establishment of an international trusteeship over Palestine. That same day, I commented:

> The American announcement does more harm to the UN—its standing and authority —than it does to us. The change in the American position indicates that the US has surrendered to Arab terror. But this does not basically change the situation here or impede the establishment of a Jewish State.
>
> The establishment of a State does not depend on the UN resolution of November 29, though that resolution had great moral and political value. It depends, instead, on our ability to emerge victorious. If we have the desire and the time to mobilize all our resources, the State will still be established.
>
> I was not among those who were overjoyed on November 29 and I am not depressed today, even if the American announcement has created a sense of depression in the Yishuv.
>
> We are masters of our own fate. We have laid the foundations for the establishment of a Jewish State and we will establish it. We will not agree to a trusteeship, temporary or permanent. We will no longer accept foreign rule in whatever form, and we will devote ourselves even more intensely to defending ourselves. The Jewish State exists and will continue to exist if we are able to defend it. The Jewish State will find a way to achieve mutual understanding with the Arabs.

The representatives of the Soviet Union also opposed the trusteeship proposal and demanded that the November 29 resolution be implemented.

Then came a proposal for a three-month truce. The Agency Executive in Jerusalem announced that it would agree to a truce if the Arabs 'ceased their attacks on Jewish settlements. The attacks did not cease. Meanwhile, the Hagana won impressive successes. The first city won was Tiberias. On the night of April 16–17 Hagana forces (consisting of a Palmah unit and a Golani unit) stormed the lower town. The hotel that controlled the Tiberias-Migdal road and was the headquarters of the Arab Command was captured by the Hagana, and on April 18 all the Arabs of Tiberias were evacuated by the British Army, even though the Hagana commanders announced that they would safeguard the lives and property of the members of all communities.

Haifa was next. Hagana units captured most of the positions held by the Arab bands, and the Arab commanders fled the city. The Hagana announced that all Arabs could remain in their homes; if they turned over their arms, their lives and rights would be safe. On April 22, at 4 P.M., representatives of the Arabs and the Hagana met in the presence of the British Governor of Haifa. The local Arabs of Haifa accepted the Hagana demands, but the Mufti, who was in Egypt, ordered the Arabs of Haifa to reject the demands and to leave the city. They would be able to return, he said, with victorious Arab forces three weeks or so later. Most of the Arabs fled; only some four thousand remained in the city. Those who stayed received documents from the Hagana entitling them to continue at their work and to move from place to place like other citizens.

At the beginning of May, Safad was captured and all its Arab residents fled, even though they were then a majority of the inhabitants. Beit Sha'an followed Safad on May 12, 1948. The same thing occurred in Jaffa in the last days of the Mandatory regime. When the Hagana captured Jaffa, the great majority of Arabs fled on instructions of the Arab High Committee.

These important Hagana victories were preceded on April 13 by the Arab massacre of Hadassah Hospital employees on their way to Mount Scopus by way of the Sheikh Jarrah Quarter. The British police officer responsible for the area had given his assurance that the road was open and safe. Dov Joseph tells of the tragedy in his book *Faithful City*:

> The convoy started at 9:30 A.M. It was made up of two ambulances, three armored buses, three trucks with food and hospital supplies and two small escort cars. The responsible British police officer had given the usual assurance that the road was clear. On the way from Sheikh Jarrah to Mount Scopus, the convoy struck a mine. One ambulance and two buses were damaged and could not be operated. The rear car turned around and managed to get away. A hail of fire, including grenades and Molotov cocktails, hit the cars from both sides of the road. The firing continued throughout the morning.
>
> The attack took place less than two hundred yards from the British military post responsible for the safety of the road. The soldiers watched the attack, but did nothing. At 9:45 General Gordon H. A. Macmillan, who was the ranking British officer in Jerusalem, passed nearby in his car; later he said he had the impression that the attack was ending. Twice later, at 1 P.M. and at 2 P.M., British military cars passed and were hailed by Dr. Chaim Yassky, director of the Hospital. Neither of them stopped.
>
> When the Jewish Agency liaison officer appealed to the British military headquarters to let us send Hagana men to the scene, he was told the Army had the situation in hand and would extricate the convoy. Hagana intervention would only make the fighting worse. Finally, two Hagana cars which tried to reach the convoy were ambushed and two cars which tried to come down from Scopus were mined, but all their occupants engaged the attacking Arabs. At noon the Arabs were reinforced. By 1:45 Dr. Judah Magnes, president of the university, telephoned General Macmillan with a desperate plea for help. The reply was that military vehicles were trying to reach the scene, but that a large battle had developed. By three o'clock the two buses were set on fire and most of the passengers who had not already been killed were burned alive.
>
> The attack had lasted for seven hours. It was 4:30 P.M. before the Arabs were finally driven off and the killed and wounded taken out. Only 28 persons were saved, eight of these unhurt. The 77 dead included Drs. Chaim Yassky, Leonid Doljansky and Moshe Ben-David, who were the founders of the new Faculty of Medicine at the university, Dr Guenther Wolfsohn, the physicist, and Professor Enzo Bonaventura, head of the university's Department of Psychology.

Convoys of doctors and nurses ascended to Mount Scopus from time to time in accordance with guarantees given personally both by the High Commissioner and by the Colonial Secretary, Arthur Creech-Jones, that medical and civilian transport to Mount Scopus would be guarded by the British Army and police. Those British promises cost the lives of seventy-seven doctors, nurses, researchers, teachers, and students.

On April 18, 1948, the National Administration held its first meeting. Only ten members were present: Ben-Gurion, Bentov, Bernstein, Rabbi Fishman, Zisling, Kaplan, Remez, Rosenbleuth, Shitreet, and Shapira. Those absent were Shertok (who was in the US), Gruenbaum, and Rabbi Levin. Among the matters discussed were the names to be given to the institutions of government that functioned under the National Administration and the Provisional State Council. Administrative problems included transportation, posts, telegraph, railways, fuel, supplies to the army and the civilian population, and the organization of manpower to meet the needs of the economy during the emergency. British rule, and with it government services, disintegrated rapidly. The most important concern of the National Administration was, of course, defense.

As the person entrusted with responsibility for defense by the Jewish Agency, I pointed out:

> The Hagana, which has been in existence for decades, has left us a considerable inheritance. It mainly consists of garrisons in each locality, which have consistently proven themselves by repulsing the attacks that have so far taken place. There were also the first small beginnings of military training, initially in the Palmah, and later also in the Field Forces. The Hagana left us a very devoted group of commanders and an extraordinary volunteer spirit, which for many years was the primary motivation within the organization. Because of the war in which we are now engaged, we have been forced in recent months to begin organizing our forces in a manner similar to that existing in a regular army. I say "similar" because without a state there cannot be a real army.

By the end of 1947 the Jewish Agency and the National Committee had called up people in the seventeen to twenty-five year age group. Recruiting offices were opened all over the country. The first group to be drafted were the seventeen to nineteen-year-olds. Agudat Israel demanded that women be exempted from military service, and it was agreed that any woman of military age who wished to be excused from duty on religious or family grounds would be released. Young people responded to the call and joined up. Dr. Benjamin Avniel, chairman of the National Service Command, reported that by the middle of January 1948, 72 percent of those who were supposed to report had already done so. The remaining 28 percent included members of the dissident organizations. All this was done without any compulsion.

A mobilization order issued in February 1948 called on young people in the seventeen to twenty-five-year age group who were overseas to register at the Zionist offices in their temporary countries of residence, ready at any moment to return for military service. In the month of March members of the twenty-six to thirty-three-year age group were called on to register. The mobilization process gathered force in April.

The National Administration met again on April 26, 1948. Only seven members were able to participate (Ben-Gurion, Bentov, Bernstein, Zisling, Rosenblueth, Shitreet, and Remez). Remez proposed the following division of posts within the National Administration: Ben-Gurion—Prime Minister and Minister of Defense; Bentov—Minister of Public Works; Bernstein—Minister of Commerce and Industry; Gruenbaum—Minister of the Interior and Labor Relations; Rabbi Fishman—Minister of Religious Affairs and of Jerusalem; Zisling—Minister of Agriculture; Kaplan—Minister of Finance; Remez—Minister of Communications and Transportation; Shertok—Foreign Minister; Shitreet—Minister of Police. The Ministers of Education, Culture, Health, and Social Welfare were not yet chosen.

Ben-Gurion declared that he could not yet accept the Defense Portfolio. He would, he said, continue in his task on behalf of the Agency Executive pending a final decision in the National Administration. The Agency Executive decided, in advance of a meeting of the National Administration on May 3, 1948, to transfer all defense matters to the National Administration. In view of this, Ben-Gurion stated that he would no longer participate in the National Command of the Hagana as an Agency representative and that the post of Head of the National Command had been abolished.

Zisling suggested that the National Administration reappoint the Head of the National Command as its representative.

Rosenblueth asked how the National Command is made up, and what is the task of the Head of the National Command and to whom is he responsible?

Ben-Gurion replied: The National Command of the Hagana was formally appointed by the National Committee, but in fact half of its members were appointed by the Histadrut and half by the Citizens' Union. The Jewish Agency supposedly exerted authority over the Hagana. After the last Zionist Congress in 1946, the chairman of the Executive was made head of the Agency's Defense Department, and he in turn appointed the Head of the National Command, who was then Moshe Kleinbaum [Sneh]. After the bombing of the King David Hotel, Sneh was forced to go into hiding and left for Paris. His post was taken by Zeev Feinstein [Shefer] from Ayelet Hashahar. At the last Zionist Congress, I named Israel Galili to replace Feinstein, who was unable to continue his work. The Head of the National Command was asked to pass on decisions of the Jewish Agency to the National Command. After the establishment of the National Administration and the Provisional State Council, when the Zionist General Council decided that the Agency should no longer deal with security matters, the post of Head of the National Command was abolished and the Agency's representative on the National Command was withdrawn. Henceforth, all defense matters are to be handled solely by the National Administration.

Bentov argued that the dismissal of the Head of the National Command meant letting go of a man who had been a central figure for ten years. He had been both an administrator and a military commander. The arguments used to justify his dismissal were purely formal. This would create problems among the soldiers as well. It was simply not good enough to justify the dismissal on formalistic grounds.

Ben-Gurion: To say that the Head of the National Command directed the war effort or was a military commander is not correct. I myself composed his letter of appointment and I did not give him those responsibilities. He was authorized to chair meetings of the National Command and to transmit the instructions of the Jewish Agency to it. He informed the Hagana High Command of the decisions of the National Command. The army received orders from the Chief of Staff, Yacov Dori. There was no such post as Commander of the Army. The National Administration is now free to arrange matters as it sees fit. If it wants to reappoint him to any task, it certainly can do so. We will discuss the organization of our defense effort, and whatever is decided will be carried out.

The National Administration took up these matters again on May 12, 1948.

Ben-Gurion: Two years ago, after the 1946 Zionist Congress, I was entrusted with defense affairs. They were then turned over to the National Administration following the decision of the Zionist General Council in April 1948. It was suggested that I become Minister of Defense. If defense matters are going to be handled as they were until the decision of the Zionist General Council, I will not accept the Defense portfolio. The lack of a single authority constitutes a grave danger. I will not be responsible for defense unless two basic principles are accepted. (1) The army and all its component parts must be subject to the authority of the people, which at this point means the authority of the National Administration. In another few months, I hope this will be an elected government. (2) All activities of the Hagana, or of an army, must be in accordance with the decisions of the elected authorities. This is true in regard to the activities of a platoon commander, a brigade commander, and the chief of staff. The organizational structure that has existed until now constitutes, under present conditions, a grave threat to our existence. Anarchy and a state are contradictory conceptions, especially in time of war, and even more so when it is a war of survival.

As one who has had his share of difficult experiences in this country, I know that there is no more trying responsibility than that of defense. It involves the lives both of individuals and of the people as a whole. When this responsibility was entrusted to me after the last congress, I did not feel that I had the right to refuse the heavy burden. But changes have taken place. In my opinion we will not be able to fight a war if there is anarchy inside the country. We must decide. But let it be clear, I will not be partner to any arrangement under which soldiers — members of the Hagana, of the Palmah, or whatever the name — are not subject to a single authority, enjoy the same conditions, and operate within the limits set by the Provisional Government, and when there are elected institutions, by those institutions. For forty-two years I have dealt with defense matters, but they can be handled by someone else. Choose whomever you like. For my part, I will not accept the task unless the two conditions I have mentioned are fulfilled, for they are vital to our success. But you are free to do whatever you please. This is my last word on the subject.

Shapira suggested that further discussion of the subject be postponed. A final decision was reached after the departure of the British and the start of the Arab invasion. The Defense portfolio was entrusted to Ben-Gurion on the basis of the principles of military unity and the supreme authority of the government.

On May 12, 1948, the National Administration discussed the Declaration of Independence. Some members had grave doubts as to whether independence should be declared. Shertok, who had returned that day from the US, proposed that the Declaration be issued. Rosenbleuth [Rosen] argued that the right of the Jews to a State had been clearly affirmed on November 29, 1947. However, a State had to be proclaimed within the boundaries laid down in the UN resolution. Boundaries were impossible to define at present.

Ben-Gurion took issue with the words "laid down in the UN resolution." He said there was no need to define the country's boundaries.

Shitreet supported Rosen's demand that the country's borders be defined. A State could not be proclaimed without a clear definition of its boundaries. Its laws applied to the areas under its jurisdiction, which therefore had to be understood clearly.

Ben-Gurion: The American Declaration of Independence contains no mention of territorial boundaries. Nothing obligates us to mention them. A nation declaring its independence does not have to define its boundaries. We should say nothing about them because we don't know what they will be. We accepted the UN resolution, but the Arabs did not. They are preparing to make war on us. If we defeat them and capture western Galilee or territory on both sides of the road to Jerusalem, these areas will become part of the State. Why should we obligate ourselves to accept boundaries that the Arabs don't accept in any case?

The question of defining the country's borders was put to a vote. A majority of five to four decided not to mention boundaries in the Declaration of Independence.

A five-man committee was established to prepare the Declaration. It consisted of Rosenbleuth, Shertok, Zisling, Shapira, and Remez. A meeting of the State Council was called for Friday noon to approve the Declaration, and at 4 P.M. in the Tel Aviv Museum to proclaim officially the establishment of the State.

At a meeting of the National Administration on May 13 Ben-Gurion reported the fall of the Etzion bloc, the surrender of the Arabs of Jaffa to the Hagana, and the appointment of Yitzhak Chizik as Military Governor of Jaffa.

Shertok, in the name of the committee, presented a draft of the Declaration of Independence, which began, as did the Mandate, with "whereas":

1. Whereas the Jewish people were exiled by force from their Land, to which they remained faithful through all the generations of exile and in all the countries of their dispersion;

2. Whereas in every generation, the Jews have striven to renew their roots in their ancient Homeland;

3. Whereas the British government which was given responsibility for the Land of Israel by the League of Nations has on this day renounced the Mandate and its responsibility for governing the country, we, members of the Provisional State Council, representatives of the Zionist movement and the Jewish people in the Land of Israel, who have gathered today on this solemn occasion, in accordance with the resolution of the United Nations Assembly, do hereby proclaim to the Jewish people in all corners of the Diaspora and to the world as a whole, the establishment of a Jewish State in the Land of Israel—the State of Israel.

There were twenty-two clauses in the Declaration. There was criticism of the term "whereas," of undue pomposity, of the absence of several points, and of the presence of a number of unnecessary points. A four-man committee—Ben-Gurion, Rabbi Fishman, Zisling, and Shertok—was appointed to work out a final formulation of the Declaration.

That evening Ben-Gurion prepared a revised draft and asked the other members of the committee to discuss it with him. Shertok was unable to be present. Rabbi Fishman and Zisling approved the draft, after a prolonged discussion on the final passage, which stated: "with trust in the Rock of Israel and his redemption." Zisling demanded that those words be completely removed. Finally the two agreed to leave the text unchanged, and the next day it was approved by the State Council, only one word being added to Section 13, which dwells on freedom of religion, conscience, education, and culture. At the suggestion of Grabovsky, the word "language" was added after the words "freedom of religion, conscience."

In regard to other proposed changes, involving criticism of the Mandatory Government or other political comments, the Council accepted Ben-Gurion's suggestion that Council members express their opinions at a meeting to be held after the departure of the British. He asked that the Declaration, with the word "language" added, be put to a vote. If a draft was approved by a majority of Council members, a unanimous vote would then be requested, so that the Declaration could become an expression of the views of the entire body. After the Declaration had been approved by a vote of sixteen to none, with eight abstentions, it was put to a second vote and approved unanimously.

Ben-Gurion announced that the Council would meet again in the afternoon to express publicly its unanimous approval of the Declaration. The oldest member of the group, Rabbi Fishman, would recite the she'heh'yanu benediction after which all members would be asked to sign the Declaration in alphabetical order. The meeting would end with the singing of "Hatikva." Space was to be left for the signatures of the Jerusalem members of the Council who could not attend the meeting.

Rosenblueth put the Declaration into legal form. The Provisional State Council adjourned.

II

DANGERS FROM WITHIN
AND WITHOUT

From the Establishment of the
State to the First Truce

Section 1. Declaration of Independence

A T 4:30 on the afternoon of May 14, 1948, the fourth session of the National Council was called to order in the Tel Aviv Museum.

Those present included members of the Council, representatives of the Jewish Agency, the Zionist Organization, the National Committee of Palestinian Jewry, the Jewish National Fund, the Foundation Fund, writers, artists, and journalists, heads of parties, the Chief Rabbis, members of the Tel Aviv Municipal Council, the chief of the Hagana's General Staff and other staff members, venerable pioneers, and representatives of leading economic bodies.

David Ben-Gurion announced: "I will now read the Declaration of Independence of the State of Israel, which has been unanimously approved by the National Council":

> In the Land of Israel the Jewish people came into being. In this Land was shaped their spiritual, religious, and national character. Here they lived in sovereign independence. Here they created a culture of national and universal import, and gave to the world the eternal Book of Books.
>
> Exiled by force, still the Jewish people kept faith with their Land in all the countries of their dispersion, steadfast in their prayer and hope to return and here revive their political freedom.
>
> Fired by this attachment of history and tradition, the Jews in every generation strove to renew their roots in the ancient Homeland, and in recent generations they came home in their multitudes.
>
> Veteran pioneers and defenders, and newcomers braving blockade, they made the wildnerness bloom, revived their Hebrew tongue, and built villages and towns. They founded a thriving society, master of its own economy and culture, pursuing peace but able to defend itself, bringing the blessing of progress to all the inhabitants of the Land, dedicated to the attainment of sovereign independence.

In 1897 the First Zionist Congress met at the call of Theodor Herzl, seer of the vision of the Jewish State, and gave public voice to the right of the Jewish people to national restoration in their Land.

This right was acknowledged in the Balfour Declaration on November 2, 1917, and confirmed in the Mandate of the League of Nations, which accorded international validity to the historical connection of the Jewish people with the Land of Israel, and to their right to reestablish their National Home.

The holocaust that in our time destroyed millions of Jews in Europe and proved beyond doubt the compelling need to solve the problem of Jewish homelessness and dependence by the renewal of the Jewish State in the Land of Israel, which would open wide the gates of the Homeland to every Jew and endow the Jewish people with the status of a nation with equality of rights within the family of nations.

Despite every hardship, hindrance and peril, the remnant that survived the grim Nazi slaughter in Europe, together with Jews from other countries, pressed on with their exodus to the Land of Israel and continued to assert their right to a life of dignity, freedom and honest toil in the Homeland of their people.

In the Second World War the Jewish community in the Land of Israel played its full part in the struggle of the nations championing freedom and peace against the Nazi forces of evil. Its war effort and the lives of its soldiers won it the right to be numbered among the founding peoples of the United Nations.

On November 29, 1947, the General Assembly of the United Nations adopted a resolution calling for the establishment of a Jewish State in the Land of Israel, and required the inhabitants themselves to take all measures necessary on their part to carry out the resolution. This recognition by the United Nations of the right of the Jewish people to establish their own State is irrevocable.

It is the natural right of the Jewish people, like any other people, to control their own destiny in their sovereign State.

Accordingly we, the members of the National Council, representing the Jewish people in the Land of Israel and the Zionist Movement, have assembled on the day of the termination of the British Mandate for Palestine, and, by virtue of our natural and historic right and of the resolution of the General Assembly of the United Nations, do hereby proclaim the establishment of a Jewish State in the Land of Israel—the State of Israel.

We resolve that from the moment the Mandate ends, at midnight on the Sabbath, the sixth of Iyar 5708, the fifteenth day of May 1948, until the establishment of the duly elected authorities of the State in accordance with a Constitution to be adopted by the Elected Constituent Assembly not later than October 1, 1948, the National Council shall act as the Provisional Council of State, and its executive arm, the National Administration, shall constitute the Provisional Government of the Jewish State, and the name of that State shall be Israel.

The State of Israel will be open to Jewish immigration and the ingathering of exiles. It will devote itself to developing the Land for the good of all its inhabitants.

It will rest upon foundations of liberty, justice, and peace as envisioned by the Prophets of Israel. It will maintain complete equality of social and political rights for all its citizens, without distinction of creed, race, or sex. It will guarantee freedom of religion and conscience, of language, education, and culture. It will safeguard the Holy Places of all religions. It will be loyal to the principles of the United Nations Charter.

The State of Israel will be prepared to cooperate with the organs and representatives of the United Nations in carrying out the General Assembly resolution of 29 November 1947, and will work for the establishment of the economic union of the whole Land of Israel.

We appeal to the United Nations to assist the Jewish people in the building of their State, and to admit the State of Israel into the family of nations.

Even amidst the violent attacks launched against us for months past, we call upon the sons of the Arab people dwelling in Israel to keep the peace and to play their part in building the State on the basis of full and equal citizenship and due representation in all its institutions, provisional and permanent.

We extend the hand of peace and good-neighborliness to all the states around us and to their peoples, and we call upon them to cooperate in mutual helpfulness with the independent Jewish nation in its Land. The State of Israel is prepared to make its contribution in a concerted effort for the advancement of the entire Middle East.

We call upon the Jewish people throughout the Diaspora to join forces with us in immigration and construction, and to be at our right hand in the great endeavor to fulfill the age-old longing for the redemption of Israel.

We trust in the Rock of Israel, we set our hands in witness to this Declaration at this session of the Provisional Council of State, on the soil of the homeland, in the city of Tel Aviv, this Sabbath Eve, the fifth day of Iyar 5708, the fourteenth day of May 1948.

After reading the document, I declared, "Let us rise to indicate our support for the Declaration of Independence." The entire audience rose.

"Please be seated," I said. "Every member of the National Council who wishes to make a statement may do so at the Council's next meeting, which will be held, we hope, on Sunday evening. There is one more announcement to be made, but before I make it I would like to call on Rabbi Yehuda Leib Fishman."

Rabbi Fishman intoned the traditional blessing: "Blessed art Thou, O Lord our God, King of the Universe, who has kept us and preserved us unto this day."

"The Jerusalem members of the National Council, who for reasons of which you are all aware were unable to reach this hall," I announced, "have gathered at the offices of the Jewish Agency in Jerusalem to express their unanimous support for our decision. I will now read the Proclamation of the Provisional State Council":

In accordance with the Declaration of Independence, providing for a Provisional Council and a Provisional Government for the State of Israel, the Provisional State Council proclaims the following:

1. The Provisional State Council is the legislative branch of the Government, but is entitled to delegate some of its legislative authority to the Provisional Government for the purpose of urgent legislation.

2. The regulations emanating from the 1939 White Paper are hereby declared null and void. Sections 13 to 15 of the Immigration Ordinance, 1941, and regulations 102 to 107C of the (Emergency) Defense Regulations, 1945, are hereby abolished. [*Stormy applause.*] The Land Transfer Regulations, 1940, are abolished retroactively to May 18, 1939. [*Stormy applause.*]

3. As long as no laws have been enacted by or on behalf of the Provisional State Council, the laws which existed in Palestine on May 14, 1948, shall continue in force in the State of Israel, insofar as this is consistent with the contents of this proclamation, with future laws and with changes arising from the establishment of the State and its authorities.

The Provisional State Council
May 14, 1948

The proclamation was approved by a standing vote.

Ben-Gurion: The members of the State Council should come forward to the podium in alphabetical order to sign the Declaration. Room will be left at the appropriate places for the signatures of the Jerusalemites.

The secretary, Ze'ev Sharef, read the names of the members of the Council and, after Ben-Gurion signed, they all signed in turn.

The names appear in the following order:

DAVID BEN-GURION

DANIEL AUSTER	RABBI WOLF GOLD
MORDEKHAI BENTOV	MEIR GRABOVSKY
YITZHAK BEN-ZVI	YITZHAK GRUENBAUM
ELIYAHU BERLIN	ABRAHAM GRANOVSKY
PERETZ BERNSTEIN	ELIYAHU DOBKIN
MEIR WILNER-KOVNER	DAVID ZVI PINKAS
ZERAH WARHAFTIG	AHARON ZISLING
HERZL VARDI	MOSHE KOLODNY
RACHEL COHEN	ELIEZER KAPLAN
RABBI KALMAN KAHANA	ABRAHAM KATZNELSON
SAADIA KOVASHI	FELIX ROSENBLUETH
RABBI YITZHAK MEIR LEVIN	DAVID REMEZ
MEIR DAVID LEVINSTEIN	BERL REPETUR
ZVI LURIA	MORDEKHAI SHATTNER
GOLDA MYERSON	BEN-ZION STERNBERG
NAHUM NIR	BEHOR SHITREET
ZVI SEGAL	MOSHE SHAPIRA
RABBI YEHUDA LEIB HACOHEN FISHMAN	MOSHE SHERTOK

Ben-Gurion: The State of Israel has been established. The meeting has ended.

The gathering concluded with the singing of "Hatikva." The people of Tel Aviv danced in the streets.

From My Diaries:

March 31–May 15, 1948

March 31, 1948

The General Staff came to me in the evening to clarify several questions. I told them that now there is only one central issue: keeping the Jerusalem road open. The manpower allocated for this purpose by Yigal Yadin is insufficient. We are facing a decisive struggle. The fall of Jewish Jerusalem might prove to be a death blow to the entire Jewish cause. The Arabs understand this very well, and will concentrate large forces in an attempt to cut the road. It is up to us to take all people who are not absolutely essential in the center of the country, Tel Aviv and the south, and to send them, with their weapons, to the Hulda–Bab el Wad–Jerusalem road. We have to keep pouring in reinforcements and to ask the commanders to find their best men and dispatch them now, tonight.

We immediately went back to the office to get to work on the project.

Tonight the first plane arrived safely (it brought rifles, machine guns, and ammunition).

April 1, 1948

I called on Nahum Verlinsky, the head of the Tnuva Marketing Company, and demanded he devote the following week—a "week" that could last more than seven days —to gathering supplies for Jerusalem, so that the efforts we were making, and the casualties we were sustaining, in an attempt to keep open the road to Jerusalem, would not be in vain. He accepted the task.

The weapons received the previous night, including fifteen machine guns, are already being used in the battle for the Jerusalem road. I told Yigal Yadin that some of the "spare" machine guns should be sent by air to Jerusalem, a symbolic gesture that would encourage the Jerusalemites.

April 5, 1948

Fritz Eisenstadt [Shalom Eshet] came from Jerusalem. He told me they have 25 machine guns, 250 rifles, 500 submachine guns, 35 small mortars, 4 big ones, 250 legal rifles, 130,000 rounds of 303-mm. ammunition, and only 8 mortar shells for each of their 2-inch mortars. They have one full company on paper, but it is scattered, with some men tied down in static positions, others in the Old City and 106 now in the Kastel-Tzuba region. Company B, with 153 men, is concentrated around Atarot and Neveh Yacov. It is almost without ammunition. There were 80 men at the northern end of the Dead Sea. There had also been 80 at Sodom, but they had been sent away by the Potash Company after an Arab had been killed by mistake. Seventy-six men had returned from the Etzion Bloc, and 150 had been sent to take their place. There were 70 men in Motza, 68 in Hartuv. A third company, consisting of 65 men in Jerusalem, 70 in Motza, and 68 in Hartuv, was being established. Two hundred men were on the way to Jerusalem, while 100 more were being held in reserve. Our boys lack field training. Our commanders are untrained as well. There is no discipline. The Palmah doesn't take any notice of the area commander: it receives its orders from Tel Aviv. There is no coordination. The population is hysterical. There are no reserves of food. The water pumps were out of action for 2 days, and Romema was without water before Fritz left Jerusalem.

In the Atarot area, there were some 1500 members of Arab gangs (Iraqis, Syrians, etc.). Our central problems: food and leadership for Jerusalem.

April 6–9, 1948

Meeting of the Zionist General Council. On April 8 I lectured on the security situation. In the meantime there have been battles in the Judean Hills and around Mishmar Ha'emek. Abdul Kadar El-Husseinei was killed on the Kastel after our withdrawal. We later recaptured the Kastel.

April 12, 1948

The Zionist General Council met until 5 A.M., but failed to complete its discussions.

April 13, 1948

Our airplane reported that our convoy reached Jerusalem. It included 165 trucks, with 800 tons of food, as well as escort vehicles and equipment. The convoy stretched over a distance of 10 kilometers. We hope that another convoy will leave tomorrow.

April 14, 1948

Yigal Feikovitz [Allon] returned from Hulda and Na'an. We lost 34 men in the Judean Hills fighting, 26 at the Kastel, and 8 in other actions. Abdul Kadar El-Husseinei had not been killed by a mine as we thought, but by one of our platoons. He had come at the head of a four-man unit to a position which was still being held by one of our platoons. Our boys immediately shot down three of the four. Abdul Kadar remained. He raised his hands and pleaded for his life. Our boys didn't know who he was and they shot him. Only when they had checked his papers did they realize whom they had shot.

Ehud Avriel signed a third agreement with the Czechs for 10,000 rifles, 3400 machine guns, and 30 million rounds of ammunition. We will receive the goods at the end of May. The prices paid under the terms of the second agreement were cheaper than those in the first agreement: 12 percent less for weapons and 6 percent less for ammunition. The third agreement calls for still lower prices in all categories.

In Yadin's opinion our units are 40 percent short of manpower, 75 percent short of transport, and 50 percent short of equipment.

Lehrer [Zadok] reported the following distribution of manpower: Palmah, 5200 men (1000 of them in the Negev); Golani, 1800; Carmeli, 2100; Alexandroni, 2100; Kiryati, 800; Givati, 3100; Jerusalem, 2000 (aside from 1000 Home Guards). There are 1800 men in the various service units. Altogether, we have 18,900 men. As far as vehicles are concerned, Operation Nahshon has 35, plus another 35 armored cars, while the Quartermaster Corps has 600 vehicles. We won't take a chance with them yet. They are being fixed up; 250 will be ready in five weeks. There are 72 vehicles in the ports and on the high seas. Zvi Eyalon thinks we should mobilize another 10,000 men. A mobilization order for the 25–35 age group must be issued.

April 18, 1948

Yitzhak Sadeh returned yesterday from Mishmar Ha'emek. Kaukji was given a real thrashing, but at the same time our units are exhausted. We were outmanned 3 to 1, outgunned 8 to 1. (Kaukji had 7 cannon and 13 armored cars. He had three brigades, each of them numbering 700 to 800 men. We had Palmah people, and another 300 members of the Field Corps.)

April 20, 1948

I reached Jerusalem at eight in the morning. We were shot at as we entered Sha'ar Hagai, but no one was hurt. Over 200 food-laden trucks arrived.

The manpower situation in Jerusalem is as follows: 3470 paid, well-trained soldiers. All our forces in the city pinned down (at the Hebrew University, in the south, in the Old City). Seventy men arrived as reinforcements from Tel Aviv. There are three British brigades in the city. The Arab gangs seized the Augusta Victoria Hospital while the English were still there, and now they are sniping at the university.

The Hadassah tragedy occurred today. The convoy set out at 9:10. There were 10 vehicles, over 70 passengers. Webb, the British police commander, was asked whether everything was in order and he answered: "The way is clear." At the crossroads between the university and Sh'hem Road, a car went up on a mine. The British Army, stationed nearby, did nothing to interfere with the Arab vandals. The cars were set on fire and most of the passengers were burned alive. About 30 bodies could be identified. Nothing remained of the others but ashes. The British Army did not allow the Hagana to go to the aid of the convoy.

April 21, 1948

620 combat soldiers and 80 members of service units reached Jerusalem.

In accordance with the decision of the Jewish Agency Executive I appointed a committee to deal with civilian affairs in Jerusalem. It is headed by Dov Joseph, who will serve as Governor. Its other members are Reuben Shriebman [Shari], Chaim Solomon, Daniel Auster, Yitzhak Werfel [Rafael], David Abulafia, and Charles Passman. They will handle supplies, the distribution of food, water, fuel, and transport, the prevention of profiteering, housing refugees, and internal security.

The Zionist Executive has decided that after the Histadrut's decision to turn over security matters to the National Administration, there is no point in having a person in charge of such matters in the Jewish Agency or serving as its representative in defense matters.

Agudat Israel has decided to join the National Administration. Its representative will be Rabbi Y. M. Levin.

In Jerusalem 3361 men have been mobilized; 252 of them are in training courses, while 3109 are in combat units.

April 23, 1948 (eve of Passover)

Our operations in the north were not successful. Our commander and eight of his men were killed. The others were forced to retreat.

In the afternoon, Yitzhak Sadeh came with more bad news. Yosefele Tabenkin sent out three armored cars as a rescue unit. The armored cars and the weapons fell into the hands of the Arabs. Fifteen of our boys were killed, among them the commander, Yo'hai.

April 24, 1948 (first day of Passover, the Sabbath)

We received our first artillery.

I cabled to Yigael Yadin to come to Jerusalem. He informed me that the city of Haifa is now completely in our hands. The port is two-thirds under our control, while the British Army occupies the other third. The workshops are also in our hands. Tonight we will attack Acre in order to open up a pathway to upper Galilee. The British Army will not interfere.

I was invited to visit the High Commissioner. He requested a cease-fire. I replied that we had agreed to a cease-fire for more than three weeks but that the Arabs had rejected such an arrangement. The High Commissioner admitted I was right. He asked only that we do not interfere with the supply lines of the British Army as it withdrew. We agreed. At five in the afternoon, I left for Tel Aviv.

April 26, 1948

I asked Israel Galili to come in for a talk. I told him that for a long time I had not been satisfied with the state of affairs in the Hagana, which was not operating in accordance with the defense needs of the country. As far as possible I had tried to avoid making any changes that were politically contentious. However, we had now reached a decisive stage in our struggle, and changes had to be made without concern for political consequences. We must do something because: (1) the Palmah is a private, political, and sectarian army; (2) some commanders are unsuitable, and the talents of others are not being fully exploited; (3) there is not enough military discipline and training.

Another shortcoming, perhaps not political in origin, is our lack of aggressiveness, our failure to exploit available manpower for offensive action. The abandonment of Lydda was a disaster, and perhaps unnecessary. The failure to attack Dir Ayule was not justified by a lack of manpower; we keep too many soldiers tied down in holding operations. We did not send sufficiently strong units to take Nebeh Yusha or Zarin. These mishaps stem from our undue emphasis on static defense. I told Israel Galili of the decision of the Zionist Executive to abolish the post of the chief of the National Command in the Jewish Agency, but added that I had not yet released this information.

In the evening, Galili returned to me with several proposals.

1. The Palmah was, in his opinion, no longer in need of its own national command. It should instead be divided into a number of independent brigades in various areas of the country. However, these brigades should be under the control of the General Staff, not the area commanders.

2. As regards commanders: Nahum Sarig and Moshe Zalitsky are good commanders. Moshe Montag should perhaps be moved to the General Staff. Ben Artzi's abilities will be tested now (he will be in charge of the Hometz Operation). Shlomo Rabinowitz [Shamir], and Mordekhai Makleff should be promoted. Itzhak Rabin is also a good man. Yosefele Tabenkin is arrogant but a good commander.

3. Galili agreed to the tightening of military discipline.

4. As far as Galili himself is concerned, he sees no point in his work unless he has the authority to intervene in various matters. However, if he should be charged with putting out an Army newspaper, he would accept the responsibility. He is knowledgeable and highly regarded. In his opinion, the Chief of the General Staff should not receive his orders directly from me. Someone should serve as an intermediary and he thinks that he would be a suitable go-between.

I asked him why he thought I should be in charge of security matters. Over the years I had never been one of the leaders of the Hagana, although I had always been vitally interested in its work. He answered that many central things would not have been achieved without my leadership. My advice was necessary on such crucial issues as the procurement and distribution of weapons, the struggle for the Jerusalem road, the decision to hold out or withdraw from particular points, etc. Though the Army people don't like my tough attitude on administrative matters, they accept my views because they need my strong moral support. While Galili may understand the situation, he does not have the strength to withstand pressure and keep his eyes firmly fixed on our central objectives, as I do.

I told him: (1) I will not assign him any work that will not give him a sense of moral satisfaction; (2) I doubt if I am completely fulfilling my responsibilities, because I sometimes avoid struggling for essential administrative reforms in order to maintain peace within the Executive; (3) the reforms that he suggests are not sufficient. If I were free (both from internal and external viewpoints) to act as I please, I would build up three armies—a Negev army, a Jerusalem army, and an army for the other parts of the country —each equipped to meet its specific responsibilities.

Yesterday I received information from Lehrer on the distribution of manpower. I noted that the high command fails to give serious consideration to the proper distribution of our forces. Of the 20,000 men at our disposal, only 1000 are in the Negev (by April 15, 1948, 1061), and 1680 in Jerusalem. This is absurd. We must defend both men and territory. We have only 1000 men defending an area of 3 million acres in the Negev. I am uncertain whether I would be carrying out my responsibilities to a greater degree by remaining outside the Defense sphere and criticizing actions taken by others, or by taking over the Defense portfolio.

April 27, 1948

I called in the members of two political parties: Aharon Zisling, Mordekhai Bentov, Yitzhak Ben-Aharon, Berl Repetur, Israel Galili [Mapam]; Levi Shkolnik [Eshkol], Golda Meir, Yosef Yisraeli [Mapai]. I began: My opinion has always been that the Defense portfolio is the most important one in the Executive. I regard this as a position without party or class overtones. We are not talking here about the establishment of a state or of an army—these may indeed have class aspects. But now the central question is the defense, indeed the very existence of the Jewish community. The Hagana, with its present equipment, organization and educational structure, is not ready to meet the needs of the new situation. There is a lack of military training and discipline. The changes to provide necessary reform have met with resistance—conscious and subconscious. Some of the changes that I knew were necessary were not carried out because I feared the political conflict that would have ensued. There have been tragedies and mistakes—some could not have been avoided; others were simply the result of amateurish methods (Nebi Daniel, Nebi Tusha). There were additional mishaps: Lydda, Dir Ayub. We are not fully exploiting our manpower, which is illogically distributed. There is a civilian approach, the result of historical circumstances, which does not meet military needs. There is a High Command, which is not a proper high command, as well as a Security Committee. All this results in a cloudy division of responsibility. In the military area: there is the Palmah—a sectarian organization with political ties. There is insufficient military training, a lack of discipline. Not every commander is suited for his task. The General Staff is not sufficiently aggressive. I will not take responsibility for defense if I am unable to introduce the reforms I know are necessary.

Israel Galili said, in part: The main reason for all the shortcomings you mentioned is the absence of a Jewish government with real authority. We lack a fully mobilized force because we failed to evaluate properly the political situation, and to allocate the necessary manpower, funds, and supplies. We have only 50 percent of the forces we need. Minor reforms will not change the situation. What we require is a clear definition of the responsiblities of the people who will take over. There is no Chief of Staff and there is no person in charge of military affairs. The Director of Military Affairs has no clear authority. The division of responsibility must be well defined. We must know who has the right to dismiss commanders at various levels, to decide on the structure of units and how they should be distributed, to allocate weapons to the various fronts, etc. I suggest that the Palmah be divided into three brigades responsible to the High Command and not to the regional commands. If the person who is in charge of defense lacks real authority, his office should be abolished. I do not believe he should be in direct contact with the Chief of Staff. This would not be effective.

I feel that I should be the person to deal with all matters. I asked Galili whether, if he took over defense, he would agree to having somebody else give orders to the Chief of Staff. He said he would not.

Ben-Aharon disagreed with me. Every party, he said, believes it serves the community as a whole through its own efforts. The Hagana has a clear working-class character. The pioneering elements have been responsible for the entire military establishment. We should not create an army along the lines of the British armed forces. The Palmah is an instrument of the pioneering spirit. If some party has been discriminated against, the discrimination should be eliminated. We need not only a General Staff but also a Military Command. The Defense portfolio is not an operational post. The person in charge of defense should concern himself with supplies and general policies, not with personnel changes.

A six-man committee was chosen to continue the discussion.

May 2, 1948

I called in Israel Galili. I told him that I wanted to make final arrangements for defense matters, in accordance with the decisions of the Zionist Executive, before the meeting of the National Administration and the National Council. The joint meeting with his party has been extremely enlightening for me. I have come to the conclusion that it is necessary to agree upon a clear division of responsibility. The post of Chief of the National Command should be abolished. I wanted him to work with me and I suggested that he formulate a plan outlining how authority should be divided. I laid down only two hard and fast rules:

1. I absolutely reject the Ben-Aharon doctrine of a political or a workers' army. It is an extremely dangerous one. We need a total national mobilization effort, not a military-political coalition. (Israel said that he disagreed with Ben-Aharon on this point.)

2. If I am to head the defense effort, I will give orders to the General Staff. Israel promised to come back with written proposals in a few hours. He didn't.

May 3, 1948

I sent a letter to the General Staff announcing that the post of Chief of the National Command in the Jewish Agency had been abolished.

I discussed Galili's future work with him. He told me that he had not succeeded in putting his proposals in writing. He was ready to concern himself with the procurement of weapons. I rejected this suggestion because of his lack of experience in the field. He asked me what I thought would be appropriate. I suggested he take over the running of the Army newspaper, which had a staff but no editor. The man in charge of defense would have direct contact with the Chief of Staff, and would be the only one to give him orders. He would be in complete charge of defense matters. He would have three aides—a number that could be increased or decreased—one responsible for manpower, one for equipment and supplies, and one for operations. The third would have to be a trained military man. The others might not necessarily be experts. All matters would be discussed by the group as a whole. This would be along the lines of what we had done at the beginning. Then Israel Galili, Yohanan Ratner, and I would meet each week to decide on important matters. Now the meetings would have to take place on a daily basis. The Defense chief, acting on the basis of the decisions of the National Administration, would have the ultimate authority. Israel said he wanted to consult Yitzhak Sadeh and would give me his answer as soon as possible. I told him that I must have it before my afternoon meeting with the National Administration.

May 5, 1948

I demanded that Galili continue serving as Chief of Staff until other arrangements could be made. He set one condition, that I appoint him Chief of the National Command. I explained to him that this position had been abolished and I had no authority to reestablish it. I suggested that we work out a plan for joint activities and he again set as a condition that he be intermediary between the Chief of Staff and myself. I told him that this was impossible. The situation in the Hagana is unsatisfactory, and only a proper legal structure will make possible the reforms that are really necessary.

May 7, 1948

A meeting with the General Staff. The operation to open the road to Jerusalem would be named Operation Maccabee, after Maccabee Metz, a commander killed in action. Seventeen hundred men will participate tonight. The attack will begin on Beit Maksir near Dir Ayub and Beit Jan. Tomorrow the engineers will repair the road. The day after tomorrow the convoy now in Jerusalem will be able to return to the coast. On May 10 a new convoy will go up to Jerusalem. According to Henry Yaffe, it will consist of only a hundred vehicles.

Last night three companies attacked Safad. They captured the entire citadel except for the top of the hill, where there is a pillbox occupied by Arabs. The struggle will continue today. We sent piats [mortars] to the Galilee. Hirbet Beit Daras has fallen to our forces. Sejera is also in our hands. But battle against the Zaviakh tribe ended in failure. Our men stumbled into an ambush; we lost eighteen killed and seventeen wounded.

Katara surrendered. We captured forty-six rifles (together with those captured at Akir, this gives us one hundred Arab rifles). Yesterday Na'an was attacked for three-quarters of an hour, either by the English or by the Arab Legion.

Upper Galilee is in great danger from Lebanon and Syria. We have reports that four thousand soldiers with tanks and artillery are massing in that area. Our patrols found hundreds of Arab soldiers with armored cars and artillery in the Malkia-Banat el Jubel region. Syrians with collapsible bridges have been seen near Mishmar Hayarden.

In the Galilee we have three brigades with a total of twenty-one hundred men, sixteen hundred of them in combat units. In addition, there are twenty-five hundred armed settlers. Next Sunday they will have six artillery pieces, as well as piats and flamethrowers.

Yigal Yadin informed me that, with the agreement of Chief of Staff Dori, changes will take place in the General Staff: Yohanan Ratner will be put in charge of planning and Yigal will deal solely with operations.

In the afternoon we went over our situation with the approach of May 15. The Mandate clearly will come to an end. Will we have to fight the neighboring nations? There are doubts regarding Trans-Jordan. Norman told our people that Abdullah wants to meet us. I suggested that we arrange such a meeting quickly but that it be secret and unofficial. Although we have been told that four Arab League states—Syria, Lebanon, Egypt, and Saudi Arabia—oppose a war, we must be ready for invasion from the north, east, and south. Our situation, as May 15 approaches, is as follows:

	Combat Troops	Armed Settlers	Total
The north	2000	2500	4500
Valley of Jezreel	1500	3000	4500
Carmeli Brigade	2000	—	2000
Alexandroni Brigade	2200	3000	5200
Tel Aviv	600	800	1400
Givati	2000	3000	5000
Negev Brigade	1200	1200	2400
Jerusalem	3500	—	3500
Harel Brigade	1400	—	1400
	16,400	13,500	29,900

Only 60 percent of our fighters are armed properly. There is a shortage of weapons: 3-inch shells, TNT, etc., and we need another four thousand rifles. We are short of vehicles. I called in Slavin and asked him if it was possible to speed up the production of 3-inch shells. He promised to drop everything else in the military industries and produce three thousand shells.

May 8, 1948

Hai Yischarof told me that Rothenberg had seen King Abdullah yesterday in Amman. He thinks that the King wants to meet with Golda Meir and that she should immediately be brought to Haifa for that purpose. I ordered that an airplane be put at her disposal, but, as luck would have it, the airplane broke down.

Maurice Fischer cabled [from Paris] that he knows of an English–Trans-Jordanian agreement with a secret clause, according to which the crown of Palestine will be given to Abdullah.

Saudi Arabia, Syria, and Egypt have decided: (1) Abdullah will enter the war in Palestine; (2) they will murder him; and (3) a government headed by the Mufti will then be established in the country.

We sent Golda Meir from Jerusalem to Haifa to enable her to meet with the "friend," our code name for Abdullah. We have decided in the meantime that there should either be an agreement on the basis of the UN decision or a mutual revision of borders.

May 9, 1948

I asked Israel Galili to come in at 3 o'clock. He came. I told him that he should return to work immediately and that over a period of time we would decide on a division of responsibilities. He promised to give me his answer today.

I received the account from Ehud Avriel. It shows:

Contract A: 4500 rifles, 200 machine guns, 6 million rounds of ammunition—$991,314.

Contract B: 10,000 rifles, 1421 machine guns, 16 million rounds of ammunition—$2,528,000. The two amounts have been paid in full.

Contract C: 10,000 rifles, 3400 machine guns, 30 million rounds of ammunition—$4,467,000. $1,983,973 paid on account.

The goods supplied under Contract A have already been received. Contract B goods are in port. Contract C goods are on the high seas.

Contract D: 10 Messerschmitts at a cost of $1 million. Of this sum, $900,000 has been paid (including payment for all auxiliary equipment).

Contract E: 75 37-ZB heavy machine guns, 1 million armor-piercing bullets, and 5 million regular bullets—$700,000. This sum has not yet been paid.

Contract F: 100 37-ZB heavy machine guns at a cost of $210,000. This sum is also yet to be paid. 20 Normand planes, costing $165,000, have already been paid for. Two of them have reached the country, and another three will arrive by May 15. Two ships costing $350,000 have been paid for. The total costs of all contracts is $11,216,373, of which $6,923,296 has been paid. We owe $4,293,027.

The Allon account includes the following:

Order A: 20 Hispano-Suiza antiaircraft guns at a cost of $1,025,000. This sum has been paid.

Order B: 50 65-mm. artillery pieces, plus 50,000 shells, 15 Hotchkiss machine guns and 300,000 rounds of ammunition, 200 Sten guns, 3 million Sten gun bullets and 1 million bullets for the Hotchkiss guns, 10 tanks (12.5 tons each), 25,000 7.5-mm. tank shells, plus another 10,000 37-mm. shells, 10 75-mm. antiaircraft guns, 12 120-mm. mortars, 12,000 shells, 500,000 7.92-mm. armor-piercing bullets, 5000 rifles, 5 million 7.91-mm. bullets, 1000 8-mm. Hotchkiss cartridge cases. This equipment cost $3,910,800. It has been paid for.

Order C: a light bomber, ammunition and auxiliary equipment for airplanes, at a total cost of $249,000, which has not yet been paid. Also airplanes—$607,000, some of which has already been paid. Another 200 bazookas for $20,000 and 200 tons of TNT for $25,000—both paid. We still owe $70,000 for 100 rifles. Together with miscellaneous expenses, these orders come to $7,931,300, of which $6,641,500 has been paid.

May 10, 1948

Yigael Yadin reports: The outposts around Beit Mahsir have been taken. Our airplanes are encountering difficulties, but in the evening they managed to drop their bombs on target. At 2 o'clock our units went into action. There was a counterattack at Beit Mahsir, which was repulsed with enemy losses.

I had lunch with Stone [Marcus] and Captain Martin, a non-Jewish expert in military training. General Hildring also saw Stone, who told him that we should hold on to the borders as of May 15 and be prepared for any eventuality. If there is an outside threat or attack across these borders, we should cross them ourselves; otherwise we should stay put.

May 11, 1948

Safad is in our hands. Beit Mahsir has fallen. Today a convoy may go to Jerusalem. Many Arab weapons were seized in Safad.

A meeting of the Central Committee. I surveyed the situation, pointing out both achievements and dangers. In the middle of the meeting Golda [Meir] arrived and gave me a note which read: "I had a friendly meeting [with Abdullah]. He is very worried and looks terrible. He did not deny that we had agreed on a mutually satisfactory arrangement. According to his plan, this would mean a united country with autonomy for the Jewish section, and then, after a year, he would take over the Arab section. But now he is only one of five [heads of Arab states]. It will be one country under his rule."

May 12, 1948

Yosef, a Hagana commander, was freed this evening by the Lehi [Freedom Fighters] Group. Lehi had seized a number of Hagana members. He was very well treated. He found extreme hatred of the English among the Lehi men. "There is no need to fight the Arabs," they argued. They returned him blindfolded to the Tel Binyamin area. He thinks they held him in Zikhron Yacov or the vicinity. There are former Palmah members among the Lehi people.

The Defense Committee met at 11 o'clock. Berl Repetur began with an attack, along pure *Al Hamishmar* lines, on the decision to abolish the post of Chief of the National Command. I told him that I had not been offered the Defense portfolio by the National Administration and would accept it, in any case, only on the following conditions: (1) the Army would be solely responsible to the people; (2) all military units would operate in accordance with a centrally determined policy; (3) security considerations, and only security considerations, would influence policy decisions. I pointed out that baseless charges were being leveled in certain quarters, but added that I would not argue the issues in public because defense considerations demanded that I remain silent.

In the afternoon there was a meeting of the National Administration. It was decided to proclaim the establishment of a State and of a Provisional Government. Peretz Bernstein suggested that we establish only a Government. Rosenblueth and Shitreet demanded that we define the borders of the State, but we postponed a final decision on the matter.

May 13, 1948

The situation in the Etzion Bloc is grave. The Arabs renewed their attack in the morning. There were 550 people in the entire bloc. In Kfar Etzion alone 40 were killed. Weapons and ammunition were sent by plane, but they may not have reached the defenders because the airfield was occupied by Arab tanks. The Etzion Bloc settlements have weapons for 400 men. A strong Egyptian attack continued against Kfar Brir.

The Jerusalem road situation is also fairly difficult. There are large Arab forces in the Ramallah-Latrun area.

4:30: Kfar Etzion has fallen. Our pilot saw Arab tanks in the kibbutz courtyard, and large concentrations of Arab troops on the road and by the crossroads. Michael Bengal, the Hagana commander in Tel Aviv, brought me the agreement formalizing the surrender of Jaffa to the Hagana. At six there was a meeting of the National Administration to discuss the text of the Declaration of Independence as prepared by Moshe Shertok. In the evening the text was given a final editing.

May 14, 1948

In the morning the General Staff met. I said that from now on our main objective was to hit hard at the enemy, not to defend static positions. The Alexandroni Brigade captured Arab Kfar Saba, advanced as far as Kalkilea, and then returned to Kfar Saba. Kfar Brir has been captured by Nahum Sarig. Sixty Arabs were killed and Arab weapons were captured.

At 11 A.M. Katriel Katz announced that the Etzion Bloc had fallen. The women were sent to Jerusalem and the men taken prisoner. At 1 P.M. the National Council met. The text of the Declaration of Independence was approved. At 4 o'clock independence was declared. The country went wild with joy. But, as on November 29, I refrained from rejoicing. The State was established. Our fate now rests in the hands of the defense forces.

Immediately after the ceremony I returned to military headquarters and discussed the worsening situation. There are disturbing reports about Arab Legion armored columns and enemy concentrations at Mafrak, in Syria, even around Lydda. On the other hand, our forces have reached the isolated Jewish settlements in western Galilee. Ahziv and Batza have fallen. The Police School and other important outposts in Jerusalem have been captured.

We have decided to requisition the rifles in the settlements in order to equip a new brigade. The production of tank traps will be speeded up.

Almost all the members of the General Staff opposed my plan to use more manpower for a greater effort to capture the Hulda-Shaar Hagai section of the Tel Aviv-Jerusalem Road. They argued that we do not have sufficient forces and are unaware of enemy plans. I do not want to overrule the General Staff without the backing of the Government, but I feel that we are losing valuable opportunities, which may affect the fate of Jerusalem and perhaps the entire campaign.

In the evening there were also very disheartening reports from the Negev. Will Tel Aviv be bombed tonight?

May 15, 1948

I was awakened twice during the night: at 1 A.M. to be told that President Truman had recognized the Jewish State, and again at 4:30 A.M. (I hadn't slept in the interval) to be informed that our people in America had demanded that I immediately make a radio broadcast to the US. I went with Yacov Yanai to the Hagana studio in Camp Yona. It took until 5:15 to make the necessary technical arrangements. Tel Aviv was being bombed as I spoke. I then traveled to the airfield, which had been under attack. One cabin was on fire, several wounded had been taken to the Hadassah Hospital, and a number of airplanes had been put out of action. The Reading Power Plant was also hit. For some reason, our antiaircraft guns stopped operating, and so the four or five enemy planes swooped low to drop their bombs.

Pajama-clad people looked out from all the houses. They did not seem to be excessively frightened. I had the feeling that they would stand up to the challenge.

I clarified our manpower situation. The Palmah has 6000 people: approximately 1300 in the Harel Brigade, 1300 in the Negev Brigade, 1200 in the north, and 1000 girls. Golani has 3573 men, plus 525 paid employees. Carmeli has 2238; Alexandroni, 3588; Kiryat, 2504; Givati, 3229; Etzion, 3166. There is a total of 24,000 men in these brigades. In addition, there are 398 men in Training Command, 659 in the Artillery, 675 in the Air Force, 150 in the Engineers, 168 in other construction units, and 1097 in Transport. Altogether there are 4161 in service units, and 1719 additional men in training. This gives us a total force of 30,574.

I called in Stone [Marcus] and asked him how many men were needed to capture the road to Jerusalem and nearby villages. He said that he would go and ask Yitzhak Rabin, and tomorrow at 10 would be back with an answer.

Our boys at the Tel Aviv airfield knocked down an Egyptian plane. The Egyptian pilot is in our hands.

Section 2. Arab Invasion and First Labors of Provisional Government

First Sessions of the Provisional Government and the State Council

THE STATE was established on Friday afternoon, May 15, 1948. The Provisional Government therefore was unable to meet until Sunday, two days later. But, of course, the Arab armies did not respect the Sabbath. The invasion began exactly at midnight, with the end of the British Mandate, eight hours after the creation of the State. Tel Aviv was bombed by Egyptian planes that night for the first time. The next day, Saturday, we brought down an Egyptian plane and captured the pilot. In the course of the interrogation he said that Arab refugees were spreading atrocity stories about the Jews: tales of butchery, rape, and theft. At the same time, the refugees claim the Jews are about to collapse, that the Arab armies will conquer the entire country in a matter of days.

On Saturday evening Prime Minister Ben-Gurion broadcast the following message to the nation:

> Something unique occurred yesterday in Israel, and only future generations will be able to evaluate the full historical significance of the event. It is now up to all of us, acting out of a sense of Jewish fraternity, to devote every ounce of our strength to building and defending the State of Israel, which still faces a titanic political and military struggle.
>
> Now is not the time for boasting. Whatever we have achieved is the result of the efforts of earlier generations no less than those of our own. It is also the result of an unwavering fidelity to our precious heritage, the heritage of a small nation that has suffered much, but at the same time has won for itself a special place in the history of mankind because of its spirit, faith, and vision.
>
> At this moment let us remember with love and appreciation the three generations of pioneers and defenders who paved the way for later achievements, the men who created Mikve Israel, Petah Tikva, Rishon LeZion, Zikhron Yacov, and Rosh Pina, as well as those who recently established settlements in the Negev desert and the Galilee hills; the founders of Hashomer and the Jewish Legion, as well as the men who are now locked in fierce battle from Dan to Beersheba. Many of these about whom I have spoken are no longer among the living, but their memory remains forever in our hearts and in the heart of the Jewish people.
>
> I will mention only one great person of those who are still among us. Whether or not he holds an official position, and whether or not we agree with his ideas, he remains our leading figure; there is no other single person who has contributed so much to the political and settlement achievements of the Zionist movement. I refer, of course, to Dr. Chaim Weizmann.
>
> The State of Israel was established yesterday and its Provisional Government has already turned to the nations of the world, great and small, in the East and in the West, announcing its existence and its desire to cooperate with the United Nations in the interests of international peace and progress. We have received unofficial reports that several countries have recognized the State of Israel. The first official recognition came from the government of the United States of America. We hope that other nations in the East and

in the West soon will follow suit. We are in contact in this matter with all members of the United Nations and with the United Nations itself.

But we should not deceive ourselves by thinking that formal diplomatic recognition will solve all our problems. We have a long thorny path ahead of us. The day after the State of Israel was established, Tel Aviv was bombed by Egyptian planes. Our gunners brought down one of the planes. Its pilot was taken prisoner, and the plane added to our fledgling Air Force. We have also received reports that our country is being invaded from the north, east, and south by the regular armies of the neighboring Arab states. We face a troubled and dangerous time. The Provisional Government has already complained to the Security Council about the aggression committed by members of the United Nations, and by Britain's ally, Trans-Jordan. It is inconceivable that the Security Council will ignore these wanton acts, which violate the peace, international law, and UN decisions. But we must never forget that our security ultimately depends on our own might.

It is the responsibility of each one of us, and of every municipal body, to take appropriate defensive measures, such as constructing air raid shelters, digging trenches, etc. We must concentrate in particular on building up a military striking force capable of repulsing and destroying enemy forces wherever they may be found.

Finally, we must prepare to receive our brethren from the far-flung corners of the Diaspora; from the camps of Cyprus, Germany, and Austria, as well as from all the other lands where the message of liberation has arrived We will receive them with open arms and help them to strike roots here in the soil of the Homeland. The State of Israel calls on everyone to faithfully fulfill his duties in defense, construction, and immigrant absorption. Only in this way can we prove ourselves worthy of the hour.

The Provisional Government* held its first meeting on May 16. Two members, Gruenbaum and Rabbi Levin, were unable to come from Jerusalem.

Foreign Minister Shertok [Sharett], who had arrived from the United States only five days earlier, reported that the State Department and the Pentagon had been absolutely opposed to the establishment of a State. The White House was closed to American Zionist leaders. The only Zionist who could see President Truman was Dr. Chaim Weizmann. He met Truman before Senator Austin presented an American proposal to the UN that Palestine be made a Trust Territory. This proposal had been prepared without President Truman's knowledge. Judge Sam Rosenman, who had been a close friend of the late President Franklin D. Roosevelt, saw Truman twice in recent weeks and asked him to recognize the Jewish State when it was established. Shortly after Truman was informed of Israel's establishment, he published the following statement: "The American Government recognizes the Provisional Government of the State of Israel as the de facto authority in the new State."

When the report of American recognition was received, Foreign Minister Moshe Shertok prepared a message to be sent to other governments. It included a copy of the Declaration of Independence and an announcement of the establishment of a Provisional Government. Messages were sent to the Soviet Union, France, Canada, Australia, South Africa, Poland, Czechoslovakia, Guatemala, New Zealand, Norway, Sweden, Denmark, and Belgium.

Ben-Gurion proposed that messages be sent also to the Arab States.

* From this point forward, with the formal establishment of the State, the author refers to the Provisional Administration as "the Government" or "the Provisional Government," and occasionally as "the Cabinet."—EDITORS.

Zisling suggested that they be supplemented by a demand that the Arab states cease their acts of belligerency. The Ben-Gurion proposal was adopted with the Zisling amendment.

Ben-Gurion reported on the situation at the various fronts: Tel Aviv was bombed. Four port laborers were killed, but work at the port continues. Ships carrying weapons purchased before the establishment of the State are now being unloaded. There is bad news from the Negev. Egyptian columns are advancing. The Egyptians are scattering leaflets demanding that the Jews surrender. A convoy of two hundred Arab vehicles reached Beersheba. Jewish settlements in the Jordan Valley are under artillery fire. The pressure on the road to Jerusalem has been eased. We captured Latrun, were thrown out, then recaptured it. Almost all of Jerusalem's New City is under Jewish control. Our troops have the Old City surrounded, but the small Jewish community inside the walls of the Old City is under Arab siege. Our forces have evacuated Atarot and Neveh Yacov to the north of Jerusalem, and not a single Jewish family remains in Kfar Etzion. The Revadim and Ein Tsurim settlers have been taken prisoner. There was still resistance at Massuot Yitzhak this morning.

Thirty thousand people are now mobilized, but only 40 percent of them are armed. We have thirty airplanes abroad, but transferring them to Israel is difficult. They can't be flown non-stop from where they are presently located, and we are not yet sure whether we will be allowed to land for refueling along the way. Therefore they must be dismantled and carried in transport planes that can fly non-stop. Their absence is strongly felt, as the Egyptians are attempting to bomb the airfields under our control. Meanwhile we possess only small planes, which we are using to supply besieged settlements. So far we have signed agreements in Europe for the purchase of $19 million worth of weapons; $15 million of this sum has already been paid. We began purchases after the Paris meeting of the Zionist Executive in August 1946. We now need much larger sums to finance them and thus it is necessary to send Golda Meir to America immediately to raise the necessary funds. Our activities in this sphere before the establishment of the State were very successful. With the money Golda collected, we were able to purchase rifles, light machine guns, heavy machine guns, and artillery pieces—all of which are en route here. Now we need planes and tanks. We will be able to hold out until we get those weapons. Eighty percent of the arms we require have already been purchased, but we will have a hard time until they arrive.

We may be forced to evacuate several settlements. Be that as it may, our main objective now is not the defense of one village or another, but the destruction of the enemy's forces. We can hold out for a considerable time if we receive 80 percent of the weapons we have already purchased. Meanwhile, the situation remains very grave.

There was also a discussion at the meeting on the distribution of Cabinet portfolios, which will be continued at the next meeting. Ben-Gurion proposed that the State Council elect Dr. Chaim Weizmann President of the State. Zisling and Bentov objected. By a vote of nine to two the meeting recommended to the Council that Dr. Weizmann be elected President.

Rosenblueth brought forward a number of legal proposals dealing with the Council, the Government, the budget and taxes, legislation, the courts, and transitional arrangements. After a discussion and several amendments, his proposals were passed on to the Council for its approval.

That same day the Provisional State Council met for the first time at the Jewish National Fund House in Tel Aviv. The Minister of Justice proposed that Dr. Weizmann be elected president of the Council. His proposal was adopted by a majority of thirteen to two, with Mapam and the Communists abstaining.

The Minister of Justice also presented a draft of the Law and Administration Ordinance for discussion. It was decided to appoint a five-man committee, consisting of Meir Grabovsky, Rabbi Kalman Kahana, Nahum Nir, David Zvi Pinkas, and Mordekhai Shattner, to discuss it and bring a revised version of the ordinance to the next meeting.

Prime Minister *Ben-Gurion* recalled his promise at the National Administration meeting on Friday. This was that members would have an opportunity to make statements on the formulation of the Declaration of Independence at the first session of the State Council.

Segal, speaking on behalf of Hatzohar, said that this party objected to the section proclaiming that the State of Israel was ready to cooperate with the United Nations in carrying out the November 29, 1947, decision of the UN General Assembly, because this section hinted at partition.

Levinstein, a spokesman of Agudat Israel, said that the secular phrasing and form of the declaration offended the religious sensibilities of Orthodox Jewry.

Shmuel Mikunis, a Communist Party representative, stated that the declaration had not emphasized the British maintenance of a colonial regime, and had not avowed that Israel would remain independent.

Luria, speaking on behalf of Mapam, raised no objections to the declaration as such. But he emphasized Mapam's views both before and subsequent to the establishment of the State. Mapam, he declared, would stand shoulder to shoulder with other progressive and democratic elements in the struggle to achieve true independence for Israel, and would safeguard the new State against any form of political, military, or economic dependence on the imperialistic powers, and against exploitation of Israel for interventionist purposes. Mapam would be in the forefront of the struggle for a true alliance with the Arab masses inside and outside the borders of the State of Israel, full equality for Arabs and Jews alike, the promotion of the forces of social liberation in Arab society, a joint Socialist pact with the Arab workers, peasants, and progressive intellectuals, and the integrity of the Land of Israel on the basis of full equality.

Rabbi Kahana (Poalei Agudat Israel) regretted that his party was not shown the Declaration before it was read out.

The Prime Minister responded that none of the statements in any way detracted from the sense of Jewish unity that was expressed on May 14. The existence of differences of opinion on matters of secondary importance shows how united the Jewish people are on the central issue—the establishment and determined defense of the State.

The next day Soviet Foreign Minister Vyacheslav Molotov informed us of his country's recognition of the State of Israel. While American recognition was de facto, Russian recognition was de jure.

That same day the American Ambassador in the Security Council, Senator Austin, called for a thirty-hour cessation of the attacks on Israel. The Arab states paid no attention to the request, and the Security Council failed to take any action on it.

First Law and Administration Ordinance

At the second meeting of the Provisional State Council, on May 19, 1948, Law and Administration Ordinance No. 1—1948 was adopted after a brief debate.

By virtue of the power conferred upon the Provisional Council of State by the Declaration of the Establishment of the State of Israel, of the 5th Iyar 5708 (May 14, 1948), and by the Proclamation of that date, the Provisional Council of State hereby enacts as follows:

CHAPTER ONE: THE ADMINISTRATION

The Provisional Council of State
1. (a) The Provisional Council of State consists of the persons whose names are set out in the Schedule to this Ordinance. Representatives of Arabs being residents of the State who recognize the State of Israel will be coopted on the Provisional Council of State, as may be decided by the Council; their non-participation in the Council shall not derogate from its power.

(b) The Provisional Council of State itself prescribes the procedure for its meetings and business.

The Provisional Government
2. (a) The Provisional Government consists of the persons whose names are set out in the Schedule to this Ordinance. Representatives of Arabs being residents of the State who recognize the State of Israel will be coopted on the Provisional Government, as may be decided by the Provisional Council of State; their non-participation in the Provisional Government shall not derogate from its power.

(b) The Provisional Government shall act in accordance with the policy laid down by the Provisional Council of State, shall carry out its decisions, shall report to it on its activities, and shall be answerable to it for its activities.

(c) The Provisional Government shall elect one of its members to be Prime Minister, and shall prescribe the functions of each of its members. A member of the Provisional Government shall be called "Minister."

(d) The Provisional Government may confer any of its powers upon the Prime Minister and upon any of the Ministers, insofar as that is not repugnant to any of the Ordinances of the Provisional Council of State.

(e) Decisions of the Provisional Government in respect of the division of powers among the Ministers shall be published in the *Official Gazette.*

(f) The Provisional Government itself prescribes the procedure for its meetings and business.

District Administration
3. The Provisional Government may divide the area of the State into districts and sub-districts and shall demarcate their boundaries.

Local Authorities
4. The municipal corporations, local councils, and other local authorities shall continue to act within the areas of their jurisdiction and scope of their authority.

CHAPTER TWO: BUDGET AND TAXES

Budget

5.   The budget of the Provisional Government shall be fixed by an Ordinance of the Provisional Council of State.

Taxes, etc.

6.   No government taxes or other obligatory payments to government the imposition whereof has not yet been authorized by law may be imposed, and no government taxes or obligatory payments to government the imposition whereof is authorized by law may be increased, save in accordance with an Ordinance of the Provisional Council of State.

CHAPTER THREE: LEGISLATION

Ordinances

7.   (a) The Provisional Council of State is the Legislative authority. The laws shall be called "Ordinances."

(b) Every Ordinance shall be signed by the Prime Minister, the Minister of Justice, and the Minister or Ministers charged with the implementation of the Ordinance.

Regulations

8.   Each minister may make regulations for the implementation of the Ordinances which are within the scope of his authority, insofar as such Ordinances confer power to make regulations.

Emergency Regulations

9.   (a) If the Provisional Council of State deems it expedient so to do, it may declare that a state of emergency exists in the State, and upon such declaration being published in the *Official Gazette*, the Provisional Government may authorize the Prime Minister or any other Minister to make such emergency regulations as may seem to him expedient in the interests of the defense of the State, public security, and the maintenance of supplies and essential services.

(b) An emergency regulation may alter any law, suspend its effect, or modify it, and may also impose or increase taxes or other obligatory payments.

(c) An emergency regulation shall expire three months after it is made, unless it is extended or revoked at an earlier date by an Ordinance of the Provisional Council of State, or revoked by the regulation-making authority.

(d) Whenever the Provisional Council of State thinks fit, it shall declare that the state of emergency has ceased to exist, and upon such declaration being published in the *Official Gazette*, the emergency regulations shall expire on the date or dates prescribed in such declaration.

Official Gazette

10.   (a) Every Ordinance shall come into force on the date of its publication in the *Official Gazette*, unless it has been provided therein that it shall come into force on an earlier or a later date than the date of publication. The date of the *Official Gazette* is deemed to be the date of publication.

(b) The publication of an Ordinance in the *Official Gazette* shall be evidence that such Ordinance has been duly enacted and signed.

(c) The provisions of this section apply also to regulations and emergency regulations.

CHAPTER FOUR: THE LAW

Existing Law

11. The law which existed in Palestine on the 5th Iyar 5708 (May 14, 1948) shall remain in force, insofar as there is nothing therein repugnant to this Ordinance or to the other laws which may be enacted by or on behalf of the Provisional Council of State, and subject to such modifications as may result from the establishment of the State and its authorities.

Termination of Dependence on Britain

12. (a) Any privilege granted by law to the British Crown, British officials, or British subjects is hereby declared to be null and void.

(b) Any provision in the law whereunder approval or consent of any of the Secretaries of State or the King of England is required or which imposes a duty to do anything in pursuance of his directions is hereby declared to be null and void.

(c) Any power assigned by the law to judges, officers, or members of the police force by reason of their being British, shall henceforth vest in judges, officers, or members of the police force who are holders of the same office or rank in the State of Israel.

Repeal of Enactments of the White Paper of 1939

13. (a) Sections 13 to 15 of the Immigration Ordinance, 1941, and regulations 102 to 107C of the Defense (Emergency) Regulations, 1945, are hereby repealed. Any Jew who at any time entered Palestine in contravention of the laws of the Mandatory Government shall, for all intents and purposes, be deemed to be a legal immigrant retroactively from the date of his entry into Palestine.

(b) The Land Transfers Regulations, 1940, are hereby repealed retroactively from the 29th Iyar 5699 (May 18, 1939). No judgment given on the basis of such Regulations shall be a bar to the lodging of a new claim in the same matter.

Devolution of Powers

14. (a) Any power vested under the law in the King of England or in any of his Secretaries of State, and any power vested under the law in the High Commissioner, the High Commissioner in Council, or the Government of Palestine shall henceforth vest in the Provisional Government, unless such power has been vested in the Provisional Council of State by any of its Ordinances.

(b) Any power vested under the law in British Consuls, British consular officers, or British passport control officers shall henceforth vest in consuls and officers to be appointed for that purpose by the Provisional Government.

Further Adaptations of Law

15. (a) "Palestine," wherever appearing in the law, shall henceforth be read as "Israel."

(b) Any provision in the law requiring the use of the English language is repealed.

Authorized Text

16. The Minister of Justice may issue a new text of any law which existed in Palestine on the 5th Iyar 5708 (May 14, 1948) and which is still in force in the State. Such text shall contain all the modifications resulting from the establishment of the State and its authorities, and upon its publication in the *Official Gazette* no other text of such law shall have effect.

CHAPTER FIVE: LAW COURTS

Law Courts
17. As long as no new law concerning the law courts has been enacted, the law courts existing in the territory of the State shall continue to function within the scope of the powers conferred upon them by law.

CHAPTER SIX: ARMED FORCES

Armed Forces
18. The Provisional Government may establish armed forces on land, on the sea, and in the air which shall have authority to do all lawful and necessary acts for the defense of the State.

CHAPTER SEVEN: TRANSITIONAL PROVISIONS

Validity of Orders
19. (a) Any order, direction, notice, demand, certificate, instrument, authorization, license, patent, design, trade mark, and any other right or concession, and any debt, obligation of liability made, given, or imposed by the High Commissioner, the High Commissioner in Council, the Government of Palestine or its authorities or officers, and which was in force in the territory of the State on the 5th Iyar 5708 (May 14, 1948), shall continue in force until varied, amended, or revoked, unless otherwise provided in any of the Ordinances of the Provisional Council of State.

(b) Regulations, orders, notices, and directions published between the 16th Kislev 5708 (November 29, 1947) and the date of publication of this Ordinance, by the Jewish Agency for Palestine, the General Council (Vaad Leumi) of the Jewish Community in Palestine, the People's Administration, or by any of their departments, in order to secure the maintenance of supplies and essential services or other economic objects, shall continue in force until varied, amended, or revoked by or on behalf of the Provisional Council of State.

Companies, etc.
20. (a) Any company, partnership or cooperative society which on the 5th Iyar 5708 (May 14, 1948), was registered in Palestine and which had on that date a registered office or place of business in the territory of the State, shall henceforth be deemed to be registered in the State.

(b) Any company, partnership, or cooperative society which on the 5th Iyar 5708 (May 14, 1948), was registered in Palestine but did not have on that date a registered office or place of business in the territory of the State, may apply for its registration in the State without payment of fees within three months from the date of publication of this Ordinance.

(c) This section also applies *mutatis mutandis* to societies under the Ottoman Law of Societies, registered business names, and registered ships.

(d) The Minister of Justice shall make regulations for the implementation of this section.

Payment of Taxes, etc.
21. The taxes and payments of every kind whatsoever which had not been paid to the Government of Palestine by the 5th Iyar 5708 (May 14, 1948) shall be paid to the Provisional Government.

Title

22. This Ordinance may be cited as the Law and Administration Ordinance, 5708–1948.

Commencement

23. This Ordinance shall have effect retroactively as from the eve of the Sabbath, 6th Iyar 5708 (May 14, 1948), and its provisions amplify and interpret the provisions of the Proclamation of the Provisional Council of State of the 5th Iyar 5708 (May 14, 1948).

MEMBERS OF THE PROVISIONAL COUNCIL OF STATE:

DR. CHAIM WEIZMANN
DAVID BEN-GURION

DANIEL AUSTER	ELIYAHU DOBKIN
MORDEKHAI BENTOV	HERZL VARDI
YITZHAK BEN-ZVI	ZERAH WARHAFTIG
ELIYAHU BERLIN	RACHEL COHEN
PERETZ BERNSTEIN	RABBI KALMAN KAHANA
RABBI WOLF GOLD	SAADIA KOBASHI
MEIR GRABOVSKY	RABBI YITZHAK MEIR LEVIN
YITZHAK GRUENBAUM	MEIR DAVID LEVINSTEIN
ABRAHAM GRANOVSKY	ZVI LURIA
GOLDA MYERSON	DR. ABRAHAM KATZNELSON
SHMUEL MIKUNIS	FELIX ROSENBLUETH
NAHUM NIR-RAFALKES	DAVID REMEZ
ZVI SEGAL	BERL REPETUR
RABBI YEHUDA LEIB HACOHEN FISHMAN	MORDECAI SHATTNER
DAVID ZVI PINKAS	BEN-ZION STERNBERG
AHARON ZISLING	BEHOR SHALOM SHITREET
MOSHE KOLODNY	MOSHE SHAPIRA
ELIEZER KAPLAN	MOSHE SHERTOK

Section 3. The War of Independence

Arab Armies Advance into Jewish Sections ★ "Burma Road" to Jerusalem ★ Conflict Until the First Truce

THE British High Commissioner left the country at midnight, May 14, but the evacuation of British forces began earlier. An Implementation Committee had been established by the United Nations to ensure an orderly transfer of authority to the Jews and Arabs respectively. The Mandatory Government, however, had refused either to recognize or cooperate with the UN body. As early as February 1948 the British Army and police began to evacuate certain parts of the country, starting with Jewish Tel Aviv and the Arab Triangle. Most of Palestine was no longer under British control by the end of April 1948. Even so, the British refused to recognize the institutions of the organized Jewish community, and several police and army buildings in Jewish areas were turned over to the Arabs. Only when British rule ended completely were we able to deal with the chaos created by the Mandatory Government, and to drive the Arab invaders from police and army buildings in Jewish districts.

In the four months between the partition decision of the UN General Assembly on November 29, 1947, and March 1948, when we embarked upon Operation Nahshon—our first organized offensive designed to open up the road to Jerusalem—over 900 Jews were killed. From Operation Nahshon until the May 15 invasion of the country by regular Arab armies, we lost 753 soldiers and over 500 civilians. During this period two gravest setbacks occurred: the slaughter of dozens of doctors, nurses, and university personnel on April 15 near Sheikh Jarrah, as previously described, and the Arab Legion capture of the Etzion Bloc in the final days of the British Mandate.

On the positive side, we had saved Jerusalem from conquest by the Arabs. The New City of Jerusalem became an almost completely Jewish entity. Even before the establishment of the State, we gained control of Tiberias, Haifa, Safad, and, two days before the end of the mandate, Jaffa and some nearby villages. Beit Sha'an had also been conquered, as had villages near Haifa, Safad, Tiberias, and in the south and in western Galilee. All this had occurred when the Hagana faced Arab bands, rather than armies. With the end of the Mandate the country was invaded by the regular, well-armed forces of the Arab states—Egypt, Jordan, Iraq, Syria, and Lebanon. The Hagana units at that time still lacked heavy weapons—artillery, tanks, and war planes. Many of our men also lacked military training and experience. Only those who had served in the British Army during the Second World War and, to some extent, those who had served in the Palmah, were properly trained. Our forces did not understand the significance of centralized military planning, subject to civilian authority. Only one of the dissident groups (Lehi) officially disbanded with the establishment of the State. The other (Etzel) continued its independent existence, in violation of the agreement reached with its leadership prior to May 14.

The month of battles, from the Arab invasion of the country until the first truce on June 11, 1948, was the most difficult and dangerous period of the War of Independence. For the most part, the Arabs enjoyed the initiative. Operations that we initiated were not always successful. The weapons purchased overseas trickled in slowly. Heavy weapons, the arms in which the Arabs had the greatest advantage, took longest to arrive because of transport difficulties. The invading forces received most of their equipment from the British government, and their training was mainly in the hands of the British.

Until the end of the Mandate an attempt was made to disguise the true state of affairs. Even the Arab governments did not accept open responsibility for the gangs, while the Mandatory authorities pretended to be neutral. But on May 12, 1948, two days before the British evacuation, the Political Committee of the Arab League adopted the following resolution:

1. A state of emergency is to be proclaimed in the member states of the Arab League.
2. The Arab states will absorb only women, children, and elderly people from among the Palestine refugees.
3. Every Arab state is to bear the cost of maintaining its forces in Palestine.
4. Arab Foreign Ministries are to exchange information in regard to all aspects of the Palestine war.

On Saturday, May 15, the invasion began.

In the Jordan Valley we had, in addition to local defense units in the settlements, an undermanned battalion from the Golani Brigade, with four hundred soldiers. One company defended the Zemah-Tiberias sector, a second held the Ashdod Yacov-Gesher sector, a third was tied down near Sejera and Kfar Tabor.

In eastern upper Galilee the Yiftah Brigade of the Palmah went into action even before the Arab invasion. After the liberation of Safad it attempted to seize Malkia and Kadesh, which fell on the morning of May 15. But a determined Lebanese counterattack inflicted casualties on the brigade and forced it to retreat.

The most important objective to fall into Arab hands was the Palestine Electric Works at Naharyim. Thirty employees were taken prisoner and sent to Mafrak in eastern Trans-Jordan. The generating station itself was destroyed and its equipment stolen. Twenty years of pioneering effort and investment went up in smoke. This area, the southern Jordan Valley, was the invasion route of the Iraqi Army. When we realized that we could not hold Naharyim, our forces blew up the two bridges across the Jordan near kibbutz Gesher. The Iraqis put up a temporary bridge, and brought across armored cars south of the kibbutz, where the oil pipeline from Iraq to Haifa crossed the Jordan River. On May 16 the Iraqis stormed Gesher, but were met by heavy fire and retreated, suffering severe losses. A second Iraqi force tried to advance south of Gesher in the direction of the Crusader fortress of Belvoir. It was confronted by a Golani unit and retreated in disorder, leaving behind thirty dead and numerous weapons.

Four of the first artillery pieces to arrive in Israel after the establishment of the State were sent to the Jordan Valley. These 65-mm. guns, which reached the area on May 20, enabled us to repulse a Syrian assault that had brought the enemy practically to the gates of the kibbutzim Degania Aleph and Beth.

The main enemy force active in the central region was the Arab Legion. As mentioned previously, the first aggressive act of the Legion, then under the command of British officers, was carried out at the Etzion Bloc several days before the end of the Mandate.

On the eve of British withdrawal the Arab Legion began to move toward Jerusalem. On May 14 it attacked Atarot, north of the city, and our forces retreated to nearby Neveh Yacov. The next day a strong attack began against Neveh Yacov as well. Our men were forced to retreat again, after suffering twenty-six casualties: four killed, twelve badly wounded, and ten lightly wounded.

We had to abandon positions east of Jerusalem, the potash works at the north end of the Dead Sea, and kibbutz Beit Ha'arava. North and east of Jerusalem no barrier remained between enemy forces and the city. Attacks began simultaneously from the north and the south. Jerusalem was bombarded by 25-pounder guns and 81-mm. mortars. The shelling went on almost continuously for a month, until the first truce. Jewish Jerusalem's suffering and heroism are described in exemplary fashion by Dov Joseph, appointed Governor of Jerusalem by the Provisional Government, in his book *The Faithful City*. Sheikh Jarrah and the Police School, seized by the Hagana on the departure of the British Army, fell to the Arab Legion because our forces were unable to hold out against the pressure of enemy armor. But the strenuous, month-long Arab effort to conquer the New City failed, though the Legion was aided by reinforcements, irregular Moslem Brotherhood units from Egypt. Ramat Rahel, south of Jerusalem, changed hands several times, with Jewish forces in control at the end. Our bitterest blow was the fall of the Jewish Quarter of the Old City.

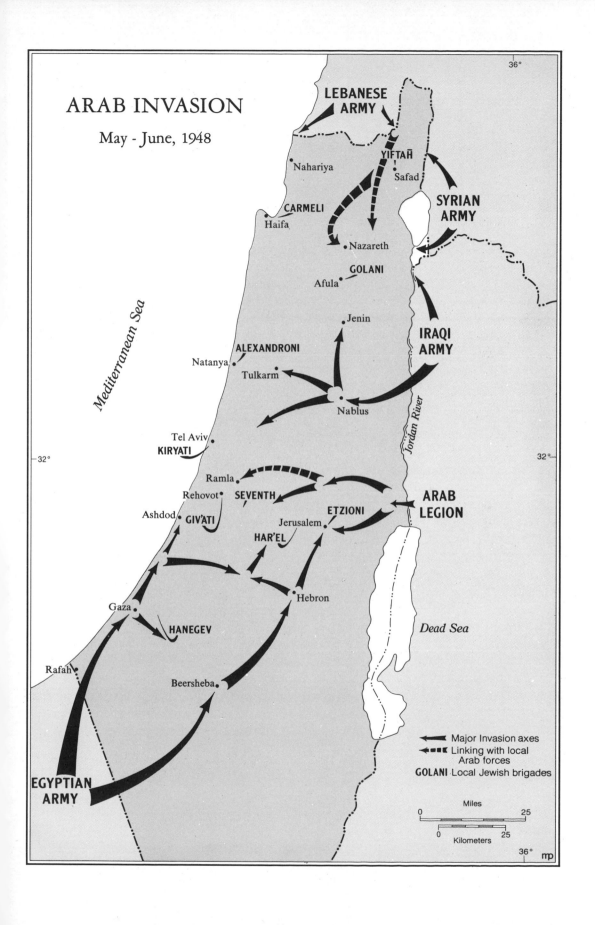

ARAB INVASION

May - June, 1948

LEBANESE ARMY

Nahariya

YIFTAḤ

Safad

SYRIAN ARMY

CARMELI

Haifa

Nazareth

GOLANI

Afula

Jenin

ALEXANDRONI

IRAQI ARMY

Natanya

Tulkarm

Nablus

Mediterranean Sea

Tel Aviv

KIRYATI

Ramla

SEVENTH

Rehovot

ETZIONI

Ashdod

GIV'ATI

Jerusalem

ARAB LEGION

HAR'EL

Jordan River

Gaza

Hebron

HANEGEV

Dead Sea

Rafah

Beersheba

EGYPTIAN ARMY

Major Invasion axes
Linking with local Arab forces
GOLANI Local Jewish brigades

Miles
0   25

0   25
Kilometers

36°

32°

32°

36°

np

Only eighteen hundred Jews, many of them children and old people, remained there by the autumn of 1947. At the time twenty-five thousand Arabs inhabited the Old City. During the period of the Mandate, when the British, responsible for maintaining order in the Old City, prevented us from sending reinforcements and equipment to the Jewish Quarter, no Jewish convoy could enter the Old City without permission of the British, who searched our shipments thoroughly for weapons.

Tension in the Old City lessened in May when it was decided to turn the area into a demilitarized zone. A Committee of Consuls was given responsibility for supervising the agreement. With the departure of the British the Arabs violated it by opening heavy fire on the Jewish Quarter from the east and north. Fierce fighting broke out inside the Old City. When the defenders of the Jewish Quarter announced on May 16 that they could no longer hold out, preparations were made at Jerusalem Military Headquarters to link up with them. Units of the Harel (Palmah) Brigade, which had been sent from the city to the Jerusalem Corridor at the beginning of May, returned to take part in the operation. A reserve unit of the Etzioni (Jerusalem) Brigade also prepared an assault on the Old City. The operations of the two groups were not coordinated because each had its own commander; so that there were, in fact, two separate attacks. The Etzioni group gathered in the recaptured Commercial Center, from which they hoped to penetrate Jaffa Gate. The Harel forces went from Yemin Moshe toward Mount Zion, where they planned to push through Zion Gate into the Old City.

Because of an administrative error, the Etzioni men waited opposite the walls for the entire day of May 18, thus alerting the Arabs to the attack. When our soldiers set out for Jaffa Gate on the evening of May 18, the Arabs were ready for them; our sappers were wounded or killed before they could reach the walls. Our armored cars were scattered. The commander of the attacking platoon was badly hit. The removal of our dead and wounded continued all night.

The same night Company D of the Harel Brigade set out from Yemin Moshe to take Mount Zion, an operation carried out almost without losses. The next day, May 19, Etzioni units again attempted unsuccessfully to penetrate into the Old City from Jaffa Gate. The Harel men managed to break through at Mount Zion and link up with the Jewish Quarter. The commander announced: "We have carried out our momentous mission and reached the Jews in the Old City, saving seventeen hundred of them. Our losses: one dead and eleven wounded." That night, members of Jerusalem Home Guard units were sent to reinforce the defenders of the Jewish Quarter. They brought with them supplies, ammunition, and several dozen rifles.

An Arab counterattack began in the early hours of the morning. Our men were forced to retreat to Mount Zion. Zion Gate was recaptured by the Arabs, and contact with the Old City was severed again.

That same day the first Arab Legion forces reached the Old City, replacing local units. Pressure on the Jewish Quarter grew ever more intense. In the evenings that followed, our forces tried again and again to break through to the Jewish Quarter, but without success. As a result of mounting Arab pressure, most of the northeast section of the Quarter was captured, and the Bater Mahse went up in flames.

A large-scale operation designed to break through to the besieged Quarter from Mount Zion and from the New Gate was planned for the dawn of May 29. Early on May 28, however, a delegation of rabbis from the Jewish Quarter went to the Arab Legion to discuss surrender terms. After negotiations, our soldiers were taken prisoner, badly wounded men and all civilians were allowed to cross over into Jewish Jerusalem, weapons were turned over to the Legion, and the Legion assumed responsibility for the safety of every Jew in the Quarter until evacuation had been completed. At 2 in the afternoon resistance ceased. Most of our officers and many of our enlisted men had already been put out of action. When a Legion officer saw our soldiers and their weapons he said: "If we had known what weapons you had, we would have attacked you with sticks. You managed to wrangle reasonable surrender terms after you had, in fact, already been conquered."

This first success of the Arab Legion in Jerusalem was also its last. The Legion continued to bombard Jewish Jerusalem, but the New City remained in our hands.

After the departure of the British we managed on May 16 and 17 to bring through two food convoys to Jerusalem. But the Legion, which advanced on the city from all directions, captured Latrun and again blocked the road to Jerusalem. A new unit, Brigade Seven, was established, composed for the most part of immigrants who had come straight from the Cyprus camps. A battalion from the Alexandroni Brigade joined it for an attack on Latrun. At dawn the battalion had reached only the site from which it was to advance on Latrun, so enemy forces were aware of its presence, and poured a deadly barrage of fire upon the unit.

The attempt to capture Latrun failed, and the road to Jerusalem remained blocked. The supply situation inside Jerusalem became so grave that another attempt to capture Latrun was imperative.

Col. David Marcus [Mickey Stone], an American-Jewish officer who had served during the Second World War under General Eisenhower and had come to Israel as a volunteer when the fighting started, was appointed by the Minister of Defense to command the forces operating in Jerusalem and the Jerusalem Corridor, including Brigades Seven, Harel, and Etzioni. One battalion from the Givati Brigade also was attached to his command. An armored force of Brigade Seven, led by Chaim Laskov, broke into the courtyard of the Latrun police station, but the operation failed when the infantry units that were to storm the station in the wake of the armored force did not arrive.

We then decided to open the "Burma Road" to Jerusalem. A unit of Brigade Seven, in the course of the attempt to capture Latrun, had gained control of the villages of Beit Jis and Beit Susin. Thus we had a continuous stretch from Hulda to a place near the Hartuv-Sha'ar Hagai road. A dirt track ran from that point to Beit Mahsir and then to Saris on the road to Jerusalem. The path from Beit Susin to the Hartuv road went along a very steep incline, but it had the advantage of concealment from enemy observation. We were able to send weapons, ammunition, and food by truck from Tel Aviv to Beit Susin; from there supplies were carried by porters or mules to a point on the Hartuv Road where they could be picked up by trucks from Jerusalem. Laborers from Jerusalem and Tel Aviv worked on the road secretly, at night. We also laid another water pipeline in this area in case the pipeline running through Latrun to Jerusalem should be cut.

To pin down the Arab Legion forces at Latrun, take pressure off Jerusalem, and divert attention from the Burma Road operation, we decided to make a third attempt to capture Latrun. The task was entrusted mainly to the Palmah brigades, Yiftah and Harel. The objective was not identified properly and the third attempt to take Latrun also failed.

A few hours before the first truce on June 11 Colonel Marcus was killed by accident. At 3:50 A.M. he left his camp near the Abu Ghosh Monastery, wrapped in a sheet. When a guard challenged him, Marcus replied in English. The guard did not hear. He fired one shot in the air. When Marcus failed to stop, another shot killed him. Marcus was the last man to fall before the first truce. We thus lost a fine commander and a fine man. In accordance with his will, he was buried at the US Military Cemetery at West Point, where he had received his military education.

The most poorly defended section of the country was the Negev—from the Gulf of Eilat to north Beersheba—constituting more than 60 percent of the area of the State. Only twenty-seven small settlements were in the district. The five largest were the kibbutzim Nir Am, Gvar Am, Dorot, Ruhama, and Yad Mordekhai. Defending the area, in addition to the settlers, were two battalions (eight hundred men) of the Negev Brigade, equipped with light weapons, and a few machine guns and mortars. The heavy weapons of the Negev Brigade were merely two 20-mm. guns, two locally manufactured mortars (Davidkas), and ten shells.

The two battalions were tied down defending the settlements, supply convoys, and the water pipeline from the Yarkon River. One battalion was responsible for the area north of the Gaza-Beersheba road, and the other for the vast area south of the road. A few days before the establishment of the State, these battalions, together with the Givati Brigade, captured Breir, Hulikat, and Kauhaba. They did not advance farther as most of the Givati Brigade was transferred to the Jerusalem Corridor.

Even before the establishment of the State members of the Moslem Brotherhood, a fanatic pan-Islamic organization, had invaded Israel, the first Egyptian unit to do so. When the Arab states decided to invade, the Egyptian command took the Moslem Brotherhood units under its wing. Their first attack was against Kfar Darom, ten kilometers away from the nearest Jewish settlement, and was defended by only thirty people. Artillery, mortars, and incendiary shells were employed. The defenders allowed the Egyptians to advance up to Kfar Darom's barbed-wire fence, and then opened fire on them. The attackers were also hit from behind by Egyptian artillery fire aimed at the settlement. The Arab unit retreated, leaving seventy dead and fifty wounded. News of Kfar Darom's valiant stand soon spread through the Negev and served to encourage its beleaguered defenders.

Regular Egyptian Army units invaded the country early on the morning of May 15, immediately after Tel Aviv had been bombed by Egyptian planes, and advanced along two routes, north along the Coast Road and east toward Beersheba, Hebron, and, finally, the outskirts of Jerusalem. The Egyptian press trumpeted news of the great triumphs, the conquests of Gaza, Majdal, and Beersheba, without hinting that these were all purely Arab towns. The Egyptians were certain that they would reach Tel Aviv in a few days. Meanwhile, they attacked Kfar Darom again. As before, the defenders allowed the Arabs to come within close range of the kibbutz, and then opened fire on them with every weapon available. Again the enemy retreated, and for weeks afterward did not dare to attack the village again, though it was kept under siege.

That same day Nirim was shelled from Rafah by artillery and mortars. As in the case of Kfar Darom, the Arabs were badly hit when they came close to the kibbutz. They left thirty bodies behind when they retreated. The victory was also a costly one for Nirim; seven of the forty settlers were killed.

The Egyptians then decided to concentrate on the conquest of Tel Aviv, and began to move north. They were confronted, on May 19, with kibbutz Yad Mordekhai. Attacks on the kibbutz continued for six days. Our losses were heavy: eighteen killed and twenty wounded. On May 22 the defenders of Yad Mordekhai announced: "We are losing strength and fear that this may become another Kfar Etzion." Reinforcements were sent, but Egyptian attacks increased and Yad Mordekhai fell on May 24. This permitted Egyptian forces to move freely toward the north. The Moslem Brothers reached the Hebron region and then Bethlehem, where they were soon in conflict with the Arab Legion, which was also in the same area.

The Egyptian column moving northward reached Ashdod. We sent four planes to attack. They were our first Messerschmitts, received in crates from Czechoslovakia and reassembled here. Our planes were met by heavy fire and one was shot down. We concentrated a large force for an attack on Ashdod. The attack failed, but it held up the Egyptian advance to the north. The Egyptians dug in around Ashdod, and cleared out areas behind their lines. On June 7 they attacked kibbutz Nitzanim, which was held by a hundred and forty people, half of them settlers and the rest from the Third Battalion of the Givati Brigade. The defenders had only light weapons, plus four Bren machine guns and one mortar. The Egyptians threw in an entire battalion, a platoon of tanks, another of armored cars, a battery of 25-pounders, and a unit of antitank guns. The bombardment continued for the entire night of June 6. In the morning the Egyptians attempted to break through into the kibbutz, but were repulsed. At 11 o'clock they tried again. Their tanks, followed by infantry, penetrated into the kibbutz. The battle continued inside the settlement. Radio contact was cut off. Members of the kibbutz tried to break out through nearby orange groves, but found themselves completely surrounded. Thirty-three settlers and soldiers were killed; a few succeeded in escaping; all the rest were taken, through Majdal, to prison in Egypt. On the night of June 9 a Givati battalion attempted to recapture Nitzanim, but lost its way. Not until the eve of the first truce did Givati units succeed in gaining control of Yasur (Hatzor) and the nearby village of Batani-el-Sharki, thus enlarging the Jewish-held corridor between Gan Yavne and Be'er Tuvia. A second attempt made that night by Battalion Seven of the Negev Brigade to capture the Iraq-Suedan police station failed.

Units of the Negev Brigade were more successful deep in the south. They captured the Bir Asluj police station and the nearby army camp. In this way the road was cut for some time between Ujah and Beersheba. But on the morning of June 11, before the first truce came into effect, the Egyptians entrenched themselves at the crossroads of the Negev road and the Mijdal-Faluja road, thus cutting off our access to the Negev.

Settlements not attacked directly by the Egyptians were nevertheless subjected to Egyptian air raids. Up to the first truce Egyptian planes bombed Tel Aviv sixteen times, Rehovot four times, and Rishon LeZion twice. On the day of the truce Ruhama was hit seven times from the air with incendiary bombs and machine-gun fire. Various settlements within artillery range of the Egyptians were hit but not conquered. These included Beerot Yitzhak, Saad, Nir Am, Gvar Am, Mekorot, Bet Eshel (near Beersheba), and Nevatim.

The following settlements were abandoned or fell during the first month of fighting:

In the south: Yad Mordekhai and Nitzanim, which were recaptured in the course of the war.

In the center: Hartuv, which was later retaken. The Etzion Bloc, Atarot, the northern part of the Dead Sea, and the Jewish Quarter of the Old City, which were not liberated until the Six-Day War in 1967.

In the north: Mishmar Hayarden, which was returned to us at the end of the war. The Naharayim power station, which remains in enemy hands to this day.

The settlements of Gezer, Masada, Sha'ar Hagolan, and Geulim, also evacuated at that stage, were recaptured a few days later.

From the establishment of the State until the first truce, 876 soldiers and some 300 civilians were killed. But in that month the military situation changed—we obtained more equipment, our soldiers were trained, and our arms industry grew larger and more sophisticated.

Israel Defense Forces Ordinance ★ *Arrival of Ships Carrying Weapons* ★ *Volunteers from Abroad* ★ *Israel's Air Force Develops*

At a meeting of the Provisional Government on May 23, 1948, Prime Minister Ben-Gurion presented the draft of an Ordinance on the Israel Defense Forces. Shapira opposed the insertion of the word "hagana" (defense), but no one supported him. In accordance with the request of several members, a final decision on the Ordinance was postponed until May 26, 1948. On that date it was approved. The Ordinance reads:

> In accordance with Section 18 of the Law and Administration Ordinance No. 1–1948, the following Ordinance is issued:
>
> 1. Herewith are established the Israel Defense Forces, consisting of ground, air, and naval units.
>
> 2. In times of emergency, conscription will be enacted for all formations and services of the IDF, with ages of those liable for conscription to be determined by the Provisional Government.
>
> 3. Every person serving in the ranks of the IDF will take on oath of allegiance to the State of Israel, its laws, and its lawful authorities.
>
> 4. The establishment or maintenance of any other armed force outside the IDF is hereby prohibited.
>
> 5. All orders, declarations, and regulations in regard to national service promulgated between November 29, 1947, and the date of this Ordinance by the Jewish Agency, the National Council for Palestinian Jews, the National Administration, the Provisional Government or one of its departments, will remain in effect until such time as they are changed, amended, or canceled.
>
> 6. All actions carried out in accordance with this Ordinance will be considered legal, even if they are in conflict with another section of an existing law.
>
> 7. The Ministry of Defense is responsible for carrying out this Ordinance.
>
> 8. This will be known as the Israel Defense Forces Ordinance—1948.
> May 26, 1948
>
> > The Provisional Government
> > David Ben-Gurion
> > Prime Minister

The publication of the Israel Defense Forces Ordinance could not in itself eliminate all the problems that resulted from the transformation of an underground army and dissident organizations into the regular army of a democratic state. But it did strengthen national unity and discipline, and it removed the moral basis for the existence of the dissident groups. Nevertheless, Etzel maintained its separate structure until September 1948. Lehi disbanded immediately upon the establishment of the State, though a secret terrorist nucleus of the group remained for some time. A marked improvement in the equipment available to the Defense Forces was made after the first month. When the invasion began, our entire artillery consisted of two dozen light 20-mm. guns, used against both planes and tanks. While the Arabs had whole squadrons of fighters and bombers, we had only light planes for communications purposes and a few transport planes. The latter, which could be used only at night, were carefully hidden during daylight hours.

Our armored units boasted a few dozen homemade armored cars, and two Cromwell tanks that had been "received" from the British. Understandably, we were at a considerable disadvantage when attacked by Arab planes, tanks, and artillery. In the first days after the establishment of the State, forty-one people were killed in an Egyptian air attack on the Tel Aviv Central Bus Station. The Egyptians also bombed the airbase at Ramat David, unaware that it had not yet passed into Jewish hands. The British, in retaliation, brought down four Egyptian planes.

Our situation improved with the arrival of ships and planes carrying weapons purchased abroad. Three such ships docked before the first truce. They contained artillery, mortars, rifles, ammunition, heavy machine guns, and planes. Four of the six 65-mm. artillery pieces which arrived at Tel Aviv port on May 15, 1948, were sent immediately to the Jordan Valley and played a crucial role in saving the kibbutzim there from being overrun. Artillery taken straight from the port was also used in the attack on Latrun.

Many Mahal (volunteers from outside the country) came from abroad during the first month of fighting. Among them were pilots, tank men, and other experts from South Africa, Canada, the United States, and elsewhere. Their professional knowledge and experience made them extremely valuable. A turning point was reached at the beginning of June when initiative in the air passed into our hands. On June 3, we won our first victory over the Egyptian Air Force, with the aid of Dakotas and Messerschmitts that had recently reached the country. The enemy's air superiority ended. During the month the Arabs lost two Dakotas, four Spitfires, and one Harvard; three Egyptian pilots were taken prisoner.

On May 31 the Prime Minister and Defense Minister published the following Order of the Day on the establishment of the Israel Defense Forces:

> With the establishment of the State of Israel the Hagana was transformed from an underground organization into a regular army. The people of this country and Jews everywhere owe an enormous debt to the Hagana for its accomplishments over the years, from the period when it consisted of a few isolated individuals in Petah Tikva, Rishon LeZion, Gedera, Rosh Pina, Zikhron Yacov, and Metulla, through the days of Hashomer, the Jewish Legion, the First World War, the defense of Tel Hai, the period of constant growth between the two World Wars—including the establishment of the Jewish Auxiliary Police during the 1936–39 riots—the setting up of the Palmah and the Field Units, the mass volunteering for service in the Second World War and the establishment of the Jewish Brigade,

up until the decisive struggle which began on November 30, 1947, and has continued until this very day.

Without the Hagana's experience, loyalty, and bravery, we could not have withstood the terrible and sanguine test of these last six months, and would not have survived to see the establishment of the State of Israel. The story of the Hagana will shine forth forever in the annals of Jewish history.

Now a new chapter has begun with the establishment of a regular army, the Army of a free and independent Israel, which will act in accordance with the policies laid down by the Provisional Government.

The security of our people and our Homeland will henceforth be entrusted to this army, which will be guided by the goals set forth in our Declaration of Independence.

"The State of Israel will be open for Jewish immigration and for the ingathering of the exiles; it will foster the development of the country for the benefit of all inhabitants; it will be based on freedom, justice, and peace as envisaged by the Prophets of Israel; it will ensure complete equality of social and political rights to all its inhabitants irrespective of religion, race, or sex; it will guarantee freedom of religion, conscience, language, education, and culture; it will be faithful to the principles of the Charter of the United Nations."

The Regular Army of the State of Israel will be composed of land, sea, and air forces, as well as the required service units.

The Israel Defense Forces will consist of all those who have served up to June 1 in various units and participated in the defense of Israel's freedom, as well as all those who will be mobilized again on the basis of the Israel Government's Ordinance.

All soldiers will be required to take the following oath of allegiance:

"I pledge to remain faithful to the State of Israel, its laws and its lawful authorities, to unconditionally accept the discipline of the Israel Defense Forces, to obey all orders given by authorized commanders, and to devote all my strength, even to sacrifice my life, in the defense of the homeland and of Israel's freedom."

The moral and physical commitment, as well as the personal devotion, of every officer and enlisted man will enable the Israel Defense Forces to be a firm bastion safeguarding the people and the land of Israel.

From My Diaries:
May 16–June 16, 1948

May 16, 1948

At 11 A.M. Israel Galili and Shkolnik were called to Menahem Begin. He proposed that their [Etzel's] ship be purchased for a quarter of a million, and that the money be used to buy arms.

The Carmeli Brigade reached Rosh Hanikra, where it blew up houses and bridges. Bridges on the northern road leading to Malkiya were blown up at Hanita as well. Acre is ready to surrender, but the situation in the eastern section of upper Galilee is quite bad. The battle for Malkiya was hard fought, with both sides suffering heavy losses. We have a hundred and fifty wounded in a battalion of five hundred men. An enemy unit holds the police station at Nebi Yusha. All the Arabs have left Safad. Two hundred men of the Carmeli Brigade have gone from the west to the east. Seventy men have reached there from Tel Aviv to replace the wounded. The first artillery pieces are now being unloaded. Among the immigrants was a French (Jewish) officer.

The Jordan Valley is under bombardment. They are asking for ammunition. The Syrians have descended from the hills. One of our planes is operating there with great effectiveness. The Alexandroni Brigade is facing an attack from Kalkilya, where some of Kaukji's men are now located. The morale of the field units is very low, as a result of the losses they have suffered. Nahum, in the Negev, demands that a high-ranking person be sent to discuss the situation in the area. Yigal Yadin is not certain about the situation there himself. Yesterday there were heavy attacks, led by tanks, on Nir Am, Nirim, and Kfar Darom. Our people don't think that they will be able to hold out. There are also reports of Egyptian columns along the coast, between Gaza and Mijdal. A large force of Abdullah's men have entered Beersheba. Nahum has only two and a half companies that are not tied down. The south is wide open. Stone [Marcus] visited the Jerusalem road. Stone and Mundik [Moshe Ben Tikva-Pasternak] have agreed on a plan of operations. Latrun was to have been attacked tonight, but I have not yet received a report about what happened. The Givati Brigade has established a Home Guard battalion of five or six hundred men. They are in Gedera digging trenches. We are holding all of our Jerusalem outposts, except in the Old City. We captured Allenby Barracks and Sheikh Jarrah. We are about to capture Su'afat. David Shaltiel says that if he is given piats, artillery, and other equipment, he will be able to stand firm against the Arab Legion.

Yitzhak Sadeh feels that we should evacuate all settlements below Nir Am. In my opinion, there is no rush. Whatever time can be gained is important. Perhaps by Thursday units will be ready for offensive action in the Negev. An engineer has gone to the south to deal with fortifications and tank traps.

Yohanen Ratner is afraid that the Arabs are planning to seize the Akir airbase and says it is necessary to fortify it. We have one Sherman tank to operate against all enemy tanks. In the course of the week our brigades will suffer losses and we must establish new units. People should be taken from the settlements. We lose an average of one brigade per week, and need a brigade to hold in reserve. We should also send replacements to units suffering casualties.

Operating procedures for the Air Force have been worked out with Aharon Remez.

A delegation consisting of Yacov Haft, Zekser, and Eli Bahir [Geller], has come from the Jordan Valley. Iraqi troops are attacking the Jordan Valley settlements. The attack on Ein Gev has ceased. Armored cars, and perhaps tanks as well, lead the way, followed by Iraqi infantry.

We must immediately dispatch machine guns, piats, and mortars to the Jordan Valley. Mordekhai Makleff should be sent there.

Tel Aviv was bombed again at 11:30.

Stone presented his plan for gaining control of the Tel Aviv-Jerusalem road. (1) Two battalions should entrench themselves along the ridges in order to prevent the enemy from reaching the road. (2) The enemy has four 75-mm. field guns and we need similar weapons (65-mm.) for operations in the Negev. Each company should be supplied with four mortars and four piats. The road must be kept in good condition. An engineering platoon and four armored cars should be ready to deal with problems arising out of air attacks, road blocks, or enemy ground action. (3) There should be a strong, motorized striking force at Sha-ar Hagai to defend convoys should they be attacked. The convoys should travel only at night. The General Staff accepted the Stone plan. The convoys will be organized tonight and tomorrow.

May 17, 1948

An attempt was made to bomb us again at 5 A.M., but our antiaircraft batteries drove off the "brave" pilots.

Tonight twenty-eight trucks are being loaded with supplies for the Harel and Etzioni Brigades.

Yigael Yadin reports: There is fighting within the Old City. Who started it? Yigael says the Arabs violated the cease-fire. The convoy carrying supplies to the Negev has been held up because the Arab Legion has entered the Iraq-Suedan police station. Stone flew to the Negev today. The Arab Legion has entered the Triangle with airplanes and armored vehicles. There is a report that Nebi Yusha has been conquered. Legion units at Sarafand attacked Rishon LeZion yesterday. The Etzel attack at Ramle is not going well. There is much Arab activity at the Lydda airfield. We are getting ready to bomb Lydda.

Beit Yosef in the Jordan Valley is under artillery bombardment. Radio Cairo announces that one Egyptian plane is missing. Radio Damascus announces that three Syrian planes have been shot down. An immigrant ship arrived this morning. An ammunition ship has been unloaded. Three cargo planes have arrived so far. Four piats, dynamite, and other matériel have been sent to the Jordan Valley.

Weapons are being collected from the settlements. Givati has already gathered 350 rifles, while Alexandroni expects to obtain 600. There are no reports yet from the Valley of Jezreel or from Galilee.

I asked Yigal whether we can fight on for another two weeks even without additional weapons from abroad. He is not certain. It will depend on the speed with which we can mobilize our own resources. Ratner reports: Kaukji's forces have been strengthened by the Arab Legion. If they are successful, local Arabs will join them. A commando operation must be carried out behind Arab lines. Moshe Dayan has been given responsibility for organizing a commando group in the central region. Ratner doubts whether we can hold out if we do not receive additional airplanes within two weeks. We are struggling against a coalition of states, which is a different matter from fighting a single nation. One side or the other will be knocked out.

Berl Repetur and Ben-Aharon came to see me; they quote Moshe Sneh and Israel Barzilai to the effect that airplanes can be obtained from Czechoslovakia and Poland if these countries are approached by the Provisional Government. When were Sneh and Barzilai there? Ten days ago—I asked Sneh to come and see me. Speaking on behalf of Berman (one of the heads of Left Poalei Zion), he told me that Poland would supply us with food (wheat from Danzig) for dollars or for goods that she needs. We will be able to receive full assistance from Yugoslavia and Czechoslovakia only if Russia approves. Sneh met with a Polish (Jewish) general, who told him: Poland's arms production is very small; everything was destroyed by the Germans and there is nothing much we can promise in the way of weapons. I asked: Were you there together with Barzilai? No, Barzilai was there before me. Did they promise Barzilai more? No, Sneh told Barzilai what he had been told and Barzilai had nothing to add. Sneh was also in Czechoslovakia, but he did not deal with these matters.

There was refreshing news in the evening: Molotov answered Moshe Shertok's message by according us recognition (de jure). Austin, in the Security Council, demanded at a Council meeting that the Arabs cease their attacks on Israel for thirty-six hours. Air raids have begun again.

May 18, 1948

Twenty trucks with supplies for the army went to Jerusalem during the night. A twenty-five truck convoy to the Negev arrived safely. Armored cars accompanying Givati came back from the Negev without losses. The situation in the Old City is critical. But in the Jordan Valley it remains stable; the Arabs have retreated and are digging in. They are also digging in upper Galilee. Moshe Dayan has been appointed commander of the Jordan Valley front. The late-afternoon bombing of Tel Aviv wrecked the Central Bus Station: dozens of people were killed and more than a hundred were wounded.

Aryeh Bahir, a member of Afikim, called me from Haifa in the evening. He told me that the situation in the Jordan Valley is getting worse all the time. The settlements are under artillery fire. A great deal of assistance is necessary. A Palmah company from upper Galilee has arrived, but this is not sufficient.

Apparently David Namiri of Ashdot Yacov has arrived from America. Good opportunities exist for purchases in Mexico, but only in lots of at least $1 million. Al Shwimmer, who is very capable, has gone into action. We must obtain two-engine bombers, single-engine fighters, cannon, and other equipment.

May 19, 1948

Ephraim Visnitski wired that we had taken all of western Galilee.

Bahir came from Haifa. He had been in contact during the night with all the Jordan Valley settlements. A bridge over the Jordan was built opposite Kinneret. A Palmah company arrived from the Galilee. Our counterattack began at midnight. It was made in an attempt to take the Zemah police station. The members of Masada abandoned their settlement and went to Afikim. The members of Sha'ar Hagolan left theirs and went to Bet Zera. In both cases the settlers acted on their own initiative, without orders. They said that they had only eighteen rifles, which just was not enough.

May 20, 1948

There are 5000 members of the Arab Legion in action: 1500 between Jerusalem and Bet Gubrin, 300 near Latrun, 1500 to 2000 in the Triangle, 300 to 400 in the Jordan Valley and 400 to 500 in the Ramle-Lydda area.

We have a battalion of 500 ex-soldiers in Ein Shemer. They have 460 rifles, 460 Sten guns, 8 2-inch mortars (each one with 96 shells), 2 3-inch mortars, 20 machine guns, 560 Mills hand grenades, 140 mines, 3 piats, and 46 shells. There is also an armored battalion at Ein Shemer composed of 9 halftracks and 360 men, half of them trained. Their weapons are included in the previous list. Laskov is at Ein Shemer.

At Tel Litvinsky, there are a unit of armored cars, 60 people, the battalion of Zvika Horowitz, 700 trainees, the heads of the Training Branch, 250 rifles, 15 machine guns, and 6 mortars.

The situation in Jerusalem: one column of the Arab Legion has reached Sheikh Jarrah. The Etzel unit there has fled. A second column has reached the Mount of Olives, and a third is at the Damascus Gate. Our forces are in control of Mount Zion. We have sufficient men and weapons there. Harel has 4 infantry companies and a heavy weapons company, altogether 700 men, but they are exhausted. On their return from Mount Zion they had an accident in which a truck overturned and 40 men were injured. They have 2 Davidkas, 4 machine guns, 2-inch mortars, heavy machine guns, and 18 armored cars. All the outposts west of Latrun are in our hands. Kiryati has 250 men there, and Givati has a reserve unit.

I have discovered that the orders I gave Israel Galili about the appointment of commanders were not carried out.

May 21, 1948

The first Messerschmitt, a German plane built in Czechoslovakia, has arrived. Our planes tonight bombed Su'afat, as well as Gaza and Dir-Sunid in the Negev . All our pilots returned safely.

Four artillery pieces were sent to the Jordan Valley, where they raised the morale of the settlers. Gad (Machnes), Jacobson, and Chizik (the Governor of Jaffa) complain about theft and anarchy in Jaffa.

May 22, 1948

A heavy attack was made yesterday on the Degania settlements. Six enemy tanks were put out of action. One of them is in our hands.

Eleven men have gone to Czechoslovakia to participate in a pilots' course. They are dressed in Czech Air Force uniforms: They have been given English-speaking instructors.

A ship is scheduled to arrive with weapons purchased by Ehud Avriel under the terms of Contract B: 10,000 rifles, 1421 machine guns, 16 million rounds of ammunition— altogether 800 tons of material costing $2,528,000.

In the evening a second Messerschmitt and a cargo plane arrived.

I was shown an urgent cable announcing that the Arab Legion had surrounded the Hadassah Hospital. Negotiations with the consuls and the Legion are under way. The Legion demands that the Hagana surrender, turn over its weapons, and allow its men to be sent as prisoners to Amman. I refuse to accept the Legion's conditions. I have cabled Yadin to mobilize a larger force and go on fighting.

May 23, 1948

A messenger arrived with a report from Stone [Marcus]: The situation is critical, but there is no reason to panic. Yad Mordekhai, defended by 80 settlers and 25 other people, has suffered 50 casualties: 20 killed and 30 wounded. An Egyptian battalion is attacking. A motorized Egyptian brigade is operating in the Negev, where it has renewed its attacks on Bet Eshel and Nirim. Egyptians, not Arab Legionnaires, are in Beersheba. The Arab Legion has gone to Bet Gubrin. Heavy attacks were made on Kfar Darom (where we have 50 people). Our men went on the offensive and inflicted heavy losses on the Egyptians, who sustained about 100 casualties: several of their tanks were damaged. They retreated.

An emissary reports that the Iraq-Suedan police station has not been captured. It is held by Egyptians and not by the Arab Legion.

The Arabs of the Negev are not active; a few of them are working for us.

Two hundred children were evacuated from the Negev tonight. Only in Dorot and Ruhama (with a total population of 350) have youngsters remained. Stone demands 300 rifles, 150 Sten guns, 30 to 40 heavy light machine guns, 15 heavy machine guns, 7 mor-

tars, 50 piats, 100 flamethrowers, and smoke and tear-gas grenades. 250 Palmahniks have
gone to the Negev; they have had a little training, and 70 percent of them are armed.

Yigael Yadin: After I left my office in the evening, a message was received from the
Harel Brigade. Two companies have remained in outposts. We were asked to bomb
Sheikh Jarrah at midnight. The message arrived late, but two planes nevertheless went
out at midnight, by way of the university, and returned safely. Our forces were unable
to break through into the Old City, or to reach the university. The Arabs are in control
of Mount Zion.

Benny Dunkelman [a Canadian] volunteered to deal with the production of 6-inch
mortars. I gave him the necessary authorization to undertake the project.

Israel [apparently referring to Israel Amir-Zovlotsky] reported from Ramat David
that four Egyptian Spitfires had attacked the British airfield there, thinking we had taken
it over. All four were shot down. Perhaps two can be salvaged.

I asked Nahum Kirschner to cable Cecil Margo in South Africa and request that he
come to serve as an adviser on aviation to the Provisional Government.

8 P.M.: The situation at Yad Mordekhai is extremely grave. A column comprising
dozens of Egyptian tanks and armored cars has arrived at Iraq-Suedan. Givati has sent
another company to the Negev. Givoni cables that the Arab Legion has conquered Ramat
Rahel and is entrenching itself in Sur Bahur. The Arab Legion has also moved into Ein
Kerem, Bet Safata, and El Malha.

I have demanded that men under the command of Shlomo Shamir and Eliyahu
Ben-Hur, who are trained and armed, be sent to Jerusalem. Those who are not trained
should be dispatched to the Alexandroni Brigade and replaced with experienced men.
These battalions should be provided with all available weapons: twenty-five guns, three
hundred Molotov cocktails, ten piats, eighteen mortars, etc. The armored cars should
be transferred immediately from Ein Shemer to Hulda. Latrun and all the villages in the
vicinity should be taken and the road to Jerusalem opened up.

Our forces presently are distributed as follows: five thousand in service units, two
thousand in the Central District, two thousand in Tel Aviv, twenty-five thousand in
Givati, fifteen hundred in the Negev, three thousand in Jerusalem, twelve hundred in
Harel, two thousand under the command of Shlomo, a thousand under the command of
Eliyahu, three thousand in Golani, fifteen hundred in Carmeli, and two thousand in Galilee
Palmah units.

May 23, 1948

Shaul Avigur cabled: Ehud Avriel has begun negotiations with the Czechs for the
purchase of airplanes, tanks, and artillery on credit. But $1 million must be paid imme-
diately and $5 million more in six months.

Another Messerschmitt arrived tonight; now we have three. Each plane has two
cannon, two heavy machine guns, and bombs. Two of our planes attacked Napoleon Hill
and Kfar Azariya tonight. The pilots returned safely.

The English are leaving Ramat David tomorrow. Our men will move in immediately. Engineers are already there. Vivian Herzog came from Jerusalem. He reports that
the Arab Legion is in Sheikh Jarrah, the Police School, Mount Scopus, and has reached
as far as the Damascus Gate. How many men do they have? We don't know. Both the
Legion and the Iraqis are in the Old City. Rabbis Meisenberg and Hazan cabled the

following message at 3 o'clock yesterday afternoon to Rabbi Isaac Herzog and Yitzhak Ben-Zvi: "The community faces total annihilation. This is a desperate call for help. Synagogues—Or Chaim, Sukat Shalom, Bet Hillel, Tiferet Israel, Nissan Beck, Porat Yosef, the Brisk Yeshiva, Ohel Moshe, etc.—have been destroyed and Torah scrolls burned. Misgav Ladah is under heavy fire. Bring our desperate plea to the attention of the entire world. Save us."

Two platoons of the Field Forces captured Ramat Rahel yesterday. We lost twelve men. Arab losses ran into the dozens. Six enemy armored cars were put out of action. We control all of Jerusalem except the Old City, Musrarah, the American Colony, Sheikh Jarrah, Wadi Joz, Bab El-Sahara, and Augusta Victoria. An attempt is now being made to penetrate the Old City by using flamethrowers. Mount Zion is in our hands. The enemy is bombarding Jerusalem day and night with shells falling everywhere. Morale is very low. People find it impossible to sleep and have practically nothing to eat. There is enough bread only for another two weeks, and no other food at all. Water is being distributed in the streets: a half tin per person every two days. There are plenty of seekers of peace, namely people willing to surrender. They are putting pressure on Rabbi Herzog.

We tapped a telephone conversation between Williams, the British Consul, and a BBC reporter. Williams said: "Amman doesn't make a move without first receiving orders from the Foreign Office." Dov Joseph is doing an excellent job. If there is any food at all, it is thanks to Dov Joseph. Our bombing raids have encouraged the population. All the members of Kfar Etzion were killed; settlers from other villages were taken prisoner. The Arab Legion has treated them very decently.

Almogi reports from Haifa: 250 immigrants arrived and disembarked on Friday. The [British] Army then ordered them to return to their ship. Abba Hushi responded by calling a strike in the port. The stevedores surrounded the British Army units and told them to shoot. The British backed down and allowed the immigrants to leave the port. The next day another ship, the *Providence*, arrived with 960 immigrants of military age. The British Army did not interfere.

There was a meeting of the Provisional Government from 4 to 9 P.M.

I fell into bed dead tired, after forty-eight hours of constant strain.

May 24, 1948

Yesterday's experiment with 6-inch mortars was a success. Three have already been made, and two more are manufactured every day. They have a range of three and a half kilometers.

Yesterday an airplane arrived loaded with bombs.

Pressure on the Negev is very heavy. Dorot was shelled yesterday—its arsenal was hit. Yad Mordekhai is still holding out. An airplane of ours bombed Iraq-Suedan and Mijdal. Egyptian armored cars advanced on Bet Mahsir but were repulsed.

The enemy bombardment of Jerusalem continues day and night. Our pressure on the Old City goes on. Ratner has returned from the central region and lower Galilee. We have taken Tantura, which has a good port. The Alexandroni Brigade has eleven hundred men from the Home Guards and eighteen hundred from the Field Forces.

There is no defense worthy of the name on the Jordan front. Kinneret miraculously holds out.

I met with a Mapam delegation on Israel Galili's role in defense matters. Ben-Aharon demanded that Israel have the right to issue orders to the General Staff. I replied that while I would not oppose Galili's being given the Defense portfolio, if I were to be responsible for defense, it was on condition that I alone give orders to the General Staff. Ben-Aharon argued that Israel would in fact be giving orders in accordance with my instructions. I rejected this approach, after which Israel announced that there was nothing more for him to do in the circumstances.

A freighter is being unloaded. Tomorrow we will have forty-five more artillery pieces and five thousand rifles—an important landmark.

Mikunis came to see me in the afternoon. He immigrated to this country in 1921, and became a communist in 1936. He has just returned from a visit to Rumania, Yugoslavia, Czechoslovakia, Poland, and Bulagria. While there he discussed arms supplies. In Bulgaria he spoke to Dimitrov (they have no weapons themselves). In Yugoslavia he met Ramkovitch, in Rumania Luka, in Czechoslovakia Clementis, and in Poland Berman and Modolsky (both of them Jews). He asked whether we were unwilling to turn to the East for assistance, as *Al Hamishmar* had reported. I told him the report was untrue. We had asked for and received assistance from the East even before the establishment of the State.

May 25, 1948

The commander of Yad Mordekhai came out of the settlement with eighteen wounded men in armored cars. Yad Mordekhai is surrounded by Arab villages. According to kibbutz members who also fought in Stalingrad, there is no comparison between that struggle and the present one.

May 26, 1948

Two Messerschmitts arrived last night. I asked the members of the General Staff whether a truce would be to our advantage. All of them (Yigal, Sadeh, Ratner, Zvi Ayalon, Lehrer) agreed that it would.

Yacov Hazan came to me to speak about Galili. He said it was imperative that I should continue to handle defense matters, and have all the necessary authority to do so, but I could not handle everything myself. I should therefore have Galili coordinate matters under my direction. I would retain control of appointments. He believed that Mapai has been discriminated against in the High Command (almost all our commanders are Mapam members). I told him that I wasn't worried about discrimination and didn't care to which party the commanders belonged. It was my firm conviction, I added, that the Army should be absolutely nonpolitical. I told Hazan I would not agree to Israel's giving orders to the Army. I was unable to complete the discussion because of the pressure of other matters. We decided to meet again the next day. After four Cabinet meetings, the Israel Defense Forces Ordinance I drafted was approved.

Large Arab forces are concentrating around Kiryat Anavim and Ma'ale Hahamisha. It appears they want to conquer Jerusalem at all costs.

Simha Blass, one of the heads of our arms industry, is producing seven piats and five to seven hundred shells per day. He fears that the 6-inch mortars may not be effective.

May 27, 1948

Ratner inspected fortifications in the south and found them satisfactory. However, they are not properly camouflaged, and can be detected easily.

Yehuda [Prihar-Friedberg] has come from Prague. Our representatives there are about to purchase another thirty Messerschmitts, thirty Spitfires, and nine Mosquitos. The Mosquitos are capable of flying directly to this country without refueling. The Czechs are also willing to sell us thirty sixteen-ton tanks now and thirty at the end of June, as well as twenty nine-ton tanks. Perhaps they will give us a $10 million credit for six months, if we pay 20 percent of what we owe them in cash.

Shmurak [a former British Army officer] came from Jerusalem this morning with a message from Dov Joseph. All the outposts that were in our hands, including Ramat Rahel, are still being held. Sheikh Jarrah and the Police School are under Arab control. Yesterday the Arabs delivered an ultimatum to the Jews in the Old City to surrender within twelve hours or the Hurva Synagogue would be bombarded. The Arabs are at Mar Elias. There is bread, sugar, and tea for another ten days and enough water for another three months. Our soldiers are waiting for ammunition; they think they will be able to hold out. The civilian population displays great courage. Rudi Klein [special operations officer in the General Staff] came to me from Sodom. All the members of Bet Ha'arava and the North have been transferred to Sodom. They took all their weapons with them. The seven hundred people in Sodom have food for a month. There are sixty Arab Legionnaires in Safa, and a hundred or so in Mizra. There are four hundred rifles, eleven Lewis guns, three machine guns, one Spandau, three 311 mortars, six 211 mortars, four piats, and a great deal of ammunition.

Dov Joseph cabled from Jerusalem: each week the population requires a hundred and forty tons of bread, three tons of powdered eggs, ten tons of powdered milk, ten tons of dried fish, ten tons of lentils, ten tons of barley, five tons of yellow cheese, and five tons of jam.

May 28, 1948

Beit Susin has been captured. A large transport plane arrived last night with bombs and propellers. Only 20 percent of the goods on the ship have been unloaded; the process goes forward very slowly. There is no news from the Negev.

Stone came. We raided Gaza. We destroyed the Egyptian artillery. With fifteen hundred men we could have captured the town. Our army is excellent. The Egyptians have weapons, which we must seize. I sent Stone to Latrun to speed up the capture of the town and the liberation of Jerusalem. With Yigal's approval, I have appointed Stone as commander of the Jerusalem Front. He will be in charge of the Harel Brigade, plus the troops serving under David Shaltiel and Shlomo Shamir.

May 29, 1948

At 10:30 I attended a meeting of the Mapai Central Committee for the first time since the establishment of the State. I gave a report on internal arrangements and on the security situation. I proposed that we halt negotiations with other parties about the appointment of government officials, as this was not a subject for interparty haggling.

Yitzhak Rabin came to see me. Seven hundred Old City Jews were freed by the Arabs and allowed to cross over to the New City. The Arab Legion occupied the Jewish Quarter on May 28, 1948, after its leaders decided there was no alternative to surrender. The conditions of surrender were: (1) weapons, ammunition, and military equipment to be turned in; (2) all men capable of bearing arms to be imprisoned; (3) all other residents, women, children, and wounded, to be transferred, under the supervision of a UN representative, from the Old City to the New City; (4) the officer signing the agreement on behalf of King Abdullah to be responsible, together with other Legion officers, for the safety of the civilians and wounded being evacuated from the Old City; (5) the Arab Legion to be given absolute control of the Quarter.

The Jewish Quarter was ablaze in the morning. The Legion treated the Hagana men and the prisoners very well. There is now tremendous pressure on Kiryat Anavim and Ma'ale Hahamisha. Women, children, and cows have been evacuated from the settlements. The New City is under heavy bombardment. One hundred and fifty trained men will join the Harel Brigade tonight. The bombing of Ramallah was successful; 75 percent of the men in one Harel Company and 50 percent in another have been put out of action. Three hundred soldiers remain, not counting those in outposts. According to Rabin, the Arab forces are concentrated at Bet Nuba, Imans, Yalu, and Latrun. Dir Ayub is almost empty.

I have drafted an oath of allegiance for the Israel Defense Forces.

Nahum Sarig arrived by plane from the Negev. I asked him whether it would be possible to conquer Beersheba. His answer: if we can leave the west undefended and concentrate all our forces on that objective, Beersheba can be taken. But he must have a decision by tomorrow if he is to carry out the operation.

May 31, 1948

Chaim Laskov penetrated into Latrun with his armored force, killing some hundred and fifty Arab soldiers. But the two companies of Brigade Seven ordered to support him were frightened by the enemy bombardment and failed to move. Thus Chaim was forced to abandon Latrun. Our losses were moderate: some twenty killed and thirty woulded.

Harel reports: The enemy is using poisoned mortar shells: two men who were scratched by shell fragments died of poisoning six hours later.

I was visited at 6 P.M. by Count Folke Bernadotte accompanied by Dr. Ralph Bunche. If an armistice is arranged, peace talks will be possible. During a cease-fire the Arab forces would be prohibited from moving from their positions. Food would be brought to Jerusalem by the Red Cross. Bernadotte realizes the problems involved in preventing the movement of arms across the borders, but hopes to overcome them after a period of time. Abdullah's entrance into Jerusalem after a cease-fire would be considered a violation of the cease-fire.

At 8 o'clock Chaim Laskov and Shlomo Shamir came from Latrun. Yigal Allon came in from Galilee. If there is no cease-fire, we will prepare an operation to free Jerusalem. We have decided to bomb Amman and Cairo.

Laskov, who hadn't slept for eight days, reported on the Latrun operation. According to the battle plan, Prulov's battalion was to take Yalu, while Laskov's unit advanced toward the village of Latrun, the monastery, and the police station. In doing so, Chaim lost about one hundred men killed, wounded, or missing. Four of his halftracks remained inside the police station; most of his drivers were killed or wounded. One of Zvika's companies went up with Prulov to the hills.

Two hundred men remain in the armored battalion, but they are in no condition to go into action immediately. Five hundred shells were pumped into Latrun in the course of the night. Had infantrymen from Brigade Seven advanced as they were ordered, the town would have been taken. Two companies occupy Beit Jis and Beit Susin, which permits us to open a new road to Jerusalem.

June 1, 1948

Three of our airplanes bombed Amman at 5 A.M. The town was all lit up; lights were not extinguished for eight minutes. Three-quarters of a ton of bombs were dropped. Fires were started. All our planes returned safely.

In the evening, we bombed Amman, Latrun, Tulkarm, Dir Ayub, and Salu.

There was a Cabinet meeting at my [Ramat Gan] office at 11 o'clock. At that very moment, it was hit by bombs and machine-gun fire from Arab planes. Apparently a spy in Bernadotte's party had informed the Arabs of the location of my office. Perhaps it was hit in retaliation for our bombing of Amman.

The Government agreed to the truce arrangements.

Abraham Sabarski [Manager of the Workers' Bank] gave me an account of expenditures during the first twenty days of May. The total, PL1,459,560, was divided as follows: maintenance of the brigades, PL415,000; food supplies, PL112,000; equipment for individual soldiers, PL118,500; salaries of administrative staff, PL60,000; payments to families, PL30,000; military industries, PL35,000; military orders placed with outside firms, PL125,500; chemical production, PL42,500; science, PL8000; transport, PL90,000; fuel, PL80,000; fuel for Air Force, PL180,000; Air Force, PL28,000; soldiers, PL35,000; fortifications, PL133,500; storage, PL41,000; medical services, PL10,000; Engineering Corps, PL25,000; purchases, PL20,000; Intelligence, PL14,000; communications, PL17,000; miscellaneous, PL1500.

A delegation from the Jordan Valley reported: seven people were killed in Degania Aleph, nineteen in Dagania Bet, eight in Kinneret, five in Afikim, and a number in Ashdot Yacov as well. The Golani Brigade withdrew a battalion yesterday and the delegation demanded that it be returned. In addition, it asked for thirty more soldiers for every settlement.

Five thousand people normally live in the Jordan Valley; 2026 children, together with 1283 mothers and elderly people, have been sent to Haifa; 1200 adults (among them 200 women) have remained. Bahir demands another 200 people to dig trenches from Kinneret to the Yarmuk. It is impossible to meet all the demands for manpower.

June 2, 1948

Yigal woke me at 3 A.M. to tell me that Reuters had reported that the Arabs had agreed to a truce. In the morning, however, I found that a truce had not yet gone into effect. Egyptian planes bombed Hulda and an Egyptian force attacked Negba. Golani captured several villages north of Jenin (Mukeibla, Edna, and Jelama) but not the town itself.

I don't know whether or not there is a truce. Alternative plans must be prepared for the month, so that we will be ready for a truce or the absence of one.

A. *Feeding Jerusalem.* Most of the road to Jerusalem is in our hands, except for a few kilometers around Latrun. However, a temporary road from Beit Susin to Sha'ar Hagai, over which to send food convoys every night, can be built. Shkolnik [Levi Eshkol], Koslovsky [Pinkas Sapir], and Yosef [Avidar] have been asked to make the necessary arrangements. The entire New City, except for Sheikh Jarrah, Bab-el-Sahara, the American Colony, and Wadi Jos, is in our hands.

B.   *Stepping up Arms Production.* I called in Slavin, of our arms industry. It has stopped producing rifles. Each day it is turning out 700–800 3-inch mortar shells (if there is enough TNT), 1200 Mills hand grenades (soon 1500), and 250 2-inch mortar shells (soon 500). It had manufactured 7000 Sten guns by June 1 and by June 15 expects to turn out 5000 more. Twenty 3-inch mortars have been produced every week; during the next four weeks the industry hopes to make 150 more. Six thousand 303 bullets are manufactured each day. Daily production soon will reach 12,000. The industry will be able to make 120-mm. mortars if it receives thick pipe from America. The Dror (light) machine gun will be ready for testing in four or five weeks.

I will still try to find out what can be done about chemical production by Yitzhak Volenchik.

C.   *Training Officers and Enlisted Men.* The Training Section must be reactivated and courses organized again for commanders of special units as well as of brigades.

D.   *New Settlements.* We must establish as many as we can and as soon as possible.

E.   *Immigration.* It must be increased.

The Harel Brigade reports that for the last three hours (from 9 A.M.) everything has been quiet on the Jerusalem front. Last night the brigade attacked the Radar outpost but was driven off by enemy fire. It lost four men.

Some misunderstanding exists in regard to the truce. The question was to have been settled by 3 A.M. but there is still no truce.

My Ramat Gan residence has been bombed again. Three employees were killed, and two of my bodyguards were wounded. This was the third bombardment since the Bernadotte visit. I will have to move. One of our planes brought down a British-Egyptian bomber over Tel Aviv.

June 4, 1948

The Golani Brigade is attacking Jenin. The enemy is putting up stiff resistance. Zalitsky [Moshe Carmel] told Yigal yesterday that once captured, Jenin could be held only if Tulkarm was also bombarded and captured.

The Yiftah Brigade will attempt to capture Latrun tomorrow. One of our Messerschmitts over Jaffa hit an enemy plane which went down in flames near Nebi Rubin. A second enemy plane was hit near Rehovot and crashed in Arab territory.

Moshe Shertok spoke to Bernadotte. There will be no truce before next Monday.

June 5, 1948

Last night we captured Yibne and Kakun.

Yosef Weitz brought me a plan to deal with the situation created by the de facto transfer of populations that has taken place. According to Weitz, 123,000 Arabs from 155 villages have left the territory of the State, while 22,000 Arabs have left 35 villages outside the borders of the State. Also 77,000 Arabs have left five towns inside Israeli territory (Haifa, Beit Sha'an, Tiberias, Safad and Semah), while 73,000 have left cities outside the borders of the country (Jaffa and Acre). Forty thousand Arabs have left Jerusalem. Altogether 335,000 Arabs have departed, 200,000 from towns and villages inside the boundaries of the State. Weitz suggests that we discuss with Arab governments the possibility of settling them in the Arab states. I don't think this is possible in the midst of a war. At the same time, we must make immediate preparations for settlement of the abandoned villages with the assistance of the Jewish National Fund.

The Alexandroni Brigade has captured 150 rifiles, 5 heavy machine guns, and 3 food-laden trucks. David, the son of Joseph Sprinzak, and Matti, the younger brother of Yigael Yadin, were in the plane that crashed yesterday after attacking Egyptian ships off Tel Aviv. Both of them drowned. I visited Sprinzak today.

June 6, 1948

One of our planes exploded at the Tel Aviv airfield between 5 and 6 A.M. Two people were killed and a number wounded.

The Syrian offensive in the Galilee has begun. The Customs House at Malkiya has been captured. Lehavot Habashan and Ayelet Hashahar have been attacked. I discussed with the General Staff the possibility of further mobilization orders. There are now over forty thousand people in uniform: five thousand in central service units, twelve thousand in battalion service units, and the remainder, combat soldiers. About four thousand men are in the north (including about nine hundred to a thousand in upper Galilee). There are thirteen hundred in the central region, a thousand in Tel Aviv, twelve hundred in Jerusalem, fifteen hundred in the Givati Brigade, seven hundred in the Negev Brigade, eighteen hundred in the Yiftah and Harel Brigades, seven to eight hundred in Shlomo's Brigade, seven hundred in Yitzhak Sadeh's Brigade, a thousand in the Engineers, a hundred in the Air Force, six hundred in the Navy, thirty-five hundred in heavy weapons companies, and five thousand in Home Guard units. We will certainly need to call up more.

June 7, 1948

The settlements in the central region demand that we mobilize the thirty-six to thirty-eight-year-old age group. That will give the region two more companies. Zyamah [Zalman Aranne] came in to tell me that the situation in Jerusalem is very difficult. There is food enough only until Friday (another three days). The bombardments of the last three days have inflicted heavy damage on the city. In the last eighteen days three hundred people have been killed and a thousand wounded. Arab artillery units stationed outside the Damascus Gate bombard the New City incessantly and with grave consequences.

June 8, 1948

Bernadotte proposes that the truce begin on June 11 at 6 A.M., Greenwich Mean Time. He demands our agreement by Wednesday noon, after which he will make a final announcement to both sides.

June 8, 1948

The food convoy reached Jerusalem via the new, secret Beit Susin route. Only the jeeps carried the food all the way; the mules did not. They are expected to go up tonight. The planned attack against Latrun this evening did not materialize.

June 10, 1948

Yitzhak Rabin came from Jerusalem this morning. Last night supplies were carried to the city by jeeps, mules, and porters. They included 9.5 tons of flour and 1300 gallons of gasoline (660 of which went to the Harel Brigade). Thirty head of cattle will be sent tonight. Stone and Yigal F. [Allon] believe that an attack on Latrun cannot take place tonight either. If there is a truce tomorrow, Latrun will remain in Arab hands. Yitzhak blames the situation on our weaknesses. We clarified a possible alternative solution, of opening a road via Beit Jin and Beit Susin. In order to do this, we must capture Tsora and Maisalun. Rabin is opposed to the plan. I suggested to Yigael [Yadin] that he undertake the operation himself, using all the forces he needs for the purpose. He told me afterward that the operation was carried out with the forces on hand.

Ehud arrived last night. A third ship has loaded for us in a Yugoslav port—rifles, machine guns, and ammunition. Everything will be transferred to one of our ships, which will depart between the 14th and 16th, reaching Tel Aviv eight to ten days later. The ship is supposedly an Italian vessel, but our men will be aboard.

We have bought planes that will be flown nonstop from Prague. Another arms agreement has been signed. It involves tanks, artillery, rifles, airplanes, and ammunition. We have purchased 120-mm. mortars in France. They will arrive by plane. We have bought artillery in Switzerland. The Czechs are willing to train our pilots, tank men, and paratroopers. They will also accept Israelis at their academy for high-ranking officers.

June 11, 1948

The following reports have been received from the fronts. Our assault on Iraq-Suedan failed. The Legion attacked Sarafand, Safariya, and Yehudiya. The Legion was beaten back at the first two places, but captured Yehudiya. Our offensive operations in western Galilee have begun. A convoy has gone to Jerusalem. Various outposts in the area have been seized. Damascus has been bombed. Our pilots met no resistance. They found the city lit up, located and bombed their "targets," deposited incendiary material, and returned safely. The truce will begin shortly.

The Syrians continued the attack in the Rosh Pina area until the evening hours. I gave orders for a full-scale attack on them during the night. Should the truce supervisors begin asking questions, we will reply that we continued to attack because they had not stopped firing at 10 A.M. as had been agreed, but at 8 P.M. We saw no reason to honor an agreement that had already been violated by the Syrians.

June 12, 1948

The Jerusalem Electric Company has been captured. The Arab workers have left; only the Jewish workers have remained. The bakeries have fuel for only three or four more days. We have been asked to supply generators to keep the bakeries operating. Jerusalem has enough water for about three months. I asked Verlinsky to collect food and fuel for the city. In a meeting with Efraim Ben-Artzi, Nahum Verlinsky was made responsible for supplies and transport as far as Kfar Bilu, and for civilian porters at Kfar Bilu who transfer the goods from one vehicle to another. The Quartermaster Corps will transport the goods from Kfar Bilu to Jerusalem, where it will turn them over to Dr. Dov Joseph or his representative. The Army will provide trucks to Verlinsky for bringing supplies to Kfar Bilu.

Yigal Feikovitz [Allon], who came from Jerusalem, reported that he has one battalion in the Sha'ar Hagai and Beit Susin outposts, and another in the vicinity of Kubab. The outposts from Sha'ar Hagai to Jerusalem are being held by Jerusalemites.

Yitzhak Dobkin reports that the Old City was lost because of dissension within the Hagana in Jerusalem. Ramat Rahel was destroyed for the same reason. Our commander must be replaced.

David Shaltiel complains that there is no discipline. Thefts are rampant. Commanders refuse to fight. There is no military tradition. There are three types of soldiers:

1. The veterans of the British Army who are well disciplined, but who, in making demands, act as if they were still in the British Army.

2. Veterans of the Hagana, who have enthusiasm and have carried out very serious operations.

3. The younger people, including young company commanders, who cannot stand up to the harsh reality of the situation, particularly insufficient sleep and water. They just can't take it. They will attack, but they don't know how to absorb a setback. Only at Kfar Etzion did they do their duty. In the Old City and at Neveh Yacov this was not the case. Despite clear orders, they fled.

The talk about thefts is exaggerated. There is hunger and thirst in the city. People lose their self-respect in such a situation. Seven hundred soldiers have been killed in Jerusalem since the beginning of the war. The Palmah does a lot of boasting, but does not act in a responsible manner.

June 13, 1948

I have decided on seven ranks for officers: *segen-rishon* (second lieutenant), *segen* (lieutenant), *seren* (captain), *rav-seren* (major), *sgan-aluf* (lieutenant colonel), *rav-aluf* (brigadier general). Zvi thinks that there should be a two-rank difference between the commander of a battalion and the commander of a brigade. He also believes that the Chief of Staff should be two ranks higher than any other officer. A committee composed of Zvi, Lehrer, and Ratner, in consultation with Yacov, will determine the ranks to be awarded. Zuckerberg [Tsur] told me he can obtain fully equipped Mosquito airplanes at a cost of £35,000 for a pair. Payment must be made in England. He can also buy new and fully equipped Spitfires at £15,000 each, but payment must be made in hard currency, dollars or Swiss francs. I told him to purchase the planes. We will find some of the money in England, and Shaul will give him the rest.

June 14, 1948

We lost many men in the capture of Bir Asluj on the day before the truce. Our casualties were caused by a mine outside the police station and explosives hidden inside it. All those who entered the building were wounded. The station itself collapsed. Our losses: thirteen killed, nine wounded, and two missing. At least thirteen Arabs were killed and fourteen captured (seven Egyptians and seven Palestinians). There was a great deal of booty.

At 10:30 Yigal came to tell me that the entire Harel Brigade had left Jerusalem. Yitzhak Rabin said that his men had to leave because they could not be welded into a cohesive unit within the demoralizing atmosphere of the city. The Brigade included many new immigrants.

Matters the Army must deal with include: transfers and replacements, training, discipline, procedures for appointments, departments in the Ministry of Defense, the structure of the General Staff, the structure of the units, ranks and insignia, flags, new brigades, reinforcement of existing units, the fronts, supplies, manpower, further callups, the production and purchase of arms, science, communications, rest periods and leaves, Home Guard units in the cities and settlements, reinforcements for the settlements, work arrangements, contact between the General Staff and the Ministry of Defense, the distribution of weapons, reserve service, the Air Force, the Navy, and advanced training overseas.

Slavin came to tell me that during the truce the arms industry will be turning out two hundred 3-inch mortars and seven hundred mortar shells each day. Another six to seven weeks will be required before 2-inch mortars can be manufactured. About thirty thousand Mills hand grenades have been produced in the last four weeks. They will finish making the other Sten guns, ninety-one hundred of which have already been turned out. Production of .303 bullets will be stepped up by beyond the present rate of six thousand per day to twelve thousand by the end of the truce. We lack steel for the 120-mm. mortars, and use iron instead, which weakens the impact of the shells, making them effective against people, but not against buildings.

There was a meeting of the government in the afternoon.

June 15, 1948

The ship sent by Allon arrived two days ago. It contains, according to Shaul: 10 75-mm. guns (the ammunition is already in the country—four guns have been unloaded so far); 10 Hotchkiss tanks (with 37-mm. cannon and 7.5-mm. machine guns, as well as ammunition for them); 19 65-mm. artillery pieces (which have already been unloaded); 4 Hispano-Suiza 20-mm. antiaircraft guns with spare parts, and 44,950 shells.

The shipment sent by Ben-Avni [Israel Dickenstein] includes 110 tons of TNT, 10 tons of cordite, 1,050,500 9-mm. bullets, 350,000 French bullets, 200,000 detonators, and 4000 electric detonators. Ehud has purchased, under the terms of Contract C, 10,000 P-18 Mauser rifles, 3400 34-MG machine guns, 30 million 7.92-mm. bullets. He acquired, within the framework of other agreements, 37 ZB-machine guns (in addition to the 145 already in the country) and ammunition for them. Also included are 10 9.5-ton tanks with ammunition, 12 16-ton tanks with ammunition, 10,000 bayonets for P-18 Mauser rifles, 2 million rounds of 7.92-mm. bullets, 250 9-mm. pistols and ammunition for them.

Yehuda Arazi and Benjamin [Munya Meridor] purchased 21,000 7.92-mm. rifles, 100 tons of smokeless dynamite, 15 20-mm. cannon and 50,000 rounds of ammunition for them. The former has purchased from Netter [in the Hagana code Netter meant France] 12 120-mm. mortars, 4000 mortar shells, 50,000 shells for 65-mm. cannon, and 300,000 rounds of ammunition for Hotchkiss machine guns.

Ehud has purchased 30 fully equipped planes for the Air Force (there is final agreement on 15 of them). Teddy Kollek has obtained (after negotiations which were begun by Allon) 3 B-25s, 2 B-17s, 6 P-47s, and 20 1.50s—altogether 31 planes.

I discussed the manpower situation with Bentov, Lehrer, and Israel. There are about 111,000 men in the seventeen-to-twenty-five age group, of whom 90,000 have reported for service. Of these, 40,000 have been taken into the armed forces, 2000 have been sent to police and other units, 7000 have been deferred because they are doing vital work, 15,000 are in settlements, 10,000 have been rejected for reasons of health, 3000 are abroad, 12,000 are dissidents or are appealing their classifications. Another 22,000 have been deferred because they have more than two children. Of the 5500 to 6000 men in each age group, 2400 to 2500 will be given military training. We have decided that all men under thirty-five with more than two children will be sent to work, while those from thirty-six to forty will go to the Army. Anyone not drafted will have to work.

Lehrer, Zvi, Peretz, and I have agreed on military insignia, and the ranks of officers who will head various sized units.

Epstein [Eliyahu Elath] cabled on June 7, 1948: "An informed source reports that Truman will support our request for a loan and will reject any attempt to revise our borders. When the new British Ambassador presented his credentials to the President, Truman informed him in no uncertain terms that he is very dissatisfied with Bevin's Palestine Policy."

Fischer cabled (June 11, 1948) that Colonel Queru, a French UN observer, is a loyal friend. Bernadotte told the French Ambassador to Iraq that the Arab armies are out of breath.

June 16, 1948

I called in Verlinsky, Yosef R. [Rohel-Avidar], and Hillel Cohen to discuss how to facilitate the flow of food to Jerusalem. No food at all was sent to the city the day before yesterday because the road was occupied by members of the Harel Brigade leaving Jerusalem for Sarafand. Yesterday one hundred tons of food were sent to Jerusalem; 85 percent of the shipment consisted of flour while the rest included cheese, milk powder, and cigarettes.

Preparations are being made to send another hundred tons tonight. Twenty-two trucks will come down from Jerusalem to pick up the goods. Tuv'yahu and Yulish, the Solel Boneh engineers, are repairing the road. Repairs will be completed in a few days. By Friday or Saturday we hope to travel along the new road to Jerusalem without the assistance of tractors. There are three UN men at Sha'ar Hagai, but they are not interfering with the movement of our goods. Yesterday 6-mm. mortars were sent to Jerusalem. Henceforth, Verlinsky will be responsible for collecting food for Jerusalem, while Solel Boneh will handle its transport. Yosef Rohel says that when the Beit Susin road is repaired, one hundred trucks can use it daily, with three tons of food on each one. Jerusalem needs four thousand tons of food each month, which works out at a hundred and thirty-five tons per day. I insisted that vegetables be sent immediately to Jerusalem. Verlinsky promised that tomorrow fifteen to eighteen tons of beets, carrots, potatoes, and oranges (Valencia) will be dispatched in addition to the other hundred tons of food.

Yigal Feikovitz [Allon] came to protest my order that the Harel and Yiftah Brigades must maintain direct contact with the General Staff, which now reaches them through the National Command of the Palmah. The Quartermaster Corps and the commanding officers are overworked, and there must be decentralization. Larger units are also necessary. At the same time, one must recognize the importance of *esprit de corps* and avoid unnecessary disruptions. I explained to him that the need for decentralization was a general one, adding that anything of benefit to the Palmah would certainly benefit the entire Army. To supply Palmah units in the Galilee through special Palmah channels would be absurd. They must use the channels that supply other units operating in the Galilee. At a particular front units should be an organic part of that front, regardless of their organizational background. We plan to establish larger units at the fronts under a single unified command. If there are good quartermasters at Palmah headquarters, they should be working for the entire Army. Sectarianism breeds such phenomena as the Harel Brigade's theft of weapons from Levite. Yigal admitted that he would certainly have shot anyone who tried to steal weapons from him. He promised to send a letter of apology. He also agreed that it was ridiculous to supply Palmah units in Jerusalem and in the Negev through Palmah headquarters. In the end, his only complaint was against the order to separate the Harel and Yiftah Brigades. I explained that the order was based on a mis-understanding. If the brigades are in one area and want to operate as a single unit, they may do so; contact will be maintained with the unified formation.

Section 4. Backround of First Truce

Distribution of Portfolios in Provisional Government

Despite the fierce struggle with Arab armies immediately after the establishment of the State, which in fact endangered Israel's very existence, we were not spared quarrels within the Provisional Government. At its first two sessions of the Provisional State Council, on May 16 and 19, argument arose over the passage of a miniature constitution. This Law and Administration Ordinance, prepared be Rosenblueth, the Minister of Justice, had been given final form by a five-man committee.

At the third meeting, on May 20, disagreements developed over the distribution of portfolios. Rabbi Fishman, who was not present, sent a short letter condemning "dis-crimination against Mizrahi and Hapoel Hamizrahi." He wrote: "Hapoel Hamizrahi has been thrown a few crumbs in the form of an important Immigration Ministry and the Mizrahi has not been given anything." He also was highly critical of the decision to appoint as Minister of Justice "a man whom I personally respect very highly, but who does not have a deep understanding of Jewish Law." Rabbi Fishman concluded by tender-ing his resignation.

Shapira complained that his party [Hapoel Hamizrahi] had been discriminated against in the distribution of Defense Ministry posts, as well as in other ministries. He also stressed the special interest of religious Jewry in the Justice portfolio.

I pointed out that the distribution of Cabinet portfolios had not yet been completed. I proposed the establishment of a three-man committee to investigate all the appoint-ments that I had made in the defense sphere since I had been entrusted with the Defense portfolios at the December 1946 Zionist Congress. Of the sixteen commanders I had named at the suggestion of Galili, only one was a member of my own party, one had no party affiliation, and most of the others were members of Mapam. But I had never been interested in the party affiliations of the men whom I appointed. I stated again that I would not deal with defense matters unless the entire Army was responsible solely to the Govern-ment, all soldiers and military units had the same rights, and all commanders operated only within the bounds of the authority entrusted to them by the Government.

Remez stated that in a four-man committee (Bernstein, Repetur, Remez, and Rabbi Fishman) that had discussed the distribution of portfolios, no differences of opinion existed except on the question of a ministry of religious affairs, about which no decision had been taken. The committee members had agreed on the allocation of the other posts.

Zisling suggested that a committee investigate not only the appointments made by Ben-Gurion in the defense sphere, but also his other appointments.

Bernstein confirmed that there had been no differences of opinion in the four-man committee about the distribution of Cabinet posts, except in regard to religious affairs, but complained that the administration was made up almost entirely of people drawn from a particular section of the population.

Rosenblueth pointed out that until a final decision was reached on the distribution of Cabinet portfolios, no minister had the right to sign official documents. He said that at least a Prime Minister must be appointed. Therefore announcement was made that, in accordance with Section 2(C) of the Law and Administration Ordinance No. 1—1948, the Provisional Government had chosen David Ben-Gurion to serve as Prime Minister. On the suggestion of Kaplan, a four-man committee—Bentov, Bernstein, Kaplan, and Rosenblueth—was appointed to prepare for the next meeting of the Provisional Government a plan for the distribution of Cabinet posts, organizational arrangements, the make-up of the administration, and a review of administrative actions already carried out.

At the next meeting, on June 23, 1948, Shertok announced that, following its recognition by the United States and the Soviet Union, Israel had also been recognized by Poland and Guatemala. The Czech consul had stated that his government was about to recognize Israel, Dr. Weizmann was negotiating with General Smuts in regard to South African recognition. The French National Assembly had adopted a resolution welcoming the establishment of the State of Israel. Its Foreign Affairs Committee and the French Socialist Party had expressed their support for the recognition of the State of Israel, but the French government hesitated because of pressure from the British government. Uruguay had been very friendly, but had not reached a formal decision on recognition.

We had contacted the Soviet government about the possibility of obtaining planes and artillery. An American embargo on the shipment of weapons to Israel remained in force. The United States had suggested to the UN Security Council that the Arab states be ordered to stop their invasion, and that if they refused to do so, sanctions be imposed on them. However, only Soviet Russia, the Ukraine, and France had supported the American initiative, and the proposal was defeated.

The sole resolution adopted called for a cease-fire. It was passed by a majority of ten to one, with only Soviet Russia voting against it. The Government decided that if the Arabs ceased hostilities, we would also do so. However, the Arabs did not honor the UN decision and therefore the truce did not come into effect until June 11.

After the Government approved the establishment of a Ministry of Religious Affairs, the four-man committee's proposal for the distribution of portfolios was accepted: Bentov, Labor and Reconstruction; Bernstein, Commerce and Industry; Gruenbaum, Interior; Rabbi I. M. Levin, Social Welfare; Rabbi Y. L. Fishman, Religious Affairs and War Victims; Zisling, Agriculture; Kaplan, Finance; Rosenblueth, Justice; Remez, Transport; Shitreet, Police and Minorities; Shapira, Immigration and Health; Shertok, Foreign Affairs. After the adoption of the Israel Defense Forces Ordinance, there was also a final decision on the Defense Ministry. The Army was placed under the control of the Government and the Ministry of Defense. Zisling announced that he accepted the three principles outlined by Ben-Gurion.

Israel Will Agree to Armistice If it Remains in All Areas Under Its Control and Immigration Continues Unimpeded

The Special Representative of the United Nations General Assembly, Count Bernadotte of Sweden, arrived at the end of May, accompanied by Dr. Ralph Bunche of the United States and six other assistants. At a June 7 meeting with Israel's Prime Minister and the Foreign Minister, Bernadotte announced his responsibility to investigate the possibility of persuading Israel and the Arab states to agree to a settlement and peace. If an armistice were arranged, he would see to it that its provisions were honored. He had already held preliminary discussions in Cairo, and after his first meeting with Israel's Prime Minister and Foreign Minister had gone on to confer with other Arab representatives. I told him that there was no need to preach to the Jews about the importance of peace, because the achievement of Israel's goals—the absorption of immigrants and the building of a new economy—depended on peace. In her Declaration of Independence, Israel had stressed the need for peaceful and cooperative relations with the Arabs inside her boundaries and in the neighboring states.

Shertok wanted to clarify what would happen, alternatively, if an armistice were agreed upon and if it were not. He wanted to know what might occur if during the armistice Abdullah entered Jerusalem with the Arab Legion. Would this be a violation of the agreement? The city had not been given to Abdullah; therefore Israel would have the right to drive him out. Bernadotte answered immediately that if we tried to prevent the Arab Legion and Abdullah from entering Jerusalem, he would consider it a serious violation of the armistice. Shertok asked about freedom of movement to Jerusalem. Bernadotte said that he was well acquainted with the problem of supplying food and water to the city, and that he was determined to deal with the matter in his role as representative of the Red Cross (he was, by the way, dressed in a Red Cross uniform). We did not accept his reply, demanding freedom of movement to Jerusalem without regard to the Red Cross. Bunche pointed out Count Bernadotte's responsibility to supervise the armistice agreement and that he would deal with issues as they arose; he could not announce decisions in advance. We declined to accept this viewpoint and demanded freedom of movement. We also raised the question of arms shipments, since we were aware that controls imposed on us would be effective. There were only a few places where we could receive goods, while the Arab states had many airfields. Bernadotte said he would recruit a large number of observers and had already contacted the Swedish government in this connection. His staff, he hoped, could begin operations in a few days.

We asked what would happen if there were no armistice. He answered that he would still have a mission to carry out, though his chances of success would not be very great. He would still make every effort to foster negotiations between the two sides. His elderly father had sent him a Bible to read during his trip, and he read it every evening. He was particularly fond of the Book of Psalms.

Bunche appeared very perturbed when he left the discussion. He sensed our lack of faith in the United Nations, and our bitterness because the UN had taken no action against the invaders. He heard our complaints against the English, who were training an Egyptian company in England and allowing the British airfield at El Arish to be used by the Egyptian Air Force. The Egyptians had complained to Bunche that we interfered with their purchases of weapons (we had seized a ship with Czech arms that had been sold to Syria, brought it to Jaffa, and unloaded it). Bunche said that the Arabs were very much afraid of us and that we exaggerated the quantity of arms at their disposal.

We learned more about America's attitude toward us. Until President Truman recognized Israel, there was considerable confusion among the American authorities, and a strong tendency to nullify the UN decision of November 29, 1947. After Truman acted a decisive change took place. Now a feeling spread that America knew what she was doing, and there had not been a single mistake since then. The United States consistently attempted to achieve the goals she set for herself. Other countries followed America's lead. Colombia, for example, revised her attitude toward Israel. The British continued plotting against us, but they met resistance from the United States and France.

In Bunche's opinion, we will play into England's hands if we reject the armistice agreement. There are differences of opinion within the British government. Not every Cabinet minister agrees with Bevin's policies. There is a great deal of criticism of the British in the American Congress. According to Bunche, France will soon recognize Israel. If there is an armistice agreement, hundreds of observers will be recruited from European countries (Sweden, Belgium, Norway, etc.) but not from England. American ships will patrol the coasts, and there will be observers at every airfield and at every port. This arrangement will cover the Arab states as well as Israel. Shipment of weapons from England to the Arab states will also be supervised. If the British have stores of arms in Egypt and in Iraq, they will be forbidden to transfer them to the Egyptians and Iraqis.

Measures will be taken to ensure that there is no change in the Jerusalem situation while an armistice agreement is in effect. After an agreement has been reached, an effort will be made to arrange for negotiations between Israel and the Arab states at a neutral site, such as one of the Mediterranean islands or aboard a ship. The Arabs argue that the Jews are divided among themselves, with factions that hate one another, and include terrorists and communists. Israel will be a constant source of trouble for the entire Middle East and will also set out to conquer other countries. In Bunche's opinion, Israel must abide by the November 29 decision of the UN General Assembly and relieve Arab fears about her supposed territorial ambitions. He warned us against a refusal to accept an armistice agreement. He was certain that the Security Council would impose sanctions on either party, Jews or Arabs, that refused to sign such an agreement.

John Reedman, Bunche's assistant, previously had told Shertok that the UN Secretary General [Trygve Lie] was insistent on an armistice agreement. Shertok informed him that we demand freedom of movement to Jerusalem, unlimited immigration, and a stabilization of the military situation. Bernadotte expressed interest in developments at the battle fronts. He was given a general review of the situation.

We asked our representative in the United States to clarify the following questions: (1) Would an armistice agreement ensure freedom of movement for civilians everywhere in the country, particularly to and from Jerusalem, and permit the dispatch of food to the city? (2) Would the movement of troops inside the country be permitted? (3) What measures would be taken to ensure that arms were not brought into the neighboring states? (4) Would the Egyptian blockade of Israeli merchant ships be ended?

We received an affirmative reply in regard to our question about freedom of movement. Count Bernadotte would be responsible for preventing the shipment of arms to the neighboring countries. As far as military movements within the country were concerned, the armistice agreement would prohibit any changes in the existing front lines, but would not prevent movement of military forces within the areas under the control of the two sides. Therefore, the Arab Legion could enter the Old City of Jerusalem. By the same token, we could transfer troops from Tel Aviv to the New City.

After a discussion the Government decided unanimously to accept the armistice agreement, provided that all the positions held by our forces remained in our hands, that there would be no interference with the movement of ships carrying nonmilitary goods, and that nothing would be done to prevent the immigration of Jews to Israel. By that time the new secret road to Jerusalem had been laid out (the "Burma Road") and an additional water pipeline had been constructed from Rosh Ha'ayin to Jerusalem. The old pipeline passed through Latrun, which was under Arab control. Finally, I announced negotiations with the countries selling arms to Israel for a $10 million credit. The proposed agreement called for payment of 20 percent of the purchase price immediately, and the other 80 percent six months later. The credit was to be used for the purchase of heavy weapons: airplanes, artillery, and tanks. To that time we had bought thirty Messerschmitts, thirty Spitfires, and ten Mosquitos.

Kaplan stated that such an arrangement would force us to keep funds frozen in America, because otherwise we would not be able to find the $8 million when it was needed.

Agreement with Dissident Organizations ★ Discussion of Military and Political Matters

Prime Minister Ben-Gurion reported on negotiations with the dissident organizations. Lehi had already announced that its members of military age would join the Israel Defense Forces, and had turned over its arms and war materiel—rifles, submachine guns, machine guns, and dynamite.

There were problems with Etzel. At a meeting on June 3 between the Commander of Etzel and a representative of the Minister of Defense the following points were agreed upon:

 1. Members of Etzel will be drafted into the Israel Defense Forces on the basis of mobilization orders issued by the Israel Government and will take the customary oath of allegiance.
 2. Members of Etzel who are called up will belong to separate battalions, within the framework of brigades and fronts, and operate in accordance with the decisions of the General Staff.
 3. Etzel weapons will be given to the Israel Defense Forces.
 4. Facilities for the production of war matériel will be turned over to the Army.
 5. A temporary headquarters staff, composed of Etzel officers, will act on behalf of the General Staff of the Israel Defense Forces to facilitate the rapid integration of Etzel

members into the Defense Forces and the activization of the aforementioned Etzel battalions.

6. Etzel and its Central Command will, of its own free will, cease to exist and operate inside the State of Israel and in all spheres of Israel Government activity.

The Defense Ministry representative who took part in the negotiations said it was understood that the term "sphere of Israel Government activities" included relations with world Jewry and therefore Etzel did not have the right to raise funds from Jews overseas. There were two addenda to this agreement:

1. All purchases of arms and military equipment by Etzel are to cease and the contacts established by Etzel in this sphere are to be turned over to the Israel Defense Forces for the benefit of the war effort.

2. Facilities for the production of arms which belong to Etzel, and which are needed by the Israel Defense Forces, are to be evaluated and appropriate compensation made for them.

Agreement was reached that the temporary Etzel headquarters would remain in existence for only a month at the most.

The Provisional State Council met for the third time on June 3, 1948. It was the first occasion on which political as well as military matters could be discussed. I pointed out that the Arabs had intended to strangle the infant State of Israel in a lightning operation. According to a plan that fell into Israeli hands, Haifa was to have been captured on May 20, with Tel Aviv and Jerusalem to follow on May 25. That same day King Abdullah was to have entered Jerusalem, to be crowned as ruler of his enlarged kingdom.

My review of the situation was to the following effect: We cannot say after what had happened in the last three weeks—a short but significant time—that the dangers facing us have passed. On the contrary, we may face still greater perils in the days ahead. After we bombed Amman the British consul ordered the Mayor of Haifa to inform the appropriate authorities that if Amman were bombed again, the Royal Air Force would destroy every Jewish plane in the skies of Palestine, since Amman was the nerve center of British aviation in the entire region.

While there is reason for concern about the future, there are also grounds for considerable self-satisfaction. The plot to destroy Israel by sending in heavily armed invasion forces from the north, east, and south has been foiled. The invasion is no closer to success than it was three weeks ago. The armies of Israel hold a larger contiguous area than they did before the attack. The entire expanse of the State of Israel allocated to us under the terms of the UN resolution is in our hands, and we have conquered several important districts outside those boundaries.

All of Jerusalem's New City, western Galilee, and a large part of the Tel Aviv-Jerusalem road are under control. Two small but vitally important areas of that road, the section between Sha'ar Hagai and Jerusalem, and some sections of the Coast Road east of Hulda, are not in our hands. We cannot ignore the severe losses we have suffered in the Jerusalem fighting. Following a courageous struggle that will stand out forever in the annals of Jewish military history, the Etzion Bloc fell. After a crushing siege of many months, during which a tiny group of defenders stood against masses of attackers, the Jewish Quarter of the Old City also fell.

The struggle continues in all parts of the country. Special mention should be made of the harsh battles that have taken place in the Jordan Valley. Tribute is due not only to the valor of the Army, but particularly perhaps to the determined settlers who, though few in number and almost unarmed, fought off an enemy equipped with planes, artillery, tanks, and armored cars. The danger has not passed in the Jordan Valley, just as it has not passed elsewhere. But in the Valley, as elsewhere, at least temporarily, we have the upper hand.

I singled out the extraordinary struggle of Jewish Jerusalem, a struggle characterized by both suffering and bravery. The city has been cut off from all other Jewish sections of the country. It has been confronted by the specter of thirst and hunger. It has been mercilessly bombarded day and night, with a complete and cynical disregard for the sanctity of a city regarded as holy by Christians and Moslems as well as by Jews. The Arab hirelings of the Bevin government, using British planes and guns, have shown a callous disregard for the Holy Places; meanwhile the Anglican Church has maintained a silence pregnant with significance. Jewish Jerusalem has stood the test with unparalleled valor. The people of Jerusalem know that the State of Israel is behind them, and that our finest sons will give their lives to free the city.

In the last three weeks our armed forces have done an excellent job. They are striking at the Arab Triangle and they stand at the gates of Jenin. Tulkarm is under attack and Nablus quivers with fear. While for us this is a defensive war—we did not seek it and are only fending off aggressors—we will not fight only with defensive tactics. To the greatest possible extent, we will remain constantly on the offensive, which will not be confined to the borders of the Jewish State. We have already struck at enemy concentrations in Syria and Lebanon; Amman, Abdullah's capital, has received its first warning in the form of an Israeli air attack.

We have grown stronger over these weeks. A Jewish Air Force has been created, as has the skeleton of a Jewish Navy. But we are only at the beginning of the road. The greatest and gravest tests lie ahead. The enemy has not yet thrown all his resources into the struggle. We certainly cannot be certain that the Arabs will display the same lack of resolve in the future that they have shown on various occasions in the past. At the same time we have yet to mobilize all our resources, in Israel and among world Jewry.

The two giant powers that supported the November 29 resolution calling for the establishment of a Jewish State have recognized the State of Israel. But our enemies are busy. In many capitals overt and covert attempts are being made to prevent the recognition of our existence. The military and political obstacles that confront us have positive as well as negative implications. They make us realize that we are not regaining our independence as the result of international charity, that our existence is not dependent on the good will of others. We have built this community over the last seventy years with our own sweat and toil. Though we never ceased appealing to the conscience of mankind, and will never cease to demand our just rights from the community of nations, we should constantly remind ourselves that our existence, freedom, and future depend on our own efforts, abilities, and will power. Two things will sustain us: our own strength and the justice of our cause.

The Security Council proposed a four-week truce. The Government appraised the proposal and decided to accept it. We informed the Security Council of our understanding that the decision has implications in five spheres that are of vital importance to us:

1. The halt in hostilities also presumes a halt to the Egyptian naval blockade of our shores.

2. The ban on the entrance of military forces under no circumstances implies a ban on Jewish immigrants of any age. We agree that if immigrants of military age arrive during the four weeks, they will not be given military training during that period.

3. Measures will be taken to supply Jerusalem with food and to protect people traveling on the roads.

4. The truce involves maintenance of the military status quo in all areas that have been conquered. This means, for example, that if the Arab Legion occupies the road between Ramallah and Sheikh Jarrah when the truce begins, it has no right to advance any farther and we have no right to drive it from the road. The same conditions hold true for us. Our forces in western Galilee retain control of the area they hold, but have no right to continue to the north.

5. The prohibition on the shipment of weapons to any of the following countries— Israel, Trans-Jordan, Lebanon, Syria, Iraq, Egypt, Saudia Arabia, and Yemen—also implies that weapons inside these countries belonging to a foreign power cannot be turned over to the local authorities.

When the Security Council fixed a four-week truce, the decision included the appointment of a UN Mediator (Count Bernadotte). We understood that he will determine the terms of the truce and when it has been violated.

We have heard that the Arab states attach two conditions to their acceptance of the Bernadotte mission: a ban on Jewish immigration and the abolition of the Jewish State. We assume that the Mediator has enough common sense to realize that if the rumors are correct, there is no point in his presenting such ridiculous demands to us. We have always been interested in peace. We have no quarrel with the Arab peoples. But the peace must be one in which the State of Israel maintains her full sovereignty. Anyone unwilling to accept this fact will find himself confronted by the full military might of our young nation, which will not rest until it has emerged victorious.

The State of Israel was not established to serve a military purpose. Its principal mission is the ingathering of Jewish refugees and the fructification of the desert. However, for another few weeks or months our State must devote all its energies to winning this war. Yet even during the conflict we have constructive tasks to perform. The Mandatory Government left us a legacy of chaos in every sphere of administration. In the midst of the fighting we have had to reestablish public services. We cannot claim that they are functioning again on a proper level, owing to the emergency and our lack of resources. Nevertheless, Bevin's malicious plan has not succeeded. More order and better services exist now than before the departure of the Mandatory Government. Not only have we set up regular public services; we have also devoted ourselves to the two tasks at the core of Israel's mission: settlement and immigration. More immigrants have entered the country during this short span than during any equivalent period in the previous generation. A considerable number of new settlements will be established in various sections of the country whether or not there is a truce.

Finally, I announced to the Provisional State Council that the two dissident organizations have agreed to disband. Their members will be called up for service in the Israel Defense Forces as will every other Jew in this country. We hope that, this time, the agreements will be carried out.

Repetur criticized the Government for not convening the Provisional State Council to discuss the question of an armistice. He praised the Government for transforming the Hagana—which for decades had safeguarded the Jewish community and in the months before the establishment of the State had been steadfast on all the fronts—into the Israel Defense Forces. But he regretted that the State Council had not been made a partner in that momentous decision. He also criticized the American government because it had failed to offer assistance to Israel in her struggle after officially recognizing our State. Moreover, he saw clear signs of maneuvers aimed at reducing the size and strength of the State. The Security Council, he pointed out, had not reacted to the ban on the departure of Jewish refugees from Cyprus. Also while the United States had voted with the Soviet Union and her allies in the Security Council, she had been responsible for decisions that weakened the State of Israel and aided the invaders. There was reason to fear that a truce might bring with it a proposal to reduce the land area allocated to Israel in the November 29 decision; the Government must oppose any such proposal. The war effort required the immigration of tens of thousands, and there was need to mobilize more people for military and economic tasks. While Israel's own strength would determine the outcome of the struggle, support must be enlisted from those who had stood by her in the UN on November 29 and subsequently. The support Israel needed might depend on contacts with the Soviet Union and its Peoples' Democracies. It was therefore imperative that the Government swiftly appoint diplomatic representatives to those countries in order to foster friendship with them and obtain their military and political assistance.

Wilner (Communist Party): Our situation remains difficult, even though it is more favorable than either our friends or enemies have imagined possible. Our difficulties do not stem from the fact that the Arab High Committee of Palestine, King Farouk of Egypt, and Abdullah of Trans-Jordan are fighting against us, so much as from the fact that the British are fighting us and that Truman's America covertly, and sometimes even overtly, is also arrayed against us. This understanding must guide the policy decisions of the Provisional State Council. We would all be happy if a great many world powers were in favor of a Jewish State. But facts are facts; we must not deceive ourselves. The State of Israel was established despite the attempts made by Truman's America to prevent it from happening. Our own military efforts and the political support we have enjoyed from the Soviet Union and other states in the United Nations are what really count. It is incorrect at this point to say that both the United States and the Soviet Union have recognized us. The US has recognized us only de facto. This simply means that they see no alternative to recognizing a situation that they do not like but which nevertheless exists. There is a great difference, therefore, between the recognition of the United States and that of the Soviet Union.

Wilner criticized the reported negotiations between Berl Locker and Nahum Goldmann on the one hand and the British government on the other. He demanded that they cease immediately. He also scorned the attempts being made by Dr. Chaim Weizmann in the US to obtain a most dubious kind of loan, which would make Israel politically dependent on a foreign power. He suggested that we turn to the Soviet Union, democratic countries such as Poland and Czechoslovakia, and, if we wished, to all the countries that had granted us official recognition with a proposal for treaties of friendship and opposition to aggression. Such an initiative would deal a heavy blow to the political machinations of the US and bring military assistance to the Jewish State in its just struggle for independence. The Arab League had advanced a provocative scheme for a cessation of immigration, and we had shown undue haste in accepting the truce on the terms offered. Communist Party contacts with progressive Arab circles in Haifa, including the League for National Liberation, have shown that some Arab groups recognized the right of the Jewish people to its own state, and supported the UN decision of November 29, 1947. It is in Israel's military and political interest to encourage such forces, he said. We must make every effort to mobilize our own resources. But how can we talk about placing our trust in our own efforts when Dr. Weizmann is asking for a $100 million loan from the United States? We need allies. Anyone who favors neutrality is actually favoring a misguided policy of faith in America and Britain.

Dr. Altman (Hatzohar-Revisionists) suggested that the armed forces be called simply the Army of Israel. With all due respect for the achievements of a particular body before a national army was established, the contributions of other bodies of fighters should be recognized. He said the time had come for the world to know that the current struggle was not between Jews and Arabs, but against the British. The Provisional State Council should make the family of nations aware that Britain is one of the belligerents. A Ministry of Propaganda should be established, as propaganda was one of the most important instruments of war. He asked whether, as reported in the press, Dr. Weizmann had already expressed a willingness to return to the Arabs some of the areas that had been captured.

Shattner (Mapai) declared that the guiding hand of the Government was apparent in the advances that had taken place in the last few weeks. But he complained that the Council did not meet often enough. He demanded that the Government prepare a plan for the economic mobilization of the community. He agreed with Dr. Altman on the need to step up propaganda efforts, though he doubted whether propaganda was as important as Dr. Altman believed it to be. He justified the choice of the name Tzva Hagana L'Yisrael (Israel Defense Forces), denying that this title implied anything vis-à-vis a particular organization, though it did emphasize the link between the contemporary State and the proud traditions of the past.

Idelson (Mapai) criticized the way in which foreign property had been mishandled during the fighting. She demanded that the Government act to prevent similar incidents in the future. She also stressed the need to care for the families of soldiers, and dwelt on the meaning of the term Tzva Hagana (Defense Forces). We are a people whose only aim is peace, and thus it is appropriate that we have an army dedicated to defense.

Cohen (Ha'oved Ha'tzioni) called for the maintenance of a proper balance between military and settlement needs. He criticized the establishment of a Ministry of Police. The police should have come under the jurisdiction of the Ministry of the Interior. He defended Goldmann's trip to London, adding that an effort should be made to prevent the British from sabotaging our work.

Weinstein (Hatzohar) criticized the journey of Goldmann, who was not a citizen of Israel. A member of the Jewish Agency had no right to negotiate on behalf of the State of Israel. He also asked whether Dr. Weizmann, who had been chosen President of the Council, had turned in his British passport.

Pinkas (Mizrahi) paid tribute to the extraordinary valor of the defenders of the Old City of Jerusalem and of the Etzion Bloc. He applauded the choice of the name Tzva Hagana L'Yisrael in appreciation of the Hagana's exploits before the establishment of the State, and because "Hagana" (Defense) indicated that Israel's armed forces were not established with aggressive acts in mind. He demanded that every minister present a plan of action to the Council and that, in general, the Council be made more of a partner in the work of the Government.

Grabovsky (Mapai) answered about Dr. Weizmann's passport. Dr. Weizmann's life and work, and not his passport, would determine his place in the State. In fact, no foreign passport had yet been exchanged for an Israeli one. He reminded Mr. Wilner that the Soviet Union was also asking for an American loan, and that the Russian Ambassador did not hesitate to meet with the Pope.

After the discussion, the Prime Minister assured Mr. Wilner and Dr. Altman that the Government did not pursue a policy of neutrality, but strove for international unity and loyalty to the United Nations. It wished to have diplomatic representatives in every country, even Britain, as did the Soviet Union. He told Mr. Weinstein that Israel was a Jewish State and so could be represented by any accredited Jew, if other countries were willing to accept him. The "passport" that counted was a man's Jewishness and his loyalty to the State of Israel. With respect to the dissident organizations, we are willing to forget earlier activities undertaken in opposition to the views of the Jewish community.

Replying to the painful question of theft raised by Idelson, the Prime Minister announced that the Government was determined to combat all such disgraceful acts, with the most extreme means if necessary. As to the discussion in London, Israel was anxious to maintain good relations with all the peoples of the world, and to improve her relations even with a government that had previously been hostile to her. No differences of opinion existed in regard to the anti-Jewish policies of the Bevin government. But that government had not declared war on Israel and Israel had no reason to declare war on Britain. There was no need to be as extreme a Jewish nationalist as Council Member Wilner. The interests of the State demanded that good relations be fostered with all countries, where that was possible, even if they had been hostile in the past. Israel was willing to forgive and forget; of course, this policy depended on the other side as well. Israel's position was not one of "neutrality." It was based on the belief that men everywhere were essentially interested in peace and mutual cooperation. Israel did not examine the regimes of other countries too closely. She wished to live at peace with all of them, if that were possible. She had hostages in almost every land and wanted them to emigrate. Her policies were thus aimed at fostering the unity of mankind and universal peace.

Israel Raises Serious Objections to Bernadotte's Proposals

At the June 4 Cabinet meeting Foreign Minister Shertok reported on his negotiations with Count Bernadotte in regard to a truce. The issue in dispute was immigration during the truce period. Bernadotte said that the Security Council's resolution on the matter was not sufficiently clear; he asked for an authoritative interpretation. A cable reply came from this month's President of the Council, Faris el Houri, which stated: "I hereby confirm that the Security Council intended in its May 29 resolution to ensure that neither side would gain a military advantage from the truce. The introduction to the resolution states that 'it is meant to bring about a cessation of hostile acts in Palestine without prejudice to the rights, demands, and status of the Arabs or the Jews.'"

This means, Shertok argued, that it is forbidden to bring in trained men, but not men of military age. At the same time, this must be done in a manner that will not accord a military advantage to one of the parties. Bernadotte pondered the matter for a considerable time, then presented a document to Shertok which, he said, would not be shown to the Arabs. It read:

1. The only question in dispute concerns the unrestricted entry of people of military age into Israel and the Arab states.

2. Israel's right to accept immigrants is not in dispute. Each side clearly has the right to accept as many immigrants as it sees fit, before or after the armistice. The problem is to ensure that neither side gains military advantage from the entry of men of military age during the truce.

3. The Arabs are willing to accept limitations on the entry of people of military age into their countries. This is less important to them than it is to the Jews, for they have an abundant supply of manpower, while the Jews have only limited manpower resources.

4. The two main goals of the truce, as defined in the Security Council resolution and confirmed in the June 4 cable from the President of the Council, are to bring about a cessation of hostilities without prejudicing the rights and status of the Jews and Arabs, and to ensure that neither side gains military advantage from the truce. The latter consideration influences all truce arrangements.

5. It is my firm intention, as UN Mediator, to ensure that truce arrangements are consistent with the aforementioned goals.

6. The right of people of military age to enter Palestine is not an immigration question in this context; no one doubts that the Jews may accept immigrants It is rather a question of military advantage.

7. It could be argued that if there were no truce, many men of military age would be among the immigrants. At the same time, you stated at our meeting in Haifa that immigration at this time involves certain dangers and irregular methods must be employed. Moreover, the question of Jewish immigration is the central issue in the whole dispute, and it is clear that the Security Council resolution was not intended to give one side or the other a military advantage. The acceptance of the principle of Jewish immigration for the first time by the Arabs is in itself a considerable achievement.

8. Therefore, if there were unrestricted Jewish immigration during the period of the truce, with a considerable number of immigrants of military age among the newcomers, and without it being necessary to use irregular methods to bring them in, this would accord a distinct military advantage to the Jews. This is true even if the aforementioned immigrants are kept in camps, under supervision, during the period of the truce. Israel's military potential would grow without the usual accompanying difficulties. This would violate the spirit of the resolution.

9. I intend to pursue the following policy in regard to immigration to Israel:

A. The appropriate Jewish authorities will be asked to inform the Mediator whenever a large group of Jewish immigrants is expected to leave a particular port for Israel. The information must be relayed far enough in advance to permit the Mediator to send observers to the port in question, where they will be authorized to gather information about the immigrants.

B. No military personnel will be allowed to enter the country.

C. The Mediator will have the right to send observers on all boats carrying a considerable number of Jewish immigrants to Israel.

D. All the immigrants will be carefully examined by observers on their arrival in Israel.

E. In regard to immigrants of military age, the Mediator will determine whether they are entering in sufficient numbers to give the Jewish side a military advantage. If he decides that this is the case, he will prohibit their entry.

F. Immigrants of military age permitted to enter the country will remain in camps during the period of the truce under the supervision of the Mediator's observers. They will not be mobilized, or given military or paramilitary training.

G. There will be no immigration for a week after the truce has come into effect in order to permit immigration controls to be set up.

H. Immigrants who are aboard ships on their way to Israel at the time that the truce comes into effect, and who reach the country during the first week of the truce, will not be permitted to come ashore until the appropriate supervisory arrangements have been made.

I. All men between the ages of eighteen and forty-five will be considered of military age.

J. Finally, the principle of Jewish immigration will remain unaffected; the aforementioned limitations will apply only to military personnel and men of military age. The entry of people of military age will be limited whenever their entry would, in the opinion of the Mediator, give the Jewish side a military advantage.

Shertok informed Bernadotte that his statement has caused grave misgivings because it represented a clear departure from the Security Council's truce resolution. The President of the Security Council has no right to speak in its name. He is the ambassador of a government that has attacked us and we need not take his views into consideration. After discussing the immigration of people of military age, the Council accepted the French amendment on the subject which prohibits the entry of military personnel, but not of people of military age. The conflict between the neighboring states and ourselves is not over the question of immigration. There has always been Jewish immigration, and the surrounding countries never sent in their armies to interfere with it. We cannot agree to a formula whereby if the Arabs stop shooting, we will halt immigration. Shertok also opposed the cessation of immigration for a week. In a Jewish State, he declared, there will be no stoppage of immigration.

The Mediator took our reply very badly, charging that we don't want a truce. You have no faith in me, he said. You are afraid that the week will turn into ten days and then into two weeks. I understand what it is for your people to be turned away from the shores of their Homeland. I will take this moral factor into consideration. As far as the reply of the Security Council President is concerned, I am certain it was formulated in conjunction with the UN Secretariat and is not simply a reflection of his personal opinion. Bunche has confirmed this fact.

Shertok pointed out that the Arabs had military advantages that the resolution did not prevent them from exploiting. They could mobilize more men. It was a question of six nations against one. He was aware of all those factors, Bernadotte replied, and would base his decisions on the dictates of his conscience. What will happen if there is no truce? Then everything will be endangered. If there is a truce, there will be immigration—with the approval of the Arabs. Moreover, he added, he did not say that people of military age will not be permitted to enter the country. Finally, it would be well if you ask your friends what effect an Israeli rejection of the truce proposal would have on international public opinion.

Bernadotte returned to Cairo to prepare a final formulation of his proposals.

Shapira (Hapoel Hamizrahi) asked whether the introduction of a truce depended on our approval, or could be initiated even without our approval. He assumed, Shertok answered, that the matter would be brought to the Security Council.

Ben-Gurion said: All our military experts are for a truce. It will give us an opportunity to train our Army, a large part of which is untrained. When we had to contend only with gangs, this didn't matter; but now we have to fight regular armies. Most of the people who have been called up are not trained. A month is not enough, of course, but in a month they can receive some training and our situation will improve. Nevertheless, I favor a clear-cut rejection of the Bernadotte proposals. He tries to make them look favorable by saying that the Arabs will agree to immigration. We don't need their agreement.

There is no mention in the Security Council resolution of a ban on the entrance of people of military age. It simply states that if such people come in, they cannot be given military training. Bevin has forbidden Jews of military age in Cyprus to come to Israel, and this has set the tone for the Arabs. His attitude certainly doesn't obligate us in any way. We will also refuse to accept the ban on the shipment of weapons. The Arabs have nothing to lose by not receiving arms for four weeks, because they have been receiving them for years. For us, the four weeks can be decisive. One of our representatives who sent a ship with arms asked that the truce be delayed. I wouldn't delay it just for that reason. But we cannot be treated in the same way as the Arab states. They already have weapons of all kinds. We do not. There is another, very basic question involved: national sovereignty. The proposed arrangements seem to strike at both sides, but they do not have the same effect on both sides. The Arabs don't need people from the outside, though no one will prevent a thirty-year-old Englishman from entering Lebanon, even if he happens to be a military officer who has come to teach the local people how to make dynamite. There will be no supervision in such instances.

I am not concerned with the political consequences of our refusal to accept the Bernadotte proposals. The Security Council is not a homogeneous body; every member has his own policies. The military consequences, however, may be more serious. Be that as it may, I suggest that we reject the Bernadotte proposals. There are two elements basic to our existence, immigration and independence. We must determine what happens in our own country. Why does Bernadotte think we have to trust him? Did we choose him? And why is he preparing his final draft in Egypt? Let him go to Cyprus. He is under constant Arab pressure. Why does he think we should have faith in him? We must reject his proposals because they conflict with the Security Council resolution. There was no mention in the resolution of a week's halt in immigration. That is Bernadotte's own inspiration. If he needs time, let him postpone the truce for a week. We will not postpone immigration.

Rabbi Levin (Agudat Israel): If all our military experts are agreed, as the Prime Minister says, that a truce is desirable, we must take this fact into consideration. All the non-Jews hate us. The Jerusalemites are hungry. They have already been under fire for six months. Thousands have fallen. We do not know what the results of the war will be. God watches over us, but we cannot put our trust in miracles. Ben-Gurion was right. We are always right. But one cannot ignore reality. If there is the possibility of a truce, and a hope for peace afterward, this is very important, even if the arrangements are not completely satisfactory.

Bentov (Mapam): We must inform Bernadotte that we cannot accept limitations on men and arms until we are certain that the Arabs are also under effective supervision. It is not good tactically just to say No. But we must tell the Mediator that the position of the two sides must be equal between the cease-fire and the beginning of supervision.

Shapira: The determining factor so far as I am concerned is the military situation. The Arabs don't need a truce; they have large reserves of manpower. In the past three weeks they did not capture Tel Aviv or Jerusalem. The truce is a blow to their military strength. If they agree to a truce, it is because they have no alternative as members of the United Nations, not for military reasons. In our case the military situation is the determining factor. If there are only five or six thousand trained men at the front, while other men are untrained, and if it is necessary to call up the thirty-five to thirty-eight age group, then the situation is very serious indeed. To tell you the truth, the Jerusalem problem weighs very heavily on me. There is no food in the city. It is true that the children of Jerusalem were happy when they saw jeeps arrive with arms rather than with food, but we know that most of the population is hungry. If, God forbid, Jerusalem should fall, I don't know how we would recover from the blow. There is also the territorial status quo to take into consideration. We have captured 189 Arab towns and villages, some of them outside the borders of the State. The biggest cities are in our hands, as is a very large area of the countryside. Maintenance of the status quo is to our advantage. Bernadotte's interpretation of the Security Council resolution is not to our liking, but it is not entirely without a basis in fact. There is need to clarify the question of transportation to and from Jerusalem. There is also another grave issue: only limited amounts of food can be sent to Jerusalem. There is no possibility of storing food for possible eventualities. If there is no alternative, we will simply have to accept the evil edict.

Bernstein (General Zionists): It is not for us to decide whether a truce is desirable, but whether it is a necessity. The issues of Jerusalem and of arms shipments are part of the overall equation. The immigration of people of military age is not a decisive question; there are many people already in the country who have yet to be trained. I am afraid that there are plans to develop a scheme for supervision in the future as well. It is certainly not a good idea to have observers in our ports. I suggest we proclaim our willingness to accept Bernadotte's plan, on condition that the supervision of Arab activities is as strict as the supervision of our own.

Rosenblueth (Progressive) proposed that the matter be brought back to the Security Council, for we have strong arguments on our side in regard to immigration. He suggested that if the Council supports Bernadotte, we should accept the Mediator's scheme. The fact that our military experts regard the truce as absolutely necessary, because many of our people are insufficiently trained, is what counts. I don't know if Ben-Gurion's evaluation of the Security Council is correct. That weak body may display enough strength to impose sanctions on us. I doubt whether we can bring in arms for our soldiers in the four weeks anyway.

Rabbi Fishman (Mizrahi): It would be very sad indeed if twenty-three days after the creation of the State we agreed to foreigners' limiting or even stopping immigration. With all that, I am not sure the road to Jerusalem will be opened.

Remez (Mapai) agreed with Shapira. The military experts apparently believe there is more danger in fighting than in accepting a truce. There would also be a great political danger in our turning down a truce. We must decide in favor of an immediate truce.

The Prime Minister and Minister of Defense reported on the military situation at the June 6 meeting of the Government. When the war began, we had twenty-five hundred trained men in the Palmah. It was our only fully mobilized group, though there were also thirty-five hundred trained men in the Field Units. In other words, we had about five to six thousand more or less trained men available. In the intervening three weeks twenty-five hundred soldiers have been killed or wounded. Generally speaking, we have lost our very best men, including a large percentage of our officers, who led their units at the fronts. Therefore only about three thousand of our "veterans" remain.

Forty thousand people are now in uniform, but only twenty-three thousand of them are combat soldiers. The rest are in service units. Not all of our combat soldiers have been trained, and we are facing trained armies. The Arab Legion is very well trained. So are the Egyptians. The Arabs have commanders with a military education and years of military service.

There was a great controversy over whether to send trained or untrained battalions to Latrun. We finally sent untrained men because the trained battalions were needed elsewhere. The untrained battalions were not equal to the task. So from a purely military viewpoint, the truce will be a blessing. It will give our combat soldiers, who haven't slept for a week, a chance to rest. It will allow us to train thoroughly our half-trained men. At the end of the month, we will have a combat-ready force of twenty thousand people.

"I haven't reached a conclusion even after what Ben-Gurion said," Kaplan commented. "When Shertok spoke, my reaction was negative. But like Shapira, I am troubled by the Jerusalem situation. Ben-Zvi cabled me today: 'With all due respect for the courage of Jerusalem's population, you must realize that there are limits to our endurance, which, if passed, may cause us to collapse.' I suggest that the Government meet tomorrow with the military men. We require not only numbers, but an evaluation of our chances of saving Jerusalem."

After several formal questions had been settled, the following resolution was adopted: "The Mediator should be informed immediately that the Government supports the views expressed by the Foreign Minister, namely, that Bernadotte is misinterpreting the Security Council's resolution. We reserve the right to appeal to the Security Council after receiving the final version of his proposals."

The Government also decided: (1) to draft seventeen-year-olds for two months' training, on condition that they would not be sent to the front without a specific decision to that effect; (2) to draft people in the thirty-six to thirty-eight-year-old age group for military service, and to mobilize men up to the age of forty-two to dig fortifications; (3) to draft married men up to the age of thirty-five, even if they have more than two children.

Bernadotte's reply to Shertok's message on the truce, received on June 8, announced that it was scheduled to begin on June 11 at 10 A.M. Should one of the sides reject the truce proposal, or accept it only conditionally, the Mediator would immediately turn to the Security Council to take whatever action it saw fit. In order to prevent either side from gaining military advantage from the truce, the following conditions were set forth:

A. No military unit can enter the Arab states or any part of Palestine.
B. The Mediator will decide about the entry of immigrants of military age on the

basis of whether their arrival will give one side a military advantage. If this is the case, they will not be permitted to enter. If they are allowed to come in, they will remain in camps under the supervision of observers. They will be forbidden to undergo military or para-military training during the truce period.

C.   The Mediator will keep watch on all the ports from which immigrants depart, and therefore must be informed in advance about any ship bringing immigrants.

D.   The Mediator will use his own judgment about permitting the entry of immigrants, no matter what their age or sex, during the first week of the truce.

E.   The movement of troops or war materiel from one belligerent state to another, closer to the borders of Palestine, or to the battle fronts in Palestine will be prohibited during the period of the truce.

F.   All battle lines will remain unchanged. Troops along those lines will not be rein-forced nor will the shipment of arms to the lines be permitted. Normal rotation of troops will, however, be allowed.

G.   War materiel will not be allowed into Palestine or into any of the belligerent states.

H.   Assistance to the civil populations of urban areas badly hit in the battles, such as Jerusalem and Jaffa, will be under the supervision of the International Red Cross. The Red Cross will ensure that the quantity of supplies available at the end of the truce will not be significantly greater or less than at the beginning.

I.   All belligerent acts on land, on sea, or in the air will cease during the period of the truce.

The Provisional Government discussed the Bernadotte proposals for two days, finally adopting Rosenblueth's suggestion that Israel accept the truce unconditionally. Nevertheless, the Government felt several comments necessary in regard to Shertok's reply to the Mediator. Its major points were: (1) The Security Council resolution places no limits on the immigration of people of military age, merely prohibiting their mobiliza-tion and training during the truce period. Yet Section B. of Bernadotte's communication speaks of his authority to ban immigration. (2) The Government is willing to cooperate with the Mediator in order to ease his burden in the sphere of supervision, but will consider as unjustified any attempt to interfere with the entry of Jewish immigrants, whatever their age or sex.

A day before the truce came into effect Ben-Gurion made the following broadcast to the people of Israel:

> After a discussion during which various factors were taken into consideration, the Government of Israel has decided to accept the truce despite its shortcomings and discrima-tory aspects. There are two main reasons for our acceptance of the truce: (1) we have declared from the moment when fighting started that we were willing to do so; (2) the State of Israel follows a policy of cooperation with the United Nations. Therefore, we will observe the four-week truce if the enemy does so.
>
> We must have absolute discipline, and absolute support for the country's legal au-thorities. The Government will not permit any violation of the truce, and will deal with anyone who attempts to violate it as one deals with an internal enemy in times of emergency.
>
> The truce comes four weeks after the establishment of the State of Israel. The treach-erous attack of five neighboring states, which enjoyed the overt and covert support of a great power, only served to strengthen the State established after nineteen hundred years of Jewish wanderings. We not only hold the area allocated to us by the United Nations

General Assembly, but have also taken sections of the Homeland outside those borders. New Jerusalem is almost completely in our hands. Our strength on land, in the air, and on the sea has grown during these four weeks. We have in large measure overcome the legacy of chaos left us by the Mandatory Government. Public services have been established and immigration has grown in the very midst of the war. Immigration will not cease during the truce, and the upbuilding of the country will continue with even greater impetus.

All the areas captured by our armies will remain in our hands. During the truce period Government services will be improved, the economy strengthened, immigration increased, and settlement expanded. We will also pay due heed to the military situation. During three generations we demonstrated our imaginative creativity. During these last six months we have demonstrated our fighting strength. We are always anxious to promote peace, but we will always stand ready to defend ourselves if that again proves necessary.

We will observe the truce with a full sense of our strength and the justice of our cause. These two elements will enable us to stand firm until peace is assured and the vision of redemption fulfilled.

The Government met again on June 14, 1948, three days after the truce came into effect. The Defense Minister reported on several Arab truce violations, including an attack on Sejera. But the worst violation was in upper Galilee, where there was a general assault on Mishmar Hayarden, which was captured by the enemy after the truce came into force. A severe artillery and air attack on Kfar Szold and Ein Gev also took place.

There was concern that the truce was violated in upper Galilee by our own forces in an attempt to recapture Mishmar Hayarden. A special person was sent to investigate the situation and on his return reported that he was convinced it was the Syrians who had violated the truce.

While these all-important military and political events necessarily absorbed our time and energy, the Prime Minister requested that the Provisional Council turn its attention to the practical problems facing it. The Minister of Justice presented the draft of the Days of Rest Ordinance—1948. It stated:

1. The Sabbath and the Jewish holidays—the two days of the New Year (Rosh Hashana), the Day of Atonement (Yom Kippur), the first and eighth days of the Feast of Tabernacles (Succot), the first and seventh days of Passover (Pesah), and Pentecost (Shavuot)—are the scheduled days of rest in the State of Israel. Non-Jews have the right to observe their own days of rest and holidays.

2. This Ordinance will form part of the Law and Administration Ordinance No. 1— 1948.

3. This Ordinance is retroactive to May 15, 1948.

The Ordinance was adopted by unanimous vote. The Minister of Justice then proposed a (provisional) Income Tax Ordinance. It was accepted in principle, with the provision that it be formulated more clearly and simply, and brought back to the Council for final approval. He also submitted the draft of an ordinance on the status of British Mandatory Government employees.

Section 5: Problems of the Truce Period

Ben-Gurion's Five-Point Plan of Action

As Prime Minister, David Ben-Gurion presented a five-point plan of action for the truce period:

1. *Jerusalem.* The successful defense of Jerusalem depends on the solution of complex organizational, engineering, and political problems. On the organizational front, we face the difficulty of finding vehicles to transport food to Jerusalem. On the engineering front, there is the question of the road to Jerusalem. In the midst of the war, we opened an alternative route to Jerusalem. Like any conquest, it cost a great deal of blood, and still leaves us with some unsolved problems. Along one stretch of a hundred and fifty meters it is now necessary to raise and lower wagons by heavy chains. Either we must improve that segment of the road or provide an alternative in the area. Politically, there are objections, from both the Arabs and the UN Observers, to the transport of foodstuffs over our new route. Meanwhile, however, shipments continue normally. The quantity of food transported grows larger day by day. If we can bring more food over this road during the next twenty-eight days, we undoubtedly can supply Jerusalem's current needs and build up a reserve.

We must prevent people from leaving Jerusalem. "Desertion" is a nasty word and I prefer not to castigate anyone. Considering the dangers faced by Jerusalemites in recent weeks—hunger and the fear of more hunger, day-and-night shellings that killed hundreds and wounded thousands, etc.—we have no right to criticize those who wish to leave or to call them deserters. Nevertheless, we must make every effort to prevent an uncontrolled exodus from the city. If we fail, the Arabs will accomplish in this way what they could not accomplish by their bombardments and their attempts to starve us out. Simply preventing an exodus, however, will not solve Jerusalem's problems. The only real solution is to improve Jerusalem's basic situation. We must ensure that Jerusalem is strengthened on a long-term basis, so that people will want to stay there.

2. *Strengthening the armed forces.* (a) Training must be improved. The present situation in this area causes great concern. As I have pointed out at previous meetings, most of our Army is untrained. Very few of our soldiers were trained before the fighting began, and many of those few have since fallen. We have also lost a large percentage of our commanders. The first priority, therefore, is training. (b) We must improve discipline, essential to the existence and effectiveness of any army. An undisciplined army is not only ineffective, but also dangerous. An underground movement does not become a disciplined army overnight because the Minister of Defense issues an edict to that effect. People do not easily change attitudes developed over many years of underground activity. But these attitudes must be changed. My views on this subject are shared by senior officers. (c) The structure of the Army must be changed. Let me give you just one tragic example of why this is necessary:

Gezer was attacked on the last day before the truce came into effect. The attack began at 12:30 P.M. and the settlement fell at 6 P.M. All of us are more or less acquainted with the spot. Gezer is not far from the Jerusalem road or from the Arab village of Kubab, which we now hold. It is not far from Hulda, where the headquarters of the Shlomo Brigade is located, or from Na'an, where there also are elements of the Shlomo Brigade. Near Gezer itself is Tel Gezer, which overlooks the entire area and where we have artillery emplacements. Radio contact with Gezer was operating all the time. Nevertheless, no help was sent to the settlement, and it fell. Twenty people were killed and all the others, except for the few who managed to escape, were taken prisoner. Twelve girls were captured and one was killed. The Arab attackers were commanded by an Englishman. He brought the girls to Ben Shemen, where they were released.

This sorry spectacle can be explained at least in part by the fact that there are independent commands in the Army. There was one commander at Kubab, a second at Hulda, and a third at Na'an. Gezer was recaptured, but we lost far too many people there. Moreover, the fact remains that the defenders fought on for six hours without receiving reinforcements, despite the presence of large units in the vicinity. This kind of situation, and even more basic considerations, necessitate a change in the structure of the Army.

Four weeks ago we were fighting only Arab bands; we had never confronted a regular army. We were not organized or trained for battles with regular armies. To the extent that our men were trained, it had been within the framework of the Hagana and its operations. It is not easy to overcome deeply ingrained habits, particularly when they are part and parcel of an ideology; the interests of public organizations, too, are involved.

I must offer a word of praise of the enemy—to the Arab Legion. It is a trained, disciplined, and brave military force, and one respected by our boys. The Legionnaires know what an army is; they don't run away; and they can storm a position when necessary. The Legion has good commanders and weapons. It will be a long time before we have the same kind of weapons. The Egyptian soldier also fights. True, his commander has to keep pushing him, but he does fight. And a regular army must be confronted by a regular army. Partisans have an important role to play, but on their own they cannot take on a regular army.

Training, discipline, and structure are the three keys for us. We must assume that the truce is temporary and that fighting will start again. We cannot allow ourselves to be less prepared at that time than we could and should be.

3. *Increasing war production*. Since it is difficult to obtain weapons from abroad—this is a major drawback of the truce, a period when we had hoped to receive important arms shipments—we must increase our own arms production. There is, after all, no UN control over local production of weapons.

4. *New settlements*. We must always be active in this sphere, and particularly now. I am sure that I don't have to explain why. But I would like to make one minor observation. In my opinion, we should avoid publicizing our settlement work at this time. Publicity will do us more harm than good. We can and should erect new settlements faster and at more places, but we should keep quiet about it. The same holds true in regard to immigration. We must bring in more people without calling attention to the fact.

5. I must comment on one matter that has been raised in the press, namely *Al Hamishmar*'s charge that "Ben-Gurion is dissolving the Palmah." I am busy building an army, and I have not concerned myself with dissolving military units. But strange things have occurred, and I have investigated them. There was supposed to be an attack on the central front, and for some reason it did not take place. When I asked why, I was told that it was because supplies had not arrived. I checked to see why they had not arrived and was informed that supplies were not sent directly to that brigade (a Palmah brigade) but through another place. I asked why supplies had to go to another place first and was told that this was the custom in the Palmah. I ordered the abolition of this practice and the shipment of supplies directly from Tel Aviv to the Palmah brigade in the Jerusalem hills. This is what *Al Hamishmar* calls the dissolution of the Palmah.

The agitation of one newspaper or another will not make me alter my policies. We are concerned here with one of the two principles that I laid down as a condition of my accepting responsibility for defense. There must be one set of rules for all military units, all soldiers, and all commanders.

We are working to create a trained, disciplined, responsible military force that knows what it is fighting for. Our Army is usually superior to enemy armies in a number of respects. In general, it enjoys moral and intellectual superiority. We must see to it that our discipline, training, and equipment are also up to those of the enemy—better, if possible. We must have a real sense of comradeship in the Army. Every Jewish soldier must be equal to every other; every brigade must be equal to every other. The pioneering spirit is not the sole preserve of a particular military unit. All of our soldiers are fighting for the security of the State and all must be equally devoted, as indeed they are capable of being.

A three-man committee was chosen to deal with the problem of supplies to Jerusalem: its members: Zisling, Kaplan, Shapira, with Kaplan as chairman.

Debates on Mediator's Proposals ★ Military and Political Implications ★ Struggle for Jerusalem

The Cabinet meeting of June 16, 1948, in accordance with the request of several members, was mainly devoted to a discussion of political and military problems. Foreign Minister Shertok reported on the questions raised by the UN Mediator, who was trying to arrange for talks between Israel and the Arabs.

Perhaps, Bernadotte said, the question of Israel's existence would not be raised, but the question of her borders certainly would be. Not only the Arabs and Jews were concerned, but others as well. Foreign Secretary Bevin and the American Ambassador in London had talked about it. We do not know all of the details of their discussion. The Foreign Office denied that an agreement existed between the American and British governments in regard to Israel's borders. But we do know that the U.S. government has discussed the question, and asked us whether we accepted the November 29 borders. The British representative, Harold Beeley, asked whether we see a parallel between western Galilee, which, according to the November 29 resolution was to go to the Arabs but is now in our hands, and the Negev, which is in Egyptian hands. He also asked if we see a parallel between Haifa (with its Arab population), which we hold, and Jerusalem (with its Jewish population), where we may be asked to accept Abdullah's rule.

The Foreign Minister stated that we agreed to the November 29 scheme, but only if it were carried out in its entirety. Otherwise, we would feel free to act as we saw fit.

There are four basic elements in the plan: (1) a Jewish state in a certain part of the Land of Israel with certain borders; (2) an independent Arab state, in a certain area and with certain borders, not to be attached to Trans-Jordan, and certainly not to Syria; (3) an internationalized Jerusalem, with an effective international regime that will guarantee equality, free access to the Holy Places, etc.; (4) an economic union of the Jewish state, the Arab state, and internationalized Jerusalem. The Foreign Minister then went on to say:

> It would be very good if we could achieve two things: (1) not give up any of the land allocated to us under the November 29 resolution; and (2) hold on to those areas that we have conquered in a struggle that was forced upon us; bitter experience has shown that these areas are vital to the defense of Jewish settlements. I refer to western Galilee, the road to Jerusalem, and Jerusalem itself. Our presence in Rosh Hanikra will allow us to sign a

pact with Lebanon. The gravest issue is the road to Jerusalem. How will we decide about Jerusalem? We may finally conclude that internationalization would be the best answer. We cannot agree to any solution that does not guarantee our position in Jerusalem, even if it is internationalized! We cannot agree to the arrangement in the November 29 resolution whereby a large sovereign Arab area separates Jerusalem from the State of Israel. We have conquered a corridor from Tel Aviv to the Romema quarter in Jerusalem and the Arabs moved out. Jerusalem's future will be determined by what happens at the western entrance to the city. This is one of the territorial changes that we must safeguard at all costs.

Since some areas allocated to the Jewish State are in Arab hands, we may be faced with the possibility of mutual exchanges of territory. The first suggested exchange involves giving the southern Negev in return for western Galilee. This problem must concern us.

I distinguish between the northern and the southern Negev, even though I know there are those who reject such a distinction. I am not an expert on the Negev. Even before Lake Success, I said that we should base our policy on the opinion of our experts (Lipschitz, Weitz, etc.). They told me that there is a considerable difference between the northern Negev, with an area of 4 million dunams (1 million acres), and the southern triangle, with 8 million dunams (2 million acres). While agricultural development in the northern Negev is limited only by the availability of water, in the southern Negev both water and suitable land are lacking. Nevertheless, we demanded that the State of Israel be given the southern Negev and our demand was accepted. However, should we have the possibility of exchanging western Galilee for the southern Negev, we should consider the proposition very seriously.

Besides the question of borders, that is, the area of the State, there is also the problem of the Arab community that was inside Israeli territory before the fighting began. Can we possibly accept a return to the status quo ante, or should we fight to maintain the present situation?

I am particularly amazed by the flight of the Arabs. This is a more extraordinary episode in the annals of this country than the establishment of a Jewish State. The latter, while enormously important in the history of the world and of the Jewish people, is not really surprising after three generations of Jewish settlement, a Jewish National Home, and war. It came about because the world was convinced that such a State in fact already existed and accorded it official recognition. Truly astonishing is that the Arabs have disappeared from a whole section of the country. Does anyone know clearly how many Arabs there are in the entire State of Israel? In my opinion, there are no more than a hundred thousand. (Ben-Gurion: "I'd be surprised if there were even a hundred thousand.")

We must explore the enormous impact of this change on settlement and security, as well as on our ethnic structure and the grave social and political problems we face. This transformation has occurred in the course of a war initiated by the Arabs. Moreover, the Arabs fled; they were not driven out. This is one of those revolutionary events that alter the course of history. There can be no return to the status quo ante, just as there was no such return after the war between Turkey and Greece.

We must be ready to pay for the Arab land. This does not mean that we will purchase land from individuals. Negotiations must take place between the governments concerned. Our compensation for Arab land and property can be used to resettle them in other countries. But they will not return. This is our State, and we will not allow that to happen.

This program, if accepted, will have a far-reaching effect on territorial questions, both internal and external. An Israel with a 350,000 Arab minority, and one that controlled a substantial section of the country, would be more vulnerable to pressures to reduce the size of the State than an Israel that had freed itself from this Arab minority that had occupied their abandoned land. This well-watered land is at least as important as the Negev (I'm not saying that we should give up the Negev, for we must also consider the ingathering of the exiles). There remains the question of an Arab Palestine, or, more specifically, the question of Abdullah. If Arab Palestine should become part of Abdullah's kingdom, opening the way to a link with Iraq, we would face an entirely different situation than if there was a fully independent Arab state. An economic union is possible only with an independent Arab state. We agreed to a certain degree of cooperation, but not with some other partner.

The discussion was taken up by the Prime Minister:

We have three objectives: Security, a Jewish State, and a pact between the Jews and the Arabs. Our goal must be not only the achievement of the first two, but eventually of the third as well. A pact between Jews and Arabs would, I believe, guarantee the fulfillment of Zionist aspirations and cause a revolutionary change in the Arab world. In any case, it would be extremely important for us.

I start with two basic assumptions: (1) The November 29 resolution is dead, or so it appears to me. Perhaps we may find ourselves in a situation where there is no alternative but to accept the November 29 resolution as the basis for a settlement, but I fail to see any enthusiastic supporters of the resolution, and if there are none, then it is indeed dead. (2) The dispute will be settled by force. The political question now is really a *military* one. This is so even in the unlikely event that fighting is not renewed. In any circumstances, military considerations will be dominant.

The major developments that have occurred—the entrance into the struggle of the Arab states with their regular armies, the ability we have shown to repulse the attacks of these armies, and the flight of the Arabs—may appear surprising, but they have not surprised me. On the other hand, I have been bitterly surprised by our own grave moral shortcomings.

The political issues will be decided by our ability to triumph militarily should war break out. Our internal shortcomings must be remedied immediately. No one should defend the looting in Jaffa and elsewhere. I was shocked to hear of these things. I could not believe that the reports were true. I asked Yacov Riftin to investigate the situation. His findings shook my confidence in our ultimate triumph. Anyone who says that he is certain of our victory must have better sources of information than are available to me. I have never doubted until now that we had a chance to win, but today I am less certain about our internal moral strength in a war. In this sphere we have not done too badly, but not too well either.

The war is not yet over; there is only a truce. If war begins again, it will be a life-death struggle *for us*, but not for them. We will obviously not exterminate the Egyptian people or the Syrian people. We could, I believe, destroy the Trans-Jordan Army and that part of the Egyptian Army sent here. But it is not our intention to slaughter the Egyptian people. However, if we are defeated, they will annihilate us. The Arabs have already arrested some hundred Jewish merchants in Baghdad on the charge that they were trading with Russia, though there is no law against trading with Russia. (*Shertok:* "We have just received a list of Zionists imprisoned in Cairo.") If they were to invade Tel Aviv, I am not at all sure that they would show mercy to its inhabitants. If war does begin again, we will be fighting for our lives. We cannot allow the Arabs to return to those places that they left.

The truce will be of value to us if it lasts for two months. We cannot accomplish a great deal in a month. We would also lose something by a two-month truce, but at its conclusion we would have a better organizational structure, as well as a trained and disciplined army.

I shall begin my discussion of other political questions with the Negev. Shertok told us that the experts distinguish between the northern and southern Negev. I disagree with the experts; not only that, I doubt whether they are really experts on the Negev. An expert on the Negev is someone who has carried out many drillings and soil studies there. These so-called experts did neither. (*Shertok:* "They said they did.") Others did. They read what others wrote. They didn't work in the Negev. I am not an expert on the Negev, but I have also read everything that has been written about it, and I assure you that they are talking nonsense. There is no basis for differentiating between the northern and southern Negev.

The Negev differs from every other section of the country for a very simple reason: it is a 12-million-dunam (3-million-acre) area which is both empty and desolate. In ordinary circumstances, this would certainly be no great advantage. A settled area would ordinarily have been better, but not from our point of view. From a Zionist viewpoint, an empty and desolate area is better, because we can turn it into a flourishing center of Jewish settlement. We are dealing here not only with the Negev, but with the Dead Sea. You do not have to be an expert to realize the value of the Dead Sea.

(*Shertok* interjected: "But that is part of the northern section." Ben-Gurion denied this) No. It is part of the southern section, because the northern section is, de facto, in the hands of the Arabs. It was given to them. The Dead Sea is a vast treasure house, particularly the southern part. The exact location of the Dead Sea is not important. The important thing is what we can extract from it and *take somewhere else.* South of the Dead Sea lies a flat area, the Arava, and then, finally, the Red Sea.

It is only natural that the Arabs should want Eilat, but we also want it. The Negev is an enormous Zionist asset, and there is no substitute for it anywhere else in the Land of Israel. First of all, it is half of the Land of Israel. There is no such thing as the northern and the southern Negev. The Negev is barren and empty now, and that is why it is important. We can create there a densely populated Jewish area, perhaps with room for millions of people. Moshe Smilansky thinks that it would be possible for 2 million Jews to make a living from farming in the Negev. If he is correct, then an additional 3 million could make a living from industry. The Jews who might be settled there are, unfortunately, not yet with us. Even so, the Negev still offers very great opportunities.

The central military issue is the struggle for Jerusalem. In my opinion, the outcome will determine the fate of the Land of Israel as a whole. This is true not only because of Jerusalem's historic importance, but also because of its strategic importance. (*Bernstein:* "Its historic importance stems from its strategic importance.") It is not only the road to Jerusalem that is at stake. The war has shown us that Jerusalem cannot survive unless it is linked geographically with the Jewish State.

A third key area as we all understand, is western Galilee.

We must begin working in Jaffa. Arab workers must be employed there, and at the same wages as Jewish workers. An Arab should also have the right to be elected President of the State. If a Jew or a Negro does not have the right to be President of the United States then I, for one, doubt the existence of civil rights there. But war is war. We did not start the war. The Arabs attacked us in Jaffa, Haifa, etc.; and I do not want those who fled to return. Everything that happens after the war will depend on the results of the war itself. While I oppose the return of the Arabs, I am for a pact with the Arab states after the war.

Our most serious potential problem is posed by Britain. I believe that we can stand up to the Arab world and the regular armies of the Arab states. But I doubt whether we could hold our own against the British Army. Therefore, I have always been against entering into a conflict with the British Army. Even as things stand, the British government is trying to strangle us. There were British commanders in Gezer and in Jerusalem, and the Arabs are using British weapons. The British are conducting a political campaign against us, because they feel that they have the Arabs in their pockets.

We will not solve our problems with the British unless we can win their political friendship. The British are a fine people, but they have suddenly turned against us because of the country's foreign policy. Eventually they will be forced to abandon their centers of power in the Middle East, and when that happens, we will be able to establish closer relationships with our Arab neighbors. If the Arabs are willing to negotiate, we should not stipulate territorial preconditions that would make it impossible for them to do so. The very meeting with the Arabs would be of value, even if it did not achieve any positive results. It is important that the Syrians, Egyptians and Lebanese know what we want. It is vital that we meet, and therefore no preconditions should be set. I don't know if such a meeting will take place, but we must try to bring it about. However, it will become possible only when the Arabs and Bernadotte understand that two things are not negotiable: we will not consider either abolishing the State or restricting its independence. If they are ready to sit down with us, it is important that we should meet. Therefore, no hard-and-fast rules should be set as prerequisites to a meeting.

Zisling: The matters before us are extremely varied and we will not get to all of them. While we had our doubts about the truce, I believe its continuation would be to our benefit, even with the restrictions, if they are not made more severe. We would gain militarily from a continuation of the truce. I agree with Ben-Gurion about the link between the political and military struggles. Our most important task, therefore, is to strengthen our military forces. We have no absolutely dependable friendships, but there are potential friends with whom we have common interests. We must do nothing to lose the good will of the Soviet Union and the United States. I have nothing to add to what has already been said by Ben-Gurion about the Negev. It is, as I pointed our during the Lake Success period, basic to the fulfillment of Zionism. So far as the Arab people are concerned, we will not be able to establish friendly relations with them through Abdullah, for he is a puppet of the English.

I would not like to cast aspersions on the defenders of the Old City, who surrendered when they had no possibility of continuing to fight. By the same token, I would not criticize the defenders of Yad Mordekhai, who abandoned the settlement. I would like to say something very unpopular. I still favor the internationalization of Jerusalem. This would not conflict with our attempt to widen the corridor to the city. If Jerusalem were part of the Jewish State, the city would be divided and Abdullah would rule part of it. Even if we controlled a road to the city, Jerusalem would still be surrounded by Arab areas and might be cut off. With all its drawbacks, an internationalized Jerusalem would still be better than a divided Jerusalem.

No resolutions were adopted at the meeting, because the Prime Minister had to leave before it ended. A discussion of political questions was postponed until the next meeting.

Addressing a meeting of the Provisional State Council on June 17, six days after the truce began, Ben-Gurion dwelt mainly on the struggle for Jerusalem in the four weeks before the truce:

> For hundreds of years Christians and Moslems have claimed that Jerusalem, sanctified in our history and in world history by the Prophets of Israel, had become holy for them as well. It was therefore decided, on the establishment of the Jewish State, to internationalize the city. Yet the Holy City has been bombarded for four weeks by Moslem desert warriors.

The cynical and brutal shelling has demolished many Holy Places, including a dozen synagogues. Nevertheless, the entire Christian world has stood by in silence. The Church of
England, the guns of whose country have been responsible for the basest acts of murder
in the Holy City, has lost its tongue. The other churches have also remained silent. Jerusalem's holiness has been forgotten. The memories that link the city with all the world's
religions have vanished into oblivion.

Only one small isolated people, left defenseless by the Mandatory Government, has
stood up to the attack. Its extraordinary suffering and valor have shown the world who
truly holds the city dear, and for whom the holiness of Jerusalem is not simply an empty
phrase.

I would like to mention only one military operation, which did not become known
to the public at the time. Even the few who heard about it did not realize its real significance,
for it was not a great success. I refer to the operation of Brigade Seven on the Latrun front.
During the last days of May, Brigade Seven was sent to one of the crossroads to Jerusalem
in the Latrun area. Not only had the city of Jerusalem been under brutal assault for weeks,
but an attempt had also been made to cut off the city from the Yishuv and to starve it into
submission. Thanks to the actions of the Mandatory Government, and later of the British-
officered and -subsidized Arab Legion, the plot almost succeeded. Brigade Seven did not
capture Latrun, though its armor, under the command of Chaim Laskov, penetrated into
the village of Latrun and set fire to the police station. But our infantry did not have enough
strength to hold it.

However, Beit Jis and Beit Susin, two villages which most people have never heard of,
were captured. Our commanders were told subsequently to send in reinforcements—but
also road construction equipment to lay down a second road to Jerusalem. While the fighting around Latrun was still in progress, our engineers and workers, covered by the fire of
our soldiers, built a road parallel to the old Jerusalem one. Thus we were able to open up a
new road to Jerusalem, even though Latrun remained in enemy hands.

We have held, since the beginning of the truce, a continuous front from Rosh Hanikra
in the north to Tel Aviv, and from Tel Aviv through settlements in the south—Na'an,
Hulda, Deir Muhezin, Kubab, Beit Jis, Beit Susin, and Beit Mahsir—to Sha'ar Hagai and
then on to the western entrance of Jerusalem. From there the front continues south straight
to Talpiot and north to Sanhedria. The front runs, therefore, from the Lebanese border to
the northern and southern sections of Jerusalem.

The struggle for Jerusalem will determine the fate not only of the country but of the
Jewish people. We must use this truce to prepare ourselves for both peace and war. We
cannot be certain of any outside assistance. We must depend solely on ourselves. I can find
no better description of the present situation than the words uttered thousands of years ago
by the Prophet Isaiah (63:2-5): "Wherefore art thou red in thine apparel, and thy garments like his that treadeth in the winevat? I have trodden the winepress alone; and of the
peoples there were none with me . . . . For the day of vengeance was in mine heart, and
my year of redemption was come: and I looked, and there was none to help; and I wondered,
and there was none to uphold: therefore mine own arm brought salvation unto me; and
my fury, it upheld me."

At the same session Shertok again reviewed foreign policy issues connected with the
truce:

As you know, he said, the truce imposes certain limitations on Jewish immigration.
Until now, these limitations have had no practical effect; a boat with immigrants has
already arrived during the truce and now we must wait and see what will happen in

regard to other immigrants. There is no question about the continuation of immigration in general, though limitations have been imposed on the entry of men of military age. The Mediator has the right to forbid their immigration if he feels that this would give a military advantage to us. People of military age must remain under supervision during the truce in order to ensure that they will not be called up or given military training during that period. Both the Arabs and we have been forbidden to bring in war matériel. The Mediator has stated that the Arab countries are already under supervision in regard to the entry of people of military age and the importation of weapons. He says that stockpiles of British arms in the Middle East are also being supervised so as to prevent their being turned over to the Arabs. The Mediator has been asked to investigate the possibility of a peaceful settlement of the conflict, one agreeable to both sides.

Several basic guidelines on negotiations were then listed by the Prime Minister. He did not think that any Council member would disagree with him. Israel, he said, has been recognized by a number of Latin American countries, Eastern European countries, and one Anglo-Saxon country. Recognition by Western European countries has been held up, because negotiations supposedly will take place between Israel and the Arabs on the initiative of the Mediator. Britain has played a major role in fostering the war against us and in enlarging its scope. The Iraqi units fighting against us are under British command, and not only on a senior level. British officers were in charge of several fronts, and themselves led attacks. All this is based on central British planning. Almost all the weapons being used against us were supplied by the British some years ago or in recent months. Britain's political and diplomatic influence is also being brought to bear against us to the greatest possible extent.

One must assume, nevertheless, that the effective establishment of the State of Israel has made an impression on the British government. The elements in Britain critical of current government policy have been supplied with a convincing argument, and the confidence of the ruling party itself has been shaken to some extent by the new facts in spite of violent British opposition. The British, moreover, apparently see little possibility of substantially altering these facts.

Just as we must strengthen ourselves to the greatest possible extent militarily, the Prime Minister went on, so must we make a major effort during this truce period to overcome the political dangers, and to tighten our hold on the territory we have conquered. The Arab armies that invaded us from every side have been repulsed; a link has been established between Jerusalem and the State of Israel; large sections of territory that are outside of the partition borders, including important cities, have been captured; and a large proportion of the Arabs who were living in the territory allocated to the State of Israel and captured by Israel have fled—all these facts must be forcefully expressed in the campaign that lies ahead.

We must continue to base our policy, as in the past, on the United Nations. As before, we must seek understanding and assistance from all the great powers, and attempt to establish friendly relations with all peoples, large and small, near and far, while maintaining our full national and political independence.

The Council adopted a code for its meetings as presented by Justice Minister Rosenblueth, though with certain amendments. It provided that the Council choose a chairman and three deputy chairmen to preside over its meetings, until then chaired by the Prime Minister.

Meeting with Brigade Commanders

On June 18, 1948, one week after the start of the truce, Ben-Gurion, as Minister of Defense, called together all brigade commanders to discuss the military situation and the lessons to be learned from the four weeks of fighting against regular armies. The meeting lasted from nine in the morning until seven in the evening. Here are some notes on the discussion:

Moshe Zelitski noted the advantages of the truce. The Army was weak and weary after many battles and severe losses. One hundred men had been killed in every battalion; there had also been desertions. The conquest had forced us to set up static garrisons in many places. This had weakened the units. The morale level had declined in the course of the month. The men who had to remain in the outposts were also adversely affected. The enemy's strength had brought us face to face with a tactical crisis. The firepower of the Arabs had increased in recent weeks and they had plenty of ammunition and heavy equipment. The Iraqis had fired an enormous number of shells in Jenin and forced our troops to abandon their outposts. Enemy morale had improved in recent weeks. Despite our bombardments and their severe losses, the Arabs had not fled. If we do not obtain better weapons, we will have to fight a guerrilla war. The enemy bombardments have forced us to dig in. Unless we receive airplanes and heavy equipment, we will not be able to engage in conventional warfare.

We lack a national strategy and proper coordination on the national level. We should operate on the basis of our own strategic plan and not simply react to enemy actions. The commanders on the northern front have proven themselves. We have increased our mobility by organizing our forces on the basis of an entire front, rather than within the framework of brigades. Particular units do not have to be used exclusively on a particular front. We need not be entirely on the defensive or the offensive. There should be defensive action in a large part of the country, based on the settlements, and an offensive where it is called for. People desert one brigade for another. Heavy weapons are needed. Men lost must be replaced. There should be ten-day courses to train platoon commanders for work as company commanders.

Michael Schechter [Shaham] complained about the induction of recruits without prior medical examinations. They were a burden and could not be used in operations. Recruits had first to be trained in a special camp. One of the reasons for desertion was the lack of training. Some recruits threw down their weapons and ran away. There were criminals in the Army. In the battle for Sejera soldiers broke into Jewish homes and looted them. Weapons had to be distributed to the settlements. We had not returned weapons to the settlements because there were not enough weapons for the Army. There were extraordinary examples of devotion both in the Army and in the settlements.

Uri Jaffe: Keeping our men tied down in static positions deprives the Army of its fighting power. Staying in outposts destroys an army. We must strengthen the settlements by giving them weapons so that they can repulse enemy attacks and free the Army to operate as a mobile force. The enemy's planes have done enormous damage. We must camouflage the Army's movements. The open retreat of Yiftah did us a lot of damage.

Dan Epstein [Even]: Until now we have not fought according to accepted military doctrine. We have sought to conquer territory rather than to destroy the enemy. We did not concentrate sufficient forces in order to achieve the latter objective. We did not strike at the enemy's weak points, but directly at his strong points. A real army is built on discipline and responsibilities, qualities we are lacking. Death sentences must be imposed on soldiers who desert before or during an operation. Imprisonment is not enough. In my district there have been no deserters, but there might be. In one battalion there were a hundred deserters who fled back to their old brigades. My brigade has not received replacements for the men it lost in battle. There was great weariness before the truce. There is no indication of a similar weariness in the ranks of the enemy. There is no clothing. Sometimes our men went out to fight in pajamas. This affects morale. There is a crisis in all battalions because of lack of assistance for soldiers' families and similar phenomena.

You need six months to train a soldier, or, at a pinch, four months—certainly not three days. Taking untrained recruits into battle is like leading sheep to the slaughter. Our Training Branch is not operating properly. It would be better to use sixty bullets in training and have only forty for actual operations, that to save ninety for the war and use only ten for training. As far as commanders are concerned, we must adopt one of two systems: either a central pool of commanders who can be sent wherever they are needed, or every brigade should train its own. Our soldiers are no fools. They know everything that is going on in the brigade and among the commanders. They know that some brigades are favored over others. Companies that were loaned out to other brigades saw that in the brigades to which they were assigned the soldiers were well-equipped and well-clothed, while they had only pajamas. I have men under my command who have been in the Army for seven months and still do not have weapons. There are cases where a soldier has run off to the induction center and come back with everything he needed. An army requires uniforms, ranks, and military law (law not for youth battalions but for a regular army).

The truce period should be exploited in order to establish a proper military framework. There should be a division between the regional commands and the brigades. Districts should be headed by a local command, which would have at its disposal the garrisons and the members of the settlements.

James [Michael Bengal]: The very small grants given to soldiers' families hurt morale. The age of the soldiers in Tel Aviv is high. There is also the problem of seniority in the Hagana. We wouldn't suffer by giving youngsters more of a chance. Decorations should be awarded. We take an erroneous view of the time factor. We should not send soldiers to fight before they have been trained. If we do, they will either run away or be killed. There is no shortcut. Maybe training can be carried out in less than four months. We should use older people where possible in order to free the younger ones for the actual fighting.

Simon Koch [Avidan]: 70 percent of our forces are tied down; there is no sense in talking about training and reorganization in these circumstances. Morale is satisfactory, and morale is our source of strength. But there can be no morale without shoes, without support for the families of the soldiers, without backing from the civilians. I don't believe in punishment. At first the Egyptians were nervous, but afterward they calmed down and dug in. The truce is a good thing. It was a mistake to have removed all the weapons and people from the settlements. We must give our settlements the weapons and the people they need if they are to hold out. Our fortifications are not good enough. We must entrench ourselves more securely, and we need the tools to do this. The present Table of Organization is not suited to the needs of a military unit. There must be new services on the company level, such as men responsible for sanitation. The press carries stories praising the conduct of the Arab Legion and the good conditions in which our prisoners are being held. Our settlers and soldiers behaved traitorously by allowing themselves to be captured.

Nahum: The situation in the Negev differs from that in all the other areas. The Regional Command is not in contact with the units. We don't know enough about the area or the enemy. This information is very important, particularly in view of our numerical weakness. No plan was prepared on how to meet an enemy invasion. We did not know whether the enemy was planning a quick thrust through the Negev or would try to conquer the whole area. What are the enemy's plans now? To strike deep into the country? We were not strong enough to strike at the enemy's lines of communications. What is the objective of the Egyptian Army? Tel Aviv? Perhaps. The enemy has use of the railroad, the roads, and the sea. Enemy forces did not penetrate into the depths of the Negev, in the area allocated to a Jewish State. This was apparently in order to avoid extended and vulnerable supply lines.

Enemy forces attacked us only along the line of their advance. The battle for Yad Mordekhai lasted seven days. The operations of the Egyptians during the truce period— the seizure of outposts—shows that their planning is confused. When the truce is over, the Egyptians will presumably strike at new areas or seize outposts all through the Negev. What has been done in the Arava? We know that there are two companies of the Arab Legion in Aqaba. We hold the police stations at Asluj, Imara, and Huzul. The Egyptians have two infantry companies in Beersheba which came in from the south under the cover of artillery fire. They brought food from Uuja el-Hafir. Now that Asluj is in our hands, they are bringing food from the north: Mijdal and Faluja. There is no artillery in Beersheba. It should be easy to take, but it would be hard to hold. It is not worthwhile capturing it while we control Asluj.

There is no real truce, but rather warfare within the framework of a truce. We must exploit the truce for planning on a national level. Every brigade must know its own task and that of the other brigades. A week has gone by without preparations. A distinction must be made between a striking force and a garrison force, but we must base our operations on regional forces. The various regions have fought with bravery and wisdom. No summary has been made of the battle experience we have gained. We have not exploited our 20-mm. artillery sufficiently; it has not been used against tanks. We should combat the enemy's air superiority with our own light weapons. With fighting on a regional level, the staying power of the soldiers is the decisive factor. We need commissars from the movement; we also need weapons for the settlements. There is not sufficient coordination. What is the role of the Negev, offensive or defensive, within the overall plan? This depends on transportation problems. Our men have not received leave for months.

Meir Sharvit (Jerusalem): Our military manpower has been depleted by our being cut off from the rest of the country. Food is also short. We lack vitamins, milk, eggs, and vegetables. Only bread and canned goods are available. Jerusalem is surrounded by enemy artillery. There have been three weeks of random shelling. We have lost some of our younger soldiers in the nearby settlements (Etzion, the Dead Sea, etc.). We have almost no Field Forces, except for two companies, and they are in bad shape psycholog-ically. Home Guard units were set up with men up to the age of 45. We have twenty-five hundred such men in seven units. Can they fight? Some of them were attached to the Field Forces and fought. The road between Jerusalem and Sha'ar Hagai was held by Jerusalemites and the Harel Brigade before the truce; now our men are holding it on their own. All our soldiers are tied down. They fought well when the pressure was high, but now there are desertions. The youngsters were killed, wounded, or captured. There are six hundred prisoners in Amman. Manpower has been exploited in Jerusalem to a greater extent than anywhere else. The enemy forces are led by Englishmen. The English appeared during the truce. The morale of the Arab Legion is high, though they would be glad if the fighting ended. Now they are basing their hopes on a prolonged siege and on Jerusalem being cut off. There is looting, dissension within the ranks, and a wide-spread feeling that political rather than military considerations are decisive. There are bad relations with the Palmah.

Fritz [Eshet]: Newman's battalion has eighteen artillery pieces. The Legion has 25-pound guns at Nebi Samuel, cannon on the French Hill, two more at Silwan, four 75-mm. guns, etc. The last few days the Egyptians have also brought up artillery. In Beit Jallah there are apparently 100-pounders. There are fifty artillery pieces in all, aside from 3-inch mortars with unlimited ammunition. They shoot four hundred shells a day. In a period of three weeks 7-8 million shells fell. The enemy has a large artillery unit and a small infantry unit.

Yigal Allon: Opportunities for decisive victories in western Galilee, Malkiya, and Jenin were not exploited. The Nahshon operation gave us very little to cheer about. Public pressure caused us to embark upon operations before we were ready. There are two reasons for the weariness of our troops: the prolonged fighting (such as at Beit Mahsir and the truce itself. Our ability to fight on level ground is very limited. In the hills, on the other hand, we have the opportunity to undertake combined operations, using both guerrilla and conventional tactics. We have overlooked excellent opportunities for carrying out sabotage in the Arab countries. New frameworks must be established. Two Yiftah battalions have not had leave for nine months. There are no desertions. Without additional forces, we will not be able to go into battle after the truce. We must make a supreme effort to mobilize more men. Brigades must be combined into divisions.

Rabin: There is a shortage of middle-level officers, between the brigades and the General Staff. From among the members of the two Harel battalions, 617 men were wounded, 220 were killed, and 200 are suffering from severe fatigue. A great many men were in outposts. There were strong counterattacks, but no outposts were abandoned. There were very few desertions. seven hundred front-line soldiers are left, without taking into consideration the service units.

Mulla Cohen (son of David Cohen): We are not operating behind the enemy's lines. Yiftah has lost 250 men killed and 300 wounded. It will not be ready to go into action again after the truce. Only 70 men were given leave; the rest remained at their posts. There is a lack of communications, equipment, beds, etc.

Yosefele Tabenkin has come up against the men of the Mufti, the Iraqis, the Egyptians and the Legion. The Legionnaires are by far the best soldiers. They have abundant fire-power, unlimited supplies of ammunition, and English officers. They never go into action without being certain of numerical superiority. The Arabs of Palestine could not resist for two days, the Iraqis for no more than four. The Legion depends on having regular supplies. We could have beat them at Latrun had we hit their supply lines to that outpost. But the Legion's superiority in weapons is not decisive. They could not destroy our emplacements, but hit at the slum neighborhoods instead. There is no need for a middle-level command between the brigade level and the General Staff. Harel requires another seven to eight hundred men to fill out its ranks; they can be trained in three weeks.

Shlomo Shamir: Discipline is not up to standard. It must be more severe in the higher ranks. Twenty-six officer candidates deserted for other units. I was given untrained men for the attack on Latrun. We should use the truce period to strengthen our forces. It must be decided whether the Manpower Branch mobilizes soldiers for the brigades, or whether every brigade looks out for itself. There must be proper arrangements for supplies. There is not enough intelligence work, without which it is difficult to fight. The commanders are not properly supervised. There is a lack of direct communications with the Operations Branch. The officers must be responsible for training; that indeed is their major responsibility.

Yitzhak Sadeh: Our lack of information on the enemy is undermining our war effort. Many men of military age have not yet been mobilized. Only women and children should remain behind to do civilian work. The shirkers lower morale in the forces. I very much value 3-inch mortars; they are the key to victory. There is no discipline in the Army. In the Palmah there is battle discipline but no administrative discipline. There is no battle discipline among the high-ranking officers. Forces must be concentrated as needed. If we intend to strike at a particular point, we must gather together mortars from other fronts as well. We must hit at the supply lines of the Legion; for example, we should blow up the Damia and Allenby Bridges.

Yadin: There is a lack of discipline on the higher levels. Additional men must be mobilized while there is still time. We now have more artillery pieces than people who know how to use them.

Dan doubted whether there can be real discipline under the present structure of the General Staff. It is not properly organized. It has too many branches. Orders issued by one branch contradict those issued by another. There is a lack of centralization and of a proper division of responsibility. It is not clear who is responsible to whom. The Operations Branch, in its present form, is unable to give binding commands. A commander must first survey the front. We need proper commanders, and then we will have discipline. The Chief of the Operations Branch doesn't visit the fronts, and doesn't give commands. There is no officer dealing with communications.

Michael: We must strengthen our fortifications. The settlements need manpower, and they cannot obtain it. We must train people to destroy tanks before they have penetrated into the settlements.

Rohel: We haven't sufficiently exploited the truce period. We must speed up mobilization. We must build up new service and operational units, and train commanders. We lack equipment and food. We must bring them in. Local production is suffering from the recurrent air-raid alarms and other factors. We may find ourselves short of fuel. We must strengthen the settlements. We need a reserve of soldiers, rifles, and munitions. There must be more discipline in the High Command. We don't know how many weapons the battalions have, for the commanders are concealing this information. Every battalion must receive the rifles—406—to which it is entitled. If we multiply that number by the number of battalions—33—that means 13,398 rifles. We should also supply weapons to the regional Field Forces. There should be supply depots in various districts.

Allon: There are more than enough rifles for forty battalions, all the Field Forces, and all the settlements.

Eliyahu [Cohen-Ben-Hur]: We need information, planning, orders, and the carrying-out of these orders. We are weak all along the line. We can achieve victory only by a maximum concentration of our forces at particular points. We are not paying enough attention to intelligence and espionage. We have lost 251 commanders and not gained a single new one. We should have a course for company commanders—with 300 partici-pants, as well as courses for men to operate heavy equipment, snipers, demolition experts, and mortar men.

Lehrer [Zadok]: If we mobilize the seventeen-year-olds, we will gain 3000 men. By taking in recruits up to the age of thirty-five, we will gain 2000, not counting the 1060 now being trained. There are good soldiers in the Home Guard units (Alexandroni Home Guard, 2000; Carmeli Home Guard, 1000). The Field Forces must be relieved from duty on the district level. This should be turned over to the Home Guard units.

Ben-Gurion: If fighting starts again, and we must assume that it will, we will be entering into a decisive phase of the campaign; the most important question then is how we are going to win. The military struggle is linked with the political struggle—the conflict with England—and there is no way of knowing how far the English will go in support of the Arabs. Leaving that element aside, we do have a chance of winning. We must decide where we can strike the decisive blow and against whom. At various periods, there were different strategic centers: Megiddo, Acre, Jerusalem, and Hittin.

At present there are three fronts: the north, where we are fighting the Lebanese and Syrians; the center where we are fighting the Arab Legion; and the south, including the Negev, where we are fighting the Egyptians. We do not have enough forces for decisive attacks on all three fronts, and so we must decide where we should concentrate our efforts. A look at the map gives us the answer. From a Jewish viewpoint the crucial area is the Tel Aviv-Haifa-Jerusalem Triangle. The fall of those centers, or even two of them, would mean our complete defeat. The Arabs have their own crucial Triangle. The very best Arab military force—the Arab Legion—is concentrated in that Triangle and it can count on the support of a densely populated Arab area. We could ensure victory by striking a blow at this force and conquering the Triangle. After breaking the back of the Legion, we could mop up the Lebanese Army and drive out the Syrians, perhaps also bomb Damascus. This would leave only Egypt.

Theoretically, Egypt could go on fighting for a long time. Egypt's population, army, and budget all exceed our own. But it is doubtful whether the Egyptians would go on fighting, unless the English saw to it that they did. Therefore, if the war starts again, we should concentrate our units, to the greatest extent possible, in the north and in the south, while preparing a force to break the Arab Legion and conquer Nablus. This requires a single command over the area of the entire Triangle (Jenin, Tulkarm, Latrun, etc.), with its headquarters in Jerusalem. The struggle for Jerusalem and its environs—apart from the sentimental factors involved—will be decisive militarily. If we win there, we will have won altogether. Of all our Army's shortcomings, its lack of discipline, particularly in the higher ranks, is probably the worst. If there were proper discipline, we would have begun the truce with upper Galilee free of enemy forces, and the entire road to Jerusalem in our hands. Perhaps we would have also captured Lydda and Ramle, which are an enormous danger to us.

The Vision that Guided the Fighters ★ The Palmah Problem

The next day David Ben-Gurion surveyed current problems in a talk to the Mapai Council. He told them of the previous day's meeting attended by the commanders from all of the fronts—the Negev, the south, the Hills of Judea, Jerusalem, the Valley of Ayalon, Tel Aviv, the Sharon and Samaria, the Valley of Jezreel, the Beit Sha'an Valley, the Jordan Valley, Haifa, and western, eastern, lower and upper Galilee. Those men gave a detailed report on our military situation, including both failures and successes, he said:

I will not recall the events that occurred during the six months before the establishment of the State, or even those of the last four weeks. The facts are known, and what is not known *should not yet* be known.

You are aware of what has been accomplished by our outnumbered Army, by youngsters who came forward, unprepared, during the course of the war itself. But without trying to belittle their achievements, their bravery, or their conquests—and I would be the last to do so—I must still point out that, were it not for the great historic vision that guided the pioneers of the last three generations over seventy or eighty years, from the days of the first agricultural settlements (Mikve Israel, Petah Tikva, Rishon LeZion, Zikhron Yacov, and Rosh Pina) until this very day, our recent achievements would not have been possible. Were it not for the personalities of the first pioneers and those who came after them, were it not for the vision that guided them, our military strength, in itself, would not have been sufficient. We would have been unable to hold out in the Negev, the Jordan Valley, or upper Galilee. If it had not been for the epic courage of the Etzion Bloc, an episode which ended so tragically with the slaughter of almost all of the members of Kfar Etzion, who knows whether Jerusalem would still be free? I am not saying this in order to allocate credit—the time for that has not yet come. We are still in the midst of a struggle, which may continue for a very long time.

During this truce period we must make our forces ready for the next stage, which may be decisive. We are not experienced in the arts of warfare. But seventy years ago we knew nothing about agriculture either. Centuries of exile did not prepare us to become the builders of a state or warriors fighting for its independence. But we had to defend ourselves, and so we established a military force for this purpose. While we suffered setbacks in the settlement sphere, we were able to learn from them and to correct our mistakes. We still have a great deal more to learn. We have made mistakes in our military operations and we must now ensure that they are rectified, for our very existence is at stake.

We have still not learned the arts of war. Neither our soldiers nor our commanders have acquired the necessary skills, and they must be acquired now, in the midst of the struggle. Learning also involves forgetting things that are outdated, abandoning practices that are no longer relevant. Not everything that was valuable within the framework of the Hagana is still valuable today, or will be tomorrow. The situation is new; the conditions are different; we are fighting a different kind of war. What was appropriate during the defense of Petah Tikva, Sejera, and Tel Hai will not work in defending Jerusalem, holding the Negev, or liberating the Galilee. We must learn new doctrines of a regular army and of modern war, which were previously alien to us.

At the beginning of the struggle, we scattered our forces and defended every settlement. That was in contradiction to every accepted military doctrine. After holding out for over five months everywhere, we were finally forced to abandon a number of settlements: Beit Ha'arava, the northern Dead Sea, Atarot, Neveh Yacov, and Naharayim. Shortly before the establishment of the State, the Etzion Bloc fell, and on the last day before the truce, nine days ago, the Syrians captured Mishmar Hayarden.

Nevertheless, if we survey the entire campaign, the balance sheet is not negative. True, we have paid dearly for what we have achieved. Hundreds of our best sons have fallen. There are bereaved parents in every section of the community, and a sense of sorrow that knows no political, social, or ideological boundaries pervades the nation. I do not want to mention specific names here, but I will make one exception. I want to say something to Shlomo Lavie, a dear comrade, boyhood friend, founder of one of our largest settlements, and prophet of the kibbutz movement: We share your grief, Shlomo, at the death of your one son in the Valley of Jezreel and your other son in the Negev. Lavie is not the only one mourning. In villages and in cities, among all communities and classes, there are grieving parents. But never have Israel's sons and daughters fallen for a cause more precious, or given their lives more willingly. Their parents have every right to be proud of them.

We have no reason to regret the fact that we tied down forces to defend every single settlement. The settlements actually defended us more than we defended them. Those settlements that fell will be retaken. Nothing is final in a war.

I would like to say a few words to the Army as a whole. An army, by its very nature, is not a democratic body or an idyllic one, for its mission is to frighten, to destroy, to kill, and to sustain losses. However, until we reach that paradise about which our Prophets spoke—where people will not lift up sword against people, nor learn war—there is no way to avoid having an army. No other country in the world is surrounded by neighbors who, like ours, are bent on its destruction.

Not all of our military problems can be discussed publicly. I will therefore go into only a few of them. An army requires equipment, weapons, and training. Without them, there is no army. But these elements alone are not sufficient. The principal, decisive, weapon of an army is its *moral strength*. We were able to hold our own against armies that were larger, better trained, more fully equipped, and led by more experienced officers (the Arabs were led by extremely experienced British officers) only because of our *moral primacy*.

A good many Hagana members served in regular armies, some of them in the Jewish Legion of the First World War. These include the late Eliyahu Golomb, Dov Hos, and others who are still with us. Many Hagana members served in Jewish units of the British Army during the Second World War, particularly in the Jewish Brigade. A few served as volunteers in foreign armies during the First or Second World Wars. A small percentage of these ex-soldiers occupied important posts in the Hagana. But, generally speaking, Hagana members were without military experience, and *the Hagana was far from being an organized military force*. Most of its members received little training, certainly not enough. Some of the men who gained military experience during the Second World War remained outside the ranks of the Hagana for various reasons, or else were not given tasks appropriate to their backgrounds. There appeared to be some conflict between Hagana veterans and men trained within the framework of a regular army.

The situation that we faced with the establishment of the State forced us to create a military force whose training, organization, equipment, and structure would enable it to meet the challenge posed by the regular armies of our enemies. This was not easy. But we started, at least, with a tradition, a glorious tradition, of which we have no reason to be ashamed—the tradition of the Hagana.

The Hagana was not established by a government and therefore was not subject to a government's orders. It was an underground army of volunteers, self-established and self-governed. Its sense of responsibility conferred a great moral strength on the Hagana, making it a creative and pioneering body. Without this moral strength we could not have met the test of the five and a half months of fighting before the establishment of the State. Who knows, indeed, whether there would have been any trace of Jewish settlement left had it not been for the Hagana. The establishment of the State did not, or course, bring with it the peace we longed for; it brought, instead, the invasion of enemy armies. This development was to have been expected, and we should have prepared ourselves militarily to meet it.

I would like to say something about the Palmah. Before the outbreak of the war, the Palmah was the only fully mobilized unit within the Hagana. The Hagana included thousands of other veteran, dedicated members, but they were called up only when they were needed for some operation; they were not mobilized on a full-time basis. The Palmah was not large: it had two to three thousand members. But it differed from all the other Hagana units in two respects: (a) its members were mobilized on a full-time basis; (b) half of its members' time was given over to military training, while the other half was devoted to agricultural work. It was, therefore, the best-trained unit in the Hagana and was not unlike a battalion in a regular army. As an illegal military force it could not receive full and open military training, but in several respects it was as good as the best units of any other army. This force, together with the veterans of the Jewish Brigade, formed the backbone of our defense effort. It is to the credit of the Kibbutz Hameuhad that it established and nurtured the Palmah. I would like to recall our comrade Eliyahu Golomb, who was one of the men who initiated the Palmah. Eliyahu and the Kibbutz Hameuhad Secretariat deserve our thanks for doing what they did. It is unfortunate, however, that one must add a reservation. Instead of establishing a pioneering force that would be at the disposal of the whole community, an attempt was made, and is still being made, to create a sectarian unit under the control of a single party. At the time of the Palmah's establishment it was not even an entire party, but only a faction within a party.

The situation changed completely with the outbreak of the war. The Palmah was no longer the only fully mobilized unit. There was also a transformation within the Palmah itself. When the fighting started, its members stopped doing agricultural work, and the Palmah became like any other mobilized unit; its members devoted themselves solely to military tasks. Not only members of the Palmah were called up; thousands and then tens of thousands of young people were mobilized. The Palmah itself was reinforced by thousands of newcomers who had received no agricultural training, only military training. There are now several Palmah brigades which devote themselves solely to training and fighting. There is no difference, as there once was, between Palmah units and other units of the Hagana. With the establishment of the Israel Defense Forces, all units have come under the jurisdiction of the General Staff and the Provisional Government. With all due respect to its glorious past, the Palmah is now part of the Defense Forces and must share the same status as other Army units.

But Siya Bet (Faction B)—which meanwhile united with Hashomer Hatzair to form a new party—has not abandoned its attempt to gain political control over the Palmah. A new Palmah National Staff was established without the knowledge of the Army or the approval of the Government (or, before that, of the Jewish Agency). Palmah ideologists term it the army of the working class. In fact, they want to make it the army of a political party.

Many citizens like myself, who are members of Mapai and of the Histadrut, stand ready, as I do, to fight for the interests of the party and the Histadrut. But there is one body where no political divisions can be allowed, and that is the Army. Within the Defense

Forces one must act as a Jew and only as a Jew. The Army was established to safeguard Israel's security. There will be no security if we do not mobilize all of the resources of the people.

The establishment of the State and of the Israel Defense Forces makes it ncessary for every person called up to receive first-rate military training and to be ready to go wherever he is needed. It necessitates changes in our defense organization; some changes have indeed already taken place. Our young people have answered the call. World Jewry has answered the call. The Yishuv has answered the call. And the transformation of the Hagana from an underground movement into a regular army, subject exclusively to the authority of the Government, has taken place without undue difficulties. But there have been problems in one important area: the faction that formerly saw the Palmah as its private army has made vigorous attempts to maintain its control over the Palmah. Despite defense and political needs, this faction stubbornly continues efforts to put its political stamp on part of the Army. Political control of part of the Army undermines its efficiency. The attempt to make it the preserve of one party harms the Palmah, one of our outstanding units. The Army is based, as it must be, on internal equality. Even in a country where there are class and social differences, an army is organized on the basis of equality. Every soldier must obey orders and give his all. An army requires unlimited discipline, and this discipline must emanate from a single body, responsible for the entire war effort. There cannot be an army in which most of the soldiers are under the control of a central elected authority, while the others are under the control, open or disguised, of a sectarian organization.

I have been asked whether we still need a striking force with special training. Obviously we need soldiers with special training, and are therefore organizing special units: the Navy, the Air Force, the Tank Corps, and others. They are being recruited and trained in accordance with technical requirements, not ideological ones. There are technical and professional differences among military units, depending on the tasks they are called upon to perform. But there are no ideological or class differences.

An army's only ideological goals are national security and safeguarding the peace. The small Palmah demonstrated what Israeli youth, motivated by the vision that stems from our creative enterprise, are capable of accomplishing. This vision should not be the exclusive property of individuals or of a particular unit. It belongs to our entire Army.

There are no noblemen and serfs among us, no master race and inferior beings. Every Israeli boy—Yemenite, Ashkenazi, or Moroccan—is capable of great valor if he is treated with love and trust, enjoys fraternity and equality, and is armed with both the weapons of war and a spirit of devotion. An army's spirit is its most important asset. A soldier must know what he is fighting for. A soldier acts on orders, for without discipline there can be no army. At the same time, giving orders is not enough. A commander will succeed only if he gains the trust of his men and is able to guide them by his own example. It is not fear of an officer, but faith in him, that ensures discipline in an army. Our commanders will gain the faith of their men if they employ the secret weapon that has always stood by us and will stand by us in the future—our moral primacy.

Section 6. The Dissident Underground: Financial Problems

Etzel and the Altalena *Affair*

YITZHAK GRUENBAUM, appointed Minister of the Interior when portfolios were distributed, had been in Jerusalem and for various reasons unable to reach Tel Aviv. He attended his first Cabinet meeting only on June 20, 1948.

At the beginning of that meeting the Prime Minister and Minister of Defense reported on his discussion with Army commanders two days before. Mainly he stressed two short-comings in the Army—the lack of training and the lack of discipline—which had seriously impaired the war effort. The soldiers were now very tired and needed a rest. It was necessary to exploit the truce period to improve training and mobilize additional men. All members of the Government, with one exception, supported a resolution to call up men in the thirty-six to forty-year-old age group, with the physically fit going to the Army and the others being sent to do essential work. Zisling proposed that seventeen-year-olds also be called up, but his proposal was turned down.

In a survey of the political situation, Foreign Minister Shertok dwelt upon a grave incident that was soon to stir up controversy throughout the country. "We may now be facing a blatant, public violation of the truce by Jews, without our being personally responsible for it," he said. "I am speaking here of an Etzel operation. Etzel has sent from overseas an immigrant ship with weapons, and this ship is scheduled to reach the shores of Israel tonight. It was supposed to have arrived last night, but apparently not everything went according to plan, and its arrival was delayed by twenty-four hours. This morning Etzel mobilized hundreds of people. According to a report we have received, five hundred Etzel members broke into one of our camps in the Shomron and took over control. They explained to the people at the camp that they planned to use it as a reception center for their immigrants. They thought that the whole affair would be over that night. But since the landing has been postponed, they have settled down in the camp and intend to carry out the operation tonight. I myself have not spoken with the Etzel people, but Bahar, from the Immigration Department, gave me a report on the situation in that camp. The story about the ship is already known around the world, and there is no way of being sure that it will escape the attention of the United Nations. We must decide how we are to react."

At that same meeting, the Prime Minister received a letter from Israel Galili about the Etzel ship, *Altalena*, which, he said, carried 800 people, 5000 rifles, 250 machine guns, and ammunition. The Prime Minister recalled an agreement that had been reached on June 3 between an authorized representative of the Minister of Defense and the Commander of Etzel, according to which Etzel agreed, among other things, to put all its weapons and military equipment at the disposal of the High Command of the Israel Defense Forces. It was also agreed that the Etzel and its Command would be disbanded and cease operations within the State of Israel and *all areas under the jurisdiction of the Government of Israel.*

"Only a temporary staff made up of Etzel officers," Ben-Gurion said, "was to operate *on behalf of the General Staff* until all of the members of Etzel had been inducted into the Army, an operation which was to be completed swiftly. It was agreed that they would be called up for service in the Israel Defense Forces on the basis of orders issued by the Government of Israel, and would take the same oath of allegiance as other soldiers. Members of Etzel taken into the Army were to have their own battalions, which would form part of brigades and fronts, as decided by the High Command. It was stated that Etzel would cease all arms purchases and that the contacts it had already established would be turned over to the Israel Defense Forces for the benefit of the war effort. It was agreed that the temporary Etzel Command would operate for a month at the very most."

It was proposed by Shertok that five hundred men be sent to the coast to break up the Etzel concentration, as well as to disarm and arrest all the people coming off the boat. Bentov suggested that Menahem Begin [Etzel leader] be arrested. Ben-Gurion asked for an immediate meeting with two members of the General Staff, Galili and Yadin. Perhaps they would have additional information on the movements of the boat.

As soon as the two men arrived, the Defense Minister asked them if they had any information about where the Etzel people planned to unload the ship. They were also asked whether it would be possible to gather a force large enough to handle the situation. Galili said that it was almost certain that the boat would arrive at about 9 P.M. at the Kfar Vitkin shore. Yigal Yadin declared that he had six hundred men there and could bring up two battalions. This would be sufficient if it proved necessary to use force. Yigal asked: What are our orders? Should the brigade commander be told to concentrate his forces and simply threaten to use them, or should he concentrate his forces and go into action if the threat does not work? In his opinion, the Commander must have a member of the Government at his side, unless his orders are crystal clear.

Bentov proposed that the Minister of Defense act in this matter in accordance with the laws of the country. Ben-Gurion responded that he was ready to act in accordance with the law, if he had enough forces at his disposal to do so. To act meant to shoot, he said, a very grave matter indeed. It was necessary to find out whether a sufficiently large force could be mobilized to dissuade Etzel from going into battle, or, should a battle begin, to win it. Rabbi Fishman asserted that a battle would be dangerous to both sides. Nevertheless, if it is possible to concentrate a sufficiently large force to seriously threaten Etzel, this should be done. To this Ben-Gurion commented that "A threat is meaningful only if it is backed up by a willingness to carry it out." The demand that a member of the Government be with the commander is understandable. It is therefore necessary to make a clear decision, namely, if there is enough time to mobilize the necessary men and weapons, the High Command should be given full authority to do so. Bentov agreed. What happens tonight, he stressed, may determine our entire future. If this Etzel operation succeeds, we will be faced with much graver clashes later. By acting tonight, we will prevent blackmail tomorrow. Therefore, the order must be clear: the Etzel people must be disarmed at all costs. If our men have no alternative but to fire, they should do so. If they can avoid it, so much the better. This is a military order and it should be clear.

It was *unanimously* decided to authorize the High Command to take action, if a sufficiently large unit could be assembled in time. The local commander was to try to avoid force, but if Etzel rejected his orders, he was to use it. That meeting took place at 9 P.M.

The next day, Monday, June 21, 1948, the Government Press Office issued the following announcement:

> The High Command of the Israel Defense Forces, on learning that a ship carrying weapons for Etzel was about to reach the country's shores, brought the matter to the attention of the Provisional Government. The Government decided to take all necessary measures to prevent Etzel from unloading those weapons. The Government regards this attempt by an independent group to bring in arms, particularly during the truce period, as a grave violation of Israel's laws and of her international obligations, as well as an infringement of the clear agreement reached recently with the heads of Etzel. According to its terms, Etzel was to cease its existence as an independent military body within the borders of the State of Israel, to mobilize its members for service in the Israel Defense Forces, and to end all independent arms purchases. The heads of Etzel were to accept the authority of the State.

> When the Government learned that the ship had reached the shores of Israel, it ordered the Israel Defense Forces to prevent the unloading of the weapons, by force if necessary. Troops were concentrated at the spot where the ship was to be unloaded, and vessels of the Israel Navy sailed up to the Etzel vessel. When the members of Etzel, who had come to unload the ship, refused to accept the authority of the State, an order was given to use force against them.

> The Provisional Government and the High Command of the Defense Forces wish to make clear that they are determined to stamp out immediately this traitorous attempt to deny the authority of the State of Israel and of its representatives. The Provisional Government and the High Command will not permit the enormous efforts made by the Jewish people in this country to secure their independence and sovereignty, while fighting a bloody conflict forced on them by external enemies, to be undermined by an underhanded attack from within. Jewish independence will not endure if every individual group is free to establish its own military force and to determine political facts affecting the future of the State. The Provisional Government and the High Command call on all citizens and soldiers to unite in the defense of national unity and the authority of the people.

The morning papers of June 22, containing the Government's statement, also carried a statement from Etzel:

> Large concentrations of the Defense Forces have been concentrated for an attack on the soldiers of Etzel, who are carrying out a mission of the greatest importance. The commanders of the Defense Forces did not hesitate to open fire at one point along the front. Blood has already been spilled and a number of Etzel men killed or wounded. We warn those agitating for a civil war, and their supporters, that if such a war begins, it will not be limited to a single area.

That same morning the Prime Minister informed the Government that, according to the Commander of the Central Region (Alexandroni), the ship had reached the Kfar Vitkin shore and many Etzel soldiers serving in the Israel Defense Forces had deserted their units and gone to Kfar Vitkin. Most of the passengers had been taken off at Kfar Vitkin, but some had remained on the ship and were trying to unload the weapons with the assistance of their Etzel comrades on shore. Galili, acting on behalf of the Minister of Defense, called on the heads of Etzel to turn over the ship and its arms to the Israel Defense Forces, but they refused to do so. Shooting began, but the revolt failed.

At that point it appeared as if the Etzel rebellion had ended. But the arms ship slipped away from Kfar Vitkin after most of the immigrants had been taken off.

At 2 A.M. Ben-Gurion was informed that the ship had reached Tel Aviv and was anchored opposite the Gat Rimon Hotel. In the morning there were discussions with the men on the *Altalena*. We demanded that they allow a Government representative to board the vessel and present them with its demands. They announced that they would not receive a representative of the Government until they had been given an opportunity to consult with the commanders of Etzel. We refused to bring the Etzel commanders. At that point the Prime Minister ordered the concentration of all the forces deemed necessary to gain control of the ship. However, he instructed our units to stand by for instructions from the Government.

Shertok asked: Do you know what happened to the ship's cargo? Ben-Gurion replied that some of it was unloaded at Kfar Vitkin and is now in our hands. Asked by Bentov to review the events of the previous two days, Ben-Gurion recalled that representatives of the High Command had participated in the meeting of the Government two days before and had received clear instructions based on a unanimous decision of the Cabinet. The Chief of the Operations Branch had himself gone to supervise activities in the field, which meant that the Prime Minister had nothing to do himself yesterday.

Then he learned for the first time that Gruenbaum, on his own initiative, had been negotiating with Etzel, and dispatched someone to Gruenbaum to clarify the matter. He sent back a note with Zvi Maimon stating that he had met with one of the Etzel people, by the name of Avraham, who had been actively involved in the negotiations. According to Avraham, Galili had not given an accurate report to the Cabinet; Gruenbaum therefore felt there was room for negotiations. Ben-Gurion sent him back a note declaring that there should be no negotiations, since the Government's decision made no mention of them. Gruenbaum had proposed to Etzel that the weapons be transferred to warehouses guarded by Etzel and by our men, and that they be distributed to Etzel battalions. It was pointed out to him that he was engaging in negotiations while Etzel was shooting. They had fired on Avihayil and cut telephone lines. Moreover, many members of Etzel battalions in the south had deserted to the north with their weapons.

Zisling asked whether it was true that Etzel battalions in the south have left their positions and was told that it was true. They had left their positions near Ramla and seized vehicles to take them to Kfar Vitkin.

Gruenbaum explained that he had voted for the proposal unanimously adopted two days before on the assumption that the force mobilized would be strong enough to prevent bloodshed and to dissuade Etzel from rebelling. He had been under the impression that the Government's goal was not to force Etzel to surrender at all costs, but to end the affair. Etzel knows that it cannot win if it comes to a test of strength. However, if it is possible to settle the matter by negotiations—which would mean that the weapons would be turned over to the Defense Forces—that would be good enough.

"I realize," Gruenbaum added, "that we cannot allow a group to violate the truce, or to bring in and use weapons as they see fit. The Government must prevent this from happening with all the means at its disposal. I don't think there are any differences of opinion on that subject. At the same time, I don't think that any of us want Etzel to go underground again and carry out terrorist acts against us. These are the basic guidelines. I intervened for two reasons: first, because I was approached and I thought that the matter was sufficiently serious to inform the Prime Minister about it. The Prime Minister told me that it was not desirable for a member of the Government to meet with representatives of Etzel. Had I known that this was the Government's opinion, I may not have acted as I did. But, I did not know. I thought the Prime Minister was simply presenting his own opinion. I intervened also in my capacity as Minister of the Interior. While the police are not under the jurisdiction of the Ministry of the Interior, the Ministry has something to do with internal security. Though I have no armed men at my disposal, I have, as Minister of the Interior, the right to act in matters involving the internal security of the country. I understood from my talks with the Etzel representative that his organization was mainly concerned with how the arms brought in by the ship were to be distributed."

Shertok: The main question here is the sovereignty of the State of Israel.

Gruenbaum: I'm not talking about what we consider to be the most important, but about the issues under dispute.

Ben-Gurion: The State's authority is the main principle involved in the negotiations.

Bernstein: Two evenings ago we unanimously adopted a resolution. I voted for it because I believe there cannot be two rival military authorities, and that decisive measures were necessary to avoid this possibility. It is true that, formally speaking, we gave the Prime Minister the authority to act in this matter in accordance with the law. However, it is clear from the discussion which preceded the decision that our intention was to mobilize a force that would be sufficiently strong to persuade the Etzel people to surrender without bloodshed. While I've not yet received details of the operations, I am under the impression that we were not able to concentrate the necessary force.

Ben-Gurion: We did succeed, and there was very little bloodshed.

Zisling: The Government's decision was very clear and anyone who voted for it should have been aware of its implications. It was intended to preserve the authority of the Government of Israel. A concession on this issue would have been the first step to much graver civil strife. The consignment of weapons to groups that do not accept national discipline is the issue at stake. A retreat now would mean a further worsening of the situation later on. A representative of the General Staff asked us to state clearly our intentions. We replied that we wished to prevent the Etzel operation from being carried out, without bloodshed if possible, but by force if necessary. There can be no possible misunderstanding on this point. Bringing the ship to Tel Aviv is clearly a provocative act.

Bentov: Before the establishment of the State it was possible to believe that its establishment would solve all our problems. But now we have no alternative: either the Government acts as a government should, or it will be clear to the entire world that it is helpless. We cannot retreat.

Shertok: I was both sad and angry at the way that Mr. Gruenbaum presented the matter. It was almost as if he were referring to two gangs quarreling over the control of a store of weapons. Even if he were not a member of the Government, I would have been amazed at what he said. What are we talking about here, two gangs? Hardly! In reality we have the Government on one side, and an organization that has violated an agreement and is now trying to benefit from its action on the other. The question is whether there will be a Government at all. Gruenbaum talked about a "private agreement between the two sides." A member of the Government speaks of two sides, though he is a member of one of the sides. I think that we must use every means at our disposal, including military force, to make Etzel accept Government policy.

Rabbi Fishman: I had talks yesterday and this morning with Mr. Shapira, and we both agree that Etzel has committed a crime. But we have our own responsibilities. We must find a way to settle the affair. I fear not only an underground movement, but open rebellion by the people.

Kaplan: I agree with those who say that a real tragedy has occurred. I want to tell Rabbi Fishman that it was for this reason that I did not participate in the discussion, but did vote for the decision. I saw no alternative. The entire Etzel operation is built on deception and provocation. I saw no alternative two nights ago and I certainly see no alternative now. This very talk about negotiations, as if there were two sides, is harmful.

Ben-Gurion: This matter is much too grave for us to deal with personalities and personal complaints at this stage. The things that have occurred endanger the war effort and the whole State. There can be no State without an army under the control of the Government. This was an attempt to destroy the Army and to kill the State. These are the two issues at stake, and in my opinion there can be no compromise where they are concerned. If there is no alternative, then we should use force. If the Army and the State surrender to an independent force, the Government might just as well pack up and go home. I opposed the agreement with Etzel made by the Zionist General Council. But it was accepted by a majority of the movement and is therefore binding. I think that a majority decision must be loyally carried out, and I will be faithful not only to its words but to its spirit. Etzel was offered numerous concessions to persuade it to dissolve, but it violated the agreement and did not dissolve.

Mr. Gruenbaum wants to make a synthesis out of what we say and what they say. That is a mistake. I thought it was a grave error for him to begin negotiations on his own initiative, though I am certain he did it with the best intentions. Nevertheless, he was wrong. We are not discussing internal security, but the very existence of the State, and we have decided on our course of action. Perhaps each one of us had his own reasons for supporting the resolution, but that doesn't matter. Everyone said that force should be used if necessary. This situation endangers the entire war effort. An army is the most dangerous thing in the world. Therefore, it must be kept under civilian control. When an army dictates to a government, that government ceases to exist.

I am as much a compromiser as the rest of you. But there are things on which there can be no compromise, for the very soul of the State is at stake. They must agree to turn over the ship, to accept the authority of the Government. Once they agree, we will be generous; we will not harm anyone. At the most, there will be a few arrests. All of us want to avoid bloodshed. But there is no room for negotiations. They must turn over the ship to the Government and accept the authority of the Army. It is our Army. If they do so, there will be no battle. If the affair is really over, there will be an amnesty. But there is no room for compromise or negotiations. The future of the war effort is at stake.

I have just received the following report from the Commander of the Alexandroni Brigade: "The struggle at Kfar Vitkin ended an hour ago with the unconditional surrender of Etzel. Meridor, the local Etzel commander, has agreed to turn over all his weapons. We suffered eight casualties, two killed and six wounded. Six Etzel men were killed and eighteen wounded. They are returning our prisoners and equipment. They are surrounded and have no way out."

There still remains the question of the ship. We can appoint a two- or three-man committee to carry out negotiations, or we can demand that the ship be turned over to

the Government immediately, and if necessary use force to back up that demand. Whatever happens, after this affair, the agreement with Etzel should be considered null and
void; they should be subject to the same laws as everyone else. There should be no special
battalions and no special command, for they did not fulfill their obligations under the
terms of the agreement.

Gruenbaum proposed that if the ship left the country, it should be allowed to depart
in peace. If it attempted to approach the shore, it should be dealt with as were the men at
Kfar Vitkin.

Ben-Gurion: I want you to understand the military significance of your proposal.
It would obligate us to keep our naval vessels ready to intercept the ship and to maintain
a large military force along the entire coast. It would mean tying down our entire Navy
and a large proportion of our land forces as well.

Three resolutions were put to a vote.

1. A resolution to appoint a committee to deal with the controversy and bring its
conclusions to the Government for final approval was defeated by a vote of six to four.

2. Gruenbaum and Shapira proposed that the ship be allowed to sail away if it did
not try to approach the shores of the country, but attacked if it did. Their resolution was
defeated. It was decided by a majority of seven to two to demand that the ship be turned
over to the State.

3. By a vote of nine to one (Rabbi Fishman dissenting), it was agreed that if the
owners of the ship removed it from the shores of the country, and pledged not to return
without the Government's prior agreement, the Government would reconsider the
matter.

Etzel Defies the Government

Early on Tuesday, June 22, 1948, the *Altalena* reached the shores of Tel Aviv. The
Minister of Defense heard details on its movements the next day from Paul Shulman,
an Israeli naval officer who had served in the American Navy during the Second World
War, and had arrived in Israel as a volunteer. He reported that on Monday, at 2 A.M., the
ship was off the coast at Kfar Vitkin, and he had sent small boats to identify it. His men
informed him that the ship *Altalena* was discharging immigrants. Shulman was instructed
to issue a warning to the Etzel vessel, but not to attack it before receiving additional
orders from Tel Aviv. At 6 A.M. he ordered his two ships (the *Wedgewood* and the *Eilat*)
to come as close as possible to the shore.

When they approached the Etzel vessel, they saw that both equipment and people
were being unloaded. On Monday morning the Etzel ship was a hundred meters from
the shore. There were about forty men on deck. They had a machine gun on deck for use
against airplanes. Menahem Begin, in civilian clothes, was on the bridge. About two
hundred people were working in the hold of the ship. Arieh Kaplan circled around the
Altalena in a small boat, and spoke to the people on board. They were unloading equipment into two rowboats and one motorboat in preparation for landing it on the shore,
where some hundred armed Etzel men were waiting. They had about twenty-five
machine guns, but were not drawn up to defend themselves. They worked slowly and

in a disorderly manner. The rifles and ammunition they were taking out of boxes were left lying in the sand instead of being loaded onto vehicles.

The previous evening, the Etzel people had asked members of kibbutz Mihmoret to help them take off the immigrants, and help was given. At first the Etzel members were friendly toward our people in the boats, but at four in the afternoon the situation changed. Apparently something had happened on shore. Actually, our troops had arrived and surrounded the area. Kaplan spoke to the captain of the Etzel ship, an American Jew, asking him whether he had received orders to shoot. The captain said no. At four o'clock shooting began. The men on board our ship saw military movements. At 9 P.M. the Etzel people began shooting at our ship from the *Altalena* and from shore. One of our Hotchkiss machine guns fired back. Our men were ordered to shoot only when fired upon and to stop shooting when the Etzel people did.

It became apparent before sundown that the *Altalena* was headed north. Shulman ordered the *Eilat* to shoot over the *Altalena* in order to force it to go south. He also ordered his ship to be lit up, and this was done immediately. Until that time there had been complete darkness. The *Eilat* fired and the Etzel ship turned south. Shulman ordered the *Eilat* to stop firing, then reported to Tel Aviv that the Etzel ship had turned toward the city and asked for further instructions.

While the ships were sailing Shulman asked the *Altalena* whether it needed medical assistance. He received a negative reply. Near Sidni Ali, the *Wedgewood* (his ship) drew within a hundred and fifty meters of the Etzel vessel. He informed its captain that it was within Israel's territorial waters, and therefore had to obey the Government's direction. He ordered the *Altalena* to move to the west. Its captain answered that he had run out of fuel. Shulman again ordered him to move westward. This was near the Reading Power Station. When his orders were not obeyed, Shulman told his men to fire over the ship. As the Etzel vessel neared the shore, he was instructed to prevent it, at all costs, from reaching Tel Aviv, but it was already too late. Shulman was thereupon ordered to proceed to Caesaria and to bring back a smaller ship from there [capable of approaching the shore]. At noon he returned with it to Tel Aviv. Already there was shooting from the shore. Some of the bullets struck his ship. He ordered it to move toward the west and remain there until 5:30 in the afternoon. Our ships did not fire a single shot all through the day. They were three to four miles from the shore.

Tuesday afternoon the Prime Minister received three Mayors—Israel Rokah, Oved Ben-Ami, and Avraham Krinitzi—as well as Messrs. Sapir and Ariav. They proposed that we negotiate with the Etzel ship and that a cease-fire be arranged. While the discussion was going on, the Prime Minister received a report that the *Altalena* was on fire, after having been hit by an artillery shell.

At a press conference after the Etzel ship had reached Tel Aviv, the Foreign Minister announced: "The Government is resolved to maintain its sovereignty and its ability to fulfill its international obligations. It will not permit undisciplined armed groups to foster political and military anarchy. The Etzel ship must be turned over to the Government immediately and unconditionally."

Galili also spoke at the press conference: "This crisis has broken out over an arms ship that reached the country during the truce, without our knowledge or approval, and only a short while after the Commander of Etzel had signed an agreement providing for the integration of his men in the Israel Defense Forces, their swearing of allegiance to the State, and an end to the purchase of weapons by Etzel. The weapons already in Etzel's possession were to be turned over to the Defense Forces. Yet among those who participated in the unloading of this ship were soldiers and high-ranking officers who had deserted the Israel Defense Forces, into which they had already been integrated. It is clear that Etzel's promise to observe the terms of the agreement was not sincere."

The Provisional State Council was convened that day. For the first time all thirty-seven members were present. Before it met we had a brief meeting of the Government, at which Rabbi Fishman and Shapira demanded immediate release of the Etzel prisoners. Gruenbaum proposed that a judge be appointed to investigate the charges against those arrested and that a three-man committee—consisting of the Minister of Justice, the Minister of Interior, and the Defense Minister—be established to consider what measures were necessary to ensure the maintenance of law and order, the unity of the Defense Forces, and the pardoning of prisoners. The proposal was accepted. Rabbi Fishman and Shapira presented their resignations and left the hall.

The State Council was called to order by the Prime Minister. He spoke at first about the obligations accepted by the Commander of Etzel under the terms of the June 1 agreement, which provided for mobilization procedures, the turning-in of weapons and war matériel held by the organization to the Israel Defense Forces, and the cessation of all purchases of arms and other military equipment. He also described what had happened when the *Altalena* reached Kfar Vitkin on June 20, 1948, and mentioned the desertion of Etzel soldiers from Defense Forces units, which had obliged the Government to concentrate a large military force at Kfar Vitkin to put down the rebellion.

He took note of the "wise and effective action taken by the Commander of the Central Region, *i.e.*, of the Alexandroni Brigade, who had carried out his mission with a maximum of efficiency and a minimum of bloodshed." The terms of surrender at Kfar Vitkin, signed by the Etzel Commander there, were as follows:

A. The Etzel forces in the area must immediately stop all hostile acts.

B. All Etzel weapons, ammunition, and military equipment in the Kfar Vitkin area must be turned over to the local commander of the Israel Defense Forces units.

C. All the officers and men of Etzel must give their names, addresses, and all other relevant details; this information would be turned over to the Government.

D. Afterward, the officers and men of Etzel will be free to leave the area.

E. The Etzel officers and men of Etzel must declare their readiness to report for duty, if called upon to do so by the Israel Government.

F. The vehicles used to transport military equipment must be returned to their owners; private vehicles would go back with the Etzel forces.

G. Prisoners held by the Israel Defense Forces would be freed under the same conditions; prisoners held by Etzel at Kfar Vitkin must be returned to the Israel Defense Forces.

This appeared to be the end of the Etzel revolt. At that moment, however, the Etzel ship slipped away and headed for Tel Aviv; once there, it refused to comply with our orders to leave the city and turn over its cargo of weapons to the authorities. The Government had previously decided that if this was not done, force would be used against the vessel, and so it was. One of the artillery shells of the Israel Defense Forces hit the ship and it began to go up in flames. The crew asked our men to help remove the wounded, and they immediately complied. The ship continued smoking off Tel Aviv.

The Prime Minister added: "An armed uprising against a state or an army can be repressed by military force, but military force is not sufficient to eliminate the danger. The chicanery of the dissidents was in large measure the result of the support given to them in various quarters. At one time it might have been possible to explain, though difficult to justify, this support. Now it is difficult even to explain. We are in the midst of a life-and-death struggle. At the moment there is a truce, but the war has not ended. Enemy armies are entrenched inside the country. Jerusalem is surrounded by the Arab Legion and its artillery. The Negev road is in the hands of a large Egyptian force. Mishmar Hayarden is held by the Syrians. Moreover, additional Arab forces are poised on the borders. The arrogant action of armed gangs inside the country gravely endangers our ability to defend our own future and the future of the entire Jewish people. This danger will not end until the citizens of this country and Jews everywhere understand the tragic significance of the very existence of such organizations. Not only the Army, but the entire people, must help to uproot this evil."

Rabbi Berlin [Bar-Ilan], a Mizrahi representative, declared: "If we were able to confine ourselves to the bare facts, to state simply that there has been a *rebellion* (which no one for a moment doubts), then the situation would be very simple. It is not only the Government's right but its duty to put down any rebellion with all the power at its disposal. But what really interests us is our situation after this terrible episode is over. It involves, after all, not only a weapons ship, but also the killing of Jews by other Jews. This is bound to affect our war effort. It will be said that the State is weak and its future is threatened. In my opinion, it would be far better for the Government to appear weak and the State strong, rather than vice-versa. Please permit me to speak frankly and firmly.

"I hope the Minister of Defense will forgive me if I tell him to his face that his actions were excessive, and should not have been taken solely on his own initiative. I regret to announce that the ministers representing Mizrahi, Rabbi Fishman and Mr. Shapira, have felt impelled to resign. Mr. Prime Minister, I would like formally to announce these resignations and make two proposals: (1) A truce should be put into effect until the release of the prisoners; (2) a committee should be appointed to investigate the matter."

Immediately after Rabbi Berlin spoke, the Prime Minister announced: "I regret that I failed to include two items of information in my statement on behalf of the Government: (1) The Government has decided to appoint a judge to study the list of prisoners; any new immigrants found among them will be released immediately. If there are men who were not armed and did not carry out any criminal act, they will also be released immediately. The possible guilt of the other prisoners will be investigated. (2) The Government has decided to appoint a three-man Ministerial Committee to consider measures to eliminate armed separatist units, violations of State laws, and the independent purchase of weapons. At the same time, there will be an amnesty for all crimes committed in this sphere until now. The Minister of Defense, the Minister of Justice, and the Minister of Interior will serve on this committee."

Luria (Mapam): I would like to ask Rabbi Berlin: Who held secret trials against the members of the Yishuv all these years? Who ambushed and murdered people? Why were the weapons not turned over immediately? Why was it necessary to desert battle stations opposite the Iraq Army and leave the front exposed? From whom were they trying to save these weapons—from the Israel Defense Forces? I believe that we should commend the Government and the Minister of Defense for their firm stand, which, I am certain, will be approved by our fighting men. I propose that the Council declare its support for the Government's action against Etzel, an organization which has challenged the very sovereignty of the State of Israel and the authority of the Israel Defense Forces, violated its agreement with the Government, and brought in arms, not for a campaign against the enemy, but to strengthen the dissidents. In my view of what has happened, it is necessary to disarm Etzel, abolish separate Etzel units in the Army, and punish all those attempting to undermine the Israel Defense Forces.

Kolodny (Ha'oved Hatzioni): Today we have a State which enjoys complete sovereignty; there can be no compromise on this point. There cannot be several armies in one country. The Yishuv wholeheartedly supports the Government. I am concerned by the resignation of the Mizrahi ministers because this undermines national unity, which should be dear to all of us. I admire the Government's patience and its willingness to offer amnesty to the rebels, if they agree to adopt new policies. The authority of the State and of the Israel Defense Forces should be the same in Jerusalem as it is elsewhere in the country.

Kosoy [Yona Kessel] (Mapai): Yesterday I heard a speech by the commander of Etzel. He boasted that, had he wanted to, he could immediately have killed the Prime Minister. How can we permit such a hostile force to exist, a force whose commander can, if he so desires, give orders to kill, and turn to our soldiers and say: "Don't shoot, don't kill, the time has not yet come." At this fateful meeting the Provisional State Council must tell the Jewish people in simple and clear terms about our internal enemies. They are capable of gravely harming the Jewish State, its armed forces, and its ability to defend itself.

Rachel Cohen (Wizo): I ask Mizrahi and Hapoel Hamizrahi to reconsider what they have done. I fear that the path they have chosen will serve to paralyze their conscience — personal, public, and political. The Prime Minister was correct in saying that military force alone will not be enough to uproot this evil; public opinion must also play its part.

Weinstein (Hatzohar): From the moment it began participating in the Council, my faction fully recognized the Provisional Government and its sovereignty, for we sincerely wish to nurture the nucleus of national independence. However, we demand the appointment of a parliamentary inquiry committee, made up not only of ministers, but of Council members who will explore all the facts, including those not made public. Everything must be revealed. Some people believe that the Government did not act to prevent a rebellion, but to pave the way for a new political sellout to other countries. I therefore propose, in the name of the Hatzohar faction, that the Council choose a parliamentary inquiry committee to investigate how the arms ship came to be shelled, as well as other aspects of this episode.

Repetur (Mapam); The agreement signed by the Zionist General Council was based on the assumption that, on the establishment of the State of Israel and of the Provisional Government, the dissident organizations would be dissolved. The agreement clearly states that all weapons are to be placed at the disposal of the people, and that no group has the right to private arms. If Etzel has really agreed to its own dissolution, why does it need such large quantities of weapons?

Warhaftig (Hapoel Hamizrahi): The real problem is how to eliminate the underground. I agree that this has to be done, but how are we to go about doing it? The experience of the postwar era in the countries where there were underground movements indicates that they cannot be eliminated in a month, or even in a year. But we are an impatient people. We have had a great deal of difficulty with these bodies, and they continue to trouble us. However, we must have patience. An investigating committee must be appointed by the Council. The arrests should also be investigated. The acceptance of these two proposals would pave the way for reestablishment of peace and quiet in the country.

Shertok: For many years we dreamed of a Jewish State, with emphasis on the first word—Jewish. Now, with its establishment, we must shift our emphasis to the second word—State. When I listened to Rabbi Berlin, I realized that the State, as such, doesn't interest him at all. He seems to think in metaphysical terms, distinguishing between the State and the Government. He thinks that the Government can be weak and the State, at the same time, strong. I don't believe it is possible to have a strong State guided by a weak Government. What value is there to this Council if the laws it adopts are not worth the paper they are written on? After all, we are not at the beginning of this controversy; an agreement already exists, but even the minority that opposed it accepted it in the end. We kept our part of the bargain, but they did not. Etzel was to stop the purchase of weapons, but arms purchases went on. It was to turn its weapons over to the Government, but the weapons were not turned over to the Government.

Rabbi Berlin felt it necessary to introduce another, completely irrelevant, matter into the discussion, namely, whether or not there should be a special Cabinet committee dealing with defense matters. He knew that that day there had been a special meeting of the Cabinet, called by the Minister of Defense, as well as a regular Cabinet meeting. But he did nothing. A report on the situation was given, on the initiative of members of the Government—not always the Minister of Defense—and it was agreed on what action should be taken, and when. The commander at Kfar Vitkin was ordered to use force to the extent that this was necessary. The next day, at another extraordinary meeting, the Government decided how the Etzel ship should be handled. And it was on the basis of this policy that our forces acted. Why did Etzel refuse to turn over the ship and its weapons to the Government? Was there any justification for its refusal? Anarchy will not be permitted in this country.

Shapira: We did not resign, heaven forbid, out of a desire to weaken the Government. We are aware of what is happening; we are cognizant of the enemy at our gates. Indeed, our resignations were meant to emphasize the seriousness of the situation. Instead of mobilizing all our resources to confront the enemy from without, we will now be forced to establish concentration camps and guard them. I believe that the Council and the Government should make a last-minute attempt to prevent civil war, which may, Heaven forbid, destroy the State at its very inception. I hope that we will find a way to establish peace within the country, so that we can concentrate entirely on our adversaries from without.

Grabovsky (Mapai): No one here can guarantee that, had the Jewish Government surrendered yesterday, Etzel would have been satisfied with its achievement and avoided taking a second step. Let us recall for a moment the days and nights of terror through which we passed. Let us remember how they mocked us, our resolutions, our proclamations, the statements of our rabbis—oh, how they mocked us! What makes you think they would pay heed to us now? How good is persuasion with them? Yesterday they announced on the radio (I heard the entire broadcast myself) that they regard this Government as a band of traitors, prepared to go to Rhodes to sell out. After a speech like that any young man of their ideological persuasion would consider himself entitled to murder the members of such a Government. It has happened before. Rathenau was murdered. If our Government had not acted as it did, it would have been lost. Do you think this problem will be solved automatically? Yesterday, under terrible stress, the Government proved itself. We must now give it our full support.

Ben-Zvi (Mapai): One thing is clear. If the Etzel weapons had been brought to serve the needs of the State and of the war effort, they would have been turned over to the Jewish Government immediately. But they were not, a fact which speaks for itself. The other events followed naturally. I would like to say something to the members of Mizrahi and Hapoel Hamizrahi: You, who have built and supported the State, should not be leaving now. You have no right to do so. I propose that we refuse to accept their resignations.

After the Prime Minister had replied, a resolution offered by Weinstein and Warhaftig was voted upon and defeated.* It was decided to discuss the Government's proposals at the next meeting of the Provisional State Council. The Council met next day, June 24, 1948. In roll-call votes, two resolutions were adopted:

> 1. The Council expresses its support of the actions of the Government aimed at preventing Etzel from bringing in weapons without Government permission. This would have been a grave violation of the State and of the obligations assumed by Etzel under the terms of the June 1, 1948, agreement. (The vote was twenty-four in favor, four opposed, five abstentions.)
>
> 2. The Council was pleased to learn that a Ministerial Committee has been established to foster the unity of the Defense Forces, as well as the equality of rights and obligations of every soldier. When this is guaranteed in practice, it will be possible to forgive past transgressions in this area.

Four members of the Council were added to the Ministerial Committee: Beba Idelson, Rabbi Levin, Repetur, and Shapira.

Special Character of Jerusalem

At the same June 24 meeting, devoted primarily to the Etzel ship, a discussion took place on Jerusalem. All Jerusalem members were present and did most of the talking. The subject was whether Jerusalem was part of the State of Israel. The Prime Minister declared: "At the moment, one can speak only of the areas where the Jewish Army exercises *de facto* control. Until there is a peace settlement acceptable to both sides and enjoying international approval, what counts are the places under the authority of the Jewish Government. Jerusalem is under the authority of the Government (though not, I regret

---

* The Prime Minister's reply and the other speeches appear in the minutes of the Provisional State Council and also in his book *Israel at War*, pp. 169–179.

to say, the Old City) just as much as Tel Aviv. There is no distinction between Jerusalem and Tel Aviv, or between Haifa, Hanita, and Asluj. They are all under the control of the Jewish Government."

Ben-Zvi noted that Jerusalemites had displayed extraordinary bravery not only at the front, but also behind the lines. In fact, all Jerusalem had been in the front lines and had suffered gravely—80 percent of those killed in the city were civilians; only 20 percent were soldiers. Jerusalem had faced not only enemy attack but economic collapse. Even during the truce, when there was no shelling, the central streets of the city remained half empty. There has been insufficient contact between the military forces and the public. In Jerusalem, cut off from the Government and the General Staff in Tel Aviv for an extended period, the civil authorities have not enjoyed a proper relationship with the military. Both teachers and underage youngsters were called up and, as a result, the upper grades of the schools were closed. Weapons sent to Jerusalem were seized by the Palmah at Kiryat Anavim.

There was no clear delineation of army authority. There was looting in the abandoned neighborhoods. Etzel began the looting, but "decent" people, and even members of the armed forces, were subsequently involved. An order outlawing looting was issued, but was not observed. The National Committee has demanded an investigation of the terrible Hadassah convoy tragedy, in which 110 people were killed. However, a committee of inquiry has not been appointed. We must learn the causes of that failure in order to avoid similar tragedies in the future. If there is a state of emergency in Jerusalem, then the Military Command should have a department dealing with civil affairs, the usual arrangement in every well-organized state. The Government should define the areas of responsibility of the military and civilian authorities.

Rabbi Berlin criticized the Government and all its members for not finding the time to come to Jerusalem during the past five weeks. People don't believe that there were no planes. The authorities have also failed to provide the Jerusalemites with air transport so that they could come to Tel Aviv to tell what was happening. It should be remembered that during those five weeks there was no mail or telegraph contact between the two cities; the only contact was by short-wave radio, to which the enemy could also listen.

Various bodies were competing with one another in Jerusalem, he said. These included the Municipality, the Community Council, the Jerusalem Committee (which was supposed to be dealing with political matters), the Jewish Agency Executive (only two or three of whose members were in Jerusalem), and the remaining members of the Provisional State Council (ten members of the Council and one member of the Government remained stranded in Jerusalem). Jerusalem's status was clear. It had been a terrible mistake not to have set up an international political executive for Jerusalem at the time the State was established. No one can accuse me of wishing to underestimate Jerusalem's holiness and our right to make it our capital. But I am convinced that, at this point, we cannot control Jerusalem, particularly if there is talk of dividing it between two authorities.

Another great tragedy exists in Jerusalem, namely, the frantic attempts being made by the citizens to leave the city. There are those who say that if people were allowed to leave, not a soul would remain. I am not so pessimistic, but I do not regard it as exaggerated to say that 50 percent of the Jerusalemites would leave if given the opportunity. Many officials are being taken out of Jerusalem. I feel this should be done as little as possible. If the officials are transferred, they should leave their parents, wives and children behind. We cannot allow Jerusalem to become a ghost town. When an official leaves, the whole city says: "As an official, he knows what the real situation is, and that's why he's getting out. It means that things are really bad." Even the leaders of the community are guilty of such talk.

People in Jerusalem are very depressed. They have been without food, fuel, water, electricity, candles, radio, newspapers, or contact with the outside world. They are hungry: some more, some less. Even the well-to-do are hungry, and in the slum neighborhoods, where there is little to eat in the best of times, the situation is far worse. Many Jerusalemites have known hunger in the past, and that is what makes them so fearful now.

Jerusalem is surrounded by hills. Ordinarily this is a blessing, but it is a curse when the city is being fired upon incessantly from every hill. A man who has escaped injury in one place does not know whether he will be hit in another. We very much appreciate what the Minister of Defense and his colleagues have done to open the road to Jerusalem. But there is also something that has not been done. A clear statement should have been made in regard to the status of Jerusalem and its relation to the State of Israel. Perhaps this would have helped the city. Whenever this matter is considered, a Jerusalemite should be called in to speak. At this moment, when Jerusalem has suffered greatly and is depressed, work must begin on building up the city. The Jerusalemites must be shown that we are not discouraged. We must make it plain that we will build and defend Jerusalem, not only militarily, but economically. Jerusalem is ours. Anyone who devotes himself to building up the city now is carrying out a particularly blessed act.

Dr. Granovsky: We must encourage Jerusalem, and not only by declarations. We must make Jerusalemites feel that they are an integral part of the State of Israel. An enormous amount of damage has been done in the city, and if we don't begin immediately to strengthen it economically, Jerusalem will become a backwater. When we were under siege, we tried to do something with our own meager resources. The Jerusalem Economic Authority, as well as two subsidiaries, were established on the initiative of the national institutions. One of the companies, to promote air transport between Jerusalem and the rest of the world, was set up the day before the truce, when the city was still being shelled. A second firm will construct industrial buildings in the city. This activity should be of interest not only to Jerusalemites but to the country as a whole. Jerusalem is capable of providing economic opportunities for a large number of Jews. We must strengthen the cultural and educational institutions in the city, particularly the Hebrew University. The university can serve as a great cultural center for Israel and world Jewry, and also provide a livelihood for hundreds of Jerusalem families. We cannot carry out these plans by ourselves. We need the active support of the Government of Israel. A special administrative and economic body should be set up to deal with Jerusalem's problems and to plan its reconstruction.

Kobashi: There is a spirit of defeatism among the poor Jews of Jerusalem. They feel that they are not receiving adequate military protection or economic support. Some poor families in Jerusalem are without sufficient bread and water. There are families with ten or more members who fled from outlying neighborhoods during the shellings to other places that seemed safer. There is no one to care for them. This situation must be rectified. If we make these people feel that we are concerned about them, there will be no need to fear an exodus from the city. The poorer elements of the population must receive economic support, for they are important to Jerusalem.

Dr. Katznelson: Jerusalemites know how to suffer in silence; perhaps that is their special valor. As it happens, I spent days on end in the blood bank. I was amazed to see women from the Oriental communities standing by the shattered bodies of their dear ones without even crying. The women of Jerusalem displayed particular bravery. They had to use wood instead of kerosene for heating. They had to stand in line in the midst of heavy shelling to receive water rations. I do not think that the Jerusalemites felt isolated. We were well aware that the entire Yishuv was with us. We knew what was happening on the road to Jerusalem. We saw what took place in the Old City; we saw the Palmah battalions; we saw the struggle for the Etzion Bloc. There was isolation in one sphere only: our relations with the Government. Why was Jerusalem entrusted to political or military district officers? Why was there no military or political leadership with real authority, one that would work closely with the local population, and allow the Jerusalemites to express their opinions on policy matters? Only now, after thirty days of shelling, is a sense of shock passing through the city.

Warhaftig: In Jerusalem we felt that we had been forgotten. It seemed as if our voices were drowned out by the explosions of the shells that rained on the city day and night. (10,500 shells fell on Jerusalem over a period of several weeks; 250–300 people were killed and at least 1500 wounded.) Every young man who came to defend the city served to encourage us, making us feel that it was not only Jerusalem's war, but that of the entire country. But why was Jerusalem discriminated against when it came to the mobilization of men? In Jerusalem, we have been mobilizing everybody up to the age of forty-five for a long time, while in Tel Aviv forty-one-year-olds are only now being called up.

Ben-Gurion attempted to sum up the challenge of the Sacred City:

> We understand why our Jerusalem comrades feel it necessary to express their feelings at this time. But they are wrong when they say that they have been discriminated against. Their argument does a disservice to the hundreds and thousands who fought for Jerusalem and, in so many cases, died for it. The problem of Jerusalem is, first and foremost, a question of military capabilities. Will we have the strength (a) to conquer the Old City; (b) to conquer a wide corridor from Tel Aviv to Jerusalem, which will be more than a narrow pathway, but a closely settled area connecting Jerusalem with the other sections of the Jewish State; (c) to destroy the Arab Legion in the Triangle. Without doing these three things, we will not be able to eliminate the dangers facing Jerusalem. These goals must be achieved not only inside Jerusalem itself, but also, indeed mainly, outside Jerusalem. To a limited extent, some of them have already been accomplished. Those comrades who had the privilege of being in Jerusalem during the siege should not ignore what has been done.
>
> Military strength will not in itself, however, solve Jerusalem's problems. Even after the Jewish forces have freed the heart of Jerusalem—the Old City—captured the areas between Tel Aviv and Jerusalem that are not yet in our hands, and destroyed the Arab Legion, it will still be necessary to provide a healthy economic foundation for Jerusalem, to give employment to its present inhabitants and to the immigrants who will come to the city. The other problem facing us, and by far the most urgent—since we don't know how much time we will have to solve it—is the stockpiling of water, fuel, food, and other supplies in the city while the truce continues.
>
> These are Jerusalem's central problems. I regret to say that the arrangements made until now for the internal organization of the city do not satisfy the Jerusalemites. When a particular man was appointed to run the city, they objected. When a committee was appointed, they objected again. When a military regime was established, again there were

objections. And if we set up a civilian regime, there will be objections once more. I don't blame the representatives of Jerusalem. The Jerusalem community has a very special character, and I am afraid that no organizational arrangements will satisfy the Jerusalemites, particularly until we gain control of the Old City and of the road to Jerusalem, and stop enemy shelling.

The Government must decide whether to appoint a governor to rule Jerusalem. The need is clear. I only hope for some wise man among us who will devise a plan that will satisfy the Jerusalemites. We should not criticize our Jerusalem colleagues for not bringing constructive proposals. We must concentrate now on military preparations to gain control of a corridor to Jerusalem and liberate the city completely. We must also concern ourselves with Jerusalem's economic development. Education and culture are among the city's natural "industries": Hebrew science, culture, and art should all be imbued with the spirit of Jerusalem. We must provide the largest possible stockpile for the city. If the fighting should begin again, we cannot allow Jerusalem to be in the kind of situation that it was when the State was established.

King David chose one of the most difficult places in the country for his capital. Those who returned to Zion in recent generations did not pay heed to the need for a physical link in Jerusalem. By some miracle, a Jewish majority was maintained in the city, and recently it has grown larger. But it is not enough to have a Jewish majority inside the city; there must also be a Jewish agricultural hinterland and a road to Jerusalem lined with Jewish settlements. We are now paying for our past errors, and we must compensate during the war for the mistakes we made during the peace. It is up to our Army—and this time, only our Army—to do so. I hope that it will. A beginning has already been made. So far, we are in control of a very narrow corridor. It must be enlarged in the north and in the south, and strengthened by the establishment of agricultural-military settlements. This will be accomplished if we can increase our military efforts, which will benefit us both during the fighting and in the days of peace to follow.

Military strength is now the key to our existence and future. The fate of Jerusalem depends on it, perhaps to a greater extent than anywhere else, because of Jerusalem's particular geographic situation. To secure Jerusalem we must secure the road to Jerusalem, which in turn depends not only on conquests, but also on construction. We need men both to fight and to settle the land.

It is not desirable or possible to talk about every problem at this moment. In time of war, many things must remain secret. Let us not reopen old wounds; instead, let us support our soldiers.

I do not understand the complaints of the Jerusalemites about the fact that we have not mobilized men up to the age of forty-five all over the country. There was simply no need to mobilize them. We require men for work as well. Jerusalem needs supplies, and supplies come from outside the city. They must be produced, stored, loaded, and transported. Craftsmen, farmers, drivers, mechanics, porters—all are working on behalf of Jerusalem. The entire country is behind Jerusalem. Moreover, we do not want the State of Israel to be supported solely by the Jews of the Diaspora. Work must go on in agriculture, industry, construction, and transport if the economy is to keep moving. Consequently, we cannot mobilize every person for military service. In Jerusalem it was possible to call up more people for digging fortifications and other defense preparations; this should not be regarded as discrimination. Let us try not to balance Jerusalem against the rest of the country. We all share in the struggle.

Jerusalem has suffered more than most places, but let us not underestimate the suffering of settlements in the Jordan Valley, upper Galilee, the Negev, the Coastal Plain, and other areas. Their sacrifices will be remembered forever. In any case, the time has not yet come to make distinctions on this score. The struggle continues, and we will still be called upon to make enormous spiritual, physical, economic, and military efforts. Shortcomings remain, but they will only be corrected by a joint endeavor, not by backbiting.

Asked to comment on the rumors about the demilitarization of Jerusalem, the Foreign Minister warned that not everything in the press should be regarded as absolute truth. He doubted whether any member of the Government is discussing proposals for the demilitarization of Jerusalem without informing the Foreign Ministry. He had no knowledge, he said, about the possible demilitarization of the Old City, though a proposal to that effect may have been made. The Foreign Ministry, in any case, did not make it. He knew that those close to the UN Mediator think that, even if there is no agreement on the central questions, perhaps agreement can be reached on the demilitarization of Jerusalem— not of the Old City alone, but of Jerusalem as a whole. So far, there have been no formal proposals or negotiations on the subject.

The meeting concluded with an announcement by the Prime Minister that Jerusalem was under the jurisdiction of the Jewish Government to the same extent as Tel Aviv.

The next day, June 25, 1948, the Prime Minister went up to Jerusalem via the "Burma Road."

From My Diaries:
June 24–July 29, 1948

June 24, 1948

I discussed how we should handle the Etzel people with Yigael Yadin, Israel Galili, and Ben-Zvi. In my opinion, those who take an oath of allegiance should be treated like all other soldiers, until such time as it becomes clear that the trust placed in them was not justified. Those who refuse to take an oath of allegience should either be sent to work in the Negev or the Galilee, or turned over to the police. We must make special efforts to see that the VIPs don't escape. This job has been entrusted to Issar "Hakatan" (little) Harel.

Sini (Arnon Azriyahu), reporting on behalf of Zvi Ben-Yacov, said that 2,080,000 English cartridges, 1473 English rifles, 30 to 40 Bren guns, 5 English piats, 3300 English piat shells, and 60 boxes, which apparently contain either rifles or Bren guns, were taken at Kfar Vitkin. Our armored cars left the scene loaded with weapons. Ben-Yacov assumes that our soldiers also took arms (Bren guns, piats), as did members of settlements. It is possible that the Etzel people also managed to bury a large quantity of arms. (A search is now going on.)

June 25, 1948

I left for Jerusalem this morning at 8 A.M., by way of Beit Jiz, Beit Susin, Beit Mahsir, and Saris. I reached the city at 11:30.

I went with Joseph Rohel [Avidar] and Dov Joseph to see the neighborhoods that had been captured. We left from Rehavia, and went through Katamon, the Greek and German colonies, Baka, Allenby Barracks, Talpiot, and the ruins of Ramat Rahel.

At 5 P.M. I met with the members of the Jerusalem Committee: Joseph, Aboulafia, Werfel, and Auster (Solomon and Shreibman-[Shaari] were in Tel Aviv). Aboulafia, who was in charge of requisitions, complained that the armed forces and the Civil Guard were continuing to seize things without permission. Aboulafia is also responsible for electricity, raw materials, and building. Auster is responsible for war victims, Solomon for housing, and Passman for the Old City and the refugees. When Passman went abroad, he turned over his responsibilities to Solomon. Werfel takes care of fuel and information, while Shreibman deals with manpower and internal security (the police and the Home Guard). Joseph handles supplies.

Joseph said that while we had conquered most of the city, we still lacked artillery, ammunition, and a spirit of aggressiveness. The food situation is improving. Jerusalem, until yesterday, received 2250 tons of food; another 600 tons arrived yesterday. Hillel Cohen and Yulish, who had been in Jerusalem, expressed concern at the possibility that they might not be able to gather enough commodities in Tel Aviv for Jerusalem. They had obtained 7000 tons of fuel. During the period of the truce, Jerusalem was supposed to receive 2800 tons of different types of petroleum. The Electric Corporation requires 600 tons a month. A third of the fuel received was kerosene, a third gasoline, a third consisted of other varieties.

There are 112,000 people in Jerusalem, 100,000 civilians and 12,000 soldiers. (Included in the population figure are 1000 non-Jews and 1000 prisoners.) Gorhovsky [Shraga Goren] said to Rohel that a shortage of cash was responsible for the limited shipments of fuel. Verlinsky informed Joseph that he could only send 100 tons of yellow cheese to Jerusalem. I demanded that 400 tons be sent and suggested that people in Tel Aviv and Haifa do without cheese. There is a similar controversy over eggs. Verlinsky suggested 1 million eggs, while I demanded 2 million. Some things cannot be obtained in Tel Aviv. Sufficient fresh vegetables are now available. Powdered milk is important, but there is none in Israel. However, planes could be sent to bring it from the United States. If the fighting starts again, it will be necessary to send 20 tons of flour per day by way of the new road. At one time every home had its own stock of supplies, but they have been used up. The question is how individuals can restock without interfering with public requirements. Rokah asked the UN people for the necessary permission, but they refused on two counts: (1) an excess supply could be sent in; (2) weapons could be brought in with the food.

Is there any control over Arab food shipments? The UN personnel say that they are checked at the Allenby Bridge and at Ramallah. Auster has demanded, on behalf of the Municipality, that it be a partner in the UN discussions on Jerusalem. I declared that there should be three authorities in Jerusalem: the Military Commander, the Governor, and the Municipality.

Werfel said: Jerusalem is weary; the truce saved the city. The last two days before the truce were a nightmare. Jerusalemites do not want to again stand defenseless in the face of enemy artillery. The people would be encouraged if we had our own artillery. The Tel Aviv press is not doing a proper job in regard to Jerusalem. Relations between the Army and the public are bad. The Army looks down upon civilians. Werfel does not share the concern of others at the possibility that Jews might leave Jerusalem.

I asked Aboulafia if the Sephardim tended to run away. Absolutely not, he replied. Two weeks ago the Jerusalem Committee started to register people who wanted to leave the city. 700 families (less than 2000 people) signed up; 250 of them left. The Jerusalem Committee (i.e., Werfel) is responsible for issuing exit permits. The French Consul is responsible, on behalf of the UN, for the entry and departure of people. The Belgian consul deals with the removal of goods. I asked the others present whether Werfel's view was correct. Auster believes that people are affected by a mass psychosis that makes them wish to leave. Aboulafia disagreed. Joseph supported him. Werfel said that since he was dealing with the situation he could say authoritatively that Auster's anxiety was exaggerated. Werfel and Aboulafia demanded the appointment of a governor.

In the evening I received a communication sent at 6:15 P.M. from Tel Aviv by the Intelligence Branch. It said: The Egyptians have violated the truce with air raids on Kfar Warburg and Be'er Tuvia. Reinforcements sent to help came under severe attack. One soldier was wounded. The convoy that was to go to the Negev, in accordance with a UN decision, was blocked by Egyptian forces and had to return to its base. Bernadotte's Chief of Staff declared in writing that the Egyptians had violated the truce, and the Jews were therefore free to act as they saw fit.

Nehemia told me that there would be a plane waiting for me at the Jerusalem airport the next morning.

June 26, 1948

I took off at 8:45 A.M. and landed in Tel Aviv forty minutes later. The plane flew at an altitude of forty-five hundred feet. We were afraid of enemy aircraft after what had happened in the south the day before, but we did not see any planes.

Epstein [Eliahu Eilat] cabled on June 23, 1948, that, in accordance with his request, Joseph Jacobson (a personal friend of Harry Truman) had spoken with the President. Truman said: (1) The United States will not support the Arabs and the English in their attempts to reduce the territory allotted to Israel in the November 29 resolution; (2) The US will accord Israel de jure recognition immediately after the truce. During the truce period this cannot be done. Israel will receive a loan for constructive purposes, mainly for the settlement of displaced persons. The President is very angry at Bevin and attacked the devious British attempts to undermine the efforts being made to solve the Palestine problem.

The day before yesterday Shitreet met with Daud el Issa, the editor of *Falestin*. Also present were Eliahu Sasson, Gad Machnes, Ezra Danin, and Yitzhak Chizik. Issa said that 150,000 Arabs had left the country for the surrounding states. The remainder had moved to other places within the country: Nablus, Ramallah, etc. Many Arabs will want to sell their property and leave the Jewish State. All sorts of wild stories about the Jews are being spread among the Arab population. Issa's remarks made it clear that the Arabs are well informed about what is going on in our midst.

Shaul wrote (on June 29, 1948) that he has 15 Norsemen planes, which must be equipped with auxiliary fuel tanks if they are to reach the country. He has purchased 5 million .303 bullets.

Ehud reported: We are about to sign an agreement in Switzerland for 50 25-mm. field guns with 50,000 shells, as well as 150,000 shells for the 20-mm. guns we already have. In France we will obtain 50,000 shells for 65-mm. artillery pieces, 12 120-mm. mortars with 4000 shells, 12 47-mm. antitank guns with 25,000 shells. We might also get 6 105-mm. artillery pieces with 6000 shells. We hope to obtain an additional 15 airplanes. Until June 21, 1948, we have received $6,825,000 from Golda [Meir]. Yesterday we asked for $5 million more.

Verlinsky reported: From the 18th until today 5000 tons of food have been sent to Jerusalem, including almost 3000 tons of flour (this does not square with what I heard in Jerusalem). Yesterday and today 1500 tons of food were sent; 3000 tons of flour will last Jerusalem for four and a half months, at a rate of 350 grams of bread per person per day. There are only 360 tons of yellow cheese in Israel; 140 tons will go to Jerusalem; 220 will go to the Defense Forces. It is impossible to obtain 2 million eggs for Jerusalem.

I cabled Teddy Kollek and Rose Halpern (in America) to immediately send a transport plane with 100 tons of powdered milk and 50 tons of powdered eggs for Jerusalem.

At 8 p.m. I was visited by Leon Simon and Melech Neustadt of the Hebrew University. They said that the English are beginning to accept the fact that there is a State of Israel, though without enthusiasm. They want the university to be neutralized.

Shaul has arrived. We have purchased 50 German-made 75-mm. artillery pieces together with 1000 shells for each gun. Every gun costs 33,252 Swiss francs, and every shell 65 francs. If there are no financial difficulties, the shells will be sent in two weeks' time. We have an option on another 50 such guns, but we will not be able to obtain them before August or September. We have purchased more mortars, artillery and shells in France. We have obtained American-made tanks in Mexico.

June 29, 1948

Today we received Bernadotte's suggestions. Those who suspect that he is a Bevin agent are not too far off the mark. He proposes a union of both sides of the Jordan in which there would be two partners, the Jews and the Arabs. The union would promote economic development, provide economic services (including customs), and coordinate foreign and defense policy. It would be headed by a Central Council or other bodies, in accordance with the decision of its members. Immigration initially would be the responsibility of the individual members. But after two years, each member could demand that the Council consider the other member's policies and make decisions on the basis of their joint interests. If the Council did not succeed in reaching a conclusion, the matter would be transferred to the UN's Economic and Social Council for a final decision, based on the country's economic absorptive capacity. Every resident would have the right to return to his former home and get back his property.

Bernadotte also included several items for "consideration": (1) partial or complete inclusion of the Negev in the Arab area; (2) partial or complete inclusion of the Galilee in the Jewish area; (3) inclusion of Jerusalem in the Arab area, with municipal autonomy for the Jewish population and a special committee to protect the Holy Places; (4) reconsideration of the position of Jaffa; (5) establishment of a free port in Haifa, to include the refinery and the terminals, as well as (6) a free airport at Lydda.

June 30, 1948

Abba Hushi called from Haifa to report that the last Englishmen would be leaving Haifa at 12:30. All the British barricades have been removed. Our Navy will enter the port at 2:30.

I decided to go to Haifa. I reached the city at 6:15 and went straight to the port, where celebrations were taking place. There are five thousand workers of military age (eighteen to thirty-five) in Haifa who are healthy and capable of fighting. They don't even go out to dig fortifications, though there is an order to that effect.

July 11, 1948

I was able to return to my office only today. A continuous six-month effort, without a single day of rest, finally took its toll.

In the meantime, the truce has ended and, as was to be expected, the decisive phase of the struggle has begun. We have won a number of victories (easy, but important ones), including those at Lydda and Ramle. The two cities are completely surrounded; at noon there was a rumor that Ramle had fallen, but that was only wishful thinking.

Our forces have met stiff resistance at Beit Naballah, and it is still difficult to know how and when the struggle will end. In the meantime, Egyptian pressure in the south grows stronger, despite the fact that the Egyptians have suffered considerable losses. We have also suffered losses (wounded).

I was contacted in the early evening by Yigal Allon whose forces have penetrated into Lydda. Beit Naballah has been taken and we are advancing on Ramle.

July 12, 1948

We received news that Lydda had surrendered. Actually the civil population has surrendered, while Arab soldiers continue to hold out in the police station. The civil population in Ramle has also announced its willingness to surrender; it is not clear what the Arab soldiers will do.

At 9:30, a meeting of the General Staff: Migdal Zedek has been captured by our forces. The Arab Legion has retaken Beit Naballah, where the struggle goes on. The situation in the Galilee is tense; in the south it is grave. A strong Arab Legion unit is on its way to Lydda and Ramle. It is approaching Gamzu.

Averbach arrived tonight from Jerusalem. He went by way of the new road and met convoys going up to the city with food. He reported that the Arab Legion is in the Old City, Sheikh Jarrah, Nebi Samuel, and on the French Hill. They are bombarding us from all those locations, though not as heavily as before the truce.

On Friday, before the end of the truce, the Arabs were firing from the walls of the Old City. On Sunday, at 12:15 P.M., we began to dynamite (there are forty tons of dynamite in Jerusalem) the café near Jaffa Gate. The Arab Legion replied with a bombardment from Damascus Gate and Herod's Gate in the Old City. On Saturday night (July 10) the Egyptians began to shell Talpiot and Ramat Rahel from the south. On Friday night our boys captured Hirbet Beit Hamama (on the road to Ein Kerem). It was defended by the Arab Legion and local Arabs. That night the Egyptians opened artillery fire on Beit Hamama (a monastery on the road to Bethlehem, opposite Mar Elias). The Arabs who tried to recapture Hirbet Beit Hamama suffered heavy losses.

Arab civilians have begun fleeing from Ein Kerem. They have begun to flee from Malha as well. Only soldiers remain. Our shells are hitting home. We have also bombarded Nebi Samuel. It is quiet on Mount Scopus; 150 Etzel members are cooperating with our forces, but there are some 600–750 Etzel members in the city.

Morale in Jerusalem is good.

A delegation from the Valley of Jezreel reported that the military situation there is disturbing. They need more men and equipment. The settlements have already given 1100 soldiers. Now they have been asked for another 360. This is the upper limit. 60 percent of the men from the settlements have been called up. They have not a single piat in their possession. They have insufficient weapons. I told them that we would not be able to send them reinforcements immediately, but that I would discuss the question of additional arms with the military bodies concerned.

July 13, 1948

A meeting of the General Staff. The Arab soldiers in the Lydda police station ceased their resistance in the middle of the night. This morning our troops entered Lydda. By 9:30 A.M. the enemy had not yet attacked Gamzu. We have captured Tzora and Tzuba. What are we going to do with Arab prisoners? We already have 3000 of them.

This morning another 300 men were sent to the south. The Givati Brigade has suffered 500 casualties—50 killed and 450 wounded—in the course of the war. The men are in good spirits. The Egyptians mounted a sustained 12-hour attack yesterday, using 3 battalions, artillery, and planes. We have artillery for defensive purposes, but lack infantry units for an attack. We are also without antiaircraft guns.

Zabarsky informed me that he will need PL5,150,000 ($25,750,000) for the July budget. About 60,000 men are under arms.

July 14, 1948

Vanya (Zeev Hadari) came to see me shortly after his return from Paris. He says that the French Prime Minister helped the *Altalena*. The boat was also assisted by British agents who were anxious to hurt the Government of Israel. A ship with 1800 people aboard will leave from Yugoslavia in four days.

I spent one day visiting Jerusalem. I found a sense of Jewish brotherhood that never existed there before. The organization of the city is excellent and morale is high.

I went to the Lydda Airport with three of Yitzhak's armored cars, passing Salame, Kfar Ana, Yehudia, and Wilhelma on the way. Our achievements in the few days since the truce ended are almost unbelievable. The airport is in our hands. I saw the two Cromwell tanks that we "inherited" from the British on the last day of their stay in the country. The airfield was conquered with these tanks.

July 15, 1948

Fighting has begun. The Arabs in the vicinity are fleeing. In the south we have reconquered Beit Afa and Hata. We have captured a great deal of equipment, including artillery pieces.

Some 30,000 refugees have left Lydda and Ramle. They are complaining about the Arab Legion. There have been anti-government demonstrations in Amman.

Severe measures must be taken to stop the looting.

Moshe Dayan came to see me. There were 400 men in his battalion, 250 combatants and 150 in service posts. He entered Lydda with 150 men in 8 jeeps, 6 half-tracks, and one armored car with a 2-pound cannon, which he had captured two hours before from the Arabs at Beit Naballah. He lost 16 men at Lydda, 4 killed and 12 wounded. This evening he is proceeding to the south with 120 combat troops, aside from service personnel.

I have ordered Moshe Carmel and David Shaltiel to take stern measures against theft in Nazareth or the Old City, should the culprits be captured.

July 16, 1948

The Flying Fortresses have arrived. One of them bombed Cairo, near the King's palace. It dropped 8 250-kg. bombs and 8 70-kg. bombs. The pilots are satisfied. Two Flying Fortresses went to hit El Arish and Gaza. They may have bombed Rafiah by mistake. This morning they took off for El Arish again. They returned at 7:30 to Tel Aviv. Our pilots are very enthusiastic. Tonight they are going to bomb Damascus.

An armored unit (under Laskov) together with an infantry unit will attack Nazareth.

At 11 Yigal Yadin called to say that Dan Tolkovsky returned with the Flying Fortresses. This morning they bombed El Arish, giving the airfield a good pasting. They dropped seven and a half tons of bombs and returned safely.

At 12 Moshe Shertok called to say that the American proposal had been adopted and that the second truce was to begin on Monday morning.

Gershon Zak informed me that the "Navy" has 3 corvettes, 3 police boats and 2 250-ton vessels. There are 1600 men in the Navy: 500 on board our ships, 500 in shipyards, 100 guarding Haifa Port, and 500 in various services. The Navy's July budget is PL80,000 ($400,000).

Trygve Lie cabled that the Security Council has decided on a cease-fire. It is to go into effect in Jerusalem 24 hours after the adoption of the resolution (tomorrow morning at 5:45). It will encompass the rest of the country 48 hours later (Monday at 5:45 A.M.), unless the Mediator sets an earlier time.

Yigael Yadin reports that a large-scale Arab offensive has begun in the Galilee. Our attack on Latrun tonight was not successful. The Harel Brigade ran into withering Arab Legion fire. On the other hand, the Yiftah Brigade captured Dir Maon (without resistance). Yigael went out to see whether we would be able to take Latrun tonight.

The Flying Fortresses will hit Syrian positions and Damascus tonight. Tomorrow and the next day they will concentrate on the south.

Moshe Carmel called to say that Nazareth had been taken at 8:30.

July 17, 1948

I received a message from the Etzioni Brigade at 6:30 A.M. stating that the previous night the Brigade had attempted, in cooperation with Etzel and Lehi, to capture the Old City. The operation began at 9:30 P.M. with a mortar and artillery bombardment of the Old City. Five hundred shells were fired in the course of an hour. Our forces, however, failed to break through the Wall, and at 5:30 A.M. retreated to their bases. This morning our men retook the Mandelbaum houses, the corner of Shmuel Hanavi Street and Saint George, which had been seized by the enemy the previous night.

In Nazareth our forces captured five "slightly damaged" armored cars. The Arabs fled. Interference from G. caused the cancellation of the air raid planned for the night on the Syrian camps and on Damascus. I gave Yigael permission to arrest him. Tira, near Haifa has been captured.

At 3 A.M. we bombed Damascus, using Dakotas rather than Flying Fortresses; they dropped three tons of bombs. The city was lit up, but the lights went out as soon as the first bombs fell.

July 18, 1948

The capture of Nazareth went smoothly. The places taken are being well protected. There are 16,000 people in the city, including 10,000 Christians. We destroyed 5 enemy armored cars in Nazareth.

"Sea-wolf" purchased two landing craft at PL10,000 each, two motor boats at PL2000 each, a tanker at PL6500, six other landing craft at PL13,000 each, ten small boats (five meters long and weighing one ton), and antiship mines—with 300 kg. of dynamite each—at PL700 each.

Yoel Palgi returned last week from South Africa. Two hundred volunteers have already arrived, some seventy for service in the Air Force. Three thousand more are waiting to come, but there are no funds to bring them. Palgi demands that a thousand South Africans, most of whom are young and some of whom are veterans, be brought to the country; 1.2 million pounds were raised by the Defense Appeal.

July 19, 1948

Though there is still sporadic fighting, the truce has really begun. If it continues for a long period (as I think it will) we will find ourselves in the midst of a difficult and danger-ous political struggle. Our military capacities will be an important factor in this contest, and we must strengthen them. However, we cannot afford an increase in the enormous financial burden we are already carrying. During the coming four weeks we will certainly not be able to cut down the number of men under arms, but we must find a way eventually to reduce this number and to increase the effectiveness of the remainder.

Future policy should be based on the following principles:

1. Officers and enlisted men with specialized tasks—platoon commanders, company commanders, artillerymen, wireless operators, etc.—must be given more training.

2. Every soldier must be given a minimum of a month's training.

3. The quality of locally produced arms must be improved.

4. More heavy equipment—artillery, airplanes, tanks, and automatic weapons—must be purchased.

5. New fortifications must be built along the entire front.

6. We must work out a plan that will permit us to mobilize reservists within a few hours. In another month's time it will be possible (and necessary) gradually to discharge men.

It was decided to hold a parade on July 27. Shlomo Shamir will be in charge of arrangements.

Yigael said that an enormous quantity of pipes, compressors, and other machinery worth millions was found at Beit Naballah. There are also many locomotives and railway cars at Lydda. I went to Ramle, Lydda, the Lydda railway station, and Beit Naballah. The tremendous stores left there must be salvaged, and quickly.

July 21, 1948

The battles have ended. Mishmar Hayarden has remained in Syrian hands. Seven hundred Arabs were killed or wounded; 50 of them deserted. During the 10-day period the Egyptians suffered 2000 casualties, including 700 dead. They have suffered 4000 casualties since the beginning of the war.

We have 65,000 men in the Defense Forces (besides the 830 being held prisoner by the Arabs). By the end of the month we will have 82,000 men under arms in 40 Field Force battalions, 22 Home Guard battalions (with 750 men each). Additional manpower will come from the normal call-up, from the mobilization of young people, and from among the new immigrants.

July 22, 1948

Last night I was visited by M., a top pilot from South Africa who arrived in Israel at 2 P.M. Within a few hours he became well acquainted with the problems of the Air Force. He praised the pilots from the US and South Africa, but said that we would only really have an Air Force when our own boys had taken over. Pilots gradually become less effective after the age of thirty.

At 11, M. and Ziv visited me. M. said that the main aim of our Air Force should be the destruction of the enemy air forces, after which it could be used to aid the Army. The choice of targets until now has not been satisfactory. An air force is a very complicated, technical organization. Proper facilities on the ground are of prime importance. Improvisation is not a good thing. There cannot be a proper air force without a strong administration and first-rate training, both in the air and on the ground. Only Sabras [Israel-born citizens] and immigrants will be trained. The men doing the job are excellent, but call-up procedures are very haphazard. There are numerous redundant people, and many who previously failed elsewhere. Supplies are also provided on a haphazard basis. There is no clear policy on the purchase of planes. There are very small ones and Flying Fortresses, nothing in between. Discipline exists in the higher echelons but not in the lower ones. Privileges are being exploited. A person who is strong, but not domineering, must be appointed to enforce discipline. The Army is not fulfilling its responsibilities to the Air Force; planes are being shot at. Our aircraft must have an identifying color and number. After the enemy air forces are destroyed, we must hit their water pipelines. We should use incendiary bombs. The head of the Army and the head of the Air Force must meet daily.

M. does not want to deal with appointments, but someone must have the authority to appoint an Air Council, a Training Officer, an Operations Officer, a Maintenance Officer, an Airfields Officer, a Personnel Officer, and above all, a Commander of the Air Force. Every branch head must be responsible for the activities in his own sphere. We need more training, better administration, better coordination between the Air Force and the Army, and a clear policy. I sent a letter on this matter to the Air Force.

July 25, 1948

M. brought me his proposals in the morning. He said that there should be 3 squadrons of fighter planes with 15 planes each, and another 10 in reserve, 55 planes altogether; a squadron of 18 medium bombers; a squadron of heavy bombers (8 Flying Fortresses); and an Air Transport Command with 15 Dakotas or 8 DC-6s. These planes and accompanying equipment will cost L1 million. Another L100,000 will be needed for spare parts and L500,000 for instruments. The Air Force will number 5000 men, though only 800–100 during peace time.

The Air Force goals will be: 1. to destroy the enemy air forces; 2. to assist the Army and Navy on all levels; 3. to attack the enemy's strategic points, in an attempt to cripple him militarily and undermine his desire to go on fighting; 4. to provide air transport inside the country and to other countries; 5. to train Sabras.

M. proposed that we eliminate the post of Air Force Chief of Staff and replace the present Commander of the Air Force. He suggested that we appoint a Commander of the Air Force who will serve as his own Chief of Staff, holding the same rank as all members of the General Staff, namely one rank lower than the Chief of Staff. He suggested that Aharon Remez be appointed Commander of the Air Force, with Hyman Schechtman serving as his Deputy. I told M. that, in general, I agreed with his proposals, but that I had to consult with the General Staff about separating the Air Force from the Army.

Aharon Remez proposed that Hyman be appointed Commander and that he be Hyman's Deputy. M., whom I saw afterward, agreed.

July 27, 1948

I asked Yigael how soon we would be ready for battle should fighting break out again. He told me that once the Government had decided on the size of the army and the General Staff had decided on its structure, it would take another month to complete preparations.

July 29, 1948

Golda Meir has returned from America. Over $50 million was raised. We will receive 66 percent of $45 million.

Swearing In the Army ★ Financial Situation Critical ★ Proposal to Establish Work Camps for Immigrants

The Israel Defense Forces had three *formal beginnings*. On May 26, 1948, the Provisional Government issued an ordinance establishing an army "consisting of land, naval, and air forces." It prohibited "the establishment or maintenance of any military unit outside the IDF." On May 30, 1948, the Prime Minister and Minister of Defense published an Order of the Day signaling the establishment of the Israel Defense Forces. On June 27, 1948, soldiers began to take their Oath of Allegiance, based on Section 3 of the Israel Defense Forces Ordinance: "Every man serving in the IDF must pledge allegiance to the State of Israel, its laws, and its legally constituted authorities."

The words "formal beginnings" are emphasized for two reasons: (1) the Defense Forces were an outgrowth of the Hagana, which had existed for decades, and of other military units, particularly the Jewish Brigade, which had been established within the framework of the British Army during the Second World War; (2) the unification and permanent organization of the Defense Forces began during the War of Independence and was accomplished mainly after the adoption of the Military Service Law in September 1949. It was impossible in a single day, particularly during the heavy fighting that preceded the establishment of the Defense Forces, to overcome all conflicts of authority, dissident tendencies, and lack of discipline, of which the majority of commanders complained when they met with the Defense Minister on June 18.

The first swearing-in ceremony took place on June 27, after a meeting of the Defense Minister with twenty-one senior officers (heads of General Staff branches and leading commanders). Before the ceremony, the minister called on every officer present to adopt a Hebrew name. Dan Epstein changed his name to Even, Yigal Feikovitz to Allon, Yigael Sukelnik to Yadin (his Hagana code name), Yehezkel Saharov to Sahar, Israel Zavlo-dovsky to Amir, Michael Rabinovitz to Bengal, Michael Schechter to Shoham, Moshe Zalitsky to Carmel, Moshe Lehrer to Zadok, Zvi Leshziner to Ayalon, Fritz Eisenstadt to Shalom Eshet, Shlomo Rabinovitz to Shamir, Shmuel Rappaport to Admon, and Shmuel Koch to Avidan. On the same occasion, two people who already had Hebrew surnames adopted new ones: Eliahu Cohen became Ben-Hur, and Joseph Rohel became Avidar. Only one commander, Chaim Laskov, was allowed to keep his previous name, out of respect to his mother.

The Chief of Staff, Yacov Dori (formerly Dostrovsky) was absent because of illness. The Oath of Allegiance was as follows: "I hereby pledge to remain faithful to the State of Israel, its laws and its legally consituted authorities, to accept unconditionally the discipline of the Israel Defense Forces, to obey all orders and instructions given by authorized officers and to devote myself, even unto death, to the defense of the Homeland and of Israel's freedom."

After the commanders had gathered next to a blue-and-white flag, the Prime Minister read the text of the Oath. Then his aide-de-camp, Nehemia Argov, called on them one by one. Every commander in turn stepped forward toward the Prime Minister and, while standing at attention, called out "I so pledge." The Prime Minister then shook his hand and the commander returned to his place. At the end of the ceremony the Prime Minister declared:

> Commanders! You—and your soldiers—are enjoying a great honor denied to tens and hundreds of thousands of the Children of Israel in all the countries of Exile over many generations, namely to serve in the Army of Israel, in Israel's Homeland.
>
> The Oath that you have just taken links you with the Hebrew commanders from the days of Joshua, the fighting and liberating Judges, the Kings of Israel and Judea, Nehemia, the Maccabees, the heroes of the war against the Romans in the days of the Second Temple and afterward. This chain was broken with the death of Bar Kokhba and Rabbi Akiva, but it has now been reforged. The Army of Israel stands ready again to go to battle for the freedom of our people in their Homeland, the ingathering of the exiles, and the upbuilding of a country based on the principles of equality, justice, and peace as enunciated by the Prophets of Israel.
>
> The Jewish people returning to their land look forward to peace and friendship with their neighbors and to a more united mankind within the framework of the United Nations. But a cruel war and rearmament, forced upon them by international troublemakers and their hirelings among the rulers of the Arab states, has made it necessary for them to put aside this vision until the final victory of the Israel Defense Forces and the achievement of a true, stable, and just peace.
>
> You will be supported by the devoted, loyal, and able men and women who serve on land, on the sea, and in the air, who, moreover, strive to bring salvation to our people, as well as peace and progress to all the countries of the Middle East.

The commanders were authorized to administer the Oath of Allegiance to their men, and on the next day there were swearing-in ceremonies in the various units.

At a meeting of the Government after the ceremony, the Prime Minister reviewed the successes and failures of the struggle for Jerusalem. The Old City had been lost; the thirty-five had fallen;* the Etzion Bloc had been overrun. But the victories had been at least as important. Some neighborhoods in New Jerusalem, where no Jew had ever ventured, are now in Jewish hands. Our victories in Jerusalem have not been properly appreciated, he said. Even if the situation had been reversed, and Arab forces in the city had been twice as large as the Jewish forces, not one Jewish neighborhood would have been abandoned. At this point there are no Arabs left in Jerusalem, except in the Old City, where the Jews are a small minority, mostly members of the old Yishuv.

The enormous achievements in Jerusalem have been overshadowed, to some extent, by the slaughter of the members of the Hadassah convoy in Sheikh Jarrah. The Mandatory Government was responsible for that disaster: it neither prevented it nor allowed the Hagana to come to the assistance of the convoy. We cannot ignore a third, very important factor, namely, that Jerusalem is surrounded by Arab territory. This was the source of Jerusalem's weakness, and is a grave accusation against our settlement efforts. But we would be committing a serious injustice if we looked upon Jerusalem as a city of failures. We have enjoyed enormous successes, and our conquests may be of decisive historical importance, paving the way for an eventual change in Jerusalem's situation.

Shertok declared that Kol Yisrael [radio station Voice of Israel] should broadcast the story of what happened in Jerusalem. A campaign of slander was being carried out against the Provisional Government over Jerusalem, as over the Etzel ship. It is being intimated that Etzel was responsible for the successes in Jerusalem, while all the failures were the fault of the Hagana and the Israel Defense Forces. Since our soldiers will pledge allegiance to the Israel Defense Forces tomorrow, they should be told the real story of what occurred in Jerusalem.

As far as the *Altalena* incident is concerned, the Foreign Minister said, public opinion in general and Jewish public opinion in particular have supported the Government. This immediate and decisive reaction, particularly, raised its prestige in the eyes of the United States government and of the representatives of the major powers in Washington. The only person to express concern over the events in Kfar Vitkin and Tel Aviv, to claim that these constituted a violation of the truce—since immigrants had entered and arms had been received without either being supervised by the Mediator—was a representative of Bernadotte. The Foreign Minister sent a sharp protest. A cable we subsequently received from Rhodes indicated that Bernadotte disagreed with his representative's letter and appreciated the Israel Government's stand.

As to the Negev: the Egyptians, moving just before the second truce came into effect, seized the crossroads to the Negev. After discussing this matter with the Egyptians, Bernadotte declared that we had the right to send convoys along the road. On June 25 we sent a convoy led by Bonde, Bernadotte's Chief of Staff. The Egyptians refused to permit it to proceed. At that moment a plane belonging to Bernadotte's group hovered overhead. The Egyptians fired at it and forced it to land. These shots led to the rumors that Kfar Warburg and Be'er Tuvia had been attacked from the air.

---

* On January 17, 1948, a company of thirty-five Hagana men, attempting to reinforce hard-pressed fighters, were all slaughtered—EDITORS

When the Egyptians refused to allow our convoy to pass, Bonde tore out a page from his notebook, wrote something down, and gave the paper to his communications officer, who brought it to us. Bonde had written that the Egyptians violated the truce and the Israeli forces, therefore, were free to act against the Egyptians. At 10:30 A.M. on June 25, 1948, after the Foreign Minister had consulted with Yigael Yadin, the Chief of Operations, he announced to the press that the Defense Forces would utilize the permission given to them at the appropriate time and place. (The Minister of Defense was then in Jerusalem.) The General Staff felt that it would take at least four or five days to prepare our forces for action against the Egyptians. There was a minor violation of the truce in the north by Kaukji, who paid dearly for it (fifty of his men were killed and fifty wounded). The Arab armies apparently are not ready to violate the truce. The Rhodes talks have not yet brought any progress toward peace.

Finance Minister Kaplan reported on the State's grave financial problems. The economy approaches a crisis point because of the lack of funds inside the country, he warned. The liquidity ratio of the banks has dropped far below a reasonable minimum, and they find it difficult to lend money even to their best customers. The Electric Corporation and the Nesher Cement Company could not obtain the PL135,000 they needed for fuel, and the Government had to give them the required credit. PL3.5 million will be needed for defense and PL5 to 6 million for other purposes during June.

Expenditures during July will exceed PL5 million, mainly because of increased defense spending. We must discuss the national budget. The State will have an income of PL1 million in June. The Finance Committee of the Provisional State Council has agreed to increase excise taxes and customs, which will bring in another PL250,000. This means that we will be PL4 million short in July. We will be able to cover this with the PL5 million Popular Loan, of which PL4 million has already been received. We have also been helped by funds from the Jewish Agency in the United States and to a certain extent by abandoned property. Overseas income is being used entirely for the purchase of arms, and is not included in the budget. In the present situation, the banks are unable to provide credit. Temporary currency must be issued if we are to prevent financial strangulation. This can give us some PL10 million, which will balance the budget for two or three months. We have encountered many difficulties in our attempts to print currency in the United States, Switzerland, and England. We began preparations as early as October 1947, but were told then that we could not prepare currency until we had a government. In the meantime, the Anglo-Palestine Bank has made preparations to issue banknotes, which can be made available in substantial sums, for use as legal tender, within a week or two.

According to our advisors, we should be able to establish a national bank responsible for the issuance of currency. This institution, the Bank of Israel, would have no commercial functions, but would serve as a central bank. Meanwhile there is still the problem of keeping the economy moving for the next five or six months. Since we do not have the time to wait until the Bank of Israel can be established, Kaplan suggested that we authorize the Anglo-Palestine Bank to print banknotes, and that, in the interval, these serve as legal tender. We will pledge to exchange them for Israeli pounds once the Bank of Israel is established. From a certain date the present pound will cease to be legal currency. People will be given three to four weeks to exchange it for the new banknotes.

The Anglo-Palestine Bank agrees to such an arrangement on two conditions: (1) that we proclaim its banknotes to be temporary currency; (2) that they be kept in circulation for at least five years. The minister would favor a period of six months to a year, until a government is established that can decide otherwise. The Finance Committee has approved of this plan, and Kaplan proposed that its implementation be entrusted to Mr. Bernstein, Mr. Horowitz, and himself, so that the banknotes could be issued within two or three weeks. Some of the Palestinian pounds will be transferred to England, where they will be exchanged for sterling. The British government must agree to this arrangement. The sterling will be used for purchases in Britain.

The Kaplan proposal was accepted in principle and will be brought up for final approval after two points are clarified: (1) whether it would allow Britain to gain control over us, because theoretically the Anglo-Palestine Bank is a British institution; and (2) whether, alternatively, we could print our own currency within a short period.

The Minister of Immigration reported on the immigration picture. It had been planned to bring in twenty thousand immigrants—twelve thousand from Cyprus and eight thousand from Europe—during the month of the truce. But this plan fell through when the British decided to prohibit the departure of our people from Cyprus, even those who are not of military age. Nahum Goldmann cabled Shertok that the British had agreed to allow the departure from Cyprus of people who are not of military age, but no such information has reached the authorities in Cyprus. The *Pan Crescent* and the *Pan York*, which brought fifteen thousand "illegal" immigrants—albeit not in very comfortable conditions—were subsequently seized in Haifa by the British, who still controlled the port. The ships were released only today.

An emissary has been sent to Cyprus to determine whether the authorities have agreed to the departure of people not of military age. If so, these two ships could bring in three thousand immigrants. There are also problems in regard to immigration from Europe, as ships did not want to sail until the truce conditions had been accepted. Thirteen hundred immigrants have arrived since the beginning of the new truce. Another twelve hundred are expected by the end of June. Three ships are now on their way to the country. Immigrants are also being brought in by plane. Three of our vessels, originally used to bring "illegal" immigrants, were sent from this country. Each of the three—the *Ayalon*, the *Lo Tafhedenu*, and the *Yehiam*—can carry five hundred people. Two other ships, *Medinat Israel* and *Lanitzahon*, can each carry three hundred passengers. Up to five thousand immigrants may arrive by the end of the truce on July 9.

Half of the immigrants who have already come are of military age and have been sent to camps. They remain idle, being forbidden to receive military training.

Rosenblueth asked whether immigrants are also coming from Western Europe and South Africa. He was told that they were coming from all countries. Important military experts have arrived from South Africa and Canada. Some non-Jews wish to join the Israel Defense Forces.

Several Cabinet members stressed the importance of purchasing ships, because of British influence on European shipping companies, which might be dissuaded from transporting immigrants. It was also proposed that the newcomers be sent to work camps as soon as possible, since they were prohibited only from receiving military training, not from working. The Minister of Immigration said that selective immigration was necessary as long as the war continued, in order to increase Israel's military and economic strength. This was not the time for sick people and social cases, or an undue percentage of children and old people. The Foreign Minister and the Minister of Immigration were charged with investigating the possibility of establishing work camps for new immigrants, while the truce provisions remained in force.

Section 7. British Evacuation; Another Bernadotte Plan

Mandatory Regime Ends ★ Haifa Port Comes Under Jewish Control

THE Mandatory Government left the country on May 15. The High Commissioner departed, taking with him his entire administrative staff and most of the British military forces. But part of the British Army remained in Haifa, where it established enclaves in the city and in the port.

On June 29 there were obvious preparations for an end to these last vestiges of British rule. British camps in Tira, Bat Galim, etc., were systematically demolished. Explosions were heard all day long in Haifa. The British destroyed weapons and equipment which they did not manage to load on their ships or which could not be removed. Work in the civilian section of the port went on normally, since it was not subject to British Army control. In the military section, however, activity was feverish as the British began to move in their military stores.

At 6:30 A.M. British soldiers at the Haifa-Acre-Nazareth crossroads stopped all vehicles, demanded identity cards from the passengers, and then took them to a nearby field. They were eventually released, but were not allowed to continue their journey. The soldiers explained that they were searching for two heavy tanks that had been stolen from the airfield during the night. General Macmillan told the Mayor of Haifa, Shabtai Levy, that he would not participate in the Municipality's farewell dinner at the Zion Hotel until the two tanks were returned.

At 4 P.M. the British Army transferred the buildings and facilities that had been under its control to the Haifa Municipality in the presence of UN Observers. Only foreign correspondents were invited to the ceremony. The British commander announced that he would leave the country, and British control over the enclaves would end on July 1. From that date not a single British soldier would remain on the soil of the Land of Israel.

At 8 A.M. June 30 management of the entire port was finally turned over to Israel. General Macmillan stated in his Bulletin Number 8 that his legal jurisdiction over the military enclaves and military rule would end on July 1. There was great commotion that morning in the port. All equipment that could be transferred was loaded on the ships; the last soldiers boarded them as well. The sole remaining British bastion in lower Haifa, the giant Hayat Building (which overlooked the entrance to the port and housed Regional Police Headquarters), was turned over to the Israeli authorities at 9 A.M. The building and nearby houses had been surrounded by a six-meter-high barbed-wire fence, creating a kind of Haifa "Bevingrad." The British turned over the area to an American colonel on Count Bernadotte's staff, who then presented it to the Acting Commander of the Haifa District Police, Baruch Gofer. Israeli policemen hastened to check all the rooms, then hoisted a giant national flag on the roof to the accompaniment of stormy applause.

The last British flag on Israeli soil was lowered at 2:30 P.M., when General Macmillan left the city. He was preceded by fully armed British naval commandos, who reached the port in battle formation. Planes from a British aircraft carrier hovered overhead. Macmillan shook hands with the British and American consuls, and then departed. The absence of the Jewish Mayor and Jewish community leaders was conspicuous. On Macmillan's departure the Jewish policemen quickly took over control of the port. On that last day twenty-five hundred British troops left the country.

At 2:30 the Israeli Navy entered the Haifa Port.

After Abba Hushi had informed him that the last British soldier would leave Haifa Port at 12:30 P.M., the Prime Minister decided to go to the city. He reached Haifa at 6 P.M., while the Army, Navy, Air Force, Police, and Municipality were holding a celebration in the port. Israel Air Force planes flew overhead. The ships of the Israeli Navy sailed through the harbor. The Prime Minister brought the greetings of the Government to the liberated city of Haifa. Israel, he said, would not forget either the assistance she had received from Britain thirty-one years before, nor her British friends, the Balfours, Wedgwoods, and Wingates. If the British people and the British labor movement could force their government to stop its dirty war against Israel, she would be prepared to forget the disgraceful White Paper episode. The Prime Minister declared that Haifa was second in importance only to Jerusalem, Israel's eternal capital. The heroes of the Hagana, he added, had the privilege of conquering Haifa, while the British were still the rulers of the country. Israel is far stronger now than she was on the day that the State was established, he went on. The Army, Navy, and Air Force are ready to repel the invading armies, and, should fighting begin again at the end of the truce, they will accomplish all over the country what the Hagana accomplished in Haifa.

Israel's Membership in the United Nations ★ Reactions to the Bernadotte Proposals

While the Prime Minister was in Haifa (June 30, 1948), the Provisional Government met under the chairmanship of Kaplan to discuss two urgent matters: a report from Dr. Mordekhai Eliash, who had returned from a Government mission to Lake Success, and the far-reaching proposals of UN Mediator Bernadotte.

Dr. Eliash had dealt with the question of Israel's membership in the United Nations. Friends of Israel in the US State Department, who were also close to Secretary of State George C. Marshall, had suggested that Israel present her request for membership before the autumn, when the General Assembly was scheduled to meet. Dr. Eliash was of the opinion that Israel stood no chance of being accepted as long as she had only a Provisional Government.

An East-West dispute had meanwhile developed over Italy's application for UN membership. Soviet Russia had made it clear that she would not vote for Italy's admission unless East European communist states were admitted as well. The question of setting political conditions for UN membership, raised by this dispute, was referred to the International Court in The Hague. It decided, by a vote of nine to six, that no political conditions, aside from those in the Charter, could be set for UN membership. The minority of six, including representatives of both East and West (England, France, Russia, the United States, Poland, and Yugoslavia), said that membership was a political question; that the conditions laid down in the UN Charter therefore were not, in themselves, sufficient.

The Charter stipulates that an application for membership must be initially approved by the Security Council, and only afterward brought to the General Assembly for a final vote. There are five large states with veto power in the Security Council. If there is no veto, a resolution must be supported by at least seven of the eleven members if it is to be adopted. Dr. Eliash believed that there was reason to fear a British veto. Even if Britain abstained, he doubted whether it will be possible to obtain the necessary seven votes as long as Israel lacks an elected government capable of guaranteeing the country's fidelity to the UN Charter. Dr. Eliash recommended that the election of a regular Government by a constituent assembly should be the first step—only then Israel would stand a chance of acceptance by the UN. True, India was taken into the UN while she still had a Provisional Government, but she was already a member of the British Commonwealth.

There were two other major stumbling blocks: Israel's borders and the status of Jerusalem, which, according to the UN resolution, was not to be part of the Jewish State. Dr. Eliash thought that we should uphold Jerusalem's international status, because otherwise the Arabs may be given control of the city.

No decisions were taken in regard to his report, as, in the meantime, Foreign Minister Shertok arrived with the Mediator's proposals. The Foreign Minister announced that four documents had been received from Count Bernadotte: (1) a private letter; (2) an introduction to his proposals; (3) the proposals, which Bernadotte calls suggestions; (4) addenda to these suggestions.

In his letter, Bernadotte states that his sugestions are only food for thought. He asks us not to take any public stand on them until we have discussed them with him. He also sent the same letter and addenda to the Prime Minister of Egypt, who heads the Arab League committee charged with discussing the Palestine question with the Mediator. In the second document Bernadotte explains how he regards his UN mission. He believes that the truce, which he successfully arranged, creates the proper atmosphere for negotiations. His proposals, he says, take into account the hopes and fears of both sides. He realizes that he cannot demand that either side compromise on matters of principle, but he does see two issues which provide a common denominator: peace between the Jews and the Arabs, and cooperation in the economic sphere.

The third and main document, containing his suggestions, consists of nine brief clauses. In the first, he proposes that the original area of the Mandate be combined in a bilateral Union of two members, Jewish and Arab. The second clause, dealing with the borders, proposes that they be determined in negotiations between the two sides, with the Mediator's assistance and on the basis of his proposals. The third clause states that the Union will deal with economic matters of common interest to both sides, including customs duties and excise taxes, and carry out joint development projects. It will also coordinate foreign and defense policies. The fourth clause provides that the Union be headed by a joint council or by other organizations acceptable to both sides. The fifth clause defines the limits of the Union's authority; each member, it says, will enjoy full freedom in its foreign relations, though the policies of the two will be coordinated. The sixth clause, concerning immigration, proposes that each member will be free to act as it sees fit in this sphere for the first two years after the establishment of the Union. Subsequently, each member will have the right to demand that the Union council discuss the immigration policy of the other. If the council cannot reach a conclusion, the issue will be turned over to the UN's Economic and Social Committee, which will make a final and binding decision on the basis of the country's social and economic absorptive capacity. The seventh clause states that there will be freedom of religion and conscience. The eighth concerns protection of and access to Holy Places. The ninth declares that people uprooted as a result of the hostilities will have the right to return to their former homes and to receive their property back.

The addendum to the main document dwells on the borders. It is, again, presented as material for discussion. The proposals to be considered include: (1) inclusion of the Negev, in whole or in part, in the Arab area; (2) inclusion of western Galilee, in whole or in part, in the Jewish section; (3) inclusion of Jerusalem in the Arab section, with municipal autonomy for the Jews and protection for the Holy Places; (4) reconsideration of Jaffa's position; (5) establishment of a free port in Haifa, including the refineries and the oil pipeline terminal; (6) establishment of a free airport at Lydda.

The Foreign Minister told the Mediator's representative, who brought the proposals to him, that two clauses were sufficient in themselves to make the whole plan unacceptable, namely, those on immigration and on Jerusalem. While the Jews might agree to the internationalization of Jerusalem, despite their bitter experience, they would not agree under any circumstances to Arab control of the city and would fight to prevent it.

It was regrettable that the Mediator made the mistake of putting his proposals in writing. Representatives of the Israel Government who were in Rhodes with the Mediator learned privately that his proposals were actually a compromise between the conflicting approaches among the members of the UN delegation. Ralph Bunche and John Reedman are relatively friendly, while Stravropolis and Mohan are hostile. Our friends understand that we cannot accept this plan, but they suggest that we should not be the first to reject it; we should leave that to the Arabs.

The Foreign Minister announced that the Prime Minister, who had to go to Haifa, had left his written comments on the Bernadotte proposals, as follows:

> 1. It is very desirable from our point of view that the truce last for four to six weeks (I doubt whether this will be possible, and we should be ready for a renewal of fighting at any time).
>
> 2. Therefore, we are interested in a *rapid end* to Court Bernadotte's mission.
>
> 3. His suggestions (whether he knows it or not) are basically a reflection of Bevin's viewpoint.
>
> 4. We can accept the advice of our friends to delay our reply until after the Arabs have reacted.
>
> 5. There is no need to comment on every specific proposal, but we must make it clear to Count Bernadotte (orally and in writing) that under no circumstances will we consider any proposal that diminishes Israel's sovereignty, permits outside interference in her immigration policy or envisions placing Jerusalem *in any way at all* under an Arab regime.

6. We are not obligated to argue with him about other territorial questions until such time as there is agreement on sovereignty (and immigration).

7. We should make it crystal clear that our *absolute* rejection of his proposals on sovereignty, immigration, and Jerusalem does not imply our acceptance of his proposals on other matters.

8. We should express our willingness to hold direct talks with the Arabs.

9. I doubt whether it is worth our while to accept Count Bernadotte's suggestion that we go to Rhodes, though we should not make this a question of principle.

Shertok spoke of his argument the previous day with Rabbi Berlin, a proponent of the internationalization of Jerusalem. Perhaps, he said, this is the most desirable solution, the only one that will safeguard the city. But it must be clear that we will fight against an Arab Jerusalem. We will not go to Rhodes to see Bernadotte if he consults with the Arabs in their own countries, he said. But if the Arabs are willing to go to Rhodes, then we will also go.

The Bernadotte documents did not mention an extension of the truce. The Arabs favor an extension, as do the British and the Americans. The Russians, the Foreign Minister believes, will do anything we ask them to do in this matter. The Arabs favor a truce because they are afraid that they will suffer setbacks in further fighting and that England, for fear of American public opinion, will not support them to the extent they desire. It is reported that Azam, the Egyptian Prime Minister, told the British in Cairo: if the fighting starts again and you do not back us to the hilt, all the Arab governments will fall and I will disappear. The British are interested in a truce because, in its absence, they will be forced either to betray the Arabs or to support them in opposition to the United States. The Americans also are against a renewal of the fighting because they want to drag out the truce until after the November elections.

Zisling suggested we announce that, in the absence of the Prime Minister and other members of the Government, we have decided to postpone the discussion until Sunday. Only after the Government's conclusions have been considered by the Provisional State Council can there be a meeting with Bernadotte. He also suggested that Shertok's position on traveling to Rhodes be adopted. Finally, he urged the Government to announce that preparations were being stepped up for a possible renewal of fighting at the conclusion of the truce.

It was decided to bring the Mediator's proposals to the next meeting of the Provisional Government on July 2. The State Council meeting scheduled for July 1 would not be postponed, but devoted to other topics. Meanwhile the Mediator's proposals would not be published. At the July 1 meeting of the State Council the Prime Minister announced that, since the Government had not yet discussed Count Bernadotte's proposals, they could not be brought to the Council. The Government, he added, would consider them in a few days.

The Council retroactively accorded the Israel Defense Forces Ordinance of June 26, 1948, the status of a Provisional State Council Ordinance and gave retroactive approval to the activities of the Prime Minister and other ministers before they were given legal authority by the Provisional Government.

The Government met again on July 2 to discuss the Bernadotte ideas. The Foreign Minister announced that he had told Bernadotte's representative that we are ready to go to Rhodes to discuss his proposals with him if the Arabs go there as well, but that we will not travel to see him if he travels to see the Arabs. Our friends at the UN had also suggested to us that we should not be the first to comment on the proposals. According to the press, the Arabs have rejected them and are unwilling to go to Rhodes.

The Foreign Minister's opinion that an extension of the truce would be to our advantage was reinforced by his visit to Jerusalem. His view was shared by the Army and by the Jerusalemites. In light of the situation, the Prime Minister suggested that, despite the negative aspects of some of Bernadotte's proposals, Israel should not break off contact with him. The Foreign Minister was not certain that it would be possible to avoid breaking off negotiations, though he did not believe this should frighten us. Even if Bernadotte announced to the Security Council that he has failed in his efforts, the Council presumably will call on both sides to continue to observe the truce. Both Britain and the United States are interested in a continuation for reasons mentioned at the previous meeting. Britain's economic situation is very weak, and she needs American financial assistance. According to our information, the British Ambassador in Washington wrote to the Foreign Office that the American government's sympathy for Israel was not an election gesture, but reflected the attitude of the American public. According to the American Ambassador in London, Bevin's position in general, and in regard to Israel in particular, was weakening. The British, therefore, favor a continuation of the truce. The State Department wants it to go on because a renewal of the fighting would obligate America to give greater assistance to Israel, and thus come into conflict with the Arabs; this, the State Department is loth to do. Despite the opposition of the State Department, President Truman was determined to send James MacDonald as Ambassador to Israel. Truman will have to go so far as to extend de jure recognition to Israel. The Americans were also about to give us a $100 million loan. They know that we are receiving arms from Czechoslovakia, now a communist state.

The Foreign Minister read a cable received from our representatives in Washington: "Lebanon and Egypt recently asked Britain for guidance. She sent on the request to the State Department and suggested that the United States and Britain work jointly on the problem. The State Department refused to offer any suggestions. It announced that it would be ready to work together with Britain within the framework of a plan based on the following principles: (a) recognition of a compact State of Israel (this seems to imply criticism of the borders); (b) American and British approval for an exchange of populations in the area; (c) support for a customs union between Israel and Trans-Jordan; (d) support for Israel as a bulwark against the penetration of foreign influences into the Middle East."

The message also stated that England has agreed that, should the truce fail, action be taken in accordance with Section 7 of the UN Charter (dealing with the imposition of sanctions). The Americans are very interested in Israel's being recognized by other countries before the General Assembly meeting in September, which would greatly strengthen their position.

The Foreign Minister suggested that the Mediator be informed that Israel cannot accept any limitations on her sovereignty or on immigration. Moreover, an Arab Jerusalem is out of the question. He proposed that Israel express her opposition to some of his other ideas, particularly a free port in Haifa and a free airfield at Lydda. These and other questions involving relations with the Arabs should be taken up solely in direct negotiations between the two sides.

The issue of immigration while the truce continues should also be raised, he said. We have three problems to take up with Bernadotte: (1) How do various governments interpret his instructions on immigration? Switzerland, for example, has banned the departure for Israel of Jews between the ages of fifteen and fifty-five. Other governments have given far-reaching interpretations to the Mediator's restrictions. Though we are, in fact, overcoming the difficulties involved, there have been delays. (2) We cannot agree to a continuation of the situation in Cyprus. While Bernadotte has approved the immigration of a limited number of persons of military age, the British have refused to allow the Jews in Cyprus to depart. (3) The position of the immigrants of military age must be reexamined if the truce continues. They lived for years in Nazi concentration camps, and then in other camps after the victory over Nazism. Now, in Israel, they are again in detention camps for an unlimited period, that is, for as long as the truce continues. Some will obviously escape, and then we will be accused of violating the truce. We should announce, therefore, in advance that we do not agree to these conditions.

Bernstein argued for a continuation of the truce, not because of Jerusalem or other domestic considerations, but because new fighting would not bring new victories, while defeats could cause incalculable losses. Bernadotte's proposals represent, in fact, British views. Britain wants to keep an outpost in the Middle East, under Abdullah, rather than under other Arabs. The Bernadotte plan places the economic burden of maintaining Abdullah on Israel. This is what his proposals actually mean. We should announce, Bernstein went on, that we have nothing against links with Abdullah. While we are ready to accept a civil union, this does not mean a division of income but rather a single tariff. We would be willing to allow Trans-Jordan to use Israeli currency, and to reach an agreement on roads and the railway. In that way we could maintain our complete independence, and at the same time help Trans-Jordan. This interests the British more than the borders.

The Prime Minister agreed that a continuation of the truce was desirable, but not absolutely necessary. We must be ready for war at any moment, he warned. We will be capable of dealing with the Arabs, unless they receive open military support from a Great Power. Barring that possibility, we will be ready, in another four to six weeks, to confront and defeat all the Arab states, even though we have had considerable difficulty in obtaining certain kinds of heavy equipment because of the British naval inspection system.

The sea, he explained, will play an important but not a decisive role in the struggle, particularly if it lasts for an extended period. The Arabs will not hesitate to sink an immigrant ship, and every immigrant will be taking a risk. No one criticized the Arabs when they bombarded Jerusalem—something even Hitler didn't do during the war. No one said anything about the destruction of the synagogues in the Old City and in the New. In this situation our naval strength is extremely important, both militarily and with regard to immigration. One of the difficulties facing our enemies is their lack of communications. This is Trans-Jordan's Achilles' heel. But the Egyptians have sea transport. They can bombard Haifa and Tel Aviv from the sea. We must obtain the necessary naval guns which are not influenced by the rocking of a ship. It is reasonable to assume that we will be properly equipped in four to six weeks. One cannot speak with absolute certainty in this matter; anyone who says he is absolutely certain is being irresponsible. Insofar as one can predict future events, it appears that we will be able to crush Trans-Jordan, Lebanon, and Syria. We will not conquer Egypt, but Egypt, in isolation, will find it hard to go on fighting.

Unlike Mr. Bernstein, the Prime Minister saw nothing to be gained from talks with Abdullah. If the UN had the power to give us what was allocated to us in its November 29 resolution, we would accept it; but the UN has proven its helplessness.

During the fighting several points, which should have been clear in advance, have become self-evident. Jerusalem is paralyzed. Theoretically, it could exist as an internationalized city, but we now know what an international regime means. It did not prevent the bombardment of the city or even try to do so. Had the Arabs conquered New Jerusalem when they conquered the Old City, nothing would have been done against them. We cannot ignore this situation, nor the fact that our country is made up of narrow strips of land, except in the Negev, which is a single unit. We have held on to these strips, which is certainly one of the miracles of the situation. None of us would have declared war in order to improve our borders, but war was declared on us, and in this war we have held our own. There are things that cannot be decided upon before the proper time arrives. There are hours of great significance that influence the course of history for many years to come. The period in which we are living will be remembered for a very long time. What we do or fail to do now, whether we succeed or fail, will determine the pattern of events for the next generation or two.

The present British government is not likely to fall, Ben-Gurion said: "I do not believe that Bevin's position is threatened. As far as I know, it is quite strong, both in England and in several European countries. We should not depend on miracles, but solely on ourselves. Only if we invest great efforts and enthusiasm will great miracles take place."

A state will not be created without resort to force, he went on. We must accept this fact, and use it to our advantage. The section in the old Peel Commission report on the difficulties faced by Britain in carrying out the Balfour Declaration makes a significant point. The Commission says that had the Declaration been implemented immediately, in the course of a war, it could have been completely fulfilled; but it proved impossible to implement it over an extended period. We did not want a war, but one was forced upon us. Now we are being threatened with the specter of an Arab invasion in order to persuade us to agree to a reduction in the size if the State. We will not accept the conditions that they are trying to impose on us. We can and will prepare ourselves for the decisive contest.

There is no reason to oppose a pact with the Arabs. There is also no justification for opposing a customs union, on condition that we have the upper hand and that immigration will be under our control. We can also join a federation, but only as a completely independent State. Our links with the Arab world can benefit both ourselves and all mankind. But what happens in this sphere does not depend on us. If all the Arabs feel the same way as Azam Pasha, and he is their most important independent leader, there is no hope at present of reaching agreement. We must be ready for a decision by force of arms if we cannot achieve our aims by peaceful means.

The Prime Minister was not speaking here of our maximum demands, because they are far from clear. If we make significant progress in our generation, that will be achievement enough. But unless we can obtain the minimum conditions that will permit us to go on with the ingathering of the exiles in a quiet and orderly manner for at least fifteen years (the period during which we can expect peace in the world), our accomplishments will not have lasting consequences.

Shertok: Not everyone believes that there will be ten to fifteen years of world peace. Churchill feels otherwise.

Ben-Gurion: We have a historic chance to establish a State. It is up to our generation to exploit this opportunity to the maximum, and that involves the use of force.

Gruenbaum violently opposed the views of Bernstein and the Foreign Minister. He said that we should not adopt a defensive attitude in our relations with Bernadotte, but should go on the offensive. We don't need people to tell us that we are good children; we must show them that we are capable of being bad children as well. All the restrictions and limitations are directed against us. We have been much stronger than the British and Americans expected; now we must speak in an entirely different tone. He agreed with Ben-Gurion's view that the contest will not end in a diplomatic and peaceful manner, but will be settled by force. The same is true in regard to Jerusalem.

We have a strong legal basis for our demand, namely the November 29 resolution, he said. Though this basis has been shaken, it still exists. Count Bernadotte cannot deny that fact. We must make it clear to him that he is obliged to adhere to the November 29 resolution, and that his current proposals are not in accord with that resolution. What will we achieve by my approach? It will guarantee the support of the Soviet Union and her satellites. This will, in turn, put the United States in a difficult position. The South Americans will also support us. If we do not do as I suggest, we will lose the assistance of the Soviet Union. She will say that if Israel deviates from the November 29 resolution, there is no reason why Russia should fight to uphold it. It has become clear to me that the Christians are not in the least interested in Jerusalem. No Christian state, not even the Vatican, is willing to fight for an international Jerusalem. They would be more than happy to give the city to the Arabs, just to get it out of the hands of the British. Let's not fool ourselves. If we lack a territorial link with Jerusalem, it will wither away, whatever its status. Our political offecsive should also take into account revisions of our borders.

Shertok: Not on the basis of the November 29 resolution.

Gruenbaum: I accept the November 29 resolution as a starting point, but I don't feel bound to abide by every detail. The Minister of Defense says that we need four to six weeks more to prepare ourselves. If I knew all the details, perhaps I would favor an extension of the truce for a longer period. But I see no sign that time is working in our favor. I believe that we should: (a) go on the political offensive, basing ourselves on the November 29 resolution; (b) demand that the future of Jerusalem be determined by the results of the war; (c) make it clear that we do not fear an end to the truce, even today or tomorrow.

Rosenblueth said that there were no differences of opinion in regard to Jerusalem, immigration, or the maintenance of Israel's independence. But he did not agree with Ben-Gurion that the issues could be settled only by force. The British and Americans, he said, will not let us achieve a final and decisive victory. It is also questionable whether we will be in a position to triumph decisively in a few additional weeks' time. Like Bernstein, I doubt whether we will be able to add to the victories we have already won.

Bernstein: I didn't say that. I only said that additional military victories will not help much in the political sphere.

Rosenblueth: In the military sphere our resources have been stretched to the breaking point, more so than is usual in other armies, and it is doubtful whether we can remedy the situation in four to six weeks of truce. The Israel Defense Forces achievements have indeed been extraordinary, but they have led to disorganization and very loose discipline. We face regular armies, which will gain in strength during the truce period. There is great danger in a continuation of the war. We are interested not only in a truce, but also in an end to the war. Negotiations are necessary. We should emphasize political activities, based, of course, on our military achievements. The November 29 resolution is where we begin. While there can be no compromise on three things—immigration, sovereignty, and Jerusalem—everything else is negotiable.

Rosenblueth favored the Galilee over the Negev, even if oil should be discovered in the Negev. Oil brings riches to a large nation, but disaster to a small and weak one, he said. A small nation with oil becomes a political football among the Great Powers. Nothing was to be gained from oil in the Negev, but a great deal was to be gained from western Galilee. He supported Bernstein's proposal for a customs union with Abdullah. In the political sphere, he said, we must strive for guarantees from the three Great Powers— Soviet Russia, the United States, and Great Britain—and not depend on our membership in the United Nations.

Zisling: There is no possibility at this point of an agreement between the Jews and the Arabs, the Jews and the British, or the Jews and the Americans. We must be ready for a decision by force of arms. In this respect, I agree with Ben-Gurion. We do not want our way only in regard to sovereignty, immigration, and Jerusalem. If we give up western Galilee, we will be endangering Haifa. At the same time, we cannot forego the Negev, where there are greater settlement opportunities than in the Galilee.

I am against a union with Abdullah. He is a British puppet and his country is the most backward of all the Arab nations. We must clearly state that we will not countenance a union with Abdullah. Arab rule in all or part of Jerusalem is out of the question, even if Jewish Jerusalem is attached to the State of Israel and a corridor is added between the city and the rest of the country. Jerusalem is surrounded by Arab villages, and a corridor would be an illusion. We must base our policies on one foundation, a willingness to fight. A truce of four to six weeks would be desirable, but this should not obscure our basic demands: sovereignty, immigration, Jerusalem, the Negev, and no Abdullah.

Shitreet reported on his talks with Monsignor Hakim and Daud el Issa. He believes that there is some change in the position of the Arabs. They are willing to accept the State if it does not have a distinctly Jewish character. They want the Jews and the Arabs to be equal in numbers and in rights. They are also willing to accept immigration, as long as it is not specifically Jewish immigration. Hakim, for his part, is primarily interested in the return of Christian Arabs. Arab attitudes have changed as a result of Jewish victories. We cannot afford to forego the Negev, which may have oil. Oil is not a disaster to a small country, as Mr. Rosenblueth believes. We should agree to an internationalized Jerusalem if we are guaranteed free access to the city. An exchange of populations would be of benefit to Jews and Arabs alike.

Rabbi Levin: I believe in miracles, but one does not depend on miracles. God will help us if we are realistic in our aims. We should not break off contact with the Mediator, because the truce serves to strengthen our position.

Bentov: I agree with Ben-Gurion that military strength is a very important factor, but it is not the only one.

Ben-Gurion: I also don't think it is the only one.

Bentov: Politics are also a weapon. A policy which lessens opposition is worth millions of bullets. A truce is clearly desirable. We must tell Bernadotte that we favor the November 29 resolution, perhaps with certain modifications. A union with Trans-Jordan is acceptable, but both partners must remain members of the UN. A coordinated foreign policy is possible, on condition that Abdullah foregoes agreements with foreign powers. We must oppose the granting of bases to other countries. This is a very important point. The British and their bases must be eliminated from the Middle East. There should be three Jews and three Arabs in the Council of the Israel-Trans-Jordan Union, with no outside members. I believe that we need part of western Galilee, but I think that it is not crucial that the southern part of the Negev be included within our borders.

Shapira: Shertok fears that the Arabs, under the influence of the British, will resume the war. While one does not depend on miracles, numbers alone are not the whole story in war. If we had added up the numbers on May 14, we would have concluded that there was no possibility of establishing a State of Israel. Our military situation then was much graver than it is now. There were many who wondered, particularly during the first week, how we could keep going. We survived because we had our backs to the wall. We felt there was no alternative to victory, and that helped us.

If we must choose between a peace settlement involving certain concessions (I know what I would be willing to concede, and what I would want in return), or a war, with incalculable results, then we should choose peace. But there are things about which there can be no compromise: sovereignty, immigration, and Jerusalem. The issues of sovereignty and immigration are clear to everyone, but the situation on Jerusalem must be clarified. If we obtain in Jerusalem what was decided upon in the November 29 resolution, we will have achieved a very great deal. We have recently heard talk about the need for a Jewish Jerusalem. People have suggested that the Government should be transferred to that city. This is a fine idea, but unrealistic.

I do not think we should turn down every item in Bernadotte's plan. The future of the Galilee and the Negev should be the subject of negotiations. I think that both Bernadotte and the British will accept the November 29 resolution with respect to Jerusalem. But I have the impression that they will not modify their views on the Negev. The exchange of territory must be dealt with in the negotiations; we cannot simply say no. We should investigate where it is possible to develop agriculture, and where it cannot be done. If we can achieve peace by exchanging territory, then we should do so.

Kaplan: Everyone longs for a peaceful solution, but Bernadotte's proposals do not raise the chances of such a solution. The Foreign Minister must make our disappointment and dissatisfaction clear to Bernadotte. His plan makes it seem that we have suffered a defeat and must now sue for peace at any price. I am for a truce, but not for an unlimited period. My reasons are economic, among others. Even during a truce, the army costs us P£4 million a month. This is a very heavy burden and one we cannot bear indefinitely. It undermines the foundation of our small and weak economy. This week we allocated P£210,000 to soldiers' families. The sum, though far from sufficient, is only one item in the defense budget. The 4 million pounds a month is just what we spend in this country; there are extremely large expenditures abroad. We should be very careful about a union with the Arabs. We should cooperate with many countries. A union with the Arabs involves grave dangers, for we would be under close supervision by those who stand behind Abdullah. Even without Bernadotte's intervention, we can allow Trans-Jordan, perhaps even Iraq or Iran, use of Haifa as a free port. But it cannot have extraterritorial status. We must ensure contiguous borders, and also a common border with Lebanon.

Ben-Gurion concluded with some remarks on Jerusalem: A Jewish Jerusalem is, of course, desirable, but it is a subject about which there are differences of opinion. True, Christianity has proven its bankruptcy on this issue, but this does not mean that the Christian world has abandoned Jerusalem. It should be clear that we will fight against an Arab Jerusalem, and those who want an internationalized city should realize that this can be achieved only by struggling against an Arab Jerusalem. Negotiations are now going on in connection with Mount Scopus. It has been suggested that the UN flag fly over the Hadassah Hospital and the buildings of the Hebrew University, and that our military forces be replaced by a 120-man police unit. I propose: (1) complete rejection of limitations on our sovereignty and on immigration, as well as any plan for an Arab Jerusalem; (2) support for the November 29 resolution, with such adjustments as were made necessary by the attack on us in violation of a UN decision, and our victory in a war that was forced upon us; (3) cooperation with Trans-Jordan, the nature of which will be the subject of negotiations.

It was decided to postpone a vote on all the issues until the regular meeting the following Sunday.

The next meeting of the State Council took place on July 7, 1948. The Prime Minister was unable to attend because of illness. Kaplan was in the chair.

The Foreign Minister reported on two talks with Count Bernadotte. At the first, Shertok presented him a letter expressing the Government's opposition to his proposals on Jerusalem, immigration, and sovereignty. Bernadotte said that he would reply in writing. They discussed the truce and the demilitarization of Jerusalem. When they met again, Bernadotte said that he was flying to Cairo to obtain the Egyptian reply, and would return in the afternoon. If both sides opposed a continuation of the truce, he would still suggest that it be extended for an additional three days, to give him an opportunity to evacuate his men and equipment. Shertok believes that Bernadotte wants three days' leeway to give the Security Council an opportunity to act.

Shertok told Bernadotte that the immigrants could not be kept in camps after they had already lived through Nazi concentration camps. That, Bernadotte replied, was why he had opposed their immigration. Shertok answered that from a humanitarian point of view they were in agreement, but differed on the conclusions that were to be drawn. He proposed that every immigrant of military age be given a card stating that he could not be mobilized or given military training, and that UN inspectors be allowed to visit them in their homes or places of work. Bernadotte agreed to release the immigrants from the camps and to avoid a similar arrangement in the future. But he requested that immigrants be kept in a central place so that they could be checked if necessary. Shertok agreed, adding, however, that there were times when the immigrants wanted to be with relatives or when work took them elsewhere. Bernadotte consented to take these factors into consideration.

Shertok complained that the water supply to Jerusalem had been cut off, a violation of the truce that caused suffering to the residents of the city. Bernadotte said that he had heard we were about to open a new pipeline to Jerusalem (by way of the "Burma Road"). David Horowitz, who was present at the discussion, said that the pipeline would be operative only in twenty days. He had informed the Jordanian Prime Minister in Cairo,

Bernadotte said, that the Arabs were violating the truce, and had been promised a reply from the Jordanian government. But there were other violations of the truce, he noted. Etzel had brought in men of military age and weapons during the truce. Bernadotte realized that the Government had done everything it could be prevent this from happening, but it had not achieved its objective. The Arab Legion was willing to allow Jews to visit the Western Wall, but it did not want to take responsibility for their safety. Snipers might shoot at them. This meant, Shertok argued, that the Legion did not have control over the snipers, and the Legion should let *us* guard the Jews going to the Wall. What good will it do if your people fire back? Bernadotte asked; meanwhile some will have been killed.

Shertok declared: This is a clear violation of the Security Council's instructions. Shertok tried to clarify what Bernadotte meant by the demilitarization of Jerusalem and the creation of a free port in Haifa.

Bernadotte explained: In Jerusalem there will be no military force, Jewish or Arab. An international army of five hundred men, composed of Americans, Belgians, and Frenchmen, will enter the city. The administration of Jerusalem will remain unchanged. Shertok asked about supplies for the city. Bernadotte answered that the UN would ensure that weapons did not enter the city, but that civilian supplies were received. If there was an agreement on the demilitarization of Jerusalem, but not on a continuation of the truce, he would ask for an extension of the truce in Jerusalem alone, because it would take him more than three days to prepare the force he needed.

No attempt would be made in Haifa to diminish Israel's sovereignty in the port, he said. The management of the port would remain, as would the customs officials. The loading and unloading of ships would continue as before. But no military units would be allowed in the port. In the Jewish section, there would be Jewish police, while in the Arab section, there would be Arab police. There would be UN units in the port. Shertok asked whether it would be possible in such circumstances to bring in weapons through the port. Bernadotte became embarrassed. A colleague remarked that one of the goals of demilitarization was to ensure that the port would not be bombed. It was impossible to bring in weapons through a demilitarized port. The refineries would also be under UN supervision. It was assumed that, should the refineries be demilitarized, Iraq would agree to allow its oil to flow through the existing pipeline to the refineries. The refined products would then be distributed to Jews and Arabs alike, and, of course, exported. This was the aim of the demilitarization of the port. If it were not for the refineries, he said, demilitarization of the port would not have been suggested. The same situation pertained to the train between Haifa and Jerusalem. It would be turned over to the UN. This would not mean, however, that the operation of the train would undermine Israeli or Arab sovereignty. It would pass through both Israeli and Arab territory at a time when there was no regular service on the line.

In the afternoon Bernadotte brought his reply to the Foreign Minister's letter. He complained about our lack of fairness. He was not trying to undermine our sovereignty, he said. He did not intend to impose a solution. He had only suggested that we agree to negotiations of our own free will. He had also asked that we offer counter-proposals, which we had not done. Shertok replied that his only counter-proposal was that the Arabs make peace with Israel.

Shertok suggested that we agree, at least in principle, to the demilitarization of

Jerusalem. We should also agree, he said, to an extension of the truce. He believed, however, that there were strong arguments against the demilitarization of Haifa port, the refineries and the railway, as they were all of great strategic importance.

Shapira asked whether the demilitarization of Jerusalem was connected with that of the railway. Rabbi Levin supported the internationalization of Jerusalem, but Gruenbaum expressed doubts. We should not agree to the demilitarization of Jerusalem, Bernstein cautioned, before consulting with defense experts. Perhaps the hills of Jerusalem were of vital military importance. He opposed the Haifa demilitarization scheme—perhaps it would ensure oil for the entire world, but not for us. Shapira agreed to the demilitarization of Jerusalem and of the railway to the city. While it is true that we have the "Burma Road," he declared, we cannot allow a demilitarized city to be without an assured supply of food, which can come only by the railway. He opposed the demilitarization of Haifa. Bentov expressed doubts about the demilitarization of Jerusalem. Who could guarantee, he asked, that the UN army would not eventually leave the city and turn it over to the Arabs? Rosenblueth supported the demilitarization of Jerusalem. Zisling was for a continuation of the truce, but had doubts about the demilitarization of Jerusalem. If there was no alternative, he would agree to demilitarization, but not in Haifa. Kaplan wanted to hear the Army's view on the demilitarization of Jerusalem, and also opposed the demilitarization of Haifa.

Shertok suggested we inform Bernadotte that he would not receive a reply on the demilitarization of Jerusalem for another day or two, and that we regarded the demilitarization of Jerusalem and of Haifa as two separate issues. We would agree to a truce in Jerusalem, but could not accept his proposal in regard to the refineries.

The final decision of the meeting was to support a maximum extension of the truce, and to oppose the demilitarization of Haifa, the refineries, and the Haifa-Jerusalem railway. If Jerusalem was demilitarized, the UN would be allowed to bring a supply train from Haifa to its forces in Jerusalem. The Government would be ready to accept the demilitarization of Jerusalem only after consultation with the military authorities. It was decided to hold another meeting of the Government that same day (July 7, 1948), after the Foreign Minister had met with Bernadotte.

The second meeting took place at 6:30 P.M. The Prime Minister was again unable to attend because of ill health. Shertok reported on his meeting with Bernadotte. The Count, who had come with a larger group than ever before, announced that he had not yet received an answer from the Arabs, because the Egyptian Parliament had been occupied the entire day with the Sudan problem. The Egyptians had promised a reply that evening. Bernadotte told Shertok that he would pass on their response the next morning. Shertok complained about Jerusalem's water supply being cut off, which he called a grave violation of the truce. Bernadotte replied that the Arabs believed Jerusalem was receiving more supplies that it was supposed to receive. Some, they said, were coming through Arab-held areas, while others were sent by a parallel route.

Shertok informed Bernadotte that the Israeli Government opposed the demilitarization of the refineries. As for the demilitarization of Jerusalem, the Government felt it necessary to clarify a number of matters and would only be able to adopt a stand in a day or two. If Jerusalem were demilitarized, arrangements must be made to transport food and supplies for the UN forces in the city. Shertok asked Bernadotte unofficially what he knew about the attitude of the Arabs. It appeared to him, the Count replied, that the Arabs would reject a general extension of the truce, but would agree to a three-day extension and to the demilitarization of Jerusalem.

The Government met again the next day, July 8, 1948, once more in the absence of the Prime Minister. The Foreign Minister announced that he had been in contact that morning with Bernadotte and Bunche, who had received an answer from the Arabs. The Arabs opposed an extension of the truce, even for a three-day period. They agreed to the demilitarization of Jerusalem only with respect to the Old City. Their reply on Haifa was completely unacceptable. Bernadotte had already ordered his men to leave the country.

The Foreign Minister said he would consult with the Prime Minister and with the Chief of Operations, Yigael Yadin, with the aim of beginning operations in the evening. This information had been relayed to Abba Eban, who was instructed to inform all members of the Security Council. He was to explain that Israel favored a continuation of the truce but that the Arabs did not, and that the Arab armies had already begun operations. Israel consequently had to take immediate counter-measures.

An agreement had been reached on the demilitarization of Mount Scopus. It would be guarded by eighty-five policemen armed with rifles, pistols, and Bren guns. The Augusta Victoria Hospital would also be demilitarized, and guarded by forty Arab policemen. Both sides agreed not to open fire on one another.

In answer to a question by Rabbi Levin, the Foreign Minister stated that Israel was continuing to receive weapons.

III

BETWEEN CAMPAIGNS

War Renewed, Israeli Victories, and Second Truce

Section 1. Strengthened Israel Expands Territory

Provisional Government Reviews Its Objections to Bernadotte Report ★
UN Security Council Calls for Extension of Truce

ACCORDING to the previous agreement, the first truce was to end on July 9. As the date approached, Count Bernadotte's demands for an extension grew steadily more insistent. On July 5 he asked our Foreign Minister again whether Israel would be ready to prolong the truce for a period acceptable to both sides.

At a meeting of the Provisional State Council that evening, the Foreign Minister, Shertok, presented the Government's views on the Mediator's proposals regarding Jerusalem, economic unity, immigration, and the area of the Jewish State. The Provisional Government had expressed its surprise at the fact that the Mediator in his proposals had not made a single reference to the General Assembly's historic November 29 resolution. He had also failed to take into account two key facts: (1) the existence of a sovereign Jewish State within the territory allocated to it by the UN resolution; (2) territorial changes that have resulted from Israel's success in repulsing attacks by Palestinian Arabs and the surrounding Arab States.

The November 29 resolution was accepted by the Jewish people as a compromise, and a painful one, for it demanded significant concessions. The area allocated to the Jews by the resolution is an absolute minimum, and cannot, under any circumstances, be further reduced. Moreover, the Arab attacks on the security and integrity of the Jewish State revealed the need for a revision of the boundaries set in the resolution. The Provisional Government, Shertok emphasized, cannot accept any limitation on its sovereign rights. While the State will continue to strike for good relations with her neighbors in every field, the practical expression of this desire must be decided upon in free negotiations with the Arabs.

The Government then turned its attention to the question of an economic union. The representatives of the Jewish people accepted the plan for such a union, as set forth in the November 29 resolution and were ready now to keep their word, provided all aspects of the original plan were put into effect. The Mediator's proposals indicate that this would not be the case. He has suggested, instead, that Israel accept a completely different partner for economic union, different in both geographical and political terms. The previous agreement cannot simply be altered to bring in the new partner. Israel regards it as her right to conclude an economic or other pact with any country she chooses. She will determine her own relations with her neighbors.

The Government particularly emphasized the question of immigration, rejecting any attempt to limit Israel's independence and sovereignty in this connection. Israel demands complete freedom to determine the size and composition of her immigration. This is one of the reasons the Jewish people sought sovereign status. The community of nations has recognized the Jews' right to a State, and no Israeli Government will agree to a limitation on its sovereignty as regards immigration or to sharing that sovereignty with another country or an international body.

As to Jerusalem: Israel has been deeply hurt by the proposal to put the city under Arab rule. The belief that an Arab-ruled Jerusalem would contribute to world peace shows a complete disregard both for historical facts and current reality. It overlooks the historic link between the Jews and Jerusalem, the central role of Jerusalem in Jewish history, and the fact that, when the fighting broke out, the Jews made up two-thirds of Jerusalem's population, a percentage that has grown with the Arab evacuation. Moreover, all of New Jerusalem (aside from a few isolated pockets) is now under Israeli control.

The United Nations, after intensive study of the question, decided that Jerusalem must be under international rule. The Provisional Government has announced to the Mediator that the Jewish people, the State of Israel, and the Jews of Jerusalem will not, under any circumstances, agree to Arab rule in Jerusalem, no matter what formal arrangements are made for municipal autonomy or access to the Holy Places. They will oppose the imposition of Arab rule with all their strength. Israel, the statement went on, regrets to announce that the shocking proposal, which reflects Arab ambitions and strikes at the hearts of the Jews, will lessen rather than enhance the chances for peace in Jerusalem.

Shertok added that the Government had limited itself to commenting on the Bernadotte proposals and that its replies would be presented in writing to the Mediator before there was a discussion, if he wanted a discussion at all. The Government had also clarified questions that were not included in its written answer. Certain policies had been adopted on the question of Jaffa, the return of the Arabs, the exchange of populations, etc. Israel, said Shertok, was aware that the Arabs had rejected the Mediator's proposals and had put forward counter-proposals. While their content was not yet known, it could be assumed that they called for making Palestine an Arab state. The Government felt the Mediator's proposals were strongly influenced by the British Foreign Office. It had information from the United States, which might or might not be accurate, that the American State Department did not support the proposals.

Participating in the discussion were Interior Minister Gruenbaum (who demanded a territorial bridge between Jerusalem and the State of Israel), Wilner (Communist Party), Dr. Altman (Hatzohar), Warhaftig (Hapoel Hamizrahi), Repetur (Mapam), Kosoy

(Mapai), Lemberger (Agudat Israel), Mintz (Polaei Agudat Israel), Weinstein (Hatzohar), Rabbi Berlin (Mizrahi), Dr. Katznelson (Mapai). The speakers did not dispute the Government's position, but offered various amendments. The Council voted down all of them and approved the Provisional Government's position by a vote of twenty-seven to four.

The Mediator, who had received the Provisional Government's reply on July 6 (the reply of the Arab States had come in earlier), cabled the Security Council that same day suggesting that it take steps to extend the truce. His cable went to the current chairman of the Security Council, Dmitri Manuilsky, of the Ukraine. Syria opposed a discussion of an extension of the truce; the United States, France, Belgium, and Britain demanded a discussion of the Mediator's proposal. Andrei Gromyko, the Soviet representative, did not oppose an extension of the truce, but insisted that the Mediator's new plans could not be ignored, since they contained proposals contradicting UN resolutions. Manuilsky similarly declared that an extension of the truce was desirable, but charged that the truce had been used as a cover for various schemes that ran counter to UN decisions: the Mediator had made suggestions that he had no right to make, and it was impossible to discuss the truce without noting that he had exceeded his powers.

The Security Council debate was adjourned to the next day, July 7. An incident of significance took place that day. At the opening of the session the chairman addressed Abba Eban as "the representative of the State of Israel" and invited him to sit at the Council table along with the Arab delegates. Until then, Eban had participated in the sessions as "the representative of the Jewish Agency."

The Syrian spokesman, Faris el Houri, protested that the chairman had not acted properly. Lord Cadogan, for Britain, declared that the chairman's use of the phrase "State of Israel" would not influence his government with respect to recognizing the State established by the Jews. The representative of the Arab Committee, Jamal el Husseini, left the meeting in protest. Manuilsky stated that the Syrian representative was in error. When Faris el Houri himself had served as chairman of the Council, he had called on members to speak of the Indonesian Republic, although it had not yet been formally recognized by the UN. There were three reasons, Manuilsky added, why the term "State of Israel" was more appropriate than the term "Indonesian Republic" had been: (1) the Jews of Palestine were never a part of Syria or any other Arab state; (2) the November 29 resolution calling for the establishing of an independent Jewish State was still operative; (3) at the end of the British Mandate, Israel did establish a State, which was recognized by a number of UN members, including the United States and the Soviet Union. He saw no reason, therefore, why the representative of the State of Israel should be denied the opportunity to appear as such.

China and Egypt supported the Syrian position. Canada suggested retaining the old title, "Jewish Agency," or using the term "Jewish Authorities." The United States argued that all of the delegates were aware of the existence of the Provisional Government of the State of Israel. Besides, the chairman's action did not obligate other delegates, who could use whatever term they considered appropriate. Manuilsky then called on Eban, again addressing him as "representative of the State of Israel." The Egyptian delegate thereupon interrupted the proceedings, asserting that the chairman's conduct did not improve the chances of a successful discussion. The Arabs, he declared, would not agree to the formulation "representative of the State of Israel."

At Gromyko's suggestion, the question was put to a vote. Five members—Belgium, Britain, Syria, China, and Canada—opposed the use of the term "State of Israel." According to the UN Charter, a resolution must be supported by at least seven Council members to be adopted. The chairman therefore ruled that the term "State of Israel" could be used in Security Council discussions. Canada and Belgium expressed dissatisfaction with his decision, then went on to a discussion of the resolution under discussion, namely, an extension of the truce.

In the ensuing debate Gromyko argued that the Mediator had ignored UN resolutions, without being empowered to do so. Instead of working for a peace settlement, he had added fuel to the fire. The suggested union between Trans-Jordan and Israel was contrary to the General Assembly's decision to establish two independent states in Palestine. Supporters of the Mediator's plan could not hope to annual the partition resolution, he said, since one of the states to be established was, in fact, already in existence and successfully pursuing independent economic and political policies. The plan put forward by the Mediator was an attempt to increase hostility between the Jews and the Arabs and to encourage Arab belligerency. The very fact that it had been suggested to add the Arab areas to Trans-Jordan revealed the character of the proposals.

Trans-Jordan, Gromyko said, was ruled by a puppet king in the pay of the British, who had no right to a single inch of Palestinian soil. World public opinion had already expressed its opposition to Arab aggression and British policies in Palestine. The British had begun a military adventure through the Arab Legion, which was under their command and enjoyed their full support. They were aided by certain Western nations, including the United States. They were trying to serve their own ends by working against the State of Israel, and, in fact, against the real interests of the Arabs as well. All supporters of the UN resolution must admit the need to expose the Mediator's real motives, Gromyko declared. It is no wonder that some believe that his proposals originated in the British Foreign Office. The proposals stir up trouble between the Jews and the Arabs, and serve to undermine UN resolutions, at the expense of the State of Israel and of the Arab state that is supposed to be established. An extension of the truce under the conditions set forth on June 29 harms those who support the UN and its decisions, while aiding those who would nullify those decisions. Despite its support of the idea of a truce, the Soviet government will therefore adopt the same attitude toward an extension under present conditions as it did four weeks earlier when the subject was last discussed.

The Syrian delegate, replying to Gromyko, denied that the partition resolution was still binding. The Mediator, he said, is free to make whatever proposals he sees fit, and the parties to the dispute are free to accept or reject them. There was no point in extending the truce, he went on, unless there was a good chance of a just and satisfactory solution.

China, Argentina, and Canada announced their support of an extension of the truce. Finally, the truce resolution was adopted by a vote of eight (Argentina, the United States, Belgium, Britain, China, France, Colombia, and Canada) to nothing, with the Soviet Union, the Ukraine, and Syria abstaining. Following the vote, Gromyko announced that abstention did not indicate Soviet opposition to extending the truce, but only to the conditions laid down by the Mediator. The Syrian representative announced that he had abstained because he thought the matter should be left to the two sides to decide for themselves. He was certain, he said, that the Arab states would reject a truce if they were not given guarantees against further violations, such as the *Altalena* episode.

The resolution as adopted stated: "The Security Council, taking note of Count Bernadotte's cable of July 5, urgently calls on the parties concerned to accept his proposal for an extension of the truce for a period to be determined in negotiations with the Mediator."

Egypt Violates the Extended Truce ★ Resumption of Fighting ★ Israel's Gains in Military Power ★ Mass Flight from Arab Villages

On July 8, while the Security Council was considering an extension of the truce, the Egyptians attacked Be'er Tuvia and Beit Daras and were repulsed by our forces. An assault on Julis by Egyptian infantry, supported by a number of tanks, was also thrown back with heavy losses to the enemy. The truce was violated in the north as well. Israeli vehicles were attacked on the Jezreel Valley Road near Ginnegar on the afternoon of July 8. That evening the Provisional State Council held its ninth meeting.

The Prime Minister, who had risen that day from his sickbed, pointed out that the Council was meeting on the eve of the end of the truce. If fighting is resumed, he said, the results may well be decisive. Our enemies have undoubtedly learned the lesson in the last four or five weeks. They now realize that they underestimated our strength when they thought they could conquer the State of Israel in a few days. We should not belittle either their intelligence or their strength. Undoubtedly they have prepared a more sophisticated plan, while mobilizing additional men and equipment during the truce period. We may now be facing a more difficult campaign—perhaps the final one.

In various respects our forces too will be in a much stronger position than at the beginning of the truce. For obvious reasons, he said, he would not go into detail here, but he had not the least doubt that the Army will continue to fulfill its mission, as it has over the past six months. Let us hope that the people will support the Army with all their strength and determination. We had no basis for differentiation between the front lines and the rear in our situation. Every Jewish settlement is part of the front. With the British departure from Haifa, the front was extended still further. The city has not been attacked since the establishment of the State, but there is reason to fear that it will now be attacked from both the sea and the air. Jerusalem, which suffered more than any other city in the last six months, may not have drained the last drop from its cup of suffering. We hope that the nation will meet these challenges with the same spirit of devotion that it has shown over the last six months, and particularly in the four weeks after the invasion by Arab regular armies.

The Foreign Minister then reported on developments in foreign affairs since the Council met on July 5. At that meeting, Shertok said, the Council had approved the Government's suggested reply to the Mediator's proposals. Meanwhile, we have been faced with the grave question of the truce. The Government favored an extension of the truce over the entire country. We agreed to a thirty-day extension starting tomorrow, July 9, at 10 A.M. Our agreement is conditional on Arab acceptance of the arrangement. We announced that we saw no possibility of continuing the present immigration regulations, under which immigrants of military age are forced to remain in camps. The Mediator has agreed to allow immigrants of military age to circulate freely throughout the country. We have promised that they will not be taken into the Army. All immigrants now in camps will be released tomorrow, whether or not the truce is extended. As to the water situation: Trans-Jordan controls Latrun, while Iraqi forces control the Rosh Ha'ayin springs. Neither will allow us to receive water. The Mediator regards this as a violation of the truce, but the situation has not been rectified. We know that Trans-Jordan is acting on British advice.

The Government has not yet made a final decision on the demilitarization of Jerusalem, but has announced its opposition to the demilitarization of the Haifa-Jerusalem railway where it runs through Israeli territory. The Government has also come out against the demilitarization of the port of Haifa and of the refineries. Even if an international army is sent to Jerusalem, we will not agree to the stationing of a non-Israeli military force inside the State or in areas now under the control of the Government of Israel.

The Arabs apparently oppose an extension of the truce. Despite the fact that they have been responsible for innumerable violations over the past four weeks, they charge us with responsibility for such violations. Arrangements have been made for the demilitarization of Mount Scopus, including both its Jewish and Arab sections. In the Hebrew University-Hadassah Hospital area there are eighty-five Jewish policemen and twenty from the UN. This morning we received a cable from Trygve Lie, Secretary General of the UN, in the name of the Security Council; he demands an extension of the truce. At the very moment that his cable arrived we received reports of renewal of Arab aggression in the south.

The Arabs have refused to accept an extension of the truce, though the American representative in the Security Council suggested, on July 8, that if one side agrees to an extension and the other side does not, the Council should consider the imposition of sanctions on the side rejecting the truce. Faris el Houri asked why sanctions had not been imposed on Indonesia and Kashmir, and called for sanctions against the Jews because Jewish terrorists had violated the truce. The United States and Russia were encouraging the Jews, he charged, and the Arabs would not take this situation lying down—even if they were attacked with atom bombs, they would go on fighting. The Council chairman, Manuilsky, declared that the situation was serious and that a decision had to be made by next day, July 9, on steps to halt Arab aggression in Palestine. In Cairo, Prime Minister Azzam Pasha announced that the Arabs would not agree to continuing the truce, even for three days.

On Friday, July 9, fighting was renewed. The Israel Defense Forces concentrated at first on the central front, the Lydda-Ramle area.

Refusal of the Arab rulers to extend the truce as demanded by the Security Council, was even more disappointing to the UN than the Arab attitude toward the November 29 General Assembly resolution. On May 15 the Arab armies still had a good chance of defeating the Hagana forces, since they enjoyed an enormous advantage in heavy weapons—artillery, tanks, planes, and ships. The Arabs had many artillery batteries, while we had only two dozen 20-mm. light artillery pieces for use against both tanks and planes. While the Arabs had fighters and bombers, Israel on the eve of independence had only transport planes and light planes, the latter used for communications and observation. The Egyptians, the Iraqis, the Syrians, and the Jordanians had British tanks; our only armor consisted of homemade vehicles and two Cromwells "transferred" to us on the eve of the British departure from Haifa.

But our situation had changed since the eve of the Arab invasion. The first arms ship reached Tel Aviv port with 65-mm. field guns immediately after the establishment of the State. Some of the guns were sent immediately to the Jordan Valley, where they affected the outcome of the battle for the Degania settlements. A few days later another arms ship arrived bringing artillery, 120-mm. mortars, and rifles. Artillerymen who had served in the British Army during the Second World War immediately prepared for operations all over the country. A third ship, which arrived recently, brought us 75-mm. artillery pieces, comparable to Egyptian and Jordanian 25-pounders. Bringing the Messerschmitts from Czechoslovakia was much harder. It was impossible to fly them directly to Israel and there was no place where they could be refueled en route. We were forced to dismantle the planes, ship them in large transport planes, and reassemble them here. The Egyptians therefore enjoyed control of the air until the first truce. Tel Aviv was bombed on May 15, immediately after Israel proclaimed her independence. That day we brought down our first Egyptian plane. The Egyptians also launched an air attack on Ramat David, unaware that the airfield was still in British hands. Thus British Spitfires piloted by Egyptians hit three other British Spitfires. British planes pursued the Egyptians. One of the Egyptian pilots made a forced landing near Dalia, in the Hills of Ephraim, and was captured by our forces. He was our first Egyptian prisoner.

During the first month our light planes could operate only in the evening. Other planes, purchased overseas before the invasion, could not reach the country during the first weeks of the struggle; but we did acquire some first-rate manpower—volunteer pilots from South Africa, Canada, and other countries—during that period. By the beginning of July our Messerschmitts were flying and on July 3 we won our first air battle, bringing down two Egyptian Dakotas that had come to bomb Tel Aviv. One Dakota crashed on the shore, south of Bat Yam. Its crew perished. The second Dakota had tried to escape to the south, to Gaza, but was also brought down. Egyptian control of the air was ended. The next day our planes attacked three Egyptian warships approaching the shores of Tel Aviv and forced them to flee toward Gaza. We also succeeded in bombing two Arab capitals, Amman and Damascus, before the truce. In the first month of fighting, the enemy lost two Dakotas, four Spitfires, and one Harvard; three Egyptian pilots were taken prisoner.

Between the establishment of the State and the end of the first truce, our equipment increased in both quantity and quality. The level of training was raised and new brigades were formed. However, many officers were lost in the fighting. The shortcomings in our military organization, which were discussed at the June 18 meeting between senior commanders and the Minister of Defense, were rectified in large measure during the four weeks of the truce. When fighting began again on July 9, our forces were better trained, better equipped, better disciplined, and more sure of themselves than they had been during the first month of the war.

The Navy, too, was strengthened during the truce. When Haifa was evacuated by the British on June 30, it became the home port of the Israel Navy. At that time we had two vessels, the *Wedgewood* and the *Eilat*, each equipped with one 65-mm. and two 20-mm. cannon. We also had a number of coast guard craft armed with light weapons.

The Egyptians, as already noted, launched an attack one day before the end of the truce. They attempted to take Be'er Tuvia and Beit Daras, but were thrown back. Our commando activities in the south, planned during the truce period, were a great success. Heavy losses were inflicted on the Egyptians. During the first two days of fighting three hundred Egyptian soldiers were killed and two hundred were taken prisoner. We also captured a great deal of enemy equipment: armored cars, artillery, mortars, rifles, machine guns, and a large quantity of ammunition. Nevertheless, the Egyptians continued to attack. They surrounded Negba and assaulted Julis, Beit Daras, Ibdis, and Be'er Tuvia. They did not succeed, however, in capturing a single place, and after six days, they took up defensive positions. In several places they were forced to retreat.

The Israel Defense Forces began a large-scale attack on Friday, July 9, with the conclusion of the truce, on the central front, in the Lydda-Ramle area. It was a combined operation, in which units from the infantry, armored corps, artillery, and air force took part. The two cities were swiftly surrounded. On the first day of fighting Lydda Airfield and several nearby villages—including Yehudia, Renta, Inaba, Gimzu, Daniel, and Deir Tarif—were captured. On July 11 the Arabs of Lydda surrendered to the Israel Defense Forces, after our units had linked up with the defenders of Ben Shemen, which had been under siege for six months. The next day Ramle fell. The Arab Legion fled from the area. The Iraqis at Rosh Ha'ayin, the source of the Yarkon River, were also dislodged. A large quantity of arms fell into our hands in Lydda and Ramle.

The Arab Legion again began to shell New Jerusalem, while Egyptian planes bombed the city for the first time. By this time, we had artillery to return the Arab fire. We shelled the Old City, taking all necessary precautions to avoid damage to the Holy Places. The shelling caused a mass flight of Jerusalem Arabs. On July 12 the Arab Legion attempted to come to the assistance of Arabs who had entrenched themselves in the police station in the Beit Naballah area, between Lydda and Ramle; but it was driven back and we captured the police station on July 13.

The Security Council met at Lake Success on July 14 to discuss the American proposal for a cease-fire. It was predicated on the proposition that the Palestine situation endangered the peace. The Syrian representative proposed that the question of Palestine's future be turned over to the World Court. The British offered two amendments to the American proposal: (1) that the Council speak of "the opposing side" rather than the "State of Israel"; (2) that the Mediator be instructed to investigate truce violations that had occurred after June 11, when the first truce had gone into effect.

Gromyko, for the Soviet Union, announced that his government had not altered its view of the situation since proposing that the two sides be ordered to cease hostilities. The Mediator's optimism with regard to the earlier truce had not been justified, Gromyko said. It had not put an end to the fighting. The entire world knew who was responsible for this situation in Palestine. The establishment of a Jewish State did not conflict with Arab interests, he went on. The provocative acts of Abdullah, the puppet king, were public knowledge. The Soviet government supported the American proposal in principle, but saw no need for amending it with respect to Jerusalem. There, both sides should be asked to withdraw their forces, so that an international regime, based on the General Assembly resolution, could be established. It was necessary to decide clearly which forces would control Jerusalem; authority should not rest in the hands of one country, he said.

The Syrian proposal to turn the controversy over to the World Court was turned down, as was the British proposal to cease using the term "State of Israel." The latter was supported only by Belgium, Britain, and Colombia. The American cease-fire resolution was accepted, to take effect within three days, at a time to be determined by the

Mediator. Argentina asked whether three days was long enough to arrange a cease-fire. Count Bernadotte said that this would not be long enough to prepare the required administrative machinery. Canada then suggested that the Mediator immediately specify the time at which the truce was to begin; he decided on July 18 at 7 P.M.

While the Security Council was discussing a cease-fire, the struggle inside the country grew fiercer. The Israel Defense Forces assault on southern and western Jerusalem led the Arab villagers in the area to flee. The Air Force was strengthened by the arrival of three American Flying Fortresses brought from Mexico by way of Czechoslovakia. They were instructed to bomb Cairo and military targets in the Sinai Desert on their way to Israel on July 15. Two days later Damascus was also bombed. Twelve enemy planes were brought down during this period, making it thirty-two since the beginning of the invasion. Ground attacks were also stepped up. A special IDF force was sent to the north to drive out Kaukji's units and to liberate central Galilee.

Shfaram, northwest of Nazareth, was captured on July 14. An enemy attack on Sejera was repulsed; one hundred and twenty Arab bodies remained on the field of battle. The villages of Zippori and Ein Ma'ahal, near Nazareth, were captured. At 6:15 P.M., July 16, a delegation of Nazareth notables, carrying a white flag, came out to meet our commanders. An armored company was immediately sent to take the Nazareth police station. According to our information, the police station was by then completely deserted, and that, in fact, is how we found it. We discovered there a great many of Kaukji's documents and plans. The Nazareth notables signed a surrender agreement at 10 P.M. The Commander of the Seventh Brigade, Chaim Laskov, had received strict instructions that the town's Holy Places and inhabitants were to remain untouched. This order was carried out in full. Our total losses in the conquest of Nazareth were one man wounded. The enemy lost sixteen dead, including one Englishman, one German, and one Iraqi. A Jewish governor was appointed for Nazareth.

The capture of Nazareth ended Arab resistance in lower Galilee. The residents of Iksal, near Nazareth, loaded their weapons on wagons and came to our forces to surrender. The residents of Daburiya, at the foot of Mount Tabor—where Wingate had led his Night Squads into battle—raised white flags as soon as they saw a Jewish jeep approach. The village of Lubya, controlling the Nazareth-Tiberias road, fell without a fight, thus opening the road to Tiberias. The flight of Arabs from the villages around Jerusalem increased. Our forces captured Malha, Tsora, and Ein Karem; their residents fled.

Beginning of the Second Truce

The second truce began on July 18 at 7 P.M. It had been accepted by both sides the day before, July 17, at 5:30 A.M. We had failed in our efforts to liberate the Old City of Jerusalem before the truce began.

The second truce differed from the first in two important respects: (1) it was not limited in time; (2) the truce resolution, presented by the American delegate, seemed to imply the possibility of sanctions, since it spoke of "ordering a cease-fire." At a meeting of the Provisional Government on July 16, Foreign Minister Shertok announced that he had just received a cable from Lake Success, with the full text of the resolution adopted by the

Security Council at its thirty-eighth meeting on July 15, 1948, at 8:45 P.M., New York time:

The Security Council,

Taking into consideration that the Provisional Government of Israel has indicated its acceptance in principle of a prolongation of the truce in Palestine; that the member states of the Arab League have rejected successive appeals of the United Nations Mediator, and of the Security Council in its Resolution of 7 July 1948, for the prolongation of the truce in Palestine; and that there has consequently developed a renewal of hostilities in Palestine;

Determines that the situation in Palestine constitutes a threat to the peace within the meaning of Article 39 of the Charter;

Orders the Governments and authorities concerned to desist from further military action and to this end to issue cease-fire orders to their military and paramilitary forces, to take effect at a time to be determined by the Mediator, but in any event not later than three days from the date of the adoption of this Resolution;

Declares that failure by any of the Governments or authorities concerned to comply with the preceding paragraph of this Resolution would demonstrate the existence of a breach of the peace within the meaning of Article 39 of the Charter requiring immediate consideration by the Security Council with a view to such further action under Chapter VII of the Charter as may be decided upon by the Council;

Calls upon all Governments and authorities concerned to continue to cooperate with the Mediator with a view to the maintenance of peace in Palestine in conformity with the Resolution adopted by the Security Council on 29 May 1948;

Orders as a matter of special and urgent necessity an immediate and unconditional cease-fire in the City of Jerusalem to take effect 24 hours from the time of the adoption of this Resolution, and instructs the Truce Commission to take any necessary steps to make this cease-fire effective;

Instructs the Mediator to continue his efforts to bring about the demilitarization of the City of Jerusalem, and to assure the protection of an access to the Holy Places, religious buildings and sites in Palestine;

Instructs the Mediator to supervise the observance of the truce and to establish procedures for examining alleged breaches of the truce since 11 June 1948, authorizes him to deal with breaches so far as it is within his capacity to do so by appropriate local action, and requests him to keep the Security Council currently informed concerning the operation of the truce and when necessary to take appropriate action;

Decides that, subject to further decision by the Security Council or the General Assembly, the truce shall remain in force, in accordance with the present Resolution and with that of 29 May 1948, until a peaceful adjustment of the future situation of Palestine is reached;

Reiterates the appeal to the parties contained in the last paragraph of its Resolution of 22 May and urges upon the parties that they continue conversations with the Mediator in a spirit of conciliation and mutual concession in order that all points under dispute may be settled peacefully;

Requests the Secretary General to provide the Mediator with the necessary staff and facilities to assist in carrying out the function assigned to him under the Resolution of the General Assembly of 14 May, and under this Resolution; and

Requests that the Secretary-General make appropriate arrangements to provide necessary funds to meet the obligations arising from this Resolution.

Answering Rabbi Fishman's question about whether the resolution spoke of sanctions, the Foreign Minister said: "It states that if one of the sides does not comply, the Security

Council will meet to discuss appropriate action in accordance with Chapter 7 of the UN Charter."

Kaplan asked whether the question of sanctions applied only to the truce. The Foreign Minister replied in the affirmative.

Zisling inquired whether the talk of compromises in the resolution did not indicate a retreat from the November 29 resolution. Shertok answered that it could be so interpreted.

Ben-Gurion pointed out that the resolution draws a distinction between the cease-fire and the demilitarization of Jerusalem. The cease-fire is clearly to be regarded as mandatory, whereas the section on the demilitarization of Jerusalem speaks only of efforts by the Mediator to bring it about. Commenting on the situation at the various fronts, he stated that, as members knew, Cairo had been bombed. It had been decided that one of the three Flying Fortresses would bomb Cairo, while the other two would hit Gaza and El Arish. Radio Cairo announced that the town had been hard hit, and according to our reports the damage was not extensive. The plane tried to hit the Royal Palace with eight quarter-ton bombs, but they landed only in the vicinity. The plane assigned to bomb El Arish bombed Rafiah, an English base, by mistake. The third bomber hit Gaza, with as yet unknown results. All the planes returned safely. The Flying Fortresses reached El Arish the next morning, and dropped seven and a half tons of bombs on its airfield. The Prime Minister also reported on developments in the Galilee, on the central front, and in the south.

Shertok reported that, after difficult negotiations, the Mediator had agreed that we would have the right to send supplies to the Negev during the truce, though the Egyptians controlled the Negev crossroads. We would agree to an unconditional truce in Jerusalem the next morning, Shertok said. There is not representative of the Mediator in Jerusalem, but there is a Consuls' Committee responsible for coordinating affairs. We should also agree to a truce on July 18, if we are certain that the Arabs will agree as well. We should make it clear to the Mediator that the Security Council resolution does not place any restrictions on the immigration of people of military age. We must be very firm about this matter, he added. The Foreign Minister favored concentrating on military operations in the Negev in the two days before the truce.

Gruenbaum instead urged concentration on Jerusalem and vicinity, stating that "unless Jerusalem is in our hands, there is no hope that it will be internationalized."

Rosenblueth wanted to emphasize the Galilee: "If we still have the opportunity of capturing all of the Galilee, that would seem most important to me."

Zisling stated: "The Negev is our chief concern. We have the road to Jerusalem and we have no hope of conquering the Old City, but the conquest of the Negev would be decisive."

Ben-Gurion: "If we have only three days left, there is not much freedom of choice in regard to the Negev. We have no chance of transferring large forces from the Galilee. The only remaining possibility is to make use of our Air Force, and this will be done. We will not stop firing ourselves until the Arabs announce their willingness to accept a cease-fire. There is no point deciding on a specific hour. If the Arabs announce their acceptance, we will also order our forces to stop shooting."

The truce was to have begun at 7 P.M. on July 18. When the Provisional Government met that day for several hours, however, no word had as yet been received from the Arabs on whether they would stop shooting at the appointed hour.

There are two possiblities, the Prime Minister said, and we must prepare for both of them: (1) the truce will begin as scheduled, but just before it does the Arabs will attempt to gain control of additional areas; (2) the truce will not begin today, and the Arabs will continue fighting in order to gain additional territory. Then, in another day or two, they will announce their willingness to accept a truce, on the assumption that sanctions will not be imposed on them merely because they delayed the acceptance. Their assumption is entirely reasonable, especially in view of their five defenders in the Security Council: Britain, Argentina, Belgium, Syria, and China.

There are signs, he added, that the Arabs are preparing to strike. They have brought up reinforcements to Majdal and are now advancing on Asluj. The situation in western Galilee gives cause for concern. Our forces have been completely engaged during the past ten days, and we must make certain that we are not faced by an unpleasant surprise this evening at 7. The direct road to the south is in our hands. We have captured many places in recent days and are digging in. The new road passes near Faluja, but is closer to Beit Gubrin. It is our intention to gain control of this entire area, and thus far we have been quite successful. We bombed Majdal several times this morning. If there are no unforeseen developments, our situation will not be too bad. However, there may be surprises. Saudi Arabian forces have entered the fighting.

At the Latrun front, Kula has passed from one side to the other ten times. At the moment we control it. Our units continue to advance and have Latrun surrounded. The Arabs do not have strong forces there but they do have plenty of artillery and are well entrenched. The central front is quiet, which is rather surprising. We have scarcely any troops there. Our men are at Rosh Ha'ayin and in western Galilee. Aside from Rosh Hanikra, now held by the Lebanese Army, that front is safe. But we may have surprises in store for us if the Arabs attack at the last moment. Mishmar Hayarden, which is in Syrian hands, has been bombed many times. Our men saw armored cars advancing toward Kuneitra. The battles on this front are continuing. We may have difficulties in store for us in the Jordan Valley, where there is a large, hidden Arab force; in the Mishmar Hayarden area, on the Lebanese border; and particularly on the central front. There may also be an Arab attack on Lydda. We have intercepted an Arab message indicating that the Legion is planning to advance on Lydda.

We must use our reserves. We have decided to take part of the police into the Army. A battalion now in training in Tel Aviv and Tel Litvinsky can, if necessary, be used in the area between Lydda and Latrun. Since there is already a truce in Jerusalem, we have ordered the heavy weapons there to be used to capture Batir. We want to gain control of the entire railway track. We already hold most of the stations: Ramle, Wadi Sarar, and perhaps Hartuv by now. The Batir station is the only major one not yet under our control.

The most exposed front is the vicinity of Wadi Milik, Wadi Ara, and Ein Shemer, Ben-Gurion continued. The Seventh Brigade, previously stationed at Ein Shemer, was sent to Nazareth. A few weeks ago we decided to train seventeen-year-olds, and they are now training in Pardess Hanna. It has been suggested that we use them as a defense force in that area if there is a local attack and there are no other units on hand. He was speaking here only of an Arab attack in that particular area. This unit would be used solely to defend the Pardess Hanna Natanya district. The Government must decide on this matter, because the General Staff has been informed by the Minister of Defense that it does not have the right to use this force without special permission from the Government. The unit has fifteen hundred men. We have often wondered why the Arabs do not attack in the area between Natanya and Haifa. Perhaps they are also keeping units in reserve for fear of an attack from us.

Bentov: Arabs, apparently Iraqis, are attacking in the Mishmar Ha'emek–Megiddo district. They came from the hill of the Triangle.

Ben-Gurion: We are afraid that the Arabs will make last-minute attempts to conquer new territory just before the truce comes into effect. Therefore, our Government must decide about the seventeen-year-olds. The Government agreed that the seventeen-year-olds could be used to defend the northern section of the Central District if necessary.

The Foreign Minister said it had been learned from Arab sources that on July 12 the Egyptian Prime Minister asked his representative at Lake Success to inform Faris el Houri, a member of the Security Council, that he would not agree to a truce under any circumstances, even if public opinion favored one. A report received yesterday (July 17) indicates that both the Egyptians and the Syrians are on the verge of despair as a result of our military victories. They now argue that the Arabs should not renew their attack because this might bring about further defeats, such as occurred in Lydda and Ramle. Nevertheless, they are finding it difficult to accept the Security Council truce resolution.

In a discussion one of our people had with the Mediator and Dr. Bunche, Bernadotte said that the Arabs had already lost the war. By accepting the truce solution, they accepted, in effect, the partitioning of the country; by rejecting it, they committed suicide. Abba Eban also participated in this discussion. The Mediator asked how we felt about the extension of his mission. Eban replied that the Mediator's previous proposals had caused Israel to lose faith in him. His mission, Eban went on, could be successful only if it were aimed at creating treaty relations between sovereign states.

The Foreign Minister reported that at first he had told the Mediator's representative that Israel would order her forces to stop firing only when she knew that the Arabs had given such an order. The Mediator's representative replied that though he would transmit the answer, he wished to call the Foreign Minister's attention to the fact that it was not in accordance with the Security Council decision, which provided that each side must order a cease-fire at a time set by the Mediator, without waiting to hear what the other side had done.

Following this discussion, the Foreign Minister revised his formulation to read: "An order has been given to our forces to stop firing immediately after being informed that firing from the other side has stopped."

Since no reply was received from the Arabs, the General Staff announced that it was ordering the Defense Forces to stop firing at 7 P.M., as the Mediator ordered; but Israeli forces were to reopen fire at places where the Arabs continued to shoot. This statement was wired to the Mediator. Bentov objected to the formulation, demanding that our forces continue firing all night, until there was an announcement that the Arabs had agreed to a truce. Gruenbaum supported this proposal, but it was voted down.

As we learned later, the Political Committee of the Arab League, meeting in Lebanon, decided to accept the Security Council resolution and to order Arab units to stop firing at the time set by the Mediator. Arab circles emphasized that this did not signify Arab acceptance of a Jewish State in Palestine. Be that as it may, the Jewish State and the Israel Defense Forces entered into the truce with a string of victories to their credit and with confidence in their own strength.

Changes in Provisional State Council ★ *Evaluation of Military–Political Situation* ★ *First Supreme Court Chosen*

At a meeting of the Provisional State Council on July 15, a few days before the start of the truce, an important change was made in the Council Executive. Until then, meetings of the Council had been chaired by the Prime Minister; now a Presidium was chosen. A proposal to that effect had been made at the previous Council meeting on July 8, when it had been suggested that the Presidium be composed of the president of the Council (Dr. Weizmann, who was not yet in the country), a chairman, and three deputy chairmen, chosen from among Council members who were not members of the Government. The chairman, it was decided, would be a representative of Mapai; his three deputies would be representatives of the other large factions: the General Zionists, Mapam, and Mizrahi and Hapoel Hamizrahi. Weinstein (Hatzohar) proposed that one of the deputies be elected from his faction, but the proposal was rejected.

The following Presidium was chosen by the Council on July 15: Yosef Sprinzak (Mapai), chairman; Dr. Abraham Granovsky (General Zionist), deputy chairman; Nahum Nir-Rafalkes (Mapam), deputy chairman. The Mizrahi and Hapoel Hamizrahi did not present their candidate at that meeting.

The Prime Minister thanked the members of the Council for the patience they had shown during his chairmanship and for the assistance all, without exception, had given him. He expressed the hope that they would display a similar attitude toward the new Presidium. He then turned over the gavel to the new chairman, Sprinzak.

Sprinzak thanked the Council for electing him. The Council, he pointed out, is a provisional body and has the responsibility of paving the way for an elected legislature representing the people. All of us, he went on, are interested in having these elections as soon as possible. The present period is one of training, during which we are preparing for normal parliamentary life and laying the foundation of a parliamentary tradition based on the greatest degree of objectivity. He fervently hoped that with the help of the members of the Council, and in close cooperation with the Government and the president of the Council, we would justify the faith placed in us.

Speaking on behalf of the committee which decided on the composition of the Presidium, and on behalf of his own faction, the Mizrahi, Pinkas thanked the Prime Minister for chairing the Council's sessions and wished him continuing success. Weinstein (Hatzohar) and Mikunis (Communists) explained that they had abstained from voting for the members of the Presidium because their representatives had not been included.

A national flag and emblem were discussed, but no consensus was reached. The subject was postponed until the next session. A budget of PL 700,000 was adopted for the month of July. This sum did not include the defense budget, which was decided on the basis of a Government proposal and was not publicized.

At a meeting of the State Council on July 22, a few days after the truce began, the Prime Minister reported on the military and political situation:

> We again enter a truce period, and this time one of undefined duration. We cannot be certain that the military struggle is over. In any case, we face an extremely grave, perhaps

decisive, *political* struggle. The situation obligates us, first and foremost, to be ready for battle at any moment; only if we are militarily prepared will we be able to meet both the military and the political challenges facing us.

There have so far been three phases in our struggle. The first, when we were faced with Arab bands, lasted for five and a half months, from November 30, 1947, to May 14, 1948. In the second, from May 14 to June 11, we confronted the armies of Syria, Lebanon, Iraq, Trans-Jordan, and Egypt. The third, from July 9 to July 19, saw another Arab army, that of Saudi Arabia, enter the war. All three phases strangely resemble several chapters from Joshua and Judges that might have been written today:

"And it came to pass, when all the kings which were on this side of Jordan, in the hills, in the valleys, and in all the coasts of the great sea over against Lebanon, the Hittite and the Amorite, the Canaanite, the Perissite, the Hivite, and the Jebusite, heard thereof; That they gathered themselves together, to fight with Joshua and with Israel, with one accord" (Joshua 9:1–2).

"And these are the kings of the country which Joshua and the children of Israel smote . . . in the mountains, and in the valleys, and in the plains, and in the springs, and in the wilderness, and in the south country . . . all the kings thirty and one" (Joshua 12:7–24).

Only the names of the kings have changed. But there is one great difference. In Biblical times the Children of Israel fought only the inhabitants of this country. This time we are fighting all the neighboring countries. Our foes of recent weeks are no strangers to our history. We have more than once met Egypt and Assyria, Babylon and Aram, Canaan and Amalek, but always singly; never in thirty-five hundred years was the whole Middle East united against us.

There is another similarity between this war and one of the Biblical wars, that of Saul and Jonathan against the Philistines. They were certain then that "there was no smith found throughout all the land of Israel; for the Philistines said, Lest the Hebrews make them swords or spears. So it came to pass in the day of battle, that there was neither sword nor spear found in the hand of any of the people that were with Saul and Jonathan" (I Samuel 13:19–22).

No less vindictively did the British take care that there should be no smith in Israel, neither sword nor spear. They blockaded us by land and sea so that no arms might reach us. Their police tried to stamp out local arms production. Who will forget the searches by massive detachments of troops and police in our villages, our schools, and synagogues, to uncover every sword and spear of Israel? Drastic laws were passed against military training, and it was at the Yishuv that they were aimed. I cannot tell you at this time how we were able, nevertheless, to equip our military forces. However, I can say that the enemy no longer doubts the power of the Army of Israel.

I don't know how many of those sitting in this hall would have been ready nine or ten months ago to declare their belief in the Jewish community's ability to repulse a united attack by all the regular Arab armies without outside assistance. The experience of recent months, and particularly of the ten days between the two truces, shows that this was possible. But the struggle is not over.

Deprived of the lightning victory which they had planned and expected, the conspirators could not see, or would not admit, the facts, and so when the United Nations envoy called for an extension of the cease-fire, and we agreed, the Arab states did not. Some thought our agreement a sign of weakness, the Arab refusal a sign of self-confidence. The ten days that followed July 9, ten glorious days in our history, have given the Arab peoples and leaders and the whole world the plainest and most final of answers. Despite an intensified embargo, designed to prevent either sword or spear from coming into our hands, our Army opened a general offensive against all Arab concentrations as soon as the truce ended, and laid low the "kings" of Lydda and Ramle; the "kings" of Beit Naballah and Deir Tarif; the "kings of Kola and Migdal Zedek; the "kings" of Tsora and Eshtaol; and the "kings" of Artuf and Ain Karim in the lowlands; the "kings" of Chatah and Kretiya in the south; the "kings" of Shfaram and Zippori, the "kings" of Ein Ma'ahal and Kfar Kana, Nazareth, and Nimrin in the Galilee; the "kings" of Lubya and of the Horns of Hittin where Saladin vanquished the Crusader hosts. And during the same ten days it smote the hosts of Egypt and Trans-Jordan, Babylon which is Iraq, Syria and Lebanon and the famed Kaukji, and slew more than five thousand men. A thousand square kilometers were added to the State in the south, along the road to Jerusalem, in the Lydda-Ramle area, south of Haifa and in central Galilee, including Nazareth.

I hope the day will come, and in the not too distant future, when it will be possible to tell the wonderful tale of how we established, organized, equipped, and trained the Jewish forces which accomplished so much. At this moment I will limit myself to mentioning a secret weapon, which, more than anything else, was responsible for our ability to meet the challenges of these eight months, and which was also responsible for our conquests. I speak of the *spirit* of the individual Jew, of the Jewish pioneer and the Jewish fighter, a spirit of faith and devotion which is found in the hearts of our youth, our settlers, and our Army. This was the spirit that enabled us to carry out our constructive activities over a period of seventy years, during which we created Jewish soil, a Jewish economy, Jewish culture, and Jewish strength. This spirit made it possible for us to emerge victorious until now. It will, I feel certain, enable us to win again if we are faced with another military challenge.

We are in the midst of a truce of undefined duration. At this stage we must devote even greater efforts to preparing ourselves to meet the challenges of the future, and not only the military ones. The State of Israel was established in the midst of an armed struggle. But the State was not established in order to do battle or to win territory. It was not even established simply to ensure the peace and prosperity of its citizens. The State of Israel has a unique mission, unique at least in contemporary history, a mission which gives it its *raison d'être*. The State was created to make the land flourish, gather together the Jews from all over the world, and carry out a large-scale settlement program. These are our major tasks. Now that we are in a truce period of uncertain length, we must increase not only our military efforts, but also our efforts to organize large-scale immigration and settlement. These two activities are of vital importance, politically and militarily.

I want to make only one more remark: the UN General Assembly chose a man to mediate between the Arabs and us. The Provisional Government and the State Council have already made clear their attitude toward the Mediator's proposals and there is nothing to be added at this point, particularly in view of the recent evidence of our military capabilities, as well as our territorial conquests. If we are forced to fight again, we will go into battle with greater self-confidence.

Yet despite our increased confidence in Jewish military strength, we must exploit every opportunity, perhaps without the assistance of the Mediator, to reach a *modus vivendi* with the Arab peoples. This would not be at the expense of our rights, aims, or conquests, but rather an accord based on the great opportunities that exist for Jews and Arabs alike if they can work together as free and equal partners in an alliance to benefit the Middle East, and perhaps contribute to the peace and fructification of the entire world.

The Arabs will be able to free themselves of dependence—open and concealed—on forces of exploitation and repression only if they cooperate with the State and people of Israel, and we will have peace in this country only if we cooperate with our neighbors. We should do no less for peace than we have done—and will if necessary continue to do—for war.

I do not know if the Arabs are ready to accept cooperation with Jews on the basis of an alliance of equals, but this cooperation is a historic necessity. Having proven our strength on the field of battle to friends and enemies alike, we must not miss any opportunity—if any exists—to lay the foundations for cooperation between the Jewish State and the Arab states.

Sprinzak, presiding, said that he had been informed that the Government wished to conclude with the Prime Minister's remarks. But he asked whether members favored a discussion. Weinstein commented that they were waiting for a survey of the whole complex of political problems facing the State of Israel, and that a debate should take place after the survey had been presented.

The Council chose the Justices of the Supreme Court in accordance with the Courts Ordinance, which states: "The Justices of the Supreme Court will be appointed by the Provisional Government on the basis of a list prepared by the Minister of Justice, and with the approval of the Provisional State Council." Moshe Zmora was named Chief Justice, with Isaac Olshan, Menahem Dunkelblum, Shneur Zalman Heshin and Rabbi Simha Assaf as Justices.

"Please permit me to congratulate the first Justices of the Israel Supreme Court in the name of the Provisional State Council," Sprinzak said. "We have entrusted them with a great moral responsibility. We hope that they will make it clearly manifest that justice reigns in the State of Israel."

Israel's First Military Parade

The truce was not fully observed by the Arabs during the first few days. There were fierce battles in Galilee. A heavy Arab attack began near the Banias, in the north, on the morning of July 19 and continued until the next day. The Arabs also attempted to conquer Susita, overlooking Ein Gev. The Syrians were active in the Mishmar Hayarden area, and the Egyptians in the Negev. The truce was also breached by the Arab Legion in Jerusalem. Truce violations occurred continually even after the meeting between the Jewish commanders and the commanders of the Arab Legion. Not until July 21 was an agreement signed between the IDF Commander in Jerusalem, David Shaltiel, and the Legion Commander, Abdullah el Tal.

When the battlefronts finally quieted down, the Minister of Defense [Ben-Gurion] ordered Aluf [General] Shlomo Shamir to organize a military parade in Tel Aviv on July 27, the anniversary of Theodor Herzl's death. General Yacov Dori, as Chief of Staff, issued the following order of the day: "Herzl's vision of a Jewish State in 1896 has become a reality. The anniversary of his death, which falls today, is not yet a holiday celebrating final victory. We still face a long struggle. This is not a day to boast of our triumphs, but to express faith in our growing strength and in the fearless spirit of our young Army. This spirit will bring freedom, peace, and security to our people, as well as equality and friendship with all the peoples of the world."

The preparations for the large parade, the first in our history, were in evidence from the morning hours. Armed soldiers arrived in Tel Aviv from all over the country, including a unit from Jerusalem, to symbolize the link between that city and the State of Israel. Flags were hoisted over public buildings as well as outside many private homes.

A few hours before the start of the parade, scheduled for 5 P.M., rejoicing multitudes lined the route and stood on the balconies and roofs overlooking it. Ropes were stretched all along Allenby Road from the Moshavot Square, where the parade was to begin, up to November 2nd Square, then down Ben-Yehuda Street to the entrance of the stadium on the banks of the Yarkon River in North Tel Aviv. Traffic was diverted to side streets. The organization was perfect. Scarcely any supervision was required. The public displayed great self-discipline and enthusiasm. There was no need for ushers.

The standard-bearers led off the parade to the music of a military band. They were accompanied by a unit carrying rifles topped with bayonets. These were followed by the participants in a Company Commanders course, a Palmah unit (including girls), a Palmah commando unit, the Police Orchestra, a Women's Corps unit, a Navy unit (headed by a bearded sailor in a white uniform), followed by a company of sailors in an amphibious jeep with a giant projector, a Communications unit, the Firemen's Orchestra, a Military Police unit, a Mule Corps unit (with the mules carrying machine guns for operations in the hills), an Armored Corps unit, Artillerymen, engineering vehicles, and representatives of all the brigades which had fought in the Nazareth-Jenin area, the Haifa-Tira area, the Lydda-Ramle area, the brigades which had fought in the south up to Ashdod, in the Negev, the Etzion bloc, Jerusalem, the road to Jerusalem, and the Hartuv area.

This was the first time that the public had seen Israeli tanks, artillery, armored vehicles, fighter planes, and bombers. The planes provided an aerial umbrella over the stadium. Blue-and-white flags in profusion waved in the breeze. The soldiers marched into the stadium in perfect order. As each unit entered, the enormous crowd applauded fervently.

Among those present were members of the Provisional Government, the State Council, the Tel Aviv Municipality, the Histadrut, the national institutions, political parties, and various organizations. Representatives of foreign governments and UN Observers were present. This was the first occasion in which the heads of General Staff branches appeared publicly in their uniforms and with their insignia of rank.

When the troops had been called to attention, the Prime Minister, accompanied by Chief of Staff Yacov Dori, entered the stadium. The entire crowd stood up and the national flag was raised. After "Hatikva" had been sung the men and women present bowed their heads in memory of those who had fallen on land, at sea, and in the air. It was an awe-inspiring moment, as tens of thousands remembered the soldiers of the Israel Defense Forces who had defended the Homeland with their very bodies, whose blood had soaked into its soil. These men had paid for Israel's freedom with their lives.

The Prime Minister began his address by quoting from an entry Herzl had made in his diary after the First Zionist Congress in 1897: "If I were to sum up the Basle Congress in one sentence—and out of caution I shall not utter it in public—it would be this: *at Basle I founded the Jewish State*. If I were to say this today, I would be the object of universal mirth. But perhaps in five years' time, at all events in fifty years' time, everyone will acknowledge it." Ben-Gurion went on to say:

> Fifty years have passed since then, and Herzl's vision has come to life. Why did Herzl believe that he had founded the Jewish State in Basle? It was, as he noted in his diary, "because the State is based upon the will of the people for a State."
>
> Herzl was not fated to witness the results of his creation. He spent only seven years in the work for his great mission, for his life was cut short at the early age of forty-four. The constructive policy which he developed for the national will for a State, however, provided

us with our two great political achievements in the international sphere: the Balfour Declaration of November 2, 1917, twenty years after the First Congress, and the United Nations resolution for the establishment of a Jewish State on November 29, 1947, thirty years later.

But the Congress and the Zionist Organization, and the political activity which came about through them, were not the only expression of the national will to statehood. Several years before the First Zionist Congress, a new channel was opened up for the yearnings of the people and for its ardent desire to make its redemption a reality. This was the immigration of settlers and pioneers, who created tangible values and *put the Zionist idea into practice.*

The builders of the first agricultural school at Mikve Israel in 1870; the Jews from the Old City of Jerusalem and from Hungary who laid the foundations of the first Jewish village at Petah Tikva in 1878; the first pioneers who founded Gedera, Rishon LeZion, Zikhron Yacov, and Rosh Pina—they and their successors opened up the first and principal channel, one which has constantly grown and widened, for the national will to statehood. Three generations of pioneers and toilers have transformed the appearance of the Homeland. They have brought into being a body of Jews whose freedom, independence, and strength is unparalleled in any other part of the world. It is a community rooted in its soil, its farms, its villages, its cities, its language, and its culture. It is rooted in its distant past and closely linked to the future to which it aspires. It embodies not only a desire but a capacity to build a State; and in fact it forms the ever growing nucleus of the Jewish State.

Without the early efforts of the pioneers of immigration and settlement we should never have achieved our present position. When the great leader breathed his last, forty-four years ago, it seemed as if the dream of a Jewish State had been dealt its death blow, as if political Zionism had reached an impasse. But at that juncture there welled up the never failing spring of the Second Aliya, which revived the pioneering venture with a mighty and youthful force. It was then, too, that a third channel was opened up for the national will to statehood, side by side with that of creative pioneering. This was the Jewish armed force.

It was at Sejera, a little Jewish village in Galilee, one of four isolated Jewish villages in that area, that the first nucleus of a Jewish self-defense force was formed over forty years ago. This force was known at the time as Hashomer. Once again the chain of Jewish valor was reforged on the soil of the Homeland. This chain grew in strength following the establishment of Hashomer. There was the Jewish Legion, which fought in the First World War. There was the formation of the Hagana following the defense of Tel Hai. There was the formation of the Jewish Settlement Police during the disturbances of 1936–39, after which came the Palmah, the Jewish battalions, and the Jewish Brigade of the Second World War. All these prepared the way for the heroic and glorious defense by our Army in this war. Without that chapter of Jewish armed heroism, we should not have attained our present position.

These, then, are the three channels through which flowed our nation's will to statehood, and all three derive from one unfailing historic mission. This faithfulness is obstinate; it does not flinch from suffering, persecution, expulsion, slaughter, or annihilation. It does not give way before cruelty, compulsion, or violence, however great the physical force applied. The faithfulness of the Jew was manifested in countless instances, from Medieval martyrdom to the awe-inspiring revolt of the ghettos in our own day. It reached its peak in the pioneering, political, and military effort in the Homeland, which has brought us to the greatest event of our generation—the proclamation of the Jewish State on May 14 which marks a decisive turning-point in Jewish history and an important milestone in world history.

Our generation has been privileged to witness the end of our subjection and the beginning of our redemption. *But we should not be unduly boastful.* It is not due to us alone that we have been granted the Jewish State. Had it not been for the profound faith and ancient heritage of generations of the Jewish people, to whom the vision of redemption was ever present, and whose hearts throughout the centuries were bound in love and yearning to their ancestral Homeland; had it not been for the early efforts of our pioneers and fighters in immigration, settlement, self-defense, and international political activity, the State of Israel would not have arisen in our day.

But the debt that we owe to our forefathers is not the only reason it behooves us to display modesty. The State of Israel arose in the storm and stress of battle, at a time when a dual war was forced upon us—a political and military war. The Mandatory Government sought to bequeath us a legacy of chaos, but we overcame it, achieved our independence, and established the State of Israel.

The battle, however, is not yet over. We have *thus far* emerged victorious from our military encounters. We have stood up successfully, without any help from the United Nations, against Arab aggression, which tried, with the help of the British government, to frustrate the UN decisions. We have succeeded not only in preserving almost in its entirety the area of the Jewish State as outlined by the General Assembly decision of November 29, 1947, but have also made enormous territorial gains outside those boundaries. Our military forces have occupied nearly all the quarters previously held by the enemy in modern Jerusalem: Romema, Lifta, Sheikh Bader, Katamon, Bak'a, Allenby Barracks, Musrara, and other places. With the exception of the Old City, Jerusalem has become Jewish to an extent unprecedented since the destruction of the Second Temple.

We have occupied Safad, Tiberias, Haifa, and Acre. Following the occupation of Aziv, Batsa, and other points, our forces in western Galilee have reached the Lebanese frontier. In the Jerusalem area we have occupied Kastel, Beit Mahsir, Tsuba, Saris, Malha, and Ein Karem. On the road to Bab al-Wad and in the Jerusalem corridor we have taken Beit Jiz, Beit Susin, Sar'a and Artuf. In the south we have taken Yibna, Kubeiba, Masmiya, Sumeil, Zeita, Hatta, and Karatiya. We have taken Jaffa and its satellite villages of Salameh, Yazour, and Beit Dajan. We have taken Lydda and Ramle, Beit Naballah and Ras al-Ein, Kawkab and Salbit, Barfiliya, Bir Ima'in, and Bourj, the airfield and railway station at Lydda. We have liberated Ben Shemen, and have reached Modi'in, the birthplace of the Maccabees. In the Valley of Jezreel we have occupied Zar'in, Nouris, and Mazar. We have occupied Beisan, the heights of Gilboa, Shfaram, Zippori, Nazareth, Kfar Kana, Lubya, and Hittin in central Galilee. On the road to Haifa we have taken Ein Hod, Jaba, and Tira. Our Air Force has rained down heavy blows on Amman, Damascus, and Cairo, and on all enemy concentrations. Our Navy has also helped.

But we are not yet entitled to congratulate ourselves that victory is ours. *Only victory in the last and final battle will be decisive*, and we cannot say as yet that our victories in the recent engagements were those of the last battle. No one can tell as yet with any certainty whether this truce is the end of the war or merely a temporary break in hostilities. Unless we are prepared, keyed up, properly equipped and ready for action on land, in the air, and at sea, so that we can deliver the knockout blow *in the final battle*, should the war be resumed, no final and decisive importance can attach to the gains and victories we have hitherto achieved.

We may have to fight a difficult political battle, for in addition to our declared enemies we have many secret and camouflaged foes who will miss no opportunity to curtail our rights and narrow down our achievements and gains. The act of May 14 will not be consummated *as long as our army and government do not assure the State of Israel peace, security, and sovereignty* within just and enduring boundaries, that will take into account not only the compromise of November 29 but all that has taken place between that date and now. *It will not be consummated until the pioneering effort of our nation in Israel and in the Diaspora gathers all the exiles into the liberated Homeland—until the desolation of this country is reclaimed to the maximum extent.*

We still have a long and difficult road ahead of us. Our historical goal—the ingathering of the exiles and complete redemption—will not be achieved without further suffering, effort, and sacrifice. We look forward to tomorrow with vigilance, tension, and increased preparedness, but also with strength and faith. We place our trust in the Rock of Israel, and our trust has not failed us. Herzl said: "The Jews who wish it will attain their State, and they will be worthy of it." Let us loyally fulfill our duty, and we shall be worthy of our State.

The first military parade in Israel made an enormous impression and gave a glimpse of the power and equipment acquired by the Defense Forces in the ten weeks since the establishment of the State. These, in turn, were the results of efforts made during the two previous years.

The enthusiasm of the crowds along the parade route and in the stadium rose to a fever pitch as captured enemy armored vehicles drove past. The ships of the young Israeli Navy also took part in the celebrations, putting on a show off the Tel Aviv shore on Herzl Day.

Talks with UN Mediator ★ Provisional Government Debates the Ending of the Truce

On July 28, the day after the parade, at a meeting of the Provisional Government, Foreign Minister Shertok reported on his July 26 meeting with Bernadotte. The Mediator complained that Israel's representatives at Lake Success had stated that she had no faith in him. Moreover, Bernadotte added, the Prime Minister had said that Israel favored direct negotiations with the Arabs, which meant that in her opinion there was no need for a Mediator. He wanted to know whether Israel would cooperate with him.

The Foreign Minister replied that since Israel had not appointed Bernadotte, the question of confidence in him did not arise. He was accepted by Israel as an agent of the United Nations. The Prime Minister's statement, Shertok added, had been of a positive character, apprising the Arabs that the Jews were ready to negotiate with them. If the Mediator could facilitate such negotiations, so much the better.

Bernadotte then brought up the question of the demilitarization of Jerusalem. Shertok informed him that Israel rejected the idea completely, and that she opposed also the authority assumed by the Consuls' Committee with regard to immigration to Jerusalem. The Jewish public increasingly felt that Jerusalem should be included in the Jewish State and hoped that the UN could be convinced of the justice of this demand. Bernadotte appeared very disappointed. He asked: Do you accept the principle of demilitarization? The Foreign Minister answered him in accordance with our Government's decision, namely, that we cannot under any circumstances agree to the principle of demilitarization. "Does that mean that you reject it?" Bernadotte asked. The Foreign Minister replied: "If I may give you a suggestion, don't push us too hard on this question. There is a truce at the moment, and therefore no need for an immediate decision." The Mediator remained unmoved. He requested an answer, "if not today, then tomorrow or the day after tomorrow." In another discussion between the Foreign Minister and two members of Bernadotte's staff, they told him that the UN proposal of July 13 had been based on the assumption that there would be no truce.

On the day of the parade the Foreign Minister received an inquiry from Bernadotte as to whether we accepted the principle of demilitarization. Whatever our answer, he declared, it will not obligate us in regared to a final settlement.

Bernadotte also raised the question of the Arab refugees. There are 300,000 to 350,000 of them, living in poverty and deprivation. As far as possible, they must be repatriated, he said. Bernadotte wanted to know whether we were ready to cooperate with him on this problem. The Foreign Minister replied that there was no possibility of admitting the refugees during the war period. The Arab states were trying to force us to accept the refugees, because they regarded them as a weapon to be used against us, a fifth column to destroy Israel from within. The Mediator did not show any flexibility on this issue.

The Count asked another question: Are we ready to consider the possibility of going from a truce to an armistice? The Foreign Minister asked, in turn, whether an armistice would be a stepping-stone toward peace—that is, would the Arabs be willing to negotiate with us as equals?

The Foreign Minister suggested the following three-point reply to the Mediator's demilitarization proposal: (1) the Provisional Government reiterates its absolute rejection of the demilitarization proposal presented to it by the Mediator on July 22, 1948; (2) the Government's attitude to the Mediator's plan is incvitably influenced by his suggestion—never retracted—that, in the final analysis, Jerusalem should be put under an Arab regime; (3) the Provisional Government is ready, as it always has been, to discuss any reasonable plan to save Jerusalem from further destruction, if fighting should begin all over the country; any plan, to be acceptable, must safeguard the vital interests of the Jewish people in Jerusalem. The proposed reply was approved after a short debate. So was the Foreign Minister's statement on the return of the refugees: "As long as the war continues, there can be no repatriation of refugees."

On August 1, 1948, a few days after the military parade, the Government met to discuss the military situation. The meeting was opened by the Minister of Defense, Ben-Gurion, who warned that the public had an exaggerated notion of our victories. Then he said in substance:

> We certainly should not underestimate what has been accomplished; at the same time, we should not delude ourselves by taking an unduly optimistic view. Considerable cause for concern still remains. We suffered three setbacks; one of them was not too important, but the others were very important indeed. The fact that we did not liberate Mishmar Hayarden was not of undue consequence, but our failure to capture Latrun and open the main road to Jerusalem, as well as our failure to gain free access to the Negev, may have very grave consequences.
>
> True, when the truce began twelve days ago, Egypt lacked an east-to-west road from its forces in Majdal to those in Faluja and Beit Gubrin, just as we lacked a road from north to south. But its forces in the Negev are much stronger than ours. If we block a road at a particular point, they can easily make a detour. We, on the other hand, have no such alternatives. At one stage the Egyptians agreed to allow our convoy to proceed to the south, but when a convoy reached their lines, it was not allowed to pass. We captured Bir Asluj before the first truce and are still holding on. However, it is encircled by the Egyptians and we find it almost impossible to get through to that outpost.
>
> An undeclared war is under way in the south. The Egyptians have apparently decided to take the entire Negev. They are grabbing new areas all the time, since they are not under

surveillance. In our case, the more we gain, the more trouble we have. We have captured additional areas, and now we must hold on to them. If our Army is forced to remain indefinitely—or even for a month or two—in the filthy, insect-ridden places that it has captured, without the possibility of rest, reorganization, or training, it is liable to fall apart. In any case, we have no justification for entrusting our existing forces with this task. We need nine thousand more men for garrison duty. The Defense Forces have lost many men in the course of the fighting, and these losses must be replaced. Some units have received only limited training, and their training must be completed. Our soldiers also need leave. We have no way of knowing how long this truce will last. We heard that Bernadotte will leave on August 15 for a month's rest at home. It is very hot here now; the climate in Sweden is certainly much more pleasant during this time of the year. The UN General Assembly will meet at the end of November, and only then will it hear a report on the situation in this country. The United Nations has time; this matter can drag on for months. It is unlikely that we can accept such a situation, if only for financial reasons. We must keep every one of our units up to full strength, and we must establish at least one reserve brigade.

As for Jerusalem: the Old City is now in Arab hands, as is Sheikh Jarrah. Bernadotte has suggested demilitarization of the city. Because he represents the United Nations, his proposals carry weight. This has created a political situation that serves the needs of our enemies, and all those who are not our friends. Perhaps the Arabs are also having difficulties, but that doesn't make our own situation any easier. Meanwhile, a new status quo is created and the world learns to accept it. We are not a nation like all other nations. We are under supervision. There are supervisors here who do not even require our visas. The world is getting used to the idea that Israel is a dubious, problematical country.

We cannot possibly know what surprises the Arabs have in store for us. We must view the situation clearly, without illusions. We won because the Arabs were extraordinarily weak and cowardly. Normally, they should have won. They had more men, better equipment, and a reasonably good officer corps. They had British, German, and Yugoslav commanders. Their human resources, true, are not on the same level as ours; we have a great moral advantage. But we should not put too much trust in these factors. We cannot foresee what will happen in a large country like Egypt, one of our most serious enemies. It is a homogeneous nation, unlike Syria and Iraq, which have many minorities. Egypt, moreover, is a rich state—the people are poor, but the nation as a whole is rich.

If the present situation continues for an extended period, our international position will worsen. Our military strength may decrease and our economic strength may be undermined. There is no reason why we should accept a truce of unlimited duration. We must inform our friends, to the extent that they exist, as well as world opinion, that such a situation cannot be allowed to continue indefinitely. The invaders must be forced either to leave the country or to make peace. Otherwise, we will drive them out ourselves. There is no political justice or wisdom in making us accept a state of affairs in which we suffer all the disadvantages of war and do not enjoy any of the benefits of peace, stability, independence, and tranquillity. The Security Council did not decide on a truce of unlimited duration. It simply decided not to set a specific time limit. The Council will continue to discuss the question. We have the legal right to demand an end to the truce. If we do not succeed in persuading the Security Council to fix a date, we will act on our own, explaining that we cannot accept the continued presence of foreign invaders on our soil, in violation of the UN Charter. We must drive them out. We have less to fear from sanctions than from a continuation of the present condition.

We will not have an easy time of it. The enemy has great advantages; that is why we did not liberate Mishmar Hayarden, conquer Latrun, or open the road to the Negev. But if we have two more brigades, we will be able to strike a decisive blow against the Egyptians, defeat the Iraqis from Ramallah to Bethlehem, mop up in the Galilee, and throw out the Syrians. If our armies are sufficiently trained, if we have reserves, and if we can obtain the necessary heavy equipment, we will be able to end the war in a month or six weeks. The truce must conclude by the end of August or, at the latest, the middle of September. We must announce to the UN that if the foreign invaders do not leave the country by then, we will throw them out.

Shertok stated that we should concentrate militarily on the Negev. He supported the Prime Minister's view that a truce of unlimited duration might create unbearable political, military, and financial burdens. But there are important questions of tactics: (1) We should not set a date for an end to the truce as yet, but simply demand that such a date be set, adding that if our demand is not accepted, we will renew the struggle on a particular date. (2) We should emphasize the fact that foreign forces are on our soil; this means that there is a state of war, and this gives us the right to demand their withdrawal. The Egyptians periodically violate the truce, and we can retaliate.

Gruenbaum agreed that there were considerable difficulties in a truce of unlimited dura-tion, but opposed an attempt to drive out the invaders single-handed. We do not demand all of the Land of Israel, and the invaders who are outside our borders are not violating our sovereignty, he said. Only if they continue their attacks in the Negev or in the vicinity of Jerusalem, should we reply with a concentrated counterattack. This we should do when we are ready, at a date that cannot yet be set.

Shapira commented that the war could be lost both in battle and during a truce. He saw more danger of suffering a substantial defeat in battle, however, than during a truce. We have no chance of capturing Damascus, Cairo, Baghdad, and San'a; consequently out situation will not have improved even when we reach the borders of Egypt or Syria. Thus in present circumstances a truce is better than rushing into a new war.

Bernstein thought that the Prime Minister's analysis of the situation was accurate. A truce of unlimited duration was an attempt to impoverish us financially, he believed.

Bentov suggested that, in the meantime, we limit ourselves to military and political preparations, rather than deciding definitely to go into action at the beginning of Septem-ber. He also thought that contact should be established with opposition elements in Egypt, Iraq, and Syria. We must seek allies, he said. Consideration should also be given to the possibility of establishing a government in exile for the Arab state in Israel.

Rabbi Levin supported the views expressed by Shapira.

Rabbi Fishman disagreed. We cannot accept a truce that will go on indefinitely and for no purpose, he said. Increasing our forces in the Negev does not have to be accomplished at the expense of Jerusalem. We must strengthen our position in Jerusalem economically, militarily, and in terms of manpower during the month to six weeks at our disposal. We must also prepare for war. We cannot depend on miracles.

Kaplan remarked that he was more fearful of sanctions than other members of the Provisional Government.

Rosenblueth, asserted that Ben-Gurion's proposal had come as a surprise to him and he wished to think about it. "I do not believe in a decisive victory, namely, the destruction of the enemy armies," he said. While we are gaining strength during the truce period, so are the Arabs. If the proposal aims to make the Arabs negotiate, it is logical; but if its purpose is to end the truce and renew the war, then it is terribly dangerous.

Remez admitted that his past fears had been unfounded. "I am happy," he said, "that we were victorious, and that I was wrong. I prefer a victory that contradicts my views to a defeat that confirms them. But any decision about war or peace is a grave matter, and what happened in the past may not happen again in the future. Thus far time has been on our side. Thanks to the truce, there has been time for training, rest for our soldiers, and the acquisition of new equipment. Why would time cease to be on our side in the future? The Arabs are not in such a good situation either. There are many splits in their ranks. Why should we renew the war and reunify them? The whole picture should be examined carefully.

Shertok responded to Bentov's suggestion that an attempt be made to seek new approaches to the Arabs. Foreign Ministry representatives in Paris, he indicated, are making great efforts in this direction, but the results have been in inverse proportion to the energy invested. People in Egypt, Lebanon, and Syria have been approached. There were also attempts to contact Arab personalities now in Europe. But the results to date have not been encouraging. The officials concerned have considered adding a group of prominent local Arabs to the Israel team, but decided against it. The one thing we must not do is establish a government of Quislings.

Bentov: Would an Arab government necessarily be a government of Quislings?

Shertok: Any Arab government that lacked roots in Arab society would be considered a Quisling government by the Arabs.

Ben-Gurion summarized the discussion:

> If peace could be achieved on the basis of the status quo, even though it is not ideal I would readily assent. But the UN has not respected its own decisions. When the Arabs announced that they would not accept them, there was no one to defend these decisions, not even the decision calling for an internationalized Jerusalem. What are they doing now? A truce has been proclaimed in order to provide an opportunity to find a way to peace. This is logical, but there is no logic in a truce of unlimited duration.

> What happens during the coming months will determine our future for many generations. Thus we cannot simply settle for what is easiest for us at this time. I cannot promise that if we fight we will win, though I believe we will. We must therefore try to determine what course of action is, on balance, least dangerous. It is clear to me that we may lose much more from a continuation of the present situation than from a renewal of the conflict. On several occasions we have fought and lost. This does not alter a number of basic facts: we enjoy a moral advantage. Moreover, when one of our soldiers is wounded or taken prisoner, he can be replaced within a period of three weeks. No Arab people can do that.

> Our most serious enemy at the moment is Egypt. If we concentrate sufficient land forces, and if we use our air power, we can destroy the Egyptian invasion force and liberate the Negev.

> I would like to turn now to a very painful matter, Jerusalem. I see Jerusalem from a Jewish viewpoint: it contains a hundred thousand Jews and is extremely meaningful to the Jews of the world. We do not have many concentrations of a hundred thousand Jews in this country, or other places like Jerusalem. We should certainly try to ensure that Jerusalem and the road to the city remain in our hands. We have, in fact, a good chance of achieving these goals. Then, if the Arabs don't want peace, there may not be peace, but there will certainly be a State. We will be able immediately to transfer the Government to Jerusalem. If Latrun had been in our hands, I would have suggested such a transfer immediately after the truce, without a formal annexation of the city. There should be no declarations, there should be deeds! Facts should be created. If Jerusalem had already been in our hands, would we have transferred the Government here [Tel Aviv]?

Our chances are good. A comparison of our forces and preparedness with those of the Arabs shows that we can break the back of the Egyptians and conquer a corridor to Jerusalem; this will drastically improve our position. Afterward, we will be able to reduce the size of the Army; we will have created a new situation in the eyes of the world. The dangers of an unlimited truce would be much greater, politically as well as economically.

We do not have to decide now when to end the truce, but we must carry out our political and military activities with a clear aim in mind, as enunciated by the Foreign Minister in Document No. 18. Our representatives must explain why a date must be set for an end to the truce, and we must make all the necessary military and economic preparations so that we will be ready for battle when that day comes.

I will try to summarize the views expressed in this debate: (a) We all agree that a truce of unlimited duration is undesirable, and that this point should be stressed by our representatives to the UN, to the United States, to the Soviet Union, and to other countries. (b) We must convince the UN to set a date for an end to the truce. (c) We must prepare ourselves for the possibility that the truce will end.

No member of the Government disputed this summary.

From My Diaries:

August 2–September 9, 1948.

August 2, 1948

Nahum Sarig came to see me. During the ten-day period the Egyptians tried to cut off the Negev completely, but did not succeed. At first the Egyptians had their eyes on the country as a whole. However, when they failed to achieve their original aim, they concentrated on the Negev. They are now taking control of new strongpoints without opposition. They have surrounded our outpost at Bir Asluj. There is an Egyptian battalion in Beersheba which receives supplies from the Hebron hills and from Egypt.

The Egyptians have good intelligence, good administration, good organization, and a great deal of equipment; but they lack battle experience. They are skillful at defense. They have organized the Arab civilian population into (tribal) Home Guard units charged with guarding the railway and military bases. Local people are also being used for such projects as harvesting and digging fortifications. After the Egyptians take over an outpost, two or three hundred Arabs are brought to dig fortifications and erect a barbed-wire fence. Good administrative work is evident everywhere. By our standards they have unlimited supplies of ammunition. Two or three thirty-car trains arrive daily with troops and equipment. Ships are also used for transport.

The Egyptians are undoubtedly the most serious force opposing us. They have an estimated 20,000 men in their army, not counting local auxiliaries.

Our most serious problem is the lack of a unified command. The Egyptians do have a unified command. Egyptian communications are excellent; ours are very bad. Every Negev Brigade operation demands the appointment of an officer to coordinate it with the Givati Brigade.

We have 1,700 soldiers in the Negev. This figure does not include the members of the settlements (among them 600 combatants). There are 650 soldiers now training for service in the Negev. We lack transport to the Negev. The soldiers and settlers in the region are very tired and under great tension. The settlements have almost ceased to exist as economic entities. There are no people to harvest the crops. The water pipeline is still operating and remains completely under our control, but we do not have the men to prevent the Egyptians from seizing it.

We must quickly send reinforcements to the Negev. Two infantry battalions, one for general operations and one for garrison duty, are required. We must find 700 people in addition to the 650 now in training. The settlements require additional manpower for both military and civilian tasks. Reinforcements can be brought in without the Arabs noticing, but more people in the region would increase the severity of our supply problems.

The war in the Negev has not ended. The cessation of operations in the north led to an increase in Egyptian activity in the Negev. Air communications in the region immediately after the truce were unimpeded. Now it is possible to send planes only at night because of increased Egyptian air activity.

We need more transport, more manpower for the settlements, a full brigade, and a unified command in the Negev. Yigael Yadin and I have worked out a series of operations to be undertaken against the Egyptians.

August 4, 1948

In the morning I traveled to Natanya to watch a combined maneuver, involving infantry, artillery, mortars, heavy machine guns, and air planes. It took place within the framework of a Company Commander's course directed by Chaim Laskov.

August 5, 1948

Tsur came to see me. Yesterday he brought four bombers (Beaufighters) to the country. They are two-engine planes and each of them is equipped with four cannon and six machine guns. A fifth plane crashed and a sixth is on the way. Ten more Spitfires are scheduled to arrive.

The General Staff met at 5:30. There are four sources of additional manpower: The 5000 Chen [Women's] members, 5000 thirty-six-to-forty-year-olds, immigrants, and young people. It has been suggested that we send a military delegation overseas to mobilize 10,000 men. Until now, they say, only the worst elements have come from abroad. The immigrants are now being placed in Home Guard units.

I clarified the question of priorities in the purchase of weapons. Avidar believes that we need 10,000 more rifles, 60 million bullets, and 300 heavy machine guns. We require tanks (10 tanks are better than 4 airplanes), as well as antiaircraft, antitank, field, and naval guns.

I talked with Yosef Yacobson about the organization of the Ministry of Defense, including accounting, purchases, industry, mobilization, overseas volunteers, aid for soldiers' families, disabled veterans, widows and orphans, rehabilitation, the air force, the navy, intelligence, military law, transportation, expropriation, government in conquered areas, youth, physical culture, and fortifications. Yosef promised to prepare an organizational code.

In the last four and a half months 10,000 immigrants with a modicum of physical and military training have come to the country via Marseilles. There are an additional 600 to 700 people in the Marseilles camp. Some 2000 people have come from Western Europe. There is a linguistic problem; they speak Hebrew, Yiddish, French, English, and

German. They range in age from seventeen to twenty-six. It is possible to mobilize another 10,000 men in Western Europe, but this will demand considerable effort. There has been no real mobilization in England. North Africa provides an important source of manpower, though the cultural level of those who come is low.

August 9, 1948

There are demands from all the pioneering youth movements (Bnei Akiva, Maccabee Hatzair, Hashomer Hatzair, Mahanot Haolim, Hatnuah Ham'uhedet, Hanoar Haoved, Hatzofim) that we provide military training, within the framework of settlement groups, from the age of seventeen. These groups would include girls. I suggested a straight three-month period of military training, to be followed by agricultural training in the settlements, during which time the youngsters would take off an additional two or three days each month for military training.

I met with Assaf Simhoni of the Palmah's Yiftah Brigade. He has just been appointed commander of its First Battalion. The brigade commander is Mulla Cohen. Assaf has spent seven years in the Palmah. In other words, he has been in since the beginning. I asked him if he had been appointed battalion commander by chance, or did his appointment represent a change in policy? Neither, he answered. There is a constant debate in the Palmah. Some commanders are gradually coming to realize that they have fallen behind other units, though at the outset they were better trained. Their training is far from complete, and they lack proper military organization. Assaf is among those who demanded that the Palmah learn from other units, and as others began to share his opinion his prestige rose. Most of the men in his battalion are members of the party. The Palmah commanders are meeting today to discuss whether a National Palmah Command is necessary. It is indicative of changing attitudes that they now realize the need for ranks and for discipline.

I was visited by Rabbi Shlomo Goronchik [Goren], whom Rabbis Fishman and Herzog had proposed as Chief Chaplain of the Defense Forces. I told him that the rabbis had to be able to earn the respect of the nonreligious, and to influence the heterogeneous population of the Yishuv. If they were not respected, they would do more harm than good. Goronchik agreed. He himself was in the Hagana and holds a university degree in Philosophy and Classics. I sent him to Yacov Dori.

August 11, 1948

I had a discussion in the evening with the General Staff on the situation in the various units. Yigael, Yosef, and Zadok, who had toured the fronts, found the situation quite satisfactory. Our men are confident. They have equipment and it only remains to bring the brigades up to full strength.

August 12, 1948

A report from Egypt (from the end of July) indicates that the Egyptians are running out of ammunition. They received their last shipment two months ago (from England); it cost E£4 million. It was, in fact, short-range training ammunition. This explains why Egyptian guns have a range of 8000 yards instead of 12,000. The same holds true with regard to ammunition for antiaircraft guns and 37-mm. cannon. Bombers flying over Cairo at 12,000 feet are absolutely safe. Since the end of the first truce, England has not supplied Egypt with a single piece of artillery.

The Egyptian Navy consists of a merchant ship armed with six cannon, five mine-sweepers of American manufacture, two auxiliary ships, and six light vessels. The Egyptians have no torpedo boats. Their Navy numbers 1200 officers and men, with another 6000 in reserve.

August 13, 1948

Assaf came to see me. Water is already flowing to Jerusalem through the "Burma Road" pipeline.

The defense budget for August is PL5,338,000 (not including overseas purchases). Maintenance requires PL1,906,000 (the salaries for 1320 men in the administration take PL58,000). PL210,000 are needed for the 70,000 men in camps, PL140,000 for the 7000 men under arms outside the camps and 35 pounds each for the 8000 men on garrison duty. This last item adds up to PL280,000. The other money is spent for miscellaneous purposes.

August 16, 1948

In the afternoon I was visited by James McDonald, the American Minister, together with his assistant Charles F. Knox. They showed me a letter from the President asking about the possibility of full recognition, a cessation of the embargo, and financial assistance to Israel. McDonald spoke all the time. There was an air-raid alarm in the middle of our conversation and we were forced to go into the shelter.

August 17, 1948

In the morning there was a reception at the Kirya for the Soviet Minister, Pavel Yershov. When he came into the room, Yershov turned to me even before being introduced. He said that he had been sent by the Presidium of Soviet Russia. I replied in Hebrew, and Moshe [Shertok] translated. Yershov then handed me his credentials, which had been signed by President Shvernik, the successor to Kalinin, and approved by [Vyacheslav] Molotov. Then he presented his party and Moshe presented ours. We sat down at a small table to talk. Yershov told me that he had heard that I had come to the country as a manual laborer. I told him of my visit to Moscow in 1925, and he said that I would no longer recognize the city. A great deal has been built, not skyscrapers, but fifteen-story buildings. He expressed amazement at seeing how Tel Aviv had been built on sand dunes. I said that two factors had been responsible for our accomplishments: work and vision. We parted after a brief conversation.

In the afternoon I went to the Ekron Airfield, which was being rededicated. There was an impressive display of airpower, including fighter planes and bombers. Mock air battles were staged. We have developed an air force.

August 18, 1948

The enemy armies are in a state of alert. The Iraqis have received reinforcements. They have eight battalions now instead of their former five. The Egyptian radio has ordered Egyptian troops to be ready to go into action at any moment. The irregular forces of the Mufti and Kaukji are active. There is also activity at Beit Jallah, around Beit Naballah and in the north. About 1000 supporters of the Mufti are being organized at Deir Ballut. There is nervousness on both sides. Perhaps the Arabs fear that we will attack them.

August 19, 1948

Twenty-three 75-mm. field guns and two 75-mm. mountain guns are on the way from Mexico. Items purchased but not yet sent include thirty-two 75-mm. cannon from France, eighteen 75-mm. cannon from Switzerland, fifteen 20-mm. cannon from Italy, and twelve 120-mm. mortars from France. Fifteen million German bullets arrived today; 10 million bullets are on the way from Mexico.

August 27, 1948

According to Rabinov, the family status of soldiers is as follows: 45,190 bachelors (66 percent), 8106 married men without children (12.2 percent), 601 married women (0.1 percent), 9856 married men with one child (14.2 percent), 5010 with two children (2.5 percent), 372 with three children, and 107 with four children—altogether 69,242. Monthly payments come to PL581,906.

August 31, 1948

In the morning I went to Haifa to visit our young Navy. We have three motorboats and four warships. Our naval personnel make quite a good impression, but there is insufficient equipment. There is not a single naval gun, and the few pieces of ordinary artillery are not suitable for use on ships. There is no antiaircraft defense and only one gunnery officer. Three questions were raised at my meeting with naval officers.

They pointed out: (1) People working for the Mosad [organization with dealt with "illegal" immigration during the British Mandate] are of military age, and yet they receive PL31 a month in addition to maintenance costs. They also travel to Europe. This causes demoralization and leads to desertions. The officers believe that all the people working in the Mosad should be taken into the Defense Forces, and the Mosad should become a branch of the Navy. I promised to take up this matter with the Mosad. (2) Every warship needs two 75-mm. cannon and twelve 20-mm. antiaircraft guns. There should also be an expert gunnery officer for every ship. (3) They suggested ranks for the Navy.

Paul Shulman, who was an officer in the American Navy, has returned. He recruited a number of naval experts. They will be arriving during the next two weeks.

I came home in the early evening.

In the evening I was visited by N, who had served as an officer in the Intelligence. He has come to train our Intelligence Corps. He suggests that we appoint a director for every Intelligence branch, on condition that the overall Director of Intelligence should not belong to any particular branch. He would coordinate all the branches.

September 5, 1948

Military manpower at the end of August included: 78,348 men in the armed forces (not including 280 deserters, 103 in military prisons, 2083 sick and wounded, 806 prisoners held by the Arabs, 541 missing).

I was visited in the evening by Andrew Summers, a Catholic Congressman from New York. He is returning to the United States tonight. He promised to tell the President that Jerusalem should be in Israeli hands. He was told this by the Catholic priests in the city.

September 6, 1948

Meeting of the General Staff. The Arabs are active on all fronts. They are reinforcing their units. The Iraqis have doubled the number of their troops; they now have 12,000 in the field. The Egyptians have rotated their units; irregular forces and troops from Saudi Arabia have joined the Egyptians. The Arab Legion has cut down the number of its men at the front and concentrated its forces. Depleted units have been brought up to strength. The Iraqis have brought in a force of Gendarmerie, numbering perhaps 2000 men. They have two large concentrations, in the north and at Mafrak.

The Mufti is making great efforts to establish his own units. The Iraqis are encouraging him. Fortifications are being built at a feverish pace from the north to the south; the work is done by the local population. In the south, the Arabs are using building material received from the English. The Iraqis have brought building material from their country. The Arabs have strengthened their artillery and their air forces. There are twenty Iraqi airplanes at Mafrak. Remez believes that they have very good modern planes. We have reports of heavy late-model tanks.

In the evening there was a strong attack on our Ma'ar outpost. Four of our men were killed. Several of our outposts have been taken.

Yigael Yadin believes that we must concentrate on building fortifications. He suggests that we proclaim a Fortifications Week. I expressed my doubts as to whether this was really the most important problem facing us. If the fighting is renewed—let us say during the first half of October—we may drive the Arabs out of their positions or they may throw us back. The present front lines will not necessarily remain. What point is there in building fortifications along these lines? It will also be hard to find the necessary manpower. There is no sense of tension. Even in government circles, it is not understood that the war has not ended. My many warnings have had little effect. The public is pleased with our victories and acts as if our security and our future existence were guaranteed. The government and the public must be made aware of the gravity of the situation. The General Staff must do its part.

Our most urgent requirement now is heavy equipment. There is not much chance of our obtaining tanks, therefore we must secure antitank guns. We must also speed up the purchase of airplanes and artillery.

September 7, 1948

Yacov Dori met with Yigal Allon, Uri Brenner, and Eliezer Shoshani about the question of the Palmah Command. Zadok and Laskov were also present. Zadok said that if the Palmah's manpower had to be carefully selected, it should be done by the Manpower Branch of the General Staff. Yacov doubted whether the Manpower Branch would be able to deal with this matter, though it could appoint a special person to handle it.

Allon and Brenner suggested a 180-man Palmah Command to deal with the training of all Palmah recruits and platoon leaders.

Yacov asked whether there was need for "loyal" brigades. A distinction should be made, he said, between what was done in the past and what should be done in the future. The Palmah had been outstanding in several spheres—though not in all those in which it claimed distinction—but this was no justification for the creation of two armies, one made up of "loyal" units and the other of unreliable ones. This would undermine the foundations of both the State and the Army. Pioneering values and loyalty could be inculcated in all soldiers; 100 percent success might not be achieved, but the Palmah was not 100 percent successful either. There was enough fragmentation already; no need to add to it artificially. I promised Yacov a decision by next week.

Ben-Aharon came to see me. Israel Galili, he said, is asking his party to release him from his work in the Ministry of Defense. The party has refused. I told Ben-Aharon that Galili is now working with me as a representative of a political party, and therefore, I will not discuss this matter with the party. I will discuss it with him only if he raises the question himself. Ben-Aharon added that Yacov had asked him to arrange for a meeting between them on military matters. I told him that I would accept an invitation to such a meeting, but I would not be among the sponsors.

Ben-Aharon claimed that his party is being discriminated against in the General Staff. I asked him whether he thought members of his party were also being discriminated against on the senior command level, where they hold 90 percent of the posts. He answered that the question of appointments to the senior command was a purely military one, while the composition of the General Staff showed whether there was cooperation or a lack of it.

September 9, 1948

The Mexican ship arrived with twenty-three 75-mm. field guns and two 75-mm. mountain guns. The ship was passed by UN officials. Unloading will begin tonight. A ship carrying 1600 people who will serve in the army left Europe the day before yesterday. Three thousand volunteers have registered in South Africa; over 500 are already here. Some have been disappointed, particularly because of the truce. About ten have returned home.

At 12:30 I had a meeting with all the newspaper editors. I explained to them that the war had not yet ended and that our gravest tests might still be ahead of us. I pointed out that the Arabs were bringing in reinforcements and additional arms. They were building fortifications and mobilizing the local population for military and civilian work. Our civilian population is not sufficiently concerned about the situation. People do not live austerely. They are unwilling to make sacrifices. They feel that everything is all right now that we have established a State, defeated the Arabs, and overcome the chaos left behind by the British. But, in fact, we are far from secure, and we should not underestimate either the enemy's strength or his will to win. Dori and Yadin gave further details on Arab preparations and answered questions put to them by the editors.

2. Military Discipline, Hagana, Palmah

Provisions for Personal Needs of Soldiers and Their Families

D URING THE prolonged truce period we were able to turn our attention to our soldiers' personal needs. Complaints had already been heard about the large number of deserters. In most cases desertion was due not to the soldiers' unwillingness to serve in the Army and to fight, but to family problems. A large percentage of the soldiers were married, and they had left their families without means of support.

A special committee to deal with the problem was established, consisting of Shattner (chairman), Repetur, Benjamin Mintz, Rahel Kogen, and Kobashi. The military budget rises from month to month. Income during the first months after the establishment of the State was very low and we had to draw on Zionist funds, which created technical difficulties. Contributions to these funds are tax-exempt in the United States and other countries because they are used for charitable purposes; they could not be turned over to the Provisional Government. It was suggested that the care of soldiers' families be entrusted to a public committee that could use money from the funds. Others believed that responsibility for the families should be held by the Government, despite the financial problems involved. Whether family allowances should go to every soldier or only to those who were in special need of such support was also discussed. The Army proposed that we follow the practice of the British Army, which gives a regular allowance to every soldier's family. In July PL750,000 was spent on assistance to the families of soldiers. Not all those who had the right to assistance, however, actually received it. Another suggestion was that every soldier's wife receive PL12 monthly, plus PL4 for every child. We had seventy-two thousand people in the Army by the beginning of August and the number was growing day by day. Most of those now being called up were married men with two children. It was estimated that we will need PL1.25 million a month for family assistance when the army numbers ninety thousand.

The problem was referred to the Provisional State Council, which considered it on August 5, 1948.

The Prime Minister expressed regret that nothing had yet been done to make decent and practical arrangements for soldiers' families. It is difficult, he said, to demand of a man that he devote himself completely to the task entrusted to him, that he give all his strength, time, and even his life—and this is what is demanded from every soldier—when he is not certain whether his wife and children are properly cared for. There have been several cases of extreme disobedience, when commanders felt unable to impose appropriate penalties since the soldiers had acted because their families were going hungry. Until now an investigation has been made to determine the condition of a family before it received assistance. This was not fair either to the soldier or to his family.

The committee set up to study this matter reached the conclusion, later approved by the Government, that the families should receive regular payments automatically, without any attempt to determine whether they required the assistance. The Government suggested that a minimum level of support for the wives and children of soldiers be set, the amount to be determined by a special committee appointed by the Ministers of Defense and Finance. The Government would be responsible for this sum, just as it is responsible for calling up soldiers. However, the committee must estimate the burden that this would impose on the State. For obvious reasons, neither the number of men called up nor the number of dependents can be disclosed. Obviously, the numbers involved are quite large, and the burden imposed on the State is great, greater than it could bear even in normal times. We are in the midst of a war with no end in sight, and our financial burdens will grow.

The government reached two conclusions:

(1) Financial responsibility for the families of soldiers rests on the State, which must find the necessary means, just as it finds the means to meet all defense needs, namely, by levying taxes, obtaining loans, etc.

(2) It is clear, to our deep satisfaction, that we do not stand alone in this struggle; the Jewish people are giving us their assistance. Never before has the unity of Jews all over the world been as evident as since the war began. The small Jewish community of South Africa raised over a million pounds for defense needs in a very short period. I cannot give figures on the sums raised by larger Jewish communities, but the response throughout the Diaspora has been quick and generous. Without it we could not have continued. We will not be able to care for soldiers' families without outside help. However, in view of the legal and political regulations in a number of countries, we must make certain that the Government of Israel does not receive any money from Zionist funds directly. While the State will be responsible for providing allowances to the families, payments will be made by a public committee.

The Government decided to handle another vital matter separately from assistance to soldiers' families, although both are connected with the war. I refer to help for disabled soldiers, widows, and orphans. Two thousand soldiers have already been killed; hundreds have lost arms or legs. It is our sacred responsibility to rehabilitate disabled veterans and to provide a decent living for the widows and orphans of our fighting men. It is not a question of a dole, but of arrangements enabling the people concerned to earn a decent living. Since this problem will not end when the Army is demobilized, we decided to separate it from the payments to families of soldiers which will be handled by a special committee. A separate body will be formed to deal with the problems of disabled soldiers, widows, and orphans, but it will also be the responsibility of the Government. We will not be doing these people a favor—only repaying a small part of the debt we owe them.

Grabovsky [Meir Argov] (Mapai) raised the question of the parents of soldiers. There are many bachelors in the Army, including recent immigrants who have been supporting their parents or other relatives. What will happen to them? He also asked about civilian casualties. There are people who were killed in the air raid on the Tel Aviv Central Bus Station, as well as civilians who fell during the Jerusalem shellings. No distinction should be made, he urged, between civilian war victims and soldiers killed or wounded in battle.

Beba Idelson (Mapai) disagreed with Grabovsky. A distinction should be drawn, she thought, between caring for the families of soldiers and for those of civilian war victims.

Levinstein (Agudat Israel) then raised the problem of the Home Guard. Ben–Gurion affirmed that members of the Home Guard would be treated in the same way as every other soldier.

Harari (General Zionists) suggested that the families of soldiers should enjoy the same reductions as soldiers in the price of movie tickets, bus tickets, etc.

Warhaftig (Hapoel Hamizrahi) claimed that the kibbutzim are being discriminated against. When bachelors are called up from the kibbutzim, no support is given to the kibbutz, though the men involved are sometimes the main kibbutz breadwinners.

Wilner (Communists) demanded that payments to soldiers' wives be raised from PL 16 to 30, and those for children from PL 4.50 to 10. This was an absolute minimum, he contended.

Kaplan (Finance Minister) replied on behalf of the Prime Minister, who had to leave to attend an urgent meeting on defense matters. He suggested that a division be made between the problem of civilian war victims and that of soldiers' families and wounded soldiers. He promised a special debate on civilian war victims, and said that he would shortly submit the draft of a law dealing with the families of soldiers. Perhaps assistance for the ill, the wounded, and the disabled should be entrusted to an independent civic organization in order to permit assistance from world Jewry, but ultimate responsibility would rest with the Government. State laws and regulations were therefore necessary.

The Council approved the following proposals:

(1) The Government will establish a special office in one of the ministries to deal with soldiers' families.

(2) A public committee will also be set up for this purpose.

(3) The Government will be responsible for financing this activity.

(4) The public committee will propose a minimum payment for every dependent and will make the payments. In special cases, the committee will consider supplementary payments.

(5) The Government, in consultation with the public committee, will make provisions to ensure the right of soldiers to their civilian jobs and to deal with the welfare of their families.

(6) All arrangements must be made during the month of August, with payments retroactive to August 1.

Shertok and Bernadotte Discuss Truce Violations ★ Israel Announces Willingness To Enter Peace Negotiations

The Foreign Minister reported to the State Council on his meeting with Count Bernadotte which had taken place that same day (August 5). The Swedish General Aage Lundstrom, who is in charge of supervising the truce, participated in the meeting. The Count criticized Shertok's statement about constant Arab violations of the truce, and his warning that if they were not stopped, Israel would feel free not only to repulse the attacks on the local level, but to launch an attack anywhere along the front against the Arab army that had violated the truce.

Bernadotte argued that the current truce was different from the first truce, which had been based on an agreement between the two sides, whereas the current truce had been imposed on Arabs and Jews alike by the Security Council. Moreover, the Security Council had made it clear what would happen to either party if it violated the truce. The Security Council had stated that should one side violate the truce, the other had the right to defend itself at the place where the attack occurred, but did not have the right to initiate an attack elsewhere. In addition, he said, the party attacked must turn to the Security Council, which was charged with clarifying the matter and taking measures against the attacking party.

The Foreign Minister disagreed with this interpretation of the truce resolution, adding that if Israel acted as he suggested, the Arabs would be free to violate the truce at any place convenient to them. They could concentrate a force large enough to give them an advantage at a particular point, forcing Israeli units to withdraw. If the Israelis were prohibited from launching counterattacks elsewhere, and the enemy were aware of this fact, the result would be obvious. The only effective defense against attack was the freedom to launch a counterattack at any suitable spot, Shertok said.

Bernadotte indicated that he would submit those views in writing to the Security

Council. Shertok said that Israel's interpretation would also be submitted in writing to the Security Council.

The Mediator then turned to the problem of the Arab refugees. He knew that we had expressed unwillingness to discuss the return of the refugees until after the end of the war, but argued that even if we were not ready to accept a large number of refugees, this should not prevent us from negotiating about the return of certain categories of Arabs. There was no possibility of discussing repatriation of any groups of refugees while the war was still going on, Shertok insisted. There might be cases calling for special consideration, such as members of a family that had been separated; this was not a subject for negotiations, but one to be settled on the local level.

Bernadotte then took up the demilitarization of Jerusalem. He repeated his statement to the press, that Israel had accepted demilitarization in principle. Shertok denied this: Israel, he declared, had not accepted the principle of demilitarization. She had only expressed her willingness to discuss any plan that would save the city from further destruction—should the fighting begin elsewhere in the country—without prejudicing the general interests of the Jewish people. Israel had not denied that demilitarization might serve the aforementioned purpose, but she had not accepted it as a solution.

Dr. Dov Joseph, Governor of Jerusalem, who was present at the discussion, said that the Arabs were constantly violating the truce in the city. Jerusalem's nights echoed with the sound of exploding shells. The Mediator, should put an end to these violations.

After further discussions, Shertok suggested that the Mediator inform the Arab states of Israel's willingness to begin peace negotiations. Bernadotte promised to do so.

Unified Control of Israel Defense Forces ★ Glories and Shortcomings of the Hagana ★ The Palmah Problem

Most members of the Government were aware of the dangers of a truce that continued indefinitely and without peace negotiations. This meant that the invading armies remained inside the State of Israel, free to concentrate their forces at any of our weak points, in the south, north, or center. They would win a local victory and then begin observing the truce again, since according to Bernadotte, the right of self-defense was limited to the particular place where the attack had occurred. The majority of the Government felt that we should not end the truce on our own initiative; there were good reasons for this view. It was therefore clear that the truce would continue for an extended period, though not forever.

The Minister of Defense urged that the truce period be used to clear up unfinished business in the Army left over from the pre-State era. The Provisional Government had accepted the view—which he made a condition for his acceptance of the Defense portfolio—that the Defense Forces must be under the sole and undisputed control of the State's elected institutions, and that all units must be equal. The ordinance issued on May 26, 1948, upon the establishment of the Israel Defense Forces, included sections guaranteeing the unity of the Army and the exclusive authority of commanders appointed by the Government. One section specified that no military or similar organization could be established or maintained outside the framework of the Israel Defense Forces and that no weapons could be kept without the authorization of the Government. Another section declared that every person serving in the Defense Forces must pledge allegiance to the State of Israel, its laws, and its legally constituted authorities.

But it had been obvious from the beginning that a unified and disciplined army could not be created simply by issuing an order, particularly in a country where dissident organizations that did not accept the principle of national discipline had operated for many years. It was impossible to change the attitude of the Hagana at one fell swoop. The Hagana generally had shown respect for the decisions of the Yishuv and of the Zionist movement. But it had been an underground organization for thirty years, with units that varied in quality, tasks, and discipline. There had been conflicting authorities in the defense sphere: the Histadrut, the Citizens' Union, the Vaad Leumi (National Committee). The Vaad Leumi was formally charged with choosing the Hagana High Command. Besides representatives of the Histadrut and the Citizens' Union, this body included people from several political parties. The Jewish Agency appointed the Head of the National Command, and transmitted its instructions to the Hagana Command through him. An underground organization does not, overnight, become a regular army, accepting the jurisdiction of a new authority; it does not easily throw off its old habits of making decisions, to a large extent, by itself.

Even before the establishment of the Israel Defense Forces, the chairman of the Jewish Agency Executive had received serious complaints about improper conduct by several Hagana and Palmah men. On February 10, 1948, he appointed Yacov Riftin, of Mapam, to investigate the matter. In his letter of appointment the chairman warned that "these acts are a grave political and moral danger to the Hagana and to the Yishuv; drastic measures must be taken to put an end to them." Some improper actions were revealed, though it should be borne in mind that, in general, members of the Hagana were the very epitome of decency and devotion. Yet there were a fair number of incidents which did not do credit to those responsible. In the course of the struggle against regular Arab armies grave shortcomings become apparent, and during the first truce, when the Minister of Defense called together all the senior commanders, nearly all of them complained bitterly about desertions, lack of discipline, and other difficulties.

As has already been pointed out, many Hagana members had previous military experience. Some had served in the Jewish Legion in the First World War, among them the late Eliyahu Golomb, Dov Hos, and Zeev Shefer Feinstein. Many more had served in the Jewish units of the British Army in the Second World War. Finally, there were officers with considerable battle experience in the British, American, South African, and other armies: men like Colonel Cecil Marcus, M. of the South African Air Force, and Paul Shulman of the American Navy. Some veteran Hagana members, without experience in any regular army, had proven excellent commanders in the Israel Defense Forces, including men like Yigael Yadin, Moshe Dayan, and Yigal Allon.

Nevertheless, the fact that most of the men called up at the beginning of the War of Independence lacked military experience had its effect, though it did not prevent us from emerging victorious. At the same time, it would be difficult to exaggerate the value to the Israel Defense Forces of its heritage from the Hagana's various units, and especially the Palmah, as well as from the Jewish Brigade and the artillery unit in the British Army, whose officers included such men as Laskov, Ben-Artzi, and Makleff.

The Hagana had many advantages. It was a volunteer force, a factor not only of moral, but also of military importance. A volunteer has enormous advantages over a man drafted into military service. The Hagana was based on bonds of friendship. There are such bonds in every army, and they are stronger in a good army than in any other organization, because in an army men depend upon one another for their very lives. Friendship imposed from above on a man, however, cannot be compared with friendship based on free will and a shared vision.

Hagana members were distinguished by their almost limitless devotion to the security of the Yishuv. The strength of an army depends not only on its equipment but on the willingness of its men to fight on, unflinchingly, to the end. The Hagana's extraordinary sense of devotion was one of the significant attributes that it passed on to the Israel Defense Forces.

The Hagana was based on a vision, a vision which had moved its members, or their fathers, to come to the Land of Israel. It was this vision for which they constantly worked, which they defended and for which they were willing to sacrifice their lives. It was the secret of the Hagana's strength. During the 1936 Arab riots the chairman of the Zionist Executive in Jerusalem met with the British military expert Captain B. H. Liddell Hart to discuss what measures could be taken against the Arab rioters. He described the character of Jewish youth in the Land of Israel, young people devoted to work and to peace, anxious to create and hating bloodshed, but willing to fight to the end against any attempt to strike at the thing most dear to them, the reestablishment of a Jewish presence in the historical Jewish Homeland. If that description of his men was correct, the British expert said, the Jews would have the best army in the world, for an outstanding army was one that knew what it was fighting for.

The vision that guided our pioneers, that brought them to this country and gave them a reason for living and for dying, was the most precious inheritance received by the Israel Defense Forces from the Hagana. Its influence was evident in the IDF's victories during the War of Independence. But the Hagana lacked some of the basic foundations of an army, not because it was unaware of their value, but because as an underground movement it did not possess the conditions or the resources of a regular army:

(A) The Hagana was well aware of the importance of arms, but its ability to obtain them or produce them was extremely limited, because of a lack of funds and, to an even greater extent, because of political conditions. The Hagana had rifles, submachine guns, two-inch and three-inch machine guns, hand grenades, and high explosives. The purchase of more weapons, their transfer, and storage demanded bravery of a high order. Local production of arms, though on a primitive level, began before the Second World War. Here again there were extraordinary acts of devotion. But the arms obtained were sufficient in quality and in quantity only for confrontations with bands of thieves, not for repulsing the attacks of armies, regular or irregular.

When the chairman of the Jewish Agency Executive checked on the Hagana's arms in April 1947, he found that it had 8720 rifles in the various settlements for local defense and 1353 rifles for national defense (336 at Hagana headquarters, 656 with the Palmah, and 361 with the Field Forces). At that time the Hagana had 1900 submachine guns, 633 machine guns, 672 two-inch mortars, 96 three-inch mortars, and a quantity of hand grenades. It goes without saying that there was not a single piece of artillery or a heavy machine gun. There were no antiaircraft or antitank weapons. There were no armored cars and not a hint of either air or sea forces. There was even very little in the way of vehicles for transport.

(B) The Hagana, as an underground movement, could not operate regular military schools. It did manage in the years of foreign rule, and in particular during the White Paper period, to give thousands of its members some understanding of military problems and weapons. But there was no possibility of training on anything higher than the company level or with heavy weapons. Maneuvers could not be held, and most of the instructors were self-taught. They had learned a great deal by themselves, but they lacked the background of real officers, except for those few who had served in foreign armies or who could learn from books.

The art of war had reached a high level. It involved not only military knowledge in the restricted sense of the term, but knowledge of the natural sciences, engineering, mechanics, psychology, economics. No man could be a military commander worthy of the name without a systematic education and advanced training. This required special military academies, which could not be established during the days of the Hagana.

(C) The Hagana did not have military discipline. Such discipline does not suddenly come into being when a man joins an army. It is based on tradition, example, and law. The members of the Hagana were volunteers, serving in its ranks for several hours every week or every month. There can be no army without discipline, just as there can be no State without a government and a body of laws.

(D) The Hagana was geared to defense, generally static defense. In the natural course of events, operating under a foreign regime, it devoted itself to repulsing the assaults of robber bands or terrorists. But in a war, even a defensive war such as ours, the best defense is a good offense. The Hagana had extraordinary achievements to its credit in the defense sphere. The events of Tel Hai, Tirat Zvi, Yehiam, Hulda, the outskirts of Tel Aviv, Jerusalem, and particularly the Etzion Bloc episode and the tragedy of the thirty-five were almost without parallel in the history of self-defense. Even before the establishment of the Israel Defense Forces we moved from defense to offense; the key turning point was the Nahshon Operation at the end of March 1948. Without this transformation, it is unlikely that we would have reached the establishment of the State and of the Israel Defense Forces.

(E) The Hagana, by force of circumstances, was limited to land forces. There was no possibility of creating units to operate in the decisive arenas of the air and the sea.

(F) The Hagana was unable to strive for the principal goal of any army, the destruction of the enemy army. In the nature of its tasks the Hagana reacted to an attack, driving out attackers from Jewish areas, which were like little islands scattered about in an Arab sea.

The Israel Defense Forces received a rich inheritance from the Hagana, without which they probably would have been unable to meet the challenges that faced them. But the Defense Forces are not an extension of the Hagana, just as the State of Israel is not an extension of the Vaad Leumi or the Zionist Executive. The State would not have been created without the longings for redemption in Jewish hearts for thousands of years, and without the settlement activities over three generations, starting with the establishment of Mikve Israel and Petah Tikva in the 1880s. Yet the State opened an entirely new chapter, not only in the history of the Land of Israel, but in the history of the Jewish people. Our Defense Forces were not simply an extension of the Hagana; they represented a new departure in the saga of Jewish heroism, in the same way as did the wars of Joshua, David, and the Maccabees.

Just as the establishment of the State did not immediately uproot Galut exile customs in the life of the Yishuv, so the establishment of the Israel Defense Forces did not immediately eliminate the shortcomings that had long existed in the Hagana. In addition to the plague of desertions—mainly the result of our failure to look after the families of soldiers—there was a lack of discipline stemming from the absence of military tradition, as well as problems deriving from the Palmah's claim to special status and the actions of Etzel and Lehi dissidents. I would not, of course, equate the Palmah with the dissidents in any respect.

The Palmah was the most selective, daring, and devoted unit in the Hagana. It was established in 1941 when Hitler's forces were at the gates of the Land of Israel. One of its founders and builders was Eliyahu Golomb, the uncrowned commander of the Hagana. Hakibbutz Hameuhad played a larger role than any other settlement organization in the development of the Palmah. Had the Kibbutz Artzi, Hever Hakvutzot, and the Moshav movement given to the Palmah the kind of support given by Hakibbutz Hameuhad it would undoubtedly have achieved a great deal more. Be that as it may, the Palmah, despite its limited size, had extraordinary accomplishments to its credit. It played a vital role in the struggle against the White Paper regime, in the organization of "illegal" immigration, and in the battles that preceded the establishment of the State. It was the Hagana's real striking force—no other unit could compare with the Palmah.

A few months before the establishment of the State, however, the Vaad Leumi and the Jewish Agency began large-scale mobilization; the Palmah was no longer the only fully mobilized unit. The men in the new brigades devoted all their time to training and military operations, so that there was no difference between them and the Palmah brigades. The Palmah and its command were subject to the authority of the Hagana's National Command, like other brigades before the establishment of the Israel Defense Forces. After the establishment of the State, they came under the authority of the Minister of Defense. Nevertheless, an attempt was made by the Deputy Palmah Commander to ensure that Palmah members accepted orders only from the Palmah Command. This move was defeated by the Minister of Defense. A special Palmah Headquarters was established without the necessary State approval, and attempts were made to create special conditions for the Palmah. This was done despite the fact that after the large-scale mobilization and the establishment of the Navy, the Air Force, and the Armored Corps, the Palmah ceased to be a special striking force different from other infantry brigades. It is to the credit of the Palmah commanders that they did not violate military discipline. After many discussions an order was given to abolish the National Palmah Command, and that order was carried out. Mapam leaders, seeking to have the order rescinded, took up the matter with the Histadrut rather than with the Provisional Government of the Provisional State Council.

It was not easy to give the Palmah brigades (Yiftah, Harel, and Negev) the same character as other Defense Forces brigades. A rumor spread among Palmah members that the Minister of Defense had decided to discriminate against them, to prevent them from receiving weapons, even to starve them. Such complaints were received by the Minister from the parents of Palmah members. On July 29, 1948, *Davar* published an article by Shlomo Lavie of Ein Harod entitled "A Message to the Youth Being Influenced by Agitators." It said in part:

While we are in a period of great joy—and what could be cause for greater joy than the beginning of Israel's redemption—storm clouds are already gathering. Our cruel enemies, supported by the forces of darkness, surround us on all sides, and are anxious to wipe us off the face of the earth. At this very moment, we are also faced with internal intrigues comparable only to the intrigues of the Second Temple period.

I am not referring to the dissidents. I hope that we will know how to get rid of them in time. I refer instead to those who are flesh of our flesh.

I admit that I speak of a matter about which I have learned from the gossip that is widespread among our wonderful youth—gossip that they accept as absolute truth and which leads them to blind and unreasoning hatred.

On the lawn in back of my house, there were two wonderful young men of the type willing to volunteer for the most dangerous missions. One of them told the other: "Ben-Gurion is plotting to destroy the Palmah. He keeps food from the Palmah and prevents it from receiving even the most necessary clothing. Its members are denied shoes for their bare feet and talented Palmah commanders are dismissed. Worst of all, the Palmah is not given the weapons it requires, despite the fact that there are weapons available. All this is being done in order to ensure that the Palmah will fail in its mission."

When I read Freud's book in which he suggested that Moses had been killed by the Hebrews themselves, this idea seemed quite reasonable to me. The great liberating spirit that he brought to his people was too onerous a burden for the masses. It shocked them and in the wake of this shock there arose a group anxious to take over the leadership of the people. A sect of priests came forward and built a golden calf so that the masses could dance around it. And when this was not enough to defeat the leader, they agitated against him, stirring up the masses who could not understand his doctrines, and they murdered him.

I am not saying that Ben-Gurion is Moses, the great leader and law-giver; no such comparison is possible. Ben-Gurion is a product of our time. But the same process is apparently taking place. Innocent youngsters, who are ready to believe any bit of gossip, will find more than enough.

My young friends, there is no need for me to defend the man you are now slandering. His actions are enough to defend him, as is the fact that he forced us to accept a Jewish State, despite the opposition of so many wise men. But if there is no need to defend him, there is great need to defend the youth, who are our future, to prevent them from falling into the net of the many politicians who have found their way into the ranks of the Palmah in the guise of cultural officers.

This argument could be a simple human one, without all the rancor. Hakibbutz Hameuhad could argue that since it created the Palmah, the Palmah belongs to it just as do its settlements. The Government of Israel could argue, for its part, that there can be no Government or State if each political party has its own private army. Just as fire and water cannot mix, so it is impossible for independent armies to live together within the framework of one nation.

But the Opposition is not interested in an open clarification of the issues; it is interested in agitation, and its emissaries are very good at it. They do not stick to the issues; they simply spread gossip on the assumption that if there is enough of it, some will be believed. It is obvious that fine young men who hear that the Minister of Defense is trying to destroy the Palmah, which they so admire, will be consumed by anger. It was an outburst of such anger that I heard on the lawn in back of my house, and which I find so hard to put down on paper.

From My Diaries:
September 14, 1948

September 14, 1948

I met with the commanders of the Palmah at Naan; all sixty-four of them were there. Sixty of the sixty-four were members of Mapam. I asked them what distinguished the Palmah militarily from other units and why it needed its own National Command. Until the outbreak of the war—a war which began immediately after the November 29 UN resolution—the Palmah was the best trained and most devoted of the Hagana units. Palmah members volunteered to serve for a full year and went to the settlements, where they worked for half a month and trained during the other half. Before the general mobilization began, the Palmah had twenty-five hundred members. After the UN resolution calling for the establishment of the Jewish State, the Vaad Leumi called up young people in the seventeen-to-twenty-five-year-old age group. Tens of thousands were mobilized. Over five thousand of them went into Palmah units. Since that time, all the men mobilized have been training constantly, not just half the month, as in the past. What is the difference between the men drafted into Palmah brigades and those who were sent to other brigades? Is there an ideological difference? a class difference? a political difference? a moral difference? a party difference? or perhaps a professional difference?

You know, I told them, that I am not a professional soldier. Two years ago, after the 22nd Zionist Congress in December 1946, I accepted the Defense portfolio for the first time. Until then I did not have any specific portfolio. I took up the responsibility because it was clear to me that the Mandate period was coming to an end, and that when the British left the country we would have to meet an attack by Arab armies, not an attack from the Arabs of this country, but one in which Arab armies would attempt to turn this into an Arab state. There was reason to fear the destruction of the Jewish community, for only by destroying the Jews would it be possible to turn the Land of Israel into an Arab state. And in fact, eight hours after the State was proclaimed, shortly after the British High Commissioner left the country, Arab armies invaded the country and began a war that is still raging.

I had many discussions with Hagana leaders after I was entrusted with responsibility for defense. I asked them whether we would be able to stand up to the Arab armies. They answered in the affirmative. I received an affirmative answer from Yigal Allon, more hesitant replies from others. Most of the answers did not satisfy me because I thought that these people did not realize the gravity of the situation, did not understand the kind of preparations that were necessary, the new type of organization that was required if we were to withstand the attack of regular armies, especially in view of our numerical inferiority. Our need was for far-reaching changes in weapons, training, and organization and more than anything else, for full national unity, a unified army, strict discipline, and the fraternity of fighting men. I had tried to explain the new situation and the new demands to the Yishuv and to the Zionist Movement. But until the November 29 resolution, and the events that followed, my remarks were not taken seriously.

We decided on a general mobilization in December 1947. I asked the General Staff for a budget estimate. Perhaps for the first time in history, those requesting a budget demanded less than the man who had to supply the funds. The General Staff submitted a PL1 million budget. I returned it, saying that it was not large enough. With the aid of a number of colleagues, I prepared a PL3.5 million budget, which was realistic only until the real war began with the invasion of the Arab armies.

I have already asked what difference there is between the men taken into the Palmah and those taken into other units, and how the Palmah differs from the Armored Corps, the Artillery, the Air Force, and the Navy, which did not exist and could not have existed in the Hagana and the Palmah while they were underground organizations.

The Palmah differed from other bodies up until the war because it was constantly under arms. Its men were better trained than other members of the Hagana and it was composed of pioneering youth. But how does it differ from all the other units now that there is general mobilization, and all men are being constantly trained and learning skills that could not have been learned during the underground period?

I was a soldier during the First World War. I served together with other young men from the Land of Israel, the United States, Canada, Argentina, and Britain. I knew—and British officers confirmed this—that a Jewish soldier learns more quickly than a British soldier. But what is special about the Palmah? I know what is special about an artilleryman or a pilot; I know the difference between a Jewish soldier and an Egyptian, Iraqi, or a Syrian soldier. But what is the difference between a soldier serving in a unit called the Palmah and in a unit called by another name? Is the name Palmah [Striking Force] appropriate now when we have special striking forces in the air, at sea, and on land? In the Hagana, between 1941 and 1947, it was the only striking force; there was no better trained or more devoted unit. But what is the special character of the Palmah now? And why does the Palmah need a special headquarters when Palmah units are scattered all over the country, in the north, center, and the Negev, and such headquarters could not give them operational instructions?

The first one who tried to answer my questions was Yissahar Shadmi. The Palmah, he said, was not established because an order was given to that effect; it arose out of the force of circumstances. There is no need for a special Palmah at this stage—what is needed is an army that is entirely along Palmah lines. But it is impossible to force an entire army to operate in the spirit of the Palmah. The Palmah has seven years of experience, which is more than the Jewish Brigade had. It has more operational experience than any other unit in the country. The Brigade fought overseas; now we are fighting inside our country, and only the Palmah has experience in this kind of fighting.

Shalom Hevlin, who for a time served as Deputy Commander of the Palmah, restated Shadmi's views in other words. The Palmah has its own special military character; it has seven years' experience. The Palmah fighter is capable of doing more, and more can be demanded of him. The Palmah is based on work, and not on training. Eighty percent of the Palmah's upkeep was financed by the work of its members.

It should also be remembered that there is Jewish fascism, Jewish reaction, he added. These things exist and they cannot be ignored. We saw evidence of it in the *Altalena* incident. Could the *Altalena* have been handled without the Palmah?

Eliezer Shoshani, a member of Mapai, said that the Palmah's special character stemmed from the fact that it was the first pioneering venture created by the youth of Israel. The First and Second Aliyot [waves of immigration] gave impetus to settlement in general, and in border areas in particular. But the Palmah was the creation of the Sabra. It was a pioneering society. If Palmah Headquarters, with its very special character, were made into an ordinary headquarters, it would lose all meaning. Without the Palmah, there would be no sense of mission. The Palmah is also necessary because of danger from the political right. The Palmah would prevent a civil war within the Jewish community.

Yehuda Drexler said that he was not a Sabra and that Shoshani's remarks therefore did not apply to him. He thought the Palmah was necessary because of the danger of fascism. The Palmah was needed to safeguard democracy.

Zerubavel Gilead declared that the Palmah does not see itself as something special within the Hagana, but simply as a higher stage in its development. The Palmah's achievements are the result of its superior training and greater dedication to national authority. It was the Palmah that brought in immigrants and opened the roads to Jerusalem and the Negev. The Palmah is not a political army but a part of the Israel Defense Forces, and a loyal part; its acts have proven this. It differs from the Army as a whole because the Army has not sprung from the same roots. The Palmah includes men who did not come from the labor movement. They were members of Hapoel Hamizrahi, the Scouts, or Maccabee Hatzair. The Defense Forces need an example. The Palmah can set an example for the entire Army, and thus guarantee that the Army will follow in its path.

Yosef Tabenkin asserted: The Palmah was the beginning of the Army. It set an example by the speed with which it absorbed people, trained them, and sent them into battle. When an operation had to be carried out against Etzel and Lehi, the Palmah was sent. He dispatched people to the Navy, Tabenkin said, and they want to return because they do not feel at home there. He sent men to the Air Force, but they did not continue there; they did not find the framework to which they were accustomed. In the Palmah settlement and immigration go together with defense and security. The Palmah gives young men a chance to express themselves; it is a reflection of these young men.

Benjamin Marshak said: "I pursue two goals, goals which all of us share: to defeat the enemy and to settle the Land of Israel. David Horowitz, speaking at a meeting of cultural officers, said that work and military service do not go together. He did not realize what the Palmah had achieved by combining the two."

Yigal Allon: "The Palmah has been in existence for seven years. During this period there have been several attempts to dissolve it for all sorts of reasons. By some miracle, we did not give in. I am sure that if it is decided today to dissolve the Palmah, in a month's time an attempt will be made to reestablish it."

I interjected: "You will be doing all of us a great favor if you explain what you mean when you speak of dissolving the Palmah."

Allon: "If you abolish the Palmah's National Command, you abolish the Palmah. No army can forego the establishment of special units, in which more is invested and from which more is expected. The Palmah was set up as a striking force in order to carry out particularly daring missions. At the time, we spoke in terms of companies, now we must speak in terms of brigades. The Palmah of today is on a slightly lower level than it was two years ago, particularly the rank and file; but the officers are actually on a higher level.

"There is no contradiction between the need to raise the general level of the Army and the need for elite units. I am speaking here only of the military aspects and ignoring the social and political aspects. The Marines should be returned to the Palmah, so should the Paratroopers. The Manpower Branch is not capable of dealing with a striking force;

it has large-scale, general tasks. One gains the impression that the Palmah has a National Command of its own parallel to the General Staff, but actually its headquarters is exactly like that of the Artillery.

"I would like to say a few words about the political and social side of the question. I believe that the Army must be loyal to the coalition government. Some time ago, I talked with a man serving as a diplomat overseas. After a few drinks had loosened him up a bit, he spoke of his work as a diplomat. Today he serves Ben-Gurion, tomorrow he may be serving Gruenbaum. What would happen, I asked him, if Menahem Begin became Prime Minister? He was taken aback. Finally, he replied: If Begin seized power, I would not serve him; if he were elected, that would be different. I told him that I would never accept Begin as Prime Minister.

"I don't want to talk about a possible civil war, when the Palmah would be needed. We should not go into this argument until the end of the war; it is destructive. I do not feel that the existence of the Palmah within the Defense Forces depends on the question of a civil war. Perhaps its existence will prevent a civil war. So far as I am concerned, Yacov Meridor's slip of the tongue at a press conference, when he said that he could take over the government with a hundred men, was enough.

"The Palmah is essential both for military and political reasons. It represents a source of strength. If its members are scattered throughout the Army, they will cease to have any influence. But as a concentrated group they will influence all the other units. There is scarcely a unit in the Army without an ex-Palmah commander. A unified Palmah guarantees the character of the Army; a scattered Palmah could not do so."

In summing up the discussion, I said that in organizing it I had in mind three goals: (1) either you would convince me that the Army needs brigades organized in a special manner, having special tasks, and with special ideologies; (2) or I would convince you that there was no such need; (3) and if neither of these occurred, at least you would learn what I really thought. I regret to say that I have failed in all three goals.

I did not receive a convincing explanation why an institution that had a *raison d'être* in the past must be continued at a time when requirements are different. You did not understand what I oppose and what I do not oppose. This was evident in the remarks of Tabenkin and Marshak. Shadmi attempted to prove something that needed no proof, namely, that the Palmah had special tasks and many advantages in the period before the establishment of the Defense Forces. I understand and accept this. I am not arguing about the past; I have repeatedly said that the Palmah was the outstanding unit in the Hagana in every respect. It is true that I favored having a number of Palmah members join the Jewish Brigade and opposed the attempt to create a gulf between the Palmah and the Brigade. Moreover, I regret that there were not more volunteers for the Brigade, men who could have helped destroy the Nazis and meet with the remnants of European Jewry. In any case, I am proud of the Palmah and far from ashamed of the Brigade.

The men who served three to seven years in the Palmah understandably stood at the forefront when the Israel Defense Forces were established at the end of May. But I am not as certain as Tabenkin that those Palmah members who were called up in December 1947 and afterward are better than other soldiers called up at the same time. What is the point of keeping secret a method of developing military superiority at a time when every soldier must be given the best possible training? I asked what professional and ideological factors differentiate a Palmah brigade from any other brigade. Yigal Allon said that men drafted for service as paratroopers should be sent to the Palmah. How will a paratrooper unit in the Palmah differ from a paratrooper unit organized as a separate entity?

I do not accept Tabenkin's description of the Navy and the Air Force, I went on. Though these units are young—much younger than the Palmah—there is no reason to be ashamed of them. I don't know if the men who fled were really in the Air Force or the Navy. The great majority of our units are very young, mostly established only four months ago. Yet the Jewish people have no reason to be ashamed of them, and I doubt whether Yosef Tabenkin's "evaluation" of the Navy and the Air Force is accurate.

I did not receive an answer to my question about the professional uniqueness of the three Palmah brigades, but I am at least grateful to Allon for telling me what was meant by the liquidation of the Palmah. This does not mean breaking up its brigades or scattering its members; it means the elimination of the special Palmah Command. I doubt whether Palmah members who hear talk about its liquidation understand that it is the liquidation of the Palmah National Command that is under discussion.

Be that as it may, I want you to understand that there is no intention of liquidating the Palmah or of destroying its pioneering values. What we are discussing is a strictly professional question. Do these brigades have a specific military task and therefore require their own organizational structure, their own special training, and their own special equipment? That is the issue. Anyone who hears Tabenkin or Marshak would think that all Palmah members will join settlements after receiving military training, while I am fighting against settlements and pioneering values. I would be very happy if demobilized soldiers would establish settlements in the Negev, in the south, and elsewhere in the country. But I don't see any connection between the National Command of the Palmah on the one hand, and pioneering values and the settlement of the Negev on the other.

I asked another question that remained unanswered, namely, whether the Palmah had some special military or ideological uniqueness. We have always opposed dissidents, those who joined Etzel and Lehi. We are fervent supporters of a regime based on the will of the people and we have no need for military units with a special ideology. We can find our place within the community as a whole, under all conditions and at all times. It is only the right wing that is not always satisfied with the will of the community, though there are exceptions like Ussishkin. On the other hand, Smol [Left Labor Zionist] refused to participate in the Zionist Congress and regarded the Jewish National Fund as a bourgeois instrument designed to exploit the working class. We split the movement for that reason in 1920, but a few years later the Left Labor Zionists returned to the Zionist Congress.

If the unique aspect of the Palmah is its pioneering character, why should we not try to give the entire Army and all the youth such a character? Do we really want pioneering values to be the sole preserve of a particular army unit? Are the seven or eight thousand men who were taken into the Palmah after December 1947 really all pioneers, and those taken into other units hostile to pioneering? The little I've seen of the Army—and I have seen little, for it has been in existence for only a few months—has given me great faith in its ability and loyalty. Though it still has serious shortcomings, we can be proud of it. I am not at all sure that every person serving in the Palmah will join a settlement; at the same time, I see no reason to assume that the members of the other units will not establish settlements. In any case, it should be understood that there is no argument over pioneering values or the importance of settlement.

We must have the best army in the world; otherwise we will lose. This kind of army can be developed only over a period of time. From the very beginning I have tried to create an army that would not be intellectually or morally inferior to any other in the world. This applies equally to all units. Each unit has its special task, and each must reach the highest possible level, and this is as true in the moral and pioneering realms as in any other. The structure of our Army must be suited to these goals.

Chief of Staff Issues Order on the Palmah ★ Objections Raised at Histadrut Central Committee

At the meeting with the Palmah commanders at Naan on September 14, 1948, as recorded in my diary, nine of them tried to explain the special character of the Palmah, and almost all had a different special character in mind; none could find a convincing argument for a special Palmah National Command. Subsequently the Minister of Defense presented his conclusions to the General Staff.

With the establishment of the State, he emphasized again, the entire Army became responsible solely to the Government and its organizational structure was adjusted to the requirements of a war against regular armies. Special units with professional tasks were established: the Infantry, the Artillery, the Air Force, and the Navy. A headquarters staff was established for each battalion and brigade, and the General Staff was put at the head of the whole organization. Within the framework of the General Staff, branches were established to deal with such matters as supplies, training, manpower, operations, and culture. The infantry brigades, as well as other units, are no longer linked to a particular geographical area, but are transferred from one place to another as the need arises. All the brigades are given the best possible military training, a task which has been facilitated by the prolonged truce periods. In the last few months considerable progress has been achieved in this sphere. Central courses for company commanders have been organized, while the training of privates and platoon leaders has been carried out within the framework of individual brigades. The Training Branch in the General Staff is responsible for these courses. Thus there is no need for a special training branch in the Palmah, any more than in other brigades.

The National Command of the Palmah cannot and should not deal with the distribution of supplies to Palmah brigades, he continued. All Palmah brigades, whether in the Galilee, the Negev, or the central region, should receive their supplies from the Quartermaster Branch of the General Staff, just as other brigades do. It is inconceivable that two Palmah brigades, one in the Galilee and one in the Negev, should receive their supplies through channels different from those used by other brigades in the same area.

The Palmah National Command can no longer give operational instructions to Palmah brigades. The Army is now organized on the basis of three fronts. Each front has its own command, which gives orders to all the brigades under its jurisdiction, in accordance with a plan decided upon by the General Staff and on the instructions of the Minister of Defense. Moreover, the Palmah Command cannot mobilize people as it sees fit, as was the case before the general call-up began. Before the establishment of the Defense Forces everything was done on a voluntary basis. Now tasks are carried out on the basis of orders from the Ministry of Defense. The General Staff has a Manpower Branch which deals with all the men called up and sends them, as needed, to various units. During the first months after general mobilization began, it is true, there was still some "kidnapping" because of competition between various units. But little by little proper procedures were established. Now no brigade is allowed to take the men it wants. The same situation holds true in the cultural and social welfare spheres. Only a few individuals argued that the Palmah has a special ideology, and no one argued, at least openly, that the Palmah has a special political role. All soldiers should participate in the same cultural programs.

The argument of some individuals that there should be a special Palmah Command because the Palmah fought the dissidents is very damaging. It may give the struggle against the dissidents a political character. As far as it is necessary to fight the dissidents, this must be done by the Government on behalf of the country as a whole.

Each Palmah brigade must have its own staff, as in all brigades. But this brigade staff must be subordinate to the General Staff of the Defense Forces. The Palmah has no need for its own separate National Staff.

This being the case, the Chief of Staff, Rav Aluf [Brigadier General] Yacov Dori, acting on the instructions of the Minister of Defense, sent the following order to the Palmah:

> The three Palmah brigades do not form a single operational and administrative unit within the framework of our military forces. Moreover, as nearly as can be ascertained at the moment, the needs of the war effort will continue to necessitate a direct line of authority between the General Staff and each of the individual brigades, so that the brigades can be shifted on the basis of general military considerations. Therefore, the tasks carried out at this moment by the Palmah Command—the absorption of new manpower, the training of privates and NCOs, and ideological education—create duplication and confusion. The aforementioned functions must be transferred to the appropriate branches of the General Staff and of the various fronts.

The Palmah Staff carried out this order immediately and without complaints. The Mapam representatives in the Histadrut, however, raised objections to it at a meeting of the Histadrut Central Committee. Ben-Aharon, speaking on behalf of Mapam, said that the Central Committee should "demand that the Minister of Defense postpone dissolution of the Palmah National Command until after the war, when the issue could be reconsidered; it should also set up a committee to discuss the strengthening of the Palmah and the Histadrut's role in its guidance."

The discussion in the Histadrut took place on October 14 and 15, 1948, under the chairmanship of Sprinzak.

Repetur of Mapam stated: There is no need to explain to the Histadrut, or to the members of its Central Committee, the value of the Palmah to the labor movement. After outlining what the Palmah had done over the previous seven years, he said that the Histadrut members in the Army and in the Government should be instructed to hold up the execution of the order and that a meeting of the Histadrut Council be called to discuss the future of the Palmah and how the Histadrut could prevent its dissolution.

Uri Brenner, a Palmah officer, pointed out that this issue was brought to the Histadrut Central Committee not by the Palmah, but by Histadrut members who, over the years, were accustomed to bringing defense questions to the Histadrut. The issue was not simply technical and organizational—the character of the Army was at stake. There were differences of opinion as to whether the Palmah's special role as a striking force continued after the establishment of the Defense Forces. Opinion was divided between Hagana veterans on the one hand, and people who had been trained in regular armies on the other. The Palmah embodied pioneering values and social concepts of the labor movement, although not all Palmah members were members of the Histadrut. The Palmah had inculcated pioneering values in all the youth of Israel.

Ben-Gurion declared that certain things had become evident at a meeting of the General Staff with representatives of the Palmah: the Palmah National Staff had been established without the authorization of the Government of Israel and the institutions of the Israel Defense Forces. It had been created, according to Uri Brenner, the current chief of the Palmah Staff, "in line with practices that existed before the establishment of the Israel Defense Forces." No responsible military or governmental institution had determined the tasks, structure, or authority of the Palmah Command. The present head of this Command had been appointed by Yigal Allon, his predecessor. Neither had been approved by the Army.

On May 24, 1948, Ben-Gurion recounted, Shalom Hevlin, who was then the acting head of the Palmah brigades, announced to all army institutions that these brigades would accept orders only through their own National Command. On May 26 the Minister of Defense informed him that his order was a violation of military law and that Palmah brigades, like all other brigades, must receive their instructions from the General Staff or the Provisional Government and its authorized representatives, without the intervention of the Palmah's National Command. Hevlin rescinded his May 24 order. Subsequent developments show that it was rescinded only in theory; in many instances, the Palmah has acted on the basis of the original communication.

In a discussion with the Minister of Defense on June 18 Yigal Allon agreed that the Palmah Staff should no longer deal with supplies and operations and that each Palmah brigade should be subject to the authority of the General Staff in these matters. However, he suggested that the Palmah National Command continue to deal with training and mobilization until final arrangements were made in these areas. The Minister of Defense replied that this matter would be taken up by the General Staff.

At a meeting of the General Staff on September 21 the head of the Manpower Branch said that there was no room for a special Palmah Command within the framework of the Army. At the same meeting Allon and his comrades stated that there was no link between the Palmah Command and the youth movements except with regard to the settlement groups within the ranks of the Palmah. At the conclusion of that discussion, the Chief of Staff issued an order abolishing the Palmah National Command, adding that discussion of this strictly military matter could not appropriately take place within the framework of the Central Committee of the Histadrut.

Others joined the debate:

Hazan asserted that he would not forego a public struggle over this question, though even if his view was not accepted, he would not foment a military revolt. There should be a solution that would not cause dissension. An attempt must be made to reach an agreement, to prevent a storm from erupting. No one would deny the fact that the Army is not the Hagana; things must be handled differently. But it still must be decided what kind of new structure should replace the old one. Who prevented Etzel from taking over Tel

Aviv? he asked. It was the Palmah National Command. There is a fascist underground in Israel, and it cannot be stopped unless there is a force capable of stopping it. They speak lightly not only of murdering non-Jews, but of murdering members of the Government and other Jews. Can we ignore this? I am against the Palmah's proclaiming its superiority over other units. There is arrogance in the Palmah—it is one of its weaknesses, though natural in view of the fact that Palmah units have borne the brunt of the war. We must end this arrogance. But can anyone criticize the Palmah from a military point of view?

The Right is unscrupulous. Should the time come when they are in a position to seize power, they will do it. Their candidate is Begin. I dream of the day when the entire Army will be like the Palmah. This will not be accomplished by abolishing the Palmah, but by giving the Army the kind of character we would like it to have. From the moment that the Palmah is abolished, there will be a leftist underground in the Army, something that is certainly unnecessary at this point. There will also be a fascist underground. The Army will be torn apart by internal dissension. By abolishing the Palmah, the Israeli labor movement will destroy one of the bulwarks of our security, undermining our role as a pioneering and fighting Zionist movement.

Galili: With the establishment of the Israel Defense Forces, and even before that, several features of the Palmah became characteristic of the nation as a whole. How, then, is the Palmah different today? Its special character stems from the fact that it contains some three thousand men who served at least three years before the outbreak of the war. The Palmah is the special creation of Jewish youth in this country; it is the only one. Sabras were not responsible for the kibbutz, the moshav, the Histadrut, or the Histadrut's youth movement (Hanoar Haoved).

It would be very bitter indeed if the Histadrut had to depend solely on the Palmah to deal with threats from antidemocratic forces. This would be an admission that the Histadrut lacks influence in the Army as a whole. The workers do not need their own brigade, since the entire Army should be under the influence of the working class. But to the extent that the security of the Histadrut depends on the Army, should we abolish a military unit which has not harmed the war effort, but on the contrary has proven itself over and over again in battle? The abolition of the Palmah's National Command is liable to result in the abolition of the Palmah brigades themselves. He was certain, Galili concluded, that the Histadrut, the Government, and all of us will regret this step. It will serve only as an encouragement to the enemies of the Histadrut.

Shaul Meirov Avigor: I would like to make my opinions quite clear. In my view, the Army is endangered by interparty conflicts. This was true even in the days of the Hagana, for both the Hagana and the Army are part of the community as a whole. We did not succeed in overcoming political dissension in the Hagana and we have not succeeded in doing so in the Defense Forces. The important thing is not the Palmah or some other unit. We are destined to live as an armed people for many years—a hundred thousand men and women under arms.

There was a time when the Hagana was under the hegemony of the labor movement, which wished, justifiably, to give it the character of a popular defense organization. The Palmah has indeed fulfilled an extremely important function. But I don't know what our situation would be like today if it were not for the men who served in the Jewish Brigade, and the others who were in the British Army. There were tens of thousands of men who served in the British Army, and we certainly benefited from having them there.

THE PROMISED LAND IS REDEEMED! On May 14, 1948, before the Provisional Parliament in Tel Aviv, Prime Minister David Ben-Gurion reads the Declaration of Independence, which he himself drafted, proclaiming the rebirth of Israel. A portrait of Theodor Herzl looks out at the historic scene that fulfilled his prophecy.

The First Zionist Congress, in Basle, Switzerland, 1897. Dr. Theodor Herzl is shown clasping hands with another great Jewish leader, Dr. Max Nordau.

SIR MOSES MONTEFIORE   BARON EDMOND DE ROTHSCHILD

Montefiore, an Italian-born English Jew, and Rothschild, a French Jew, gave generously of their treasure and zeal to Jewish agricultural pioneering in Palestine in the second half of the nineteenth century.

THEODOR HERZL (1860–1904). Born in Budapest, Theodor Herzl grew up as a thoroughly assimilated Jew, a noted Viennese journalist. A witness to deepening anti-Semitism, and especially horrified by the Dreyfus persecution, he turned to the cause of his people. The Zionist movement had been gathering impetus for decades, but Herzl is regarded as its practical founder. His book *Der Judenstaat* (*The Jewish State*), published in 1896, gave ardent and persuasive form to the plans for a Homeland. A magnetic and prophetic personality, Herzl dominated the First Zionist Congress in 1897. After its close he wrote: "In Basle I created the Jewish State. In five years perhaps, in fifty certainly, everyone will see it." The State was reborn 51 years later.

BEN-GURION IN RISHON LEZION, 1907. Arriving in Palestine from his native Poland, the 21-year-old Ben-Gurion joined this old settlement, founded in 1882. He is the bare-legged young man (*front, center*) above the "X".

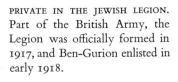

PRIVATE IN THE JEWISH LEGION. Part of the British Army, the Legion was officially formed in 1917, and Ben-Gurion enlisted in early 1918.

LABOR LEADER. Ben-Gurion became Secretary of the Jewish trade-union federation, Histadrut, in 1920. Here, in 1924, he speaks at the laying of the foundation of the Histadrut Building in Jerusalem.

THE "YOUNG TURKS". Ben-Gurion (*left*) and Yitzhak Ben-Zvi, law students in Turkey around 1911, were destined to be, respectively, the first Prime Minister and the second President of Israel.

Nearly half a century later, in 1959, as Prime Minister and President, they greet a foreign statesman, the Burmese Prime Minister, General Ne Win.

Above: Petah Tikva, one of the earliest pioneer settlements, began in 1878 as a tent colony in a desolate land. It is today a flourishing town.

Right: Stampfer Street in modern Petah Tikva.

Below: A Jewish family from the Caucasian Mountains in southern Russia on arrival in Palestine, 1870.

Above: Bilu pioneers on a rock-infested field, their tents in the background. Bilu—an acronym for "House of Israel, come and let us go!" (*Isaiah*)—was formed by Russian Jews in 1882 for the purpose of emigration to Palestine. Its first contingent, that very year, consisted of fifteen men and one woman.

Left: Fascinated Sabras hear tales of the heroic past from Sara Henkin, an aged Bilu veteran.

Below: Hashomer, local groups for defense against marauding Arabs, evolved in all settlements. Men and women at work always carried weapons. Here is one such formation in 1921.

In 1908 on a stretch of sand dunes outside the Arab city of Jaffa, a meeting of men and women decided to establish an all-Jewish city on this site, to be called Tel Aviv. Here, 40 years later, the State of Israel was proclaimed.

Right: An aerial view of Tel Aviv, built on the dunes.

Below: Seaside promenade in Tel Aviv.

Ein Hashofet—"Spring of the Judge," named for Justice Louis D. Brandeis—was founded in 1937 by Jews from the United States. In 1946 (*right*) it counted about 100 souls; today the kibbutz has some 600 members.

Arab discontent, a perennial problem, erupted in violence during critical periods. *Left:* Arabs riot in Jerusalem, 1921. *Right:* Rioters burn and loot Jewish houses in Jaffa, 1936.

A mounted Hashomer unit in the late 1930's, after "Aussie" hats had replaced the fez and tarbush.

Right: Unauthorized immigrants stealing ashore, 1939.

Below: An "illegal" transport. On sighting British ships or planes, a tarpaulin would be thrown over the "cargo" to disguise the vessel's purpose.

Bottom: Having evaded British vigilance, European refugees brought by the *Sussana* are escorted on a forsaken beach, March, 1947.

Above: The ordeal of the *Exodus* in 1947 is an enduring legend of Jewish suffering. The jam-packed ship, intercepted by the British, was forced to sail to Haifa. After a tantalizing glimpse of the Promised Land, the passengers were forcibly loaded onto a prison ship to Cyprus. *Left:* Passengers resist disembarcation in Haifa.

Below left: A night landing of another contingent of "illegals", helped by underground activists, 1947. *Below right:* Mother and son "caught in the act" in Haifa await deportation.

Above: DR. CHAIM WEIZMANN. Weizmann's scientific contributions to Britain's war effort played a role in obtaining the Balfour Declaration on November 2, 1917. Elected President of Israel in 1948, he served until his death in 1952.

Above right: Dr. Weizmann and Emir Feisal at Amman in 1918, during the continuing Jewish-Arab talks. *Right:* Weizmann, Sharett [Shertok], Ben-Zvi, and other Zionist leaders with Arab notables, 1933.

Below: THE JEWISH LEGION. A unique sight in Jerusalem—Jews in British uniforms at the Western (or Wailing) Wall, in World War I. Recruits from all Diaspora centers joined Palestinian Jews to man the Legion.

Below right: Ladies of the Palestine Yishuv bid farewell to Legion volunteers. The formation fought in the Middle East under General Allenby.

War of Independence, 1947–1949. The UN Partition Resolution in 1947 touched off Arab riots in towns and attacks on settlements, followed by full-scale invasion on May 15, 1948, when Israel proclaimed its Statehood. *Left:* Arabs burn and loot in Jerusalem.

Above: Soldiers of the Hagana sprang into action throughout the Holy Land. *Above right:* Hagana night patrol in the Tel Aviv–Jaffa area, December, 1947. *Right:* Armed boys and girls of the Irgun Zvai Leumi deployed on a roof; Jaffa is seen in the background. These irregular formations were later absorbed by the Israel Defense Forces.

Left: In Tel Aviv, a huge demonstration against pro-Arab policies of the British Mandatory Government, late 1940's.

Below left: Soldiers in the trenches celebrate Succoth, 1948.

Below: Bread is distributed to the Jewish population besieged in Jerusalem.

Bottom: Jewish forces on the attack in Upper Galilee in the War of Independence.

Israel's flag is raised at the United Nations, 1949. Present are (*left to right*) Fiorello La Guardia, Mayor of New York; Knesset Member Hacohen; Ambassador Abba Eban; Foreign Minister Moshe Sharett.

Below: Thousands from all parts of Israel and from abroad throng the streets of Tel Aviv to celebrate the first anniversary of independence, May, 1949.
Below right: Young Israelis everywhere dance the traditional "hora".
Bottom: Military parade on the third anniversary, May, 1951.

Above: Dr. Chaim Weizmann addresses the Knesset for the first time as President.

Above right: Yitzhak Ben-Zvi, second President, is inaugurated in the Knesset in 1952. He served until his death in 1963.

The third and current President, Zalman Shazar, took office in 1963. *Right:* President and Mrs. Shazar at a reception given by President and Mrs. Lyndon B. Johnson, 1966. (*photo by Eli Attar.*) *Below:* Shazar and one of the Chief Rabbis with Pope Paul VI in Jerusalem, January, 1964.

I played a major role in the struggle against Hashomer, despite the fact that the members of Hashomer were my teachers and mentors. Were we fighting against the principles of Hashomer when we fought against the organization? No, we were fighting against an organizational framework that had become outmoded. No one questions the positive values of the Palmah or the importance of the link between the Army and physical labor. The issue is an organization which is no longer appropriate. I believe that a Palmah National Command is militarily anachronistic and absurd. The sooner it is eliminated, the better for the Palmah itself. Any framework which has become irrelevant must be eliminated, no matter how noble its original inspiration. Hashomer, the Hagana, and other bodies are no longer relevant.

One of the major functions of the Palmah Command has been in education and culture. I have many friends in the Palmah, but I was terribly shocked when I met with its naval units, which played an important part in "illegal" immigration. The influence of the poison that they have imbibed every day in letters and rumors is terrible. I do not wish to say that everything that I saw was the result of a conscious effort at indoctrination, but I will say that positive pioneering values are being lost because of a crude disregard for the things that are most dear to us. We cannot allow people to carry out educational and cultural activities in the Army as they see fit. We cannot allow army channels to be used to create dissension.

It should be understood that we are not criticizing the positive values of the Palmah, but rather a framework that was created under specific circumstances and which is no longer relevant.

Zvi Yehuda: I hear from members of labor settlements that the Palmah is being starved while other Army units are being given good food, that the Palmah is being sent to the most dangerous places so that its members will be killed, that the Palmah is going barefoot while other units are given shoes. I heard this from my own nephew. Who is responsible for this agitation? I have no way of knowing. If I did not feel that this talk was causing demoralization, I would not have chosen to speak, for, in point of fact, the decision on a Palmah National Command cannot be made here.

At the end of the debate, the following resolution was adopted by a majority of sixteen to eight:

> The Histadrut Central Committee believes that the Israel Defense Forces must be built as a unified and popular army under the guidance of the non-political leadership of the nation and its authorized institutions, while, at the same time, the pioneering Zionist character of the Army is maintained. The Central Committee declares that it is not competent to deal with the question of whether there should be a Palmah National Command.

Yosef Bankover of Mapam made the following statement after this resolution was adopted: "Since the decision taken will vitally affect the character and development of the Army, as well as the role of the labor movement within it, we demand that it be reconsidered at a meeting of the Histadrut Council at the earliest possible moment."

At a second session of the Central Committee of the Histadrut on October 27, 1948, a Mapam resolution on the Palmah was defeated. Mapam, which at that time also included Ahdut Haavodah, was chiefly responsible for the problems that arose in connection with the Palmah. Breaches of discipline occurred in a number of brigades, not only in the Palmah. The argument over a Palmah National Command took place only with Mapam.

The commanders of the Palmah, led by Aluf [Colonel] Allon, immediately carried out the order abolishing the Palmah National Headquarters. Only the representatives of Mapam raised objections in the Histadrut, which decided that the matter was not within its jurisdiction. The Histadrut, moreover, by over a two-thirds majority, expressed the view that the Israel Defense Forces must be built as a unified and popular army under the control of the nation and of Israel's legally constituted authorities.

Negotiations with Etzel Units in Jerusalem ★ The Assassination of Bernadotte ★ Etzel in Jerusalem Dissolves After Ultimatum by General Staff

Bringing about the dissolution of the dissident organizations, Etzel and Lehi, was much harder. Their leaders had announced that they would dissolve the two groups upon the establishment of the State and the setting up of a Jewish government. Lehi in fact disbanded immediately after the Declaration of Independence and its members were inducted into the Defense Forces in the same way as all other men were called up, although there remained a secret Lehi group under another name. The leaders of Etzel fulfilled their obligations only in part. During the first truce, as we have seen, Etzel brought in the *Altalena* and refused to turn over to the Government the weapons it was carrying.

At a meeting of the Provisional Government on August 11, 1948, Interior Minister Gruenbaum stated that relations with Etzel were being arranged satisfactorily in Tel Aviv and within the borders of the State, particularly after Etzel decided to become a political party. Etzel units had agreed to turn over their weapons to the Defense Forces—within the borders of the State. Arrangements had also been made in regard to mutual financial claims. But in Jerusalem the situation was not satisfactory. Etzel members in the city had announced that they accepted the authority of the Military Governor, on the assumption that they would be treated like members of the Defense Forces. They were pleased with the Government's statement that all of the laws of the State of Israel applied to Jerusalem as they did to other parts of the country. But they were not convinced that this decision would be carried out in the end, and therefore did not want to dissolve and accept the authority of the Government as they had done within the borders of Israel. A situation might arise, they felt, when they would be called upon to play the same role in Jerusalem as the Polish General Zilkovsky had done in Vilna.

The Minister of Interior suggested that Etzel members be treated like all other citizens of Jerusalem, namely, that they be supplied with food, but as citizens, not as soldiers. Most of the members of the Committee of Seven on Jerusalem, including the Prime Minister, disagreed with the Minister. Gruenbaum admitted that the existence of a separate army was very dangerous, but pointed to the dangers of trying to impose a decision by force. He favored a policy of continued tolerance.

The Prime Minister supplemented Gruenbaum's report. It is not the job of the Committee of Seven to reach a settlement with Etzel, he said, but to ensure that the country has a unified army, subject to a unified command. The committee has not yet tried to achieve this by force, since Gruenbaum believed that it could be accomplished peacefully, and the Prime Minister agreed to let him try. But he has not been successful. Gruenbaum believes that our show of patience did no harm. If the experiment had ended successfully and Etzel had dissolved, the show of patience would, indeed, not have been harmful. But since it failed, our patience did a great deal of damage.

Gruenbaum's report convinced most members that there was no chance of an agreement consistent with the Council's call for a unified army subject to a single authority. The Committee of Seven should inform the Government that there are, in fact, two independent military organizations in Jerusalem, Etzel and Lehi. Gruenbaum's assumption that the situation would be satisfactory in other parts of the country may also prove mistaken. Etzel in Jerusalem maintains contact with the man who was Commander of Etzel in the country as a whole.

We cannot be certain that Etzel has indeed turned over its weapons in other parts of the country to the Defense Forces, as Gruenbaum believes. We are now responsible for Jerusalem, and we have declared that Israeli law applies to Jerusalem as well. Jerusalem should accordingly be treated like other parts of the country. If we are incapable of exercising our authority in Jerusalem, it means that we are not capable of exercising it elsewhere. The situation is particularly grave in Jerusalem because the city is in the international spotlight. We will be judged by what we do there. We cannot act like the Zionist Organization, and I am not saying this out of any disrespect for the organization. The Zionist Organization is a voluntary body. It has no way of enforcing its decisions. In a state there is an army subject solely to its authority; if such authority is lacking, then the state ceases to exist. In Jerusalem two armies exist that are not subject to the authority of our State.

Something very grave could have happened yesterday, Ben-Gurion declared. Bernadotte was in Jerusalem and Lehi sent out some jeeps—nobody knows why. There are those who say that they wanted to kidnap him. I am not among Bernadotte's admirers, but he is a representative of the United Nations. The Commander of the Defense Forces in Jerusalem, Moshe Dayan, went out to meet him with a jeep with a gun mounted on it. His aide, also from Nahalal, went out in a second jeep carrying a gun. When the Lehi people saw the two jeeps, they quickly departed.

We want Jerusalem to be part of the Jewish State. This cannot be achieved unless there is a single authority and a single army. Terrible things have already happened in Jerusalem—consulates have been looted. Perhaps this was not done by the dissidents. ("The Czech Consulate was robbed by Etzel," Shertok interjected.) When negotiations were being conducted with Etzel, we did everything we could to make it easy for them. But the negotiations failed. This I regret, but since they did fail, we must demand that Etzel turn over its weapons within twenty-four hours and instruct all members to report for military service in the Defense Forces.

Shertok: If I shared Gruenbaum's views, I would have suggested delaying a decision about whether to proclaim Jerusalem as an area under the control of the State of Israel until the situation in regard to Etzel has been clarified. I would have supported a continuation of the status quo, so that if anything happened, we would not be held responsible. If I am not mistaken, Gruenbaum also agreed that we should declare Jerusalem to be under Israeli authority. Please forgive me, Gruenbaum, if I say that your attitude is almost childish. We told the world that we are the legal government in Jerusalem, then we say that ours is a government that does not govern.

I have very little to add to what Ben-Gurion has said. We are now attempting to gain membership in the United Nations, basing our claims on our de facto control of various areas. We have told the world that we are in control of Jerusalem, yet we ourselves are adjuring responsibility for the city. Everyone knows that we regard Jerusalem as an integral part of the State of Israel, yet we allow Etzel in Jerusalem to do as it sees fit. It must be one or the other—either we do not have the strength to subdue Etzel or our claims to Jerusalem are unjustified, and so are our demands for the recognition of the State of Israel. Etzel and Lehi have a radio station. They use it to fill the airwaves with screams and slanders, gossip and lies. We have abdicated our authority in this sphere was well. Anarchy exists. We bear a heavy responsibility.

Zisling: I support the views expressed here. We must ensure that the State Council's decision, calling on Etzel to dissolve and turn over its weapons to the Army, is carried out. The situation in Jerusalem is particularly clear; elsewhere the same things are going on, but beneath the surface. I don't know why conduct prohibited elsewhere is permitted in Jerusalem. If anything, it should be the other way around. Gruenbaum is making a very grave error and may saddle us with a civil war at the worst possible time and under the worst possible conditions. You can count on them to choose the most difficult time and conditions.

Rabbi Fishman: Etzel exists not only in Jerusalem. There is Etzel in Tel Aviv, Haifa, and elsewhere. I agree with Zisling, but we cannot afford an internal war as long as we are threatened by external forces. We should wait, even if this causes difficulties. Let us not antagonize anyone. Let us wait another month, until the situation becomes easier, until the State is more firmly established. I, too, believe that there should be a single army, but we are living in a period when the State is surrounded by enemies. We should do nothing at this moment to foment the spilling of blood in a civil war.

Bernstein: We continue to forget that we have a certain inheritance with which to live. We are now in the midst of a truce, something that I always feared. While the war is on, at least this question does not have the same urgency. We will certainly not gain strength by plunging into internal wars, particularly in a Jerusalem surrounded on all sides. I agree with Gruenbaum that the issue should be set aside for a little while longer.

Gruenbaum: The country is calm; there are no clashes; Jerusalem is quiet. Is it really necessary to disturb this situation? Certainly not! We showed our strength when we were forced to do so. But what state, on its own initiative, sets out to antagonize a section of the population when everything is calm? This is absolutely unnecessary. I do not believe that the negotiations failed. If it were not for the negotiations, there would be explosions every week. In what way does their existence imperil us as this point? When the *Altalena* arrived, it could be argued that they were threatening our sovereignty. But why do we have to present them with an ultimatum now?

The first result of tomorrow's debate in the Provisional State Council will be that former Etzel members will refrain from turning over their weapons to the Army. There will be a public debate, which will force the Revisionists to leave the Council. Other members will leave as well. I will be the first to leave the State Council if such a decision is reached. What's more, I will suggest to my General Zionist colleagues that they do the same. I would like to propose: (1) that we continue with the negotiations to reach an agreement aimed at the eventual elimination of their organizations; (2) that the matter should not be discussed tomorrow at the State Council.

Rabbi Levin: The existence of two armies does indeed endanger the State, but who knows what will happen if there is civil war and bloodshed in Jerusalem? I suggested yesterday in the Committee of Seven that another attempt be made to negotiate with them. They must be made to realize that this would be our last attempt at negotiations, which might be followed by more extreme measures.

Ben-Gurion: We have before us Gruenbaum's proposal that the matter should not be brought to the State Council and that the committee should continue negotiating with the members of Etzel who have accepted the authority of the State and should present them with an ultimatum. This would be without a specific deadline, and leave Gruenbaum free to take further steps.

Gruenbaum: Mr. Ben-Gurion knows that I have not made any move in this matter without consulting him in advance. I will continue to do so. If he informs me that we have reached a point where it is impossible to continue, I will bring the issue to the Government for a decision.

The decision reached was that the Minister of the Interior present an ultimatum to the dissident organizations demanding that they dissolve, turn over their weapons, and join the Army. Otherwise, the Government would use force against them. The Minister of the Interior was instructed to report on the negotiations after he returned from Jerusalem. The members of Mapam abstained from voting; while they wanted to give Gruenbaum a chance, they did not believe that he would achieve anything.

Gruenbaum's discussions with the dissident organizations dragged on and on, while the General Zionists and the Mizrahi threatened to resign from the Government if any firm action were taken. The dissidents demanded that the Government agree not to remove them from Jerusalem, even if the Government itself left. Most members of the Committee of Seven did not agree with the proposals Gruenbaum had made to the dissidents. When he brought them to the Government on September 5, 1948, several members asked for time to consult their parties. Zisling argued that the Gruenbaum proposals contradicted the decisions of the Provisional State Council: "While I have every respect for Mr. Gruenbaum, I have a strong feeling that he is leading us down a very dangerous path. We are being asked to surrender to Etzel."

Because of pressure from the Mizrahi and the General Zionists, the Government failed to reach a decision—until disaster struck. On Friday, September 17, 1948, at 6 P.M., the Minister of Defense received a telegram from the Military Governor of Jerusalem, Moshe Dayan, stating that the UN Mediator, Count Bernadotte, and the French Colonel André P. Serot were murdered in Katamon by Jews while they were on their way to a meeting with the Governor of Jerusalem, Dov Joseph. A few hours after the murder, sealed envelopes were left at various Jerusalem consulates with an announcement that a new underground organization, The Fatherland Front, was operating in Jerusalem and assumed responsibility for the murders. An immediate investigation showed that The Fatherland Front was in fact a name assumed by a group of Lehi people who had committed the murders.

Dov Joseph immediately came from Jerusalem to give us details of the crime. At the spot where the road from Katamon comes into Rehavia, a jeep blocked the way to three UN cars. Three boys with automatic weapons jumped out of the jeep and fired at the UN vehicles. One of them went up to Bernadotte's car, where he shot first Serot and then Bernadotte. General Lunstrom and the Belgian driver, who were also in the car, remained untouched. Gruenbaum telephoned the Prime Minister at 11 P.M. to say that an Etzel representative had come to him in Jerusalem to declare that Etzel had not been involved. This was confirmed by the Secret Service.

On Sunday, September 19, 1948, the Government met. The central question, of course, was how to deal with the dissidents. Gruenbaum suggested that Etzel members should join the Defense Forces and take an oath that would obligate them to serve only in Jerusalem. He was asked: If the State of Israel decides that Jerusalem is to be internationalized, will Etzel be free to do as it pleases? Yes and no, he replied. As long as the Army remains in Jerusalem, Israeli law will operate there. If we leave Jerusalem and our law ceases to operate there, then they would, of course, be free to act as they see fit.

Gruenbaum's proposal was rejected and the Prime Minister's was accepted instead. It provided that Etzel forces in Jerusalem be informed that all the laws of the State in regard to the Army, mobilization, and arms applied to those who live in or come to Jerusalem, exactly as they did for residents of every other part of the State; and that Etzel members must obey those laws without further negotiations. This Ben-Gurion proposal was supported by Bentov, Rabbi Fishman, Zisling, Kaplan, Rosenblueth, Remez, Shitreet, and Shertok. Three members abstained: Bernstein, Gruenbaum, and Shapira. Three members—Ben-Gurion, Zisling, and Shertok—were entrusted with carrying out the decision.

On September 20 a representative of the General Staff presented the following ultimatum to a representative of Etzel:

> 1. Etzel in Jerusalem must accept the laws of the State of Israel in regard to the Army, mobilization, and arms.
> 2. All Etzel members of military age must join the Israel Defense Forces.
> 3. All weapons must be turned over to the Israel Defense Forces.
> 4. Every person joining the Army must take the usual oath of allegiance.
> 5. Members of Etzel will be treated in the same manner as every other Jew.
> 6. If in the course of twenty-four hours, starting on Monday, September 20, 1948, at 12, you accept these conditions—dissolve Etzel and its special battalions, turn over your weapons, and join the Defense Forces—none of you will suffer for previous violations against the laws of Israel and you will be treated in the same way as every other Jew.
> 7. If the aforementioned conditions are not carried out in full during these twenty-four hours, the Army will take every necessary measure to implement this decision.

Etzel accepted the demands of the Government. Its weapons were surrendered to the Defense Forces, which Etzel members joined as individuals. They were treated in the same manner as all other soldiers.

Israel Defense Forces Expand Manpower and Equipment During the Second Truce

As has already been pointed out, the second truce differed from the first in that it was not limited to a fixed period of time and that it did not depend upon the agreement of the two sides, but involved a threat of sanctions against either side if it violated the truce. The second truce began on July 19 and ended on October 15.

The two truces brought great benefits to the Defense Forces, though there were certain difficulties during the first truce in transferring weapons and equipment purchased before the establishment of the State, or afterward. At the end of the first truce, on July 9, the UN Inspectors left their posts and the new equipment could be transferred without interruption. After a period of desperate defensive battles before the first truce, the Israel Defense Forces went over to bold attacks and conquests when the truce ended.

We were not everywhere successful. For example, the Syrians were not thrown out of their bridgehead at Mishmar Hayarden. However, all of lower Galilee was liberated and our forces reached the Beit Netofa Valley. In the Gilboa region, the Defense Forces retreated from the Jenin Valley to a more easily defended line, but the little Triangle remained in our hands. We had considerable achievements to our credit in the Central Region. We captured Lydda and Ramle and the area around Latrun; we enlarged the corridor to Jerusalem to the south and west. In the south we drove the Egyptians from Masmia, Kastina, Tel Asafi, and Hartia, but the Egyptians seized strongpoints controlling the movement from Majdal in the west to Beit Gubrin in the east, and almost succeeded in cutting off our contact with Defense Forces units in the Negev. The Arabs were unable to wrest the initiative from the Defense Forces, but because of their superiority in armor and in the air several IDF attacks were driven off. The dangers facing the State of Israel were not eliminated.

No one knew how long the second truce would last, but the period was fully exploited. The Defense Forces were trained, expanded, and equipped. They grew constantly stronger.

Army manpower on May 15, 1948, was as follows: in nine infantry brigades (Golani, Carmeli, Alexandroni, Kiryati, Givati, Etzioni, and the three Palmah brigades)—24,000; Artillery—659; Air Force—675; Engineers—150; Transport—1097; Training Staff—398; Military Police—168; in basic training—1719. The total—29,266.

By the beginning of October the number of men in uniform reached 79,889. There was a considerable increase in the Navy (2417), the Air Force (4377), and the Artillery (3718). The new manpower came from three main sources: a further call-up of local people, Mahal, and Gahal.

Mahal was the name given to volunteers from abroad who came to fight but not to settle in Israel. Some twenty-four hundred of them fought in the War of Independence: five hundred each from England and France, over three hundred each from South Africa and the United States, smaller numbers from Latin America, Canada, Scandinavia, and other countries. There were some non-Jews among them. Mahal's special contribution was qualitative. Most Mahal members had military skills almost unknown in Israel. They had been trained as pilots, sailors, artillerymen, tank men, etc. They included the late David Marcus, M. (the crack pilot from South Africa), Ben Dunkleman from Canada (who commanded the force which liberated the Galilee at the end of October), and Professor Jack Penn (a well-known surgeon from South Africa). Without the Mahal people, it would have been extremely difficult to establish an Air Force and Navy of the size and quality we attained.

Gahal was the name for new immigrants to the country in the second half of 1948. Some arrived directly from the camps in Germany, from other European countries, or from North Africa. Most came from the detention camps in Cyprus, where they had been interned after trying to enter the country "illegally." Some Israelis, who had accompanied the "illegal" immigrant ships, were interned as well. These captive Israelis, mostly members of the Palmah, began training detainees in Cyprus in 1946 under the guise of youth activities.

Some fifty thousand people, many of them young men capable of doing military service, were in the Cyprus camps. They included veterans of the Russian and Polish Armies. The Hagana emissaries had smuggled a small quantity of weapons into the camps. The British and the UN Observers tried to prevent young people of military age from coming to Israel, but some managed to get through. Particular efforts were made to bring in those with military experience in vital fields such as the artillery and the tank corps.

Miltary equipment also increased. The first efforts to obtain such equipment were made in 1946 after a meeting of the Zionist Executive in Paris, attended by its chairman, Ben-Gurion. The purchase of arms was the responsibility of two emissaries, Ehud Avriel and Yehuda Arazi, and their devoted assistants. They procured rifles, machine guns, tanks, artillery, and planes. Most of the weapons were bought in Czechoslovakia and France, some indirectly in other countries as well.

The purchases in Czechoslovakia began when Jan Masaryk was Foreign Minister, but continued during the regime of Vlado Clementis, the first Communist Foreign Minister, Rudolf Slansky, the Jewish Secretary of the Communist Party, was violently opposed to the sale of weapons to Israel. He was afterward sentenced to death, together with Clementis, for allegedly aiding the Zionists.

The first tanks were purchased in France. They were light, eleven-ton Hotchkiss tanks with 37-mm. cannon. These tanks were antiquated, but in the first days after the invasion they at least enabled us to deal with Arab tanks. We obtained rifles, machine guns, and airplanes from Czechoslovakia. The planes were of the worst possible type—Messerschmitts—but they also made it possible for us to take to the air against the Egyptian Air Force. As has been mentioned, the Messerschmitts could not be flown nonstop from Czechoslovakia. At first we were forced to fly them to Corsica, and from there to Israel, which added about a thousand miles to the journey. With great effort, we obtained a base closer to the country. Later we were able to purchase Spitfires, which were much better than the Messerschmitts, but again we had difficulty bringing them to Israel. Spitfires, even with auxiliary fuel tanks, could not fly for more than three hours at two hundred miles an hour, but they had to fly 1400 miles to reach Israel. Then our engineers and technicians succeeded in putting additional fuel tanks on the planes, permitting them to fly for seven hours straight.

Thanks to the increased strength of the Air Force, we were able to overcome the problems of contact with the Negev. We had twenty-six settlements and several army units in the south and the Negev, on the other side of the Egyptian line running from Majdal to Beit Gubrin. Using transport planes, Dakotas, and Norsemen, and with the help of a former American Air Force man (a Christian), we succeeded in supplying the settlements and military units. We shipped 2225 tons of supplies and brought back 2000 men from the Negev.

Our naval force also grew during the second truce. We purchased vessels abroad and repaired "illegal" immigrant ships in the country. In October, before the renewal of fighting, the Navy had sixteen vessels of about seven thousand tons. We had four warships, the *Wedgewood*, *Hagana*, *Maoz*, and *Noga*. The first two had one 75-mm. cannon, one 65-mm. cannon, and two 20-mm. cannon, as well as four heavy machine guns. The other two had only two 20-mm. cannon. Actually only the first two were suitable for battle. There were also three service vessels: one, the *Eilat*, was armed with a 65-mm. cannon and two 20-mm. cannon; the other two, the *Dromit* and the *Itamari*, had no cannon at all. We had a few coast guard vessels. Despite Egyptian naval superiority, our small Navy was able to take on their much larger fleet.

During the first weeks of the second truce, we purchased field guns, antitank guns, and tanks. We had difficulty unloading the tanks, for we found that there were no cranes in Israel strong enough to unload a fifty-ton Sherman tank from a ship. The problem was solved when we located a foreign ship near the coast of the country, the cranes of which, together with the cranes on shore, could unload the Shermans.

Proposed Retaliation Against Jordanian Destruction at Latrun Is Turned Down ★ Final Bernadotte Plan for Palestine

Under the terms of the truce neither side had the right to carry out hostile acts. The first to violate this condition were the Jordanians, who destroyed the pumping station near Latrun that had helped bring water from Rosh Ha'ayin to Jerusalem. We had secretly laid a second pipeline not dependent upon the Latrun pumping station, but this did not justify its destruction. Knowing that our forces had grown stronger, I concluded at the beginning of October that we should react militarily to this open violation of the truce by the Arab Legion, the purpose of which was to make Jews of Jerusalem die of thirst. I discussed with the General Staff how large a force would be necessary to storm Latrun and then continue on to Ramallah, Jericho, and the Dead Sea, as well as liberate the Hebron region and Bethlehem in the south. The General Staff thought that a week would be needed for such an operation with the forces that would be at our disposal in the middle of October. This proposal I brought to a meeting of the Government on September 26, but it was rejected by a majority vote.

Those opposed to it emphasized the fact that the assassination of Bernadotte had stirred up enmity toward Israel in several European countries. In such an atmosphere, they feared, a military initiative could undermine our international position. There was also concern about the situation that might develop in the UN General Assembly, which was scheduled to discuss the Bernadotte Plan at its next meeting. The plan had been completed by Bernadotte on September 16, 1948, the day before he was murdered, and presented to the Secretary General of the United Nations. In it Bernadotte laid down the principles which could, in his opinion, solve the Palestine problem. The points of the plan were as follows:

1. Peace must be achieved in Palestine, and every measure must be taken to ensure that hostilities are not renewed.
2. The Jewish State is an established fact.
3. The borders of the State will be determined by a formal agreement, or by the United Nations.
4. Geographical unity should be the criterion for determining Israeli and Arab borders;

it is not desirable therefore to remain absolutely committed to the territorial arrangements set down in the November 29, 1947, resolution.

5. The rights of the Arab refugees must be safeguarded; those who wish to return should be allowed to do so, and those who do not should be given appropriate compensation.

6. Jerusalem should be dealt with separately because of its religious and international significance, and because of the conflicting interests involved.

7. International responsibility should serve as a means of allaying existing fears, particularly in regard to the borders and human rights.

If the two sides did not reach an agreement on the borders, Bernadotte suggested the following revisions of the November 29 resolution:

1. The Negev, south of the Majdal-Faluja line, should be defined as an Arab area.
2. Ramle and Lydda should be included in the Arab area.
3. The Galilee should be defined as a Jewish area.

The decision concerning the future of the Arab section of Palestine, in the Mediator's opinion, should be made by the Arab states. There were three possible solutions: (1) creation of an independent Arab state west of the Jordan; (2) division of the Arab area among the Arab states that had participated in the war; (3) annexation of the entire Arab area by Trans-Jordan. Count Bernadotte recommended the third solution, because Palestine and Trans-Jordan were linked historically and had common interests. He proposed that Haifa Port together with the refineries and the terminus of the pipeline, as well as the Lydda Airfield, be made free zones, open to the Arab countries.

The Mediator withdrew his earlier proposal on Jerusalem, submitted during the first truce, and again recommended that the UN be given effective control of the city. At the same time, maximum autonomy would be granted to the Arab and Jewish communities.

Bernadotte recommended the establishment of a UN Conciliation Commission, to take all necessary steps to foster a peaceful solution of the Palestine problem and the development of friendly relations between Arabs and Jews, as well as to supervise arrangements decided upon by the UN as to borders, roads, railways, a free port, minority rights, etc. He placed special emphasis on the refugee problem, involving 360,000 Arabs and 7000 Jewish refugees. Since they were citizens of a former Mandated Territory, the international community had a continuing responsibility for them. Bernadotte underlined the "desperate urgency" of the problem, stating: "The choice is between saving thousands of souls immediately or allowing them to die," and concluded: "I am certain that the participation of the international community in caring for the Palestinian refugees is a key precondition to the establishment of peace in that country." The Mediator went on to warn:

It would be dangerous complacency to take it for granted that with no settlement in sight the truce can be maintained indefinitely. Each side contends that the indefinite truce works to the advantage of the other. The strain on both sides in maintaining the truce under the prevailing tension in Palestine is undoubtedly very great. I am convinced that neither side really wished to resume the fighting, but on the other hand, neither side appears to be prepared, openly and voluntarily, to surrender its position or to make fundamental concessions. There is the constant danger, which must be faced, that the accumulated irritation from daily incidents, war of nerves, the economic strain of maintaining large armies in the field, the pressure of public opinion, and the tendency to despair of a peaceful settlement, may provoke one or the other party to take the foolhardy risk of resuming hostilities in the vain hope of a quick victory. There is also the danger that under the constant pressure of tension, mutual suspicion and recrimination, and in the absence of any enforcement ability by the United Nations representatives, the truce, if too long prolonged in its present indefinite form, will deteriorate into virtual resumption of hostilities through a mounting number of local incidents widely spread.

The second truce differs from the first in that the Security Council imposed it on the parties, using the threat of sanctions as outlined in Article 7 of the UN Charter. Therefore, it is not limited to a specific period of time. This introduces a new element into the situation, as compared to the first truce. Both sides tend to regard any act by their adversaries as reason enough for calling on the Security Council to intervene. Each side complains that the borders set by the truce agreement are harmful to its interests. This attitude finds its expression in the position adopted by both sides vis-a-vis the Observers and vis-a-vis truce obligations in general. The truce is undoubtedly a heavy burden on both sides, but a war is liable to be a still heavier burden.

The truce is not an end in itself. It is meant to prepare the way for peace. There is most chance of constructive action during this period, action based on the fact that the truce is the result of international intervention. But if it appears that there is no chance of replacing the present arrangements by permanent ones, which will give a realistic assurance of peace, then international intervention will become gradually less effective and international supervision will be viewed with great cynicism. If the present period is not exploited in order to reach a solution to the problem, then the opportunities inherent in international intervention are liable to disappear completely.

The day after the Provisional Government debated and rejected Bernadotte's proposal, the State Council met (on September 27, 1948) to consider it. Meanwhile the Mediator had been killed by The Fatherland Front.

Shertok and Ben-Gurion Analyze Situations as UN General Assembly Session Approaches

Discussion of the Bernadotte Plan in the Provisional State Council on September 27, 1948, opened with a report by Foreign Minister Shertok:

We approach the UN General Assembly, holding a larger section of the Land of Israel than was allocated to us in the November 29 resolution. We appear before the Assembly backed by an army, created from scratch in a single year, actually in much less than a year— an army which is perhaps the most important military force in the Middle East. Nevertheless, we do not approach this meeting in a state of overconfidence.

The Assembly has before it the report of the late Count Bernadotte, who wished to revise the arrangements laid down in the November 29 resolution. There is no doubt that Bernadotte's report was prepared by its author jointly with very important elements on the international scene. The full and immediate approval of the report by the American and British governments testifies to this fact.

There are several positive elements in the Bernadotte report, along with the considerable number of negative ones. On the positive side, the report speaks of Israel as an established fact. The assumption that the truce must end with a peace settlement is also positive. There are two positive aspects on the territorial questions: (1) the proposal that all of the Galilee be included in the State of Israel; (2) indications that Jaffa should be included in the State of Israel; this is not said directly, but hinted at.

On the other hand, the report has extremely negative aspects. It suggests that every Arab individual has the right to decide whether he will return to his former home in the State of Israel. We do not believe that this is a decision to be made on an individual basis. It is a matter for negotiations between nations. The report also speaks of international supervision of certain areas within the country, which opens the way to an expansion of such supervision to the point where Israel would become a trusteeship. The gravest aspect of the report is its suggestion that the Negev be removed from the State of Israel. Israel's southern border, according to the plan, would run north of the Majdal-Faluja line. There is also mention of a special regime in the Port of Haifa, including the refineries, as well as the Lydda Airport. Then comes the section on an international regime in Jerusalem. Finally, mention is made of a Conciliation Commission, which would not only arbitrate on behalf of the UN, but exercise governmental powers backed up by international authority; this would limit our sovereignty.

My mission at the UN General Assembly will be to prevent the acceptance of Bernadotte's proposals by a two-thirds majority; this would leave the November 29 resolution as the legal basis for an international arrangement in the Land of Israel. I am not saying that we should regard the November 29 resolution as immutable. There was no contradiction between our demand for all of the western section of the Land of Israel as the Jewish State and our agreement to establish the State in part of the country. The initial demand was justified; so was the compromise. We demanded what was our due, and accepted what we could obtain. But we never said that what we accepted was our maximum demand; on the contrary, we made it clear that it was our minimum demand. If the November 29 resolution had been carried out in full, on the basis of cooperation between the two sides, we would have had to accept the obligations involved. But this did not happen. The partition plan was not put into effect; the only provision carried out was the one calling for the establishment of the State of Israel. Experience has shown the justification, the need, and the possibility of making revisions in the November 29 plan. We now demand Jerusalem and a corridor to it, Jaffa, and all of the Galilee.

The Government decided, before the publication of the Bernadotte report, not to raise the question of the borders. If the question arose, it was decided to demand the entire area allocated to the Jewish State under the November 29 resolution plus certain additional sections of the country. We will not agree to abandon the part of the Galilee that is in our hands; and, of course, we will not give up the Negev. The Government has decided to demand inclusion of New Jerusalem within the Jewish State, as well as a corridor to Jerusalem, the corridor we now hold. There is still the question of Haifa. We oppose making Haifa a free port. As far as the refugees are concerned, we must carry out a determined information campaign to explain the need for a fundamental solution to the problem, based on the settlement of these Arabs, or at least most of them, in the neighboring states. This would be a blessing to their descendants, the neighboring countries, and the Jews of Israel.

The Prime Minister stated that the Foreign Minister had presented the views of the Government and there was little to add. But he thought it necessary to clarify a number of basic assumptions that formed the foundation for Israeli foreign policy:

First of all, we are in the midst of a combined political and military campaign, and we should not consider one phase without taking the other into account. Neither will be decisive on its own. Secondly, two groups of interests are involved: those of the Arabs and the Jews of the Middle East on the one hand, and those of the Great Powers on the other. If only the interests of the Jews and Arabs were involved, the military factor would be decisive. The Arabs believed that their military strength would settle the issue, but they were wrong. They lost the military struggle. Indeed, were military factors in the Middle East to determine the outcome, then we could speak in terms not only of the November 29 resolution, but perhaps also of the Biltmore Program. But developments in the Middle East will not be decisive on their own. The larger world arena, with friendly and hostile forces, is also involved. In the present period, *our military position is stronger than our political position*, for not all the Great Powers are supporting us. Therefore, it seems to me, we cannot depend solely on the political struggle. At the same time, the military struggle *alone*, even if it develops to our advantage, will not be decisive; there are forces in the world that will see to it that it is not decisive.

It is incorrect to divide the world simply into two parts, East and West. The East is largely monolithic, the West much less so. There are differences between England and America, between England and France. There are even differences within the United States itself.

As the time for the meeting of the General Assembly approaches, we must ask ourselves whether a final decision will be made in that body rather than the Security Council. I doubt it. Perhaps there will be a two-thirds majority supporting a particular resolution. But will this resolution determine the course of events in Israel? I doubt that, too. The forces supporting the resolution are certainly strong enough to ensure that it is carried out, but will they want to do so? We must make a careful distinction between two completely different things: the attitude of governments and statesmen on the Palestine problem, and their ability and willingness to use the forces at their disposal to ensure that a resolution is put into effect. In other words, we must differentiate between the *political* and *military* positions of various governments.

Let me recall two instructive examples from the experience of the past year. The UN resolution of 1947 was supported by more than a two-thirds majority, including the US and the USSR; nevertheless, it was not implemented. The Arabs utterly disregarded the wishes of the UN. If they had had the military power to carry out their nefarious plans, nothing would have remained of the UN resolution. The Jews might have disappeared from the Land of Israel and there certainly would not have been a State of Israel. Yet no one at the UN would have uttered a word. Look at what happened when the Arabs defeated us in the Old City. Not a voice was raised against the desecration of the Holy City or the violation of the UN decision about Jerusalem's special status. It was not the UN decision that left New Jerusalem in our hands.

A second example: At the beginning of May, some of the great world figures, including General Marshall, warned us not to establish the State of Israel. And there were good friends who told us that we had no alternative but to accept Marshall's views. It seems, superficially, that these advisors were right. Marshall was backed by a gigantic force, which no Jewish force in Israel or elsewhere in the world could withstand. We would not have had the least chance if we had gone to fight the American Army. When we failed to accept Marshall's views, it was not because we thought our forces were stronger; we could not have been so foolish. We acted as we did because we doubted whether Marshall was willing to utilize the forces he represented to prevent the establishment of the State of Israel. The State was set up in opposition to Marshall, and the American Army was not used against us. Had it been, the State would have been destroyed at once. However, the very opposite happened: the United States immediately accorded de facto recognition to the State of Israel, although it has not yet recognized Israel de jure.

If we had not been able to differentiate between what a government *said* and what it was willing and able *to do*, the State of Israel would not have been established. Those who advised us not to establish the State did not err in their evaluation of the forces that stood behind Marshall; they did not exaggerate in the least; they erred in that they could not differentiate between what the American representative *said* and what the American government *would do*.

Now we face another struggle on the international scene. There are, theoretically, three possible means of solving the Palestine problem: by an agreement between the Jews and the Arabs, by a UN decision, or by a military decision in a struggle between the Jews and the Arabs. There is scarcely any chance of an agreement between the Jews and Arabs *at this time*. A UN decision would certainly give us much more than the Arabs would be willing to give us *at this time*. But this raises two questions: (1) If the Arabs oppose a UN decision, and there is every reason to assume that they will, *even if we are also dissatisfied with it*, how will the situation be different than it was on the November 1947 UN resolution? No matter how successful our information program, is there any chance that we can convince the UN to give us the Negev, a corridor to New Jerusalem, Ramle and Jaffa, central and western Galilee, at least the new section of Jerusalem, the port of Eilat, a continuous land area running up to the Dead Sea, and not impose external control on Haifa? And if, by some miracle, such a resolution is adopted by a two-thirds majority, won't we still have to fight to implement it, just as we had to fight this year for the November resolution? Is there any reason to believe that the UN will employ the necessary force to implement whatever resolution it adopts?

This brings us to the third possibility: *a decision achieved by our military forces in this country*. In the meantime, we have had the experience of a truce period. The truce has two consequences: it prevents the UN from enforcing its own decisions and it prevents the Jews and the Arabs from using force to achieve their aims. It remains open to doubt, however, whether a truce can solve the problem to the benefit of the Jews or of the Arabs. It only proves that there are elements in the outside world who wish to ensure that our military superiority does not allow us to *tip the balance in our favor*. If their attitude is strictly *political*, and they are not willing to use their *military might to enforce it, there is no reason why we have to give in to this truce policy*.

We are now about to begin a new stage, perhaps a decisive one, in the political struggle. We should not forget at this time the basic premise about which I spoke when I began my remarks, namely, that this is a *combined* struggle. In view of the military situation in the country at this moment, it is unlikely that the UN will adopt a resolution that meets our requirements with respect to the Galilee, the road to Jerusalem, Jerusalem, and the Negev. There is no reason to believe that political factors alone will solve this problem or solve it to our satisfaction. Our influence in the *international arena* is simply not adequate. If we do not take measures ourselves to make territorial adjustments, or at least the most vital ones, they will not be made at all. We will not achieve what we require in the Negev, on the road to Jerusalem, and in the Galilee simply through a political struggle.

The UN Observers declared that water had to be sent to Jerusalem. This was a basic condition of the truce. Nevertheless, the Arabs blew up the pumping station at Latrun, and until this very day no water is flowing via Latrun to Jerusalem. We did not depend on the UN. Instead, we laid a new water pipeline and saved Jerusalem. A UN committee decided that we had the right to send convoys to the Negev during certain hours. The Egyptians have refused to honor this decision, and our settlements in the Negev would be dying of hunger if we had not found other ways of bringing in supplies. But these alternative routes are not safe. If the UN lacks the desire or the strength to carry out its decisions, must we sit by and accept the impotence of the UN? The conclusion of all this is clear: we cannot depend solely on political activity, or on political decisions, even if the decisions are desirable ones from our point of view. We must be ready to exploit the military factor whenever and wherever necessary.

The Government's position was approved.

Deciding Whether To Break Through to the Negev

After the meeting of the State Council, the Foreign Minister left for Paris to attend the UN General Assembly session. Ben-Gurion left to meet with the commanders in the south, to assess the size of the Egyptian forces and determine the Israeli force required to open the road to the Negev. His proposal for opening that road was the main item on the agenda of a meeting of the Government set for October 6, 1948. In preparation, he decided to meet not only with the General Staff and commanders of the fronts but with members of his party in the Government.

Until then, he had brought military problems solely to the General Staff and the Government. But when his plan for opening the road from Latrun to Jericho and the Dead Sea had been rejected on September 26, three members of his own party were among his opponents. Consequently, he now considered it necessary to discuss the new proposal with members of his party in the Government in advance. One of them, Transport Minister David Remez, at first opposed the plan for breaking through to the south with great vehemence. Israel so far had won miraculously, he argued, but that did not mean we should depend on miracles.

Ben-Gurion replied that it was not a question of miracles. Our Army, despite its tender age, was superior to the Arab armies in its spirit, and there was reason to believe that the past victories would be repeated in the future. He also stressed the dangers posed by a continued truce that allowed the Egyptians to seize new strongpoints from time to time—a process that might result in complete isolation of our settlements and military forces in the south and the Negev. As winter approaches we will not be able to bring in supplies by air as we have done since the truce began. Although the UN Observers say we should be permitted to pass through the Egyptian lines for several hours each day, the Egyptians have refused to let us through. We therefore have the right to break through by force.

Ben-Gurion then met with the General Staff and the commanders of the fronts. He asked them how large a force would be needed to defeat the Egyptian invaders in the south, if Trans-Jordan, Syria, and Iraq did not intervene. There were differences of opinion. One of the finest commanders doubted whether hostilities could take place with Egypt without the other Arab countries intervening. He admitted that it was easier to defend the corridor to Jerusalem from the south, but added that it was easier for the Arab Legion to attack the corridor from the north. Trans-Jordan and Iraq would then attack our forces in the center of the country along a fifty-kilometer front, which could not be defended without mounting an attack on the entire Triangle. The Commander of the Palmah, Yigal Allon, supported the Defense Minister's proposals. The Commander of the Air Force, Aharon Remez, thought that our forces should attack the Triangle and entrench themselves in the hills. The fact that Israel only held a narrow strip of land along the sea endangered the

Jewish community. The Minister of Defense expressed his doubts about whether a battle with Egypt would bring about fighting on all the fronts, pointing out that relations between Egypt and the other Arab states were very tense.

On the afternoon of the same day (October 6) the Provisional Government met to deal with the Prime Minister's proposal to force open the road to the Negev. The Egyptians, he pointed out, do not permit our convoys to reach our settlements and military forces in the south, despite the decision of the UN committee granting us free passage for three hours a day, from 9 A.M. to noon. We have twenty-six settlements and several army units on the other side of the Majdal–Beit Gubrin line, held by the Egyptians. We must supply them with food and all their other requirements. With the approach of winter, the airlift will be far more difficult and the quantity of supplies required much larger, because the settlements will be sowing their fields after the rains and will need seeds from the north. The Air Force has been airlifting seventy tons a night. It will not be able to do this during the winter, and certainly not to increase the amount. It will be necessary to send a convoy in another few days during the hours specified by the UN; if the Egyptians refuse to let it pass, we will be forced to break through their lines. One should not ignore the possible consequences of such a step. The first result would be the renewal of fighting all through the south. A road runs from the Egyptian border and El Arish along the seashore up to Isdud. This entire line is held by the Egyptians. The end of the line is north of Isdud, between Isdud and Yibne.

An Egyptian brigade is encamped between Majdal and the area north of Isdud. A second Egyptian brigade is between Majdal and Beit Gubrin a third between Majdal and El Arish. The largest number of troops are concentrated in that last area where there are additional Egyptian companies. Apart from the regular army, volunteers from the Sudan and Libya are there, organized on a paramilitary basis. They are mainly east of Beit Gubrin and the road to Jerusalem. In addition, local Arabs have been mobilized as well as members of the Moslem Brotherhood. They hold Hebron, Bethlehem, and the area up to the southern part of Jerusalem. But these are not of very great importance. The major Egyptian force consists of the three brigades, armed with field guns and antitank guns. There are ten field guns along the Isdud–Majdal line. The road back to Egypt is not safe because we have settlements and military forces behind the Egyptian lines in the south. The only clear path for the Egyptians is by way of the sea, but our naval forces are now strong enough to prevent them from reinforcing their army by sea.

It is possible, of course, that the fighting will spread to the other fronts, though this is not likely in view of the worsening relations between Egypt and Abdullah. Abdullah does not recognize the government established by the Egyptians in the Gaza Strip, since it is made up of supporters of the Mufti. Nevertheless, the importance of Arab rivalry should not be overestimated. Perhaps the Arab League will meet and decide that all the Arab armies must fight. Even if the struggle is confined to the Egyptian front, it will not be an easy one. We have three brigades in the south, apart from a Home Guard brigade. The Commander of the southern front demands an additional brigade, and, indeed we have one brigade (Brigade Eight) in reserve. The commanders in the south believe that we should be able to destroy the Egyptian forces within a week.

If the fighting remains confined to the south—that is, if the Iraqis, Syrians, and Trans-Jordanians do not intervene—then we will be able to gain control of the entire Negev as far as the Dead Sea and on down to the Red Sea. We may also be able to capture Hebron and Bethlehem, if Arab forces do not come down from the north. If the other Arab armies do not intervene and the situation at Latrun and in Sheikh Jarrah remains static, our situation in Jerusalem will improve. We control the railway to Jerusalem, and we are paving a new road to the city, so that we will not need Latrun and will enjoy more secure access to Jerusalem. The Arab armies have torn up the tracks to the city at several points, but it will not be difficult to repair the damage.

A renewal of fighting is liable to provoke the bombing of Tel Aviv, the Prime Minister recognized. However, our situation in the air is now much better than it was before—we can do more damage to Cairo than the Egyptians can do to Tel Aviv.

We would have to begin such a campaign even if the UN were not discussing the removal of the Negev from the Jewish State. Incidentally, according to reports that we have received from Paris, where the General Assembly is meeting, our situation is quite favorable. Public opinion is not enthusiastic about the Bernadotte Plan. American circles say that there is no possibility of removing the entire Negev from Israel and that a compromise is required. We would have to capture the road to the south if it were only because we have twenty-six settlements on the other side of the Egyptian lines.

Bentov asked: What will we do if the Egyptians allow our convoy to pass through their lines?

The Prime Minister replied: We demanded that the UN allow us to send through convoys twice a week, and every time a request was submitted the Egyptians turned it down. There is a decision in writing giving us the right to send through convoys, and we also have a document from the UN Observers stating that the Egyptians have refused to allow our convoys to pass.

Shitreet: Won't our attempt to force our way through the Egyptian lines make things more difficult for Shertok at the United Nations?

The Prime Minister: In my opinion, our operation will make it easier for Shertok. It is not enough just to capture the road, for the Egyptians are scattered all over the Negev around our settlements.

Bentov: Did the General Staff accept the plan?

The Prime Minister: One might say, if it were possible, that the plan was accepted more than unanimously. The only discussion was about whether the reserve brigade should be kept in the north or sent to the south.

Gruenbaum suggested that Shertok be asked for his opinion before a final decision was made; another four or five days were required in any case to make the necessary preparations. They could go on while Shertok's reply was awaited.

David Remez listed four reasons why he would support the proposal: (1) we have many settlements on the other side of the Egyptian lines and contact with them must be maintained; (2) the Minister of Defense and the General Staff believe that we have a good chance of winning; (3) there is a clear decision of the UN's according us the right to pass through the Egyptian lines, and the UN has done nothing to carry out its decision; (4) Shertok is in Paris and is aware of this plan; if he feels that it creates difficulties at the United Nations, he would certainly hasten to warn us of this possibility.

Bernstein: I opposed the Latrun operation at a meeting of the Government on September 26 because I regarded it as an open provocation against the United Nations. The issue here is an entirely different one. We must maintain contact with our settlements. At the same time we must determine whether this operation will cause a general outbreak of fighting all over the south; if so, we may be accused of embarking upon it as an excuse for reopening the campaign.

Zisling: We cannot, of course, ignore the dangers involved in such an operation; but the truce is only an illusion and it is also dangerous to allow the situation to remain as it is.

Rabbi Fishman: I voted for the operation at Latrun, and I certainly support this one.

The Prime Minister: I believe that Shertok was among those who opposed the Latrun offensive at the previous meeting of the Government. I spoke with him afterward and he said that he had opposed the idea of a general offensive, but not an attack on Latrun itself.

Rosenblueth expressed surprise at the change in attitude of some members since the discussion on the Latrun proposal. What had happened since that meeting to justify the change? When we discussed the Latrun matter, it was clear to me that we were talking about a renewal of fighting everywhere. If we embark upon this campaign in the south, I am certain that the Arabs will renew the war along all the fronts. If I understand the General Staff and the Minister of Defense correctly, they believe that we should continue the war because only in that way will we be able to win. This, in Ben-Gurion's opinion, is the surest way to peace. He has lost faith in the United Nations. I do not share his pessimism or his exaggerated despair. I am against the operation, for it would mean violating a UN resolution. It would be a gross provocation against the UN, particularly now, while the UN is meeting to discuss the matter. The reaction in Paris will be very hostile and damaging to our cause.

Kaplan: I was extremely surprised by Ben-Gurion's statement that Shertok had agreed with those who supported an attack on Latrun. I find this very difficult to understand in view of Shertok's speech at the meeting on September 26. I believe that we should ask his opinion about this scheme as well.

Gruenbaum suggested that the Government wait for Shertok's reply, though, he added, it would not influence him. Even if Shertok opposed the operation, he would vote for it.

The Prime Minister answered Mr. Rosenblueth: What will happen if the Security Council calls for a cease-fire? We will cross that bridge when we come to it. When we have cut off the Egyptian forces, then we will accept the UN's decision or we will put off our acceptance for an additional day. I have not lost faith in the UN, but what counts is what we do here. There are forces in the world who will help us. History is made not by talk, but by action. We are acting not out of despair, but out of faith in our strength and in the conscience of humanity. Our success in the south will influence opinion at the United Nations.

Only two members supported a resolution opposing the operation. Remez's proposal was accepted instead. It said: (1) the plan for breaking through to the south has been adopted in view of the fact that the UN Observers, in the face of Arab opposition, have failed to implement their own decision; (2) the Foreign Minister will be informed of this decision, and if he opposes it, the matter will be brought up again for discussion by the Government; (3) if there are no objections, the Committee of Five (the Cabinet Security Committee) will be authorized to implement the decision.

Ben-Gurion immediately cabled the Foreign Minister in Paris, asking him to send his comments as quickly as possible. The operation was set for October 14, 1948, the day after Yom Kippur.

Dr. Ralph Bunche, who had been appointed to succeed Bernadotte, talked with

David Horowitz on October 7, 1948. A continuation of the truce, Bunche said, was a life-or-death matter for the British and Americans. This is not 1936, he said, when no one intervened [in the war between Italy and Ethiopia]. This time there may be intervention by the two blocs that could trigger a world war. If it should be necessary, the UN will impose sanctions on the side responsible for the renewal of fighting, or on both sides. Bernadotte's report has become, after his assassination, a sacred "Last Testament." At first Bernadotte had suggested the 31st Parallel (south of Sodom) as the southern border of Israel. Later, when he heard that the Jews wanted to trade the Negev for the Galilee, he changed his opinion for the worse and proposed the Majdal-Faluja line.

Horowitz told Bunche that he had a heavy responsibility. You must, he said, reach agreement with the Jews or you won't have an agreement at all. For there can be no agreement with the Arabs. Bunche concurred. The American delegation at the United Nations was flexible, he said, and hinted that it would agree to the 31st Parallel. As far as Jerusalem was concerned, there were two possibilities: an internationalized Jerusalem, with an international force, or a division of the city, based on an agreement with Abdullah, in which case the Jews would receive a corridor to Jerusalem. Bunche believes that the question of the Negev is more difficult than the question of Jerusalem, for Bernadotte's "Will" deals with the Negev. As to the refugees, it is clear that a majority will not wish to return; that is why there is a section about their resettlement and the granting of compensation. Bunche believes that Bernadotte was mistaken on this point.

Bernadotte was not a brilliant man, but he was decent. He was not serving the English, Bunche said, and had met with them four times to convince them that the State of Israel was an established fact that could not be eliminated. He had not done this out of a love of Israel, but out of a desire to succeed, since he knew that it was vital to his success. He accused the British of making both the Jews and the Arabs hate them, and advised us to be reasonable. Even if we conquered the entire country as far as the Jordan, the Arabs would not accept the situation. Their fears would grow and the war would go on. This was not November 29th. Now the Security Council was meeting, and the Council had teeth. The Council would invoke sanctions if one of the parties to the dispute refused to abide by the UN decision. The Bernadotte report accepted two Jewish points, Bunche said: it stated that there could not be an unlimited truce and that a Jewish State was necessary.

The same day (October 7) the Minister of Defense met with the Chief of Staff, Yacov Dori, and with the Chief of Operations, Yigael Yadin. He said that two factors had to be taken into consideration. (1) If fighting began on the day after Yom Kippur, it could be assumed that it would not last more than four or five days, for the Security Council would intervene immediately; it might be possible, at most, to continue the fighting for up to seven days. (2) Under these circumstances, it was reasonable to assume that the Iraqis and Trans-Jordanians would not have time to intervene. Abdullah was at odds with the Egyptians, and the others would not intervene unless the Egyptians asked them to do so. Even if there were such an Egyptian request, the fighting might be halted by the Security Council before they had a chance to intervene.

This led to two military conclusions. (1) The *maximum* possible force has to be concentrated in the south so that a great deal may be accomplished in a very short period, even if this did not include the destruction of the entire Egyptian Army. (2) We must hasten to capture the railway stations in the south, and free the southern section of Jerusalem; therefore, we should send another brigade from the north to the south. The Chief of

Operations strongly opposed the suggestion, considering it certain that once fighting broke out in the south, the war would start again along all the other fronts. Nevertheless, additional men, supplies, and weapons immediately began streaming to the south.

At a meeting on October 10 the Prime Minister informed the Government that the Foreign Minister, in Paris, had approved the plan and that all necessary preparations were being made so that the operation could begin immediately after Yom Kippur. As it happened, the Egyptians had stepped up their operations in the south and had mounted serious attacks from time to time. They had suffered severe losses and Egyptian equipment, including artillery and armored cars, had been captured. These were immediately pressed into service against them. The Prime Minister said that in recent days he had met twice with the Security Committee of the State Council in accordance with the Government's decision. He had not informed the Committee of the decision to open the road to the south, but the majority of its members had recommended that the Government end the truce.

Section 3. The Road to Armistice Agreements

The Campaign in the South Begins ★ The Security Council Demands an Immediate Cease-Fire

ACCORDING to the plan, a convoy was to begin moving south on Thursday noon, October 14, the day after Yom Kippur. Rabbi Herzog, who had been informed of the undertaking, ruled that all soldiers could work and eat on Yom Kippur, but in order to maintain secrecy did not explain why. Because of delays in the organization of the forces assigned to follow the convoy—if the Egyptians did not allow it to pass—its departure was delayed until Friday noon. The UN staff was so informed. At first the Egyptians did nothing to stop the convoy, but when it was within three hundred meters of one of their outposts, they opened fire on it. In compliance with previous orders, the convoy turned back. Two vehicles had been hit, but no one was hurt.

The Air Force immediately went into action. Since the other fronts were quiet, the entire Air Force could be used for this operation. Gaza, Majdal, and El Arish were attacked. The Egyptian Air Force base at El Arish was hit with twelve tons of bombs. Five tons were dropped on Gaza, four and a half on Majdal, and two on the town of El Arish. We hit a number of Egyptian airplanes at El Arish and destroyed the airfield. Our Flying Fortresses carried out the raid on Majdal. All our planes returned safely. The attack on El Arish was particularly successful, as was evident the next day when not a single Egyptian airplane appeared over Israel.

The general attack began, as planned, on the night of October 15. The attacking forces had more artillery and heavy mortars at their disposal than had ever been used in a Defense Forces operation.

The Negev Brigade, which had been in the Negev for a very long time, was sent to the north. Some of its members had not visited their homes for eight months. The Brigade left its equipment behind for the Yiftah Brigade, which replaced it. The Yiftah Brigade had had considerable battle experience in the Valley of Jezreel and the Galilee, and on the Latrun front during the "Ten Days."

As night fell on October 15, 1948, the Ninth Brigade began its first operation: the railway on the Egyptian border was blown up; the Rafia-Khan Yunis road, west of Nirim, was mined; and fire was opened on Egyptian camps and units behind the front. That same night a wedge was driven into the Egyptian lines. Units of the Yiftah Brigade left from Nirim and captured outposts east and northeast of Beit Hanun. Sappers blew up the bridges over the road, and on the morning of October 16 our forces began hitting at Egyptian transport traveling along the road. A second wedge was driven into the Egyptian lines by the Third Battalion of the Givati Brigade between Iraq-el-Manshia and Beit Gubrin. Hirbat-Samara, north of the road, and Hirbit-e-Rahi, south of the road, were taken without a fight. The road to Beit Gubrin was cut.

The attack on Iraq-el-Manshia began the next day. It was unsuccessful. The raids by our Air Force did not take place on schedule. The shelling by our artillery and mortars also started late, at 6:20. It was then that our infantry and tanks were to launch a coordinated attack on the Egyptian positions, but because of our lack of experience, the attack was not properly coordinated. The company that struck at the school was met by fierce resistance and was forced to retreat. This shocked the second company, which was on its way to the hill. At the same moment, the Egyptian artillery in Faluja opened fire and within a few minutes a third of our men were hit.

It became necessary to revise our plans, for it was no longer possible to surprise the Egyptians. We concentrated on the western sector rather than the eastern. An attempt was made to capture the Egyptian outposts between the crossroads and Breir. This very difficult mission was entrusted to veteran Battalion One of the Givati Brigade. Two outposts, 103 and 100, controlling the north-south and east-west crossroads, were captured at midnight.

By October 16 the UN Observers already ordered us and the Egyptians to halt operations and return to the positions we held on October 1. Both sides rejected this demand.

The next morning the Egyptians began shelling the outposts we had captured, but our casualties were very light because the Egyptian fortifications were well built. The Givati Brigade had been entrusted with capturing Huleikat between Julis and Bror-Hayil. By the 29th Huleikat and all of the surrounding outposts were in our hands. We did not succeed in taking the Iraq-Suedan police station. After the road to the south had been opened with the capture of Huleikat, our troops were ordered to take Beersheba. At 9:15 A.M. on October 21 a message was received at Operational Headquarters: "Beersheba is ours!".

The third truce began that morning. The previous day we had received a communication from Mohan, Dr. Bunche's personal representative, in which he wrote: "In its resolution of October 19 on the situation in the Negev, the Security Council demanded an immediate and unconditional cease-fire. In accordance with this resolution, and on the basis of instructions received from the Acting Mediator [Bunche], I wish to request that you immediately inform me of the date and hour when the Israel Army will be ordered to stop firing. Steps required to carry out the other sections of the Security Council resolution will be taken immediately on the cessation of fighting."

The Prime Minister replied that a special and urgent meeting of the Cabinet had been called to discuss the matter.

A cable had previously been received from Abba Eban in Paris. It stated: "The unanimous cease-fire resolution was adopted on the initiative of the Soviet Union. It presumes that the places we have captured will remain in our hands and be the subject of negotiations. It seems imperative to me that we obey this order. The reaction of the Security Council was very weak. The failure of the United States to participate in the discussion was striking (Austin, the American representative, opposed the decision), but a refusal on our part to accept the cease-fire would precipitate strong international action." The UN decision thus did not obligate us to abandon the places that we had captured, as had been demanded previously, but called instead for a cease-fire and discussions between representatives of the two sides on the entire problem of the Negev.

At a meeting of the Government on October 20, the Prime Minister proposed that a cease-fire order be issued the next morning at 10. Gruenbaum asked whether we could continue our operations on the road to Jerusalem. Ben-Gurion replied that a cease-fire would apply to that area as well.

Three resolutions were offered on the time of a cease-fire. Bentov suggested that it begin twenty-four hours after Israel had been informed that Egypt had accepted a cease-fire. Kaplan proposed six hours after Egyptian acceptance, while Shapira proposed twelve hours. Shapira's suggestion was accepted.

At a Cabinet meeting the following day, the Prime Minister announced:

> I delayed replying to Bunche until this morning because, following yesterday's session, I met with the members of the General Staff to discuss what they regarded as the most important objective still to be accomplished. They said it was the capture of Iraq-Suedan. By taking that police station, they declared, we would control access to the Negev. Appropriate orders were given. However, for some reason, the attack did not take place; moreover, the Commander of the southern front was not informed of this fact. We are now attempting to determine who is responsible for this mishap. The second matter discussed at the General Staff was Beersheba. It was decided to continue the attack on the town. The first information on the progress of our forces came from an Arab radio station, which announced that battles were going on in Beersheba. An hour ago we received word that it had been taken, though the police station remained in Arab hands. We were subsequently informed that the police station was captured as well.
>
> This is the text of the letter which I am sending to Bunche: "The Government of Israel, in accordance with its consistent policy of working for peace, and in accordance with the resolution adopted by the Security Council about which we were informed on October 20, has issued a cease-fire order. In order to ensure that it be fully and effectively observed, as demanded by the Security Council, the Provisional Government requests that the Acting Mediator inform it as soon as possible of the decision of the Egyptian government in regard to a cease-fire, to be observed by all forces in the Negev, including the irregular units operating in the area. The cease-fire order given to the Israel Defense Forces will be put into effect no more than twelve hours after an announcement is received from the Acting Mediator that the Egyptian government is abiding by the Security Council resolution."

Before the twelve hours had passed, the Prime Minister ordered the Navy, in accordance with a previously prepared plan, to sink the *Farouk*, an Egyptian ship anchored off Gaza. The order was carried out on the evening of October 21.

Reactions in the UN General Assembly to the Battles in the South ★ Debate on Shertok's Report

After the battles in the northern Negev, which had gone on for seven days, were concluded on October 22, Foreign Minister Shertok returned from Paris. He reported to the Government at its October 26 meeting on the General Assembly's reaction to the fighting. He said:

> The operation undoubtedly made an enormous impression, and from a legal viewpoint we have come out of the affair very well; it has been regarded as a reaction to Egyptian provocations. Our cause was greatly aided by the British press, which helped bolster our military and political prestige. Never has the British press, and particularly *The Times*, shown such appreciation for the Defense Forces' victories.
>
> It is not yet clear how our military victories will affect the political situation. It would appear that we have ended Egyptian control over the northern Negev. In any case, we now have a very convincing argument against the Bernadotte Plan vis-à-vis the northern Negev. At the same time, there are those who argue that the very enormity of the Arab defeat will engender support for the Bernadotte Plan. When one of our representatives met recently with British Deputy Foreign Secretary Hector McNeill, who previously had stated that there was no chance of the Bernadotte report's being suppported by a majority of UN members, he said that the United States might now support the report, and that it might be accepted by the Arabs as well.
>
> It seems to me that while our victory saved the northern Negev for us, it has increased the danger to Eilat. The very fact that we do not hold Eilat undermines our demands for it. This is not to say that our chances of obtaining it were so very good before that. In any case, we must carefully consider how we are going to win the struggle for Eilat.
>
> The most fervent supporters of the Bernadotte Plan are the British. It has become clear, beyond the shadow of doubt, that the report was not a compromise between the Jews and the Arabs, but between the British and the Americans. We know for a fact that when Bernadotte wrote the report in Rhodes, he had with him a high British official and a high American one. The Britisher had come from Cairo, the American from Washington. After the report had been prepared, Bunche told his colleagues that a common Anglo-American approach to the Palestine problem had been agreed upon. When one of them expressed surprise at the fact that Israel's border had been moved northward, Bunche said that this change was made in order to persuade the British to support the plan. They regarded it as an absolute necessity, while the Americans did not particularly care one way or the other.
>
> Some of the other delegations are influenced by the British, while some are sympathetic to our arguments. There are delegations which say it is unfair to detach the entire Negev from the State of Israel. The Eastern Bloc stands behind us. The Soviets have a firm policy on this matter. Suggestions in our press that the USSR will not budge from its demand for an internationalized Jerusalem, or that she will not accept our view on the Arab refugees, are incorrect. The Russians are acting in the Security Council as if they were our emissaries.
>
> The Bernadotte affair has not been forgotten. We still are being condemned for it. Everyone feels that we were at fault. They do not blame the Government for the murder, but the fact that we did not keep proper watch over our prisoners—who fled from Jaffa prison—and that we have not discovered the murderers is interpreted to mean that we do not care very much about the affair. Sweden is particularly affected.

The Government has decided that we should apply for UN membership. The Russians favor wholesale admission of all countries requesting it. They will benefit from such an arrangement because there are seven or eight Eastern applicants as opposed to three Western. We face very severe difficulties in relation to the West. The French say they will not support us unless the British agree to do so as well. They also oppose our admission before Italy is admitted. John Foster Dulles told us that we have a very good chance of being accepted by the UN. State Department officials have said that we must first agree to defined borders, and pledge not to use force to achieve a territorial solution unless we are attacked. No answers were given to these questions, but we should prepare answers, if the members of the Government are agreeable.

Eliyahu Sasson had a talk with a representative of one of the Arab states who admitted that the Arabs had no hope of winning a military victory. They would like to persuade the UN to make an anti-Israel decision, but their chances are not good. Their only real option is to undermine Israel's economy. They believe that we will not be able to maintain ourselves economically. The one thing that can save us is an American loan. Once it is received, the last lingering Arab hopes will have been dashed.

Gruenbaum: Mr. Shertok has told us that our victories in the Negev made a considerable impression. Does he believe that we acted wisely in ordering a cease-fire almost immediately after having received the demand to that effect?

Shertok answered: "First of all, I don't think you are presenting the situation in a true light. We categorically rejected the first demand for a cease-fire, and continued fighting for several days. We accepted the second demand, but delayed implementation as long as possible. I was very concerned about those delaying tactics, for our international position would have been very precarious indeed had we not agreed to a cease-fire."

The Prime Minister commented: "The Security Council made its decision on Tuesday. We were informed by cable on Wednesday. Since it arrived in the form of an announcement, we said that we would not reply to it. Afterward Bunche said that we had not been advised of the resolution just for informative purposes, but in order that we agree to a cease-fire. We said that we could not reply until the Government had discussed the matter. Only the next day (Thursday) did we send our answer. The fighting continued until Thursday night. As you can see, we did not hasten to observe the cease-fire. On Thursday, Shertok cabled to say that in Paris we were being accused of causing great tension by our refusal to abide by the cease-fire."

Shertok: "We stopped firing seventy-two hours after being asked to do so. Anyone who was at the General Assembly knows that our delaying tactics were widely discussed."

Zisling said that, in his opinion, we could have held out for a longer period without creating an untenable situation. He inquired about the Jerusalem area, and about the orders given to our forces in the Negev.

Gruenbaum asked whether the cease-fire on the Egyptian front concerned only the Negev, or other places as well.

The Prime Minister: "The cease-fire affects the entire Egyptian front. The Egyptians remain bogged down at Majdal, Isdud, Iraq-Suedan, Faluja, Iraq-el-Manshia; and Beit Gubrin. They have no way of supplying their troops—numbering at least three battalions —with food. They will certainly demand that we allow them to reoccupy their former positions; and we will just as certainly reject such a demand. If they try to use force to regain their positions, we will open fire. There has already been some firing. The Egyptians broke through from Majdal to Gaza. They lost a great many vehicles—twenty-seven in all—in doing so. We will not allow them to move from place to place.

"During the truce period, we enlarged our corridor to Jerusalem. The area is empty and we have set up new settlements. The 'Burma Road' is already outside the range of Arab guns. We control a good many places on the other side of the road, and the railway up past Batir. If the Arab Legion interferes with our sending supplies to the Hebrew University on Mount Scopus, there will be trouble there.

"The Arabs have learned a great deal from us. They have built their own 'Burma Roads.' The Egyptians fought with great bravery at Outpost 113, and at Huleikat. The battle for Beersheba continued for almost ten hours. The Arabs also displayed extraordinary valor at Iraq-Suedan. The best soldiers were the Sudanese and the Saudi Arabians. The Egyptians fought at Iraq-Suedan as they had never fought before.

"Kaukji [in the north] has launched an attack, apparently on the assumption that all our forces are tied down in the south and that the time is therefore propitious. He struck at three outposts. We tried to hit back, but were unable to do so. Manara is cut off. The entire road as far as Metulla is within the range of his guns, which have been set up on a nearby hill. If full-scale fighting breaks out, it will be in the west.

"There have been false rumors about the extent of our losses in the Negev. In fact, we lost a hundred and eighty men killed and three hundred wounded, most of them only lightly."

Ben-Gurion then raised the problem of finances. We purchased, he said, $9.5 million worth of weapons from Czechoslovakia. We gave the Czechs $3 million in cash and agreed to pay the other $6.5 million on November 1, namely, in another six days. We must keep our word.

Kaplan (Finance Minister) added: "The situation is more serious than Ben-Gurion indicated. PL1 million a week has been spent so far on defense, and the Ministry of Defense argues that this sum does not cover even minimal expenses. We owe the Czechs over $6 million, $6.3 million to be exact. I asked Henry Montor, in America, to obtain an urgent loan for us. At this moment we have $4 million. It is doubtful whether this sum will cover the cost of even such essential items as bread, fuel, and raw materials. We have negotiated for a $2 million loan in Switzerland. This sum, together with what we already have, will give us almost $6 million. If I do not obtain other funds, and we turn over this entire amount to the Czechs, tomorrow we will not be able to purchase a single thing, neither food nor weapons. We are perched on the edge of an abyss. Perhaps I will have further details tomorrow or the next day, and I will then be able to bring the matter to a special meeting of the Government."

It was decided to take up the question again at the next meeting of the Government.

Liberation of Upper Galilee

Our attention then turned to liberating upper Galilee from Kaukji's forces. In the ten days before the second truce came into effect, all of lower Galilee, including Nazareth and Shfaram, had been liberated. Kaukji moved his headquarters to upper Galilee. Kaukji did not recognize the United Nations. Since his army was not an official force of one of the

Arab states, he felt that he was not bound by the truce arrangement. This turned out to be a mixed blessing for him—it certainly made things easier for us as far as international law was concerned. Now that the Egyptian forces had been defeated in the northern Negev, the time had arrived to launch an attack on Kaukji.

His Liberation Army continued to hold out in upper Galilee and in part of central Galilee. The front ran from Hanita in the north along the hills of western Galilee to Berva, and from there to the western edge of the Beit Netofa Valley. In the south the front ran along this valley up to its eastern edge, and from there turned north along the Eilabun Marar-Meron line to Malkia.

While our forces were occupied in the south, Kaukji launched an attack on October 22, and gained control of the Sheikh Abd outpost north of Manara. Our attempts to dislodge him were unsuccessful. At that time the Commander of the northern front had the following forces at his disposal: Brigade Seven, including an armored battalion, two infantry battalions, and a company of Circassians; the Oded Brigade, which had returned from the southern front, and included a Druze company; part of the Golani Brigade and part of the Carmeli Brigade.

Kaukji had three brigades with a total of thirty-one hundred men. The Israel Defense Forces, however, had to take into consideration the Lebanese Army, which had four battalions, one at Rosh Hanikra, a second a Marj Ayun, a third along our northern border, and a fourth in reserve. The Iraqi Army, numbering four brigades, was encamped in the Triangle. Our Northern Command was given the assignment of destroying the Liberation Army, freeing central and upper Galilee, and establishing a defense line along the Mandatory border of Palestine. Brigade Seven was to operate in the eastern part of the sector, the Oded Brigade in the western part. The Golani Brigade was to defend the southern part of the front against the Iraqis, while the Carmeli Brigade engaged Kaukji's forces around Manara, as well as the Syrians.

The operation began on the night of October 28 and was completed within sixty hours. Our Air Force bombed Arab bases all through the area on October 28. Leaflets were dropped on Lebanon, stating: "We have no quarrel with you. If you do not intervene, nothing will happen to you. If you intervene, we will invade your country."

At zero hour Brigade Seven moved out of its Safad base in three columns. One column, composed of an armored unit and a Circassian company, captured the villages north of the Safad-Meron road. But the column which attacked Meron failed to take it, and only after an armored unit had attacked and captured Safsaf in the early hours of the morning did Meron fall as well, following a brief battle. Most of the enemy company holding Meron was destroyed. Immediately after the capture of Safsaf, an attempt was made to take Jish, the ancient Gush Halav. Kaukji's men fled from Jish toward the western side of the Jermak. That same evening a four-hundred-man Syrian battalion was brought to Jish. It lost two hundred men in the battle. All the Liberation Army's attempts to retake Safsaf and Jish ended in failure.

In the early hours of October 29 the Oded Brigade was to capture the outposts controlling Tarshiha from the west. A Druze company was entrusted with the mission of taking Yanuah, a Druze village south of Tarshiha. It was well organized for defense, since there had been many clashes in the area during the months of the truce. The Israel Defense Forces had therefore concentrated a large number of artillery pieces to shell the village. But the outposts controlling Tarshiha were not taken. The battalion that was supposed to capture them returned to its base. Only the next evening, when the Golani Brigade advanced toward Sasa, was the village taken. There was practically no resistance. When the sun rose in the morning, white flags fluttered from the houses in Tarshiha, which had been shelled during the night. The Liberation Army had fled, leaving behind most of its heavy equipment. The village surrendered to the Israel Defense Forces. Golani units captured Eilabun on the evening of the 29th.

The Druze company, which had captured the village of Yanuah the evening before, lost contact with the Oded Brigade and failed to receive the order to withdraw. When morning came, the Army of Liberation inside Tarshiha had gained heart and a unit of Kaukji's men captured Yanuah. The Druze company was forced to flee, and suffered considerable losses; ten of its men were killed, including a Jewish doctor and two commanders. Only toward the evening was contact reestablished with the company, and it was extricated under the cover of artillery fire.

Some of the Arab forces retreating from the south were surrounded by Golani units when they reached the Suhmata crossroads on the Tarshiha road. All of their vehicles and supplies fell into our hands, but the Arab soldiers themselves managed to escape. Initially, there was resistance at Suhmata, but it was eventually captured.

Defense Forces units continued to advance toward the north, despite the fact that our men were very tired. The Oded Brigade moved from east to west along the northern road, and Brigade Seven moved from south to north toward Malkia and Nebi Yusha. Our men met very little resistance. Two villages along the road, Ikrit and Tarbiha, surrendered. The armored company of Brigade Seven reached Malkia, which was expecting an attack from the east. The attack from the south thus surprised the village and there was no resistance, though heavy battles had previously taken place there. The Air Force helped to drive out the Liberation Army. Resistance at Sheikh Abd collapsed completely, and the Carmeli Brigade crossed the Mandatory border to capture villages in Lebanon. The Brigade penetrated as far as Wadi Duba in the west and the Litani River in the north. Operation Hiram [after Hiram, King of Tyre, who had been King David's friend and ally] was completed.

The UN Observers, who had not prevented Kaukji's attacks on October 22, arrived on October 29 and demanded that we accept a cease-fire and withdraw to the positions we had held on October 21, before Kaukji's attack. The Minister of Defense ordered the IDF to continue operations. On October 30 the Observers again demanded a cease-fire, and the General Staff announced that firing would stop the next day. It ended between 5 and 6 p.m. on October 31.

The entire Galilee had been liberated. All roads running from west to east and from north to south in upper Galilee were opened up to the peaceful movement of all the inhabitants of the area. The Arabs lost four hundred killed, and some five hundred Arab soldiers were captured by the IDF. Fifteen hundred rifles, five artillery pieces, two armored cars, ten other cars, four medium machine guns, and a quantity of ammunition and food were also taken.

Forty of our men were wounded and nineteen killed, including nine Druze. Some thirty thousand Galilee Arabs fled; another thirty thousand remained.

Money To Cover the Expenses of the State

The Prime Minister again raised the question of the debt to Czechoslovakia, due on November 1, at a meeting of the Government on October 26. Minister of Finance Kaplan said he preferred to discuss the whole range of financial problems at a special meeting. It was called for October 27, at which time he reviewed the financial situation and the loan:

The regular budget for October is PL1.25 million. The extraordinary budget presently consists of three sections: overseas expenses, local expenses, and income. The IDF branches have requested PL6 million in October. The Finance Ministry allocated between PL4.3 million and PL4.5 million to the Ministry of Defense. This caused great tension among the various finance officers, particularly since they have meanwhile come forward with additional demands not included in the original budget. This is the case, for example, with the Negev. That area, while certainly an asset, also involves us in a great many expenses. As the saying goes, "the more you have, the more you have to worry." We must provide for outposts, fortifications, and the maintenance of personnel.

On what basis did the Ministry of Finance decide on this sum? We receive PL1 million a week from Treasury bills. It was decided to allocate PL1.2 million for the entire regular budget. In point of fact, the sum of PL1.2 million has already been spent. This means that there is no more money left for defense purposes. The Ministry of Defense demands, during the next three months, at least PL15 to 18 million. We need an additional PL2 million in the very near future. PL1 million are required to repay foreign debts. Internal debts, arising from expenditures on defense, have reached a total of PL5 million. We will owe PL3 to 4 million overseas, as a result of weapons purchases.

The Ministry of Defense has a minimum ($15 million) and a maximum ($25 million) program for purchases.

As far as income is concerned, we are receiving PL1 million a week from the Treasury bills. We will apparently be able to reach a maximum figure of about PL19 million. So far, PL16.5 million has been received. Today there was another issue of PL1 million in bills. In other words, we've used up almost this entire source of funds.

Tomorrow $3 million will be transferred overseas. Negotiations are going on about raising additional dollars. I would like to add that what we need overseas are dollars, not pounds. There is very little that one can do with pounds.

In all countries, aside from the US, Canada, and England, there are special emergency campaigns (in accordance with the decision of the Zionist General Council). Funds from these campaigns are divided as follows: 50 percent for defense, 25 percent for the Keren Hayesod [Colonization Fund], and 25 percent for the Jewish National Fund [Land Reclamation]. There must be a special discussion in regard to the US, Canada, and England.

Since I wish to cover the debt to Czechoslovakia on a temporary basis, we will require another source of funds to meet the PL15 million in internal defense costs during the next three months. Defense requirements call for a minimum expenditure of PL13.5 million. How are we going to raise this sum? There are also other demands for funds. The Municipalities are in the forefront. They are asking for long-term loans. Enterprises connected with the State, such as the railway, also want money. The railway is asking for PL1 million or PL1.25 million. There are others as well.

We will not be able to raise these funds, at least not as fast as necessary, simply by levying new taxes. A property tax has been proposed. When it was first suggested, I countered with a proposal for a compulsory loan instead. I requested that every member of the Government receive a copy of the memorandum presented to me by a number of economic bodies: the Manufacturers' Association, the Merchants' Association, and others. After the memorandum was submitted to me, I discussed it with the Anglo-Palestine Bank. If the loan had been received in September, a sum of PL10 to 12 million would have been enough. Meanwhile, another month has passed and we need PL4 to 5 million more.

I was opposed to a property tax for a very simple reason. I was afriad that it would have a negative influence on the import of capital, and reports from overseas indicate that this is so. I therefore favored a compulsory loan, on the assumption that this was the best way to raise additional funds. The economic organizations, together with the Anglo-Palestine Bank, have suggested that instead of a compulsory loan, we try to raise the same amount of money by threatening such a loan. They propose that the three groups participating in the discussion (the Manufacturers, the Landlords, and the Merchants) raise PL5 million for us. They suggest that we use compulsion only if they do not succeed in obtaining the money on a voluntary basis. In point of fact, these groups intend to use compulsion with their own members. An Appeals Committee will be established by them, or by the Government, and every member will be assigned a quota. It will be made clear that if payment is not forthcoming, his property will be reevaluated. They suggest that this be a ten-year loan at 3 percent interest, and free of income tax. Mr. Hoofien has proposed that we give the banks 3.5 percent interest, and not free them of income tax. In fact, it would be better to pay the 3.5 percent interest and eliminate the tax exemption. They suggest that all the banks provide PL3 million and that PL2 million be raised through a popular loan.

I recently stated that PL10 million would not be enough, that we need more. The banks have suggested to us that in addition to the funds still available from the Treasury bills and the Popular Loan, we can obtain about PL15 million. How? PL5 million from a ten-year loan, repayment on which would begin after five years; PL3 million on a one-year loan; PL5 million worth of Treasury bills are also being offered. The bankers argue that even if a national loan is necessary, it should not be made compulsory. They suggest the threat of a compulsory loan instead.

Let me now turn to the question of the Appeals. We are interested in the Appeals from two viewpoints: some of the money raised is used for defense purposes, while other funds cover Jewish Agency activities in the areas of immigration and settlement. Ben-Gurion has told me that these two matters are not always handled properly. Nevertheless, progress is quite rapid. Today we established two new settlements, and as far as we can obtain release of the necessary people, we will be in a position to establish more.

Ben-Gurion: We have established thirty-four settlements during the war.
Shapira: How many settlements have been established on the road to Jerusalem? The Minister of Finance went on to say:

The immigration situation is unsatisfactory. There are fourteen thousand immigrants in the camps. The success of the Appeals is a life-or-death matter for us. We need foreign currency. There is a controversy in the US between two groups over fund-raising. The leadership of the Palestine Appeal, because of the pressure from Rabbi Abba Hillel Silver, has accepted the resignation of Henry Montor. They want to organize the Appeal by themselves, and carry out negotiations with the local communities and the Joint Distribution Committee. But the communities and the JDC have refused to negotiate. A second group, the so-called Montor Group, has expanded and been joined by people who, in fact, are responsible for fund-raising in the various localities, both as heads of the local communities and as professionals. They held a meeting in which eighty people participated, and at which, according to the participants, $50 million were raised.

At one time Rabbi Silver suggested to this opposition group that the UJA be reorganized, so that two-thirds of the leadership would consist of representatives of the Keren Hayesod and the Keren Kayemet [Jewish National Fund], and a third of representatives of the communities. The opposition rejected Silver's proposal, which was supportd by only four people. They suggested that all the money raised in the US be transmitted to the Jewish Agency in Israel which would decide how to spend the money in Israel and also decide whether any of it should be spent in the US. The opposition argued that money intended for Israel was being spent in America. Israel vitally needs the money, and yet it is being held in the US. Some of it is being used for *local* Zionist purposes, a practice which the Montor group opposes.

In the meantime, there are negotiations between the Jewish Agency Executive in the US and the Jerusalem Executive. There was a meeting of the leadership at which it was decided to invite me to arbitrate between the two sides. The Montor group agreed, the Silver group did not. The members of the Executive in the US have asked the Jerusalem Executive not to intervene. This is an American matter, they say, and Israel has no right to intervene. A cable to this effect was received from Silver.

The Agency Executive in Jerusalem asked Kaplan if he would be willing to travel to the US. Kaplan said that he was not willing to go there as a representative of the Jewish Agency, because he agrees with most of the demands of the Montor group.

Henry Morgenthau, who is here, has had a meeting with the Jewish Agency. He says that attitudes toward Israel have changed in recent months. He does not understand the task of the Jewish Agency. He is not a Zionist, but a Jew concerned about the possibility that Israel may be destroyed. He says that if, God forbid, Israel were defeated, Jews all over the world would be adversely affected. "Your victories changed the attitude of the peoples of the world, not only to you, but also to us," he declared. "Israel's triumphs have strengthened our position in America," he added.

Morgenthau is interested in the elimination of the displaced persons camps in Germany. Anti-Semitism, he says, is growing in the US. In his opinion, there are two central tasks: supporting the State of Israel and eliminating the DP camps. He wants all money raised to be used to achieve these goals. Otherwise, he will not devote himself to fundraising in the United States.

The Jewish Agency in Jerusalem received a cable from America, asking it to persuade Morgenthau to serve as chairman of the UJA. Morgenthau told Kaplan that he is unwilling to accept the position unless he is assured that all money raised in the US will be sent to Jerusalem, where it will be decided how to divide it.

Kaplan said that there was need to reduce the military budget. The Government, he went on, had to decide how funds were to be raised in Israel and whether, if it did not itself intervene in the dispute in America, it would allow him to intervene—though not in its name.

He also announced that the Presidential election campaign in the United States had brought renewed discussion of a $100 million loan to Israel. The Americans were demanding information on specific projects—such as the irrigation of 40 million acres—in which the money was to be invested. Kaplan declared that he would be willing to travel to the US if the loan materialized and if the two sides involved in the UJA dispute would invite him. He was willing to go despite the fact that it was very difficult for him to absent himself from the country.

Shapira asked: How much will the Government get from the Appeals in the US, Canada, and England?

Kaplan replied that one of the reasons he wanted to travel to the US was finally to clarify this very point.

Ben-Gurion: The Jewish Agency is not a hostile body. Let us meet with the Executive at a joint session and clarify the questions in dispute.

Zisling: The question of a compulsory loan inside the country has nothing to do with the Agency Executive.

The decision reached was to hold a joint meeting with the Agency Executive, and afterward decide about the loan and the Appeals.

Bunche Demands that Israel and Egypt Return to Their Previous Positions ★ Ben-Gurion's Visit to Galilee ★ Egyptian Feelers for Settlement by Negotiation

Dr. Bunche had informed the Security Council of his request that both Israel and Egypt return to the positions they had held before the recent battles in the Negev, and that passage through the lines be guaranteed. Abba Eban cabled that the Security Council was expecting a reply from the Israel Government.

Reporting this UN demand, the Prime Minister suggested that our reply convey a willingness to discuss all existing problems with the Egyptian government, without mentioning Bunche's proposals or expressing an opinion about them. If we state specifically that we will discuss Bunche's proposals, he said, it would suggest a readiness to withdraw to our former positions. We will not, in fact, evacuate any place that we have taken, and we will not allow the Egyptians to extricate their forces unless they surrender.

When the Egyptians wish to move men or supplies from Majdal to Gaza, they can go by road as far as the village of Herbia, and then must travel along the seashore (we control the Herbia-Gaza road). Our guns can reach them along the shore, but they are not very effective, because of the distance. The Egyptians in the Majdal-Faluja area are completely surrounded.

When we received word that Beit Gubrin was deserted, we sent in a unit to occupy it. Later, our men at Beit Gubrin were attacked by either Egyptians or the Arab Legion, probably the latter. The attackers came from the direction of Hebron and used armored cars, some of which we set afire, while the others retreated. Beit Gubrin remained in our hands. We suffered three casualties. The Egyptians were unable to escape from Faluja, Iraq-el-Manshia, and Iraq-Suedan. It is rumored that there are Germans in Iraq-Suedan.

The Government approved the Prime Minister's suggestion that Israel inform the Security Council of her willingness to negotiate with Egypt on all questions affecting the two sides.

At the same meeting the Government also discussed the cost of living. A five-man committee, including the Minister of Agriculture (Zisling), the Minister of Labor and Construction (Bentov), the Minister of the Interior (Gruenbaum), the Minister of Finance (Kaplan), and the Minister of Commerce and Industry (Bernstein), was appointed to consider measures to combat rising prices.

Bernstein later reported that the Committee of Five had persuaded Eliezer S. Hoofien to head a new body that would coordinate the war against rising living costs. Hoofien was to be officially appointed by the Government of Israel, and would be responsible to the Committee of Five. He would act within the context of the economic policy to be worked out jointly with the Committee. Activities that directly concerned specific ministries would be carried out by the ministries themselves. Activities that concerned several ministries would be coordinated by the new body. Economic policy would be determined by the Ministerial Committee, which would be joined by Hoofien, as head of the Coordination Center, and David Horowitz, as Secretary of the Committee. Hoofien said that he would accept the post only if the aforementioned guidelines were approved by the Government as a whole. After a short debate they were so approved.

The Provisional Government met on October 31, 1948, the day on which the Hiram Operation ended. The Prime Minister reported on the operation and noted its success, then enlarged on the situation:

Our problems in the Galilee are over. So, apparently, is the truce. The truce is, in fact, dead. The Arabs are in a desperate situation. The Syrians have ten battalions altogether. One of them was destroyed, while three or four more are engaged at Mishmar Hayarden. They are holding the settlement. Kaukji sent desperate pleas for help to the Syrians, but their battalions did not move. Lebanon has also failed to come to Kaukji's assistance. It is true that Lebanon does not have a large army—only three battalions—and that if we wanted to conquer Lebanon, we could do it very easily.

I have just returned from the Galilee. Our troops there need a rest. The commander says that they require at least a week off. The Galilee victory has made it possible for us to withdraw two brigades from the area. The other two brigades are occupied, one in holding the main road and the other in patrolling the area, for there are still many Arabs in Galilee.

I visited the south to survey the situation of our forces there and to determine to what extent additional men are required. I had an argument with the commander. In my opinion, it is possible to release many men for activities further south, but the commanders are extremely cautious. I want our forces to take Kurnub, Ras-Zuveira, and Ein Husub (the first police station in the Arava, some thirty kilometers below the Dead Sea). Our patrols have reported that the station, which lies on the Trans-Jordan border, on the road to Aqaba, is unoccupied. The largest spring in the Negev is at Ein Husub.

There is another interesting place from an archaeological viewpoint. In the Bible it is called Punon (Numbers 33); it is where Moses made his copper snake (Numbers 21:9). It was once the site of copper mines belonging to King Solomon. Copper was taken to Etzion Gever to be smelted, as Nelson Glueck discovered. Near Punon there is a large spring called Ein Husub. I was afraid that it would be occupied by the Trans-Jordanians, but our patrols found that it was deserted. Despite the spring and the trees, it contained only a police station. Another police station is at a very important place called Kurnub, located on a broad plain. The soil is similar to that in Petah Tikva or Rehovot, but there is no water. A third place, Ras-Zuveira, lies midway between Masada and Sodom. It is possible to pave a road from Ras-Zuveira to Sodom.

The problem now is to establish a link between Beersheba, which is in our hands, and Sodom. We should hold at least two of these three places in order to maintain contact with the southern Negev. The commander in the south says that so long as the "pocket" (Faluja, Iraq-Suedan, and Iraq-el-Manshia) exists, he cannot release men for operations in the Arava and at the Dead Sea. We assume that there are three Egyptian battalions in the "pocket." Four days ago an officer at Iraq-Suedan asked us under what conditions we would allow the

Egyptians to leave. When we told him that they would have to turn over their weapons and accept the status of prisoners, he announced that these conditions were unacceptable. (Gruenbaum interjected: "I would release them with their weapons.")

Then they could go back and attack Beersheba. Our commander feels that they will not be able to hold out more than two weeks in the "pocket." A great many things can, of course, change in a week. If the Egyptians cannot supply their troops with food, it is unlikely that they will be able to hold out for two weeks. There are some Bedouin tribes in the south that have expressed a desire to establish peaceful relations with us. They are willing to do whatever we ask, if only we allow them to return to their former homes. I suggested that we foster relations with these tribes, but the local commanders say that so long as Beersheba is still endangered and the Egyptian Army in the "pocket" has not yet surrendered, the Bedouin may still help the Egyptians; therefore, they cannot yet be allowed to return to their former homes.

In my opinion, we must hasten to seize Kurnub, and perhaps Ein Husub as well. The three hundred people in Sodom are not soldiers. They should all be evacuated and replaced by soldiers, perhaps a larger number. We have captured another village, the second largest after Dahariya, south of Jerusalem. This cuts off the Egyptians in the "pocket" from Hebron. We hold Lahish, which in Arabic is called Kubeiba. It is about half a kilometer away from ancient Lahish.

Gruenbaum: What is the situation south of Jerusalem on the road to Bethlehem?

Ben-Gurion: Our forces are threatening the Bethlehem-Jerusalem road. The Egyptians still hold the road, but they are unable to move from Hebron to the south or to the west. They are apparently evacuating Majdal and planning to transfer their forces to Gaza. Our armies in the north and in the south need a truce, a brief rest, but the UN truce has become ridiculous.

The fact that the Egyptians were so hard hit in the south, without receiving any assistance from other Arab armies, prompted them to put out unofficial feelers about the possibility of a settlement. At a meeting of the Provisional Government on November 4, which the Prime Minister could not attend because of ill health, the Foreign Minister reported on these feelers. It was not clear at first whether they were made with the knowledge of the Egyptian Prime Minister, Nokrashy Pasha, or of the King, or whether they were unofficial. Recent information led the Foreign Minister to the conclusion that they were official proposals. Shertok announced:

> The new aspect of the plan is that (the emissary) is willing to suggest that we meet with an Egyptian representative. I think this shows that the proposals presented to us are indeed official. The fact that the Egyptians are ready to send an official representative means that Nokrashy has given his approval, or at least that he is not interfering. They have set two conditions: (1) we must withdraw from all captured areas in the south that are not within the boundaries of the State of Israel; (2) we must agree *in advance* that the entire coastal strip from Isdud to Rafiah, including Gaza, as well as the strip from Rafiah southeast along the border, will remain in Egyptian hands
>
> What is meant by the term "in advance"? They are suggesting not a peace settlement but an armistice, not a cease-fire but an armistice. They are demanding that we agree in advance, so that when there is an eventual peace settlement, the area will belong to Egypt. Those are the two tough nuts. It remains to be seen whether we will be able to crack them.
>
> In point of fact, we have not gone beyond the area allocated to Israel under the terms

of the November 1947 resolution. Majdal is still in their hands. We have taken Isdud. The area below Isdud is under their control. The Egyptians hold most of the strip along the shore, except for the northern section, which we hold. But we have made a spectacular advance further to the east. We have taken Beit Natif, Dir Nahas, and Beit Gubrin. We have driven deeply into the southeastern section of the Negev. The Egyptians want us to evacuate the entire area. They are not demanding that we turn it over to them, but simply that we leave it. They demand the entire coastal strip for themselves.

I suggest that in our reply we make a clear distinction between the eastern and northern borders of the Negev on the one hand, and its western and southern borders on the other. We are ready to discuss future boundaries with the Egyptians.

Mr. Ben-Gurion believes that we cannot agree to Egypt's having the Rafiah-Gaza-Isdud Strip, because this would open the way for Egyptian expansion into Israel. Egypt is a very heavily populated country, with an estimated population of 17 or 18 million. The Egyptians themselves claim 20 million. It is certainly desirable that there be a desert separating us. If they strike roots here, on the other side of the desert, their population will begin moving to the fertile area. The Arabs accuse us of expansionism—we must argue that *they* are expansionists. I agree with Mr. Ben-Gurion and am willing to defend his position. I would like to add another argument: as long as the future of the western section of the Land of Israel is not clear, we cannot make any final decisions about Gaza. If we reached an agreement with Egypt, this would mean that we were denying, in advance, a port to an Arab state in Palestine. If we do not give them Jaffa, Haifa, or Acre, then they will remain without an outlet to the sea. Such an argument makes us appear to be very harsh vis-à-vis the Arabs.

I said that I accept this position and am willing to defend it, but I would not like the Government to overlook the practical problems involved. First of all, the Egyptians are holding Gaza and there is no indication that they are planning to leave. On the contrary, they are digging in. They have recently brought in reinforcements. The men withdrawn from Majdal are being taken to Gaza. The Egyptians have sent in two fresh battalions, and there is every indication that they intend to hold the town.

It is therefore doubtful whether we gain anything by refusing to agree to Egyptian control of Gaza, unless we intend to drive them out. We could agree, with great magnanimity, to allow them to hold something they already possess. On the other hand, Ben-Gurion's very convincing arguments must also be taken into account. I would therefore suggest that, initially at least, we refuse to agree in advance to the coastal strip remaining in Egyptian hands.

Rosenblueth: What was the status of the strip according to the November resolution?

Shertok: It was supposed to be in the Arab state. I refer to the area from Gaza to Rafiah along the coast—the non-desert area. We must demand that they agree to borders based on the November resolution. This would mean their acquiescence to our presence in Eilat.

Gruenbaum: If Gaza should eventually be given to Trans-Jordan, might not this bring a demand for a corridor?

Shertok: Today Gaza is the port of the Arab state; when we point this out, we are not changing the situation in any way.

Shapira said that the Egyptian willingness to negotiate with us would strengthen our position vis-à-vis the British and the Jordanians. The reply suggested by the Foreign Minister would prevent negotiations with the Egyptians.

Remez agreed with Shapira's remarks.

Bentov commented that he tended to accept the position adopted by Ben-Gurion and Shertok. We are faced with a demand for the area between Majdal and the Egyptian border. This area is divided into two approximately equal sections. The first, from Majdal to Rafiah, runs along the seashore. The second, comprising approximately half a million acres, goes from Isdud to the Egyptian border. We cannot claim that there is no room for any type of negotiations. We can agree to some of their demands, namely, in regard to the desert area. As far as their other demands are concerned, we need not hasten to react to them. Negotiations can continue.

Gruenbaum suggested that opportunities be sought for negotiations without pre-conditions. If the Egyptians want to talk, by all means, we are ready and willing; if they want us to promise anything in advance, we cannot agree.

Zisling: We regard Gaza as the port that will serve Arab Palestine, and at the same time relieve the pressure for Arab use of Haifa. If the Arabs of Palestine do not have Gaza, they will either be denied access to the sea, or we will be forced to provide such access for them. It is very important that we open negotiations with the Egyptians.

Bernstein: I am not worried about the possibility that Gaza may remain in Egyptian hands. On the other hand, if Trans-Jordan demands the internationalization of Gaza, there is no reason why we should oppose them on this issue. We can agree to Egyptian control of Gaza, plus a few kilometers beyond the town, but no more than that. In return the Egyptians must agree to permit us freedom of actions vis-à-vis the other Arab states, or at least promise that they will not interfere after we have reached an agreement with them. Egypt is the largest country in the area. She is also important economically. A settlement with Egypt would solve many of our economic problems.

Rosenblueth: I understand Ben-Gurion to say that, in fact, he wants this strip of land within the borders of the Jewish State, because if it should be in Arab hands—Trans-Jordan, Egyptian, or others—it would not serve as a barrier against the surge of Egypt's population toward this area. If, on the other hand, we accept the November 1947 resolution, I cannot see much difference in whether the area belongs to an independent Arab state, Trans-Jordan, or Egypt. I agree with Bernstein in this respect: if we can win over the Egyptians by agreeing to their control of the area, then it would be desirable to do so.

Shertok: Before I summarize the discussion, I want to read you a cable sent to me yesterday by Abba Eban. He states:

> I had a long discussion this morning with McNeill. I explained to him the effect that British support for the Security Council resolution would have on future relations between Britain and Israel. I said that a deep and burning resentment was felt by the entire population of Israel against British policy and I explained in detail why we opposed the decision. He thanked me for my frankness. The British believe it will be impossible to carry out the Bernadotte Plan unless we withdraw from our positions in the Negev. He repeated this several times. I expressed surprise at his frankness and said that his arguments were not likely to convince us to withdraw from the Negev. In point of fact, I added, the Government and people of Israel were united in their opposition to a withdrawal for just those reasons. He said that Britain had not supplied arms to the Arabs during the truce, but that Arab pressure was growing and it might not be possible to withstand this pressure for a fulfillment of British obligations if the truce were to fail. Israel's presence in the Negev, he added, was harmful primarily in the political sphere. I replied that we would lose politically by withdrawing from the Negev; this would settle the outcome of the political struggle in advance. There were no practical results to the discussion, but it was most revealing.

Eban subsequently met with three representatives of the State Department, members of the American delegation in Paris. He told them in general terms about the Egyptian feelers. Should the Security Council adopt the proposed resolution, he said, it would bring this development to a halt. [The pending resolution called for Israel and Egypt to withdraw to positions held before the Negev battles and for sanctions if either side refused.] The Americans felt that there was very little chance of the last provision, on sanctions, being adopted. They will not vote for it, which in turn guarantees that it will not be supported by a majority of members. They argued that our temporary withdrawal from the area would not lessen the possibility of a negotiated settlement. Eban then told them about his talk with McNeill. They were shocked. They said that they would consider postponing the passage of a Security Council resolution until the possibility of negotiations had been investigated.

When the Security Council debate began, and it appeared that the American delegation would support the resolution calling for a withdrawal to the former positions held by the two sides, Shertok cabled Marshall, the American Secretary of State, asserting that Israel would be committing suicide if she agreed to a withdrawal, and no country would willingly commit suicide. He emphasized the absurdity of allowing the Egyptian Army to reoccupy its former positions. Eban informed our Ambassador in Washington about his talk with McNeill. The Ambassador, Eliyahu Epstein, spoke to Lovett, the American Under-Secretary of State, and explained how the adoption of the Anglo-Chinese resolution calling for a withdrawal to positions held before the battles began would reduce the chances of peace.

Shertok, summarizing, declared that it was necessary to meet with an official Egyptian representative; meetings until then had been with unofficial representatives. The following summation was adopted by the Government:

> Our representatives will meet officially with representatives of the Egyptian government and will explain our attitudes, which are designed to foster negotiations, rather than to end them. It should be borne in mind that:
>
> A. A distinction must be made between the northeastern section of southern Israel (Beersheba, Faluja, Beit Gubrin, etc.) and the southwestern section (Isdud, Gaza, Rafiah). The northeastern section is not the subject for negotiations with Egypt, but with the Arab state that will be established.
>
> B. The Government of Israel is not favorably disposed to the annexation of the Gaza area by Egypt; it fears Egyptian expansionism and believes that the future of Gaza should not be decided upon until there is some decision on the future of the Arab section of Palestine.
>
> C. The Government of Israel would be favorably disposed toward Egyptian control of the desert area extending southeastward from Rafiah, which under the November 1947 resolution was to be part of the Arab state.
>
> D. Egyptian agreement to Israel's borders as defined in Section C, and southward from there to Aqaba, in accordance with the November 1947 UN resolution, is demanded by the Israel Government.
>
> E. The representatives of the armies concerned must clarify the question of Egyptian withdrawal from Jerusalem and vicinity, as well as from the Faluja "pocket." There is no point in trying to determine at this stage whether the Egyptians will be allowed to leave with their weapons.

Review of Achievements and Shortcomings of Israel Defense Forces ★ *We Can Be Saved Only by Qualitative Advantages*

The first course for company commanders was completed at the beginning of November 1948. In addressing the graduates, the Minister of Defense took the opportunity to review the achievements of the IDF, which was less than a year old. He put particular emphasis on the problems that it still faced, including the shortcomings of both officers and enlisted men.

The Israel Defense Forces, he said, were mobilized, organized, trained, and equipped in the midst of the fighting that followed the establishment of the State. Generally speaking, they stood the test successfully. The Nahshon operation, the ten days of fighting after the first truce, the week in the south, and the sixty hours in the Galilee were sagas of courage and triumph. But we have yet to reach the Promised Land—to achieve final victory and peace.

Only one section of the country, the Galilee, has been completely liberated. Jerusalem is still partly under siege and is bombarded night after night. Sharon and Samaria are under attack from time to time, as is a considerable section of the Negev. This area, where we achieved glorious victories in the third week of October, is still largely controlled by the Egyptian enemy. Military and political plots are still being woven against us, and the Security Council is now discussing an Anglo-Chinese resolution to force Israel, under threat of sanctions, to withdraw to the positions she held before the enemy violated the truce in the middle of October. Our existence, freedom, independence, and security, as well as our final boundaries, depend mainly on the Israel Defense Forces. We cannot allow ourselves to become overconfident as a result of past victories. The Army has yet to complete its mission. We must constantly reexamine the efficiency of this instrument for the salvation of Israel.

The Israel Defense Forces have proven themselves on the battlefield and shown extraordinary devotion, Ben-Gurion said, but there have also been a number of shortcomings that cannot be ignored. The very prestige of the Army and its many responsibilities make it imperative that we mercilessly uncover all its shortcomings and work unceasingly to eradicate them as quickly and completely as possible. The most glaring shortcoming is in the area of discipline. Discipline is not what it should be, *neither among enlisted men nor among officers, of whatever rank.* Discipline is an army's very breath of life. An army without discipline cannot carry out the tasks imposed on it. Moreover, it is dangerous.

The reason for the lack of discipline in the Defense Forces is clear. Our Army is young and lacks a military tradition. It inherited many fine, indeed wonderful, qualities from the Hagana, but the Hagana, as an underground movement, could not develop or promote military discipline. Besides, a disciplined army cannot be created overnight. But time is running short. We have none to waste, and what others accomplished in a generation we must accomplish in a single year. Our commanders must give the Army an understanding of the importance of strict discipline. They can do this only by setting an example themselves.

Discipline is required not only in major things—on the battlefield—but in simple daily matters such as cleanliness and orderliness during training and elsewhere.

The Army is not sufficiently thrifty. Both combat and service units fail to show proper concern for saving food, fuel, vehicles, time, and ammunition. Public property is precious; it is costly in terms of both money and blood. There is waste because of a lack of proper order. We must organize an army that in our terms is very large, and do it in a brief time. We must make enormous efforts to equip, clothe, house, and arm this force, as well as supply it with the tools and transport it requires.

We are a small and impoverished people. The burden that has been placed upon us is almost unbearable. Nevertheless, the commanders and enlisted men do not yet realize how careful they must be to avoid all waste in our camps, huts, tents, vehicles, kitchens, dining halls, warehouses, and training grounds. It is not that people are purposely wasteful; waste stems, rather, from poor administrative arrangements and a lack of effective supervision.

An army's ability is measured not only by its willingness to fight and by its enthusiasm, but also by its orderliness and its ability to deal with a thousand minor matters. Such matters can be as crucial as willingness to fight. A lack of concern for such matters may undermine an army's strength and prevent a nation from maintaining it under suitable conditions. One does not win victories simply by devotion. Good organization and a concern for details are perhaps three-quarters of the secret of victory.

Reckless driving is still very common in the Army. The General Staff has set a speed limit, but it is not honored either by enlisted men or by officers. As a result there are many tragedies—as if the tragedies on the field of battle were not enough. Not only is there loss of life, there is also a waste of valuable military vehicles. This in turn reduces the military capabilities of our units.

The Army has not always shown a proper respect for the civilian population, Jewish and Arab. There are enlisted men as well as officers who are boastful and aggressive in their contacts with civilians. Fortunately this is very rare, but even rare incidents of this sort can cast a shadow on the Army as a whole. Our men must show respect not only for their fellow soldiers but also for every human being, Jew and Arab alike.

The Army is the only framework in Israel where members of all communities and all classes meet on an equal basis. It provides the only opportunity to overcome many of the shortcomings in our national life: the many divisions, not only political and ideological, which are largely artificial, but also the divisions that stem from profound social, economic, communal, and educational differences.

The public sincerely believes in political equality; nevertheless, we have in our midst an aristocracy cut off from the life of the masses. Though public officials on the national and local levels belong to different political groups, they have for the most part the same kind of educational background, read the same kinds of books, and live more or less the same kind of lives—lives that have little in common with those of the masses who live in poor neighborhoods, suffer privation, and may not even know how to read and write. The only place where youth from all strata of society meet is the Army.

There young people from labor settlements (kibbutzim and moshavim), high schools, and universities come together with youngsters from poor neighborhoods, with the common people of all communities, those who do not read books, and may not even know how to read and write. The period of Army service offers an extremely valuable opportunity to unite the nation and eliminate differences between various groups. It permits us to create Jewish unity and fraternity, not on a basis of words or ideologies, but by deeds, by eliminating illiteracy, by raising the educational level—Jewish and general—by showing concern for youngsters from the poor sections of the population, by giving them a greater sense of their own value and inculcating in them the ideals of our pioneering youth, not on the basis of philanthropy, but on the basis of the fraternity of fighting men who share dangers and triumphs. Our commanders have a fruitful role to play in eliminating communal barriers and raising the cultural and moral level of our soldiers, so that men on leaving the Army will be better Jews and better human beings than they were when they entered it.

Our military problem is unique. We are few and our enemies are many. In this war we have prevailed—seven hundred thousand or eight hundred thousand of us against thirty million enemies. If we have to fight again, and no one can deny this possibility, we will again face such a situation. Even if our community grows, and it will grow—it is growing now in the midst of the war, thanks to increasing immigration—we will again be facing a numerically superior enemy. There is no objective possibility of our reaching numerical equality with our enemies, actual or potential. Numbers are an important factor and generally a decisive one in the military sphere.

How, then, have we held our own until now and how will we continue to hold our own in the future? *Our success depends on our qualitative superiority, expressed in moral and intellectual terms.* We must concern ourselves not only with physical training, with the ability to withstand suffering, to move swiftly, to adjust to modern weapons, to adopt efficient organizational methods and discipline, to learn the history of war in Israel and other nations, to understand the internal, personal, social, political, and technical factors involved, to exploit all the newest developments in science, technology, and transportation—all these alone will not be enough. In the final analysis, it will not be the tank, the cannon, or the airplane that counts, but *the man who operates them*, and this man is a creature not only of muscles, though his muscles are very important, but also a creature of *spirit*. There is immense significance in his spiritual and intellectual fitness, his sense of determination, his loyalty, his willingness to face every danger and difficulty, his initiative, and that undefinable factor, deep within the human soul, that is stronger than death itself.

This is what gives man, created in the image of God, his moral strength, and constitutes a decisive factor in times of war, just as it is basic to creativity in times of peace.

The Jewish people's future will not be safeguarded by the sword. War has been forced upon us and we will fight as long as we are in danger, but we will not build our future on armies and wars. Our future depends on our creativity and our labor, on our settlements, factories, shipping, and aviation, on our advances in science and technology, our development of art and literature, and the vision that we impart to our youth and to future generations, the vision of the Prophets of Israel, a vision of justice and truth, of human fraternity and freedom. The political and social regime for which we strive can be summarized in five words: "Love thy neighbor as thyself."

UN Debates Proposed Withdrawal to October 14 Positions ★ Ben-Gurion Reports on Fighting, October 15–22

The victory of the Israel Defense Forces in the Negev and in the Galilee during the second half of October raised Israel's international prestige, but British Foreign Minister Bevin regarded the Egyptian defeat as an opportunity to strengthen Britain's position in Egypt and the Sudan. He negotiated with the Egyptian Ambassador to this end, promising to help Egypt in the Security Council to force the Jews to withdraw to the positions they held before their advances in the October 15–22 period.

The October 26 meeting of the Security Council opened with a report from Ralph Bunche on the situation at the fronts in Palestine, with particular emphasis on the Negev and the Lebanese border. The ensuing debate was opened by Hashaba Pasha, Egypt's Foreign Minister, who argued that the Jews had gained military and political advantage from violating the truce in the Negev. This, he said, ran contrary to the spirit of the Security Council resolution, and demanded that the Council take decisive action to safeguard the peace. It should order the armies, he said, to return to the positions they held on October 14.

Fuad Amun, for Lebanon, complained that the Security Council was encouraging the Jews to embark upon aggressive activities, for they had learned that the UN acquiesced to any *fait accompli*. Faris el Houri, for Syria, accused some members of the Security Council of supporting Jewish demands for the Negev, and exclaimed: "Is the right of conquest recognized in the twentieth century?"

In his rejoinder Abba Eban pointed out that the Egyptians had not heeded the demands of the UN Observers to allow Israeli convoys to pass through the Negev, and the Israel Defense Forces had to use force to break through the blockade. Egypt had no rights in the Negev, he said, and no part of it could change hands without Israeli agreement, which would not be forthcoming.

Two days later, on October 28, an Anglo-Chinese resolution threatening sanctions was presented. Representatives of Canada, Syria, and Belgium supported it, as did France with certain reservations. It was opposed by the USSR and the Ukraine. Voting was postponed for a day.

That same day, at a meeting of the Provisional State Council, the Prime Minister gave a brief report on the fighting in the south between October 15 and 22. He said:

> This operation was of importance in relation to the authority of the UN, the balance of forces in the Middle East, and the future of our country. It provided a test of the actual value and effectiveness of the truce; the usefulness of the truce observation machinery, and its ability to implement its decisions; the unity and effectiveness of the Arab League; the reality of the "Gaza government:" and the respective capacities of the Egyptian and the Israeli armies. With the exception of the Jewish forces, none of the other factors concerned stood the test.
>
> We objected to the truce in the past and we still maintain that stand. However, we accepted it when we were ordered to do so by the UN. We object to the truce because it gives the invading forces international status. This truce equates the aggressors with the aggrieved; it prolongs the war unnecessarily; it is harmful both to the Jews and Arabs. As we have seen during the three truces we have experienced so far, it in no way serves as a pathway to peace.
>
> We accepted the truce because our policy is based upon the UN. We were not unaware of that organization's weakness. But we regard as shortsighted any attempts to exploit that weakness. As human beings and as Jews we believe it to be in our interest to strengthen UN authority and effectiveness. We believe in international cooperation; we are interested in cooperation between the East and West; we are interested in the universal rule of law and in the settlement of disputes among nations by peaceful means. But we did not, and shall

not, accept a one-sided truce. It became clear to us from the first moment that the truce that both we and the Arabs were ordered to abide by was indeed one-sided. Hardly a day passed without some violation—in the south, the east, the north, and in Jerusalem.

During the truce the Egyptians—and in this instance I speak only of the Egyptians— brought up a constant stream of arms from Egypt, the Sudan, and other countries. Additional arms were constantly arriving.

The UN Observers decided that both sides had the right to use the roads: the Egyptians, from west to east through our lines, and the Jewish Army from north to south through their lines. The Egyptians rejected this decision. They acted on two assumptions: (1) that the UN Observers had neither the desire nor the ability to implement this decision; (2) that the Israeli Army had neither the desire nor the ability to implement it by its own efforts. Their first assumption regarding the attitude of the UN proved justified. Week after week we made representations to the organization, but the only reply we got was: "You are quite right, but the Egyptians don't agree!" Their assumption in regard to the Israel Defense Forces, however, was wrong.

On Friday, October 15, a convoy set out for the Negev, even though the UN had not yet received the agreement of the Egyptians. The events that followed are now history. There was complete coordination between our air, land, and naval forces. Our Air Force was in on the beginning of the fight, and our Navy was in on the end. Our Army completely fulfilled the mission with which it had been charged, to open the road to the Negev and to assure our forces freedom of movement.

This was the first time in the course of our long history—and Jewish history begins with a meeting between Jews and Egyptians, for the first Jew who was taken down to Egypt saved that country from starvation and destruction; and in our relations with the Egyptian people, which date back thirty-five hundred years or more—that the soldiers of Israel had encountered the soldiers of Egypt.

In the interests of truth, it should be pointed out that in the numerous wars we fought with the peoples of the East, we had fewer quarrels with the Egyptians than with any other nation. There was once an unsavory incident with Shishak, King of Egypt, who despoiled the Temple and the Royal Palace. We also had an encounter with a Sudanese Army near the scene of that engagement, which our forces now occupy, Beit Gubrin. The Bible refers to them as Kushim. They were headed by Zerah and the Kushi (2 Chronicles: 14, 11–14), and we beat them. But the real military encounter took place in the time of King Josiah, when Pharoah Necho went out to fight Assyria. He said that he had nothing to do with the Jews; but Josiah, who had a pact with Assyria, went out to fight him at Megiddo, and met his death there (2 Kings: 23; 2 Chronicles: 35).

Aside from those isolated incidents, in a three-thousand-year history this clash in the south was the first between the armies of Israel and of Egypt. We hope that it will also prove to be the last. We see no reason for a dispute between ourselves and our neighbors to the south. Those who urged the Egyptians to fight us were not doing a service to the Egyptians or the Arab peoples. They simply wanted to embroil Egypt in a controversy that was not her affair in order to divert her attention from vital matters in other places. Nokrashy Pasha, the Egyptian Prime Minister, was serving the national interests not of his country but of her enemies when he involved her in a sorry adventure in the Negev.

We want cordial relations with Egypt, not only because of past memories, but also because of future needs. Egypt must still make enormous efforts—economic, social, cultural, and political—to transform her formal independence, achieved in this generation, into a reality. These efforts are also required to make the great Egyptian people—numerically the largest Arab people—healthy, in the most literal sense of the term, as well as free, progressive, and truly independent. Peace and friendship between Israel and Egypt will benefit both peoples. We hope that the Egyptian rulers will now realize that they have nothing to gain from pursuing their present course and will work together with Israel for peace and neighborly relations.

Of course, we have no right to ignore what is happening on the fronts, and the schemes that might now be in the planning stage, not only in Cairo, but also in Amman, Baghdad, and elsewhere. The campaign is not over. Foreign armies are still encamped on our soil, and we are still insecure. Until there is final victory and peace, the Israel Defense Forces must be ready for any eventuality. I trust that they will stand the test in the future as they have in the past.

The day after the meeting of the Provisional State Council the UN Security Council decided to establish a five-member subcommittee to formulate a draft resolution based on the various ideas that had been presented in connection with the Anglo-Chinese proposal. The French representative, Alexandre Parodi, expressed opposition to a number of sections in the proposal. He was emphatic about the elimination of the section on sanctions. Warren Austin, the American Ambassador, serving for the last time as President of the Security Council, took delaying action—perhaps because the American Presidential elections were only a few days off. The two candidates for the Presidency, Truman and Thomas E. Dewey, had expressed sympathy for Israel during the campaign, but President Truman had spoken more clearly and decisively in Israel's favor. Almost the entire world was certain that Truman would be defeated, as indicated by all pre-election polls. It was the view held by most American and European newspapers.

It appears that US Secretary of State Marshall, then in England, had reached an agreement with Bevin on the Anglo-Chinese resolution. However, there were rumors that John Foster Dulles, who was expected to become Secretary of State under the Republicans, was opposed to the Anglo-Chinese resolution. Lord Cadogan, British representative in the Security Council, was willing to make some minor changes, in order to meet French objections. But Parodi was not satisfied with Cadogan's revisions. He suggested that the word "demand" be replaced by "request," and that if the request was not accepted, the Security Council be called to reconsider the matter. He also demanded the elimination of the threat of sanctions. He said that the side that had advanced should be asked to retreat, but that the side that had retreated should not reoccupy its former positions. Instead, a no-man's land should be created.

Abba Eban recalled that the October 14 situation—which the English were so anxious to restore—had developed out of Egyptian violation of the truce through many months. When they were taking place, Cadogan had shown no interest in the truce violations and in Egypt's refusal to obey the directives of the Mediator; he had not then spoken about sanctions. If there was talk of asking the armies to withdraw to their former positions, these should be the positions of May 14, Eban said. The UN Charter prohibited the entrance of the Egyptian Army into Palestine— if it had not been permitted into the country, the whole question would not have arisen.

Yakov Malik, the Soviet representative, supported the views expressed by Eban. Gen. Andrew J. MacNaughten, the Canadian delegate, recalled that Bunche had spoken of the need to replace the truce by a permanent settlement, and suggested that a committee be established to work out a plan agreeable to all. He proposed that the committee be composed of representatives of Britain, China, Belgium, France, and the Ukraine. Cadogan supported Canada. Manuilsky, however, opposed the entire Anglo-Chinese resolution.

The Canadian plan was supported by nine members of the subcommittee, and was there-fore adopted.

At the end of October Dr. Bunche sought to persuade the Arabs to begin direct negotiations with Israel. He asked the subcommittee to suggest to the Security Council that it back his efforts to bring about peace negotiations between the Jews and Arabs. France and Canada showed interest in Dr. Bunche's proposal, but the Council decided to postpone discussing it until after the US Presidential elections. In the meantime, the sub-committee had prepared the following proposal for submission to the Security Council:

> On July 15, the Security Council decided that, unless there was a new Security Council or General Assembly decision, the truce would remain in force until a peace settlement was reached, in accordance with the resolution of May 19, 1948. It decided on October 19 that neither side would be allowed to violate the truce on the basis of the argument that it was simply reacting against the other side, and that neither had the right to gain military or politi-cal advantages from truce violations. It decided on May 29 that should the truce be rejected or violated by either side, the Security Council would reconsider the Palestine situation with a view to taking action in accordance with Section 7 of the UN Charter. The Council hereby reaffirms its support for the request of the Acting Mediator on October 26, sent to the Egyptian Government and to the Provisional Government of Israel, following the Security Council resolution of October 19. The Council asks the Governments concerned to do the following:
>
> 1. Withdraw those forces that had advanced beyond the positions they held on October 14. The Acting Mediator will have the right to determine demarcation lines beyond which no military movements will be permitted.
>
> 2. Establish, on the basis of direct negotiations between the two sides, or if this does not succeed, through the UN Mediator, permanent truce lines delineating neutral de-militarized zones, in a manner that will ensure that the truce will henceforth be carried out in full. If there is no agreement, the truce lines will be determined by the Acting Mediator.

Liberation of Yad Mordekhai ★ Israel Refuses To Withdraw Before Start of Peace Negotiations

The American Presidential elections were held on Tuesday, November 2. The results became known only the next day. Despite the predictions of experts, polls, and newspapers in America and Europe, Harry Truman was reelected President. Arab representatives to the United Nations received the results with great dismay.

The subcommittee proposal was brought to the Council on November 3. The sec-tion on sanctions was removed at the request of the Americans. The amended proposal was supported by France, the United States, Britain, Argentina, Canada, Belgium, Colom-bia, Syria, and China. It was opposed by the Ukraine, while the Soviet Union abstained. The Ukraine suggested that the Council demand a renewal of direct negotiations between Egypt and Israel. The suggestion was supported only by the Ukraine and the Soviet Union, and opposed by Syria. The other members abstained. Since it lacked the minimum seven votes, the proposal was defeated.

The amended resolution adopted by the Security Council was identical with the subcommittee's draft up to the words "taking action in accordance with Section 7 of the UN Charter." Beyond that, the revised resolution called attention to the demands presented by the Acting Mediator to the Egyptian Government and the Provisional Government of Israel on October 26, calling for the withdrawal of all military forces to the positions that they held on October 14, without this in any way prejudicing their demands or rights in a final settlement of the problem. It provided for the appointment of a subcommittee composed of the permanent members of the Council (the United States, USSR, Britain, China, and France) together with Belgium and Colombia, to advise the Acting Mediator, should he request such advice, on the measures to be taken if one of the sides failed to act in accordance with the resolution within the time limit set by the Mediator. This committee would then swiftly examine the situation and suggest to the Council what steps should be taken in accordance with Section 7 of the Charter. A British suggestion that the Galilee be included in the resolution was voted down.

The meaning of the resolution was not clear. The Americans had succeeded in toning down the threat of sanctions, but not in eliminating it completely. Gen. William Riley, the American appointed to head the UN Observers, showed deep sympathy for the young State of Israel and admiration for the strength and courage of its Defense Forces. He arrived in Paris after the Security Council had adopted the resolution, and explained the real military situation in the country to its members. A cable from Abba Eban in Paris, received by the Foreign Ministry on November 7, reported: "Riley's report had considerable influence on Bunche's position."

General Riley also met with representatives of the Arab states and suggested that they enter peace negotiations with the Jews if they wished to avoid crushing defeat. Bunche, Eban said, had taken it upon himself to convince the Security Council that the time for peace had arrived. The British reaction was negative. The representatives of our Foreign Ministry in Paris (Shiloah and Eban) told us it was necessary to establish new settlements in the Negev in order to prove that Israel really controlled the area.

On November 6 the Prime Minister met with Yosef Weitz and Levi Eshkol to discuss the settlement of the first three hundred Jews in Beersheba (until that time there had not been a single Jewish civilian in the town), as well as the establishment of settlements in the vicinity. They also discussed the setting up of new villages in upper Galilee, along the seashore as far as Rosh Hanikra, and along the Lebanese border in the north. The establishment of settlements in the Negev and Galilee was no less important than the military conquest of those areas. Weitz asked where people would be found for the new villages. Among the new immigrants, the Prime Minister replied. They would be released from the Army and would go, together with instructors, to form the settlements.

The General Staff was ordered to clear out the Faluja "pocket." Yigael Yadin, the Chief of Operations, was sent to Paris to explain to our representatives at the UN General Assembly and, if necessary, to Bunche as well, that we intended to consolidate our hold on the Negev and that the demand for a withdrawal to the positions we held on October 14 was absurd and unjustified. Yadin's mission was to coordinate our political activities in Paris with our military activities inside the country.

The Egyptian Army retreated of its own volition from the Majdal "pocket" and moved toward Gaza. The Israel Defense Forces took over the area on November 5. In the Hebron district the Egyptians were gradually replaced by the Arab Legion. But the Egyptian units in the Faluja "pocket" did not move.

With Egypt's withdrawal from the Majdal "pocket," Yad Mordekhai was retaken, and its surviving members returned to their kibbutz. They had beaten off the Egyptians for six days. Their settlement was destroyed and twenty-four of its defenders were killed. Yad Mordekhai's stand prevented the Egyptians from advancing through the south and the coastal plain. They vented their anger on this stubborn kibbutz. Thirty thousand shells were rained on it in the six days. Sixty Egyptian tanks took part in the assault. When the members returned, they found that the kibbutz had been demolished. The agricultural buildings, the water tower, the diesel engine, and the reservoir had all been reduced to rubble; only the houses remained, because Egyptian soldiers had been living in them for five and a half months, but they were also in bad shape. When soldiers of the IDF reentered the settlement, they raised the Israeli flag on the wreckage of the water tower; it bore the legend: "Yad Mordekhai has been redeemed."

On November 6 the Prime Minister sent the following message to Marshal Stalin, Chairman of the Soviet Council of Ministers:

> On behalf of the State of Israel, and on my own behalf, I wish to extend warm greetings to you on the occasion of the October Revolution, which gave national equality to the peoples of the Soviet Union, guaranteed food and work to all the laboring masses, paved the path to social and spiritual progress for people in the cities and in the villages, and created the powerful Red Army, which played an extraordinary role in the war against Nazism and Facism. We will never forget the assistance that the Soviet Union extended to the Jews, victims of Nazism, and her consistent support for the people of Israel in their war for freedom and independence in their historical Homeland. I wish the peoples of your country the successful completion of the economic reconstruction which began after the war, as well as economic and cultural advancement, and international peace and understanding.

The arrival of General Riley in Paris and his description of the achievements of the IDF made a strong impression on the members of the Security Council and also confused them. Our forces in the south had, in the meantime, received orders to capture the Iraq-Suedan police station, which had already been stormed seven times without success. In view of the earlier failures, it was decided to concentrate a large number of heavy weapons for the attack, so that our firepower would be superior to that of the Egyptians, and so that we could penetrate the walls of the station, which stood at the eastern edge of the Faluja "pocket."

To ensure accurate artillery fire, the attack was made in the daytime, on November 9. The sustained shelling had its effect. By three in the afternoon the Egyptians were already fleeing to the village of Iraq-Suedan. Our infantrymen, riding on halftracks and accompanied by tanks, approached the station. Our sappers blasted a hole through the barbed wire, then through the wall of the police station itself. The Egyptians fled and the building was captured. The units that had captured the station did not suffer a single loss, but a number of our men were killed in the diversionary attack on the village of Iraq-Suedan.

The fleeing Egyptians gathered in the area between Faluja and Iraq-el-Manshia, which remained in Egyptian hands until the armistice agreement. They were supplied by air, and from time to time received reinforcements from Gaza and Hebron. Several Egyptian convoys that attempted to reach the "pocket" were intercepted by our forces.

Despite our ground and air attacks, the Egyptians refused to surrender. They suffered serious losses, but held the "pocket" until the end of the fighting.

British pressure on Bunche grew stronger. The Middle East expert of the British Foreign Office met with Bunche in connection with Riley's statements and to consider the sanctions that they wanted the Security Council to impose on Israel if she did not withdraw. At a closed session of the Security Council on November 8 Bunche suggested declaration of an armistice, with the establishment of large demilitarized zones under UN supervision to separate the forces involved, after Jewish and Egyptian forces had withdrawn to their former positions. The Council should demand, he added, that the Acting Mediator and the two sides make arrangements to assure a restoration of peace.

The Prime Minister received a letter from Bunche in which he demanded that Israel retreat and that an Egyptian Governor be appointed for Beersheba. Malik announced that the plan was not acceptable to the government of the Soviet Union. First of all, he declared, the committee had to invite the two sides to meet for direct negotiations; the proposal to establish demilitarized zones was a political one, and the Acting Mediator had no authority to make it.

The Prime Minister told foreign correspondents (Sidney Gruson of *The New York Times*, Kenneth Bilby of the New York *Herald Tribune*, and Mrs. Gruson of the London *Observer*) that Israel would not surrender her gains in the Negev unless compelled to do so by force. Israel would not agree to the establishment of an international regime in Jerusalem. Finally, the Prime Minister said, it was neither justified nor realistic for the UN to impose sanctions on Israel.

On November 14 Dr. Bunche's personal representative, Dr. Mohan, presented the following letter from Bunche to the Director of the Israeli Foreign Ministry:

> Following the Security Council's resolution of November 4 about the Negev, a number of steps must be taken by your Government in order to permit the establishment of demarcation lines between the Egyptian and Israeli forces in the Negev; no movement of military forces will thereafter be permitted beyond those lines. They have been worked out in consultation with the committee established by the Security Council under the terms of its November 4 resolution. The representatives of the two sides testified before the committee, and their views were given serious consideration. November 19 has been set as the date on which these temporary demarcation lines will come into effect. You are hereby requested to announce the name of the officer or officers of the Israel Army with whom the Chief of the UN Observers, General Riley, will be able to discuss the necessary arrangements. Among the matters to be clarified are the military movements required to carry out these arrangements. Both the Chief of the UN Observers and I will do everything we possibly can, after temporary demarcation lines have been decided upon, to facilitate negotiations between the two sides—in accordance with the Security Council resolution—aimed at reaching an agreement of permanent boundaries, and neutral or demilitarized zones, as the case may be.
>
> We wish to emphasize on this occasion that the arrangements about which we speak are temporary ones, within the framework of the existing truce. They will be in effect only until such time as permanent truce lines are decided upon. I sincerely hope that the problem of permanent truce lines will be solved soon by negotiations between the two sides. The temporary demarcation lines were set down in the following memorandum:
>
> 1. In order to carry out the provisions of the November 4 Security Council resolution calling for an orderly withdrawal of military forces in the Negev, in order to establish effective means of supervising the truce, and to set up a broad zone in which no military movements will be permitted, the following plan has been approved: (a) temporary demarcation lines

are to be decided upon; no military movement or military supplies will be permitted beyond these lines; (b) military forces are to be withdrawn to positions behind the temporary demarcation lines; (c) machinery to supervise the truce arrangements in the area between the temporary demarcation lines is to be created.

2. In accordance with Section 5 (1) of the November 4 Security Council resolution, the temporary demarcation lines will be as follows: (a) the temporary demarcation lines for the Israeli forces on the southern front will begin from the intersection of the truce line of October 14 with the Hata-Julis road, and go from there southeastward to Julis, then east to Ibdis, Jisar, Zita, and up to the October 14 truce line next to Baal Huseima; there will be a full retreat of all military forces in other places to the truce lines of October 14. Only those units that were stationed at Israeli settlements in the Negev for defensive purposes before October 14 will be allowed to remain. (b) The temporary demarcation lines of the Arab forces in the Negev will begin in the western section along the coastline next to Wadi Hasi, to the eastern side of the Dir Sunid road, which crosses the Gaza-Majdal road, to a point three kilometers east of the main road, and from there southward parallel to the Gaza-Majdal road down to the Egyptian border. In the eastern section, the line will begin from the Arab positions south of the neutral area of Government House by Tsur Bacher, and then to Mar Elias, Beit Safafa, Shuafat, Beit Jallah, El Kada, and Hussan; from there it will continue southward by way of Nachlin, Surif, Beit Ula, and Tarhia; it will then go southeast as far as Dura and Dahariya; from there it will continue eastward by way of Samua to the Dead Sea. All military forces on both sides, except for those mentioned in Section 2A to 2C (4), will be prohibted from remaining in the aforementioned areas.

3. Beersheba will be demilitarized. Israeli forces will withdraw from the city and an Egyptian Governor will be appointed to handle its affairs.

4. The two sides will be prohibited from carrying out scouting in the area between the temporary demarcation lines. No military movement or military supplies will be permitted except with the agreement of the supervisory bodies, and under their control. Civilian supplies for normal use of the residents of the area will not be limited in any way.

(Signed) R. Bunche,
Acting Mediator

Meanwhile Canada had offered a resolution in the Security Council calling for a replacement of the truce by an armistice agreement, to be drawn up in direct negotiations, or negotiations through the good offices of the Acting Mediator. The Security Council approved this resolution on November 16, with Soviet Russia and the Ukraine abstaining. The Soviet representative suggested that the Jews and the Arabs be forced to carry out formal negotiations aimed at achieving a peace settlement. This proposal was supported only by the Russians and the Ukranians. All other members of the Council abstained; thus it failed of passage. Most members felt that the question of a settlement was an affair of the General Assembly and the Security Council.

Bunche had demanded a reply to his proposals by November 19. A meeting of the Provisional State Council on November 18 rejected the Bunche proposals as well as any withdrawal before the start of peace negotiations. This decision was adopted after the matter had been clarified by Reuven Shiloah, appearing on behalf of the Foreign Ministry, and Yadin, speaking on behalf of the Ministry of Defense.

Yadin had returned from Paris with General Riley on November 17. He explained to Riley that Israel had military forces in the Negev even before October 14. Moreover, all the units sent to the area in order to break through Egyptian lines had returned to their bases. Riley pointed out that there were no Israeli military forces in Beersheba before October 14. Yadin answered that after the breakthrough, Israel had a new military frame of reference. Riley in turn asked that UN Observers be attached to all Jewish military units in the Negev, a suggestion that was opposed by Yadin and Shiloah on security grounds. UN Observers, they said, have the right to be in the Negev and to supervise the truce, but not to be with our troops. Riley requested that the Egyptian forces in the Faluja "pocket" be allowed to join up with other Egyptian units. Our representatives said that this was impossible from a military viewpoint, because it would give the Egyptian Army in the Negev an additional full brigade. If Egypt will discuss peace with us, we will be ready to discuss the release of the forces in the Faluja "pocket," they declared.

Section 4. Arab Defeats and Conclusion of Armistices

Celebration of the Seventieth Anniversary of Petah Tikva

O N November 9, 1948, Petah Tikva celebrated its seventieth anniversary. A military parade was held in the presence of the Chief of Staff, General Dori, and the Prime Minister and Minister of Defense. Among those sitting in the front row was Moshe Raab, one of the surviving founders of the Mother of Settlements; next to him sat Avraham Shapiro. The Mayor, Yosef Sapir, presented the flag to the commander of the parade.

"This flag," he said, "is a symbol of our appreciation of your bravery in all the campaigns in the Petah Tikva area. Soldiers of the Israel Defense Forces! Petah Tikva's holiday is the holiday of Israeli courage. The first seeds of independence were sown with the first plowing. Petah Tikva was not only the first Hebrew settlement, but also a bastion of the defense of Hebrew territory. The courage of the founders of Petah Tikva was not the courage of martyrs, but that of heroes who conquer their Homeland with sweat and blood."

The next speaker was the Prime Minister, who said in part:

> The founders of the first Hebrew settlement led the way in defense as well. We extend our salutations to Bar Kochba, Yohanan of Gush Halav, the Maccabees, Ezra and Nehemia, the Kings of Judea and Israel, the Judges and Prophets, those who forged the shining chain of Jewish history.

> Forty-two years ago I was a Hebrew laborer on the soil of the Homeland in this village. I will never forget that privilege. It is particularly meaningful for us and for the founders of the first Hebrew village to be celebrating its founding during the greatest and most wonderful year in Jewish history. Four extraordinary things have happened during this year: the Israel Defense Forces have been created and equipped; the State of Israel has been reestablished; we, who are numbered in the hundreds of thousands, have courageously withstood the attack of millions; we have liberated large sections of our country, and the Israel Defense Forces are still at work.

> One might have wondered how such a military force came to be established. Today we have the answer. It did not spring suddenly, full-grown, into existence. It was, rather, the result of strenuous efforts over many decades by those who came before us. The pioneers of seventy years ago established the first village in the revived Homeland. Our military

strength stems from those pioneers and the others who followed in their footsteps. It is hard for us to imagine how a handful of young men—Salomon, Guttman, Shtamfer, and Raab—could have had the courage to come from behind Jerusalem's walls and from Hungary to create the first village in the wastelands of the Yarkon, fighting nature, the wilderness, and malaria, living as isolated individuals in an untamed desert. They had no army, only their two hands and the courage of their convictions. Their spirit nurtures the thousands and tens of thousands who form the Israel Defense Forces.

Our generation can be proud of its achievements, and I hope that future generations will do even more. But there is one sphere in which we cannot compete with those who founded this village—they had the privilege of being the first. The first to return to Zion were characterized by modesty and humility. Though our generation has great achievements to its credit, we should not be vain. We could not have accomplished what we did had it not been for those who came before us. We are only beginning. This celebration has served to convince us that we will succeed, and that the long chain of Jewish creativity will never be broken.

Security Council Calls for Permanent Armistice ★ Again Demands Israeli Withdrawals ★ First Census ★ Election Law for Constituent Assembly

On November 16 the Security Council called on the Jews and Arabs to negotiate a permanent armistice in Palestine, and again demanded that the Jews withdraw from the areas they had captured in the battles between October 15 and 22.

At a meeting of the Provisional State Council on November 18 the Prime Minister, commenting on this Security Council decision of November 16 and on Dr. Bunche's letter of November 14, said:

> We cannot, for obvious reasons, disclose the movements of our military forces, but I would like to announce today that all the additional forces sent to aid our units in the south to penetrate the Egyptian blockade—which was a violation of the UN decision and of the terms of the truce—have returned to their former positions. The forces we have in the Negev now are the same that were there before October 14, and all of them will remain to guard the Negev against a possible attack by the Egyptian units stationed south of Rafiah.

He wished to make one more comment on the Security Council, Ben-Gurion said:

> In its decision of November 16 there was a new element that we heartily welcome. It appears that at least some members of the Council finally understand that the truce does not lead to peace; on the contrary, it may serve to fan the flame of belligerency, which will benefit neither Jews nor Arabs. The resolution adopted two days ago by the Security Council, while not as strong as it should be, nevertheless marks a turning point in the Council's comprehension of the problem of war and peace in this country. The Council decided on November 16 that there was need for direct negotiations, or negotiations through the good offices of the Mediator, between the two sides. These would not be negotiations about a truce but about an armistice, which would be the first step toward permanent peace.

> We heartily welcome this decision. The Israel Government is ready to begin negotiations with all Arab states, with individual Arab states, or with those states that have already concluded that there is no way of defeating Israel. We will inform the Mediators and the

Security Council that we regard such negotiations as the only path that can lead to peace between the Arab states and Israel. We do not place much value on the boastful talk that is still heard from various Arab statesmen.

We have reason to believe that a large proportion of the Arab peoples have concluded that the war they tried to wage against the establishment of the State of Israel has failed, and that the Arab states have nothing to gain from its continuation. We are convinced that there are no irreconcilable conflicts between the interests of Israel and the just interests of the Arab states. We are pleased at this request from the Security Council, which has urged the two sides to make peace. We will give the Security Council every possible assistance and support in this sphere.

At midnight on November 18 the Government's reply to Dr. Bunche's memorandum of November 14 was handed to Dr. Mohan. It said:

A. The Government of Israel understands that it was not the Security Council's intention to order the withdrawal of military forces from positions they held before October 14.

B. The Government has taken note of the Acting Mediator's announcement that the withdrawal of military forces north of a predetermined line does not affect the units stationed in Israeli settlements in the Negev for defensive purposes prior to October 14.

C. The Government would like to use this occasion to point out that since May 15, 1948, there have been motorized units in the Negev moving freely through the area, in addition to the forces engaged in static defense.

The Government expresses its satisfaction at the fact that the Security Council did not order the retreat of forces that were in the Negev before October 14 in order to guarantee the independence and security of the State of Israel and to defend its inhabitants.

D. The withdrawal of our units from the central part of the area, including Beersheba, would invite pillage by irregular forces which constitute a constant threat to the security of the residents living there. If Beersheba is left undefended, the pathway to Jerusalem will be open and it will no longer be possible to guarantee its defense from the south.

E. The Government hereby announces that the forces that entered the Negev on or after October 14, in order to reestablish transport facilities that had been disrupted by the Egyptian Army, in violation of the truce and of the decision of the Chief of the Observers, have been withdrawn to their previous positions.

F. As far as the coastal area is concerned, the Government is ready, in consultation with the Observers, to order the withdrawal of its regular forces to the area north of Sunid, on condition that arrangements are made for local security, in a manner to be agreed upon with the UN Observers.

G. The Government sees a contradiction between the Acting Mediator's proposal to establish demilitarized or neutral zones, and his decision that Egyptian forces may remain in the Bir Asluj area and that his "supervision of the road from Bir Asluj to Rafiah will continue." The Government retains the right to raise this point again in negotiations with the UN Observers.

H. Finally, the Israel Government wishes to reiterate its concern for the decisions and recommendations of the Security Council and its willingness to do whatever it can to foster a peaceful settlement of the dispute that broke out in the Land of Israel as a result of Arab aggression. In accordance with the request of the Acting Mediator, the Government has appointed Yigael Yadin and Reuven Shiloah as its representatives in discussion with the Chief of the UN Observers. The Government reiterates its urgent request to the Acting Mediator that he immediately announce the time and place of a meeting with authorized representatives of the Arab governments. It expresses the hope that this meeting will result in the opening of direct negotiations designed to establish peaceful and neighborly relations, a goal that the State of Israel has constantly sought since this unfortunate dispute began.

The reply was signed by Walter Eytan, the Director of the Foreign Ministry.

That day the Prime Minister received a reply to his message from Stalin. It read: "Please accept my thanks for your greetings and good wishes on the occasion of the thirty-first anniversary of the October Revolution. (Signed) Stalin."

The first Israeli census took place on November 8, 1948. In order to carry it out, a seven-hour curfew was ordered. The census showed that there were 713,000 Jews and 69,000 non-Jews in the area under the jurisdiction of the Israel Government on October 14 (before the conquest of the south and the Negev). A corrected estimate of Mandatory Government figures indicated that at the end of 1946 there were 608,225 Jews in the country; the Jewish Agency estimated the Jewish population at 625,000. The fact that in the interval natural increase had added 19,000 souls to the population, and that there had been 83,000 more arrivals than departures, accounted for the increase of 102,000 in the Jewish population. (In 1882, there had been 24,000 Jews in the country; in 1900—50,000; in 1914—85,000; in 1922—83,790; in 1931—174,610; and in 1941, according to a Jewish Agency estimate—502,000.)

The following population figures for Jews (outside of soldiers) emerged: Jerusalem—68,000; Tel-Aviv-Jaffa—213,000: Haifa—90,900: Tiberias—5000: Safad—2100; Petah Tikva—23,300; Rishon LeZion—9800; Rehovot—9000; Holon—7,900; Ramat Gan—15,400; Bnei Brak—10,300; Givatayim—8300; Herzliya—4900; Kfar Saba—4400; Natanya—7000; Hadera—7500. Figures for other areas showed: Judea and the south—19,200; the Sharon and Hefer Valleys—53,800; the Valleys of Jezreel and Beit Shaan—22,800; the area around Haifa—19,200; the Jordan Valley and Galilee—13,200. The total population included 616,300 civilians and 96,500 soldiers. Of the non-Jews, 16,800 were in Nazareth, 2900 in Haifa, 3700 in Jaffa, and 2000 in the Lydda-Ramle area. The rural non-Jewish population included 1900 in the Jerusalem area, 23,500 in the vicinity of Haifa and Shfaram, 16,600 in lower Galilee, 500 in upper Galilee, and 100 in other places. This made a total of 68,600. Not all the Arabs in the Galilee were counted.

At the aforementioned Council meeting (November 18) an election law for the Constituent Assembly was finally adopted. The Provisional Government had begun dealing with the matter in July. The law, which is still on the books and which has aroused considerable controversy in the Knesset [Parliament] over the years, includes Section 2, which states: "For the purpose of counting votes and determining election results, the entire area of the State will be considered one district"; and Section C: "Elections will be general, direct, equal, secret, and proportional." These two sections were adopted only because it was impossible in wartime to divide the country into electoral districts and adopt the British system (in which one member is elected for each district), or the Scandinavian system (in which three or four members are elected on the basis of proportional representation for each district). Our electoral system has caused an exaggerated degree of fragmentation and the creation of many small factions that, taken together, form a majority in the Knesset. It is unlike any other system in the world.

Elections to the Constituent Assembly were scheduled for January 25, 1949.

The Council, at its next meeting, on November 25, 1948, adopted the following regulations to govern election propaganda within the Army:

A. Meetings, speeches, lecturers, and propagandists—whether sponsored by parties or by election lists—are prohibited.

B. All written propaganda, be it election platforms or other material, will be permitted in the camps and measures will be taken to facilitate its distribution to every soldier. The form of the material will be subject to the supervision of the General Staff, or of a special body established for this purpose.

C. No announcements, films, placards, or slogans will be permitted in the camps.

D. Every effort will be made in the two weeks before the elections to grant leaves to soldiers who wish to participate in the campaign (this matter will be dealt with by a special committee).

E. Every officer and enlisted man will have the right to appear as the representative of a party on a political platform providing that he does not wear his uniform and that he is on leave.

These regulations were approved by a vote of twenty to thirteen.

Agreement in Jerusalem ★ All Egyptians Driven from the Negev ★ Cairo Announces Readiness To Negotiate ★ Five British Planes Shot Down by Our Air Force

Israel's reply to the Acting Mediator, at midnight on November 18, on his request for the withdrawal of her forces in the Negev was welcomed by Dr. Bunche. The British continued to demand the imposition of sanctions on Israel if she refused to evacuate the Negev, including Beersheba, but their only support came from the Arabs. The American delegate, Philip Jessup, announced on November 19 that the United States opposed any reduction in the area of the State of Israel without Israel's agreement. But if Israel wished to hold territory outside the borders set down in the November 29 resolution, he said, she must negotiate with the Arabs for an exchange of territory. In general, he expressed support for direct negotiations between Israel and the Arab states. The Soviet representative, Syropkin, opposed the Bernadotte Plan and demanded the implementation of the November 29 resolution.

Three different programs thus emerged at the UN: the British demanded that the Negev be given to Trans-Jordan, in return for which western Galilee would be given to Israel; the Americans demanded that there be negotiations between the Arabs and Israel regarding both the Negev and western Galilee; the Soviets demanded the implementation of the November 29 resolution.

In the meantime, talks began in Haifa between the Chief of the UN Mission, General Riley, and the Israel Liaison Officers, Yigael Yadin and Reuven Shiloah. There were also meetings in Jerusalem between Moshe Dayan and the Military Governor of the Old City, Abdullah El-Tel.

Dr. Bunche on November 26 informed the Arab governments that Israel was willing to open peace negotiations. Israel, he said, would prefer direct negotiations; if this was not possible, she would be willing to negotiate through mediators appointed by the UN. No reply to his memorandum was received from the Arab governments. The seven-man committee appointed to consider the imposition of sanctions on Israel, should she refuse to withdraw from the Negev, failed to reach agreement on the issues.

On November 29 the Israel Government submitted an official request to the Security Council for membership in the UN. In a letter to Trygve Lie, the Secretary General, Foreign Minister Shertok wrote: "On May 14, 1948, Israel declared her independence on the basis of the natural and historic rights of the people of Israel and in accordance with the decision of the UN General Assembly of November 29. Since that time, the State of Israel has established itself administratively and has successfully repulsed the attacks of the neighboring states. Israel has already been recognized by nineteen states. On behalf of the Provisional Government of Israel, I have the honor to request that we be accepted as a member of the United Nations in accordance with Section Four of the Charter."

At a meeting with Israel journalists on the eve of the anniversary of the November 29 resolution, the Prime Minister said:

> We must base our lives on new foundations if we are to carry out two tasks: (1) defend ourselves against external danger, even after peace has been achieved, for there has never been a peace which was not followed by a war; (2) absorb large-scale immigration and develop those parts of the country that have been liberated. Last week five-thousand immigrants arrived in a single day. This fact shows that we require not only large-scale immigration but also the strength and capacities to absorb the immigrations. This, I might add, is no simple matter. We have yet to display either the desire or the ability properly to organize absorption. The Army has liberated the Negev and Galilee, but the Army cannot hold the Negev and Galilee. If we do not develop those areas, we will be failing in our historic mission.

At the end of November an agreement calling for a cease-fire in Jerusalem was signed by Maj. Moshe Dayan and Col. Abdullah El-Tel, to go into effect at 8 A.M. on December 1. However, sniping and shelling ceased a day earlier, immediately after the signing of the agreement. Arab Legionnaires near Notre Dame left their positions on the walls of the Old City, laid down their weapons and began unofficial "peace talks" with Jewish soldiers. At the same time, several Legionnaires continued to snipe at the northern Jerusalem neighborhoods. As a result of this sniping Shlomo Mansor was wounded and, despite the doctors' efforts, died of his wounds.

On October 30 the British representative in the Political Committee of the UN General Assembly announced that Britain was withdrawing its support of the Bernadotte Plan, but had not yet accepted the partition plan in its present form. Syropkin for Soviet Russia declared that the existence of a Jewish State was proof that the November 29 resolution could be implemented.

Meanwhile the General Staff of the Israel Defense Forces, in accordance with instructions from the Minister of Defense, prepared a plan to drive the Egyptian Army out of the Negev, following the refusal of the Egyptians to discuss an armistice agreement with Israel.

General Riley had demanded during the latter part of November that Observers be attached to our military units, since, he said, these units did not have the right to move about. He also demanded that we agree to the appointment of an Egyptian Military Governor for Beersheba. With regard to the Faluja "pocket," he asked that we either allow the Egyptian units to leave or to receive food. We replied that we were willing to discuss supplying the Egyptians with food from our own sources. We absolutely refuse, however, to allow the stationing of Observers with our units in the Negev. The task of the Observers was to safeguard the truce, not to prevent the movement of our Army. As to the demand for an Egyptian Military Governor in Beersheba, we insisted that the Egyptian invaders had no rights in the country, and no Egyptian representative would be allowed to enter Beersheba or any other place we held in the Negev. In regard to Faluja, the Prime Minister cabled Shertok in Paris, asking him to inform Bunche that we could not allow the Egyptian units there to join the forces fighting against us in the Negev. Moreover, as things stood, the Faluja situation might help persuade Egypt to enter peace negotiations. Bunche told Shertok that he hoped negotiations would begin soon.

In the first convoy that we allowed to bring food to the Egyptian Army in the Faluja "pocket" the UN Observers discovered spare parts for weapons in the food boxes. On these boxes it was clearly written "To Haifa." We seized the spare parts and the food and announced that if there were no negotiations for an armistice, we would feel free to prevent food shipments to the Faluja "pocket."

At a meeting of the Government on December 8 the Prime Minister announced that the Egyptians had attacked several outposts between Gaza and Rafiah, but had been thrown back. Two days previously the Egyptians had attacked with twenty-two tanks. In the subsequent battle they lost five tanks, while two of our artillery pieces were put out of action. "Yesterday," the Prime Minister said, "the Egyptians attacked in battalion strength, but were repulsed and lost one hundred men. It is unlikely that the conflict has ended with this incident; we must drive the Egyptians from the Negev."

The Prime Minister held talks with Bunche, who told him that he had been in Egypt and in Trans-Jordan, where he had met with Nokrashy Pasha and Abdullah. He was certain that the two countries wanted peace. The Egyptians realized that they were in great difficulty but did not know how to extricate themselves. The people inside Egypt did not yet know that their army had suffered a severe defeat in Palestine, and Nokrashy Pasha was fearful of Egyptian public opinion. Bunche mentioned three problems that awaited solution: a final settlement, the way to reach a final settlement, and the matter of Beersheba and Faluja. He agreed that the truce was absurd, that permanent peace was required. He said that we should allow the Egyptians to send food to Faluja and that we should leave Beersheba, which had not been included within Israel's borders under the terms of the November 29 partition plan.

The Prime Minister told him: we will not leave Beersheba. We had the right to send convoys to the south; the United Nations was unable or unwilling to guarantee the passage of these convoys and we were forced to fight. It is impossible to discuss a return to the status quo ante at this point. The Egyptians are here as enemies, in a country that does not belong to them, and as long as there are no peace negotiations, we will not allow them to remove their troops from Faluja. Bunche tried to appply pressure on this point, but he was informed that Israel would not compromise. On hearing our strongly worded rejection of his proposal that we withdraw from Beersheba, he dropped the issue.

Afterward the Prime Minister talked with Riley. He asked him: "If you were in our place, wouldn't you act in the same way?" Riley replied: "Of course, you have no alternative." He asked about our attitude toward a permanent settlement. The Prime Minister replied that we were ready for peace, but would not accept foreign armies in our country, which endangered our security and existence. He explained the importance to us of the Negev and of access to the Red Sea. The Arabs, he said, had plenty of deserts and they did not need the Negev. As far as Jerusalem was concerned, a year ago we would have agreed to an internationalized Jerusalem but in the meantime various events had taken place, and the Jews of Jerusalem would no longer accept foreign rule. Finally, the Galilee and Haifa were Jewish, and would remain Jewish. Riley replied that he was no longer thinking about a foreign regime in Jerusalem. There was no intention of sending an international force to the city, only of establishing international supervision in Jerusalem.

After Bunche had returned to Paris, Riley told us that the Egyptians had withdrawn their agreement to participate in peace negotiations. There could be no peace negotiations, they had announced, until the Security Council decision of November 4 had been carried out, namely, until our forces had withdrawn to the positions that they had held before the campaign and until Beersheba was evacuated.

At a November 15 meeting of the Government the Prime Minister reported on his talks with James MacDonald, who had returned from Paris. The American Ambassador thought that Israel had been very successful at the meeting of the UN General Assembly. The Bernadotte Plan had been removed from the agenda, and the only delegation that had earned respect at the Council was the Jewish one. The Arab representatives had not bothered to speak to Council delegates, but only to newspapermen from their own countries. This had caused considerable criticism in the Council.

General Marshall had been replaced by Dulles, a Republican, as head of the American delegation. The Americans, Dulles said, had learned three things that year. (1) They had discovered the real balance of power in the Middle East, namely, that the Arab forces were nonexistent and the Jews were the only real force. (2) They now understood that the English had led them astray; either the English did not know what the situation was, or they were willfully misleading the Americans. (3) While America had to work together with England, this was possible only if the Americans led and the English followed, not vice versa.

The Prime Minister informed the Government that all necessary preparations had been made to drive the Egyptians from the Negev in another few days. Unsuitable weather conditions caused a postponement of the operation to December 23; it was completed on January 7, 1949. We threw the invaders out of Bir Asluj and Auja el-Hafir. The entire Beersheba road, as far as the Egyptian border, is in our hands. There is not a single Egyptian soldier in the entire area.

This operation involved enormous transport difficulties. The only road to the south and the Negev was the Beersheba-Auja road, and it was held by the Egyptians. We were forced to find new paths through the desert, paths that had never been traversed by motor vehicles. This demanded a great deal of work and the preparation of a track for the passage of tanks. Time was short and it was impossible to pave a road through the sand. We covered the sand with metal sheeting. The Engineering Corps and the Transport Corps played a decisive role in this campaign.

We also had enormous supply difficulties. The battles took place at great distance from our bases. We were forced to stockpile huge quantities of food, ammunition, and fuel in case our transport lines should be cut. We therefore had to commandeer a great many civilian vehicles, though the population was unaware of the operation until the very last moment. The transport of supplies was extremely arduous, because the road from the north ran only as far as Breir. The Gaza-Beersheba road from Breir to Saad was in very bad shape. As it happened, there was also heavy rain during the period that had been set for the operation, and the entire area was turned into a sea of mud. It was necessary to tow the vehicles with tractors, and even the tractors did not have an easy time of it.

The Egyptians were very well dug in, and we knew that we could not defeat them except by surprise assault. A diversionary attack was launched on Gaza. But the Egyptian forces there were very large and well equipped with tanks and heavy artillery. After we had captured a number of outposts in the Gaza area, the Egyptians launched a heavy counterattack. Our 13th Battalion, one of the best we had, was cut off and could not be reached with assistance. The battalion, forced to withdraw, lost thirteen men killed, twenty-five wounded, and about ten missing.

The battles around Gaza continued for four days and led the Egyptians to believe that we were aiming to take the town. Our main attack against Auja was postponed because of weather conditions. On the date when it was to take place, there was heavy rain around Beersheba, and it was delayed for one day. Auja was captured in a surprise attack, and then Bir Asluj was taken as well. The Egyptians were driven from the road. A large proportion of their men were captured and the rest fled. There were a number of high-ranking officers among the prisoners. They told us that they could not conceive of an attack from the eastern side, which was completely covered with sand and rocks and seemed impassable.

Three days after the attack began, our forces moved into Sinai and the next day reached Abu Ageilah. The Egyptians were left with only one means of transport, the railway, which our planes successfully hit. At the same time, we attacked the Faluja "pocket" with artillery and airplanes. One of our battalions broke into Iraq-el-Manshia, but the Egyptians launched a strong counterattack, inflicted heavy losses on the unit, and recaptured the town. Our shelling of Faluja continued. The Egyptian stand at Faluja was worthy of respect. Though their supplies were running out and they were in a hopeless position, they refused to surrender.

All three arms of the Defense Forces participated in the Negev attack. Our Navy shelled the Egyptian coast and carried out reconnaissance missions as far as Port Said, without running into a single Egyptian ship. Our Air Force almost destroyed the Egyptian Air Force. Only once did six enemy planes appear near Faluja: one of them was shot down, two others were hit, the rest fled. After we shot down a number of Egyptian planes in a second air battle their Air Force disappeared from the skies.

Egyptian land forces operated in great strength. There was danger that our units, on crossing into Sinai, would clash with British units. The Minister of Defense therefore ordered them to return to Abu Ageilah, in order to capture Rafiah and cut off the Egyptian Army in Gaza. After they had recrossed the border they were told that they could go across the border on the Rafiah-Auja road to attack Rafiah. The Egyptians, however, were too well entrenched along the Gaza-Rafiah line, and though we captured a number of outposts we were unable to cut off Gaza and capture Rafiah itself. The Egyptians resisted stubbornly. They were equipped with heavy weapons and their fire pattern was exceptionally effective.

On January 6, 1949, the Egyptian government announced its willingness to open armistice negotiations. Eight days earlier the Security Council had ordered an armistice. A cease-fire went into effect at 2 P.M. on January 7. The final battle took place over an outpost blocking the Rafiah-El Arish road. The clash, in which halftracks and armored cars participated, concluded at 7 P.M. that day.

A few hours previously, just before the end of the fighting, an event occurred that, for a moment, appeared to presage an all-out battle with the British, which the Israel Defense Forces had always striven to avoid. Five British warplanes from the Canal Zone, hovering over the battlefield to determine whether Israeli forces were really on Egyptian soil, were shot down by our planes near Nirim. The British Foreign Office demanded an explanation and compensation from the State of Israel. British forces in Aqaba were reinforced. The Egyptians, encouraged by this development, announced that they would not begin negotiations until the Israel Defense Forces had left Egyptian soil. But Ernest Bevin had gone too far this time. The American government expressed its disagreement with his actions; President Truman strongly criticized the flight of British planes over a battle zone, as well as the reinforcements sent to Aqaba. There was also criticism of the Foreign Secretary in Britain itself for needlessly endangering the lives of British fliers.

Our General Staff ordered all units still on the other side of the border, even a short distance on the other side, to return to the border itself, along the Auja-Rafiah road. At 2 P.M. on January 7 the armistice came into effect. The Negev had been liberated and only the Gaza Strip remained in Egyptian control.

At this time it was still not certain that the war had really come to an end. Firing continued here and there both by the Egyptians and by our forces. But by midnight of January 7 the Prime Minister was apprised that quiet reigned on all fronts, and the next morning at 10, when he went to Tiberias, he wrote in his diary:

> A great revolution in the history of our people has taken place during the past year: we have established a Jewish State and gone from slavery to freedom. We have created the Israel Defense Forces and defeated the Arab armies that invaded our country. We have liberated the Negev and Galilee, so that the land there can be used for large-scale settlement. We have brought in over 120,000 immigrants in a single year, as the first step toward the ingathering of the exiles. We have become a factor in the Middle East and in the entire world.
>
> Two things have made our achievements possible:
>
> 1. The settlement and defense activites by three generations of pioneers from the days of Petah Tikva until this very day.
>
> 2. The political and military guidance of our movement, imbued with daring, wisdom, and vision, which mobilized the Zionist movement and the Jewish people in these years of trial.
>
> Our movement, combining bold vision with an understanding of reality, a profound political analysis of future developments with a sense of loyalty to the historic needs of our people, found itself in conflict with men of little faith, men who were guided by a false realism, who denied our right to a State and our ability to create it. We also struggled against our verbose maximalists, who were very good at talking but not at carrying out positive activities, and who, by trying to accomplish too much, stood in danger of accomplishing nothing at all. Our movement brought international recognition to the Jewish State and allowed us, through our own efforts, to write the greatest saga in the history of our people for over two thousand years.
>
> At a time when the military danger threatening our existence was scarcely evident,

our movement prepared the means to defend ourselves against the Arab armies, established the extraordinary defense force, which, it seemed later, had sprung out of the ground to defeat six Arab States with a population forty times as large as that of the State of Israel.

The great revolution is not yet over. We have scarcely begun to address ourselves to the positive tasks that await us. We must, in the near future, lay the foundations that will serve us for decades and perhaps for centuries. We must shape the character of the State of Israel and prepare it to fulfill its great mission of gathering together the exiles and building a society based on freedom, equality, and justice.

While the war and its dangers have not yet passed, and security remains our central concern, we must also deal with the two major tasks facing the State, immigration and settlement. The security of the State of Israel depends on:

A. A constant and rapid increase in immigration, and the integration of the immigrants in the country.

B. Planned settlement activities and the populating of the empty expanses with people, who will constitute a human wall against the dangers of invasion.

C. A foreign policy based on peace in the world and cooperation with our neighbors.

D. The development of industry, agriculture, air transport, and shipping, which will provide the economic basis for our plans.

E. A popular army.

Armistice with Egypt Negotiated in Rhodes ★ Liberation of the Southern Negev ★ Israeli Flag over Eilat

After arguments about where Israel and Egypt should meet to discuss an armistice, the island of Rhodes was agreed upon. On January 12, 1949, the Egyptian and Israeli delegations arrived, as did Ralph Bunche and his advisors. All the delegates were housed in one hotel. The discussions began on January 13. At first there was an enormous gulf between the two sides. The Israeli delegation demanded the withdrawal of Egyptian forces to the other side of the Mandatory border, while the Egyptians, pointing to the November 4 resolution, demanded a withdrawal of the Israeli forces to the positions they had held before the battles began in the Negev. Dr. Bunche handled the negotiations with great skill and gradually brought the two sides closer to agreement, initially on minor questions, and then on major ones as well.

As a first step, the two sides agreed not to renew hostilities. Israel assented to the evacuation of the Egyptian brigade from Faluja, provided there was an overall agreement by January 23. When that day came and an agreement had not yet been reached, Israel refused to permit the evacuation, though it did allow food to be sent to the brigade. The Egyptians demanded that no Israeli troops be allowed to remain south of the Majdal-Faluja line. This would have meant foregoing the Southern Negev, as well as Beersheba. The Israeli delegation, of course, refused. It was agreed, finally, that only Auja, from which the Egyptian Army had invaded the country, and through which the Israel Army had broken through to Abu Ageilah, would become a demilitarized zone under UN control, and would serve as the headquarters of the Armistice Commission.

Initially the Egyptians also demanded that the southern part of the Negev, up to the

Eilat area, be declared a no-man's land. In the end they agreed that it would be under IDF control.

The last difficult point in dispute concerned Beersheba. The Egyptians had not admitted up to that time that the city had fallen to the Jews, and therefore demanded that the town have an Egyptian Governor. The Israeli delegation, of course, refused to discuss the proposal, insisting that Beersheba be considered a part of the State of Israel. The Egyptian delegation left for home. On February 23 it finally returned with instructions to compromise on this point.

The next day, February 24, an armistice agreement between Israel and Egypt was signed in Rhodes. It was the first in a series of agreements between Israel and her neighbors: Egypt, Lebanon, Jordan, and Syria. The preamble to the agreement stated that the negotiations took place in order to facilitate the transition from a truce to permanent peace, and obligated the two sides to cease using military force to solve the problems in dispute between them. It also stated that the armistice lines would not affect the rights of the two sides, which would be determined within the context of a final solution of the Palestine problem. But the agreement prohibited the two sides from moving their armed forces beyond the line. The Auja area was demilitarized of both the Egyptians and the Israelis and designated headquarters of the Armistice Commission, which was to meet whenever it proved necessary. All the Negev, except for the Gaza Strip, remained in Israeli hands.

We were represented at Rhodes by Col. Yigael Yadin and Walter Eyran, Director of our Foreign Ministry.

After the agreement had been signed, the Defense Minister ordered the Army to liberate the southern Negev, part of which was controlled by the Arab Legion. This area had been allocated to Israel under the terms of the November 29 resolution, but neither the Hagana, nor afterward the Israel Defense Forces, had taken physical control of it, since it was far distant from Israel's centers of supply and military bases. The Egyptians agreed, under the armistice terms, that their forces would not cross the Mandatory border; consequently only the Jordanians remained. The Legion held the area from Ein Viba (Ein Yahav) to the Gulf of Aqaba, along the whole length of the Arava.

The Golani and Negev Brigades were entrusted with the task of liberating the Negev. The Negev Brigade was supposed to advance through the middle of the Negev, while the Golani Brigade proceeded down the Arava. The operation began on March 5, when an advance unit of the Negev Brigade left Beersheba for the south, along the Beersheba-Auja road and by a sand track up to Avdat. From there it continued to the Rimon Crater, and then turned south. The going was very rough; large boulders blocked the way and it was not easy to find a passageway through the area. In the difficult sections our forces advanced no more than two kilometers an hour. At 6 A.M., the advance guard of the Negev Brigade, riding in jeeps and accompanied by Air Force men, reached Abraham Field, the spot that had been designated as a landing strip. In the afternoon, planes were seen flying south at a great distance from the landing strip. The members of the Negev Brigade, not realizing that these were our planes, did not try to attract their attention. At about 6 P.M., our soldiers recognized two Commando transport planes, which were able to land at the airstrip without difficulty. Planes arrived one after another with members of a company that was to capture the heights overlooking the pathway to Eilat. They brought equipment and supplies.

At the same time, a unit of the Golani Brigade proceeded down the Arava, and by March 7 had come to Ein Husub, which we call Hatzeva. There is a large spring there. After the first planes landed at Abraham Field, jeeps left for the south to capture Ein Yahav. We knew that the Legion had been encamped there, but when our forces arrived at the spot, they found it deserted. A race developed between our two units to determine which would be the first to reach Eilat. The advance guard of the Negev Brigade was within fifty kilometers of Eilat, but it was confronted by grave natural obstacles. The Golani Brigade, with an advance unit in Ein Yahav, was a hundred and twenty kilometers from Eilat. However, it was much easier going in the Arava, despite the fact that clashes with the Arab Legion were expected. Ten kilometers from Ein Yahav, a Golani unit came up against a Legion unit, but the Legionnaires were driven away with a flanking movement, without our soldiers having to fire a single shot. The Golani men stopped on seeing a cloud of dust, until it became evident that it was caused by a strong wind rather than the movement of enemy forces. The unit reached Nahal Paran, which runs into the Arava from the mountains of the Negev. The same day the Golani Brigade captured Bit Miliha, which we now call Be'er Menuha.

The western arm of our forces, the Negev Brigade, progressed very slowly because of the difficult terrain. The brigade entrenched itself fifteen kilometers south of Abraham Field. An aerial reconnaisance carried out over Um Rashrash, which had been a police station under the British, revealed the positions held by the Legion northwest of the station.

On March 9 the eastern wing (Golani) continued southward and reached Gerandal. The emplacements at Gerandal had been abandoned. The members of Golani assumed that the path down to Ein R'dian (today known as Yotvata) was open, but they soon learned that the enemy soldiers had not gone over to Trans-Jordan, but had entrenched themselves at Mount K'tora. There the Legion, equipped with tanks and mortars, was preparing an ambush. While the Legionnaires opened fire first, they did not cause us any casualties. The road to Ein R'dian was blocked, but not for long. When night fell, Golani dispatched lightly equipped units to outflank the enemy, after which the Legion withdrew. On the night of March 8 and the next day, March 9, the Golani units sent out men to seek a pathway to Eilat.

On March 10, we learned that the Legion had evacuated Ras a-Nakeb and Um Rashrash, and moved its forces to Aqaba. An aerial reconnaissance flight showed that the Legion posts on the hills overlooking Um Rashrash had been abandoned. Men from the Negev Brigade immediately rushed to seize the Ras a-Nakeb positions, and at noon they reached a peak from which, for the first time, they were able to see the Gulf of Eilat. The members of the company continued toward the gulf, and at 3 P.M. entered the abandoned police station, where they found a blue sign with *Police* written in English, Arabic and Hebrew.

Two hours later, after Golani had captured Ein R'dian without a battle, the advance guard of the brigade reached Eilat as well. A makeshift flag, white cloth on which a Star of David was drawn in ink, was raised. The following cable was sent to the Command of the southern front: "Please inform the Government of Israel that, on the occasion of Hagana Day, the Negev Brigade of the Palmah and the Golani Brigade present the Gulf of Eilat to the State of Israel.

The Arab Defeat as Seen by an Iraqi Inquiry Committee of Iraq Parliament

The Iraqi Parliament decided, after the fighting ended (on February 12, 1949), to set up a parliamentary inquiry committee to study the Palestine problem. Specifically, the committee was to investigate the failure of the Arab invasion. It was headed by Abdullah Dumlug; the other members were Jamil Urpali, Saad Amar, Ahmed el-Amar, Ahmed Hafez, and Ali Kamal.

The report in due time presented by the committee to the Iraqi Parliament included a historical survey of the period between the two World Wars. It dwelt on the British agreement with King Hussein, the Balfour Declaration, the Palestine riots, the 1938 Round Table Conference, the 1939 White Paper, the situation and activities of the Jews during the Second World War, American assistance to the Jews, the appointment of the Anglo-American Inquiry Committee and its decisions, the meeting of the Arab Legion Council at Bludan in June 1946, the talks between representatives of the Arab countries and the British government in September 1946, the meetings of the Arab League Political Committee in Lebanon on September 16, 1947, and in Egypt on December 8, 1947.

According to the report, the following secret resolution had been adopted at Bludan:

A. The Palestine situation is developing in an alarming manner as a result of the activities of the Zionist military organization and the terrorist groups, and because the Zionists tend to use force to achieve their aims. The Arabs of Palestine are liable to use the same means to defend themselves, in which case the situation of the Arab states will be very delicate, since they will not be able to prevent their citizens from offering their Palestinian brethren assistance in the form of money, arms, and manpower.

B. If the American and British governments approve the recommendations of the political investigating committee, and if these recommendations are implemented, relations between the Arab governments and those governments will worsen. The Arab states will defend themselves by carrying out the following measures: (1) No new economic concession will be granted to the United States, Britain, or their citizens. (2) The Arab states will not support the interests of the Americans or the British in any international organization. (3) A cultural boycott will be declared, (4) A study will be made of the possibility of canceling the concessions already granted to these states, (5) A complaint will be made to the UN Security Council.

The main activity of the parliamentary committee was to describe "military operations in Palestine." It thus provided an Arab version of the events recounted in the foregoing pages:

From the time the General Assembly approved the partition plan, and Britain announced that she was withdrawing her military forces from Palestine in May 1948, there was an increase in the activities of the Jewish bands, and their attacks became very serious. The Arab states remained complacent and continued their endless hand-wringing. If they had intervened at the proper time, they would certainly have saved themselves a great deal of difficulty and incalculable damage to the peaceful Arabs of Palestine.

Not only did the Arab states fail to make important decisions, they also failed to carry out the decisions that they made. In October 1947 the Political Committee decided that a Military Committee would be appointed to obtain urgent assistance for the fighters in

Palestine. The committee gave each Arab country a quota of weapons, and asked that they be supplied with the maximum possible speed. One country denied the validity of the decision and another sent outdated weapons that were unusable. There was a long series of such incidents. This situation continued despite the Iraqi communication and the many warnings which appeared in the reports of Emir Leva Ismail Tzafot.

The situation in Palestine became particularly serious with the withdrawal of the British forces. The areas evacuated by the British were immediately captured by the Zionists, who were thus able to strengthen their military position. In addition, they perpetrated atrocities in order to frighten the peaceful Arabs and force them to abandon their towns and villages. The Zionists hoped to confuse the Arab states, to keep them occupied with the refugees, and to dissuade them from carrying out their military plans. The Arab states filled the air with bombastic pronouncements about their ardent desire to free Palestine, but in fact no serious military preparations were made. In Iraq, in any case, the war was not felt. Thus units sent into battle suffered from shortages of equipment and ammunition. It is extraordinary how the Arabs, though they knew the bitter truth about Palestine and the determination of the Jews *to establish their State by force*, allowed themselves to lose so much valuable time.

Public opinion in the Arab world began to demand decisive action to save the Arabs of the Holy Land from being slaughtered by the Jews. It was against the background of this general enthusiasm that a meeting of the commanders of the Arab armies took place at the end of April 1948, fifteen days before the conclusion of the Mandate. The participants studied the situation from all sides, and after hearing a report by Emir Leva Ismail Tzafot, adopted the following decision: "After a discussion on the military situation, those present decided unanimously that, in order to defeat the Jewish forces, it is necessary to make available at least five well-equipped divisions and six wings of warplanes. In order to ensure their maximum efficiency, these forces must operate under a unified Arab command, on the basis of an advance plan."

This decision was made known to the Political Committee, which was meeting at the same time in Amman. But the Political Committee regarded the estimates of the generals as exaggerated and the number of soldiers demanded as too large. It demanded that operations begin with existing forces, and with the approval of the Arab governments. The members of the Committee apparently felt that if Arab forces were concentrated on the borders of Palestine, where they would shout menacingly, this would be sufficient to persuade the Great Powers to intervene on behalf of the Arabs and force the Jews to accept Arab demands. It was for this reason that the Arabs began their operations with only half the forces they really required.

On May 11 and 12, 1948, the Political Committee met in Damascus and adopted a great many decisions. Measures called for included the declaration of a state of emergency in the Arab countries, the imposition of press censorship, plans to deal with the refugee problem, etc. In addition, Emir Lua Rachan Nur Aldin Muhamed was appointed senior commander of the regular and irregular forces. But this appointment never actually went into effect.

Shortly before May 15, 1948, the Arab armies moved toward Palestine, and prepared to cross the borders of the country on that great day, which might have opened a new page in Arab history if the Arab states had been properly prepared. Instead, to our great regret, a disastrous period for the Arab nations began that day. In order to clarify a number of matters, we must first list several important factors which greatly influenced the pattern of events. On April 17, 1948, the UN Security Council adopted the following resolution:

1. The Security Council asks individuals and organizations in Palestine in general—and particularly the Arab High Committee and the Jewish Agency—to take the following measures to ensure peace in Palestine, measures which will not prejudice their rights or demands: (a) Stop military and semimilitary operations as well as the activities of terrorist

groups; (b) prevent the entrance of armed bands or groups of fighters into Palestine; (c) ban the import of weapons and military equipment into Palestine; (d) avoid any political activity which might harm the interests of the two sides, until such time as a form of government for Palestine is decided upon; (e) cooperate with the Mandatory authorities to maintain law and order as well as essential services, particularly transport, communications, health, foodstuffs, and water; (f) prevent any activity that might endanger the Holy Places or dissuade people from visiting them.

2. The Security Council asks the British government to persuade the two sides to accept this decision and to use its forces in the Holy Land to carry it out. The British government should inform the Security Council and the General Assembly of all developments in the country. Every state, and particularly those bordering on Palestine, should take measures to facilitate the implementation of these instructions, especially in regard to the entry of armed bands, ammunition, and other military equipment into the Holy Land.

Here we must point out that, after the UN statement, there was in Amman a gathering of Arab military men, who agreed to abide by the aforementioned decisions. As was stated before, during February, Emir Leva Ismail Tzafot was present at a meeting of the Political Committee in Cairo, where he reported on the military situation in Palestine. On March 23, 1948, he also presented a detailed report which said, *inter alia:* "While the Jews are receiving enormous quantities of weapons from overseas, the Arab armies lack vehicles. If they are really planning to save Palestine, they must prepare themselves properly and in time.

All the aforementioned details lead us to two important conclusions:

(1) The Arab governments knew that the UN partition resolution was contrary to the interests of the Arabs of Palestine. They realized that the Holy Land could not be saved, except by military intervention and that success in such an effort depended on the superiority of the Arab armies over the Zionist organizations, so that those organizations could be smashed and the UN presented with a *fait accompli.* (2) The Arab states also knew that the Jews had enormous forces and that time was working to their advantage. They realized that Arab military intervention would not be successful if it did not come as quickly as possible. The Arabs should have taken these factors into consideration, but they did not. They entered the fray with small, weak forces and this led to defeat on the field of battle. We must ask ourselves today: who can guarantee the safety of the Arab armies if the Jews should decide to concentrate their force for a strong attack aimed at destroying them?

The Arab armies crossed the borders of Palestine on the morning of May 15, 1948. At first they advanced through Arab areas and took them without resistance. But they met with very strong resistance when they came to the Jewish areas. Despite the courage of the Zionists, our units achieved important victories: the Jordanians captured the Old City of Jerusalem and our troops reached the outskirts of Tel Aviv. However, when the Jews saw that their situation was worsening, they turned to their American friends and asked that they intervene to bring about a cease-fire. The United States suggested to the United Nations that it declare the situation in Palestine a danger to peace in accordance with Section 39 of the UN Charter. The UN did not agree. The United States then made other proposals, which were the subject of the well-known debate.

Finally, a resolution was adopted calling for a cessation of military activities. At that point Count Bernadotte, the UN Mediator, appeared on the scene. It was decided that the truce should go into effect on June 11, 1948. The Arab states were not enthusiastic, and agreed only on condition that the borders be delineated according to the military situation of that date. There is no need to point out here that the Jews should not have been believed when they said that they would abide by the conditions of the truce. No force in the world could have stopped them from arming themselves and smuggling in troops who would join their ranks with the renewal of the fighting. It is now realized that the Arabs' agreement to the truce was their biggest mistake.

The reasons for their agreement are unknown, but it can be assumed that they were political rather than military, since the Arabs had the upper hand on all the fronts. The question of accepting the first truce was discussed by the Iraqi Parliament and at one meeting of the government as well. However, we cannot give the details of that meeting since it was secret. At another meeting the Foreign Minister, Natzrat el Parsi, said: "We accepted the truce in order to safeguard Arab unity." In any case, a great change in the military situation took place as a result of the truce. More than that, the whole front was undermined, as had been noted by the responsible military commanders. In the third part of the eleventh answer in the Ministry of Defense report, it is written: "As far as the second truce is concerned, it was only natural that we would agree to it, since we had agreed to the first one. It is known that the Jews exploited the truce to strengthen their military position. They received enormous quantities of weapons, ammunition, planes, and particularly, men. The Arabs were unable to coordinate their military operations. Thus, they were not in a position to embark upon any operation at the conclusion of the first truce."

In the second part of the Iraqi report presented to the Ministry of Defense on August 15, 1948, four days after the truce, it is stated: "The military situation was favorable to the Arabs until the truce. We believe that if the Arab states had made greater efforts, it would have been possible to tighten the noose around the Zionists and to capture their vital centers; perhaps the whole operation could have been completed soon thereafter. We must warn those concerned that if the Zionists are able to complete their preparations during the truce period (and they may be able to do so), they will be in a position to surprise the Arab armies, or some of them, with very forceful moves before the end of the truce, or immediately after it ends. The situation is made even more serious by the fact that, as we know, they are violating the truce in many ways."

In a report submitted to the Prime Minister on August 15, 1948, by a parliamentary delegation that had visited the front, it is stated: "The military operations in Palestine can be divided into four stages: (1) The first stage lasted from May 15, 1948, until the first truce on June 11. During that period, the Jordanian Army displayed extraordinary valor in Jerusalem, Bab el Wad, and Latrun. The Iraqi Army fought well in the Jenin and Mishmar Hayarden areas. Many Iraqi soldiers and enlisted men alike fell on the altar of honor. The Egyptian Army advanced as far as Isdud after a bitter struggle in which it lost many men. Generally speaking, the Arabs held the initiative; the Jews lacked artillery, airplanes, and tanks, Jerusalem and the Jewish villages suffered from severe shortages of food and ammunition. (2) The second stage—the period of the first truce—lasted for a month. During that time the Jews received considerable reinforcements and different types of weapons, which they used to strengthen their positions in the New City of Jerusalem, in other cities, and in their villages. During this period, the Arabs did not receive any reinforcements worthy of mention. (3) In the third stage the initiative passed to the Jews, who captured Lydda, Ramle, Safad, Nazareth, and a large number of Arab villages. The Arabs began to flee in ever larger numbers. (4) The fourth stage was the period of the second truce, which was violated by the Jews before the very eyes of the UN Observers. The Jews are continuing to fight in Jerusalem and threaten to capture it."

This is only a tiny excerpt from what was written and it shows how great a disaster befell the Arabs.

During the first truce, Count Bernadotte was unable to find a solution to the Palestine problem that would be acceptable to Jews and Arabs alike. Before the end of the truce the Security Council asked to extend it, but the Arabs refused since they were disappointed by the actions of the Security Council and decided to renew hostilities on the day and at the hour previously decided upon. The Arab public, which was expecting a quick victory, was very pleased with the decision of the Arab governments. It did not know that in the meantime military initiative had passed into the hands of the enemy.

In the first part of the seventh answer in the Defense Ministry report, it is stated: "The Jews were able to improve their military situation in violation of the truce conditions. They carried out constant local attacks along the entire front in order to obtain information on Arab units and their plans. Their planes carried out constant reconnaissance flights over our lines for the same purpose. They succeeded in photographing our positions. In addition, the Jews cleaned out Arab pockets of resistance, which had remained here and there in the areas under their control. They captured villages and drove out the residents, thus assuring themselves unimpeded lines of transport. The most glaring violation of the truce was their attack on isolated Arab villages: Jiba, Igzim, and Ein Razil (June 16, 1948)."

In the same section of the same answer, in the same report, it is stated: "The Jews gained great military advantages from the first truce. They doubled the number of their soldiers, trained them, and equipped them with the very best weapons. They used every possible means to achieve this end, including illegal ones, and spent enormous sums of money. They also employed secret agents all over the world, who provided them with the weapons and manpower that they required. Many of their soldiers were trained outside of Palestine. They also used a number of their ships to transport war supplies to their shores. When the fighting was renewed, they threw men and equipment into the battle that they did not have before the truce."

In the third part of the same answer it is stated: "The Arabs gained nothing at all from the first truce in view of the *small forces that they had at the front*, and because of the dissolution of the Arab Command, which, had it existed, could have coordinated the operations of the Arab armies. Moreover, *the Arabs, generally speaking, acted in accordance with the truce regulations and they did not send additional forces to the front for fear that they would be accused of violating the truce.* Nevertheless, Iraq sent eleven convoys with weapons and equipment to Trans-Jordan and Palestine during the truce. As was stated, when the battles began again, initiative had passed to the Jews, who conquered large areas, and when a second truce was suggested, all the Arab states agreed, except for Syria and Iraq, who opposed it for political reasons. In point of fact, their opposition was meaningless, for the fighting stopped on July 8, 1948."

The second truce. Various events which occurred during this period seemed to undermine the position of the Arab armies in Palestine. But this did not justify the fear that gripped the Arab states. They accepted the *status quo* and the possibility of peaceful compromise; in the end they participated in the Lausanne talks. This final step implied a recognition of the partition plan and of the State of Israel. Since they had abandoned the armed struggle and returned to appeasement, the Arab states approached the Palestine problem in a completely different manner than they had previously. Their demands at Lausanne concerned the borders of the State of Israel, the Jerusalem problem, and the return of the refugees.

During the period of the second truce, the UN General Assembly reconsidered the Palestine problem in view of developments there, and also took into consideration the reports it had received from Count Bernadotte. The Assembly accepted the existing situation, with minor adjustments, such as the internationalization of Jerusalem, special protection for the Holy Places, etc. The Arab governments did not agree with the UN position, but since Iraq was the only Arab country that did not take part in the Lausanne talks, and did not sign the armistice agreement, we see no reason to go into detail about this stage of the Palestine problem. As has been stated, Iraq remained an active enemy of Israel, but she could not maintain her armies where they were in the absence of military operations in Palestine. This was particularly the case after Trans-Jordan, which provided the base for the Iraqi

Army and protected its left flank, signed an armistice agreement with the Jews. Iraq therefore decided to withdraw from the area that she had conquered and turn them over to the Arab Legion. Since Iraq's attempts to unify the Arab states are presented in detail in a special and secret document, we saw no need to review them in this report.

Armistice Agreements with Lebanon, Trans-Jordan, and Syria ★ Iraq Withdraws Its Forces ★ Tasks Facing Israel at the War's End

The armistice with Egypt was signed on February 24, 1949. A week later, on March 1, talks began with Jordan and Lebanon. Lebanon participated in the war with Israel without enthusiasm and with limited forces, which were all she had. Moreover, the Christian section of the population was not interested in taking part in the conflict. Nevertheless, the Lebanese were not courageous enough to explore the possibilities of peace. Only after the Egyptians had signed an armistice agreement did talks begin with Lebanon.

They were concluded very quickly. After five meetings, an armistice agreement was signed at Rosh Hanikra, along the line of the accord with Egypt. Israel was in a superior bargaining position, because her forces had taken fourteen Lebanese villages during the last days of October 1948 when the Galilee was being liberated. Before discussing an armistice, the Lebanese demanded that these villages be evacuated. Our representatives, in turn, demanded that the Syrians evacuate the areas they had conquered around Mishmar Hayarden, and that armistice negotiations be carried out jointly with Syria and Lebanon. The Lebanese argued, not without justification, that these villages had been captured during the truce. Dr. Bunche supported the Lebanese and opposed making the evacuation of the Lebanese villages dependent on the evacuation of the Mishmar Hayarden area by the Syrians. Our representatives then demanded the withdrawal of Syrian units from Lebanon, and a prohibition of "military activities by a third party operating out of the territory of one of the signatories of the armistice agreement." After this demand had been accepted, the armistice agreement with Lebanon was signed on March 23, 1949. It resembled the agreement with Egypt.

Negotiations with Jordan began in Rhodes on March 1. The points in dispute with Jordan were more numerous than those with Lebanon. The front lines at the time of the negotiations were the same as they had been during the second truce. There had been several clashes between the Legion and the Israel Defense Forces during the second truce, the gravest of them in Jerusalem, but there had been no operations similar to those that had taken place in the south and in the north. On the eastern front we faced not only the Legion but the Iraqi Army. Moreover, the front was longer than either in the north or the south. Part of the railway line to Jerusalem was in Jordanian hands. The entire Old City of Jerusalem was held by the Legion. Mount Scopus, site of the Hebrew University and the Hadassah Hospital, had been demilitarized during the first truce, but the road to Scopus was controlled by the Legion.

In preliminary secret talks, Jordan demanded the return of the refugees to Lydda and Ramle and the free use of the port of Haifa, which would have freed Jordan of her dependence on Lebanese ports and on transport through Syria. Jordan also demanded the return of certain neighborhoods in the New City of Jerusalem to the Arab residents who had fled during the war. One agreement, on the convoys to Mount Scopus, was reached on December 25, 1948. The presence of the Iraqi Army in the center of the country created another problem. It was not clear whether the Iraqi Army would remain where it was, in the areas seized by Abdullah, or whether it would turn over these areas to the Legion. Jordan also demanded a discussion on the return of the refugees. Moreover, she protested against Israeli seizure of the western part of the Arava and the southern Negev.

The Iraqis hesitated for some time about whether to remain in the areas they held or to turn them over to the Legion. Finally they decided to withdraw. Abdullah saw a real chance of enlarging his kingdom on the western bank of the Jordan. He wanted to send the Legion immediately to take over the positions held by the Iraqi Army, but the Government of Israel protested that this step was a violation of the truce. The Legion was unsure about whether it would be able to conquer these areas by force.

While the negotiations with Jordan were going on in Rhodes, the Alexandroni Brigade, based in Beersheba, was charged with seizing the outposts on the southern and eastern slopes of the hills of Judea and moving toward Ein Gedi. An infantry company and a platoon of sappers left Sodom at nightfall on March 8. Despite the intense darkness, they identified the Ein Gedi shore. One unit entrenched itself by the spring, while a second took control of the ancient *tel* [hill] nearby. The third climbed up along a steep path to the edge of a cliff. The night was dark and rainy, the path narrow and slippery, but the unit reached its destination. When morning came, Ein Gedi and the surrounding slopes were in our hands. Subsequently, when the area south of Ein Gedi was placed within the boundaries of the State of Israel, we also gained control of Masada, bastion of the last desperate fighters against the Romans who continued to resist after the fall of Jerusalem to Titus, and who chose death rather than fall into the hands of their besiegers. This final Jewish stronghold, after the destruction of the Second Temple, was the final place captured by the Jews during the War of Independence of the Third Temple.

The decision of the Iraqis to withdraw their forces from the country was welcome to both the Jordanian and Israeli Governments. Our representatives in the negotiations, headed this time by Moshe Dayan, did not agree to Jordanian forces taking the areas evacuated by the Iraqis. They demanded, instead, that the border line be moved to the east, and that Wadi Ara, which connected Hadera with Afula, as well as part of the triangle in the east, be placed under the jurisdiction of Israel. Agreement was reached on free access to the Holy Place in Jerusalem's Old City, the use of the ancient cemetery on the Mount of Olives, the reconstruction of the pumping station at Latrun—which had been sabotaged by the Legion after the truce—the renewal of normal activities at the Hebrew University and the Hadassah Hospital on Mount Scopus and free access to them, freedom of movement along the Latrun-Jerusalem road, the supply of electricity to the Old City, and the renewal of travel along the railway line to Jerusalem. Except for the last item, namely, travel along the railway line to Jerusalem, not one of these provisions was put into effect until after the Six Day War.

A large proportion of the talks with Jordan took place at Abdullah's palace in Amman, but the armistice agreement was signed at Rhodes on April 3, 1949. Soon thereafter Israel Defense Forces entered Um el-Fahm, Baka el-Garbiya, and the other villages in the Wadi Ara area, as well as Beit Safafa and Batir, near the railway line to Jerusalem. Thus the whole line from Tel Aviv to Jerusalem was inside the boundaries of the State of Israel.

At the same time, our forces evacuated the area around Dahariya, on the road between Beersheba and Hebron.

The negotiations over the first three agreements lasted two months; but the negotiations with Syria alone took more than three and a half months, and were the most difficult of all. Syria's was the only Arab army that succeeded in capturing and holding, until the time of the truce, a part of the country that had been allocated to Israel under the terms of the November 29, 1947, resolution. Israeli representatives were not willing, under any circumstances, to forego this area around Mishmar Hayarden. The Syrians insisted on retaining it. Finally they agreed to withdraw, but in return they demanded compensation east of the waterline—the Jordan, the Hula, and the Kinneret. Under the Anglo-French agreement the waterline had been set as the eastern border of the country. During the negotiations with Syria a military revolution took place in Damascus, and Colonel Zaim took power. Zaim was supported by France, and this strengthened Syria's position in the negotiations, which began on April 5. All the compromises suggested by General Riley and the Acting Mediator, Dr. Bunche, were rejected, and on May 17 the talks ceased completely.

The deadlock lasted for a full month, until Bunche returned from the United States and presented a new compromise proposal: instead of having the truce lines run along the international border, this border would serve as the armistice line. In places where the two lines were not equivalent the armistice line would run between the truce lines of the two sides, and the area between the armistice line and the international border would be demilitarized. The purpose of this demilitarization, according to Dr. Bunche's proposal, was to ensure territorial rights until a final peace settlement could be reached, and meanwhile to separate the two opposing armies, which would evacuate the demilitarized zones and allow normal civilian life to begin again.

On the basis of these proposals the talks were resumed on June 16, 1949. The question then arose as to who would serve as the civilian authority in the demilitarized zones. Dr. Bunche said: "Civilian administration in the demilitarized zones, including the police, will be on a local basis, without reference to general administrative questions, the administration of justice, citizenship, and sovereignty. In places where Israeli citizens live, or to which they will return, civilian administration and the police will be Israeli. The same pattern will hold true in regard to Arab villages in the demilitarized zone. The chairman of the Mixed Armistice Commission will supervise the administration and will have the authority, in consultation and in cooperation with local residents, to restore civilian life and to safeguard their interests. But he will not bear direct administrative responsibility for the area."

This vague proposal, which laid the foundation for numerous future conflicts, provided the basis for an agreement. Another crisis developed when the Syrians demanded the inclusion of Zemah in the demilitarized zone, arguing that it had supposedly been captured by the Jews after the truce. But this argument was disproved and the Syrian claim was rejected.

The armistice agreement with Syria was signed on July 20, 1949, a date that marks the formal end of the War of Independence. But peace did not yet reign between Israel and her neighbors.

In the weeks that followed, the Syrians withdrew their forces beyond the international

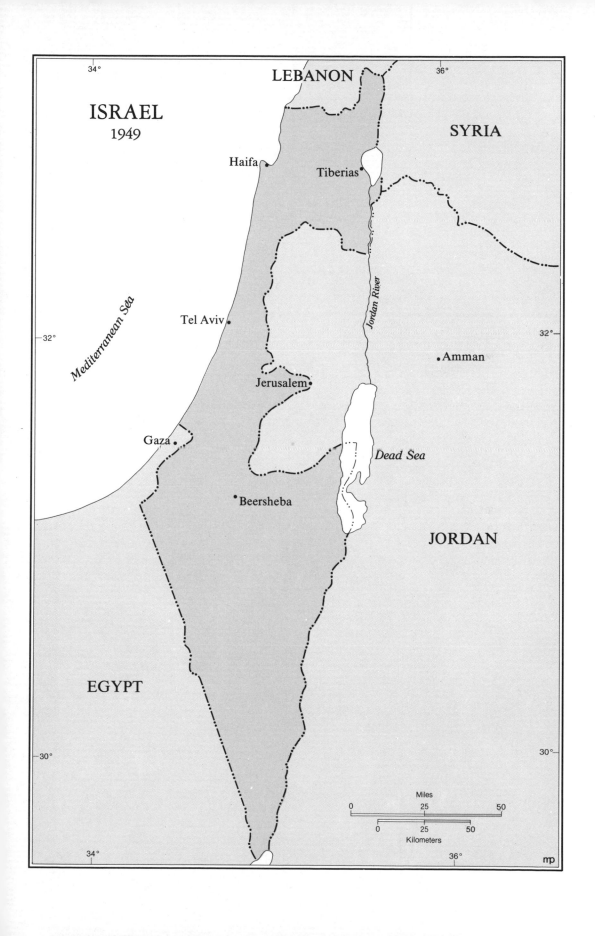

ISRAEL
1949

LEBANON

SYRIA

Haifa

Tiberias

Mediterranean Sea

Tel Aviv

Jordan River

Amman

32°

Jerusalem

Gaza

Dead Sea

Beersheba

JORDAN

EGYPT

30°

Miles
0   25   50

0   25   50
Kilometers

34°

36°

32°

30°

34°

36°

np

border, and Israel demilitarized the Ein Gev and Dardara areas, which remained under Israeli administration.

The Arab invasion of Israel, which took place without opposition from the United Nations, proved the weakness and bias of that organization. The two great powers, Soviet Russia and the United States, that supported the November 29 resolution calling for the establishment of a Jewish State, did nothing to prevent the Arab invasion, and did not even demand that the Arabs withdraw from the State of Israel. Without trying to underestimate the value of the November 29 resolution, it can be said without exaggeration or boastfulness that only the courage of the Israel Defense Forces permitted the establishment and guaranteed the existence of the State of Israel. The Defense Forces, moreover, were responsible for increasing the territory of the State. The UN resolution called for an Israel of 14,900 square kilometers. After the end of the fighting and the signing of armistice agreements with Egypt, Lebanon, Trans-Jordan, and Syria, Israel encompassed an area of 20,662 square kilometers. The New City of Jerusalem, Lydda, Ramle, Jaffa, and Beersheba, which had not been included within the boundaries of the Jewish State, were now Jewish cities within the State of Israel; in addition, a corridor was opened to Jerusalem.

Eight months after the establishment of the State, and a week after the fighting ended, on January 15, 1949, the Prime Minister spoke to a meeting of intellectuals—writers, teachers, scientists, and others. He said:

> For many years we must continue to devote our best efforts to safeguarding the security of the State. At the same time, it must be realized that security is only a means of ensuring our existence and independence. The State of Israel has another special goal: the salvation of the people of Israel and the ingathering of the exiles.
>
> Even in a period of national emergency, as for example during the first eight months of our national life—when we had to defend ourselves against the armies of five Arab states and establish an orderly regime and public services out of the chaos left behind by the Mandatory Government—there was no interruption in the flow of immigration; from the establishment of the State to the end of 1948, 101,825 immigrants reached Israel.
>
> With the cessation of fighting we are faced with the task of bringing in masses of immigrants and integrating them into the economy—in agriculture, industry, and trades; as well as building new cities and villages to absorb the hundreds of thousands of Jews who will be coming to Israel during the next four years. We must emphasize our settlement activities—the establishment of cities and villages on a scale unprecedented in the last seventy years. We must rapidly afforestate the hills, put in irrigation systems, fructify the soil, build houses, schools, factories, and laboratories. We must develop large-scale transport on sea, on land, and in the air. We must organize exports and imports, build roads and railways, etc., etc.
>
> But this is only one side of the coin. We are not bringing in herds of animals who have only to be transferred, fed, and housed. We are bringing in masses of Jews, who cannot live on bread alone. We are bringing in a unique people, scattered all over the globe, speaking many languages, steeped in foreign cultures, divided into numerous tribes and communities. *We must take this heterogeneous mass and mold it into a new nation.*
>
> We must remove the geographical, cultural, and linguistic barriers that separate the various sections of the population and give them one language, one culture, one citizenship, and one loyalty. We must provide them with new laws and a new system of justice. We must promote culture, literature, science, and art. We must develop new cultural and political frameworks; we must give the newcomers a sense of attachment to our past and a belief in our future. We must prepare them for the life of an independent people, a life based on

national sovereignty and self-rule, one endowed with freedom, Jewish unity, mutual assistance and collective responsibility. At the same time, we must concern ourselves with their security, the security of the State, its freedom and its place in the world. All this must be accomplished in a complex and dangerous period, at a time when the peace of the world is in the balance and we are surrounded by rivals and enemies.

How will we accomplish this great and difficult task? How will we bear the related economic, political, cultural, and organizational burden—we few? The entire Jewish people is very small. We have, with great difficulty, accumulated a small measure of material wealth in this country. But it will not be enough to provide for the large-scale immigration. We must accomplish in a short period of time, and with minimal resources, something we have never done before. We will be able to accomplish this mission *only if we mobilize to the fullest the one advantage that we do have—the moral and intellectual uniqueness of the Jewish people.*

Only if we mobilize to the fullest our moral strength and our intellectual abilities will we be able to overcome the enormous difficulties that we face in achieving the goals that we have set for ourselves. This means that we will not be able to depend solely on official bodies, on the members of the Government and of the Parliament. Official bodies will be required, but in themselves they will not be sufficient.

We must activate all the pioneering fervor within us and mobilize all the qualities in the Jewish heart and mind. I speak not only of the qualities of a few exceptional men, who have been richly endowed, but of the masses. For every man and woman has great powers hidden within him, and one has only to know how to reach and activate them. We revealed these powers when we established the pioneering movement. The young people who were responsible for one of the most fruitful revolutions in human history and who established a unique enterprise were not geniuses, but ordinary young men and women. The independence that we have attempted to create in the midst of war cannot be limited to the political sphere alone. The revolution that came with our independence will not be fulfilling its aims if it is limited to the political and military arenas. *The decisive revolution still lies ahead.* We must transform our land, our people, and our entire way of life.

Only if we remain loyal to our historic Jewish mission and to our vision will we prevail. As far as intellectual and moral qualities are concerned, the small but wonderful Jewish people is the equal of the greatest nations, and our educational system must be designed to foster these qualities. Only if we possess them will we be able to survive in a world of competition and hatred. *If we possess them, we will be able to blaze new paths for the world,* paths to peace, justice, freedom, and human fraternity. We can lead the way not by preaching, but by setting an example in our own lives, for the State of Israel must be an ideal state. It can be one if there is cooperation between the pioneering working class and the intellectuals.

IV

LINKS IN A CHAIN

Birth Pangs of Parliamentarianism; Coalition Cabinets; Relations with Communist Nations

---

Section 1. First Elections and Coalition Government

Election of the Constituent Assembly ★ *General Amnesty* ★ *The First Parliament Convenes*

SEVERAL months before the end of the war, the Provisional State Council and the Government began to discuss elections to the Constituent Assembly—afterward called the First Knesset. The discussions began on July 1, 1948, when the chairman of the State Council's Committee on Committees, David Zvi Pinkas (Mizrahi), proposed the establishment of an Election Committee, including representatives of all parties, each having the same number of votes as in the Council. On July 8 a thirteen-member Election Committee was chosen.

At the October 28 meeting of the Council the chairman of the committee, David Bar-Rav-Hai, presented a draft of an Election Code. The committee, he said, had been guided by the traditions of Zionist democracy. Some members had favored a system of constituency elections; others favored constituencies within which elections would be held on the basis of proportional representation. However, almost all agreed that, with a war in progress and most of the citizens under arms, such proposals had only theoretical significance. If they were to be held quickly, elections could take place only on the basis of nationwide proportional representation. All other systems would demand much more complex preparation than could be made in a short time, Bar-Rav-Hai explained.

Within the committee heated controversy developed as to the size of the Constituent Assembly. The majority view was for an Assembly of 171 members; the Government suggested 101. The committee finally accepted the Government's view, but allowed the minority who opposed it to bring the issue, if they so desired, to the State Council for a final decision. After some discussion, it was decided to set eighteen as the voting age. Members felt that if a young man was taken into the army at eighteen, he should also vote at that age. At first the committee suggested that twenty-five be set as the lower age limit for candidates to the Assembly; but after further discussion, the majority decided to accept the Government's proposal to set the age of eligibility at twenty-one. A minority favored eighteen instead of twenty-one.

A question was then raised about the voting rights of Cyprus internees, *i.e.*, the "illegal" immigrants who had been sent by the Mandatory Government to camps in Cyprus and who were still there. Despite the opposition of the Government, represented by Interior Minister Gruenbaum, the committee decided to give them the right to vote.

Gruenbaum explained that while all Israelis would have liked to see the internees in their midst, and sharing their rights, this could not be accomplished. The law clearly stated that elections could not be held outside the area subject to Israeli law. There was a special reason for this. The law accorded voting rights to residents of Israel, residents, that is, of that part of the Land of Israel—of the former British Mandate—ruled by the State of Israel. Some of these were outside the area where Israeli law prevailed. If voting rights were accorded to such people, outsiders would ask why these were extended to Jews and not to Arabs. It was also questionable whether the British would allow elections in intern-ment camps under their control. Certainly, Gruenbaum went on, we do not wish to go now to the hostile British government, which does not yet even recognize us, and ask it to permit us to arrange elections in the camps.

The Government decided that the Election Committee should be headed by a non-political personality representing law and justice, namely, someone designated by the members of the Supreme Court chosen on July 22. The Council accepted Warhaftig's proposal for a 120-member Constituent Assembly. Election Day, declared a holiday, was set for January 25, 1949.

Twenty-one parties participated. There were 506,867 eligible voters out of a total population of 782,000; 440,095 (87 percent of the eligible voters) cast their votes. Election Day was quiet and orderly. Nine lists failed to receive even one mandate (Hatzohar, Lema'an Yerushalayim, Hagush Ha'oved, Alcutla el Amala, R'shimat Haraidim, R'shimat Yahadut M'soratit, Hapoalot v'Ha'isha Hadatit, Ha'rishima Hameuhedet shel Poalim Datiim, Hagush Ha'amami Ha'aravi). The following parties gained seats: Mapai—155,274 votes, 46 seats; Mapam 64,618 votes, 19 seats; United Religious Front—52,982 votes, 16 seats; Herut—49,782 votes, 14 seats; General Zionists—22,661 votes, 7 seats; Progressives —17,786 votes, 5 seats; Sephardim—15,287 votes, 4 seats; Communists—15,148 votes, 4 seats; Democratic List of Nazareth District—7387 votes, 2 seats; Fighters' List—5363 votes, 1 seat; WIZO—5173 votes, 1 seat; Yemenites' Association—4399 votes, 1 seat.

About two weeks after the elections, on February 10, the State Council met for its fortieth and last session. First of all, the Council approved the proposal of the Emblem and Flag Committee. The Zionist flag had already been approved as the national flag by the Council at its meeting on October 28, 1948. At the previous meeting of the Council, the chairman of the Emblem and Flag Committee, Mrs. Beba Idelson, presented its proposal for a national emblem: a seven-branch Menorah on a broad base, with olive leaves at its sides and the word "Israel" engraved on it. The proposal was unanimously accepted.

Then the Council committees gave reviews of their work. The chairman of the Security Committee, David Zvi Pinkas, summarized its activities from its birth on August

12, 1948, some three months after the establishment of the State. It had replaced the Security Committee of the Yishuv. The committee's discussions had not reached the floor of the Council, since they took place in complete secrecy. At every meeting of the committee its members heard a report on the military situation from the Minister of Defense.

The Security Committee discussed, among other things, the budget of the Ministry of Defense and payments to soldiers. It held a searching discussion on the dissolution of the Palmah and on military censorship. It also considered the question of military organization. On several occasions the committee heard reports from the Chief of Staff, Brigadier Yacov Dori, and representatives of the Defense Ministry. Pinkas emphasized the harmonious relations at all times between the Minister of Defense and the Security Committee. The chairman expressed his thanks to the Israel Defense Forces and to the veterans of the Hagana.

Berl Repetur, chairman of the Immigration Committee, organized on October 9, 1948, pointed out that its activities had been limited by the fact that the Zionist General Council had entrusted the Agency Executive with the problems of immigration and absorption. His committee had concerned itself mainly with those areas for which the Government was also responsible. It held joint meetings with the Jewish Agency, chiefly on questions of absorption and immigration.

The work of the Finance Committee was reviewed by its chairman, Dr. Granovsky. The first discussion on the budget had taken place on May 19, 1948. It had been decided to authorize the Government to determine its own expenditures until July 1, at which time it was to present a six-month budget to the committee and the Council. But this proved extremely difficult. The Minister of Finance, Eliezer Kaplan, thereupon asked the Council to authorize a monthly budget not exceeding IL 700,000, with the committee deciding how the money was to be allocated. Only on September 30 was there a discussion of a six-month budget, running from July to December 1948, and totaling IL7.8 million. This was exclusive of the defense budget, which was not brought to the Council. At the meeting of the State Council on December 30 the Minister of Finance suggested that it adopt only a three-month budget, leaving it to the Constituent Assembly to adopt a long-term budget and to decide on the principles on which it would be based. Meanwhile, the Council adopted a one-month budget (for January 1949). It was set at one-sixth of the budget allocated for the last half of 1948, plus IL150,000. The Finance Committee was to allocate these funds. At the State Council meeting on January 27, 1949, the Minister of Finance proposed a three-month budget (to March 1, 1949) totaling IL4,835,000 (not including the defense budget).

Warhaftig reported on the work of the Constitutional Committee. Reports were also made by Nir-Raffalkes of the Legislation Committee, Kol of the Foreign Affairs Committee, Grabovsky of the Interior Committee, Dr. Altman of the Public Services Committee, Shattner of the Dependents of Soldiers Committee, and Pinkas of the Committee on Committees, which coordinated the work of all the committees and settled differences among the Knesset factions.

A brief survey of the events of the nine months (less four days) that had passed since the establishment of the State was then offered by the Prime Minister. He spoke of the suffering and courage of Jerusalem, almost without parallel in history; the ten-day battles, which had upset the political and military status quo in the Middle East and transformed the young State of Israel into the most important military power in the lands of the Bible;

the seven-day campaign in October, which had liberated the northern Negev; the sixty hours in the Galilee, which had liberated the whole area; and, finally, the last campaign, when the Egyptian invader was driven out of the entire Negev, opening the road to an armistice agreement.

"Having recalled all these proud developments," Ben-Gurion declared, "let us now bow our heads in memory of those fighters who gave their lives so that we might enjoy freedom and independence, and whose bereaved mothers and fathers can never be adequately comforted." Everyone present stood at attention.

The Prime Minister continued:

> During this period we overcame the chaos left behind by the Mandatory authorities and established the administrative, economic, and cultural organs of government. Special mention should be made of one of these, the one that has borne the brunt of the great historic revolution of the past year—I refer to the Israel Defense Forces.
>
> In this period we have thwarted attempts to violate the sovereignty of the State and eliminated military dissidence. We have taken in over 145,000 Jewish immigrants and set up 52 new agricultural settlements. We have transformed a number of abandoned cities into Jewish municipalities and we have been granted diplomatic recognition by 38 states. Finally, we have held democratic elections to a Constituent Assembly which took place in an orderly manner, reflecting self-respect and political maturity equal to that found in the most advanced countries.
>
> The Government proposes that the transition to orderly parliamentary life be marked at the final session of the State Council by granting amnesty to all citizens and residents who have committed crimes, whether or not they have already been sentenced for them, except in the case of such grave offenses as murder and treason, namely, offenses for which the penalty is death or life imprisonment.

After amendments offered by Nir, Riftin, and Warhaftig had been rejected, the Government's proposal was adopted unanimously.

The Minister of Justice, Rosenblueth, suggested that the President of the Provisional State Council read the following oath of office to the delegates at the opening session of the Constituent Assembly: "I swear to be loyal to the State of Israel and faithfully to fulfill my obligations as a member of the Constituent Assembly." After this oath is read each of the delegates, whose names would be called in alphabetical order, would rise and say: "I do so pledge." This formulation was accepted without dissent.

The chairman of the Council, Sprinzak, closed the meeting with the following remarks:

> This evening marks the end of the first stage in the life and the organizational structure of the State of Israel. It was from this chamber that the message of the State went forth. We learned to deal with the complex problems of political organization. We worked together in mutual friendship, a sense of collective purpose and responsibility. We took the first step; other steps will follow. The people of Israel will go on to win world respect for the way in which they organize their lives, for their creativity, and for their success in the ingathering of the exiles.

The entire audience rose and sang "Hatikva." The session concluded at 8:37 P.M.

Four days later, at 4 P.M. on February 14, 1949, the first session of the Constituent Assembly was held at the Jewish Agency building in Jerusalem. It was opened by the President of the Provisional State Council, Dr. Chaim Weizmann:

> It is with a feeling of reverence and awe that I rise to open this meeting of the Constituent Assembly of the State of Israel, the first Knesset of Israel in our era held in the Eternal City of Jerusalem. This event was made possible by the gigantic awakening of national will in recent generations. The first clarion call was sounded some seventy years ago. The very best of the nation's sons, the outstanding men of their generation, arose to fulfill the dream of many generations, the dream of a return to Zion, and the revival of our national independence.
>
> There were two paths to this revival. The first, the spiritual one, involved a return to the wellsprings of Judaism, a revival of the Hebrew language and Hebrew literature, mobilization of the scattered forces of the people into a united body, and finally, concerted educational and informational work. The two key way stations along this path were the Kattowitz Convention and the First Zionist Congress.
>
> The second path was the one chosen by the men of action who were unwilling to wait for a slow mobilization of forces in the Golah and for the rights of the Jews to be recognized by others. They surged forward to the Land of Israel, seeking to bring salvation by their own efforts, their own sweat and blood. They were the first pioneers, the Biluim, the pathfinders who laid the foundations for everything that was to follow. In their footsteps came generations of immigrants and settlers, until finally this vital community was created. Their heroism and sacrifices paved the way for the State of Israel.
>
> All my life I have striven to make science and research the foundation stone of our national enterprise. But I have always realized that there were values more sublime than those of science, values essential to healing the ills of mankind—I speak of justice and integrity, peace and brotherhood.
>
> "Zion shall be redeemed with justice, and they that return to her, with righteousness."
>
> The first Knesset of the State of Israel is hereby called to order.

After all the members (except for six who were absent) had taken the oath of office, Yosef Sprinzak was elected Speaker of the Constituent Assembly, and two Deputy Speakers were chosen. A thirty-three-man steering committee was also elected. The session concluded with the singing of "Hatikva."

That same day a forest was planted in Sha'ar Hagai in memory of those who had fallen in the war. Brigadier Dori read an Order of the Day. At the entrance to the pass there was a sign proclaiming: "Refrain thy voice from weeping, and thine eyes from tears; for thy work shall be rewarded." Bereaved parents and relatives, wounded veterans, comrades of those who had fallen, military units, the Chief Rabbis, the Diplomatic Corps, Military Attachés, IDF commanders, and members of the Knesset were present at the ceremony. The Prime Minister and the Chief of Staff were invited to plant the first trees. The Prime Minister said:

> The memory of the heroes who fell to save their people and their Homeland will not be preserved by the trees that we plant or the monuments that we erect. It will be preserved, rather, in the hearts of the Jewish people, and of every single Jew, in this generation and to the end of all generations. They will remember the awe-inspiring courage of the heroes who accepted the challenge of history and triumphed.
>
> Dear bereaved parents, and particularly you, the mothers: we realize how heavy a burden of grief you bear, but dear mothers and fathers, you have a privilege denied to tens

of thousands of mothers and fathers through all the generations of exile. Their sons were slaughtered without reason and without purpose. Your precious sons fell so that the Jewish people might enjoy independence in its Homeland.

Law Governing the Operation of the Knesset ★ Weizmann Elected President of Israel ★ He Calls on Ben-Gurion to Form a Cabinet

The Constituent Assembly held three more sessions, from February 15 to 17, during which it passed a series of basic laws to facilitate its operation.

The first speech by an Arab member was delivered at the end of its second day of work. Amin Salim Jarjura, representing the Nazareth Democratic Party, praised the credo embodied in the Declaration of Independence: "The State of Israel will be based on the principles of liberty, justice, and peace. It will uphold the full social and political equality of all its citizens, without distinction of religion, race, or sex," he said, and concluded with the following statement:

"We are pleased to see the first signs of an end to the struggle in the Holy Land, which will, we hope, be followed by treaties fostering neighborly relations between Israel and the surrounding Arab states. The fact that the young State of Israel has been recognized by the nations of the world is a source of pride to us. Support for Israel grows larger day by day. We must prove by our actions that we believe in justice and integrity, that we strive for freedom, tranquillity, and neighborly relations. We must serve as an example in the cultural sphere, by working for the benefit of all mankind."

On February 16 the Law of Transition proposed by Justice Minister Rosenblueth was adopted after having been considered in the Legislation Committee. Only two minor changes were made in the draft, which reads:

LAW OF TRANSITION, 5709–1949

Chapter One: The Knesset
1.   The legislative body of the State of Israel shall be called the Knesset. The Constituent Assembly shall be called "The First Knesset." A delegate to the Constituent Assembly shall be called "a member of the Knesset."
2.   (a)   An enactment of the Knesset shall be called a law.
      (b)   Every law shall be signed by the Prime Minister or Ministers charged with its implementation.
      (c)   The President of the State shall sign every law, except laws concerning his powers.
      (d)   Every law shall be published in the *State Records* within ten days from the date of its being passed by the Knesset.

Chapter Two: The President of the State
3.   (a)   The President of the State shall be elected by the Knesset by secret ballot.
      (b)   The candidate who obtains the votes of more than half of all the members shall be considered elected.
      (c)   If no candidate obtains a majority of votes as aforesaid, there shall be a second

ballot. If no such majority is obtained in the second ballot, voting shall continue, and in the third and any further ballot, the candidate who obtained the smallest number of votes in the preceding ballot shall not stand again for election. The candidate who in the third or any further ballot obtains the votes of more than half the members of the Knesset taking part in the ballot shall be considered elected.

4.   Within four days of his election, the President shall make and sign in the Knesset, or before the Chairman of the Knesset, the following declaration: "I, (name), pledge myself as President of the State of Israel to be loyal to the State of Israel and to its laws."

5.   The President of the State shall hold office for the duration of the term of office of the First Knesset and until the expiration of three months from the convening of the new Knesset.

6.   The President of the State shall sign treaties with foreign states which have been ratified by the Knesset; appoint, upon the recommendation of the competent Minister, the diplomatic representatives of the State; receive diplomatic representatives of foreign states who have been sent to Israel, and approve the appointment of consuls of foreign states; he shall also be empowered to pardon offenders and to reduce punishments.

7.   Every official document signed by the President of the State shall be countersigned by the Prime Minister or by such other Minister as may be designated in that behalf by the Government.

Chapter Three: The Government

8.   Immediately upon the election of the President of the State, the Provisional Government shall render to him its resignation, but it shall continue to exercise its functions pending the constitution of a new Government.

9.   After consultation with representatives of the party groups within the Knesset, the President of the State shall entrust a member of the Knesset with the task of forming a Government.

10. The Government shall consist of the Prime Minister and of a number of Ministers, who may or may not be members of the Knesset.

11. (a) As soon as the Government has been formed, it shall present itself to the Knesset, and after having obtained a vote of confidence, it shall be considered as constituted.

   (b) Within seven days of the date on which the Government obtains such a vote of confidence, the Prime Minister and the other Ministers shall read and sign before the Knesset the following declaration: "I, (name), as a member of the Government, pledge myself to be loyal to the State of Israel and to its laws and to comply with the decisions of the Knesset."

   (c) The Government shall be jointly responsible for its activities to the Knesset, shall report on its activities, and shall hold office as long as it enjoys the confidence of the Knesset.

   (d) A Government that receives a vote of non-confidence from the Knesset, or that has decided to resign, shall immediately tender its resignation to the President of the State, but it shall continue to exercise its functions pending the constitution of a new Government in accordance with the provisions of this law.

Chapter Four: Further Provisions

12. The Government shall have all the powers vested by law in the Provisional Government.

13. Everything required by law to be published in the *Official Gazette* shall henceforward be published in the *State Records*; every reference in the law to the *Official Gazette* shall henceforward be deemed to be a reference to the *State Records*.

14. Section 1(c) and (d), section 2(b) and(c), the second sentence of section 7(a), and section 7(b) of the Law and Administration Ordinance, 5708–1949, are hereby repealed.
15. This Law shall have effect from the date of its being passed by the Knesset.
Passed by the Knesset on the 15th Shevat 5709 (16 February 1949).

David Ben-Gurion
Prime Minister

On February 16, 1949, the Assembly discussed the election of a President. Speaking on behalf of the Steering Committee, Rubashov [Shazar] announced that there were two candidates for the Presidency, Professor Chaim Weizmann and Professor Yosef Klausner.

Peri (Mapam) declared: Our faction has decided to support the candidacy of Dr. Chaim Weizmann. In so doing, we demonstrate our appreciation of Dr. Weizmann's personality and his labors over the years on behalf of the Zionist enterprise, as well as his loyal cooperation with the pioneers in the Land of Israel. We particularly favor Dr. Weizmann over the candidate of the Herut Movement, founded by Etzel, whose character and ambitions are well known. At the same time, we wish to make it clear that our support for Dr. Weizmann does not indicate support for his political program.

Ben-Eliezer (Herut) said: The President of the State must represent the Hebrew State, its greatness and glory. His personality must symbolize the dream of freedom and independence of many generations, as well as the renewed traditions embodied in the War of Independence. He must be a wise and devoted man who reflects the tradition of those who paved the way for their people. The Herut Movement cannot, therefore, support Chaim Weizmann. We will cast our votes instead for Yosef Klausner, who, in his writings, has told the glorious story of our earlier wars of liberation, and who has provided the basic texts for a whole generation of fighters and rebels. As for what was said a moment ago, I have only one comment: we have never argued with collaborators, and we don't intend to begin now.

(Ben-Eliezer's last remark touched off an uproar in the hall. There were cries of "Boo! Fascists! Followers of Mussolini! Collaborators!")

Wilner, for the Communists, announced that they would vote for neither Weizmann nor Klausner.

Friedman-Yellin (Fighters' List) announced that he would not vote for Weizmann.

Dr. Weizmann was elected by a vote of eighty-three to fifteen. Six members (four of whom were abroad) did not participate and fifteen blank ballots were cast.

The Speaker invited all members of the Knesset to be present the next day at 11:30 A.M., when the first President would take his oath of office at the Knesset. A special delegation representing the Presidium went to Dr. Weizmann in Rehovot to invite him to the session.

The next day, February 17, 1949, the Speaker, presiding at a meeting held in the Jewish Agency building in Jerusalem, told how a delegation had left for Rehovot at 7 A.M. It had been composed of himself and the two Deputy Speakers, Nir and Burg, as well as Knesset members Rokah, Dr. Granovsky, Elmaleh, Rabbi Nurok, Kahana, Rachel Cohen, Mrs. Ada Fishman, Smilansky, Tabib, Said Mohamed Seif el Din El Zabi, Hazan, and Rubashov. The road to Jerusalem was lined with people as they returned with Dr. Weizmann. At Motza, on the outskirts of Jerusalem, the President was greeted by the Mayor and handed the key to the city.

A shofar was blown at 12:35 and, at the same time, Dr. Weizmann entered the hall. The members of the Knesset and the public rose to their feet.

The Speaker declared: "Chaim, son of Ozer and Rachel Weizmann, please raise your right hand as I read to you the oath you will take as President of the State of Israel: 'I, Chaim, son of Ozer and Rachel Weizmann, hereby pledge, as President, to be faithful to the State of Israel and its laws.' " Dr. Weizmann raised his hand and declared: " I hereby pledge to be faithful to the State of Israel and its laws." The Speaker exclaimed, "Long live the President!" The audience broke into wild and prolonged applause. Rabbi A.H. Shaag proclaimed: "Blessed be our Father in Heaven who has honored those who fear him." The audience responded: "Amen."

"I wish to thank you for the great honor that you have bestowed upon me by electing me First President of the State of Israel," Dr. Weizmann said. "I will strive with all my heart and soul to fulfill this exalted mission to the benefit of my people and of all the citizens of the country. I have been entrusted with a momentous task. I am only a human being and I may, God forbid, fail; but if I do, it will not be for want of trying.

"At this great moment in my life, in the lives of all of us, I wish to send my warmest greetings to all the citizens of Israel and to the Jewish people all over the world. I know that anything we do or fail to do in this country will affect our entire people. It is with a sense of heavy responsibility that I assume the office of President of Israel." (Prolonged and stormy applause.)

The Speaker then declared: "I hereby close our sessions in Jerusalem, where we have fulfilled the dream of generations, a dream that did not die despite suffering, expulsion, torture, and *autos-da-fe*. The provisional stage in the life of the Knesset has now been completed. The representatives of the people of Israel have come together to establish and shape the independent State of Israel, to strengthen and safeguard it so that all our far-flung exiles can be gathered together in this land. At this session we have chosen a President. In the sessions to follow we will choose a permanent Government. We have taken the first step toward building our lives. Israel's salvation is at hand."

There was a stormy applause. The members of the public and the Knesset sang "Hatikva."

On February 24 the President informed Ben-Gurion that after consulting political parties, he was entrusting him with forming a Government. The Provisional Prime Minister was at that time confined to his bed. But even earlier, on January 29, when the results of the elections to the Constituent Assembly had become known, he had broadcast some remarks over Kol Yisrael about the composition and goals of the new government:

> It appears that I will be entrusted with establishing and heading a Government. I believe it will be of benefit to the public if I enumerate, even before talks begin, the principles that will guide me in my discussions with all those who wish to participate in the Government. There are four points to which I attach particular importance:
>
> 1. The acceptance of collective responsibility for the policies of the Government by all parties participating in it.
>
> 2. A foreign policy aimed at achieving friendship and cooperation with the United States and the Soviet Union; a pact between Jews and Arabs; loyal support for the United Nations; and a strengthening of world peace.
>
> 3. A labor majority in the Government and cooperation with constructive forces.

4. Complete civil equality for women—Jewish, Christian, and Moslem—and the abolition of all existing discrimination against women as embodied in Turkish and Mandatory laws that are still on the books. These laws deny women full equality and civil rights. On the day we established the State we proclaimed that it would accord equal rights to all its citizens without regard to religion, race, or sex. Let us be faithful to that declaration.

It seems to me that these four points reflect the feeling of a decisive majority of the citizens of the State of Israel, and they will obligate any government that is to be established. But one thing is clear, the Constituent Assembly will make the final decisions—and its sovereign wishes be respected.

Six days later, on February 4, 1949, the Prime Minister spoke at a meeting of workers; he added two more points to the four he had enumerated in his broadcast to the people:

1. Even more than before we need a partnership between the State of Israel and the Jews of the Diaspora. The existence, development, and security of the State depend on a common effort by the entire Jewish people—Zionists and non-Zionists alike—to carry out the tasks imposed upon the State. There must be another partnership inside the country itself. *I speak of a partnership between the workers and the other constructive forces among the people, to the extent that they exist.* The tasks that lie ahead are so great and difficult, and the time at our disposal is so short, that we cannot overlook the constructive forces that exist outside the labor movement. *The mission we have taken upon ourselves is not an easy one, and it will not be accomplished if we are unable to mobilize the assistance of all the Jews in the Diaspora and all the constructive forces in Israel.*

We have not borrowed values from others. We did not adopt the approach of the German Social Democrats when they were still the leading force in the international labor movement before the First World War. We did not copy the ideas of the British Labour Party when it grew in importance and influence. We did not follow in the footsteps of Soviet Communism. *We paved our own path; it is along this path that we have moved forward and will continue to do so.* We are the sons of a people whose fate differs from that of all other peoples, and we are faced with a task that was not imposed upon the workers of any other country.

2. We must raise the standard of living and improve cultural conditions. This is not only a matter of laws. Unless we raise the productivity of the worker, improve vocational education and upgrade the quality of our work, we will not be able to improve our standard of living. And unless the workers learn how to manage the economy, unless they understand all aspects of production and accept responsibility for the organization and success of the economy, we will not be able to create a new society.

Our standard of living will depend first and foremost on our productivity. We will obtain from the economy only what we put into it. Our ability to produce will determine the economic condition of the country, and productivity will determine the workers' standard of living. One does not create a new society by revolutionary declarations or simply by gaining political power.

Negotiations for Coalition ★ *General Zionists and Mapam Withdraw* ★ *Religious Front, Progressives, and Sephardim Enter the Government*

Immediately after the President asked him to form a Government to be presented to the First Knesset, Ben-Gurion turned to all the constructive parties—from Mapam to the General Zionists, as well as Hapoel Hamizrahi and Agudat Israel—to discuss the establishment of the Government on the basis of the aforementioned principles.

That day (February 24, 1949) the Provisional Prime Minister, having left his sickbed and returned from Tel Aviv to Jerusalem, met with three factions: The General Zionists, the Religious Front, and Mapam. All three discussed the program of the Government and the distribution of Cabinet posts. It was difficult to judge what was more important to these parties, the program or the portfolios. The General Zionists, who had seven members in the Knesset, demanded two portfolios; the Religious Front, with sixteen members, demanded three; Poalei Agudat Israel asked for an additional portfolio; Mapam, with nineteen representatives, wanted three posts.

The General Zionists were the first to meet with Ben-Gurion. Their delegation consisted of Sapir, Mrs. Shoshana Persitz, and Israel Rokah. Mrs. Persitz asked the Prime Minister how he expected the Government to operate. The Prime Minister quoted the memorandum that had previously been sent to the General Zionists:

> The Government of Israel, if it is to fulfill its responsibilities, must encourage private, government, and international capital, as well as foster all creative enterprise, private and collective, rapidly and efficiently to exploit the country's natural resources and economic possibilities so as to facilitate the absorption of mass immigration. Just as we must save the remnant of Israel from the Diaspora, so must we save the remnant of Jewish capital—without these two things we will be unable to build up the country.
>
> The Government must also promote the development of rural and urban labor enterprises, the expansion of labor settlements and cooperatives of all types; the development of the trade union movement—encompassing all workers; the enactment of progressive labor, land, and social welfare laws; the uprooting of illiteracy, overcrowding, and illness in the slum neighborhoods; the amelioration of the social conditions of Oriental Jews and the removal of barriers between communities; and the improvement of the standard of living and conditions of work, education, and health of the entire population without reference to nationality.

His party represented the little man, the small merchant, craftsman, and grocer, Rokah said. Sapir explained that the General Zionists opposed giving the collective sector of the economy preference over the private sector. He did not believe that there were any basic differences in the sphere of foreign policy. However, the General Zionists opposed Mapai's view that the Government should be based on an economic program aimed at achieving Socialist Zionism, which meant that the collective sector of the economy would be favored, both in law and in practice. They demanded equality between the collective and private sectors.

Mrs. Persitz declared that the experience of the nine months since the establishment of the State showed that their fears were well founded. Laws were adopted, she contended, though temporary, without the public being allowed to express its opinion about them. Our Government should follow the example of the British Government. In Britain every law is discussed in Parliament during the first reading, and then there is time between the first and second readings to discuss it again.

Ben-Gurion indicated that he was not sure whether it would be possible to follow British practices. Britain was already developed; Israel was not. There were many urgent problems facing Israel. It had been impossible during the months of the war, he said, to tell the Egyptians and their compatriots: wait until we have a chance to train our Army.

For the lack of any alternative, untrained men were sent into battle and, as a result, Israel suffered setbacks. Such things might happen in other spheres as well. The Government must lead the Parliament, it must take the initiative. This did not mean that the Government presented its views on a "take it or leave it" basis. There was opportunity for discussion and clarification, and the Government was obligated to heed the views of others. Moreover, its draft laws could be amended. But after discussion had taken place and a decision reached, every party in the Government would bear responsibility for carrying out this decision, even if, deep inside, the party was opposed to it. A particular party would simply have to decide whether it was worth sharing responsibility for a policy that it did not like in order to share responsibility as well for vital matters. Agreement had to be reached on a program for a specific period of time.

Mrs. Persitz: What period of time?

Prime Minister: In my opinion, a program should be worked out for a four-year period. It would aim at bringing in an additional million Jews, which is absolutely necessary for security reasons, as well as justified in its own right. If the fighting were not renewed, most of the soldiers would be released from the Army. This is not such a simple matter. We could not simply throw out people who saved us from destruction. We must take care of them. There will also be new immigrants. These are the most pressing issues. We will have to act quickly and energetically. It is no simple matter to fight a war, develop a country, and absorb mass immigration. If we find after a year that we have made mistakes, then we will correct them.

Mrs. Persitz: There is a controversy over wages and productivity. We must, first of all, know the Government's attitude on these questions.

Prime Minister: I am not ready to discuss these matters. Do you mean to say that there is an ideological gulf separating us, and that there is no possibility of establishing a coalition?

Sapir: We must find out how the gulf between us can be bridged.

Prime Minister: The bridge must be a common desire to carry out the ingathering of the exiles. This must be the basis for common action.

Mrs. Persitz: You have spoken about a coalition and not about the make-up of the Cabinet.

Prime Minister: I favor a Cabinet with eleven or twelve ministers. That is the number of basic tasks. I intend to establish a coalition encompassing the General Zionists, the Progressives, the Sephardim, Mapam, the Religious Front, and Mapai.

Mrs. Persitz: How many portfolios do you intend to give to each party?

Prime Minister: I am in favor of a one, one, one, two, two, five distribution.

Mrs. Persitz: You mean to say that the Progressives, the Sephardim, and we will each have one portfolio? I doubt whether we will be able to participate on such a basis. If there were to be twelve portfolios, we should have two.

Prime Minister: How large a coalition do you foresee? If I give you two portfolios, how many will I give to the others? You must take into consideration the Government as a whole.

Sapir: If we are to bear responsibility in a government in which we will be a minority, then we will have to have at least two Cabinet posts.

Prime Minister: You must tell me how many members there will be in the Cabinet! In my opinion, we need eleven or twelve ministers. If you refuse to budge from your demand for two portfolios, I think we will have very grave difficulties.

A second meeting was scheduled for the next day. That afternoon there was a meeting with the representatives of the Religious Front: Kalman Kahana, Rabbi Yitzhak Meyer Levin, David Z. Pinkas, and Moshe H. Shapira. They divided the portfolios into three categories: major, intermediate, and minor, asking one portfolio of each type. They knew that Ben-Gurion favored that the State supply religious needs, and opposed religious or antireligious coercion. They were satisfied with the arrangements for Kashrut (dietary laws) in the Army, but what bothered them, aside from the distribution of portfolios, was Sabbath observance and the use of the Jewish law as the basis for the laws of the State.

Pinkas said that the Religious Front did not want to impose all aspects of Sabbath observance on the general public, but was interested in the character of the Sabbath in Israel. He demanded that the Religious Front be given four ministers, so that Poalei Agudat Israel could be represented in the Cabinet, perhaps by a deputy minister.

The *Prime Minister* responded that Jewish law could be adopted where it met the requirements of modern life. The Sabbath would undoubtedly be a legal holiday, but it was also necessary, to put it brutally, to desecrate the Sabbath, for example in the case of the telephone and telegraph. An internal railway might not run on the Sabbath, but an international railway, if it existed, would have to run on the Sabbath. The State certainly had to be given a Jewish character, without harming the Moslems or the Christians. The most difficult problem was the distribution of portfolios. The General Zionists had demanded two and spoken about relative weights. But if every party considered its own relative standing, according to the General Zionist scheme, the Religious Front should have five portfolios, Mapam almost six, and Mapai fourteen. We cannot set up such a large government. There are also the Sephardim and the Progressives to consider; each should have a least one portfolio. This country does not need more than twelve ministers.

Shapira suggested a Cabinet with fourteen or fifteen members, divided as follows: three to the Religious Front, three to Mapam, one to the General Zionists, and seven to Mapai.

It was decided to continue this discussion at a second meeting.

That same evening Ben-Gurion met with the representatives of Mapam, Yitzhak Ben-Aharon and Yacov Riftin. He told them briefly about his talks with the General Zionists and the Religious Front, and suggested that the Mapai platform serve as the basis for the coalition. He had read part of the platform to the General Zionists (on economic questions), and the part on religion to the Religious Front; now he read the section beginning with "constructive efforts to promote the ingathering of the exiles" and ending with "improving the standard of living, education, and health of the entire population, without reference to nationality" to the representatives of Mapam.

Ben-Aharon: Can these goals be achieved?

Prime Minister: That depends on you.

Riftin read an excerpt from the Mapam platform: "Taxes should be levied mainly on the well-to-do sections of the population (*i.e.*, there should be an increase in property taxes and direct taxes, together with a reduction in indirect taxation)."

The *Prime Minister* remarked that he could not accept something that was in Mapam's platform, but not in Mapai's.

Riftin said that the Prime Minister had made no reference to the position of the Histadrut.

Prime Minister: Reference is made to a single labor organization.

Riftin continued to read from the Mapam platform: " Inflation must be combated by reducing the profits of the industrialists and merchants, imposing severe penalties on speculators, rationing, the distribution of goods according to fixed prices and in fixed quantities, subsidies to lower the cost of vital commodities, a government monopoly on imports, and a rejection of any proposal to freeze wages." Riftin then added: "We are presenting an ultimatum. We must reach agreement on a program acceptable to the labor majority in the Government."

Prime Minister: There must be an agreement among all members of the coalition. Perhaps only our two parties will be in the coalition, but if there are other parties, they must also agree to its platform.

Riftin: In education there is the question of having parents decide on the type of school to which their children will be sent. Matters of personal status must be governed by civil law and there must be an independent foreign policy.

Ben-Aharon suggested the appointment of a joint committee of the two parties to discuss economic policy.

Prime Minister: Until now I have left economic matters to Kaplan because I was primarily interested in the war. From now on, I will not depend solely on him because I am now concerned with bringing in a great many Jews in a short period of time. We will eventually establish a socialist regime, but for the immediate years ahead our main concern must be immigrant absorption. Our national income is very small. It must be increased by raising productivity, using more modern machinery, introducing improved management techniques, and restraining the greed of the capitalists—all this demands planning.

Ben-Aharon again suggested a meeting between two representatives of Mapai and two representatives of Mapam to discuss the plan.

The *Prime Minister* said that he first had to discuss the matter with his party.

Riftin raised the question of foreign policy.

The *Prime Minister* answered: We favor friendship with the two powers, an alliance between Jews and Arabs, strengthening the United Nations and world peace.

Riftin voiced suspicion of the US. The Americans, he said, had not accepted the borders of the State of Israel. James MacDonald, the American Ambassador, had not come to the opening of the Knesset, while Pavel Yershov, the Soviet Ambassador, had come. There was also the question of the Marshall Plan.

The *Prime Minister* said that he did not reject the Marshall Plan as such. If Israel were asked to join, she would discuss the conditions.

Ben-Aharon turned to the composition of the Cabinet.

The *Prime Minister* said that he would suggest what he had already suggested to the other parties: a broad coalition with a twelve-member Cabinet—one each for the Sephardim, the Progressives, and the General Zionists, two each for Mapam, and the Religious Front, and five for Mapai. This would mean a slight injustice for Mapam, and a much greater one for Mapai. It would give a small bonus to the Religious Front, as well as to the Sephardim and the Progressives. The General Zionists also gained a bit. One could not divide portfolios with mathematical exactitude, he said.

Ben-Aharon: Why do we need the Sephardim?

Prime Minister: I know that the Oriental immigrants will not vote for the Sephardim, but then we cannot have a Cabinet in which a whole section of the population remains unrepresented.

Ben-Aharon: Isn't there room for the Communists as well in a broad coalition?

Prime Minister: The Communists cannot be compared to the Sephardim. The Communists are capable of supporting the Mufti, as they did during the Mandate period.

The rest of the discussion was devoted to the distribution of Cabinet posts.

Ben-Aharon demanded three portfolios for Mapam. "Let us assume that we reach agreement on a common program concerning both domestic problems and foreign affairs," he said. "Nevertheless, there will still be the question of our role in the Government. We must be the number-two faction in the Government and must have three portfolios. Three for us will mean seven for Mapai, which will be discriminated against only to a slight degree. However, I suggest such a discussion with a clear conscience, because you will have the Premiership, the Finance Ministry, and the Foreign Ministry."

Ben-Aharon asked that either the Defense portfolio or the Labor portfolio be assigned to Mapam. Ben-Gurion replied that he still hadn't discussed the matter with Mapai. There was need, he said, for a four-year plan covering housing, settlement, finances, the standard of living, vocational education, productivity, and the efficient management of the economy. Government planning was required. At the same time there was also room for free enterprise. Ben-Aharon thereupon announced that he would put Mapam's conditions in writing and that his party would also inform the Prime Minister as to which portfolios they demanded. It was decided to meet again two days later, on February 27, 1949.

In the interim, on February 25, there was the second conference with the General Zionists, who were again represented by Sapir, Shoshana Persitz, and Rokah. Mrs. Persitz stated: We have two portfolios in the present Government, and we must have at least that many if we are to participate in the next Government; otherwise we will not be able to fulfill our tasks properly. How many cabinet members did she envisage altogether, Ben-Gurion asked. She answered: That's for you to decide; we do not favor a twenty-member Cabinet.

Rokah: We must have at least two portfolios. We will not be able to arrange matters among ourselves unless we do. I spoke yesterday with Shenkar (the head of the Manufacturers' Association), who said: It is true that we have only twelve hundred members, but they employ forty or fifty thousand workers. You want to provide work for another five thousand people by establishing new industries. What will one poor representative be able to do? In the agricultural field, we have links with the citrus growers. They want us to defend their interests. We have not come to ask for charity; in point of fact, you need us.

Prime Minister: If the growth of industry and citrus—two very important branches, which I hope will be even more important in the future—are endangered by the "gang" that will be running the Government, what good will two ministers be? Just consider the consequences of your proposal. Yesterday, I met with representatives of the Religious Front. They demand three portfolios. They also have three representatives in the Provisional Government. Why should this number be reduced? They speak on behalf of the Torah, while you speak on behalf of the citrus growers. The Torah is also important. I do not agree with what they say, but I understand them. They argue that they have three members in the Provisional Government, and that they represent Orthodox Jewry, the wellspring of Judaism. They want the country to be governed by the laws of the Torah. In the meantime, they are willing to compromise on that point, but they want three portfolios. If you have two Cabinet posts, they will demand four. Your party received 22,661 votes, while they received 52,982. If it is a matter of votes, they should have five representatives. You speak of economic weight, they speak of religious weight. I offered them two representatives within the framework of a twelve-member Cabinet. They are ready to accept a fifteen-member Cabinet. If your proposal is adopted, there will be a twenty-five-member Cabinet.

Rokah: There are many justified demands from various circles, ones which the Religious Front cannot represent. I speak of the small merchants, the middle class. How can we properly defend these groups if we do not have at least two Cabinet posts? Their interests cannot be safeguarded by any other group, not by the Sephardim, and not by the Yemenites. I envision a fourteen-member Cabinet: Mapai—five representatives; Mapam—three; the Religious Front—three; the General Zionists—two; and the Progressives—one. You want to bring in another million Jews over the next four years. These ministers will then be responsible for one million Jews. It won't be so terrible if there are fourteen members in the Cabinet; this number would satisfy everyone.

Prime Minister: You do not realize how this arrangement will appear to others. You say it is not numbers but wisdom that counts. The trouble is that everyone has his own conception of wisdom. Mr. Pinkas claims to represent the merchants and the citrus growers as much as Rokah. Can we tell the religious parties that they should not have more than twice as many representatives as the General Zionists? They argue that they are not only more numerous but on a higher level. Then there are my friends on the Left, who won over 64,000 votes, almost three times as many as the General Zionists. Will they agree to having only one and a half times as many representatives as you have? They believe that every one of their supporters is worth several General Zionists. The Sephardim received 15,287 votes, as against your 22,661. Can we leave them without a minister? You won only 2500 votes more than the Progressives. Finally, will the Mapamniks agree that two of their votes should be worth only as much as one of your votes? They argue, not without justification, that they are pioneers, that they fought in the Hagana and in the Palmah; if you receive two portfolios, they will demand six.

Sapir: There is a certain logic in what you say. But Mapai and Mapam together constitute a majority, and even if we have two portfolios, their majority will remain intact.

Prime Minister: Mapam regards itself as a completely independent entity, not as part of Mapai. If you are given two representatives, that will mean one portfolio for about ten thousand votes. The Progressives will then have about six thousand votes left over; let us assume that they won't ask for another portfolio, and that neither will the Sephardim. But the religious parties won almost as many votes as you did, Mapam almost six times as many, and Mapai fourteen times as many. This shows you the absurdity of the suggestion.

Mrs Persitz: You were able to overcome Jewish logic on other occasions, for example in regard to a unified army.

Prime Minister: Then the majority was with me, but when it comes to forming a government, I must negotiate with political parties. I know that the other parties—I've not discussed the matter with my own—will not accept your logic. I will do everything I can to include you in the coalition, but if I have to choose between having you, and having Mapam, then there will be nothing I can do to bring you into the coalition.

On the same day there was a private discussion between the Prime Minister and Felix Rosenblueth of the Progressive Party. On February 27 there was the second meeting with the representatives of Mapam, Ben-Aharon and Riftin.

Ben-Aharon announced that his party was unwilling to forego either of the portfolios that it had held in the Provisional Government, Agriculture and Labor and Construction. Moreover, it demanded a third portfolio, Defense or Interior. Mapam also opposed giving jurisdiction over land to the Ministry of Finance instead of the Ministry of Agriculture, and jurisdiction over the rehabilitation of soldiers to the Ministry of Defense instead of the Ministry of Agriculture. In any circumstances, he said, Mapam wanted to be properly represented in the Foreign Ministry. And if a planning office was established comprising economists and union leaders, then Mapam should also be there. Mapam did not want its participation in the Government to be limited to some kind of ghetto. It did not want to have just two ministries in which it could place its people.

Prime Minister: How large do you think the Cabinet should be?

Ben-Aharon: We would like a Cabinet without the General Zionists. Then it would be divided seven, three, two.

Prime Minister: The ratio between you and the religious parties, however, is not three to two.

Ben-Aharon: If they demand three portfolios, we don't object. The important thing is our representation in the Civil Service, and whether our people will serve as heads of departments. That is part of the question of partnership.

Prime Minister: I find it very difficult to accept the principle of having the heads of departments in the various ministries appointed according to parties — very difficult indeed. If you had to accept personal responsibility, you would see the need for a broad coalition. We must carry out tasks that do not confront any other nation. We must absorb mass immigration while we are still faced by the threat of war. There is also need to promote large-scale construction, fight rising living costs, increase agricultural yields, step up industrial production, and maintain a proper standard of living. These things are not simple. I asked Rosenblueth if he would be willing to participate in a narrow coalition with the two labor parties. He said he would not be willing to do so.

Ben-Aharon: We want a reply about our participation in the Ministry of Defense and in the Foreign Ministry. To us in Mapam this is no less important than the question of portfolios.

Prime Minister: I have not yet discussed this matter with my party.

There were three more talks with Mapam at which no further progress was achieved. The Mapam Council, meeting on March 3, decided by a majority vote (the members of Hashomer Hatzair ranged against the members of kibbutz Hameuhad) not to participate in the Government. They sent a brief message to the Prime Minister, signed by Riftin and Ben-Aharon, saying that "The Mapam Council has decided that the party cannot enter the Government under the proposed conditions."

In the end the Progressives, the Sephardim, the Religious Front, and Mapai joined the coalition. There were twelve members in the Cabinet. The coalition was supported in the Knesset by seventy-three members, as follows: Mapai—48, including two Arab members representing the Democratic List of Nazareth; the Religious Front—sixteen; Progressives—five; Sephardim—four.

Government List Presented to Knesset ★ Debate on Government's Basic Principles ★ Vote of Confidence

The seventh session of the First Knesset opened in Tel Aviv on March 8. Five members who had not been present at the opening (Golda Meir, Yehudit Simhonit, Benjamin Mintz, Eliezer Kaplan, and Shmuel Merlin) took their oaths of office and the Prime Minister-Designate reported on the composition of the Cabinet and its program. He proposed: Ben-Gurion—Prime Minister and Minister of Defense; Dov Joseph—Minister of Rationing and Supply; Rabbi Y.M. Levin—Minister of Social Welfare; Mrs. Golda Myerson (Meir)—Minister of Labor and Social Insurance; Rabbi Yehuda Leib Hacohen Fishman—Minister of Religious Affairs; Eliezer Kaplan—Minister of Finance; David Remez—Minister of Transport; Pinhas Rosenblueth—Minister of Justice; Behor Shitreet—Minister of Police; Zalman Shazar—Minister of Education and Culture; Moshe Shapira—Minister of the Interior and Immigration; Moshe Shertok—Minister for Foreign Affairs.

The Prime Minister-Designate, introducing his program, declared:

> We may be in transition today from a "grand period," marked by heroic military and political values—which changed the course of Jewish history and "renewed our days as of old"—to a "humdrum period," which will be characterized by the slogging workaday effort of economic construction and the organization of the State. This new period may lack the dramatic moments of glitter and glory; it will be a period of hard, concentrated, and devoted labor; it will involve building homes for the new immigrants, fructifying abandoned and derelict soil, establishing new industries and workshops, developing land, sea, and air communications, maintaining educational and health services and creating and improving social insurance schemes, mobilizing financial resources on an unparalleled scale for security, the absorption of immigrants, and the provision of services.
>
> It would be a grievous and dangerous error to suppose that the undramatic tasks required of us today are easier to accomplish, less vital, or less decisive than the great demands of the preceding period. The economic and organizational test that confronts us now is no less grave or significant than the test of war through which we have passed. On the contrary, it will be more prolonged and in many respects more difficult.
>
> The establishment of the State of Israel was merely the first stage in the fulfillment of our historic vision. The ingathering of the exiles is a prerequisite to its full realization. Israel's principal task today is, therefore, to gather in the exiles. In the first nine months of our existence as a state, in the midst of a life-and-death struggle, more than 150,000 immigrants entered the country, nearly four times as many Jews as returned from Babylon in ancient days. And this is only a beginning. Everything that is humanly possible will be done to ensure that this stream of immigration does not slacken, but swells.
>
> Immigration is not merely a matter of transporting Jews from the Diaspora to Israel. The problems begin here, in the country itself, and we dare not blind ourselves to the enormous difficulties involved in absorbing immigration. Let us remember that these immigrants do not come to a consolidated, peaceful, and orderly country. They come to an infant state that has risen from chaos and the bloody conflict of war and international aggression. They come to a country whose small and impoverished community must quickly absorb an immigration that exceeds it in size.

History has never witnessed such a phenomenon. In the brief period since the establishment of the State, immigration has increased the Jewish population by 25 per cent. In American terms, that is the equivalent of an immigration of 30 million people a year. Even housing this immigration is almost a superhuman task.

Each individual—the worker, the soldier, the immigrant, the craftsman, the member of a cooperative, the shopkeeper, the merchant, the foreman, the industrialist, the farmer, the clerk, the civil servant, the teacher, the doctor, the lawyer, every man and woman without exception—every group and institution, public, economic, social or cultural, every trade union, collective and cooperative, every settlement and village, the General Federation of Labor and the Manufacturers' Association, the Farmers' Federation and the Chamber of Commerce, the Municipalities and Local Councils, all private and public bodies, local and national, will have to contribute to the effort. I believe that our community is capable of responding to this tremendous call, for I am sure that it is a much better community than its press and parties represent it to be.

The Government of Israel must be positive and dynamic. It must initiate, control, encourage, plan, direct, and push forward in every sphere of economic, cultural, and social life. It must begin development plans, encourage the increase of production, reduce the cost of living, and raise the standard of living, improve equipment and work methods in agriculture, industry, building, and every other branch of our economy, control imports and prices and endeavor to attract Jewish and international capital for productive investments which will assist the speedy and effective development of the economic possibilities of this country, expand its absorptive capacity, and raise the standard of living of its inhabitants.

These tasks will require a planned economy, adapted to security requirements, the absorption of masses of immigrants, and the development of a progressive and independent nation.

On the 25th of Shevat, the President called on me to form a government. I immediately approached all the parties that in my opinion belonged in one degree or another to the category of "constructive forces," from Mapam to the General Zionists, including the Sephardim. I suggested that we form a coalition government. All the parties agreed to join the coalition, but to my regret Mapam and the General Zionists made demands that did not, in my view, accord with the formation of a coalition nor with the will of the people as expressed in the election results. All my proposals to Mapam were turned down. And so, for the time being, we have established a small coalition comprising the Sephardim, the Progressive Party, the Religious Front, and Mapai. In this Government the Sephardim have one member, the Progressives one, the Religious Front three, and Mapai seven.

In a supplementary statement to be made in the coming weeks or days I will announce the allocation of the portfolios of Trade and Industry, Health, Agriculture, and Minorities. For the time being the Government as a whole is responsible for these matters.

Had the State of Israel arisen in 1937, with control of immigration and defense, European Jewry might have been saved from destruction. Throughout the magnificent messianic enterprise in which we have been engaged these seventy years, we have consistently placed emphasis on the individual human being, on man the creator, the builder, the worker, the defender, the immigrant, and the fighter. We do that now in the State of Israel. It was not the rifle, the cannon, or the fighter plane that saved Israel. Our enemies possessed these as well. It was the Jew who held the rifle, who fired the gun, who piloted the plane who won the day. It was not the plough, the hoe, or the machine that brought our community into existence, but the pioneer who guided the plough, wielded the hoe, operated the machine, and with these tools converted the desert into fruitful soil, built factories and schools, and implanted in the hearts of the people and the youth a vision and courage, loyalty, and devotion, love of country and of nation, of justice, liberty, and equality.

The capacity of man, his spirit, his vision, his creative ability, and stubborn initiative—these are the pillars of our entire enterprise. In our State it will be man who will control the economy and not the reverse.

If I am asked whether we have at hand any tried and proven means to overcome with ease the enormous difficulties involved in implementing the three great tasks before Israel today, I confess that we have none. The work will not be easy for us, members of the Government, or for you, members of the Knesset, nor for those who sent us here. And it may well be that we will make mistakes. But even so we shall not waver in the discharge of our duties. For we have something on which we can rely.

We can rely, firstly, on the wellspring of creativity and love of the Jewish people throughout the world. For a long time this source was largely blocked. But the establishment of the Jewish State, with its daring fight for liberty and its assumption of its present mighty task, have, as it were, rolled the stone from the mouth of the well. Today the entire Jewish people, Zionists or not—with the sole exception of tiny groups of irreconcilables—share a strong love and devotion for the State of Israel. Secondly, we rely on the constructive pioneering spirit of our youth, both here and abroad, a spirit that can move mountains and bring fruitfulness to the desert.

There is a third thing that will bring this marvel to pass—science and technology, which will be part and parcel of every aspect of our work. We are witnessing what is perhaps the greatest revolution humanity has ever experienced, no mere change in government or regime, but a revolution in man's relations to the mighty hidden forces of nature, his harnessing of atomic energy, his conquest of the air, of space, and of the secrets of creation. We cannot compare ourselves to many nations in strength, wealth, numbers, or possessions, but there is no reason why we should lag behind any of them in our intellectual and moral power, which constitutes our one great legacy from centuries of persecution, suffering, and spiritual courage.

Together with the most advanced nations in the world, we must devote ourselves to pure and applied scientific research. It will not merely be the special preserve of individual genius, but a public concern, shared by the workers and builders, influencing the economy and the culture we create in this country. Everything we do in the realm of matter and of spirit to strengthen our security and expand our economy, to educate our sons and absorb our immigrants, must be based on the most advanced scientific research and technical methods, so that our products will be equal to those of the most advanced and industrious peoples of the world.

This is our mission. We shall strive to carry it out to the best of our ability.

The following is a summary of the Government's basic principles presented by the Prime Minister to the Knesset.

Section A—Collective responsibility of all members of the Government and of the parties of which it is composed.

Section B—Equal rights and responsibilities for all citizens, regardless of religion, race, or nationality; complete social, economic, and legal equality for women; State supply of public religious needs, but no religious coercion; proclamation of the Sabbath and the Jewish holidays as the official rest days in Israel, with non-Jews being allowed to observe their own holidays.

Section C—Foreign policy: fidelity to the principles of the UN Charter; friendship with all peace-loving states, and particularly with the United States and the Soviet Union; efforts to achieve a pact between Jews and Arabs; support for all steps designed to strengthen peace and ensure equality among peoples; assurance of the rights of all Jews who so desire to leave the countries in which they now live and settle in their historic Homeland; effective safeguards for the full independence and sovereignty of the State of Israel.

Section D—Security: compulsory mobilization of all citizens in those age groups designated by law.

Section E—Immigration: ingathering of the exiles; channeling of immigrants to agricultural settlement; development of vocational education for immigrants and their integration into the cultural, economic, and social life of Israel.

Section F—Development: doubling of population in four years; rapid and balanced populating of the unsettled sections of the country and prevention of excessive urbanization; special attention to the development of Jerusalem; encouragement of private capital and of both free and cooperative enterprise in villages and cities; emphasis on the development of labor enterprises; a consistent war against the high cost of living and the assurance of a decent standard of living for the workers and the poorer sections of the population; exploitation of the latest achievements of science and technology to foster economic development; progressive taxation, inheritance taxes, and luxury taxes; elimination of illiteracy, overcrowding, and disease in the slums; insurance for all citizens against illness and old age, as well as social benefits for widows and handicapped people; elimination of slums; encouragement of a higher birthrate; the promotion of tourism.

Section G—Education: free education for all children up to an age to be determined by law; translation of the treasures of human culture into the Hebrew tongue; establishment of a special Ministry of Education and Culture; education in Arabic for all Arab citizens, who will also learn Hebrew; scholarships for capable young people so that they may continue their studies in high schools and universities; a minimum course of studies at all schools, including the Hebrew language, Jewish and general history, Israeli and general geography, the Bible and Jewish literature, the sciences, work in agriculture, industry, or crafts, pioneering values.

Section H—Rehabilitation of soldiers: guarantee of the right of demobilized soldiers to return to their previous place of work and of priority in obtaining employment; vocational education courses for demobilized soldiers.

Section I—Labor laws: freedom of labor to organize; a minimum wage in various trades, encouragement of collective bargaining; freedom to strike; establishment of institutions for social insurance against unemployment, accidents, disability, old age, orphanhood, and widowhood; protective legislation to ensure the welfare of factory workers; vocational training for youth; banning of employment of women in jobs that are harmful to their childbearing capacity; paid birth leave; a ban on night work by women; a ban on the employment of children under the age of fourteen; a single labor exchange that will distribute work to all job-seekers, without regard to their community, nationality, or party affiliation.

Section J—Government employees: to be appointed on the basis of tests given by an independent committee.

Before the debate began Finance Minister Kaplan announced the receipt of a $100 million fifteen-year loan from the US Export-Import Bank, to be used to carry out a development program in various branches of the economy. During the first three years only interest is to be paid. $35 million of the $100 million are for agricultural development, $20 million for industrial development, $25 million for building, and $20 million for transportation.

A prolonged debate began in the evening, after the speeches of the Prime Minister and the Minister of Finance. The first speaker was Meir Yaari (Mapam). He pointed to the danger of "interventionist pacts against the Soviet Union and the peoples building socialism," as well as the danger of "growing pressure by world reaction and the Marshall Plan on the countries of the East and on Israel." He warned that "the integrity and sovereignty of Israel are under constant attack by the Western powers." He criticized the Prime Minister for forming a "reformist, clerical coalition subservient to the pressures of internal reaction and the economic and political dictates of foreign forces." He complained about the candidate for Prime Minister, "who feels that his party is the only one that can carry out the ingathering of the exiles and achieve socialism." Yaari expressed concern at the "supposed equal degree of friendship for the United States and the Soviet Union." The Government presented to the Knesset, he said, was "unfaithful to its own declarations and to its natural class allies." It had broken its word, he went on, "to those who with their own bodies and without any real arms had stopped the advance of the Egyptian invader on Tel Aviv, at Yad Mordekhai, Revivim, and Nirim." Yaari warned that he and his comrades "would not allow the Knesset to be turned into an arena of clownish demagoguery."

Warhaftig (Religious Front): "The next four years will be one of the most glorious periods in the history of our people. The dangers facing us make it imperative that we achieve a maximum degree of unity. Therefore we were the first to support a broad coalition, even though it meant being together with those who are less than friendly toward us, those who direct all their fire at us. I would like to say a few words about that party which, for some unknown reason, is trying to prove that some kind of a war is going on between Ein Harod and Tirat Zvi. I don't know what makes us less genuine members of the working class than they are. We have a pure pioneering, working class past. We have established settlements from Dan to Beersheba, and we suffered many losses in the War of Independence. I simply do not know why and by what right they deny us our place in this country. Why is it perfectly all right for Yaari to be in a coalition with the Revisionists, while he rejects us as reactionaries?"

Menahem Begin (Herut) complained that "the Government's foreign policy purposes ignore the UN plan to divide the Homeland. Our official foreign policy is based on our present, artificial borders. The talks that took place at Rhodes with Egypt also led to the withdrawal of our forces from areas of the Homeland—which were effectively put under a foreign regime—in contradiction to the pledge given by the Foreign Minister at the Journalists' Convention in Jerusalem that there would be no demilitarized zones in the Negev."

Pinhas Lubianiker [Lavon] (Mapai): "Our appeal was a sincere, comradely one. We set only three conditions: we demanded loyalty to Zionism, not in words but in deeds, loyalty to democracy, and loyalty to the State, to its authority and to its authority alone, to its laws and its laws alone. We did not accept the view that the Government should be based on a labor front. We have no need to base our program on ideas that were discarded five or ten years ago in Europe. We cannot have a government within a government. On some matters our party is less in agreement with Mapam than with the other parties. This is well known. Until now there has been little real disagreement with the Prime Minister's program. Meir Yaari said he was expressing a lack of confidence in the Government, but I did not hear one specific objection to its program."

Dr. Herbert Foerder (Progressives): "The Provisional Government was successful. It frequently displayed courage and dynamism. We hope that the new Government will show courage in economic matters in view of the fact that our balance of trade is absolutely negative. One can talk about austerity; we support the idea ourselves. But the people must be supplied with food. Moreover, we want to build and we want to earn profits, both within the country and from the export of our products. There can be no mass immigration without industry and no industry without exports. Large-scale investments from abroad are a precondition to an improvement in our balance of payments."

Sapir (General Zionists), referring to the achievements of the section of the population that he represents, declared: "During the entire period of the Hagana, and even before it, our people were in the front ranks. They voluntarily provided most of the funds required to maintain public security and carry out the struggle against foreign rule. Even today, the private sector accounts for almost half of the mixed-agricultural economy, 80 percent of the citrus-growing branch, 90 percent of trade and industry, and the overwhelming majority of construction and other branches of the economy. It is on behalf of these people that we speak. Though we were not authorized to do so, we also speak for the eighty thousand members of the middle class who voted for Mapai, mainly because the man who heads it has great personal achievements to his credit. Our past work, under all circumstances and at all times, is guarantee enough of our standing in Israel today, even if we are not in power. Unless the Government gives proper representation to the broad middle class, it will not be truly representative and it will not be capable of carrying out the enormous tasks that fate has thrust upon it in this decisive period of our national life."

Mikunis (Communists): "Mr. Ben-Gurion is offering us a government that distorts the desires of the workers of Israel. The government he presented is typical of those existing in areas under the influence of American imperialism. His program for foreign policy is overflowing with contradictions. He speaks of friendship with all peace-loving states, and particularly with the United States and the Soviet Union. But any intelligent person immediately realizes that the end of the sentence contradicts the beginning. When the United States, with its present rulers, is singled out as a peace-loving state and equated with the Soviet Union, which is also apparently peace-loving, then this whole 'foreign policy' looks very strange indeed. It attempts to group together the America of Truman and Marshall—the America that foments war and enslaves people—with the Soviet Union, the bastion of world peace since its establishment thirty years ago, the land of socialism and international fraternity, the steadfast defender of the Jewish people from the establishment of the USSR until this very day."

Mrs. Beba Idelson (Mapai): "One of the hallmarks of a progressive state is the condition of its women, its working mothers and their children. We, the women workers of Israel, believe that we should have rights and responsibility equal to those of the rest of the population. We have never demanded only rights; equality means both rights and responsibilities."

Tewfik Toubi (Communists): "The attempts of the imperialists to undermine the November 29 UN resolution calling for the establishment of two independent states in Palestine, Jewish and Arab, as well as the military attacks made by their agents, the reactionary Arab rulers, in an attempt to prevent the establishment of the State of Israel, were also attacks against the interests of the Arab masses in Palestine and in the Arab states, and against the establishment of an independent and democratic Arab state in Palestine. This is why the imperialistic intrigues and military adventures were not supported by the Arab masses of Palestine and the surrounding countries. Under the leadership of the democratic forces and the Communist Parties, a strong movement developed in these countries against the interventionist war in Palestine, as well as for cooperation between the Jewish and Arab peoples of Palestine and for the establishment of two states. Abandonment of the idea of an independent Arab State in the other part of Palestine serves to strengthen reaction in the Middle East and denies to the Jewish people in Israel the possibility of having a friendly neighbor. We will be faithful guardians of Israel's independence and freedom, her democracy and equality. Israel must become a bastion of peace and freedom in the Middle East."

Nathan Friedman-Yellin (Fighters, formerly Lehi): "The Israel Defense Forces are strong enough to liberate all sections of the Homeland, to drive out the invading armies and to inflict defeat on those who sent them. Must we wait until a sword is pressing on our necks before we act? Were there not also 'realists' who feared the liberation of western Galilee as well as areas in the center of the country and in the Negev? Was it not necessary for the Prime Minister to overcome the opposition of the 'realists' to the pro-clamation of a State? Where, if not in the Knesset, can we give notice to the simple truth that the Motherland is one, and any partition or division of it is both illegal and purely temporary?"

Ben-Zvi Dinaburg (Mapai): "The Government has made it crystal clear that its central goal is to double the Jewish population of this country within four years. This goal must serve as a yardstick for all our actions. I would like to call attention to the problem of the spiritual integration of the immigrants, which is a prerequisite to the success of our work. We must determine how the educational system can be used to promote spiritual unity, the integration of the various communities, and the strengthening of those new characteristics that were created here and that enabled us to withstand the Arab onslaught. We must promote the cultural unity of the nation."

I. Idelson (Mapam) complained that the candidate for Prime Minister had devoted only eight words to the question of security: "This means that he will do as he pleases. The Palmah was dissolved without our being asked. We are being told that our opinion will not be asked in the future either."

Elyashar (Sephardim) spoke of the special problems of the Oriental communities and particularly of the degrading poverty in which the Jewish slum-dwellers lived. Our hope and prayer, he said, is that the Prime Minister's pledge to uproot illiteracy, over-crowding, and illness in the slum neighborhoods will be carried out. We call for immediate efforts to bring in Oriental Jews while there is still time. We must train them in those countries where it is possible. Differences developed between the various com-munities over the many generations of dispersion, and as the Prime Minister says, these must be removed.

Mrs. Persitz (General Zionists): "The General Zionists did not join the coalition because the Prime Minister rejected their demand that a joint program be worked out in advance. The coalition program presented yesterday by the Prime Minister is indeed comprehensive, but it is far from clear."

Yacov Hazan (Mapam): "We were asked to join a Government that had, in fact, already been established by Mapai and the Religious Front. After this Government falls, and fall it will, I would suggest that the members of the largest party negotiate with Mapam, their natural partner, in a different spirit. We suggested that Israeli neutrality be defined in terms of a willingness to fight against any attempt to transform this country into an interventionist base. Why didn't you agree? We know that there is a basic difference between our attitude and yours toward the Soviet Union. We regard the Soviet Union as the bastion of world socialism, our second socialist homeland. We have not asked you to agree with us on this question. The fact that there is only one small section on the Army in the Government's program gives reason for concern about the future character of that Army."

The Knesset debate lasted for three days. In his reply, the Prime Minister said:

I tried with all my strength to establish a broad coalition government, though this meant concessions and compromises. However, I could not disregard the desires of the voters and the vital interests of the State, I am very sorry that two parties that participated in the Provisional Government have not joined the coalition. I regret having to bid farewell to two colleagues who took part in the great work of the last nine months. While nine months is hardly a significant period in the history of a people as ancient as ours, I doubt whether there has been a similar period in all of Jewish history. People who were with us during those nine months certainly do not find it easy to leave now. So why did they?

The General Zionists made three demands that I found unacceptable. After they had received my rejection of their demands, they decided to drop two of them. The first was for a government statement that socialism and Zionism were incompatible. I did not agree with them, but said: "Do you really think that you can come to me with such a demand?" The second demand, also later dropped, was that a two-thirds majority be required to adopt a constitution. I know of countries in which a constitution can only be repealed by a two-third majority, but such a majority is not required to pass it. The third and apparently central demand was for two Cabinet posts. The explanation for General Zionist difficulties was given, I believe, by Mr. Sapir here in the Knesset. He argued that they represented not only their twenty-two thousand voters, but also the middle-class voters who supported Mapai or Ben-Gurion. I explained to them that if they were given two portfolios, then there would have to be at least a twenty-five-member Cabinet. (Serlin interjected: "There is no justification for establishing a coalition on the basis of the relative strength of the various parties." And Mrs. Persitz: "We thought in terms of the weight of the various parties.") Every citizen in Israel has the same weight. That was why I did not accept your demand. All Jews, whether they have been in this country seventy years or seven weeks, are equal when it comes to elections; all of them have only one vote. There can be no compromise on this democratic principle.

A representative of the General Zionists has stated that our program is liable to frighten off private capital. I can reply to this charge only by reiterating what I have already said on many occasions to both the General Zionists and to my own colleagues, namely, that we must encourage private capital and free enterprise, particularly since the ingathering of the exiles is and will remain our central task. It is our Zionist duty.

A Mapam member has argued that the section on security is unclear. It is indeed unclear, but not for the reason stated by Mr. Idelson, who claimed that the Minister of Defense would do whatever he pleased. He brought such examples as the Defense Minister's unilateral decision to dissolve the Palmah Command. Did the Palmah ask anyone's permission when it established the Command? Neither the Government nor the Provisional State Council was asked; nor the Ministry of Defense. Not a single person in the Israel Defense Forces was asked. (Zisling: "We established the same kind of command in the Hagana with the approval of the Zionist Organization.") The section on defense was purposely left vague, for reasons that should be clear to every Knesset member. I was not interested in giving military secrets to the enemy. But policy will be determined by laws, and laws are passed solely by the Knesset. So what are you frightened about?

I explained why, to my regret, the General Zionists did not join the coalition. Now I would like to say a few words about something no less regrettable—the absence of Mapam from the coalition. I discussed the coalition program with Mapam as I did with the other parties, but it is my impression that the negotiations failed over the question of portfolios. In the last discussion with Mapam—during which the party's representatives informed me that they were going to recommend that Mapam does not participate in the coalition—the only matter discussed was portfolios.

Comrade Yaari uses arguments similar to those of Knesset member Sapir. He claims to speak not only in the name of the 64,000 people who voted for Mapam, but also in the name of the 162,000 men and women who voted for *us*. No one authorized him to do so. Those 162,000 men and women failed to support Mapam not because Mapam rejected their support. Mapai certainly wanted the 64,000 Mapam voters to vote for it, but they did not. We cannot speak for them and Yaari has no right to speak on behalf of the people who cast their votes for Mapai. We live in a country in which the voter is absolutely free to choose whom he wishes.

In our country he does not simply vote for personalities. He is offered a particular program. We will not abandon our program even if we remain isolated. It was not pulled out of a hat on the eve of the elections, and we have no intention of abandoning it immediately after the elections. It is the path that we have followed during these nine historic months, and it is the path that we will continue to follow. We have reason to believe that it brought benefits to the workers and to the people as a whole. We do not accept the theory of Knesset member Yaari, who says that since both Mapai and Mapam failed, the Government should adopt a program midway between the programs of the two parties. We are not capable of doing such a thing. We doubt whether Mapam is capable of doing it either. Moreover, Mapam's "failure" is not similar to the "failure" we have suffered.

Yaari accuses my comrades and myself of not being Marxists. According to his testimony, he in any case is a real Marxist. He divides the Yishuv into two parts, the workers and the bourgeoisie. We did not lose among the workers. They gave us a majority of their votes, both in the Knesset and in the Histadrut. We failed only among the bourgeois. They did not give us a majority of their votes.

Mapam calls this a coalition with clerical elements. Perhaps this is a sin. If it is, we refuse to repent. We have been in a clerical-right wing-reformist coalition for fifteen years in the Zionist Executive. One could hardly accuse that coalition of not doing anything. Things were accomplished to the benefit of the Jewish people and the Jewish workers. There have been accomplishments in the spheres of immigration, settlement, education, and defense. A Jewish State has been established. All this was the work of a clerical-right wing coalition. The Jewish workers did not suffer as a result.

Mapam joined this clerical-right wing coalition during the period of the Provisional Government. Three representatives of Jewish clericalism—Rabbi Fishman, Rabbi Levin, and Moshe Shapira—sat together with Mapam in the Provisional Government, which also encompassed the bourgeois right, which has not joined the present coalition. Mapam, in my opinion, has no reason to regret participation in the Provisional Government. On the contrary, I am certain it will eventually boast about its contributions to the clerical-right wing Provisional Government. Even today Mapam is part of a clerical-right wing coalition, lacking a socialist majority, in the Zionist Executive.

You tell us that this Government will fail. You may very well be right. I am extremely afraid that it will fail, not because it is a bad government, but because the tasks that it has assumed are almost beyond the ability of human beings to carry out. We do not think that we are the only ones that count. We realize what was accomplished by those who preceded us in this country. We also appreciate the contribution of those who laid the foundations for private industry. When I meet with workers, I tell them that we need the support of the entire Jewish people and that we need private capital. I know that Yaari and Idelson are fervent supporters of a certain Great Power, and call themselves revolutionaries. What kind of a revolution did Yaari and Idelson carry out here? In what way is Knesset member Shlomo Lavi less of a pioneer, less of a farmer, and less of a fighter than Yitzhak Tabenkin? I know that you struggled to achieve several things that we did not favor. You struggled for a binational State—and we did not. You struggled for an international trusteeship, an international mandate; you wanted to be governed by the US, the Soviet Union, and England—and we did not.

My main task as Prime Minister will be to stir the people into action so that we will be able to accomplish the historic task that we have taken upon ourselves. Our goal is a common one, and so is our path. There could have been a broad coalition based on a program of bringing in more Jews and still more Jews.

In a roll-call, the first vote-of-confidence test, the Government was supported by a majority of seventy-three to forty-five.

Knesset Approves $100 Million American Loan and Economic Aid to Demobilized Soldiers

The first elected Government, which won the confidence of the Knesset on March 10, 1949, inherited an important economic and political achievement from the Provisional Government—namely a $100 million loan from the American Export-Import Bank. The money was allocated for agriculture development ($35 million), industrial development ($20 million), construction ($25 million), and transportation on land, on sea, and in the air ($20 million). Finance Minister Kaplan had gone to the United States during the days of the Provisional Government to arrange for the loan. On February 17, 1949, he signed an agreement for a $35 million loan, subsequently increased to a $100 million.

On the day the elected Government was presented to the Knesset, Kaplan proposed the establishment of a small Knesset committee to study the loan. On March 17, 1949, Fritz Naftali (Mapai) presented a four-section draft law on the subject:

1. The Minister of Finance is hereby authorized to accept a $100 million credit from the Export-Import Bank in Washington, an agency of the American government, on behalf of Israel.

2. The Minister of Finance is hereby authorized to sign agreements with the Export-Import Bank on behalf of the Israeli Government in connection with the aforementioned credit. The Finance Minister may sign these documents himself or assign this task to one of his representatives.

3. The authorization given in the first two sections is hereby made retroactive to February 10, 1949.

4. The Minister of Finance is responsible for carrying out this law.

Kaplan had informed the Knesset on March 8, 1949, that the $100 million had to be spent in the United States, which meant that the loan would cover only a small part of the cost of the Government's development program. The $35 million spent on agriculture would necessitate an overall agricultural development program of $90 to $100 million. The main goals in agriculture were the establishment of sixty-five hundred new farm units, together with seven regional irrigation schemes to provide water for them; the rehabilitation of citrus farming, which had suffered during the war; and the strengthening of existing mixed farming. The $25 million allocated for construction was to be used to build houses for immigrants as well as public buildings required because of the growth of the Yishuv and of immigration.

In the debate that followed the Naftali statement, *Mikunis*, for the Communists, opposed the loan, charging that it was meant to enslave Israel and to open the way for American political intervention in the country. It would, he added, make Israel's capitalist economy even more parasitic.

Repetur (Mapam) expressed grave doubts about the desirability of accepting a loan from a bank that was an agent of the American government and its policies. Even the explanantions offered by the Minister of Finance had not put an end to his fears that the loan involved political obligations.

Ben-Eliezer (Herut) said that he feared that the $35 million for agriculture would be turned over to the Jewish Agency, since the Provisional Government had decided that settlement would be left to the Agency. What guarantee was there, he asked, that the Agency would not discriminate against certain elements? Perhaps the Agency would only help people who belonged to the Zionist Organization or to elements represented in the Agency. He demanded an amendment to the law, stating that the Minister of Finance had no right to sign the loan agreement without the approval of the Knesset Finance Committee.

Sneh, then still in Mapam, complained that Israel had not discussed her economic development plan with the Soviet Union or asked for Soviet assistance. This could not be given, to be sure, in dollars, but the Russians had worked out a program to help their genuine friends. The Soviet Union had not been approached, although negotiations with the US had been going on for over a year. After all, the Government's basic principles stated that Israel's foreign policy was based on friendship with the two Great Powers. It was no coincidence that the favorable American reply had been announced one day before the elections to the Knesset. Since the Government in accepting the loan denied the existence of American plots, the Communists could not support it.

Zisling (Mapam) challenged Naftali's assertion that the loan had been supported by all members of the Provisional Government. The Provisional Government, he said, had never discussed the conditions of the loan. While it is true that we need a great deal of money, he went on, we cannot allow ourselves to be dictated to by any country.

Naftali poited out to Zisling that the loan negotiations had begun during the period of the Provisional Government with the agreement of all its members; this was admitted by Zisling.

Kaplan stated in his reply: "The American Government cannot tell us what we can or cannot do, but it can determine which enterprises will benefit from the loan. Anyone who thinks that the loan will cover all our economic requirements is making a mistake." Commenting on Sneh's allegation that Israel had turned only to the US, Kaplan pointed out that Israel had signed two trade agreements, one with Holland and one with Hungary. Moreover, Israeli trade delegations were now in Czechoslovakia and Poland. We need, he said, not $100 million but at least $500 million for the regular budget. We must use every available means of raising this enormous sum. There is no foundation for Ben-Eliezer's fears about how the money will be spent, for all agreements will be brought for discussion to the Knesset's Finance Committee.

The Government's proposal was approved by a vote of eighty-five to three, the three being the representatives of the Communist Party. Nineteen members, most of them from Mapam, abstained. The loan law was supported, among others, by twelve members of the Knesset who were not in the coalition. The vote took place two months and ten days after the end of the fighting.

On March 22, 1949, the Prime Minister presented a Demobilized Soldiers Law, aimed at guaranteeing the right of a demobilized soldier to return to his former job. If a soldier died or was badly injured and could not work, the law guaranteed the job to a member of his family. The State assumed a heavy responsibility in calling up citizens for military service. The law was meant to ensure, to the greatest possible extent, that when released they could return to their former places of work, and would not have to waste a single day searching for employment. It was the responsibility of private and public employers, factories and offices, the Jewish Agency, the Municipalities, the cooperatives, and the kibbutzim to give the demobilized soldier his job back.

After a debate that continued until April 25, the law was passed. It came into effect on May 15, 1949, exactly a year after the establishment of the State. By that time immigrants were streaming in and they were finding it difficult to obtain employment.

On September 5 the Prime Minister presented the Invalids (Allowances and Rehabilitations) Law. It was designed to guarantee the right of every disabled veteran to an allowance from the Ministry of Defense for himself, his wife, and his children, according to the degree of his disability for the entire time that he suffered from it. Some thousand disabled soldiers had already been demobilized before the law was presented, while others had remained in the Army. The latter included some very badly injured men who required and were receiving the best possible medical care.

We have, the Prime Minister declared, an outstanding medical service, both in professional qualifications and personal devotion. Jewish specialists from overseas, particularly surgeons from South Africa and other countries, have answered our call; together with the finest doctors in Israel, they have treated our fighters with devotion and love. This same spirit was shown by the service personnel, the nurses, and other employees.

The law adopted by the Knesset on the day of its submission provided that every invalid with at least 40 percent disability was to receive a grant of IL5 (a pound was then worth $4) for each percent of disability. An invalid whose degree of disability was more than 40 percent and less than 50 percent was to receive a grant of IL7 for each percent of disability. An invalid whose degree of disability was at least 50 percent and less than 100 percent was to receive, throughout his life, in accordance with the number of his dependents, allowances proportionate to his degree of disability. If his disability was 100 percent, he was to receive throughout his life, the following allowances: (1) IL12 a month for himself; (2) IL3 a month for his wife; (3) IL2 a month for each additional dependent: (4) a cost-of-living allowance equal to the cost-of-living allowance granted to government employees with the same size family and with a basic salary equal to the total amount paid to the invalid under paragraphs (1), (2), and (3). A medical committee was to reexamine the demobilized soldier from time to time in accordance with the provisions of the law.

By March 16, 1950, applications for assistance from 2539 demobilized soldiers under the terms of the Invalids Law had been approved, out of a total of 3721 submitted.

By March 16, 1951, 100,000 soldiers had been released from the Army. Ninety thousand requests for assistance had been received by the Ministry of Defense, including 74,314 from the cities and towns, 1977 from the settlements, 5882 from wounded soldiers, and 2827 from bereaved families. Aid was given to all those who asked for it. Of the 55,000 who requested help in obtaining work, 50,000 were provided with permanent employment, and the rest were given temporary jobs. By March 16, 1951, 7060 demobilized soldiers settled in 53 new agricultural settlements as well as in existing ones; 1800 veterans had organized themselves into 170 different cooperatives; 1300 were absorbed by the transport cooperatives; 4500 were given vocational training and afterward helped to obtain employment; 1500 received loans for study at institutions of higher learning; 15,000 received initial assistance; jobs were found for 2172 disabled veterans.

The Ministry of Defense spent IL6,564,000 by March 16, 1951, on this program— IL2.3 million for grants to demobilized soldiers, invalids, and bereaved families; IL600,000 for settlement activities; IL464,060 for vocational training and higher education; IL2,450,000 for loans to promote rehabilitation, membership in cooperatives, and housing; and IL750,000 for loans to wounded men and bereaved families.

Israel Joins the United Nations ★ Problems of Immigrant Absorption ★ Struggle Against High Living Costs

Israel was accepted as a member of the United Nations Organization on May 11, 1949, almost a year after her establishment. Only three of the Arab states that had attacked Israel had signed armistice agreements with her at that time: Egypt on February 24, 1949, Lebanon on March 23, 1949, and Jordan on April 3, 1949, Iraq had refused even to discuss an armistice, and the agreement with Syria was signed only on July 20, 1949.

Had the Arab states accepted the UN resolution of November 29, 1947, as Israel did, the Jewish State on the day of its establishment would have had a population of 450,000 Arabs and 650,000 Jews. It would have encompassed an area of 14,920 square kilometers, while the Arab State in what had been Palestine would have been slightly less than 11,000 square kilometers. The Arabs, however, decided to use military force to nullify the resolution, despite the fact that it had been supported by over two-thirds of the UN members, led by the Soviet Union and the United States. When the British High Commissioner left the country at midnight of May 14, the Arab armies moved in. Actually, of course, the undeclared war between Jews and Arabs had begun on November 30, 1947, the day after the UN decision.

A noted American military expert asked his Jewish friends in Washington and New York to warn their colleagues in Israel against the establishment of a Jewish State. He was acquainted with the size of the Arab armies, the quality of their weapons, and the capabilities of the British commanders; he also knew that the Jewish defense forces, which operated on an underground basis prior to the establishment of the State, lacked military training and the weapons of modern war—artillery, warplanes, tanks, and ships; he knew that the Jews in Israel were outnumbered forty to one by their Arab enemies, and he was certain that if a Jewish State were established under such conditions, within a few weeks not a Jew would remain alive.

This was also the view of Col. Rosher Lund of Norway, who was in Israel that year and aided the Hagana. He knew what the Hagana possessed and what it didn't possess. The British commanders of the Arab armies were no less certain that within ten to fourteen days after the invasion there wouldn't be a trace of a Jewish State or a Jewish settlement.

Actually, the Arab aggressions resulted in an increase in the area of the Jewish State—instead of the 14,920 square kilometers set by the resolution, it was 20,666 square kilometers at the end of the war. Obeying instructions of the Arab High Committee, almost all the Arab residents of Haifa, Safad, Tiberias, and Jaffa left these cities even before the establishment of the State; this despite Hagana assurances that they would be guaranteed full rights if they remained. Arab leaders ordered them to leave, promising that within a few weeks the Arab armies would throw all the Jews into the sea, after which Arab civilians could return and take over the homes of the Jews. At the end of November 1947 the Arabs began to leave the areas allocated to the Jews by the UN resolution. The November 8, 1948, census, the first in the Jewish area after the War of Independence, showed a population of 782,000—713,000 Jews and 69,000 non-Jews. By the end of September 1949, Israel had a population of 1,135,000—965,000 Jews and 170,000 non-Jews.

The task that the first elected Government had set for itself, "doubling the Yishuv in four years," was more than fulfilled. Between May 15, 1948, and the end of December 1951, 689,275 immigrants arrived in the country, as compared to 363,914 during the thirty years of the British Mandate. Natural increase accounted for 97,208 in the expanding Jewish population. In order words, the Yishuv grew by 120 percent in a period of three years, seven and a half months.

The first arrivals were the "illegal" immigrants, who had been interned in Cyprus by the Mandatory Government. On the day the State was established 24,000 people were in the Cyprus camps. The "illegal" immigrants came together with the Jewish survivors of the German concentration camps. Within a year of Israel's establishment (by the end of April 1949), she had absorbed 203,581 immigrants, most of them from Europe, including "illegal" immigrants from Cyprus and Displaced Persons from Germany. They were joined by immigrants from Bulgaria, Rumania, Czechoslovakia, Hungary, and Yugoslavia. The largest number of immigrants came from Poland (56,057); they were mostly people who had been in camps in Germany. During that year the first immigrants arrived from Asia (Turkey, the Arab countries, and Afghanistan). There were many more immigrants from Asia and also Africa in the second year. Almost the entire Jewish community of Yemen was redeemed, as was the Jewish community of Libya.

Immigration from Poland and Rumania also increased—125,162 Jews came from those countries in the first two years of the State; 16,388 immigrants arrived from Czechoslovakia, 6903 from Yugoslavia, 3107 from the Soviet Union. In the two years between May 15, 1950, and May 15, 1952, immigration totaled 304,457, mostly from Asia and Africa. Almost the entire Jewish community of Iraq, the most ancient in the Diaspora, was saved in this period. Jews had lived in Iraq for over 2500 years, from the time of the destruction of the First Temple. Only 6910 Jews came from Iraq during the first two years of the State, but in the two following years 112,464 arrived in Israel. This was the largest immigration from one country in the period immediately after the establishment of the State (several years later Moroccan immigration exceeded Iraqi). Some 70 percent of the Iraqi immigrants were small merchants without specific training; about 15 percent were professional men, and another 5 percent were men of property. That wave of immigration also brought to the country many intellectual elements, men and women who contributed a great deal to the absorption of the members of their own community. Over 500 Iraqi immigrants were teachers, and as soon as they had learned Hebrew at special courses they were sent to teach their fellow immigrants in the transition camps.

As was to be expected, the large-scale immigration in the first four years caused great economic difficulties. Some members of the Provisional Government had opposed unlimited immigration, and they offered quite weighty arguments. The majority of the Government, however, justifiably regarded the ingathering of the exiles as the major task of the State and opposed any limitation on immigration. The difficulties were not felt so severely during the first year of the State, as many workers were called up for military service and there was a resultant labor shortage. Almost all the new arrivals capable of working were thus able to find employment. The housing problem was also less severe than it later became. Immigrants were settled in abandoned villages and cities, such as Jaffa, Ramle, Lydda, Tiberias, Safad, Beit Sha'an. But after the end of the War of Independence tens of thousands of soldiers were demobilized and it became necessary to find jobs for them. This put a strain on the labor market, which was in poor shape to begin with.

Immigration reached its peak in the second year after the establishment of the State. In 1949, the year in which the Army began demobilizing men, 239,076 immigrants arrived in Israel. The fighting ended on January 7, 1949, and a few months later armistice agreements were signed with Egypt, Lebanon, Jordan, and finally Syria. Immigration came to 169,405 in 1950 and 173,901 in 1951. Absorption problems, hardly felt during the first year of the State, became almost unbearable in the three years that followed. There were grave shortages of housing, food, and employment. Some 20 percent of the immigrants were unable to work because of their age or the state of their health. There were cripples, as well as people suffering from tuberculosis, heart trouble, nervous diseases, and so on. There were also the blind, the aged, and the deaf-mutes. At the end of 1949 the (American) Joint Distribution Committee, in cooperation with the Jewish Agency and the Government of Israel, established Malben, an organization to handle these social cases.

A special effort was made to settle the maximum number of immigrants on the land. In the first year only 662 families were settled in immigrant moshavim set up on the soil of abandoned villages. By the second year 5700 families were given homes in immigrant moshavim and in work villages. After the abandoned villages had been settled the establishment of new, planned settlements began. The heads of families would go to the site where the settlement was to be built, set up tents, and begin building houses and preparing the land for planting. A few months later they would be joined by their families. Such settlements were established all over Israel, in the Galilee, Samaria, Judea, and the south. In addition, some 400 families joined veteran moshavim and some 8000 immigrants, half of them from Oriental countries, entered kibbutzim. About 20 percent of them left the kibbutzim after a short stay.

Most of the immigrants who came after the establishment of the State differed from those who had arrived before the Second World War, before the extermination of 6 million Jews. The post-1948 immigrants had not received either agricultural training or a pioneering education before coming to Israel. In the Diaspora they had been merchants and craftsmen; yet they responded in an unexpected degree to the call for establishment of farming settlements. Contact with the soil of the Motherland, national initiative, and the guidance of veteran settlers transformed them from townspeople into tillers of the soil and builders of settlements. The love of Israel felt by Jews in every country and in every generation was undoubtly one of the factors responsible for this transformation.

More settlements were set up during the first 4 years after the establishment of the State than during the 40 years of Ottoman rule or the 30 of the British Mandate. During the last 40 years of Ottoman rule 32 Jewish agricultural settlements were established; these included 26 villages based on private property and hired labor, 4 kibbutzim, and 2 moshavim. During the 30 years of British rule 222 agricultural settlements were established, a few of them on private land and by private capital, most of them with the aid of national (Keren Hayesod and Keren Kayemet) capital and on the soil of the nation. During the first 4 years of the State (1948–1951) 273 agricultural settlements were set up, among them 170 moshavim and 86 kibbutzim. From the middle of May to the end of December 1948 alone, 22 kibbutzim and 14 moshavim were established. In 1949 the total was 48 kibbutzim and 70 moshavim; in 1950, 7 kibbutzim and 70 moshavim; in 1951, 9 kibbutzim and 12 moshavim.

The agricultural economy became more diversified. Settlers began growing such industrial crops as tobacco, sugar beet, flax, and later cotton (with the help of Sam Hamburger, the agricultural pioneer from California who had been educated at the Hebrew Gymnasium in Jaffa). The citrus groves that had suffered during the rioting and fighting were restored and expanded. The acreage devoted to olives, grapes, figs, bananas, peaches, and apples was also increased. More vegetables were grown and there was a tripling of the area under irrigation. The settlers were mainly immigrants from Asia, Africa, Latin America, and Europe (Poland, Rumania, Germany, etc.), but Israeli youth also made important contributions to agricultural development. The Army, through Nahal, played its part as well.

During the 70 years of settlement activity from 1878 to 1948, we reached a cultivated area of 500,000 dunams (125,000 acres). By the end of 1951 almost 1 million acres were being cultivated (125,000 of them by Israeli Arabs). The whole agricultural enterprise was the work of the new immigrants from Yemen, Morocco, Iraq, Turkey, India, Tunisia, Libya, Poland, Rumania, and the other countries of East Europe —together with pioneers from North and South America, South Africa, and Western Europe.

During the entire Mandate era the Government and the Jewish National Fund, together with private individuals, planted 12 million trees on some 15,000 acres. In less than 4 years after the establishment of the State, from mid-May 1948 to the end of 1951, the Jewish National Fund, the Israel Defense Forces, the Ministry of Agriculture, and private individuals planted 25 million trees on 31,000 acres.

The rapid growth of immigration in the initial four years of the State was accompanied, at first, by a drastic decline in agricultural production, particularly of vegetables, milk, eggs, and chickens. This decline was caused by the flight of Arabs from villages in the center, the south, and to a certain extent in the north, the mobilization of young members of Jewish agricultural settlements, and disruptions resulting from military operations. Many areas that had been cultivated until that time were abandoned. About 40 percent of the citrus groves were badly hit. The raising of cattle and sheep declined. Banana plantations also suffered. Rising immigration during the first years of the State was thus accompanied by an increasing shortage of agricultural produce. For this and other reasons the Government stated in its Basic Principles that it would encourage immigrants to settle on the land.

There was no shortage of land. With the establishment of the State the White Paper restrictions that had blocked Jewish agricultural settlement in 90 percent of the western part of the Land of Israel were abrogated. The Israeli conquests in the Galilee and in the Negev opened vast new areas for settlement, areas that had been abandoned by their Arab inhabitants even before the establishment of the State. There were particularly large tracts in the barren wastes of the Negev.

Only a small percentage of the immigrants, however, became farmers. Most of the newcomers settled near the cities in temporary housing. At first they lived in immigrant camps. There were 100,000 immigrants in such camps by August 1949. It was a demoralizing experience, since many of the people became used to living on charity. The problems caused by mass immigration became evident even before the establishment of the first elected Government, and the Prime Minister-Designate, in presenting his Government, asked the Knesset whether the young and tiny State of Israel, surrounded by mortal enemies, could bear the terrible burden of security and the absorption of mass immigration. Answering his own question, he said: "We have no alternative. It is vital to our existence. We must do our best to foster immigration, for the ingathering of the exiles is both our *raison d'être* and a prerequisite for our existence."

About six weeks after the first elected Government had been voted into office, it was obliged to inform the Knesset of absorption difficulties and of the necessity to introduce austerity and to fight against the high cost of living. The chances of peace increased to some extent after armistice agreements had been signed, but it was still necessary to keep most of the Army under arms, while at the same time taking in tens of thousands of immigrants, housing them, and finding work for them. Only about 160,000 immigrants had been housed up to that time (out of a total of over 210,000). Tens of thousands lived in conditions of extreme overcrowding in the immigrant camps, and not all the immigrants who were housed were also given employment.

As immigration continued, deprivation grew steadily more pronounced. Speaking on April 26, 1949, on the decision to introduce austerity, the Prime Minister declared: "The desperate efforts made last year to repel the Arab invaders must be made again if we are to absorb the rapidly growing immigration. The Government cannot promise quick or easy victories. But during the transitional period, until sufficient capital comes into the country to permit industrial and agricultural development, restrictive measures will also be necessary. We must introduce austerity as a temporary expedient in order to reduce our dependence on imports and our expenditure of foreign currency. We must reduce or eliminate the consumption of luxury goods and make it possible for every family to reduce its expenditures, without lowering its standard of living or foregoing basic material and spiritual requirements."

The Minister of Supply and Rationing, Dr. Dov Joseph, informed the Knesset that the Government had decided to combat rising living costs by imposing effective controls on imports and on the prices of imported goods, as well as on production costs and prices of Israeli products. The Government also planned to control prices of transport and services, and introduce a strict system of rationing food, clothing, and other essential commodities. It would take other measures to reduce the cost of living, Dr. Joseph declared:

During the first stage of the struggle against the high cost of living the following measures will be taken: a reserve of food and other essential goods will be built up; a list of essential foodstuffs will be prepared and only these items will be made available to the public; a list of clothing, footwear, furniture, and household goods for sale at minimal prices will be compiled, and efforts will be made to ensure that consumers can obtain these goods.

There will be a reduction of prices for certain foodstuffs. This will be accomplished by: (a) imposition of excise taxes on such nonessential commodities as white flour in order to reduce the prices of such vital ones as standard bread; (b) funds from excise taxes and from the profits earned on goods imported by the Government itself; (c) determination of prices for locally produced industrial and agricultural goods on the basis of a careful analysis of the cost of production and services, such as transportation, to ensure that the consumer will not have to pay for unjustified expenses; (d) consideration by the Government of the possibility of eliminating duty, or reducing it, on certain essential goods, as well as subsidies to permit reductions in the cost of the most essential ones; (e) permission of the production of luxury goods only when they are destined for export or will replace imports; (f) a one-year import-and-export plan designed to provide basic foods; (g) appropriate measures to facilitate the production of commodities that are nourishing and inexpensive.

Five factors, not all of them necessarily compatible, will be taken into consideration in determining the program for local production: (a) the austerity regime; (b) the reduction of living costs; (c) the replacement of imported goods by local products; (d) the saving of foreign currency; (e) the expansion of agricultural and industrial production to meet the needs of the local market and to facilitate exports, in order to develop the economy of the country and absorb new immigrants.

The national menu will be devoid of luxury products; it will include the least expensive commodities, but will be designed to ensure an individual's health and ability to work. It will give every person 2700–2800 calories a day. This menu, prepared in consultation with nutrition experts, is similar to the one that obtained in England in 1944; it is on a higher level than the usual European standard. The foodstuffs included in the menu will be rationed. Special concern will be shown for the needs of children, the sick, pregnant women, nursing mothers, etc. The rationing program will go into effect at the beginning of May.

It is estimated that each person will be able to save I£1 per month by the correct choice of foods. This will mean yearly savings of I£12 million on food alone.

All imports will require licenses from the Ministry of Supply and Rationing. The importers will be permitted to sell their foods only to wholesalers designated by this Ministry. Every wholesaler will be linked to a certain number of retailers and will be able to sell his goods only to them, on the basis of Ministry regulations and at the prices it will set. A number of consumers will be linked to each retailer and they will be able to buy their rations only from him. Retailers will receive goods in accordance with the number of consumers they serve. When there is a drop in the price of food, there will be a concomitant reduction in the cost-of-living index. We expect to cut the living costs of a four-member family by IL1.25 during the month of May.

Imports will be handled by a limited number of importers who have the necessary expertise and will be satisfied with limited profits. This will facilitate the control of imports. Anyone who engages in profiteering will have his import license withdrawn. Public committees will be established all over the country to help the Government in its war against profiteering and the black market.

After the debate, which continued until May 11, 1949, the following resolution presented by Meir Grabovsky (the Mapai Whip) was adopted by a vote of fifty-seven to thirty-three:

> The Knesset welcomes the Prime Minister's statement on the efforts being made by the Government to prepare the economy to meet the great challenge of immigrant absorption. The Knesset expresses its general approval of the plan presented by the Minister of Supply and Rationing and regards it as the first step in a Government effort to combat high living costs and to promote industrial and agricultural production. This plan, and additional proposals, will be discussed by the appropriate committees. The Knesset welcomes the Government's statements regarding further measures to aid all branches of the economy.

Rationing helped in no small degree to alleviate the shortages caused by large-scale immigration, though at the same time it gave birth to a large black market. Considerable industrial development and an increase in national income were in evidence. Nevertheless, the deficit in the balance of trade increased as well.

During the first 20 months after the establishment of the State 2350 plants employing 15,400 workers were established in the metalworking, textile, food, and clothing industries. In March 1950 the Investment Center was established, and by the end of 1951 it had approved the launching of 650 new plants with an investment of IL85 million.

From the end of 1948 to the end of 1951 national income increased from IL150 million to IL440 million. The number of gainfully employed rose from 240,580 in November 1948 to 505,000 at the end of 1951. The wage-earners were divided as follows in 1951: agriculture—70,000 (1950—59,000); crafts and industry—119,000 (1950—112,000); building and public works—48,000 (1950—27,000); transportation—35,000 (1950—30,000); trade and finance—85,000 (1950—70,000); the professions—40,000 (1950—35,000); public services—58,000 (1950—50,000); other services—50,000 (1950—39,000). But simultaneously the deficit in the balance of trade grew from year to year: it was IL21 million in the second half of 1948; IL77.4 million in 1949; IL88.5 million in 1950; and IL105.9 million in 1951.

Economic difficulties were accompanied by educational difficulties. There were not enough teachers or schools for immigrant children. Adult education also became a much more serious problem, since adult immigrants had to learn Hebrew as well. There was a large-scale expansion of "Ulpanim" (National Hebrew Study Centers for Adults). They were particularly important for immigrants in the professions: doctors, engineers, lawyers, accountants, and the like. Special vocational training courses were also organized in such fields as construction, carpentry, metalwork, sewing, embroidery, etc.

The problem of immigrant housing was particularly grave. As stated earlier, we made do with abandoned houses, in which 160,000 people were placed during the first year. But 582,382 immigrants arrived in the 1949–1951 period, and it was necessary to provide housing for them in three stages. (1) At first they were housed in immigrant centers or transient camps, where the idle inhabitants were supported by public funds; about 100,000 people were in these camps at the end of 1949. (2) Immigrants were later housed in "ma'abarot" (temporary quarters), where they supported themselves. (3) Finally, permanent housing was built. In 1949, 843,000 square meters of construction was carried out, 749,000 of it for housing, the rest for industrial, commercial, and other purposes. This rose to 1,240,000 square meters in 1950 and to 2,137,000 square meters in 1951 of which 1,946,000 was for housing. But this rapid rise in construction was not adequate to meet the housing needs of the expanding community.

First Annual Budget ★ Ben-Gurion Analyzes Israel's Unique Security Needs ★ Knesset Debates Defense Services Law

The first annual budget was presented to the Knesset by Finance Minister Kaplan only on June 14, 1949, thirteen months after the establishment of the State. Until that time budgets were adopted for a few months at a time: from May 15 to the end of June 1948— IL2,128,484; from July to December 1948—IL 12,455,626; from January to the end of March 1949—IL14,300,672. For ten and a half months this amounted to a total of IL28,884,784 (not including all defense expenditures).

In presenting the budget for 1949–1950 (from the beginning of April to the end of March), the Finance Minister pointed out that there were really three budgets involved: an ordinary budget (including State services), a defense budget, and a budget for immigrant absorption. For security reasons only the ordinary budget and the budget for immigrant absorption and development were presented to the Knesset. The Finance Committee both discussed and decided on the defense budget. It was right, indeed necessary, Kaplan said, to obtain credit to cover the cost of security and development. The need to win a military victory justified placing burdens on future generations. And the development budget, by promoting the growth of the economy, would result in the creation of income producing assets. But where the ordinary budget was concerned, it was necessary to cut costs and to keep expenditures within the bounds of anticipated income.

After a debate that lasted for over two months, until August 31, 1949, a IL 40,178,000 budget was authorized. It included IL6.3 million for the rehabilitation of soldiers and IL2 million for health, welfare, and the vocational training of immigrants.

The ordinary budget for 1950–1951, adopted on August 10, 1950, totaled IL59,450,000. The development budget that same year was IL65 million, of which IL18 million was for immigrants housing, IL1.5 million for housing soldiers, IL11.3 million for agricultural development, IL8.7 million for industrial development, and IL6 million for the expansion of transportation.

For 1951–1952 the budget totaled IL113,637,000. The agricultural development budget for that year was IL24.5 million, IL3.6 million of which was for the construction of housing in new settlements. The ordinary budget of the State of Israel increased nearly threefold over a three-year period.

Two weeks before the first annual budget was approved by the Knesset, Ben-Gurion presented the Defense Service Law to the Knesset, which was afterward the subject of vigorous debate. In his statement to the Knesset, Ben-Gurion said:

The Israel Defense Forces Ordinance was published on May 26, 1948. But only after the last armistice agreement had been signed (with Syria) on July 20, 1949, was it possible to consider the proper organization of the Israel Defense Forces. In planning for the future, we cannot simply be satisfied with the methods that brought us victory in the past. What was sufficient at one stage may not be sufficient in the future. We must consider our potential enemies not as they were in the war that has ended, but as they might be in some future war. First of all, we must make it absolutely clear that security is not a matter for the Defense Forces alone. Many factors are involved.

The first and most important factor is large-scale, rapid immigration. Immigration is not only a means of achieving the central goal of the State, the ingathering of the exiles, but also the most effective way of ensuring its security. We cannot allow economic factors to impede immigration.

Another factor in our security, almost as important, is the establishment of settlements and a balanced distribution of our population. Our security is endangered because less than 10 percent of the Jewish people live in Israel, less than 10 percent of the area of the State is under cultivation, and there is an undue concentration of population in one region. We must pursue a settlement policy aimed at populating all sections of the country. Sending immigrants to agricultural settlements in the east, the south, and the Jerusalem area is not only a biological and economic necessity, but also of great importance from a security viewpoint. There is no need to recall the important role played by the border settlements in the defense of upper Galilee, the Jordan Valley, the Jerusalem Hills, and the Negev. A settlement program designed to strengthen our security will not be possible without a great pioneering drive. However, the Government cannot depend solely on pioneering initiative. It must give every possible assistance to agricultural settlement by enacting appropriate laws, providing financial aid, and ensuring proper planning. The State must see to it that settlements are established along the borders, where they will serve as our first line of defense.

Our security demands that we develop our industrial and agricultural production. This involves a tremendous creative effort based on modern equipment, scientific methods, high productivity, and efficient and thrifty management. Economic power is one of the decisive factors in contemporary military struggles. Our economic strength played an important role in our recent victory.

We cannot afford to overlook our unique geographical situation. Should we be in conflict with our neighbors again, we will lack overland contact with the outside world. This grave fact obligates us to draw a number of conclusions. (a) Our agriculture and fishing must make the country self-sufficient from the point of view of food. (b) We must promote the production of weapons so that we will not be dependent on outside sources. (c) We must foster Israeli shipping and expand our maritime links with all corners of the world; special emphasis must be placed on swiftly obtaining merchant ships and on educating a new generation of seamen. (d) We must facilitate the development of internal and external air transport, which will involve the purchase of planes, the training of ground and air crews, and the development of an advanced radar system.

Scarcely any country can be so economically independent that it remains unconcerned about its foreign trade; for a small country like ours foreign trade is particularly important. We must remember that it will depend mainly on sea and air transport. Moreover, in case of war, our only connection with the outside world will be by sea, or perhaps only by air.

Our independence and security depend to a significant extent on our scientific and technological research. Technology is particularly important in the security sphere. If we fall behind the rest of the world in technological development, our security will be imperiled.

In the course of the general mobilization during the war we became aware of the painful fact that a large percentage of our young people were not completely healthy. Moreover, the immigrants who have arrived recently are in much worse shape. The health of our young people and of the nation as a whole is a vital factor in our security.

Finally, one cannot ignore another element of great importance in the security sphere: our foreign policy must be based on a sincere desire for peace with our neighbors and with all the nations of the world. We must make an active effort to promote friendship with all nations, great and small, in both the East and the West. We must also support all measures designed to bring regional and international peace. Such a policy will, in itself, contribute to our security. The world's recognition of our genuine desire for peace will strengthen our position. But as long as there is a possibility of war, our security will also depend on our army.

Our army will necessarily be a small one, because we have a small population and need our manpower to carry out the basic tasks of our State—the absorption of immigrants and the creation of a new culture and economy. Therefore, our army must achieve the *highest qualitative level*. We will require, no less than any other State, the most advanced professional and technical information available to the most modern armies in the world. But this alone will not be enough. In view of our special geographical and historical situation, our army must also have its own special characteristic, *pioneering fervor*. Only by exploiting our moral and intellectual excellence to the fullest will our army play its proper role in maintaining the security of the State.

When war was declared on us, before we had even gained our independence and at a time when our hands were tied by a hostile foreign regime, we mobilized our resources as best we could. There was no possibility of going into details in an hour of danger. Our only goal at the time was to throw back the enemy and to emerge victorious. The experience that we had gained in the Hagana and in the Jewish military units during the Second World War, as well as the loyalty and valor of our youth, enabled us to win. Now we are entering a more or less prolonged truce period, and we have the possibility of properly organizing our army without being rushed by the presence of an enemy at our gates. In doing so, we must avail ourselves of the most advanced military know-how in the world, at the same time taking into account the special needs and conditions of the State of Israel and the people of Israel.

We must rid ourselves of the misconception, inherited from backward countries, that an army is a degrading thing. There are such armies in the world. But they are the products of backward regimes, which are bound to establish armies in their own image. The army of a progressive nation can be, and in our case must be, an instrument for raising the level of the population. Our army will not be fulfilling its mission, externally or internally, if a soldier's period of military service does not enrich him physically, culturally, and morally. Our security needs, as well as the need to build up our nation, will not be met if our army is not a bastion of pioneering youth, who are healthy in body and spirit, endowed with initiative, courage, energy, and a willingness to overcome every difficulty and face every danger. It must not be forgotten that we are not yet a normal people. The veteran sections of the population, those who lived a life of Jewish independence even before we had gained political independence, are liable to overlook the fact that they are only a small percentage of the Jewish people, and that the overwhelming majority of our people are without a common language, traditions, or roots, and lack an understanding of what it is to be part of an independent national society. They must be absorbed, not only economically, but also socially and culturally. We must unite those who, in the Diaspora, were far apart in time and in space. We must mold them into a unified nation.

We must not overlook the fact that here, in the State, there are still factors that operate to separate us. Our political and ideological differences are as pronounced as in the most backward of nations. The constant struggle among parties and factions does not promote unity. Aside from the schools, which are not completely free of factionalism themselves, only the army can serve as a unifying force, one that can facilitate the proper absorption of immigrants in Israel's developing society. The army's educational task is not only important internally, but it is also vital to our security. An army of mercenaries, who are not an integral part of a people and do not share its vision of the future, will not be able to win a struggle in which the few are pitted against the many. Not only intellectuals, but also military geniuses and professional soldiers like Hannibal and Napoleon realized the *decisive military importance of the spirit of man.* And we are more dependent on this factor than any other army in the world because we are so few.

Our soldiers must be, first of all, citizens of their State in the most exalted sense of that term. They must be rooted in the Homeland, in the nation's past, in its culture and language. They must be acquainted with its creative heritage and share its vision of the future. Our army must be based on the fraternity of fighting men. At the moment it is the only institution in the country without communal, political, class, or other barriers. Every soldier is equal in his position, his rights, his food, his housing, and his uniform. We cannot allow this military fraternity to be simply a formal matter; it must be endowed with real meaning; it must reflect a shared mission.

During the mass mobilization of the war period young men and women from all communities, from settlements and factories, from slums and wealthy neighborhoods, met for the first time. It was then that one could see the enormous gulf separating them. It was not the ideological and political gulf fostered by the parties, but a gulf resulting from a different way of life. On the one hand there were young people from the groups that run the Yishuv and all of its parties; on the other there were young people who, from their very birth, were denied the opportunity to receive a proper education, who grew up in ignorance and filth, unacquainted with the basic values of Judaism and of mankind.

The young people in this latter group also proved their courage during the war, but they did not receive what they should have received from the army. At a time when our very existence was in the balance, we could not devote sufficient attention to educational and cultural activities. There can be no justification for such neglect in the future, for now we are in a position to plan the systematic development of our army.

The Defense Service Law that is now before you is intended to endow our army with the two basic characteristics essential to our security: military capability and pioneering fervor. The first year of military service will be devoted primarily to a pioneering education within the framework of the army; after the soldiers receive their basic training, extending over a period of one and a half to three months, they—the Sabras and the immigrants, the boys and the girls—will be sent for agricultural training. This will be accompanied by an intensive cultural program designed to give the immigrants a knowledge of Hebrew and to acquaint the youth who did not go to school, or who were not interested in their studies, with Hebrew culture. This period will prepare every young person for group life, responsibility, discipline, outdoor living, and a period of fighting and creative service.

The agricultural training given to every young person, including immigrants up to the age of twenty-six, will serve both military and settlement needs. In the opinion of military experts with whom I have consulted, including important experts from abroad, we will not be able to create an efficient army in this country, a country of immigration, if the young people, and particularly the immigrants, do not first receive an agricultural education that will serve to integrate them into the life of the Homeland, get them used to physical work, and give them a knowledge of the nation's language and culture.

This agricultural training will facilitate the establishment of border villages, which are essential to the security of the State. These border villages will serve as Israel's first line of defense, not a line of fortifications, but a line of human beings. The State cannot force its citizens to settle on the border. A man is not made a pioneer because of an order to that effect. The entire educational system in Israel, inside and outside the schools, as well as our literature and press, must work toward developing a pioneering generation devoted to building up the country, overcoming natural perils on land, on sea, and in the air, as well as creating an economy, society, and culture that will attract Jews from all the Diaspora, and serve as an example to the world.

Jewish history has not been too kind to us. We have not inherited from former generations, as have other peoples, riches, strength, and natural resources. For over forty generations our people have known only persecution and suffering. But we have one precious legacy— great moral strength and intellectual ability. In those spheres we are the equal of any people in the world. We must exploit our moral and intellectual heritage to the fullest; we must pass it on to the young people who grow up in this country and to those who will come to join us.

For three generations we have witnessed in this country the unique phenomenon of "Halutziut" [Pioneering], which was responsible for everything that has been accomplished, from the foundation of Mikve Israel and Petah Tikva to the establishment of the State and our military victories over our enemies. "Halutziut" is not confined to a few extraordinary people; it is found in the soul of every human being. Every person has within him hidden resources and spiritual treasures, most of which never find expression. The pressure of historic needs together with an educational program designed to stir the hearts and souls of men can bring forth these characteristics and elevate every human being to the highest levels of courage and pioneering.

Every talented military commander is aware of this secret. He knows that our army, made up of simple men and women, can be transformed into an army of heroes. The challenge of our historic mission in this country awakened the pioneering fervor that was hidden in the hearts of Jewish youth in the little towns of Lithuania, Poland, Galicia, Rumania, and America. The immigrants who will arrive during the coming years will be mostly from the Oriental countries, the lands of Islam, the nations of Asia and Africa. The Jewish communities in these countries did not have the opportunity in recent generations to avail themselves of the cultural treasures of mankind and of the Jews, even to the same degree that this was possible in Europe.

But there is no reason to believe that the Jews of North Africa, Turkey, Egypt, Iran, or Aden differ basically from the Jews of Lithuania, Galicia, and America. They also have hidden within them the rich springs of pioneering, work, and creativity. If we invest in them only a fraction of the efforts that we invested in the Jewish youth of Europe, we will achieve the desired results.

The year of agricultural training provided for in the Defense Service Law is intended to foster our educational work and to create a generation of pioneers, builders, and defenders. As far as I know, this section of the law is unique, existing only in Israel. But for us it is essential to our security and our existence. It applies to young men and young women alike.

During the War of Independence we were forced to send men into battle after they had received only a few weeks of military training, and sometimes even less. But we should not hasten to draw conclusions from this experience, assuming that basic military training is of no importance. We cannot depend on miracles. The Allied invasion of Europe during the Second World War was delayed for a long period of time because the United States did not want to send its soldiers into battle before they had been properly trained.

Our young people, who come mainly from the Hagana, have a particularly good background in guerrilla warfare. A future war, if it breaks out, will also demand partisan skills. Every soldier will have to show initiative and be able to deal with new situations as they arise in the mountains and in the plains, in built-up areas and in the countryside, during every hour of the day and night, in the heat and in the cold. A knowledge of the country, an ability to cope quickly with any unexpected difficulty, will still be required. As in the past we will sometimes operate in small units, even on an individual basis, on land, on sea, and in the air. Every soldier must be trained to act as his own commander in time of need. But this is not sufficient.

A contemporary army's strength depends primarily on its ability to carry out large-scale operations, using battalions, brigades, or divisions. Moreover, these operations often involve the combined employment of land, sea, and air units. The army must train its men both to show individual initiative — when that is called for — and to work with others in combined operations. An army without discipline turns into a mob endangering both the external and internal security of a nation. Discipline does not imply a denial of individual freedom. Discipline is based on mutual responsibility, on a common belief in the community, the State, and the nation. Pioneering qualities and discipline are the two foundations upon which our Army must be built if it is to carry out the tasks imposed upon it.

The Hagana, the Palmah, and the Jewish units in the British Army gave the Israel Defense Forces a large number of devoted, daring, and experienced commanders. Moreover, I am pleased to add, only a very few of them believe that they have nothing more to learn from the regular armies of the advanced countries.

Everything demanded of an ideal military officer in the most advanced countries is required of our commanders as well. But we also have an additional requirement: *our commanders must serve as models for their men*. It is not enough for them to possess technical and professional know-how, to be endowed with military and administrative abilities, to be loyal and devoted, though all these qualities are essential; in view of the human material from which our army has been and is being built, as well as the historic circumstances in which we live, they must also be capable of serving as an example for their men.

The commander is entrusted with supreme responsibility for both the security of the State and the lives of his men. A real commander does not educate only, or mainly, by giving orders and explanations. His primary educational tool is his own conduct, system of values, and vision of life, a vision worth living for and dying for. The commander must win the love and trust of his soldiers. There cannot be an army without commands and discipline, but the courage that is demanded of an army, the unlimited devotion unto death itself, can stem only from the spirit of man, and only a commander who is able, by his own example, to arouse trust, respect and appreciation can evoke devotion and courage in his own soldiers; only such a commander can succeed in his task. This war, as well as the fighting that preceded it, has proven that we have marvelous human material, from which it is possible to create outstanding commanders and fighting men.

Commanders worthy of the name never complete their studies and training. They continue to learn and progress during their entire lives. We must create military schools on all levels to provide the necessary training. We will also send men overseas to special courses. We are negotiating with several governments in the East and in the West on this matter, and we have already received favorable replies from some of them, though at the moment only a limited number of men are involved.

The Defense Service Law is intended to prepare the entire people to be a fighting people if the need arises, to give Israeli and immigrant youth pioneering values and military training, to maintain under arms a force large enough to repulse a surprise attack until the reserves can be mobilized, and to create, within a military framework, a united, peace-loving, and confident nation that will assume its rightful place in the family of nations.

Not all the Knesset parties agreed with the program proposed by the Government. Some demanded thirty hours for the debate, but a ten-hour debate was finally agreed upon. It began on August 29, 1949.

Riftin (Mapam) complained that the Prime Minister had not sufficiently emphasized the fact that we must have a "People's Army," but had stressed instead the supposed conflict between democratic life and the goals of the Army. He regarded Ben-Gurion's remarks about Israel's excessive political fragmentation "as a grave blow to the democratic Yishuv." In particular he disagreed with the powers given to the Defense Minister by the proposed law. "The Prime Minister's speech does not indicate that the pioneering character of the Army will be properly safeguarded," he said.

Sapir (General Zionists) doubted that the Army was as non-political as the Prime-Minister claimed. In addition, he opposed the period of compulsory agricultural service, arguing that the nine months devoted to it would cut into effective military training.

Rabbi Levin (Agudat Israel) opposed military service for women, which he called "an absolute contradiction to the spirit of Israel." (Several others attacked the section of the law granting exemption to girls on religious grounds.)

Meridor (Herut) said the Prime Minister seemed to believe that "history began in Sejera, where the Hebrew Air Force and Navy were formed." He charged Ben-Gurion with responsibility, directly or indirectly, for halting an attack on Latrun when the town was about to fall into Israeli hands. He also accused the Defense Minister of preventing an attack on the Old City of Jerusalem.

Galili (Mapam) disagreed with the Defense Minister's views on the character of an army. He dwelt on the negative influences in an army. "Militarism," he said, "opens the way to sloth and reaction. These are in the very nature of an army." There are, he added, "disturbing developments in our own Army. These developments threaten our security because they may undermine the basic character of the Defense Forces." It was for this reason that he opposed the regulation forbidding soldiers to participate freely and actively in public life. He saw this regulation as an example of the pernicious spirit in the Army. He told the following story: "When one of our boys, applying to join the Air Force, was asked about his profession and said that he was a farmer, he was rejected. This is because there are books which say farmers are ignorant and have limited intelligence and poor judgment." Such, he added, "apparently are the texts that shape the character of the Israel Defense Forces."

Shaag (Religious Front) declared that the National Service Law was in keeping with Jewish tradition. Our people, he said, was the first, or in any case one of the first, to institute compulsory military service in ancient times. Our first commander declared: "From the age of twenty and above, every man must serve in the army." This continuity is important. We need not think that we are doing something new; we are merely restoring old traditions. With the renewal of our political life we are renewing these values.

Mohamed Seif el-Din el-Zoubi (Nazareth Democratic List): "There are those who say that we are still at war with the Arabs, and therefore cannot yet trust our own Arabs with weapons. There may be some justification for this view. But a great deal depends on the arrangements that the Government makes about the return of a number of refugees. If the Government sees to it that corrupt elements are not allowed in, there will be an increase in security and in cooperation. We will fight with all our strength against anyone, whatever his language, who invades our country. We have not yet forgotten the declaration by one of the important figures in the Jordanian government, Falah Pasha el Madadha, who stated that every resident of Israel would be considered an enemy. Having heard many such statements from various Arab leaders, we know that it is impossible to cooperate with them.

"I am resolutely opposed to the mobilization of women. As a Moslem, I regard this as an absolute violation of our principles, customs, traditions, and religion. It is true that women participated in military campaigns during the first period of Islam, but not as fighters. They walked behind their husbands, brothers, or relatives to inspire them with songs. They carried water and helped to quench the thirst of the fighters and to bind their wounds. Women were not created to bear arms. We have enough men to establish an army worthy of the name."

Amin Salim Jarjura (Nazareth Democratic List): "Compulsory mobilization of women violates the laws of nature and of religion, and undermines the foundations of society. Such mobilization conflicts with the customs of Eastern peoples and particularily of the Arabs."

The Defense Minister, replying to Galili, said that the atmosphere outside the Army was being poisoned and that there were disturbing signs of an attempt to carry the same atmosphere into the Army. As to the claim that a young man was rejected by the Air Force because he was a farmer, the Commander of the Air Force denied the whole story. He knew of no Air Force officers, who felt that a farmer was necessarily unsuited to join that service and he knew of no book that defined farmers as narrow-minded or stupid.

The Commander had pointed out that "there are four stages in the selection of pilots: (a) a medical examination; the Air Force did not rely on the general examination because flying demands higher standards of health; (b) an aptitude test; (c) a general educational test; (d) a final selection process following these tests. When the candidates appear for their medical or aptitude tests, no inquiries are made into their social backgrounds or professions. Those who pass the first three stages successfully appear before a selection committee, whose members choose the most promising candidates solely on the basis of the tests and of the impression they make."

The Defense Minister continued:

> Galili, it seems, was told that a number of young farmers among candidates for pilot training had been rejected. That much is true. But the statistics show the following complete picture: 119 of the 270 candidates for flight training, that is, almost half, were rejected before or during the course. Of the 18 candidates from labor settlements, 6 were rejected, 2 before the course began and 4 during the course itself. In other words, a third of the candidates from the labor settlements failed, as opposed to almost half of the others. It is on the basis of such material that Israel Galili, who is regarded as a military expert in his own party, is ready to pass judgment not only on the Air Force, but on all those responsible for the Israel Defense Forces.
>
> I would like to say a few words about Mr. Meridor's arguments. He criticizes my original sin—preventing an Army attack on July 19. It is very strange that a man like Meridor should think that I committed my first sin on July 19. There were three attacks after July 19, with decisive, historic results. An attack for which the Minister of Defense bears some measure of responsibility took place on October 15; another on October 29; a third one on December 23. They affected the very fate of the country. Mr. Meridor also spoke sarcastically about the "extraordinary preparations" made before May 15. It is a little difficult to argue with him on this point; the two of us are not free to speak to the same extent. Mr. Meridor talks about things he doesn't know; and I know things I can't as yet talk about.

I'd like to comment briefly on the points raised in regard to agricultural training and the compulsory mobilization of women. We have a tendency to regard the Army and security as one and the same thing. This is incorrect; for while there is certainly a connection between the Army and security, security does not end with the Army. The defense needs of every people are different. Our security does not depend on fortifications, weapons, or the Army— it depends on the entire people. If the entire people are unable to meet the challenge facing us, fortifications, weapons, and military units will be of no avail.

And since everything depends on the entire people, we must ask ourselves a question that no other people asks: Are we really a people? As I see it, we are not yet a people. I am not speaking in ideological terms. I refer rather to a people as a unified group of individuals rooted in their Homeland and their culture, ready to fight to the last man to defend themselves. With the passing of time, I am certain we will be shaped into such a people in the crucible of the Homeland. We will acquire a common language as well as a sense of our independence and integrity. But this historic process, which is only just beginning, is a very prolonged one.

Jews are coming from everywhere and they lack a common language in the most direct and immediate sense of that term. When a dozen Jews meet, they cannot communicate with one another. Will men and women without a common tongue be able to face grave challenges? We have people from fifty-five countries in the Army, and a wide gulf separates them from one another. If we had a great deal of time, there would be no cause for concern. After all, our people are all sons of Israel, and with the passage of time they or their children will learn the Hebrew tongue, will become rooted in the Homeland, will link up with one another to become a unified nation. But who knows how much time we have, and when we will be called upon to face a challenge to our existence?

The year of agricultural training is intended, in the first place, to help build a people, to mold it from broken men who have come together from all corners of the earth into a single national entity. The schools cannot do this, because many of the newcomers are no longer of school age. We must give immigrants in the 18-to-25-year-old age group a knowledge of Hebrew and of the country. We must initiate them into a national framework, so that we can create a people united in language and consciousness, a people rooted in the soil of their land. We must give our Army a pioneering character—this can be accomplished during the period of agricultural training. Since the creation of the State, 130 agricultural settlements have been set up; in the 70 years from the foundation of Petah Tikva until the establishment of the State we founded 320 settlements; and yet 90 percent of the soil of the State remains untilled. Agricultural training for every boy and girl will give an enormous impetus to pioneering settlement; settlement and immigration are the two keys to our security.

Now for the question of women in the Army. When one discusses the position of women, two factors must be taken into consideration. First, women have a special mission as mothers. There is no greater mission in life, and nature has decreed that only a woman can give birth to a child. This is the woman's task and her blessing. However, a second factor must be remembered: the woman is not only a woman, but a personality in her own right, in the same way as a man. As such, she should enjoy the same rights and responsibilities as the man, except where motherhood is concerned. There are members of this House who feel differently. That is their privilege, but the majority of the community accepts the basic principle that women cannot be allowed to occupy a lower position in society than men. The arguments heard here against taking women into the Army were heard thirty years ago from the representatives of Mizrahi when they opposed the participation of women in elections to the National Assembly. They, too, appealed to tradition. Now the members of Mizrahi and of Agudat Israel sit together with women in the Knesset and in the Government.

We are told that women are not drafted into any other army in the world. We, too, have no intention of putting women into combat units, though no one can be sure that, should we be attacked and have to fight for our lives, we should not call on the services of every man and woman. But the law in question deals with a peacetime situation, and we want to give women only the most basic military training.

I certainly agree with those who stress the significance of childbearing, but for this very reason it is important to give women agricultural training, for there will be no children born in the new settlements if they are inhabited solely by men. The opposition of the Religious Front is motivated not by religious but by moral considerations. Boys and girls work together in the religious kibbutzim. Is there a lack of morality among them? Why should we fear sending girls for training to Tirat Zvi or Hafetz Hayim? How will this undermine their morality? Why shouldn't we pay attention to the morality of men? After all, a woman cannot go wrong without the assistance of a man.

I believe that if the young people mobilized for military and agricultural training are handled with love and devotion, the Sabras and the immigrants coming together in the settlements and in the camps, they can be taught the value to work and of discipline. They can be inculcated with a love of country, courage, loyalty to their comrades, and mutual assistance. These young people will be capable of fructifying the wilderness and overcoming the perils of nature on land, on sea, and in the air. The Israel Defense Forces will be the crucible of a pioneering, fighting, and creative nation, a nation steeped in pride, courage, and faith in its future. I see no reason why our Army should not be one of the best in the world, if not the best. We can establish an army that will be a source of pride and a bastion of security for the reborn State of Israel.

The Defense Service Law was sent to the Foreign Affairs and Security Committee on September 5, 1949, and approved by the Knesset on September 8, 1949, with only twelve abstentions.

After the law had been adopted Knesset member Esther Raziel-Naor (Herut) asked the Prime Minister: "In your speech to the Knesset you said: 'The strategy of our Army will be an offensive rather than a defensive one.' This being the case, hasn't the time come to change the name of the Army and call it the Israel Army rather than the Israel Defense Forces?"

Ben-Gurion replied: "The questioner does not differentiate between a name, which symbolizes our foreign policy, and military methods, where effectiveness is the central consideration. By calling our Army the Israel Defense Forces, we emphasize that Israel has no aggressive designs on her neighbors, and that we are a peace-loving people. But if we are attacked, we will defend ourselves in the most effective way, which is to mount the strongest possible offensive in enemy territory. So we will continue to use a name symbolizing our desire for peace, and employ a strategy that will ensure victory."

The Transfer of Herzl's Remains to Israel

On August 10, 1949, the chairman of the Knesset Committees, Izhar Harari, presented the draft of a law calling for the transfer of Dr. Theodor Herzl's remains to Israel. The law, unanimously adopted that day, said:

The last will and testament of the seer of the Jewish State, Theodor (Binyamin Zeev) Herzl, of blessed memory, that his remains be reinterred in the Land of Israel, will be carried out on the twenty-second day of Av 5709 (August 17, 1949) in Jerusalem, Eternal Capital and Holy City of the Jewish people.

2. The Government will place at the disposal of the Jewish National Fund a plot of land in Jerusalem as a burial place in which Herzl's remains will be laid to rest.

3. The Executive of the World Zionist Organization, which is engaged in carrying out the aforementioned last will and testament, will receive every assistance that is my require for this purpose from the Israel Defense Forces and the other State organs.

4. The State and the World Zionist Organization will bear, in equal shares, the cost of carrying out Herzl's testament.

5. The Prime Minister is charged with the implementation of the law.

An Israeli delegation left aboard a special El Al plane for Vienna. The delegation included a representative of the Government, David Remez; a representative of the Jewish Agency Executive, Yitzhak Gruenbaum; a representative of the Israel Defense Forces, Col. Yosef Avidar; as well as officers from the Infantry, Artillery, Navy, Air Force, and the Chaplain's Corps. On Sunday, August 14, 1949, the remains of Herzl and his parents were disinterred from the Debling Cemetary and taken to the synagogue in the First District of Vienna, where thousands of Jews paid their last respects. The plane returned to Lydda Airfield on August 16, 1949. It was met by the Prime Minister, other Ministers, the Speaker of the Knesset, the Chief of Staff, and representatives of the Zionist Organization. The coffin was transferred in a military vehicle to Tel Aviv and placed in front of the Knesset, where tens of thousands of people came to pay their respects. Sprinzak and Ben-Gurion spoke in the Knesset.

Sprinzak read a statement sent by Chaim Weizmann, who, because of illness, was recuperating outside of Israel:

We, the elected representatives of the State, hereby receive the creator of the Zionist Organization and the seer of political revival, the man who awakened the collective desires of the people in order that they carry out what was, as he put it in his book, an "old idea." Theodor Herzl left us while he was still a young man, but his message did not die with him; rather it grew and developed until it became the hymn of a new life that developed in the land of our forefathers.

The Prime Minister said:

The remains of the greatest prophet of our period were interred for forty-five years in foreign soil, in the place where Herzl developed the idea of a Jewish State and created the machinery for its establishment. Herzl wrote in 1898, six years before his passing: "I do not know the hour of my death, but I know that Zionism will not die. From the days of Basle, the people of Israel have had their own popular representation, and the Jewish State will be established in the Homeland." His vision has been fulfilled. When we bear Herzl's remains to Jerusalem, it will not be a funeral march. It will be a victory march, the victory of a vision that became a reality.

On August 17, the coffin reached Jerusalem and was transferred to the courtyard of the Jewish Agency. Masses of Jerusalemites filed by the coffin and at 4:30 P.M. it was taken to a grave that had been dug in the stony soil of Mount Herzl.

*UN Assembly Votes To Internationalize Jerusalem ★ Ben-Gurion
Declares That This Decision Cannot and Will Not Be Carried Out*

The same year that Herzl's body was reinterred in Jerusalem, the Knesset and some Government offices were transferred to the Eternal Capital of Israel, in defiance of the UN General Assembly resolution demanding that the city be placed under the jurisdiction of an independent UN body.

On December 10, 1949, the General Assembly, by thirty-eight to fourteen, with seven abstentions, voted to uphold its resolution of November 29, 1947, which called for treating Jerusalem as a separate entity under UN rule. The thirty-eight votes were provided by the Arab countries, a number of Moslem countries (Afghanistan, Iraq, Pakistan), the Communist bloc, Chiang Kai-shek's China, and a number of European and Latin American Catholic countries. The fourteen votes were cast by the United States, Turkey, Britain, Yugoslavia, Denmark, Canada, Sweden, Costa Rica, South Africa, Uruguay, Iceland, Guatemala, Norway, and Israel. Under the terms of the resolution, Jerusalem was to include the area of the city itself together with a number of neighboring villages, going down as far as Bethlehem in the south, Abu Dis in the east, Ein Karem in the west, and Shuafat in the north, as had been indicated on the maps attached to the November 1947 UN resolution.

The original resolution was offered by Australia, and amended by the Soviet Union and Lebanon. The Lebanese representative, Charles Malik, declared that the decision symbolized a new and wonderful beginning for Jerusalem and the entire State of Israel: "There is every chance that the UN will be able to carry out this resolution. There is no basis for the fear that our Israeli friends will not obey it."

He and those who voted with him apparently forgot that the UN had failed to carry out the 1947 resolution with regard to the establishment of a Jewish State, though it was supported by more than two-thirds of the UN membership, headed by the Soviet Union and the United States. When the State of Israel was established notwithstanding, and the Arab armies invaded it, the UN did not raise a finger to interfere. Had it not been for the bravery of Jewish youth, there would be no trace of the State nor of its Jewish residents. Malik and his friends also ignored the announcement made by the Prime Minister of Israel in the Knesset on December 5, 1949, five days before the UN General Assembly resolution on internationalization, when he said:

> As you know, the UN General Assembly is now discussing the problem of Jerusalem and the Holy Places. The State of Israel is a member of the UN and as such must make its other members, and all those who love peace and justice in the world, aware of what she has felt about Jerusalem since she became a national entity under the leadership of King David three thousand years ago. She must also inform them of her views on the relation of other religions in the city.
>
> When the restored State was established on May 14, 1948, it proclaimed: "The State of Israel will guarantee freedom of religion, conscience, education, and culture; will safe-

guard the Holy Places of all religions; and will loyally uphold the principles of the United Nations Charter."

At the same time it must be made clear that Jewish Jerusalem is an integral part of the State of Israel, just as it is an integral part of Jewish history, Jewish faith, and the Jewish spirit. Jerusalem is the very heart of the State of Israel. We are proud that Jerusalem became holy to other religions, and we will certainly make all the necessary arrangements to ensure that adherents of other religions will be able to satisfy their religious needs in Jerusalem. Moreover, we will cooperate with the UN to ensure that these arrangements are made.

But we cannot conceive of the possibility that the UN should attempt to tear out Jerusalem from the State of Israel, or to strike at the sovereignty of Israel in her Eternal Capital.

On December 13, the Prime Minister announced in the Knesset:

A week ago I presented a Government statement on Jerusalem. The views expressed in that statement have not changed and will never change. As you know the UN General Assembly has in the meantime voted by a large majority that Jerusalem should be placed under an international regime. This decision cannot be carried out, if only for the determined opposition of the residents of Jerusalem.

We respect the desire of interested states for freedom of religion in Jerusalem and free access to its Holy Places, as well as their desire to maintain established rights in regard to Holy Places and religious buildings in the city. Our pledge to safeguard these rights still stands, and will be fulfilled. However, we cannot allow Jerusalem to be forcefully torn apart. This would be a denial of the natural rights of the people who dwell in Zion.

When the First Knesset opened in Jerusalem on February 14, 1949, normal life had not yet been restored in our capital city. In the meantime life has returned to normal and there is no reason that the Knesset should not return to Jerusalem. We suggest that you make a decision to that effect.

This Government recommendation was vigorously supported by one representative after another. Yitzhak Ben-Aharon said: "At this grave hour in Israel's history, we feel it to be both our right and responsibility to support the Government in its efforts to ensure the sovereignty of Israel over an undivided Jerusalem, and to defeat any attempt to cut Jerusalem off from the rest of the nation." Yosef Sapir said: "We reiterate the statement that we made a week ago—we are determined not to be influenced by any decision aimed at cutting us off from Jerusalem." The Knesset Speaker, Sprinzak, declared: "I can safely say that almost the entire Knesset supports the Prime Minister on this matter. I wish to announce that the Knesset will again meet in Jerusalem after Hanukah." (Applause).

Foreign Minister Sharett on January 2, 1950, reported on the Jerusalem struggle in the General Assembly. "The debate on Jerusalem," he said, "was one of our most difficult international challenges. The Assembly resolution surprised and shocked us. It was as if we had been struck by an arrow shot from what we regarded as our sanctuary. We were not the only ones hurt by that vote. It lowered the prestige and impaired the moral authority of the United Nations. The supporters of the resolution cast their votes for it without considering whether or not the UN could carry it out. A great many delegations even refused to believe that it could be passed. World public opinion was generally hostile to it. The worst aspect of the resolution is the irresponsible way in which it was adopted. Its supporters voted for it despite being well aware that it was not likely to be implemented."

Several speakers accused the Minister of Defense of abandoning Jerusalem. In his response on January 4, 1950, the Prime Minister informed the Knesset for the first time about preparations that had been made for the War of Independence. The time had not yet come to publish all the details, he said, and limited himself to mentioning two dates of special importance. The first, July 1945, was when somewhere in the world (now it can be told—it was in the United States) the first preparations were made for the development of an arms industry in Israel, an industry that was to play an important role in the War of Independence. The second date was August 1946, when the Zionist Executive, meeting in Paris, decided that Zionist funds should be used for arms purchases and the development of an arms industry. Two years later the Arab armies invaded the country in order to destroy the restored State of Israel.

No one man can claim credit for the extraordinary things that were done and for the glorious achievements of the Hagana and of the Defense Forces. The enterprise was a collective effort, the work of anonymous men and women who invested their efforts over a long period of time in the production and purchase of weapons, beginning with simple and primitive ones, and ending with the most complex and modern arms.

He would like to say something about Jerusalem in the War of Independence, the Prime Minister continued. Jerusalem was twice destroyed in our history. We have very few details about the destruction of the First Temple, but we do have details about the destruction of the Second Temple by Titus. The Romans knew what it meant to fight a war. They did not begin the struggle in Jerusalem; they left Jerusalem to the last. First they fought in the Galilee and in Judea, and only after they had conquered the rest of the country did they turn to Jerusalem. They knew that Jerusalem could not be held if the rest of the country had not fallen.

The Hagana and the Israel Defense Forces were charged with defending the entire country, including every Jewish settlement. This was the task of the Hagana even before the creation of the Defense Forces. The Hagana did its job without publicity or public demonstrations. All the settlements were under attack and if the Hagana had not succeeded in defending them—in defending hundreds of villages and cities, in defending the roads—Jerusalem would have been wiped out. Jerusalem was saved because the rest of the country was saved. There cannot be a Jewish Jerusalem without a Jewish country. There cannot be a Jewish Jerusalem without Jewish transport. Jerusalem's existence was dependent on the defense of all the Jewish settlements while the Mandatory regime was still in power, and on freedom of access to the city.

When the second truce began on July 18, 1948, enemy forces were in control of the heart of the Galilee, they were encamped in the entire Negev and in most of the south. The Jewish settlements in the south were endangered by the Egyptians. So we devoted our major efforts at that time not only to the defense of Jewish Jerusalem but to the liberation of the south, the Negev, and the Galilee. But at no time was Jerusalem forgotten. The "Road of Valor" ["Burma Road"] was completed on December 2, 1948, and this made possible the opening of the First Knesset in Jerusalem. When the armistice agreement with Trans-Jordan was signed on April 3, 1949, we gained control of the railway in the Jerusalem area that had been in the hands of the Legion. After the tracks had been repaired and the bridges rebuilt, we could send the first Israeli train to Jerusalem on August 7, 1949. These efforts paved the way, in turn, for the transfer of Government offices to Jerusalem.

When our delegation at the United Nations informed us that our Jerusalem resolution might receive only one vote, our own, the Prime Minister cabled back that, in his opinion, the one vote was sufficient in this instance. The fate of Jerusalem was decided by the military, economic, and settlement activities that began on November 30, 1947, and have continued until this very day: the defense of communication lines; the Nahshon and Latrun operations; the conquest of neighborhoods inside Jerusalem itself (Lifta, Romema, Katamon, etc.); the taking of the Jerusalem Corridor; the establishment of settlements in the Corridor; the construction of the "Road of Valor"; the Israeli railway; the stand of the Jews of Jerusalem; the arrival of new immigrants—all these factors played their part.

The struggle for Jerusalem is not only political. The Jewish nation is unique in the annals of history and this country is unique among the countries of the world—if not of the entire world, at least in that part of the world where the Jewish people have lived for two thousand years: the Christian and Moslem part. China and India have had no contact with Jerusalem, and they make up half of mankind. But the other half of mankind, among whom the Jews have lived, has a link with this land. There are two elements— political and spiritual—in the struggle for Jerusalem. They are interdependent, and yet independent of one another.

The vote on the internationalization of Jerusalem, in which the Soviet bloc, the Catholic bloc, and the Arab bloc joined together, did not surprise us. These blocs have nothing in common; they were united only by their opposition to a Jewish Jerusalem.

We know what Jerusalem has meant to us over a period of three thousand years, from the days of King David to the present time. There is no city in the world, not even Athens or Rome, that has played such an important role in the life of a people for such a long period as has Jerusalem in the life of the Jewish people. But something that happened in Jewish Jerusalem less than two thousand years ago transformed it into a religious center for hundreds of millions of people, for the inheritors of Greco-Roman culture among whom we lived. The tidal wave that swelled out of Jerusalem engulfed all the leading peoples of the world, all, that is, except the Jewish people. They remained "stiff-necked," though they paid dearly for their stubborness.

When, in the seventh century, a new force emerged from the Arabian desert and spread like wildfire over the entire region, the Jews were the only ones who did not surrender to it. Individual Jews and whole branches of the Jewish people were lost. Of the many Jewish tribes in the Arabian Peninsula, only the Yemenites remained Jewish. All the others were converted or killed. But the Jewish people lived on.

Taken in the context of Jewish history, what has just happened in the UN General Assembly was no suprise, Ben-Gurion continued. We are certainly alone, though here and there we have friends and supporters. Our very nature makes us both the most isolated and, at the same time, the most universalistic people in the world. This apparent contradiction is what makes the Jewish people and the State of Israel unique. This "contradiction" is what earns us both friends and adversaries among the nations of the world.

No, the vote in the UN General Assembly was no surprise. But it was based on mistaken assumptions, as will soon become clear. If we emerge from this struggle successfully, as can be expected, we will be stronger than ever before. The history of Jerusalem and its presentday reality will operate in our favor. Our struggle for Jerusalem did not begin in the UN General Assembly, but encompassed a contructive effort extending over many decades. Moreover, our military and economic achievements of the last two years have changed the face of Jerusalem. Both justice and power are on our side in the struggle for Jerusalem. We will be able to win if we exploit these two factors. Power alone is not enough to win a city, particularly not Jerusalem. We will succeed in Jerusalem if we show the utmost respect for the rights of our neighbors.

The Christians and Moslems must understand that the Jews will not bow their heads to those who hate Israel, but will respect the religious feelings and Holy Places of others. The error of the UN will be rectified, for the UN is bound to realize that a mistake was made. But we must see to it that we don't make our own mistakes. Jerusalem will be ours if we show proper respect for the rights of others, the rights of other religions.

Some three thousand years before the creation of the UN General Assembly, King Solomon built the first Holy Place in Jerusalem. When he finished his work and prayed for the well-being of his people, he added a prayer on behalf of the stranger, saying: "Moreover, concerning the stranger that is not of Thy people Israel, when he shall come out of a far country for Thy name's sake—for they shall hear of Thy great name, and of Thy mighty hand, and of Thine outstretched arm—when he shall come and pray toward this house; hear Thou in heaven Thy dwelling place, and do according to all that the stranger calleth to Thee for; that all the peoples of the earth may know Thy name, to fear Thee, as doth Thy people Israel, and that they may know that Thy name is called upon this house which I have built" (I Kings 8:41–43).

"The State of Israel must remain true to the spirit of Solomon's prayer," the Prime Minister concluded.

Israel Bar-Yehuda, speaking on behalf of Mapam, then offered the following motion: "Since the Government has not promised to oppose any attempt to allow the annexation of the Old City of Jerusalem or conquered parts of the country by Trans-Jordan, and in view of its hapless foreign policy, the Knesset hereby express its lack of confidence in the Government." His motion was defeated, sixty-three to twenty-eight.

On behalf of Herut, Yacov Meridor presented another resolution: "The fact that the Government has systematically avoided issuing a declaration that Jerusalem is the capital of Israel, and that its policy is designed to perpetuate the partitioning of the Homeland and British-Arab control of parts of it, including sections of the City of David, has led to Israel's isolation in the international sphere and a renewed UN decision to tear Jerusalem from the body of the State. This grave failure reflects, in particular, the activities of the Foreign Minister. But since the Prime Minister is closely connected with those activities, and since he has announced that the entire Government is responsible for them, the Knesset hereby expresses its lack of confidence in the Government."

This resolution was also rejected, by a vote of sixty-three to eleven.

Compulsory Free Education Law ★ Crises in the Government ★ Conflict with Syria over the Hula Swamp

The mass immigration from all corners of the globe, from countries with a high educational level and from others with a low level, multiplied Israel's educational problems.

On July 13, 1949, fourteen months after the establishments of the State and seven months after the end of the War of Independence, the Minister of Education and Culture, Zalman Shazar, presented to the Knesset a draft law for compulsory free education. He pointed out that even in the time of the First Temple children from every city and village were given an education, and that before the establishment of the State 90 percent of the Jewish children went to school—even without a law. However, a survey carried out in 1937 by Dushkin and Brill showed that not all children completed the eighth grade. In 1940 seven thousand children were receiving no education at all, and every year another three thousand were added to the roll of the unlettered. Only in the settlements in which a free education was offered did children remain in school from the first to the eighth grades. In the beginning of 1948–1949, four months after the establishment of the State, there were six thousand Jewish children of elementary-school age who were not studying (a figure that did not include the children in the immigrant camps).

In accordance with the Compulsory Education Law adopted by the Knesset on September 21, 1949, compulsory education was to include every child up to the age of fourteen and every young person from the ages of fourteen to seventeen who had not completed an elementary education. Compulsory education embraced all children between the ages of six and eleven in 1950–1951; between five and twelve in 1951–1952; and thereafter all children between the ages of five and thirteen. Starting in 1950–1951, the law also covered those youngsters who had not yet completed their elementary educations.

The law recognized four school systems or "trends": General, Workers, Mizrahi, and Agudat Israel. The division among the various types of schools in 1951–1952 was: 43.3 percent in the Workers Trend (in 1950–1951, 37.3 percent); 28 percent in the General Trend (32.7 percent in 1950–1951); 18.4 percent in the Mizrahi Trend (18.5 percent in 1950–1951); 7.7 percent in the Agudat Israel Trend (6.6 percent in 1950–1951). The choice of school to which children were sent was left up to the parents.

In 1949–1950, 100,743 Jewish boys and girls studied in elementary schools, as did 15,400 non-Jewish children. In 1950–1951, the figure was 133,016 Jewish and 21,480 non-Jewish children. In 1951–1952, it was 181,093 Jewish and 23,126 non-Jewish children. The shortage of teachers grew more and more severe from year to year. Five-month teacher-training courses for high-school grades were organized. There was also a severe shortage of buildings and equipment; in some immigrant settlements school buildings were decidedly substandard.

The four school systems and the registration arrangements caused a Government crisis, the second during the tenure of the First Knesset. The first crisis began when the Prime Minister felt it necessary to add a minister to the Government. The first elected Government had only twelve ministers, and the coalition was composed of four parties: Mapai, the National Religious Front, the Sephardim, and the Progressives. The Prime Minister had wanted to add Mapam and the General Zionists, but as he pointed out earlier, they refused to join, and thus a number of ministries were assigned temporarily to other members of the Government, who were already busy.

In November 1949, with the opening of the second session of the Knesset, the Prime Minister turned again to Mapam and the General Zionists and also formulated principles that he hoped would permit all the parties to work together in a coalition. The spokesman of one of the parties asked him why he wanted more parties to join the coalition at a time when he already had a sufficiently large majority—75 out of the 120 Knesset members. The Prime Minister replied that he favored enlarging the coalition because the State of Israel was created not only for its inhabitants, but for the ingathering of the exiles, a task perhaps more difficult than both the establishment of the State and the War of Independence put together. Earlier, under Ottoman and British rule, the gates of the Homeland had been closed to immigrants; now there were several countries that Jews wished to leave and come to Israel, but were not allowed to do so. At the same time, many Jewish communities in the Diaspora still felt that they could live happily outside of Israel—and it made no difference whether or not they called themselves Zionists. There were also economic difficulties. Israel was a small, poor, and ravaged country that had to absorb an enormous number of immigrants in a short period of time, since its first elected Government had set as its goal the doubling of the Jewish community in two years. This was being accomplished, but not without enormous economic difficulties caused by lack of money, lack of housing, and a lack of jobs.

There were also cultural problems. The Jewish people were unlike any other people. They were, in fact, a collection of tribes distant from one another not only geographically but historically. Some had lived in countries with a seventeenth-century environment, while others lived in twentieth-century lands. One tribe did not know the language of another, and almost all were cut off from their people's culture, language, history, and national movement. It was necessary to create a nation out of shattered human beings, just as it was necessary to create a Homeland from a country that was deserted and for the most part desolate. All this required a pioneering effort from all sections of the people and of the economy. There was need for private initiative and private capital, just as there was need for group initiative and national capital.

The two parties did not answer the Prime Minister's call. During the parliamentary recess that began in August 1950, the Government discussed the difficult economic problems that had arisen in consequence of mass immigration. The Prime Minister concluded that it was necessary to add another Cabinet member to head a Ministry of Commerce and Industry. In progressive countries with constituency elections, where there are only two or three parties and no need for a coalition with a multiplicity of parties, the Prime Minister can replace ministers in his Government as he sees fit. But when there is a coalition with several parties, the division of offices among them must be taken into account. The addition of a minister, even if it is really necessary, immediately brings demands from the other parties for additional ministers.

The Prime Minister therefore decided that he should add a Minister of Commerce and Industry who was completely non-political. Several days before the opening of the third session of the First Knesset, he brought a proposal to that effect to the Government. The parties said they would consider the matter. Legal experts informed the Prime Minister that he could not add a new member to the Cabinet without its resigning and then being presented again, with the new minister, to the Knesset for its approval. The Prime Minister informed the Government of the situation the day before the opening of the third session of the Knesset (October 15, 1950), and found the National Religious Front unable or unwilling to agree to the addition of a Minister of Commerce and Industry. On the day the Knesset was to meet the Prime Minister gathered together the entire Cabinet, but failed to gain the approval of the religious parties.

He therefore announced his resignation at the opening of the Knesset (October 16), adding that if all the parties would agree to the addition of a non-party minister, he would present a new thirteen-member Cabinet at once. If not, he proposed the creation of an eight-member all-Mapai Transition Government (Ben-Gurion, Joseph, Golda Meir, Kaplan, David Remez, Shazar, Shitreet, Sharett). If no other party could form a Government, he suggested that arrangements be made for elections to a Second Knesset.

After a two-day debate Knesset Speaker Sprinzak put the question of the Transition Government up to a vote; it was rejected by a majority of fifty-seven to forty-three, with eight abstentions. The Speaker thereupon announced that the previous Government would remain in office until a new one had been established.

In less than two weeks, however, the religious parties had agreed to the addition of a non-party Minister of Commerce and Industry, and the Prime Minister presented a thirteen-member Cabinet to the Knesset on October 30. Some changes were made in the composition of the Cabinet and in the distribution of portfolios. They were allocated as follows: Ben-Gurion, Prime Minister and Minister of Defense; Yacov Geri, Minister of Commerce and Industry; Dov Joseph, Minister of Transportation; Pinhas Lubianiker [Lavon], Minister of Agriculture; Rabbi Y. M. Levin, Minister of Social Welfare; Golda Myerson, Minister of Labor and Social Insurance; Rabbi Y. L. Maimon [Fishman], Minister of Religious Affairs and of War Victims; Eliezer Kaplan, Minister of Finance; Pinhas Rosen [Rosenblueth], Minister of Justice; David Remez, Minister of Education and Culture; Behor Shitreet, Minister of Police; Moshe Shapira, Minister of the Interior, of Health, and of Immigration; Moshe Sharett [Shertok], Foreign Minister.

While he was reading out the list of Cabinet members, the Prime Minister expressed the hope that Lubianiker and Mrs. Myerson would adopt Hebrew names. [They did: Lavon and Meir, respectively.]

After a two-day debate the Government was approved by a vote of sixty-nine to forty-two with two abstentions. It also proved short-lived because of a controversy that arose over the registration of children to attend schools of the various trends.

Section 10 (a) of the Compulsory Education Law, adopted on September 12, 1949, states:

> Parents discharging the duty imposed on them under Section 3 to register a child or adolescent may, at the time of registration, declare that they wish the child or adolescent to attend an institution for elementary education belonging to a certain recognized trend or that they wish him to attend some other institution for elementary education. Where no such declaration is made, the parents shall be deemed to have declared that they wish the child or adolescent to attend the official institution for elementary education which is nearest to the place of residence of the child or adolescent.

On March 29, 1950, an amendment to the law was adopted providing that the regulations in Section 10 would not apply to immigrant camps, where the Minister of Education and Culture was given the right to determine registration arrangements. Immigrant camps meant any place where immigrants were accommodated while awaiting temporary or permanent housing.

This amendment was adopted because of the unbridled competition that had developed between representatives of the various educational systems or trends, particularly in the immigrant camps. Actually there were not four trends but more, and the disputes and mutual recriminations created havoc in the camps. For this reason David Remez (who because of Shazar's state of health was Acting Minister of Education, and on October 30, 1950, replaced Shazar) offered an amendment to the law stating that "in immigrant camps there will be transitional classes directed by the Education Branch of the Ministry of Education and Culture." On February 5, 1951, Remez, as the new Minister of Education and Culture, presented to the Knesset a survey of education in the immigrant camps.

Inflammatory leaflets had been distributed in the camps, declaring, for example: "The evil instructors and clerks are forcing you to turn your children, of the holy seed, over to the Devil, who will train them to abandon the ways of the righteous and become part of the unclean life in Israel." Those leaflets were distributed by Yeshiva students and others sent by religious fanatics to the camps, though the Government had organized religious schools for all Yemenite children, on the assumption that all of them were religious, and had sent all children whose parents had expressed a desire to that effect to religious schools.

The central issue in dispute was whether the Workers Trend had the right to establish religious schools run by the Religious Workers faction in the Histadrut.

At the end of the debate, on February 14, 1951, the Prime Minister announced that he had informed the coalition a week previously of the Government's decision on educational matters: (1) religious education would be given to every Yemenite child; (2) religious education would be given to every immigrant child whose parents wished him to receive such an education; (3) the Government would not accept the proposal of the Religious Front that this religious education (in immigrant centers) would be under the control of four supervisors—one each from the Mizrahi, Agudat Israel, General Zionists, and Histadrut. Rather, the same arrangements obtaining in regular religious schools would obtain in the schools for religious immigrants.

There was no mention in the law of religious or secular schools; the difference, for example, between the Mizrahi Trend and the Agudat Trend was not between religion and secularism. Moreover, there was nothing in the law stating that the Workers Trend should be either secular or religious. The Workers Trend and the General Trend had full right to operate either religious or secular schools. The law stated that it was up to the parents to decide which type of school their children would attend. The Prime Minister said he had informed the coalition that the Government's decision was final, and that should it be rejected by a majority vote the Government would resign. This would probably necessitate the holding of new elections, because it was unlikely that another stable Government could be established without new elections.

Rokah (General Zionists) presented the following resolution: "The Knesset rejects the Government's proposal as it was presented by the Minister of Education and Culture on February 5, 1951." It was passed by a vote of forty-nine to forty-two with three abstentions. The Prime Minister immediately announced that he regarded this as a vote of no-confidence in the Government, which was therefore resigning. He informed the President of the situation that same day, stating that if no one else was able to establish a Government, as would obviously be the case in view of the make-up of the Knesset, the present Cabinet would remain in office as a Transition Government.

On March 5, 1951, the Knesset Speaker read a message he had received from President Weizmann, as follows:

The Prime Minister, Mr. David Ben-Gurion, has submitted the resignation of the Government. In accordance with the Transition Law, I invited representatives of the various factions for consultations on the situation. The representatives of most of the parties said that there seemed to be no possibility of reestablishing a stable Government and that it would be necessary to hold new Knesset elections. The hope was expressed that these elections would result in the creation of a majority that would ensure a stable Government for an extended period; such a Government was necessary to carry out the great tasks of gathering in the exiles and of strengthening the country internally and externally.

As a result of my consultations with the factions, I called on Mr. Ben-Gurion and asked him to make another effort to establish a stable Government, but he saw no possibility of doing so, and presented convincing arguments to support his contention. In view of Mr. Ben-Gurion's reply and of the results of my consultations with the Knesset factions, I have reached the conclusion that the Government that has resigned should continue in office in accordance with the Transition Law until a new Government is established after the elections.

I therefore request that you inform the First Knesset of the situation.

On June 19, 1951, the Knesset adopted the law for elections to the Second Knesset. The elections were set for July 30, 1951. Even before the First Knesset had completed its term of office Minister of Education and Culture David Remez suddenly died. On May 21, 1951, a day after the funeral, he was eulogized in the Knesset by the Speaker, by Deputy Speaker Nahum Nir-Raffalkes, Yitzhak Ben-Zvi, Yohanan Bader, Shoshana Persitz, Idov Cohen, Avraham Elmaliah, and Tewfik Toubi. The acting Prime Minister, Foreign Minister Sharett, declared in his eulogy: "We have lost a colleague and friend who for more than forty years stood at his post as a worker in the vineyards of Samaria, as one of the first organizers of the labor movement, as one of those responsible for developing labor economy, as a distinguished representative of the labor movement in the Zionist Organization, as Chairman of the National Committee, and as a minister in the independent State of Israel. The Government of Israel mourns the loss of a dear comrade, whose noble spirit, broad understanding, and pleasant ways earned him a special place among his fellow ministers. His death removes one of the bulwarks of our State. May his memory be blessed!"

The Prime Minister was not in the country during that period (April–June 1951), having been invited to the United States to open the drive to sell State of Israel Bonds.

At the beginning of May 1951 a dispute broke out with Syria over the draining of the Hula Swamp, control over which had been purchased by the Zionist Organization during the period of the British Mandate. The armistice agreement with Syria stated that a certain area was to be regarded as a demilitarized zone. An armed Syrian force composed of members of the Syrian Army and local Arab residents attempted to seize positions in Israeli territory in the central section of the demilitarized zone, and outside it. An Israeli Army unit opened fire on the Syrians. On the morning of May 6, an Israeli Army unit attacked the major Syrian outpost on the border of the demilitarized zone and drove out the Syrian unit holding it.

The Israel Government officially complained to the Security Council, charging Syria with violating the Armistice agreement. On May 8, the matter was discussed in the Council, where Israel's position was presented by Abba Eban. The Council unanimously adopted the following resolution: "The Security Council asks the parties and individuals in the areas concerned to cease the fighting and to fulfill the obligations that they had accepted." The Israel Government pledged to honor the cease-fire on the clear and obvious assumption that the other party would also honor it.

In a statement to the Knesset on May 14, 1951, Foreign Minister Sharett declared: "Two questions continue to concern the Government: the security of the Jewish villages in the demilitarized zone of Israeli territory, and the presence of armed Syrian or armed Arab forces in the zone. Just as Israel has no intention of crossing the border into Syria, so it is resolved to defend with all its strength every inch of its soil against Syrian incursions. Those interested in the situation should take cognizance of the determined stand of the Government of Israel."

Section 2. The Four Years of the Second Knesset

Election of a Second Knesset ★ New Coalition Government Formed ★ United States Grant to Israel ★ Death of Weizmann and Choice of Ben-Zvi as Second President

THE period of tenure of the First Knesset was not stipulated either in the Constituent Assembly Election Ordinance of the Provisional Council of State or in the Transition Law of 1949. It was left to the Knesset itself to decide. When the first elected Government was presented to the Knesset on March 3, 1949, the Prime Minister submitted a four-year plan of action that the Knesset confirmed. This expressed the desire of the coalition majority that the First Knesset serve four years, something the Prime Minister reiterated in the Knesset on various occasions.

Yet before this could be embodied in legislation, two crises developed, as we have seen: the first on October 16, 1950, as a result of which a thirteen-member Government was set up on October 30, replacing the first twelve-member Cabinet; the second on February 14, 1951, as a result of conflict on education in the Ma'abarot (transit camps). Elections for the Second Knesset were set for July 30, 1951.

Despite the reduction of its term, the First Knesset succeeded in enacting 117 laws, including the Women's Equal Rights Law, 1951. This provided that "A man and a woman shall have equal status in respect to any legal act; any provision of law which discriminates, with regard to any legal act, against women as women, shall be of no effect." It enacted a Marriage Age Law prohibiting the marriage of "a female person under the age of seventeen years." It passed the Fallen Soldiers' Families Law, providing a monthly pension for the widow of a fallen soldier for her lifetime, if before the date of his death she had attained the age of forty-six; only for six months, if before the date of his death she had attained the age of thirty but was under forty-five; and for only three months, if before the date of his death she was under the age of thirty; even if she had not attained the age of forty-five or thirty years, she would be paid a monthly pension as long as she was unfit to earn her living and without means sufficient for her subsistence. The Hours of Work and Rest Law, 1951, provided that the working day shall not exceed eight working hours, and seven in night work; and that a working week shall not exceed forty-seven working hours. In addition, the Annual Leave Law, 1951 entitled every employee to fourteen days' leave with pay in each working year.

A total of 695,007 persons voted in the elections to the Second Knesset. Mapai received 256,456 votes, 45 seats; Mapam—86,013 votes, 15 seats; the Mizrahi—10,383 votes, 2 seats; Agudat Israel—13,799 votes, 3 seats; Poalei Agudat Israel—11,194 votes, 2 seats; Hapoel Hamizrahi—46,647 votes, 8 seats; Herut—45,651 votes, 8 seats; the Sephardim—12,002 votes, 2 seats; the Yemenites—7965 votes, 1 seat; the Progressives—22,171 votes, 4 seats; the General Zionists 111,394 votes, 20 seats; the Communists 27,334 votes, 5 seats. There were also three Arab lists: the Democratic List—16,370 votes, 3 seats; Kidman V'Avodah: 8067 votes, 1 seat; Hakla'ut u Fituah—7851 votes, 1 seat.

The new Knesset was convened on August 20, 1951, by its oldest member, Chaim Boger, because President Weizmann could not attend due to ill health. In a letter to the Knesset read by Boger the President praised two basic laws enacted by the First Knesset, the Law of the Return and the Compulsory Education Law, and expressed the hope that like its predecessor this Knesset would concern itself with the defense of the State and the ingathering of the exiles and effective absorption of masses of immigrants.

Sprinzak was again chosen Speaker by 103 votes, with Hannah Lamdan and Yosef Serlin as Deputy Speakers. The Knesset began work only on September 10, 1951. After the committees were organized the first question dealt with was the agricultural situation and the food supply.

Minister of Agriculture Lavon noted that 1951 had been marked by a heavy drought that affected field crops, fodder, and non-irrigated fruit and vegetables. The Korean War had also had a detrimental effect on our economy; as a result certain prices had risen by 20 to 50 percent. There was a shortage of foreign currency. The Ministry of Supplies had received less foreign currency from January to July than the State expended during the same months in the previous year, despite the arrival of 250,000 new immigrants and the fact that prices had risen. A drastic cutback in allocations was therefore called for.

On the other hand, the area of sown crops had increased. In 1950–1951 1.2 million dunams had been sown, and in 1951–1952 1.6 million dunams. In addition another 540,000 dunams, mostly in the Negev, had been plowed, and would be sown in 1952–1953. Though attempts to increase the area under irrigation had encountered a shortage of steel and piping as a result of the Korean War, 60 to 70,000 dunams of irrigated land had been added in 1951—40,000 in new settlements and 30,000 in established settlements. Long-range fishing had been increased. Forty modern fishing boats had been acquired, enlarging the fishing fleet from 750 tons to approximately 1500 tons. The provisions situation was difficult and had deteriorated even further during August and September. There was a serious shortage of sugar and meat and the black market had grown. This was offset in part by imports by immigrants and the shipment of food parcels from abroad.

On September 11, 1951 the Prime Minister announced that after consulting with the parties, the President had asked him to form a Government. Dr. Weizmann had told him, "I see the need to form a stable Government with the participation of the majority of the parties, from Mapam to the General Zionists," because in the coming four years we would face difficult tests and it was essential to mobilize the nation's maximum forces.

Six parties with a total of ninety-seven Knesset members announced their willingness to participate in the Government. Though there were considerable differences among them—some grave, others imaginary and inflated—the majority of the nation was united on the following four principles: state security, ingathering of the exiles, construction of the Homeland, and the strengthening of world peace. If the parties gave these principles priority over anything else, a national concentration would be possible for the achievement of our objectives.

Debate on agriculture and provisions continued until September 18, when it was decided to refer all the proposals that were made to the Economic Committee.

On the same day Minister of Finance Kaplan spoke on the Transition Budget (October–December 1951). Despite the bleak outlook for agriculture, the information on the growth of national income from April to September 1951 was encouraging. Instead of an anticipated IL 35,850,000, income during those months had reached IL 38 million and perhaps several hundred thousand pounds more—two thirds greater than in the same months in 1950.

Income tax receipts had been estimated for the six months at IL 12.5 million and IL 9.6 million had already been collected in the first five months. Luxury taxes for the the six months had been estimated at IL 2.8 million and IL 3.6 million had already been collected. Income tax receipts had increased because of both the growth of the economy and improved collection methods. Increased income from customs and excise had also been noted. On the other hand, the education budget would increase during the second half of the budgetary year (November–April 1951–1952) as a result of the large-scale immigration and the implementation of the Compulsory Education Law. After a lengthy debate the Transition Budget, as formulated by the Finance Committee, was adopted on September 26, 1951. In the three months from October to December 1951 the Government was authorized to expend IL 27,440,000.

In fact the income for 1951 was IL 68,602,000 compared to an estimated IL 63,664,000, and expenditures were IL 62,683,000 compared to an estimated IL 63,564,000.

It should be noted that income exceeded estimates in the two previous years as well. In 1949 the estimate was IL 16,738,000, actual income IL 18,931,000; in 1950 the estimate was IL 42,555,000, the actual income IL 43,007,000. In 1949 the expenditures (IL 17,575,000) had exceeded the estimate (IL 16,738,000), but in 1950 the actual expenditures (IL 42,260,000) were below the estimate (IL 42,555,000).

The new Government was presented to the Knesset on October 7, 1951. The hope of creating a stable body in which all the parties that had participated in the Provisional Government, from Mapam to the General Zionists, was not fulfilled. The parties had not yet overcome their unfortunate heritage of exile and a life of dependence; morbid and excessive fragmentation derived from a life devoid of independence and national responsibility. They had not yet surmounted traditions and habits detrimental of the life of the State. Not all of them understood that the State, far from making our lives easier, would impose upon its inhabitants heavy burdens and tremendous responsibilities such as they had not previously known.

To the nation in exile the State was a source of relief and deliverance but upon the generation of its founders it would impose long-drawn-out difficulties and grave obligations. The State would open wide the gates of the Homeland to every individual Jew or Jewish group wishing to be delivered from the hardships of exile. It would give us the key to the country's upbuilding and development, and would enable the people of Israel to enjoy equal rights in the family of free nations. But independence involved heavy and difficult responsibilities; the ingathering of the exiles would require tremendous efforts, perhaps beyond the capacity of the young and small State.

The State demanded of its representatives national responsibility, foresight, adherence to principles, and compromise on secondary matters. With the exception of a few, however, the first generation of people in the State was unaccustomed to thinking and acting in national terms. It tended to focus not on the central problems of the nation as a whole, both in Israel and the Diaspora, but on the needs and concepts of its immediate environment and the circles in which it lived. The lesson of ten months of joint action and responsibility in the Provisional Government had not yet taught all parties that their ideological differences did not preclude them from jointly bearing the burden of the nation's major needs.

In presenting the new Government to the Second Knesset, the Prime Minister stated:

> In the past weeks I had fifty-five meetings with Mapam, General Zionists, Progressives, Hapoel Hamizrahi, Poalei Agudat Israel, Hamizrahi, and Agudat Israel. Some of the talks went on for many hours. It was necessary to hold comprehensive and exhaustive programmatic consultations on all questions of State, both internal and external; on matters of the economy, culture, education, religion, the civil service, the structure of the society, and foreign relations. Unfortunately, and to my great surprise, these consultations have ended in failure. The two largest parties after Mapai—Mapam and the General Zionists—rejected my proposals.
>
> A considerable amount of time went to waste in this strenuous effort to rally a larger force. Not only time was wasted. A tremendous amount of energy and high tension was invested in negotiations without letup or respite. I considered it a sacred duty to exploit every opportunity for maximum cooperation of forces in the government and I do not regret the effort even though it did not succeed. I did my duty as I saw it in accordance with the will of the people and the course in which I believed.
>
> After receiving negative replies from the two large parties, I saw no other possibility than the creation of a small coalition. The Government I present to you consists of the following members: David Ben-Gurion, Prime Minister and Minister of Defense; Levi Eshkol, Development and Agriculture; Joseph Burg, Health; Ben-Zion Dinur, Education and Culture; Dov Joseph, Commerce and Industry and Justice; Rabbi Yitzhak Meir Levin, Welfare; Golda Myerson [Meir], Labor; Peretz Naftali, without portfolio; David Zvi Pinkas, Transportation; Eliezer Kaplan, Finance; Behor S. Shitreet, Police; Moshe Shapira, Interior and Religious Affairs; Moshe Sharett, Foreign Affairs.
>
> The basic policy is practically identical with that of the first elected Government, with three innovations. (1) An Economic Council with advisory powers, composed of representatives of both the private and collective economic sectors, will be appointed to work with the Prime Minister. This council will examine all the economic problems of the State and will endeavor to achieve more efficient administration and increased production. It will also examine grievances and complaints of economic partiality and discrimination. (2) Compulsory social insurance for the entire population will be introduced in stages, covering hospitalization, childbirth, sickness, old age, widowhood, disability, unemployment, etc. (3) A Government commission will draw up a program for the inclusion of all the elementary schools in the State education system based on a standard compulsory minimum curriculum obligatory for all schools. The rights of parents to decide the complexion and enlarge the scope of the education provided will be recognized as long as it does not affect the obligatory minimum. Religious education will be guaranteed to all children of parents who wish it.

The Prime Minister concluded his address with the following words:

> We do not promise easy answers. In our twenty years of work and struggle in this country we have not believed in easy answers. Only by dint of intense and constant effort

have we achieved all that we have and opened a new chapter in the history of our people and the country. However, we have had not only conquests and wonderful achievements; we have also known failures and mistakes. We do not ignore the faults and blemishes. We have assumed a heavy repsonsibility. With the approval of the Knesset and the constant participation of all sectors of the nation, both old and new, we will attempt to meet it to the best of our ability.

After a two-day debate the Knesset on October 8 confirmed the Government, fifty-six to forty with four abstentions. On the same day it approved the proposal by Meir Agrov, chairman of the Organization Committee, concerning the chairmanship of the nine Knesset Committees; Mapai would chair the Knesset Finance, Foreign Affairs and Security, and Labor Committees; Mapam, the Economic Committee; the General Zionists, the Internal Affairs, and Education and Culture Committees; Hapoel Hamizrahi, the Law Committee; and Herut, the Public Services Committee.

At the end of the day's session Ben-Gurion spoke in praise of the four outgoing Ministers: Yacov Geri, Pinhas Lavon, Pinhas Rosen, and Rabbi Maimon. Concerning the last-named he said:

> Last but not least I wish to say a few words about my colleague and dear teacher, Rabbi Maimon. I have had the privilege of working with him for over sixteen years, though I have known him for over forty years. It has not been easy to work with him, for Rabbi Maimon is a tough, stubborn, zealous man who defends his views vigorously and militantly and in this respect has not changed to this day. It is amidst strife and conflict that we have learned to appreciate him. I know no other man among the veteran members of the Movement who arouses any greater feelings of respect and trust in his exalted faith and moral views, which would do honor to any good socialist.
>
> I have had the privilege of working with him not only for many years in the Zionist Executive but in the Government of Israel ever since the formation of the Provisional Government, and perhaps no one in the Government has caused me more headaches than Rabbi Maimon. But never have I accepted troubles with more love than those he caused, for I love this man with all my heart for his profound Zionist faith and his pure and perfect love of Israel, his unbounded loyalty to the State, and his great concern for the well-being of the nation and the State. He has often told me how one should love the State, not only with body but with soul, and I am afraid to give his definition of soul lest his opponents interpret it the wrong way. This is indeed an admirable Jew, erudite and learned in all the fine points of the Law, blessed with a wonderful memory, lover of the literature of Israel—not only the religious but the enlightened and critical as well—even when he opposes the views it expresses.
>
> He is a wonderful representative of Judaism and the Law of Israel, overflowing with love for both and deeply concerned with the honor of the State. He dared to rebuke those rabbis in America who slandered Israel and considered themselves the custodians of religion in this country. I was very sorry to learn that he would not run for reelection to the Knesset. I feel that the absence of this man is a great loss to the nation's elected governing body. Despite his external appearance and, as it were, halting manner of speech, he ennobles every gathering. I remember once when I attended a convention of the Israel Workers Party in Rehovot before World War Two. I arrived late, but upon my arrival—immediately after the departure of Rabbi Maimon—I found the entire convention in exceptionally high spirits. This was thanks to his inspiring influence on all present, old and young alike. Although the majority of the delegates were non-believers, Rabbi Maimon's words aroused feelings of respect, admiration, and affection.

I greatly regret his departure from the Government, more than I am prepared to express, and I am glad that his departure does not mean that he has left the affairs of the State. I am confident of his continued love and concern for and loyalty to our endeavors. Even if he should oppose any specific measure, he will desire with all his heart the success of the State and the Government. On behalf of all those present here and in the name of all the members of the Knesset, I wish to extend to Rabbi Maimon my sincere and heartfelt good wishes for a long life and to express my admiration for him. May he continue to enlighten the readers of his excellent and instructive articles, books, compilations, and memoirs, and be an honor and blessing to Israel.

This was the last meeting before the holidays (Rosh Hashanah and Succoth). In his speech on foreign policy at the first meeting after the holidays on November 4, 1951, Foreign Minister Sharett said that in addition to the loan of $100 million through the Export-Import Bank during the days of the Provisional Government and an additional loan of $35 million through the same bank, the American government had allocated to the State of Israel surplus food valued at $20 million. Now, after Israel's inclusion in the list of states benefiting from technical aid under Article IV, the United States Treasury had, by a decision of Congress confirmed by the President, granted Israel the sum of $64,950,000. This grant followed an appeal by the Government of Israel for assistance in the absorption of mass immigration. The request enjoyed the support of an important bloc of members in both Houses of the United States Congress. The administration had originally proposed a grant of $25 million to Israel and $100 million to other countries in the Middle East and Africa. After lengthy consideration at every level, the grant to the Middle East and Africa was set at $160 million, of which $65 million were earmarked for Israel.

Meanwhile the President's term of office was drawing to a close. The Transition Law of February 6, 1949, by the Constituent Assembly, as the First Knesset was originally called, said in Section 5: "The tenure of office of the President of the State shall be for the duration of the First Knesset and until the expiration of three months after the convening of the new Constituent Assembly." The term of office of the first President, Dr. Weizmann, had therefore ended on November 19, 1951, and on that day the Speaker of the Knesset announced that elections would be held for the Presidency.

Dr. Weizmann was nominated by Itzhak Ben-Zvi on behalf of Mapai, Chaim Boger for the General Zionists, Zerah Warhaftig for Hapoel Hamizrahi, Seif el-Din el-Zoubi for the Democratic Israel Arab List, Fares Hamdan for the Haklaut u Fituah, and Israel Bar-Yehuda for Mapam. Arieh Ben-Eliezer on behalf of Herut, and Shmuel Mikunis for the Communists opposed Dr. Weizmann's nomination, but they did not nominate anyone else. In a secret ballot eighty-five members of the Knesset voted for Dr. Weizmann and eleven against him; three ballots were blank and twenty-one members did not participate in the voting. The Speaker therefore announced that "on Monday, the 25th day of Heshvan 5712, the Second Knesset elected Chaim, son of Ozer and Rachel Weizmann, President of the State of Israel."

Two days later the Knesset enacted an amended Presidential Tenure Law according to which (Section 2) "The tenure of office of the President of the State shall be five years from the day on which he assumes office. The election of the President shall take place within ninety days, but not later than thirty days before the expiration of the term of office of the preceding President. Should the term of the preceding President expire before the end of the period stipulated in Section 2, the election shall take place within thirty days of the date on which the term expired."

Unhappily Dr. Weizmann did not complete his five-year term. On November 9, 1952, he died after a protracted illness. The next day he was eulogized in the Knesset by Speaker Sprinzak and the Prime Minister. Seven days later, on November 17, 1952, he was eulogized by representatives of the various parties: Zalman Shazar on behalf of Mapai, Israel Rokah for the General Zionists, Aharon Zisling for Mapam, Moshe Shapira for Hapoel Hamizrahi, Esther Raziel-Naor for Herut, Meir Wilner for the Communists, Pinhas Rosen for the Progressives, Rabbi Levin for Agudat Israel, Seif el-Din el-Zoubi for the Democratic Israel Arab List, David Lifshitz for two members who had seceded from Mapai, and Mordekhai Nurock for Hamizrahi.

In accordance with the amended Presidential Tenure Law the Knesset proceeded on December 8, 1952, to elect a new president. There were four candidates: Yitzhak Ben-Zvi, Peretz Bernstein, Yitzhak Gruenbaum, and Mordekhai Nurock. In the first ballot Ben-Zvi received forty-eight votes, Bernstein, eighteen, Gruenbaum seventeen, and Nurock, fifteen. Twelve ballots were blank; a hundred and ten members of the Knesset had participated in the voting. The Speaker announced that "in accordance with Section 5 (2) of the Presidential Tenure Law, 1951, we shall proceed to a second ballot." The same results were obtained. A third ballot, also secret, followed. Knesset members Yacov Uri, Shoshana Persitz, Israel Bar-Yehuda, Michael Hazani, and Binyamin Avniel were requested by the Speaker to open the ballot box and count the votes. When the counting was completed the Speaker announced, "I have the honor to reopen the meeting and to notify the members of the results of the third ballot. Knesset member Yitzhak Ben-Zvi has received sixty-two votes, Knesset member Nurock, forty votes, Yitzhak Gruenbaum, five votes; five ballots are blank, a hundred and twelve members took part in the voting, and eight members were absent. I hereby announce that Yitzhak Ben-Zvi, Knesset Member, has been elected second President of Israel. I wish for him and for us that during his term of office the State of Israel may flourish and Progress." The announcement was greeted with general applause.

At 10:40 A.M. on Wednesday, December 10, 1952, a Knesset delegation set out for the home of the President-elect to invite him to the swearing-in ceremony. At 11 A.M. he arrived at the Knesset building in the company of the Chief of Protocol, his military aide-de-camp, and an escort of mounted policemen preceded by a group of motorcycle outriders. When he entered the building the shofar was sounded and the members of the Knesset and invited guests rose. At the end of the shofar blast the President entered the hall and was led to his place at the right of the Speaker by the Officer of the Knesset. The Speaker announced the opening of the inauguration ceremony and read the declaration of the President-elect. Yitzhak Ben-Zvi covered his head, laid his right hand on the Bible, and declared: "I, Yitzhak, the son of Zvi Ben-Zvi, pledge my loyalty to the State of Israel and its laws and pledge to faithfully fulfill my duties as President of the State."

The audience remained standing while the declaration was made. Then the Presidential flag was unfurled over the building and a twenty-one-gun salute was fired. The Speaker invited the President to address the Knesset.

The new President of the State said:

Knesset of Israel: I wish to express my deep gratitude to the Members of the Knesset for the confidence they have reposed in me and the honor they have conferred upon me in electing me to be President of the State of Israel.

It is no easy thing to occupy the seat of the first President of Israel, that uniquely great man, the man of trial and action, who brought the ship of Israel to its appointed shore and who in the work to which he dedicated his life laid the foundations for the translation of the vision of the Prophets of Israel in the days of old, and that of the creator of political Zionism, Binyamin Zeev Herzl, in our own day.

Great are my misgivings lest I am not found fit and proper for the task; and my doubts whether I shall command the strength to fill this office of supreme dignity and great responsibility—the task of representing the young State in the difficult days we are facing. The ingathering of the exiles is the pivotal and most sublime idea of the State of Israel. We shall not be deflected from this function by anything, regardless of the waves of hatred and slander breaking against us. Our enterprise was one of peace from the start and is designed to bring peace to the entire world and peace, near and far, to all the inhabitants of this country, Jews and Arabs and all the other communities. We shall pray for peace and we shall do our part to bring it to the world.

The fate of the nation, its future, and its honor, are in the hands of this Legislature in which I have had the great privilege of serving as a member. It is with no light heart that I take leave of the Knesset, and I shall always follow its work day and day with concern and confidence. Before I take leave of the Knesset I should mention Jerusalem, the eternal capital of Israel. We have been privileged to reestablish in this city the center of our political life but much must still be done to fulfill the ancient precept: "Walk about Zion and go round about her" (Psalms 45:13). And in conclusion I pray before the Rock of Israel and its Redeemer that He may grant us success and that in our days Judah may achieve eternal salvation and Israel dwell in safety.

American Jewish Leaders, in Jerusalem, Approve Billion-Dollar Popular Loan ★ Stormy Debates in Knesset on German Reparations ★ West Germany Agrees to Pay $750 Million to Israel Over Twelve Years

In the third year of the State of Israel it became clear that the tasks it faced could not be carried out by the State alone, not even with the help of the Zionist funds, the Keren Kayemet, and the Keren Hayesod (which were in effect included in the Combined Jewish Appeal).

In the first two years alone, that is, the first nineteen and a half months, over 340,000 new immigrants had arrived. Unlike the immigrants before the Second World War, most of these newcomers were penniless and many were afflicted with various diseases, especially ringworm. The needs for housing, employment, health, creation of new settlements, erection of workshops and factories, improvement of transport, paving of roads, provision of free education for all children, and the necessity to maintain and augment the deterrent strength of the Israel Defense Forces and improve its equipment led the Government to conclude that the means at its disposal from national income and voluntary contributions by the Jewish people in the Diaspora would not be sufficient.

The Prime Minister proposed organizing in the United States, and perhaps in other countries, a popular loan of $1 billion for twelve to thirteen years (State of Israel Bonds).

Financial experts consulted by the Prime Minister and Minister of Finance, among them U.S. Senator Herbert Lehman of New York, thought that such a project would not succeed. They reasoned that such campaigns succeed only when a large part of the contribution is deductible from income tax, that few would contribute to a loan in which every cent came out of the donor's pocket. Popular loans that had been attempted in America by several European heads of state had failed. The Prime Minister, not because he did not value their financial knowhow but because he did not rely on the Jewish sensitivity of these experts, did not accept this view. In September 1950 he invited the leaders of America Jewry, both Zionist and non-Zionist, to Jerusalem.

Almost all of those invited came. Among them were representatives of the American Jewish Committee, leaders of the Zionist movement, members of the various Jewish councils and federations, and Jewish financial and economic experts. The convention was opened by the Prime Minister on September 3 at the King David Hotel in Jerusalem. President Weizmann, unable to attend for reasons of health, sent a letter noting that the State of Israel had taken upon itself a task that had no parallel anywhere else. In addition to the burden of security and of reconstructing the ruins of the war it was called upon to absorb hundreds of thousands of impoverished immigrants who had been cut off from agriculture and other productive work for centuries. If the tremendous capacity of American Jewry were not harnessed to this end, it would be practically impossible to carry that burden.

Finance Minister Kaplan, addressing the meeting, pointed out that from the formation of the State until March 31, 1950, besides the tremendous defense expenditure that could not be published, we had spent over IL 120 million on liquidating the chaos left by the British Mandate. We had been compelled to institute a regime of austerity and rationing and to impose heavy taxes. The defense budget in the past year had been covered completely by taxes. Up to now 460,000 immigrants had arrived; some 18,000 of these had subsequently left. According to an American economic expert, it cost $2500 to absorb one immigrant, so that the absorption of 600,000 immigrants would require $1 billion. Until now we had spent IL 165–170 million, which was less than half that amount (the rate of exchange at the time was $2.8 to IL 1). The population had increased 70 percent and agricultural output 60 to 65 percent, while industrial output had risen only 35 percent. Consequently we required a large amount of imports, and the economic situation in Israel was very tense.

Apart from the Jewish Agency and municipal authorities, the Government itself up to now had spent IL80 million on absorption of immigrants. Most of this had been spent during the past two years. We had IL140 million on deposit in the banks. Due to rationing and austerity only 5 percent of this, or IL7 million, had been withdrawn during the past month. In the next three years we might well have to absorb 600,000 Jews and possibly the number would be greater. That depended not on us but on the international situation, but we had to be ready just in case. The Evian Conference—called in 1938 by President Franklin D. Roosevelt to deal with the absorption of Jewish refugees—had been a complete failure. Not one country had been prepared to open its gates. Our own country was at that time closed by the Mandate Government and the Jewish people had paid a horrible price, one which had no equal in our history of suffering.

To absorb 600,000 Jews $1.5 billion would be needed. The State would underwrite one-third, half a billion, and the Jews of the United States and other countries of prosperity would have to provide the other two-thirds in the form of loans. Before creation of the State the ration of capital brought in by immigrants to that demanded from the public was 85–15, as most of the immigrants brought capital in with them. The ratio now was 33 percent private capital to 67 percent public capital.

Robert Nathan, one of the greatest economists in American Jewry, noted the similarity between the position of the Israeli Prime Minister and Minister of Finance now, and that of the American President in the fall of 1941. At that time Roosevelt realized that if the war against Hitler were to be won, a hundred thousand planes and fifty thousand tanks a year would be needed, figures that seemed fantastic and impossible to many people. If you take a close look at your absorption needs, he said, you will arrive at figures that will seem fantastic at present. Mr. Kaplan has told us that the cost of absorbing one immigrant is $2500, not including the expense of bringing him over. For six hundred thousand this comes to $1.5 billion. The cost of absorbing one family of four is $10,000. Now the average Israeli produces $600 a year. That is to say, in order to absorb one person, four years of production have to be invested.

This, Mr. Nathan observed, was not very different from the American experience. The annual national income of the United States is $250 billion. The national wealth is four times the national income. In other words, the investment of private and public capital has to be four times the national output. This indicates the magnitude of the absorption needs. In the United States the annual Gross National Product is $280 trillion; savings and accumulated capital amount to approximately $45 trillion. One-sixth of the product, that is to say, is saved and invested in new or renewed capital. Thus it is obvious that out of the savings and production of the present population, Israel is unable to provide the capital required to absorb immigrants.

Though in the past three years the Israeli population has produced more than it has consumed, he continued, the difference is not sufficient for the absorption of immigration. The question is, can Israel absorb two hundred thousand immigrants a year? Since the creation of the State four hundred thousand immigrants have arrived and only fifty or sixty thousand of them are still in immigrant camps. It would be a mistake, however, to assume that these four hundred thousand have already been absorbed. Each of them in effect produces only two units of output instead of the ten units required. And with the arrival of additional immigration the problem will be exacerbated. The question is, can the objective undertaken by the State of Israel be implemented? Will it be able to absorb two hundred thousand immigrants a year?

In 1943 a group of Jews, both pro- and anti-Zionists, asked Robert Nathan and two other economists how many people the Land of Israel would be able to absorb. In 1946 the three published a booklet entitled "Palestine—Problem and Promise." Mr. Nathan now pointed out that various British commissions sent to Palestine had claimed that there was no possibility of settling more immigrants. Immigrants who came during the war brought with them five-sixths of the amount needed for their absorption; outside help was required only for the other sixth, and in the past twelve or thirteen years the Jewish community in Israel had been practically self-supporting. As far as we knew the country was not rich in natural resources, its greatest resources perhaps being the creative ability and pioneering initiatives of its inhabitants. If the required capital were found, Israel could absorb two hundred thousand immigrants a year. The one-third that the State of Israel has promised to provide would be a considerable burden. Though it would not be achieved without a massive effort and continuing sacrifices, it was not impossible that the country could provide this $500 million.

The other $1 billion would have to come from the United States in four ways: contributions, private investments and loans, government grants, and bonds. Though one could not say beforehand how much the American government would provide, most of the funds would necessarily come from American Jewry. The average income of America's Jews was greater than that of the nation as a whole. Not all the Jews were well-off and a large number were poor, but the Jewish community's share of income and wealth was higher than the American average. Until now the Jews of America had given only contributions, though generously; now they would be called upon to invest part of their capital in the form of loans. If over the next three years the Jews of America would put aside 10 percent of their savings, the $1 billion could be raised.

Would Israel be capable of paying its debts? At present it owed the American Export-Import Bank $100 million, and there were other debts as well. If Israel borrowed $1 billion, or $1.5 billion, would these loans be repaid? The US government had a national debt of $260–$270 billion. This would not be repaid in one day or at any given time and the US would continue to borrow. The same applied to Israel. The actual problem facing it was not to pay off its debts but to become self-sufficient. There was another question: Would the American Jewish Community do its bit? Not *could* it, because of that there was no doubt, but would it *want to*? Could it be certain that its loans would be repaid? Some doubted that they would be. It should be said openly that Israel will pay off its debt, even while it continues to borrow, just as America does. Ben-Gurion had said that the national resurgence has two motivating forces—hardship and vision. What American Jewry has will be vision and love of Israel.

The convention discussions went on until September 6. Participants included representatives from all parts of the United States, Nikolai Kirschner, representing South African Jewry, and Harry Sacher, representing British Jewry. Americans who took part in the exchange of views included Nahum Goldmann, Stanley Myers, Judge Morris Rothenberg, Julian Venezky (chairman of the United Jewish Appeal), Harold Linder, Herbert Abeles, Joseph Shulman, Joseph Hoodin, Meyer Weisgal, Louis Myers, Rabbi Herbert Friedman, Moses Leavitt, Joseph Schwartz, Mrs. Matilda Brailove, Adolph Robinson, Abraham Feinberg, Benjamin Browdy, Rudolph Sonneborn, Rose Halprin, Monroe Goldwater, Sam Rothberg, Julian Freeman, Dr. Linman, Emanuel Neumann, Ralph Wechsler, Edward Mitchell, Philip Bernstein, Fred Monosson, Joseph Myerhoff, and Louis Lipsky.

The Jerusalem conference unanimously decided to mobilize American Jewry and the Jewish communities in the other prosperous countries to implement the $1-billion Independence Loan. It adjourned on September 6 with the singing of "Hatikva."

The Bond Drive, opened in New York on May 10, 1951, by the Prime Minister, met with remarkable success. In the first year (from March 1951 to the end of March 1952) $65,124,000 worth of bonds were sold; in the second year (1952–1953), $42,012,000; and in the third year (1953–54), $36,869,000. In that year we redeemed bonds worth $4,861,000. By the end of 1965 $827,562,000 worth of bonds had been sold and $337,621,000 redeemed. No bond drive in the United States by any foreign government has ever been as successful.

We have already mentioned the first $100 million loan by the US government, obtained during the Provisional Government. Others followed. By the end of 1960 Israel had received a total of $447 million from the US government, some of it in loans, the greater part in outright grants.

Of great help in Israel's development were the reparations payments by Germany that had aroused unprecedented controversy in the Knesset and in the Israeli press.

On March 12, 1951, Foreign Minister Sharett submitted to the four occupying powers in Germany (USA, USSR, Britain, and France) a note on behalf of the Israeli Government that presented and justified a demand for $1.5 billion from Germany (both West and East). "A crime of such vast and fearful dimensions as that committed by the Germans in the destruction of one-third of the Jewish people cannot be expiated by any measure of material reparation," the note said. "All that can be done is to secure the indemnification of the heirs of the victims and rehabilitation of the survivors." The three Western powers expressed sympathy for Israel's demand, but took exception to the amount demanded. No reply came from the Soviet Union.

The West German Chancellor, Dr. Konrad Adenauer, in a statement on September 27, 1951, in the Plenum of the Bundestag (the West German Parliament) in Bonn, indicated his government's willingness "to arrive at a solution to the problem of material reparations by means of negotiations with representatives of the Government of Israel which has absorbed such a large number of homeless Jewish refugees, and with the representatives of the Jewish people."

A three-day debate on this question began in the Knesset on January 7, 1952. In all its years the Knesset had never known such a stormy exchange of views. In opening the debate, the Prime Minister said among other things: "The State of Israel has set the amount it demands from both parts of Germany at $1.5 billion because this is the minimal sum required for the absorption and rehabilitation of half a million immigrants from the countries subjected to the Nazi regime."

The General Zionists, who at the time had twenty-three seats in the Knesset (to the twenty members elected on their list had been added two Sepharadim and a Yemenite who had been elected on separate lists), as well as Mapam (fifteen members), Herut (eight members), and the Communists (five members), were firmly and fervently opposed to any negotiations for German reparations. Agudat Israel and Poalei Agudat Israel (five members) abstained. Mapai (fifty members), Hapoel Hamizrahi and Mizrahi (ten members), and the Progressives (four members) were in favor. The General Zionists' spokesman claimed that reparations would destroy the nation's moral backbone and spiritual uniqueness.

The most extreme in their opposition, however, were Mapam and Herut. Hazan (Mapam) said: "On November 5, a fateful foreign-policy debate took place here [on the American loan]. What the Government proposal and the motion adopted by the majority of the Knesset amounted to was a surrender of our political independence. Today there is a sequel which is sevenfold more grave. Now the Government is proposing the surrender of our spiritual independence, the sale of our souls to follow the sale of our bodies." Manahem Begin (Herut) went even further. He claimed the negotiations with Germany on reparations were "the ultimate abomination, the like of which we have not known since we became a nation."

While he was raging and threatening, masses of incited persons whom he had addressed earlier that day arrived at the area in front of the Knesset, hurled stones through the windows, attacked with sticks and stones the guards who came to the defense of the members, knocked them bleeding to the ground and trampled them underfoot. The situation was only saved by the Army, called in by the Minister of Defense to protect the Knesset building.

As reported in the newspaper *Herut* the next day, Begin had told the crowd in Zion Square, "When they fired on us with their cannon I gave the order—No! Today I give the order—Yes! This will be a war of life or death."

In his speech in the Knesset, Begin also began to make threats, and the Acting Speaker, Yosef Serlin, was forced to adjourn the meeting. When the Knesset reconvened, Begin resumed his attack:

> In Zion Square, to fifteen thousand Jews, I said: "Go, surround the Knesset, as in the days of Rome. When the Roman procurator wanted to set up an idol in the Holy Temple, the Jews came from all corners of the country, surrounded the building and said, 'Over our dead bodies!' " And to the Knesset I say, there are things in life that are worse than death. This is one of them. For this we will give our lives. We will leave our families. We will say goodbye to our children, but there will be no negotiations with Germany. I know that you have power. You have prisons, concentration camps, an army, a police force, detectives, artillery, machine guns. It makes no difference. On this matter all this force will shatter like glass against rock. I know you will drag me off to a concentration camp. Today you have arrested hundreds. Perhaps you will arrest thousands. We will sit together with them. If necessary we will die together with them but there will be no reparations from Germany.

At the end of a debate unprecedented in the annals of the Knesset, the roll was called and the Government proposal was adopted by vote of sixty-one to fifty. When the Acting Speaker announced the results, Herut member Landau cried, "All the same, you won't get the money. Just wait and see!" For his unruly behavior, Begin was suspended from the Knesset for three months.

Following a decision by the Foreign Affairs and Security Committee, the Government on February 18, 1952, decided to enter into negotiations on reparations with West Germany. Complete coordination was achieved between the Government of Israel and representatives of all the Jewish organizations abroad, and the negotiations were opened in the Hague, capital of Holland, on May 21, 1952. They were concluded on September 18 with the signing of an agreement whereby the West German government agreed to pay 3 billion marks ($715 million) in goods to Israel and 450 million marks to an all-Jewish committee [representing organized Jewry throughout the World]. The payments would be spread over twelve years. The agreement was ratified by the Bundestag on March 18, 1953, and by the Israeli Government on September 22. By the end of 1965 Israel had received $822 million in German reparations. Members of the parties that had opposed the payments willingly benefited from the goods received.

Government Crises in the Second Knesset ★ *Retirement of Ben–Gurion* ★ *His Later Co-option as Defense Minister* ★ *Education Law and Zionist Organization Law*

The First Knesset, as we noted, did not complete its entire term of office. The Second Knesset did, but its four years were agitated by many Government crises.

Understandably, the few years of our renewed independence could not overcome the centuries-old experience of life in the Diaspora. Two thousand years of dispersion among foreign nations—most of them hostile and inimical, all of them alien to us in language, religion, traditions, ways of life—did not implant in the Jewish heart an inner psychological tie to the states in whose shelter they had gathered. Life in strange lands and long periods of wandering negated all sense of statehood. Instead of the needs, goals, and problems of a state that depended on him, the Jew focused his conceptual thinking on "eternal" problems independent of place and time. Without solid ground to stand on, he floated in a vacuum and argued matters whose practical outcome did not depend on himself, nor did he learn to distinguish between fundamental and trivial, substance and transience, or among priorities in time and space.

Lacking a national framework, which united people whether or not they are conscious of or desire it, Jewry became fragmented, clustered in myriad frameworks to suit every convolution of thought. And we continued in this unhealthy game even after the renewal of the State with its great prospects and great difficulties. To the parties that had existed in the Zionist movement were added those outside of it and numerous splinter groups. By the nature of their capacity, needs, spheres of influence, and source of inspiration small factions were concerned first and foremost with their own specialized interests—with the important or unimportant, that distinguished them from their fellows. They stressed that which is important only to a circle limited in quantity and quality.

When such groups are in the Opposition, their policy in relation to the Government is devoid of restraint and national responsibility, and if they join the Government it is in return for concessions to their factional concerns that would have no chance of acceptance if the majority of voters had their way. All this led to an inflation of group differences. Factions thrived on such differences because they did not have to make the decisions, naturally claiming that they acted in the national interest. Yet what counted with them was primarily some factional consideration.

In the elections to the First Knesset there were twenty-one lists; to the Second, seventeen; and to the Third, twelve. The mischief of fragmentation was abetted by the proportional election system, whereby the entire State was treated as a single constituency. In the elections to the First Knesset, planned during the War of Independence, there was good reason for this: with tens of thousands of citizens mobilized in the Army and several areas still occupied by invading forces, it was not possible to divide the country into many constituencies, either according to the British system, in which each constituency returns the single member who receives the largest number of votes, or the Scandinavian system, in which each constituency returns a number of candidates chosen by proportional balloting.

Efforts by the Prime Minister–Designate to bring into the Government all the constructive forces, from Mapam to Agudat Israel and the General Zionists, did not succeed even once, although there were no differences of opinion among those invited to form a coalition on fundamental issues: security, ingathering of the exiles, upbuilding of the country, fructification of the wasteland, elevation of the cultural and economic levels of all inhabitants, efforts to achieve peace with our neighbors, encouragement of all fruitful initiative whether private, cooperative, or nationally owned, the preclusion of religious or antireligious coercion.

The Prime Minister, who was carried over in office from the First Knesset, announced on September 11, 1951, that he was negotiating with Mapam, Mapai, Agudat Israel, Poalei Agudat Israel, the Mizrahi, Hapoel Hamizrahi, the General Zionists, and the Progressives on the formation of a broad coalition. Talks with the General Zionists (twenty-two members) and Mapam (fifteen members) produced no results; the Progressives refused to join a limited coalition. Despite six weeks of effort, the first Government in the Second Knesset was joined only by Hamizrahi, Hapoel Hamizrahi, Agudat Israel and Poalei Agudat Israel, and of course Mapai.

This Government was formed on October 7, 1951, when a thirteen-member Cabinet was presented, consisting of Mapai and the religious parties: nine members of Mapai, one of Agudat Israel, two of Hapoel Hamizrahi and one of Hamizrahi. (The assignment of portfolios has been listed in preceding pages.)

The basic policy of this Government remained essentially unchanged from that of its predecessors, but there were two important innovations. (1) A program for State education in all primary schools based on the principles listed earlier: ending the affiliation of schools to parties and organizations; a minimal curriculum for all schools; assurance of religious education for all children of parents who desire it; recognition of the parental right to shape and expand education, under the supervision of the Ministry of Education and without affecting the obligatory curriculum. (2) Provision for the Government to place before the Knesset amendments to the Electoral Law aimed at preventing divisions that prevent the integration of the immigrants and stultify the democratic regime.

The second item was not implemented because of the changes of membership in the new Government, confirmed by the Knesset on December 23, 1952, and joined next day also by Hapoel Hamizrahi; Shapira and Yosef Burg returned to the Government with Knesset approval.

On January 22, 1952, the Prime Minister announced revisions in the Government made necessary by Eliezer Kaplan's relinquishment of the Finance portfolio because of illness, and the resignation of the Minister of Justice, Dov Joseph. In the reorganization Kaplan remained as Minister without portofolio; Levi Eshkol took over the post of Minister of Finance; Peretz Naftali became Minister of Agriculture; Chaim Cohn became Minister of Justice. The Knesset approved these changes. The death of Kaplan brought a further change. On August 18, 1952, after the thirty-day period of mourning, the Prime Minister announced the co-option of Pinhas Lavon as Minister without portfolio.

Several months later, on September 18, Rabbi Levin of Agudat Israel, Minister of Welfare, resigned owing to pressure from his party's extremist wing. In his letter of resignation he wrote: "For my part I wish to preserve decency and friendly relationships in the future as well. I will try to conduct every activity, even outside the coalition, in the spirit of love of Israel." It was not empty rhetoric. Though he never returned to the

Government, he was faithful to his pledge. Rabbi Levin had resigned during the Knesset recess, on the eve of Rosh Hashanah. The Prime Minister could make the announcement only at the opening of the second session on November 3, 1952, at which time he also reported the co-option of Rabbi Nurock of the Mizrahi as Minister of Posts (Until then the postal department had been part of the Ministry of Transport.)

The Government was compelled to dissolve on December 19, 1952, following the resignation of two ministers of the Hapoel Hamizrahi and a minister of Mizrahi. Three days later, however, the Prime Minister succeeded in bringing in the General Zionists and the Progressives. On December 22 he presented to the Knesset a Government slate consisting of five members of Mapai, four of the General Zionists, two of Hapoel Hamizrahi, and one of the Progressives.

On that occasion Ben-Gurion reviewed all the crises that had erupted until that time. "Each of the Government crises," he pointed out, "had its special causes, but they all stemmed from one source: the crisis that had marked the State from the first moment to this day—the one inherent in the inflated and morbid fragmentation we have inherited from our unhappy past, from a life of dependence devoid for thousands of years of statehood and national responsibility. In this Knesset we have no fewer than eight small parties totaling only thirty-four members, without taking into account five factions, that have only one or two members each."

In late 1953 Ben-Gurion reluctantly chose to retire to the Negev, "for a year, two, or more." First, however, he requested and received two months' leave in order to study the nation's defense requirements for the next three years before leaving the Government. In his absence Sharett was appointed Acting Prime Minister and Pinhas Lavon Acting Minister of Defense. On October 18, 1953, Ben-Gurion delivered an address on the security situation and requirements for the ensuing years. The Government approved his program. In November he wrote to President Ben-Zvi, explaining his reasons for retiring:

My dear Mr. President:
I consider it my duty to advise you in writing, as I have already done in person, of the reasons that compel me, to my great and profound regret, to retire from my work in the Government in the near future.

For six years I have been working under extreme tension and with great effort, something I doubt anyone will understand even after I have explained it. Fateful problems crop up constantly and every difficult question has weighty arguments, both pro and con. Some think that for this it is sufficient to have a "line" that, if once drawn, will automatically lead along the straight and easy path. I must admit I have had no such "line." I have been guided rather by a "point," *the point of the desired target*. To the best of my knowledge there is no ready-paved road leading to a desired end, but amidst the endless fluctuations and changes of a reality that never repeats itself, one must continuously and unceasingly hew out a difficult pathway toward the target. There are steps that, though correct yesterday, may be disastrous tomorrow. I am not qualified to state whether I have succeeded in finding the proper path toward the target every step of the way, but this I can say: I have not spared mental, intuitive, or cognitive effort in each and every case to find the right step, and you can believe me if I tell you that all these years I have worked under supreme mental tension, knowing full well the gains and losses involved.

This crushing tension, however, did not begin six years ago. Ever since 1936, when as chairman of the Jewish Agency I met with the Peel Commission, I realized that the promise of the British Mandate, *i.e.*, aid by England for the creation of the "National Home," had come to an end and no legal or political claims of international obligation, even if justified, would change this fact or be of any avail, and henceforth the entire Zionist policy would have to be different. From that time on, a period of sixteen to seventeen years, I have been working under the greatest tension, as I have attempted to describe it to you. I need not tell you that I have done it out of love. Nor would I conceivably claim any credit for myself. You know that in my world there is nothing dearer than the State of Israel, nor any privilege greater than to serve it faithfully. It is not only a privilege but a duty, and I am not afraid to say a sacred duty, a duty that must be done until one's last breath.

However, for a year now I have felt unable to bear any longer the psychological strain under which I work in the Government—the tension without which I cannot and am not entitled to work. This has not been just ordinary fatigue; on the contrary, when I leave my work in the Government for a few days I feel practically no tiredness and am capable of working, from both the physical and psychological standpoints, as I did twenty or thirty years ago. But there seem to be limits, at least in my case, to the psychological effort one can make. I have come to the unfortunate conclusion that I have no choice but to leave this work for a year or two or more. A close friend, whom I have consulted on this matter, has advised me to request from the Government an extended leave of absence of a year or two. I have weighed the matter carefully and concluded that even if it were permitted constitutionally, an extended leave for the Prime Minister is inconceivable.

There is one thing that has bothered me especially, and that is my departure from the Ministry of Defense. I have devoted many weeks to a thorough examination of the problems of security and the structure and needs of the Army, and have come away encouraged and heartened. At two special meetings devoted to that purpose I have submitted to the Government a detailed report on the problems of the Army and security, as well as a three-year program of action. I have given you a summary of this plan orally and will not go into it in this letter. The Government has approved it. Let me merely say this: the security of the State is in good hands: the Israel Defense Forces are built on a firm foundation and its corps of commanders and tens of thousands of soldiers on land, at sea, and in the air are worthy of their mission.

Ben-Gurion submitted his formal resignation on December 7, 1953. According to the law, a resigning Prime Minister is required to remain in office until a successor Government has been approved by the Knesset. Together with the resignation, therefore, he asked for a leave of absence until the new Government was chosen, so that he might go to the Negev immediately. That day Sharett informed the legislature as follows:

Yesterday, at the Government meeting, Prime Minister David Ben-Gurion announced his decision to retire from his Premiership and the post of Minister of Defense. He announced that he would submit his resignation to the President today, and today the resignation was submitted, which according to the Transition Law is tantamount to the resignation of the Government as a whole. According to the Transition Law, when a Government resigns, the resigning Government is obliged to carry on its function until the creation of a new Government. As long as the existing Government remains in power, therefore, David Ben-Gurion remains Prime Minister. However, he requested at yesterday's meeting, and the Government agreed, that he be granted leave until the formation of a new Government. The Government has decided to entrust the Premiership temporarily to the Foreign Minister, and to appoint Minister Lavon as Acting Minister of Defense.

Both the resignation and the leave of absence were approved. In a broadcast to the nation the same day Ben-Gurion said:

I have today submitted my resignation to the President. No words of mine can adequately express what I feel toward the nation for having had faith in me and entrusted me with the exalted and fateful mission of heading the Government of Israel ever since its establishment. I have endeavored to fulfill my mission, as far as lay in my power, with devotion and in all humility. But I do not claim to have been free from fault and error. With complete sincerity I can repeat literally the words of the Psalmist in the first verse of Chapter 131: "Lord, my heart is not haughty, nor mine eyes lofty; neither do I exercise myself in things too high or in matters too wonderful for me."

I must confess: I find it difficult to take leave of the Defense Forces of Israel—stronghold of the State and creative center for uplifting the youth and welding together the nation in Israel. I saw the early shaping of our armed force many years ago, during the Ottoman regime, when I went forth with my friends to plow in the fields of Galilee with a rifle over my shoulder, spending nights on guard at a lone and exposed Jewish village. I kept pace with it as a soldier in the First World War, when the first Jewish legions of our generations were formed. I followed its silent growth and its heroic adventures during the British Mandatory period. I had something to do with training and equipping it in preparation for what was likely to come with the end of the Second World War. I was privileged to be at its head as Prime Minister and Minister of Defense when it boldly emerged from the underground, with the birth of the State, as the Defense Forces of Israel, arrayed before all the Arab armies, achieving remarkable victories on land, at sea, and in the air. And in the last four years I have been closely concerned with its reorganization and training, the improvement of its equipment, and its educational and pioneering activities—the training of our youth, the education and integration of our immigrants, and the establishment of frontier settlements. It is indeed very difficult to leave. I hope and pray that the new Minister of Defense and the corps of loyal and gifted officers will not rest content with what has been achieved until now, but will strive unremittingly to raise the standards of training and equipment, to intensify the pioneering drive, to strengthen the Forces' roots in the Homeland and in the Hebrew heritage, and to keep them constantly ready and prepared for whatever may come.

I have derived much satisfaction from the support of the minorities in Israel—Moslems, Christians, and Druze—of the Governments that I have been privileged to head.

On leaving the Government, I must express my profound appreciation to all the colleagues who have served with me in the Provisional Government and in the Governments that have followed. I owe a profound personal debt of gratitude to the band of assistants, civilian and military, in the Prime Minister's Office and the Ministry of Defense. They have shared loyally in all my efforts and difficulties. Their work has been enthusiastic, devoted, and efficient. If all State employees will be like this, no harm can befall us.

From the bottom of my heart I send best wishes to the next Government: may fortune crown all its actions and may it succeed in everything to which it lays its hand.

We did not receive Statehood as a gift. Our beloved and devoted sons and daughters gave their lives for the revival of Israel. May we be worthy of their sacred memory.

Upon leaving the Government, Ben-Gurion settled in Sde Boker, a young kibbutz in the Negev.

More than six weeks passed before Sharett was able to present a revised slate. The new Government was installed on January 25, 1954, with Sharett as Prime Minister and Minister for Foreign Affairs. The other members of his Cabinet were Zalman Aranne, Minister without portfolio; Eshkol, Minister of Finance; Burg, Minister of Posts; Bernstein, Minister of Commerce and Industry; Ben-Zion Dinur, Minister of Education and Culture; Dov Joseph, Minister of Development; Lavon, Minister of Defense; Golda Meir, Minister of Labor; Naftali, Minister of Agriculture; Sapir, Minister of Transportation; Serlin, Minister of Health; Rosen, Minister of Justice; Rokah, Minister of the Interior; Shitreet, Minister of Police; and Moshe Shapira, Minister of Welfare and of Religious Affairs.

This, unfortunately, was not the end of changes in the Government during the Second Knesset. On February 21, 1955, Sharett informed the Knesset that Minister of Defense Lavon had tendered his resignation because he "did not see the possibility of continuing in his post after his proposal for changes in the structure of the defense organization had been turned down by the Prime Minister." It was vital, Sharett said, to fill the vacancy "with the greatest possible dispatch, practical effectiveness, and moral weight."

He was certain, he added, "that no candidate could have more prospects of filling the post with success, and enjoy greater confidence of the nation, than the man who established the Israel Defense Forces, presided over its campaigns and its gravest days of trial, consolidated its foundations for the future, and is bound to it with love and loyalty with every fiber of his being. Through a special envoy I have asked the First Prime Minister and Minister of Defense, Knesset Member David Ben-Gurion, now a member of Sde Boker, once again to accept this difficult task. David Ben-Gurion has responded favorably to the appeal, though, I know, not without reluctance and soul-searching. My proposal to co-opt him for the Defense portfolio was approved by the Government yesterday."

There was a short debate, in which representatives of Mapam and the Communists objected to the co-option but the change was confirmed by a vote of seventy-five to twenty-two. Ben-Gurion was once more the Minister of Defense. (*The circumstances of my return, involving a crisis of confidence in the Defense Ministry, will be recounted later in connection with the so-called "Lavon Affair."*)

Scarcely four months later, on June 29, the Prime Minister told the Knesset of another change:

Yesterday there occurred in the Knesset something beyond the bounds of every framework of accepted parliamentary conduct—the General Zionists' abstention from voting against a motion of no-confidence in the Government submitted by the Herut party. Even the General Zionist members of the Government saw fit not to vote against the no-confidence motion. Before the voting I told these members that if they could not find it possible to vote against the motion, I would consider myself compelled to demand their resignation. Their answer was that ministers could not be compelled to resign if the way was open to the Prime Minister to submit his own resignation to the President, which is tantamount to the resignation of the entire Government.

I have decided to take this course and therefore this morning at a special meeting of the Government I announced that decision. In accordance with the Transition Law, the President at once began consultations with the various factions in the Knesset and at 6 P.M. imposed on me the task of forming the new Government. These are its members: Zalman Arrane, Minister of Transport; Levi Eshkol, Minister of Finance; Yosef Burg, Minister of Posts; David Ben-Gurion, Minister of Defense; Ben-Zion Dinur, Minister of Education and Culture; Dov Joseph, Minister of Development and of Health; Golda Meir, Minister of Labor; Peretz Naftali, Minister of Agriculture and of Commerce and Industry; Pinhas Rosen, Minister of Justice; Moshe Shapira, Minister of the Interior, of Welfare, and of Religious Affairs; Moshe Sharett, Prime Minister and Minister of Foreign Affairs.

That evening the Government received a vote of confidence, sixty-six to thirty-two—the first time that a Government resigned and a new one was formed on the same day, and as it happened, at the very end of the Knesset's four-year term. The following day, June 30, 1955, the Second Knesset held its final meeting, set elections for July 26, and adjourned.

Changes had occurred in the make-up of the political parties in this Knesset. In the elections the General Zionists received twenty seats, compared to seven in the First Knesset, and in time they were joined by two members from the Sephardi list. On the other hand, the Mapam list practically disintegrated. It won fifteen seats, but three of its Knesset members—Moshe Sneh, Avraham Berman, and Rustum Bastouni—resigned from the party on January 29, 1953, to form a Left Faction. Then, on October 30, 1954, Berman and Sneh joined the Communists, while Bastouni returned to Mapam. Two members, Hannah Lamdam and David Lifshitz, resigned from Mapam on January 25, 1952, and on January 13, 1954, they joined Mapai. On August 23, 1945, Kibbutz Hameuhad members Ben-Aharon, Bar-Yehuda, and Aharon Zisling, as well as Poalei Zion (Left) member Erem withdrew from Mapam, leaving that party only seven members, this after the return of Bastouni.

The Education Law and the Zionist Organization Statute

The outgoing Knesset had enacted the State Education Law (passed on August 12, 1953) in order to fulfill Section 8 of the Government's Basic Policy of December 22, 1952, regarding the elimination of affiliation of schools to parties, the determination of a minimum curriculm applicable to all schools, the assurance of religious education for all children of parents who desire it, and the recognition of the rights of parents to shape and expand education without effecting the obligatory curriculm. Section 2 of the State Education Law declares: "The object of State Education is to base elementary education in the State on the values of Jewish culture and the achievements of science, on love of the Homeland and loyalty to the State and the Jewish people, on practice of agricultural work and handicraft, on halutzi (pioneering) training, and on striving for a society built on freedom, equality, tolerance, mutual assistance, and love of mankind."

The law attests that the first things to be inculcated in the young are the values of Israel's culture, a culture created and developed in the course of four thousand years. Whether it can be transmitted in full to children aged six to fourteen and even older is doubtful, so we must of necessity give the youth only its choicest essence, namely, the Bible. Though we created important works afterward, the Bible has remained the summit of Hebrew creation and has left its mark on the majority of the human race. It is an undeniable fact, however, that in the days of the Bible our culture was one-sided, and therefore the new law provides that the achievements of science must be taught as well. Without the conquests of science and its practical applications we could not maintain an economy, defend ourselves, foster culture, or mold a new society.

The law also calls for the inculcating of loyalty to the State. In every other nation this goes practically without saying, but not so in Israel. For two thousand years we had had no sense of statehood and the mere proclamation of a State does not remedy the situation. Loyalty requires much cultivation, in Israel more than in any other new country, because Israel is not only the State of its inhabitants but of tens of thousands of Jews still dispersed throughout the world, and its supreme objective is the ingathering of the exiles. The law therefore speaks of loyalty both to the State of Israel and to the people of Israel. As the great majority of the people of Israel are scattered in countries all over the world, we must deepen both the attachment of the younger generation to the Jewish people as a whole, and the attachment of the Jewish people to Israel. This will come about if Israel will be a magnet for the Diaspora by serving as a model state, that is to say, a society based on freedom, equality, mutual aid, and love of one's fellow man.

That is why the law also stresses pioneering—the key to our future and the secret of the revolution that has taken place before our eyes, the beginning of the period of the Third Temple. The young State of Israel is the result of pioneering that transformed people without ground under their feet, at the mercy of foreigners, into persons of labor and settlement, defense and arms, the creators of the culture and the values of a new society. Through pioneering effort we have withstood wilderness and natural disasters, enemies and the habits of exile, and only by dint of pioneering effort will we survive in days to come. Just what is pioneering? It is an awareness of the historic mission and a dedication to its service, unconditionally and unflinchingly, in spite of difficulty and danger. Pioneering is the moral capacity and the strength of soul to live day by day according to the dictates of conscience and the requirements of historic destiny. Pioneering is the demand a man makes of himself; it is a personal realization and implementation of the values of truth, justice, and love of one's fellow man; the desire and the capacity to carry out acts of creation.

The Education Law in itself, of course, is no guarantee that the education will be the kind desired and needed. Implementation of the law depends first of all on the talent, capability, and moral qualities of the teacher, and such teachers are as yet in short supply.

Another legislative act of special significance was the Zionist Organization Status Law, a bill the Prime Minister presented on May 5, 1952, during the first session of the Second Knesset. It has not been implemented as those who adopted it had intended. The bill, as the Prime Minister pointed out at the time, was a twin and a complement to the Law of the Return, enacted during the First Knesset. It aims to give legal force and State recognition to the basic fact of the Jewish people's experience, its historic continuity, unity, and aspiration; to give the impress of the State and the law to the fact that the State of Israel is the creation of the Jewish people as a whole, not only in this generation but in preceding generations and those to come.

This continuity is rooted not only in the common heritage of the past but in a common historic destiny. It evidences the fact that not only the Jews living in Israel but the State itself as a sovereign entity have a connection with the Jewish people, and that the destinies of both are intertwined. For the State of Israel is the product of the Jewish people's vision of redemption throughout the generations; if, with the emergence of the State, that ideal has not been fulfilled, it is because most of the Jewish people are still dispersed among the nations. The establishment of the State provided the practical basis for the ideal of Jewish redemption; hence the State has become an integrating and unifying force for the Jewish people abroad like nothing else before it. As long as the ideal was theoretical, few rallied around the banner of the vision that at the end of the nineteenth century became known as Zionism—an aspiration not born at that time, having existed for hundreds of years, ever since the destruction of the nation's independence in its Homeland.

Dr. Herzl, the founder of the Zionist Organization, effectively and succinctly defined this vision in a way that has been forgotten and neglected by the majority of Zionist workers since. He said, "Zionism is the Jewish people on its way"—on the way back to its land. This profound and fateful definition was later mutilated and transformed into something meaningless—"The Zionist Organization is the State on its way." In effect the majority of its leaders alienated themselves from the State and adhered rather to the Zionist Organization. Immigration to Israel existed before the Zionist Organization and it was this and this alone that gave the Zionist Organization its *raison d'être*, ultimately building the State. The difficulties and obstacles that stood in the way of immigration before the creation of the State were not removed afterward; during the first four years the problems were no fewer, though different from those encountered previously.

The Zionist Organization Status Law, adopted by the Knesset on December 5, 1952, declares:

> The State of Israel regards itself as the work of the whole Jewish people and its gates are open to every Jew who wishes to come. The ingathering of the exiles, the essence of the tasks undertaken by the State of Israel and the Zionist movement in our days, calls for continuous efforts by the Jewish people in the countries of the Diaspora. Therefore the Jewish State expects that all Jews, both individuals and groups, will participate in the upbuilding of the State and in assisting large-scale immigration, and regards as essential the unification of all Jewish communities for this purpose. The Jewish State expects the World Zionist Organization to make efforts to arrive at this unification.

Only in the first four years of the State did annual immigration exceed 100,000. A sharp decline was manifest in 1952, when only 23,375 immigrants arrived; in 1953 the figure was 10,347; in 1954, 17,471; and in 1955, 36,303—87,496 in all during the second four years. (Jewish departures from Israel in these four years after 1951 totaled 32,500). Meanwhile the natural increase of Jewish population in the four years 1952–1955 was 134,700 compared to 88,100 in the initial four years. At the end of 1951 the Jewish population was 1,404,400; at the end of 1955 it was 1,590,500.

Achievements in the First Four Years ★ Three Rates of Exchange To Attract Foreign Capital ★ Efforts To Reach Economic Independence

In the first four years the main objective of the first elected Government—to double the Jewish population—was completely achieved. Quantitatively, it was exceeded. To the population of 650,000 on the day the State was proclaimed (May 14, 1948), 684,275 immigrants and a natural increase of 97,208 had been added. Of these we must deduct 27,767 yordim (emigrants), making the overall addition 753,706 persons. In these four years 132,000 housing units were erected, 75,000 permanent and 57,000 temporary units, at a cost of IL72 million. An aggregate of 550 kilometers of new roads were built in the Galilee, on the coastal plain, and as part of the road to Jerusalem; over 500 kilometers of existing roads had been widened and improved. In 1951 1.32 million tons of imports arrived at Haifa port, compared to 236,000 tons in 1948—a more than fivefold increase. The airfield at Lod, which was transferred to the State of Israel by Israel Defense Forces, became an international airport after the loss of the airport at Kalandia. In 1948 1700 planes landed there and in 1951 31,000. In 1948 the merchant marine consisted of 4 ships with a tonnage of 6000 tons and 100 seamen. At the end of 1951 we had 34 ships comprising 120,000 tons, and the number of seamen had risen to 1200. When the State was created, we had 18,000 farm units collectively and privately owned (excluding orchards). In October 1952 Jewish farming units came to 41,000, and the Arab sector had 15,000. Yet Israel was still far from self-sufficient in food production.

In the same years the area under irrigation was doubled. The 200,000 dunams under irrigation in 1948 expanded to 400,000 dunams by 1951. The vegetable and fodder area increased from 104,000 to nearly 340,000 dunams. Industry and crafts had not expanded at such a rapid rate: at the end of 1949 80,000 breadwinners were employed in industry and crafts and at the end of 1951 119,000. Nevertheless, factories were erected for the manufacture of automobiles, tires, pipes, plywood, textiles, fruit concentrates, chocolate, glass, household utensils, etc. The glass industry had imported glass sand bought with foreign currency. After the creation of the State, however, glass sand of the highest quality was discovered in the Negev and by 1951 we were using 5000 tons of it annually. After the conquest of the Negev, which accounts for 60 percent of Israel's terrain geological studies proved that it was not the desolate wasteland that had been supposed. Apart from glass sand, rich deposits of phosphates were discovered and immediately put to use in local industries. Export possibilities were found for the copper lodes at Timna; kaolin, manganese, sulphur, and other minerals were also found. The fertilizer plant in Haifa began using phosphates from the Negev.

In the three years from the end of 1948 to the end of 1951 the national income increased from IL 50 million to IL 440 million. The number of breadwinners in agriculture, industry, transportation, services, commerce, and finance grew from 200,000 to 510,000. Though the daring innovation introduced in the Defense Services Law—to transform the Army into a workshop for fighting, pioneering youth (Nahal)—had had many opponents in the Knesset, it proved successful. During the two years after the enactment of the law the Nahal set up fifteen new settlements, mainly on the Syrian and Egyptian borders, the frontiers that had seen the greatest number of violations of the armistice agreements. These settlements constituted a defense chain of human steel at the country's weak points. Nahal settlements were also formed in the Arava at the southern tip of the Negev near Eilat and on the shores of the Dead Sea.

Yet the trade deficit had increased from year to year. The raw materials, food, implements, machines, equipment, vehicles, etc., imported for absorption and development work from the end of the War of Independence early in 1949 until October 1951 cost us $828,601,572 while our exports were only $104,824,980. In less than three years the gap between imports and exports thus reached $732 million, an amount that was made up by contribution campaigns, bonds, grants, and imported capital. While a large part of the import-to-export surplus was invested in basic means of production in agriculture, industry, and transportation, thereby increasing the State's productive capacity, a considerable part went into consumer goods. This deficit has been and remains one of the young State's gravest problems.

This, however, was not the most serious problem of the initial four years—the greatest four-year period in Jewish history since the Hasmoneans defeated the Greeks

2113 years earlier. The most serious problem was posed by the absorption of immigrants and continued ingathering of the exiles. Despite the slowdown in immigration after 1952, many years passed before the mass immigration of the first four years had taken root, economically and culturally. These immigrants were almost completely penniless and in the large part bereft of Jewish and general education. Nevertheless, the bleak forecasts of the spokesmen of those parties that refused to join the first elected Government did not come true. The mass immigration, without parallel to this day (and perhaps unequaled at any time in history), proved a great blessing and in due time was absorbed, economically and culturally. Despite the limitations and restrictions on nutrition imposed by the austerity program, the infant mortality rate declined from 51.7 per thousand in 1949 to 46.5 per thousand in 1950 and 39 per thousand in 1951. The health budget, less than IL 1 million in 1948–1949, reached IL 6,316,000 in 1952, and the education budget increased from IL 595,000 to IL 8,280,115.

What was accomplished in these years could not be measured or weighed solely by numbers of people, by a count of settlements, or by a census of capital, machines, factories, and schools. Without question, the quantitative side of this great creation was important; but no less important was the qualitative aspect, which could not be expressed in figures and scales. A profound and fundamental transformation was taking place in the lives of hundreds of thousands of Jews, more than six hundred thousand, that cannot be evaluated by any quantitative criterion. Here we were witness to one of the profoundest revolutions in the fate of man and nation, not a revolution in regime and government—which, in effect, concerns only a few—but a revolution deep down in the character and nature of the Jews and in the land to which he is returning.

The mortal clay of Jewry existing in foreign climes, dependent, ever wandering, in bondage, its life hanging by a thread, was hardened on entering its Homeland into a sovereign and independent organism, implanted and enshrined in the great past and at one with the vision of the modern days, the vision of national and human redemption. Long severed from work and soil, cut off from the sources of nature, torn away from the primary branches of economy, these Jews returned to their land and were changed into tillers of the earth, workers in mines, in factories, in the harbors and upon the seas, on the railroads and in civil aviation; and they created a new, a free, and an independent basis for a diversified and deeply rooted national economy.

Born into a variety of languages and subjected to the influence of foreign cultures, cut off from the sources of the Jewish spirit and the language and literature of their people, the immigrants returning to Zion renewed the tongue of the Prophets. A language silent for centuries became once again the lingua franca of ingathered exiles; on the trunk of the ancient Hebrew culture there sprouted the foliage of its modern Hebrew counterpart, steeped in Jewish and human values and making no distinction between Jew and any decent human being. Jewish Man in Israel was evolving and renewing his inner sensations, his capacity for practical achievement and creation, his Jewish and human awareness, his material and spiritual strength, his bond with his people, his past and his future, his rootedness in the soil of his Homeland, and his liberation from dependence on alien and inimical forces.

This human revolution, almost unparalleled in history, applied to all those who returned to Zion, whether from Europe and America or the countries of Asia and Africa. Especially radical and profound was the transformation that took place in the Jewish daughter and mother returning to her Homeland from the countries of Islam. The degradation of human dignity practised against women in backward and degenerate countries came to a stop when the Jewish women set foot on the soil of the Homeland. The women of Israel from Yemen, Iraq, Persia, Morocco, like those from Poland, Germany, South Africa, and the U.S., were free and equal in the State of Israel. All fields of endeavor in work, culture, education, science, army, management, and government were open to them no less than to their sons, brothers, and husbands.

And this profound human transformation was bound up with a thorough revolution in nature, uncovering its hidden treasures and resources, rebuilding its ruins, increasing its fertility and yield, and restoring its ancient crown of glory.

When the first elected Government appeared before the Knesset, soon after the end of the fighting in the War of Independence, the Prime Minister declared, as cited earlier:

> It may well be that we are passing from the phase of great things, the phase of epic courage and victory in the military and political spheres to a phase of little things, the phase of the dusty and protracted struggle toward domestic construction and national organization perhaps lacking in lustre, in the lightning flash and dramatic heroism. All it has to show is painful exertion, unremitting and loyal. But anyone who considers that the little things now demanded of us are less vital, less decisive for our destiny, than the great things, is making a bitter and dangerous mistake. The ordeal we shall have to undergo now is no whit less serious than the ordeal of war, and it is more drawn-out and, in many respects, more difficult.

The facts of the three years after the War of Independence showed that this was no overstatement. The military victories were the prelude to a regime of austerity, stringent rationing, as well as determined efforts to increase the influx of capital in various ways.

On February 13, 1952, the Prime Minister announced in the Knesset:

> In order to encourage the flow of foreign capital, to stabilize the currency, increase export of our agricultural and industrial produce, and halt the rise in the cost of vital commodities, the Government has decided to fix three rates of exchange to the pound: $2.80 per pound for bread and other vital food products; $1.40 per pound for money from appeals, tourists, diplomatic legations, and also for a number of commodities such as meat, fish, coffee, tea, medicaments, and fertilizer; and $1 to the pound for capital investment.
>
> In view of this change in the rate of exchange, the Government will prevent any rise in the prices of goods in stock. If it is proved that the goods were bought in accordance with the new rate and if the seller receives a certificate to that effect, only then will he be allowed to raise the price by a suitable amount. Every foreign investor will be permitted to import an automobile, equipment, building materials, and raw materials for his approved enterprise without payment of foreign currency. Every immigrant and foreign investor will be permitted, on the basis of import licenses, to import goods, if he produced or dealt in such goods abroad. The proceeds of the sale of goods imported by a foreign investor of this kind will be placed under the supervision of the Ministry of Finance for investment locally. The rate of exchange for such imports will be a pound to the dollar, but the importer will not, as was the case hitherto, have to hand over to the Government an additional dollar for every dollar's worth of imports. An interministerial committee will be empowered to allow an importer of this category expenses not exceeding 15 percent of the sale price. The commodities will be sold only under a permit of sale given by the competent authority.

In these ways, the Government hopes to facilitate the flow of capital into the country in the form of currency or goods and to check the flight of capital and the profiteering malpractices that have done grave harm to our economy and to the value of the Israel pound.

However, the crux of our drive toward economic independence is, in the opinion of the Government, increased production, enhancement of productivity, and expansion of exports, as we declared in the Government's Basic Policy, approved by the Knesset at the beginning of the month of Tishri this year (8 Tishri 5712; August 10, 1951).

The Government is confident that all sectors responsible for the Israeli economy—be it laborers, farmers, foremen, factory owners, bankers, craftsmen, or contractors—are interested for their own sake and that of the State in increasing productivity, in improving the quality of products, in managerial efficiency, and in increasing the competitive worth of Israeli products on the international market. Unless we increase the productivity of labor, not by sweatshop methods but by establishing efficient working conditions, improving equipment, reducing the cost of administration and making it more efficient, we will not be able to maintain our economy and security.

In view of all this, the Government has decided that, from now on, the price of products and profits will not be calculated mechanically by adding a percentage to the cost of production. This leads to the lowering of the productive level and in many cases to exorbitant and unjustified profits, which cripple the competitiveness of our products. Prices and profits will be fixed in the light of economic efficiency and the improvement of production processes, which should reduce the costs of production, increase productive capacity, and improve the quality of the product. Higher profits will be linked from now on to increased efficiency in the factory. Raw materials will not be allocated mechanically either, according to past privileges. Here, priority will be given to undertakings that increase exports, manufacture at low costs, and look after the quality of their goods.

We regard the right to work as the first right of man. The Government has in the past taken heed and will continue in the future to take heed for full employment. But the right to work entails an obligation. And we recognize equally the right to a fair profit for the promoter and capitalist, who help to develop the country and to absorb immigration. This right, too, entails obligations.

I note with satisfaction the resolution passed by the Executive Council of the General Federation of Labor (Histadrut) on January 6, 1952, "to introduce into every branch of labor, where possible, a wage system based on norms and premiums, and in certain other kinds of labor, the piecework system of measuring a minimum daily wage. Additions to the wage will in general be linked with productivity and efficiency, in line with the resolutions of the Seventh Congress of the Histadrut (May 1949)." I also mention with pleasure the Histadrut Executive's decision of the same date which reads: "In view of the scarcity in manpower, there is need to refrain from shortening working hours at this stage."

The responsibility for the fate of labor and the workers, and for the fate of Israel's economy, implied in these decisions does honor to the supreme council of the largest federation of labor in the country. Responsible managers of industry have also expressed their concern for the need to enhance the quality of our products and ability to compete on international markets.

We know and we understand that the cure of our economy, checking inflation, stabilizing the currency, and our drive toward economic independence cannot be attained by the economy and its makers alone. Only the goodwill which harmonizes the interests of the individual and of the public, which realizes that only with the peace of the State, its security and its comfort, can there be also the peace and security of the individual—only that kind of goodwill can serve as a guarantee of our future, in the political as well as in the economic field. We believe that such goodwill is alive among the majority of our citizens, old-timers and new im-migrants, and that it can be brought into action.

We have set up an Economic Council, comprising representatives of all economic circles, to deliberate upon all the economic problems of the State; to clarify methods of efficiency and managerial administration and the means of increasing output and expanding production; and to examine grievances and complaints of deprivation and discrimination. This Council will not diminish the sovereign powers of the Knesset, for it will act only as an advisory authority. We do, however, believe that, in concerted discussion with representa-tives of the various circles and organizations, from both the private and the cooperative sectors of the economy, a common language will be found for the fortification of Israel's economy and its expansion, and for carrying the State of Israel rapidly forward by joint endeavor along the road to economic independence, just as our sons did in the War of In-dependence, sons of fathers from all circles and every class, to assure the independence of Israel and its political sovereignty.

After a three-day debate, February 18–20, four motions of no-confidence submitted by the General Zionists, Mapam, Herut, and the Communists were rejected. The following motion by the Coalition was adopted: "The Knesset accepts the Prime Minister's announce-ment of February 13, 1952, of the Government's program in economic and financial matters."

Section 3. Israel and the Communist World

Debate on the Anti-Zionist Trial in Prague ★ Communists in the Knesset Defend the Czechoslovak Regime

ON November 24, 1952, during the second session of the Second Knesset, the Minister of Foreign Affairs, Moshe Sharett, made a declaration about an international event that shocked the entire civilized world, one that affected Judaism and Israel in general and two Israeli citizens in particular:

> The entire world these days stands aghast at a farce in the form of a legal trial, performed this time on the stage of a Czechoslovak court. Leaders of a party and heads of a regime who but yesterday stood at the helm, shaping the policies of their country and dominating her destinies, are today exhibited as a treacherous gang of conspirators, swindlers, and saboteurs. Even more astounding is the fact that the accused revel in incriminating themselves by confessing to every possible abomination of which they are accused. This exhibition of moral suicide and self-degradation must shock everyone who still believes in the sanctity and spiritual worth of human personality.
>
> In one respect the shameful spectacle constitutes an innovation. The majority of the accused are Jews, and the prosecution has spared no pains in highlighting their racial origin and in tracing their alleged crimes to this prime cause. The indictment, the court proceedings themselves, as well as the publicity given to the trial in the official Czechoslovak press, are all permeated with a spirit of rabid anti-Semitism.
>
> The prosecution has unfolded a dark screed of criminal plotting, of acts of conspiracy and subversion that these Jewish enemies of the Czechoslovak people have either perpetrated

or sought to perpetrate. Not satisfied with impugning their Jewish origin, it has denounced them as Zionists. Men who had never had any connection with the Zionist movement—some of whom, indeed, have persecuted Zionism with a vengeance—have themselves been branded with that stigma. The Zionist movement as a whole, that movement of liberation and of return to the Homeland, has been smeared and slandered as a band of intriguers and spies, bent on undermining the very foundations of the Czechoslovak regime, seeking the ruin of that country, and dishonestly exploiting the property of its citizens for its own nefarious purposes. The attempts of the Jewish survivors of the Nazi inferno to recover a tiny fraction of the immense quantity of Jewish property that had been plundered, have been denounced as acts of deceit and robbery. Israeli citizens who sought to serve the interests of the Czechoslovak Republic and her allies have been ensnared in this judicial plot and forced to admit charges of subversion and sabotage.

Finally, libelous allegations have been made against ministers and accredited representatives of the Government of Israel, charging them with having conspired with the enemies of Czechoslovakia, both within the country and outside, and seeking to destroy her economy and undermine her security.

The Government of Israel holds it utterly superfluous to attempt any detailed and factual denial of the tissue of libels and fabrications regarding activities of its members and emissaries, produced by the fertile imagination of the Czechoslovak Secret Police and Public Prosecution. These slanders are self-contradictory in the light of simple reason. Their falsity is obvious to the naked eye, refuted by patent facts. Israel has always entertained a sincere sympathy for the Czechoslovak people. Israel has sought to establish and foster friendly relations with the present Czechoslovak state. Israel obtained valuable aid from Czechoslovakia during her War of Independence for which she paid in full. This was arranged with the full knowledge and authority of the heads of the Czechoslovak state, some of whom still occupy high seats of power. At one stage Israel concluded a commercial agreement with Czechoslovakia, upon terms that proved suitable to both parties. Israel admitted thousands of Jews officially authorized to leave Czechoslovakia after they left most of their property behind them.

Israeli representatives have never served as agents or spies of any foreign power. Only those to whom espionage and sabotage come naturally as a matter of daily practice can invent such stories of sinister plotting about the ministers of Israel.

History had already passed judgment upon those regimes that had resource to the bogey of anti-Semitism in order to divert the attention of their masses from their own troubles and the failures of their rulers, and to turn their hatred against the Jews chosen as scapegoats. The liberation of Czechoslovakia from Hitler's Storm Troopers stands desecrated before the whole world by this attempt to revive Hitler's vile spirit within her borders.

This campaign of vilification is calculated to serve as a threat to the Jews of Czechoslovakia and of neighboring countries. Its object is to discredit the State of Israel in their eyes and to stamp out from their hearts their Jewish pride. It seeks to make them hated by the masses around them and to provide in advance justification for any future acts of discrimination and persecution of which many may become victims.

In this hour our hearts are with the multitudes of our Jewish brethren, cut off from the main body of the Jewish people and from any contact with the State of Israel—those forced to bear the burden of their destiny in isolation and solitude. Our voice may not reach them, but our hearts are heavy with anxiety for them, for their well-being, and their future fate.

Our people has a long memory. It will never forget any act of help and kindness in its hour of need. It will ever recall all aid received for its salvation and the defense of its freedom. Yet the Prague trial has cast a dark, ugly blot on the glorious record of friendship between the peoples of Israel and Czechoslovakia. It has imposed a heavy, a grievous burden on the memory of the Jewish people.

The Prime Minister was frequently interrupted by Esther Wilenska and Meir Wilner of the Communists. Acting on a proposal by Knesset Member Israel Rokah, it was decided to hold a debate on the Prime Minister's report. It took place the next day, November 25, 1952. Peretz Bernstein on behalf of the General Zionists said: "The most shocking aspect is that this time the accusations are to a large extent based on the fact that most of the accused are Jews and have been marked out as such, to the point where the concept of Jewishness, Jewish origin, and Zionism are in themselves elements of guilt." Eliezer Peri for Mapam made the following statement:

> The United Workers Party is shocked at the attempt in the Prague trial to implicate Zionism as a whole which in its very essence is a movement for the rescue and liberation of the most persecuted of nations in its historic Homeland. Mapam firmly rejects the broad accusations that have been hurled against Zionism. The fact that in Zionism, as in every national liberation movement, there are reactionary forces at work does not invalidate the progressive substance of our liberation movement. At the same time the Mapam faction in the Knesset rejects outright the announcement by the Foreign Minister on behalf of the Government that exploits the Prague trial for purpose of anti-communist agitation, to serve the forces of imperialism in their anti-Soviet aggression. We utterly reject the charge of Nazism hurled against the force that played a decisive role in the overthrow of Hitlerism and rescue of the survivors of the Holocaust.
>
> Mapam considers itself an integral part of the world revolutionary camp headed by the Union of Soviet Socialist Republics. We will stand unflinchingly behind the lands of Socialism and Popular Democracy in their struggle for the realization of Socialism and defense against enemies without and within. No attack or provocation will make us budge from the position with which we have kept faith for an entire generation and which has survived the most severe of trials. With upright stature, with firm determination, with pioneering dedication we will fulfill our Zionist-Socialist mission just as we will keep faith with our revolutionary Socialist path.
>
> The State of Israel arose as a result of the national Jewish liberation movement in the midst of an anti-imperialist war of liberation with the decisive help of the Soviet Union and the People's Democracies and for the purpose of serving as the beginning of the ingathering of the exiles of the Jewish people. The Socialist countries and People's Democracies have written a brilliant chapter by the very fact of the State of Israel's foundation, by their assistance in its struggle for independence, and by providing the arms that saved us and opened the gates for Jewish immigration.
>
> The activity of the forces of reaction in the Zionist movement and in the State of Israel has had a share in the distortion of the image of the Jewish people's national liberation movement. But we stress once again that the existence of these reactionary forces against whose policy of submission to imperialism we will continue and will intensify our struggle, does not give the prosecution in the Prague trial the right to besmirch the progressive path of our liberation movement or to link Zionism with accused persons who have detached themselves from their nation and have always fought bitterly against it.
>
> We stress and stress again to the forces of peace and socialism throughout the world that our struggle for the Zionist solution to the Jewish national problem through territorial concentration of the Jewish nation in its Homeland and for democracy and the independence of the State of Israel is in line with the interests of freedom and peace of all progressive humanity and is worthy of a positive attitude and the greatest support on its part.

Mapam stresses again that to the best of its knowledge our comrade Mordekhai Oren, who was carrying out a public mission, is innocent of any crime. We are convinced of the innocence of his intentions and do not conceive the possibility of malicious action on his part against the Czechoslovak government. We are certain that only a fortuitous entanglement of tragic circumstances led to the accusations that have been made against Mordekhai Oren, and we hope for his liberation and speedy return to the Homeland.

The next speaker was Mordekhai Namir on behalf of Mapai. He noted, among other things, that:

There is a unique psychological side to this trial, one that would confuse concepts and the common language shared by human beings and eliminate the elementary possibility of people conversing with one another in human society. This did not begin with the Prague trial. We know that the same language that knows how to praise dictatorship as a way of life and government and to disparage the democratic form of rule also knows how to call dictatorship democracy, war peace, etc. In this trial there is also a systematic effort to confuse concepts and ideas. One of the main points in it is the besmirching of Zionism and of the State of Israel, though among the accused who have been branded with the sin of Zionism there are people who have been sworn enemies of the Zionist movement for years. It is a good question, deeper than the abyss, how that regime arrived at the use of anti-Semitic provocation. (Esther Wilenska interrupted: "That is not true. There is not nor has there ever been any anti-Semitic provocation in the Socialist countries!")

Members of the Mapam, have you not yet made a reckoning with yourselves? Have you had no part in this trial? Have not your slanders, calumnies, and defamations of the State of Israel, its Government, and its policies which you have reiterated on this rostrum scores of times provided some of the ideological and political equipment for the impresarios of this trial? This is a sin that will never be forgiven you. (Yitzhak Ben-Aharon of Mapam interrupted: "That is a very foul piece of demagoguery!") Knesset member Peri's statement on behalf of Mapam was not a demurrer but a desertion from the line of defense of the entire Jewish people at this time.

Meir Wilner then spoke on behalf of the Communists:

In Prague, the capital of the People's Democratic Republic of Czechoslovakia, which is in the process of building Socialism, a trial is now being held against the Slansky* and Clementis gangs of spies and traitors. As is usual when spies are detected in the service of the imperialist warmongers and their scheme to overthrow a People's Democratic regime is frustrated, the imperialists and their hangers-on begin a hypocritical jackal-wailing. With this wailing the imperialists and their agents in Israel are trying to sow confusion in the nation. But disgrace is in store for them since all the accused have confessed their guilt, because guilty they are, a guilt that has been proved by evidence so extensive and convincing that they could not avoid confessing.**

The Prime Minister, Ben-Gurion, then addressed himself to the issue:

---

* Slansky: Secretary of the Communist Party of Czechoslovakia, a Jew but an extreme anti-Zionist who opposed the sale of arms to Israel during the War of Independence: he was accused of Zionism at the Prague trial. Clementis: Czechoslovak Foreign Minister. He aided Israel with arms, with the approval of his entire Communist government—EDITORS

** After the death of Stalin the Czechoslovak rulers would admit that the accused were innocent—EDITORS

I have before me the editorial of *Al Hamishmar* of November 23, 1952, titled "False Accusation," apparently written and edited with the approval of the Mapam governing bodies after considered examination and deliberation. The party and its organ identify themselves with the party regime holding the trial, the frightful frameups of loyal members of the Communist regime, the inquisitional methods used to extract "confessions," the anti-Semitic accusations and the arousing of base instincts against Jews as such among the Czechoslovak people. In the face of this moral atrocity, outrageous both from the human and the Jewish standpoint, we find not one word of denunciation, and silence in this respect is without doubt tantamount to admission of guilt, since neither the editorial staff nor the Mapam party are passing over the trial in silence. On the contrary, they have devoted to it an editorial that certainly has been weighed on the scales of the party's conscience. This editorial expresses reservations regarding the trial, but only as to the guilt of the members of Mapam (Oren and Ben-Shalom) and the Zionist movement. These two reservations imply in the clearest possible manner identification with all the other slanders and defamations in this staged "trial."

To avoid any misunderstanding I will say at once that I am prepared to concur in the opinion of the editorial board that Mordekhai Oren did not commit any sabotage in the Czechoslovak state. I do not for one minute believe Oren's "confessions," which were either forged or extracted from him by torture or other means of duress or deceit. But I ask: How could the people of *Al Hamishmar* and Mapam lend a hand to similar frameups and accusations hurled against the heads of the Communist Party of Czechoslovakia, who no less than Oren and Ben-Shalom were loyal and devoted to the Communist movement and the Communist regime in that country? Does any member of Mapam imagine that Slansky was any less of a Communist than Oren? And if Oren is innocent because of his "profound friendship for the countries of socialism," why do they not acknowledge that Slansky and his colleagues are likewise innocent for the same reason? Is not this double standard in the nature of hypocrisy and malicious evil?

Does anyone in Mapam doubt the loyalty to "revolutionary socialism" of Communist Party Secretary Slansky, who was loyal to the Kremlin all these years; of Franck, the Deputy Secretary, of André Simon, the editor of *Rude Pravo*, the official organ of the Communist Party; of Vlado Clementis, the Foreign Minister of the Communist government; or of Karl Schwab, the Deputy Minister of Defense in that government? If Oren's "confessions" are false why are those of Slansky and his colleagues valid? If Oren's evidence about Slansky and his colleagues being saboteurs is invalid because *Al Hamishmar* assumes that it was not given at his own free will, why is the testimony of Slansky and Clementis against themselves trustworthy? And must we assume that measures to compel him to testify falsely were used only against Oren?

In the Prague trial the Jews Slansky, Avriel, Sharett, Morgenthau, Oren, and others were represented as international monsters, a gang of stateless pirates scheming to exploit and impoverish the poor land of Czechoslovakia. *Al Hamishmar* does not find any fault with this anti-Semitic presentation. What, then, is the paper defending? Two things—Oren and Zionism. It does not defend the other Communists who have been falsely accused. It does not defend other Jews. This calls for explanation.

I am certain that members of Mapam know as I do that Communism has been fighting Zionism all through—not just one flank or another but the movement as a whole, without making any distinctions between right and left, between bosses and workers; that in every country where Communism has come to power all the Zionist parties and Zionist movements have been outlawed, and that Mapam can exist only in countries outside the Soviet bloc. In the *Soviet Encyclopedia*, published by the Soviet government under the supervision of the top leaders of the Russian Communist Party, the Zionist movement is defined as "a reactionary bourgeois nationalist stream" and the World Zionist Organization—not one party or another but the Zionist Organization as a whole—as "a reactionary organization." Dr. Weizmann is described as an agent of British imperialism who helped England exploit Zionism to buttress its colonial rule in Palestine; who, after England's positions were weakened, went over to serve American imperialism. "According to the instructions of the American imperialists," the *Encyclopedia* says, "Weizmann implements a policy of suppression of the Jewish working forces and the Arab national minority, and likewise according to these instructions, Weizmann strangles the forces of peace and democracy in Israel."

These statements were made not in a showcase trial but in the chief scientific organ of the Soviet Union and world Communism. To pretend that the Prague trial was the first time the Zionist movement was attacked by a Communist regime is nothing but political pettifogging.

Minister Pinhas Lavon said as the debate continued:

> Though the organizers of the Prague trial harp on the Jewish theme and try to besmirch Zionism and the State of Israel, it is not really a trial of the Jewish people, of Zionism, or of Israel. In actual fact this horrible, nightmarish trial is a trial of Communism itself, Communism as a doctrine, as a method, as a way of life. And to make this slightly more understandable, let us imagine the following nightmarish scene:
>
> Mapam has managed to achieve its aim in this country and set up the "happy regime." As is the way of such regimes, it will be ruled by a Leader. I do not know who he will be. I suspect he will not be from the traditional leaders of the various sections of the party. Then imagine that the Leader puts the entire Knesset faction of Mapam on trial with the exception of himself. Meir Ya'ari appears at the trial and declares himself to be the scum of the earth, a traitor even before he was born. He proclaims himself an agent of the American CIA or any other intelligence system and accuses himself of every horrible thing conceivable. What will we say, if we will be able to say anything? And if we cannot speak, what will we think when after Ya'ari, Erem and Bar-Yehuda appear and play the same record over again, one after the other? What kind of a trial will this be? An historic, moral, spiritual trial of Mapam, its path and the doctrine on which it is based!

It is worth noting that after the statement by Eliezer Peri no member of Mapam took part in the debate but merely heckled the others who spoke. Thus Yacov Riftin shouted, "Perhaps you could talk a bit more intelligently."

When the Minister of Labor, Golda Meir, asked, "Why are you relinquishing your right to speak?" Riftin replied, "We have not relinquished it. You are engaging in cheap provocation!" Lavon went on to quote an excerpt from a newspaper article signed by one of the persons present:

> And more about the tactics of the Soviet authorities against the Zionists: In Bialystok one of the leading Zionists was summoned to the NKVD [Secret Police]. He was ordered to submit a report on the political activities of the Zionists exactly as the Gestapo had done in the areas conquered by Germany. They told him he was to continue his work in the Zionist movement and even to strive to increase it as much as possible and report to the Soviet authorities everything that was done and who did it. They demanded that he make a declaration in writing to this effect. Naturally he did not want to do so, but they threatened that if he did not comply he would not leave the room alive. He was ordered to sign it with a pseudonym and chose the name Maranno. The Russian official did not perceive the implication of this penname. He ordered him to submit a report of his activities in one week.

The conversation took place late at night and since there was a curfew he was given a special permit in order to go out.

Everything had been especially staged. When he arrived at the NKVD building, he was led through dark chambers. In the room in which he sat only one small light was burning, shining right on his face. Everything else was in darkness. The man who spoke to him was practically invisible and in this way an artificial atmosphere was created in an attempt to intimidate him. He signed the declaration and the next morning was already in Vienna. He came to me and told me what had happened. He was crying like a baby. To soothe him I explained that to make a false report to the authorities was no offense.

The author of the article was Dr. Moshe Kleinbaum (Sneh), in those days a Knesset member for Mapam. While Lavon read this, Sneh was present but did not say a word.

At the close of the debate the Communists submitted the following resolution: "The Knesset considers the Foreign Minister's statement of calumny against the People's Democratic Republic of Czechoslovakia a stratagem to prepare the people of Israel for participation in the war being planned by the Atlantic Bloc against the camp of Peace and Socialism. The Knesset rejects the Foreign Minister's statement." Eliezer Peri in addition proposed: "In summation of the debate in this matter the Knesset confirms the statement by Mapam."

Both resolutions were voted down. The proposal by Meir Argov on behalf of the Foreign Affairs and Security Committee was accepted:

> The Knesset expresses its sense of shock at the trial now proceeding in Prague, that has struck at the Jewish people, in attempting to bring into disrepute the good name of the State of Israel, in undermining the traditional friendship between the Czech people and the Jewish people, and in endeavoring to besmirch the Zionist movement—the liberating movement of the Jewish people.

Explosion at the Soviet Legation in Tel Aviv ★ The Soviet Union Breaks Diplomatic Relations with Israel

On Tuesday, February 10, 1953, Prime Minister Ben-Gurion rose in the Knesset for a solemn announcement:

> It is with very deep regret that I have to report to the Knesset on an abomination committed in Israel last night: an explosion in the courtyard of the Soviet Legation which caused damage to the building and injured some of the Legation personnel, including Mrs. Yershov, wife of the Minister, who sustained light injuries; the wife of a member of the staff, whose injuries are more severe; and the Legation chauffeur. All three were immediately brought to the hospital where they received medical treatment, and the wife of the Minister was able to return home shortly afterward. In the name of the Government, I extend to the injured our sincere wishes for their speedy recovery, and I am certain that the Knesset and the people of Israel join us in these sentiments.
>
> The premises of several Legations, including the Soviet Legation, are guarded by the police. The courtyard that was the scene of last night's explosion is guarded by the Legation itself. Although the Government had offered the Legation a police guard there, the offer was not accepted by the Legation, and therefore Israel security forces have no access to the

courtyard. Immediately after the explosion high-ranking police officers reached the scene. Mr. Yershov, the Soviet Minister, showed them what had happened in the courtyard and in the premises, but did not permit police experts to investigate immediately whether there were any vestiges of the explosive material in the courtyard or traces of the perpetrators of this crime. The police investigation is of course proceeding and will be continued with the utmost vigor.

The Ministry for Foreign Affairs transmitted the following note to the Soviet Legation this morning:

"The Israel Ministry for Foreign Affairs presents its compliments to the Soviet Legation in Israel and has the honor to bring to its notice the following:

The Ministry for Foreign Affairs:

1. Expresses to the Legation of the Soviet Union the deep regret and apologies of the Government of Israel for the dastardly crime perpetrated last night against the Legation, its staff, and its premises.

2. Affirms the readiness of the Government of Israel to pay compensation for the injuries and material damages sustained.

3. Notifies the Legation that the Government of Israel last night published the following declaration: 'The Government views with horror and detestation the dastardly outrage committed this evening at the Soviet Legation in Tel Aviv. This act of criminal folly stands condemned in the eyes of all decent citizens, who will recognize it as directed not merely against a foreign diplomatic mission, but at the heart of the State itself. Every effort will be made to find the perpetrators of this foul deed, and when found they will be brought to swift justice. The Government expresses its profound sense of affliction and deep regret to the Soviet Minister and the members of the Legation staff and, in particular, to the injured who are now being tended in the hospital.'

4. Requests the Legation to give permission to police experts to examine as soon as possible the scene of the explosion in the courtyard of the Legation in the hope that they may find fragments or other clues that may be helpful in the discovery of the criminals who carried out this outrage against the Soviet Legation last night.

The Ministry for Foreign Affairs takes this opportunity to assure the Legation once more of its highest esteem."

After receiving this note the Soviet Minister agreed to permit police experts to examine the scene of the explosion. To the note of the Ministry for Foreign Affairs I consider it my duty to add the following to the people of this country:

The hooligans who committed this dastardly crime are more the enemies of the State of Israel than haters of a foreign state. If self-styled Jewish patriotism was the motive of their foul deed and if their intention was to fight for the honor of Israel, then let me say that they themselves have profaned the honor of Israel by this senseless crime.

The State of Israel maintains and will continue to maintain normal relations with every peace-loving country. The missions of states, great and small, accredited to our country enjoy a special status of honor, safety, and privilege in our midst, not only by virtue of international and Israel law and custom, but also by virtue of their being the guests of the nation and the State. He who harms them harms first and foremost the honor and prestige of the State of Israel. Our State is based on the rule of law and only the responsibly chosen representatives of the State may determine its internal and external relations. The criminal and wicked act committed in the Legation courtyard last night undermines the sovereignty of the State of Israel and besmirches the honor of the Jewish nation.

We cannot ignore the fact that the foul crime perpetrated in the courtyard of the Soviet Legation last night is not the first. Criminals placed a bomb in the house of one of the Ministers of the Government of Israel, the late Mr. Pinkas. Then there was an attempt to plant a time bomb in the Ministry for Foreign Affairs of the State of Israel. And now a bomb has been placed in the Legation of a powerful state with which Israel has maintained normal relations almost from the day of its establishment.

The Government considers it its duty to do everything possible to discover the source of crimes that are endangering the security of the State, and to eradicate the cancer of violence directed both internally and externally. We must now let the police continue their searches and investigations so that the culprits may be discovered, brought to justice, and punished with the full severity of the law.

Yosef Sprinzak, the Speaker: "It will be accurate if I say that we are all shocked by the vicious attack on the Legation of the Soviet Union in Tel Aviv. The entire Knesset is united in denouncing this barbaric act and in expressing its opinion of the perpetrators of the abhorrent deed as savages, devoid of national responsibility and civic conscience. The Knesset expresses its profound sorrow at what occurred, and wishes the Minister's wife and the members of the Legation's staff who were hurt a full and speedy recovery."

Bentov: "We cannot absolve the Government of responsibility for the developments that led to this crime and therefore we wish to express no-confidence in the Government."

Sprinzak: "Motions for the agenda have been submitted. The Foreign Affairs and Security Committee dealt with this matter and expressed the opinion that no further deliberation was necessary. Nevertheless, since a motion for the agenda was submitted and there are objections, I have decided together with the Deputy Speaker that in accordance with the Rules and Regulations the question whether or not there will be a debate shall be referred today to the House Committee.

Yohanan Bader (Herut) and *Meir Wilner* (Communists): "This is contrary to the Rules and Regulations."

Sprinzak: "The House Committee will decide in accordance with the Rules and Regulations and with the law."

Wilner: "You are trying to cover up the Government's responsibility for this atrocious act of gangsterism."

Sprinzak: "Knesset member Wilner, you have not been denied the chance for a debate but it will be in accordance with the law."

Wilner: "You are responsible for the outrage that took place."

Sprinzak: "I have duly replied to the motion for the agenda and we shall now proceed to the next item."

Wilner: "You are responsible and you are bringing disaster upon Israel. You are politically and morally responsible for what took place."

The Speaker then gave the floor to the Minister of Transport, in connection with a bill to amend the Ports Ordinance. The House Committee decided to hold a debate on the bombing the following week. On February 16 the Prime Minister informed the Knesset as follows:

Three days after the explosion in the yard of the Soviet Legation, on which I made a statement in the Knesset last Tuesday, the Foreign Minister of the Soviet Union handed our Minister in Moscow a note informing him that it had been decided to withdraw the Soviet Legation from Israel and demanding the withdrawal of the Israel Legation from Moscow.

The Government learned of this step by a Great Power with amazement and grave concern. In the note handed to our Minister we could find no justification for this astonishing step since the reasons indicated in the note have no basis in fact, and the practice of the Soviet Union itself in international affairs is not in keeping with them.

The Government rejects with all vigor the contention that the explosion took place with the connivance of the police. The Foreign Ministry offered to set a police guard in the yard of the Legation some time ago, and it was the Soviet Minister who rejected the proposal. The absence of police in the yard no doubt facilitated the commission of the crime. Even the police in the Soviet Union are not always able to prevent crimes. The envoy of a foreign state was murdered in Soviet Moscow and the Soviet government did not lay the responsibility for the crime at the door of its own police.

Attacks on legations have taken place in many countries. Attacks have taken place even on Soviet legations, and the government of the Soviet Union has not in consequence broken off diplomatic relations. We may recall, for example, the murder of the Soviet Minister in Warsaw in 1927, the laying of a mine in the Soviet Legation in the same city in 1930, the attack on the Soviet Legation in Riga in 1926. In none of these cases were diplomatic relations severed.

The Soviet note declared that the expressions of regret of the Israel Government were intended only to cover the tracks of the criminals and evade responsibility for the act; that they were contradicted by incitements to acts of enmity against the Soviet Union carried by the press of the Government parties and members of the Knesset and the Government. In this connection particular mention was made of the address of the Foreign Minister of Israel in the Knesset on January 19, 1953, which contained, according to the note, open incitement to acts of enmity against the Soviet Union.

There is not a shadow of truth in this description of the Foreign Minister's speech. There is not a single word or a single implication in the speech that constitutes, directly or indirectly, any incitement to acts of enmity against the Soviet Union.

The Foreign Minister rejected in his speech—and it was his political and moral duty to do so—the slanders published in the Soviet press against Jewish doctors who were accused of having carried out horrifying and abominable murders on the instructions of a great and distinguished institution of the Jews of America and of the Zionists in the world. The Foreign Ministry rightly stated at the time that the Government of Israel could not be silent when anyone attempted to cast a slur on the name of Jewry. We are not prepared to accept in Israel the practice that accused persons should confess to crimes that they have not committed, and I am not aware of any movements in the world more upright than the Jewish people's movement for revival and rehabilitation, which is known as the Zionist movement; nor are there many institutions in the world more deserving of praise and appreciation than the "Joint"* for its humanitarian work in assisting uprooted, oppressed, and downtrodden Jews in all countries including the People's Democracies.

There is no foundation to the contention in the Soviet note that conditions for the normal diplomatic functioning of the Soviet Legation do not exist in Israel. This Legation has been assured in our country a degree of freedom of action that our Legation in Moscow has never dreamt of demanding for itself. We are not aware that in any country the Soviet Union has made it a condition of the maintenance of diplomatic relations that the Communist Parties of those countries should be given a monopoly of political and social propaganda and comment on international relations. As in all countries where freedom of thought and expression exist, it is permissible in Israel to criticize Communist ideology and the defects of totalitarian regimes.

We are unable, therefore, to find any justification for the severance of relations in anything that has been done by the citizens of Israel or its Government. Nor are we able to

---

* *Joint Distribution Committee,* a Jewish charitable and relief organization in the US—Editors

find any precedent for this act in the practice of the Soviet Union in its relations with other states in which, as in Israel, a democratic regime exists.

Wilner: "This is a blood libel against the Jews of the Soviet Union. If only we were as free as they are! If only Israel were free!"

Ben-Aharon: "We cannot disregard the background that led up to this step on the part of the Soviet government. The dispute of the Zionist movement with the Communist world for scores of years over the solution of the Jewish problem and the concentration of the masses of Israel in their historical Homeland—this is a debate that has not known a lull for even one day. However, the moment the Government of Israel abandoned its policy of nonaligment, violated the principle of the neutrality of the State of Israel in the interbloc struggle and thereby made it an integral part of the anti-Communist, anti-Soviet front, at that moment we knew that the Government of Israel and the forces it represents were assuming responsibility for the disaster that sooner or later would overtake our people. What have the Prime Minister and Minister of Defense done in the fateful days since that turnabout came into effect? Thus this Government bears full responsibility for the present development."

Zalman Aranne (Mapai): "In the past few days two serious things have happened. I am referring to the anonymous physical bomb that was planted in the Soviet Legation in Tel Aviv and the political bomb the Soviet Union has thrown at the State of Israel. It is not known as yet who committed the physical crime. But as long as it has not been proved otherwise, we may assume that it was done by Jewish hands. They have made it easy for the Soviet Union to break off diplomatic relations with Israel. We have conducted an ideological struggle against the Communist Party in Israel in which we have seen first the spectacle of Jewish apostasy in the nineteenth century and then a pogrom movement as well. With the increase of Communist missionary activity in Israel, which was also joined by Mapam, we expanded our ideological struggle against the phenomenon known as World Communism. And then, after a generation and more of Soviet estrangement from the Zionist movement, when we heard a speech by Gromyko [in the UN Assembly] in favor of the creation of a Jewish State, a heavy burden was lifted from our hearts and we thought the turning point had finally arrived.

"Yet half a year after this historic speech Ilya Ehrenburg, the Jew Seuss of the Soviet Court, wrote his programmatic, pogromatic article against recognition of the Jewish people's existence, against Zionism, and against Aliya (Wilner interrupts: "Out-and-out lies!"). And about that time there began the liquidation of the remnants of organized Jewish public life in Soviet Russia, the liquidation of the remaining books in Yiddish and authors who wrote in Yiddish, the liquidation of the Jewish theater, Jewish schools, any element of Jewish public life; and this the entire world knows. (Esther Wilenska shouted, "Sholem Aleichem and Peretz are read more in the Soviet Union than here!") In his accusations against the Government, Knesset member Ben-Aharon has gone even farther than [Soviet Minister] Vishinsky's note. He implies that the reason for breaking off diplomatic relations is the political stand we have adopted in the international political arena. There are scores of states that are thoroughly hostile to the Soviet Union, yet the Soviet Union maintains regular diplomatic relations with them. Have the positions we have adopted in the United Nations been the reason for breaking off diplomatic relations with Israel? Nothing of the sort! Those who claim that the Government of Israel and the

Knesset are responsible for the severance of relations are trying to mislead. If you members of Mapam think that by a multitude of slanders against the Government of Israel you will rescue your party from disintegration, you are mistaken."

Elimeleh Rimalt (General Zionists): "The Prime Minister rightly noted that in international diplomatic relations, and even in connection with Russia, things much more serious than this have occurred. Russia did not break off diplomatic relations with the Greek people nor with Tito's Yugoslavia. And I ask Ben-Aharon and his colleagues: Does Tito's Yugoslavia not slander Russia? It is the biggest besmircher of all."

Golda Meir (Minister of Labor): "Knesset member Ben-Aharon has said that this is a sad and bitter day. I say that it is bitter and sad to hear Ben-Aharon defend a Great Power in this way and to present thus what it did to the Jewish people, the Zionist movement, and the State of Israel. I would suggest to Knesset member Erem not to try to protect Ehrenburg or Ben-Aharon. Only a month or two ago you were heckling in defense of Knesset member Sneh. It is a sad and shocking thing to hear Knesset member Erem being shocked by something said against Ehrenburg.★

"I have no words that can describe that Jew. This person who has lost all semblance not only of a Jew but of a self-respecting human being. (Wilner: "You are slandering him even though you do not reach his ankles.") A Jew who knows one thing and one thing only: to carry out the orders of his masters and disavow everything Jewish and the language of the Jewish people; in the presence of a non-Jew to deny that he is Jewish, to disavow all Jewish history, the Jewish future, the Jewish present. About a week or ten days after our arrival in Moscow, when Mapam members Bentov and Zisling were still in the Provisional Government, this 'valiant fighter' wrote that there is no such thing as a Jewish people because the various groups of Jews in their different places of exile throughout the world now had nothing in common. This was written in September 1948. And at the beginning of January 1949 the sign was taken down from the anti-fascist Jewish Committee—apart from the synagogues, the last Jewish institution in the Soviet Union. In those very days the Jewish newspaper in Moscow and Jewish newspapers throughout the Soviet Union were being shut down. This was when Mapam was still participating in our Government as a guardian of neutrality and friendship with the revolutionary world. At the same time the Emess Book Publishing House [in Moscow] was closed down, the Jewish writers disappeared.

"Are there not represented in the Soviet Union countries which by law do not permit Communist Parties to exist? Is the Soviet Union that sensitive? After the Prague trial we conducted ourselves as would any self-respecting people. True, there are elements in our country, though fortunately small ones, that feel compelled to justify everything a priori. And immediately afterward came the Moscow trials and the 'Doctors Plot.' Why did we not hear a strong, self-respecting Jewish-Zionist word against this from Mapam?"

Moshe Sneh (who had left Mapam and founded the Left Faction): "Not only can I not absolve the Government of responsibility but in cases such as this it must be declared forthrightly that the entire responsibility devolves upon Ben-Gurion and Sharett for the severing of diplomatic relations by the power that was the first to support the creation of the State."

★ Ilya Ehrenburg's anti-Zionist article appeared approximately one week after Golda Meir's arrival in Moscow as Israel's Minister to the USSR.

Yonah Kesse (Mapai): "This won't help you. In Prague they're already saying you're a spy."

David Libshitz (who together with Hannah Lamdan had also resigned from Mapam): "Behind this proposal [to express no-confidence in the Government] by eighteen representatives of the Communists, Mapam, and the Left Faction there is no responsibility whatsoever — whether from the point of view of labor, Israel or the Jewish people. In the present situation, in view of the sharp changes in Soviet policy, we must assemble and mobilize our fullest responsibility in order to develop a policy based on the bitter and tragic reality of the present situation of the State of Israel and the people of Israel."

Sharett (Foreign Minister) responded the following day, February 17: "In concluding this debate I have nothing to add by way of explaining the Government's position and appraisal, for this has been done by the Prime Minister at the opening of the discussion. However, I wish to reply to a few points that were made in the course of it.

"Knesset member Sneh has tried to dredge up the forgotten past. He claims that the Soviet Union rescued thousands of Jews from extermination. I do not know at what date we should start keeping accounts. For instance, what would have happened if at the outbreak of the Bolshevik Revolution in Russia in 1917 the ax had not fallen on the Zionist movement, if a way had been found to reconcile that regime with continued emigration to Israel; if the masses of Russian Jewry had been permitted to go to Israel as they wanted to; if a broad channel had been opened before the Halutz movement in Russia? What would have been the result? The 1920s would have passed quite differently and we would have been arrayed differently to confront the Holocaust of World War Two — perhaps we would already have achieved independence in the '30s and then it is doubtful whether European Jewry would have been exterminated. When a World War broke out and the Holocaust was menacing European Jewry, what role in its outcome was played by the pact concluded then [between Hitler and Stalin] and what possibility did it open for the unobstructed domination of Europe by Hitler and his Storm Troopers and the doom of the Jewish people throughout the world?"

Bentov for Mapam, Wilner for the Communists, and Sneh for the Left Faction each submitted a motion of no-confidence. Each of the resolutions received eight votes in favor and eighty-five against. A motion by the Coalition Faction that "the Knesset identifies with the Prime Minister's statement" was adopted, seventy-nine to sixteen. Begin had announced that Herut would abstain.

On July 20, 1953, four months after Stalin's death, diplomatic relations between Israel and the Soviet Union were resumed at the latter's initiative. A. N. Abramov was named Soviet Minister to Israel and Dr. Shmuel Elya Yashiv resumed his post as Israeli Minister in Moscow.

The "Lavon Affair" ★ Investigation by the Olshani-Dori Committee Fails To Reach Firm Conclusion ★ Background of Ben-Gurion's Return to Defense Post

The final year of the Second Knesset saw an event that agitated the country and left an unpleasant aftertaste. In the language of the censorship it was the "Security Mishap" or the "Unfortunate Affair"; in the language of the newspapers, the "Lavon Affair."★ Whatever the label, it referred to an order given, or at any rate carried out, in July 1954 by the person whom the censors called the "Senior Officer," as a result of which several persons lost their lives.

The unnamed Senior Officer claimed that he received the order from the Minister of Defense, at that time Pinhas Lavon, and several days after the mishap informed me in writing that those involved had been arrested and would be put on trial. Lavon did not react at all to this information. The Chief of Staff, Moshe Dayan, was not then in the country. On his return he demanded a report from the Senior Officer. After receiving it on November 1, 1954, Dayan announced at a Staff meeting that the operation in question had been carried out on orders from the Minister of Defense, and that an officer was obliged to obey the Minister without hesitation.

The Minister of Defense did not participate in Staff meetings but his secretary, Ephraim Evron, who was present, undoubtedly reported to him what Dayan had said. In the middle of December, Lavon called in Dayan and the Senior Officer, and told them that the Government or the Knesset's Foreign Affairs and Security Committee or both would most likely summon them to a hearing into the security affair. He therefore proposed that they testify that the order had been given to *plan* the operation, not to *execute* it. When the two men did not reply, Lavon understood that they did not agree to say what he suggested.

The "security mishap" occurred in the second half of July 1954. A few days earlier, on Tuesday, July 13, 1954, Shmuel Dayan [father of Moshe], Kadish Luz, and Mordekhai Namir had come to see me at Sde Boker, with the idea of drawing me back into the Government. The visit had been initiated by Shmuel Dayan, who consulted several other Mapai members. Luz had not taken part in the consultations but the members wanted him included as a representative of the kibbutzim, with Dayan representing the moshavim and Namir as spokesman for the cities. At Sde Boker, Namir did most of the talking. "The public has no feeling of security," he said in substance. "There is no authority. Though the apprehensions at the time of your resignation have proved false, they now are growing worse. We have come to ask you to return."

I replied that I did not intend to return just then because, though a private citizen, I was busy with two very important matters. One was the mobilization of young members of the well-established moshavim to settle with their families in the new immigrant moshavim. (An enlightening book on this project, *Movement Without a Name*, was later written by Braha Habas, published by Davar in 1964.) The other was the creation of a "regional settlement" in the desolate south of the country, in an area later known as the Lahish Region.

Toward the end of the month, on July 28, while I was undergoing treatment at Tel Hashomer Hospital, I had a visit from Golda Meir, Zalman Arrane, and Levi Eshkol, who spoke about difficult relations within the Ministry of Defense. I suggested that they speak forthrightly about Pinhas Lavon. Back home at Sde Boker, on August 24, Moshe

---

★ Lavon Affair: An Israel Intelligence operation abroad, the details of which have never been officially disclosed, proved unsuccessful. Whether a Senior Officer (his identify never officially revealed) undertook the operation, as he claimed, on the order of Defense Minister Lavon or on his own authority as Lavon claimed, was the crux of the "affair." — EDITORS.

Dayan, the Chief of Staff, came to see me. He told me about the astonishing order issued by Lavon while he, Dayan, was abroad. The operation ordered failed, he said, and it should have been known that it would fail.

Namir paid me a second visit on the morning of November 20, 1954. In recent weeks, he claimed, the sense of national security had weakened further, the situation of the country and the Mapai party had deteriorated. There was a lack of authority and discipline in the Government, the Histadrut, and Mapai.

On January 27, 1955, Shaul Avigur, visiting me, said he had been informed by Prime Minister Sharett that he had appointed a private commission (the Olshan-Dori Committee) to investigate who had given the order. Either the Minister or the Senior Officer had exceeded his authority and had acted on his own. The committee had not found judicial proof, but its clear impression was that the order had come from Lavon. Avigur said the Army had no confidence in Lavon, and it was known that he did not like the Army. He therefore urged that I return to the Ministry of Defense.

In the first days of February 1955 I received from Lavon a copy of a letter he had sent to Prime Minister Sharett, tendering his resignation. It complained that the Olshan-Dori findings were submitted to Avigur over Lavon's opposition; that he had been "kept at arm's length" during hearings; that members of the Government avoided him as if he "were afflicted with a loathsome disease." He felt himself "excluded from the group and from collective responsibility" and therefore was resigning.

The copy of the letter indicated that copies were also sent to Golda Meir, Arrane, and Eshkol.

Two weeks after the receipt of this copy, on February 17, 1955, I was visited by Golda Meir and Namir. They had come on behalf of the Prime Minister, to ask me to return to the Ministry of Defense. Their report on the gravity of the crisis in the Ministry and the lack of confidence inside the Army shocked and upset me. I knew that in our situation the Army was the most precious body in the State. Though I had intended to remain in Sde Boker for at least another year, I felt that this time I had to yield to the Prime Minister's wishes. Security and the Army came before all.

The next morning, February 18, I was surprised when Paula, my wife, said that she had heard of my appointment as Minister of Defense on the 11-o'clock news broadcast the previous evening. On Monday, February 21, I went to Jerusalem and was present in the Knesset when the Prime Minister announced Lavon's resignation and Ben-Gurion's co-option as Minister of Defense. No debate was held, but a number of members—Ya'ari on behalf of Mapam, Ben-Aharon for the Kibbutz Hameuhad members who had left Mapam, Shmuel Mikunis for the Communists, and Chaim Landau for Herut— announced their opposition to my co-option. By a vote of seventy-four to twenty-three with one abstention (myself) the co-option was approved and I immediately signed the declaration of allegiance.

On returning to the Ministry of Defense, Ben-Gurion read the conclusions of the Olshan-Dori Committee which said in part: "We regret that we are unable to answer the question posed by the Prime Minister: we can only say that we have not been convinced beyond a reasonable doubt that he (the Senior Officer) did not receive instructions from the Minister of Defense; at the same time we are not certain if the Minister of Defense actually did give the orders attributed to him."

Ben-Gurion knew both Olshan and Dori, and esteemed them highly. Both men had been members of the Hagana for many years. Olshan was a Justice of the Supreme Court and Dori the first Chief of Staff of the IDF. Since they had not been able to establish the truth, Ben-Gurion decided not to deal with the affair at all. He did not even read through the entire report of the committee. It was necessary, he felt, to give Lavon the benefit of the doubt and to continue to treat him as a colleague, for he possessed qualities and talents that Ben-Gurion considered important. As for the Senior Officer, the Defense Minister felt it necessary to be strict, since he served in a unit calling for a high degree of trustworthiness because it guarded State secrets; in view of the doubt, he decided to transfer the man to a different post. Ben-Gurion spoke about this with Moshe Dayan, who concurred, as did the Prime Minister. The new Defense Minister refrained from asking Lavon, Sharett, or any other member of the Government what he thought about "the Affair," and none of them told him anything they might have known about it.

Only later in the year did Ben-Gurion find letters in the Ministry of Defense, addressed by Sharett to Lavon, that seemed somewhat surprising.

In a letter dated August 14, 1953 (when Sharett was still serving as Acting Prime Minister and Lavon as Acting Minister of Defense, Ben-Gurion being on a leave of absence):

> Between the Prime Minister and Minister of Defense (Ben-Gurion) and myself there was a practice of providing advance notice of every serious act of retaliation against any of the neighboring countries, or any forceful step against the Arab population of the State. This procedure was not followed with regard to the curfew and the search in Tira or the operations carried out on the night of the 12th of this month. Therefore I must request you henceforth to give me sufficient advance notice of any serious operation of the types I mentioned, which you have ordered or which have your approval.

In the second letter on August 19, Sharett wrote to Lavon:

> Your refusal to participate in collegial consultations is very surprising and creates a very serious problem. If the intention is to bring about my resignation as Acting Prime Minister, there could be nothing simpler. Is that what you desire?

A letter dated May 25, 1954, when Sharett was already full rather than Acting Prime Minister, and Lavon full Minister of Defense, Sharett wrote:

> Security measures are not being reported to me as they should be. Things occur that are not being brought to my attention. I hear announcements on the radio and later read about them in the papers without knowing the true background. The proper arrangement would be for me to know the facts, if at all possible, before the official version is released. I should know the facts, and it is up to you to take the initiative.

Even while living and working at Sde Boker, Ben-Gurion had heard of the strained relations between the Government and the Minister of Defense, as well as within the Ministry of Defense itself. Since the Prime Minister did not find it necessary to tell him about these things after his return to the Ministry of Defense, Ben-Gurion did not press him. Nor did he ask the other members of the Government after the elections to the Third Knesset when he again became Prime Minister and Minister of Defense, in a coalition he had formed of Mapai, Mapam, Ahdut Haavodah, Hapoel Hamizrahi, and the Progressives—the Government confirmed by a vote of seventy-three to thirty-three on November 3, 1955. Meanwhile the Senior Officer, in his new assignment, carried out his duties to

Ben-Gurion's satisfaction, and with Lavon Ben-Gurion continued to maintain the same friendly relations as before he had retired to Sde Boker.

Through all his years of service, from the formation of the Israel Defense Forces until his resignation from the Government at the end of 1953, there had been, to the best of Ben-Gurion's knowledge, no case when officers exceeded their authority and carried out military operations on their own. There had been other offenses and during the War of Independence a few episodes of insubordination, but he was certain that the Army was completely immune to the dangerous maladies infecting the Arab armies both then and now: usurpation of power and failure to submit to the civilian authorities. After what happened in 1954, however, he saw the need of sending the following instructions to the Chief of Staff:

I consider the nation's complete confidence in the Army a most valuable asset. The undermining of this trust constitutes a danger to security and a serious stumbling block to the Army. I assume that you and all of your associates will help me to augment this trust. The nation and its representatives must of necessity be completely certain that the Army is the executive arm of the State and *not the director of its policy*. Israel policy is determined by the Government and the Knesset and by them alone.

Soldiers and officers, like all other citizens, are free to belong to any lawful organization in the State, nor is the military or civilian authority entitled to restrict their freedom of thought and of civilian action, apart from restrictions legally imposed on the political activity of soldiers. Nevertheless, soldiers and officers receive from the State training, equipment, and information earmarked for State security. These are not private property of the soldiers and commanders, who may use them only according to the instructions and with the knowledge of the authorized bodies. Here of necessity discipline must be very strict and unqualified. A soldier or officer who misappropriates any of these three things is betraying his nation and comitting a grave offense. The higher his rank, the greater the responsibility and the graver the restrictions.

An officer may not divulge the information he receives by virtue of his military duties even to his closest and most trusted friend. This applies all the more to staff officers. Anyone who cannot meet this requirement would do better to resign from his post of his own free will. The transmission of information to unauthorized persons is a crime of no lesser magnitude than the handing over of arms and explosives to civilians for their private use or for the commission of crimes.

As a citizen a soldier is subject to the laws applicable to every citizen. As a soldier he is at the command of the State and its authorized bodies and them alone, and is subject to severe discipline. The Army and the entire nation must be made aware of this. Despite differences of opinion on every other matter, it is vital that on the question of security there be a maximum unity among the entire nation. Even if we have controversies in matters of defense, the entire nation must have full confidence in the IDF, because the IDF, its men, and commanders exist only for the security and welfare of Israel.

As Minister of Defense from the creation of the Army until the end of 1953, and again from February 1955 until June 1963, Ben-Gurion knew that the Army had been conducted along these lines; he assumes that this has continued.

There have been cases of desertion and a very few instances of inaccurate reporting. At the very beginning there were some cases of insubordination, as well as of weapons stolen and sold. In all these cases the guilty were punished (apart from a very few times during the War of Independence, when it was practically impossible to detect and punish such things). When two generals committed an error by announcing complete mobilization over the radio—an error, not a crime—both were dismissed after an investigation by the entire Government had shown that it was indeed an error. The Security Mishap of 1954, as far as Ben-Gurion knows, has had no parallel in the Army from the day of its birth to the present. Consequently, he had no interest in dealing with this "affair," which concluded with the private investigation by Olshan and Dori. Though the members of that committee had no formal authority, they were wise and just men on whose actions and findings he could rely without reservation.

Appeal to Youth To Cultivate Zionist Ideals ★ Controversy Over Regional Settlement

The year of the so-called Security Mishap, 1954, was also a year of soul-searching by the younger generation. Youth was yearning for an inner consolidation and did not always find it. The steep decline in Aliya that began in 1952 and reached its lowest point in 1953— 10,388 immigrants; 12,500 emigrants—inevitably brought the best elements of the nation to a profound reckoning with themselves. The bitter fact could not be ignored that the sources of immigration having dried up for the time being, our forces had to be strengthened from within, especially among the young.

Israel at that time had about a hundred thousand young people in the fourteen to eighteen age group, only 20 to 25 percent of whom were attending academic or vocational high schools. The various youth movements concerned themselves chiefly with those in schools, so that some seventy-five or eighty thousand boys and girls of this age category were being neglected. These were youths who had already passed the elementary-school age or young people from slums and backward districts, condemned to grow up without education, training or involvement.

Israel's first Minister of Defense, who had meanwhile resigned from the Government, did not agree with the bleak appraisal of our youth being made at this time. In his work with the Army during the State's first six years he had come to know young people from all walks of life—children of old, established settlers, native-born youths, new immigrants, urban and rural youngsters, rich and poor, educated and uneducated, for the Army takes in even illiterates, persons completely without education or training, teaches them how to read and write, and gives them their first knowledge of the Jewish nation and the Jewish people. It accustoms them to order and cleanliness, discipline, courage, and esprit de corps. It was obvious to Ben-Gurion that there are no real differences among various communities and tribes.

The attempts made during the first years to appoint officers to the highest and most responsible posts at an extremely young age had proved no error. Generals and Chiefs of Staff under the age of forty or even thirty-five had not failed us, not would any army in the world have been ashamed of them. But the most important thing the Army showed was that there was no natural difference among communities or persons from different countries of origin with respect to valor and devotion to the State. The Army indeed had proved that we were one people. Its officers had been born in Afghanistan, Persia, Bulgaria, Turkey, Yemen, Morocco, Egypt, India, Germany, Poland, England, and America.

Nor was everything accomplished merely by compulsion. The Army educated through personal example, through Jewish brotherhood, and the personal qualities of the best of its commanders. The strength of its framework lay in its unity and in the universality of its application. Had a single, united, universal youth movement come into existence for service to the nation as a whole, dedicated to the national security, fructification of the wasteland, and education of new immigrants, even the deprived young people of the slums would have been uplifted and would have manifested latent treasures of pioneering capacity and inspiration. Pioneers must be trained to serve not merely one group or another but the nation as a whole. Not necessarily the "well-connected" youth, those attending high school, had to be reached, but the young people in the transit camps and slums.

In May 1954 an attempt to do this was made by Ben-Gurion, with the help of the Ministry of Education and the Teachers' Union. They convened students of the upper high-school grades in Sheikh Munis, where he posed to them the question "A Career or a Mission"? For despite all the victories of the War of Independence, won through our spiritual superiority when we stood 650,000 against 30 million, the longed-for redemption—of the country and of the people—had not yet been achieved. Neither had the scattered parts of the nation been reunited, the ruins of the Homeland rebuilt, economic independence assured, or security attained.

The victory in the War of Independence had given us only *a first taste of redemption—Jewish sovereignty in the Homeland.* In the few years after that we had known the great blessings of this first portent: the tremendous accomplishments in the ingathering of the exiles; the grand deeds of fructification of the wasteland; the creation of hundreds of agricultural settlements; the erection of thousands of factories and workshops and tens of thousands of housing units; the early development of shipping and aviation; compulsory free elementary education; the cultivation of literature and science and the raising of Israel's stature throughout the world. But we were still only at the beginning of the road. And it was a long and difficult road, crowded with obstacles; much work over a long period awaited us that could not be done by the State and its laws alone without voluntary work of a pioneering nature.

The decisive factor in our future, in the fulfillment of our historic mission, was *the image of the man in Israel:* his spirit, character, initiative, vision, courage, and loyalty. And that image meant first of all the image of the youth. Young people with an eye only to career, easy profits, and a parasitic existence would be the secret weapon of our enemies, with which the people of Israel would easily be defeated. Only the dedication of our youth to its historic mission—to its creative ability and pioneering initiative, its capacity to make demands of itself—a youth free of the afflictions of exile, valiant and daring, standing up bravely to any foe capable of dominating the forces of nature, fructifying the wastelands, conquering the sea and the air, working creatively for the achievement of Israel's economic independence and the formation of a new Hebrew society—only such a youth would not shame our past or fail the messianic longings for redemption, *Jewish and human redemption,* of many past generations.

Such was the vision Ben-Gurion tried to evoke for the young people:

(1) *Working Together.* In a free nation every citizen is entitled to think, say, and write what he pleases. Free men have opinions of their own, opinions that are therefore different from

and opposed to one another. There are also conflicts of interests, both real or imagined. But the fragmentation among our youth and in the Knesset is morbid and excessive. It makes a shambles of our public life, politically and socially, because it really derives not from justified differences and practical contradictions but from the habits of exile of a people bereft of a sense of national responsibility. There is no reasonable justification for such divisions in the youth movement. These are said to reflect class conflicts. Yet the best of our youth have overcome them. Can the fragmentation of the pioneering settlement movement itself be explained by class differences? If not artificially inflated, valid differences of opinion can be a blessing. What unites the nation is greater than what divides it, and this is true especially of the young. Youth, working together, must be a uniting, elevating, purifying, and strengthening element in the nation.

(2) *Integrity*. History has deprived the Jewish people of many things: we have not inherited a large country, nor have we been many in number or granted much political power. One thing, however, that has been granted to the Jewish people since the very beginning is a moral power perhaps without equal among other nations. It is through this power that, even in days of antiquity, we withstood mighty states that exceeded us not only in numbers, material, and military strength but in many respects culturally as well. Our people succeeded in preserving its uniqueness and identity for two thousand years. We possess an inherent moral strength not found among most nations, and this is what has brought us to where we are now. In our wanderings through the world we have also acquired the modern cultural and scientific attainments of the peoples of Europe and America, and in recent centuries have participated in their creation. Only with *full mobilization of our qualitative advantage*, that is our moral vitality and intellectual capacity, will we be able to overcome the tremendous difficulties of realizing the ideal of our State. In your own day-to-day lives do all that you would want the entire nation to do. Make your own lives an example for the nation, because a living example is the most effective.

(3) *Integration of the Exiles*. The greatest accomplishment since the War of Independence has been the absorption of three-quarters of a million immigrants from all parts of the world, the majority of them from the most depressed places of exile in Eastern Europe, North Africa, and backward countries of Asia. This tremendous exploit was accompanied by a tremendous failure: the fact that the established community ignored the new immigrants, relying solely on the State to absorb them. But the State alone cannot achieve integration of the exiles at the rate and on the scale required. What is needed is good will on the part of the entire nation, and that, alas, had not yet been manifested to a sufficient degree. It is as if two different nations have come into being in Israel. And in the integration of exiles and the elevation of man—every man in our midst—youth must serve as an example for the entire nation. Our spiritual superiority will stand us in good stead if it will be shared equally by all the tribes and communities.

(4) *Settlement of the Border and Wasteland Areas*. This is perhaps the biggest and most difficult mission facing the new generation. We have liberated tremendous tracts of land that are still uninhabited. This free territory will be really ours only through labor and settlement—settlement not dissociated from science, art, literature, and spiritual values. Primitive settlement will not succeed here. Only by harnessing the forces of science and technology will we be able to populate and settle the wilderness and wasteland of the Negev and the wilderness of the Galilean Hills.

(5) *A New Society*. In the world balance of power the State of Israel is numerically insignificant. But *we have the ability to show the world a new way of life*, one that is both the heritage of our Prophets and the achievement of the best of our pioneers ever since we began the building of the Third Temple. We must put into practice what is set forth in the second section of the State Education Law: "The object of State education is to base elementary

education in the State on the values of Jewish culture and the achievements of science, on love of the Homeland and loyalty to the State and the Jewish people, on practice in agricultural work and handicraft, on Halutz (pioneer) training, and on striving for a society built on freedom, equality, tolerance, mutual assistance, and love of mankind." This is the image the State has prescribed for the united nation developing in its midst. The young generation will mold this image if it will light torches of power and radiance, Jewish and human brotherly love, integrity, and pioneering sentiments. If youth will say, "We will make the attempt," history will reply, "You will succeed."

A sharp complaint against the organizers of the youth convention was heard in the Knesset. Esther Raziel-Naor (Herut) protested the appearance of Knesset member Ben-Gurion at a convention of high-school students held on the initiative of the Ministry of Education and Culture. "If the Ministry and the Minister who heads it wish to address the youth," she said, "that is not only their right but their duty, because the Minister is in charge of education and culture in the State. If, for some reason, he feels that youth should hear another speaker as well, he certainly can choose someone engaged in education or questions of culture and the spirit — there are still such people in the State of Israel who do not have the mark of party affiliation on their forehead. If, however, the Minister of Education invites a party man, then the question arises: Why only one, and why this one and not another? Does the Ministry of Education consider it its function to introduce political propaganda into the schools? The Knesset has decided that State education shall be free of any connection with political and party organizations. This step is uneducational and immoral and one that cannot be reconciled with concepts of integrity."

Mrs. Raziel-Naor was supported by Knesset member Avrahan Berman (who together with Moshe Sneh had joined the Communist bloc). "Why did the Minister of Education invite Mr. Ben-Gurion to the Student Convention?" he asked. "Neither in the Government nor in the Ministry of Education does Mr. Ben-Gurion hold any official position that gives him the right officially to address a convention of students or teachers. It is no secret why Ben-Gurion wanted to address the convention. His plan to create a single framework for youth and a national youth movement is well known. Experience in various countries shows that this leads to fascisization of the youth. There is no doubt that Ben-Gurion's program is clearly of a fascist nature. It holds great danger for all Israeli youth."

The Minister of Education and Culture, Ben-Zion Dinur, answered: "The convention of Grade 11 and 12 students which I organized and am responsible for was called on the initiative of the principals of high schools of every type throughout the country." He told the Knesset, "I brought the proposal for the convention to them and the idea was accepted unanimously. A special delegation of principals, including those of Herzlia High School in Tel Aviv, the Reali School in Haifa, and Beit Hakerem High School in Jerusalem held two consultations with Knesset member Ben-Gurion, who agreed to take part — this is the fact of the matter. Formally speaking, I think it is the absolute and unquestioned right of the Minister of Education to hold a conference, and in my opinion he is obliged to invite as speaker the person he feels most suitable in relation to the problems he intends to examine."

He then proposed to proceed to the next item on the agenda, which was done.

On June 11, 1954, about a month after the convention of high-school students, young members of the well-established moshavim were invited to Nahalal, the first of the moshavim erected after the First World War. At this gathering Ben-Gurion called upon them to rally to the aid of the immigrants in the desolate areas.

We have two great things at our disposal: a million and a half Jews and all the land of the State. These million and a half Jews are mainly concentrated in a few urban areas while the largest part of the land is empty and desolate. This holds great danger, both for those Jews and for the land. The only way to guard against it is to disperse the population through the expanses of the Negev and northern Galilee, to achieve the integration of the exiles in the shortest possible time. This cannot be done through the resources of the State alone, but must be accomplished mainly by voluntary work and pioneering endeavor.

We cannot have two Jewish nations that differ from one another in every aspect of their lives. We are all together in the same boat on a stormy sea, and if we won't row together with equal energy there is the danger that the boat will be wrecked by the waves. In a few short years we have created four hundred new settlements. This is mostly the work of the new immigrants and it attests to the creative ability latent in this population. But a barrier still exists between the established community and the new Aliya. It holds social and moral threats and makes integration of the exiles a vital necessity. The founders of Nahalal, Degania, Ein Harod, Tirat Zvi, Mishmar Ha'Emek, and Hafetz Hayim were prepared for pioneering endeavor by the education of generations. Yet we must not abandon the immigrants of Iraq, Rumania, Yemen, and Poland. The immigrant settlements are capable of becoming like Degania and Nahalal in a short time if the sons and daughters of Degania and Nahalal will get together with them, not as instructors and teachers from outside but as members inside. It is incumbent upon us to develop and populate the wasteland to the maximum. This will not be done by preaching but by a living example—if the youth from the pioneering moshavim will get up and create border settlements in the Negev and Galilee.

The call was heeded. In 1954–1956 hundreds of young people from the old established moshavim as well as a number of youths from the kibbutzim of the Ihud Hakvutzot ve Hakibbutzim together with their wives and young children went to live in the immigrant moshavim in the north and south in order to guide their brethren, distant yet near, not by issuing instructions but by a living example in managing farmsteads, mutual aid, educating the young, and training for defense. The young volunteers from the moshavim and kibbutzim spent at least two years in the immigrant settlements. They worked together and trained together with the immigrants and breathed new life into the settlements. Their moral and educational influence was felt especially among the younger generation of new immigrants.

Two of these volunteers gave their lives in this work of integrating the exiles: Varda Freedman of Kfar Vitkin and Ben-Ami Malkiman of Kfar Yehezkel. The story of these two youngsters who fell at their posts, uniquely dramatic in the annals of Jewish valor in Israel, and of their comrades who remain alive has been recorded in the book *Movement Without a Name* by Braha Haba, published in 1964.

Some weeks after the convention of the young moshav members in Nahalal Ben-Gurion, speaking in Beersheba, challenged young people from all over the country to create a regional settlement system in the desolate part of southern Yehuda. Before the creation of the State, he pointed out, we were compelled to build individual settlements, because the acquisition of every strip of land involved immense difficulties and loss of time. The picture had changed, he went on:

Now, when practically all the vacant and desolate areas of the State are national property, regional settlement systems must be set up. Every settlement will be autonomous in its internal life and in the choice of its form of settlement. But they will all be connected through joint cultural and economic enterprises that will ensure the maintenance of the conditions required for integration of the exiles and the molding of a new society. Educational and industrial centers such as no individual settlement is capable of providing will be set up, and will serve the needs of the entire area.

This settlement system will be free from any political or party definition. One of the serious afflictions of important parts of the pioneering settlement system is that of ideological and party totalitarianism known as "ideological collectivity." It is a fact that there is no party in Israel that binds all its members to pioneering realization, while every labor party has pioneering settlements. We must separate and make a distinction between unity of ideology and party and the work of settlement. And just as there must be political freedom, there should be freedom of definition, freedom in choosing the form of settlement.

In every regional settlement system there will be a place for kibbutzim, moshavim, and cooperative settlements to suit the taste of every settler. Every such settlement will have to be geared to the integration of the exiles, embracing at least a large minority of well-established inhabitants with a maximum of new immigrants. If we create settlements that consist solely of immigrants on one hand, or solely of high school graduates or descendants of well-established settlers on the other, this will serve merely to consolidate the barrier between the two Israels.

The regional settlement system should aspire to an integration of manual and intellectual work. Every such system region will require teachers, doctors, engineers, natural scientists, and the like. The pioneering work of the present need not be like that of the Second and Third Aliya. Science and scientists must be an organic part of the undertaking. Only the habits of exile and careerism are responsible for the fact that professionals employed in developing the Negev and the Dead Sea and in planning irrigation are not living on the site, but in Tel Aviv and other cities far from the place of work. To the credit of the new immigrants, it should be noted that it is they who have built the majority of the settlements founded since the creation of the State, thus refuting the vain words of so-called "progressives" from Russia and Germany who believed that the only people capable of pioneering work were those who read Pushkin and Goethe.

The regional settlement in the Lahish area must serve as a bridge to the "second part of the country"—the empty and desolate Negev. Though inhabitants of the north consider anything south of Beer-Tuviah to be "the Negev," the Lahish area is not the Negev. Its regional settlement will, in effect, serve as a bridge between the north and the Negev.

While both the State and the Jewish Agency favored the Lahish area regional settlement plan, newspapers supporting pioneering endeavor and published by kibbutz Ha'artzi and kibbutz Hameuhad (after the split in Mapam) printed long and bitter attacks on the proposal. *Al Hamishmar*, on October 1, 1954, published an "Open Letter to David Ben-Gurion" by Eliezer Hacohen:

> It has recently become known that you have proposed plans for settlement. You have come up with a new idea: regional settlement. You protest against "party settlement" and demand the unification of settlers without any party barriers. You have not yet succeeded in proving that there is any substance or importance to this idea. What urgency, strategical or settlement-wise, is there in concentrating reserves in this middle part of the country? I can imagine the diligent advisers with a ready-made answer: we will reduce the amount of water in the north in order to close gaps in the south. But such a solution means cutting

away the roots of the existing settlements in the north and center of the country, which for many years will remain the center of production and a stronghold of the spirit.

A month later, on November 24, *Al Hamishmar* published an editorial by Alexander Pereg entitled "Regional Settlement—Truth and Falsehood," in which the man singled out for castigation was Ra'anan Weitz, who had undertaken the planning of the Lahish area. Then on December 1, *Lamerhav* ran an editorial captioned "Empty Slogans," which attacked Ben-Gurion, claiming that the real purpose of the "non-party settlement" was to keep Kibbutz Hameuhad and Kibbutz Ha'artzi out of the new settlement blocs. "Indeed" the editorial said, "it is not for nothing that the bourgeois press has received Ben-Gurion's slogan with such enthusiasm. It immediately seized upon the 'generous, non-party' aid which Ben-Gurion was extending to its aspirations and appetite for reducing the power of the workers in the State. It is doubtful if the settlers of Nahalal, Kfar Yehoshua, Dagania, and Geva will consider their leader's new proposal for non-labor, non-independent, non-Histadrut settlement as the acme of wisdom and the way to 'unite two countries and two nations into one.'" On December 8, *Al Hamishmar* struck once more: "The hypocrisy of the slogan of non-political settlement," it said, "is evident for all to see. Comrade Ben-Gurion would offer Sde Boker as an example of the new form of settlement. This is a case of counting one's chickens before they are hatched."

To the credit of the settlement agencies, it must be recorded that they disregarded such attacks. They gave the regional settlement project their full support and built scores of settlements in the Lahish area as well as the city of Kiryat Gat. Immigrants from dozens of countries were transformed into settlement builders. Moshavei ovdim, Moshavim shitufim, and Kibbutzim (both Hashomer Hatzair and Hakibbutz Hameuhad) came into existence. The Lahish was one of the most successful undertakings of 1955 and became a "center of creation and stronghold of strength," not necessarily for the north and central part of the country as Eliezer Hacohen had advocated in *Al Hamishmar*, but as an expansion of the Pale of Settlement southward in the form of a bridge to the Negev. At this writing the Lahish region has already celebrated its tenth anniversary and in its wake the Ta'anahim area was built in the north.

Egypt Closes Suez to Israel ★ British Evacuate the Canal Area ★ Knesset Protests Arms to Egypt and Rearmament of West Germany

In 1954 an alarming change in relations was evident among the Middle East states; it was destined to culminate in the dramatic events of 1956. The focal point of trouble was the Suez Canal.

The canal was built by the French to provide a waterway from the Mediterranean to the Red Sea, through the Straits of Suez and thence to the Indian Ocean. Early in the nineteenth century the Turkish ruler Mohammed Ali (an Albanian) gained control of Egypt, which in theory had been an Ottoman province since 1517. In 1854 his successor, Mohammed Said, signed a contract with his friend Ferdinand de Lesseps to form the Universal Suez Canal Company, and work on its construction began.

Because it would provide easy access by sea from Europe to India and Asia as a whole, Great Britain feared French competition in that area and for a long time pressed the Turkish government to delay the project. Since Ottoman dominion over Egypt was to a large extent fictitious, the digging continued. On November 17, 1869, the first ship passed through the canal: the French luxury liner *Aigle*, with Empress Eugenie, the wife of Napoleon III, aboard. Britain became reconciled to the accomplished fact, honored de Lesseps in London—and eventually acquired most of the shares in the canal.

The contract with the Suez Canal Company stipulated that the waterway would be open to the merchant ships of all nations. After the effectual takeover of Egypt by the British Army in the 1880s an international convention met in Constantinople on October 21, 1888, attended by Britain, France, Germany, Austria-Hungary, Italy, Russia, Spain, Holland, and Turkey. The first section of the treaty worked out at this gathering provided that "The Suez Maritime Canal shall always be free and open in time of war as in time of peace to every vessel of commerce or of war, without distinction of flag." Nearly sixty-one years later, on February 24, 1949, Egypt signed an armistice agreement with Israel that did not alter this international rule. Yet one year later, in 1950, ships going to and from Israel were forbidden the use of the canal.

The Government of Israel protested to the United Nations Security Council, which on September 1, 1951, adopted a resolution explicitly affirming Israel's full right to freedom of navigation in the Suez Canal. Egypt, ignoring the resolution, continued the blockade, but the Security Council took no action to enforce compliance with its decision.

Meanwhile Egypt had undergone political turbulence internally. A revolution by the so-called "Free Officers," in 1952, exiled King Farouk. A military government was installed, provisionally headed by General Naguib. On June 18, 1953, the monarchy was officially abolished. The junta designated Naguib as President and Prime Minister, with Col. Gamal Abdel Nasser as Deputy Prime Minister and Minister of the Interior, while Nasser's close friend Major Abdul Hakim Amer succeeded Naguib as Chief of Staff. General Naguib remained in power only until 1954, when Nasser became Prime Minister.

The main objective of the "Free Officers" was the expulsion of the British Army, which had been in Egypt for 72 years, ever since 1882. On July, 1954, the British government agreed to withdraw its forces within twenty months. A number of bases at the canal would be retained for an additional seven years and Britain would have the right to bring in forces if Egypt, one of the Arab League nations, or Turkey were attacked. (The final treaty embodying these points was not signed until October.) This understanding between Britain and Nasser completely ignored Egypt's violation of international commitments in closing the Suez Canal to Israeli ships and ships bound for Israel, in open defiance of the Security Council declaration that the ban was illegal and its demand that it be lifted.

On August 30, 1954, the Prime Minister and Minister of Foreign affairs, Moshe Sharett, addressed himself to this problem in the Knesset. He said in part:

> The Government of Israel is not aware of any concrete guarantee given by or even demanded of Egypt to ensure her compliance with the Security Council decision, in a treaty that gives her such tremendous gains. Yet Britain and the United States were among the foremost sponsors of the Security Council with regard to the canal. Only a few days ago the government of the United States reiterated its support of this resolution, and proclaimed its desire to see it implemented. But the powers have not yet taken any effective step to ensure implementation.

The question is: Are they not putting these efforts to open the canal to naught, by fulfilling most of Egypt's desires, by failing to call that country to account, while there is still time, for her violations of international law? Are they not in effect approving these violations?

The transfer of the Canal Zone to the military control of Egypt increases, at one stroke, and to a very substantial extent, her effective military strength and her capacity for aggression against Israel. Suffice to mention the airfields with which the Zone is well supplied to make clear what is here involved. Large-scale material reinforcements are falling into the hands of a state which invaded the Land of Israel in defiance of the United Nations; which, as a result of that invasion, still occupies an area to which she has no sovereign title; which constantly reiterates the existence of a state of war with Israel, and its intention of carrying out the plans at which it failed on first attempt.

In recent days it is true, we have heard from the rulers of Cairo words that seem to hint at readiness for a peaceful settlement with Israel. In spite of all our yearning for true signs of peace, we must, in the light of our experience, beware of being led astray by deceptive tactics. Only time will tell whether Cairo's words were sincerely meant, or whether it was merely an attempt to lull and mislead the authorities in Washington, and to frustrate our efforts to win American public opinion to our side.

We are far from falling into panic, but we shall avoid illusions. We have been in grave situations before, when our entire future hung by a hair, and came out unscathed. We should be able to endure new trials if such are in store for us. But we shall not exempt from responsibility those who by their policies may bring nearer or aggravate these orders. Today we are isolated in our region, but we are not alone in the world. Millions of our fellow Jews will stand by us in this struggle and will continue to support us with a brotherly hand. The more we here in Israel do with our own strength what is incumbent upon us, the more will we enjoy loyal and united support by Diaspora Jewry. The more firm and united we stand on the political and military fronts, while at the same time strengthening our moral structure and the spiritual quality of our undertaking, the more will the best elements of humanity show sympathy for Israel, faith in its future, and willingness to help.

The ensuring debate lasted three days. Meir Wilner on behalf of the Communists declared that the policy of the American and British governments was a most serious blow to the political, economic, and security interests of Israel; that it endangered peace in the Middle East and sabotaged prospects for a peace treaty between Israel and the Arab states. Yacov Hazan for Mapam stated that American negotiations with Egypt on military aid, as a sequel to its military agreement with Iraq, would turn the Middle East into a base for American aggression. Moshe Erem (Ahdut Ha'avodah-Poalei Zion) proposed that the Knesset express dissatisfaction with the announcement by the Prime Minister and Minister of Foreign Affairs, claiming that it embodied no response whatsoever to the revolutionary developments in Israel's international position. Aryeh Altman (Herut) maintained that the Government's foreign policy, based on denial of our nation's historic rights to its integral Homeland, had failed and if continued would lead to catastrophe. The demand to unite the divided Land of Israel [Israel and Jordan] should be raised immediately in the international arena.

In the end the proposal adopted was the one put forth by Meir Argov on behalf of Mapai, the General Zionists, Hapoel Hamizrahi, the Progressives, Agudat Israel, and Poalei Agudat Israel: "The Knesset, having heard the statement of the Prime Minister and Minister for Foreign Affairs, supports the Government in its efforts to prevent the supply of arms to the Arab states and the upset of the balance of military strength that leads to the undermining of the security situation in the area."

The agreement between Britain and Egypt negotiated in June was signed on October 19, 1954. It provided that the British Army would be evacuated within twenty months. On the same day the British Foreign Secretary, Sir Anthony Eden, sent a note to the Israeli Ambassador in London. Her Majesty's Government, he stated, attached great importance to friendly relations with Israel; it was prepared to do everything in its power to help bring about a peaceful settlement in the dispute between Israel and the Arab states, and the Government of Israel could count on the sympathy of Her Majesty's Government in its efforts to promote the peaceful progress and welfare of the Israeli people. Nevertheless, Israel was not included in the list of countries which, if attacked, would permit Britain to restore her forces to the bases at the Suez Canal.

The treaty was debated in the British House of Commons on November 2. Several speakers from all parties expressed admiration for Israel's constructive achievements and demanded guarantees for Israel's security that would be more binding that those included in the Tripartite Declaration [Britain, France, United States] of 1950.

In his reply Eden said that the 1950 declaration obliged not only England but also the United States and France to prevent any acts of aggression against Israel or the Arab states. The document established the principle of an arms balance between Israel and the Arab states, and this Her Majesty's Government together with the allies intended to maintain. Eden's assurances, however, did not correspond with reality. The United States signed an agreement for financial aid to Egypt which was not made conditional on the lifting of the economic blackade against Israel in violation of international law and the express decision of the Security Council supported by the United States. The Anglo–Egyptian agreement (Section 8) stipulated that the Suez Canal, though "an integral part of Egypt," was "an international, economic, commercial, and strategic waterway," and that the signers "declare their absolute resolve to honor the convention of October 29, 1888, guaranteeing freedom of navigation." Yet on September 28, only three weeks before the agreement was signed, the Egyptian government detained the Israeli vessel *Bat Galim*, arrested her captain and crew, and kept them imprisoned even after the signing of the treaty with Britain.

The Egyptian Premier made no secret of his attitude toward Israel. Early in November he declared to a correspondent from an Arab paper published in the Old City of Jerusalem that "There will be no solution to this problem, nor will there be peace between the Jews and ourselves, as long as a single crumb of what belongs to you remains in enemy hands." Similar statements were made by other Arab leaders. In his throne speech on the opening of the new parliament, the Jordanian King Abdullah said: "There will be no peace and no negotiations with Israel." The Prime Minister of Syria, Faris el Houry, in an address to his parliament on November 4, said: "Peace with Israel is unthinkable. Some Arab statesmen are accustomed to saying erroneously that there will be no peace with Israel before Israel implements the UN resolution. I am opposed to such statements. There is no connection between the return of the refugees and implementation of the rest of the UN resolution and peace with Israel. Even if the refugees are returned to their lands, we will not make peace with Israel on any account. The Arabs will not agree to peace as long as Jews live in the heart of the Arab states and sow unrest and fear in our midst. The first round unfortunately was unsuccessful. There is no doubt that the Arabs will prepare for a second round with all their energy."

In the political debate in the Knesset on November 15 and 16, the Opposition dwelt mainly on the danger involved in the rearming of Germany.

Hazan said: "There is no more shocking proof of the dangers inherent in the policy of our Government—which is willing to forego its independence—than its approval of the Tripartite Declaration by Britain, the US and France. It was in London that the revival of Germany's neo-Nazi army was in effect approved. This is one of the most dangerous steps towards a third World War. The greatest threat to the world is not the atomic bomb or the hydrogen bomb. The Soviet Union also has the hydrogen bomb and the West is an easier target than the East and knows it well. American strategy is more and more moving away from the insanity of a preventive war and a surprise atomic or hydrogen attack on the socialist world. It knows that a Soviet response would be inevitable, several times more powerful than the American. The most concrete and gravest peril to peace at present lies in the creation of the neo-Nazi army, which threatens the destruction of the world and of our nation."

Aryeh Altman: "The rearming of Germany is one of the West's most serious mistakes. A rearmed Germany will fight alongside the Russians against the West. The German nation itself is a danger, as Nietzsche once said."

Mikunis: "The two most important matters in the world today—the two things that bring out the abysmal contradiction between Anglo-American global policy and Israel's vital national interests—are the arms race in the Middle East and the danger of a rearmed Germany. In violation of the Yalta and Potsdam Agreements not to permit the revival of German militarism, the American, British, and French governments have concluded a separate agreement with the neo-Nazi West German government on German remilitarization. The revival of German militarism is a terrible danger to the nations of Europe and all humanity—and especially to Israel and to Jews everywhere. What has and is the Israeli Government doing in the face of this terrible danger? The Government has been collaborating and is intensifying its collaboration with the Nazi leaders of West Germany."

Ben-Aharon: "The ground is now being prepared for the establishment of diplomatic ties with Germany which not only we but British Lords, German democrats, and French Social Democrats consider neo-Nazi. The overwhelming majority of Western opinion views Adenauer's Germany as the flimsy and transparent veil of an old man on the face of renewed neo-Nazism."

Sneh: "All of Israel's vital interests are consistent with Soviet policy. First of all, the opposition to the revival of German militarism. The Soviet plan calls for disarmament of all Germany. The matter of Germany's future is the link that binds the destiny of the Jewish people with that of the Soviet people. The Soviet Union vanquished the Nazi beast of prey but now America wishes to bring it back to life."

Sharett acknowledged that he had not referred to the German question in his opening remarks, but the question was on his mind, and the process of Germany's rearmament must arouse the deep concern and resentment of the Jewish people. On the other hand, he noted: "This beginning that is about to be made in West Germany was preceded by four years if not more of rearmament in East Germany. Two and a half years ago, in the summer of 1952, we heard a declaration by the East German President, Otto Grotewohl, at a convention of the National Democratic Party, as the Communist Party there is known, that the East German Army was in the process of formation. And this is being carried out at an ever increasing rate. Why did we hear no protests about this from certain benches at the time? Why object to German armament and its dangers only now? Does this not show that those benches are concerned here not merely with the Jewish people and its historic account with Germany but something else entirely?

"In considering the problem of the future of Germany and our relations with it," Sharett went on, "I am obliged to note that the Reparations Agreement, brought by the head of the West German government, Dr. Adenauer, is being carried out fully and punctually. This is the situation at present and there is reason to believe that it will continue. All the sinister prophecies and scorn regarding the 'naïvete' of the previous coalition Government have now been fully disproved. The country's entire economy in all its branches, regardless of class and party affiliations, is benefiting from these payments. What should be our overriding consideration in this case? To immerse ourselves in memories and sacrifice the present and the future to the past? Are not the survival of the State and the elevation of its stature supreme injunctions for Jewish survival and Jewish honor both present and future?"

A call by Riftin of Mapam for a vote of no-confidence in the Government was rejected, as was a similar motion by Herut, Ahdut Haavodah, and the Communists.

In the wake of the agreement between Britain and Egypt, Israel's security situation did not improve. Instead of the danger that members of the Opposition, right and left, foresaw in the rearmament of West Germany, it was the danger from the Egypt of "Free Officers" that loomed large.

On October 18, 1955, Foreign Minister Sharett made the following declaration in the Knesset:

> The renewal of Egyptian aggressive actions along the Gaza Strip has jeopardized the security of our settlements in that border area and deeper in the country. The Egyptians have resorted to the odious tactic of sending gangs deep into Israel to commit acts of murder and destruction. Vigorous reaction became imperative and the Israel Defense Forces struck against one of the nests of the gangsters. With the cessation of attacks in the south, however, similar gangs began to operate in the northern sections of the country.
>
> According to information in our possession, these too were organized primarily on the criminal initiative of Egypt, assisted by other Arab elements, particularly Syria. We must once more warn Egypt that it will be considered responsible for the continuation of such murderous activities, though this warning in no way absolves from responsibility those other Arab countries bound by the Armistice Agreements to prevent the penetration into Israel of armed forces from their territory.
>
> The Army of Israel and our border police stand on watch, and are alert and vigilant. Meanwhile the Egyptian acts of lawlessness in the frontier zone along the Sinai border forced us to create certain physical and political facts. The situation in that region was restored to normal, though it has apparently again deteriorated. We reserve to ourselves the freedom to act in accordance with the requirements of the situation.
>
> In relation to all these questions we are anxious to act in full cooperation with the competent organs of the UN in accordance with the Armistice Agreements. But we shall insist upon bilateral fidelity to these agreements. We will not agree to their being observed by one side, while the other side feels free to violate them at will.
>
> A most conspicuous violation of the Armistice Agreements is implicit in the recent Egyptian regulations regarding entry into the Gulf of Eilat, aimed to obstruct the passage of Israeli ships to the southern harbor of our country. Here, too, we reserve for ourselves full freedom of action at the time and in the manner we shall find suitable.

After two days of debate the following resolution was adopted on behalf of all the parties in the Knesset, with the exception of the five opposing votes cast by the Communists.

The Knesset expresses its profound anxiety in the face of the large arms shipments to Egypt and the continuation of the arming of Iraq and other Arab states which proclaim that they are in a state of war with Israel; they will be used by her enemies in a war of obliteration against her, and they endanger the peace of the region and of the world.

The Knesset directs the Government to marshal the people and the State against the danger, to increase the strength and the equipment of the Israel Defense Forces, and to demand of the Powers that weapons for defense be supplied to Israel. The Knesset votes with pride the voluntary action of the masses of Israeli citizens to acquire arms for the Israel Defense Forces.

V

SUEZ CRISIS, 1956–1957

Czechoslovak Arms Deal; Sinai Campaign; American and United Nations Intervention

Section 1. The New Knesset and the New Government Face

Soviet Hostility

Elections to the Third Knesset ★ *Ben-Gurion Again Prime Minister* ★
Aliya from Africa ★ *New Government Is Organized*

THE fourth session of the Second Knesset ended on June 30, 1955. In the six years from 1948–1949 to 1954–1955 the national budget had increased almost ninefold. In 1948–1949 the ordinary budget came to IL28,885,000 of income, and expenditures of IL27,529,000. In 1954–1955 the equivalent figures were IL344,296,000 for income, IL391,498,000 for expenditures. The development budget for 1948–1949 was IL35,201,000; in 1954–1955 it was IL293,141,000.

The foreign trade balance for 1949 was: net imports of $251,906,000; net exports of $28,494,000—an excess of imports over exports of $223,411,000. In 1955 net imports came to $334,453,000, net exports to $86,300,000; the excess imports over exports was $245,397,000, The trade deficit per person in 1949 was $214; in 1955 only $141.

Aliya, which had reached a low ebb in 1953, began to increase again but did not attain the level of the first four years after the creation of the State. In 1954 17,485 persons arrived (compared to 10,388 in 1953) and in 1955, 36,327. Emigration also showed a decline after 1953; it dropped from 12,500 emigrants in 1953 to 1000 in 1954; and in 1955 the figure was 6000. By the end of 1955 the total population of Israel was 1,789,000, of whom 1,590,500 were Jews. The national income, IL1.497 billion in 1954, rose to IL1.75 billion in 1955. The real national income per person had grown by 6 percent. By the spring of 1956 the number of Jewish rural settlements reached 740.

444

The elections to the Third Knesset took place on July 26, 1955. There were 1,057,795 registered voters, of whom 876,085 cast their ballots; valid votes totaled 853,219. Mapai received 274,735 (32.2 percent); Herut, 107,190 (12.6 percent); General Zionists, 87,099 (10.2 percent); Mizrahi and Hapoel Hamizrahi, 77,936 (9.1 percent); Ahdut Ha avodah, 69,475 (8.2 percent); Mapam, 62,401 (7.3 percent); the Minorities List (affiliated with Mapai), 42,261 (4.9 percent); Agudat Israel, 39,836 (4.7 percent); Communists, 38,492 (4.5 percent); Progressives, 37,661 (4.4 percent); other parties, 13,685 (1.6 percent). Mapai received 40 seats, Herut 15, General Zionists 13, Mizrahi and Hapoel Hamizrahi 11, Ahdut Haavodah 10, Mapam 9, Communists 6, Agudat Israel and Poalei Agudat Israel 6, Progressives 5, Minorities List 5.

The Third Knesset was opened on August 15, 1955, with an address by the President, Yitzhak Ben-Zvi; Yosef Sprinzak was reelected Speaker by acclamation. Nine committees were elected: House, Constitution, Finance, Economic, Foreign Affairs and Security, Interior, Public Services, Education and Culture, Labor.

The first problem on the agenda of the fourth session of the Knesset was the immigration from North Africa. As Prime Minister Sharett pointed out, this community of Jews had long been "one of the darkest exiles on our nation's world map of wandering." Under the yoke of Islam the condition of the Jews there was pitiable. Sharett said:

> With the introduction of French rule, the economic and cultural situation of this community improved considerably, but large portions of it have remained in deep poverty and ignorance, and the legal standing of the Jews in general has remained inferior. Love of the Land of Israel and a yearning for redemption had always glowed among these Jews. The Magrebian Aliya, centered in Jerusalem, began at the start of the 1880's,* almost at the same time as the Russian and Rumanian immigration that built the first agricultural settlements in Judea and Galilee.
>
> News of the creation of the State of Israel aroused enthusiasm among all North African Jewry, manifesting itself in increased Aliya. By August of last year this had totaled sixty-five thousand persons from Morocco, Tunisia, and Algeria. The Moroccan independence movement is directed against French rule and colonialism, but in some places its unrestrained wrath is poured out on the helpless Jewish communities. Jewish homes and shops have been looted, neighborhoods and villages abandoned by their Jewish inhabitants; a number of Jews have been murdered with frightful savagery, and it is rumored that several Jewish children have been abducted. There is no way of knowing what the future will bring, but it would be difficult to exaggerate the imminent and long-term dangers. The Moroccan Nationalist Movement has taken pains to stress that it is not directed against the Jews and that it seeks their well-being. However, it is not able to guarantee that events will not take a sudden turn for the worse.
>
> In this situation it is incumbent upon Israel to speed assistance to every Jew who wishes to immigrate. To this we must apply all our energy, over and above any normal effort. Actually for a year now we have witnessed intensified Aliya from North Africa and especially Morocco, compared to previous years. In the first eight months of 1954 a total of 6457 Jews arrived in Israel from all countries of the world, an average of 800 a month. Immigrants from North Africa accounted for less than 40 percent of this figure. By comparison, from mid-August 1954 to mid-August 1955 there arrived 32,000 immigrants, or 2700 a month, of whom 18,400, or 57 percent, were from Morocco and 6700 from Tunisia, Algeria, and Spanish

---

* The first Jewish settler in Jaffa in 1838 came from Morocco.

Morocco, making a total of 26,000, or 80 percent, from North Africa and only 6500, or 20 percent, from all other countries. We do not intend to content ourselves with these figures. Plans call for bringing in a total of 45,000 Jews from October 1, 1955, to the end of September 1956, of whom at least 40,000, or nearly 90 percent, will be from North Africa.

Actually immigration proved greater than Prime Minister Sharett hoped. In 1955, 36,327 Jews arrived; in 1956, 54,996; and in 1957, 71,000. In 1958 another slowdown began—in that year there were only 26,093 immigrants and in the following year, 23,045.

Three days after the opening of the Knesset the President called upon Defense Minister David Ben-Gurion to form the new Government. Negotiations over its organization and the controversies touched off by the Prime Minister-Designate's program continued for two and a half months. The inordinate number of parties and the consequent mushrooming of party politics, as well as the attempt of the small factions to impose their will by their ability to prevent the formation of a Government, encumbered the process of negotiation.

Ben-Gurion made efforts to bring seven parties into the Cabinet: Mapai, the General Zionists, Mizrahi and Hapoel Hamizrahi, Ahdut Haavodah, Mapam, Agudat Israel, and the Progressives. He proposed to them a general program of Government policy.

The General Zionists replied immediately in the negative. The Prime Minister-Designate appealed to the party at a meeting with its representative, but its position was unchanged. Peretz Bernstein, chairman of the General Zionist Party, said in a letter that the proposed program "cannot serve as the basis for negotiations." Agudat Israel also put forth demands that Ben-Gurion could not accept, because he felt that they were contrary to the wishes of the large majority of the nation. The five parties that finally agreed to the program were Mapai, Ahdut Ha avodah, Mapam, Hapoel Hamizrahi and Mizrahi, and the Progressives. Negotiations were completed by October 7, but because of Ben-Gurion's illness the Government was presented to the Knesset only on November 2, 1955.

The program was no different from that of the first elected Government. In the first section the Prime Minister-Designate formulated nine objectives for Government activity over the next four years. (1) The ingathering of Jews from the countries of distress and encouragement of Aliya from other countries. (2) Progress toward economic independence. (3) Settlement of the empty and wilderness areas in the north and in the Negev. (4) Diligent striving for security, peace, and friendly relations with all nations. (5) Closing the gap between the veteran population and the new immigrants. (6) Strict observance of integrity and the encouragement of voluntary pioneering work. (7) Full employment for longtime residents and new immigrants alike, and a decent standard of living. (8) Promotion of education and cultivation of sciences and research. (9) Consolidation of democracy and national independence.

Addressing the Knesset, Ben-Gurion expressed his esteem for Prime Minister Sharett, "who has stood at the helm of State for two years, ably and in good taste, and is gifted with fine qualities and talents not possessed by the first Prime Minister." He also praised Ministers Dov Joseph and Ben-Zion Dinur who had not joined the proposed new Government. Then he read and explained the fifteen sections of the outlined policy, dwelling at length on the security situation:

> Our problem is not simply the security of our independence, our territory, our borders, our regime, but the security of our simple physical survival. Our enemies are scheming

not only against our territory and independence. Their plan, as many of them state frankly, is to throw us all into the sea. Let us not forget that during World War Two the majority of Arab rulers admired Hitler and looked forward to his victory. Five years ago, on November 1, 1950, the Prime Minister and Minister of Defense announced that he did not share our public joy over past victories. The danger ahead of us now is no less grave than it was three years ago, and perhaps even more so. I am still filled with anxiety, perhaps more than I am prepared to say at this time.

The aspiration to destroy Israel was reiterated not long ago by Radio Cairo, which says nothing that has not first been cleared with the ruling military junta. Our security problem is the problem of our survival—our physical survival, plain and simple. The entire future of the Jewish people now depends on the survival of the State of Israel. And just as our security problem is different from that of other countries, our means and needs for security are greater than those of any other country. We must view the crucial difference between ourselves and our enemies with brutal clarity. Our enemies believe that they can solve the problem of Israel absolutely, once and for all, by our total destruction. We cannot and would not wish to achieve a security of this nature. It is not our wish, not our right, and not within our capacity, to liquidate millions of Arabs in the Middle East. Our security lies in constantly building up our strength in every area and on all fronts.

At this moment the nation is deeply concerned by the large quantities of arms pouring into the enemy countries, Egypt in particular. Yet precisely at this time the security of Israel must not rely solely on armed forces and arms, though without them there can be no security. The security of Israel means Aliya. In Egypt alone there are over twenty-two million inhabitants. In Israel, only one and a half million. Aliya is not only the supreme historic objective of our State but a security need of the highest order. Aliya means not only bringing Jews from North Africa or other countries to the shores of Israel, but giving them roots in work, in the soil of the Homeland, the economy, the Hebrew language, the values of our heritage, national responsibility, Jewish fellowship, a sense of national pride and security, and the desire and ability to be a builder, a defender, and a molder of the image of the Homeland.

Security means settlement and first of all settling the wilderness. Concentrating on industry and the great majority of the population in the central coastal plain carries grave dangers—in terms of security and otherwise—for the future of the nation. Upper Galilee and especially the empty expanses of the south and the Negev are the weak points. No military force can keep them in our hands if we do not settle them as soon as possible with the greatest density. Our surplus water, our surplus manpower, from the new Aliya and the youth reaching majority, our new workshops and factories, development projects, and research and scientific institutions must be diverted to the south. It is out of the empty south that the evil will break forth, and it is the south, and especially a populated and highly industrialized Negev, that will ensure our security and our economic independence. It is on these that our economic ties with the Asian continent will depend to a large and perhaps an overwhelming extent.

Security means conquest of the sea and air, to make ourselves a maritime power and a force to be reckoned with in the air. Settlement is not limited merely to land, to the soil. There can also be settlement of the sea and of the air, and the great advantage here is that there are no territorial limitations and curtailing borders. Directing a large part of the youth in the coastal cities—Naharyia, Acre, Haifa, Jaffa, Migdal, Ashkelon, Eilat—to fishing and seafaring is a national economic and security requirement of the first order.

Security is the cultivation of research and scientific ability at the highest level, the apex of knowledge, in all the physical, chemical, biological, and technological sciences. We will never enjoy quantitative superiority in manpower, equipment, or material means. Let us work toward intellectual and spiritual superiority. We must elevate our moral and intellectual ability to the highest degree. Our scientific capacity and our moral image will determine our international standing, our national image, our defensive might, and above all our influence on the Jews of the Diaspora and the attraction to Israel.

Security is modern vocational training of youth in agriculture, crafts, industry, construction, seafaring; equipping them to turn out high-quality work that is competitive in the international markets.

Finally, security requires that the youth, the nation, its savants volunteer for difficult and vital objectives in settlement, in security, and in the integration of exiles. Our entire undertaking in this country would not have come into being were it not for this wonderful quality of adventurous pioneering that we showed during the three generations that preceded the creation of the State. Through the State, the law, and compulsion alone we will not reach the great goals that lie ahead of us. The outstanding symbol of pioneering and exalted love of Israel in our days is Varda Friedman of Kfar Vitkin, who, together with other young members of the veteran settlements, went out to live together with distant brothers— Kurdish immigrants from Persia—in the remote village in the distant south called Patish. Her purpose was to instruct the immigrants in work, education, and defense, and on this mission she gave her life.

Two weeks ago Prime Minister Sharett spoke of the deteriorating security situation following the developments at the Suez Canal, and I have nothing to add to this. However, we must not pass over in silence Nasser's declaration over Radio Cairo on September 27 in which he said, "Last week we signed a commercial treaty with Czechoslovakia by which that country will supply us with arms in return for cotton and rice." Two days later, on September 29, it was announced that ships had set out for Egypt loaded with tanks, guns, planes, and submarines. And Radio Cairo proclaimed, "The day of Israel's destruction is coming closer. There will be no peace on the borders, for we demand revenge and revenge means death to Israel!"

There is no doubt that the Czechoslovak government knew full well for what these arms were earmarked. Not for the improvement of the conditions of labor and the life of the masses of Egyptian workers, not for the improvement of the material conditions of the fellahin. The Czechoslovak communist paper, *Rude Pravo*, wrote that "the peace-loving policy of the Arab countries is universally known," but the views of the Egyptian rulers are voiced by the Egyptian press, not by newspapers in Prague. And the Egyptian press declares that "it is inconceivable that Egypt will conclude peace with or recognize Israel." One Egyptian paper puts the matter even more bluntly: "The Arabs regard Israel as an artificial State that has to be destroyed." And Radio Cairo a short while back was equally blunt: "The day of Israel's destruction comes ever closer. This is our resolve: this is our faith. There will be no peace on the borders, for we demand revenge and revenge means death to Israel." The Foreign Minister of Egypt tries to tell the American public that Radio Cairo pronouncements are not official proclamations, but he fails to note that Egypt is fully controlled by a military dictatorship. Obviously this is known to the Czechoslovak government.

It is my duty to tell all the powers that rule the world, with the modesty becoming a representative of a small nation in political affairs but with the moral force of a son of the Jewish people: "The people of Israel in the Land of Israel will not be led like sheep to the slaughter. What Hitler did to six million helpless Jews in the ghettos of Europe will not be done by any foe of the House of Israel to a community of free Jews rooted in their own land."

On the very day when we renewed our national independence seven years ago we were attacked by the Arab states who invaded our country. We would have been destroyed but for the heroism of our sons and daughters. When the fighting was over, we did not harbor any hostile feelings toward those who attacked us. Our hand was stretched out for peace. Our neighbors, however, refused to make peace and only armistice agreements were concluded. Even these agreements they have not observed and the war against us has been carried on in other ways: through boycott, blockade, and frequent incursions by murderers and saboteurs.

It is Egypt that recently took the lead in this guerrilla warfare. Raids from the Gaza Strip alone in the first nine months of 1955 have caused a hundred and fifty-three casualties in dead and wounded. The spokesmen for Egypt at the United Nations have openly declared that the state of war between Israel and Egypt continues. The Egyptian government has violated the basic international law of freedom of navigation in the Suez Canal, reaffirmed by an explicit resolution of the Security Council. It is this Egypt that now seeks to block the passage of Israeli ships through the Red Sea Gulf in contravention of the international principle of freedom of the seas. This unilateral warfare must cease, for it cannot remain unilateral indefinitely.

The Israeli Government is prepared, as in the past, to observe faithfully all the provisions of the Armistice Agreements in every detail, both in the letter and the spirit. But this obligation is also binding on the other side. An agreement that is violated by the other side will not be binding on us either. If the armistice lines are regarded as open to the passage of saboteurs and murderers, they cannot remain closed to the defenders. If our rights are affected by acts of violence on land or sea, we shall reserve freedom of action to defend them in the most effective manner.

Our aim is peace—but not suicide. We wholeheartedly want peace and good-neighborliness, and we are willing to cooperate with all our neighbors for the prosperity and well-being of the Middle East and for the strengthening of peace in the world. We do not covet a single inch of foreign soil, just as we will not permit anyone to deprive us of a single inch of our territory as long as we live. We can see no real reason for conflict between us and Egypt. On the contrary, we see a basis for fruitful cooperation between the two peoples and there is certainly no lack of good-will on our part.

In order to overcome the dangers inherent in the present unstable situation, I am prepared to meet with the Prime Minister of Egypt and with every other Arab ruler as soon as possible, to achieve a mutual settlement without any prior conditions. The Government of Israel is prepared for a lasting and enduring peace settlement and for long-term political, economic, and cultural cooperation between Israel and its neighbors. If the other side is not yet ready for that, we would also agree to limited settlement providing for guarantees of the complete implementation of the Armistice Agreements, mutual elimination of all incidents and acts of hostility, boycott, and blockade, observance of freedom of the seas, and any further terms agreeable to both sides.

To our people at home, I would like to say: no complacency, but no depair. Although we cannot rely on verbal guarantees, let us not despair of the conscience of mankind and of enlightened world public opinion. Good men, and they are not few all over the world, can distinguish between a dictatorial regime built on force, aggression, and abasement of the dignity of man, and states devoted to the values of freedom, the transcendent worth of the individual, justice, and peace. We have given our support to the United Nations out of loyalty to the heritage of the Prophets of Israel and to their vision of peace among nations and the love of man that has been enunciated again in the United Nations Charter. But the United Nations Organization does not absolve its members from the duty of looking after themselves. Our task is first and foremost the maintenance of our security, and that is a job that will not be done for us by others. We shall have to do all that is incumbent upon us to attain peace and assure our security. If we do that, we need fear no evil.

It is my privilege to request that the Knesset approve the Government's program and express its confidence in the proposed Cabinet consisting of the following members: David Ben-Gurion, Prime Minister and Minister of Defense; Zalman Arrane, Minister of Education and Culture; Levi Eshkol, Minister of Development; Israel Barzelai, Minister of Health; Israel Bar-Yehuda, Minister of the Interior; Moshe Carmel, Minister of Transport; Kaddish Luz, Minister of Agriculture; Golda Meir, Minister of Labor; Peretz Naftali, Minister without portfolio; Pinhas Sapir, Minister of Commerce and Industry; Pinhas Rosen, Minister of Justice; Behor Shalom Shitreet, Minister of Police; Moshe Shapira, Minister for Religious Affairs and Minister of Social Welfare; Moshe Sharett, Foreign Minister. With this I will conclude. Thank you for your attention.

The debate lasted two days. *Menahem Begin* (Herut) quoted the strong criticism by "Yariv's Grandfather" [a pseudonym used by Ben-Gurion, whose grandson was named Yariv] of Mapam's adherence to the Soviet Union. He praised Sharett for his fine qualities and his courtesy to the opposition, but criticized his seeking defense guarantees from the United States, something that, in effect, amounted to patronage. He objected to his use of the term "preventive war" (Sharett denied using this), when in effect it would be a war of self-defense, and concluded with the opinion that the proposed Government would be unable to solve our problems. It was doomed to failure, he said, because it was based on exploitation, eviction, corruption, and the concentration of the national assets in the hands of a single-interest group.

Bernstein (General Zionists) congratulated Ben-Gurion on his recovery, "because today we can congratulate ourselves on nothing else." In his view the proposed Government was a labor grouping. He complained that the Sharett Government had canceled the minimum percentage [of participation] and claimed that he had refused to join the Government because there had been no discussion of the problem he considered more important than all the talk about basic outlines, namely, the composition of the Cabinet and a distribution of functions. He saw in this Government "a class struggle" and was "surprised at the Progressives who joined such a Government." Finally, he expressed hope that the Government would not survive long.

Sneh (Communist) agreed with Ben-Gurion that the defense issue was the most important, but complained that Mapam and Ahdut Haavodah had "not gained even one of the conditions they had set forth before the elections as a basis for entering the Government," and that "all they had contributed to the Government was ministers, not principles." He stated that "the Soviet Union has extended and is extending its hand in friendship to Israel and all the nations of the region and that the Government of Israel is rejecting it," and he concluded by warning "the Social Democrats—Mapai, Mapam, Ahdut Haavodah—and the bourgeois democratic parties" of the danger of fascism in public life and in the Government.

Seif el-Din Zoubi (Arab Democrat): "I will not forget the time when Mr. Ben-Gurion addressed the Knesset immediately after the revolution by the present regime in Egypt. Mr. Ben-Gurion expressed satisfaction and welcomed this movement, which put an end to the Farouk regime by deposing him from the throne. He expressed his hope that the revolution would prove a blessing to the Egyptian people, the Egyptian peasant, and the Egyptian worker, and would blaze a new trail different from that of the previous regime. Unfortunately, these hopes which we all fully shared have been disappointed, for the revolutionary leaders in Egypt have deceived their people and now seek to embroil them in a war with Israel.

Serlin (General Zionists): "I know two Ben-Gurions: one who is an asset of the entire nation, the other who is the head of Mapai. I regret that it is the second Ben-Gurion who has presented the new Government." He added that the Government in its present form would be bad for ordinary times and very, very bad in times of emergency.

After the Prime Minister-Designate replied to the speakers on November 3, 1955, the Knesset confirmed the new Government, seventy-three to thirty-two with three abstentions.

"The Knesset has hereby voted for a Government of Israel under the leadership of David Ben-Gurion," Speaker Sprinzak announced, then gave the floor to Sharett.

"With the conclusion of the term in office which the Knesset delegated to me slightly over one year and nine months ago," Sharett said, "I wish to express my profound gratitude to the honorable House for the degree of confidence and patience it has shown me. If at any time during my term of office I may unfortunately have hurt any member of the Knesset, I request his forgiveness. It was without intent. May I wish my comrade and my friend David Ben-Gurion strength and courage in body and soul to support the heavy burden that has been imposed upon him. All his comrades will assist him to the fullest of their abilities in the fulfillment of this great and highly responsible task. 'Go with this might of yours, and deliver Israel.'"

All members of the Government (except Carmel and Sapir, who were absent that day) submitted declarations of loyalty which they duly signed.

Egyptian and Syrian Aggressions ★ Syrian Guns Silenced ★ The Security Council Notes Syrian Guilt But Censures Israeli Reprisal

On the night of Thursday, November 3, 1955, while the debates over the formation and the program of the new Government were under way, a battle erupted in the Nitzana area in the South between an Israeli Defense Forces unit and an Egyptian unit that had entered Israeli territory and refused to leave despite demands by the United Nations representatives. The Armistice Agreement with Egypt had provided for the demilitarization of the Nitzana area, which lies within Israeli territory, and that a certain area on the Egyptian side be limited as to the number and types of Egyptian forces in it.

The Mixed Armistice Commission decided on January 3, 1955, that the two sides would jointly mark out the international boundary. The Egyptians, however, refused to comply. When a mixed group of UN observers and Israelis began to mark the border, on August 5, 1955, the Egyptians opened fire. It was discovered that two Egyptian outposts were already on the Israeli side of the border. Defying demands by the UN observers, the Egyptians not only refused to evacuate the Israeli territory but proceeded to destroy border markers already in place. As a result an Israeli Army unit was posted to the Nitzana area, but was withdrawn on October 2 under an agreement with the UN observers. The agreement provided that the Egyptian outposts be removed from Israeli territory; that Egyptian forces on their side of the border be limited in accordance with the Armistice Agreement; that Egypt desist from interfering with the marking of the border; and that Israeli police checkposts be located within the demilitarized area of Nitzana to defend the lives of civilians there. The Egyptians refused to comply with the Armistice Commission; border-marking operations had to be stopped when they again threatened to open fire.

In mid-October the Egyptians fired on two United Nations cars driving along the border and ten days later they attacked the Israeli police checkposts at Be'erotayim. A policeman was killed, three were injured, and two taken prisoner. About the same time the Egyptians crossed the border in the Nitzana area and dug themselves into the southern corner, inside Israeli territory. After repeated United Nations demands that the Egyptians withdraw were ignored, the IDF was ordered to expel them from Israeli territory. Since the ending of hostilities in the War of Independence on January 7, 1949, this was the first time the Israeli Army had been required to use force to drive a foreign army from Israeli territory.

The order of the day of the Commander of the Southern Command, issued on November 3, 1955, by Aluf Mishne Meir Amit, read as follows:

> A striking force of the IDF broke through into positions of the Egyptian enemy in the Be'erotayim area and smashed it utterly. The enemy troops were swept out of Israeli territory without leaving a trace. Enemy losses are fifty dead, forty-nine prisoners—including two officers—and considerable booty. Our losses: five killed, eighteen injured. With bowed heads we stand before our heroic comrades who fell in the storm of battle. The number of Egyptian dead and the prisoners taken confirm the weakness of the Egyptian army when confronted with the IDF. All honor and glory to those who have crushed the enemy but let not our alertness slacken. Let us be prepared. Let us not be complacent. The time of rest is not yet at hand. Let not the Fighters of the South replace their swords in their sheaths. The Egyptian is not a fast learner and much work remains to be done. Remember, the eyes of the nation are upon you in love, in preparedness, and in anticipation of what is to come.

The Egyptian unit that had moved into the Nitzana area was covered by Egyptian positions on the other side of the border, expecially in El Sabha, well dug in on a hill and equipped with anti-tank guns, 8-mm. mortars, light machine guns, and personal weapons that were to a large extent automatic. The Israeli force took the hill and dispersed the enemy in a battle that lasted one hour, from 10 to 11 P.M. The Egyptian force at El Sabha beyond the Kouseima-Abu Agheila line was there in violation of Article 8, Paragraph 3, of the Armistice Agreement. Immediately after expelling the enemy from Israeli territory and from the area beyond the border forbidden to the Egyptian Army, the Israeli force retired beyond the demilitarized zone and the Israeli police entered the zone. The Egyptian prisoners were transported via Beersheba to a prison camp and were treated in accordance with the Geneva Convention.

After the battle, before replying to those debating his program in the Knesset, the Minister of Defense said: "First allow me to express the heartfelt sympathy of all members of the present and future Government and I hope of the entire nation, to the mothers and fathers of the five warriors who fell yesterday in the defense of the Homeland. I have no words to console them for their hard loss. We have not the power to restore to them the youthful bloom of their dear and heroic sons but perhaps it may be of some comfort to them to know that the entire nation will remember them forever in pain and sorrow but also with pride. I regret, too, the fact that fifty Egyptian soldiers were killed, for they were the victims not of their own evil intent and will but of the aggression of a dictator who plays with the lives of his countrymen."

This time Egypt submitted no complaint to the Mixed Armistice Commission or to the Security Council. Nevertheless, Radio Cairo consoled the Egyptians with imaginary communiqués about the fighting continuing until 3 P.M. on November 4, 1955 (though it had, in fact, ended at 11 the previous night) and two hundred Israelis killed and scores taken prisoner.

Three days after the expulsion of the Egyptians from the Nitzana area the Secretary General of the United Nations, Dag Hammarskjöld, after consulting the governments of the United States, France, and Britain, submitted five proposals to the two sides. (1) Withdrawal of the military forces of both Israel and Egypt from the demilitarized zone. (2) A clear demarcation of the western boundary of the zone, coinciding with the Mandatory border of Palestine, by means of large white stones, the entire length of the border. (3) The Egyptian forces to take up position west of this line. (4) Israel to be allowed to maintain a thirty-man police force within the zone. (5) Israel to continue to maintain the civilian settlement set-up within the zone.

A few days later, speaking at an annual banquet in honor of the Lord Mayor of London, the British Prime Minister, Sir Anthony Eden, criticized the Soviet government, which had chosen to "inject a new element of danger into the delicate Middle East situation and to deliver weapons of war, tanks, airplanes, even submarines to one side only." He claimed that "it is impossible to reconcile this Soviet action with protestations that they wish to end the Cold War in the new spirit of Geneva," and "fantastic to pretend that this deliberate act of policy was an innocent commercial transaction." (That was how the "transaction" of flooding Egypt with Soviet weapons had been described by the Czechoslovak government.) The British Prime Minister, however, completely ignored the danger that the supply of weapons to "one side only" involved for Israel. He put the main responsibility on the suppliers rather than the recipients, as if Egypt had purchased the arms just for decoration.

Sir Anthony Eden, complaining that the Soviet Union was supplying arms to one side only, apparently forgot that for a long time his own government had been supplying arms to one side only. Nor was there any indication in his statement that it would not do so again in the future, though he dwelt on the seriousness of the Middle East situation and even put forth a "compromise" solution. The Arab states, he said, took their stand on the United Nations decision of November 29, 1947, and "it is not right" that United Nations resolutions should be ignored; Israel took its stand on the frontiers set out in the Armistice Agreement of 1949. Therefore, he concluded, it was necessary to find a compromise between the two frontiers, by cutting off part of Israel's "excess" territory and handing it over to the neighboring states.

In this "compromise" proposal and in the reasons he gave for it Eden ignored not only the fact that thirty years prior to the United Nations resolution the League of Nations, headed by the British government under Lloyd George and Balfour, had acknowledged the historic link between the Jewish people and the Land of Israel, but the fact that this link was not brought into existence by the Balfour Declaration but had existed throughout the generations. He also ignored more recent facts:

1. The British government was the only non-Arab state that declared at the United Nations General Assembly that it would not implement the United Nations decisions on the Palestine problem, thereby encouraging the Arab states to oppose the UN partition resolution. Britain refused to hand over the administration of Palestine to the UN Commission during the transition period and abandoned the country to chaos. Only the establishment of a Jewish State on May 14, 1948, eight hours before the British with-

drawal, saved the Jewish community from annihilation and the country as a whole from ruin.

2. The Arab states—Egypt, Syria, Iraq, Lebanon, Trans-Jordan, and Saudi Arabia—according to Sir Anthony Eden, took their stand on the United Nations decision of November 29, 1947. In fact they did not content themselves with publicly announcing their opposition to that resolution, but invaded the country immediately after the departure of the British in order to destroy the State of Israel, the reestablishment of which had been supported by more than two-thirds of the UN members. All the states that had raised their hands in favor of the creation of a Jewish State did not lift a finger to defend the young nation against attack by neighbors forty times the size of the Jewish community.

3. The UN Assembly had never decided to do what Sir Anthony Eden proposed—to enlarge the territory of neighboring countries at Israel's expense. To what reward were Egypt, Syria, Lebanon, or Jordan entitled for their invasion of Israel in violation of the UN Resolution? The only state in the Middle East entitled to redress was the one that had been criminally attacked by its Arab neighbors. What the British Prime Minister was proposing, then, was to reward aggressors and violators of international treaties.

Meanwhile, the situation on the Egyptian border grew worse. On December 5, 1955, the Prime Minister summoned General E.L.M. Burns, gave him a copy of Israel Government policy as formulated in the Knesset on November 2, 1955, and asked him to clarify with the Egyptian rulers whether they were willing to order an absolute cease-fire, to promise to uphold the Armistice Agreements, or to agree to the proposals of the UN Secretary General.

General Burns was very "precise." He did not say that the Egyptians had rejected the cease-fire, refused to uphold the Armistice Agreements, or rejected the Secretary General's proposals, but merely that they had not committed themselves to the cease-fire (and, in fact, at that very time were continuing to fire on Israeli forces and border settlements), nor promised to abide by the Armistice Agreement nor indicated a willingness to implement the Secretary General's proposals. From statements Burns made to journalists it was also clear that no change had come about in Egypt's negative position on an overall security arrangement along the Israeli-Egyptian borders or on Hammarskjöld's proposals for a demilitarized zone in the south.

The situation along the Syrian border, too, had deteriorated following the signing of an Egypt-Syrian military pact. On December 10, 1955, Syrian armed forces opened artillery fire on Israeli fishing boats and their police escort. Although the entire Lake Kinneret, including a ten-meter-wide strip on the Northeast coast, is sovereign Israeli territory, the Syrians on repeated occasions had attacked Israeli fishermen who approached the northeastern side of the lake. The Truce Commission repeatedly requested the Syrians to desist from these attacks; they did not comply. The fishing season each year had been transformed into an extended period of Syrian aggression that resulted in loss of lives and severe property damage.

When it had gone too far, the Israeli forces were ordered to silence the batteries responsible for the attacks and to ensure the safety of the fishermen lawfully engaged in their work.

The previous Chief of Staff of the Truce Supervision Organization, General Benicke, no friend of Israel, had ruled that Israel had exclusive sovereign rights over the entire lake and its shores, and demanded that the Syrians stop their attacks. At the same time he had required that Israel dismantle the heavy guns from the escort launches, on the grounds that the Armistice Agreement forbade the maintenance of a "naval force" within a zone of several kilometers from the east bank of the Kinneret. Israel complied. The boats guarding the fishermen went out without heavy guns. On December 10 the Syrians, who until then had been using machine guns, opened fire with artillery, causing heavy damages to the launches. The IDF were thereupon ordered to silence the aggressors' artillery. The operation succeeded. The Syrians suffered heavy losses in lives and weapons. Fishing was resumed. The Commanding Officer of the Northern Command, Chaim Zadok, at a news conference on December 12, declared that the situation following the retaliatory action was quiet, but probably we would hear over Radio Damascus of a Syrian counter-attack and great victories. "We will make do with our victory on the battlefield and let the Syrians win victories over the airwaves," he said at 12:30 P.M. Sure enough, two hours later Radio Damascus announced the death or wounding of two hundred Israeli soldiers.

Ahmed Shukeiry, Syrian representative in the United Nations, demanded that Israel be expelled from the UN. In his response Abba Eban said: "The clash on the shores of the Kinneret is both an index and a result of the tensions prevailing between the two countries. Ever since the signing of the Armistice Agreement, Syria has persisted in efforts to achieve its aim—to turn Israel into a wasteland by preventing utilization of its water resources." He cited a long array of Syrian acts of violence against Israel and the denunciations of Syria by the Mixed Armistice Commission. "In the first eleven months of 1955," he summed up, "Syria violated the Armistice 108 times, or an average of once every three days, on a border no more than 22 miles long." The Egyptian dictator, Gamal Abdel Nasser, in a letter to the Secretary General, warned that "Egypt and Syria will attack Israel in the event of further aggression." A majority in the Security Council voted to condemn Israel on the Syrian retaliation action.

Aluf Mishne Yuval Ne'eman, Deputy Chief of Israel Intelligence, told military and foreign correspondents on December 20 that documents discovered in the Syrian positions by Israeli troops "established beyond any doubt that the Syrian Army attacks against fishing in the Kinneret were not accidental. They were part of a calculated plan drawn up by Syrian Army headquarters which for years has deliberately ignored the Armistice Agreement and in particular the article establishing Israeli sovereignty over Lake Kinneret. The documents confirm that the firing was not a localized act by Syrian fishermen or civilians but resulted from an explicit order by the military high command. The Syrian intention to penetrate Israeli territory was a flagrant violation of the Armistice Agreement, which provides that in this zone the demarcation line coincide with the Mandatory border, with no demilitarized zones. Typical is the order signed by the Syrian Chief of Staff, General Shukeiry, designating Israeli territory as Syrian territorial waters. The captured documents also confirm that the Syrians mounted weapons inside the ten-meter shore zone that belongs to Israel."

Ne'eman read to the correspondents orders signed by Shukeiry claiming territorial waters for Syria in the Kinneret, and the order to open fire on any Israeli boat entering the 250-meter zone of these supposed territorial waters.

These documents were submitted to the UN Truce Supervision Commission and also forwarded to the Security Council. General Burns, in his report to the Security Council, declared that Israel had "violated the Armistice Agreement in the attack carried out on the night of December 11." Nevertheless, he noted that "In the past year and a half Syria has violated the Armistice Agreement a number of times with serious provocations against Israel." The Security Council postponed consideration of the Kinneret incident to the start of the following year, in January 1956.

At the end of 1955, General Burns filed a supplement to his report on the Kinneret matter, in which he said:

A UN military observer interrogated in the prison of Acre a Syrian cadet taken prisoner on the night of December 11–12. This officer said that he was the commander of El Douga and that on December 10 he had fired at an Israel police boat on Lake Tiberias with a bazooka. The distance of the police boat from shore at the time was 80 meters. The prisoner also referred to telephonic instructions he had received from the company commander, who was then at El Koursi, to fire at the Israel police boat if it got closer than 200 meters from shore. The prisoner recognized as belonging to him a map of the Douga sector and orders from the commander of the sector that the Israel police officer of Acre stated had been captured during the Israel attack on December 11–12. Photostatic copies of the Arabic documents in question were sent to me on December 21 by the Israel Foreign Ministry. Assuming the authenticity of the documents and the accuracy of the translation into English, which I have studied, I should like to submit the following comments:

The first document dated March 14, 1954, is an order from the Syrian Chief of Staff. After referring to repeated incidents between Syrian posts and Israel military boats and fishing boats and to the fishing rights of Arab inhabitants along the shore, the Chief of Staff issued instructions to the effect: (a) that the limit of the territorial waters off the Syrian shore in Lake Tiberias should be considered to be 250 meters from shore; (b) that fire should be opened on Israel military boats approaching closer than 250 meters; (c) that no fire should be opened on fishing boats unless they took part in landing operations.

While, according to Article II, Paragraph 2, of the General Armistice Agreement, no provision of this Agreement shall in any way prejudice the rights, claims, and positions of either party in ultimate peaceful settlement of the Palestine question, *the GAA contains no clause authorizing Syrian authorities to consider any particular area in Lake Tiberias as Syrian waters.* The eastern part of Lake Tiberias and a ten-meter strip of land on the northeast shore are in the Israel-controlled defensive area.

The Armistice demarcation line follows the international boundary between Syria and Palestine, and orders to fire at Israel military boats on Lake Tiberias would be orders to contravene Article I, Paragraph 2, unless such boats are used in military operations against Syria. It would be noted, on the other hand, that the Syrian order was issued in March 1954, when so-called Israel police boats armed with machine guns and cannon were considered by the Mixed Armistice Commission to be naval craft prohibited by the GAA in the defensive area. Continued use of such boats in the vicinity of the northeastern shore of the lake may have been considered provocative or threatening after the MAC decision. However, it appears from a minute on the document transmitted by Israeli authorities that this March 1954 order was still valid in June 1955 and is presumably still valid, though in September 1954, Israel, by my request, agreed to modify the craft it was using as police boats. Shooting at such police boats because they are closer than 250 meters from the shore is a violation of the Armistice Agreement.

The second document contains instructions given by the Syrian commander of the southwestern front in connection with fishing season 1955–1956. According to the instructions dated November 8, 1955, which refer to a letter of the Senior Syrian Delegate dated November 2, fishing by Syrians shall be prohibited until new orders are received.

The Syrian commanders of the southern and middle sectors were to convey this order to the Syrian fishermen of the Betiha and El Koursi regions. Israel fishermen were not to be prevented from fishing unless they came nearer than 250 meters from shore.

Other documents contain instructions for the defense of the Douga post against an Israel attack. Such instructions are for any army a matter of routine. My attention, however, has been drawn to the position of a bazooka "in front of the Syrian post at 6 meters from the shore," that is, in the 10-meter strip on the Israel side of the Armistice line. The Syrian cadet who was interrogated at Acre stated that, owing to the terrain, he had to emplace his bazooka farther than 6 meters from the shore. However, the order to emplace a bazooka in the 10-meter strip contravened the Armistice Agreement."

The Security Council debate on the Israeli retaliatory action lasted five weeks. On January 10, 1956, the Soviet delegate, Arkady Sobolev, introduced a strongly worded draft resolution condemning Israel; it ignored completely the Syrian attacks as well as the incriminating documents reported by General Burns. The proposal included a threat of sanctions against Israel as well as the obligation of Israel to pay compensation to the Syrians. This draft proposal found practically no supporters in the Security Council. Neither was a less severe motion by Yugoslavia found acceptable; it was not even put to a vote.

In the end an American compromise resolution was passed unanimously. It condemned "the attack of November 11 as a flagrant violation of the cease-fire provisions, of the terms of the General Armistice Agreement between Israel and Syria, and of Israel's obligation under the Charter," and expressed the Council's "grave concern at the failure of the Israeli Government to comply with its obligations." Unlike the Soviet proposal, however, it noted in a preamble that "according to the reports of the Chief of Staff, there has been interference by the Syrian authorities with Israeli activities on Lake Kinneret in contravention of the terms of the General Armistice Agreement between Israel and Syria."

After "calling upon the Israeli Government to take effective measures" to uphold the provisions of the cease-fire, the Armistice Agreement, and its obligations under the Charter, the resolution "calls on both parties to comply with their obligations under Article V of the General Armistice Agreement to respect the armistice demarcation line and the demilitarized zone," and "calls on both parties to cooperate with General Burns in this and in all other respects to carry out provisions of the Armistice Agreement in good faith and in particular to make full use of the Mixed Armistice Commission's machinery in the interpretation and application of its provisions."

A few days after the passage of the Security Council resolution, Moshe Sneh (Communist Party) asked for a vote of no-confidence in the Prime Minister and Minister of Defense. In defending the motion he said, among other things: "Ben-Gurion may be implementing American policy, but Israel lies in Asia and we must not overlook what is happening here. On this continent a revolutionary liberation movement directed against colonialism and against military juntas is now under way. Ben-Gurion is of the belief that he can be a bulwark against this rising tide. The imperialists first impel him to certain actions and then abandon him; therefore the Knesset must remove Ben-Gurion from power."

Sneh was answered by Finance Minister Eshkol, who explained that the Prime Minister was engaged in conferring with Dag Hammarskjöld, who had come to Jerusalem and Cairo in connection with the demilitarized zone on the Negev border and Sinai.

Eshkol pointed out that two or three weeks earlier the Knesset had held exhaustive debates on this issue that had ended with a vote of confidence for the Prime Minister and the entire Cabinet.

Not one Knesset bloc, even in the Opposition, could be found to support Sneh's proposal and it was voted down, seventy-six to four.

The Prime Minister Surveys the New Political and Security Situation and Praises Israeli Fighting Men.

The Knesset debate mentioned by Eshkol in replying to Sneh had taken place from January 2–9, 1956. The following members participated: The Prime Minister and Minister of Defense, the Minister of Foreign Affairs, Menahem Begin, Peretz Bernstein, Yitzhak Raphael, Yigal Allon, Meir Argov, Yacov Hazan, Shmuel Mikunis, Ishar Harari, Benjamin Mintz, Herzl Berger, Mordekhai Nurock, Z. Ben-Yacov, Elimeleh Rimalt, Berl Locker, Shlomo Hillel, Ehud Avriel, Chaim Landau, David Hacohen, Yacov Greenberg, Avraham Herzfeld, and Yitzhak Ben-Aharon. The Minister of Foreign Affairs replied. On the conclusion of the debate, the Communist members called for a vote of no-confidence, which was defeated, seventy-nine to six with eight abstentions.

At the start of the debate on January 2 the Prime Minister and Minister of Defense recalled something he had said in the Knesset seven years earlier, on January 12, 1949, five days after the end of the War of Independence:

> Let us not be intoxicated with victory. To many people and not only among ourselves, it would appear to be a miracle: a small nation of 700,000 persons (at the outset of the campaign there were only 640,000) stood up against 6 nations numbering 30 million. However, none of us knows whether the trial by bloodshed has yet ended. The enemy forces in the neighboring countries and in the world at large have not yet despaired of their scheme to annihilate Israel in its own land or at least to pare away its borders, and we do not yet know whether the recent war, which we fought in the Negev and which ended in victory for the IDF, is the last battle or not, and as long as we cannot be confident that we have won the last battle, let us not glory.

Seven years have passed since then, he said, and we have stood the test of all the great and growing efforts involved in building and defending the State. Fifteen times more people had returned to the country than in the days of Zerubavel, Ezra, and Nehemiah. We were faced with enormous difficulties in absorbing immigrants bereft of everything, remnants of the Nazi slaughter in Europe and refugees from the Arab countries. In this short period we had to rebuild the ruins of the country and to rectify the misdeeds of conquerors and foreign rulers from the days of Rome down through the British Mandate.

Our aim was peace. We did not bear enmity against the aggressors and invaders and we were prepared to enter into an alliance of peace with our neighbors and to co-operate with them to make the Middle East blossom and to strengthen the cause of peace in the world. However, peace requires goodwill on both sides. For war it was enough to have goodwill on one side only.

At the conclusion of hostilities Armistice Agreements were signed with Egypt,

Jordan, Lebanon, and Syria. But these agreements, too, have been broken by our neighbors with the exception, perhaps, of Lebanon, which carried out its obligations more or less, sometimes more and sometimes less.

Like the truces that preceded them, the Armistice Agreements were intended as a step toward lasting peace. The first paragraph of the four Armistice Agreements begins with the words: "With a view to promoting the return of permanent peace in Palestine, the following principles are hereby affirmed." And in the first and second Articles these principles are formulated as follows:

> No aggressive action by the armed forces—land, sea, or air—of either party shall be undertaken, planned, or threatened against the people or the armed forces of the other. No element of the land, sea, or air military or paramilitary forces of either party, including nonregular forces, shall commit any warlike or hostile act against the military or paramilitary forces of the other party, or against civilians in territory under the control of that party; or shall advance beyond or pass over for any purpose whatsoever the Armistice Demarcation Line set forth in Article VI of the Agreement, and elsewhere shall not violate the international frontier. After this Agreement has been in effect for one year from the date of its signing, either of the parties may call upon the Secretary General of the United Nations to convoke a conference of representatives of the two parties for the purpose of reviewing, revising, or suspending any of the provisions of this Agreement other than Articles I and II. Participation in such conference shall be obligatory upon the Parties.

These Articles are included in all four Agreements. In addition, each Agreement contains further clauses applying particularly to the relations with Egypt, with Jordan, with Syria, or with Lebanon.

The first state to violate the Armistice Agreements was the Hashemite Kingdom of Jordan, as it is officially termed in the Agreement. Article VIII of the Agreement with this State stipulates:

> 1. A Special Committee composed of two representatives of each party designated by the respective governments shall be established for the purpose of formulating agreed plans and arrangements designed to enlarge the scope of this agreement and to effect improvements in its application.
>
> 2. The Special Committee shall be organized immediately following the coming into effect of this agreement and shall direct its attention to the formulation of agreed plans and arrangements for such matters as either party may submit to it, which, in any case, shall include the following, on which agreement in principle already exists: free movement of traffic on vital roads, including the Bethlehem and Latrun-Jerusalem roads; resumption of the normal functioning of the cultural and humanitarian institutions on Mount Scopus and free access thereto; free access to the Holy Places and cultural institutions and use of the cemetery on the Mount of Olives; resumption of operation of the Latrun pumping station; provision of electricity for the Old City [which we were willing to supply but which the Jordanian government refused to accept]; and resumption of operation of the railroad to Jerusalem.

The Jordanian government refused to comply with Article VIII, refused to set up a Special Committee, and up to the Six Day War of 1967 interfered with freedom of movement on the Latrun-Jerusalem road, blocked free access to the Holy Places and the cultural institutions, prevented use of the cemetery on the Mount of Olives, and did not permit resumption of the work on the pumping station at Latrun, which it destroyed in violation of the truce as early as the middle of 1948.

But the Jordanian government was not alone in violating the terms of the Armistice Agreement. In contempt of the principles of the UN Charter, all four of our neighbors organized a boycott of Israel and blockaded her since the end of the fighting in January 1949. In violation of international law, of the Armistice Agreements, and of a Security Council resolution, Egypt closed the Gulf of Suez and later also the Red Sea Straits to Israeli shipping. We took our complaints to the Security Council, which on September 1, 1951, adopted a resolution expressly reaffirming our full right to freedom of navigation in the Suez Canal. Egypt ignored this resolution. A case in point was that of our ship *Bat Galim*, seized first on the false excuse that it had opened fire on the Egyptian Coast Guard; then, when this charge was proved baseless, Egypt persisted in its disobedience, and the Security Council resolution remained a dead letter.

Not contenting themselves, however, with violations of the principles of the UN Charter and the rights guaranteed to us in the Armistice Agreement, our neighbors organized guerrilla warfare against the citizens of Israel. Here, too, Jordan took the first step. Gangs of saboteurs and murderers used to cross the border and lay ambushes for any Israeli citizen who crossed their path. Such incidents took place as early as the first year after the conclusion of the Armistice Agreement, but increased especially from 1951 forward.

In 1951, 137 Israeli citizens were killed or wounded by these terror gangs. In 1952 casualties rose to 147, and of these Jordan alone was responsible for 114. In 1953 Egypt began to compete with Jordan in acts of murder and the casualty figure rose to 180. Of these Jordanians took the credit for 117 and Egypt for 50. (In the previous year there were only 26 casualties caused by Egypt.) In 1955 Egypt took the lead. Of the 258 Israeli casualties by the murder bands, only 37 were due to attacks by Jordanians and 192 were inflicted by Egyptian gangs especially organized by the Egyptian dictator under the name of "Fedayeen." At the beginning their function was to fight the British at the time of the Suez Canal dispute; when that conflict was over, the marauding bands were transferred to the Gaza Strip. According to the Egyptian dictator's own admission, as well as reliable information from the ambassadors of countries friendly to Israel, the Fedayeen were sent also to Jordan and Lebanon, whence they infiltrated into Israel, though the authorities of these two countries did not view this operation with favor. The Egyptians also became expert in mining Israel's lines of communication, as a result of which in 1955 alone 49 disasters occurred.

In the past five years regular and irregular military forces have caused us 844 casualties, 258 of which took place in the last year (1955) alone. This guerrilla warfare did not attract sufficient world public attention for a simple reason. The murders and minings were not carried out en masse and at the same time. The killing of Israeli citizens two or three times a week was not sufficiently sensational for the world press and did not make the headlines.

Egyptian representatives to the UN General Assembly and the Security Council (Mahmoud Fawzi on June 16, 1951, Abdel Hamid Galeb on February 16, 1954, and Asmi Bey on March 14, 1954) expressly declared that Egypt continued to maintain the state of war with Israel and for that reason Egypt would not comply with Security Council resolutions or decisions by United Nations Observers.

Nor was Syria idle. In May 1951 a Syrian Army unit crossed the border to the north of Lake Kinneret and attempted to occupy Israeli territory at Tel Mutilah. In the ensuing battle with the Israel Defense Forces, forty Israeli soldiers were killed. The Syrian unit, of course, suffered greater losses and was forced to withdraw to its own territory. One might also recall the premeditated attack against the northern shore of Lake Kinneret, all of which, including ten meters of shore on the Syrian side, was sovereign Israeli territory.

More than three years ago a military coup took place in Egypt. A group of officers under the leadership of Mohammed Naguib deposed King Farouk and assumed power. At that time the Prime Minister had declared (August 18, 1952):

> The tensions and conflicts inside the UN deprive the community of nations of the ability and authority to decree peace; and the situation in the different countries of the Middle East foreshadows, not stability, quiet development, and projects of peace, but the opposites. Apart from two stable and strong countries in the Middle East—Israel and Turkey—all Near Eastern countries are immersed in a whirlpool of disturbances, revolts, political chaos, political assassinations, deposition of monarchs, and constant contests for power between adventurers and dictators.
>
> It is possible that these stormy developments may also contain some positive trends for recovery and progress. Wherever such trends exist, we view them with favor. No doubt some of the events in Egypt in recent weeks in connection with the seizure of power by Mohammed Naguib may be welcomed. We can accept the testimony of Mohammed Naguib, the head of the military revolution, who declared that he and many of his colleagues in the Army had been opposed to the invasion of our country, and that the man chiefly responsible for the war against us was the deposed King Farouk.
>
> The reasons for Naguib's opposition to the invasion may have been merely military, but there is no doubt that there was not then, nor is there now, any ground for a quarrel between Egypt and Israel. A vast expanse of desert stretches between the two countries and leaves no cause for frontier conflicts. There never was nor is there now any reason for political, economic, or territorial conflict between the two neighbors.
>
> The State of Israel wishes to see a free, independent, and progressive Egypt. We bear Egypt no enmity for what she did to our forefathers in the days of the Pharaohs, nor even for what she did to us four years ago. We have proved our good-will toward Egypt—in spite of the foolish conduct of the Farouk government toward us—throughout the months when Egypt was involved in a serious conflict with a great world power. It never occurred to us to exploit Egypt's difficulty in order to attack her or take revenge upon her, as she did to us when our State was established.
>
> Yet we cannot ignore the fact that even this Egypt does not show any signs of goodwill to make up for the grievous offenses of the deposed King Farouk, and none of us can tell with certainty what Egypt is aiming at: peace or war.

The Egyptian dictator published a booklet called "The Philosophy of the Revolution." It is not my concern to discuss the nature of the revolution and of the philosophy in this booklet, but the author frankly tells of three ambitions that guide his policy: (1) to stand at the head of the Arab peoples; (2) to be the leader of the Islamic nations; and (3) to be the spokesman for the African continent. In order to achieve hegemony over the Arab peoples the rulers of Egypt apparently concluded that the easiest and cheapest means would be an attack on Israel. The Fedayeen gangs that had initially been organized to fight the British in the Suez Canal were sent into the Gaza Strip and penetrated with their acts of murder as far as the approaches to Tel Aviv in the vicinity of Nes Tziona; eventually they were even sent to Jordan and Lebanon to strike at our frontier settlements in the east, the north, and the west. Recently Egyptian units were sent to seize Israel territory at Nitzana, and Egypt's new ally, Syria, tried to do the same at the northern part of Lake Kinneret.

In view of these grave assaults, the new Cabinet upon being presented to the Knesset on November 2, 1955, declared: "The Government of Israel is prepared, as in the past, to observe the Armistice Agreements faithfully, but this obligation is equally binding on the other side. An agreement that the other side violates will not be binding on us either. If our rights are violated by acts of violence on land or on sea, we shall reserve our freedom of action to defend them in the most effective manner."

The situation of the State of Israel is unique. It is doubtful whether there is another state in the world which, like Israel, is subject even in normal times to constant danger to its security. This uniqueness is what has made it difficult for Israel's friends—and they are many among the world's freedom- and peace-loving nations, large and small—to understand our peculiar situation and the methods of self-defense forced upon us by the attacks of our neighbors. Condemnation by UN observers of these acts of sabotage and murder—more than that they could not do—did not detract one iota from the gravity of the situation. We had to declare before the whole world that the blood of Israeli citizens was no less precious than the blood of the citizens of Britain, the Soviet Union, or any other country. No British, Soviet, or American government would tolerate the planned and continuous killing of its citizens by gangs organized by a neighboring government for purposes of sabotage, murder, and frontier violation.

It is the duty and the right of the State of Israel to defend the lives of its citizens and its territorial integrity like any other free and sovereign state. It must and will do so with every means at its command for as long as necessary. In so doing, the State of Israel would not strike, like its neighbors, at civilians, but would maintain active and energetic self-defense only against regular or irregular enemy forces assigned to acts of sabotage and murder within its territory—as stated by the Government of Israel upon being presented in the Knesset; and this declaration was approved by the representatives of the people of Israel.

The guerrilla warfare of our neighbors has been an organic part of their systematic and ceaseless acts of hostility aimed at undermining and destroying Israel's existence without risking a frontal attack for fear of the IDF. Indeed, there is no doubt that the Israel Defense Forces was and remains the most efficient army in the Middle East in organization, training, devotion, and morale. Although the morale of an army is an inestimably precious asset, and many years will pass before the armies of our neighbors can be compared with ours in this respect, no army can fight with its bare hands. As in agriculture and industry, the importance of machines, tools, and instruments, which are being perfected from year to year, is steadily growing. Armaments in our day are no longer the primitive weapons handled by armies in days of old, or even the weapons used by armies in the nineteenth century or the First World War. The weapons of today—heavy self-propelled equipment, armor, and tanks, and above all enormous progress in the perfection of aerial weapons, fighter planes, bombers, and guided missiles—have given military equipment a determining and decisive value such as it never had in former times.

Throughout the years since the end of the fighting all the Arab armies, and even Egypt alone, have enjoyed a quantitative superiority in armaments in all services—on land, at sea, and in the air—even apart from their huge quantitative advantage in manpower. In the number of cannon, tanks, aircraft, and ships we have never equaled our neighbors, all of them together or Egypt alone. But aside from naval armament, where Egypt also has a qualitative superiority, our armament has not until recently been inferior in quality to that of the Arab armies; and we have been able to rely confidently on the moral and spiritual superiority of the Israel men and fighters, though they are incomparably inferior in numbers and their weapons were fewer than those of their enemies.

Various moral exhortations had been directed against the IDF Command, asserting that the Army has no right to act on its own initiative, being merely an executive arm of the State and subject to the orders of the Government, which can give it orders to act in certain cases. However, the IDF and its commanders have no need for such exhortations. Given orally or in writing by people not familiar with the situation, they are liable to present the Army in a false and misleading light.

Since its foundation the IDF has had four commanders in chiefs—Yacov Dori, Yigael Yadin, Mordekhai Makleff, and Moshe Dayan. Each differed from the other in various personal qualities and characteristics, yet all four were identical in two respects: in boundless devotion to their difficult task and their responsible mission to the Army, and in their absolute loyalty to the competent authorities of the State. The same may be said of all the higher officers in the Army. To a large extent the Israeli Army is the creation of the underground Hagana, though the volunteers who served in the British Army during the Second World War had a large share in its formation and training. An underground organization must of necessity operate on its own initiative to a large extent, and upon the transformation of the Hagana into a regular army at the start of the War of Independence, there was considerable difficulty in enforcing the supreme and sole authority of the State over the Army. The IDF was, in fact, organized properly only after the adoption of the National Service Law at the end of 1949, and I do not know any army in the world more loyal to the supreme authority of the State and its democratically elected representatives than the Israel Defense Forces.

Even the rulers of Egypt have admitted that throughout these years the Israel Defense Army was superior in quality to the armies of Egypt. On the other hand, the Arab rulers, including the rulers of Egypt, never concealed the fact that their aim was war with Israel, once their strength increased and it was within their power to overrun and destroy us.

The Czechoslovak weapons deal with Egypt in 1955 transformed the situation in the Middle East in the gravest and most dangerous manner. The character and political objective of this deal, at first disguised as an innocent commercial transaction, was clarified explicitly and unreservedly in a speech by Nikita Khrushchev, Secretary of the Communist Party of the Soviet Union, at a meeting of the Supreme Soviet in Moscow. My duty was to draw the attention of the Knesset and the people of Israel—and as far as possible decent public opinion in the world (and there *is* such a public opinion)—to the terrible danger and the pernicious objective of the flow of Soviet arms to the military junta in Egypt, constantly augmented by a flow of British arms as well. No man in his senses believed that Nasser and his associates might use the Soviet arms for a war against the West or the British arms for a war against the East.

On June 4, 1955, Radio Cairo, which was at the beck and call of the Egyptian ruler, declared: "The Egyptian revolution was born on the soil of Palestine. Egypt is able to join battle in accordance with the will of the Arabs, to carry out its mission to the end and to vanquish the enemy. Egypt has established a strong army, at the back of which there are 22 million citizens, for the purpose of restoring Palestine and rooting out criminal Zionism. In the second round the Arabs will be able to avenge their honor, to restore their country, and to purge Palestine."

Three days later the same Radio Cairo declared that "the leaders of the Arab States are bound to know that if they do not fight Israel, Israel will fight them, and if they do not put an end to Israel, Israel will put an end to them. We must be in a state of war with Israel, and this requires us to mobilize all the resources of the Arabs for Israel's final liquidation."

On October 16, 1955, Nasser himself told an editor of the *New York Post* that he was "not fighting Israel alone but international Jewry and the wealth of the Jews." The tone of his statement was reminiscent of Hitler's *Mein Kampf*. Abdullah Taeema, secretary of the "Freedom Movement" founded by Nasser and his colleagues as the government party in the coming elections, made the following declaration to a delegation of El Azhar teachers in Cairo: "We are today involved in a military conflict with an enemy. Israel and Zionism are an enemy; they are the first enemy that has to be liquidated."

We could have adopted an attitude of scorn and contempt for such boastful and threatening words, just as we did to the tale the Egyptian dictator invented about the two hundred Jewish dead in the Nitzana battle. But the flow of Czech and British arms to Egypt lent these threats a dangerous and tangible reality, which we would have been grievously at fault to ignore. What we demanded, and had a right to receive, were defensive arms not inferior in quality to the aggressive arms pouring into Egypt. Even more than we had to direct our demands at that fateful juncture to the outside world, we had to address them to *ourselves*. Despite the seriousness of the hour, there was no need to encourage fear and spread panic. We had to be prepared *at home*. We had to establish within our midst a regime of mass voluntary effort.

In the War of Independence we mobilized 18 percent of the entire population. This was perhaps the highest mobilization percentage in any country in recent times. The preparedness of our people reached its peak at the time, and it was natural that the tension could not be maintained after the war. It slackened and gave way to relaxation. The great pioneering effort glowing on our horizon was that of the younger generation of the old established settlements, volunteering to serve in the new immigrants' villages, from 1954 on. This movement had an almost revolutionary educational effect. Since the establishment of the State, 382 new agricultural settlements had been founded, 63 by veteran inhabitants of the country and the remaining 319 (83.5 percent) by new immigrants. Before they came here these immigrants had received no pioneering training, and many of them not even a general and Jewish education. On the day of reckoning the strength of these settlements might be just as important as that of the Army.

The immigrants, even those who came from backward and impoverished countries, proved their ability in work, in building farms, and settling in the desert, and there was no doubt that they would show the same vitality in self-defense. In 1955 they began to build up the hitherto empty and desolate Lahish area as a bridge to the Negev. We had to give them, as a matter of Jewish and human brotherhood, all assistance and guidance. In every immigrant settlement we had to provide a permanent team—capable teachers and instructors, a doctor and a nurse—to accelerate to the maximum the process of integration of exiles and to bridge the cultural and material gap between the established community and the new immigrants.

In recent months we witnessed a spontaneous awakening of volunteering for the Defense Fund. Leadership of this work was taken over by the first two Chiefs of the IDF, Generals Dori and Yadin. Impressive results were achieved, and the moral value of the voluntary movement was worth more than its weight in gold. The large-scale popular voluntary effort was necessary to overcome the ill effects of the laxity in the postwar period.

We could not allow ourselves to raise the living standards of those wage–earners and self-employed persons who had attained a minimum subsistence without hardship. More than ever we had to strive for the recovery of the economy and for financial stability. Above all we had to increase our productivity and make the economy more efficient, to reduce prices and make our products competitive on the world market. In order to stand fast in the hour of reckoning we had at the same time to increase both our military potential and our moral and economic strength. This was the triple-stranded cord that must not be torn asunder. Our duty in that fateful hour was summed up in one verse by the sweet singer of Israel: "The Lord will give strength unto His people, the Lord will bless His people with peace." If, by the efforts of the State and the people, we could raise Israel's strength morally, militarily, and economically, we would guarantee peace for the nation as well. All our efforts therefore had to be devoted to ensuring these two things: strength and peace.

Consequences of the Czech Arms Deal ★ Foreign Minister Reviews Political Situation ★ Israel Seeks Arms To Restore Balance

Our security situation after the Czech arms deal, clearly instigated by the Soviet Union, deteriorated still further because of harsh attacks in the Soviet press. This was the main theme of the Knesset speech on January 2, 1956, by Foreign Minister Sharett, who said in part:

I attach particular importance to my meeting with the Foreign Minister of the Soviet Union. We regard that country as principally responsible for the crisis that had arisen. We had, of course, a serious accusation to make against the British government, which had sold to Egypt arms of a kind it had refused to sell to us and had thereby upset, to our detriment, the military balance between us and Egypt even before the Czechoslovak deal. But the Czech deal, which we had every reason to suppose was based on policy laid down in Moscow, gave Egypt, a country threatening aggression, an overwhelming military superiority over an Israel called upon to defend herself. It confronted us with a danger such as had not menaced Israel since the end of the War of Independence.

At a time when we thought that serious discussions between Israel and the Soviet Union, undertaken in Jerusalem and Moscow and continued in Geneva, had not yet ended, an event took place that imposed an additional heavy strain on our relations with the Soviet government. A few days ago we heard from the exalted rostrum of the Supreme Soviet a definition of the policy of Israel such as had never before been uttered by the official spokesman of any state maintaining normal relations with us. This is what was said, according to the officially published text: "Worthy of condemnation are the actions of the State of Israel, which from the first days of its existence began to threaten its neighbors and to pursue a hostile policy toward them." Evidently there are persons and political parties in whose hands undisputed historical facts are like clay in the potter's hand, given certain forms and discarding them according to the needs of the hour.

This Soviet declaration about the supposedly menacing attitude of Israel toward her neighbors aroused not only deep regret, grievous offense, and bitter ridicule among the people of Israel, but amazement and revulsion in the hearts of lovers of truth throughout the world. The world well remembers what happened in the first days of Israel's existence and it knows what has happened from that day to this. It remembers, too, what distinguished representatives of the Soviet Union said in those fateful days when they spoke in the hearing of all in the highest international forum.

Here, for instance, is what a delegate of the Ukraine, Tarasenko, said in the Security Council on May 15, 1948, the day on which the regular armies of the Arab states invaded our country: "What does the Government of Egypt consider to be its objective in invading Palestine? At the end of its declaration Egypt asserted that her intervention has no other object in view than the restoration of security and order to Palestine. It is known, however, that according to the rules of the international community, each government has the right to restore order only in its own country."

And here is Mr. Tarasenko again, two days later, that is, on May 20, 1948: "We are concerned with the plain fact that a number of Palestine's neighbor states have sent their troops into Palestine. Our knowledge of that fact is based not on rumors or newspaper reports, but on official documents signed by the governments of those states informing the Security Council that their troops have entered Palestine. I refer, in particular, to the documents signed and sent by the governments of Egypt and Jordan." And further on, in the same speech: "There is the State of Israel. The existence of that State is now a reality. . . . Eight governments have already recognized it. This new State has its own armed forces. It has decided to defend its territory. In view of these facts, can there be any doubt that a threat to peace exists in Palestine? . . . I should like to point out in passing that none of the states whose troops have entered Palestine forms part of its territory. It is an altogether separate territory without any relationship to the territories of the states that have sent their troops into Palestine."

And on the following day, Andrei Gromyko declared: "The USSR delegation cannot but express surprise at the position adopted by the Arab states in the Palestine question, and particularly at the fact that those states have resorted to such action as sending their troops into Palestine and carrying out military operations aimed at the suppression of the national liberation movement in Palestine."

And here is Mr. Tarasenko speaking a week later, on May 28: "I would point out, in the first place, that we do not know of a single case of the invasion of the territory of another state by the armed forces of Israel except in self-defense, where they had to beat off attacks by the armed forces of other states on Israel territory. That was self-defense in the full sense of the word. Secondly, can the entry of a certain number of Jewish immigrants appreciably affect the balance of forces when the surrounding Arab countries, which had declared war on the State of Israel, have a population numbering tens of millions?"

I shall skip several of the sessions of the Security Council and come to Mr. Gromyko's appearance at its meeting of July 14, 1948. These are significant words, which have a direct bearing on the question of the "threat": "The Arab states have no reason to consider the creation of an independent Jewish State in Palestine a threat to themselves. Seven hundred thousand or one million Jews cannot represent any danger to 26 million Arabs. A Jewish State cannot be a threat to the Arab east."

A month later, at the meeting on August 18, Yakov Malik, the Soviet Delegate, declared: "It is now an obvious and undeniable fact that the failure to solve the problem of Jewish displaced persons in Europe and the development of the new problem of Arab refugees in the Near East result from the sabotage of the General Assembly resolution on Palestine. Those who have contributed to that sabotage are directly responsible for the suffering of these people."

At the meeting on December 2, 1948, Mr. Malik said, referring to Israel: "This state has already shown that it fulfills the conditions laid down in Article IV of the Charter. Ever since its birth this State declared that it wished to live in peace and entertain peaceful relations with all its neighbors and with all the nations of the world. It is not to blame for the fact that this appeal did not meet with any response from its neighbors." And on the 17th of the same month, Malik said: "Sir Alexander Cadogan's attempt to cast doubt on the peace-loving character of the State of Israel, and at the same time to present Trans-Jordan as a model peace-loving state, speaks for itself and needs no comment. It is clear to all that it was foreign aggression that forced the State of Israel to concentrate its whole strength and attention on self-defense."

These are admissions by the Soviet Union, and their significance lies in the fact that they were actually made in those days—the first days and weeks and months of the existence of Israel—while last Thursday's speaker in Moscow completely ignored the evidence. Who in the Middle East at that time threatened whom, and who threatens whom today? Who is hostile to whom, whose hand is stretched out in peace, in whose heart are there thoughts of war? These are basic axioms of contemporary history that require no proof.

The same degree of falsehood revealed in the attempt to make history fit the needs of the hour was revealed also in the attempt to define Israel as a State exploited by "imperialist powers" to serve as "an instrument against the Arab peoples." Here we find them refurbishing the stale discredited Communist slogans about Zionism and putting them into circulation in the new Soviet market in the Middle East.

With what degree of elasticity it is possible to handle historical events can be seen in the fact that about the same Arabs, and in particular the Arabs of Trans-Jordan, with whose struggle "for complete liberation from foreign dependence" such unreserved sympathy was expressed last Thursday, the Soviet delegate in the Security Council said in July 1948 that they "were in fact playing into the hands of those who hoped to exploit for their own economic and strategic aims the situation that has arisen in the Near East owing to the Palestine question."

The distortion of Israel's position as, surrounded by enemies, she fights for life and aspires to peace; the presentation of her as a threat to her neighbors; this slander of Israel, a tower of freedom for the Jewish people, as a state which for low purposes offers itself as a tool for others—all of this intensifies our anxieties about the new Soviet policy that is expressed in the arms deal with Egypt. We shall not shrink from any attempt to bring home to the Soviet Union the truth and its responsibility, but it is well for us to see with unshaded eyes what lies in store. No distortion can disguise the plain fact of Arab aggression in the past and present, nor close our eyes to the danger of its intensification in the near future.

Our demand for the arms we need for self-defense—and first and foremost to make others think twice before attacking us—grows more urgent with every passing day. It was the central subject in our talks with the representatives of the Western Powers. The British government, which gave Egypt preferential treatment as against us in arms and air forces even before the Czech deal, has not seen fit to correct the balance since that deal. There is some prospect of a response on the part of certain nations in Western Europe, but it must be remembered that they are subject in certain respects to the discipline of NATO, or regard themselves as obliged in general to harmonize their arms-supply policy with the United States. Our main demand is consequently addressed to the American government.

I must place on record the lively awareness of our problems on the part of the American public, aroused by Israel's request for arms, and the sympathy and support evinced by large and significant groups in the United States for meeting this request and for granting Israel a security guarantee.

Along with the increase in our military preparedness, we shall continue to work for peace. But we shall not buy peace at the price of concessions that sap our ability to live and encourage further encroachments and schemes to destroy us. We consider ourselves bound to say again in all clarity that Israel is not prepared under any circumstances to make one-sided territorial concessions of any kind, nor to return and resettle refugees. We have no reason today to fear that the United States will demand that we give up Eilat or our uninterrupted territorial access to Eilat, but the possibility still exists that we may be asked to make other territorial concessions. We are determined to reject them.

The country that laid it down that negotiations for the relaxation of international tension must be conducted from a position of strength (since otherwise it would be bound to end in failure and further retreat) cannot, without involving itself in self-contradiction, deny our right to an increase in strength, primarily for defense against aggression, but also to pave the way for the possibility of effective negotiation. I would like to add that authority can be found in the Book of Psalms for the principle of negotiations from a position of strength—the Prime Minister has quoted chapter and verse.

Until peace comes, and for the sake of peace itself, preparedness for defensive war is the supreme duty. At this hour, too, it behooves us to strengthen every bond that binds us to countries that cherish friendship for us, and to strive without pause to forge new bonds—in Europe, in Asia, in America, and in all other parts of the world.

The Knesset debate on the ominous political situation and the Government's policy lasted four days, January 2, 3, 4, and 9.

Menahem Begin indicated surprise that "the Foreign Minister used Soviet quotations to dispute with Nikita Khrushchev." The quotations would not be of much help, he said, and contributed a Soviet quotation of his own, one he had heard in a Soviet prison in the second week of June 1941: "All the accounts in the foreign press about German military concentrations on the frontiers of the Soviet Union are groundless, and their aim is provocative. While certain German forces may be marshaled in this area, it is only a natural result of the conclusion of the Cretan campaign." This was in the second week of June 1941, and we all know what happened a few days later [German invasion of the Soviet Union]. He dwelt on alleged differences between the Minister of Defense and the Foreign Minister about the Kinneret operation. Had this occurred in a normal country, one of the two would have had to resign, but in his opinion it would be better if both resigned. He strongly denounced the Government for its abstention in the UN vote on "Jordan's" application for membership. This he considered sacrilegious. In his opinion the present Government of Israel "has brought military, political, moral, and economic disasters upon us; it has led us from failure to failure and from bad to worse; it has taken the people of Israel to the brink of disaster. In saying that if we are attacked we will fight, has the Foreign Minister told us anything new? Any child in Israel could say that. The question remains: with what will we fight, how will we fight, and when will we fight?

Peretz Bernstein called upon the Government not to wait any longer but to go to war. Nevertheless he was opposed to retaliations like the Kinneret operation. "Retaliatory actions don't provide defense; they are incapable of providing defense." He was especially angry with the Prime Minister, who had chosen this time to bring the Leftist parties into the Government.

Yigal Allon denied that an armistice existed between Israel and its neighbors. Actually a state of war existed between Israel and the Arab states. In his words, "The new Soviet move is endangering Israel's welfare, pure and simple." He agreed with what the Prime Minister said about not spreading fear and panic, and noted with approval that Ben-Gurion had said a few weeks earlier that the coming summer would decide our fate, because the nation had to be told the truth.

Yacov Hazan took issue with Allon's statement that we were in a "state of war." Allon's entire speech, in effect, had been an attempt to prove that we were already at war. Hazan felt that "we are still living in peace; true, a dangerous peace, but peace nevertheless. We are still building the country. We are still establishing new settlements. We are still bringing in immigrants. Given another seven years of such a peace and we will have over 2 million Jews in the country, and hundreds of additional villages. One might ask, 'Do you believe it is still possible to save the peace?' True, this is not entirely in our hands, but something does depend on us as well." In conclusion he stated: "I must regretfully reject the statement of Nikita Khrushchev regarding the character of the State of Israel."

Mikunis (Communist): "Mr. Hazan's groundless onslaught against the statement by the First Secretary of the Soviet Communist Party, Khrushchev, and against Soviet policy in the Middle East compels me to quote a few sentences from official Mapam documents which prove that Mr. Hazan's intention in this attack has been to justify the policy of the Israeli Government. In Mapam's platform for the elections to the Second Knesset we read: 'The Ben-Gurion Government identifies itself with the capitalist bloc and its anti-Soviet intrigues in the Middle East. The government of Ben-Gurion has expanded the rift and built higher the wall between the two peoples, the Jewish nation and the Arab nation.'

"And now," Mikunis continued, "I will quote to you from the platform of one of Mapam's sister parties, Ahdut Haavodah. The platform for the Third Knesset reads, and I hope Mr. Allon is listening: 'Siding with the selfish interests of the Western powers in the international arena has resulted in worsening relations with the Soviet Union, the People's Republic of China and the other People's Democracies. By playing a part in imperialist policy, Israel has taken a stand against the freedom and independence of the awakening nations of Asia.'

"These quotations suffice to show that their platforms run counter to all their provocative statements against Khrushchev and against Soviet policy in the Middle East. The words of Khrushchev fully confirm the correctness of the view and positions of the Israel Communist Party. It has always warned the nation against a policy of dependence on the American rulers, which merely serves the enemies of peace and the peace-loving nations and which brands Israel as an aggressor throughout the world. Owing to this policy, a policy running counter to the interests of peace and of our national security, the Communist Party calls for a motion of no-confidence in the Government."

To the Foreign Minister's citations from Soviet spokesmen in 1947–48 and their current contradictory statements, Berl Locker added a quote from a Soviet delegate to the first International Workers Congress held after World War Two (London, 1945). There the Histadrut delegates called for a Jewish state in Palestine. Kuznetsov, the Soviet delegate, said that the Jewish problem could be solved in two ways: (1) by granting the Jews equal rights in every country; or (2) by giving permission and every assistance to those Jews who wished to found a state of their own. Whereupon the Congress adopted the motion of the delegation of the Confederation of Jewish Workers in the Land of Israel to the effect that the labor movement supported the Jewish people's demand for a country of its own, and in this, Locker said, we were aided considerably by the position of the Soviet delegation, no doubt guided by its government.

The debate ended on January 9. Six members voted in favor of the Communist motion of no-confidence, seventy-nine opposed it, and six abstained. Motions of Herut and the General Zionists were also rejected. Meir Argov's proposal on behalf of the coalition parties was adopted. It read: "The Knesset notes the statement by the Prime Minister and Minister of Defense and by the Foreign Minister in connection with defense and foreign policy, and refers the debate for summation to the Defense and Foreign Affairs Committee."

Our Security Position Worsens ★ The Weapons Gap Between Egypt and Israel Widens ★ Eisenhower and Ben-Gurion Exchange Notes ★ Cairo Avoids Commitments to Peace

For Israel 1956 began under a triple threat. There was the deteriorating security situation: guerrilla attacks by Jordan, Syria, and most of all Egypt; the Czech arms deal of November 1955 under which, at the behest of the Soviet Union, Egypt was being saturated with the weapons of aggression; and the falsified description of Israel policy in the Supreme Soviet, alleging that "from the very first days of its existence, Israel began to threaten its neighbors and wage hostile policy against them." This was an open contradiction not only of the facts but also of statements made by the Kremlin's own spokesmen in the UN, as quoted by the Foreign Minister in the Knesset on January 2, 1956.

Almost all the parties in the Knesset were agreed on the danger. Some, like Begin and Allon, went so far as to argue that we were already at war. And indeed it would be difficult to call the situation of Israel during its first seven years a state of peace. The Arab countries that had invaded Israel on the day our State was established refused to maintain peaceful relations as Israel had urged, and as required by the UN Charter and the Armistice Agreements. These agreements were being continuously violated; the neighboring countries sent bands of saboteurs and murderers across the border to destroy the lives and property of Israeli citizens along with Israel's territorial integrity, as Egypt did in Nitzana and Syria at the northern Kinneret. Nevertheless, the Government of Israel was able to distinguish between the absence of peace and actual war, though the difference is not very great. Actually, the offensive by Egypt, Syria, Lebanon, Jordan, and Iraq had not begun with the invasion by their regular armies on the night of May 14–15, 1948, at the end of the British Mandate. The war had broken out unofficially one day after the UN General Assembly Resolution of November 29, 1947.

It was not easy to continue for long in that limbo of no-peace. But here too Israel was unlike other states; even in the unstable condition of continuous violation of the Armistice Agreements she had to cope with the absorption of immigration and the opening up of a desolate wasteland. Despite the absence of peace in the first seven years of the State, more was accomplished in these two areas than in the seventy preceding years. Israel had no more important and precious objective than constantly to build up its strength through Aliya and construction—both material and moral. In those seven years we had also created a military force with no equal in the entire Middle East; an army that had been organized, trained, and equipped mainly in the years of no-peace.

This was not the first time in our history that we had been required to build, while one hand did the work and the other held the weapon. In the Declaration of Independence we had stated: "We appeal—in the very midst of the onslaught launched against us now for a month—to the Arab citizens of the State of Israel to preserve peace and participate in the upbuilding of the State, and we extend our hand in peace to all the neighboring states and their peoples in an offer of peace and good-neighborliness, and appeal to them to establish bonds of cooperation and mutual help with the sovereign Jewish people settled in its own land." And it should be noted that there were Arab minorities, Bedouins and Druze, not large yet not inconsequential, who had lent a hand in the defense of Israel. The ruler of Trans-Jordan had not entirely ignored Israel's call for peace, but he had been overcome by pressures from the other Arab states, especially Egypt, Iraq, and Syria.

Since that time considerable change has come about in the attitudes of our neighbors, especially Egypt. A revolt took place in that country. The corrupt royal government was overthrown and power passed to a military junta with imperialistic ambitions vis-à-vis the other Arab countries, which felt that the elimination of Israel was the easiest way to gain the Arab hegemony it sought. Egypt then had a population of 22 million, almost fifteen times the Jewish population of Israel (1,526,000). She was receiving arms from two Great Powers, the Soviet Union and Britain, to both of whom it was obvious that the weapons could be intended only for use against Israel.

Blessed with an abundance of land and water, Egypt had been the earliest center of culture and civilization in the Mediterranean area. Yet now it was one of the poorest of nations. Few peoples in the world were so afflicted with all kinds of diseases and so sunk in ignorance and poverty. At first it looked as if the country's new rulers had the welfare of the people at heart and intended to improve the lot of the urban and rural laborer. In fact, a beginning was made in this direction. But such an undertaking is not easy; it demands a prolonged effort, perhaps over generations. It would seem that the military man in the saddle, growing impatient, decided to realize Egyptian imperialist ambitions in a shorter and easier way, by war against Israel.

For two years the Egyptian forays over the border have been numerous. No less grave was the blocking by Egypt of Israel's routes to Asia and East Africa, both through the Suez Canal and the Straits of Eilat, in contempt of international law and resolutions of the UN Security Council. We did not repay Egypt in kind by attacking civilians on her side of the border, but dealt heavy blows to the staging centers of the paramilitary terrorists. Not wanting even this "small-scale" warfare, we called upon the Chief of the UN Truce Supervision Observers to go to Cairo and demand that Nasser abide by the Armistice Agreement, since Israel was willing to maintain it in every detail and to order a cease-fire, as in fact we had done. In Cairo the Chief of the TSO could not obtain the necessary undertaking from the ruling junta. Meanwhile Soviet and British arms were continuing to flow into Egypt, and Radio Cairo and Nasser himself had announced unequivocally that their aim was war against Israel. The looming danger could no longer be ignored. Egypt still needed a few months more to "digest" the new weapons. Czechoslovak specialists and instructors were hard at work in Egypt, and Egyptian officers were being sent to Czechoslovakia for training in the use of these new arms.

In Britain considerable opposition developed to Eden's policy of arming Egypt, especially in the Labor Party led by Hugh Gaitskell. The bulk of the arms, however, was coming from Czechoslovakia, and the dangerous arms gap was increasing from week to week. It was no secret that ever since the creation of our State, Arab neighbors enjoyed a quantitative preponderance in all types of weapons, over and above their manpower advantage. Egypt alone possessed more arms of all types—land, sea, and air—than we did. Nevertheless, until the Czech arms deal we had not been in real danger, for two reasons:

1. There was no qualitative preponderance. Though the Egyptians had more planes, tanks, and guns than we did, these were generally the same types that we possessed. They did have a qualitative edge in two categories: they possessed two destroyers, which we did not, and Centurion heavy tanks, which the British government had refused to sell us. All the same, until the Czech arms deal, the qualitative gap was not decisive.

2. We had supreme quality in the most important "weapon" of all—the morale of our fighting men. It was thanks to this superiority of spirit that we had achieved victory in the War of Independence, when we stood seven hundred thousand against invading armies numbering three million, with superior equipment. Nor had our human advantage declined since then. On the contrary, the Army's homogeneity, subordination to the elected authorities of the State, discipline, and level of training had improved since then. At the same time, however, the fighting capacity of the enemy was not to be scoffed at, for he too had not been marking time.

The Czech intrusion changed the state of affairs decisively. Not only was the quantity of arms flowing into Egypt now immeasurably greater, but the Soviets were supplying equipment of a quality we did not have: jet fighters, jet bombers, first-line tanks, and (so it was said) submarines as well.

The IDF could hold off its enemies with fewer arms and men, provided its weapons were not inferior. Egypt and the other Arab states appreciated this strength of the IDF. Without a quantitative and qualitative advantage they would not dare to attack us. Hence our most pressing problem was the acquisition of arms not inferior to those of the Arab states. Even our victory in the War of Independence had not been gained easily or at a low cost. Many remembered the brilliant victories, but people familiar with the events also knew of the failures and the losses. Those entrusted with Israel's security could not allow themselves for one minute to forget the serious losses: Beit Arava, Naharayim, Neveh Yacov, Atarot, Kfar Etzion, and above all the Old City of Jerusalem. Nor could they have forgotten that the war had cost us hundreds of millions of dollars and, more important, thousands of the best of our youth, the most terrible and dearest price of all. Since then the concern of those responsible for security has been primarily to obtain equipment to enhance the strength of our military forces.

It will be recalled that the first Minister of Defense retired from the Government temporarily at the end of 1953. In the fourteen months he remained at Sde Boker, until called upon to return to the ministry by the internal security situation following certain events of 1954, he had given his attention to two civilian needs of no small significance to security. (1) The strengthening of the new immigrant settlements morally and educationally by hundreds of young volunteers from the well-established settlements; they came with their families to live and work in these villages for at least two years, and with brotherly assistance and by personal example to raise the competence of new settlers and their involvement in the economy, in labor, in the Israeli way of life, and in bolstering local security. (2) Populating the empty and desolate south by regional plans like the one that had proved so successful in the Lahish area, thus building a bridge between the north and the empty Negev, which, being the greater part of the territory of the State, was both its Achilles' heel and its greatest opportunity.

Before retiring, the Prime Minister and Minister of Defense had reviewed security and military needs and submitted to the Government a plan for improving and strengthening the defense system over the following three years. The Government had adopted it unanimously. Indeed, from 1953 on many changes for the better came about in the Army's capacity, both under the second Minister of Defense and after the return of the first. The Egyptian Army, however, had also been improving, while the Czech deal created a menacing gap in arms. The people of Israel were summoned to renewed efforts, not only compulsory but freely voluntary.

Addressing a meeting of the Executive of the Histadrut and the Trade Unions in Tel Aviv on January 5, 1956, during the Knesset debate on security, the Prime Minister and Minister of Defense declared:

> In our primary concern for the immigrant settlements and for increased Aliya and its settlement in the expanses of the south and the Negev, and our obligation to prepare for the danger of war, it would be an unforgivable sin at this time for us to try to raise the standard of living of the established community concentrated in the cities and the large settlements. By doing so we would widen the dangerous gap, both material and spiritual, between the established community and the new immigrants, and thus undermine our main opportunity to populate the empty expanses and to make the wilderness bloom. For how will we be able to resist the enemy—and this time the evil will break out from the south, not the north—if the southern regions remain empty and desolate?
>
> The choice before us is between increased wages and standard of living, and Aliya and new settlement. This becomes the more serious when we take into clear consideration our vital and ever increasing defense needs. I do not know if our public properly appreciates the extent of the financial effort required at this grave juncture. Our land frontiers are 1080 kilometers long. In the War of Independence we had but few settlements along these borders. In the past seven years, fortunately, the number of border settlements has grown, and we have to safeguard and strengthen them and make them capable of withstanding the enemy on the day of trial.
>
> The question is: Shall we properly equip IDF units on land, air, and sea, fortify immigrant settlements, strengthen all the border settlements in the south, in the east, and in the north, or shall we raise the standard of living of the established community in the cities and large towns? Nor should we forget that in view of the approaching danger of war, we cannot permit ourselves to settle only for military preparedness in the narrow sense of the word. We must continue with and expand the settlement of the south and the Negev itself, for this will provide our blessing of strength for a long time to come, as well as enhancing our security in the short run.
>
> I know that I have said things that are not popular. However, all my life I have had faith in the pioneering destiny of the workers of Israel and the historic mission they have shouldered without any orders from outside, and I do not believe they will fail us at this time either. We shall arm ourselves to the full extent of our moral, economic, and military capacity, even though we reject the harmful idea that there is no escape from war. Peace is also possible, but peace is not up to us. We cannot force peace upon our neighbors. They, on the other hand, can force war on us and therefore—readiness, readiness to the highest degree of our capacity and effort is demanded of us.

The laboring public and the community as a whole did not disappoint us. A Defense Fund was organized voluntarily and many workers contributed six days' wages to the fund. Many volunteered to work in fortifying the settlements close to the border.

On January 24, 1956, the UN Secretary General, Dag Hammarskjöld, arrived in Jerusalem. It was his first visit to Israel. He came following his visit to Egypt and talks with Nasser, and remained only one day. The official communiqué issued the next day read:

> The United Nations Secretary General was received yesterday by Prime Minister David Ben-Gurion. The Foreign Minister, Moshe Sharett, was present at the meeting. The problems discussed were those connected with peace and security in the Middle East and especially matters concerning the relations between the parties signatory to the Armistice Agreements. Also considered was the complex of international problems engaging the United Nations.

At a press conference Hammarskjöld said that he had obtained from Egypt and Israel an agreement on the Nitzana question by which both sides would remove their armed forces from the area and from the defense zone on the Egyptian side of the border, and by which the international border in the Nitzana area would be marked—something the Egyptians had formerly opposed.

In conversation with the Prime Minister, Hammarskjöld related that he had spoken with Nasser about observing the armistice and the cease-fire, and that Nasser said he was interested in these things, but refrained from giving any assurances that he would maintain them. And indeed, the shooting from the Gaza Strip went on almost daily, and in the months of February and March we suffered thirty-seven casualties (thirty-one wounded and seven killed).

In April the problem grew even more acute. The Egyptian Army began to cross over the border, shelling settlements along the Gaza Strip: Kissufim, Ein Hashlosha, Nahal Oz, Nirim, and others. In that month, too, the Fedayeen stepped up their activity; hundreds of these thugs infiltrated Israeli territory to kill and to destroy. Naturally, we could not sit idle, and each bombardment was answered by one of our own. From April 1 to 19 we had eighty-two casualties among our soldiers and civilians: eighteen killed and sixty-four wounded, including the despicable murder of children in the synagogue of Shafrir. During that time our Army and police forces killed eleven Fedayeen within Israeli territory, and five were taken alive. Also captured was a wounded Egyptian pilot, shot down by our Air Force in the vicinity of Sde Boker.

On April 10 the Prime Minister received a letter from the United States President, Dwight D. Eisenhower, in which he said, inter alia:

> I realize that this is a very tense time, and additional provocative acts are possible from irregular forces. I sincerely hope that in view of the terrible tragedy that general hostile actions will undoubtedly bring to this region, you will abstain, even under the pressure of extreme provocation, from any retaliatory acts which may result in very dangerous consequences.

In his reply to the President, Ben-Gurion wrote in part:

> During the past three nights, the Egyptian authorities sent gangs of murderers from Gaza to murder innocent citizens, to destroy installations and to spread fear among peaceful villagers. United Nations observers recognized the responsibility of the Egyptian authorities.

I am certain that if the entire situation were detailed for you, you would not have restricted yourself merely to expressing hope that we would abstain from military acts. I cannot imagine that in case of continual Egyptian attacks you would assume that we would abandon our country and people to the dangers and bloody consequences of a perpetual campaign of terror by the terrorist gangs of the Egyptian government.

I am certain that no other country would surrender to such a situation without appropriate action. The Government of Israel and I are fully aware of your sincere White House declaration that the United States will oppose any attack in the region. However, I would not be candid with you nor would I be fulfilling my obligation to my people were I not to say in all friendliness that such a declaration does not relieve our grave anxiety for Israel's security.

On April 12, the Prime Minister of Israel despatched a letter with Israel's Ambassador to France, Yacov Tzur, to Guy Mollet, Prime Minister of France. It read in part:

Strengthened by modern arms, planes, bombers, and tanks, which were generously provided by the Czechs, the Egyptian ruler considers this an opportune time to open a new campaign against Israel by sending armed and trained gangs to the heart of our country. The tension is great, and one cannot ignore the Egyptian danger any longer. The only hope of salvaging the situation is for Egypt not to retain her advantage and superiority in air power and armor much longer.

I am convinced that the French Government will recognize that the balance of power, recently upset to Israel's disadvantage, must be restored at this time with utmost urgency. Israel's Ambassador to France, Yacov Tzur, who is returning from a brief home visit, will give you details regarding the dangers lurking in the current situation. I have also instructed Shimon Peres, Director-General of the Ministry of Defense, to brief you concerning the problems and urgent needs of Israel's security. At this dangerous time, the small and young Republic of Israel appeals to the older and great French Republic with the certainty of mutual understanding.

In mid-April 1956 Hammarskjöld again visited Egypt and Israel, and announced that Nasser had agreed to two points: "(1) That both sides must observe all the clauses of the Armistice Agreements in letter and in spirit. (2) That one clause in the Armistice Agreements should be singled out in particular, and its observance made obligatory for all parties, even if the other clauses were not being carried out, and that this clause must not be violated on account of the nonobservance of the other clauses of the Agreement."

The reference was to Article II, Paragraph 2. This clause states that "no element of the land, sea, or air military or paramilitary forces of either party, including nonregular forces, shall commit any warlike or hostile act against the military or paramilitary forces of the other party, or against civilians in territory under the control of that party; or shall advance beyond or pass over for any purpose whatsoever the Armistice Demarcation Line set forth in Article VI of the Agreement, and elsewhere shall not violate the international frontier." On receiving this information from Hammarskjöld, Israel agreed to the two points, naturally on conditions of mutuality.

Israel Independence Day in 1956 came on April 17. In a message to the nation the Prime Minister declared:

We do not deceive ourselves. We see with open eyes the dangers that threaten us from the constantly increasing pace at which our enemies, especially Egypt, are rearming. A heavy responsibility to the history of humanity has been assumed, not only by the powers that are supplying aggressive arms to the Egyptian dictator, but by those powers that deny defensive arms to Israel. The conscience of the great powers failed when Hitler sent 6 million of the Jews of Europe to the slaughter. Will that conscience fail again, now that the Egyptian dictator and his allies are planning to do the same thing to Israel in its own land?

No matter what the answer may be, we no longer depend merely on the mercies of the nations, although we still believe in international responsibility and the interdependence of all peoples. We place our trust and our faith in the Israel Defense Forces. Our support and our strength are the State and the people in Israel itself. The Jewish people in the Diaspora is no longer what is was before the rise of the State. Our independence in the Homeland has straightened the backs of Jews wherever they live, increased the respect in which they are held among the peoples, deepened their unity, and intensified their love and devotion to the ancient Homeland. In Israel itself our roots have struck deeper, our will has been fortified, our independence has been strengthened, our spirits have been enriched—we look forward to the future in confidence and faith, in the consciousness of our ideal; with a clear insight into all difficulties and dangers that bestrew our path, but without fear or hesitation.

In our creative efforts to integrate the immigrants and revive the wastelands; in our intensified military preparedness for the defense of the State; in sincere and active endeavors for peace in the Middle East and the whole world—let us be strong and of good courage, and we need fear no evil.

Two days later Hammarskjöld announced that he had received notice from the governments of both Israel and Egypt that instructions had been issued to comply strictly with the stipulation of Article II, Paragraph 2, of the Armistice Agreement.

Czech Authorities Release the Two Israeli Victims of the Prague Purge Trials ★ Fail to Repudiate Anti-Zionist Charges

Readers will recall how Israeli public opinion was shocked when the Foreign Minister spoke in the Knesset on November 24, 1952, of "a mockery in the guise of a trial, presented this time on the stage of a court in Czechoslovakia." Among the accused prisoners were two Israelis: Shimon Orenstein, who was sentenced to life imprisonment, and Mordekhai Oren, one of the leaders of Hashomer Hatzair (a wing of Mapam), who was sentenced to eighteen years.

A Knesset debate on the Prague trial took place on November 25, 1952. Hashomer Hatzair did not participate, and Eliezer Peri merely submitted a statement in the name of Mapam, charging that the Foreign Minister's announcement "exploits the Prague trial for anti-Communist agitation and serves the purposes of imperialism in its preparations for anti-Soviet aggression."

Mordekhai Oren had been sent by Hashomer Hatzair to a congress in East Germany. From there he left for Paris, and after a short stay informed his friends that he was going to Prague. Then all trace of him vanished. On March 23, 1952, the Israeli Foreign Ministry received this telegram from its Ambassador in Prague, Dr. Aryeh Leon Kubovy: "The Czechoslovak Deputy Foreign Minister, Vastimil Burk, has officially notified the Israeli Ambassador in Prague that Israeli citizen Mordekhai Oren is under arrest in Czechoslovakia.

The Czechoslovak authorities suspect Mr. Oren of criminal offenses against the security of the Czechoslovak state."

Years passed. In the second half of October 1954, Shimon Orenstein was suddenly released. The Attorney General of Czechoslovakia issued a short communiqué that read: "This is to announce that I no longer require the continued detention of Shimon Orenstein, and I order his immediate release. With that, I order his expulsion from Czechoslovakia. My decision is final. It shall be effective immediately and not subject to appeal." The release of Orenstein, who was serving a life sentence, while Oren, who got only eighteen years, remained in prison, caused surprise. The Government of Israel thereupon made vigorous efforts to have Oren released, demanding that the Czech authorities officially acknowledge his innocence. For a long time these efforts did not bear fruit.

On April 13, 1956, the newspaper *Davar* published the following statement from Orenstein:

> On the plane on my way back I had only one thought in mind and that was to alert the Yishuv to Mordekhai Oren. I told myself that I, who had been accused of the same crime and knew the tragedy in every detail and had spent three years in prison, had the right and duty to explain, and to summon people to his rescue.
>
> I returned to Israel and kept silent. My heart was bleeding. I could not rest, but still remained silent because I accepted the opinion of competent persons in the Government who have been working for his release that any activity outside the official framework would not only not help but would be harmful. Even now I feel that his rescue can only come through Government channels. I am certain that the day is not far off when our country will manage to persuade the Czech Government that not only the State of Israel but the Zionist movement has not engaged and is not engaging in espionage.
>
> If I have decided to publish a few words at this time, it is to warn the Mapam movement and Hashomer Hatzair not to present the case of Mordekhai Oren in the wrong light. For a year and a half I have been following their various declarations and can see in them only a deliberate distortion of the truth, out of stubborn adherence to the sacred lie that Mapam is considered a revolutionary movement by the Communist world and that only "a combination of tragic circumstances involving the internal affairs of Czechoslovakia could have implicated Oren in matters in which he had no part." (From the article by Israel Hertz in *Al Hamishmar*, April 3, 1956.)
>
> Only by maintaining this sacred lie can we come to the conclusion of Bunim Shamir in the Kibbutz Ha'artzi Council: "Comrade Oren was tried because of his connections with Titoism and now that Titoism has been rehabilitated he should be released." Or the naive questions of Comrade Israel Hertz: "Why don't they release Oren? How can the leaders of Czechoslovakia explain it? By saying that behind Mordekhai Oren is a movement and a party that play a central role in Israel in the struggle for peace and the fostering of international solidarity and sympathy for the revolutionary world?" He also complains that Oren was first invited by the Czech Government and then arrested and that this was not very hospitable of them.
>
> I will try to elucidate the entire affair briefly and clearly and perhaps this will help Oren's friends open their eyes.
>
> (A) Mordekhai Oren was not invited to Czechoslovakia. He was on his way to Zurich and Israel from East Berlin, where he attended a Trade Union Congress. At that time there was no direct air connection to Zurich, so to get there he had to go via Prague. With him was Hanan Rubin, who continued on by plane to Zurich the same day, while Oren planned to spend a few days in Prague to try to obtain newsprint for his paper, *Al Hamishmar*.
>
> (B) The Prague trial was a trial against the Zionist movement in general and the State

of Israel in particular. (If it were only an internal affair of Czechoslovakia, as claimed by *Al Hamishmar* people, why was it necessary to charge the sin of Zionism to Slansky and his friends?) The object of the trial was to prove: (1) that the Zionist movement is reactionary and throughout its existence has been serving American imperialism; (2) that since the State of Israel is headed by the leaders of the World Zionist Organization, it is led and directed by that same imperialism, the aim of which is to undermine the People's Democracies. (C) Mordekhai Oren, who for years was an emissary of the Zionist Organization in Europe, was to have proved that the Zionist movement is indeed reactionary and working for American imperialism; while Shimon Orenstein, who in 1949–1950 was employed by the Israel Legation in Prague, was supposed to prove that the State of Israel is indeed controlled by imperialism.

(D) Oren confessed that during his Zionist activity in Europe he met with various European statesmen and engaged in espionage for the Americans. His connections with statesmen from Yugoslavia merely served as additional proof that there, too, the Zionist movement helped American imperialists undermine the Communist regime and put a Titoist-fascist government in power.

(E) Orenstein [the writer of this letter] confessed that while employed in the Israeli Embassy in Prague he engaged in espionage on behalf of the Americans with the object of helping to undermine the People's Democratic regime.

(F) In reading the confessions signed by Oren, I found that at the beginning, the two of us, as members of Mapam, adopted the same line of defense. We both tried to explain that, even assuming that there were reactionary elements within the Zionist Federation (to this we both agreed because we had been educated to it for years in the [Mapam] movement), we should not be suspected of subversion against the People's Democratic regime, since our party had always cultivated international solidarity and sympathy for the revolutionary world.

This explanation aroused laughter and derision. In reply we were told: "Mapam is not only not revolutionary, it is even worse than Mapai. Also, it is more dangerous because, under the guise of Leftism, it infiltrates all sorts of international revolutionary organizations like the peace movement, the revolutionary trade unions, etc., and undermines the Communist movement. While ostensibly it appears as an opposition, in fact it is working for the reactionary Zionist movement."

The Mapam people and Hakibbutz Ha'artzi are doing a disservice by trying to put the emphasis on how revolutionary they are in order to prove Oren's innocence. If they want to help him, which I believe they do, then they must state explicitly that Oren did not establish relations with Titoism, not even with American imperialism, because he is a Zionist and was working for the Zionist movement, which is engaged in the ingathering of the exiles and in rebuilding the Jewish people in its own land and is not now nor has ever been engaged in any espionage.

Oren's release can be brought about in only one way and that is by clearing the Zionist movement of false accusations, instead of the Mapam people diverting themselves with the rehabilitation of all kinds of dead people like Reik, and trying to persuade Czechoslovak leaders that Zionism is not and has never been a reactionary movement serving imperialism. On the contrary, it is our liberation movement and as such has a right to exist just like the other liberation movements of small nations. Mapam will help in his release if, through its channels, it helps explain that this is indeed so.

And finally, an answer to the question by Israel Hertz, who states: "Along with our comrade, another Israeli citizen, Shimon Orenstein, was also arrested and convicted; he received a much heavier sentence, life imprisonment; yet Orenstein was released two years ago while Mordekhai Oren remains in prison." Let me quote, word for word, the answer given to me by the authorities at the time of my release: "Shimon Orenstein was sentenced for activity against the state while employed by the Israel Legation in Prague, where he acted under the instructions of his superiors. Orenstein has spent three years in prison, and Czechoslovakia, which has meanwhile resumed normal relations with Israel, can allow itself, as a goodwill gesture, to pardon and release him. Such is not the case with Oren. Mordekhai Oren was a politician of long standing, did not act under the instructions of his superiors, but rather, according to his confessions, did everything on his own responsibility and that of his party, and hence we see no reason to release him at this time."

Last but not least, I wish to express my public thanks to Mapam and its officials, who, as soon as my arrest became known, washed their hands of me, denied I belonged to their party, and were prepared to close the book on me. What happened to them happened to Balaam: "They wanted to curse and instead they blessed." Who knows if Oren wouldn't be better off if he were treated as his "dear comrades, Riftin and his gang" wanted.

On May 12, 1956, the Czechoslovak news agency stated officially that "the Attorney General has decided to commute the sentence of Mordekhai Oren, who will be expelled from the country immediately." On the same day the Czech Prime Minister, Viliam Siroky, announced the posthumous cancellation of all charges of Titoism against Communist Party Secretary Rudolph Slansky, who was executed after the Prague trial in 1952.

Slansky had been charged with espionage, treason, Zionism, and support of the sale of arms to Israel during the War of Independence. The Communist Foreign Minister, Clementis, who had succeeded Jan Masaryk, had been indicted on the same charges and executed. One "accusation" against Clementis was correct: he had continued the Masaryk policy before the Communist takeover of selling arms to Israel when it was under attack by Arab armies. Slansky, a virulently anti-Zionist Jew, had opposed the policy. Clementis was simply acting for his government, since aid to Israel was then Soviet policy.

At the conclusion of the trial, the Israeli envoy was recalled from Prague, and the Czechoslovak envoy recalled from Israel. In both countries only *chargés d'affaires* remained. On May 12, 1956, the Israeli Foreign Ministry announced that the Israeli *chargé d'affaires* in Prague, Shlomo Kedar, had been notified officially that the Prague authorities had waived the remainder of Mordekhai Oren's term, and that he was to leave Czechoslovakia at once. The Legation was required to arrange his transportation. The Israeli Foreign Ministry at once notified Oren's family and Hashomer Hatzair. Oren's wife immediately left by plane for Zurich, where Oren was to arrive from Prague. Yacov Hazan and Menahem Bader had also planned to leave on that plane, but since there was no room, they flew on a different plane for Rome.

Orenstein related how he had heard Oren's voice only once. In a prison near Prague, when a group of prisoners were brought in, he heard the name of Oren while the roll call was being taken. Throughout his imprisonment he had never seen Oren, though they were both in the same prison. When he was released he asked a Secret Police officer if Oren had also been freed. The officer replied, "You've just been absolved of espionage, and you're starting to spy all over again." At the trial both Orenstein and Oren confessed to the charges of treason, espionage, and everything else they were accused of, though the two men were innocent.

Oren, accompanied by the Israeli *chargé d'affaires*, reached Zurich on May 13. Reporters asked him why he had confessed to treason against Czechoslovakia and espionage for Israel. He declined to answer. It was known that the prosecution made use of Oren's testimony at the Slansky trial. He told the reporters that he had had no connection with Slansky. In recent months, he said, he had been held in a prison in Prague. Before that he had been at forced labor.

That evening Oren's wife arrived in Zurich, and the next day they left by plane for Rome. As Oren declared at a news conference, the Czech authorities had given him no explanation for his release or cleared him of the charges, but had merely commuted the remainder of his term. According to the Swiss newspaper *Neue Züriche Zeitung*, the Czech Communist Party continued to oppose the new Soviet line, yet they had been compelled to release Oren under Soviet pressure, despite the fact that at the trial, on November 20, 1952, he had "admitted" to being an agent of British Intelligence and a professional spy for "capitalist Israel."

On the eve of the festival of Shavuot, May 15, the Orens arrived at Lod Airport. They were received with shouts of joy by thousands of members of Hakibbutz Ha'arzi (the Mapam kibbutz movement), Mapam ministers, and delegations of the Histadrut. Yacov Hazan and Menahem Bader had returned with him. Shimon Orenstein was also present. After Meir Ya'ari made a welcoming speech, Oren went to the microphone, took some much-erased sheets of paper from his coat pocket, and read, in moving tones, the following speech:

> Dear Comrades, dear friends: I have literally no words that can express my feelings of joy on setting foot afresh on the soil of the Homeland after a period which seemed to me a whole lot longer than four and a half years, and on rejoining my family, my movement, and the Yishuv. I consider it a pleasant duty to express my deep thanks to all those who have worked on behalf of my release, first and foremost, the President of the State, Comrade Yitzhak Ben-Zvi; to my movement, my party, and to my wife, Rega: to many groups and individuals in Israel and in the Diaspora and in the progressive international labor movement: to Israel's diplomatic representative in Prague, Comrade Kedar, to the workers in the Foreign Ministry, and last but not least, to Minister of Foreign Affairs Moshe Sharett.
>
> On my way home, it was with great excitement that I learned of how great was the interest the Yishuv took in my fate and in my release. For imprisoned along with me in the cell was my party, its immaculate image sullied. Locked in together with me was the Zionist movement, its essential purity maliciously distorted. I was compelled to hold on so that, even while imprisoned, I might continue to fight for the justice of my cause, and to see the day of my release, which I believed would come, after which I would contribute my share to the struggle to rectify the great wrong.
>
> Despite what they did to me, and the tragic experiences I have undergone, I have kept faith with my revolutionary socialist philosophy. I have remained loyal and a partner in spirit to the labor movement and its struggle for peace, national independence, democracy, and socialism. My heart, of course, holds a vigorous protest and an absolute disavowal of the manifestations of rottenness, of which it was my lot to be one of the innocent victims. However, I have kept my faith in revolutionary socialism. I was a victim, not of the regime but of those who have defiled the movement's integrity and lowered its stature. I believe that the situation will change and that the movement will overcome the manifestations, foreign to its spirit, that distort the development of the socialism that will ultimately be victorious the world over.
>
> I have been a loyal member of Mapam, the Zionist pioneering revolutionary socialist party. I am happy that today I have been given the opportunity to return to its bosom as a loyal worker. I am happy that the day of my release has arrived. Nevertheless, the cup of good wine of freedom is not without its bitter dregs. I have not been given complete vindica-

tion. The manner of my release and the restoration of my freedom, stolen from me more than four years ago despite my innocence, by no means constitute a rectification or wipe away the blot with which the image of socialism has been stained.

Freedom has been restored to me as Prisoner No. 2321, Mordekhai Oren: but the main problem is yet unresolved. My innocence has not been acknowledged. No admission has been made of the fact that I am not a criminal but the victim of a crime that defiles its perpetrators. To this day persons have not been released who were imprisoned for their Zionism, suffered together with me, and who, though as innocent as I, are still rotting in prison. The slander and calumny against our national liberation movement and our party have not been withdrawn. Those who, through methods foreign to all humanitarian and moral principles, compelled me to confess things that have no basis in fact, have not yet admitted their crimes, and that is why my release is not complete. Hence I consider it an obligation to carry on, together with my movement, the campaign for the rehabilitation of myself and of Zionism.

I firmly believe that this campaign will be crowned with victory, for it is also in the interest of the Czechoslovak democracy, which is struggling to bring to light the pollution in its midst. This will be a campaign to clear not merely my own name. I was the person who served as an object through which the Zionist movement was smeared. Though it has been my lot to undergo four and a half years of bitter suffering, I will consider that experience a great privilege if "that which is crooked is made straight." It goes without saying that I wish to return to active service as a loyal member in the Zionist movement and the labor movement. I require no rest. I will devote my humble abilities and my great loyalty to the ideal of socialist Zionism in our land.

Oren refused to give reporters details about his imprisonment and interrogation. From Lod Airport he and members of his family were accompanied by friends to his kibbutz, Mizra. But in the dining room of the kibbutz on the eve of Shavuot, Oren recounted some of his experiences in his years of incarceration.

He had been kept in a dark cell, in solitary confinement, for five months, and was served food like a baby. During the interrogations he had been abused with insults, including anti-Semitic obscenities. In prison he had not heard that Mapam had split up, but only learned about it later from Bader. He told the members that his main ordeal had been during the months of interrogation before the trial. He had been the helpless object of interrogation methods that outraged morality and debased human dignity. Only in the last year had they allowed him to read the Moscow *Pravda* and a Czech newspaper. They had not agreed to his request, before leaving, to meet with the body affiliated with the Communist Party Central Committee that recently had been reviewing the 1952 purge trials.

At about the time of Oren's release we learned that Czech arms were flowing also into Syria: they included fighters, Stalin and T-34 tanks, armored cars, and nine hundred tons of artillery ammunition.

Section 2. Weapons Gap and Mounting War Perils

Moscow Declaration for UN Action on Mideast Peace ★ Special Defense Tax and Voluntary Fund Drive for Arms ★ Ben-Gurion Addresses the World Zionist Congress

O N April 17, 1956, the Soviet Government announced in Moscow that it would give its full support to United Nations efforts to strengthen peace in the Middle East, and was ready to assist in ending the Israel-Arab dispute. It called on all interested parties to do nothing to upset the Armistice lines between Israel and the Arab states. Moscow stressed that the situation developing in the area merited the attention of all powers concerned with peace and the relaxation of tension. Its delegation, it said, would support UN action to buttress peace in the Middle East, and believed that measures to this end be taken without interference from the outside, because that conflicted with the will of the Middle Eastern states and the principles of the United Nations.

The Soviet statement urged all the interested countries to avoid anything that unsettled the demarcation lines between Israel and the Arab states as fixed by the Armistice Agreements, and to take all necessary steps to improve the hard lot of the hundreds of thousands of Arab refugees deprived of their means of livelihood and made homeless. In the interests of international peace and security, the Soviet Union considered it necessary to work toward a stable, peaceful settlement of the Palestine question on a mutually acceptable basis, taking into consideration the just national interests of both sides. The Soviet Government declared itself willing to cooperate with other nations in the solution of still unsettled problems. The most serious problem in the Middle East, Moscow said, stemmed from the Arab-Israeli conflict, which certain powers sought to exploit for their aggressive aims and the preservation of colonialism, in the perpetuation of which certain oil companies had an interest.

The 1950 Tripartite Declaration whereby the United States, Great Britain, and France guaranteed the existing boundaries in the Middle East, the Kremlin declared, aimed at intervention in the affairs of the Arab states and the restoration of the positions of colonialism. Russia, the statement went on, supported the efforts of countries in the Middle East to consolidate their independence, and considered unjustified and illegal any attempts to use the Arab-Israel conflict to interfere in the internal affairs of the independent Arab states or to station foreign troops in the area.

The same day the Soviet Foreign Minister, Vyacheslav Molotov, told Western correspondents that the new Soviet declaration on the Middle East provided a basis for discussions between the Soviet Prime Minister, Marshal Nikolai Bulganin, the First Secretary of the Communist Party, Nikita Khrushchev, and the British Prime Minister, Sir Anthony Eden. The two Soviet leaders were scheduled to arrive in London next day, April 18. In London the Kremlin declaration was viewed as a blow to the Tripartite Declaration of 1950. The Cairo paper *Al Akhbar* wrote that in the light of the Soviet pronouncement the Tripartite Declaration could be considered a dead letter.

At a meeting with the UN Secretary General, at the same time, Ben-Gurion informed Hammarskjöld of the failure of the Arabs to comply with Article VIII of the Armistice Agreement, which specifies "free movement of traffic on vital roads, including the Bethlehem and Latrun-Jerusalem roads; resumption of the normal functioning of the cultural and humanitarian institutions (the Hebrew University on Mount Scopus); use of the cemetery on the Mount of Olives; resumption of operation of the Latrun pumping station (from Rosh Ha'ayin to Jerusalem)." Mr. Hammarskjöld promised to deal with the matter.

At the Knesset meeting of April 22, 1956, the Prime Minister reviewed the security problems and political events following the Czech arms deal, as already recounted. He concluded his address as follows: "On Friday evening (April 20, 1956) I told the Secretary General that 'if he found in any of the neighboring countries a sincere inclination toward peace, he could be confident that we on our side would willingly examine all the avenues leading toward permanent peace.' And to the people of Israel let me say this: We will increase our capacity for defense without respite, and we will strive indefatigably for a stable peace with our neighbors."

Ben-Gurion was followed by Levi Eshkol, Minister of Finance, who spoke of the Defense Tax Law. In January 1956 a supplementary budget of IL 50 million for defense purposes had been approved. Half of it was to come from the Defense Fund and half from contributions from Jews in other countries and from foreign loans. The Defense Fund had come into being as a voluntary campaign for the acquisition of modern weapons for the armed forces. The quota per person had been set at six days' salary for wage-earners and 2 percent of their annual income for self-employed persons. It had developed, however, that the sum set was not enough, and the Government had decided on a special onetime Defense Tax. People with annual incomes not exceeding IL 1000, or in the case of married persons with one or more children, IL 1500, would be exempt from this tax. The rates for self-employed persons would vary from 4 to 10 percent of yearly income. A tax on commodities would also be imposed.

Debate on security and on the Defense Tax went on for two days.

Meridor (Herut) said that the present difficult security situation was a result of the faulty Armistice lines and the war that was left unfinished in 1948. "Had our lines of defense rested on the Jordan river and had we liquidated the Gaza Strip, we would not have needed tens of thousands of troops to defend them these past eight years. We have the strongest army in the Middle East. We have the advantage, and if only we had the initiative, Nasser would vanish from the horizon. Our chances of obtaining arms at this stage are doubtful."

Rimalt (General Zionists) quoted what Winston Churchill had said a few days earlier: "One does not have a moral right nor is there any sense to demand of Israel that she wait until Egypt became stronger, as long as no guarantee is provided that if she does wait, she will not lose or be defeated."

Jabber Mu'addi (Druze member of the Israel Arab Democratic List) welcomed the Defense Tax to finance urgent defense needs in order to safeguard the existence of the State of Israel in the present difficult circumstances.

Zeev Tsur (Ahdut Haavodah): "Our situation is still unchanged. It has remained as it was before, that of a small state struggling for existence and surviving at the cost of its blood. The outcome does not depend on us. To the extent that it does, it depends, as it always has, on the degree of our preparedness and strength to deter the enemy."

Hazan (Mapam) was of the opinion that "even from the international standpoint our situation today is better than it was a while ago. We welcome the initiative of the UN as expressed in the mission of the Secretary General. We should not ignore the fact that we are witnessing a transformation that may forecast a meaningful change in our international position. I refer to the announcement by the Soviet Union. We recall our anxiety, our bitterness, and our protests at the outset of the Czech arms deal; now we have this Soviet statement, which is different. It embodies an attempt to maintain a balance between ourselves and the Arab states. It speaks differently about the borders. It speaks differently about the refugee problem. We have grounds to assume, therefore—I emphasize, *merely grounds to assume*—that we are on the threshold of a new era. Anyone who compares the dark days of the Czech arms deal to the days of this present announcement cannot but admit that new political opportunities have opened up before us. I say this with the greatest caution. At the same time we must stress and stress again that a prerequisite for ensuring peace is that we be strong. For that reason I wholeheartedly endorse the Government's proposal in connection with the Defense Tax Law."

Rabbi Levin (Agudat Israel): "We are in a very dangerous situation, the likes of which we have not known in the recent history of the Jewish community in this country. Nevertheless, we should see to it that those who have contributed to the Defense Fund be exempt from the Defense Tax."

Esther Wilenska (Communists): The Soviet proposal pointed the way to solution of the Arab-Israeli conflict, and proved once again that the Soviet Union had in the past acted and was once again acting in the cause of peace. Under these circumstances, what was the political sense of a supplementary budget proposal for additional military expenditure? The way to our security did not lie in increased military outlay. It lay in responding to the news of peace and adopting an actively positive stand vis-à-vis the Soviet declaration.

Izhar Harari (Progressives) expressed surprise that Meridor considered that the solution of our security problem lay in extending the State of Israel to the Jordan River. Modern strategy has learned to overcome rivers far larger and wider than the Jordan. As far as Egypt was concerned, he believed that the moment we took the Gaza Strip, there would be a revolution there. Time, he said, did not allow him to ask Mr. Meridor what solution he proposed for the Arab refugees in the Gaza Strip. The UN, he felt, was an instrument—at times effective, at times completely ineffective—for preventing war. One thing he proposed to the Government was that henceforth in UN debates we abstain from referring to our case as the "Palestine question." If a problem existed between ourselves and Syria and Egypt, or other countries, it should not be referred to as the "Palestine" problem.

Avraham Harzfeld (Mapai): Just as we had not relied on one nation or another in the past, we should not do so today. In these matters we have to rely on ourselves, first and foremost. The outside world did not always agree with our wishes and requirements, even if they were just and honest. He had seen the biggest of all tragedies in the settlements and villages: Shafrir. He had witnessed the scene in which children were murdered and youths slaughtered at prayer, how they were murdered in their homes in the heart of the Jewish community, in the heart of the country. Having seen that, he well understood the enormity of the danger confronting us.

Nahum Nir (Ahdut Ha'avoda Poalei Zion): It has been claimed here that Dag Hammarskjöld has succeeded in easing the tension. This is something of a distortion. The very moment when the shooting stopped on the Egyptian border, it began on the Jordanian and Lebanese borders, and today (April 23, 1956) we have learned of the incident with the Kinneret fishermen. The Soviet communiqué is without doubt positive, but here too I will wait a while before welcoming it. Not because I am unhappy with it. I am very happy to have the communiqué in this form rather than the form at the Twentieth Congress of the Communist Party, when Khrushchev said that Israel has been an aggressor since the day of its birth. The danger of war is not past, and since it exists, we have to arm for it.

The Foreign Minister: The declaration by the Soviet Foreign Ministry still has to pass the test of action. Its formulations suggest a certain change for the better. Its central aim is no doubt to claim and establish for the Soviet Union the status in Middle Eastern affairs that has been a guiding purpose of Soviet policy for some time. I have to note the statement in the declaration that the Soviet Union has lent and is lending sincere and wholehearted support, so it says, to the aspirations of the Arab states—their aspirations only, that is, to a further strengthening of their independence and improvement of their economic conditions. In talking of a peace settlement between Israel and the Arab states, it makes no mention of direct negotiations, a principle the Soviet Union has always upheld in relation to the settlement of international conflicts.

These negative points, which I have covered only briefly, gain additional importance in view of an article in *Izvestia* on Saturday, April 21, that emphasizes and dwells at length on the one-sided friendship of the Soviet Union for the Arab states; it accuses Israel of what it calls "crass violation" of the UN Charter; stigmatizes us as a tool of the aggressive circles of the United States and Britain; and makes a distinction between the armistice demarcation lines and a permanent frontier. The whole intent of the article is to obscure the positive and to underscore the negative in the Moscow declaration. The declaration admits the danger of war but ignores its origin. It calls for the prevention of war but is silent on how this is to be achieved. Moreover, implicit in this statement is an attempt to justify the cause of the serious gap in armed strength that has developed between ourselves and Egypt: the Czech arms deal that is at the root of the evil we are now striving to overcome.

It is doubtful whether the authors of the declaration have given the necessary attention to the contradiction between justification for arming Egypt on the one hand, and on the other the assertion that the Soviet Union has always opposed any action in the Middle East likely to cause armed conflict. The Soviet Government claims that it has persistently sought measures for the reduction of international tension in line with the aspirations of the peoples of all countries, including those of the Middle East. In our eyes the effect of the Czech arms deal with all its ramifications directly contradicts this professed aim. As long as the wide gap in arms exists between Israel and Egypt, the danger persists; no verbal declarations can eliminate this peril and safeguard our security. Security is primarily a matter of balance of armed strength, not of modifications in the tone of political declarations. In fact, even as worded, the Soviet declaration hardly offers any correction of the situation. On the contrary, it conveys hints of further dangers.

Consequently our demand for defensive arms not only remains unaffected, but it is incumbent on us to press it with even greater force, precisely because of the danger of illusions and an unwarranted stilling of conscience. A very perilous situation would be created if the Soviet declaration were to serve as a pretext for withholding defensive arms from Israel on the ground of relaxed tension and lessened danger. The call is being heard for a freezing of all armaments in the Middle East at their present level—thus crystalizing the existing imbalance to the detriment of Israel. We will oppose this pernicious slogan with all our strength.

After Foreign Minister Sharett's speech a vote was taken. Motions by the Communists, General Zionists, and Herut were defeated. The Coalition motion was passed: "The Knesset notes the announcement by the Prime Minister and the reply of the Minister of Foreign Affairs." The Defense Tax draft law, it was decided, would be submitted to the Finance Committee. After consideration in the Finance Committee, the law was given a third reading in the Knesset on May 22, 1956.

The 24th Zionist Congress convened in Jerusalem the day after the political debate. Here the Prime Minister set forth the main problems facing Israel and the Jewry in the Diaspora. Though he considered himself a loyal citizen of the State, his primary and basic commitment was to the Jewish people as a whole. First he listed the historical problems that had been solved by Israel's renewal some eighty years ago, then the new problems that had arisen since. It was incumbent upon us, he said, to view both sides of the coin soberly:

> With the establishment of the State, Israel's independence was revived in a considerable part of the Land of Israel. On the world stage there appeared again an independent Hebrew nation, free and equal with all other peoples, whose actions are guided by her own needs, her own will and aims, without dependence on any other people or subordination to foreign rule. The State has made a substantial beginning on the ingathering of the exiles, especially from Europe, Asia, and Africa, and the course of this great enterprise has also clearly demonstrated the national unity of the various tribes of Israel scattered throughout the world.
>
> The State of Israel has placed at the disposal of the Jewish people the free and unencumbered soil of the Homeland, and has enabled it to build up the land and make the desert bloom.
>
> The State has liberated the spiritual and economic powers of the Jewish people, so that Israel's Homeland has become a progressive center of economic activity unequaled in the whole of the Middle East, and a center of learning, science, and research that has every prospect of taking a foremost place among the enlightened and progressive countries of the world.
>
> By all these achievements Israel has exalted status, honor, and self-respect for all the Jews of the world, and increased the esteem in which they are held among the peoples. The State has also united and consolidated world Jewry in bonds of love for Israel, to an extent unparalleled since the weakening and disintegration of the ties of religion and faith, which for hundreds of years served as the spiritual link between the scattered elements of world Jewry.
>
> And yet we must ask ourselves in all seriousness: *Has the revival of Israel guaranteed its own survival, the survival of the Jewish people's messianic mission, the survival of world Jewry?* This, in my opinion, is the question that ought to hold the central place in the deliberations of this Congress, and that should occupy the heart and mind of every devoted Jew, wherever he may be.
>
> Even a cursory review of the State's defense problems—apart from any particular event, such as the Czech arms deal and the stream of arms flowing to Egypt and to no small extent to other Arab countries, but from the point of view of the geopolitical conditions of its existence and the historical period in which it has arisen—is enough to arouse grave and constant anxiety as to the security and peace of Israel, and her capacity for survival. *Israel is a small island surrounded by a great Arab sea extending over two continents*—Western Asia and North Africa, from the Taurus Mountains in Southern Turkey to the Atlas Mountains on the

shore of the Atlantic Ocean. *This sea extends over an enormous and continuous area of 4 million square miles*, an area greater than that of the United States, and it has a population of about 70 million people, the great and decisive majority of whom—with the exception of Copt, Assyrian, Kurd, Druze, European, Berber, and pagan minorities—are Arabic-speaking Moslems.

Our own country alone has four neighbor states—Egypt, Jordan, Syria, and Lebanon—with a population of nearly 29 million and an area of 460,000 square miles, about 58 times the area of Israel. These four countries, together with Iraq and Saudi Arabia, took part in the attack on Israel in 1948, and since that time have boycotted, blockaded, and besieged our country.

Our enemies believe that by crushing our military power they can solve the Palestine problem once and for all—by driving us into the sea, or, in simple words, by physically destroying us. And though we are confident that if we are once again compelled to match our strength with that of our enemies we shall again be victorious, we would of course never dream of doing to the Arabs what they are planning to do to us.

The State of Israel has not placed its sole trust in the Israel Defense Forces, though these are our first and principal fortress, and they have never failed us, either in the War of Independence or in the guerrilla warfare that has never ceased since then. Israel's security depends first and foremost on the continuation of immigration and the growth of our numbers—not only quantitative but also qualitative growth, that is, the accretion of moral and intellectual vitality by the absorption of skilled workers, scientists, and men of intellect.

Parallel with the continuation of immigration is settlement—the building of new economic units in town and village and on the sea, in fishing and seafaring. First place in our defense requirements and settlement efforts is held by the need to populate the desert and make it bloom. This involves the decentralization of our population and industry in all parts of the country, and first of all in the expanses of the south and the Negev, and on our borders east and west, north and south.

One of the decisive factors in our security is the scientific and technological capacity of our people. We have always been and shall always remain a small people, and it is our fate throughout the generations to remain the few against the many. We must therefore see to it that our qualitative superiority not only be maintained for a long time to come, but be constantly increased.

The State of Israel has arisen in a period of world tension, in which the great powers are split into rival blocs for political and ideological reasons. The Arab rulers are prepared to support any side in the global conflict which will give them greater rewards or help them to consolidate their rule and their influence. In this respect, both main blocs pay very little attention to the ideologies they profess, and the Arab rulers are well able to exploit this world rivalry. This is the meaning of the grave and dangerous crisis that has become more intense in recent months, since the Soviet bloc began to direct a stream of heavy arms of all types to the land, sea, and air forces of Egypt. The United States and Britain, which themselves have not withheld weapons from several of the Arab countries, have in practice imposed an arms embargo on the State of Israel.

Though security in these days is our chief preoccupation, I shall not have done my duty as a citizen of the Jewish people unless I deal—even with the utmost brevity—with two other problems: the survival of Jewry in the Diaspora and the realization of the messianic vision. I am not using the modern terms ending in "ism," for the name of many of these "isms," both Jewish and general, is taken in vain in our day. I prefer to use an ancient and authentic Jewish term—the vision of messianic redemption, which expresses both a profound Jewish meaning and a general, worldwide human idea. No one can as yet see in the State as it is today an embodiment of Israel's messianic vision, from either the Jewish point of view or that of humanity, though undoubtedly an encouraging, significant, and hopeful beginning has been made here from both these points of view.

Our social, spiritual, and economic achievements, and the forces latent in our people, especially in the younger generation, give us faith that, in spite of internal and external difficulties in the ingathering of the exiles, in the building of economic strength, in the maintenance of security, we shall struggle with God and men—and we shall surely gain the victory. But we cannot succeed by our own strength alone. Without the devoted assistance of world Jewry we shall not accomplish the great tasks that history has imposed upon us, or overcome the obstacles that have accumulated in our path.

And the great question—to my mind, the supreme question—is this: Can we be confident of the survival of Jewry in the Diaspora and the preservation of its values, after the destruction of European Jewry and the assimilation in practice that we see taking place in all the lands of the dispersion, almost without exception? The greater part of Diaspora Jewry is now concentrated in the New World, and assimilation in practice, without any ideology, is advancing with giant strides. In the heart of every Jew anxious for the future of Judaism the question must arise: Will Diaspora Jewry long survive? I am not one of those who can think of nothing but the needs of the State of Israel. A common destiny binds Israel to Diaspora Jewry, and the reverse is also true. And you will not have done your duty unless you attempt in the course of this Congress to find effective and reliable methods: (A) to strengthen dispersed Jewry by *Hebrew education and intensification of its Jewish consciousness and unity;* (B) to intensify its attachment to the hope of messianic redemption, by the encouragement of pioneering immigration from all the countries of the Diaspora.

The greatest ideal of the Jewish people was and is the messianic ideal, which has continued from the Prophets of yore through all the generations unto the thinkers and teachers of Israel in our own days. Though at various times it has been given different names and titles, the messianic ideal holds that we are the Eternal People by virtue of our heritage and our destiny. This country of ours is the Chosen Land, and the period of greatness and redemption is not in the past but in the future. National redemption means the ingathering of the scattered sons of Israel from the ends of the earth, and the redemption of Israel is bound up with the redemption of the world, the redemption of all the peoples, by the reign of mercy and truth, justice and peace in this world of ours, peopled by men of many nations.

Those who aspired only to the Kingdom of Heaven placed themselves outside of Israel. The father of the Jewish people, after whom our State is named, saw in his vision a ladder standing upon the earth with its head reaching to the heavens. The ladder of the Jewish people's aspirations for the future is based upon reality, on the soil of the nation, but it rises high into the heavens. "Practical men" may receive these visionary words with a smile, but though in the last three generations many "practical men" have smiled at our dreams, their "practical" arguments have been proved baseless, while the dreams have become a reality. And if I am asked: What will secure the survival of Jewry in the Diaspora? I shall say: two things—*Hebrew education and a personal attachment to the hope of the messianic vision.*

Hebrew education means not only learning the Hebrew language but the study, in the original, of the Book of Books, which is the certificate of the identity, the honor, and the genius of the Jewish people. Only the teaching of this Eternal Book in the original to the younger generation in the Diaspora will enable our people in the future to be conscious of its roots and the sources of its greatness, its national destiny, and its destiny as part of the human race, and will safeguard its attachment to the aspirations of its people, and to peace among the nations and human brotherhood.

On March 26, 1956, following the talks in London between Marshal Nikolai Bulganin, Nikita Khrushchev, and Sir Anthony Eden, the Soviet and British representatives had issued the following communiqué:

> The United Kingdom and the Soviet Union have the firm intention to do everything in their power to facilitate the maintenance of peace and security in the Near and Middle East. For this purpose they will give the necessary support to the UN in its endeavor to strengthen peace in the region of Palestine and to carry out the appropriate decisions of the Security Council. The governments of the two countries consider that effective measures to this end should be undertaken in the immediate future, in accordance with the national aspirations of the peoples concerned, with the necessity of insuring their independence, and in full conformity with the principles expressed in the UN Charter.
>
> The governments of the two countries call on the states concerned to take measures to prevent the increase of tension in the area of the demarcation lines established in accordance with the relevant Armistice Agreements between Israel and the Arab states. They will also support the UN initiative to secure a peaceful settlement on a mutually acceptable basis of the dispute between the Arab states and Israel. They recognize the importance of the problem of the refugees and accordingly will support UN action directed toward the alleviation of their hardships.
>
> The governments of the two countries express their strong hope that other states will also do everything possible to help the UN in bringing about a peaceful solution of the dispute between the Arab states and Israel and thus strengthen peace and security in the Near and Middle East.

Resignation of Sharett as Foreign Minister ★ Ben-Gurion Lauds His Services and Refutes Distortions of the Event at Home and Abroad

The aggravation of the security situation led to changes in the Cabinet. On June 18, 1956, the Prime Minister made the following statement to the Knesset:

> At a special Cabinet meeting this morning the Foreign Minister announced his decision to resign from the Government. Not only the members of the Cabinet and the Foreign Minister's party colleagues but, I am certain, large numbers of Jews and non-Jews in Israel and many who are our allies and not our allies the world over will receive the news with great regret. From the time of the Provisional Government up to the present — and I have had the privilege of participating in all these Governments — there has not been one minister (perhaps I should make an exception for the Minister of Justice) who in his work of a lifetime before the creation of the State, his wide erudition, great knowledge, thorough understanding of international affairs, tact, temperament, agreeable manner, loyalty to duty, and tremendous perseverance so fitted him for his tasks as Moshe Sharett was fitted to serve in the Foreign Ministry.
>
> Sharett was not only the Foreign Minister but also the second Prime Minister of Israel. When I presented the present Government to the Cabinet on November 2, 1955, I said that "the second Prime Minister was gifted with qualities and talents not possessed by the first." I did not say this merely out of courtesy and homage to high-flown phrases, for I do not say what I do not believe, nor do I believe in distributing hollow compliments to anyone, near or far.

Were Moshe Sharett retiring from political life, I would try to recount, if only briefly, the glorious record of a son of the Biluim, a dear colleague of mine in his country's service for twenty-three consecutive years, and as the Foreign Minister of his people: his unflagging efforts since 1933 to augment immigration; his bitter struggle against the White Paper from 1939 forward; the mobilization of the Jewish battalions and the creation of the first Jewish Brigade in the British Army to fight the Nazi murderers; the saga of illegal immigration steeped in suffering and valor; the struggle for the creation of the State of Israel in the UN; the organization of the first Foreign Ministry in the independent State; his wide-ranging and fruitful activity in the international arena which led up to Israel's membership in the United Nations and its respected place in the family of nations; the procurement of large-scale aid from the American government for the absorption of our mass immigration in the first years of the State; the forging of ties with countries east and west; the training of a Foreign Ministry staff—ambassadors and envoys of whom even a Great Power would not be ashamed; the winning of friends and the defense of our cause with honor, pride, and discernment against accusers and adversaries in the international arena.

But I will not do so, because the political activity of Moshe Sharett is not over. His valued talents, his rich experience, and his vast knowledge will be placed at the disposal of the Israel legislature, and his advice will be heeded willingly and with profit by all those who will shape Israel's internal and foreign policy in days to come. I am certain that many great exploits still lie ahead for the man who has stood at the helm of our foreign policy for nearly a quarter of a century. That is why I need not try to summarize, even briefly, the manifold and fruitful activity of my friend Moshe Sharett with whom I have worked together for over forty years—at times in dispute and with differences of opinion, but by and large in intimate agreement, and always in mutual trust and respect.

I need not stress that the Government's policy as a whole will be conducted in the future, as in the past, according to its Basic Policy. Its security and foreign policy in particular will be conducted in accordance with my address to the Knesset on November 2, 1955, when the new Government was presented, and which was delivered with the approval of all members of the Government, without exception.

The Government has decided that the Minister of Labor, Golda Meir, will be the new Foreign Minister, and to co-opt Knesset member Mordekhai Namir as Minister of Labor. I ask the Knesset to confirm this in accordance with the Transition Law.

Moshe Sharett at once supplemented the announcement, as follows:

I thank the Prime Minister for his kind words of appreciation. And I wish to express my thanks to the Knesset for the measure of trust it has accorded me during my period of office as Foreign Minister and for the attention and patience with which it has favored me.

In connection with my resignation, some well-considered comments have appeared on the one hand, and much that is nonsensical on the other. In order to assist the members of the Knesset to distinguish between truth and falsehood, I wish to bring the following facts to their attention.

In August 1955, after the last elections, when the present Prime Minister proceeded to form the new Cabinet, I asked him not to include me in the list of ministers. I had well-founded reasons to fear that cooperation between my friend David Ben-Gurion as Prime minister and myself as Minister for Foreign Affairs would not be successful this time, and I believed it would be best for me to free him and the new Government from unnecessary complications. The Prime Minister rejected my refusal to enter the Government, and in view of the attitude he then adopted I had to give way. In the course of my term of office in the present Government, cooperation between us was several times subjected to most uneasy tests, which we managed to overcome by an effort to maintain a partnership that has continued between us for many decades, and in view of the emergency through which the country is passing.

In recent weeks, however, it became clear to me that my resignation was unavoidable. This situation did not arise in connection with any pending political issue or with any current event or incident. Nevertheless, in a frank conversation with the Prime Minister on the evening of Sunday, June 3, I reached the absolute conviction that it was impossible for me to remain in the Government he heads. In the middle of that week I proposed to him that he should immediately convene a special meeting of the Cabinet so that I could proffer my resignation. The Prime Minister urged me to postpone my resignation for a few weeks, and he cited weighty reasons for his request. It was only a few days later that the Prime Minister realized that it would be better to avoid any further delay, whereupon we agreed on urgent arrangements to give effect to the resignation.

This, in brief, is the true story. Any version of rumor or conjecture that has received publicity and contradicts this story either in essentials or in any point of detail is pure fabrication.

The following day, June 19, 1956, Ben-Gurion sought to clarify several points that the newspapers had misrepresented in connection with Sharett's retirement:

After what was said yesterday I must correct several distortions and errors. A silly falsehood has emerged in the local press, and especially in the foreign press, to the effect that the Prime Minister proposed the post of [Mapai] Party Secretary to the Foreign Minister in order to eliminate him from the Government. On the basis of this fabrication the foreign press has built several castles in the air. I consider it my obligation to state categorically that I have never proposed the post of Party Secretary to the Foreign Minister. The first I heard of it was from Sharett himself at the first meeting of the party's Committee of Nine, which has also been subjected lately to wide publicity by the press. After examining and considering this proposal I decided against it, and when members subsequently brought it up I rejected it categorically.

It was said yesterday that the Prime Minister had more say in foreign policy than the Foreign Minister did. Now it is true, and I think it should be, that between one meeting and the next the Foreign Minister generally consulted with the Prime Minister on foreign affairs. On the other hand, it is completely untrue that in such matters the Prime Minister took any step whatsoever without the Foreign Minister and his office or without his knowledge. I wish to say to the Knesset and to the nation that foreign policy is at all times the responsibility of the entire Government, not only for formal reasons of collective responsibility but for practical reasons as well. There is no problem to which the Cabinet has devoted so much debate, and taken decisions week after week, as in the case of foreign policy. If this policy has been good, the credit must be shared by the entire Cabinet, and if bad, the entire Cabinet is equally to blame. Hence, as one of the members of the Cabinet, it is with great satisfaction that I take full responsibility for Sharett's foreign policy.

In every Government that has arisen in Israel, and I have had the privilege of being in all of them, there have been differences of opinion. There are Knesset members here who were in the Cabinet, left it, and later returned. There are those who have remained all through; and others who have been members now and then. They know that the Cabinet has never had "one language and many utterances," not only because it is a coalition Government and must of necessity embrace differences of opinion, but because it is a democratic rather than a totalitarian Government. Even if it were made up of a single party, and that party were the one to which I have the honor of belonging, it would still embrace differences of opinion because it is a democratic party. Many issues, indeed, from the time of the Provisional Government until the present have been decided not unanimously but by majority opinion, and so I am certain it will be in the future as well.

I will not undertake to state whether all these decisions have been good or bad. There were times when I was in the majority and times when I was in the minority, and naturally, like any Cabinet member, I may be permitted to assume that I was right in both cases. Still, I feel it is proper especially in matters of vital importance, when members find themselves in a minority—as I was more than once in the Provisional Government—that they refrain from bringing on crises or resigning. If they did, the country would face a new crisis every week and soon would be in chaos. Those members who have found themselves in the minority and nevertheless submitted to majority rule deserve to be commended.

In my brief remarks yesterday I did not conceal the fact that though I have had differences of opinion with Moshe Sharett, and not only with him but with members to whom I have been even closer ideologically, I believe that at no time did these differences impair our friendship. But perhaps I did not fully express my esteem for Moshe Sharett yesterday, even if I differ in several respects with his position and views. If there is anyone of a fascist or totalitarian hue who is unable to understand or believe this, I will not force him.

Yesterday Sharett explained that when I was charged with the formation of a Government after the last elections, he asked me not to include him but I insisted. Now I did this not only despite our differences of opinion but to a large extent because of them. Like many other members, I cannot work only with "yes men." I am not one who thinks he is incapable of making mistakes and I like my opinions and views checked against those of colleagues whose outlook is different. Yet this was not the only reason I urged Sharett to join the Government, and why I was grateful to him for doing so.

Yet with the deterioration of our security and the increasing hazards of our foreign policy—which I will touch on later—I concluded that the national interest now requires as much coordination as is humanly possible between the Foreign Ministry and the Ministry of Defense, as well as new leadership in the Foreign Ministry. This is not because I feel that we should depart from the Basic Policy outlined by all those who participate in the Cabinet and who devoted much time to its formulation; nor do I feel that we should alter the defense and foreign policy, which was outlined in my speech of November 2, when I presented this Government to the Knesset, and which was delivered with the consent of all members of the Government.

I do feel, however, that at this difficult time it is essential that we have maximum co-ordination between these two ministries, Foreign Affairs and Defense, which deal in effect with one and the same thing, since any affairs of the Foreign Ministry that are not related to security are at this time of little importance. While in normal times foreign policy does not focus solely on defense problems, the present case is different. While differences of opinion on these questions are usually beneficial, it is essential that harmony now prevail between the two ministries.

This is why my colleague Sharett told you yesterday that he felt compelled to leave the Government. Though personally, as a friend of long standing, I regret it, from the point of view of the national welfare I consider it for the good of the State. At this time there is need for a change of personnel. I do not believe that the country depends on one man alone. Three years ago when I felt the need for rest from the psychological tension of more than twenty years' duration (and what twenty years they were!) I, too, permitted myself to retire from the Government. I was certain no harm would come to the country from my departure and that it would even help to educate the nation. I think the same holds true for security and foreign affairs.

This Government has declared that it is prepared, as in the past, to observe the Armistice

Agreements faithfully in every detail, both in letter and in spirit. However, this obligation is binding on the other side as well. An agreement that is violated by the other side will not be binding on us either; nor have we said this merely for stylistic effect.

When the UN Secretary General visited Israel a short while ago, our approach to the Armistice Agreements was in line with this declaration. We said that we would uphold the cease-fire unconditionally, but *naturally on a basis of mutuality*. We could not stop firing while the other side continued to fire; the cease-fire commitment did not have any strings or provisos attached, nor was it conditional on compliance with the other articles of the Armistice Agreements. We wanted the borders to be quiet, our settlements safe, without shooting and without forays across the border. This was something to which, unlike the other side, we had been committed even before the visit by the Secretary General.

But when the Secretary General brought in other Articles in which for some reason he was especially interested — Articles VII and VIII of the agreement with Egypt, requiring us to withdraw from Nitzana — we told him No, that it depends on whether the Egyptians uphold Article I, something they have been violating all these years by threatening war against us, by proclaiming a state of war in contravention of the Armistice Agreement and the resolution of the Security Council, and by imposing upon us a boycott and a maritime blockade. The agreement, we told him, was a single unit. On our part we were prepared to uphold it in its entirety, and faithfully, provided the other side did the same. Otherwise it simply did not exist. If Article I is violated, we are not obliged to uphold Article VII. The Secretary General accepted this, though he did not include it in his published report; that, however, is his business.

I wish to state here that this will be our policy in the future as well. We are prepared to observe the entire agreement, provided that others also observe it in its entirety. The only thing not dependent on the other Articles is the cease-fire, but this too must be on a basis of mutuality. I want the members of the Knesset and the entire nation to know that this is neither simple nor easy. Though it seems to be logical and straightforward, it may place us in a difficult situation. The nations of the world have not yet learned to apply to the State of Israel the same principles of honesty and logic as they do to other nations, and we may face a hard struggle over this simple, elementary point. Yet this is our determined policy, even if it brings us into conflict with bodies we respect very much, bodies that at least on the basis of their avowed objectives have great human value.

We said something else on November 2, and this too was explained to the Secretary General at length and, it seems to me, in great depth. We said that "if the armistice lines are opened on the other side of the border to saboteurs and murderers, they will no longer be closed to the people who are defending their homes." This seems acceptable to many, even if not to all of us. A small number of people among us say No — if they shoot at us we will keep silent; if they kill us we will keep silent; if they sabotage us we will keep silent. Those who say this are few; they are either foolishly pious or pretending to be. Those who are attacked must defend themselves. The right of self-defense is sacrosanct, and is also affirmed in the UN Charter.

But here again not everything accepted from the world at large is accepted from Israel. If you read the Secretary General's report, you will find that though we explained the situation and refuted all his arguments, he expressly denies our right to defend ourselves against saboteurs and killers. Our neighbors sought to overcome us in war; failing that, they imposed a boycott on us, thinking that this would undermine our economy. Not content with a boycott and blockade, they have organized gangs of murderers and saboteurs to undermine our internal security; and it is hardly conceivable that these gangs should be allowed to operate or that we should allow those responsible to go unpunished.

I do not agree with the slogan that "we are alone in the world," which is current for no good reason. I know that we have loyal friends in America, in Europe, in Asia, in Australia, and we must do everything, we must work hard, diligently, and perseveringly, both at home and abroad, to win additional friends on all these continents and in Africa as well.

The main thrust of our efforts, however, shall be along the lines of those who have built up this country and constitute its Government, though many who are not in the present Government have also played no small part in this work of construction. Constant, ceaseless, and unwearying upbuilding of our internal strength in this country—this is at the center of our foreign policy; this is the linchpin of our defense policy, this is the entire doctrine—the enhancement of our moral, economic, and military strength. It is this and this alone that in the final account will determine all the undertakings, all the disputes, and perhaps even the battles we will have to face.

Harari (Progressives) exclaimed: "We must determine what the present events were that brought things to a head and made the Foreign Minister resign. What happened?" Sharett interrupted to say: "But I said that my resignation has no connection with anything specific that happened recently. This was explained both in my speech and in that of the Prime Minister." Comments were made by Rabbi Levin (Agudat Israel), Rabbi Nurock (Mizrahi), Ben-Eliezer (Herut), and Eliezer Rimalt (General Zionists).

Then the General Zionists proposed a resolution stating that "the Knesset sees in the Government's change of personnel an admission of the failure of the foreign and defense policy for which the entire Government is responsible and expresses no-confidence in that Government." This resolution was rejected. Also rejected was a resolution by Herut stating that "in view of the resignation of the Foreign Minister and its causes, the entire Government should tender its resignation." By a two-thirds majority the Knesset adopted a Government motion that confirmed the change of personnel in the Foreign Ministry and the cooption of Mordekhai Namir. The new minister immediately submitted his declaration of allegiance.

Arms from France ★ First Two Destroyers Are Acquired ★ Ben-Gurion Reviews Security and the International Situation

An appeal by the Prime Minister to Guy Mollet, Socialist Premier of France, and talks by our Deputy Minister of Defense, Shimon Peres, with the heads of the French Army made clear the danger to Israel from the ever growing imbalance between Egyptian and Israeli armaments. They led to a tightening of friendly ties between France and Israel and to the French arms deal.

In the War of Independence France was one of the two European states that aided Israel with arms, even if at full price. The other was Czechoslovakia, both under the democratic regime when Jan Masaryk was Foreign Minister and under the Communist Foreign Minister, Vlado Clementis. The first six 60-mm. artillery pieces received from France saved the agricultural settlements of the Jordan Valley from the Syrian Army, already at the gates of Dagania. They also helped in the capture of Kastel, the hill commanding the approaches to Jerusalem, where the Arab commander, Abdul-Kadr El-Husseini fell.

The French Foreign Ministry at that time was not sympathetic to Israel; France recognized our State only several months after it had come into existence. But the French Army had always shown much support and admiration for Israel. During World War Two, when Syria was under the control of Pétain agents, Gen. Charles de Gaulle had used young Israelis to maintain contact with the French Underground in Syria and Lebanon. Both the French High Command and the French people appreciated the heroism of the Hagana in guerrilla warfare even before the creation of the State. Sympathy for Israel increased following Israel's victories in the War of Independence, when within eight hours after the proclamation of independence five Arab armies moved in to wipe the young State off the map.

With the accession to power of Guy Mollet in early 1956, the "transaction" of supplying arms to Israel was effected without the knowledge of the French Foreign Ministry but with the personal participation of Foreign Minister Christian Pineau, also a member of the Socialist Party. French arms began to arrive in Israel on July 25, 1956, and continued until the end of September.

June 20, 1956, two days after the resignation of Sharett had been announced, saw the arrival of the first two destroyers acquired by the Israeli Navy. Purchased in England, they were brought to Israel by an Israeli crew that had spent several months in training with the British Navy. One ship was named *Eilat*, the other *Yafo*, after the first two ports in Hebrew history: Eilat during the First Temple and Yafo during the Second. The destroyers, of course, did little to reduce the arms gap between the Egyptian and the IDF created by the Czech deal.

In the following three months—July, August, and September—the balance was to a large extent righted by the Socialist government of Premier Mollet which supplied Israel with tanks, guns, jet planes, machine guns, and ammunition. Twenty-four Mystère fighters had also been acquired by Foreign Minister Moshe Sharett from the preceding French government of Edgar Faure. This large quantity of arms arrived in the utmost secrecy. Since hundreds of people had to be involved in unloading and transferring it to Army camps, the Prime Minister called together the editors of every newspaper in the country and let them in on the secret, lest anything be published prematurely. To their credit, let it be said that not one paper violated its undertaking until the Prime Minister announced the transaction in the Knesset in the middle of October. Quantitatively the gap in arms was still considerable, but qualitatively it had been reduced. One night the poet Nathan Alterman was invited to observe the ships' arrival and unloading. Moved by the sight, he wrote a wonderful poem, which was not released for publication until the announcement in the Knesset. It was first published in *Divrei Haknesset*, the only poem ever to appear in that parliamentary digest. I will quote only two stanzas:

> This is a night that was or yet will be. Either way
>   it is no lying vision.
> It is a night without a name, a festival night that
>   will be remembered beyond the bounds of time.
> Happy the people with such a fate, whose faults are
>   open to the eye of friend and foe,
> Whose finest, boldest deeds are hidden till the time
>   is ripe,
> For the darkness covers them.

Perhaps this is a night of dreams, but wide-awake, and
    what it saw was the melting away of the terror gap
Between us and the forces of destruction. Iron comes
    on steadily and the bowels of the earth tremble. . . .
Let Israel's day know that it draws from the night
    power of life, the power of fire.
Let Israel's body know this. . . its spirit too will add
    its touch of steel.

After all the equipment had been received in absolute secrecy, the Prime Minister was able to announce the facts in a major address in the Knesset on October 15, 1956, when he said in part:

There has been a distinct improvement in the power of the Israel Defense Forces, although I must point out with grave anxiety that Egypt alone still has an enormous arms superiority over Israel, both at sea and in the air, and even on land. It has destroyers, and submarines; it has heavy tanks—British, Czech, and Soviet; it has Soviet jet fighters and bombers superior in quality and quantity to anything we possess. If we add the constantly increasing armament of the other Arab countries, we have still more cause for anxiety.

Nevertheless we are not as defenseless as we were at the beginning of the year. I am confident, as is every commander in the Israel Defense Forces, that any conflict with Egypt or with the rest of the Arab armies will end in our victory. Our desire, however, is to prevent war and to safeguard our rights, our position, and our security. That can be achieved in one way only: if our friends and the true lovers of peace supply us with sufficient defensive arms no lower in quality than those of the enemy, even if not in the same quantity. Only if we receive sufficient arms of superior quality will the enemy be deterred from initiating a war against us, violating our rights, and endangering our position.

Arms of this type and in sufficient quantity, even if in smaller quantity than those of our enemies—these we do not possess even now. Hence we insist upon our demand for arms —first of all from the United States, which does not desire a war in the Middle East and wishes well both to Israel and the Arab peoples. The enemy will not dare to attack us, only when he knows that we are well equipped according to his own concepts, and peace will prevail in this region. The Arab rulers cannot appreciate, as we do, the value, importance, character, and spirit of the man who does the fighting; they do not cherish human life and the values men hold apart from their own lives and their own importance. The enormous arms superiority at their disposal may intoxicate them and upset their mental balance, since they never cease to proclaim to their masses that there is war between them and Israel which can end only with our destruction.

In a speech to mark the anniversary of the British evacuation of the Suez Canal on June 19, Gamal Abdel Nasser proclaimed: "We must be strong in order to regain the rights of the Palestinian nation by force." And Abdul Hakim Amer, Nasser's confidant, Minister of Defense and Commander-in-Chief of the Egyptian Army, addressed the Egyptian forces in the Gaza Strip on February 5 as follows: "The hour is approaching when I and my comrades in the Revolutionary Council will stand in the front ranks of the battle against imperialism and its Zionist ally." After Amer was appointed Supreme Commander of the armies of Egypt, Syria, and Saudi Arabia, he said in Alexandria on June 11: "The danger of Israel no longer exists. The Egyptian Army has enough strength to wipe Israel off the map." Shukri el-Kuwatli, President of Syria and Nasser's ally, declared on April 2: "The present situation demands the mobilization of all Arab strength to liquidate the state that has arisen in our region. Israel is like a cancer, and is not content to feed only on its own manpower, but is also assisted by World Zionism." The Prime Minister of Syria, Sabri el-Asali, declared in the

Parliament at Damascus on June 28: "Our foreign policy is based on a war against imperialism, Zionism, and Israel, on nonrecognition of the theft of Palestine, on opposition to peace with Israel and on strengthening the blockade against her." And Jordan's King Hussein wired the Egyptian dictator on July 28: "We look forward to the future when the Arab flag will fly over our great stolen country."

Day after day the Egyptian, Jordanian, Syrian, Iraqi and Saudi Arabian armies listen to the hostile incitements and calls for war of their commanders and rulers; and while we are strong enough to defend ourselves and resist an attack, we are not well enough equipped to deter our enemies, bent on war and planning hostile acts against us. We are subjected almost every day to guerrilla war conducted against us by some of our neighbors, especially Egypt and Jordan, through organized and well equipped bands of killers, called Fedayeen or by other names. Under instructions they cross the borders from time to time, and murder anyone they come across: workers in the fields, passersby, worshippers in the synagogues, women and children in their sleep, watchmen in the fields or on the roads, Jews, Druzes or members of other minority communities. This is not done at random, but is thoroughly organized with the consent of the governments. Until 1953 Jordan took the lead in this type of war. In 1954 Egypt assumed leadership in the murderous enterprise, and in 1954 and 1955 Egypt inflicted on us 242 casualties in killed and wounded.

In April this year the Secretary General of the UN, Dag Hammarskjöld, came to Israel and made a great effort to secure a cease-fire on our borders, even if the other Articles of the Armistice Agreements were not observed. The Government of Israel was prepared to carry out the Armistice Agreements in their entirety, on conditions of mutuality, and it agreed to observe the cease-fire even if the other Articles were violated by our neighbors, if only they observed the cease-fire.

The first to violate this renewed undertaking were Egypt and Jordan. Egypt sent its Fedayeen from all the Arab countries to sabotage military installations and blow up public buildings in Israel. It renewed mine-laying by Egyptian saboteurs on Israeli roads in the south and the Negev. When the Suez crisis broke out the Egyptian border became quiet for the moment— yet another proof that these operations were planned by the Egyptian government; all murders and sabotage have recently emanated from the Hashemite Kingdom. But the day after the Security Council session, after the conclusion of the Suez affair, Egypt sent her gangsters into action again. Only yesterday a band of Egyptian Fedayeen sent into Israel in the Sinai area was captured near Sde Boker.

Shortly after the departure of the UN Secretary General, Jordanians blew up a two-story house at Aziz, near Kfar Yavetz. On that same day a police vehicle was attacked near Kfar Saba. A tractor driver was murdered from ambush near Kubeiba, and an Israeli citizen was murdered south of Jerusalem. Two civilians were murdered near Nir Eliyahu and one was wounded by gunfire. An Israeli car was mined near Afula and an Israeli policeman injured. A civilian vehicle was attacked near Ein Hatseva in the Arava and two of its passengers were murdered. On the outskirts of the capital, at M'vaseret Yerushalayim, hand grenades were concealed as booby-traps and Jewish workers were shot at. At Ma'aleh Hahamisha a grenade was thrown into the children's quarters. A bus was attacked on the way to Eilat; four Israelis were killed and nine injured. Near Um-el-Fahem in the "Triangle" an Israeli patrol was attacked and a soldier killed. In the Duweima area six Israeli soldiers were murdered and two injured.

At Ein Ephrayim three guards, Israeli Druze, were murdered by a Jordanian gang which is known to us. These men confessed their deeds to the Jordanian police but King Hussein himself ordered their release a few days ago. Arab Legionnaires opened fire on an archeological gathering at Ramat Rahel, killing four and injuring sixteen. A Yemenite woman picking olives in the village of Aminadav was killed by the Jordanians, and that same day Jordanians murdered a tractor driver at Maoz Hayim and wounded his comrade. A Jordanian gang again murdered five Israelis in an ambush not far from Sodom, and, finally, two Israeli workers were murdered by Jordanians last week near Even Yehuda.

After the Egyptian and Jordanian outrages, we demanded week after week that the UN representatives take substantial steps to ensure that the Arab countries put an end to these murderous attacks and loyally observe their cease-fire obligations. All our insistence was in vain. I do not accuse the UN officials of lack of goodwill, but they turned out to be helpless to compel our neighbors to keep their promises. The chain of murders continued. We had no alternative but to take action ourselves for our self-defense, which is a natural right; perhaps more than a right: the *duty* of the State.

According to the UN Charter, every member of the United Nations Organization has the right to self-defense. Article 51 of the Charter says: "Nothing in the present Charter shall impair the inherent right of individual or collective self-defense if an armed attack occurs against a member of the United Nations, until the Security Council has taken measures necessary to maintain international peace and security." Yet there are some United Nations representatives who deny Israel this right to self-defense. They give the name "reprisals" to our defense against the murders organized and encouraged by the Egyptian and Jordanian authorities, and in his report to the Security Council dated May 9, the UN Secretary General denied the right to these "reprisals." Even if the Charter had not expressly safeguarded the right of self-defense for every people, it has inherent validity. The UN has demonstrated its incapacity—I do not say unwillingness—to put an end to repeated and systematic murders of Israeli citizens. As far as I know, this is the only country in the world whose citizens are not sure of their lives owing to the dispatch of bands of murderers against them by the rulers of neighboring countries. I cannot imagine that there is a single country in the world that would leave its people defenseless against murderers organized by neighboring governments.

The UN Observers and the UN Secretary General are as well aware as we are that these gangs conduct their activities on the orders of their governments, and that Egypt holds the leading position in organizing, equipping, and training these gangs, and in planning their activities. The Fedayeen we have captured have confessed as much in the courts, and the Egyptian Minister of War, Hassan al-Bakuri, spoke as follows in a broadcast over the Cairo radio station Saut al-Arab, controlled by the Egyptian dictator: "There is no reason why the loyal Fedayeen, who hit their enemies, should not penetrate deep into Israel, and make the lives of its people a hell." The Government of Israel will not allow its country to be transformed into a hell. The murderers and those who send them will not be allowed to escape without punishment, severe punishment. We will not allow ourselves to be deprived of the right of self-defense as long as the UN and its Security Council are incapable of putting an end to these murders. As soon as the Arab rulers honor their signature to the cease-fire, there will be tranquillity on the borders, for Israel has never violated and will never violate its promise.

The UN is founded on the principles of peace and justice, which are no less precious to us than to anyone else. It is our obligation and privilege to ensure, as far as it lies within our power, that these principles should apply to us as much as to other members of the UN. It is inconceivable that Israel should consent to discrimination: one rule for ourselves and another for the rest of the world.

The first Article of the Charter declares that the object of the United Nations is to safeguard international peace and security, and to this end collective measures have to be undertaken for the prevention and removal of threats to peace. But we are subject to overt and continual threats from the rulers of the Arab countries—Egypt, Jordan, and Syria. The Arab press is full of these threats, and so are the radio and public speeches of the Egyptian dictator, the King of Jordan, the Syrian President, King Saud—in concert or each by himself.

Yet nothing is done by representatives of the UN, here or in any other place, for the "prevention and removal" of these threats.

That same Article I requires "adjustment or settlement of international disputes by peaceful means." Year after year we have demanded such a settlement. We have proposed a meeting with the Arab rulers for a peace settlement or at least for the prevention of aggression. But ours has been the voice that crieth in the wilderness. We have protested against the fact that UN member nations are organizing an economic boycott against us with the object of undermining our economy, although Article II, paragraph 4 of the Charter expressly forbids such a hostile act. How is it possible to reconcile the boycott and blockade of Israel, publicly organized and inplemented by the Arab states, with the UN Charter? And if these two things cannot be reconciled, what have the institutions of the UN done, or attempted to do, to safeguard our elementary rights according to the Charter, and to prevent and bring to an end these hostile activities?

This year we have made desperate efforts to preserve peace, in our region, even the present shaky peace, and we are always prepared to cooperate in any attempt to establish lasting peace. But the British announcement that immediately followed the declaration of Nuri Said, the Iraqi Prime Minister, designed to force on Israel a peace settlement on the basis of the 1947 Partition Plan, cannot be accepted as a step toward peace. This is a disguised attack on the integrity of our borders. I do not know what were the original sources of this doubtful peace initiative, but the Government of Israel has already expressed its determined opposition to the speech of the British Prime Minister in the Guildhall on this question on November 15, 1955.

We have not taken a single foot of soil from Egypt, Syria, or Lebanon, and they will not receive from us a single foot of our soil. Egypt still occupies the Gaza Strip, which does not belong to her, and the Hashemite government has taken over, without any legal right, portions of western Palestine, and it certainly has no claims of any kind to parts of our territory. We have said more than once that frontier rectifications here and there, through mutual agreement and for the benefit of both sides, can be considered, but this scheme, to cut up the State of Israel, which has made its way from Baghdad to the Guildhall or from Guildhall to Baghdad, will never succeed. This proposal is apparently intended only to distract the attention of the Arab world from the grave Suez problem, and to direct it toward Israel. That problem, now the focus of world public attention, has not been revived for Israel's benefit.

As for the Suez problem that has now been placed in the center of the international stage, there has been no change as far as Israel is concerned. With respect to Israel's freedom of navigation through the canal, the impotence of the United Nations has been obvious for several years. The Security Council, whose function it is to safeguard peace and international justice, has not done its duty or implemented its own decision on Israel's freedom of navigation in the canal.

Article I of the Treaty of Constantinople of 1888 says: "The Suez Maritime Canal shall always be free and open, in time of war as in time of peace, to every vessel of commerce or of war, without distinction of flag. . . . The High Contracting Parties agree not to interfere in any way with the free use of the canal, in time of war as in time of peace." Article 10 of the treaty does, it is true, give Egypt the right to take steps to safeguard the defense of Egypt and the maintenance of public order, but Article 11 immediately adds that "measures which shall be taken in these cases shall not interfere with the free use of the canal."

The UN Charter stipulates that the United Nations are determined "to establish conditions under which justice and the respect for the obligations arising from treaties and other sources of international law can be maintained." When the Soviet Union proposed the addition of a long list of countries to those to be invited, including even some that had no connection whatever with the canal, such as Jordan, she too "forgot" to add the State of Israel to the list. In paragraphs 2 and 3 of Article I it is stated that the purposes of the UN are, among other things, to foster "equality of rights" among nations. Yet in violation of both the Treaty of Constantinople and the principles of the UN Charter, Egypt has imposed a blockade on Israeli ships, as well as on other ships carrying fuel and other cargoes to Israel, depriving them of the right of transit through the Canal.

In 1951 the Security Council rejected Egypt's contention that she was in a state of war with Israel. It ruled that the Armistice Agreements put an end to the state of war, that Israel has the right to free passage through the Suez Canal, and that the Egyptian government may not violate this right. Egypt has been violating this Security Council decision for five years, and neither the UN authorities nor the Security Council itself have taken a single step in all that time to ensure the implementation of the decision, nor have UN Observers been sent to the canal to verify whether the decision was being carried out or not.

The Israel Government approached some states to demand that Israel should have the same right of navigation in the canal as any other country. We received assurances from several governments that Israel's right of navigation would be safeguarded by the establishment of a regime of free navigation for all the peoples. The President of the United States was asked by a journalist at the end of last month about the Egyptian blockade on Israeli shipping for seven years. He replied that of course the blockade was a black mark that had been in existence for a long time. It was most unjust, and he believed it was not in keeping with the Constantinople Treaty of 1888. In an earlier interview, his Secretary of State, John Foster Dulles, said that Israeli ships and cargoes, whether or not she was a member of the Canal Users' Association, would have all the facilities in the Association.

The Security Council session came to an end two days ago with the formulation of six decisions. The first says that "there shall be free and open transit through the canal without discrimination." On the surface this seems to be a satisfactory decision. But I must warn against false optimism. This decision says less than what is laid down in the Constantinople Treaty, and though the Egyptian dictator has never repudiated that treaty, he has violated it as far as Israel is concerned, and has persevered in the violation even after the Security Council expressly decided five years ago that Israel is entitled to freedom of navigation in the Suez Canal.

It is our duty, therefore, to declare from this rostrum that Israel will not submit to any discrimination in respect of her sovereign international rights, and that the *continuation of the arbitrary blockade that the Egyptian dictator has imposed on Israeli shipping in the Suez Canal and the Red Sea straits will disturb the stability of the peace in the Middle East.* International justice and peace are indivisible. The President of the United States was right when he declared a few days ago that peace is inevitably bound up with justice. Peace and justice, he said, must be carried out together, otherwise it is not peace. The Egyptian dictator endangers the peace in the region by violating international justice.

It is a common saying in Israel that we are isolated. In this there is some truth, but also some falsehood. In a certain sense we are the most isolated people in the world, by our origins, history, spiritual characteristics, and our status in the world. But in a different sense Israel has friends and admirers no less than any other small people, and we enjoy the friendship and sympathy of a number of countries in Europe, North and South America, and Asia, although from the formal point of view we have no allies. In addition, we benefit considerably from international political and material assistance. An outstanding example is the substantial help we have received from the United States in loans and grants. And we are now engaged in negotiations with the Export-Import Bank for a large loan for irrigation needs, and a delegation from the bank is to come here shortly for that purpose.

We must clearly understand how friendships and alliances among nations come into being. Some countries easily acquire friends because they are great and powerful, control rich and extensive territories, and have populations of scores or even hundreds of millions. Other countries acquire friends as a result of a common religion or language, like some of the Arab countries, the countries of Latin America, or the countries of Scandinavia. Some countries enter into alliances because they have a common enemy or object of fear. Israel does not possess great power, tremendous wealth, or broad territories; she has no common language, religion, or race with any other state; and the peoples who are closest to us from the point of view of language and race are the Arab peoples who, for historical and, I believe, temporary reasons, are at present our bitterest enemies.

What, then, is the real basis for the acquistion of friends by Israel? One factor is the Jewish Dispersion. Jewish communities in some countries serve as a bond and a bridge between Israel and the country in question. There are many countries, however, where the Jews are not an important political or public factor, or where there are hardly any Jews; this applies to almost all the countries of Asia and Central Africa. In the Scandinavian countries there are indeed small Jewish communities, but they do not have any real influence. A common enemy may at a particular moment fulfil the function of bringing two states closer together, but this negative factor is subject to change, and no *permanent* foreign policy can be built on it. In our case, almost all the great powers are anxious to win the friendship of our enemy, the Arab rulers, and some powers show hostility to Israel for the sole purpose of currying favor with the Arab states.

We must clarify to ourselves what is the permanent, enduring basis on which we can found our aspiration to acquire friends and allies. There can be only one such basis: *the light of our creative, liberating achievements, our capacity to be a model to other peoples, and our ability to assist backward peoples through scientific, technical, and cultural guidance, without any likelihood or tendency on our part to dominate others.* Instead of the common religion, language, and race which serve to cement the alliances of other nations, we can gain friends and allies on the basis of *common values,* and the interests involved in these values. As far as we have succeeded in gaining sympathy and goodwill in the world—and we have succeeded in no small measure—we have done so only because of the cultural, spiritual, and social *radiance* of our work. Any endeavor that is in the nature of a light to the Gentiles is an emissary of our little state, capable of winning sympathy, friendship, and goodwill for Israel.

Through all the generations, and in our own day as well, we have looked upon the revival of Israel as a work of redemption, creation and peace, the rebuilding of the ruins of our Homeland, the assembling of the scattered sons of our people to weld them together as a united nation, firmly rooted in the soil of the land of our fathers, in the spiritual heritage of the nation throughout the generations, in the values of Israel's prophecy, and in the spiritual and scientific achievements of our own day and the days yet to come; an independent nation cooperating on a basis of universal equality and partnership in the efforts of the human race toward material and spiritual advancement, liberty, and equality, as human beings all of whom—without distinction of nationality, color, religion, or sex—have been created in the image of God. *That is the messianic vision, which for thousands of years has throbbed in the heart of the Jewish people,* and which, it is my profound conviction, has brought us to this point. *Only if we remain loyal to it throughout our lives will our historic aspirations be realized.*

Our grave concerns about security, which will not easily or speedily be brought to an end—and which must have first priority among our needs—must not distract our attention for a moment from the *positive tasks and ideals that are the soul of our messianic vision.* The development of the country and the bringing of new life to the wasteland, the absorption and the *integration* of the immigrants, the fostering of science and scholarship, the education and the pioneering training of the younger generation, the enhancement of skill, productivity, and quality in our labor, a determined struggle for economic independence—meaning that we must earn our living only through our own efforts and liberate ourselves from our dependence on external aid—the removal of communal barriers and the unification of the various communities, the increase of the birth rate, and the fostering of national health, the liquidation of the slums and the teaching of the Hebrew language, the safeguarding of a minimum in the cultural and economic sphere for the whole people, the establishment of a regime of social justice and human freedom—all these are our daily bread. They are indispensable for their own sakes and at the same time strengthen our security and ensure the survival of the State of Israel.

It is our duty not only to sustain the State of Israel but to transform it into a magnet for the entire House of Israel. This is not too difficult for us if we all arm ourselves with goodwill and bear the burdens of the State willingly; if we lend a hand to our brothers who are returning to us from impoverished exile; if we work hard and diligently and conduct our economic affairs efficiently and frugally; if we prefer the needs of the community to those of individuals and sections; if we treat each other with respect and mutual trust; if we dare to look the difficulties and the dangers facing us boldly in the eye; if we intensify our iron determination to overcome them in a spirit of true comradeship; and, above all, if the love of Israel reigns in our midst, that wonderful source of energy that activates our dear sons and daughters who risk their lives in defense of our persons, our borders, and our independence on nights of anxiety, heroism, and self-sacrifice.

We must stand guard with open eyes, with goodwill, with foresight, with strong determination, and with increased military strength. We are faced with the need for a supreme effort in the area of security, for it is forced on us by external factors and hostile forces. We may be facing fateful decisions and events. Let us stand ready and united, and the Rock of Israel will not fail us.

For three days the Knesset discussed the new challenges. Then, by a vote of seventy-six to thirteen, it adopted a resolution submitted by Akiva Govrin in the name of all the Coalition parties (Mapai, Mapam, Ahdut Haavodah, Hapoel Hamizrahi and Mizrahi) as well as the General Zionists, Agudat Israel, and Poalei Agudat Israel. It read: "The Knesset has heard and taken note of the statement by the Prime Minister on October 15, 1956."

Section 3. The Sinai-Gaza Strip Campaign and Its Aftermath

The Military Alliance of Egypt, Syria, and Jordan ★ Israel Launches Preventive Invasion of the Sinai Desert and the Gaza Strip ★ Total Victory in Seven Days

I N THE wake of the Knesset debate, October 15–17, 1956, the Middle East picture grew more perilous. Seven weeks of relative quiet were broken when the southern front once more became the scene of Egyptian assaults.

Two of our military vehicles hit Egyptian mines on October 25 northwest of Kibbutz K'tziot in the Nitzana sector. Three soldiers were killed and twenty-seven wounded, five of them seriously. The first vehicle was thrown a long distance by the force of the explosion, killing two soldiers and injuring six, four of them gravely. The second vehicle, a Ford truck carrying twenty-five soldiers, was traveling on the left side of the road. When it came alongside the crater formed by the initial explosion, its left wheel struck another mine, planted in the gravel. The truck was blown to bits. One soldier was killed and the rest injured.

The previous month, on August 30, at exactly the same spot, a military vehicle had hit a mine; two soldiers were killed and three injured. The tracks of three persons in rubber-soled shoes led to the border of Egypt. In the same weeks the Israel Defense Forces captured two Lebanese Fedayeen employed by the Egyptians. They admitted infiltrating Israel for the purpose of espionage and terror.

New elections to the Jordanian Parliament took place on October 21, 1956. Through the influence of Egyptian bribery, a pro-Nasserite majority was returned and immediately thereafter, on October 23, a three-way military pact was concluded among Egypt, Syria, and Jordan. The armies of all three countries were placed under a united command, with Abdul Hakim Amer, Egyptian Minister of War and Chief of Staff, at its head.

A glance at the map shows the deadly danger in which Israel found itself following this tripartite alliance, whose prime objective was by no means kept secret. The three countries surrounded our small State on three sides. In a surprise attack the Jordanian Army could cut our territory in two, as the narrow belt in the central part is no more than fifteen or twenty kilometers wide. In a matter of minutes the Syrian and Egyptian Air Forces could reach Israeli population centers and prevent mobilization of the Reserves on which our security depended, since we did not maintain a large regular army. A combined attack under Egyptian command might come at any moment and leave us defenseless. Small wonder that after the conclusion of the three-way pact the commander of the Jordan Legion, Ali Abu Nawar, saw an opportunity and a need to proclaim publicly: "The time has come when the Arabs will be able to choose the time for an offensive to liquidate Israel."

In a meeting with all the parties of the coalition, the Prime Minister and Minister of Defense pointed out the inability of the UN to prevent terror and guerrilla attacks and its failure to adopt any means to secure compliance with its resolution on freedom of navigation in the Suez Canal and the Straits of Eilat. He concluded that it was up to ourselves to safeguard the lives of our inhabitants on the borders and in the interior by destroying the Fedayeen bases in the Gaza Strip and the Sinai Peninsula and at least to secure freedom of navigation in the Straits of Eilat, and that to that end the Reserves had to be mobilized. All the coalition parties agreed except Mapam, which announced that, though they opposed the use of force, they would share fully in the responsibility if the majority approved the operation.

With the consent of the Knesset's Foreign Affairs and Defense Committee, Ben-Gurion as Minister of Defense ordered mobilization of the Reserves under Section 8 of the Defense Service Law. The response was swift, full, and eager. Many persons who for economic, educational, and administrative reasons were not required to report nevertheless did so and asked to be mobilized. At the time the entire country believed we were about to undertake an operation in the east, because Iraqi forces appeared about to cross to the east bank of the Jordan and our Government had announced that, if that happened, Israel would reserve freedom of action.

The call-up of the Reserves naturally became known abroad, and the President of the United States sent two letters in succession to the Prime Minister of Israel expressing his concern. In reply the Prime Minister reminded him that the Israeli Government had loyally supported his attempt during the past years—through his special envoy, the Secretary of the Treasury—to bring about peace talks between Israel and Egypt, whereas the Egyptian ruler had obstructed this effort by openly proclaiming his intention to destroy Israel. The Prime Minister concluded with these words:

> With the Iraqi Army encamped on the Jordanian border, the establishment of a joint Egyptian-Syrian-Jordanian Command, and the renewed penetration of Egyptian bands into Israel, the Government would not be fulfilling its elementary responsibilities if it did not take all possible measures to thwart the declared aim of the Arab rulers to destroy Israel. I feel certain that your own abundant military experience allows you to understand how great a danger we are now facing.

At the regular Cabinet meeting on Sunday morning, October 28, the Prime Minister noted that though he had already conferred with all the members, only the decision taken at this session would be binding.

"As the members know," he said, "Egypt has violated the Armistice Agreement all these years. Egypt has violated the 1951 resolution of the Security Council that, with the Armistice Agreement, no state of war existed between Egypt and Israel; and that even if a state of war did exist, Israel still had the right of transit in the Suez Canal." He went on to say:

> In contravention of international law and the Security Council resolution, Egypt also prevents free navigation in the Straits of Eilat. She has organized a special force known as Fedayeen, which operates also out of Jordan and Lebanon under the guidance of Egyptian military agents, and whose job it is to wound and kill Israeli citizens and to undermine the security of their lives.
>
> After thorough consultations with the General Staff of the IDF we have concluded that it is urgently necessary to mount an invasion of the Sinai Desert and the Gaza Strip with the object of destroying the Fedayeen bases and occupying the emplacements on the banks of the Straits of Eilat—at Sharm el-Sheikh at the tip of the Sinai triangle facing the Red Sea, slightly to the south of the Island of Yotvat, which is now called Tiran.
>
> The passage from Eilat to the Red Sea between Sharm el-Sheikh and the island of Tiran is quite narrow. The sea is shallow in the area and there is only a space of 150 meters through which ships can pass. A small Egyptian force is stationed on Tiran, but in Sharm el-Sheikh there is a large force that includes artillery and aircraft armed and equipped with superior weapons. In order to secure navigation from Eilat to the Red Sea and thence to the Indian Ocean, it is essential to gain control of Sharm el-Sheikh and Tiran, and, of course, the roads leading there. Two main roads lead from Israel to Egypt—one along the coast, the other from Nitzana to Ismailiya. First, however, we will have to occupy Ras el-Nakeb, in the mountain range west of Eilat.
>
> This operation calls for a big force, since the Egyptians have large military forces as well as military airfields in Sinai and the Gaza Strip. In the Gaza Strip they have a division; a second division is stationed in the area of El Arish and Abu Agheila. The third consists of units deployed throughout the length and breadth of the Sinai Peninsula: at Ras el-Nakeb, Kuntilla, el-Thamad, Kusseima, Jabel Libni, El-Nahal, El-Tor, Ras Nasrani, and Sharm el-Sheikh.
>
> There is, of course, the problem of the two major world powers, the Soviet Union and the United States. America is now six days away from Presidential elections and some are of the opinion that it will not intervene at this time. I am not so sure of that. I know that our

operation will not find favor with Mr. Dulles. There are those who say that Russia won't intervene if America doesn't. I cannot guarantee that. Russia has enough strength to suppress the popular uprising in Hungary as well as to intervene in the Middle East. Still, we cannot be reconciled to a regime of terror and blockade contrary to international justice, decisions by the Security Council, and the Armistice Agreements. We must now decide officially on the commencement of the operation tomorrow evening.

Since not one of the neighboring countries interfered when we carried out a number of raids into Jordan and the Gaza Strip, we may reasonably assume that, despite the recently concluded alliance, Jordan and Syria will not intervene. Still, this is only an assumption and in a matter as serious as this one cannot rely on assumptions. In consultations with the General Staff, we have decided on a series of precautionary measures along the borders. The eastern border is long and there are a large number of settlements along it whose existence we do not have the right to endanger on the basis of an assumption.

We have posted forces along the eastern border—the border with Syria and Jordan— and placed them at the disposal of the Northern Command. Other forces are at the disposal of the Central Command. One force will protect Jerusalem against any attempt at a break- through. We have located a certain force at a crossroads to be directed north or south as needed to respond to a surprise attack. We have also concerned ourselves with air protection. We have trained pilots for all the jets which, as you know, have increased in number during the past two months.

"What is the ultimate objective of this invasion?" Bentov asked. "Let us assume it goes off as planned. Do we wish to annex the Sinai Peninsula or any part of it, and what will happen to the Gaza Strip? Need we not fear that the countries of Asia will make war on us?"

The Prime Minister replied: "I do not know the outcome of Sinai. We are interested, first of all, in the Straits of Eilat and the Red Sea. Only through them can we secure direct contact with the nations of Asia and East Africa. However, I can conceive that there will be forces that will compel us to leave the Sinai Peninsula. There is America; there is Russia; there is the UN; there is Nehru; there are Asia and Africa. But most of all I fear the United States. America is capable of forcing us to withdraw. It need not send an army for that purpose. It has other means that are effective—and very serious.

"The main thing, to my mind, is freedom of navigation in the Straits of Eilat. As far as the Gaza Strip is concerned, I fear that it will be embarrassing for us. If I believed in miracles I would pray for it to be swallowed up in the sea. All the same, we must eradicate the Fedayeen bases and secure peaceful lives for the inhabitants of the border areas. I am not afraid of the nations of Asia. Nehru will not make war against us. He may be angry with us, but we are angry with him and with better reason, and it doesn't matter to him. China and Indonesia won't go to war either, nor will Burma."

On the same day the Prime Minister met with the opposition parties in Tel Aviv. After committing them to absolute secrecy, he advised them of the reasons and the plans for an invasion of the Sinai Peninsula on the morning of October 30. They all received this with enthusiasm and complete agreement.

On the same day, too, the Prime Minister came down with a bad case of influenza and was confined to bed for seven days. Nevertheless, he remained in continuous contact, day and night, with the commanders of the Army and the Chief of Staff, General Moshe Dayan, as well as the staff of the Foreign Ministry.

By the time he got out of bed (against his doctor's advice) on November 7, seven days after the start of the invasion, the Israel Defense Forces controlled the entire Sinai Peninsula from Ras el-Nakeb opposite Eilat to Sharm el-Sheikh on the south coast of the Sinai Peninsula, and from the Eilat-Rafiah axis to the Suez Canal and its southern gulf—an area of nearly sixty-thousand square kilometers, almost three times the size of the State of Israel. We also controlled the entire Gaza Strip from the point opposite Yad Mordekhai in the north to Rafiah in the south, and the island of Yotvat (Tiran) about which the sixth-century Greek historian Procopius, a native of Caesarea, wrote: "The Hebrews have been leading an autonomous existence there since ancient times and only in the present reign of Justinian have they become subjugated to the Romans (*i.e.*, the Byzantines)." After remaining desolate for many centuries the island was occupied a few years ago by the Egyptians, who placed a garrison there, and on the opposite shore at Sharm el-Sheikh positioned a force equipped with artillery and planes capable of attacking any Israeli ship passing through the Straits of Eilat.

At the beginning of the invasion an IDF spokesman issued the following communiqué:

> Units of the Israel Defense Forces have penetrated and attacked Fedayeen bases in the Kuntila and Ras el-Nakeb areas and have taken up positions to the west of the Nahal road junction on the approaches to the Suez Canal. This operation comes as the result of Egyptian military strikes against Israeli communications on land and sea aimed at causing destruction and denying peace to the citizens of Israel.

On the first night of the operation, October 30, Kuntila, Ras-el-Nakeb, and Kuseima were captured; also El-Thamad, El-Basis, and El-Ofra in the heart of Sinai. On October 31 Bir Hassneh fell without resistance and El-Nahal was captured. Abu Agheila was taken after a fierce battle. On November 1 all the outposts near Rafiah and Bir Gafgafa, on the Nitzana- Ismailiya road, fell to the IDF, as well as the first enemy post on the outskirts of El Arish. On November 2 El Arish was captured against bitter resistance. Three hours later Gaza fell without resistance. The Egyptian Governor of the Gaza Strip, Lt. Gen. Mohammed Fouad, sent a statement of surrender to the General of our Southern Command, Asaf Simhoni:

> I, Liwa Mohammed Fouad, General Administrator of the Gaza Strip, on behalf of the Egyptian Ministry of War, hereby request the front-line commander of the Israel Defense Forces, Aluf Mishne Asaf Simhoni, to accept my unconditional surrender as well as that of the administration of the City of Gaza and the entire Gaza Strip.

A number of important points on the south coast of the Gulf of Eilat, including Dahab and the Ras Nasrani, were captured on November 3. On that day the entire Sinai Peninsula was effectively under Israeli control, except for Sharm el-Sheikh, the small bay on the coast of the Red Sea opposite the island of Yotvat, fortified by long-range artillery and aircraft. This last Egyptian stronghold fell into our hands in the morning hours of November 5.

In relation to the size of the operation our losses were few: 171 killed and 1 pilot wounded and taken prisoner. We captured 6000 enlisted men, officers, and senior commanders, and a great amount of matériel, including heavy armaments, ammunition, and British- and Soviet-made vehicles. Despite our knowledge of the vast flow of arms to Egypt during the year, we had no idea of the tremendous abundance and superior quality of Egyptian arms and equipment, the greater part of which now fell into our hands.

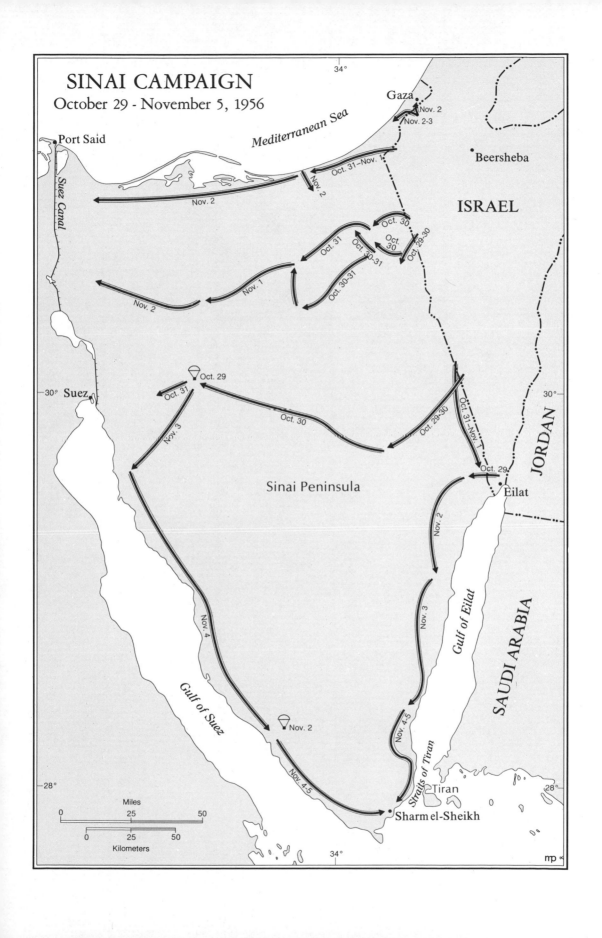

SINAI CAMPAIGN
October 29 - November 5, 1956

Mediterranean Sea

Port Said

Gaza
Nov. 2
Nov. 2-3

Beersheba

Suez Canal

Oct. 31–Nov.

Nov. 2

Nov. 2

ISRAEL

Oct. 30

Oct. 31

Oct. 30

Oct. 30-31

Oct. 29-30

Oct. 30-31

Oct. 30

Nov. 1

Nov. 2

Oct. 29

Oct. 31

Oct. 30

30° Suez

Nov. 3

Oct. 29-30

Oct. 31-Nov. 1

30°

JORDAN

Oct. 29

Eilat

Sinai Peninsula

Nov. 2

Nov. 4

Nov. 2

Gulf of Suez

SAUDI ARABIA

Gulf of Eilat

Nov. 3

Nov. 4-5

Straits of Tiran

28°

Nov. 4-5

28°

Miles
0   25   50

0   25   50
Kilometers

Tiran

Sharm el-Sheikh

34°

mp

It was unable to withstand the offensive of the Israel Defense Forces, which in a few days—seven, to be exact—wrote one of the most glorious chapters in the military history of the world.

This dry, laconic description does little justice to the wondrous epic of heroism which few previously would have believed possible. Nor did we profit from a windfall. The campaign was planned with two main objectives: rapidity of execution and minimal losses. Both these objectives were achieved beyond expectations, despite a few failures here and there.

On October 31 the *Ibrahim Al Awal*, an Egyptian destroyer sent to shell Haifa, was seriously hit by our Air Force and Navy. After its commander ran up a white flag, it was towed into Haifa port. The crew numbered 153, of whom 2 had been killed and 6 injured.

An American military historian, Gen. S. L. A. Marshall, described the Sinai Campaign as the most brilliant battle in the history of nations. This glory devolved equally on all the units of the IDF—Air Force, Armoured Corps, Paratroopers, Infantry, Navy, Artillery, and all military echelons.

Franco-British Military Intervention Against Egypt ★ The UN Orders Cease-Fire and Withdrawals ★ Threats from the USSR ★ Pleas from the US ★ Israeli Replies Justify Invasion

At the end of the Sinai Campaign on November 7, 1956, the Prime Minister addressed the Knesset, concluding with these words:

"We have in store for us a difficult political struggle, and maybe something worse than that. We have experienced difficult times in the past and have not been deterred. We will not now be influenced by the cheap boastfulness of the Arab rulers, nor will we humble ourselves before world powers when they are not in the right. In our efforts to establish peace and justice in the region we look forward to the support of people of good will and lovers of peace among all the nations. We will meet the days to come with courage, understanding, awareness of the justice of our cause and of our strength, while not disregarding our natural and necessary connection with the family of nations."

The political struggle, in fact, was well under way before the military phase was over—encumbered by the military intervention of Great Britain and France almost simultaneously with the Israeli action. On October 30, the morrow of our invasion, the British and French governments issued an ultimatum for Egypt and Israel to withdraw ten miles from the Suez Canal to permit their own forces to move in and separate the combatants. That evening the Foreign Minister issued a favorable reply, on condition that the Egyptians do likewise. Nasser announced that the ultimatum was not acceptable under any circumstances. After an additional warning the Anglo-French air forces on October 31 began to bomb the airfields across the canal and Port Said.

The UN Security Council intervened at once, and the United States proposed a strong resolution censuring Britain, France, and Israel. Though Britain and France vetoed the resolution, a majority of the Council voted to summon an emergency session of the General Assembly. President Eisenhower, on October 30, had appealed urgently to the British governments to facilitate a peaceful settlement of the current crisis; at the same time he summoned the American Congressional leaders to Washington in view of the possibility of emergency meetings at the White House.

On November 1 Egypt severed diplomatic relations with Britain and France, and an Egyptian spokesman at the UN stated that Egypt considered itself at war with these two countries. On November 2 the emergency session of the General Assembly adopted the following United States resolution, which stated:

The General Assembly.

Noting the disregard on many occasions by the parties to the Israel-Arab Armistice Agreements of 1948 of the terms of such agreements and that armed forces of Israel penetrated deeply into Egyptian territory in violation of the General Armistice Agreements between Egypt and Israel of February 24, 1949;

Noting that armed forces of France, and the United Kingdom and Northern Ireland are conducting military operations against Egyptian territory;

Noting that traffic through the Suez Canal is now interrupted to the serious prejudice of many nations;

Expressing its grave concern over these developments;

1. *Urges*, as a matter of priority, that all parties now involved in hostilities in the area agree to an immediate cease-fire, and as part thereof halt the movement of military forces and arms in the area;

2. *Urges* the parties to the Armistice Agreements promptly to withdraw all forces behind armistice lines, to desist from raids across armistice lines to neighboring territory, and to observe scrupulously the provisions of the Armistice Agreement;

3. *Recommends* that all member states refrain from introducing military goods into the area of hostilities and in general refrain from any acts which would delay or prevent the implementation of the present resolution;

4. *Urges* that upon the cease-fire being effective, steps be taken to reopen the Suez Canal and restore secure freedom of navigation.

5. *Requests* the Secretary-General to observe and report promptly on the compliance with the present resolution to the Security Council and to the General Assembly for such further action as they may deem appropriate in accordance with the Charter;

6. *Decides* to remain in emergency session pending compliance with the present resolution.

On November 3 the Israel Government announced its agreement to the cease-fire. The General Assembly, however, did not leave it at that.

The Israeli Ambassador, Abba Eban, explained to the Assembly the background and the reasons for the Israeli invasion, and his words struck an echo of understanding for Israel among Jews and non-Jews throughout the United States. The American press managed to distinguish between the Israeli and the Anglo-French actions, to Israel's credit. The sympathy intensified when the news came through of the Israeli forces' brilliant achievements in Sinai.

On November 5 Soviet Premier Bulganin sent a sharply worded letter to his Israeli counterpart. The tone of his letter was unusual even for Soviet correspondence with the tiniest countries in the capitalist world. It read:

Mr. Prime Minister:

The Soviet Government has already expressed its unqualified condemnation of the armed aggression of Israel, as well as of Britain and France, against Egypt, which constitutes a direct and open violation of the Charter and the principles of the United Nations. At the special Emergency Session of the Assembly the great majority of the countries of the world have also condemned the act of aggression that was perpetrated on the Egyptian Republic, and called on the governments of Israel, Britain, and France to put an end to the military operations without delay, and to withdraw the invading armies from Egyptian territory. The whole of peace-loving humanity indignantly condemns the criminal acts of the aggressors, who have violated the territorial integrity, sovereignty, and independence of the Egyptian Republic. Without taking this into account, the Government of Israel, acting as an instrument of external imperialistic forces, perseveres in the senseless adventure, thus defying all the peoples of the East who are conducting a struggle against colonialism and for the freedom and independence of all peace-loving peoples in the world.

These acts of the Government of Israel clearly demonstrate the value to be attached to all its false declarations about Israel's love of peace and her aspiration to peaceful coexistence with the neighboring Arab countries. These declarations by the Government of Israel in effect aimed only to dull the vigilance of other peoples, while she prepared a treacherous attack on her neighbors in obedience to a foreign will and acting according to orders from outside. The Government of Israel is criminally and irresponsibly playing with the fate of the world, with the fate of its own people. It is sowing hatred of the State of Israel among the Eastern peoples, such as cannot but leave its mark on the future of Israel and places in question the very existence of Israel as a State.

Vitally interested in the maintenance of peace and the preservation of tranquillity in the Middle East, the Soviet government is at this moment taking steps to put an end to the war and to restrain the aggressors. We propose that the Government of Israel should consider this, before it is too late, and should put an end to her military measures against Egypt. We appeal to you, to the Parliament, to the workers of the Israeli State, to all the people of Israel: Stop the aggression! Stop the bloodshed! Withdraw your armies from Egyptian territory! In view of the situation that has been created, the Soviet Government has decided to ask its Ambassador in Tel Aviv to leave Israel and return to Moscow without delay. We hope that the Government of Israel will fully understand and appreciate our warning.

Marshal Bulganin also sent threatening letters, though couched in polite terms, to the Prime Ministers of Great Britain and France, intimating that the Soviet Union would launch missiles against Paris and London if their armies were not evacuated from Egyptian soil. The UN Assembly was seized with hysteria about a Third World War, and the Afro-Asian bloc, led by India, closed ranks in full force behind the Egyptian dictator.

The two great world rivals [Russia and the US] were competing for the Afro-Asian bloc, most of whose members refused to examine the substance of the Israeli-Egyptian dispute and what had led up to the Sinai Campaign. Owing to the fact that US Secretary of State John Foster Dulles was ill and the Israeli Ambassador was away from Washington attending the UN General Assembly, a senior official of the State Department summoned another Israeli diplomat and told him in substance: We are on the brink of a World War. Israel's failure to comply with the decisions of the Assembly is endangering the peace. Israel's position will of necessity have serious consequences, such as the cessation of all government and private assistance, UN sanctions, and perhaps even expulsion from the United Nations.

On the same day, November 7, the President of the United States sent a letter to the Israeli Prime Minister, in polite terms but firmly demanding withdrawal to the armistice lines:

Dear Mr. Prime Minister:

As you know, the General Assembly of the United Nations has arranged a cease-fire in Egypt to which Egypt, France, the United Kingdom, and Israel have agreed. A United Nations force is being dispatched to Egypt in accordance with pertinent resolutions of the General Assembly. That body has urged that all other foreign forces be withdrawn from Egyptian territory, and especially, that Israeli forces be withdrawn to the General Armistice line. The resolution covering the cease-fire and withdrawal was introduced by the United States and received the overwhelming vote of the Assembly.

Statements attributed to your Government to the effect that Israel does not intend to withdraw from Egyptian territory, as requested by the United Nations, have been called to my attention. I must say frankly, Mr. Prime Minister, that the United States views these reports, if true, with deep concern. Any such decision by the Government of Israel would seriously undermine the urgent efforts being made by the United Nations to restore peace in the Middle East, and could not but bring about the condemnation of Israel as a violator of the principles as well as the directives of the United Nations.

It is our belief that as a matter of highest priority peace should be restored and foreign troops, except for United Nations forces, be withdrawn from Egypt, after which new and energetic steps should be undertaken within the framework of the United Nations to solve the basic problems which have given rise to the present difficulty. The United States has tabled in the General Assembly two resolutions designed to accomplish the latter purposes and hopes that they will be acted upon favorably as soon as the present emergency has been dealt with.

I need not assure you of the deep interest which the United States has in your country, nor recall the various elements of our policy of support to Israel in so many ways. It is in this context that I urge you to comply with the resolutions of the United Nations General Assembly dealing with the current crisis and to make your decision known immediately. It would be a matter of the greatest regret to all my countrymen if Israeli policy on a matter of such grave concern to the world should in any way impair the friendly cooperation between our two countries.

With best wishes, sincerely,
Dwight D. Eisenhower

For technical reasons the American letter reached us only on November 8. On the same day the Cabinet held two meetings and discussed the response to the letters from Marshal Bulganin and President Eisenhower. The Prime Minister, moreover, summoned the leaders of all the opposition parties (except the Communists) and informed them of the developments in the Assembly and world capitals and the line the Government was adopting in its replies to the two letters, which were sent the same day.

The reply to Bulganin read:

Mr. President of the Council of Ministers:

I have received your note of November 5, 1956. I have read it carefully and I am sorry that I must point out that some arguments are based on incomplete and incorrect information you received.

More than two years ago Egypt's ruler organized a special force called Fedayeen whose purpose is to penetrate surreptitiously within the boundaries of our country and to murder citizens working in the fields, traveling along the roads, and dwelling in their homes. At the beginning these groups operated only from areas occupied by Egypt such as the Gaza Strip. Lately he has organized such groups of murderers in Jordan, Lebanon, and Syria, and the lives of our farmers along the borders are subject daily to their murderous onslaughts. During the time of the Suez crisis the activity of these groups ceased. Three weeks ago, however, their activity was intensified.

In an Order dated February 25, 1956, by the Commander of the 3d Egyptian Division in Sinai, Major General Ahmed Salem (according to a photostatic copy attached herewith) it is said, *inter alia:* "Every commander is to prepare himself and his subordinates for the inevitable campaign with Israel, for the purpose of fulfilling our exalted aim, namely, the annihilation of Israel and her extermination in the shortest possible time, in most brutal and cruel battles."

Egypt's ruler organized, in contravention of the Charter of the United Nations, an economic boycott against Israel. He established a blockade against our freedom of navigation in the Suez Canal and the Straits of Eilat, and for five years he had violated a decision of the Security Council concerning the freedom of passage of Israel's ships in the Suez Canal. After the Security Council, on October 13 this year, again forbade all overt or covert discrimination with regard to freedom of navigation in the Suez Canal, Egypt's ruler announced that the discrimination against Israel would continue.

About two weeks ago the Egyptian ruler concluded a military pact with Jordan and Syria against Israel.

Therefore, the action we carried out at the end of October was necessitated by self-defense and was not dictated by foreign wishes as you have been told. In response to the appeal of the General Assembly of the United Nations we ceased fire and for several days past there has been no armed conflict between us and Egypt.

Yesterday I stated in the Knesset in the name of the Government of Israel that we are able to enter immediately into direct negotiations with Egypt, without prior conditions and without any compulsion, to achieve a stable peace. We hope that all peace-loving states and especially those that maintain friendly relations with Egypt will use all their influence in Egypt to bring about peace talks without further delay.

I am constrained, in conclusion, to express my surprise and sorrow at the threat against Israel's existence and well-being contained in your note. Our foreign policy is dictated by our essential needs and by our yearning for peace. It is not and will not be decided by any foreign factor. As a sovereign state we decide our path by ourselves and we join with all other peace-loving peoples of the world in striving for relations of peace and justice in our area and the entire world.

David Ben-Gurion

The same day a reply was also sent to President Eisenhower.

Dear Mr. President:

I have only this afternoon received your message, delayed in transmission owing to a breakdown in communications between the [U.S.] Department of State and the United States Embassy in Tel Aviv.

Your statement that a United Nations force is being dispatched to Egypt in accordance with pertinent resolutions of the General Assembly is welcomed by us. Neither I nor any other authorized spokesman of the Government of Israel has stated that we plan to annex the Sinai desert. In view of the United Nations resolutions regarding the withdrawal of foreign troops from Egypt and the creation of an international force we will, upon the conclusion of satisfactory arrangements with the United Nations in connection with this international force entering the Suez Canal area, willingly withdraw our forces.

Although an important part of our aim has been achieved by the destruction, as a result of the Sinai operation, of the Fedayeen gangs and the bases from which they were planned and directed, we must repeat our urgent request to the United Nations to call upon Egypt, which has consistently maintained that it is in a state of war with Israel, to renounce this position, abandon its policy of boycott and blockade, cease the sending into Israel territory of murder gangs, and, in accordance with its obligations under the United Nations Charter, live at peace with member states and enter into direct peace negotiations.

On behalf of my Government I wish to express to you our gratification at your reference to the deep interest of the United States in Israel and its policy of support for our country. I know these words of friendship stem from the depths of your heart and I wish to assure you that you will always find Israel ready to make its humble contribution at the side of the United States in its efforts to strengthen justice and peace in the world.

David Ben-Gurion

A reply in the same spirit was sent that day to the UN Secretary-General, who had transmitted to Israel the Assembly's resolutions demanding a withdrawal to the Armistice lines.

On November 5 the Knesset Foreign Affairs and Security Committee held a comprehensive debate on the political situation. The entire committee, including all the re-representatives of the Opposition except Herut (the Communists did not participate in this committee), unanimously approved the Prime Minister's reply to the American President and the Foreign Minister's reply to the UN Secretary-General.

The Herut member objected to the sentence in the Prime Minister's reply that said: "In view of the United Nations resolutions regarding the withdrawal of foreign troops from Egypt and the creation of an international force we will, upon the conclusion of satisfactory arrangements with the United Nations in connection with this international force entering the Suez Canal area, willingly withdraw our forces." According to him, "this reply renders the decision of the Knesset null and void, without even consulting it."

In the Knesset the Prime Minister repeated the speech he had broadcast to the nation on November 8, after sending the replies to Marshal Bulganin and President Eisenhower, in which he listed our three main objectives in the Sinai Campaign: (1) to destroy the forces that had been lying in wait to destroy us; (2) to liberate territory of the Homeland that had been occupied by the invader; and (3) to safeguard freedom of navigation in the Straits of Eilat as well as in the Suez Canal. Although for the time being only the first and primary object had been achieved, he voiced confidence that the other two aims would also be implemented in their entirety:

> None of us knows what the fate of Sinai will be. In my review yesterday in the Knesset it was not through inadvertence that I passed over this important problem in silence. There is no doubt in our minds that we face a combined campaign, both military and political, and no one yet knows if either of them has ended, or how. We faced difficult trials during the War of Independence as well, and though we didn't achieve then all that we wanted, never in our entire history did we achieve more than at that time. Only shortsighted people can fail to see the greatness of what we have attained at this time, though the struggle is not yet over. As I told the commanders of the Army: "No force in the world can put your victory to naught, and Israel after the Sinai campaign will not be the same as it was before this great operation. Your work will be of great historic benefit and I believe that our entire nation will be worthy of it."

The Foreign Affairs and Security Committee met the day after the Prime Minister's broadcast, and discussed some matters public discussion of which was precluded by national interest. It also considered and approved the reply to the President of the United States. The objection raised by the Herut member was dismissed by a vote of sixty-six to thirteen.

Growing Sympathy Abroad for Israeli Position ★ *The General Assembly Creates a Mideast Peace-Keeping Force* ★ *Israel's Conditional Willingness To Withdraw*

The political struggle, begun with the letters from the two Great Powers, lasted for several months. The conspicuous valor of our forces in the Sinai Campaign, no less than our victories in the War of Independence, put Israel on the map, gave prominence to its unique position in the Middle East, and directed the attention of the nations to the continuing problem of its security. Not only in the United States and France, but in the other countries of Europe as well as in Asia and Africa, people at last began to understand Israel's special position, which had practically no parallel in any other country. They also began to recognize the double standard the UN had been applying to this small young nation. Typical in this respect was an article in the American quarterly *Foreign Affairs* by Paul-Henri Spaak, the former Foreign Minister of Belgium and first president of the UN General Assembly, who at the time of the Sinai campaign was Secretary of NATO. He wrote in part:

> Let me put it in a different way. In the present United Nations setup, which is not what its founders wished and hoped it would be, everything short of war is allowed. Treaties may be violated, promises can be broken, a nation licensed to menace its neighbor or to perpetrate any sort of trick on it, just as long as there is no actual war. The attitude of Egypt during the last few months is a case in point. While Egypt denied transit through the Suez Canal to Israeli ships, sent death commandos onto Israeli soil, violated the Treaty of Constantinople, sent arms to be used against the French in Algeria and made preparations to attack its neighbor, the United Nations was powerless to intervene. Such intervention would not come within the scope of the Charter as at present interpreted. But let Israel in desperation send troops into the Sinai Peninsula and let Anglo-French forces land at Port Said, and they are sure to be condemned.
>
> Foreign Affairs vol. 35 No. 2. Jan. 1957

Mr. Spaak's article was but one expression of the growing awareness throughout the world of the justice of Israel's cause, in contrast with Egypt's mockery of international law, the UN Charter, and the undertakings to Israel in the Armistice Agreement.

The change in public opinion in America and several of the European countries did not make itself felt in the attitude of the great powers. After France and England had submitted instantly to the UN General Assembly resolution and on November 6 announced acceptance of the cease-fire and evacuation of the Suez Canal and Egyptian territory, England's voice was added to the countries exerting pressure on Israel to withdraw immediately, not only from Sinai but behind the Armistice borders. On that day, November 6, elections in the United States returned Eisenhower to the White House, though with a reduced majority in Congress. As a result of a Constitutional Amendment adopted in Truman's time, providing that a President can serve only two terms, Eisenhower was less dependent on public opinion; but the Republican Party Congressmen, having lost strength in Congress, were rather more sensitive than previously to public opinion.

A Soviet resolution in the Security Council, requiring Britain, France, and Israel to withdraw from Egypt within twelve hours, failing which the Soviet Union and the United States would be called upon to assist Egypt with weapons, volunteers, and other military help, was rejected on the night of November 5–6. It had received the votes of only the Soviet Union, Yugoslavia, and Iran. When it failed to pass, Marshal Bulganin on November 7 sent letters to the Prime Ministers of Israel, France, and Britain warning of unilateral Soviet action. In Israel's case he added a further sign of dissatisfaction by recalling the Soviet Ambassador.

The Soviet threat made itself felt in England, where virtually from the outset public opinion had been divided on Eden's military actions against Egypt. On November 5 Foreign Minister Selwyn Lloyd announced in Parliament that Britain had informed the United Nations that it concurred in the need for rapid withdrawal of Israeli forces. The next day, when France and England decided to cease hostilities and withdraw from the canal, they failed to impose any preconditions for an agreed settlement, as Israel had done with regard to the Straits of Eilat.

On the night of November 7–8 the General Assembly decided on the creation of an international peace-keeping force. Seven countries—three in Asia: India, Pakistan, and Ceylon; three in the Americas: Canada, Brazil, and Colombia; and one in Europe: Norway—volunteered part of their armies for this force. Representatives of these countries would also serve as an Advisory Committee to the Secretary-General in connection with the operation of the international force. When the Afro-Asian bloc proposed an immediate withdrawal from Egypt, it explained that this meant immediately after the arrival of the UN Emergency Force.

Herbert Hoover, Jr., acting for Dulles, who was ill, summoned our Ambassador, Reuven Shiloah, and transmitted to him orally what Dulles had told him in the hospital as a supplement to Eisenhower's letter of November 7: This is a very grave situation for the free world, not only for the future of the Middle East but that of the entire world. It is clear that the Soviets are exploiting the situation for purposes that are fraught with disaster. If the worst should happen, Israel will be among the first to perish. Israel's refusal to withdraw, as required by the overwhelming majority of UN members, makes it responsible in the eyes of many for endangering world peace. The only way to avoid this terrible danger is through the UN and the UN alone. Israel's refusal means contempt for public opinion both in the world and in the United States. Under these circumstances Israel's stand will necessarily lead to very serious consequences, such as cessation of all government and private aid, UN sanctions, and probably expulsion from the United Nations as well.

Shiloah said he would inform his Government, remarking that in their last talk, before the Secretary of State had entered the hospital, Dulles had promised there would be no return to the former situation. William M. Rountree, a State Department official who was present, remarked: "We said we could not allow the problem to remain unsolved. But we also said that the first step had to be a cease-fire and withdrawal behind the Armistice lines." In his last talk with Dulles, Abba Eban had told him that the Prime Minister would be prepared under certain circumstances to advise the Government to withdraw our forces from Egyptian territory.

After Eisenhower had received the Prime Minister's reply, the White House spokesman announced that the President was satisfied, and the US Ambassador to Israel, Edward B. Lawson, transmitted to the Prime Minister the following message from the President:

I appreciate the message you sent yesterday announcing that you would withdraw your troops from Egyptian territory. This decision will be welcomed not only by the United States, but by all other nations struggling to restore peace and security to the peoples of the Middle East.

This is an important step towards the creation of an atmosphere in which a peaceful solution will be possible.

The Knesset on November 14, following its acceptance by the Foreign Affairs and Security Committee, supported the Government's view that withdrawal was in order if satisfactory arrangements could be made with the peace-keeping force. The Minister of Defense then saw the need to clarify to the commanders of the Army the nature of the political struggle in the wake of the Sinai campaign. Both before and after the events of 1954 the IDF had been taught that policy in peace and war is determined only by the elected bodies of the sovereign people—that the Army is merely an executive arm of the Government. Nevertheless, Ben-Gurion looked upon the Army not as a passive mechanical force but as a body of responsible persons carrying out their duty with full knowledge and understanding. As UN pressure for a withdrawal increased, he convened the Officers Corps to explain the Government's policy. Among other things he said:

When the fighting ended on November 7, 1949, it was clear that our work was not over. Obviously our enemies would not become resigned to their defeat, nor would they willingly put up with our existence much longer. Our task was: (1) to prepare the Army to counter any of the Arab armies, and if necessary, all of them together; (2) to avoid a clash with a non-Arab nation by every means at our disposal. As the person responsible for security matters even before the creation of the State, I kept both these things in mind. Just as it was clear that to survive we had to be equipped to withstand all the Arab armies, we knew also that we must not become embroiled militarily with a foreign power—England, Russia, America, etc.—for it would endanger our lives.

In the War of Independence we had an important supporting weapon—corruption and dissension in the enemy camp. Let us not forget, however, the decree by history that we are a small nation and cannot match strength militarily with world powers. Even with the Arab nations we are not eager for battle, to say nothing of powers foreign to this area.

We have to realize that victory in war does not always increase the victor's strength. Certainly a defeat doesn't, but sometimes neither does a victory. England was victorious in two World Wars, both the First and the Second. Nevertheless, from 1914 on, England has steadily lost the position of a leading world power that it held in the nineteenth century. Despite two glorious victories it has become a second-rate power. Germany, on the other hand, was defeated in both World Wars, yet returned to full strength a short time later, and though since World War Two it has been divided, this is for altogether different reasons. Thus we see that wars are not always decisive, neither do victories always accomplish the victors' purpose.

In our own case we must remember that we are living in two different spheres—one is the Middle East. Within this sphere if we are not strong enough to stand up to the armies of our neighbors, we are liable to be wiped off the face of the earth. But we also live in a greater sphere—that of the entire world. And this world is now one, though not united. It may now be very much at odds within itself, perhaps more so than ever before, yet it is not divided. Formerly, the world was split into separate parts, each of which knew nothing about the others. China, for example, thought for a long time that it was the center of the world. The lands of the Bible, now known as the Middle East, were a world unto themselves. The Roman Empire thought of itself as the entire world.

At present the world may be at odds within itself; there are conflicts among nations. All the same, it is all one world. Whatever happens today in Jerusalem or in Rafiah is known five minutes later in all parts of the world, and all the nations are partners, for good or ill, in joy or fear. Our region is part of the great world and matters here are not resolved by the forces in the Middle East alone. Since the War of Independence several changes have come about here. Then there were only five independent Arab countries in the United Nations; now there are eleven, and these eleven votes carry more weight than one Israeli vote, especially if they are backed by 70 million people while we have less than 2 million.

Something else has changed as well. Many new nations, including the nations of Asia with their tens and hundreds of millions of people who till now were subjected to foreign powers, especially European powers, have gained their independence. They have grown strong and increasingly are becoming a factor to be reckoned with, not only in Asia but throughout the world. The age of these nations since independence is approximately the same as ours, eight or nine years.

There is a third factor, at this moment perhaps the most disquieting of all. Before the War of Independence, Soviet Russia along with the United States and thirty-three other countries voted for the creation of a Jewish State. In that war Russia welcomed our victory over the Arab invaders, and while not aiding us directly, did not preclude help from those subject to it. The arms we had then originated mostly in Czechoslovakia. The Russian rulers did not know at the time that the recent edition of the *Soviet Encyclopedia* would say that the War of 1948 was caused by American imperialism and that the State of Israel is an imperialist base.

We should note one other fact that has gained special prominence these days: the impotence of the UN when either of the two Great Powers (the United States or the Soviet Union—though perhaps a few years from now there will be two others, India and China) is opposed to a UN position. Everyone knows the human tragedy that is taking place in Hungary. The world's conscience was shocked and the UN called on the Soviet Army to withdraw. It was decided that United Nations Observers would go to Hungary, but these have remained resolutions on paper, because the Soviet Union opposes their implementation.

Finally, there is another factor that must not be overlooked. In the past nine years fear of a world war has reached new heights, because never before has man had such destructive powers as he now possesses. Every nation trembles when it perceives the possibility or the danger of a new world conflagration, and the fear is justified.

In the political struggle in which we are now engaged, we need time, time for the world to weigh matters calmly, not hysterically or in panic but with a clear-eyed view of the situation. We have enemies who will not change their stand no matter how much we explain and demonstrate the justice of our cause. I fear that the answers Bulganin has received from the Israeli Prime Minister have not changed his attitude. The rulers of Soviet Russia want to win the friendship of the Arabs at any cost. The cheapest price for them is enmity toward Israel.

On November 2 several UN resolutions were adopted. One called for the withdrawal of foreign troops from Egypt; the second for freedom of navigation for all without discrimination. The Secretary General was sent to Egypt and returned with an agreement that Nasser had dictated. The agreement makes no mention of freedom of navigation, but speaks only of the evacuation of foreign troops. A report to this effect was submitted to the General Assembly, which approved it. For the moment nothing has been done in connection with freedom of navigation, since this does not accord with the wishes of the Egyptian dictator. We need time to explain these things to the public in the free world. Even now we can point to a change for the better in several countries. Public opinion in the United States has changed for the better. Practically every important American paper is now on our side. They both justify our action in Sinai and support our demands now that it is over. The same is true of several countries of Western Europe and to a lesser degree in Latin America as well.

Let no one delude himself that we have already won this struggle or are close to winning. Victory is still far away, for this is a struggle for the soul of the greater part of humanity, for its understanding, honesty, and attitude toward Israel's position, rights, and future. But this, like our political needs, will require no small amount of time. Our political imperative now is to put off the end of the withdrawal as long as possible. The political struggle will be both hard and drawn out. We will wage it by explaining the justice of our cause. Israel's survival and security depend on two things: our strength and the justice of our cause. These we shall maintain to the best of our ability.

Second and More Threatening Letter from Soviets ★ Ben-Gurion's Reasoned Reply

As the Prime Minister told the Officers Corps, one letter did not suffice for Bulganin, who was not satisfied with our reply. On November 15 he addressed a second letter to Israel, in the familiar Soviet style:

Mr. Prime Minister:

I have received your letter of November 8. In addition, we have at our disposal the texts of official statements by leaders of the Israeli Government during the past few days which enable us to judge Israel's position on the present situation in the region of the Near and Middle East. The position of the Soviet Government on the situation in this region was stated in my letter to you of November 5.

Since in your answer you attempt to defend the actions of Israel against Egypt, I am compelled briefly to reply to you concerning your conclusions.

Your letter maintains that the incursion of Israel's armed forces into Egyptian territory was necessitated by considerations of self-defense, justifying this by the existence of some threat to Israel from Egypt. Actually, as is borne out by a series of resolutions of the Security Council, it was not the Arab governments but precisely Israel that has been guilty of many armed attacks on the territory of neighboring Arab states. The Security Council has expressed grave concern with regard to the nonfulfillment by the Israeli Government of its obligations under the Armistice Agreements, and has called on the Israeli Government to carry out these obligations in the future under threat of suitable sanctions against Israel, as provided by the UN Charter.

Your very contention that Israel undertook an armed attack against Egypt, allegedly because of the danger threatening from Egypt, means that the Israeli Government has no desire to abide by the provisions of the UN Charter which forbid member states to resort to force and which demand the settlement of disputes between them by peaceful means.

The Soviet government cannot disregard the fact that the Israeli Government has not only failed to comply with the General Assembly's call for an immediate cease-fire and the withdrawal of troops that had invaded Egypt, but has openly announced its annexationist claims with regard to Egypt, its plans to seize and attach to Israel the Gaza region, the Sinai Peninsula, and the islands of Tiran and Snapir in the Gulf of Aqaba. Your speech in the Israel Parliament on November 7 also mentioned the "nullification" of the Armistice Agreements concluded by Israel with Arab States.

It is worth noting that even when compelled to decide on withdrawal of its troops from Egyptian territory, the Israeli Government still attempts to make compliance with this demand provisional on a "satisfactory agreement with the UN with respect to the entry of the international force into the Suez Canal Zone," which, as is known, is an inalienable part of the sovereign Egyptian state.

All this is in glaring contradiction with the contention in your letter that the policy of the Israeli Government is dictated by a "thirst for peace" and by Israel's "vital needs." The Soviet Government is convinced that Israel's present policy, directed at fanning hostility toward the Arab Governments and at crushing them, is in fact dangerous to the cause of general peace and fatal for Israel. Actually, as has been borne out by recent events, such a policy serves only the interests of outside forces seeking to reestablish a colonial order in this region; but we are fully convinced that it is foreign to the interests of all peoples of the Near and Middle East, without exception.

The Soviet Government has cautioned the Israeli Government about the dangerous consequences for Israel should aggressive armed actions be launched against the Arab states. We regret that you did not heed this. As a result of the aggression launched against Egypt by Israel, Egyptian towns and inhabited localities have been destroyed, thousands of innocent people have been killed and maimed, and damage has been inflicted on Egyptian communications, trade, and economy. But what has Israel achieved? Only the blind can fail to see that aggression has brought nothing good to Israel either. Without doubt aggression against Egypt has undermined Israel's international position, aroused profound hatred toward it on the part of the Arab and other peoples of the East, worsened Israel's relations with many states, and given rise to new economic and other difficulties within the country.

The Soviet Government takes into consideration that the Israel Government has ceased fire and subsequently announced the forthcoming withdrawal of Israeli troops from Egyptian territory. It is self-evident that Israeli troops must be withdrawn from Egyptian territory without delay. At the same time, in order to stabilize the situation in the Near East and to liquidate the consequence of the aggression against Egypt, the Soviet government considers it essential that measures be taken to remove the possibilities of new provocations by Israel against neighboring states and to ensure a durable peace and tranquillity in the region.

Justice also demands that Egypt, as the victim of unprovoked aggression, should be compensated by Israel, as well as by Britain and France, for the losses inflicted through the destruction of Egyptian towns and inhabited localities, and as a result of interruption in the operation of the Suez Canal and the destruction of its installations. In addition, Israel is obliged to return to Egypt all property that has been removed from Egyptian territory by the Israel armed forces that invaded it.

The international armed forces of the UN, to whose creation the Egyptian government has agreed, in accordance with the UN resolutions, must be deployed on both sides of the demarcation line between Israel and Egypt established by the Armistice Agreements.

I want to express the hope, Mr. Prime Minister, that the Israeli Government will draw the proper conclusions from the lessons which the latest events indicate for Israel.

N. Bulganin.

The Prime Minister on November 17 replied as follows:

Mr. President of the Council of Ministers:

I have received your letter of November 15, 1956. In view of the statements therein, I feel compelled to draw your attention once more to the true state of affairs in the relations between Egypt and Israel which has produced the present crisis.

The basic fact of the situation is that when the State of Israel was established on May 14, 1948, the Egyptian Army, and with it the armies of the other Arab states, invaded our country for the purpose of annihilating us. Upon the termination of these hostilities Armistice Agreements were signed between Egypt, Lebanon, Jordan, and Syria on the one hand, and Israel on the other. Egypt, however, did not honor her obligations under these agreements and has continued her hostile acts against Israel to this day. I cannot but express my surprise at the fact that you do not appear to be aware of these roots of the tension in our area, and I must therefore stress the true background of the situation. The facts are as follows:

(1). When the General Assembly of the United Nations in November 1947 resolved in favor of the establishment of the Jewish State, Egypt at the head of the other Arab states declared publicly that she would not recognize and would oppose this resolution.

(2). Pursuant to this defiant declaration, the Egyptian Army, together with the military forces of the other Arab states, invaded the State of Israel on the night of May 15, 1948, for the purpose of destroying Israel.

(3). In the course of the proceedings of the Security Council after this brutal invasion, the representatives of the USSR, and of the Ukranian SSR., together with the spokesmen of other states, condemned the action of Egypt and other Arab countries in attacking Israel. At the 309th meeting of the Security Council on May 29, 1948, Mr. Gromyko, representative of the USSR, stated: "Indeed, what is happening in Palestine can only be described as military operations organized by a group of states against the Jewish State," and that "the states whose forces had invaded Palestine have ignored the Security Council resolutions."

(4). At the 366th meeting of the Security Council on July 14, 1948, Mr. Gromyko, representative of the USSR, declared that "the Arabs dispatched their troops to invade Palestinian territory and made no bones about informing the whole world that it was their firm intention to prevent the creation of independent Arab and Jewish states in Palestine."

(5). In the Armistice Agreement between Israel and Egypt, signed on February 24, 1949, it was expressly stated that the purpose of the agreement was to "promote the return of permanent peace in Palestine."

(6). In spite of the fact that Egypt signed this agreement, the rulers of that country have maintained ever since that Egypt is in a state of war with Israel.

(7). This declaration of the Egyptian government is contrary not merely to the terms of the Armistice Agreement, but also to the Charter of the United Nations, which requires all member states of the United Nations to live together in peace as good neighbors and to resolve all international disputes by peaceful means.

(8). The Security Council in its resolution of September 1, 1951, expressly denied the right of either party to the Armistice Agreement "to assert that it is actively a belligerent." Egypt defied this decision, as well, and continued to proclaim that she was in a state of war with Israel.

(9). As one of its instruments of war against Israel the government of Egypt organized an economic boycott of Israel and used intimidation to apply pressure on business under-takings in various countries to break off economic relations with Israel.

(10). In violation of the Constantinople Convention of 1888, which guarantees to all countries freedom of navigation in the Suez Canal in time of peace as in time of war, and in defiance of the resolution adopted by the Security Council on September 1, 1951, which prohibited interference with Israel's right of free navigation in the Suez Canal, Egypt has continued to maintain a wartime blockade against the State of Israel in the canal.

(11). On October 13, 1956, the Security Council unanimously adopted a resolution prohibiting any overt or covert discrimination against any state in regard to navigation in the

Suez Canal. This was immediately followed by a renewed declaration on the part of the Egyptian government that Israeli shipping would not be allowed to pass through the canal.

(12).   The Egyptian government did not limit itself to a maritime blockade in the Suez Canal, but throughout the period under consideration extended its blockade also to the Gulf of Aqaba. In violation of international law it prevented Israel shipping passing through the gulf on its way to and from the port of Eilat.

(13).   In pursuing her war against Israel, in continuous contravention of the Armistice Agreement, Egypt did not confine herself to the maintenance of the economic boycott and the maritime blockade designed to bring about the economic collapse of our country. For the past two years the Egyptian government has organized specially trained gangs of murderers and saboteurs, known as Fedayeen, and sent them clandestinely from the Gaza Strip and the Sinai desert into our villages and onto our highways. These terrorist gangs have murdered Israeli workers in the fields, travelers on the roads, and children in the schools. They have also blown up irrigation pipes and agricultural installations in our villages.

(14).   We have in our possession instructions issued to these murderers by officers of the Egyptian Regular Army; files describing the itineraries and activities of Fedayeen groups under the direct command of the Egyptian army in the Gaza Strip and the Sinai desert; furthermore, documents showing that these gangs received their arms and equipment from units of the Egyptian Army. In my letter to you of November 8, 1956, I enclosed photostatic evidence of Egypt's design to destroy Israel. If you so desire, I shall supply you with additional photostatic evidence proving the connection between these gangs of murderers and saboteurs and the commanders of the Egyptian Army.

(15).   The rulers of Egypt have repeatedly proclaimed throughout the last eight years—and these declarations have become more outspoken and more frequent during the past two years—that the time was drawing near when the Egyptian Army would eliminate Israel by force. Have these declarations never reached your ears?

In recent months matters have come to a head. A series of developments has brought home to us the imminent danger to our very existence:

(a)   A few weeks ago Egypt signed aggressive military pacts with Syria and Jordan, the purpose of which was the destruction of Israel.

(b)   During the period of the Suez crisis, when the Security Council was considering the problem of the canal, the activities of the Fedayeen ceased. As soon, however, as the Security Council had completed its deliberations on the subject, on October 13, 1956, Egypt intensified the murderous activities of these bands. Hundreds of these trained murderers were sent by the Egyptian military command to the other Arab countries—Jordan, Syria, and Lebanon—to step up their activities from bases against Israel's citizens and border villages all along our frontiers in the north, east, and south. Almost every day peaceful Israeli citizens were murdered by the terror squads sent out by the Egyptian military dictator.

(c)   In the Gaza Strip and all along our borders with the Sinai Peninsula, enormous Egyptian military forces were concentrated, equipped with tremendous quantities of aggressive weapons, poised to attack and destroy Israel.

These facts are known to the entire world. I would add that the vast quantities of Egyptian weapons and military equipment that were destroyed by our forces in the Sinai Desert clearly indicate the intentions and the preparations of the Egyptian dictator. It was, therefore, the elementary duty of our Government to take defensive measures in accordance with the right assured to every state under Article 51 of the United Nations Charter—to protect the lives of its citizens and defend the existence of the State by destroying the Fedayeen nests and the Egyptian military bases that directed their activities. Any other people similarly placed would have been compelled to do the same.

You say in your letter that in my address to the Israeli Parliament on November 7, 1956,

I stated that the Armistice Agreements signed by Israel with the Arab states were no longer valid. This is not correct. If you examine the text of my speech you will find that I said in that address that Israel on her part will observe the Armistice Agreements with the other Arab countries—even though the latter are not prepared for permanent peace—as long as they, on their part, are prepared to observe these Agreements.

What I said in the Knesset was that the Armistice Agreement with Egypt—and only that with Egypt, not those with the other Arab states—is dead and buried and will not return to life. For years the Egyptian dictator has treated the Agreement with contempt, has violated its principles and purposes, has defied the Charter of the United Nations and the resolutions of the Security Council. By his repeated declarations that a state of war existed between Egypt and Israel he distorted the nature and aim of the Armistice Agreement, whose first and fundamental article states that it was signed with a view to promoting the return of permanent peace.

In my address I stated further that "the Egyptian dictator has throughout been exploiting the Agreement as a smokescreen for his murderous attacks against Israeli citizens, and as a cover for his relentless blockade of Israel on land, at sea, and in the air. Colonel Nasser did not content himself with the Fedayeen gangs, which he organized in the territory under his control; he also directed and activated these gangs against Israel from the other Arab countries. In this way the Armistice Agreement became a harmful and a dangerous fiction, serving only the destructive plans of the Egyptian dictator. Any return to the Armistice Agreement means a return to murder, blockade, and boycott, directed against Israel, aimed at her ultimate destruction."

As for the recent resolutions of the General Assembly of the United Nations, we have announced that we are prepared to withdraw our forces from Egypt when satisfactory arrangements have been made with the United Nations in connection with the International Force mentioned in the resolution. This declaration remains fully valid.

From the mass flight and surrender of the Egyptian soldiers, peasants torn from their homes in Egypt and sent against their will to do battle in a remote desert, it is clear that these soldiers were not prepared to fight for the fascist dictator of Cairo. The first to flee were officers of the Egyptian Army. This is conclusive proof that many people in Egypt have come to understand the true character of Gamal Abdel Nasser, who at the beginning pretended that he was concerned to improve the conditions of his people—in health, education, and economic development—but who since then has shown himself to be consumed by the lust for power and the ambition to impose his rule on all the Islamic peoples. He has squandered his country's resources to increase his military power and armaments to carry through his expansionist ambitions and make himself master of the Moslem world.

I have to point out that your statements about our military operations are not accurate. We have not destroyed a single Egyptian town, nor have we caused harm to any civilian center. We have not damaged the Suez Canal; as far as we know, the canal has been blocked by the Egyptians themselves. Our forces were given strict instructions not to injure civilians, and these instructions were faithfully observed. The transport that did suffer—and this for years—was that of Israel, in the air, on land, and at sea, as a result of Egypt's illegal blockade.

If there is a case for claiming compensation, it is we who are entitled to compensation for the Egyptian invasion of our country in 1948, for the deaths of thousands of our sons and daughters as a result of this aggression, for the economic boycott and the maritime blockade maintained in defiance of the UN Charter and the Security Council's resolutions, for the hundreds of Israeli Jews and Arabs murdered by the Fedayeen, and for all the damage caused to our economy, running into millions of pounds. However, if peace is established between Egypt and ourselves, we shall be ready to forgive all past transgressions of the Egyptian rulers.

In closing, I would repeat my statement that, in accordance with Article 33 of the Charter, Israel is prepared for a settlement of her dispute with Egypt, as well as with the other Arab states, by peaceful means. It is with regret that I have to point out that several of the expressions about Israel used in your letter are not likely to be interpreted by the Arab rulers as as encouragement to the achievement of peace in our region. Nor would they appear appropriate to the accepted relations between member states of the United Nations.

I am confident that if the USSR will lend its support to bring about direct peace negotiations between Israel and her neighbors, this will be a real and significant contribution to the strengthening of peace in the Middle East and throughout the world.

David Ben-Gurion

Israel Demands Freedom of Navigation in the Tiran Straits ★ US Suggests Provisions Against Egyptian Armed Incursions from the Gaza Strip

The political struggle, touched off in the first days of the Sinai Campaign, continued for four months—from the beginning of November 1956 until the first days of March 1957. It went through three phases.

In the first, lasting until February 11, virtually the entire world demanded Israel's withdrawal behind the armistice lines without any prior conditions. Secretary-General Hammarskjöld adopted an obdurate attitude against Israel such as he had not shown to any of the Arab states when they refused to submit to UN resolutions or to comply with the verdict of the Security Council. He stubbornly refused to discuss Israel's demands, even those that had been recognized at the UN General Assembly, until the Israeli forces withdrew.

The young and small State of Israel thus found itself embroiled in a bitter controversy with two world forces for which it had no less esteem than any other country, namely, the United Nations and the United States. It was a controversy over moral questions of profound significance in international relations: Should the UN, with the support of the United States, countenance discrimination, adopting one standard toward dictatorial Egypt and another toward democratic Israel? Should those who sought to destroy us be allowed to send terrorists and saboteurs into our territory but not permit us to fight for our lives? Should the UN, with American support, subject us to sanctions because we refused to submit to the double moral standard of an Egyptian dictator who insisted that others observe all obligations to his advantage, while ignoring bilateral agreements and international obligations he considered advantageous to our side? Would the UN and the United States give the stamp of their approval to a regime of shameful and deliberate discrimination in international relations?

Even in the midst of this tragic struggle the Government of Israel was not misled into a sweeping condemnation of others. While it saw the shadows and the weak points in the UN, it also esteemed the great vision that organization symbolized. Despite the bitter and tragic controversy with the government of the United States, it did not forget that this great nation had extended a loyal helping hand to us before and after our State was created; nor, no less important, that the United States had in the course of nearly two centuries carried out a vast pioneering work of building and developing an underpopulated land, absorbing and integrating tens of millions of immigrants from many countries; had fought a cruel civil war of more than four years' duration to free the slaves; and created the greatest and strongest democracy in the world.

In the debate between the governments of Israel and the United States, we sought not to close the way to continued negotiations; and it should be pointed out that on its part the United States at all times showed no small amount of goodwill and patience. Nevertheless, American pressure on Israel to comply with the UN Assembly resolution, in the matter of withdrawal to the armistice lines, continued unabated. It was applied not only by the American delegation in the UN but also by President Eisenhower himself in a series of letters and messages to the Israeli Prime Minister.

Israel's position was made more difficult by the fact that France and Britain had quickly and completely liquidated their occupation of the Suez Canal, and complied unconditionally with the United Nations demand. The British Foreign Minister, Selwyn Lloyd, even announced in Parliament that Britain had informed the UN of its concurrence in the need to obtain the rapid withdrawal of the Israeli military forces.

When the UN adopted the Canadian resolution to set up an international peace-keeping force, an advisory committee was appointed by the Secretary General consisting of representatives from seven countries—Brazil, Canada, Ceylon, Colombia, India, Norway, and Pakistan. The Israeli delegates in the UN met with four of the members (a majority) of this committee—Brazil, Norway, Colombia, and Canada—and explained to them Israel's position and found a willing ear. The Secretary General, however, subsequently conferred but little with this committee.

On December 29 our Foreign Minister, Golda Meir, met with Secretary of State Dulles. She told him that least of all we wanted a clash with the government of the United States or a crisis with the UN. We were therefore asking him to announce support for freedom of passage in the Straits of Eilat and the nonreturn to Egypt of the Gaza Strip; to persuade Hammarskjöld to postpone any changes in Sinai and the Gaza Strip until a settlement was reached and agreed to; and to obtain a United States guarantee of freedom of navigation in the Straits.

Dulles protested that we had not consulted the United States before the invasion, which was equally his complaint against France and England. In his opinion, our action in Sinai had reduced the chances of rectifying the wrongs we had suffered. He could not do things behind Hammarskjöld's back. Although in large measure he concurred with Israel's claims, they had to be brought to the United Nations. His government supported freedom of navigation in the Suez Canal and agreed that the Gulf of Eilat was an international waterway open to navigation by all. The Gaza Strip had never been Egyptian territory, he acknowledged, but according to the Armistice Agreement it was not included in the territory of Israel either. It was incumbent upon the government of Israel to work for peace with its neighbors. While the United States felt great friendship for Israel, it could see no end to the difficulties in the Middle East from the standpoint of Israeli-Arab relations. Mrs. Meir expressed regret and surprise that Dulles had disregarded all of Israel's efforts to achieve peace. The unfortunate fact was that the Arab leaders were refusing to recognize Israel's right to exist; as he knew, even the attempts by President Eisenhower to bring about negotiations between Israel and the Arab countries had been of no avail.

On January 1 the Prime Minister wrote to Gen. Walter Bedell Smith, one of the men closest to General Eisenhower having been Chief of Staff during World War Two. He explained what had led up to and made the Sinai campaign inevitable (the specific points were those given in the second letter to Marshal Bulganin quoted above). He pointed out Israel's unceasing efforts to establish peace since the first day of its existence, and recalled President Eisenhower's attempt the previous year to send a special envoy for that purpose to Jerusalem and Cairo—a move that Nasser had set at naught.

Israel understood that the United States has global considerations that might not be identical with Israel's vital needs, the letter recognized. Even a small nation has a right to exist, however, and its citizens to live without terror and murder by gangs organized by a government that had concluded an Armistice Agreement with Israel whereby it undertook not to cross the border with regular or paramilitary forces. We were certain that had the Egyptian dictator succeeded in destroying us, many people in America would have felt regret. We believed that we have the right to life rather than to sympathy after our death, and we were certain that any other state facing similar dangers and plots would have acted as we did, so would the America of Eisenhower, about whose sincere devotion to peace no one had the slightest doubt.

On the same day Ben-Gurion conferred with Mr. Lawson, the American Ambassador to Israel. The Ambassador handed the Prime Minister an *aide-memoire* that agreed that the Armistice Agreement should not be revoked unilaterally. The Prime Minister, however, pointed out that the Egyptian leader had been violating the agreement continually, all these years, by rejecting peace, imposing a boycott and blockade in the Suez Canal and the Straits of Eilat, and organizing gangs of saboteurs and murderers whom he sent into Israel. As for Gaza, it had never been part of Egypt, and had it not been for the American intervention in 1948, we would have expelled the Egyptians from the Strip.

Abba Eban, who met with General Smith in Washington, reported that the General was highly impressed with the analysis and arguments in the Prime Minister's letter and had forwarded copies, along with a letter of recommendation and support, to President Eisenhower, Secretary Dulles, and several friends highly influential in the shaping of American policy.

An *aide-mémoire* submitted to Dulles by Eban called attention to the fact that Israel was the only littoral state on both the Mediterranean and the Red Sea, and that after the Gulf of Eilat was conquered, on November 3, 1956, Israel had opened it to all nations without discrimination. From the legal standpoint the Straits of Tiran were an international waterway, the document made clear, because:

1. They provided access to four littoral states bordering on the gulf.

2. They constituted the only passage to and from the coast of Eilat.

3. The International Court of Justice had ruled that in straits constituting a waterway serving more than one country, all states have the right of navigation, even if the straits fall wholly or partly within the territorial waters of one country or another.

4. The Security Council in 1951 had rejected an Egyptian claim of the right to search or seize ships headed for Israel.

5. The United States had declared in the Security Council that the 1951 principle applied also to the Gulf of Aqaba (Eilat).

6. In reply to a question by the US government in January 1950 Egypt had stated that passage through the Straits of Tiran would remain free as it had in the past "in accordance with international law."

Israel accordingly demanded that the debate on its withdrawal from Sharm el-Sheikh be postponed until concrete guarantees had been provided for freedom of navigation in the Straits. Its appeal proved of no avail. On February 2 the General Assembly adopted two additional resolutions. The first deplored the failure of Israel to complete its withdrawal behind the Armistice demarcation line despite repeated UN requests and called upon Israel to do so without further delay. In the second resolution the Assembly re-recognized among other things (the wording was vague) that withdrawal by Israel must be followed by action to assure progress toward the creation of peaceful conditions.

On the night of February 4 the American Ambassador handed the Israeli Prime Minister a note from President Eisenhower, which said, among other things:

> You know how greatly our people value close ties of friendship with your people, and how interested we are in continuing the friendly cooperation that has contributed to Israel's national development. I therefore feel it necessary to make the strongest possible plea to Israel that she cease ignoring the United Nations resolutions which, taken as a whole, can help, I believe, to bring tranquility and justice to your country and her neighbors. Continued disregard for international opinion, as expressed in the UN resolutions, will almost certainly lead to further UN action which will seriously damage relations between Israel and UN members, including the United States.

In his reply to Eisenhower, Ben-Gurion expressed his gratitude for the friendly relations between the two countries and added:

> In response to your request of November 7, we began the evacuation of our forces from the Sinai Desert. They withdrew from an area of more than 50,000 km., remaining only in a narrow strip along the western shore of the Gulf of Eilat, in order to ensure freedom of passage through the Gulf. We have informed the UN that we have no intention of remaining permanently in this strip, and that we will evacuate it as soon as we receive adequate guarantees of freedom of passage. I must regretfully point out that the United Nations has not treated Egypt and Israel in the same manner so far as this question is concerned. For eight years Egypt acted in violation of the Armistice Agreement and of the UN Charter. She violated a clear decision of the Security Council when she denied us free passage through the Canal and also failed to keep her word about freedom of passage through the Gulf of Eilat. I refer to the solemn Egyptian obligation transmitted to the American Ambassador in Cairo on January 28, 1950. All those who had the power and authority to intervene failed to take the necessary steps to prevent these very grave violations of international obligations.
>
> We stand ready to withdraw our forces from Sharm el-Sheikh if there is a guarantee of passage through the Straits. We are also willing, out of respect for the United Nations, to withdraw our forces from the Gaza Strip immediately, leaving behind a civilian administration and a police force. Only such arrangements will ensure peace and stability in the region, give the local population a real share in its administration and prepare them for economic independence. Such arrangements will also increase the chances of a brighter future for the refugees in an atmosphere free from Egyptian agitation.
>
> Do we not have the same right to freedom from attack guaranteed by the UN Charter to other nations? With all due respect, I must ask you, Mr. President, why did the American

Government and other governments that supported the UN General Assembly resolution fail to take effective measures to give us such security?

In your letter you spoke of the possibility that"measures"might be taken against Israel by the UN if she failed to carry out, in full, the General Assembly resolution. Such"measures" were not taken against Egypt when for many years she failed—as she still fails—to abide by the decisions of the Security Council or to respect the UN Charter; moreover, they are being contemplated at a time when public opinion in the free nations is beginning to understand the justice of our demands. Is it possible that the United States will give its support to such discrimination, and to UN"measures"designed to force us, against our will, to return to a situation where we will be subject to murder and blockade?

Mr. President, the Law which we received over three thousand years ago at Mount Sinai, and which has since become the heritage of all mankind, forbids discrimination between one man and another, or between one people and another. Despite thousands of years of persecution, we have never lost our faith in the ultimate triumph of justice, peace and human brotherhood. It is inconceivable that now, after we have regained our independence in our ancient homeland, we should submit to discrimination. Whatever the consequences, our people will never agree to do so.

Will the UN act one way towards Egypt and another way towards Israel? You, more than any living man, can help put an end to all hostility and to bring peace between our neighbors and ourselves.

Please permit me to conclude with my appreciation for your concern about my health; I value this most profoundly.

Sincerely yours,
David Ben-Gurion

The great work of our Embassy in Washington and our delegation to the UN General Assembly headed by Golda Meir and Abba Eban left its mark on American public opinion. The press, Congressional circles, and intellectuals showed greater understanding of Israel's position and the justice of its cause. The pressure of public opinion led to a change in policy that marked the beginning of the second phase of our political struggle.

On February 11, 1957, Secretary of State Dulles, on behalf of President Eisenhower, made public a note that had been delivered to the Israeli Ambassador in Washington and said, among other things:

We believe that the United Nations General Assembly and the Secretary General should seek that the United Nations Emergency Force, in the exercise of its mission, move into this area and be on the boundary between Israel and the Gaza Strip. . . .

With respect to the Gulf of Aqaba and access thereto—the United States believes that the Gulf comprehends international waters and that no nation has the right to prevent free and innocent passage in the Gulf and through the Straits giving access thereto. We have in mind not only commercial usage but the passage of pilgrims on religious missions, which should be fully respected.

The United States recalls that on January 28, 1950, the Egyptian Ministry of Foreign Affairs informed the United States that the Egyptian occupation of the two islands of Tiran and Snapir at the entrance of the Gulf of Aqaba was only to protect the islands themselves against possible damage of violation and that "this occupation being in no way conceived in a spirit of obstructing in any way innocent passage through the stretch of water separating these two islands from the Egyptian Coast of Sinai; it follows that this passage, the only practicable one, will remain as in the past, in conformity with international practice and recognized principle of the law of nations."

In the absence of some overriding decision to the contrary, as by the International Court of Justice, the United States, on behalf of vessels of United States registry, is prepared to exercise the right of innocent passage and to join with others to secure general recognition of this right.

It is of course clear that the enjoyment of a right of free and innocent passage by Israel would depend on its prior withdrawal in accordance with the United Nations resolutions.

The Government of Israel gave this document serious consideration and expressed its appreciation of the efforts by the President and his Secretary of State to find a solution to the problems of navigation in the Straits of Eilat and of the Gaza Strip. Mr. Dulles' *aide-mémoire*, however, was unsatisfactory in that it stipulated prior withdrawal to the Armistice demarcation lines in the Gaza Strip and evacuation of the coast of the Straits of Eilat. We summoned Eban to Jerusalem for consultations, and on February 18 the Prime Minister sent the following letter to Mr. Dulles:

At this last moment, before the clock strikes twelve, I turn to you personally in an attempt to prevent a fateful misunderstanding between our two peoples. I would like to request that you arrange for a temporary postponement of the Assembly debate and for the appointment of a committee comprising representatives of several disinterested states that will immediately go to Israel—and, if necessary, to Egypt as well—to facilitate an agreed settlement of the dispute over Sharm el-Sheikh and the Gaza Strip. A withdrawal in present circumstances might have disastrous consequences. I must again point out that Egypt has pursued an aggressive policy against Israel since May 15, 1948, and has publicly declared her intention to continue pursuing such a policy.

President Eisenhower, rather than Dulles, replied on February 20, stating that he would make a radio and television address on the Middle East situation that evening. He listed thirteen points that night:

1. The United States has no ambitions or desires in this region. It hopes only that each country there may maintain its independence and live peacefully within itself and with its neighbors.

2. The United States fully realizes that military action against Egypt resulted from grave and repeated provocations, but also that military force to solve international disputes cannot be reconciled with the principles and purposes of the United Nations.

3. Israeli forces have been withdrawn from much of the territory of Egypt that they had occupied. They remain at the mouth of the Gulf of Aqaba, which is about a hundred miles from the nearest Israeli territory. Israeli forces still remain outside the Armistice lines and they are in the Gaza Strip, which, under the Armistice Agreement, was to be occupied by Egypt. These facts create the present crisis. A fateful moment approaches when either we must recognize that the United Nations is unable to restore peace in this area or the United Nations must renew with increased vigor its efforts to bring about Israeli withdrawal.

4. If Israel will withdraw in response to the repeated requests of the United Nations, greater security and tranquillity for that nation will be achieved.

5. The United States was a co-sponsor of the United Nations resolution and thus sought to assure that Israel would, in the future, enjoy its rights under the Armistice and under international law.

6. Neither the United States nor the United Nations has authority to impose upon the parties a substantial modification of the Armistice Agreement that was freely signed by both Israel and Egypt.

7. Nevertheless, the United States, as a member of the United Nations, will seek such disposition of the United Nations Emergency Force as will assure that the Gaza Strip can no longer be used as a source of armed infiltration and reprisals.

8. The United States will be glad to urge and support participation by the United Nations, with the approval of Egypt, in the administration of the Gaza Strip.

9. With reference to the passage into and through the Gulf of Aqaba, we have expressed the conviction that the Gulf constitutes international waters, and that no nation has the right to prevent free and innocent passage in the Gulf.

10. Peace and justice are two sides of the same coin. Perhaps the world community has been at fault in not having paid enough attention to this basic truth. The United States, for its part, will vigorously seek solutions of the problems of the area in accordance with justice and international law.

11. The United Nations has no choice but to exert pressure upon Israel to comply with the withdrawal resolutions.

12. Egypt, by accepting the six principles adopted by the Security Council last October in relation to the Suez Canal, bound itself to free and open transit through the canal without discrimination, and to the principle that the operation of the canal be insulated from the politics of any country.

13. We should not assume that if Israel withdraws, Egypt will prevent Israeli shipping from using the Suez Canal or the Gulf of Aqaba. If, unhappily, Egypt does thereafter violate the Armistice Agreement or other international obligations, then this should be dealt with firmly by the society of nations.

On February 21 the Prime Minister informed President Eisenhower that Abba Eban, who was returning to the United States the next day, would present the Israeli Government's considered position.

American Jewry Backs Israel's Stand ★ French Proposal, Supported by the United States, Confirms Freedom of Navigation To and From Eilat ★ UN Force To Take Over in the Gaza Strip ★ Israel Vacates Conquered Territories.

President Eisenhower's broadcast on February 20 made a strong impression on public opinion and on the American Congress. The next day the influential *Washington Post* ran an editorial headed "The Last Chance for Compliance."

Israel, it said, "cannot reasonably demand that Egypt renounce belligerency while she herself remains in territory assigned to Egypt for occupation under that armistice," but she is entitled "to ask that the UN Emergency Force move into the Gaza Strip simultaneously with her withdrawal." And it concluded with these words:

> Let her declare explicitly that if Colonel Nasser does not afford her adequate protection, she will reserve the right to take whatever steps she deems necessary in her defense with a clear conscience. That will place the responsibility squarely on the UN and at the same time invite new respect for Israel in world opinion.

At the same time the President and his Secretary of State took measures to mobilize the leaders of American Jewry. Jacob Blaustein, Philip Klutznik, William Rosenwald, and others were invited to meet with Mr. Dulles on February 21. At the meeting they spoke firmly and with dignity in support of Israel's demands, and Klutznik, the president of Bnai Brith, announced publicly that the State of Israel was completely justified in demanding safeguards before leaving the conquered areas.

On the same day the problem was debated in the Knesset. The discussion was opened by the Prime Minister, who said:

> Yesterday the President of the United States told the American people that the UN would exert pressure on Israel to withdraw from the Gaza Strip and the western shore of the Gulf of Eilat. In spite of the painful feelings aroused by some of his words, I cannot forget for a moment that President Eisenhower is not only the elected leader of the American nation, but one of the most illustrious men of our generation, who personally contributed to the destruction of what was perhaps the most monstrous regime in human history.
>
> President Eisenhower's letter a fortnight ago contained the same demand he made yesterday in the message to his people. For me this constituted great moral pressure, for I was keenly conscious of the personality and the standing of the writer. If I was compelled to reply as I did, it was only under a still stronger compulsion: the pressure of my conscience as a man and a Jew, the pressure of the justice for which my people were fighting and the absolute certainty that justice is the source of the strength and survival of my people.
>
> In his speech, the President rightly declared that the United Nations and its member states must from now on make a great effort to safeguard international law and justice. These words clearly imply that until now the United Nations has not adequately done its duty in this respect—and the main victim has been Israel. For eight years the United Nations had permitted acts of hostility, boycott, blockade, and murder by the Egyptian government against Israel. The people of Israel cannot submit to discrimination in international relations. We have believed and we shall continue to believe in the conscience of humanity and we appeal to the American government and to all friends of peace and justice in the world to stand by our side and help to secure for the people of Israel its international rights, sovereign equality, peace, and security.

Our Ambassador to the United Nations, Mr. Eban, who had been called back for consultations, was instructed to make a supreme effort in Washington and the General Assembly to have the problems of freedom of navigation and of the Gaza Strip separated, in order to secure freedom of navigation before we retreated from the Strip. At least in the matter of freedom of navigation we saw eye to eye with the United States government. In a cable sent after his departure for America, Eban was requested to tell the American government that Israel required:

> (1) That her ships be permitted to sail in the Gulf and carry on trade to Eilat, including the transport of oil to Eilat.
> (2) That the United States government publicly acknowledge that if Egypt interfered with Israeli shipping in the Gulf and in the Straits after the evacuation, Israel would have the right in self-defense to adopt all forceful measures necessary to secure freedom of passage.
> (3) That the definition of "free and innocent" should include warships, *i.e.*, that Israeli warships should have complete freedom to sail in the Straits and the Gulf.
> (4) That in the event the United Nations General Assembly passed no resolution calling for the stationing of an international force on the western shores of the Straits until peace is achieved, there should be a resolution calling for a United Nations naval force to patrol the Straits and the Gulf until peace is achieved.

(5) That the United States government should obtain declarations from as large a number of states as possible, recognizing the Gulf as an international waterway and the terms of paragraph two above.

Immediately on his arrival in the United States, Eban met with Dulles and his assistants. In accordance with the Prime Minister's request, Dulles said, the United States was making efforts to have the UN debate deferred until February 25. He listened attentively to Eban's proposals and after consulting with his assistants expressed satisfaction with the "constructive program," which he considered a sincere effort by Israel to find a practical solution to the crisis. Eban cabled the Prime Minister that Dulles had accepted our proposal regarding the Gulf, had agreed to separate the problem of the Straits from that of the Gaza Strip, and that as soon as we evacuated the shore of the Straits our right of free navigation would be recognized independently of a settlement in the Gaza Strip.

Subsequently, in a meeting with Hammarskjöld, Eban encountered hostile opposition. The Secretary General refused to discuss any arrangement whatsoever that did not recognize Egypt's rights in the Gaza Strip under the Armistice Agreement.

In the Knesset debate on February 25, 1957, regarding the exchange of letters between the United States President and the Israel Government, the Prime Minister remarked: "The stationing of the IDF on the shore of the Straits was not and is not our objective. It is merely a means for safeguarding freedom of navigation. What we are fighting for is not the occupation of a strip of uninhabited, albeit beautiful desert, but a free outlet to the Red Sea and the Indian Ocean. If we got the recognition of the UN and of the Great Powers for our right to use force to defend our shipping in the Straits and the Red Sea if it were attacked by force, we would see in this the safest guarantee for freedom of navigation, at least for a fairly long period."

In the General Assembly on February 28 the Canadian Ambassador, Lester Pearson, proposed that the Assembly confirm that there should be no interference with shipping in the Straits. The Israel forces would withdraw and the UN force would move in behind them to the shore of the Straits, as well as to the other parts of Sinai; Israel would withdraw from the Gaza Strip but Egypt's forces would not return to it. Rapid negotiations would take place over the relinquishment by Israel of the civil administration. The Secretary General would appoint a UN Commissioner for Gaza to work in coordination with the commander of the UN Forces. All this would be in the nature of a provisional settlement. A permanent settlement would be dependent on the United Nations.

Meeting again with Secretary of State Dulles the same day, Abba Eban explained that Hammarskjöld's insistence on acting solely in terms of Egyptian rule in the Gaza Strip ruled out any possibility of discussing the problem. An agreement on the freedom of navigation in the Straits had to be arranged first. Dulles replied that for the moment he was not prepared to separate the two problems; however, a meeting had taken place that morning between President Eisenhower, French Prime Minister Mollet, French Foreign Minister Pineau, and himself at which the French made a proposal that in the opinion of the four might lead to a solution. He and the President supported this proposal, but he was not permitted to divulge its nature.

Abba Eban proceeded immediately to the French Embassy to confer with Pineau. Pineau said that France had no intention of exerting pressure on Israel to accept the plan, which seemed to him was to Israel's benefit. It was as follows: The United States, France, Britain, and other countries would declare—a declaration that would not require approval by a two-thirds majority—that every country had the right of freedom of navigation in the Straits to and from Eilat and that they recognized Israel's right to safeguard this against any aggression, in accordance with Article 51 of the UN Charter. In the Gaza Strip the UN Force would take over exclusively all the powers of the military and civilian administration after the Israeli withdrawal and in the interim period would fulfill the following functions: safeguarding life and property, police services, effective civilian administration, a program to assist the refugees in the Strip and its inhabitants. "The interim period" would be the time between the departure of the Israeli forces and the peace settlement. In announcing its decision in the Assembly, Israel would state that it was leaving solely on the basis of the above-mentioned assumptions. The plan had the support of the United States.

This marked the beginning of the third and final phase of the political struggle. The Government of Israel agreed to the plan, provided that the maritime powers announced their acceptance even without its being put to a vote in the Assembly, since an Assembly resolution required a two-thirds majority and it was obviously impossible to mobilize two-thirds of the UN members for this purpose.

With the participation of Abba Eban, and with the concurrence of the delegations of the United States and France, the statement that Mrs. Meir would make in the Assembly was prepared, after which the delegations of the United States, France, Canada, Britain, and other members would announce their concurrence. Henry Cabot Lodge, the American Ambassador to the United Nations, was sent to discuss this matter with Hammarskjöld.

On the afternoon of March 1 Mrs. Meir made the following declaration in the Assembly concerning the evacuation of the Gaza Strip:

> The Government of Israel announces that it is making a complete withdrawal from the Gaza Strip. In accordance with General Assembly resolution (I) of February 2, 1957, it makes this on the following assumptions: (a) On its withdrawal the United Nations Forces will be deployed in Gaza and the takeover of Gaza from the military and civilian control of Israel will be exclusively by the United Nations Emergency Force. (b) It is further Israel's expectation that the United Nations will be the agency utilized to carry out the functions enumerated by the Secretary-General, namely: "safeguarding life and property in the area by providing efficient and effective police protection, as will guarantee good civilian administration, as will assure maximum assistance to the United Nations refugee program, and as will protect and foster the economic development of the territory and its people." (c) It is further Israel's expectation that the aforementioned responsibility of the United Nations in the administration of Gaza will be maintained for a transition period from the takeover until there is a peace settlement, to be sought as rapidly as possible, or a definitive agreement on the future of the Gaza Strip.
>
> Israel is also prepared to evacuate the shore of the Gulf of Aqaba in accordance with General Assembly Resolution (II) of February 2, which contemplates that units of the United Nations Emergency Force will move into the Straits of Tiran area on Israel's withdrawal. The main function of the United Nations Emergency Force in the Straits of Tiran area will be the prevention of belligerent acts, and freedom of navigation for Israeli and international shipping will be assured following the withdrawal of the Israeli forces.
>
> The Gulf of Aqaba comprises international waters and no nation has the right to prevent free and innocent passage in the Gulf and through the Straits giving access thereto. In its capacity as a littoral state, Israel will gladly offer port facilities to the ships of all nations and all flags exercising free passage in the Gulf of Aqaba. We have received with gratification the assurances of leading maritime powers that they foresee a normal and regular flow of

traffic of all cargoes in the Gulf of Aqaba. Interference, by armed force, with ships of Israeli flag exercising free and innocent passage in the Gulf of Aqaba and through the Straits of Tiran will be regarded by Israel as an attack entitling it to exercise its inherent right of self-defense under Article 51 of the Charter.

In a public address on February 20, President Eisenhower stated: "We should not assume that if Israel withdraws, Egypt will prevent Israeli shipping from using the Suez Canal or the Gulf of Aqaba." This declaration has weighed heavily with my Government in determining its action today. Israel is now prepared to withdraw its forces from the Gulf of Aqaba and the Straits of Tiran in the confidence that there will be continued freedom of navigation for international and Israeli shipping in the Gulf of Aqaba and through the Straits of Tiran.

Following this statement, Lodge made a declaration on behalf of the American Government. It did not fully correspond to the agreement arrived at in the talks between Eban and Dulles. On the other hand, there were encouraging statements by the representatives of Argentina, the Philippines, and Spain, and an excellent speech was made by the French Ambassador, Georges Picot.

Abba Eban met with Secretary of State Dulles and pointed out the discrepancies between Lodge's speech and the agreement arrived at previously, and indicated that these discrepancies had perplexed the Israel Government and its people. After clarification and consultations Dulles announced that President Eisenhower would send the Israeli Prime Minister a letter that would say that the assumptions and hopes expressed in the General Assembly by Israel's Foreign Minister were acceptable and that the United States would work for their implementation. The letter, cabled to us immediately, read as follows:

My Dear Mr. Prime Minister:

I was indeed deeply gratified at the decision of your Government to withdraw promptly and fully behind the Armistice lines as set out by your Foreign Minister in her address of yesterday to the General Assembly. I venture to express the hope that the carrying out of these withdrawals will go forward with the utmost speed.

I know that this decision was not an easy one. I believe, however, that Israel will have no cause to regret having thus conformed to the strong sentiment of the world community as expressed in the various United Nations resolutions relating to withdrawal.

It has always been the view of this Government that after the withdrawal there should be a united effort by all of the nations to bring about conditions in the area more stable, more tranquil, and more conducive to the general welfare than those which existed heretofore. Already the United Nations General Assembly had adopted resolutions which presage such a better future. Hopes and expectations based thereon were voiced by your Foreign Minister and others. I believe that it is reasonable to entertain such hopes and expectations and I want you to know that the United States, as a friend of all of the countries of the area and as a loyal member of the United Nations, will strive that such hopes prove not to be vain.

I am, my dear Mr. Prime Minister,
Sincerely,
Dwight D. Eisenhower

On receipt of the letter that evening a Cabinet meeting was called and the Prime Minister proposed the evacuation of the Gaza Strip. A resolution to this effect was passed by a large majority. The Minister of Defense also convened the General Staff of the Army to explain that the political struggle had come to an end. The main objective had been reached: freedom of navigation in the Straits of Eilat, through the Red Sea, and into the

Indian Ocean, and the introduction of a United Nations Force outside our territory to safeguard this freedom of navigation and quiet in the Gaza Strip.

On March 8 the Prime Minister replied to President Eisenhower in the following letter:

Dear Mr. President,

Now that we have withdrawn from the Sinai Desert, as I promised in my letter of November 8, and have also withdrawn from the Gaza Strip, which I profoundly believe we should not have done for both political and security reasons, please permit me to point out that we did so in large measure because of your letter of March 2 in which you expressed your conviction that "Israel would have no reason to regret" such an action and that the "hopes and expectations" expressed by her Foreign Minister "would not prove groundless." I must tell you how much we appreciate the continuation and deepening of US-Israeli friendship, and how greatly all of us, and myself in particular, value your noble and moral personality. I must explain to you why it was difficult for us, as you acknowledged in your letter, to evacuate the Gaza Strip. During the last few months the inhabitants of our villages in the South and the Negev could, for the first time in eight years, live in peace, knowing that grenades would not be thrown into their homes at night, and that they would not be ambushed on their way to work in the fields during the day. These pioneers, our finest youth, have left well-to-do families in Haifa and Tel Aviv, interrupted their education, and gone to settle in the border areas, risking their lives in order to populate the wilderness. You will therefore understand why, since yesterday, our hearts have been heavy and our villagers have been uneasy. We are particularly concerned at the fact that the Secretary General, basing himself on his own formalistic interpretations, may try to bring the Egyptians back to the Gaza Strip, a place which never belonged to them. But we put our trust in the attitude expressed in your letter, and in your assurance that our Foreign Minister's hopes and expectations will not prove groundless.

I believe, as you have written, that we will have no reason to regret our decision.

I also believe that the declarations made by you and by your Secretary of State, Mr. John Foster Dulles, about Eilat and the Straits of Tiran will soon become a reality.

Rest assured, Mr. President, that we will cooperate with you to the fullest possible extent in your efforts to bring peace and tranquility to our region, for the benefit of all its peoples and of world peace.

With best wishes, I remain,

Sincerely yours,
D. Ben-Gurion

It should be noted that in the UN General Assembly the government of France was the most emphatic and the clearest of all concerning the Straits of Eilat and the Gaza Strip. It announced that it intended to make effective use of the right of free passage in the Straits and the Gulf of Eilat and the Straits of Tiran. It was convinced that any interference with free passage was a violation of international law and would afford the opportunity for measures envisaged in Article 51 of the UN Charter. In its view no littoral nation of the Gulf of Eilat was in a state of war with any other littoral state, and Israel's position was therefore in complete accord with international law.

The French Government, moreover, was of the opinion that Resolution II of the Assembly on February 2, 1957, as well as the Secretary-General's report of February 22 imposed the obligation on the UN Force to occupy the positions along the Gulf of Eilat hitherto occupied by the Israeli Army and to remain there until such time as a settlement between the two sides or an international agreement determining the manner of navigation in these free waters precluded any risk of resort to belligerent means. The government of France concurred with the proposal embodied in the Secretary General's report that the UN Force would take over the administrative functions in the Gaza Strip then being carried out by the Israel Forces.

The British Ambassador took issue with the view of Krishna Menon, representing India, that the Straits were international waters only like the fjords of Norway or the Hudson River in the United States. These straits, he said, traversed four states and all nations have freedom of navigation in international waters; the Israeli Government's assumptions and expectations in connection with the Gaza Strip were therefore reasonable. Speeches in the same spirit were made by the representatives of Australia, New Zealand, Canada, Belgium, Holland, and others.

Reporting to the Knesset on March 7 on the Government's decision and the General Assembly debate, the Prime Minister listed their positive and negative aspects. Despite all the declarations, he noted, there was no absolute certainty that the Egyptians would not return or be restored to the Gaza Strip, either as a civilian administration or a military force relying on the Armistice Agreement, which, in Israel's opinion, was invalidated by Egypt's claim to the rights of a belligerent party. He stressed that under any regime and administration the Gaza Strip would be a source of trouble as long as the refugees had not been resettled elsewhere, adding:

> Anyone who speaks of the Gaza Strip without understanding all the implications and dangers inherent in the makeup of the population is living in a fool's paradise. As for the Straits, there is no express United Nations resolution that the UN force will remain and safeguard free passage until a peace settlement. Only the Advisory Committee (appointed by the UN Secretary General and which, as he declared in a memorandum published on February 26, 1957, would be the first to consider any proposal for withdrawal of the UN Force) can require that the UN Force not be withdrawn or replaced by an Egyptian force without any express resolution. On the other hand, there is a declaration of all the principal maritime states (except the Soviet Union) that the Gulf and the Straits are an international waterway and that all nations have the right of free passage. In addition, all of them have taken note of our declaration that if our right to free passage is violated by forceful means, Israel will be able to defend itself by force, under Article 51 of the Charter.

Some members of the Knesset and the Government opposed the evacuation of the Gaza Strip and Sharm el-Sheikh. In so doing, however, they disregarded two consequences that would have been entailed by rejection of the French and Canadian proposal: 1. If our Army remained in Sharm el-Sheikh, we would retain a theoretical right of freedom of navigation, but in a situation of total ostracism shipping itself would be nonexistent, as no ship of any foreign nation would come to Eilat and the oil we planned to pipe to Haifa would not reach our southern port. On the other hand, at the beginning of March 1957, following the evacuation, we were able to lay a pipeline to carry oil from Eilat to the refineries in Haifa. 2. By rejecting the proposal of the most friendly power of all, which had provided the vital equipment without which the Sinai Campaign would not have been possible, we would have endangered the chances of arming the IDF in the future. As for the Gaza Strip, our alternative was to absorb either hundreds of thousands of new immigrants or the three hundred thousand inhabitants of the Strip, of whom two hundred thousand were refugees.

Had the Government of Israel not dared to take a fateful though unpopular decision with a view to the supreme long-range needs of the nation, it would not have been worthy of the heavy responsibility the nation had entrusted to it. Therefore, after reviewing the Sinai Campaign and the subsequent struggle, the Prime Minister told the Knesset on April 2, 1957: "No less than every other Jew, I am proud of the Sinai operation. I am proud of the moral courage this Government has shown in deciding on this unpopular but wise, valuable, and loyal step, which will stand out in Jewish history as one of the greatest landmarks in the progress of the State of Israel since its foundation."

What was not effected by a Security Council action on freedom of navigation in the Straits of Eilat was brought about by the declaration of the principal maritime powers (other than the Soviet Union). For more than ten years freedom of navigation prevailed in theory and practice, although there was no absolute certainty that it would not be violated. Only 10 ships, with a total displacement of 60,000 tons, had anchored in Eilat from the time the IDF arrived in March 1949 to the Sinai Campaign at the end of October 1956—a period of seven and a half years. In the first year after the Sinai Campaign 30 ships arrived at Eilat, bringing a total of 23,680 tons of imports, and 28 ships left with 19,810 tons of exports. In addition, 27 tankers brought 429,857 tons of fuel. In 1958, 35 ships brought 28,124 tons of imports and 35 ships left with 28,012 tons of exports. Tankers brought 1,081,585 tons of fuel. In 1959, only 42 ships arrived, but in 1960, 56 ships; in 1961, 76; in 1962, 93; in 1963, 59; in 1964, 57; in 1965, 54; 1966, 51; and in 1967, 66.

At the end of the Sinai Campaign a road was paved from Beersheba to Eilat, linking the two seas of our country with a network of highways. In April 1957 an eight-inch pipeline was laid from Eilat to Beersheba. In August 1958 a sixteen-inch pipeline was laid from Beersheba to Haifa. Ever since it went into operation in September 1960 oil has been flowing from Eilat to the Haifa refineries.

The freedom of navigation made possible by the Sinai Campaign had a broader significance. While the Negev, which occupies 60 percent of the territory of the State of Israel, has always been largely an uninhabited desert, it represents a geopolitical advantage of inestimable value. Being located at the crossroads of three continents—Europe, Asia, Africa—it has, through the Gulf of Eilat and the Red Sea, direct and extremely short access to the two developing continents, Asia and Africa, which embrace more than 60 percent of the human race. This geopolitical position of the Negev can be a tremendous and perhaps overwhelming factor in the State of Israel's economic future. This notwithstanding the fact that not only in the four hundred years under Turkish rule but even during the British Mandate the Negev was considered a barren desert with capacity for little more than a few tribes of primitive nomads.

Since 1882 the British had in effect controlled Egypt and hence the Suez Canal—the only direct passage from Europe to Asia—yet the canal itself had been built with French capital by a French engineer and was completed in 1869 despite British attempts at interference. King Solomon was the first of the Kings of Israel who took an interest in foreign trade, and recognized the importance of the Gulf of Eilat which opened a sea route to the lands of Asia (I Kings 9:26; II Chronicles 8:17). Access to the gulf had been made possible by King David's conquest of the Land of Edom (II Samuel 8:14; I Chronicles 18:12 –13). Israel's control over Edom and Eilat, however, did not long prevail. In the days of Yoram Ben Yehoshafat, Edom rebelled and was reconquered only in the days of King Amatzya (II Kings 8:22). Amatzya's son, Uziyahu, one of the greatest of the Kings, "built Eilat and restored it to Judah" (II Chronicles 26:2) but during the reign of his grandson, Ahaz ben Yotam, "Retzin, King of Edom, recovered Eilat for Edom and drove the Jews from Eilat, and the Edomites came to Eilat, where they dwelt to this day." In our own day the IDF amended this last verse. Following the Armistice Agreement with Egypt (February 24, 1949) the IDF was ordered by the Minister of Defense to liberate the entire southern Negev, then still occupied by the Arab Legion. On March 20 they reached the Gulf of Eilat (then known as Oum Rash-Rash), where they found only three small buildings of the Palestine Police from the days of the British. Eilat has since been completely rebuilt.

VI

YEARS OF PEACE, PROBLEMS, AND PROGRESS

1957–1962: From the End of the Suez War to the Fourth Knesset

Section 1. Governments and Election Systems

A German Loan for the Negev ★ *Aliya Increases* ★ *The Growth of the Nation's Economy*

THE Prophet Ezekiel foretold of the Negev: "And the desolate land shall be tilled, whereas it lay desolate in the sight of all that passed it by. And they shall say, 'the land that was desolate is become like the Garden of Eden; and the waste and desolate and ruined cities are become fenced, and are inhabited.' Then the heathen that are left round about you shall know that I, the Lord, built the ruined places, and planted that which was desolate; I the Lord have spoken it and I will do it" (Ezekiel 36:34–36).

To the words of the Prophet we should add a few of our own. For while the *words* of God are deeds, only Man's *acts* are deeds, and it is by our acts, not our words, that we shall be judged and shall gain strength. Even our meager accomplishment in the Negev since the creation of the State proved that a great future lay in store for it. The few studies we had made proved that it is not an empty desert. Beside the tremendous chemical resources of the Dead Sea, rich lodes were discovered of phosphates, gas, copper, gypsum, granite, kaolin, and other minerals. Though adequate studies have not yet been made, one of the great assets, perhaps the greatest, was obvious without further investigation: thanks to its proximity to Asia and Africa, the Negev has a considerable advantage over the countries of Europe in trading with these continents. The Negev has no need of the Suez Canal because through the Gulf of Eilat and the Red Sea it has access to East Africa and the Indian Ocean.

While sparse rainfall and rocky soil over the greater part of the Negev leave but few areas for the development of agriculture and pasturage, the potential for industry and trade exceeds that of every other portion of the country and, given its proximity to the Asian and African continents and its direct maritime outlet to the Indian Ocean, even that of the countries of Europe. To this day Israel's main customers are in Europe and to a lesser extent the Americas. But because Israel cannot compete with the advanced nations of Europe, its imports are several times greater than its exports. The country has no chance of gaining economic independence without constantly increasing its exports, and that will be possible only if it sells to the underdeveloped and highly populated countries of Asia and Africa. These nations too will doubtless progress in the course of time, but Israel will not be standing still either.

That was why the Prime Minister, in his meeting with the West German Chancellor Dr. Adenauer in New York on March 14, 1960, proposed that Germany lend Israel $500 million over ten years, or $50 million a year, for development of the Negev. This was two or three years before termination of the Reparations Agreement signed in Luxembourg in 1952. The Prime Minister gave two reasons for his proposal—one moral, the other economic. The economic argument was that the Negev had to be transformed into a large industrial center for export to Africa and East Asia by way of Eilat and the Red Sea. The moral one was that the German generation born after the defeat of the Nazi regime hearing of the Nazi atrocities that had no parallel in human history, would be ashamed of their nation and its deeds during World War Two; they would find some moral satisfaction in knowing that their nation had helped Israel to gain independence and develop the desolate Negev. Chancellor Adenauer agreed and, trusting in his honesty and fairness, the Prime Minister did not insist on a formal written commitment.

On his return to Germany, Dr. Adenauer faced difficulties in meeting his commitment without having a special law passed by the Bundestag, and there was considerable doubt whether such a law would be approved—even confirmation of the 1952 Reparations Agreement had run into a lot of opposition. Dr. Adenauer therefore designated Herman Abs, Director of the German Bank for Rehabilitation, to arrange the loan. Mr. Abs came to Israel and conferred with the Prime Minister, the Minister of Finance, the Governor of the Bank of Israel, and others. In a letter to Dr. Adenauer on July 29, 1960, he said:

> As far as I understood, in your talks with the Israeli Prime Minister you did not discuss details of this financial assistance, which will be given on a commercial basis. On the other hand, as you told me, you expressed to the Israeli Prime Minister your willingness in principle to agree to German aid in financing the continued rehabilitation of his country for both moral and political-economic reasons. Being familiar with the unique economic problems of Israel, from personal knowledge and observation and talks with many people in that country, I agree with you that an intensive effort at cooperation is an important undertaking for Germany. From the standpoint of the Israeli economy, the problems mentioned by Mr. Ben-Gurion seem well-founded and, in character and scope, in line with Israel's needs. However, I cannot refrain from pointing out the difficulty inherent in the fact that definite promises can be made from time to time for a limited time only, in view of the budget regulations to which the Bonn Government is subject. Further progress is now entirely dependent on the decisions which you, Mr. Bundeskanzler, intend to make.

On August 9, 1960, the Prime Minister received a letter from Dr. Adenauer, dated August 5, which read:

One of the things we discussed in our New York talk was West German economic assistance to Israel. On my return I asked Mr. Abs for his opinion about the plan to provide economic assistance, in the form of long-term credit, to promote Israel's development. Mr. Abs' views are expressed in his letter (of July 29, 1960), a copy of which I gave to Ambassador Shinnar and asked him to transmit to you. After the completion of the current vacation season, namely towards the end of September, I will do my best to obtain German financial assistance for Israeli development projects. I would be pleased to hear your opinion on this matter, and would be grateful for any comments you might have.

Since both the letters from Dr. Abs and Dr. Adenauer failed to mention the purpose for which the loan was intended—development of the Negev—the Prime Minister in his reply to Dr. Adenauer felt it necessary to reiterate the main points of their conversation in March of that year. In a letter dated September 27, he wrote, among other things:

As I explained to you in New York, I am not an economist, but the development of my country is among my major concerns, and on my return I discussed this matter with my colleagues, the Minister of Finance and the Minister of Commerce and Industry. I told them that in my opinion the long-term loan of $50 million a year for ten years should be used mainly for the establishment of large-scale development projects in the Negev (which constitutes 60% of Israel's Territory). There are two considerations involved, one economic and the other moral:

The economic consideration is that the development of the Negev depends primarily on the establishment of large-scale industrial enterprises, for the area has very little land suitable for cultivation or for grazing. Four or five major industrial centers should be established in the West, Center and South—the last meaning Eilat. These would include plants devoted to chemicals, potash, bromine, gypsum, cement, glass, quartz (there are high quality deposits near Eilat), for most of these materials are found in abundance in the Negev and the Dead Sea. The Negev is particularly important because it provides an outlet, by sea, to East Africa and Asia (by way of Eilat and the Red Sea), without resort to the Suez Canal, and I believe that our economic well-being depends in large measure on our commercial relations with the peoples of Africa and Asia, though, of course, I would not wish to minimize the importance of our ties with Europe and America. My colleagues agree with me that the funds we will receive from you in the form of a long-term loan (let us say for fifteen years) totaling $750 million, i.e. $50 million a year, will be invested in the establishment of large, profit-making industrial enterprises that will basically transform the character of the Negev, and in the creation of large population centers between Beersheba and Eilat.

The moral consideration is as follows: All of us know what happened during the Hitlerite period. You were the men who understood that the entire German people bears moral responsibility for the terrible Holocaust, and though there was no way of forcing you or Germany to do anything, you felt that your people had a moral responsibility to offer some measure of compensation to the surviving victims of Nazism.

I don't know whether the German youth of today are aware of what was done by Nazi Germany, but I haven't the slightest doubt that someday German youth will know the terrible truth, and every young German will feel sorrow and shame. So, with your assistance, I wish to establish pioneering enterprises here in Israel which—when German young people see them or read about them—will give them moral satisfaction by showing that Adenauer did as much as could be done to atone for the sins of Hitlerite Germany. It is for this reason that I want the loan agreed upon in New York to be used for the establishment of giant economic enterprises in the most barren part of our country, enterprises which will do honor and give satisfaction to the Germans who contributed to their establishment.

I was pleased to read reports about the talks between our Minister of Finance, Mr.

Eshkol, and Mr. Shinnar on the one hand, and your Economics Minister, Mr. Erhard, on the other. On September 2, 1960, my friend, the Minister of Finance, told Mr. Erhard of our intention to establish a broad-based chemical industry and related industries in the Negev.

I will not go into the technical problems involved in arranging the loan, because I am not an expert in such matters. I only wished to emphasize, Mr. Chancellor, the two aspects of the program—economic and moral—that I regard as important. Even without being an economist I was always aware of the special importance of the Negev, despite the fact that it has been a wilderness from the first six days of Creation. For I have faith in our ability to make the desert blossom as was predicted by our Prophets (Isaiah:35).

After the initial financial arrangements for the loan had been made, Ben-Gurion wrote to Dr. Adenauer on January 1, 1961:

Yesterday, in a meeting with several of the economics ministers and with Mr. Shinnar, we worked out a plan for the next few years. It calls for the construction of three urban centers in the Negev: one—near the source of natural gas in the desert—Arad. There, over a year ago, when we were drilling for oil we found instead a rich source of natural gas that will supply power to the entire region for at least the next five or ten years. The second center will be between Dimona, which we set up five years ago, and the Dead Sea Works. The third center will be at the site of the Negev's largest crater, between Beersheba and Eilat, and will be called Mitzpeh Ramon. At the outset, each center will have a population of at least five thousand families. We are already piping water to these places from the north, and after arrangements are made in regard to the annual $50 million loan, we will begin building both housing for the settlers and factories. We are also going to expand the copper plant at Timna (in the southern Negev, not far from Eilat), and to establish a large plant to produce cement for export to East Africa by way of Eilat and the Red Sea. This initial program will cost about $100 million. I was very pleased to see your letter of December 15, 1960 to my friend Shinnar, in which you reiterated the promise you gave me "to put into effect the plan to provide credit on a commercial basis for constructive projects in your country within the framework of your development plans."

The secrecy which you call for at your end will, I can assure you, be maintained at our end as well.

The Prime Minister, however, was slightly too optimistic regarding the possibility of maintaining the required secrecy in Israel.

The year of the Sinai Campaign was marked by an increase in immigration: as against 36,303 in 1955, the figure for 1956 was 54,925; for 1957, 69,773. While in 1956 the majority (47,617) of the immigrants were from Asia and Africa, in 1957 the majority (39,763) came from Europe and America. The years 1958–1960 saw a decline in Aliya. In 1958, 25,919 immigrants arrived (only 11,490 from Africa and Asia); in 1959, 22,987 (7635 from Africa and Asia); in 1960, 23,487 (680 from Africa and Asia). In these four years there was a rise in *emigration*: 11,000 in 1956 (only 6000 in the previous year); in 1957, again 11,000; 1958, 11,520; 1959, 9500; in 1960, 8500.

At the end of 1956 Israel's population was 1,872,400 (1,667,500 Jews); at the end of 1960 it was 2,150,400 (1,911,200). The aggregate increase was 278,000; the increase in the number of Jews, 239,200.

While exports increased during these five years, imports increased even faster, so that the trade deficit grew. As a result of the large expenditures for military equipment and the maintenance of a big army, 1956 and 1957 showed the greatest trade deficit of all. In 1956 it was $269,092,000, in 1957 $292,702,000. Similarly, in the next three years the deficit increased yearly: 1958 net exports were $139,103,000 and net imports $420,930,000, making an import-export deficit of $281,827,000. In 1959 net exports were $176,383,000, net imports $427,291,000, for a deficit of $250,908,000. In 1960 exports were $211,276,000, net imports $495,646,000, and the deficit $284,370,000.

The total national income in 1956 was IL 2,135,200, of which agriculture accounted for IL 281 million; industry and mining for IL 437 million; construction, IL 129 million; public utilities, water, and power, IL 36 million; transportation, IL 164 million; commerce, IL 248 million; finance, insurance, and real estate, IL 187 million; other services, IL 230 million; and government revenues, IL 420 million.

In 1959 the national income was IL3.211 billion broken down as follows (in millions): agriculture, IL 377; industry, IL 712; construction, IL 230; water and power utilities, IL56; transportation, IL232; finance and real estate, IL260; commerce and services, IL656; government revenues, IL688.

In the four-year period 1955 to 1958–1959, total land under cultivation increased from 3,685,000 to 4,105,000 dunams. This included an increase in land cultivated by Jews from 3,030,000 to 3,350,000 dunams.

At the end of 1960 Israel had 827 rural settlements, 723 of them Jewish and 104 non-Jewish. At that time the rural population was 501,278, of whom 171,544 were non-Jewish. There were 229 kibbutzim with a population of 77,950 persons, 336 moshavim with a population of 119,113, and 1213 cooperatives with 7073 members and 6651 hired employees and apprentices. The cooperative economy, both rural and urban (kibbutzim, moshavim, and cooperatives), embraced over a quarter of a million people.

The number of pupils and students also grew: In 1948–1949 it was 140,817 (129,688 Jews and 19,129 others); in 1956–1957, 471,522 (432,840 Jews and 38,682 others); in 1957–1958, 517,488 (476,273 Jews and 41,215 others); in 1958–1959, 551,262 (507,702 Jews and 43,560 others); in 1959–1960, 580,202 (532,797 Jews and 47,405 others); in 1960–1961, 599,962 (548,147 Jews and 51,815 others); in 1961–1962, 627,274 (571,827 Jews and 55,447 others).

From its birth to the end of 1960 the young State had spent a total of IL 393,021,015 on education and IL221,621,660 on health. Thanks to its good health services Israel showed one of the lowest infant mortality rates and longest average life spans in the world. Research centers, led by the Weizmann Institute in Rehovot, had done much to raise the academic level and to foster science and research.

Ben-Zvi Reelected President ★ *Security of the State Secrets* ★ *New Government Formed*

The first term of office of Israel's second President, Yitzhak Ben-Zvi, came to an end in October 1957. On October 21 the Knesset Speaker, Yosef Sprinzak, announced that two candidates had been nominated, Ben-Zvi and Yosef Yoel Rivlin. On the day set for the elections Rivlin withdrew, leaving only one candidate. According to Section 5 of the Presidential Term of Office Law, 1951, the voting is by secret ballot. Only ninety-four members of the Knesset were present. Those absent were for the most part abroad. Of the ninety-four ballots cast, sixteen were blank and the remaining seventy-six were for Ben-Zvi. The Speaker thereupon declared that "the Knesset has elected Yitzhak Ben-Zvi President of the State of Israel for the next five years for the glory and welfare of Israel. The Inauguration will take place on Wednesday, October 31."

On the day before this election, which marked the first anniversary of the start of the Sinai Campaign, a hand grenade was hurled to the floor of the Knesset from the visitors' gallery during a speech by Yitzhak Raphael. It exploded near the Cabinet table. Four ministers were injured: Ben-Gurion, Shapira, Golda Meir, and Carmel. The session was immediately adjourned. Later it was established that there was no connection between the grenade outrage and the anniversary of the Sinai Campaign.

On October 31 the President arrived at the Knesset. With head covered, he laid his left hand on the Bible, raised his right hand, and declared: "I, Yitzhak, son of Zvi Ben-Zvi, promise to be loyal to the State of Israel and its laws and faithfully to carry out my duties as President of the State." Invited to address the Knesset, the reelected President on behalf of the entire nation voiced his shock at the violence on the previous afternoon, perpetrated apparently by a person of unsound mind, and his wishes for a speedy recovery to the four injured ministers.

Ben-Zvi said he was happy that it had been his lot to be the occasion for unity in the Knesset, which represented the entire nation. When he accepted the exalted office for the first time, he had considered one of his principal tasks to be the unification of the nation in all its tribes and communities and all the parties loyal to the State, including our citizens of the minority communities. The heroic war in the Sinai desert in the past year, he said, had given the State of Israel victory over a foe ten times its size and proven the superiority of the Israel Defense Forces fighting for national and human freedom. The Sinai Campaign had achieved freedom of approach and passage by sea to our gateway to the east, the port of Eilat. This historic achievement would be inscribed in our hearts and the hearts of our children and their descendants to the credit of the Israel Defense Forces, all their men and officers, and to the credit of the Government, and the Prime Minister in particular.

During the past five years, the President pointed out, the Jewish population had increased by three hundred thousand, including two hundred thousand immigrants. The way before us was still long, but our profound faith in the historic ideals and in the Eternal Rock of Israel, Who would not be false, and our fervent aspiration for the realization of justice on earth—had sustained us and in these we placed our trust. He hoped that the coming five years would see the speedier consolidation and rebuilding of Jerusalem, materially and spiritually, as befitted the capital of Israel, and concluded with these words: "I pray to the Rock of Israel that we may yet have the privilege of witnessing with our own eyes during the next five years a true peace among all the nations of the world, the progress of Israel, the intensification of the building of our country, and the homecoming of the scattered sons of our people."

The Speaker responded: "Mr. President, in great affection, esteem, and appreciation the Knesset has reelected you for the next five years. All your life you have striven for the welfare of your people and your brethren are grateful. May this desire and this faith in you give you further strength and inspiration in fulfilling your exalted task. I wish you long life for the welfare and the glory of the State of Israel." All present rose and sang "Hatikva," and the meeting adjourned.

The second Knesset served out its four-year term but not without crises. On December 31, 1957, the Prime Minister submitted his resignation to the President, which according to the Transition Law involved the resignation of the Government as a whole. For reasons of state he conveyed most of the reasons that led to his resignation orally, and only put part of them in writing:

Mr. President,

From the full details which I have given you orally on the problems of security, the need for vital equipment for the Israel Defense Forces, the conditions for its acquisition, and the sources from which it can be obtained, you can appreciate the serious nature of the injury to the security of the State and its international standing that has been caused by the behavior of one of the parties participating in the Government. Like all the other parties in the present coalition, this party undertook in the coalition agreement "to preserve complete secrecy in all matters of security and foreign policy discussed in the Government." On the first of Tevet this year (December 24, 1957) the Cabinet resolved that it considered the publicity given last week by Ahdut Haavodah to the Government's confidential decision to be harmful to the State and a grave violation of the principle of the collective responsibility of the Government for its decisions.

At the Cabinet meeting on December 2 I abstained from voting on the censure of Ahdut Haavodah, not because I thought it was unjustified, but because I believed that we should deal not with the past, which cannot be changed, but with the prevention of such uncalled-for occurences in the future. My colleagues (including Pinhas Rosen, the Minister of Justice) and I made prolonged efforts during the last few weeks to ensure that such deplorable acts should not be repeated in the future. To my deep regret, all these efforts, which continued until yesterday afternoon, have been in vain. I accordingly submit to you herewith my resignation from the Government.

I am surprised that the Mapam Party has followed in the wake of Ahdut Haavodah in this regrettable episode. I have objected all along to the attempts made from time to time by these two parties to establish a kind of government within the Government, consisting of "the three workers' parties," to use their term. In presenting the Government to the Knesset, I said on November 3, 1955, in my comment on the debate: No justification would have been required if a workers' government had been submitted to the Knesset. But I am not submitting a workers' government—this will be a pioneering Government, devoted to all the needs of the nation and all sections of the nation—and this was agreed upon by the five parties of the coalition. I do not understand, therefore, the strange association of the two parties in this unfortunate case.

I pointed out in the Knesset on the same day that there are differences of opinion on foreign policy among various members of the Government. But there is a principle of collective responsibility and unity of action, and the Government will act even in opposition to the opinion of a minority within it. In this Government, as in its predecessors, the principle of collective responsibility ensures that there be only one policy to guide its actions. The foreign policy of this Government would be based on a desire for peace and friendship with all the peace-loving nations, without inquiring into their internal regimes. This has been clearly laid down in the Basic Principles. It is also stated in the Basic Principles that "the Government will strengthen its ties with all countries that help to promote the security and development of Israel and enable their Jewish communities to share in the upbuilding of Israel and to emigrate to it." Consequently I was shocked to see in Ahdut Haavodah's statement yesterday to Kol Yisrael (Voice of Israel, radio station) a deplorable hint that we have made an attempt to take sides against a particular state, and I immediately issued a denial of this hint.

Finally, I must point out that when I presented this Government in the Knesset, I said that "a coalition Government is not based on ideological uniformity, but on unity in practice. The Government is a single unit and what it decides is binding on all its members. Anyone who cannot accept the decision must leave the Government." I assumed, and I still incline to this assumption, that the Ahdut Haavodah ministers had no share in the perfidy of their party, and in my opinion they should have resigned after the violation by their party of a confidential decision of the Government. Since they did not do so, and I do not presume to set myself up as their judge, I felt it necessary to resign in their stead.

There is not a scintilla of truth in the stories now being spread by interested parties to the effect that I wished to expel the Ahdut Haavodah and Mapam Parties from the Government. During the discussions of the last two weeks I opposed every proposal for the dismissal of ministers, either by the Prime Minister or by a two-thirds majority decision or by any other procedure.

In resigning from the Government, I wish to express my thanks to all the members of the Cabinet who have worked with me for over two years, for the confidence they have placed in me as Minister of Defense and Prime Minister.

Later the Prime Minister, in the Knesset, declared orally:

When on 9 Tevet 5718 (January 1, 1958) the President charged me with the formation of a new Government, I informed him that I would undertake the task only if by Monday, 14 Tevet (January 6, 1958), I could make perfectly certain that the parties commanding a majority in the Knesset who were prepared to take part in the Government would undertake two obligations: to maintain the collective responsibility of the Government in principle *and in practice*, and to ensure the effective preservation of secrecy in regard to the deliberations of the Government, especially in matters of security and foreign policy.

Yesterday morning I was informed by representatives of the Israel Labor Party [Mapai], the National Religious Party, Ahdut Haavodah-Poalei Zion, the United Workers Party [Mapam], and the Progressive Party that they agreed to establish a Government that would be based on the Basic Principles and the coalition agreement of the previous Government and work in partnership in every area of Government activity. These parties declare that they are prepared to maintain the Government until the end of its term of office in July 1959 or a few months later. In order to reinforce the collective responsibility of the Government and the preservation of secrecy, the five parties have agreed to the following provisions:

"Collective responsibility will bind all the members of the Cabinet and the coalition parties to vote in the Knesset for all the decisions of the Government and the Laws proposed by it to the Knesset.

"The Government may permit a party to abstain from voting in certain circumstances. A party may also permit one or several of its members to abstain from voting. The details of such abstention and the circumstances under which it may be permitted will be determined by the Government.

"If one or more ministers feel compelled to abstain from voting without the agreement of the Government, the minister or ministers concerned must resign from the Government. A vote by a party against a Government decision shall be treated as equivalent to the abstention of a minister without the agreement of the Government.

"The ministers bind themselves in accordance with the coalition agreement to preserve

Above left: Prime Minister Ben-Gurion visiting President Dwight D. Eisenhower.

Above: President Weizmann, at the White House in 1949, presents a Torah to President Harry S. Truman.

Left: President John F. Kennedy chatting with Foreign Minister Golda Meir in the White House, 1962.

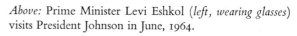

Above: Prime Minister Levi Eshkol (*left, wearing glasses*) visits President Johnson in June, 1964.

Left: Ben-Gurion with Mrs. Eleanor Roosevelt in New York, 1960.

THE INGATHERING OF EXILES

The new State removed all restrictions on Jewish immigration. From the many Diaspora lands came hundreds of thousands, full citizens of Israel on touching its soil.

Below left: From Persia.
Below center: From Rumania.
Below: Ethiopian Jew with Sabra friend.

Bottom left: The "magic carpet" aviation brought thousands of Yemenite Jews. This group has just landed at Lod Airport.

Bottom right: Language is one of the barriers faced by adult immigrants. Special courses in Hebrew are provided by the Government Ulpan program. This class in Upper Nazareth is typical.

Above left: Brokers at the Diamond Exchange in Ramat Gau. Started by immigrants from Amsterdam and other diamond centers, the industry in Israel has become one of the world's largest.

Above: An oil drill on the Dead Sea; exploration for the precious resource is intensive.

Left: Fishermen at Eilat prepare for another haul.

Below left: Teenage students of the Kfar Hayorek Agricultural School, near Tel Aviv, on their way to work in the fields.

Below: At Kibbutz Hatzeva, irrigating the Negev.

Above left: In the northern Negev, guarding his kibbutz against Fedayeen incursions.

Above: Hassidic reservist sees action in the
Sinai war.

Left: The Prime Minister with troops in
the Sinai desert.

Below: They have taken the Gaza Strip
with Torah and guns.

Observances of the tenth birthday of the State took color from the victorious Sinai Campaign less than two years before. *Above:* Reviewing the holiday parade at Ramat Gau Stadium, Jerusalem, are (*left to right*) General Moshe Dayan, Moshe Sharett, President Ben-Zvi, Ben-Gurion. *Left:* Part of what they witnessed.

Below: On this occasion the Prime Minister pins the highest military award, the Hagana Medal, on General Chaim Laskov, Chief of Staff, and on General Dayan.

ISRAELIS ALL

The country has a vividly heterogeneous population. The "ingathering of exiles" has brought together Jews from all over the world, with their distinctive looks, cultures, customs, languages, and religious practices. One of the main tasks, as the author underlines, is to integrate them as an equal and unified Jewish community, without destroying the best in their diverse backgrounds. In addition there are the native Arabs, a large minority enjoying full Israeli citizenship.

Right: A Field Command Post.

Below: Israeli tank column advances across the desert.

Bottom left: Soldiers fly their Israeli flag on the minaret of the El Kantara mosque in Sinai.

Bottom right: Taking her turn as guard at the kibbutz wall.

Above: Storming the Golan Heights, where the hardest battles were fought.
Opposite: General David Elazar, one of the conquerors of the Golan Heights.

Left: Two of the chief architects of the victory—Minister of Defense Moshe Dayan and General Yitzhak Rabin—on the final day of the war.

Below: Egyptian prisoners.

Above: The liberation of all Jerusalem completed, Israeli troops gather at the Western, or Wailing, Wall of the Temple of Solomon.

Left: On the eastern bank of the Suez Canal, Israelis stand guard.

The war was won, but peace was still remote. *Below left:* Dr. Gunnar Jarring, Swedish diplomat representing the UN Security Council as peace negotiator, with Abba Eban, December, 1967. *Below:* United States Secretary of State William P. Rogers arrives in Israel in early 1971 in search of a peace formula.

The twentieth Independence Day, in May, 1968, less than a year after the Six-Day War, turned into a dramatic victory celebration. Soviet-made tanks and weapons captured in the war stirred the vast crowds in Jerusalem. *Above:* A part of the military parade. *Left:* Israeli tankmen pass the wall of the Old City.

Below: From all corners of the country Israelis flocked to Jerusalem for the anniversary festivities.

Top: The Knesset Building, in the background, was constructed with funds provided for the purpose by the English branch of the Rothschild family. The giant menorah is a gift of the British Government.

Above left: Ben Yehuda Street in the New City.

Above right: Street scene in Old Jerusalem.

Right: In the Old City, after it fell to Israel in the Six-Day War, business as usual.

Top left: Levi Eshkol, Prime Minister from 1963 to 1969. *Top right:* Welcomed by school children at the Eilat Airport.

Above left: Eshkol with Defense Minister Dayan, General Bar-Levi, and other officers after the Six-Day War.

Above right: The Prime Minister with General Shlomo Erell on a naval patrol vessel in the Straits of Tiran, June, 1967.

Left: During an intermission at the Israeli production of *My Fair Lady*, Eshkol is surrounded by members of the cast.

GALLERY OF PORTRAITS

Left: Ben-Gurion visits with Winston Churchill, 1962.

Below left: Ex-Chancellor Konrad Adenauer with the Ben-Gurions at Kibbutz Sde Boker.

Below: The Prime Minister and President Charles de Gaulle stroll in the Elysée Garden, Paris, 1960.

Bottom: At the White House, 1970, Prime Minister Golda Meir and President Nixon appear to agree, hilariously, on an undisclosed subject.

Opposite—left to right, top to bottom: YIGAL YADIN, top general and Dean of Archaeological Department in Hebrew University; one of the discoverers of the Dead Sea Scrolls. MOSHE SHARETT [Shertok], Foreign Minister from 1948 to 1956; also Prime Minister, 1953–1955. MOSHE DAYAN, military leader, now Minister of Defense. YIGAL ALLON, top strategist; now Deputy Prime Minister. RABBI YEHUDA LEIB HACOHEN MAIMON [Fishman] served in several Cabinets as Minister of Religious Affairs and Welfare. (Died 1962.) YOSEF SPRINZAK, Speaker of the Knesset from its first session until his death in 1959. PROF. MARTIN BUBER (1878–1965), philosopher and author, for many years head of the Israel Academy of Sciences. BEHOR SHALOM SHITREET, of Moroccan origin, Minister of Police for 18 years, 1948–1966. (Died 1967.) MENAHEM BEGIN led underground Irgun, then Herut Party; joined Unity Government for the Six-Day War.

Left: The Elder Statesman, retired to Sde Boker in the Negev.

Ben-Gurion did not, in fact, turn his back on public life. He has written extensively—including this book—and is in constant and active touch with national affairs. *Below left:* Visiting Bar-Lev line at Suez in 1970. *Below:* Admiring new arrivals on his kibbutz. *Bottom:* Participating in a seminar at Sde Boker, 1968.

complete secrecy in regard to all deliberations in the Government and its committees in matters of security and foreign policy, without any exception. If the Government decides that secrecy shall also apply to its deliberations on any other matter, the ministers are bound to secrecy also in that case.

"In order to guarantee the required secrecy, a State Secrets Law, applying both to the person revealing the secret and to the newspaper publishing it, will be submitted to the Knesset at the earliest possible moment on behalf of the coalition parties. The Law will define those matters included in the category of State secrets, the publication of which is forbidden. It will in any case include the deliberations of the Cabinet on matters of security and foreign affairs, as well as such other deliberations as the Government itself does not release for publication."

At a meeting I held on Sunday, 13 Tevet (January 5, 1958), with representatives of the Editors' Committee of the daily press, I explained the reasons that made it necessary to enact a law for the preservation of State secrets, applicable both to the person revealing the secret and the newspaper publishing it. The representatives of the Editors' Committee expressed their wish, with which I concur, that after the reconstitution of the Government it should be asked to agree to consult, during the preparation of the Law in the Cabinet, with the Editors' Committee, which would express its opinion on the content and scope of the law.

In conclusion the Prime Minister asked for a vote of confidence in the Government, which in composition was the same as that presented on November 2, 1955, except for two changes: Mordekhai Namir would replace Golda Meir as Minister of Labor, and Mrs. Meir would replace Moshe Sharett as Minister for Foreign Affairs.

The ensuing debate continued until the evening of that day (January 7), when the Knesset attested its confidence in the Government by a vote of seventy-six to thirty-three. All the members of the Government immediately made declarations of allegiance, except Shapira, who had not yet recovered from injuries resulting from the grenade incident eight days earlier.

Hapoel Hamizrahi Ministers Resign ★ Registration of Children in Mixed Marriages

A second Government crisis arose when two members of Hapoel Hamizrahi, Minister for Religious Affairs and Welfare Shapira and Minister of Posts Burg, resigned because of directives issued by Minister of the Interior Israel Bar-Yehuda regarding the registration of persons as Jews. They regarded these directives as a violation of the status quo on matters of religion. The Prime Minister reported the resignations to the Knesset on July 1, 1958. Since all the other members of the Government desired the return of the two who resigned, no one was appointed to replace them and for the time being their portfolios were held by the Prime Minister. In accordance with a demand, a debate on this matter was opened on July 8, 1958. The first speaker was Shapira, who explained the reasons for his resignation. "In the directives issued by the Ministry of the Interior on March 10, 1958, regarding registration of Jews," he said, "it is stated that any person who declared in good faith that he is a Jew is to be registered as such, nor shall further proof be required." This, he went on, "meant that a Christian, Moslem, or a member of any other faith could simply declare he was Jewish and no other proof would be required. Now had this been accepted as is, we would have arrived at new kinds of Jews—Christian Jews, Moslem Jews, and so on, like the Christian Jews at the outset of the Christian Era." He then went on to say:

> The other members of the Government, however, decided to add the words, "and does not adhere to any other religion." But this too could prove an obstacle in case the person making the declaration adhered to no other religion yet was born, for example, a Christian.

> Section 18 of the directive states, "If both members of a couple declare that their child is Jewish, this shall be treated as a lawful declaration made by the child himself, for under the Equal Rights for Women Law, 1951, both parents are the child's legal guardians and can speak in his name." Here too one of the conditions is that this declaration shall be made in good faith. However, it is also stipulated that if one of the parents is not Jewish and so declares, this shall not be considered evidence of bad faith. With regard to the registration clerk, the directive goes on to say that "It is of no importance that according to religious law the child's religion is that of the mother, for it may well be that it is not rabbinical but rather civil law which applies in this case, and according to civil law the religion is that of the father, not the mother." These are problems which the registration clerk, as I have already said, is neither competent nor capable of resolving. All that is required for a child to be registered as Jewish is for parents to declare that he is Jewish.

> So much for the directives. From the quotation we see that the Minister of the Interior provides—and the Government has confirmed it—that even a child born of a Christian mother is to be considered Jewish, something that annuls and subverts the Law of the Torah by which our fathers have lived and conducted themselves for thousands of years. The State of Israel is surrounded by enemies on all sides, nevertheless it has allowed itself to declare war on the Jewish religion and the unique national character of the people of Israel.

> In our State, where one of the principal problems and concerns is the integration of exiles and their fusion into a single nation, Jews loyal to the laws of Israel and its Torah will have to start keeping geneaological records in order to assure themselves of future generations in keeping with the laws which the nation has held sacred throughout the past. Moreover, by declaring a non-Jewish child Jewish you deceive both the child and the parents. What will the child say when on reaching maturity he comes to marry a son or daughter of Israel? That he cannot enter into wedlock with a son or daughter of Israel because the law of marriage and divorce in Israel, the one to which you agreed, is according to the Torah of Israel? He will come with his identity card and claim, "You told me I was Jewish; it is written in my ID card." This will end up in scandals and in tragedies.

> Apart from that, your decision violates the status quo. Here is a directive by the Director of the Registration Division of the Ministry of the Interior dated May 14, 1957, that is, when the present Minister of the Interior, Mr. Bar-Yehuda, was already in office: "(a) if both parents are Jewish the child shall be registered as Jewish; (b) if only the mother is Jewish the child shall be registered as Jewish; (c) if the mother is not Jewish the child's religion shall be registered as that of the mother; (d) if the parents make any declaration other than the above, the matter will be decided by the relevant Registration Office or submitted to the Central Office in Jerusalem; (e) if the parents possess a conversion certificate in the child's name, he shall be registered as Jewish."

> Even earlier, on May 22, 1956, the religion registered was that of the mother. Through-

out my term as Minister of the Interior I followed the law of the Torah. I am told that Mr. Rokah, who succeeded me, issued other directives, but that they were not followed in practice. The present Minister of the Interior, Mr. Bar-Yehuda, has admitted that he himself was not aware of these directives for some time and has implemented them only now in issuing the new directives. Hence, the status quo—not only in the Coalition Agreement but that which has existed in the people of Israel since its beginning as a nation—has been violated in the most flagrant manner.

Minister Burg said: "Speaking not as a party man but as a Jew in the broadest sense of the word, I say: Let us not tear up the nation's pedigree papers. Let us not tear up our nation's unity. Let us not permit the registration of Jews without conversion. Let us not consent to separation of religion and nationality. It is our duty to strive both for our unity and our uniqueness. We cannot have one at the expense of the other. If a government has no religious faith then there can be no confidence in it. Let us not permit the registration of Jews without conversion. Let us strive to preserve our unity and our distinctiveness."

Bar-Yehuda, declared that he felt it necessary to explain the course of events:

What are these directives? My point of departure is that when citizens apply to the representatives of the Government things ought to be in order. We cannot allow every official in the Ministry of the Interior to make entries as he sees fit, depending on his party affiliation. When I discovered the extent of the disorder in these matters I felt that clear and simple instructions should be drawn up, binding on all the employees. I also assumed that I could not say anything I felt like but had to adhere to existing laws and directives and the status quo to which I am committed as a member of this Government.

After formulating the directives I met with the Attorney General. In the directives we had written that "The registration clerk lacks the authority to determine personal status nor shall he rule in legal or religious questions," and that he was obliged to warn anyone registering personal data that "such registration does not constitute legal proof of veracity but merely proof of fulfillment of the obligation of registration." When we speak of an ID card what we mean is not an identity card but rather an *identification* card. It establishes not *what* but rather *who*. After giving the abovementioned warning, the registration clerk is obliged to record all the information he is given unless he has reason to doubt it. He is obliged to accept it as the truth, and must investigate it only if there is reasonable cause to believe that the person before him is not telling the truth. Unless there is reasonable cause to believe otherwise, he must consider that every citizen of Israel is telling the truth.

After that, even before the commotion that suddenly arose, I wrote: "The decisions of the registration clerk are also valid and binding with regard to implementation of the Registration of Inhabitants Ordinance." In 1950, when the Interior portfolio was held by a religious minister, Moshe Shapira, the Chief Rabbinate issued directives to all rabbis registering marriages and divorces to the effect that mere presentation of an ID card is not sufficient but that every item therein must be verified. Regarding marriage and divorce, I wrote in my directives that "Questions of marriage and divorce of Jews in Israel who are citizens or inhabitants of the State shall come under the exclusive jurisdiction of the rabbinical courts," for this is the law in force in the State of Israel, whether I like it or not.

I have always emphasized that I am not authorized to intervene in religious matters. In Section 17 I say: "The entry 'Jew' establishes who is a Jew for the purpose of the civil law but not for the Law of the Torah." For Torah law is determined not by our registrar but by the rabbis. It is we, however, who determine who is a member of the Jewish nation.

You have done a lot of talking about Christians and Gentiles who have joined the Jewish nation. This is neither correct nor fair. We are speaking of directives in the case in which one of the members of a couple is Jewish and both have decided to come to Israel and live among us, and both say in good faith that their child is Jewish. If only one parent says so while the other says something else, we write, "Nationality uncertain." When he grows up we will see what he will be. However, if both parents say he is Jewish it means he has joined the Jewish people. Here too the Government has added a proviso, namely, that he does not belong to another religion.

Registration of inhabitants began immediately after the founding of the State, on the basis of the emergency regulations of 1948. In the first census, held on November 8, 1948, the inhabitants were requested to answer twenty questions. There were separate entries for Nationality and for Religion, and the answers given were accepted as the truth. This was during the Provisional Government, which included members of Mizrahi, Hapoel Hamizrahi, and Agudat Israel. This has been the basis on which inhabitants are registered. In actual fact the great majority of the Jewish population replies "Jewish" to both these questions. However, there were those who replied "nonreligious" or "irreligious" as requested.

On May 1, 1950, while Mr. Shapira was Minister of the Interior, a directive was issued to record newborn children according to the receipt slip of the Ministry of Health. This receipt contained no indication of religion or nationality. But two kinds of receipts were in use—one in Hebrew only and one in Hebrew and Arabic. Anyone who filled out a Hebrew one was considered a Jew and so registered. The Director of the Ministry of Health, Mr. Patish, states that in case of doubt the Ministry of Health registered the child according to the father's nationality, in keeping with directives in force during the British Mandate.

The Chief Rabbinate did not object to this during the Mandate period, nor during Mr. Shapira's term. Of the two questions referring to nationality on the ID card, only one entry was retained—that of nationality. I do not know who made the decision but this is how I found it, and ID cards were issued before my time—not once but twice—and that was how I left it.

On July 7, 1954, a directive was issued in Interpretation File Number 276 in connection with questionnaires for new immigrants which do not list information on religion or nationality. If the applicant had received permission to enter the country as an immigrant, this was to be taken as prima facie evidence that his religion and nationality were Jewish. In other words, here there was a connection between the two.

On January 26, 1955, Circular Number N/161 contained a directive on registration of newborn children: "Section 10—Religion: this should be registered as that of the parents. Section 11—Nationality: this should be registered as that of the parents." On the same day it was realized that no provision had been made for mixed marriages and on January 26, 1955—this was in the time of Mr. Rokah—Amendment 26 was sent out as a supplement: "In Section 10 the religion shall be registered as that of the parents; in the event of a mixed marriage, i.e., parents belonging to different religions, the registration shall be registered as per a declaration signed by both parents stating which religion they wish their child to have. The same holds true with regard to Section 11—Nationality."

On June 1, 1955, the registration of births and deaths was, by a Government decision, transferred from the Ministry of Health to the Ministry of the Interior. On July 8, 1955, in the interval between Mr. Rokah's term of office and my own—that is, when Mr. Shapira was Minister of the Interior—Amendment 52 was issued which, repeating the directive of January 26 of that year, says that both in respect of religion and nationality "this item should be registered as per declaration signed by both parents stating which religion and nationality their child is to have."

When Mr. Shapira handed me the keys to the Ministry on November 9, 1955, these were the instructions that were in force, having been confirmed twice, once during the terms of office of each of my predecessors.

In 1952 under Mr. Shapira and in 1954 under Mr. Rokah the question arose of whether a Jew who had converted to another religion was entitled to benefit under the Law of the Return. There is a letter written by Rabbi Dov Katz, Director of the Rabbinate and Rabbinical Court Department of the Ministry for Religious Affairs of Jerusalem, on January 14, 1952, in connection with the case of a Jewess who had converted to another religion. It states that in consultations with the Chief Rabbis of Israel, he learned that they concurred that "the method of registration of nationality should not be altered," and proposed entering under nationality "apostate Jew." In my opinion this is unacceptable. There is no such nationality. The Rabbis added that she should be "registered as a Jew, but as one who had converted to a different religion." Mr. Shapira, then Minister of the Interior, decided to recognize the apostate's right to benefit from the Law of the Return and she was issued a visa under the abovementioned Law as a Jew of the Christian religion. [Yitzhak Raphael (Hapoel Hamizrahi) interjected: "That is in keeping with the Halakha."] Why does the Halakha differ in different cases depending on who expounds it?*

To sum up, under both of my predecessors, there were directives in force under which nationality in mixed marriages is determined by the decision of both parents, and that was what I upheld. What has taken place during the ten years of the State? What is the nature of the status quo which my colleagues and I accepted in the Government's basic policy as binding upon us?

In the area of religion there are basic, harsh, fundamental differences of opinion among the various sectors of the public represented in the Government. Yet all these factions agree that the dangers facing us from outside and the necessity not only of orating about Aliya but ensuring and properly absorbing it are so important to the destiny of the State and of us all that it is better to be tolerant on both sides, for we all face difficult tasks. All Aliya is desirable. When there was immigration from Hungary that was in large part fanatically religious and non-Zionist or even anti-Zionist, we received it with open arms. There are other kinds of Aliya as well. The immigrants from Poland were unlike those from Hungary. Those from Argentina are unlike those from North Africa. But all of them must be received with open arms. Will we not receive immigration from the Soviet Union when they open the gates? That is the reason for being of the State of Israel.

Was there not an agreement among the first elected Government, in which Mizrahi, Hapoel Hamizrahi, and the Agudat Israel participated, that the State would safeguard freedom of religion, conscience, education, and culture, maintain complete and utter equality for all, and furnish the public religious needs of all its inhabitants while preventing religious coercion? Is all that in keeping with the Halakha?

The rabbis in Israel operate solely by virtue of the elected Government, the Knesset, and our laws. Outside the law anyone who wishes to obey the rabbis can do so and anyone who does not cannot be compelled to do so. The only thing binding every individual is the laws of the Knesset. You ask, what will the Jews of America say? The Jews of America say things that are contradictory and at variance with each other because they are free to say anything they wish, provided it does not violate the laws of the state. There are various different Jewish movements in the United States and there are those who do not belong to any movement. But they too are Jews. The question before us is: How can we who differ from one another in our conceptions of Jewish tradition all get together and build a united Jewish State?

---

* Halakha: Jewish religious jurisprudence.—*Editors*

This debate went on from July 7 to July 15. At its conclusion the Prime Minister surprised the Knesset by announcing that he would not say what he had intended to in this unfortunate debate but would merely announce the Government's decision, prefacing it with a statement of a few sentences:

> Nowhere in the world is Jewishness so deep-rooted, genuine, and rich as in Israel and I have stated often on behalf of the Government that this is a State of Law, not of Halakha. By their signatures to Israel's Declaration of Independence on May 14, 1948, all the parties sitting here committed themselves to freedom of conscience and religion. Now this is the Government's decision: To set up a committee of three—consisting of the Prime Minister, the Minister of Justice, and the Minister of the Interior—to consider and draw up directives for the registration of children of mixed marriages whose parents wish them listed as Jews. The committee will hear the opinions on this subject of sages of Israel both in Israel and abroad, and the resulting directives shall take into account the accepted tradition in all Jewish circles and every trend, both religious and secular, and the special conditions obtaining in Israel as a sovereign state guaranteeing freedom of conscience and religion and serving as a center for the ingathering and integration of exiles.

He proposed that the Knesset take note of the Government's decision and reject the no-confidence motion to be made by several parties.

Esther Raziel-Naor declared: "By way of summing up the debate and in view of the Prime Minister's reply, the Herut movement proposes the following resolution: "The Knesset expresses no-confidence in the Government." Similar motions were made by Israel Shlomo Rosenberg for the National Religious Party, Agudat Israel, Poalei Agudat Israel, and by Israel Rokah for the General Zionists. The no-confidence motions were turned down by a vote of sixty to forty-one, with one abstaining. The Prime Minister's proposal was adopted, fifty-nine to forty-one, with one abstaining.

The two members of Hapoel Hamizrahi refused to return to the Government even after the Prime Minister announced that a special Cabinet committee would be set up to reexamine the directives regarding the registration of children of mixed marriages. On November 24, 1958, therefore, the Prime Minister proposed the co-option of Rabbi Yacov Moshe Toledano as Minister of Religious Affairs and the transfer of the Posts portfolio to the Minister of Health, Israel Barzilai. For the time being the Welfare portfolio would remain with the Prime Minister.

On the day set for debate on this question, December 3, 1958, Herut and the National Religious Party made a motion of no-confidence in the Government. Menahem Begin claimed that a letter sent in the Prime Minister's name to Chief Rabbi Nissim constituted an insult to the Chief Rabbi. Speaking for the National Religious Party, Yitzhak Raphael said that "since the Israel Labor Party [Mapai] has broken its partnership of many years' standing with national religious Jewry and subjugated itself to the two parties of the Left, the Government has ceased to represent the totality of Israel, is increasingly taking on a one-sided sectarian character, and careening down a steep and dangerous slope in its war against Torah Judaism."

The motion of no-confidence was immediately rejected by a majority of the Knesset and the debate over the co-option of Rabbi Toledano continued. In his reply on December 3, 1958, the Prime Minister stated:

A. The Committee of Three announced on July 15, 1958, at the conclusion of the debate on the resignation of two members of Hapoel Hamizrahi and the directives regarding registration of children, that it was meeting and would continue to meet until replies were received from "sages of Israel" both in Israel and the Diaspora, at which time it would draft recommendations for the Cabinet and the Cabinet would come to a decision.

B. All directives governing the registration of children of mixed marriages issued since the founding of the State have been canceled and we were starting with a clean slate. Only after being clarified and considered anew would a decision on this subject be taken. This had also been said by the Minister of the Interior at the end of his statement in that debate. If the directives were canceled, why should the Hapoel Hamizrahi members leave the Cabinet?

C. The Ministry for Religious Affairs was not a "religious" ministry nor was it necessary that the person who headed it be religious. It was a Government ministry like any other and could be headed by any suitable person. The Minister handled the needs not only of the Jewish faith but also of the Moslems, Druze, and Christian religions and obviously he could not be devout in Judaism and Islam and Christianity.

The Prime Minister had been informed that Rabbi Nissim had decided to rectify the error in the *Jewish Observer* to the effect that Ben-Gurion had given his support to certain directives, and had done so. With this correction, which did honor to Rabbi Nissim, he considered the unfortunate matter closed.

Someone abroad had sought to create the erroneous impression that the Government was intervening in religious matters and enacting laws of a Halakhic nature. Neither this nor, he was certain, any succeeding Government, no matter what its composition—even if it consists wholly of outstanding rabbis—had taken or would take upon itself the issuance of rulings in matters of religion. This was not its function nor was it authorized to do so. Every Israeli Government, whether made up of religious or of non-religious Jews, must do everything to prevent war either for or against religion.

By a vote of sixty to thirty-eight the Knesset approved the co-option of Rabbi Toledano as Minister for Religious Affairs. The Rabbi immediately made his declaration of allegiance.

Dangers of a Proportional Election System ★ Mapai Overwhelmingly Favors Constituency Elections ★ Knesset Against the Change

The present election system of proportional elections, in which all of Israel is a single constituency and every elector votes for a list of 120 candidates, is the result of the special conditions prevailing when elections to the First Knesset were held during the War of Independence. The Provisional Government appointed a committee of three, Prime Minister Ben-Gurion, Minister of the Interior Gruenbaum, and Minister of Justice Rosenblueth [Rosen], to draft an election law. The Prime Minister proposed the British system, under which the country is divided into constituencies equal in number to the number of seats in Parliament, and every constituency returns one representative—the candidate who received the highest number of votes. His two colleagues proposed that the entire country constitute a single constituency and that elections be on a proportional basis. The majority of the Government accepted the latter system and requested Ben-Gurion not to bring the issue before the Council. He immediately acceded to the request.

On July 7, 1948, however, the Council appointed a committee composed of representatives of all the parties to draft an election law. Its chairman, David Bar-Hai on behalf of the majority of the committee, submitted to the Council a proposal for continuing proportional national elections. He explained that even those committee members who had been in favor of constituency elections as in England had concluded that at the present stage such elections were not possible because a large part of the electors in the Army were compelled to move from place to place. He stated explicitly that this was not intended to serve as the basis for future elections but merely to enable people under arms to vote.

When the Council debated this proposal on November 4, 1948, Dr. Altman (Herut) opposed a single constituency for the whole country with every voter choosing from a list of 120 candidates, with most of whom he was completely unfamiliar. This, he argued, would lead to fragmentation of the nation's forces and artificial conflicts. The public would have no influence in choosing the candidates, since the lists would be drawn up at party headquarters. The system would cut any connection between the voter and his representative, who would be dependent on his party leadership rather than on those who elected him and whom he would not even know. The ensuing party fragmentation would result in many parliamentary factions uniting to form a dominant majority, not on the basis of a common program but merely to divide up the positions of influence and the national budget. Regional elections alone could prevent this, as the deputy would know who had elected him and could maintain constant contact with them. To win a majority, the candidate would have to gain the approval of the majority of voters in his own constituency and concentrate on the problems that concerned that majority. Instead of a multiplicity of parties and election lists, a constituency system would promote national unity and an organic link between the voter and his legislative representative.

Bar-Rav-Hai replied that the proper place for Dr. Altman's strictures was the constitution committee dealing with questions of basic law and the State. In any case, his committee had been charged with preparing elections in a time of war and the Council resolved that "the entire elections area shall be a single constituency and the elections shall be proportional."

Dr. Altman's apprehensions were fully borne out after the elections to the Second Knesset. In the elections to the First Knesset there were half a million eligible voters and twenty-one party lists; though nine of these, including Gruenbaum's personal list, did not return a single candidate, the Knesset ended up with twelve different blocs, not one of which had a majority. The small factions, without whom no majority Government could be formed, were interested in preserving the proportional election system. Thus there came into being a large number of small parties whose programs held no interest for the majority of the nation, which was denied its basic democratic right of a real choice of the Government. Its composition was decided after the election by the parties alone. The elector had no connection with his representative, who in turn had no say in drawing up the list of candidates. Consequently the interests of the parties, as conceived by the leadership of their Central Committees, became paramount. In the elections to the Second

Knesset there were eight hundred thousand eligible voters and seventeen party lists, fifteen of which obtained representation in the Knesset. In the Third Knesset there were ten factions at the beginning and twelve after the split in Mapam.

The first two elections proved to anyone who could see and was concerned for the country's fundamental interests that the national proportional system distorted the principle of elective representation and resulted in excessive multiplication of parties. This tended to division in a nation that needed unity above all. When the Executive Council of Mapai, with the largest representation in the Knesset, convened on December 16, 1954, the first Prime Minister, who after each of the five elections had been entrusted with the formation of a Government, listed three basic problems confronting the State: the safeguarding of our security and independence, the continuation of immigration and development, and the nation's unity and education in national values.

The majority of the public is unacquainted with the State's true condition, and lives in a euphoria that artifically sweetens its political awareness. This majority, concentrated in three crowded cities, neither knows nor sees how empty and desolate the country is and the extent of the danger this poses even to the densely populated areas. Israel's leading spokesmen have been raised from their youth on Zionist theory. Though they do not doubt for one moment that we are one people, they do not know that, while correct from the theoretical viewpoint, their inner conceptions do not yet reflect an objective reality. Many, and perhaps most, of us are still a mixture of tribes, deficient in the values and perceptions that weld human beings into a national entity.

Through the years we have experienced the difficulties of an ingathering of the exiles and in recent years the problems of their integration as well. We know that this integration cannot come overnight. We cannot reshape in a short time what had been wrought by hundreds of years of history to make us a scattered and disintegrated people, its sons often light years apart culturally, linguistically, and in their concepts of government. Even in the Homeland this condition cannot be rectified in a few years. Let us not, therefore, add to the difficulties bequeathed by history new stumbling blocks through a poor form of national government. Let us not aggravate the internal fragmentation by a system of elections that has no exact parallel anywhere in the world—proportional national elections.

The proponents of proportional elections are under the illusion that such a system provides a fuller, more accurate, and more faithful reflection of public opinion. The truth is that no elected body can represent the voters' wishes with complete fidelity and accuracy. When thousands of voters vote for one man, it does not imply that they agree on all issues and always identify with him in every respect. Only in a totalitarian state are "representatives" supposed to reflect the opinions of the voters that are 100 percent identical with those of the rulers. This "ideal" cannot be achieved in a democratic government in which every citizen enjoys freedom of thought.

Political logic and parliamentary necessity have compelled the numerous factions, large and small, to combine into two opposing bodies—a sort of two-party system consisting of a Government coalition on the one hand and an Opposition coalition on the other. But the disadvantages of such a system outweigh its advantages, and neither coalition is a partnership based on truth and good will. The "Opposition" contains such contradictory elements as the Communists and Herut, Mapam and Agudat Israel, which vote together and even decide on joint tactics and the wording of no-confidence motions in open consultation on the Knesset floor. In a democracy opposition is natural, valid, and desirable, but even the opposition must be responsible to the State and capable of forming a new government if it succeeds in toppling the one in power. A fragmented Opposition such as ours is good only for negation, for opposition without responsibility, and it educates its public to national irresponsibility.

The Government coalition likewise cannot thrive on negation alone, being based of necessity on a joint program of activity supported by the majority in the Knesset. Yet in a situation of party fragmentation, when no one party has a majority, even a relatively large party, without which no government can be formed, requires the cooperation of smaller factions, which affords opportunity for subtle moral extortion by these groups. They appeal to a small minority only, not in the name of the needs of the nation as a whole but in the name of marginal interests with only minority appeal. Yet they are able to impose upon the majority policies it might have rejected outright had it been truly free to do so. Owing to the nature of coalition government, it has no choice. Without these small factions there can be no majority, while the opposition is incapable of forming a government. The door is thus open to improper extortion, and a proportional election system provides practically no means of correcting this grave fault.

It may be argued that even in countries with a genuine two-party system and constituency elections the two parties are merely coalitions of different tendencies and trends. Now it is true that in a democracy every party is to a certain extent a coalition of varying tendencies and views. Every man is free to join one party or the other without fear; people join together in parties, not because they share identical views in every respect, but because they hold basic principles in common; on disputed issues they try to reach a compromise or submit to a majority vote. The party framework is not obligatory. When they join together it is because their outlook on fundamental questions is the same. The existence of two such parties is a blessing to the parties themselves, to the State, and to the nation. Such parties teach their members loyalty to basic principles, flexibility in relationships among the members, and the wisdom of unifying compromise.

The election system in Israel, on the other hand, has given rise to a large array of parties, perhaps larger than in any other modern state. Most of them, besides, are characterized by inner conflicts among different trends. An outstanding example is Mapam, the "United" Workers Party. Drawn mainly from the Hakibbutz Hameuhad or Hakibbutz Haartzi movements, Mapam split up during the Second Knesset. And it would be a mistake to think that Hakibbutz Hameuhad or Hakibbutz Haartzi is itself a monolithic bloc. Zisling and Yigal Allon in Hameuhad are no less remote from one another than Ya'ari and Riftin in Haartzi. In vain does Hakibbutz Haartzi boast of ideological collectivity. It is merely trying to conceal its inner conflicts from the eyes of outsiders.

There are those who say, "There is nothing you can do—that is what the nation wants." We doubt if that is really what the nation wants. The people of Israel were never asked if they desired a proportional national election system that would divide and disperse its strength. It is highly doubtful if the small factions in the Knesset would agree to a referendum on this issue. Surely the nation does not want perpetual fragmentation and multiplicity. No election system can provide a mathematically correct reflection of opinions among the nation. A system ensuring conditions for the effective operation of democracy and maintenance of civil rights should:

(a) Provide an opportunity for the people to decide from time to time on fundamental issues. The nation need not resolve problems of an eternal metaphysical, religious, or ideological nature that are outside the sphere of practical affairs.

(b) Enable the voters to choose a representative who will be responsible and bound to them in a reciprocal relationship. From time to time he will inform his electors of matters tabled for debate in the Knesset and the electors may express their opinion in the matter.

(c) Enable the nation to choose the government it desires. Only in a two-party system can a government be chosen in which the majority have confidence.

These three essentials are ensured only under the British election system. Under the system in Israel the elector has no contact with his legislator. He must vote for a list of candidates most of whom he does not even know, and it is the party apparatus that decides who will be on the list and in what position, and whether he stands a chance of being elected. Only after the elections is the composition of the government established by negotiations among the various parties.

After a five-hour debate of the Mapai members, a vote was taken. Fifty-two favored the British election system; six were opposed.

On October 8, 1956, during the second session of the Third Knesset, the Prime Minister raised his question during the debate on the Basic Law. The Law Committee proposed that the Knesset be elected by general, national, direct, equal, secret, and proportional ballot. On behalf of Mapai, Knesset member Azanya called for regional elections in which the country would be divided into 120 constituencies by the Supreme Court and each constituency would elect one member of the Knesset. The proposal was rejected seventy-two to forty.

On February 12, 1958, the Basic Law of the Knesset was passed with an amendment to Section 4 (proportional national elections) reading: "This section can be amended only by a majority of the members of the Knesset," that is, an absolute majority of sixty-one. The amendment was approved, fifty-eight to fifty-six.

Ten months later, on December 9, 1958, at the fourth session of the Third Knesset, Member Yosef Almogi once more raised the issue of the election system. Since the majority in the Knesset which had approved the old system consisted of a multitude of small factions with no concern beyond their own partisan interests, he proposed a nationwide referendum on the matter. Joseph Serlin, on behalf of the General Zionists, also called for a referendum though rather than constituency elections on the British pattern he proposed proportional regional elections like those in Scandinavia. After a long debate it was decided, fifty-eight to forty-two, not to refer the proposal to the Law Committee, which meant in effect that it was dropped.

A New Crisis: Sale of Arms to West Germany ★ Cabinet Members Violate Collective Responsibility ★ Resignation of the Government

Shortly before the conclusion of the Third Knesset another Government crisis broke out, this time because of the sale of arms to West Germany.

On June 29, 1959, the Communist Member Mikunis called for a motion of no-confidence because of this issue. "This foul arms deal with Hitler's spiritual successors," he claimed, "has branded our country with the horrible black stain of active aid to German militarism, which is again menacing the world and Israel's welfare. The present West German regime is based upon the same forces of darkness and murderous militarism that characterized the Hitler regime. Only Ben-Gurion and his henchmen could be capable of the fiendish jest that assisting Hitler's torchbearers with Israeli arms increases Israel's security. Only this decadent militarist elite could permit themselves to assert that Israeli arms in the hands of German soldiers under the command of Hitler's generals does not clash with the feelings of our people. Only alienation from the national ideals and estrangement from the life and noble aspirations of the people could lead the power elite to prefer dollars to our nation's blood and soul, its present and future."

The Mikunis motion was supported by Menahem Begin (Herut). He declared that "between the Germany known as the Reich of Wilhelm and that known as Hitler's Third Reich came the idyll of the Weimar Republic. Can anyone of sound mind anywhere in the world say with complete sincerity that what the blind consider the Adenauer idyll is not paving the way for a Fourth Reich? Who can answer this terrible and frightening question that to this day disturbs people of good will in England, America, France, Belgium, Holland—everywhere in the world?"

Peretz Bernstein (General Zionists) announced: "Regarding the transaction that led to the motion of no-confidence, we have declared that we are against cancellation [of the arms sale]. We will therefore abstain from voting on the Communist motion of no-confidence. Yet our support for the action that inspired the motion does not alter the fact that this Government is indeed not worthy of confidence." This was the first time in the Knesset that an opposition party supported the Government solely out of national concern, without considering whether the action would win any more votes for it.

When the discussion was resumed the next day, the Prime Minister proposed the Government's resolution: "The Knesset expresses its opposition to canceling the export of arms to West Germany and proposes a debate on this question." The no-confidence motion was rejected by a vote of fifty-seven to five, with thirty-seven abstaining. But the debate continued throughout June 30, and Ben Gurion replied the following day, July 1.

The reply takes up eight pages in *Divrai Haknesset* (Volume 27, pp. 2403–2410). Here we will merely note that at the Cabinet meeting on December 24, 1958, attended by all members, including the representatives of Ahdut Haavodah and the United Workers Party (Mapam), an explicit decision had been made. The Prime Minister on that occasion reported that a large dollar order had been received for mortar bombs. The legal advisor of the Ministry of Defense had informed him that under paragraph 2 (b) of the Firearms Law, weapons could be sold abroad only with the approval of the Government, and therefore he had brought the matter before the Cabinet.

Cabinet members wanted additional information. Minister Bentov (Mapam) asked, "From whom is the order?" "From various countries in Europe," the Prime Minister answered. Minister Rosen (Progressives) said, "All the same it is worth knowing which countries." "A number of countries—Holland, Germany—perhaps also a third country," Ben-Gurion stated. "I am asking for a general approval." To which Rosen commented that "there might be exports having a political significance." The Prime Minister responded: "On several occasions there were orders in which the Foreign Ministry intervened and did not permit the sale. If there is no opposition, we are finished with this question." It was resolved, in accordance with paragraph 2 (b) of the Firearms Law 5707 (1949), to authorize the Ministry of Defense to sell arms to foreign countries in all cases in which the Ministry of Foreign Affairs had no objection.

Subsequently there was an exchange of letters with two Ahdut Haavodah Ministers; Bar-Yehuda (Interior) and Moshe Carmel (Transport). On April 14, 1959, four and a half months after the Cabinet decision had been taken in the presence of both of these Ministers, they wrote the Prime Minister:

> During the discussion on the foreign currency budget, you made a statement at the meeting of the Cabinet on plans existing in the Ministry of Defense for the sale of arms to West Germany. The Government decided at the time to hold a discussion on the matter. Since the Cabinet has not yet held a discussion on this proposal owing to other pressing affairs, we find it necessary to inform you without delay of our unequivocal opinion that we are absolutely opposed to the sale of arms to Germany, and we shall explain our opinion at the meeting of the Cabinet that discusses the question. At the same time we wish to express our hope that as long as the said discussion has not taken place in the Cabinet, the Ministry of Defense will take no step toward implementing its plans to carry out the arms deal with Germany.

The Prime Minister answered them from Sde Boker on April 29, 1959:

> I received today your letter of April 14 (I do not know why it reached me only today). I have examined the Government decision on the sale of arms and found that the decision applies to all countries without exception. For this reason the matter does not require further discussion in the Cabinet. You have, however, the right to propose cancellation of the decision, and until your proposal is adopted—if it is adopted—the decision remains in force, and the Ministry of Defense will act in accordance with it.

The Prime Minister returned to Jerusalem from Sde Boker on May 3. A Cabinet meeting was held at which the two Ministers did not mention the sale of arms. But the next day they wrote to the Prime Minister again:

> In reply to your letter of April 29, 1959 we wish to remark:
> 1. We do not recall a Government decision that can be relied upon on the sale of arms to Germany by the Ministry of Defense without prior consultation with the Cabinet.
> 2. Even if we are shown that such a decision exists, taking into consideration the fact of our opposition to the sale of arms to Germany in the present circumstances, we ask that this transaction should not be carried out before the subject has been discussed in the Cabinet.

On May 10, 1959, the Prime Minister replied:

> The decision that you do not recall exists, and it states that arms may be sold to any country if the Foreign Ministry does not object. It does not say "if the Minister of the In-

terior or the Minister of Transport does not object." The Ministry of Defense has acted and will act according to this decision.

Since then six weeks had passed and seven Cabinet meetings had taken place, but neither Ahdut Haavodah nor Mapam had posed the question of arms for Germany or proposed that the matter be discussed. After speeches by Ministers Carmel, Barzilai, and Bar-Yehuda, who took issue with the Prime Minister, the Government tabled the following proposal: "The Knesset opposes the cancellation of the export of arms to West Germany." It was adopted by a vote of fifty-seven to forty-five, with six abstaining.

The Ahdut Haavodah and Mapam members voted against it. This constituted a violation of the law of collective responsibility and the additional commitment they had taken upon themselves on December 31, 1957, to the effect that "collective responsibility shall bind all members of the Cabinet and the Coalition parties to vote in the Knesset for all Government decisions and the laws it may propose to the Knesset. If a Minister or Ministers feel themselves compelled to abstain from voting without the Government's consent the Minister or Ministers must resign from the Government. A vote by a party against a Government decision shall have the same effect as the abstention of a Minister without the agreement of the Government."

On July 5, 1959, the Prime Minister notified all the members of the Cabinet in writing: "If Ministers Bentov, Barzilai, Bar-Yehuda, and Carmel do not, before 1800 hours, submit their resignation from the Cabinet as a result of their violation of the Law on the collective responsibility of the Government and their breach of the express undertaking they assumed when this Government was established early in 1958, I will submit my resignation from the Government not later than tomorrow morning."

At the Cabinet meeting at which that letter was read the Government demanded that the four members in question resign. They failed to do so, and on the same day the Prime Minister submitted his resignation to the President of the State. He attached to it all the documents connected with the matter discussed in the Knesset on June 29–30 and on July 1, 1959; the Government's deliberations and decisions on March 16, 1958, December 14, 1958, January 18, 1959, and March 29, 1959; as well as the exchange of correspondence with the Ministers of the Interior and Transport.

In his letter the Prime Minister noted that "both the Foreign Affairs and Security Committee and the Knesset had expressed their support for the Government's decision." Therefore he was notifying the President that "my colleagues and I cannot, of course, take part in a Government, four of whose members violate the law of the State and commit a breach of the obligation they undertook in the Knesset as a condition of joining the Government. I hereby submit my resignation from the Government according to paragraph 11 (g) of the Transition Law 5709 (1949). The effect of my resignation is the same as that of a decision by the Government to resign."

On July 15 the President entrusted Ben-Gurion with the formation of a new Government that would enjoy the confidence of the Knesset. On the same day Ben-Gurion wrote to the President:

> This morning you charged me with the task of forming a new Government enjoying the confidence of the Knesset. I shall endeavor to execute this commission, although under present conditions there is hardly any prospect of success. However, I shall make the attempt, for two reasons.

1. It is the moral duty of the Knesset to put an end to the shame of the Government of Israel, so that it should not contain members who break the law of collective responsibility and violate the clear and express obligations that they undertook, and which were a condition of their entry into the Government and their confirmation in their posts by the Knesset.

2. Legal experts have informed me that unless a new Government is formed without my participation—and no such Government can be established without a compact between Ahdut Haavodah and Herut with the support of the National Religious Party and the General Zionists—I am obliged by the Transition Law to continue to participate in the Government, although this involves me in moral and spiritual difficulties.

In order to clarify the first reason, I must draw attention to the statement made by Mr. Bar-Yehuda, Minister of Interior, in the Knesset on July 1, 1959, at the close of the debate on the Communist Party's no-confidence motion and the Government motion to decide against the cancellation of the export of arms to Germany. Mr. Bar-Yehuda ended by repeating the statement that he had made in the Knesset on January 7, 1958, after the confirmation of the present Government, as follows: "In addition, I wish to state: in the future, as in the past, any Government that shall be left by one of the parties whose participation in it was a factor in the expression of confidence in the Government by the Knesset shall be obliged, whether this is expressly written or not, to resign, and to submit the new composition of the Government for the approval of the Knesset."

In this statement Mr. Bar-Yehuda ignores, and also failed to tell the Knesset, that the Government that was accepted at the time had been approved solely on the basis of a clear and express additional obligation, which no previous Government had undertaken, namely, that "collective responsibility shall bind all members of the Cabinet and the coalition parties to vote in the Knesset for *all* the Government decisions and the laws it may propose to the Knesset. If a Minister or Ministers feel themselves compelled to abstain from voting without the Government's consent, the Minister or Ministers must resign from the Government. A vote by a party against a Government decision shall have the same effect as an abstention of a Minister without agreement of the Government."

This undertaking was accepted by all the parties that entered the Government on January 7, 1958. They entered only on this condition, and on the same condition they were approved by the Knesset. This undertaking has been violated by Mr. Bar-Yehuda and his colleagues, on their own responsibility and without the agreement of the Coalition, and no Knesset can exempt them from this undertaking.

Although I am afraid that the task with which you have charged me cannot be carried out, I shall make every effort to do as you have asked, Mr. President, and next week I shall inform you of the results. I am making this hopeless attempt mainly because legal experts have told me that the law obliges me, in case a Government of a different composition is not established, to continue in this Government as Prime Minister.

Six days later, on July 21, the Prime Minister informed the President: "In accordance with your request of July 15, I undertook to form a new Government that would enjoy the confidence of the Knesset. It is now clear that there is no possibility of this."

It was then decided that the existing Government continue in office until after the elections of a new Knesset on December 3, 1959.

Section 2. "Who Is a Jew?"

James de Rothschild Bequeaths PICA Lands to the Nation and Allocates Funds for Knesset Building

D
URING the Third Knesset the possibility of erecting a permanent home for Israel's Parliament arose. The First Knesset had met on the top floor of the Jewish Agency building in Tel Aviv. After that it had been lodged temporarily in the Kessem Cinema, not far from the seashore. On July 22, 1957, the Speaker requested the Prime Minister to read a communication from the late James de Rothschild's widow, written on July 15.

Ben-Gurion introduced the document, brought to him the previous day by a special envoy, by lauding the British Jew as "one of the most outstanding personalities of our generation who did much in behalf of Israel, whose father before him also did great things for the country." Because of "its lofty content and especially because it concerns the Knesset," he said, "this letter deserves to be read here and recorded in *Divrei Haknesset*." The letter follows:

My dear Mr. Prime Minister:
I have often read and reread the noble and generous words of your cable of condolence. They give me so much comfort in my sorrow. Now I must turn from my grief and apply myself to the affairs of the PICA [Palestine Colonization organization]. My husband, over the last years, had given much thought to the work of PICA and its future. He had carefully considered every aspect of the problem, and, shortly before his death, prepared a letter to you in which he set out his conclusions. The letter read as follows:
"My dear Prime Minister: My father began his colonization work in Israel seventy-five years ago. The work which was then begun has continued to this day. When in 1924 my father set up the Palestine Colonization organization—PICA—he assigned to it the task of colonizing all his land holdings. It fell to me to preside over PICA since its inception.
"In the years that followed marshes were drained, the rocky hills and barren wastes were turned into fertile soil. All these lands were then colonized by PICA. Today there is no cultivable land left to PICA for further colonization. The task set for PICA has been fulfilled.
"As I cast my eyes back over our work, I think that I may fairly say that we have adhered to two principles which will bear restating—first, that we did our work without regard to political considerations; and second, that we endeavored to give to Israel and her people all that we could, without seeking anything in return, neither profits nor gratitude nor anything else.
"The colonization work having been fulfilled, the question before me was the future of PICA. The State of Israel has been created and national institutions have emerged to take over the major colonization effort in Israel. Weighing all the elements, I have reached the conclusion that with the completion of its task, the right course would be to terminate the activities of PICA instead of duplicating the work which is done now, on a far larger scale, by the National Institutions.
"PICA is a private association but all its efforts have been directed to the benefit of the public. For this reason I thought it right to inform you of my position first. For the same

reason I also propose to transfer now all remaining PICA lands (leased and not leased) to the National Institutions.

"I look upon the termination of PICA's work as a mark of fulfilment and not as a withdrawal. I would like to underline this by a special act of identification with the aspirations of Israel and her people. We intend to provide the sum of IL6 million for the construction of the new Knesset building in Jerusalem, which, I understand, it is proposed to set up. Let the new Knesset building become a symbol in the eyes of all men of the permanence of the State of Israel.

"With this done, PICA will withdraw from the scene of Israel with the knowledge that the work which was begun seventy-five years ago is being carried on by the State and people, supported by world Jewry.

"With this letter I meant to inform you of my decision. I do not intend, with this letter, to take leave of you or Israel. My interest in the development of Israel is abiding. Even if PICA must cease to operate, I shall remain as close to you as I have always been. Your cares will be my cares and your happiness will be my happiness. Indeed, I shall want to examine whether I shall be able to make some modest contribution, in the future, toward the advancement of science, art, and culture in Israel—all matters which, I know, are near to your heart; however, these are but thoughts for the future. I am not yet fully decided on them but may revert to them as these thoughts become crystallized in my mind.

"The foundations of the State have been well and truly laid. I am confident that, by the grace of the Almighty, the new chapter in the history of our people which began with the creation of the State, will be glorious and enduring."

Alas, with this letter, my husband took leave of you and of Israel, and it is now fallen to me and the Council to execute what he had resolved.

I need hardly say that the contribution of 6 million Israeli pounds for the new Knesset building will be provided. Let me add that this was a project to which my late husband attached special significance.

For myself, I will readily examine what contribution it will be possible to make in the fields of science, art, and culture which are mentioned in the letter. I cannot say at the moment what will prove feasible, but I can assure you that anything that can be done will be done.

Before concluding let me add that my husband always thought and spoke of you with the greatest affection and respect. In all his work for Israel he was greatly inspired by your example and by the exertions of the whole people of Israel.

Yours faithfully,
Dorothy de Rothschild

The Speaker added some words of tribute to the memory of James de Rothschild and for the widow of the deceased.

The Wadi Salib Episode ★ Torah Law and Civil Law in Determining Jewishness

About a month after the last recess of the Third Knesset, a sad occurence in Haifa agitated the entire country. On Friday, July 12, 1959 the Minister of Police, Behor Shitreet, told the story in the Knesset:

On the night of Wednesday, July 8, and on Thursday July 9, regrettable events took place in Haifa. At 6 P.M. on Wednesday a police sergeant in a patrol car encountered a drunken man obstructing traffic on Shivat Zion Street in Haifa [a quarter with largely Oriental residents]. The policeman persuaded him to leave the street and left him in the hands of local residents who promised to take him home.

A short time later a patrol car came to one of the cafés on that street. The owner of the café stated he had had trouble with a drunk who had caused damage, seized a panful of hot coals, injured one of the customers, and run away. The policemen later found the drunk imbibing alcoholic beverages in one of the nearby cafés. Two policemen asked him to accompany them to the sergeant in the car. He did so but when requested to get into the car refused, ran back into the café, and began throwing bottles at the car and at the policemen. At this point policemen fired four or five shots from two revolvers, under circumstances that are now being investigated.

The subject of the complaint, a resident of the Wadi Salib Quarter, was injured by one of the shots and was immediately taken to the hospital by the police. The disturbance and the shooting led to a gathering of local inhabitants. When a car of the Criminal Investigation Department arrived, it and the men in it were attacked by the crowd. A policeman who happened on the scene and saw the policemen in trouble fired one pistol shot in an attempt to rescue them. A local resident who lived on the top floor also fired a pistol, for which he had a permit. Additional police reinforcements arrived, including a Subdivision Commander who expressed his regret at the occurrence, announced that an investigation would be held, and asked the inhabitants to calm down, and they complied.

The next morning there was a procession of some two hundred people carrying black flags and the national flag smeared with blood. The procession reached the area in front of police headquarters and a delegation on its behalf was received by the Subdivision Commander. The Commander expressed his regret at the incident and denied all rumors to the effect that the injured man had died. He provided information regarding his condition and the delegation appeared to calm down. The crowd finally dispersed.

After this demonstration, a number of incidents of hit-and-run vandalism were perpetrated by small groups of inhabitants of the Quarter. In these disturbances a number of shops and cafés in the lower city and in the Quarter itself were damaged and a number of private automobiles were overturned and set on fire. The Mapai club and the Labor Council club in the Quarter were destroyed. In several of these disturbances the participants included young people, children, and even women. The police, quickly arriving on the scene, were stoned. They did their best to soothe tempers and were successful in many cases, while in others they were compelled to use force to disperse the crowd and had to make arrests.

Around 6 o'clock a serious outbreak occurred when a small group of youngsters from Wadi Salib ran up the steps of the Quarter and through the main streets of Hadar Hacarmel breaking shop and kiosk windows indiscriminately, injuring anyone in their way and overturning automobiles. This outbreak lasted only a very short time and its perpetrators vanished into the narrow streets out of which they had come. At 8 P.M. demonstrators armed with stones again made their way up to Hadar Hacarmel and began throwing them. The police dispersed them by force before they caused any damage.

A total of thirty-two persons, including two women, were arrested. On Friday, July 10, when things had quieted down, all the arrested persons were released. In the course of the disturbances thirteen policemen were injured; two of them required treatment though their condition is not serious. Two civilians were injured and hospitalized.

At its meeting on July 12 the Cabinet heard a report by the Minister of Police and decided to appoint a committee of inquiry headed by a judge. The other members were the Rabbi of Ramla, Yitzhak Abu Hatzeira and Knesset member Yizhar Harari. The assignment of the committee was (1) to determine how and under what circumstances the police acted on Wednesday and Thursday, July 8 and 9; (2) what factors and circumstances led bystanders to take part in the incidents; (3) whether any organization was involved in the riots.

In the debate that followed, the first speaker was Aryeh Eliezer: "This is one of the most serious events since the renewal of our political life, and one of the gravest since the arrival of the exiles in the Homeland in which they hoped to become one nation. We must call for an assuagement of tempers, the imposition of order, and the insurance of justice." He proposed that a parliamentary committee be set up instead of the committee the Government had appointed. Yitzhak Rokah suggested that the existing committee be enlarged by the addition of two Knesset members.

Yisrael Yeshayahu Sharabi said that for many years we had been worried by the possibility of just such a flareup of communal passions as had occurred in Haifa: "The ingathering of the exiles from all corners of the world has revealed a distressing situation, for though we are one nation in our historic awareness and our Jewish religion, we find ourselves after two thousand years of exile a people that not only has been dispersed among the nations but fragmented by sharp differences of language, food, dress, customs, concepts, ways of thinking, and other things. Nor is this the result of any conscious desire but a curse, perhaps the harshest one that has been imposed upon us by exile."

"The way of life developed in Israel before and especially after the rise of the State," he continued, "has generally been directed not only to upbuilding of the country's desolate areas but to the rehabilitation of its people. In actual fact our achievements in this area have exceeded expectations. From my personal experience of thirty years in this country I know that there is no comparison between the relations among the various communities thirty years ago and today. However, in three areas—economic, social, and educational—progress has not been completely satisfactory. I would request that in speaking and writing about this unfortunate incident, we do not implicate an entire community."

After the debate the Herut proposal for a parliamentary committee was rejected and the Knesset adopted the proposal by Hannan Rubin and Akiva Govrin which said: "After hearing the Government's statement, the Knesset refers the matter to the Knesset Interior Committee."

About a week before the close of the Third Knesset, Shlomo Lorentz (Agudat Israel) demanded that "before ending, the Third Knesset relieve itself of the sin and shame of raising the question of 'Who is a Jew?'" For the first time in Jewish history, he said, "a concept that has been clear and sacred since time immemorial has been called into question by directives issued by the Ministry of the Interior and the controversy that has arisen as a result." He therefore proposed that "Whereas during the term of the Third Knesset an attempt was made by the Government to call into question the concept of Jewishness, let there be added to the interpretative order the following definition : For the purposes of every law a Jew shall be a person who is a Jew according to the Law of the Torah."

The statement by Lorentz was not completely accurate, the Prime Minister delcared. The Government had not raised the question of who is a Jew. This was a malicious slander, he charged. Differences of opinion have existed as to the nature of Jewishness. The Neturei

Karta* did not accept Mr. Lorentz's concept of Jewishness because according to them he was making common cause with the enemies of Israel. Some of the members of Agudat Israel rejected the concept of Jewishness of members of the Mizrahi who called themselves the National Religious Party. Among American Jews likewise there were various communities and trends, and even in Israel there were differences of opinion in matters of Judaism. Ben-Gurion proceeded as follows:

> The Government has not claimed the right to decide whose Jewishness was better or more correct and has never raised the question of who is a Jew. On December 3, 1958, I announced, "All the directives regarding the registration of children of mixed marriages since the creation of the State are canceled and we stand before a clean slate." Why did I add the words "since the creation of the State"? Because I found that even when the Minister of the Interior was a member of a "religious" party, things had been done with which I could not agree.
>
> Apostate Jews have been given rights on the basis of the Law of Return. I might perhaps have granted them the right to enter the country, but not on the basis of the Law of Return, because this law applies to Jews only and, in my opinion, an apostate Jew is not a Jew. The Government accepted this view. It accepted the view that a Jew who belonged to another religion is not Jewish. Hence this problem does not exist.
>
> The question that has arisen concerns mixed marriages, and there have been mixed marriages among us since the very beginning. If the people of Israel began with Abraham, then he was involved in a mixed marriage. Isaac brought his wife from Aram Naharayim and Jacob took four wives from Padan Aram. Moses took a wife from Midian and even an Ethiopian wife, and Solomon took Pharaoh's daughter for a wife.
>
> (Yacov Katz of Poalei Agudat Israel interjected: "That was before we became a nation." The Prime Minister retorted: "We weren't a nation in the time of King Solomon?")
>
> As it happens, Mr. Lorentz, there was a great holocaust. Jews were saved by merciful and humane Gentiles, and there were many cases of mixed marriages in which the wives agreed to come and live in Israel. I think that if you were Minister of Immigration you would give them permission to immigrate. The problem has arisen: If the father or the mother does not wish the child to become Jewish, we cannot compel them; but if both the father and the mother want the child registered as a Jew and he is too young to speak for himself, how should he be registered?
>
> We have said that this is a question on which it is worth hearing the opinions of our sages, not only in Israel but throughout the world, for it is a question that concerns all Jews. And until a decision is taken on this matter, nothing will be determined. All the directives that have been in existence since the creation of the State—and there have been many different Ministers of the Interior since then, one from the General Zionists, another from the "religious" parties, and the present one—are null and void, and nothing is being registered. This is the situation at present.
>
> Six months ago one of the leaders of the Mizrahi in America wrote an open letter to me in the New York Yiddish paper *Der Tog*. I replied in the same paper that I could merely express my own opinion, which is that if both the mother and the father (and the question only arises if the mother is a "Gentile" and the father is a Jew) wish the child to be Jewish, then if it is a girl she should be immersed, and if a boy circumcised and immersed. I stressed, however, that this was my personal opinion and that the Government had not yet come to any decision on the matter. That is why I feel that Dr. Lorentz's bill is not really necessary in the last week of the Knesset on the eve of the elections.

* Neturei Karta: ultraorthodox religious group; literally, "Guardians of the Walls."—*Editors*

The Lorentz proposal was dropped.

Concern over the recent riots continued. Knesset member Eliezer Shostak (Herut) renewed the proposal for a parliamentary board of inquiry to look into the causes of the rioting in Haifa and other places. Hazan recommended enlarging the function of the committee set up by the Minister of the Interior to investigate also incidents in Migdal Haemek and in Beersheba, which followed those at Wadi Salib in Haifa. Bernstein, speaking as a member of the Opposition, came out against those who laid the blame on the Government. They were trying to turn a social welfare problem into a racial problem, he said.

The Minister of Labor, Mordekhai Namir, was of the opinion that provocation and agitation had played a decisive part in these disturbances. Although the welfare situation was still far from perfect, it had improved considerably in the past year, he said. Minister of Police Shitreet remarked that "too much stirring spoils the soup." As a member of the Oriental community, he urged that nothing more be said about discrimination.

Shostak's proposal was rejected.

The Speaker, Nahum Nir, adjourned the last session of the Knesset on Monday, August 6, 1959. He summed up the abundant and fruitful work of the Third Knesset.

> There were 686 meetings of the plenum; 270 laws enacted; answers given to 1911 parliamentary questions; 33 general debates, and 464 motions for the agenda considered; 12 private bills proposed by Knesset members were adopted. The Knesset, which was a faithful expression of the State's sovereignty and the bedrock of Israeli democracy, had earned a place of honor in the State, in the nation, in the Diaspora, and even among the nations of the world. Exchanges of parliamentary delegations, visits of parliamentary representatives to various countries and parliamentary representatives who came to Israel, as well as the regular participation of the Knesset delegation in the meetings of the Inter-Parliamentary Association had developed and enhanced ties between Israel and the nations of the world and had demonstrated our progress, achievements, and aims as an independent peace-loving state in the world in general and in our region in particular.

The Speaker mentioned the bequest of James de Rothschild that had provided IL 6 million for the construction of the new Knesset building in Jerusalem, as "a symbol in the eyes of all men of the permanence of the State of Israel." In closing, he also noted "the great loss to the Knesset by the death of Joseph Sprinzak, its Speaker for over ten years, from the day of its establishment until January 28, 1959. Sprinzak was one of those who laid the foundations of Hebrew parliamentarianism," he said, "and his memory will be cherished forever."

Elections to the Fourth Knesset ★ The New Government Demands Joint Responsibility of All Ministers

Elections to the Fourth Knesset were held on November 3, 1959. There was a total of 1,218,483 eligible voters, approximately two and a half times as many as the 506,567 eligible to vote in the elections to the First Knesset. A total of 994,306 ballots were cast (compared to 434,684 in the first elections) and 969,337 of them were valid.

Mapai received 370,585 votes—38.23 percent of the total, a larger share than in any previous election—and returned 47 Jewish members or, with the five members of the minority groups, a total of 52. The second largest party, Herut, received 130,550 votes and 17 seats, also more than in any previous election. Third was the National Religious Party with 95,581 votes and 12 seats (11 previously). Mapam won 69,468 votes and 9 seats, Ahdut Haavodah 38,034 votes and 7 seats. In the elections to the Third Knesset after the split in Mapam, Mapam alone had won 9 seats and Ahdut Haavodah 10; in the elections to the Fourth Knesset Ahdut Haavodah lost 3 seats. The Communists were down to 3 seats from their 6 in the Third Knesset. Also down were the General Zionists, with 8 seats compared to 13 in the Third Knesset. Agudat Israel and Poalei Agudat Israel with 6 remained the same as in the Third Knesset. The Progressives gained 1 seat, giving them 6.

The Fourth Knesset was opened on November 30, 1959, with an address by President Ben-Zvi, who noted that "The previous Knesset and the outgoing Cabinet had the privilege of playing an important role in the nation's struggle against the onslaught of destruction that menaced our Homeland three years ago, of sharing in the privilege of returning to Sinai, and securing transit through the Gulf of Eilat." He sent heartfelt good wishes to the Israel Defense Forces, "which had stood in the gap and earned the glory of heroism and victory," and conveyed his own condolences and that of the entire Knesset to the families whose sons had fallen in battle.

"The Fourth Knesset," Ben-Zvi declared, "more than any of its predecessors, includes representatives of immigrants from different parts of the world, both East and West. They have not only managed to strike roots in the country but also to identify themselves with it completely and to represent the entire nation honorably, without any communal divisions, and I look forward to the complete elimination of all such distinctions in the near future and our unification into a single nation, not only in the Knesset but in all walks of life. Though we have witnessed negative phenomena like the excessive number of party lists, the nation has shown its maturity in reducing their number considerably. Nevertheless, we must learn from experience and be aware of the need to correct the situation in the future."

The President memorialized the members of the Knesset who had passed away—first and foremost Yosef Sprinzak, the Knesset's superb helmsman, and members Chaim Ariav, Yitzhaki, Avraham Abass, Zalman Ben-Yacov, and Israel Rokah. The members of the Knesset rose and stood in silence in tribute to their memory.

The first session was conducted by the oldest member of the Knesset, Nahum Nir. He eulogized at greater length the members of the Knesset who had departed this world, especially "that dear man, one of the outstanding forces in our new parliamentary life, Israel Rokah."

Rokah, he said, "was one of those party workers who maintained a broad outlook and earned the esteem of broad circles of the general public, who esteemed his sincerity, honesty, earnestness, loyalty, and devotion to the tasks with which he was entrusted. Here was a man who was genial and well liked. Born in Israel, he was deeply rooted and committed to the life of the local Jewish community and concerned with everything that took place here. While still young he dedicated himself to public affairs in which he found his life's work and to the last was taken up with the problems and concerns of the Jewish public in Israel. Varied and manifold was his work in the Knesset as a member of various committees, as a leader of his party, and as Deputy Speaker. In recent years he devoted himself completely to the problems of erecting a permanent home for the Knesset. It was pleasant working together with him on the Presidium. While he upheld the opinions of the groups he represented, he looked first of all to the interests and the honor of the Knesset as a whole. The man was incorruptible and demanded the same of others."

When the Knesset members had made their declarations of allegiance, the Prime Minister announced that Kadish Luz had resigned as Minister of Agriculture. Akiva Govrin thereupon nominated Luz as Speaker of the Knesset. No other candidate being advanced, Luz was elected by 112 votes with only 3 abstaining.

After consulting with all the parties in the Knesset, the President on December 8, 1959, entrusted David Ben-Gurion with the formation of a new Government. Eight days later, on December 16, it was submitted to the legislature.

The new Cabinet was essentially no different from the last one confirmed by the Third Knesset. Once again the parties participating were Mapai, Mapam, Hapoel Hamizrahi, the Progressives, and Ahdut Haavodah, which this time had one Minister instead of two. The Mapam members were unchanged and retained the same portfolios as previously: Mordekhai Bentov, Minister of Development, and Israel Barzilai, Minister of Health. For the Progressives, Pinhas Rosen continued as Minister of Justice. Of the Mapai ministers the following remained at their former posts: Ben-Gurion, Prime Minister and Minister of Defense; Zalman Aranne, Minister of Education; Levi Eshkol, Minister of Finance; Golda Meir, Minister for Foreign Affairs; Pinhas Sapir, Minister of Commerce and Industry; and Behor Shitreet, Minister of Police. Moshe Dayan was designated Minister of Agriculture in place of Kadish Luz; Giora Josephthal replaced Mordekhai Namir, and Abba Eban replaced Peretz Naftali as Minister without portfolio. The new member for Ahdut Haavodah, Yitzhak Ben-Aharon, replaced Moshe Carmel as Minister of Transport. The two members of Hapoel Hamizrahi who had resigned from the Government on July 1, 1958, resumed their former posts: Shapira as Minister of the Interior and Burg as Minister of Welfare. Rabbi Toledano, who had been co-opted into the Government on November 24, continued as Minister for Religious Affairs.

The changes in the Basic Policy were few. Joint responsibility was strengthened. It was specified that the Basic Policy and Government decisions were binding on all members of the Cabinet and their parties, and that the following amendment would be introduced into the Transition Law:

> Collective responsibility is binding on all Cabinet members and their factions. Voting in the Knesset by a Cabinet member or members of his party against a Cabinet decision, or the abstention of a Cabinet member or members of his faction without Cabinet consent, will be considered as the resignation of its member from the Cabinet. The resignation will be operative with the announcement by the Prime Minister to the Knesset to that effect. Such an announcement does not require Knesset approval.

With regard to the main objectives, the only change was one of wording: the nine main objectives listed in the Basic Policy of the Third Knesset remained essentially the same. Nor was there any significant change with reference to economic and foreign policy, education, and minority rights. On religion, a section was added to the effect that "the Government will maintain the status quo in the State on matters of religion."

The Prime Minister, having read the names of the Cabinet members and their portfolios, was obliged to leave the session for reasons of health. The debate on the Basic Policy
and the composition of Government was more restrained than in the past, even on the
part of the Opposition.

Hazan (Mapam) listed the main points on which his party differed with the majority
—the sale of arms to Germany, military government, etc. He announced that if it ever
appeared that a majority in the Knesset was in favor of the aims of his party, they would
vote against the Government, but its ministers would resign before doing so, as stipulated
in the Basic Policy. Allon stated that every one naturally wanted the Basic Policy of the
Government to be identical with his party's platform, but the Basic Policy presented
by the Prime Minister-Designate doubtless covered the main points of the platforms
of all the parties who had joined forces to bear the responsibility for the Government in
the next four years. Harari noted with satisfaction that this time the negotiations over
formation of the Government had taken only one week. Only Mikunis (Communists)
maintained that Ben-Gurion's proposed policies were in profound contradiction to
Israel's national interests. He complained bitterly that though Mapam and Ahdut Haavodah had often denounced Mr. Ben-Gurion during the election campaign, they had entered
the Cabinet on the basis of his platform.

After a two-day debate the Knesset expressed confidence in the proposed Government by a vote of seventy-eight to thirty-three. The members of the Cabinet who were
present signed declarations of allegiance. On December 21, 1959, Minister of Finance
Eshkol announced in the Knesset that the Minister of Defense, with the approval of the
Cabinet, had appointed Knesset member Shimon Peres as Deputy Minister of Defense.

The following day the Prime Minister was able to come to the Knesset and sign
the declaration of allegiance. On December 28 he proposed the amendment to the Transition Law of 1949 on the Cabinet's joint responsibility to the Knesset, in the same language as
in the Basic Policy. The proposal, he said, was being submitted on behalf of all members
of the Government and their parties, a total of 86 Knesset members. He feared, however,
that the reasons and explanations he was about to give would not meet the approval
of all his Cabinet colleagues. The present proposal, Ben-Gurion said, was a direct corollary
of the announcement he had made two years ago, on January 7, 1958, when he presented
a Government with the same composition as at present, except that the parties in the coalition then held only 80 seats in the Knesset. He went on to say:

> Since the Foundation of the State, the Government has been based on a coalition for
> the simple reason that to this day no party has received an absolute majority under the
> proportional election system. Most of the parties were in favor of coalition government
> and on record in opposition to an absolute majority by any one party. What they really
> opposed was an absolute majority. There is no party in the Knesset, with the possible excep-
> tion of the Communists, which has not wanted or aspired to gain a majority of the nation's
> votes. I say "with the possible exception of the Communists" because they feel, by analogy
> with what has happened in a several foreign countries, that they will be able to rule in a
> one-party regime that forbids the existence of any other party. All the other parties aspire
> wholeheartedly to a majority; no party spokesman or newspaper has ever appealed to the
> nation at election time to give them only a small number of votes.
>
> What most of the parties in the Knesset truly and sincerely oppose is for a party other
> than themselves to gain a majority and so be able to govern without a coalition. If the majority
> of the parties in the Knesset at present favor a coalition government, not only after the

elections but even before them, it is only because they know that they have no chance of obtaining an absolute majority in the forseeable future and do not want any other party to do so and form a Government without them.

In my opinion this is also the real reason why the majority of the Knesset factions are opposed to regional elections. They know that under such a system they do not stand a chance of obtaining a majority in the foreseeable future, while another party may do so.

In my opinion there is no party that does not secretly wish to undertake full responsibility for the Government, not necessarily because of a lust for power but because they feel that their course is the correct one—provided they indeed have a course and believe in it. If not all of them say so openly, it is not out of humility but out of practical shrewdness, as they know it is not feasible in the forseeable future.

I have said all this in order to stress that every party feels that the Government should be conducted with undivided responsibility; as long as a coalition government is necessary we should aspire that it be unified and as far as possible a consolidated bloc with collective responsibility. This doubtless was the intention of the Transition Law, which in Section 11 stipulates the rule of collective responsibility. I realize that an opposition sometimes rejoices in a government's weakness and internal contradictions. This is human nature. Nevertheless, while a responsible opposition has every moral right to aspire to inherit the Government, as long as it is not capable of putting this aspiration into practice, it should be interested, for reasons of State, in the existing Government's acting with full responsibility.

The rule of collective responsibility does not provide sanctions, since the Knesset has immunity from police and the judiciary. But from experience we know that it is necessary to ensure that the Government be unified and that we cannot allow part of the Government to be both in the Opposition and the Coalition at the same time and enjoy the best of both worlds.

Clearly no member of the Government should be obliged to vote and act against his convictions and conscience. He can vote for his convictions and scruples with complete freedom upon leaving the Cabinet. There is nothing compelling him to remain in the Cabinet when his views on basic matters and matters of conscience are at variance with it. Hence the amendment we are presenting involves no violation of conscience. In the event of a contradiction between collective responsibility and inner conviction the Cabinet member should resign. To avoid any misunderstandings we are saying that the very act of voting or abstaining from voting in opposition to a Government decision constitutes departure from the Government, i.e., resignation. In such a case the law we are now proposing authorizes a Prime Minister to announce such a resignation to the Knesset. When this announcement is made the resignation comes into effect and does not require Knesset approval.

It is obvious that after leaving the Government, the members of his party are entitled, if they feel the need, to call for a motion of no-confidence in the Government, a right that the Transition Law guarantees to every member who is not in the Government and every party not in the Coalition. I propose that this Bill be referred to the Law Committee.

After a debate that lasted until December 30, the draft Bill, by a vote of fifty-five to twenty, was referred to the Law Committee of the Knesset. Two days earlier, on December 28, 1959, the Prime Minister had announced in the Knesset: "In accordance with Section 11A of the Transition Law, 1949, I hereby announce on behalf of the Government: (1) with the approval of the Government, the Minister of Education and Culture has appointed Knesset member Ami Assaf Deputy Minister of Education and Culture; (2) with the approval of the Government, the Minister of the Interior has appointed Knesset member Israel Shlomo Rosenberg Deputy Minister of the Interior."

The summer session of the Fourth Knesset convened on May 9, 1960, with a ceremonial meeting in honor of the anniversary of the birth of Binyamin Zeev [Theodor] Herzl. The Speaker, Kadish Luz, opened the meeting by saying:

> The Jewish people is celebrating the one hundredth anniversary of one of the great sons and redeemers of Israel. On the face of it he was, by his own admission, alien to the Jewish people and his inspiration from its treasures of the spirit was meager. However, the nine years that followed his emergence showed that all along he had harbored in his heart the pain and longing of generations and had been, as it were, consecrated from birth to the great calling of the leader who determined the fate of his people.
>
> Herzl was preceded by the theorists of the Return to Zion and the national resurgence: Rabbi Alkalai and Rabbi Kalisher, Moshe Hess, Yehuda Leib Pinsker, and others. He was preceded by his contemporaries, the men of the First Aliya, who laid the foundation of Jewish settlement in Israel and revived the Hebrew language. He was also preceded by that wonderful man, the "Noted Philanthropist." Yet in his combination of the qualities of prophet and leader, organizer and man of action, Herzl was unique. He raised abstract stirrings of redemption to the level of political action, molded messianic faith by organizing institutions and activities, imparted confidence in strengthened drive. It was as a herald of the kingdom of Israel and a powerful instrument toward its achievement that he created the World Zionist Organization and its national institutions as well as the Zionist Congress—the parliament of the Jewish people. He stood before kings and statesmen as leader of his people and gave the Jewish people the status of a political factor in the international arena. Despite its necessary vagueness, the Basle program was the first challenge the Jewish people threw down to the world over its rights to the land of its forefathers and its desire to return and repossess it.

Eulogies of Dr. Herzl were also delivered by the Prime Minister, Menahem Begin, Mordekhai Nurock, Yacov Hazan, Peretz Bernstein, Israel Bar-Yehuda, and Moshe Kol. The memorial session adjourned with the singing of "Hatikva."

Educational Problems ★ Bridging Educational-Cultural Gaps Between Children of Oriental and European Origin

The next day, May 10, 1960, the Prime Minister reported: "Owing to the resignation of Zalman Arrane, the Government has decided to transfer the Education and Culture portfolio to the Prime Minister for the time being. In accordance with Section 11A of the Transition Law 1949 I hereby announce that with the approval of the Government, I have appointed Knesset member Ami Assaf Deputy Minister of Education and Culture." And on August 3, 1960, he announced that "The Education and Culture portfolio, which I have held temporarily, will be assigned to Abba Eban, who has heretofore served as Minister without portfolio."

The Speaker congratulated the new Minister and wished him success in the advancement of education and the promotion of cultural life. "Mr. Speaker," Abba Eban responded, "allow me to thank you for your warm good wishes. I feel that this is not the proper forum for detailed discussion of the education system. In view of its supreme importance for the nation's advancement, however, I will ask the Knesset after the recess to hold a comprehensive debate on this subject. Today I will merely express my intention to work to the best of my ability for the progress of education and culture in Israel, in faithful cooperation with all bodies concerned, especially the teaching community that carries the main burden of educating the Generation of the Resurgence."

In reply to questions by Knesset members, Ami Assaf, the new Deputy Minister of Education and Culture, on the same day provided some interesting information regarding progress made and obstacles to be overcome in ensuring equal opportunities for the various communities in Israel:

It is estimated that the Oriental community today accounts for half the children and youth and 62 percent of all children being born at present. It is true that only 12 percent of children from Oriental communities received first-class marks in Grade 8 Seker [high school entrance] examinations, compared to 40 percent of the children of European descent. The Ministry of Education recognizes the need for special measures to accelerate the bridging of the gap between children from different social strata.

In the past four years much has been done in various directions that has already begun to bear fruit. Before describing this work in detail, let me repeat what has been said on previous occasions—that we are dealing with a wide gap resulting from a divergence of social backgrounds and communal affiliation. The Ministry now considers the problem mainly a social one and believes that with thorough work over an extended period and sufficient means, gradual improvement and progress among these underprivileged groups can be achieved. Among the many activities now under way or which have been decided upon I may note the following:

1. Attempts in recent years to improve kindergarten supervision. In the coming school year this will encompass the majority of the kindergartens attended by children of the poorer classes.

2. Experiments in developing mental capacity at an early age, prepared by the Szold Institute in collaboration with the Ministry of Education, and supported by a special grant from the Ford Foundation on the basis of a recommendation by the Research Fund Committee affiliated with the Prime Minister's office.

3. Experiments in improving teaching methods in Grade 1 carried out over the last three years in collaboration with the Szold Institute that have produced good results. For the year 1961–1962 the Pedagogical Secretariat has decided to extend these methods and materials to include six hundred classrooms in which the majority of the children in question are concentrated.

4. The preparation of appropriate teaching methods and texts in language and arithmetic. In 1961–1962 these will be introduced on an experimental basis in 100 Grade 2 classes in language and two hundred Grade 4 and Grade 5 classes in arithmetic. Preparation will also continue of experimental material for Grades 4 and 5 in language, Grades 4 and 5 in local studies, and Grades 5 and 6 in arithmetic.

5. Allocation of IL 1 million for tutoring children needing it; a special inspector has been appointed for this purpose.

6. Provision under the Norm B system for graduated school fees for 25 percent more Grade 8 pupils from the Oriental communities, raising the percentage of such children receiving financial help to that of children of European descent. To help such children keep up, the Ministry has organized coaching in small classes for all high-school grades.

7. For children unable to attend three- and four-year regular and vocational high schools, opening by the Ministry in 1959–1960 of a network of two-year high schools, which will be expanded in 1960–1961.

8. For children completing Grade 8 who do not have the opportunity to continue school full time, opening by the Ministry of secondary classes for part-time students; in 1961–1962 these will be increased to over one hundred. A special Bill for free partial secondary education has been tabled in the Knesset.

9. For gifted children of the Oriental communities who complete Grade 8, opening in 1961–1962 of an experimental live-in school. Selection will be on the basis of financial situation, teachers' recommendations, and comprehensive aptitude tests. If successful, the experiment will be expanded. In addition the Ministry plans a special fund for gifted children of the poorer classes, and negotiations with various bodies are now under way.

10. Reduction of the classroom-density ratio in immigrant settlements and urban neighborhoods by 5 percent in 1961–1962. Classroom density in general will gradually be reduced from 55–50 to 45–40.

11. Inspectors have been asked to draw up a list of schools needing special attention, and on the basis of this a Permanent Committee of Elementary Education has drawn up a comprehensive plan for special action to include increased counseling, help in obtaining textbooks, smaller classes, more time to prepare lessons, etc. For this program an additional budget is required and negotiations are now being carried on with the Ministry of Finance. As stated by the former Minister of Education, Zalman Aranne, the Ministry favors giving children of the poorer classes increased opportunity to attend kindergarten from the age of four. The problem is financial. This year's budget covers an additional three thousand such children and in the 1961–1962 budget we plan to enlarge our activities in this area.

In reply to another question, the Deputy Minister gave the following information:

The Central Bureau of Statistics estimated the total number of Jewish youngsters aged fourteen to seventeen in the State of Israel at 116,500. Of these, 64,620 boys and girls, or 55.4 percent, were attending school full time; another 13,500, or 11.5 percent, were on part-time; 78,120, or 66.9 percent, of the total were thus covered by the education system, while 38,380, or 33.12 percent, remained uncovered by the education system. The following is our program for raising the number of youngsters receiving schooling:

1. A system of graduated school fees for students in regular and agricultural high schools. This arrangement would gradually be extended to the vocational schools, where a study-grant system is now in effect.

2. The Ministry submitted to the Knesset a partial Secondary Education Bill. While awaiting its enactment, it has made a start by erecting 34 classrooms in 1959–1960, which it plans to increase to 120 in 1960–1961.

3. The Ministry is working on the improvement of evening schools for working youths in coordination with the local authorities, particularly by combining academic activities with social and educational programs. Examples are the youth clubs being operated in development areas and poor neighborhoods by the Youth Division of the Ministry of Education and activities in youth centers in immigrant settlements conducted in cooperation with the Ministries of Labor and Agriculture.

4. The Ministry is working for the expansion of full-time secondary schooling both by new two-year combined academic and vocational schools, especially in development areas (during the past year 26 such schools have been opened and in the coming year the network will be expanded), and for development of additional frameworks of integration adjusted to the needs of students in existing secondary vocational and agricultural schools.

5. The percentage of fourteen-to-seventeen-year-olds attending school full time was among the highest in the world, exceeded only by the United States, which had laws requiring compulsory education up to the age of sixteen and in some states up to the age of eighteen.

VII

THE TRIAL
OF ADOLF EICHMANN

Nazi Mass Murderer Captured
in Argentina; Tried and Convicted
Under Israeli War Criminals Law

Section 1. "Monster in Chains"

Nazi Criminal Brought to Israel ★ *Argentina Complains to the United Nations* ★ *The Two Countries Resume Friendly Relations*

Having first apprised the Cabinet of the sensational development, Prime Minister Ben-Gurion on May 23, 1960, made the announcement in the legislature: "I have to inform the Knesset that a short while ago the Israeli Security Services captured one of the greatest Nazi criminals, Adolf Eichmann, who together with the Nazi leaders was responsible for what was termed the 'final solution to the Jewish problem,' that is, the destruction of 6 million European Jews. Eichmann is already in detention in Israel and will soon be put on trial here under the Nazi and Nazi Collaborators (Punishment) Law, 1950." His words were received in complete silence. But when he came down from the rostrum, he was surrounded by Knesset members who congratulated him on the capture. "The praise should go to the Security Services, not to me," Ben-Gurion insisted.

The news immediately spread all over Israel and throughout the world, and everywhere stirred up great excitement and controversy. Professor Theodor Heuss, the former German President, who happened to be visiting Israel, said: "Eichmann is one of the chief war criminals and heads the 'wanted list' of these criminals in Germany. He did enormous evil and caused untold suffering all over Europe." Israel would handle the Eichmann case correctly and justly, Heuss felt.

On the day the announcement was made, Eichmann was arraigned before a magistrate in Jaffa. When the handcuffs were removed he stood at attention in ramrod-stiff Nazi style. Shmuel Roth, the Deputy Head of the Investigation Department at Police Head-quarters, read the charges and swore that they were well founded. He spoke in Hebrew of course, and what he said was translated into German. When asked if he was Adolf Eichmann, the accused identified himself. When asked whether he had anything to say, he replied that he did not at the moment but at the appropriate time would request the opportunity to defend himself. After being remanded into custody for fourteen days by Magistrate Yedid-Halevi, the handcuffs were replaced and Eichmann was returned to prison.

One of the most notorious figures of the Holocaust, Adolf Eichmann for a long time was also one of the most mysterious. Rumors said he had once lived in Sharona, a German colony not far from Jaffa, and could speak Hebrew. Born in Germany, he had been raised in Austria and had joined the Nazi Party even before Hitler's ascent to power. After the defeat of the Nazis and Hitler's suicide, he disappeared and various reports about his whereabouts proved false. Searches were fruitless. In 1959 rumor placed him in Kuwait. Because the alleged information originated in Germany, our Foreign Ministry instructed its envoy in Cologne to clarify whether that country was taking measures for Eichmann's apprehension, and forwarded photographic material that would assist in his identification and apprehension. Germany thereupon requested Britain to extradite Eichmann, only to be told that the British authorities had no knowledge of his whereabouts.

In view of the Kuwait reports, Peretz Bernstein on December 25, 1959, submitted the following question to the Prime Minister: "With the location of the Nazi murderer Adolf Eichmann known, the Israel authorities should take every action likely to lead to his arrest and punishment. Is the Prime Minister prepared to take suitable measures in order to bring about the murderer's apprehension and punishment?" This question re-mained unanswered, but the Prime Minister's Secretary, Yitzhak Navon, wrote to Bern-stein: "Certain measures are being taken to promote the apprehension of Adolf Eichmann. The Chief of the Security Services will be prepared to provide further information per-sonally and orally. The Prime Minister feels that a public reply in the Knesset would merely impair these measures and would appreciate your withdrawal of the question." Bernstein acceded to the request; he published the question and the answer only after the announcement of Eichmann's arrest.

Every newspaper in the world displayed the news of Eichmann's capture. In Germany his picture was published under such captions as "Greatest War Criminal of the Third Reich." The West German Government announced that it would not demand his extra-dition. The chief prosecutor (an American) at the Nuremberg trial of Nazi war criminals proposed that this Allied tribunal be revived to try Eichmann. While expressing satis-faction at Eichmann's capture, he doubted whether it was desirable for him to be tried in Israel because of the hostile atmosphere in that country.

In a letter to a friend, published in *Davar* on May 27, 1960, the Prime Minister said in part: "In my opinion the importance of Eichmann's capture and trial in Israel lies not in the resourcefulness demonstrated by the Security Services (though it would be hard to exaggerate the praise due to them) but in the fact that the entire episode of the Holocaust can now be laid bare in an Israeli court so that the youth in this country—which grew up after the Holocaust and has heard only faint echoes of this atrocity unparalleled in history, and world opinion as well—will know and remember. I have no doubt that in the service of the dictators of the neighboring countries there are scores and hundreds of Nazis, German and Arab, who took part in the slaughter of the Jews then and are now plotting the same thing for the nation of Israel in its own country. Public opinion in the world must be reminded whose disciples are those now planning Israel's destruction, and just who is aiding them, knowingly or unknowingly."

Among the foreign journalists who flocked to Israel after Eichmann's arrest there were many who, like the American prosecutor at Nuremberg, held that no Israeli court could be sufficiently objective. Dr. Nahum Goldmann, president of the World Zionist Organization, then in Israel, wrote an article that concurred in the demand for an international tribunal, though he expressed faith in Israeli justice and Israel's right to try one of the top Nazis in its own land. The Prime Minister sent Dr. Goldmann the following reply, which was released to the press:

In Israel there is complete freedom of expression, not only for its citizens but for tourists here for a short or long time. You, however, are not here now as a tourist. You have come as the president of the Zionist Organization to discuss closer cooperation with the Government of Israel. In the matter now at the political center of interest of the entire nation you did not feel the need to go first to the Government, but went straight to the press.

American journalists, who have not suffered from the Nazi atrocities, may be "objective" and deny Israel's right to try one of the greatest Nazi murderers. But the calamity inflicted on the Jewish people is not merely one part of the atrocities the Nazis committed against the world. It is a specific and unparalleled act, an act designed for the complete extermination of the Jewish people, which Hitler and his collaborators did not dare commit against any other people. It is therefore the duty of the State of Israel, the only sovereign authority in Jewry, to see that the whole of this story, in all its horror, is fully exposed—without in any way ignoring the Nazi regime's other crimes against humanity, but as a unique crime without precedent or parallel in the annals of mankind.

It is perhaps the first such episode of historic justice in history when a small nation, beset by many foes, is able on its sovereign territory to try one of its chief enemies for atrocities against hundreds of thousands of its sons and daughters. It is not the penalty to be inflicted on the criminal that is the main thing—no penalty can match the magnitude of the offense—but the full exposure of the Nazi regime's infamous crimes against our people. Eichmann's acts alone are not the main point in this trial. Historic justice and the honor of the Jewish people demand this trial. Historic justice and the honor of the Jewish people demand that this should be done only by an Israeli court in the sovereign Jewish State.

This was the decision of the Government of Israel and the opinion of the entire Jewish people in its land. The publication of your proposal in the press which, whether or not you intended it, went out to world public opinion is a grave blow at the sentiments of the people of Israel (and I believe not in Israel alone) and the honor of the State, particularly when it comes from a man who bears the double title of president of the Zionist Organization and president of the World Jewish Congress, at the time when he is in Israel to discuss cooperation with its Government.

According to an interview in *Haaretz* (June 3), Dr. Goldmann replied: "My proposal does not detract from the honor of Israel and its courts but, on the contrary, compliments them." He proposed that "since the Nazis exterminated peoples of other nations as well, judges from those nations should also be invited to participate in the trial." These judges, he said, should hold the trial in Israel under an Israeli chairman, and it should be conducted according to Israeli law. He was not speaking in the name of the Jewish Agency or the Zionist Congress, he emphasized.

The Soviet Foreign Minister, Andrei Gromyko, said at a news conference at United Nations headquarters at the end of May 1960 that he agreed with Israel's intention to try Eichmann for his war crimes. Also, the Soviet Ambassador in Washington declared that though the Soviet Union had serious differences with Israel in the matter of "imperialism," his government felt that Israel was entitled and obliged to try Eichmann. Should Israel relinquish this right, the Soviet Union would demand Eichmann's extradition to the USSR for the crimes he had committed against Soviet citizens, including numerous Jews.

Rumors abounded about where and how Eichmann had been captured. Early in June 1960 the American weekly *Time* reported that he had been apprehended by Israeli agents in Argentina, where he had arrived in 1950 with Red Cross documents issued by the Welfare Department of the Vatican. Some of the details became known. Under suspicion for a long time, he was finally identified on May 13 while he was walking home from work. A car suddenly pulled out of line; he was grabbed and thrust in before he could resist or raise a clamor. That night a coded cable went to the Israeli Prime Minister with the words "Monster in Chains." Eichmann's family searched for him the whole night, contacting many friends and acquaintances and checking the local hospitals—then went into hiding.

On June 1 Aryeh Levavi, Israeli Ambassador to Argentina, was summoned by the Argentine Foreign Minister, Drogenes Taboada, and asked for an official explanation as to the truth of the information that an Israeli commando unit had penetrated Argentine territory and kidnapped Adolf Eichmann. If it was proved that the abduction had taken place on Argentine territory, he stated, his government would be compelled to take measures against Israel. The Argentine nationalist paper *Azul y Bianco* attacked President Arturo Frondizi for "countenancing the abduction of war criminal Adolf Eichmann by Israeli secret agents—an act that violates Argentine sovereignty." On the other hand Dr. Sylvano Santander, leader of the United Citizens Radical Party, declared publicly that Argentina was being soft on Nazi émigrés and, despite their past, was granting them hospitality and freedom of movement. Nevertheless, he expressed regret over the manner of Eichmann's abduction, which "to a certain extent affronts our patriotic feelings."

Meanwhile the police of Tucumen State revealed officially that in 1952 Eichmann had been issued an identity card in the name of Ricardo Clement. According to the same source he had been living in Latin America for eight years, having arrived there from Spain with documents as a war refugee issued by the Italian Red Cross through the Vatican Welfare Department. He had landed at Tucumen City on the northwestern coast of Argentina and under the name of Ricardo Clement found work with an Argentine-German surveying company. Beginning to fear discovery, he moved to Brazil, where he worked for a year on a ranch. In 1954 he moved to Paraguay, worked for a few months under a different name, and in the same year returned to Argentina. After the overthrow of Perón in 1955 he fled to Bolivia, but returned to Buenos Aires a year later.

In Israel meanwhile, on June 5, 1960, Eichmann's remand order was extended for another fifteen days. In proposing the extension, Deputy Commander Ephraim Hofstater★ stated that Eichmann was suspected of crimes against the Jewish people under Section A (1),

---

★ [Subsequently Hebraized his name to Elrom, was kidnapped and murdered when Israel's Consul General in Istanbul, 1971–Eds.]

and crimes against humanity under Section A (2) of the Nazi Collaborators (Punishment) Law, 1950. He also requested an order forbidding publication of Eichmann's place of internment, the security precautions, or anything else that might directly or indirectly indicate the place. Such an order was issued.

At its meeting the same day the Government considered Dr. Goldmann's proposal for an international court. Its position remained unchanged, namely, that the trial would be conducted only by an Israeli court. On this the Ministers were unanimous.

Bureau 06 of the Israeli Police began Eichmann's official interrogation, which went on four to five hours a day. Eichmann replied to all questions and cooperated freely with his interrogators. The bureau consisted of thirty men in five squads. One squad unearthed and examined documents, the second handled Eichmann's personal interrogation, the third took evidence from other persons, the fourth examined thousands of documents in various archives, and the fifth prepared the evidence and investigation material for the trial.

A Diplomatic Note by the Israeli Foreign Ministry, in response to the Argentine demand, was published on June 7, 1960:

> The Government of Israel had no knowledge whatsoever that Eichmann came to Israel from Argentina, as the Israel Security Services did not inform it of this. It was only after the receipt of the cable from the Ambassador of Israel in Buenos Aires, dated June 2, 1960, that the Government ascertained the details from the Security Services, which had detained Eichmann, and the circumstances as elucidated were the following:
>
> Ever since the end of the Second World War, Jewish volunteers (among them some Israelis) had begun to look for Eichmann, the person principally responsible for the extermination of the Jews of Europe. For fifteen years these groups of volunteers searched for Eichmann in several countries of Europe, in the Arab countries, and on the American continent, without any results. Some months ago, one of the groups of searchers received information to effect that Eichmann might be hiding in Argentina under a false name, without the knowledge of the Argentine authorities but with the help of other Nazis living in that country. It was not clear to the searchers whether this information was correct or not, but they succeeded in establishing the fact that many Nazis were residing in Argentina.
>
> The searches were renewed more vigorously and the address of Eichmann, where he was living under a false name, was discovered. The group of volunteer searchers made contact with Eichmann and asked him if he was prepared to come for trial to Israel. When Eichmann realized that he had been recognized, he admitted his true identity and stated that he was living in Argentina with false papers and under an assumed name; as to the question whether he was prepared to stand trial in Israel, he requested a delay of twenty-four hours before giving his agreement to come to Israel of his own free will to be tried. He also handed the group a letter to the Argentine government written in his own handwriting (a photostatic copy of which has been forwarded to the government of Argentina). The following is the text of Eichmann's letter (as translated from its German original):
>
> "I, the undersigned, Adolf Eichmann, state herewith of my own free will: Since my true identity has now been revealed, I realize that there is no point in my continuing to try to avoid justice. I declare myself willing to proceed to Israel and to stand trial there before a competent court.
>
> "It is understood that I will receive legal counsel and I shall try to recount, without any embroidery, the facts relating to my last years of service in Germany, so that a true picture of the events may be transmitted to future generations. I am submitting this declaration of my own free will, I have not been promised anything and I have not been threatened. I want at last to achieve inner peace.

"As I am unable to remember all the details and may also mix things up, I request that I be helped by the putting at my disposal of documents and testimony to assist me in my eneavor to establish the truth.

(signed) "Adolf Eichmann, Buenos Aires, May 1960."

On May 23, 1960, the group of volunteers informed the Government of Israel that Eichmann was in their custody and the Government instructed the police and the Attorney General to prepare the case for trial. Only after that was the Government informed that Eichmann had come to Israel from Argentina.

Should it appear that the group of volunteers violated Argentine law or infringed the sovereign rights of Argentina, the Government of Israel expresses its regret. The Government of Israel requests that the extraordinary significance of bringing to trial a person who bears the responsibility for the murder of millions of our people be taken into consideration and that it be noted that these volunteers, themselves among the survivors of the Nazi Holocaust, placed this historical mission above all other considerations. The Government of Israel is fully confident that the government of Argentina will show understanding for these historical values.

On June 19, 1960, the Foreign Minister of Argentina handed the Israeli Ambassador the answer, as follows:

1. The Argentine nation, under the shelter of whose Constitution and laws all men the world over seeking to live on Argentine soil without any discrimination on grounds of race, language, or religion may establish themselves to live in peace and work, could not and cannot but express its most vehement repudiation of the mass crimes committed by the Hitlerite agents, which cost the lives of millions of innocent beings belonging to the Jewish people as well as of many others in Europe.

2. The Argentine government must regret, nevertheless, that expressions in the Note under reply do not correspond with the forms customary in communications between two friendly nations. The circumstance that one of these agents, the one accused of having planned and directed the cold-blooded execution of a vast plan of extermination, entered and established himself in Argentine territory under false name and documents, in a situation which is evidently irregular, and in no manner in conformity with the basic principles of asylum or territorial refuge, does not justify the gratuitous affirmation that "in the Argentine reside numerous Nazis."

3. The Note under reply, on the other hand, affirms the accuracy of facts relating to Eichmann's capture and to Eichmann's transfer with his full consent to Israel, and that only later did the Government of Israel become aware that Eichmann had come from Argentina.

4. The government of the Argentine Republic understands that the Government of Israel is not unaware of the responsibility it has assumed by acknowledging these facts and by the quick expression of its regrets in the event that the action of the "groups of volunteers" violated the law of Argentina. Nevertheless, that expression of regret is not accompanied by any corresponding offer of reparation which is the inevitable consequence of such recognition of responsibility. It is not necessary to prove that the ability of a state to exercise its authority over all persons and things living or being in its territory constitutes an inviolate right. The fact that a state sends its agents to the territory of another state for the purpose of there exercising, without authorization, acts of any sort and especially acts of coercion, cannot be regarded legitimately within the framework of international juridicial relations.

5. The Embassy's Note does not specify if those "groups of volunteers" can be validly

considered as organs of the State of Israel or agents in its service. The responsibility that arises for any state for the illegal acts of its organs or agents makes them violations of international law. The State of Israel has the responsibility that derives from its express approval of the acts of those individuals.

6. With respect to the circumstances referred to in the Embassy's Note as to the manner in which Eichmann was transferred, and the voluntary consent which he may have given to it, the government of Argentina is in no position to appraise them adequately, especially when contrasting them with other, more recent facts.

7. The Government of Israel has publicly announced its decision itself to try Eichmann and has also publicly rejected suggestions in any other sense. Nevertheless, if Eichmann is accused of the crime of genocide, it is difficult to understand how in his case Article 3 of the Genocide Convention ratified by the Government of Israel can be rejected.

8. If the Government of Israel or its agents had knowledge of the presence of Eichmann in Argentine territory they could have employed the legitimate means at their disposal for procuring his detention by the jurisdictional authorities.

9. The Government of Israel asks that we take into account the extraordinary significance of the fact that this man is charged with responsibility for the murder of millions of persons belonging to the Jewish people. The people and government of Argentina perfectly understand what can be the feeling of the Jewish people in relation to the man accused of the acts of extermination in the concentration camps. But at the same time it cannot refrain from asking itself if nonetheless it [the Government of Israel] should not have weighed the obligation to respect the sovereignty of a friendly state with which it maintains the most friendly relations. The Argentine state expects that the Government of Israel will accord adequate reparation for the said act—which can only be the restitution of Eichmann during the present week and the punishment of the individuals guilty of the violation of our national territory, and is confident that there will be no delay in satisfying this request. Once the said restitution has been made, there is open to the Government of Israel the way to request his delivery by the methods contemplated in international law. If not, Argentina will refer the case to the United Nations in accordance with the obligation that rests upon the members under Article 2, Paragraph 3, of the Charter.

Even before receipt of the note from the Argentine Foreign Minister, the Prime Minister on June 8 sent a personal letter to President Frondizi of Argentina:

Mr. President:

At this hour, as a result of the capture of the Nazi war criminal Adolf Eichmann and his transfer to Israel, misunderstandings may arise in the relations between the Republic of Argentina and the State of Israel, and I therefore consider it my duty to send you this direct message. I take the liberty of doing so precisely because the relations between our two governments and our two peoples are dear to our hearts and because we should regard it as a matter for profound sorrow and regret if they were to be in any way impaired because of recent happenings in connection with Adolf Eichmann.

I understand that you personally at the present time are giving due consideration to the Diplomatic Note that our Ambassador at Buenos Aires delivered to your Minister for Foreign Affairs on Friday, June 3. In that Note you will find all the elements of our case in this matter. There are, however, certain points touching the very core of the issue which transcend the confines of a Diplomatic Note. It is on these points that I wish briefly to enlarge and I do so in the conviction that only by fully appreciating them is it possible to pass judgment on the issue.

During the Second World War, Eichmann was the person directly responsible for the execution of Hitler's orders for the "final solution" of the Jewish problem in Europe, *i.e.*, the murder of every single Jew on whom the Nazis could lay their hands throughout the territories of Europe that they had occupied at that time. Six million of our people were murdered in Europe, and it was Eichmann who organized this mass murder, on a gigantic and unprecedented scale. I need not explain to you, Mr. President, what it means for any people on earth to be the victims of such a satanic murder campaign, and what profound scars such an experience must leave on a people's soul.

Never, even in the age-old annals of our martyrdom, has there been such a fiendish atrocity. Not only were millions murdered—including a million infants—but the cultural and spiritual center of our people, which until World War Two had its seat in Europe, was extirpated. There is hardly a Jew in the world who does not have a member of his family among the Nazi victims. Hundreds of thousands of the survivors are living in our midst, and hundreds of people in Israel and abroad would not rest since the end of the war until they had found the man who had been in charge of this appalling campaign of extermination. They regarded it as their mission in life to bring the man responsible for this crime, without precedent in history, to stand trial before the Jewish people. Such a trial can take place only in Israel.

I do not underestimate the seriousness of the formal violation of Argentina law committed by those who found Eichmann, but I am convinced that very few people anywhere can fail to understand their feelings and appreciate the supreme moral validity of their act. These events cannot be approached, Mr. President, from an exclusively formal point of view. Though I do not question for a moment the duty of every state to respect its neighbor's laws—and we regard the Argentine Republic of which you are the head as an outstanding example of a state founded on respect for law—yet we can appreciate the overriding motives whose tremendous moral and emotional force underlay the determination to find the chief murderer and to bring him, with his consent, to Israel.

I am convinced that Your Excellency will give full weight to the transcendental moral force of these motivations, for you yourself have fought against tyranny and shown your deep regard for human values. I hope you will understand our feelings, accept the expression of our sincere regret for the violation of your country's law which was the result of an inner moral imperative, and associate yourself with all the friends of justice in the world, who see in the trial of Adolf Eichmann in Israel an act of supreme historic justice, and that the friendly relations between Israel and your country will not be impaired.

On June 15, 1960, Dr. Mario Amadeo, the Argentine Ambassador to the UN, submitted to the president of the Security Council a note that said that the manner of Eichmann's removal had created a climate of insecurity and distrust incompatible with the preservation of international peace, and asked the Council to pass a resolution that would restore Argentina's rights.

The Security Council debate began on June 28, 1960, after all attempts to induce Argentina to withdraw the complaint had failed. The Soviet Ambassador, Arkady Sobolev, made a strong attack on Argentina, "which has not carried out expressed commitments to arrest Nazi leaders in Argentina." He recalled that in a joint statement issued in Mexico in March 1945 the American states had identified themselves with decisions taken by the Allies in connection with World War Two war criminals.

Henry Cabot Lodge, the American Ambassador, said that the Security Council should be guided in the Eichmann affair by three considerations: (1) the Council should not adopt any resolution that would further impair or complicate relations between Argentina and Israel; (2) the principles and practices of international law should be upheld; (3) the matter of Eichmann's abduction should not be considered apart from his monstrous acts, which constituted the ultimate in brutality and atrocity. He held out the hope that the dispute could be settled in a satisfactory manner. The Italian delegate declared complete sympathy with Israel's motives in capturing Eichmann, and France also took a firm pro-Israel stand.

In the end a resolution was adopted by eight to nothing (the Soviet Union and Poland abstained, while Argentina, although then a member of the Security Council, did not participate since it was a party to the dispute) to the effect that Eichmann's abduction was an offense against Argentine sovereignty and that the Council requested Israel to make "adequate reparation" to Argentina. Lodge felt that adequate reparation would consist in that expression of views by the representatives in the Security Council, together with an apology by Israel for any violation of Argentine law incurred by Eichmann's abduction.

On June 25, 1960, the Foreign Ministry in Buenos Aires announced that an apology by Israel would not be sufficient. On the same day Ben-Gurion, then on an official visit to France, Belgium, and Holland, stated in The Hague that Eichmann would not be returned to Argentina. Had he been in the place of the people who apprehended Eichmann, he said, he would most likely have acted just as they did. At the same time he voiced hope that traditional friendly relations between Israel and Argentina would not be disrupted, "Eichmann will be brought to trial in Israel," he declared. "I am convinced that he will receive a fair trial. Any country, Argentina included, that wishes to send an observer may do so."

The Ambassador of Argentina in Israel was recalled home and on July 25 the Israel Ambassador was recalled from Argentina. At the same time Shabtai Rosenne of the Israel Foreign Ministry was sent to that country to adjust the difficulties between the two governments, and on August 3, 1960, the dispute was terminated by a joint communiqué:

> The governments of Israel and of the Republic of Argentina, animated by the wish to comply with the resolution of the Security Council of June 23, 1960, in which the hope was expressed that the traditionally friendly relations between the two countries will be advanced, have decided to regard as closed the incident that arose out of the action taken by Israel nationals that infringed fundamental rights of the State of Argentina.

Police Interrogation of Eichmann ★ Reactions to the Case Abroad ★ Summary of Charges ★ Trial Begins in Jerusalem

A few days after the official announcement that Eichmann was in Israel and would be tried here, a special police investigation bureau force was set up, designated as Bureau 06, headed by Commander Avraham Selinger and a corps of German-speaking officers and policemen. The investigation lasted eight months. When Eichmann was asked by Deputy Commander Hofstater if he was prepared to describe his role in Hitler's Third Reich, he agreed.

The investigation was conducted by Chief Inspector Less. Eichmann's statements as recorded and transcribed filled 3564 pages. Each typed page was read by Eichmann, who confirmed its accuracy by initialing it. He proved to have a remarkable memory.

He could recall every detail of the books he had read, the names and dates of everyone he had met during his trip to Palestine and Egypt in 1937. Only with regard to Jewish matters was he vague. He could not recall what he had seen in the extermination centers. He did not remember when Jews had been executed. After several sesssions with Inspector Less, Eichmann read the following written statement:

"I am prepared to relate all the facts I know without exception. For a long time I have been prepared in my heart to issue such a general statement but I did not know where destiny would have me do it. On January 7 I was told by a fortuneteller that I would be put on trial during the year and that I would not live past my fifty-sixth birthday. The first has already happened and the second, it seems to me, is inevitable." (These predictions were fulfilled almost to the letter: He was brought to trial in 1961 and remained alive only two months beyond his fifty-sixth year.)

"This knowledge," he added, "has made it possible for me to state everything I know without considering myself. All my life, from kindergarten until May 8, 1945, I have been accustomed to discipline, which, during the years of my membership in the SS, reached the point of unlimited obedience. In my heart I am prepared to be punished for the black events and I know that the death sentence awaits me. I do not request mercy for I do not deserve it." Eichmann's conduct throughout the police inquiry and the trial, however, was not consistent with that statement. Nor did he yield to the entreaties of the Protestant minister William Hull to make a written confession of his guilt. "I have done nothing wrong," Eichmann told him after Hull had come to see him at his request. And Eichmann's attorney said that "Eichmann does not anticipate the death sentence." Moreover, the police findings cast doubt on the sincerity of his "confession." Eichmann admitted those things that he knew had already been proved, while denying other things or pretending to know nothing about them.

"Did you send Jews only to Auschwitz?" Less asked him. "Yes, to Auschwitz," he replied. "There were consultations about other places but I did not participate. I was somewhere else, it seems to me. And I do not know if I went to Treblinka or entered the ghetto, one of the ghettos. The truth is, I cannot say, Herr Inspector. It was other people's business. I did not participate in the consultations."

> LESS: Were these people your subordinates?
> EICHMANN: Yes, they were my subordinates.
> LESS: How many Jews did you send to Auschwitz for extermination?
> EICHMANN: To answer that I would have to check the records. By now I do not remember.
> LESS: How many Jews were asphyxiated and killed there?
> EICHMANN: Herr Inspector, I read that Hoess, the Commandant of Auschwitz, said that he had killed four million Jews. Personally, I feel this figure is exaggerated.
> LESS: Did you not speak with Hoess about the number of Jews killed in Auschwitz?
> EICHMANN: No, never. He told me once that he had set up new buildings that would kill ten thousand a day. That I remember. I do not deceive myself, but I do not know. And I do not think that I am deceiving myself. I do not remember when he said it or how he said it, perhaps I read it somewhere or so it seems to me.

At first Eichmann denied all knowledge of the conference on September 21, 1939, where the "final solution" was discussed and was shocked when told that Less had an official Nazi document proving that he had participated in it.

While Inspector Less was questioning Eichmann, Bureau 06 was engaged in intensive efforts to assemble and organize masses of documents from seventeen different countries. These revealed Eichmann's activities during ten years. Among them were German Foreign Ministry documents captured by the American Army before the Nazis had time to burn them as they had planned to. These documents weighed many tons. While the original papers had been subsequently returned to the German Government, copies remained in the United States which provided Israel's Yad Vashem Memorial Authority with thousands of documents relating to the Jews, including files on the "final solution."

Important material was obtained from other sources as well. The police officers assigned to examine the multitude of material and its relation to Eichmann's life and activity found themselves transformed into scientific researchers. Kibbutz Lohamei Hageta'ot also provided much important material. The records of all the postwar trials were collected, including forty-two volumes of the proceedings of the International Military Tribunal and fifteen thick volumes of later trials. Police Commander Selinger personally visited the documentation centers in England, United States, France, and Holland and recruited the assistance of historians in other countries. Only the Soviet Union refused to give any assistance. Yugoslavia cooperated fully and Czechoslovakia and Poland helped to no small extent. West Germany willingly complied with every request by Bureau 06 to authenticate documents and information.

Without the manifold and comprehensive work of the police under Selinger's command, the trial could not have been held. In December 1960 Bureau 06 submitted its first summaries to the Attorney General, Gideon Hausner, and throughout the trial a small unit of police officers stood at his disposal.

It was natural for Argentina to object to Eichmann's abduction and demand his return, although eventually it acquiesced to having Eichmann tried in Israel. However, many newspapers in other countries objected to the trial of Eichmann in Israel, principally because they could not imagine that Israeli judges were capable of giving the man who killed millions of Jews a fair trial. As we have seen, even a Jewish leader, Dr. Nahum Goldmann, demanded that judges from other countries at least be allowed to participate. Leading the objectors were the two most influential newspapers in the United States, the *New York Times* and the *Washington Post*. The *Post* contended that Israel was doing Diaspora Jewry a disservice by undertaking to try Eichmann. The *Times* found fault with the very fact of Eichmann's capture.

Many people rejected the Nazi and Nazi Collaborators (Prosecution) Law, 1950, on the grounds that a law could not be retroactive, forgetting that the Nuremberg Trials, which no one called into question, of necessity relied only on the law enacted after the commission of crimes for which the Nazi leaders were sentenced to death and executed. Only a few foreign papers from the outset justified having the trial in Israel. On June 11, 1960, the Paris *Le Monde* wrote: "In the present state of international affairs, with crime more prevalent than law, and the UN incapable of a uniform stand in a world ruled by anarchy, punctilious adherance to the niceties of protocol is of minor value or importance. If we seek the rule of law, we must first find the road to justice." Skepticism about the fairness of the coming trial was widespread.

The Chancellor of West Germany, Dr. Konrad Adenauer, said: "I have complete faith in the Israeli courts and the Israeli Government that they do not seek to use the Eichmann trial for political gain but wish justice done. I believe that this position will make every important contribution and will have an influence on public opinion. Eichmann will get his just deserts."

The trial began on April 11, 1961, in the Beit HaAm Hall in Jerusalem, which had been rushed to completion for the purpose. A bulletproof glass cage was installed in which the accused sat, guarded by an armed border policeman on either side. The three judges in the special session were Supreme Court Justice Moshe Landau, chairman, Dr. Benjamin Halevi, and Dr. Yitzhak Raveh. The prosecutor was Attorney General Gideon Hausner. The defense attorney was Dr. Robert Servatius, a German.

The courtroom was full to capacity. Hundreds of foreign and local newsmen were on hand, representing papers on every continent and in practically every country. Official and unofficial observers from foreign countries sat in the balcony. Numerous members of the Knesset as well as a number of leaders of the ghetto fighters in Poland were present.

At exactly 9 A.M. the three judges entered the hall. Justice Landau, as chairman, read the indictment, which had been drawn up by Mr. Hausner. The accused was charged with the following offenses: Crimes against the Jewish people—an offense under Section 1A (1) of the Nazi and Nazi Collaborators (Punishment) Law, 1950; and Section 23 of the Criminal Code Ordinance, 1936. Here only the main elements of the charges can be given:

The accused, together with others, during the period 1939 to 1945, caused the killing of millions of Jews, in his capacity as the person responsible for execution of the Nazi plan for the physical extermination of the Jews, known as the "final solution of the Jewish problem." Immediately after the outbreak of the Second World War the accused was appointed head of a department of the Gestapo in Berlin, the duties of which were to locate, deport, and exterminate the Jews of Germany and the other Axis countries, and the Jews of occupied areas. Instructions for the execution of the plan of extermination in Germany were given by the accused directly to local commanders of the Gestapo, while in Berlin, Vienna, and Prague the instructions of the accused were issued to central authorities for the direction of which the accused was personally responsible until their liquidation toward the end of the war.

In areas occupied by Germany the accused acted through the offices of the commanders of the Security Police, and through those persons especially designated to deal with Jewish affairs, appointed from the department of the accused in the Gestapo and subject to his instructions. The accused, together with others, secured the annihilation of the Jews, by their extermination in concentration camps, the specific purpose of which was mass murder. The more important of these camps were:

(1) Auschwitz—millions of Jews were killed in this camp from 1941 until the end of January 1945 in gas chambers and in crematoria, and by shooting and hanging; (2) Chelmno—an extermination camp in operation from November 1941 to the beginning of 1945; (3) Bergen-Belsen—a death camp operated from the beginning of 1942 until the spring of 1943; (4) Sobibor—operated from March 1942 until October 1943, and containing five stone gas chambers; (5) Treblinka—in operation from July 23, 1942, until November 1943; (6) Maidanek—where extermination continued from 1941 until July 1944.

Immediately after the German invasion of Poland in September 1939 the accused committed acts of expelling, uprooting, and exterminating the population in coordination with massacre squads, recruited from the ranks of the German Security Police and the

SS, known as "Operational Groups" (*Einsatzgruppen*). Groups of this nature also functioned in Russia after its invasion in 1941. They operated in the main on the Sabbath and Jewish holidays, chosen as days for the slaughter of Jews. During the first four months of the German invasion of the abovementioned areas Two Operational Groups exterminated Jews as follows: in Lithuania, more than 80,000; in Latvia, more than 30,000; in Estonia, about 4700; in Byelorussia, more than 7600; in Russia, about 2000; in the District of Tilsit, about 5500—a total of nearly 130,000. A third Operational Group, up to November 3, 1941, exterminated more than 75,000 Jews in the Ukraine, including 33,000 Jews in the city of Kiev. A fourth Operational Group, up to December 12, 1941, exterminated about 54,000 Jews. At the end of 1941 the accused ordered the deportation of thousands of Jews from Germany, Austria, and Czechoslovakia to ghettos in Riga, Kovno, and Minsk. These Jews were annihilated.

During the years 1940 to 1945 Eichmann, together with others, caused the killing of hundreds of thousands of Jews in forced labor camps, conducted on the lines of concentration camps, in which such Jews were enslaved, tortured, and starved to death. The accused, together with others, caused the death of hundreds of thousands more Jews from 1939 to 1945 by their mass deportation and concentration in ghettos under cruel and inhuman conditions in Germany, Austria, Italy, Bulgaria, Belgium, the USSR, and the Baltic States; in the part of Poland annexed to the USSR after September 1939, Denmark, Holland, Hungary, Yugoslavia, Greece, Luxembourg, Monaco, Norway, Poland, Czechoslovakia, France, and Rumania. The accused caused the extermination of about half a million Hungarian Jews by their mass deportation to the death factories at Auschwitz and other places from March 19, 1944, to December 22, 1944. All the acts mentioned in this count were committed by the accused with the intention of destroying the Jewish people.

The indictment listed a long series of other brutal crimes, such as sterilization, abortion, spoliation of Jewish property in Germany and the areas subject to German control, which the accused committed together with others. During World War Two and until a short time before its conclusion, freight trains containing the movable property of persons murdered in extermination camps, concentration points, and ghettos were run month by month from the occupied districts in the East to Germany. In Poland, then occupied by Germany, between 1940 and 1942, Eichmann caused the deportation of over a million Polish civilians from their places of residence with intent to settle German families in those places. He was also responsible for the deportation and extermination of tens of thousands of gypsies, and the deportation of a hundred children of the village of Lidice in Czechoslovakia to Poland and their murder there.

The indictment was read in Hebrew by Justice Landau, and in German by an interpreter. The reading and translation took slightly over an hour and Eichmann was asked if he understood it. He did. Asked if he wished to be represented in the trial by counsel, Robert Servatius and Dieter Wechtenbruch, Eichmann agreed.

Dr. Servatius put forth two preliminary claims: (1) that the judges had to ascertain whether they were not disqualified from sitting in judgment because of their preconceived opinions; (2) that the court was not qualified to try Eichmann: (a) because he had been abducted from Argentina by force; (b) because the Nazi and Nazi Collaborators (Punishment) Law was contrary to international law, had been enacted *post factum*, and hence was invalid. The acts attributed to the accused, he argued, were committed before the creation of the State of Israel, against persons who were not citizens of Israel, and there was no justification for putting a foreign subject on trial. An international court should have been set up to try Eichmann. The present trial, he went on, could not be compared to that at Nuremburg, which had brought suit against leaders, whereas the defendant here was not a leader but a mere functionary. Eichmann's written declaration that he had come to Israel of his own free will, Servatius charged, had been extracted by force: it was unlikely that a man who had hidden for fifteen years to avoid trial would suddenly wish to appear in court, especially in a country where he had reason to fear each and every one of the inhabitants. Servatius spoke in German and his statements were translated into Hebrew, section by section.

Section 2. Eichmann and the Holocaust

Court Rejects Objections to Its Competence ★ *Attorney General Depicts the Holocaust and Its Perpetrators*

THE Attorney General, Gideon Hausner, answered the objections raised by Dr. Servatius. First he dealt with the claim that Jewish judges could not be objective in a trial of this nature. No decent person in the world could be indifferent or neutral regarding crimes such as those of which Eichmann stood accused. Naturally the judges sympathized with the victims. Nevertheless, a fair and just trial could be assured, provided they judged according to the evidence. Hausner cited an article written fifteen years earlier by Professor Goodhart of Oxford in which he refuted objections to the right of a tribunal of the nations victorious over the Nazis to try war criminals. While judges had to be fair they need not be neutral, otherwise no decent citizen would ever be able to try a criminal.

Regarding the objection that Eichmann had been abducted and brought to Israel against his will, Hausner argued that the manner in which a defendant is brought within the jurisdiction of a given state has no bearing on the court's competence to try him. The transportation of a person from one state to another can be the subject of negotiations between the two states, and such negotiations between Israel and Argentina had ended successfully. There was no legal precedent for an accused person's claiming in his defense that the sovereignty of some state had been violated. The question of competence could be considered only in reference to the laws of the state in which the trial takes place; since Eichmann had been brought to trial by virtue of a law passed in Israel, this court had the authority to try him.

Servatius had argued, further, that a trial in Israel would make it difficult to bring witnesses for the defense, both because they might themselves be held here as Nazis or collaborators and because of financial problems. Arrangements should therefore be made, he contended, to obtain testimony under oath abroad. Hausner informed the court that he had already told Servatius that the prosecution would agree to such a procedure. If Servatius had any witnesses who were afraid or unable to come to Israel, there would be no objection to having testimony submitted in writing, despite the fact that the state would be deprived of the right of cross-examination. He was prepared to go one step further, Hausner added, even agreeing to the submission of evidence from witnesses who testified in German courts.

The first session ended a few minutes after 1 P.M. and the court reconvened at 4:30. At this second session the Attorney General cited decisions in American courts that it made no difference how an accused was brought to trial, whether by private individuals or an official agency of government. He pointed out, nevertheless, that this should not be taken as an admission that, as the defense claimed, Eichmann had been abducted from Argentina against his will. He put on record the letter signed by Eichmann in Buenos Aires in 1960.

Hausner declared that only the state from which a person had allegedly been abducted could bring suit against the state accused of the act. He submitted to the court the joint communiqué issued at the beginning of August by the governments of Argentina and Israel, confirming that they considered the incident closed. Regarding the objection that the Israeli law on Nazis and Nazi collaborators had been enacted *ex post facto*, Hausner pointed out that Nazi Germany had defiled the most sacred principles of law by a succession of unprecedented crimes. Without retroactive law, the greatest malefactor would have been immune; humanity had no alternative but to invoke retroactive laws against crimes and criminals of this nature.

He quoted a decree signed by Roosevelt, Churchill, and Stalin in 1943 warning war criminals that they would be punished. Following the defeat of the Nazis, the London agreement signed in August 1945 by the United States, Britain, France, and the Soviet Union provided that an international military tribunal would be set up to try Nazi criminals and that other courts would be set up for the same purpose. Since the end of the war, the accepted principles with regard to crimes against humanity had taken root in the judicial consciousness of the world, and even Germany had signed the last two conventions without reservation. He mentioned, among other things, the UN Declaration of Human Rights, which established the principle of fair and open trials, and the European Convention for the Protection of Human Rights and Fundamental Freedoms adopted in Rome in 1950 and ratified even by states like West Germany that were not members of the United Nations. In enacting a retroactive law for the punishment of Nazis and their collaborators, in short, Israel had introduced no innovation, except for the fact that special emphasis had been placed on crimes against the Jewish people. While the Hitler regime had come into conflict with many states in the military arena, there was only one nation that this evil regime had tried to destroy utterly—the Jewish people.

The Attorney General rejected the claim that Germany had atoned for the crimes of the Nazis by paying reparations. The Reparations Agreement could never serve as an atonement or make us forget. For such atrocities there was no atonement and no forgetting. We could hope that the sons would be different from their fathers and would not bear the guilt of their fathers, but for the persons who carried out the crimes there could be no forgiveness. Hausner took issue with the argument that Eichmann was merely an agent of his country. He was not a small cog in the machine of destruction—it was he who initiated, planned, organized, and implemented the attempt to exterminate the Jewish people in Europe. To the claim that Eichmann could not be tried for crimes committed before the State of Israel was created, Hausner countered that despite the fact that it did not yet exist at the time, the Great Powers had recognized Israel as a party to the war against Germany. He submitted a document, dated 1950, in which the governments of the United States, Britain, and France invited Israel to join them in putting an end to the state of war with Germany.

On April 17 the court announced that it ruled against the defense objections and confirmed its competence to try Adolf Eichmann. The trial was concerned with the responsibility of the accused for the actions enumerated in the indictment, the presiding judge said. In elucidating the facts the judges would have no difficulty in maintaining the guarantees of which every accused person is assured under our judicial system— that every man is presumed to be innocent and that his case is decided solely on the evidence brought before the court. "It is true that the memory of the Holocaust shocks every Jew to the core," Justice Landau said, "but now that this case has been brought before us, we are duty-bound to overcome these emotions, too, while sitting in judgment. This duty we shall discharge."

Eichmann was then asked how he pleaded. " Not guilty," he replied.

The Attorney General then began to describe the Holocaust:

When I stand before you here, Judges of Israel, to lead the prosecution of Adolf Eichmann, I am not standing alone. With me are six million accusers. But they cannot rise to their feet and point an accusing finger at him who sits in the dock and cry: "I accuse!" For their ashes are piled up on the hills of Auschwitz and the fields of Treblinka, and are strewn in the forests of Poland. Their graves are scattered throughout the length and breadth of Europe. Their blood cries out, but their voice is not heard. Therefore I will be their spokesman and in their name I will unfold the awesome indictment.

The history of the Jewish people is steeped in suffering and tears. "In thy blood, live!" is the imperative that has confronted this nation ever since its first appearance on the stage of history. Pharaoh, Khmelnitzky, and Petliura all contrived to destroy the Jewish people. Yet never in its history has any man arisen who succeeded in dealing us such grievous blows as did Hitler's iniquitous regime, and Adolf Eichmann was its executive arm for the extermination of the Jewish people. In all human history there is no other example of a man against whom it would be possible to draw up a bill of indictment such as has been read here. The most terrible crimes of Nero, Attila, or Genghis Khan, the telling of which curdles our blood and makes our hair stand on end with horror, seem almost to pale into insignificance when contrasted with the abominations, the murderous horrors, that will be presented to you in this trial.

Murder had been with the human race since the day when Cain slew Abel. It is no novel phenomenon. But we have had to wait until this twentieth century to witness with our own eyes a new kind of murder: not the product of the momentary surge of passion or mental blackout, but of a calculated decision and painstaking planning; not through the evil design of an individual, but through a mighty criminal conspiracy involving thousands; not against one victim whom an assassin may have decided to destroy, but against an entire people.

In this trial we shall also encounter a new kind of killer, the kind that exercises his bloody craft behind a desk and only occasionally does the deed with his own hands. Indeed, we know of only one incident in which Adolf Eichmann actually beat to death a Jewish boy who had dared to steal fruit from a peach tree in the yard of his Budapest home. But it was his word that put gas chambers into action. He lifted the telephone, and railway trains left for the extermination centers. His signature it was that sealed the doom of thousands and tens of thousands. He had but to give the order, and at his command the troopers took to the field to rout Jews out of their homes, to beat and torture them and chase them into ghettos, to pin the badge of shame on their breasts, to steal their property—until finally, after torture and pillage, after everything had been wrung out of them, when even their hair had been taken, they were transported en masse to the slaughter. Even the corpses were still of value: the gold teeth were extracted and the wedding rings removed. Millions were condemned to death, not for anything they had done, but only because they belonged to the Jewish people. The development of technology placed at the disposal of the destroyers efficient equipment for carrying out their appalling designs.

This unprecedented crime by Europeans in the twentieth century led to the definition of a criminal concept unknown in human history even in the darkest ages, the crime of genocide. The calamity of the Jewish people in this generation was considered at a number of the trials conducted in the wake of Germany's defeat in World War Two. But in none of these trials was the tragedy of Jewry as a whole the central concern. There was only one man who had been concerned almost entirely with the Jews, whose business had been their destruction, whose role in the establishment of the iniquitous regime had been limited to them. That was Adolf Eichmann.

The prosecutor described the phenomenon of Hitler. Many events contributed to the rise of Nazism: the defeat of Germany in World War One; the subsequent economic difficulties; lack of leadership and futile party divisons; fratricidal strife and disunion—all these impelled the German people, disoriented and groping, to turn its eyes toward the false prophet who spoke of the cult of hatred and power, of Germany's mission to rule peoples and nations, of the supremacy of the Aryan race, the master race. In place of the injunction "And thou shalt love thy neighbor as thyself," we find "Crush him that is unlike thyself!" Instead of the ideal of human brotherhood, we have the principle of race superiority. Only those of Aryan blood were worthy of citizenship—this was established by the Nuremberg laws.

They tried to show that Jesus of Nazareth was an Aryan, in whose veins no drop of Jewish blood flowed. Prof. Philip Lenard, Nobel Prize-winning physicist, undertook to establish a German physics "in opposition to the Jewish science represented by Einstein." In the hierarchical pyramid of racial superiority the Jews found themselves at the bottom of their list, followed only by gypsies and the Negroes. Hitler knew that for the success of his lying doctrines he would have to place before the German people an object to which he could attribute everything loathesome and contemptible, an object worthy of abhorrence that would be the absolute antithesis of the Aryan man, the Nazi, and whose existence and activities could be presented as the cause of all the failures and difficulties that Germany had encountered. This object was the Jew. Gideon Hausner continued:

> In order to complete the picture, we should point out that there were in Germany tens of thousands of scientists and ecclesiastics, statesmen and authors and ordinary people, who dared to help the Jews, to raise their heads in opposition to the iniquitous regime, and even to rebel against it, and among these were men whose names were famous in German science and culture. Thousands of opponents of the bloody regime were imprisoned and were later destined to suffer greatly in concentration camps before the Nazi monster was brought low. Thousands of them died without seeing the day of liberation. Hundreds of the clergy were arrested and imprisoned. There were examples of personal valor—like that of the priest who was sent by Eichmann to a concentration camp for intervening openly on behalf of the Jews. There were Germans who hid Jews, shared their rations with Jews, and who at the risk of their lives helped them to hide or obtain "Aryan" papers, and others who maintained an anti-Hitler underground. During the war there were Germans who even protested to Hitler at the disgrace the Gestapo was bringing on the German people

by acting like beasts of prey, as they described the extermination of the Jews. There were also soldiers who tried to frustrate the killings by direct intervention.

But when all is said and done, these were a very small minority. The decisive majority of the German people made peace with the new regime, and were passive witnesses of the most terrible crime ever perpetrated in human history. The majority of German intellectuals were ready to warm themselves at the bonfires of the bookburners. Anti-Semitism became an excellent article of "export" to be sown everywhere and cultivated by German ambassadors and agents abroad. The Nazis deliberately fanned anti-Jewish hostility and agitation in order to form fascist parties in various countries and to prepare the Fifth Columns that were at their disposal in neighboring countries like Norway, Holland, France, Slovakia, Croatia, Rumania, Hungary, the Ukraine, Latvia, Byelorussia, and others.

Even on the verge of defeat, in April 1944, the German Foreign Ministry convened a meeting of diplomats in the European capitals to consult on ways and means of strengthening Jew-hatred in the world. In April 1945, at the moment of his death agonies, when the Soviet cannon were thundering in the streets of Berlin, when Hitler sat imprisoned in the celler of the Reichschancellery, his entire world in ruins and his country stricken, over the corpses of six million Jews—at that moment the Führer wrote his political last will and testament in which he bequeathed the injunction of eternal hatred for the Jews. "Above all," he concluded, "I enjoin the government and the people to uphold the racial laws to the limit and to resist mercilessly the poisoner of all nations, international Jewry."

The Nazi Party created three criminal organizations to dominate Germany and impose a reign of terror on the occupied territories: the SS, the SD, and the Gestapo, to all three of which Eichmann belonged. The SS, headed by Heinrich Himmler, was designed to be a powerful fist to strike and subjugate every opponent or rebel. At the beginning this organization had only two hundred and eighty members. At the outbreak of the war it numbered about a quarter of a million who had received military training and were organized in paramilitary units. Later Himmler set up the Armed SS (*Waffen SS*), select military units to serve as a counterweight against the regular German Army, in case the latter ever showed signs of faltering in its loyalty to the Führer. The SD, headed by Reinhard Heydrich, was an internal espionage organization. The International Military Tribunal at Nuremberg stated that in its judgment the Gestapo and SD were used for criminal purposes, including the persecution and extermination of the Jews, brutalities and killings in concentration camps, excesses in the administration of occupied territories, and the mistreatment and murder of prisoners of war.

According to the Nuremberg judgment, the SS also participated in the commission of war crimes, and played a particularly significant role in the persecution of the Jews. The SS set up concentration camps, work camps, and extermination centers. In Jewish matters Adolf Eichmann was the executive arm of the SS. With regard to the Jews in the concentration camps, every means of humiliation was deliberately employed to destroy men's faith in themselves. They were whipped across the face, deprived of food until they writhed with the pangs of hunger; men and women, boys and girls were ordered to perform their excretory functions in full sight of one another; women were made to run naked before the guards; killing and butchery took place from mere caprice or for sport. The overall extermination program was kept secret for a long time. Brothels were even opened inside the concentration camps, to which those loyal to the butchers were offered admittance.

The Nazi programs and the techniques used to put them into effect varied according to circumstances. At the beginning, when the Nazis were still somewhat sensitive to world opinion, the "solution" took the form of forced emigration and the looting of property. When they found that it could be done, that for all practical purposes the world was indifferent, they went over to total extermination. In between there was a transitional phase, in which the Nazis toyed with the idea of a so-called territorial solution by the concentration of all the Jews on the island of Madagascar, for example. Eichmann took an active part in all of these programs.

From Terror to the "Final Solution" ★ Eichmann's Leading Role ★ Undergrounds Help Jews in Denmark, Holland, Norway, Belgium, and France

Having identified the Nazi organizations through which Eichmann accomplished the extermination of millions of Jews, Gideon Hausner—hour after blood-chilling hour—described the several stages of Nazi persecutions climaxed by the "final solution." Then he summed up, country by country, the tragic fate of its Jews under the Nazi blood-lust.

At the end of October 1938 Hitler's government decided to expel all Jews in Germany who had formerly been Polish citizens. The victims were crammed into freight cars, hauled to points near the eastern frontier, ordered to descend, then driven through the fields toward the Polish border. The Polish frontier guards, caught unaware, were helpless to stop the sudden surge of humanity.

In Paris, apparently after he had heard of the heartless expulsion of Polish Jews like himself, young Herschel Grynszpan attempted to assassinate Ernst von Rath, Counselor of the German Embassy. This incident was made the excuse for the first of many nights of Nazi frightfulness against Jews throughout Germany, November 9 to 10. The Brownshirt thugs broke into Jewish homes, pillaged, plundered, and destroyed. Thousands of Jews were rushed into concentration camps, supposedly to "protect them from the wrath of the people." A hundred and one synagogues were desecrated and burned and 76 destroyed; 7599 places of business were wrecked and looted. These figures are taken from an official report by Heydrich to Hermann Goering at a council of Ministers two days after the night of terror. It was at this meeting that they agreed to set up a central authority for forcible "emigration" of Jews from the Reich. Heydrich reported to the Ministers on the activities of Eichmann in Vienna to implement Jewish "emigration" from Austria.

In January 1939 Goering instructed Heydrich to use all possible means to speed up the expulsion. Thenceforth the forced-emigration program was carried out in all conquered areas, beginning with the part of Czechoslovakia that had already fallen into the hands of the Germans. Eichmann and his special section became the central authority for all the Reich ministries in connection with Jewish affairs.

Eichmann took special pains to frustrate emigration to Palestine. He had obligations on this score to the Mufti of Jerusalem, Haj Amin el-Husseini, with whom he had established close contacts even before the war. The mutual admiration of these two men was so strong that el-Husseini asked Himmler to provide him—after the war, when he would enter Jerusalem at the head of the Axis troops—with a special adviser from Eichmann's department, to help him solve the Jewish problem as "efficiently" as it was being done in the Axis countries. Eichmann offered the job to his assistant, Dieter Wisliceny. When the Foreign Ministry in Berlin interceded with Eichmann to save individual Jews, whom the occupation authorities for one reason or another wanted to keep alive, he refused.

"All Jews," he insisted, "as soon as possible and without exceptions must be included in the great program."

Forced emigration, of course, was only the first step toward the "final solution." The Nazi invasion of the Soviet Union of June 22, 1941, and America's entry into the war in December that year were turning-points in the development of the extermination program. At the end of July 1941 Goering sent Heydrich the following directive:

Complementing the task that was assigned to you on January 24, 1939, which dealt with the carrying out of emigration and evacuation as a solution of the Jewish problem, I hereby charge you with making all necessary organizational and financial preparations for bringing about the total solution of the Jewish question in the German sphere of influence in Europe. Wherever other governmental agencies are involved, these are to co-operate with you.

This was the signal. Heydrich had been selected to organize the mass murders, and he in turn appointed a cruel and fanatical man, implacable in his hatred—this evil Eichmann —for its planning and execution. In August 1941 Eichmann wrote to the Foreign Ministry that it would be advisable to cut off further emigration "in the light of preparations for the final solution of the problem of European Jewry." That summer found him in Auschwitz, arranging the many technical details with Rudolf Hoess and choosing the site for the erection of an extermination plant. In the autumn Eichmann flew to Kiev, which was in German hands, to report to Himmler. Soon thereafter, on October 27, 1941, Himmler issued a decree forbidding any emigration of Jews from the areas of German rule. Two days earlier, on October 25, an official in the Ministry of the Occupied Territories wrote that an agreement had been reached with Eichmann to use gas chambers for the solution of the Jewish problem.

The first country to savor the bitter taste of the German Blitzkrieg was Poland. Nazi race doctrine regarded all Slav peoples as inferior beings, whose historic destiny it was to serve a "higher" and "nobler" race. Accordingly the declared aim of Nazi policy was to subjugate the Polish people. Toward the Jews of Poland the Nazi policy was immeasurably harsher. They were abandoned to annihilation. Their ordeal began with the entry of the Germans in September 1939—pogroms, brutality, humiliation, burning of synagogues, plunder of property, staggering "collective fines" extorted from entire communities. Then, increasingly, Jews were kidnapped and carried off for forced labor. People were simply seized in the streets. A Jew going out in the morning did not know whether he would come home in the evening. This, however, was for the time being the period of "minor terror." The time of extermination followed. For the horrification of future generations a report by SS Gruppenführer Katzmann, exterminator of the Jews of Eastern Galicia, has survived. It conveys the information that he had already destroyed 434,329 Jews and that in a number of camps in his area only 21,156 Jews still remained.

The Warsaw Ghetto was the largest in Europe, not only because of the city's massive Jewish population but because many Jews from the surrounding districts and towns fled to Warsaw. In the middle of 1942 there were no longer any illusions in the ghetto about the purpose of even larger deportations from Warsaw. The chairman of the Ghetto Council, Adam Czerniakow, and his wife committed suicide by poison in July 1942, when the Germans ordered him to supply another contingent of Jews for shipment. In

September 1942 more than 100,000 Jews were assembled: 30,000 were "freed" for labor and the remainder dispatched to the death camps.

Then the Warsaw Ghetto uprising erupted. The Polish underground smuggled nine revolvers and five hand grenades into the walled area. A committee for underground resistance was elected, headed by Mordekhai Anielewicz, with Yitzhak Zuckerman as second-in-command. There had been isolated instances of desperate resistance before, but from now on activities were coordinated.

In January 1943 the Jewish underground acted for the first time, and the first German victims fell. When his ammunition was spent, Anielewicz fell on the nearest German soldier with his bare hands, snatched his rifle and disappeared. The contest grew more furious. It was a desperate struggle without a shadow of hope, without the remotest chance of success, but the victims would no longer go like sheep to the slaughter. The leaders divided the Ghetto into areas, and feverish efforts were made to acquire weapons from the Christian side of the city. A revolver cost thousands of zlotys. Bunkers were set up. The Nazis were struck with amazement. After wiping out the first nests of resistance, they tried their usual wiles: "All we want is to send a number of Jews to work camps. What is all the fuss about?"

Himmler gave the orders for the total annihilation of the Ghetto: "This quarter, so far inhabited by half a million subhuman creatures, who in any case are of no use to the Germans, must disappear!" On April 19, 1943, on the eve of Passover, *Waffen SS* forces, commanded by Jurgen Stroop, who had recently been appointed Police Commander in Warsaw, moved in the direction of the Ghetto. The attacking force consisted of 2100 soldiers, supported by tanks. The Jewsih underground opened fire, and many of the Germans were killed and wounded. The Germans laid siege to the Ghetto, opening up a merciless bombardment, which was followed by the entry of SS units. They took prisoners and destroyed buildings and bunkers. The tens of thousands of prisoners were wiped out, some on the spot and others in the camp at Treblinka. Stroop reported that 56,065 Jews were killed in the process. One cannot refrain from pointing out that this butcher and murderer called his victims "bandits."

Warsaw was not the only place where the Jews put up a last-stand resistance. Both before and after, similar operations were organized in the ghettos of Chenstokhov, Vilna, Cracow, Bendin, Bialystok, and elsewhere. Afterward uprisings broke out within the extermination centers. In the gas chambers of Treblinka, Sobibor, and Auschwitz hundreds of acts of rebellion took place. After the crushing of the ghetto uprisings the few survivors formed an undergound national Jewish body which in 1944 called for united action against the enemy. A manifesto they issued said: "The insurrection of the Warsaw Ghetto fighters has become the symbol of a valiant struggle unknown to Jewish history since the days of Bar Kochba. Let Israel mourn its dead—and let it train its sons in the legacy of their valor."

The extinction of the vast Polish Jewry was carried out in the camps to which, on the orders of Eichmann and his henchmen, millions of Jews were transported. The bitter end came in Auschwitz, Belsen, Treblinka, Sobibor, Maidanek, and Chelmno.

After completing the conquest of Continental Europe, Hitler in June 1941 had invaded the Soviet Union. In every country the destruction of the Jews was related in part to the treatment meted out to the local population. On July 17, 1941, the invaders were ordered to deal first of all with the professional revolutionaries, officials of the Comintern, political commissars of the Red Army, in other words with all the Soviet and Jewish intelligentsia and officialdom without distinction of profession, occupation, or politics. Then the Jews were gathered for the final act.

At first they were shot beside trenches and their corpses tossed in. As of early 1942 gas vans were sent to the "transit camps" in which the victims were assembled, ostensibly for transfer elsewhere, as they were told in advance. When the victims were packed into the vans, the doors were hermetically sealed and gas pumped in. Within ten or fifteen minutes all the occupants were dead and the vans proceeded to the burial trenches. Another triumph of German technology! In the eight months following the invasion of the USSR over 720,000 Jews were murdered. Thousands fled to the forests to join the Soviet partisans, to take up arms and fight, but not many made it. In the end most of the Jews of occupied Russia were imprisoned in ghettos and systematically destroyed.

At first the Russian Jews, like the Polish Jews before them, could not believe what was happening to them. A wounded, unkempt, barefoot, and disheveled woman with a crazed expression appeared in the streets of Vilna. When she told the doctor who examined her, in a frightened whisper, that she came from the valley of death in Punar, where Jews were being murdered, she was thought insane. The same thing happened in Kovno. Executions after inhuman tortures had begun at the end of June 1941. After that came horrors of atrocity and murder. Women were dragged into the streets naked and SS thugs conducted searches of their bodies. Jewish mothers began smuggling out their children through the ghetto fences for peasants to hide, but not many of the children found safety. When the parents were away at forced labor the SS butchers would arrive, snatch the children, and put them to death. The adults soon had their turn as well. The liquidation of the Kovno Ghetto was carried out with the same cruelty as elsewhere.

In Hungary blood negotiations (that is, the release of Jews in exchange for vehicles and other things the Nazis needed) were first conducted by Yoel Brand and Rudolf Kastner. Eichmann did everything in his power to prevent this transaction; instead, just before Germany's downfall, he ordered the infamous "death march" of Hungarian Jewry.

The Hungarian government had opposed the expulsion and extermination of the Jews. As late as April 1943, when the Regent of Hungary, Horthy, was summoned to a meeting with Hitler and his Foreign Minister, von Ribbentrop, and ordered to cooperate in the liquidation of the Jews, he refused. In March 1944, however, the German Army crossed the borders and took control of Hungary. The fate of Hungarian Jewry was sealed. Eichmann brought into the country his entire apparatus of murderers, who had already slaughtered millions of Jews and by reason of experience elsewhere knew all the tricks of persuasion and incitement of the local population. Knowing that the time at their disposal was growing short, they needed the help of the Hungarian populace. The Soviet Red Army had already reoccupied the Ukraine and was advancing on the Carpathian mountains. The killer gangs had serious grounds for fear that unless they carried out their evil assignment quickly they would never be able to complete it. They had at their disposal all the military might of Nazi Germany, and after Szalasy, a puppet of the Germans, was made Prime Minister, the Hungarian authorities as well. Eichmann personally headed this group. Determined that the Warsaw Ghetto revolt would not be repeated, he devoted particular attention to ensuring that it would never occur to the Jews to revolt or attempt to escape.

Negotiations with Jewish representatives began over the "blood for goods" deal.

Jews were to be spared in return for trucks, coffee, tea, and soap. Yoel Brand was ordered to travel to neutral Turkey to present the offer to spokesmen of Jewish organizations, and Kurt Becher, a high-ranking SS officer, was delegated by Himmler to manage these deals. Himmler told Becher that he could promise what he liked: "What we shall carry out, however, is a different matter." To facilitate the negotiations with a token gesture, Becher obtained Himmler's consent to allow one train carrying 1684 Jews to leave. The train was directed to Bergen-Belsen and from there, on two separate occasions, those released were permitted to travel to Switzerland, and so were saved from death. In the meantime all the necessary preparations were being made in the death camps, which had by now in fact almost ceased operations. Rudolph Hoess was ordered to put Auschwitz back into operation and to make all preparations for intensified extermination. And indeed Auschwitz had never witnessed a period of such feverish "production" as in the summer and autumn of 1944. At times more than 10,000 Jews were destroyed in a single day. The deportations to the slaughterhouses were carried out in secret.

Representatives of Hungarian Jewry were informed by Eichmann and his accomplices that Jews could be saved "by consignment to Austria," in return for ransom money. Some 15,000 Jews were sent to Austria in this way. There, those able to work were taken to build fortifications, the rest were dispatched for extermination. At the end of 1944 Horthy attempted to withdraw Hungary from the war on the side of Germany. But the Germans took control of Budapest by force, arrested Horthy, and put Szalasy, the leader of the fascist Arrow Cross, in power. Once again the Jews were at the Nazis' mercy.

That was when the infamous "death march" was organized. Trains were no longer available. Eichmann, with the help of his Hungarian fascist allies, organized a march of Hungarian Jews to Austria, ostensibly to provide labor for the fortifications, but actually in order to murder them. Eichmann's calculation was simple: the weak would fall by the way, the sturdy would arrive at their destination to work on the fortifications, and then would be destroyed. The march began in November 1944 in rain, snow, and cold. The Jews were lodged en route in the open or in pigsties. Not only men but the women, children, and old people were in the ranks. Anyone who found the going difficult was shot by guards. Great numbers collapsed and died. Hundreds committed suicide or died of the typhus raging among the marchers. The entire route was strewn with corpses.

The horror reached such proportions that the escorting Hungarian officers and soldiers began to mutiny, demanding to be sent to the front instead. Even Szalasy's intervention to end the march was to no avail. And then an astonishing thing occurred. Himmler himself reprimanded Eichmann for organizing this operation, and the dreadful march ended. The Soviet Army had by this time surrounded Budapest, and the remnants of the Jewish community in the capital were spared.

In the northern countries, Norway and Denmark, there were not many Jews. At the time of Denmark's capitulation, about 6500 Jews were living there. Initially the German invaders permitted the local authorities to function. King Christian remained the formal ruler of the state and the Danish government continued to govern. This explains why the anti-Jewish laws were not imposed, nor was the Jewish badge of identity introduced. But with the intensification of anti-German activities by the Danish underground, a roundup of Jews was planned, and Eichmann sent a number of men from his department to Denmark to do the job. The roundup took place in the first two days of October 1943. The barbarians broke into Jewish homes only to find most of them deserted. Having prior knowledge of the murderous action, the Danish people mustered at the ports fishing and excursion boats and any other vessel able to float. The Jews were escorted to the coast by Boy Scouts, students, and other volunteers, put on board, and secretly taken to Sweden. In this way, some 6000 Danish Jews were rescued; only a few hundred fell into the hands of Eichmann's killers.

In Norway there were about 1750 Jews, and despite efforts by the Swedish authorities to help them, nearly 800 were exterminated.

Tens of thousands of Belgian Jews were killed. Only a few survived, thanks to the assistance of the underground and the fact that the Christian population hid a number of Jews. The mass arrests started in July 1942, and in August the deportations to Auschwitz and the death ovens began.

In Holland the Nazis encountered resistance to the persecution of the Jews by the non-Jewish population. The anti-Jewish campaign in all its stages began immediately after the occupation in May 1940: anti-Jewish laws, identification of Jews by compelling them to wear the Star of David; theft of Jewish property; and finally, deportation to the death centers. In Holland, as in other West European countries, the problem of children of mixed marriages troubled the occupation authorities, for they were partly Jewish. Finally the Nazis found a solution: the sterilization of all the children of mixed marriages, in order to prevent them from passing on Jewish blood to progeny. These abominations aroused the Christian inhabitants, and in February 1941 a general protest broke out in Amsterdam and quickly spread to other cities as well. Gas and electric services were brought to a standstill and train service disrupted. The Nazis quickly brought in SS and police units from Germany, under orders to shoot at crowds to kill. Leaders of the Dutch resistance movement were arrested and put to death. Jewish children of mixed marriages were taken as hostages, dispatched to concentration camps, and tortured to death. The strike was smashed by Nazi might and terror. In Dutch cities non-Jews by the thousands also began to wear the yellow Star of David as a demonstration of solidarity with the persecuted. Eichmann's agents, however, managed to identify and isolate the Jews, concentrating them in camps and special neighborhoods, and soon their mass transportation began, first to labor camps and then to the death camps.

At first the Germans did not know what to do with the Sephardic Jews of the Spanish and Portuguese community in Holland. Did these belong to the people doomed to destruction or not? Eichmann's office resolved their doubts by ruling that they were full Jews in all respects, and subject to extermination with the rest of their brethren. Christians began to hide Jewish neighbors, as in the celebrated case of Anna Frank and her family. But the majority of the Jews were segregated, labeled, assembled, and robbed of their property. The deportations from Holland began in the middle of July 1942. By April 1943 only 68,300 had been deported and 71,000 were left. A more vigorous operation was therefore ordered. To avoid possible difficulties with Sweden, the protecting power for Holland, a special law was promulgated whereby Dutch Jews, like German Jews, would lose their nationality the moment they crossed the state frontier on the tragic journey eastward. The second half of 1943 was a period of increased activity. Trains rolled eastward loaded with their human cargo, and only isolated groups of Jews were left in Holland. These included skilled diamond craftsmen, whose services Germany needed. A number of Jews were also employed in German armament plants. These, too, were eventually deported, and only about 5000 Dutch Jews survived.

In France the Vichy authorities abandoned the Jews to the tender mercies of the conquerors. In the first instance, the stateless Jews were removed, then foreign nationals, and finally, despite Marshal Pétain's personal opposition, French citizens as well. The French underground did much to rescue Jews. Southern France fell to the Italians. Mussolini was prepared to cooperate with the Nazis in the extermination program, but a section of the Italian administration was unenthusiastic and thwarted the operations.

Eichmann was also active in Yugoslavia. Synagogues were burned down, and the Serbian and Croatian Jews were confined in camps where they died by the thousands either from disease or through direct extermination.

In Slovakia, which had been established as a separate political unit, the extermination proceded at full steam. The Nazis found Slovak allies in Prime Minister Tuka and Minister of the Interior Mach, who were among the first leaders of the satellite countries to cooperate in deporting Jews. After 55,000 Jews had already been removed, pressure was exerted by the Church, and the Slovak Government developed some doubts about continuing the deportations. Eichmann at once applied counter-pressure. New roundups began in September 1944, and again more than 12,000 Jews were deported, while many thousands of others were killed in Slovakia itself.

Operating in Rumania on Eichmann's behalf was Hauptsturmführer Richter. The deportation was to have begun on September 10, 1942. All the plans were ready in Eichmann's office. The German railway administration had made all necessary arrangements. In the meantime, however, the Rumanians changed their minds. Richter tried every kind of pressure, but to no avail. The Rumanians concentrated the Jews in camps, where tens of thousands of them died, but the deportations to the extermination camps had been circumvented.

The Jews of occupied Greece also passed through the valley of the shadow of death, especially the Salonika community, which in the days of the Turks had been the most Jewish city in the world, and where even after the German occupation the majority of the Jews in Greece lived. Deportations from Greece to death camps in Poland, in freight and cattle cars, began in March 1943. With all speed and energy about 54,000 Salonika Jews were rushed to the extermination plants.

Such, in substance, was Gideon Hausner's preliminary presentation, which had taken ten horror-packed hours. He concluded with these words: "Adolf Eichmann will enjoy a privilege that he did not accord to even a single one of his victims. He will be able to defend himself before the court. His fate will be decided according to law and according to the evidence, with the burden of proof resting upon the prosecution. And the judges of Israel will pronounce true and righteous judgment."

Prosecution and Defense Present Their Cases ★ Eichmann Guilty on All Counts ★ Appeals Rejected ★ Execution on May 31, 1962

The first prosecution witnesses, on April 18, 1961, were mainly police officials who had assembled the masses of documents that had been and would be submitted to the court.

The documentation section in Bureau 06 had been directed by police officer Naftali Bar-Shalom. The greatest quantity was that received in photostats from the archives of the German Foreign Ministry, containing records from 1870 up to the end of World War Two, which had been captured almost in their entirety and shipped to England. Dr. Meir Vashem archives center. Bureau 06 received these photostats from the director of to London to photograph documents relevant to Jewish history on behalf of the Yad Vashem archives center. Bureau 06 received these photostats from the director of Yad Vashem, Dr. Israel Karamish.

The attorney for the defense, Dr. Servatius, said that he had no objections to these materials being accepted but reserved the right to cross-examine those who submitted them. Documents were also presented that had come from a Jewish institution under the auspices of the French Government; from Amsterdam; from Dr. Lunhertz, who had headed the Viennese Jewish community during the Holocaust.

On April 20 Chief Inspector Avner Less submitted the tapes of Eichmann's interrogation, thirty-five hundred typewritten pages. Eichmann had been told that everything he said would be recorded and he had consented. The tapes contained the following statement by the accused:

> Despite everything, I know of course that I can never wash my hands clean, because the fact that I was obeying orders has no meaning today. Those who planned, decided, instructed, and gave orders have escaped from their responsibility cheaply enough through suicide; others who belong to this group are now dead or not available. At any rate, I am ready to atone personally for the terrible events and I know that I face a death sentence. I am not pleading for mercy for I am not entitled to mercy. Yes, if it were thought a greater atonement, I am ready to hang myself in public as a warning to the anti-Semites in all countries of the world.

In view of the Independence Day celebrations, advanced that year to the 4th of Iyar (April 20) because the 5th of Iyar was a Sabbath eve, the trial was recessed for several days. An impressive military parade in Jerusalem marked the first public showing in Israel of modern Centurion heavy tanks that had been acquired from Britain. Letters of congratulation were received from the Kings of Sweden, Holland, and Nepal, the Presidents of the United States and France, the Supreme Soviet in Moscow, from Burma, India, Yugoslavia, Switzerland, Cambodia, and many others. The parade for the *bar-mitzvah* [age 13] celebration of the State of Israel was watched by more than half a million persons from Jerusalem and all parts of the country, as well as large numbers of tourists.

In an Independence Day broadcast to the nation, the Prime Minister said:

> The State of Israel's *bar-mitzvah* year has bequeathed two extremely significant events to the annals of the Jewish people. While on the surface there is no connection between the two, both are the outcome of that great day which opened a new era in the life, destiny, and status of the Jewish people, the day on which the nation's renewed independence in its ancient Homeland was proclaimed thirteen years ago. These events are: (1) the meeting in the Judean desert, overlooking the Dead Sea, between the heroes of our contemporary War of Independence and those who fought for the independence of their people and homeland 1830 years ago*; (2) the trial by a Jewish court in Israel's capital of the man charged with the destruction of European Jewry—the cream of the Jewish people in the Diaspora— on behalf of Nazi Germany.

---

* The immortal siege of Massada in the first century C.E.

It was not in Israel that this abominable crime took place. Israel as a Jewish State was not yet in existence when the millions of Jews were slaughtered. Nor was this the first massacre in Jewish history. But even our thousands-of-years-old Jewish martyrology has known nothing like the comprehensive, cruel, and carefully planned murder of millions of Jews by the Nazi butchers, an operation designed to obliterate and destroy an entire people, old and young, women and infants, leaving no trace of this ancient nation on the face of the earth.

This is not an ordinary trial nor only a trial. Here, for the first time in Jewish history, historical justice is being done by the sovereign Jewish people. For many generations it was we who suffered, who were tortured, were killed—and we who were judged. Our adversaries and our murderers were also our judges. For the first time Israel is judging the murderers of the Jewish people. It is not an individual that is in the dock at this historic trial and not the Nazi regime alone but anti-Semitism throughout history. The judges whose business is the law and who may be trusted to adhere to it will judge Eichmann the man for his horrible crimes, but responsible public opinion in the world will be judging anti-Semitism, which paved the way for this most atrocious crime in the history of mankind. And let us bear in mind that only the independence of Israel could create the necessary conditions for this historic act of justice.

On the morrow of Independence Day, April 21, 1961, the Eichmann trial was resumed. The playing of tapes of Eichmann's testimony continued. In most of it the Nazi's aim was to prove that he had merely carried out orders issued by his superiors. "If they had told me at the time that my father was a traitor and I was to kill him, I would have done so without hesitation," he said. "I was blindly obeying orders. There was a war on for the survival of the German nation and it made no difference what assignment they gave me." When asked by Less if there had been cases in which people refused to carry out orders, he replied, "I don't know, I don't know, perhaps there were cases here and there but I don't know about it."

After the tapes came witnesses for the prosecution. The first was Professor Salo Baron, who gave the court a historical review of the rich contributions of the Jews to European culture from the time of the Emancipation in the nineteenth century. In 1939 the world Jewish population was 16.5 million; after the Holocaust only 10.5 million remained. Servatius tried to prove that in history irrational forces were at work and deeds did not always produce the result that the instigators intended. For example, an attempt had been made to exterminate the Jewish people but just the opposite had occurred— the creation of a Jewish State. Professor Baron replied that the question here was not historical but judicial: every man is responsible for his own actions and for his motives.

On April 25 the court heard a posthumous affidavit by Dieter Wisliceny, who was initially Eichmann's superior and later one of his subordinates. Wisliceny had made this deposition to American prosecuting officers before he was hanged by a Slovak court. He divided the anti-Jewish operations into three phases. (1) The years 1937–1940, when the policy was to accelerate Jewish emigration from Germany and Austria. After the conquest of France there was a plan to send the Jews to Madagascar which was never implemented. (2) The years 1940–1941, when the Jews were herded into ghettos and concentration camps in Poland and other conquered territories in Eastern Europe. (3) The years 1942–1943, when the Jews were exterminated.

Wisliceny related that in 1942 Eichmann had told him that according to a written order by Himmler dated April 1942 the Jews were to be exterminated. When Wisliceny expressed some reservations, Eichmann replied, "Don't be sentimental, this is the Führer's order." Wisliceny also claimed that at the end of 1944, when Germany's defeat was certain, Hitler directed that all executions of Jews were to cease but Eichmann refused to obey unless he received a written directive signed by Himmler. In February 1945 Eichmann told him, "I will laugh when I jump into the grave because of the feeling that I have killed five million Jews. That gives me great satisfaction and gratification."

The affidavit also spoke of Eichmann's ties with the Mufti, Haj Amin el-Husseini. In the autumn of 1937 Adolf Eichmann and his aides made a study of the Zionist question and spoke of meeting with the Mufti. In Cairo he met with his friend the Mufti. When el-Husseini took refuge in Germany during the war, he visited Eichmann's office in Berlin and also called on Himmler. Visiting Eichmann a few days later, Wisliceny heard a detailed report of the conversation. Eichmann said he had given the Mufti a lecture on the "solution" of the Jewish question in Europe. The Arab leader, according to Eichmann, had been highly impressed and said that he had asked Himmler that one of Eichmann's people be appointed as his personal advisor after the victorious Germans entered Palestine. The Mufti had made a strong impression on Eichmann and also on Himmler.

Wisliceny went on to say that at the end of 1942, at the request of the [American] Joint Distribution Committee, he obtained approval from Eichmann and Himmler to bring ten thousand Jewish children from Poland to Theresienstadt, where they would be exchanged for German civilians in the Allied countries. Some of the children had already arrived in Theresienstadt when Wisliceny was urgently summoned to Eichmann in Berlin. Eichmann revealed that the entire operation had been canceled, because the matter had come to the notice of the Mufti, who strongly protested against it to Himmler on the grounds that in a few years these Jewish children would be adults and would reinforce the Palestine Jewish community. Due to the Mufti's intervention, Himmler not only canceled the entire transaction but issued a blanket order against any Jews immigrating to Palestine from areas under German control. Himmler's stand as a result of the Mufti's intervention later had a fateful influence on all negotiations for the rescue of Jews, especially the ransoming of Hungarian Jewry. The efforts to save the Hungarian Jews failed, Wisliceny stressed, because the only place they could go to was Palestine and this was opposed by the Mufti.

A multitude of witnesses provided shocking information on the Nazi atrocities as well as stirring facts on the heroism of the ghetto fighters. On August 10 the prosecution wound up its case with a demand for Eichmann's conviction. Four days later Dr. Servatius concluded his case for the defense. He challenged the Israeli court's authority to try Eichmann, maintaining that since he had not been legally extradited, he could be tried only according to the laws of Argentina. He denied the validity of the Nazi and Nazi Collaborators (Punishment) Law, arguing that the destruction of the Jews had not depended on Eichmann.

The trial had lasted more than four months, from April 11 to August 14. Four more months passed before, on December 11, the judges handed down the verdict. The courtroom was as full as on the opening day: official envoys of West Germany and many foreign ambassadors were present and of course journalists from the world and local press. The tension rose as Eichmann was led into the glass cage. A few minutes later the three judges filed in. Justice Landau ordered the accused to stand. Eichmann got to his feet. Silence was deep as Landau, addressing the accused, announced: "The court finds you guilty of crimes against the Jewish people and crimes against humanity." He then turned to the nature of this case:

> Adolf Eichmann was brought to trial before this court on charges of unsurpassed gravity—charges of crimes against the Jewish people, crimes against humanity, and war crimes. The period of the crimes ascribed to him and their historical background is that of the Hitler regime in Germany and in Europe, and the paragraphs of the indictment encompass the Holocaust that befell the Jewish people during the period—a story of bloodshed and suffering that will be remembered to the end of time.

> This is not the first time that the Holocaust has been discussed in court proceedings. It was dealt with extensively by the International Military Tribunal at Nuremberg during the trial of the major war criminals, and at several of the trials that followed it. But this time it has occupied the central place in the court proceedings; and that is what distinguished this trial from those which preceded it. Hence there was the tendency, noticed in the course of and in connection with the trial, to broaden its scope.

> A desire was felt, understandable in itself, to include within the framework of this trial a comprehensive historical description of the ghetto fighters, of those who revolted in the camps, and the Jewish partisans. There are also those who wished to see this trial as a forum for clarifying questions of great import, some of which derived from the Holocaust, and others, of long standing, that have come up again, all the more acutely, because of the unprecedented sufferings visited upon the Jewish people and the whole world in the middle of the twentieth century.

> How could this have happened in broad daylight? And why was it precisely the German people from which this great evil sprang? Could the Nazis have carried out their evil designs without the help given them by other nations among whom the Jews lived? Could the Holocaust have been averted, at least in part, if the Allies had been more willing to help the persecuted Jews? Did the Jews in the free countries do all in their power to rally to the rescue of their brethren and to sound the alarm for help? What are the psychological and social causes of the group hatred known as anti-Semitism? Can this ancient disease be cured, and if so, how? What is the lesson which the Jews and other nations must learn from all this, and which every man must learn about his relations with his fellow-man. The questions are too numerous to be listed.

> In this maze of insistent questions the path of the court was and remains clear. It cannot allow itself to be drawn into provinces that are outside its sphere. The judicial process has ways of its own, laid down by law, which do not change, whatever the subject of a trial may be. It is the concern in every criminal case to ascertain whether the charges in the indictment against the accused are true, and to mete out due punishment. In order that these goals may be achieved, everything to be clarified must be clarified at this trial itself, and everything extraneous must be kept out of the proceedings—otherwise the judicial process is impaired, and that must be prevented at all casts.

> In these prefatory remarks, we are not unaware of the great educational value implicit in the very holding of this trial, for Jews living in Israel and abroad. As far as this court is concerned, however, all such considerations are regarded only as by-products of the trial.

The judges expressed appreciation to the representatives of both sides who worked so hard in the presentation of the trial. They praised the Attorney General, Mr. Hausner, and his assistants, Dr. Robinson and Messrs. Bar-Or, Bach, and Terlo, who helped him conduct the case, and displayed absolute mastery of the immense amount of legal and factual material prepared for them by the police investigators. And they had words of appreciation for the chief defense counsel, Dr. Servitius, and his assistant, Mr. Wechtenbruch. Dr. Servatius, they attested, in this great legal battle in an alien environment, always directed himself to the heart of the issues, refraining from unnecessary controversy over matters that did not seem to him vital to the defense of his client.

Justice Landau and his associates rejected the arguments of the defense that no Israeli court had the right to try Eichmann because the Nazi and Nazi Collaborators (Punishment) Law was in contravention of international law and because the crimes attributed to him were committed outside of, and before the creation of, the State of Israel. They found that there was no contradiction between the Israeli law on Nazis and international law. The crime of genocide was recognized as a crime against humanity both in decisions of the United Nations General Assembly and decisions of the International Court of Justice. With respect to the Defense Attorney's claim that the crimes charged to his client were committed outside of Israel, there were many historical precedents of pirates and other criminals being tried under universal law regardless of the place where the offenses were committed. With regard to the retroactive nature of the Nazi and Nazi Collaborators (Punishment) Law, no new crime had been created with this law. On the contrary, the offenses involved were recognized as crimes in the laws of all civilized nations, including Germany, both before and after the Nazi regime. Even the German courts had rejected the legal plea that the crimes of the Nazis were not forbidden at the time of their commission, and that their perpetrators did not have the required criminal intent.

The court rejects the defense argument that the crimes attributed to the accused were Acts of State, *i.e.*, acts for which the State alone is responsible," Justice Landau declared. "This theory was rejected by the International Military Tribunal at Nuremberg. While it is true that according to international law Germany is responsible for crimes it committed as Acts of State, this does not detract one iota from the accused's personal responsibility for his actions. Even the Convention for the Prevention and Punishment of Genocide stipulates in Section Four: 'Persons committing genocide shall be punished whether they are constitutionally responsible rulers, public officials, or private individuals.' The connection between the State of Israel and the Jewish people needs no explanation. The State of Israel was established and has been recognized as a Jewish State. It is the sovereign State of the Jewish people."

The reading of the verdict took two days. First Dr. Landau began reading it, then Dr. Benjamin Halevi continued, and finally Dr. Yitzhak Raveh completed the reading.

Adolf Eichmann was convicted on all fifteen counts in the indictment.

On December 13, 1961, Gideon Hausner and Dr. Servatius made their final pleas. Hausner demanded the death penalty. He noted that while the Israeli legislature had abolished the death penalty, it had reserved to the courts the right to impose capital punishment, and only in the case of murderers of victims of the Holocaust. "Before us stands the exterminator of a people, an enemy of mankind, a shedder of innocent blood," he concluded. "I ask you to pass sentence of death on him." Servatius, speaking immediately afterward, pleaded that Eichmann had become a different man after the war. He therefore appealed to the judges to hearken to the voice of divine mercy and not to impose the supreme penalty.

When the attorney for the defense had finished, Justice Landau asked Eichmann if he had anything to say in connection with the penalty the court was to impose on him for the crimes of which he had been convicted. Eichmann replied that he intended to appeal the verdict. He defined himself as a victim of the Nazi regime whose only guilt was that he obeyed the call of duty and had been loyal to his oath and his flag. He accused those in power in Nazi Germany of misusing his obedience. He said he understood the need to atone for the crimes committed against the Jews, but that they were committed against his will—only the political leaders were to blame for the mass murders.

The court pronounced its sentence on December 15: "Fully conscious of the heavy responsibility placed upon us, we have reached the conclusion that in order to punish the accused and to serve as a warning to others, we must impose the maximum sentence provided by law. We have found that the accused completely identified himself with the orders he received and he was motivated by an acute desire to achieve their criminal purpose." Handcuffed, Eichmann was returned to his cell and from that moment the regulations concerning persons condemned to death applied to him.

The convicted felon appealed to the Supreme Court. In the brief of appeal Dr. Servatius, admitting that the accused had been given a fair trial, reiterated his previous claims. The appeal was heard by the Supreme Court on March 22, 1962; the panel of judges included Yitzhak Olshan, the president of the Supreme Court; his deputy, Dr. Shimon Agranat; and Justices Moshe Silberg, Joel Sussman, and Alfred Witkon. The Attorney General disputed the claims on wich the appeal was based, and Servatius again replied at length.

On May 29 the court announced its decision. The first section was read by the Deputy President: "The manner in which the district court dealt with the various arguments was thorough, profound, and persuasive," it declared. "We fully concur, without hesitation or reserve, in all the conclusions and reasons of the lower court because they are fully supported by copious judicial precedents and by substantial proof abstracted out of the monumental mass of evidence produced."

Eichmann at once filed an appeal for clemency to President Ben-Zvi, who studied the request and the opinion of the Ministry of Justice. After much consideration he decided that clemency should not be granted.

On May 31, 1962, Eichmann was notified that his appeal had been rejected and that the sentence would be executed at midnight. He wrote a few letters to members of his family and was ready when Hull and Mrs. Hull came to see him. He told them that he he would go to his death calmly, believing in Nature rather than God. Mounting the scaffold, he gave his blessing to Germany, Austria, and Argentina. His body was cremated and on June 1 his ashes were carried three miles offshore by a police cutter and thrown into the sea.

VIII

ANOTHER "AFFAIR" AND A "SCANDAL FACTORY"

Echoes of the 1954 "Security Mishap"; Ben-Gurion Opposes Cabinet Role in Judicial Case

Section 1. Cohen Committee and Committee of Seven

Trial in Jerusalem Recalls "Lavon Affair" ★ *Board of Inquiry Appointed* ★
Press Rebuked for Distorting Issues

In the final months of 1960, while the public was awaiting the trial of Adolf Eichmann, an internal sensation rocked the country. Whether deliberately or inadvertently, many people connected an espionage trial in Jerusalem with the so-called "Lavon Affair" of 1954–1955, with which the writer has dealt earlier in this book.★

At the end of 1953, it will be recalled, Prime Minister Ben-Gurion retired from the Government "for a year or two or more," as he informed the President. On the urging of Prime Minister Moshe Sharett and his colleagues, he returned much sooner—first, on February 21, 1955, as Defense Minister because of a morale problem in the Ministry, and then, after the elections to the Third Knesset in July 1955, also as Prime Minister.

Meanwhile the "affair" that had caused his earlier return quieted down completely. A private inquiry set up by Sharett, the Olshan-Dori Committee, had reached an impasse, and Secretary of Defense Pinhas Lavon had resigned. Upon succeeding him, Ben-Gurion transferred the Senior Officer involved in the case to a different post. At the end of 1954

★ In accordance with restrictions imposed by military censorship, the author has withheld the names of the Senior Officer and other officers involved in the so-called Lavon Affair, as well as the name of the accused in the espionage trial in Jerusalem.—EDITORS and in 1955 Ben-Gurion was on cordial terms, both personally and publicly, with both men.

The Senior Officer carried out his new assignment in the Central District very ably. Ben-Gurion continued to treat him as a friend. He also remained on friendly terms with Lavon, giving him the benefit of the doubt. Ben-Gurion appreciated his administrative abilities and looked upon his resignation from the Defense Ministry as a final liquidation of the "affair." He even gave Lavon a civilian security assignment when the need arose.

In the Third Knesset no question connected with the unfortunate "security mishap" was ever raised. Even in the elections to the Fourth Knesset, when Mapai emerged with its greatest victory of any time before or since, no repercussions of the 1954 case were heard. In fact, until 1960 no echo of the dispute, either written or oral, had reached the Prime Minister, nor did he have any interest in it. None of the Cabinet members who had served with Lavon in the Sharett Government had told Ben-Gurion what had taken place at the time, and he had not asked for such information.

That was the situation until May 5, 1960, when Lavon informed the Prime Minister that he had heard from a certain lieutenant-colonel that Army documents related to the 1954 events had been falsified. A few hours later he sent Ben-Gurion a record in writing of what that officer had alleged. The Prime Minister immediately assigned his military secretary, Col. Chaim Ben-David, to investigate. Five days later Ben-David brought in a report, including accounts of conversations with the lieutenant-colonel, a number of other officers, and a civilian employee of the Defense Ministry.

Now we must go back a bit: to July 29, 1959, when a trial began in a Jerusalem District Court of a man who had figured in the 1954 affair and whom the press had dubbed the "Third Man," the other two being Lavon and the Senior Officer. The trial was not related to the mishap of 1954. The charge was violation of State security and the man was sentenced to twelve years in prison. More than a year later, on August 28, 1960, the Chief of Staff, Gen. Chaim Laskov, sent the Prime Minister excerpts from the verdict in Jerusalem. These embodied information that necessitated the appointment of a military board of inquiry to examine the reliability of two officers, one in the regular Army and one in the Reserves.

The Prime Minister instructed Laskov that the board was to include an outstanding jurist and that it make a thorough investigation into the allegations of falsification and concealment of documents. The Chief of Staff asked Chaim Cohen, a member of the Supreme Court and a former Attorney General, to serve as chairman. The proceedings of the Cohen Committee, as it was generally called, inadvertently gave rise to the Affair of 1960, which should properly have been termed the Ministerial Committee Affair; the content of the inquiry was entirely different from the affair of 1954. However, the new developments finally obliged the Prime Minister to examine what had happened in 1954, something that he had seen no need or purpose in doing until then.

At the time the Cohen Committee was set up, Lavon was on vacation in Europe. But he sent his secretary, Ephraim Evron, to demand that the Prime Minister have the board of inquiry dissolved. Ben-Gurion replied that it was none of Lavon's business. Suspicions having been raised against Army officers, he was obligated as Minister of Defense to obtain the facts. Lavon returned to Israel on September 24, 1960. Two days later, under the headline "Committee to Investigate Lavon's Resignation from Cabinet," *Davar* published the following piece of fiction:

A few weeks ago a high-level board of inquiry was set up to investigate the affair leading to Pinhas Lavon's resignation as Defense Minister in February 1955. It was decided to appoint the committee after new evidence came to the attention of the Prime Minister and Minister of Defense.

Similar items, without any basis in fact, appeared in all the other newspapers. They also reported that Lavon would visit Ben-Gurion that day. Lavon did call on the Prime Minister. In his diary for September 26 Ben-Gurion wrote:

I was surprised to hear Lavon's objections to a board of inquiry with regard to the Senior Officer. First he objected to Chaim Cohen. I told him that I held Cohen's ability, erudition, and fairness in great esteem. He said that as a member of the Government at the time when Cohen was Attorney General, he had tried to have him dismissed. (Later, when I related this at a meeting of the Cabinet, Pinhas Rosen said that there had been no such proposal). Lavon feared that the president of the Supreme Court, Justice Olshan, who had been a member of the Olshan-Dori Committee in 1954–1955, would be able to influence Cohen, a fellow member of the court.

When I rejected this argument Lavon demanded that I announce publicly that he had not given the order [in 1954] and had been punished unfairly. I assured him that I had never accused him, but that, on the other hand, I could not clear him, since by so doing I would be incriminating someone else. I was not a judge, nor had I ever investigated the matter. He said he would go to the Foreign Affairs and Security Committee. I advised him not to, as it too was not authorized to adjudicate in a dispute between two individuals. I also told him that when the Cohen Committee concluded its hearings, I would submit its findings to the Cabinet. The next day *Davar* printed the following misinformation:

"It has meanwhile developed that some of the testimony presented at the time [to the Olshan-Dori Committee at the end of 1954] did not support Lavon's version and was unreliable. On the basis of these developments the Prime Minister decided to appoint a new committee with authority to rehabilitate Lavon completely if, as is likely, it turns out that he was wronged. It is assumed that the committee will concentrate on the affair as it relates to Lavon's resignation, rather than the other aspect of the problem."

In this fabrication there was not one word of truth. Similar and worse things appeared in the other newpapers, especially *Lamerhav*. *Davar* accompanied its article on the purpose of the Cohen Committee with an editorial to the effect that "various public figures with detailed knowledge of the matter have long been convinced that the time has come for an official rehabilitation of Pinhas Lavon in connection with the Affair which led to his resignation." In their editorial opinion no further boards of inquiry were necessary because recently the matter had been sufficiently clarified. (It did not say where, by whom, or when.) On the other hand, the editorial went on, the announcement has to come from the Prime Minister.

On September 28, 1960, *Davar* reported that on the previous day Lavon had said, "The Board of inquiry to investigate my resignation as Minister of Defense in February 1955 does not concern me and I do not intend to appear before it." He added, however, that "if invited to the meeting of the Knesset Foreign Affairs and Security Committee," he would attend. *Davar* also reported that the General Zionist and Herut blocs had demanded that the Foreign Affairs and Security Committee be convened as soon as possible. Because of these distortions of the object of the Cohen Committee, the Prime Minister's

Office sent the newspapers an official statement defining that committee's jurisdiction and authority:

> On instructions of the Minister of Defense the Chief of Staff has appointed a three-man board of inquiry to investigate the conduct of an officer in the regular Army and a reserve officer in the light of a verdict by a civilian court which makes a new reliability check necessary. The Minister of Defense will submit the board's findings to the Government and the Minister of Justice will take every measure that is called for.

In view of the mistaken and misleading press reports about the assignment of the Cohen Committee and Lavon's conference with him, the Prime Minister on October 2, 1960, issued the following statement, published in the papers the next day:

> After my meeting with Mr. Lavon on Monday, September 26, 1960, a number of false, unfounded, and tendentious comments appeared in several newspapers. For my part, I gave no information to the press about the meeting and I assume that nothing was said by Mr. Lavon either, but someone decided to stir up trouble and gave several newspapers false and misleading reports about what took place at the meeting.
>
> I had nothing to do with what is called the "Lavon Affair." I had no reason to blame Lavon for anything done by him during his term of office as Minister of Defense, and as I told him when I met him on September 26, 1960, I see no need or obligation to exonerate him: (a) because I did not censure him; and (b) if anyone did censure him or tried to do so, it is not within my authority to exonerate him. I am not an investigator or a judge. I do not pass judgment on anyone, least of all on Mr. Lavon.
>
> As Minister of Defense I considered it my duty, in view of the material that was submitted to me by Mr. Lavon some five months ago, and the reports that reached me during the trial of a certain person in recent months, and particularly after the verdict, to instruct the Chief of Staff to appoint an inquiry board to investigate the integrity of an officer on active service and another officer in the reserves. I did not suggest to Mr. Lavon that he should appear before this board and it did not occur to me to do so.
>
> However, I told Mr. Lavon about the motives that prompted me to appoint such a board, and I turned over to him, at his request, the material in my possession, and of which he was not aware, that led me to initiate this investigation. It seems to me that he has the right to see this material.
>
> The newspapers that are dealing with this affair in good faith, out of concern for the truth and for Lavon's good name, are deserving of praise. But I am not certain that all the newspapers are dealing with the affair from such pure motives. Other persons should not be blamed, directly or indirectly—we are concerned here with two officers of the Defense Forces, but this applies to everyone—as long as they have not been proved guilty. I assume that Mr. Lavon is not in the least interested in defense or aid of this dubious kind.
>
> Through misinformation or bad faith, several newspapers are confusing two spearate matters: (1) an unfortunate incident on which an inquiry committee, appointed by Prime Minister Sharett at the end of 1954 at the request of the then Minister of Defense, Pinhas Lavon, reached no conclusion; (2) the resignation from the Government of Mr. Lavon, who was then the Minister of Defense. The then Prime Minister announced this resignation in the Knesset on February 21, 1955, in the following words: "At a meeting of the Cabinet yesterday, Mr. Lavon submitted his reasons for resignation, namely, that he did not find it possible to continue in his post after his proposals for changes in the structure of the defense organization were not accepted by the government."
>
> I have not the least doubt that the then Prime Minister made a truthful announcement

to the Knesset. I had political differences of opinion with Mr. Sharett in the Government, but I never had and I do not have today the slightest doubt as to his personal integrity and honesty, and I am certain that he did not make any statement in the Knesset that was not the whole truth. All the members of the Cabinet at the time and the Foreign Affairs and Security Committee know that Lavon himself made the same statement about the cause of his resignation, both in the Cabinet and in the Foreign Affairs and Security Committee, but at greater length. [Ben-Gurion at this point listed those present at that Cabinet meeting and at the Knesset committee meeting.]

Everyone who writes that Mr. Lavon was "dismissed" from his post is either writing an untruth on purpose—and there are such journalists—or he is writing about events without knowledge of them.

Even today I do not know what changes in the structure of the defense organization were proposed by the then Minister of Defense [Lavon], and why they were not accepted by the Prime Minister [Sharett], but neither before I left the Ministry of Defense at the end of December 1953 nor or after I returned in February 1955 did I see any need for changes in the Defense organization, and during my meetings with Lavon I did not hear from him what his proposals were. (In a letter to me on October 3, Lavon rightly pointed out that I was mistaken—that he had submitted the proposed changes to me after my return to the Ministry.) I cannot say that the structure of the Defense organization is ideal—there is no such thing—but it is, in my humble opinion, effective and suitable for our needs. I will not say that no shortcomings are possible in this structure—after all, human beings and not angels serve in the Defense Forces and the Ministry of Defense. But I do not think that the existing structure necessarily gives rise to shortcomings.

Five months ago Mr. Lavon gave me certain material. Last week, when he returned from his vacation, a discussion took place between us, at his request. Since Lavon did not tell me that I had the right to publish the contents of our discussion, I will not describe it, but I have read a series of misrepresentations of this meeting in the press. Just as Mr. Lavon did not tell me that I had the right to make this discussion public, so I did not tell him that he had the right to make it public; I assume that, like myself, he said nothing about our conversation to the press.

But I must refute certain false or inaccurate press reports. A statement has already been made with my approval by the Prime Minister's Office on the functions of the board of inquiry appointed by the Chief of Staff in accordance with my instructions. This committee does not deal with what the newspapers call the "Lavon Affair" but only with the integrity of two officers, whose investigation was made necessary by certain legal material—as Minister of Defense I must know if Army officers are trustworthy or not.

Since Mr. Lavon thought, perhaps rightly, that this material affects him, I gave him the material that I had on this question. The officers being investigated must be given every opportunity to prove their innocence; this is the elementary right of every man, even a criminal. With respect to fairness, justice, and law, all men are equal. As Minister of Defense I will not allow an officer to serve in the Defense Forces whose hands are not clean; but I will also not allow an officer to be pilloried without proof and without trial.

In *Maariv* on September 25, 1960, the following headline appeared in large type: "Ben-Gurion Orders a Reinvestigation of the Evidence That Caused Lavon's Resignation from the Government in 1955." This statement is wholly without foundation.

The report published in *Lamerhav* on September 28, 1960, by an anonymous writer, that the Prime Minister told Lavon that "this committee is not capable of reaching the *full* conclusions regarding *all* those involved in the affair, and he [Lavon] therefore objected to its composition," is not "accurate." I am not certain that Mr. Lavon told these things to the *Lamerhav* reporter, because the remarks attributed to him here contain two "inexactitudes": the Cohen Committee was chosen for a limited purpose, as was announced officially, and this, of course, was told to Mr. Lavon in my discussion with him on Monday; it was not for the reason mentioned in the newspaper that there was an objection to the composition of the committee, if there was such an objection.

Yediot Aharonot on September 28, 1960, reported that "Lavon categorically submitted to Ben-Gurion his old demand for the clearing of his name with an unequivocal declaration." I do not know how the newspaper knows what the committee is about. It was not "imposed" on Mr. Lavon; it was "imposed" (if the language of the editor must be used) upon two officers. The committee's conclusions will be submitted to the Cabinet, and if the Minister of Justice and his counsel see fit to embark upon legal action, they will do so. Mr. Lavon was not asked his views on the committee and did not have to be asked, for the two officers whose reliability the Minister of Defense saw fit to check in the light of certain data are not subordinate to him.

On September 29 *Haaretz* itself denied a news item that had appeared in its own paper on the previous day, according to which the Prime Minister's office had issued a denial concerning new findings brought to the Prime Minister's attention by Mr. Lavon.

Lamerhav and *Yediot Aharonot* of September 29 carried the information that they had heard from Lavon that the "documents" he had presented to the Prime Minister do not shed light but cast a shadow. Apparently the reference was to a document handed to me by Lavon a few months ago. For the sake of accuracy it should be mentioned that in the course of the conversation between us on September 26, I told Mr. Lavon about certain documents I had received recently—not from him—that cast doubts on the reliability of two officers. Lavon asked to see these documents. I immediately called upon my military secretary, Col. Chaim Ben-David, and asked him to transmit them to Lavon, since it appeared to me that they might possibly have some bearing on the affair in which Lavon is interested.

Lamerhav of September 30 wrote that its correspondent "learns from reliable sources that Lavon never requested that his name be cleared by Ben-Gurion's making a unilateral announcement of such a rehabilitation. What Lavon asked Ben-Gurion was the opportunity to have the matter clarified in the appropriate parliamentary public body, *i.e.*, the Foreign Affairs and Security Committee."

The "reliable sources" presented the correspondent with a piece of information that is false from beginning to end. As I have already stated, I do not regard myself as entitled to inform the public of Mr. Lavon's words to me, just as I presume that Mr. Lavon does not consider it his right to publish my words to him, without each of us having received prior permission to do so from the other. But the statement that Lavon asked me for the opportunity to clarify the matter before the Foreign Affairs and Security Committee is silly. Lavon needs no such permission from me, and he may approach that committee any day, whenever he sees fit, without my knowledge or my permission.

Finally, I wish to state that I am completely in accord with Almogi, who said that this entire matter has no connection with Mapai, the Israel Labor Party. To the extent that I am dealing with this matter, it is only in my capacity as Minister of Defense.

On the day this statement was issued the Prime Minister was invited to the Foreign Affairs and Security Committee. The Minister of Justice, Pinhas Rosen, was also present. The committee's regular chairman, Meir Argov, being out of the country, Herzl Berger took his place. The absence of the regular chairman caused considerable confusion. Argov was well versed in the Knesset rules and regulations, which he upheld strictly and resolutely; he would not permit members to overstep their authority. Berger, while perfectly honest, was not well acquainted with the committee's powers and limitations.

Ben-Gurion gave the Knesset committee a summary of his statement to the press. When certain members began to ask about the affair of 1954 and whether he believed that the Defense Minister at the time had given the famous order or the Senior Officer had acted on his own, he told them: "I do not think it is the Foreign Affairs and Security Committee's business to investigate people's guilt or innocence. It is not a judicial committee. In my opinion this is a matter to be decided by the judiciary."

Mr. Bader of Herut remarked that "there is nothing more terrible than for a person to feel he has been wronged." The Prime Minister replied: "If only one person were involved it would be much simpler, but in this matter there are two people; one cannot say simply, 'You are innocent, and you are a criminal.' This is the whole trouble."

Later in the discussion Bader said, "Sir, if you were to appoint a committee of three judges right now I would be more at ease." The Prime Minister replied, "I am not the one to appoint judges." Bader then remarked, "It would be better if the matter were cleared up here and now, but that is only my opinion." The Prime Minister commented: "I am no less interested than Mr. Bader in having the innocent man cleared but this is a matter for a court of law."

After other members asserted that what was involved was a security matter, the Prime Minister said:

> I see that you want to argue a matter that belongs to the judiciary. I will not participate in a committee that discusses matters rightly belonging to the judiciary. While I may not be a jurist, I am able to distinguish between judicial matters and matters of security. Here we have a judicial matter. There are two people; one says one thing, one says another. And though one is closer to me than the other, the obligation to seek the truth is binding on all of us. No security problem is involved in knowing who told the truth and who didn't. Mr. Berger announced that like every institution in Israel, the powers of this committee are clearly limited. In my opinion it would be in the public interest to extend the framework of its authority to the greatest degree possible. Still, there is a limit to how far it can be stretched without breaking. I would ask all members to take this into account in making proposals. The committee did not draw up the Knesset rules, but rules do exist.

Since a number of members, especially one from Herut, had further questions, the chairman postponed the discussion to an early subsequent day.

Lavon Tells His Side of the Story to the Knesset Committee ★ Peres and Sharett Refute Some of His Testimony

On October 3, 1960 Pinhas Lavon wrote to the Prime Minister as follows:

> I read your statement to the press yesterday and I will certainly reply to it. With your permission I will touch at present on one of the points you make. After stating that I wasn't "dismissed" from the post of Minister of Defense and that I resigned because the changes I recommended in the defense system were not accepted by the Government, you add, "Even today I do not know what those changes were—in my meetings with Pinhas Lavon I did not hear from him what they were." Allow me to refresh your memory:

Immediately after rejoining the Government as Minister of Defense, you invited me to inform you of my proposals and conclusions. In that conversation I told you, as I did Prime Minister Sharett before my resignation, that two men ought to be expelled from the defense organization. Likewise I told you of my various proposals regarding the structure of the defense organization. All this took place in your office in Tel Aviv on February 22, 1955. At your request, immediately after the conversation, I put my proposals in writing and sent them to you in my letter of February 24, 1955.

Lavon was right in refreshing the Prime Minister's memory. It is true that at the time of Ben-Gurion's return to the Ministry of Defense, Lavon stated his proposed changes. In the other matters at issue, however, he was mistaken. Three documents remain from the time of his withdrawal in February 1955:

1. His letter of resignation to the Prime Minister dated February 2, 1955, which states:

You have submitted the additional findings of the Olshan-Dori [Committee] to Shaul Avigur. You did this despite my opposition. During the two hearings that went on for weeks I was kept at arm's length. Neither you nor any other member tried to speak to me (except Eshkol, with whom I did not wish to speak for reasons which some worthy people may perhaps not understand), as if I were afflicted with a loathsome disease. I was anathema, I could not know what you thought, claimed, or accused. I was an object of pity or for settling accounts. Your conduct and that of the members excluded me from the group and from collective responsibility. But you are not the only ones who are free; I am also free, and this is to inform you that I am no longer prepared to be the friend of people who have liquidated their friendship with me. I hereby tender my resignation as Minister of Defense and from the Government.

There is no hint here that he was resigning because the Prime Minister did not agree to remove two people from the Defense Ministry. There is also the testimony of the Prime Minister at the time, that Lavon's resignation was influenced by the fact that bad relations obtained between Lavon and himself. At a meeting of the [Mapai] Party Central Committee, Sharett later would say: "I do not think that it is a secret to many that when I was Prime Minister and Pinhas Lavon Minister of Defense, a serious complication developed in our relationship, a complication that was very disappointing, very regrettable, and very grave. I will not go into details at this point. I am only stating the fact. This personal conflict was not without effect on Lavon's resignation as Minister of Defense."

2. The stenographic record of the Cabinet meeting of February 20, 1955, the last one in which Lavon participated. He spoke of the many mishaps that had occurred in 1954, concluding with these words: "In the light of these developments and the additional mishaps since then, I informed the Prime Minister that such failures could not be averted and complete control assured over the defense forces without the creation of a legal basis for their operations. We are the only state that lacks a definitive law in this respect. Presumably the Prime Minister had good reasons not to accept my proposals. Now that they have been rejected there is no possibility of my continuing to bear responsibility for national security and I have informed the Prime Minister of my resignation."

After Lavon left the Cabinet session, the Prime Minister said that the resignation has given rise to a serious internal situation. "How are we to understand the word 'internal'?" Sapir asked. Sharett explained: "Between myself and the Minister of Defense. Unfortunately not all these discussions remained where they belonged; they have become the property of many people, both in the Army and among the general public. Now, this has created a grave situation in the Army, a situation of disappointment, bitterness, mistrust, internal insecurity. The supreme need, in my opinion, is to fill the vacated post, and in such a way that this resignation not weaken the Army's internal stability but make it even greater than before." [The reference was to the effort to co-opt Ben-Gurion to return to that post.] The Cabinet discussion went on for a long time, but no one mentioned that a condition for Lavon's remaining Minister was the dismissal of two people from the security system.

3. Finally there is the record of the Foreign Affairs and Security Committee meeting the next day, February 21, 1955. Lavon spoke at length of the chain of events that led him to conclude that "failures such as these cannot be prevented, nor control over the security forces ensured, without changes of a rather radical nature both in the structure of the security system as a whole and the division of authority among its various branches." He added: "I did not object when the Prime Minister, for reasons which were doubtless well founded, saw no possibility of accepting my proposals. Following their rejection I did not feel it possible to continue to bear responsibility for State security and I informed the Prime Minister of my resignation from the Government."

These are the three documents. Lavon's statements to the Foreign Affairs and Security Committee and to the press in October 1960—five years and eight months later—cannot be reconciled with the records of 1955. After his first appearance before the Foreign Affairs and Security Committee on October 4, 1960, *Haaretz*, the only independent newspaper in Israel at that time, came out with a prominent headline: "Lavon Reveals Intrigues and Forgeries That Compromised Him as Defense Minister. Foreign Affairs Committee Continues Hearings." As Minister of Defense and Prime Minister for six years before and six years after Lavon, this writer knew of no deliberations of that committee ever having leaked to the press. Only statements released for publication by its chairman ever reached the public. No Government body had ever observed such strict secrecy as the Foreign Affairs and Security Committee, nor was any Government body ever as reckless as that committee during its hearings on the Lavon matter from October 4, 1960, until January 18, 1961.

Lavons's initial appearance before the Knesset committee was on October 4. Before the debate the chairman, Mr. Berger, said: "Yesterday an item appeared in *Haaretz* and was repeated in *Yediot Aharonot* that completely distorts what took place in this room. *Haaretz* writes: 'Among other things the Prime Minister said at the Foreign Affairs and Security Committee on October 2, 1960, that two versions had been presented to the investigating committee at the time—the Olshan-Dori Committee [1955]—and the committee had rejected Lavon's version in favor of the other one.' *Yediot Aharonot* put it even more clearly. Apparently they had time to formulate it better: 'It is also known that the only thing Ben-Gurion told the Foreign Affairs and Security Committee which was not included in the statement to the press was the revelation that two versions were presented to a two-man committee of Justice Olshan and Gen. Dori which in 1955 investigated the affair that led to Lavon's resignation, and the committee accepted the second one.' I hope," the chairman concluded, "that the members will have no objections if I inform the press today that the Prime Minister never said this or anything like it."

Lavon thanked the Knesset committee for allowing him to address it. "As far as

I am concerned," he said, "it is basically untenable that this is a matter for the courts. To the best of my understanding it is not a matter for negotiations at the judicial level, but belongs to a different sphere altogether. I must ask your forgiveness if I am not brief. I will be compelled to speak of several points connected with the findings of the Olshan-Dori Committee, and it was decided not to let me see its material except for my own testimony, of which I had had a stenographic record made anyway. Apart from that I saw none of the testimony."

"Even while you were Minister of Defense?" Ben-Eliezer asked.

"Yes," Lavon answered. "Even when I asked for the testimony of a particular witness they refused, claiming that that person, who was one of my subordinates, did not want me to see it."

He presented at length his version of the affair which to this day, perhaps rightly, has not been released by censorship except for a few things that can be noted here.

"One bright day in January [1955]," he said, "there appeared before the committee a letter supposedly sent on July 19, 1954, by the Senior Officer to the Chief of Staff, who was in the United States at the time."

In Lavon's opinion the reason this letter was produced was because it said that the Minister of Defense had given the order to the Senior Officer; but the letter in question, he claimed, had been forged. He stated that Knesset member Galili had told another member, an officer, to inform Lavon that forgeries had been made. Lavon asked to see the officer, but he could not be persuaded to meet Lavon.

He then related that on February 4, 1960, he was visited by an officer who had heard of the alleged forgeries; that in May 1960 he informed the Prime Minister what he had been told, and that the Prime Minister immediately assigned his military secretary to investigate the matter. (After this three-quarters of a page of the stenographic record is blank: evidently either the committee chairman or Lavon had not permitted a record to be kept.) He was surprised, Lavon said, that after the material was submitted to Ben-Gurion, on July 15, 1960, he did not do the elementary thing called for, since this material was substantial, even if, from a purely legal point of view, not sufficient. (It is not clear to the writer whether he was objecting to the formation of the Cohen Committee or to the fact that it was appointed only after the trial of the "third man" was completed.)

Lavon cited what the Prime Minister had said two days earlier to the Foreign Affairs and Security Committee: "Perhaps this investigation will lead us to the matter of the 1954 affair, or perhaps there is no connection. I do not know." And Lavon added, "I wish to say that I only hope that this was a slip of the tongue by the Prime Minister, for otherwise it is extremely serious, both for me personally and for the matter at hand— a whole lot more serious than a great many other things in this affair." (The writer can state that far from being a slip of the tongue, it was his considered opinion throughout, when he was Prime Minister and when he was not, that only an authorized court of law was qualified to investigate rumors and accusations that cast suspicion on certain people.)

Lavon followed these statements with an indictment of the Cohen Committee: "What is the object of this committee?" he exclaimed. Trials and justice do not always go hand in hand, he said. Then he complained against the Director-General of the Ministry of Defense both in his own time and under Ben-Gurion: "The Director of the Ministry of Defense, who had no connection with the affair itself and knew nothing about it except from hearsay, considered it necessary to appear before the Olshan-Dori investigating committee and give evidence which, despite my request, I have not been permitted to see to this day."

"To whom did you make the request? To the committee?" Meridor asked.

Lavon replied: "To the Prime Minister at the time, Moshe Sharett. He told me that the witness was unwilling to have me see the testimony. Hence I cannot say that no collusion was involved here." In answer to a question by Bader, Lavon declared, "I am not saying nor have I ever said—I have no evidence—that either the former Chief of Staff (Moshe Dayan) or the former Director of the Ministry of Defense (Shimon Peres) were accessories to acts of forgery and perjury. However, it is very likely—there is a good deal of logic in it. The wagon was rolling, there were accounts to settle. It was possible to climb aboard, if not the front way then around the back, and strengthen the hand of forgers and perjurers."

Shimon Peres appeared before the Knesset committee on October 23, 1960. "As I have already stated," he said, "my testimony was made up of questions from members of the [Olshan-Dori] committee and my answers. I was not asked nor did I answer questions on anyone's character. Mr. Lavon has complained publicly that I refused Prime Minister Sharett's request to show Lavon my testimony. Since then I have learned, after Mr. Sharett's statements to the committee, that this complaint is groundless. Mr. Sharett never even mentioned the matter to me. I would like to ask Mr. Lavon: Would it really have been so difficult for him to ring up Mr. Sharett and to learn in one minute that he was making false complaints?"

Returning to Lavon's testimony on October 4, 1960: "It is true," he said, "that the statement I issued was to the general effect that I demanded changes in the security system. My proposals were rejected and I resigned. Let me tell you what these changes were: one of them, the deciding factor in whether I would remain in the Government, was a change in personnel. I informed the Prime Minister at the time that I could not remain as Minister of Defense with a Director who gave evidence against me behind my back and a Senior Officer who accused me falsely—this was the minimum condition. The Prime Minister felt he could not do this."

We have already seen what Lavon wrote the Prime Minister in connection with his resignation on February 2, 1955. We have seen the reasons he gave to the Cabinet on February 20, 1955, and to the Foreign Affairs and Security Committee on February 21, 1955. These documents make no mention of a demand for the dismissal of the Director of the Ministry and the Senior Officer.

Sharett testified before the Foreign Affairs and Security Committee on October 17, 1960: "The Minister of Defense (Lavon) asked me to approve a series of measures that he considered essential. They included changes in organization as well as changes in personnel. The changes in personnel were to be two. One was the transfer of the Senior Officer from his post. Lavon did not demand his removal from the Army or the forfeit of his officer's rank but merely his transfer from the General Staff to a different post." Sharett added that such a transfer is within the authority of the Chief of Staff, not that of the Minister of Defense.

The writer can confirm this. If an officer of any rank acted without authority and then claimed that he had an order from the Minister of Defense—as Lavon contended in 1955 and now again in 1960—the Minister's duty was to have him court-martialed at once, behind closed doors. The substance of the dispute would not be made public: Israeli military courts could be trusted to keep security secrets just as a civilian court was trusted in 1959 to conduct the trial of the "third man" in secret. As for the dismissal of Director-General Peres, Sharett confirmed that Lavon had demanded it and explained why he had not complied. Such an action, he said, would have been construed as laying the blame for the affair on him and "this blame could not be hung on the Director-General."

Shimon Peres testified the following week. "I had no part personally in any discussion about Lavon's dismissal or acceptance of his resignation," he said. "The Prime Minister did not request my opinion in the matter. I did not attend any party meeting or other forum where it was considered, nor did I know anything about the proceedings except from hearsay. The first time I learned explicitly that Mr. Lavon had demanded my resignation was his statement before the Foreign Affairs and Security Committee." "Now?" asked the chairman. "Yes now, in 1960," Peres affirmed.

Another strange thing in Lavon's speech to the Knesset committee on October 4, 1960, in connection with his reasons for resigning, must be recorded. "I also wish to mention the following facts," he said. "On February 2, 1955, I sent my letter of resignation to the Prime Minister, a rather long letter. Since it was a letter between the two of us, I will not read it here, nor is it of any importance in this matter. But it gave my reasons for resigning. On February 17, 1955, the statement was broadcast over Kol Israel. I did not wish to wait for the outcome of the various investigations that were under way in different parts of the country, near and far, so I asked my friend on my left here, Mr. Evron, to give the announcement to Kol Israel. He showed it to the Prime Minister at the time and then it was broadcast. It said: 'Today, February 17, 1955, the Minister of Defense issued the following statement: On February 2, 1955, I notified the Prime Minister in writing of my resignation from the Government. In the light of negotiations since then, I informed the Prime Minister today that my resignation is final. I have decided to give the reasons therefore to the Cabinet and to the Knesset Foreign Affairs and Security Committee.' "

Copies of Lavon's letter of resignation to Sharett were sent to four people, three of them—Aranne, Eshkol, and Golda Meir—were members of the Government at the time; the fourth was an ordinary citizen living in Sde Boker, Ben-Gurion. Clearly that letter contained the real reasons for his resignation. It said nothing of changes in the defense system or a demand for the dismissal of Director-General Peres and the Senior Officer. The reason he cited for resigning was his personal relations with Aranne, Eshkol, and Sharett. Though its language was bitter, the letter complained only that the Prime Minister and his colleagues lacked confidence in him. One may doubt whether he gave the real reasons for his resignation to the Cabinet and the Foreign Affairs and Security Committee in February 1955 or to the same committee five years later, but one could hardly doubt the sincerity of the emotions expressed in the letter of February 2, 1955.

At the October 4, 1960, session of the Foreign Affairs and Security Committee the two Herut representatives, Meridor and Bader, proposed that the Cohen Committee hearings be postponed. Bader went so far as to say, "I doubt whether the public, the nation, the people, and history take seriously the recommendations of a committee before which Mr. Lavon has not appeared in this matter." The Knesset committee came to no decision, arranging to reconvene in another week.

Lavon Statement to the Press ★ *Three Conflicting Reasons for his* 1955
Resignation ★ *The "Scandal Factory"*

On the day of his first appearance before the Knesset committee Lavon made a press
statement, published the next day, October 5, in all the papers. It read:

> On October 2, 1960, David Ben-Gurion, Prime Minister and Minister of Defense,
> issued a statement which compels me to take issue on several main points:
>
> 1. The Prime Minister states that there was no connection between my resignation
> from the Government and the hearing previously conducted by the Committee of Two
> [Olshan-Dori]. The Prime Minister bases himself on the announcement in the Knesset by
> the then Prime Minister, Sharett, and on my announcement in the Cabinet and in the Foreign
> Affairs and Security Committee to the effect that I had resigned because proposals for
> changes in the structure of the defense system were rejected by Mr. Sharett. Upon reading
> the Prime Minister's announcement in this connection, I sent him the following letter on
> October 3, 1960. [The letter is quoted in full above, pages 610–11.] To this I must add that
> the only ultimative condition for my remaining in the Government was the dismissal
> of two men with whom no self-respecting person could continue working together after
> what had happened in a certain affair.
>
> 2. I was surprised to read the Prime Minister's arbitrary declaration that "if anyone
> or anything needs clearing, only a court of law has the right and power to do so." I do not
> think anyone has the right to confuse these two matters: that of the two officers which is
> being or will be investigated by a certain board of inquiry about charges of forgery and
> perjury, and that of the resignation of a former Minister of Defense. Naturally, when the
> investigation on the first matter is completed, the Minister of Defense or the Chief of Staff
> can decide to put those guilty of criminal acts on trial. This, however, is not the case with
> regard to the question of why a Minister of Defense resigned, and what the circumstances
> were which compelled him to do so. These questions are not of a judicial, or even a security
> nature. They are questions of national and public interest, and there is no logical or moral
> reason for trying to invoke judicial intervention. Even the Committee of Two, appointed
> at my request, was not a judicial body and did not have judicial authority. Obviously the
> Prime Minister and Minister of Defense, with a considerable amount of justice, does not
> consider himself suited to be the arbiter in this matter; but there are institutions and not
> merely personalities in this country. There is the Government, which under law is a collective
> body; and there is the Foreign Affairs and Security Committee. There is no reason why
> in this affair, which is of a national and public nature, both institutions or either of them
> should not consider themselves compelled to investigate and to draw conclusions.
>
> 3. On the instructions of the Minister of Defense the Chief of Staff set up a board of
> inquiry while I was abroad. I will not go into the question whether he had the right to do
> so without informing me. Formally, he undoubtedly did, but from the point of view of
> human relations and friendship there can be other opinions. I myself cannot see the need
> for such a board in view of the fact that the material in the hands of the Prime Minister and
> Minister of Defense (and I am familiar with all of it) was sufficient to be forwarded to the
> Attorney General, who in pursuing his investigation could have obtained the assistance of
> an officer or two whom the Chief of Staff would most certainly have placed at his disposal.
> It is not clear to me why this procedure was not followed instead of matters being complicated
> by setting up a committee that does not have any final arbitrating power.

4. At this point I wish to add a remark which is not included in the Prime Minister's statement, consisting as it does of "explanations" he is trying to disseminate to the effect that there is no connection, nor is any likely to develop, between the material that has recently come to light and a certain "affair." As long as it is in the nature of a security secret, I cannot divulge the nature and contents of this material, but I can state publicly and with full responsibility that all of it is connected with the affair in question and with that alone.

5. I agree unreservedly with the Prime Minister's assertion that no aspersions should be cast on the personal integrity of several of the people who have had to do with this affair. But it can happen that people of integrity make mistakes, and serious ones. The fact that such mistakes come to light has nothing to do with their personal integrity.

6. Finally, I stress once again that under no circumstances should the Israel Defense Forces be involved in this affair or in any ramifications that may develop from it. The IDF is dear to all of us. If, at and about the time of my resignation I remained silent for so long, an overwhelming consideration was concern for the welfare of the IDF. Yet nearly six years have passed since then. The IDF has changed. Great transformations have come about in its corps of commanders. For most of the IDF the affair is already a matter of history; if it is necessary to reopen it now, care must be taken not to drag in the Army. It does not concern the IDF nor will its good name be harmed by it.

Lavon appeared before the Knesset committee three more times, on October 11, 17, and 20. Never before, not even in the days of the *Altalena*, had the country been so agitated. Proceedings of the Foreign Affairs and Security Committee were always considered confidential, and had never before been leaked. But now everything that transpired was spread in the press, usually in mangled form. All barriers were dropped. Testifying on October 17, Sharett defined this "innovation" as follows: "A storm has risen in Israel, a storm now raging in the press and the length and breadth of Israel's public life. What is now under way is not a process of inquiry but a scandal factory."

The Lavon statement to the press made a number of valid points such as that the Army should be kept out of the affair. But it also contained some doubtful points and inaccuracies. Why was he so surprised by the Prime Minister's assertion that "if anything or anyone needs clearing only a court of law has the right and power to do so"? Did he not know that the crux of the 1954 affair lay in the fact there were two versions: that of Defense Minister Lavon, who denied giving the order for the unhappy operation, and that of the Senior Officer, who claimed that he had received it?

He was correct in saying that no one "has the right to confuse these two affairs"— the officers being investigated by the Cohen Committee and his resignation. But if there was any attempt to confuse the two issues, Lavon himself was to blame. In September 1960 he tried in vain to persuade Ben-Gurion to nullify the board assigned to examine the reliability of two officers. True, the question of why any Minister resigns is not a matter for the judiciary; nor can the resignation, after its acceptance, be the subject of an inquiry. But we cannot help wondering why on different occasions Lavon gave different reasons for giving up his post. And the October 4, 1960 attesting in his press statement compounded the confusion by saying that "the only ultimative condition for my remaining in the Government was the dismissal of two men with whom no self-respecting person could continue working together after what happened in a certain affair."

Press items from the "scandal factory" claimed that had Sharett known in 1955 what he learned in October 1960, he would never have "forced" Lavon to resign. Yet in a letter to Ben-Gurion on March 6, 1961 (two months after Ben-Gurion had resigned over the miscarriage of justice by the Ministerial Committee of Seven in December 1960), Sharett would write: "I have taken care to refute the assumption in various circles and newspapers that had what was known in 1960 been known in 1954, Lavon would not have been compelled to resign. The truth is that the causes of the resignation were altogether different. Serious things had happened for which Lavon was to blame and these obliged him to resign. This was the gist of my statement to the Foreign Affairs and Security Committee on October 17, 1960, my article in *Davar* on October 21, my statement to the press on October 25, and my speech to the Mapai Party's Central Committee on February 4, 1961."

From Sharett's testimony we may conclude that the 1954 affair was not the sole or perhaps even the main cause of the resignation. His emphasis on grave personal complications clearly implies that Lavon's resignation was not brought about only by the affair of 1954. On December 16, 1960, in Lavon's presence, Levi Eshkol said exactly the same thing to the Mapai Secretariat: "I want to be perfectly frank. He (Lavon) has already heard me say this. I said that unless a miracle occurred I did not see how the system of relationships Lavon had created would long survive." Turning to Lavon, he added: "There was something called the 'Affair,' and it began the day you took office." Lavon had joined the Government formed by Sharett on January 25, 1954, and the "security mishap" took place in July 1954. If Eshkol's statement was correct—and since Lavon did not deny it at the time we may assume it was—then some affair had been in existence from the moment Lavon entered the Government, at any rate before the unfortunate mishap in July. In the *Davar* article to which he alluded, Sharett wrote (October 21, 1960):

> The resignation of a Minister in a coalition government cannot always serve as the subject for a serious and purposeful inquiry by that Government itself, and certainly not by a Government formed later. Just as members of such a Government do not elect or appoint each other, so they cannot prevent one of their colleagues from resigning. In a coalition government the Ministers represent their respective parties and a resignation is something worked out on the formal level between the Minister and his party, and on the personal and political level between the Minister and the Prime Minister. At any rate, it is not a matter for "investigation" in any government framework.

> Actually, what is now taking place in our public life is not an inquiry but a scandal factory. In my appearances before the Foreign Affairs and Security Committee, I refused to contribute to this destructive process. Mischievous winds are raging in our public life. Newspapers lacking all restraint are ceaselessly stirring up trouble between individuals and trying to poison the public atmosphere. It would seem that people well acquainted with the meaning of responsibility have been struck blind and are disregarding it more and more. Others, out of spite it would seem, are rebelling and leading the public astray. Every day the press explodes with a new "revelation" to blow up the controversy and inflame a lust for virulent rejoinder and blind revenge. The majority of the public is flabbergasted by the divulgences and confused by the turmoil, which kicks up such a lot of dust while keeping the main thing hidden.

> I discern three different aspects of the affair and my conclusions are likewise threefold. First, the criminal aspect that is basically a subject for judicial inquiry. Secondly, the defense aspect of both the operation itself and the information that has come to light in its wake; this can be heard by the Foreign Affairs and Security Committee, which will do well to limit itself to this matter only and wind up its hearings as soon as possible. Thirdly, the resignation, which should be left to the judgment and appraisal of public opinion and in the final account to history.

It is hard to dispute these conclusions, but for some reason Sharett did not stick by the first of them when it was required. He did not make clear in his article that if the criminal aspect—the question, that is, of who gave the order—had been submitted to a judicial body, the scandal factory would have ground to a halt, since the judiciary enjoys the nation's confidence, and has earned it. Such an investigation was prevented by Lavon's powerful opposition from 1954 onward, as we learned from Sharett himself. At the meeting of the Mapai Secretariat on January 15, 1961, he would say: "In Lavon's place I would have declared myself in favor of a judicial board of inquiry, and the reason it was not held was not because I refused but because Lavon opposed it."

But why was Sharett as Prime Minister dependent on Lavon and his opinion? Had a judicial investigation taken place at once, in 1954, the "Lavon Affair" would never have developed and we would not have been subjected six years later to a scandal factory and a Government crisis.

One member of the Foreign Affairs and Security Committee in the period of the scandal factory, Yacov Hazan (Mapam), noted the confusion of issues. At the meeting of October 17, 1960, he said: "We are dealing with two different matters. One of them is personal, between Lavon and the Senior Officer, only one of whom can be in the right . . . . One of the two has to be cleared: either one of them committed forgery or the other lied. I think that a properly run country cannot afford to live off the blood of its citizens."

This sensible view was ignored by the other committee members, just as they had ignored the Prime Minister's plea for a judicial inquiry when the committee deliberations first began. Ben-Gurion was heeded neither by the Mapai members nor those of other parties, perhaps for the reason given by Eshkol: "Lavon's appearances before this committee have made him a magnet for all of Mapai's opponents. He has become a magnet, and all those who seek to hurt Mapai have clustered around him."

New Accusations by Lavon ★ The Cohen Committee Submits Findings ★ "Senior Officer" Requests Judicial Action ★ Cabinet Sets Up a Ministerial Committee of Seven

To this day large parts of Lavon's statements to the Knesset committee in October 1960 have not been released for publication by the censor, although the "mishap" has been described in full detail in many foreign papers. Lavon, however, did not restrict himself to that security blunder. He complained also of irregularities in the Ministry of Defense and in the work of its Director-General, Shimon Peres. He had bitter things to say about a mishap of a similar nature which had occurred earlier and in a different country.

The writer will not presume to judge between Lavon and Peres. But as Minister of Defense for fifteen years, both before and after Lavon, he considers it his duty to establish beyond doubt that Lavon's claim that a similar security mishap had occurred in 1952 in a different country was completely unfounded. What took place in that country was an intentional frameup of local Jewish youths by a hostile Arab government. One of them "confessed" his guilt after terrible tortures. In the subsequent trial he insisted that the confession had been obtained under duress, and that neither he nor his friends had had any part in the crime attributed to them. He was hanged notwithstanding. The second young Jew, also sentenced to hang, later had his sentence commuted to ten years of imprisonment. He is now living in Israel and is familiar with every detail of the episode.

None of the Jews accused implicated any of their friends or claimed they had received orders from Israel. The fact is that no Jews had any part in the crimes in question, nor was there any resemblance between what happened in that country in 1952 and what is known as the "Lavon Affair," in which the Senior Officer claimed that the Minister of Defense had given him an order and the Minister claimed that the officer had acted on his own. The truth could be discovered only by judicial proceedings, but Lavon opposed this. He even tried to call off the board of inquiry known as the Cohen Committee.

Although Lavon told the Foreign Affairs and Security Committee that the Army "must on no account be brought into this affair," in subsequent appearances before the committee he hurled serious accusations against Army officers and officials of the Ministry of Defense, if not against the Army as a whole.

"I call it corruption," he said at the October 17 session, "when officers and officials of the Ministry of Defense consider it their function to engage in talebearing, to spread rumors, and to influence the newspapers in this affair. I do not know how many they are. I am told that there are scores of people. I am told this by the newspapermen themselves to whom they speak. What business is it of lieutenant-colonels or majors or officials of the Ministry of Defense to devote days and nights to this matter? Is that what they get paid for?" And he added, "I have material even more damaging than this, but I have refrained from making it public. We have a Minister of Defense (Ben-Gurion) who is not an interested party. He ought to tell those boys to lay off—it's none of their business."

He had not yet revealed all the corruption that he supposedly knew about military officers and officials of the Defense Ministry. He went on to say that "officers at present responsible for the Army have no connection with the matter." Yet when Knesset member Chaim Landau (Herut) asked, "What people in the Defense Ministry are engaging in journalism?" Lavon replied, "I am not prepared to mention names." Nor did he refrain from intimating that the present Minister of Defense also bore responsibility for those unnamed lieutenant-colonels and majors, because he did not "tell those boys to lay off." Lavon did not make plain to the committee that he had never brought his accusations against the lieutenant-colonels and majors, or even the officials of the Defense Ministry, to the attention of the minister, and refused to mention names when requested to do so.

Naturally Lavon's charges against people in the Ministry of Defense, including Army officers, appeared in the newspapers and were the occasion for a question in the Knesset. S. Zalman Abramov of the General Zionists addressed it to the Prime Minister and Minister of Defense: "On October 14, 1960, *Davar* published an interview with Pinhas Lavon in which he says: 'If there is talebearing and the dissemination of false rumors in order to cultivate journalists and influence in certain circles, the question is, is this their function? Is it for this that they receive salaries from the national coffers?' Since no denial of this serious accusation has appeared in that paper or any other, I would ask the honorable Minister: (1) Is the abovementioned accusation true? (2) If so, how does he plan to eliminate these faults and ensure that they will not recur? (3) If the accusation is untrue and the abovementioned statements are a slander of the defense system, what action does the Minister intend to take against its author?"

Ben-Gurion replied in the Knesset on November 23, 1960:

1. The abovementioned person has elsewhere said things of an even more serious nature about "scores" of lieutenant-colonels, majors, and officials of the Foreign Ministry who spend their days and nights in talebearing and disseminating false rumors in connection with this affair. Yet when asked to state who they were, he replied, "I am not prepared to mention names." Hence, I do not see any substance of responsibility whatsoever in his accusations.

2. The employees of the Defense Ministry are among the most loyal and devoted of our civil servants, for they know that what they are serving is the nation's most vital need. If any accusation is brought against a specific person or persons among them, I will treat the matter with the utmost severity, just as I do in the case of the Army.

3. I have asked the Attorney General if the authors of statements such as these can be prosecuted for libel. He replied that unless a specific person can be identified to whom the statements apply they do not come under the definition of libel provided by law. The Attorney General feels that a new libel law should be enacted which would "put an end to the present state of affairs whereby a citizen's honor and good name can be disparaged at will."

The hearings by the Foreign Affairs and Security Committee brought no clarification or conclusions regarding the 1954 affair or any other. The majority of Lavon's claims and charges were refuted by Sharett and Shimon Peres. On January 30, 1961, the Minister of Justice denied Lavon's implication that the Senior Officer had done something else without authorization. "I will give only one example," Lavon had said in October. "There was an operation that Knesset member Hazan surely remembers—one in which five boys were sent to Syria in connection with some instrument that was supposed to be planted in some tree. As a result one boy, Feige Ilanit's son, lost his life. This was something neither I not the Chief of Staff knew about and it was done by that same person."

"That is to say," Bar-Yehuda asked, "the same Senior Officer?"

"Yes," Lavon replied, "it was folly from beginning to end."

Raphael interrupted to ask, "Was it within the Senior Officer's authority?"

"No, he needed approval by the Chief of Staff," Lavon answered. "I believe that the Chief of Staff at that time (Dayan) knew about it. I myself learned about it only after it was all over."

The event to which Lavon referred occurred a short while before the writer returned to the Ministry of Defense on February 21, 1955. On reassuming the post he inquired into the matter and read what the preceding Minister of Defense (Lavon) had told the Foreign Affairs and Security Committee. What he told them at the start of 1955 about the event in question was the exact opposite of what he now told the same committee in 1960.

In November 1960 the Minister of Justice, Pinhas Rosen, persuaded the Foreign Affairs and Security Committee to suspend its hearings because the Cabinet—overriding the Prime Minister's objections—had decided to set up a seven-man ministerial committee to deal with the subject.

When Chief of Staff Laskov on September 12, 1960, in accordance with the Prime Minister's instructions, formed the Cohen Committee, its scope was quite clear. In the letter to Justice Cohen and the two lieutenant-colonels who constituted the committee, he stated:

You are appointed to a board of inquiry the purpose of which is to investigate:

a. Whether any measures were taken by the "Senior Officer," his assistant, or any other officer in the bureau in question to induce witnesses in general and the "third man" in particular to perjure themselves to the Olshan-Dori Committee that investigated the "security mishap" or to the Minister of Defense and Chief of Staff and whether false evidence was actually given.

b. Whether any alterations were made in the documents of [name deleted by censor] or other documents connected with the investigation carried out by the abovementioned committee, and if so, by whom and at whose orders.

c. Justice Chaim Cohen will be the chairman of this board of inquiry. It will seek to establish facts and arrive at conclusions. It will begin its work by examining: (1) the material of the Olshan-Dori Committee of Inquiry; (2) the verdict of the Jerusalem District Court in the case of the "third man" written by Colonel Amiad. The board will submit its findings by October 15, 1960.

The Cohen Committee findings, presented on the specified day, read in part:

Since 1955 various accusations and suspicions have been raised to the effect that documents and records in connection with the "security mishap" had been forged. Apparently no one has yet succeeded in obtaining proof. Though we do not know if the claims of forgery that we have heard are all the claims ever made to this effect in this affair, we find that they have not been proved, nor have the suspicions, except for one matter which still bears investigation, been substantiated.

In July 1954 the Senior Officer sent the Chief of Staff, who at the time was in the United States, a typewritten two-page letter. The second page contained a paragraph beginning with the words, "according to Lavon's instructions . . . [deleted by censor] have been activated." The suspicion was raised that this letter was written not on July 19, 1954, but at a later date; or alternately that the second page was subsequently altered by the addition of a paragraph that was not in the original.

Colonel Herzog, who accompanied the Chief of Staff on that trip to the United States, has confirmed that the Chief of Staff received the Senior Officer's letter between July 23 and 26, 1954, while visiting a military base in Florida.

The officer in charge of the Police Laboratory for Criminal Identification, Avraham Hagag, has given his opinion in writing that the two pages of the document submitted are of the same age; that the dates appearing on the first page are as written originally and have not been altered; that when they were written the same second page now attached to the first page was attached to the first page; and that the document was not tampered with in any way to make it appear either more or less recent than it really was. A copy of his opinion is attached herewith: "In view of this evidence, we hereby establish that the Senior Officer's letter was sent to the Chief of Staff on July 19, 1954, that it consisted of the same two pages that make up the document now in our possession, and that it was not altered in any way."

The board then went on to state that no support was found for the testimony of the "third man" in the Jerusalem District Court that his original diary for the year 1954 had been replaced and reports altered with a view to substantiating the testimony of the Senior Officer and his assistant before the Olshan-Dori Committee. As for the claim that the Senior Officer or his assistant had tampered with documents relating to the affair, it found that "Neither we nor those who made allegations or voiced suspicions know which documents were allegedly forged, nor have we in our possession any data enabling us to assume that if any documents were in fact forged, even during the period in question, they related to the Affair and served, or could have been or were designed to serve, as evidence before the Olshan-Dori Committee. If notwithstanding all this we felt it necessary to investigate the question of those forgeries thoroughly, this was mainly in order to put an end to the discussion and the speculations that these allegations and suspicions have aroused."

The board found that documents had vanished from the office of the Senior Officer and that the frightening ease with which the "third man" (sentenced to twelve years for espionage) had been able to steal secret documents "point to serious and disquieting flaws in that unit's filing system." However, they "have not found sufficient evidence indicating the guilt of any particular person." In the board's opinion the Senior Officer had not told all that he knew and remembered. Also the board had not had time to examine four witnesses whose examination, it felt, was in order.

On October 18, 1960, the Minister of Defense submitted all the material of the Cohen Committee to Attorney General Hausner.

While the country was still rocking from the "scandal factory" and the distortions in the press, and before the release of the Cohen Committee's findings, the Senior Officer asked the Chief of Staff for a judicial committee of inquiry to determine whether he had acted on his own in 1954 or had received an order from the Minister of Defense. The Chief of Staff passed his letter on to the Minister of Defense who gave it to Minister of Justice Rosen at the Cabinet meeting of October 23, 1960. Levi Eshkol thereupon asked: "Will the Minister of Justice be the one to decide the issue?" Ben-Gurion replied: "He can appoint an inquiry committee, but not if the Cabinet should rule otherwise. That is why I am bringing the matter to the Cabinet. I have consulted the Attorney General, and this is what he advised me to do, because it is a matter of common decency; a person has the right to defend his honor. For Ben-Aharon and myself Lavon may be a very important person, but before the law everyone is equal. The Senior Officer is requesting a judicial committee with the power to subpoena witnesses and determine whether or not he gave the order."

Mr. Rosen then said: "The Minister of Interior and the Minister of Justice have the authority to appoint inquiry committees. Neither has ever been known to appoint a committee on an important issue without consulting the Cabinet. I will not do so on my own initiative." When several Ministers voiced their opposition to a judicial inquiry, the Prime Minister said:

"There will be no end to this business until a committee rules according to law. There will be no end of it if the Senior Officer's proposal is rejected. This is a country of law. I understand that there are members here who would like the Government to be the judge. To that I am completely opposed. The Government cannot be a judge in a case like this. Only a committee of jurists who have no preconceived notions in the matter or an inclination to one side or the other, and who know how to conduct a judicial inquiry, can do this. I see how a 'judicial' inquiry is developing in the Foreign Affairs and Security Committee—it is a scandal the like of which Israel has never yet known. I am opposed to the Government acting as an investigator in this matter."

"Perhaps," Minister of Finance Eshkol suggested, "the Government won't investigate but will merely come to the reasonable conclusion that we have reached the end of the line."

At that meeting the Cabinet did not reach a decision because it was busy debating whether to publish the findings of the Cohen Committee. By a vote of six to five (in which the Prime Minister did not participate) it was decided to publish the findings as edited by the Minister of Justice, and without mentioning names. The question of a judicial inquiry was postponed to October 30, 1960, the following week.

Meanwhile the Prime Minister learned that Eshkol was trying to persuade members to appoint a *ministerial* committee, rather than a judicial committee of inquiry. At the start of the October 30 meeting the Prime Minister therefore declared:

"I will participate neither in the debate nor in the voting. I merely wish to clarify my position. In my opinion there is only one question with regard to the past: Was the order given or not, and if it was, by whom? I hold that this is a question that can be resolved only by due judicial process, by objective persons with the power to subpoena witnesses and to put the person who lied on trial. There is law in this country. We must distinguish between two things. As to how to proceed tomorrow or the day after in some security question or other, there can be no differences of opinion. That is something which can be decided by a political body. But in cases in which one has to determine what has already happened, to establish facts, the entire free world provides for judicial procedures. Now that I have said what I had to say, I will merely conduct the meeting."

"The Senior Officer has submitted a request to the Chief of Staff," the Minister of Justice then said. "The Chief of Staff forwarded it to the Prime Minister and last week the Prime Minister gave it to me. The Senior Officer requests a board of inquiry, under the Committees of Inquiry Law, empowered to 'determine if I was given an order by the Minister of Defense at the time. I have said, and I repeat, that when I gave the order to carry out the operation, it was on the basis of an order from the Minister of Defense at the time.' If there is no new material, I see no reason to accede to the request. I think this is a matter that should be decided by a ministerial committee, such as I am about to propose.

"In my opinion the ministerial committee should resolve the question whether a committee of inquiry is required, after seeing all the material. The Government should decide how to proceed in this matter and how to arrive at a conclusion. This will hardly be possible unless a limited ministerial committee sees all the material, after which it will be in a position to recommend that the Government appoint a committee of inquiry with power to subpoena witnesses, and so on. It can also recommend against the appointment of such a committee. But personally I am not at all sure if we will be able to bring this business to an end without a committee of inquiry. I have said this several times. I assume that what the ministerial committee will decide on will be the procedure. It may well be, however, that on the basis of the material it will decide that the last word can be said on the subject. I doubt that this will be the case, but it is possible."

Ben-Aharon and Eshkol firmly supported Rosen's proposal for a ministerial committee. After a lengthy debate, both relevant and irrelevant, Rosen said: "I gather that the members agree that a ministerial committee should be appointed to study the material and recommend to the Government how to proceed. The committee as such—so I understand—will not make conclusions without submitting a report to the Cabinet." The proposal was adopted by a vote of twelve to nothing. The Prime Minister abstained from the voting. Opinion differed on the number of members on the committee. By a vote of seven to four the Cabinet decided on five members: Pinhas Rosen, chairman; Eshkol, Ben-Aharon, Shapira, and Shitreet. An additional session was set for the next day for final agreement on the composition of the committee. The following day, October 31, the Cabinet convened without the Prime Minister, who was busy in the Knesset. The ministerial committee, it was decided, would have seven members. Israel Barzilai and Benjamin Mintz were added to those already elected.

Meetings of Ministerial Committee ★ Rosen Drafts Its Findings ★ Police Investigation into Alleged Forgery Reports "No Case"

The first meeting of the ministerial Committee of Seven on November 3, 1960, was opened by its chairman, the Minister of Jusice, Pinhas Rosen. He defined its competence as follows: "To review the material and to tell the Government what in our opinion should be done in the future." There is no stenographic record of the first thirteen meetings— only brief summaries of the material examined.

At the third meeting (November 10) Minister Mintz asked to see documents relating to the Senior Officer in a certain trial. At first Rosen said that the material was not relevant to the matter at hand, but then he agreed to produce it. When the Prime Minister learned that this material was read to the committee, he wrote to the Minister of Justice: "I have learned that one of the members of the Committee of Seven asked to see the material of [deleted by censor] and you consented. Since I am not the Senior Officer's defense attorney it makes no difference to me whether you delve into his past, but as far as I know this is not your assigned function; nor have you asked for any material on the actions of the other party to the dispute, the Minister of Defense in 1955. Does this not constitute discrimination?"

The Prime Minister received the following answer on January 11, 1961: "We have drawn no conclusions from the Senior Officer's conduct in the matter of [deleted], as I have warned the members several times not to be influenced by this case, which occurred twelve years ago and which did not preclude his attaining the rank of a Senior Officer in the Israel Defense Forces."

The Prime Minister found the reply astonishing. The Minister of Justice recognized that this material did not pertain to the committee, then went ahead and presented it. He felt that by admonishing his colleagues not to be influenced he had rectified the error. But why did the members of the committee wish to see this material? For diversion? Later one of its members indicated that it was solely on the basis of this material that he had decided against the Senior Officer.

On November 20 the Minister of Justice wrote the Prime Minister:

> The committee's conclusions will relate to questions of procedure only. Our assignment is to review the material connected with the affair and to advise the Government how to proceed in dealing with the affair itself, and whether additional steps should be adopted to this end. Our proposals could be any of the following: (1) to empower the seven-man committee to draw findings from the material it has seen; (2) to accredit the seven-man committee as an inquiry committee; (3) to accredit the seven-man committee as an investigating committee; (4) to appoint another investigating committee in which the [Knesset] Opposition will not participate; or (5) to appoint an investigating committee in which the Opposition will participate.

Eshkol persuaded Ahdut Haavodah, Mapam, and the religious parties to agree to recess the Foreign Affairs and Security Committee and to appoint a ministerial committee because that was the only way to replace the Foreign Affairs and Security Committee hearings with something more practical and effective.

For some reason the Minister of Justice did not realize that the Foreign Affairs and Security Committee's hearings would have stopped in any case, had the Government granted the Senior Officer's just request for a judicial board of inquiry.

On November 28, 1960, the Minister of Justice announced that he had instructed the Cabinet Secretariat to ask Lavon whether he had any material relating to the affair. The material was received that afternoon, but the minutes do not disclose its nature. At the thirteenth meeting, the following day, the Secretary read a photocopy of the police experts finding, as conveyed to the Cohen Committee, that no forgery had been found in any copy of the Senior Officer's letter of July 19, 1955.

Beginning with the fourteenth meeting on December 5 there is a complete stenographic record of the proceedings. On that day Rosen apprised the members that Attorney General Hausner had flown to Paris to question the "secretary," the Senior Officer's successor, and others in connection with the matter of alleged forgery. Though by law such an interrogation was the function of the police, Rosen had insisted that it be done by the Attorney General. Barzilai asked, "Did the Cohen Committee recommend this?" Rosen replied, "First of all it was I who requested it and it is also recommended by the Cohen Committee." On the same day he said, "Though I am not inclined to a committee of inquiry—I am opposed to it—I think we ought to hear Sharett, Lavon, the Senior Officer, and the reserve officer in this matter." He also asserted that "The Senior Officer has a legitimate interest in a committee of inquiry," but failed to explain why he opposed it.

At the same December 5 meeting Rosen said, "The wording of the decision (to set up the Committee of Seven) is imprecise. In the Cabinet we spoke explicitly of procedural findings; findings, yes, but specifically the kind I'm talking of; that is to say, not fact findings." Eshkol asked, "Then what are we now?" Rosen answered, "A study committee."

Returning from Paris, the Attorney General appeared before the Committee of Seven on December 13. He had spoken with the "Senior Officer's successor" and then with the Senior Officer's secretary. The successor said that in 1955 he had heard from the secretary that she had made a change in some letter. In a confrontation with Hausner she denied saying this. Hausner then questioned her in private. She was a great admirer of the Senior Officer. On the last day of the interrogation she admitted that she had made a change in the letter. When Hausner produced the letter of July, 1954, she said, "Yes, that is the one." The secretary was now back in Israel, Hausner announced, and was being questioned by the police. Eshkol asked whether any purpose will be served by continuing the police investigation. "The secretary's testimony is of the first importance for any further inquiry," Hausner answered.

Chairman Rosen: "We have before us a request by the Senior Officer and his attorney to be heard in order to prove that Lavon gave the order. We will have to decide about this. I propose that we hear a certain officer who seems to have been present when the Senior Officer came out from a conference with Lavon and told him that he had just received the order. After that I want to hear Dayan, who has asked to be heard. We should also hear the Senior Officer and Lavon and perhaps Sharett as well."

The prospect of an appearance by Dayan worried Ben-Aharon. "I'm afraid of what happens if we start opening the door," he said.

Rosen: "I would like to hear the Senior Officer. I would like to hear Lavon and I would also like to hear Sharett."

Shapira: "Dayan ought to be heard."

Eshkol: "You want it in all the papers?"

Shitreet: "I said at one of the previous meetings that I am in favor and my opinion is unchanged. If the chairman wants to hear three or four witnesses, and they are key witnesses, they ought to be heard."

Eshkol: "I remain opposed. We are not an investigating committee."

Rosen: "Let's take a trial vote."

The vote was taken: three members were in favor of hearing witnesses, two were opposed, and one abstained.

With that the meeting ended. In opening the next session (December 15), Chairman Rosen reported that he had spoken to General Dayan: "He must find a way for the Foreign Affairs and Security Committee to know that Lavon lied in at least one respect. We have before us also a request by Advocate Salomon (the Senior Officer's lawyer) to address the committee. He has heard about the alteration in the copy of the letter which previously read 'in accordance with previous talks,' or something like that. But he feels this does not prove that Lavon did not give the order."

Unexpectedly, Rosen then informed the committee that he had already prepared a draft of its findings. The draft included the statement: "The committee has not heard witnesses. The majority of the members were of the opinion that it was not within its competence to hear witnesses." At the first meeting, it will be recalled, the Minister of Justice declared the function of the committee was "To review the material and to tell the Cabinet what in our opinion should be done in the future." In the draft of findings, however, the formulation was different: "The Cabinet set up a committee to examine all the material relating to the affair and to submit its conclusions to the Government."

The Committee of Seven knew very well that the interrogation of "the secretary" (who had returned to Israel at the request of the Attorney General) and of three other civilians and three Army officers had been turned over to the Israel police. In his directive to the Chief Inspector of the Police, on December 12, Hausner wrote, among other things:

> I request that you assign a suitably experienced officer to wind up the investigation concerning the possible forgery of a document mentioned in the deposition of the secretary. The man against whom the accusation is made, an officer in the reserves, has already been questioned and denies the said accusation. Attached is a copy of the report on this subject.

On December 26 the Deputy Commander of the Investigating Military Police submitted a Final Investigation Report to the head of the Manpower Division: "Subject: suspicion of forgery in the letter by the Senior Officer to the Chief of Staff on July 19, 1954."

The principal witness, it appeared from the report, was the secretary alleged to have altered a letter by the Senior Officer in order to stress that Lavon had given him the order for the operation in question. In her interrogation by Hausner, in Paris, she declared that she introduced the words "according to Lavon's order" in what she was "99 percent certain" was the letter of July 19, 1954. But in the first police questioning in Israel she stated that "after thinking over" her Paris testimony, given under great tension, "she had begun to doubt whether it was in the letter of July 19, 1954, that the alteration had been made." The police report added: "In a face-to-face confrontation with the reserve officer the secretary adhered to her story that among the documents the latter had given her to type there had been *some document* [emphasis in the original] in which she was to have made the change." But she remained doubtful whether it was the July 19 letter.

The report also stated: "After two days of tests, Albert Hagag, a criminal identification expert with the Israel Police, concluded that all the existing copies of the Senior Officer's letter of July 19, 1954, to the Chief of Staff, had been typed simultaneously on one typewriter. He identified the typewriter. *No traces of forgery were found in the copies of the letter.* [Emphasis in original.]" Citing the ambiguity in the secretary's testimony and the conclusion of the identification expert, the report concluded: "No Case."

Section 2. Ministerial Committee Proceedings; Ben-Gurion Resigns

Senior Officer Not Invited To Testify ★ *Peres Answers Lavon's Accusation* ★ *Ministerial Committee Makes "Material" Findings*

Most of Lavon's testimony before the Foreign Affairs and Security Committee was not released by censorship and rightly to the extent that it related to the "mishap" and its consequences. A large part of it, however, did not relate to the affair itself but to charges of "irregularities" in the Defense Ministry during his term as Minister, for which he blamed largely the Director-General of the Defense Ministry, Shimon Peres. The Knesset committee rejected the just demand by Hazan that the Senior Officer be invited to present his side of the affair, but it did invite Peres. In the course of four appearances he commented on Lavon's imputations—not as reported in the newspapers but as set forth in the shorthand record. He also refuted slanders in press reports against high-ranking Army officers.

On January 5, 1955, Peres had received a phone call from the Olshan-Dori Committee asking him to appear before it that afternoon. On his arrival he was informed that the committee's inquiry was secret and that his testimony would be kept secret. In the nearly six years since then he had not seen the records of his testimony. Only now, in late 1960, did he learn that because of this testimony Lavon had at that time demanded that the Prime Minister dismiss him—a demand based in part on the false assumption that he had refused to show it to Lavon. Peres also vigorously denied that he had testified about Lavon's character, as Lavon claimed: he had merely answered questions, none of which related to Lavon's character.

Lavon had told the Foreign Affairs and Security Committee of a plot, forgeries, wastage, and other troubles in the Ministry, and the newspapers had linked this with his demand for the removal of Peres. The press, indeed, gave the impression that Israeli democracy was menaced by defense personnel and officers—the lieutenant-colonels and majors about whom Lavon had complained, while refusing to identify them by name. Peres declared that in his thirteen years in the defense system he had come to know most of the high-ranking officers, but had never heard from them any objections to the democratic civilian control over the military. On the contrary, the magnificent Officer Corps completely accepted and supported our democratic form of government.

He had not taken part in any Cabinet discussions, if there were any, about the dismissal or resignation of Lavon, Peres testified, nor had he been asked for his opinion in the matter by Prime Minister Sharett. Lavon himself had never told him that he wanted him dismissed, which in any case was within his authority as Minister of Defense. Peres made clear that he had no connection whatsoever with the "security mishap" before, during, or after the event.

Lavon complained before the Foreign Affairs and Security Committee that the Defense Ministry had had some dealings in connection with a floating dock, which he claimed was not a defense matter, citing it as an example of the "irregularities."

"One bright day," he said, "I heard that there was a draft agreement [on the dock]: 50 percent Ministry of Defense, 50 percent Solel Boneh [a civilian company]. I asked whether the three or four or five boats we had in the Navy justified 50 percent coming out of Defense funds. Whether such a dock should be bought or not is not a question for the Ministry of Defense. There are Economic Ministers, let them do the deciding. Why does the Defense Ministry have to be a partner in it?"

It is true that the Ministry was involved in a dock purchase, but it had no such implications of "irregulaity." In October 1953 the Minister of Defense at the time (Ben-Gurion) submitted to the Cabinet an eighteen-point plan for defense policy over the next three years. Point 10 spoke of maximal utilization of the civilian economy for military supply, transport, construction, production, and other military services. Point 16 dealt with "expansion of civilian aviation and shipping," including procurement of "a floating dock at Haifa."

Asked about this part of Lavon's accusations, Peres recalled that Lavon himself, as Defense Minister, "took the initiative" on acquisition of a floating dock, and two months before his resignation proposed that it be operated jointly by the Defense and Transport Ministries, and also serve the Merchant Marine and the Navy. "The first time I heard that Lavon was opposed to it," he said, "was after his appearance before the Foreign Affairs and Security Committee on October 11, 1960."

At a subsequent hearing Lavon extended the dimensions of his charges. "At the last meeting," he said, "I gave the dock as an example. I can add several others as well. For instance, there was the matter of the maintenance plant. When I looked into it I was unable to understand why the 'gigantic' State of Israel needed three maintenance plants, one for the Air Force, one for El Al, and one set up by the Ministry of Defense. Why three maintenance plants? Why not only one? Such a plant, of course, could not be under the sole jurisdiction of the Ministry of Defence. I am mentioning this as another example of the differences of opinion."

On this point, on October 23, Peres related:

> The idea for the maintenance plant originated in 1951. On a visit to the United States, Mr. Ben-Gurion saw such a plant in California run by former Mahal people [foreign volun-

teers during Israel's War of Independence], and invited them to Israel. It was then that he put me in charge of construction. On August 17, 1952, the Government resolved (Resolution No.560) to create an aircraft maintenance plant. I handled the matter not only for the Minister of Defense but also for the Minister of Transport at the time. I also have documents consenting to the creation of the plant from El Al, from the Ministry of Transport, and from the Economic Ministers.

Disputes developed as to the nature of the plant, the relationships with El Al and the Air Force, and other things. There was also opposition to the appointment of Mr. Schwimmer, who is presently the plant's director. Mr. Lavon claims there are three maintenance plants. I am afraid he is mistaken. There are as many plants as there are airfields. Every Air Force squadron requires a maintenance plant for low-level repairs. . . .

Take the current year, for example: the Bedek plant will put in manhours of work worth IL18 million, including $2 million worth of work from foreign customers who pay for it in dollars, as well as work for the Air Force, for El Al, and for Arkia. We have dealings with the United States, England, France, and other countries. The management of the Bedek plant, which employs twenty-five hundred workers, includes representatives of the Ministries of Defense, Finance, Transport, and Commerce and Industry, as well as the Air Force and the IDF. And there are no problems of either duplication or friction. It is one of the finest outfits in the country.

Lavon had made a blanket charge of "wasteful redundancy—almost everything in the Army had its counterpart in the Defense Ministry: spokesmen, manpower departments, administration, budget, and so on and so forth." Except for the "so on and so forth," Peres dealt with each of these elements. Where there was seeming duplication, he argued, there were always different functions that made it necessary and justified.

The strangest thing about these proceedings was that the Foreign Affairs and Security Committee in 1960 was discussing irregularities that supposedly took place in 1954—discussing them with the person who was Minister of Defense in that year. Was there no Foreign Affairs and Security Committee in 1954? Were there not members of the committee in 1960 who had also served on it in 1954? No one asked the most simple question: Why had the Minister of Defense in 1954 not brought these complaints of redundancy before the committee five or six years ago?

On October 26, 1960, the Knesset Speaker tried to show that it was not within the committee's authority to deal with what happened in 1954, since it was not an investigating committee. Section 22 of the Basic Law of the Knesset and Section 13 of the Knesset Rules of Procedure made it clear that the committee had no authority whatsoever to hear of things that did or did not occur in 1954 from the Minister of Defense in that year. But only after the Cabinet on October 31 decided to set up the ministerial Committee of Seven did the Minister of Justice manage to persuade the committee to interrupt its hearings on what happened in 1954–1955 until the Government committee completed its investigation.

What the Minister of Justice who initiated the Committee of Seven failed to understand was that such an investigation was not within the authority of a ministerial committee either. The objective—to determine who gave or didn't give the order in 1954—was not within the Cabinet's authority but belonged to a judicial body. Every democratic state maintains a separation of powers; there is legislative and executive power on the one hand, judicial power on the other; the executive is not empowered to adjudicate disputes between individuals. In fact the Minister of Justice had himself informed his committee colleagues on December 5, 1960, that their findings were to be procedural rather than material, and that they were merely a study committee. He had stated the same thing in a letter to this writer dated October 20, 1960.

In the committee's last days, however, he suddenly changed his mind and presented a draft of findings, concluding with the words: "The investigation of the affair should be considered closed." His proposed findings asserted that the Attorney General's investigation in Paris had shown that the words "according to Lavon's order" were not in the Senior Officer's original letter; this was plainly untrue. Upon returning from Paris, Mr. Hausner had merely said that the testimony of the secretary gave grounds for further investigation, which was being carried out by the police in Israel.

Strangely, Rosen saw no need to await the outcome of this investigation. Perhaps it was because, when he had first heard of the "security mishap" in early 1955, he said he was certain that Lavon had not given the order. This certainty was based, it seemed, only on the belief that a smart man like Lavon wouldn't do a foolish thing like that. He did not consider that the Senior Officer was also a smart man and that for him to do such a thing would have been even more foolish. The Minister of Defense was at least authorized to give such an order, whereas the Senior Officer was not. What motive could he have had for such an operation without the Minister's agreement? If it succeeded, the Defense Minister would get all the credit, and if it failed, he could be court-martialed and expelled from the Army. Actually, had he really acted without authorization, it was Lavon's duty to put him on trial at once for undertaking an unauthorized operation that led to the loss of lives.

Yet Rosen repeated several times at one meeting, "I am almost certain that Lavon did not give the order." And he said this both before and after he had heard the Attorney General testify that the matter should be further investigated in Israel by the police. Then, incredibly, the committee did not await the final outcome of the police investigation (though the secretary's revised testimony to the police was already before it), and on December 21 produced findings that were clearly "material" rather than prodecural. In substance they cleared Lavon, which amounted to condemning the Senior Officer without even affording him an opportunity to tell his story.

After some discussion these findings were approved, with a few changes, and submitted to the Government.

Cabinet Confirms the Findings of Its Committee of Seven ★ Prime Minister Condemns the Entire Proceedings and Tenders His Resignation

The Prime Minister received the ministerial committee findings two days before they were brought to the Cabinet session on December 25. As he examined the committee's minutes and the findings, he was struck by some puzzling facts: According to Pinhas Rosen, the committee was to "examine all the material relating to the affair and submit its findings to the Government." Yet when he opened the first meeting on November 3, he defined its authority as "to review the material and tell the Government what we feel should be done in the future." When and on what grounds had the committee's authority suddenly changed? In a letter to the Prime Minister dated November 20, as already noted, Rosen had written: "The committee's findings shall be procedural only." Its findings a month later, however, said that the episode should now be considered closed.

"The committee did not hear witnesses," according to Section 3 of the report. "The majority of the committee was of the opinion that to hear witnesses was outside its competence." But the Minister of Justice had sent the Attorney General to Paris to question witnesses, and his information was brought before the committee. The chairman himself went to Mr. Olshan and Justice Cohen to clarify facts in connection with the affair and submitted their statements to the committee. Eshkol told the committee, of which he was a member, that he had heard from Moshe Dayan that Lavon had not given an order; they refused, however, to hear Dayan, who had asked to appear. It quickly became clear that Eshkol's story was mistaken—Dayan had never said that Lavon did not give the order, and Eshkol himself then asked that his statement be stricken from the record.

The Committee of Seven alleged in its conclusions that "witnesses" questioned by the Olshan-Dori Committee had lied. It noted that it had read the recent minutes of the Foreign Affairs and Security Committee; although these showed that some of Lavon's statements had been refuted by Sharett, Peres, and Rosen himself, it failed to mention this in the findings. According to Section 8, "The Attorney General's investigation has shown that the words 'according to Lavon's order' were not in the original letter." This despite the fact that the Attorney General had instituted further inquiry on the issue by the police in Israel. Despite the fact, too, that the Cohen Committee had accepted the judgment of the police experts that there had been no tampering with the letter.

The testimony gathered by the police enabled them to conclude that "there is no evidence of any forgery." The police investigation disclosed that the secretary involved had not even handled the letter of July 19, 1954. As it later developed, she had made a change in a different letter, dated November 1, 1954, that the Senior Officer had sent, at his request, to the Chief of Staff. This was the letter she had typed; this was the change, a quite innocent revision, that remained in her memory. No alteration whatsoever had been made in the letter that became the basis for reviving the "Lavon Affair": the letter of July 19, 1954, containing the words "according to Lavon's order."

The Attorney General on December 13, 1960, informed the ministerial committee of the testimony of the Senior Officer's successor. It was this man's claim that the secretary had told him of a change which had started the whole rumpus. Questioned by Hausner, he said, "In straining my memory, I find the secretary may simply have mentioned an Army document rather than the letter to the Chief of Staff and perhaps in view of what I learned later I connected the two by association." At any rate, unlike Rosen, Hausner was not convinced that the crucial letter, that of July 19, had been falsified and therefore brought the secretary to Israel for further interrogation.

Section 12 of the committee's findings asserted: "In this report we have concentrated on one question, namely, whether the Senior Officer received the order to act from Lavon." Why then, in Section 8, did they introduce something that refers not to the Senior Officer but to the reserve officer? This could mislead readers unable to distinguish between them. The reference, moreover, was based on the findings of the Cohen Committee that "the instructions given by the reserve officer at an earlier date were not merely liaison orders," though no one had claimed that the Senior Officer had given operative orders "at an earlier date." If the committee "concentrated mainly on one question," namely, who gave the order, why did it drag in the reserve officer's order "at an earlier date"?

The Minister of Justice presented the committee's conclusions to the Cabinet. When put to a vote, the findings were accepted by eight ministers; four abstained (Eban, Burg, Dayan, Yoseftal) and the Prime Minister did not participate in the voting. Immediately after this vote the Prime Minister requested a leave of absence for five or six weeks for reasons of health. Having received the Government's consent to the leave, he said among other things:

> I took no part in the discussion nor in the selection of the ministerial committee. I was opposed to the whole idea. Until two and a half months ago I had read only the findings of Olshan and Dori. I said to myself that if two such people could not ascertain the truth, it would be better to let the matter fall into oblivion. This was before Lavon came to me with objections to the judicial board of inquiry, not against himself but against Army officers under suspicion. He objected to Supreme Court Justice Chaim Cohen. I told him that Cohen was a man to be trusted. Lavon said: "When I was in the Government I proposed his dismissal." I replied: "Had I been in the Government at the time I would have voted against you." All this did not affect my attitude to Lavon, until I read the minutes of the Foreign Affairs and Security Committee and was stunned—accusations and slanders with no basis in fact, slanders against lieutenant-colonels and majors whom he refused to name. . . .
>
> You have probed and dug around to prove that the Senior Officer is capable of not telling the truth. But have you found that Lavon speaks only the truth? I asked myself: what happened? I was responsible for the Army on behalf of the State six years before Lavon and six years after Lavon. In all those years nothing occurred like what happened in 1954. When I learned that a certain captain and three soldiers had not told me the truth in connection with an incident on the Sinai border, I ordered them put on trial. Soldiers should be better than private individuals. In this lies their strength. I asked myself: what happened that year? How did a sudden transformation come about in the Army? I know now that the Minister of Defense in that year issued orders that two Chiefs of Staff, Mordekhai Makleff and later Moshe Dayan, felt should not be executed because they might bring disgrace upon the State, and prevailed upon him to revoke them. One of these Chiefs of Staff—he is now a member of the Cabinet—asked to testify to the committee about this but was refused permission. The committee also refused to hear the Senior Officer who had been slandered by Lavon, though one of its members, Yacov Hazan, demanded three times to hear him. Lavon admits that he had spoken to the Senior Officer about certain operations that led up to the "security mishap"—why did he not speak to the Chief of Staff about it?
>
> In 1954 I was an ordinary citizen living in the Negev and did not know what was taking place. In recent weeks, however, I tried to clarify what happened at the time and came across a letter written by the Prime Minister at the time, dated May 25, 1954, to Minister of Defense Lavon: "Security matters are not being reported to me as they should be. Things occur that are not being brought to my attention. I hear announcements on the radio and later read about them in the papers without knowing the true background. The proper arrangement would be for me to know the facts, if at all possible, before the official version is released. At any rate I should know the facts; however, it is up to you to take the initiative."
>
> What is the basis of the ministerial committee's main finding, Section 10? It is that "Lavon claims that nothing of the kind happened." There is no other proof that the Senior Officer did not receive an order. From his appearances before the Foreign Affairs and Security Committee, have you the impression that everything Lavon says is the truth?

I ask the Minister of Justice: He knows that there is a certain procedure and only through that is it possible to arrive at the truth. Witnesses are interrogated, each side cross-examines the other, and their lawyers probe and investigate. Why were you so afraid of a judicial board of inquiry? . . .

You have made your decision. There are findings, and there is a Government resolution that confirms them. The Cabinet has a rule of collective responsibility. I do not, nor will I, share this responsibility, not for appointing the committee, for its findings, or for the Government resolution. I am not a member of your Government.

With these words the Prime Minister left the meeting, since he had been granted the leave of absence. After Ben-Gurion left, Dayan said he wished to bring two things to the Government's attention: "One: What Lavon told the Foreign Affairs and Security Committee is not the truth. And I will request permission to appear before the Foreign Affairs and Security Committee and set things straight. The second is: When I was Chief of Staff, Lavon issued an order, at least one and perhaps more, which I found unacceptable, and instead of carrying it out I prevailed upon him to revoke it and he agreed."

The Zionist Congress on December 28, 1960, and a grave dispute with the American government delayed the Prime Minister's resignation. Only on January 31, 1961, was he able to tender it to the President of the State. The letter of resignation said, among other things:

It is not easy for me to abandon endeavors which I consider important and in which I have been engaged for many years, and plans which I have begun to implement. My understanding of my obligations toward the State forbids me to bear the responsibility for the decision adopted by the Government on December 25, 1960, as this decision is incompatible with the fundamental principles of justice and the basic laws of the State. The law of collective responsibility obligates every member of the Government to bear the responsibility for its decisions and acts, even if he is himself opposed to them. True, on several occasions the members of the Government adopted decisions with which I did not agree, and I accepted the ruling of the majority and bore the responsibility. At this session, however, the Government adopted a decision that I cannot reconcile with my conscience, and I have no alternative but to resign.

I did not take part in the voting on this decision, as I did not take part in the voting on the adoption of the conclusions on December 25, 1960. It was clear to me that if it was necessary to investigate the matter known as "The Affair," which has been disturbing the public for several months for reasons I will not discuss here, it should be investigated by legal procedure before a court or a judicial inquiry committee. In such a judicial investigation both parties should be given an equal opportunity to summon witnesses or submit documents if they find it necessary, each party cross-examining the other, and the duly constituted court should issue its verdict. It is an accepted principle that it is better to acquit ten guilty persons than to condemn a single innocent man. To acquit a suspected person, it is not necessary to prove by convincing evidence beyond a reasonable doubt that he is innocent. But in order to condemn a suspected person, it is essential to prove by convincing evidence beyond the shadow of a doubt that he is guilty.

I opposed the establishment of the Committee of Seven. It was my opinion that if it was necessary and possible to investigate what truly happened in 1954—which of the two was guilty and which innocent—this should be done only by an authorized judicial instance, according to due process of law, and not by a political body, contrary to the laws of the State. When the "Seven" submitted their conclusions to the Government on December 25, 1960, I told the Government, "The conclusions were wrong, because they acquit one of the two and convict the other without a judicial investigation and without hearing the parties." The conviction of a citizen without due process of law is a grave violation of the basic rights of the citizens. It is also a dangerous precedent for the future.

The campaign of denigration that has been organized against me during the past few months—by whomever it was organized—at meetings, in the press, in the Foreign Affairs and Security Committee, and in the Knesset cannot affect me in any way. I hold democracy in Israel no less dear than any other citizen, and democracy means, among other things, the separation of powers between the legislature, the executive, and the judiciary. My resignation from the Government at this time is due to the command of my conscience and my profound concern for law and justice in the State.

These Issues Debated by Central Committees of Mapai and Histadrut ★ Mapai Removes Lavon from Histadrut

The Eichmann trial diverted the public attention somewhat from the storm aroused by Lavon's appearances before the Foreign Affairs and Security Committee and the differences of opinion in the Government regarding the powers assumed by the ministerial committee in adjudicating a dispute between two persons. The Prime Minister was only the most conspicuous of those who contended that the committee violated the Basic Law of the State, without even observing the accepted legal procedures of fairness to both sides. Intentionally or not, the press continued to confuse the public by applying the word "affair" to two completely separate matters.

The *first* was what happened in 1954 as a result of an irresponsible order that led to the loss of lives, the origin of which was not clarified either at the time or afterward. After Ben-Gurion's return to the Government in 1955 the matter was dropped, as already recounted. Five years later, in 1959, one of the persons involved in the episode was tried and convicted of treason—on charges in no way connected with the 1954 affair. As a by-product of this trial questions arose about the reliability of two officers, one of them the Senior Officer of the so-called "Lavon Affair." The Senior Officer requested the Chief of Staff for an investigation to determine at long last who had given the disputed order in 1954.

It was this request that produced the *second* affair, climaxed by the resignation of Ben-Gurion. The Government refused to grant the Senior Officer's demand for adjudication by a court of law, setting up instead a ministerial committee that presumed to pass judgment without the due process provided in such cases. Ben-Gurion termed this "a serious blow to the basic laws of a democratic state and the basic rights of its citizens."

Obviously, had it not been for the "security mishap" of 1954 the Minister of Defense in that year (Lavon) would not have appeared before the Foreign Affairs and Security Committee in 1960, touching off a public controversy without precedent in the history of the State; nor would a Cabinet committee have taken upon itself to judge between two people who accused each other. Nevertheless, the 1954 affair and the conduct of the ministerial Committee of Seven were two entirely different matters, both in content and in the people involved. The first affair was a dispute of fact between two citizens. The second involved the right of the Cabinet to assume purely judicial functions.

A special meeting of the Central Committee of Mapai convened at Ben-Gurion's request on January 12, 1961, over two weeks before he tendered his resignation. There he again analyzed Lavon's statements and his complaints about the work of the Ministry of Defense and the Army. He said in part:

In the past three months Lavon has mobilized all the enemies of his party in the Opposition as well as in the two parties in the Coalition (Mapam and Ahdut Haavodah), as well as some daily and weekly newspapers, for an effective and virulent war against Mapai and certain Mapai members, those who, for some reason, did not find favor in the eyes of the Minister of Defense of 1954. And with the aid of his subordinates who received their wages from the Histadrut, of which I too am a member, a campaign of slander and backbiting has been organized the like of which we have never before known in Israel.

In these months he has succeeded in transforming the cause of security and the honor of the Israel Defense Forces and its leading personalities into levers for unbridled party conflict in Israel. The name of the Israel Defense Forces has been defiled. Security has ceased to be the sincere concern of all parties as it was until four months ago. For this purpose Lavon insisted categorically that the dispute should not, heaven forbid, be submitted to judicial inquiry by upright men without party prejudice. A judicial inquiry might have revealed the truth; so he insisted that the matter be discussed only in the Foreign Affairs and Security Committee, in which all the other parties would be on his side and the members of our party would be silenced. And his calculations were not mistaken.

Dr. X in the Knesset and Mr. Y in the press are trying to terrify us with the idea that we are in danger of a dictatorship by a "superior elite." This is a vile and foolish slander. Any army in the world would be proud of the Israel Defense Forces' leadership. There are no angels in our Army; sometimes some officer or soldier misbehaves and he is immediately brought to trial. Nowhere in the world is more care taken than in the Israel Defense Forces to prevent the slightest stain on the honor of the military commanders. Every boy and girl who is sent to the Army is in devoted and honorable hands. The slanders against the Army come from sullied sources. Its thousands of officers and civilian staff have done and are doing their duty loyally and devotedly, and I am full of affection and admiration for them.

Although these statements by Ben-Gurion appeared in full in the press, the "scandal factory" continued to operate, with "intellectuals" issuing manifestos about the imminent danger of dictatorship. Some even professed to see the Prime Minister's decision to resign because of the Committee of Seven's conduct as an attempt to apply pressure on Mapai to expel Lavon from the Histadrut Secretariat. On January 25, 1961, Moshe Sharett wrote to the Prime Minister as follows:

If you wish to enchance your standing in the eyes of the Israeli public and the nation as a whole, to prevent the party's disintegration, and put a stop to the internal moral degeneration of the State, you must get up and declare that you will wind up your vacation and return to your post as Prime Minister in the very near future without any preconditions; that you do not require that any member be dismissed from his post and you will content yourself with what has already been said, draw a line under it and let it go at that.

The Prime Minister replied two days later:

I have not the slightest doubt that what you say you say with sincerity. There is no ulterior motive and you have the good of the State and the movement at heart. Unfortunately I am unable to agree with your suggestion. I may finish my vacation in ten days, but on returning I will tender my resignation to the Government as I said I would when they confirmed the findings of the Committee of Seven. I will resign because there is something called the rule of collective responsibility and this I cannot share after the Government, even without bad intentions, in my view has done something that is unacceptable in declaring itself a court of law, thus violating one of the foundations of the democratic State where complete separation between the executive and judicial authorities is required, and in confirming findings which constitute half-truths and a blatant injustice.

This country cannot live by whitewashing lies, misrepresenting facts, and perverting justice. I shall bear no part of this responsibility for subversion of the moral foundations of our existence. I am not, nor have I any means of, applying pressure, nor, if I had, would I put them to use. I have never utilized means such as these, no matter what the intellectuals say. On the other hand I will not lend myself, even passively, to the grave moral error committed by the majority of the Cabinet members.

If asked, I will be prepared to form a new Government with full freedom to fight for the disclosure of the truth, for I believe in the power of truth. I believe that the truth is stronger than anything, and would cleanse the atmosphere, enhance the party's honor, and strengthen the State. I have not for one moment made my remaining in the Government dependent on Lavon's standing but rather on what has been done by the members of the Government for which I cannot share the responsibility.

While the Prime Minister did nothing with regard to Lavon's position in the Histadrut, three of Lavon's close assistants in the Secretariat of the Histadrut Executive Committee announced on January 22 that they could not continue working with him and resigned. Zeev Cohen, a member of Kibbutz Tel Yosef, wrote in his letter of resignation:

As a result of the developments and complications in the Lavon Affair, I consider it my public and personal duty to tender my resignation to the Histadrut Central Committee. When I first heard Lavon's version of the Affair at the start of October 1960, I sincerely wished for his exoneration. But the deep abyss into which the State, the Histadrut, and the party have been pushed as a result of his declarations and testimony has undermined the basis for my jointly bearing any further responsibility for the leadership of the Histadrut in the party's name.

Yitzhak Haskin, like Pinhas Lavon a veteran member of Hapoel Hatzair, wrote to the Party Secretatiat: "I am unable to continue serving as a member of the Executive of the [Histadrut] Central Committee under the leadership of Pinhas Lavon. I am informing you of my resignation, the reasons for which I will state orally." Yehudit Simhoni, a member of Kibbutz Geva and the mother of Gen. Assaf Simhoni who fell in the Sinai Campaign, wrote that for her "the basis of Mr. Lavon's moral authority has been undermined, and to work under his leadership has become unbearable."

At the Mapai Secretariat meeting on February 2, 1961, to consider the three resignations, Eshkol presented a resolution to the effect that Lavon could no longer represent the party in the Histadrut. The resolution was supported by Bar-Am, D. Hacohen, Moyal, Kargman, Surkis, and Netzer, but strongly opposed by Arrane, Hering, and Sapir. Lavon attacked the three who resigned with exceptional ferocity, venting his spleen especially on Mrs. Simhoni, to the point where the chairman, Almogi warned him to desist. Put to a vote on February 4, the Eshkol resolution was approved by a large majority, and it was referred for final decision to the party's Central Committee meeting scheduled for the next day. There it was decided that two members would speak for the resolution and two against. The speakers were Eshkol and Yoseftal for; Dr. Rotenstreich and Sharett against.

Eshkol pointed out that Mapai had made Lavon the Secretary of the Histadrut after the events of 1954–1955. Many sided with him in his struggle to vindicate himself for the period when he was Defense Minister. But now he had seriously prejudiced values and institutions as well as individuals, and done it in the public domain, where the party has many bitter enemies.

When Ben-Gurion insisted that the unsettled contradiction between Lavon and the Senior Officer could be dealt with only by the judiciary, Eshkol said, he was not opposed to that view in principle. All the same, he "fought to have it recognized that the matter could be brought to a conclusion in a ministerial committee." Thus "we set up the Committee of Seven." But, he continued, "In his appearances before the Foreign Affairs and Security Committee, Lavon seriously and needlessly prejudiced several matters and interests."

"In his performance in the Foreign Affairs and Security Committee," Eshkol added, "he managed to make himself a magnet for all the opponents of Mapai. All who sought to hurt Mapai clustered around him. Perhaps the intention was only, if possible, to get back at Ben-Gurion, who had held his central position in the life of the State for thirteen years. But the ultimate effect was, with the help of the statements and the material Lavon provided, to undermine the entire regime. A situation has now developed in which he is unable to serve as Secretary of the Histadrut."

Dr. Rotenstreich, in opposing the resolution, suddenly switched to the subject of Ben-Gurion:

> Ben-Gurion has many disputes: A dispute with Jewish history, a dispute with treasures of Jewish creativity throughout the generations, and a dispute with Zionism. The position taken by Ben-Gurion in these disputes is based on steadfast views, which made him the leader of his generation and the architect of our people's resurrection. Ben-Gurion has taken as his term of reference his standing in this generation and considers the rebirth of our nation not only as a meeting ground of previous generations but as a mirror of them as well. However, the present dispute is different: It does not pertain to Ben-Gurion's position in history or to his concept of our nation's position in history.

He appealed to the Central Committee not to be led astray by the impulse of hatred and to remove the issue from the agenda until tempers cooled down. With regard to Eshkol's statement that Lavon had been a magnet for Mapai's opponents, he argued that "There is no magnet which hasn't first been magnetized." Mapai, he said, should be guided by principles and by comradeship. "How will we be able to demand that young people show responsibility and adhere to principles?" he asked. "One can gain a moral victory yet lose in the public arena, and one can win in the public arena and lose on the moral level. A public victory that lacks a true moral foundation is not enough."

Giora Yoseftal then spoke:

> We are not sitting here as a tribunal. We are not deciding who gave the order or did not. What we are being asked to do is to make a political decision. whether or not Lavon can represent the party as Secretary of the Histadrut. I have come to the conclusion that part of the aims of his campaign is not valid, and for that reason he can no longer serve as the party's representative in such a central post in our public life.

Lavon has been fighting two campaigns, not one. The first is the campaign for his rehabilitation, in which he has had the party's sympathy. But he fought a second campaign as well, one far beyond what concerned him personally. . . . Lavon has created a condition of psychosis in this country, such as no one before him has ever succeeded in bringing about. The psychosis alleges that the Army is an independent entity in which subordination to the civilian authorities is not assured. This is the suspicion that has led to the present hysteria, the fear that democracy is endangered. We can state categorically that if there is any country where the subordination of the military to the elected civilian authorities is assured beyond doubt it is ours. We proved it in the withdrawal from Sinai where it was a well-known fact that the Army did not want to withdraw. We have proved it on other occasions as well. Lavon, on the other hand, has painted a picture of people in the Army who seek to operate without control of the Knesset and the Government. Lavon has damaged confidence in the survival of the basic and elementary foundations on which democracy is based. A public representative who fights for his rehabilitation by casting suspicion on the basic values of our social and political life can no longer represent us.

The last speaker, Sharett, said in part:

I do not think that it is a secret to many that when I was Prime Minister a problem developed between myself and Lavon, one which was very disappointing, very regrettable, and very grave. I will not go into details at this time. This personal complication was not without effect on Lavon's resignation as Minister of Defense. However, I did not maintain that the resignation was the end of the road in his public life. I was not one of those who had unqualified praise for Lavon's work in the leadership of the Histadrut. I did feel, however, that his positive points outweighed the negative.

But Lavon's appearance before the Foreign Affairs and Security Committee shocked me. He said things that to my mind were absolutely bad. I want to say that Giora Yoseftal was right in one respect about Lavon's appearance before the Foreign Affairs and Security Committee, and I agree that it was the most important one of all: that of confidence in the Army and the security forces.

Suddenly a demand comes to settle accounts with Lavon as a man working in the service of our movement. We all know what happened: One man, a member in our midst, we might call him our eldest brother, concluded that Lavon could not continue as Secretary of the Histadrut and that if he were not dismissed, he would react accordingly. Let no one deny it: this is the point of departure of the new stage in the imbroglio and the reason we are sitting in this meeting. I am firmly opposed to the Prime Minister's taking it upon himself in any way to determine who will or will not head a body that is by no means an organ of the State. In my opinion, in such cases he has no right to say "either-or." Naturally, he is entitled to demand an inquiry into whether or not a given person is worthy of holding that post but *without threats and/or ultimatums* [emphasis in the original]. In this matter the Prime Minister is not entitled to impose his opinion in any manner whatever. As for myself, I am not so certain whether Ben-Gurion is really prepared to formulate and defend his position in those terms—that is, *either-or*. I have reason to believe that he is not prepared to go all out in this; but that is not the point. The important point is that members are convinced that this basically is his position. Our guiding lights, in other words, are not honor and justice but fear and a desire to settle accounts. Such a policy will bring the party neither honor nor strength. I am expressing my opinion—is it really a question of conscience for a personality like Ben-Gurion? And if so, is he entitled to compel the conscience of others?

I do not know if adopting Eshkol's proposal will ensure Ben-Gurion's return to the Premiership, and he is no doubt entitled to propose certain conditions. In view of these unknowns I am forced to assume that serious complications are yet in store for the party. If Eshkol's motion is rejected I shall propose that the Central Committee appeal to Ben-Gurion to return to the Premiership, draw a line, and let things go at that.

The writer, who did not attend that meeting, had no part in Eshkol's resolution, though, as he told the Central Committee on January 12, 1961, his attitude toward Lavon after his testimony to the Knesset committee was completely negative. When Sharett said that Ben-Gurion was entitled to require that the person who filled a certain post be qualified but "without threats or ultimatums," he apparently forgot what Ben-Gurion had said to him in a letter on January 27, only a week before: "Not for one moment do I make my remaining in the Government dependent upon Lavon's status but rather on actions of members of the Government for which I cannot share responsibility." Had Sharett conveyed this to his colleagues in the Central Committee, it might have saved the movement a good deal of embarrassment and obviated the demonstrations and manifestos by "intellectuals.."

Eshkol's proposal, in effect removing Lavon as Secretary of the Histadrut, was adopted by a vote of 159 to 96, with 5 abstaining.

IX

THE PERIOD OF THE FIFTH KNESSET: 1961–1965

Israel Counters Syrian Aggressions; The New President—Shazar; New Prime Minister—Eshkol

---

Section 1. New Elections; Conflict with Syria

Ben-Gurion Presents Another Coalition Cabinet ★ *Growth of Aliya, Production, Employment* ★ *Engineers' Strike*

ELECTIONS to the Fifth Knesset took place on August 15, 1961. The Central Election Committee was headed by Supreme Court Justice Zvi Berenson. A total of 1,037,030 ballots were cast, of which 30,066 were invalidated. The 1,006,960 valid votes were distributed as follows: Mapai, 349,330 (42 seats); Herut, 138,599 (17 seats); Liberal Party (formerly Progressives and General Zionists), 137,255 (17 seats); Mizrahi and Hapoel Hamizrahi, 98,756 (12 seats); Mapam, 75,654 (9 seats); Ahdut Haavodah-Poalei Zion, 66,170 (8 seats); Communist Party, 42,111 (5 seats); Agudat Israel, 37,178 (4 seats); Poalei Agudat Israel, 19,424 (2 seats); Shituf v'Ahvah (an Arab list affiliated with Mapai), 19,342 (2 seats); Kidmah u'Fituah (Arab list also affiliated with Mapai), 16,034 (2 seats); Kidmah v'Avodah, 3561 votes; Lema'an Hatzedek v'Haahvah, a Religious Sephardi party, 3181 votes; and Shoarei Hademocratia, 335 votes.

The first meeting of the Fifth Knesset was opened on September 4, 1961, by the President, Yitzhak Ben-Zvi. "In recent months," he said, "the State of Israel has been deeply involved in the elections to the Knesset. Now that the elections are over, I hope the Knesset will strengthen the unifying rather than the divisive forces." The session was again conducted by the oldest Knesset member, Nahum Nir. After the members made their declarations of allegiance, Akiva Govrin nominated Kadish Luz for Speaker, and he was elected by 109 votes, with only 5 abstentions.

On November 2, 1961, two months after the Fifth Knesset was convened, the Prime Minister presented his new Government, which adhered to the Basic Policy approved by the preceding Knesset on December 17, 1959. The proposed Cabinet was as follows: David Ben-Gurion, Prime Minister and Minister of Defense; Abba Eban, Minister of Education and Culture; Yigal Allon, Minister of Labor; Yosef Almogi, Minister without portfolio; Levi Eshkol, Minister of Finance; Yosef Burg, Minister of Welfare; Yitzhak Ben-Aharon, Minister of Transport; Moshe Dayan, Minister of Agriculture; Zerah Warhaftig, Minister for Religious Affairs; Dov Joseph, Minister of Justice; Giora Josephthal Minister of Development and Housing; Golda Meir, Minister for Foreign Affairs; Pinhas Sapir, Minister of Commerce and Industry; Behor Shitreet, Minister of Police; Moshe Shapira, Minister of the Interior and of Health; Eliahu Sasson, Minister of Posts. They represented a coalition of only four parties: Mapai (11 members), Hapoel Hamizrahi (3 members), Ahdut Haavodah-Paolei Zion (2 members), and Paolei Agudat Israel (no ministers).

The debate on the Government slate ended the same day. The Prime Minister did not discuss the Basic Policy, since it remained unchanged. Of his response to the debate, we will note only what he said on points raised at the final meeting of the Fourth Knesset in connection with the validity of the conclusions of the Government and the Knesset regarding the Committee of Seven:

> The Knesset is sovereign but we must bear in mind in what respects it is so. It has no sovereignty to establish law regarding historical fact, such as whether or not Job actually existed in real life. Even if the Knesset decides unanimously that Job never existed, any Jew can come along and say he did. Neither the Government nor the Knesset has the judicial authority to determine what took place in history, nor even what happened eight years ago. Such assertions are of no value. I do not have to believe what I am told if I know otherwise.
>
> Thus there are areas to which the Knesset's sovereignty does not apply. Where it does apply is to the enaction of legislation, to making policy, to telling citizens how they should behave toward one another, what relations shall be maintained with foreign nations, what taxes we will pay, and whether or not there will be war, roads will be paved, or the Negev developed. The Knesset is not authorized to write history. The Government is not so authorized, nor does it have the power to decide disputes between individuals. For this purpose the law has provided one institution only—the judiciary.

Hanan Rubin (Mapam): "Where does it say that?"

Prime Minister: "Every civilized nation makes a distinction between the executive arm and the judiciary."

Rubin: "Where does it say that in the law of Israel?"

Prime Minister: "Is there no law regarding judges and courts? Just because it is not written that Hanan Rubin may not sit in judgment, does that mean he may do so? The law should specify who is and who is not entitled to judge. Is there no law in the Land of Israel? Is there no law stipulating how disputes between two parties should be adjudicated? Is there no law saying every man is innocent until proven guilty? This is one of the basic tenets of government, not only in the democracies but in every government endowed with a minimum of humanity. A distinction must be made between the executive and the judiciary. The executive operates differently. The executive decides which taxes to impose, whether or not an absorption tax should be imposed. It decides what the nation needs and brings it to the Knesset. If the Knesset gives its approval, there is an absorption tax; if not, there isn't."

Menahem Begin (Herut): "Didn't the previous Minister of Justice understand what you are saying?"

Prime Minister: "Ask him. A judicial procedure is provided when you want to clarify facts, when two people differ with one another, when either one or the other is a criminal. When the Government that I headed did something that contravened basic human rights, I resigned in order to bring about the resignation of the entire Government. I am proud of what I did. No decision by the Knesset can give validity to a violation of the fundamental principles of justice, and certainly the Knesset does not have the power to establish what occurred in the year 1954, especially when it didn't even make an effort to investigate it."

Many members were surprised that no one of the Coalition or even of the Opposition took issue with the Prime Minister's statement as to the Knesset's limited sovereignty and the Cabinet's lack of authority to sit in judgment. After the Speaker put the proposed Government to a vote, he announced: "By a majority of sixty-three to forty-six the Knesset expresses confidence in the Government headed by David Ben-Gurion." All the Cabinet members who were in attendance (four were absent) then signed declarations of allegiance to the State of Israel and its laws.

Though the Government Coalition was smaller than that in the previous Knesset, the Fifth Knesset, unlike the Fourth, was destined to complete its term. The four years were marked by a considerable increase in immigration compared to previous periods. While in 1960 a total of 22,847 persons arrived, in 1961 the figure was doubled to 46,650 and in 1962 and 1963 it continued to rise; 59,600 persons arrived in 1962 and 62,156 in 1963. The following two years saw a slowdown in immigration—52,456 in 1964 and 28,795 in 1965.

During this period the national budget increased as well. (The fiscal year begins on April 1 and ends the following March 31). The 1961–1962 budget was IL 1,876,350; the 1962–1963 budget, IL 2,375 million; the 1963–1964 budget, IL 2,790 million; and the 1964–1965 budget, IL 3,465 million. Thus in four years the budget practically doubled.

Exports almost doubled as well. (The export year begins in January and ends in December.) Though imports, of course, also increased, in the first three years the growth in exports far exceeded that of imports. In the fourth year (1964) the export-import ratio declined. In 1961 net exports totaled $239,082,000 and net imports $583,919,000, making the export ratio 40.9 percent. In 1962 net exports totaled $271,403,000, net imports $626,222,000; and the more favorable export ratio was 43.3 percent. In 1963 net exports were $338,295,000, net imports $663,506,000 and the ratio almost 50 percent. In 1964, however, net exports were $356,800,000; net imports $817,303,000, and the ratio was down to 43 percent.

Though 1961 was marked by expanded immigration the unemployment rate declined. There was almost full employment and even a shortage of unskilled labor. Despite the import-export gap the economy continued to accumulate foreign currency reserves as a result of increased influx of foreign capital. The real output of industry and crafts increased by 13.5 percent compared to 11.6 percent in 1960. At the end of 1961 there were 188,000 persons employed in industry and crafts compared to 170,000 at the end of 1960. In the developing areas 182 industrial plants and workshops had been added.

This expansion continued in 1962. At the end of the year a total of 197,000 persons were employed in industry. Industrial investment was IL286 million compared to IL227 million in 1961. Ninety-one industrial plants and workshops were erected in 1962 in development areas, with a total investment of IL2,608,600. The Israeli diamond industry continued its rapid growth in exports and number of people employed; in 1962 the Israeli diamond industry employed 7000 persons—one-quarter of the world's total. The export of agricultural produce also rose: $63,130,000 in 1961, $67,100,000 in 1962; as did industrial exports: from $63,606,000 to $212,370,000. Of the $280 million of exports, Europe took $170 million, America $50 million, Asia $30 million, Africa $12 million, and other countries $18 million.

In 1963 immigration reached its high-water mark for the 1960s. The number of workers employed in industry reached 210,000. Industrial exports reached $261,500,000, compared to $213 million in 1962. Industrial output grew by 14.5 percent, to $5.2 billion. A total of 955 plants in developing areas provided work for 36,000. The plantation area grew to 1,505,000 dunams from 1,440,000 dunams in the preceding year. Irrigated crops increased from 552,000 to 591,000 dunams. The total agricultural output increased from IL3.33 billion to IL3,590,000,000.

Although 1964 was marked by a slowdown in immigration, the number of persons employed in industry rose to 255,000. As the ratio of exports to imports declined, the trade deficit increased from 43 percent in 1963 to 50 percent. In 1963 the deficit was $324,794,000; in 1964 it was $452,281,000. In that year the number of villages increased to 804, a figure that included 367 moshavim and 231 kibbutzim.

In the four-year period 1960–1964, the number of students increased from 598,422 to 685,952, and in 1964–1965 to 711,274. Of this total the number of Jewish students was as follows: in 1960–1961—584,147; in 1963–1964—622,563; and in 1964–1965—643,709.

One of the rare labor disputes tabled for debate in the Fifth Knesset was an engineers' strike. On December 18, 1961, the following agreement was reached by the Histadrut [General Federation of Labor] Central Committee, representatives of the Engineers' Association, and a representative of the Ministry of Finance:

> A committee of five shall be set up composed of a member of the Experts' Committee, two representatives of the Engineers' Association, one of the Government, and one of the Histadrut Central Committee. The function of the committee is to examine and decide finally the exact rate at which the change in the engineers' salaries shall take place, bearing in mind the findings of the Experts' Committee, the objections and reservations of the Engineers' Association, basing itself upon the letter of the Histadrut Executive Council of May 26, 1958, and the decision of the Central Committee of June 23, 1961. The committee shall conclude its work by January 5, 1962.

The committee held six long meetings and arrived at the following decisions: (a) to take into account the changes in differentials that took place between the base year 1958–1959, and 1960–1961, namely 5.9 percent; (b) to accept the contention of the engineers that in calculating the differentials, the changes in the wages of foremen and permanent employees in Solel Boneh should also be taken into account, which added 7 percent to the benefit of the engineers. Summing up, the committee decided that the differentials had been reduced by 6.6 percent between 1958–1959 and 1960–1961. At the same time it agreed that in calculating salaries, the increase should be rounded up from 6.6 percent to 7 percent.

Upon learning these committee conclusions, the two representatives of the engineers announced that they would not accept them and would take no further part in the deliberations. This was followed by a decision by the engineers to strike. On January 17, 1962, the Prime Minister made the following statement on behalf of the Cabinet:

> The Government regards this behavior by the engineers' representatives and their organization, violating the undertaking accepted by them when the committee of five was set up, as a grave blow at the entire system of collective bargaining that is the basis of working and wage arrangements in this country, as in all democratic countries, and the introduction of dangerous anarchy in labor relations and labor organization.
>
> This is the first case, as far as the Government is aware, in the history of labor relations in this country, in which a workers' organization repudiates the signatures and undertakings of its representatives and tries to extort salaries that are not due to them, only because it assumes that it has the power to impose its will on the entire country by harmful acts and by interrupting the work of enterprises vital to the economy of the country and the people. The Government will not be deterred by the threats of an unauthorized strike and in its due concern both for the economy and for the integrity, responsibility, and organization of the workers, will adopt all essential and legal measures to maintain the vital services in the State and the economy and will not pay a penny to those who do not wish to work. If the Knesset wishes to hold a debate the Government has no objection.

The debate took place on January 22 and 23. A motion was then presented by Akiva Govrin on behalf of the Mapai, the National Religious Party, Ahdut Haavodah-Poalei Zion, Poalei Agudat Israel, Shituf V'Ahvah, and Kidmah u'Fituah, reading: "The Knesset takes cognizance of the Prime Minister's statement on January 17, 1962, regarding the engineers' strike." It was adopted by a vote of fifty-three to twenty-eight.

The Government Acts To Stabilize the Economy

On February 12, 1962, the Minister of Finance, Levi Eshkol, submitted to the Knesset the Government's program for the stabilization of the economy, in three chapters. The first, dealing with the rate of exchange for foreign trade, contained three sections:

I: *Rate of Exchange For Foreign Trade:*

1. The Israeli pound will be fixed at a uniform rate of three per US dollar. This rate will apply to the export of goods and services, to imports, and to capital transfers. With the establishment of the new rate, the premium system for the export of goods and services, and subsidies for capital transfers, will be abolished.

2. Most levies on imports goods will be abolished. The import of equipment and, in part, of raw materials will be entirely free of customs. Customs rates on other goods will also be considerably reduced.

3. Relying on the new exchange rate as a brake against excessive expansion of imports, we shall be able gradually to remove administrative restrictions on imports. We shall also work for the simplification of procedure in matters of foreign trade, including the abolition of the need for import permits in regard to certain categories of goods.

The second chapter contained four sections:

1. We shall gradually lower the barriers of excessive protection of local produce against imports, in order to place the branches of industry and agriculture on a basis of cheap and efficient production. It is our intention to limit the ceiling of protective duties and to abolish quantitative restrictions on imports. Outside the sphere of protection, local goods will have to face competition with imported goods.

2. The Government will continue to assist by granting development loans on easy terms; it will also help, by training of staffs and in other ways, to establish new undertakings and improve the efficiency of existing ones. However, we shall make sure that aid will be given only to those undertakings which, after a not excessive period of preparation and adaptation, will be able to face competitive conditions in both foreign and local markets.

3. The Government will soon establish the framework and the regulations for planning the development of the various branches of the economy for a period of four to five years. We will thus work for the development of the economy according to a long-range plan.

4. The Government will act in cooperation with the Histadrut to establish measures to ensure greater labor efficiency in manufacturing enterprises and Government and public services.

The third chapter contained eleven sections:

1. The Government will take measures to ensure stability of prices. It will ensure abundant supply of both local and imported products, and when necessary will provide subsidies from its budget to prevent an increase in the prices of essential products. The prices of oils will not change, and the price of sugar will not be raised. The Government will also prevent, as far as possible, an increase in the rates charged for its services.

2. The Government will take measures to prevent unjustified profits and excessive expenditures that lead to an increase in prices. We intend to intensify our activities within the framework of the Restraint of Trade Law to prevent high profits. We will also act by fiscal means to prevent excessive profits if the need should arise.

3. The Government intends, in cooperation with the Histadrut, to take appropriate steps to ensure the implementation of the principle that any rise in wages shall not exceed the rate of increase in the net national output. Accordingly, a suitable part of the additional output will be devoted to lowering the prices of our products in foreign markets and only part will be directed to increasing incomes.

4. The cost-of-living allowance system will be maintained.

5. As part of the efforts to be made by all concerned to ensure the stability of the economy, the Government will contribute its share by refraining from raising taxes, apart, naturally, from the financing of unexpected emergency needs. At the same time we shall endeavor to improve tax collections in general, and ensure the collection of just taxes from those with high incomes, especially companies.

6. The Government will endeavor to persuade recipients of personal restitution payments to continue to invest a considerable part of their compensation payments in fixed-term deposits in the banks, under conditions ensuring reasonable income.

7. We will endeavor to balance Government finances on both a budgetary and a cash basis.

8. Bank credit to the public will be extended at a rate not exceeding the rate of increase of real output.

9. We shall intensify our efforts to increase savings, in the confidence that the stabilization of the economy and the currency on a firm basis will increase the tendency of all sections of the public to save.

10. Any proposal for the acceptance of a foreign loan will be examined, before being

approved, from the point of view of the length of the term of the loan, its contribution to the raising of the level of production in the economy, and the need for foreign currency.

11. The establishment of a stable rate for the Israeli pound makes it possible to stop the acceptance and granting of loans linked to the exchange rate. The Government will, of course, honor all its obligations arising out of linking clauses in bonds that it has issued in the past and on its other debts. The Government will examine the possibility of making suitable arrangements in regard to the redemption dates of the linked loans to agricultural settlers and producers in other branches, if their incomes do not rise. The Government will examine the possibility of making concessions in accordance with need in the redemption dates of loans related to the exchange rates given to residents in popular housing schemes.

The Minister of Finance added that after conferring with the Minister of Commerce and Industry, the Manufacturers Association, and the Merchants Association, they had decided to instruct members not to raise prices apart from the few cases that were a necessary consequence of the change in the rate of exchange. Marketing organizations such as Hamashbkr Hamerkazi, Tnuva, and others would also contribute their share to the overall effort of price stabilization.

We had been able to implement this program to stabilize the economy, he said, with no fear that it would cause unemployment, with the suffering and hardship it entails. It was good that we had managed to introduce the program in a period of full employment. Our main object was to raise the competitive ability of the economy. This meant that a reduction in the price of our products both in foreign and local markets was the order of the day.

Yohanan Bader (Herut) asserted that the working public did not want devaluation. Since Friday (when the Government had decided on this program, two days before it was brought to the Knesset) a price revolution had taken place. Was this stabilization? We are in a wretched situation in which each year we consume several hundred thousand dollars that we did not earn. This would have to stop.

Yosef Sapir (Liberal Party): If we wished the Israeli economy to integrate in the European and world markets, its competitive ability had to be more or less equal to that required by these markets, in terms not only of price but in quality of production. The competitive ability of the overwhelming majority of the Israeli economy was 20 to 25 percent lower than that of other economies. The imminent problem was the danger to export production.

Yacov Hazan (Mapam): The Government should have maintained a pioneering regime—one that would not have permitted the rise of an ever growing class of people getting rich at the expense of the general public, present and future. In view of the danger of inflation the Government should have absorbed the surplus buying power of the rich by progressive property taxes and compulsory loan and savings schemes and only then imposed the burden of construction on the shoulders of people of limited means. It was the Government that had encouraged the process of fragmentation and economic polarization of Israeli society instead of doing its best to build a society whose basis would be austerity and pioneering rather than the pursuit of wealth and profit. The Government was therefore responsible for the present crisis.

Israel Bar-Yehuda (Ahdut Haavodah) replied to Hazan: The three months during which the present Government had been in office are not enough to make the citizens of Israel forget six years of participation in previous Governments, something which Knesset member Hazan had managed to do in pretending he was born only yesterday.

Debate on the economy and currency continued intermittently until February 19, 1962. On that date the Knesset adopted a proposal by Meir Argov on behalf of Mapai, the National Religious Party, Ahdut Haavodah-Poalei Zion, Poalei Agudat Israel, Kidmah u'Fituah, and Shituf v'Ahvah: "The Knesset takes note of the announcement by the Minister of Finance on behalf of the Government of the plan to stabilize the currency exchange rate and the economy." The vote was sixty-six to forty-three.

The Abduction and Recovery of Yossele Schumacher

A unique case, with both human and political implications, shook the country at this time.

In 1957 Alter and Ida Schumacher and their children arrived in Israel from the Soviet Union. Because of difficulties in getting settled and obtaining suitable housing, they gave their two children, Yosef and Zila, to Mrs. Schumacher's father, Nahman Shtarkes, on condition that he return them when the financial situation of his daughter and son-in-law had improved and they had found a place to live. At the start of the 1959 school year the parents came for the children. Shtarkes returned the girl immediately but made all sorts of excuses for holding on to the boy and even refused to let the parents see him. Eventually Shtarkes told them that the boy had been hidden and would not be returned because the Schumachers, he charged, were planning to return to Russia and cut off the child from his Jewish faith.

According to a statement in the Knesset by Minister of Police Shitreet, the grandfather claimed this right on the basis of a letter from the late Rabbi Zvi Pesah Frank which read:

> Whereas Reb Nahman Shtarkes is preventing his grandson, Yosef Schumacher, from leaving the country, and whereas his son-in-law wished to take him to Russia, where he will, as is well known, be severed from the religion of Israel, Reb Nahman Shtarkes is required by the law of the Torah to detain his grandson lest he depart the Land of Israel for the place where apostasy is decreed upon Jews; and whereas, according to the law of the Torah, what applies to sons applies equally to grandsons, Reb Nahman is required to do everything in his power to prevent the boy from becoming an apostate and an infidel, and anyone who can assist him in this is obliged to do so with all his power. In witness whereof I affix my signature. Zvi Pesah Frank has spoken.

Through their lawyer the parents applied to the Supreme Court in February 1960 for an order against Shtarkes and his wife, Miriam, and the court directed that Shtarkes restore the boy, generally called Yossele, to his parents by February 15, 1960. When Grandfather Shtarkes failed to comply, the court ordered (1) that he be imprisoned until he agreed to restore the boy to his parents, or until the court ordered otherwise; (2) that the Inspector General of the Police take all necessary measures to find the boy and turn him over to his parents.

The police took all possible steps. They questioned everyone connected with the Shtarkeses; conducted searches wherever the child might be concealed; placed informers in the grandfather's social circles; organized negotiations between Shtarkes and the child's parents; and negotiated with persons of influence who might persuade the grandfather to give up the child. On April 25, 1960, the police informed the court that they were unable to locate Yossele.

The Supreme Court on May 12 directed the police to continue the search, even if it involved the possibility of violent resistance. "The impression gained from the report," the court said, "is that the police have taken extensive action to find the boy through detective work, the gathering of intelligence, and attempts to bring the two sides to a compromise. It is also our impression that the police have encountered opposition and interference on the part of a segment of the public which supports the grandfather in his refusal to reveal the boy's whereabouts or restore him to his parents. In view of the extensive work to date, we leave the scope of the activities to be undertaken henceforth in locating the boy completely to the discretion of the Police Inspector General."

The issue was brought to the Knesset on June 8, 1960, following a proposal by two members of Agudat Israel, who to a certain extent defended the grandfather. When the debate grew heated the Minister of Police suggested that the matter be referred to the Internal Affairs Committee. On July 5 this committee declared that the police had acted with considerable restraint in its search for Yossele and noted the Inspector General's statement that in view of the Supreme Court's decision, no effort would henceforth be spared in locating him. It called upon all citizens to assist the police.

The search continued but in vain. On May 23, 1961, the affair was once again raised in the Knesset by Emma Talmi (Mapam). "This is a matter of life and death," she said. "Considerable time has gone by and every passing day deepens the pain and anxiety of Yossele's parents and the public at large. From the moment the grandfather denied knowledge of the boy's whereabouts it stopped being a family quarrel and became a matter of a felony and a dangerous moral and legal precedent." The Minister of Police agreed with her and stated that the police were making an all-out effort. They had called on rabbis, friends, and relatives to prevail upon Shtarkes to surrender the child, but the stubborn old man was supported by a group that adhered to the edict of the late Rabbi Frank, and for whom nothing else in the world—neither the law of the State nor an order by the Supreme Court—was of any value. Though the grandfather had appealed to the court to be released for three months during which time he would do everything in his power to locate and return the boy, he was not cooperating.

The problem was returned to the Interior Committee. It heard a further report by the Inspector General on June 13, 1961, on the fruitless efforts to find Yossele. A total of 852 persons had been questioned; 400 searches had encountered nothing but rigid obduracy on religious grounds. He concluded that the boy was no longer in Israel and neither was the man who had taken him out of the country. On April 5, 1962, the Minister of Police again proposed that the matter be referred to the Interior Committee, touching off a Knesset debate.

Emma Talmi (Mapam) declared: The Supreme Court verdict showed that the grandfather was a wily old fox who was taking advantage of his position. When asked for the boy's whereabouts by the President of the Court he replied, "I refuse to answer," adding, "He is among Jews." There were people in Israel who had had a hand in the shameful act of concealing a child from his parents, an act morally and legally tantamount to the atrocious crime of abducting a minor from his natural guardians. She quoted these views from the court verdict.

Baruh Uziel (Liberal Party): "This is a brutal crime and one which brings up frightful memories from days of childhood when we read *The Laughing Man* by Victor Hugo and *In Those Days* by Yehuda Steinberg, that told of children being kidnapped by the Gentiles in order to convert them to Christianity. We all feel revulsion for this crime and for the foul group that perpetrated it, for it is a group and not a single malefactor. Acts such as these will decrease respect for religion among the youth. The silence on the part of all religious elements, whom I know to be loyal to the State of Israel, has made an impression that is very damaging."

Menahem Cohen (Mapai): "I have gone to see the old man half a dozen times. I was there when his daughter came to visit him and begged with tears in her eyes that her son be returned. In my presence he drew himself up to his full height and slapped her across the face. It took a number of guards to keep him from scratching her to pieces."

Rabbi Y.M. Levin (Agudat Israel): "What we have here is a tendency evident among anti-Semites at all times and all places: when a single individual or a small group does something, everyone accuses the Jews as a whole. They ask us, Why are you silent? Maybe you should ask yourselves why *you* are silent. Since the foundation of the State a network of missionaries has been operating with the purpose of abducting children and converting them to a different faith. Have you ever raised your voices against this?"

At the close of the heated argument the Knesset adopted the proposal of Akiva Govrin on behalf of the following parties: Mapai, Herut, Liberal Party, National Religious Party, Mapam, Ahdut Haavodah-Poalei Zion, Poalei Agudat Israel, Shituf v'Ahvah, and Kidmah u'Fituah. Fifty-six members voted in favor of this proposal, two abstained, and none was opposed. It read as follows: "1. The Knesset denounces the concealment and abduction of the boy, Yosef Schumacher, from his parents. 2. It takes note of the announcement by the Minister of Police regarding the efforts being made to restore Yosef Schumacher to his parents and calls for intensified efforts on this behalf. 3. The Knesset calls on every member of the public to make every possible effort to secure the boy's return to his parents. 4. The Knesset refers the debate to the Internal Affairs Committee."

By the middle of March 1962 little doubt remained that the boy had been smuggled out of the country. The Prime Minister ordered Issar Harel, Chief of the Security Services, to find and bring him back to Israel. Less than three and a half months later Yossele was traced to the United States, in the Williamsburg section of Brooklyn, New York, a stronghold of the fanatic disciples of the Satmer Rabbi. The boy was living there under the name of Yacov Gertner.

Yossele's mother and sister flew to New York and the boy was restored to them on July 3, 1962. The dramatic reunion took place in the offices of the US Immigration authorities where the mother and sister had gone straight from the airport. When she entered the room and saw Yossele, the mother burst into tears and embraced him crying, "My son, my son!" At first Yossele stood passively, but in a little while he called Ida Schumacher "Mama" over and over again. The boy's identification was facilitated by his resemblance to photographs from a few years back which the mother had brought with her, and by his clear resemblance to his young sister, Zila.

Mr. Gertner, who had harbored the boy and given him his name, told immigration investigators that the child had been brought to him by a woman who claimed she had come from Argentina, was his mother, and would come to collect him later. On July 4, 1962, mother, daughter, and son arrived at Lod Airport in Israel, where the father and a large crowd were on hand to meet them. On the same day the grandfather was released from Ramia Central Prison. He also came to the airport but was not allowed to approach his grandson. The reunited Schumachers returned to their home in Holon. A three-years' press sensation had come to a happy end.

Syrian Position for Attacks Is Demolished ★ UN Security Council Censures Israel ★ Knesset Reaffirms Right to Self-Defense ★ The Soblen Expulsion

While the Israeli public was still agitated by the Yossele Schumacher affair, attacks were intensified on Israel's eastern and northern borders by its most implacable enemy, Syria.

Thirteen years had passed since the signing of the Armistice Agreements with the neighboring countries that had invaded Israel the day its independence was proclaimed. The first article (paragraph 2) stated that "no aggressive action by the armed forces—land, sea, or air—of either party shall be undertaken, planned, or threatened against the people or the armed forces of the other." Had Israel not been able to defend itself with its own forces, in accordance with Article 51 of the UN Charter, the lives of every citizen and resident of Israel would have been in jeopardy from the incessant attacks by the Arab states that had signed the Agreements.

The Sinai Campaign in 1956 assured us of relative peace on the Egyptian and Jordanian borders. But through all these years Egypt had continued to violate the Security Council resolutions adopted unanimously in 1951 and again in 1956, affirming freedom of passage through the Suez Canal. The UN censured Egypt for denying a UN member its international right to freedom of navigation in the canal. Nor was this the only occasion on which its discrimination against Israel called into question the moral basis on which the UN was founded.

In contrast with the relative peace on the borders of the Gaza Strip and Sinai desert, as well as on the frontier with Jordan, depredations across the Syrian frontiers increased. In the six years following the Sinai events the Syrians relentlessly attacked Israeli patrols moving within our territory and Israeli settlements along the border in the north and the east. In the final two months of 1956 there were 11 such attacks, in 1957, 125; in 1958, 100; in 1959, 50; in 1960, 67; in 1961, 25; and in the first three months of 1962, 26 episodes. These aggressions were committed mostly by regular Syrian forces, and resulted in the death or injury of 122 Israelis.

In the middle of March 1962 the Syrians opened fire several times on our settlements on the east bank of Lake Kinneret. The entire lake, including a ten-meter-wide strip of shore north of Kibbutz Ein Gev and east of the Jordan, was sovereign Israeli territory. When the attacks from a Syrian position near the village of Nukeib were stepped up, the Minister of Defense, on March 16, 1962, on the basis of a Government decision, ordered this Syrian position near Nukeib destroyed. The operation was carried out by a unit of the Golani Brigade. The Artillery and Air Force were ordered to stand by, just in case.

Ein Gev was bombarded the whole night, though all the inhabitants had taken refuge in the shelters before the raid began. Our forces encountered well-planned resistance—

mines and artillery—but overcame it and demolished the Syrian position. Five of our men were killed. A number of buildings were destroyed and the electrical system was knocked out. Our artillery fired back at the Syrian batteries.

The Syrian government complained to the UN Security Council. The Syrian leaders had no fear of being censured for their violation of the Armistice Agreement and incessant attacks on Israeli forces and border settlements. They could rely on a veto by the Great Power on the Security Council that made more use of its right to veto than all the other members put together. The United States delegation chose to formulate a resolution of censure against Israel that would meet with the approval of Egypt, at that time a member of the Security Council. In his speech on March 28, 1962, the American ambassador at the UN, Adlai Stevenson, spoke of provocation and retaliation, but did not find it necessary to point out who was responsible for the provocation; neither did he feel obliged to define Syrian attacks by machine guns and recoilless artillery on Israeli patrol boats on Lake Kinneret as violations of the Armistice Agreement, calling them "anonymous" provocations.

In his report and in replies to questions by the Security Council, the head of the UN Truce Supervision Observers, Maj. Gen. Carl Von Horn concealed every trace of the Syrian attacks on March 8, 15, 16, and 20 on Israeli patrol boats in the Kinneret. He failed to report a single case in which Syrians opened fire on Israeli settlements or on Israeli fishermen and police patrol boats on the lake. The Council, moreover, ignored Syria's constant declarations denying Israel's right to exist.

The Syrian Premier, Dawalibi, addressing his Constituent Assembly on January 8, had said: "Syria's main problem is Palestine. As long as Palestine has not been restored to the Arabs as part of free Arab life, as long as the Zionist specter has not been exorcized, as long as the parasitic State of Israel has not been annihilated, Syria regards herself as suffering a severe injury that endangers her existence and that of the Arab nation." (Soon after this speech the Syrian Parliament and the government of Dawalibi were forcibly overthrown by the military.) Zahr-e-Din, Commander-in-Chief of the Syrian Army, at the graduation ceremony of an officers' course at Latakia on January 13, spoke in the same spirit: "The Mediterranean Sea is Israel's nautical front with the Arabs. To strangle and destroy Israel, the Arabs must pluck out Israel's sea lung by means of a naval combat force that will constitute a wall of steel in the sea and deny air to this monstrous state."

On April 9 the Security Council adopted the strongly worded resolution censuring Israel, as formulated by the United States and Great Britain. Of the Great Powers, only France abstained from voting in favor of it. The next day, April 10, the Prime Minister denounced the resolution in the Knesset:

> Israel will not tolerate any attacks on Lake Kinneret fishermen or on Israeli patrol boats on the lake, which is entirely in Israel's sovereign territory. Israel will not tolerate any attack on settlements and citizens inside her territory, and she will defend herself with all the means at her disposal if any of her neighbors violate the Armistice Agreements and endanger the peace and the lives of Israeli citizens or encroach on her territorial integrity. As long as there is any danger of aggression by our neighbors Israel will continue to rely on the Israel Defense Forces, and our people knows that it can rely on them.
>
> We consider yesterday's resolution by the Security Council as based on a double standard, and an encouragement to our neighbors—even if not so intended by those who drafted

the resolution—to continue their attacks on Israel's citizens and her sovereign territory. This appeasement of Syrian aggression does not redound to the honor of the UN or strengthen peace in our area. I should like to note with profound appreciation the one country—France—that abstained from voting for this dubious resolution.

Finally, Israel will abstain from any violation of the Armistice Agreements and will comply strictly with their terms, but she will under no circumstances submit to violation of the Agreements by her neighbors, nor will she on any account waive her right to self-defense, which is reserved to every nation and safeguarded by the UN Charter.

All speakers in the Knesset debate condemned the Security Council action. The one exception was Esther Wilenska (Communists) who said that "the vote of censure represents a moral and political failure for the Ben-Gurion policy of relying on the elements of imperialism. Ben-Gurion's old cronies, the rulers of the United States and England, have denounced the raid. Even France, whom Israel admires, did not vote *against* the resolution."

At the close of the debate Meir Argov offered the following motion:

1. The Knesset categorically rejects the Security Council resolution of April 9, 1962—a resolution that displays one-sidedness, completely ignores the frequent attacks on Israel by the armed forces of Syria, and constitutes an injustice that encourages aggression and endangers peace.

2. Israel is surrounded by hostile nations that maintain a constant state of belligerency against her. The Knesset declares that Israel's right of self-defense is an inalienable sovereign right assured to every nation by the United Nations Charter.

3. Israel is loyal to the principles of the United Nations and she will fulfill all the obligations involved toward every state on the basis of reciprocity. She will not submit to aggression.

4. Israel will preserve her sovereignty in principle and in practice, over all her territory and waters.

On behalf of the Israel Communist Party, Moshe Sneh proposed the following resolution:

1. The Knesset finds that the Nukeib action was not an inescapable consequence of the requirements of national self-defense but a premeditated act of aggression.

2. The Knesset calls upon the Government to do everything in its power to maintain peace and quiet on the borders and to refrain from any military raids, reprisals, or acts of aggression whatsoever.

3. The Knesset declares that the prevailing policy of military adventurism and service to the imperialist powers is fraught with dangers to Israel.

The resolutions did not reach a vote for several weeks. In the interval another issue—the expulsion from Israel of a Jew convicted of espionage in the courts of the United States—was before the Knesset. On July 4 Knesset member Sneh (Communists) addressed some questions to the Minister of the Interior:

1. Why was Dr. Reuven (Robert) Soblen expelled from Israel despite the fact that under the circumstances [he faced a long prison term for espionage in the United States] expulsion in effect meant extradition, and even if an extradition treaty with the United States were in force, it would not apply to this category of criminal?

2. Whereas the abovementioned is a Jew and the Law of the Return applies to him and

the same Law of the Return does not give you the authority to expel someone who had entered the country as an "illegal immigrant," on what grounds did you in this case deny this Jew the right provided in the Law of the Return?

3. Why was Dr. Soblen's attorney not given time to apply to the court to delay the expulsion order and the order executed with such haste as to present the attorney with a fait accompli?

4. Why was the expulsion order issued and executed despite the fact that Soblen had previously been remanded for ten days by a Magistrate's Court? (*I.e.*, his expulsion by the executive arm was in violation of a decision by the judiciary.)

5. In issuing the expulsion order, why did you not take account of the fact that the man was suffering from a fatal illness?

The Minister of the Interior, Moshe Shapira, replied in the Knesset on July 10:

1. Dr. Soblen was expelled from the country in accordance with the Government's policy, which I have often stated, that Israel is not intended to serve as a refuge for escaped criminals. The implementation of the expulsion order, in my opinion, does not constitute extradition.

2. Dr. Soblen was expelled not under the Law of the Return but under Section 13 of the Law of Entry into Israel. The Law of the Return applies to every Jew who submits an application and expresses his desire to settle in Israel. Dr. Soblen did not request an immigrant visa under the Law of the Return nor did I receive such a request on his behalf. But even if such a request had been submitted to me, I would have rejected it, on the strength of my authority under the Law of the Return.

3. Mr. Soblen's attorney had three days in which to apply to the high court to prevent or delay the issuing of the expulsion order.

(Yacov Riftin of Mapam interjected: "Three days including Shabbat!" Shapira retorted: "If saving a life is involved, then even on Shabbat. I did not feel it was our job to guide the attorney in protecting his client's rights.")

4. The execution of the expulsion order was assigned to the police as was the remand order issued by the court. Although there had been no judicial ruling on this subject, in the view of the police and the Attorney General, a remand order under Section 10 (3) of the Code of Criminal Procedure (Arrests and Searches) does not obligate the police to detain a person but merely permits them to do so. If the police detain a remanded prisoner for only part of the period specified in the remand order, or if they waive this right altogether, this in itself does not conflict with the decision of the court.

5. Before leaving the country Dr. Soblen was examined by a physician who found no medical reason why he was unfit to travel.

Three parties, the Liberals, Mapam, and Communists, offered a no-confidence motion based on the expulsion of Dr. Soblen.

Yizhar Harari, for the Liberals, pointing out that Dr. Soblen was expelled by administrative order, contended that opportunity should be provided to debate such administrative measures in the Knesset. As long as the person being expelled has not left the country, he can be detained. But why was Soblen escorted out of Israel by a police doctor? According to the newspapers there was another escort as well in the person of an American detective. Are there American detectives posted at the gateways to the country waiting to escort anyone who is expelled?

Expulsion under Section 13 of the Law of Entry, he went on, means their expulsion from Israel and not more that that—not their delivery to a given country and certainly not one that seeks their extradition. In the case of wanted criminals there is an extradition law according to which, after a request for extradition has been submitted by another country, the person in question must be brought before a district court. We have heard that pressure was applied by American Jewry to have Soblen expelled. But our actions here in Israel must be guided by law rather than by pressure on the part of American Jewry. A section of the Law of the Return added in 1954 states that "no immigration permit shall be issued to persons with criminal records who are liable to endanger the public welfare." Though Dr. Soblen had a criminal record it is doubtful if he would have posed a danger to public welfare in Israel. The gravest aspect of this entire affair is the haste with which the authorities acted in expelling him Sunday morning without notifying his attorney.

Mikunis (Communists) held that the Government had sinned in handing Soblen over to the "American McCarthyite witch-hunters." The Prime Minister had proven himself a senior servant of the American atomic hysteria mongers and the Minister of the Interior a senior servant of Dictator Ben-Gurion.

Bentov (Mapam) said he did not wish to enter into the moral problem of whether persons who, like Dr. Soblen, had been convicted of espionage should or should not be extradited. Extradition, expulsion, or prevention of application of the Law of the Return were judicial procedures that should not be implemented without authorization by the courts. The 'Government had removed a prisoner from jail in violation of the judge's order.

Golda Meir: "Even if he was under detention, a judge's order is an order. He cannot be removed without another order being issued."

Joseph, Minister of Justice: "That's not so."

Bentov: "Sir, you are not the only jurist in this country. Soblen was not expelled, he was extradited. We don't know who or what American Jews brought the pressure to bear. There is no doubt that pressure was applied by the American representative. The United States Ambassador paid the Prime Minister an urgent visit."

Ben-Gurion: "A distinction should be made between the Law of the Return and the granting of asylum to criminals. If criminals came to Israel we would continue to expel them without applying to the courts. The law says that such a criminal should be expelled, not put on trial. If the law gave the Minister of the Interior such authority, he is responsible to see that it is upheld. It was his duty to see to it that criminals did not benefit from a windfall in Israel. The policy that this Government has had and would continue to follow will be stringently to observe the Law of the Return with all due honor and respect for Jewish and world public opinion, which knows and understands the true meaning of refuge in Israel.

"This refuge was something granted to Jews who did not wish to or could not remain where they were and wanted to come and settle in Israel and immediately on so doing became Israeli citizens, something that occurred in no other country. At the same time there existed a Law of Expulsion, so that criminals and offenders who somehow made their way to Israel would be deported. We should not falsify the State of Israel's image and should continue to expel criminals who entered the country illegally by due process of law, namely, the Law of Entry into Israel of 1952, enacted two years after the Law of the Return.

"Knesset member Bentov was either inaccurate or a victim of misleading information when he said that pressure had been applied by the United States Ambassador. The Ambassador called on me twice and asked about Soblen. I told him, "This is our affair and not yours," and he left immediately. While not belittling the attitude of any country, large or small, I take orders from no country in the world but act in accordance with our laws, weighing what is good for Israel, the Jewish people, and world peace.

"Soblen was not the first person to be expelled under Section 13 of the Entry Law. The first Jewish criminal expelled by the Minister of the Interior under this law was Frederick Grunwald, who had embezzled money deposited by thousands of not-wealthy people and when found out thought Israel would be a sure haven. But he was expelled. There was another case, that of a criminal from France named Janovice, who was expelled immediately. Soblen likewise entered the country under false pretenses with a forged passport and no visa, and was duly expelled by the Minister of the Interior. By law expulsion does not require resort to the courts. This Government will continue to expel crooks who entered Israel in violation of the law. All these cases of expulsion, Soblen's included, involved no act of extradition."

The no-confidence motion was defeated, fifty-three to twenty-eight. Three weeks later, however, on August 1, 1962, the Soblen case was once more raised in the Knesset. Yohanan Bader submitted another motion of no-confidence—this despite the fact that in connection with the earlier motion on July 11 leaders of his party had announced: "We have not made a motion of no-confidence in this matter. We are as well acquainted with this parliamentary weapon as our younger neighbors—younger in the sense of national service in the Opposition. In this decision we have been guided by the overwhelming national and moral consideration that such action might be misconstrued by people near and far, east or west, as support for the granting of asylum to persons such as Dr. Soblen under the conditions in which he came here. This was our only consideration and one that is decisive morally and from the point of view of our national interest. For this reason we will not propose a motion of no-confidence in this matter and we will not support those who have."

The reason Bader now gave for the reversal of his party's policy was that questions he had asked in the Finance Committee about the plane that took Soblen from Israel had not been answered. This, he said, violated the rules and regulations whereby a permanent committee may obtain explanations and information from a Minister. He had directed to the Minister of Transport a series of questions for which no answers had been forthcoming. According to Mr. Bader "the Minister said that some Cabinet committee composed of three interested Ministers was investigating and no answers would be forthcoming until it had completed its work."

"That's not what I said, and you know it," the Minister of Transport, Bar-Yehuda, remarked. "Then something like it," Bader answered, "The reason you didn't reply was because of that committee."

Bar-Yehuda: "Your statements do not correspond to reality."

Bader: "The fact remains you didn't answer. And for such questions to remain unanswered is a grave violation of parliamentary rights and the rights of the Opposition. Its amounts to contempt for the rights of the Opposition and contempt for the rights of the Opposition means contempt of Parliament and therefore I propose a motion of no-confidence in the Government."

The Prime Minister then entered the discussion: "Mr. Bader wants to express no-confidence in the Government because of Soblen's expulsion; but since the leaders of his party announced that they would not join in the no-confidence motion in the Soblen affair, he disguises his true intentions by trying to capitalize on the Opposition's right to ask questions in the Finance Committee.

"Now any Knesset member has the right to ask questions but this right is clearly defined in the Knesset Rules and Regulations. If the question does not come under the committee's purview the Minister is not required to reply; if it does come under its purview the Minister is obliged to reply to any committee member whether in the Opposition or the Government. The questions to which the Minister of Transport did not reply were unauthorized and in that respect I support him completely. The questions rightly pertained to an inquiry rather than the Finance Committee, and if there is any question as to a committee's purview, that is for the Knesset House Committee to decide.

"The Knesset Rules and Regulations clearly state (Section 13-b): 'The committee is entitled to require of the Minister concerned explanations and information regarding matters submitted for its consideration or which comes under its purview.' According to Section 12-a (2), the matters within the competence of the Finance Committee are 'the national budget, taxes of all kinds, customs and excise, loans, currency and foreign currency, banking and bank notes, national income and expenditure, and relations with the State Comptroller.' Soblen's expulsion does not come under these headings. Bader did well in expressing no-confidence not only in the Minister of Transport but in the Government since it fully supports the Minister's refusal to reply on matters that do not pertain to the Finance Committee."

The Bader motion was rejected fifty-eight to forty.

The two proposals relating to the UN censure were put to a vote. The one submitted by Argov on behalf of ten parties received seventy-five votes, the Communist substitute, three.

A great scholar, writer, pioneer, Zionist statesman, and revered leader of the Mizrahi movement, Rabbi Yehuda Leib Hacohen Maimon [Fishman] died on July 10, 1962, at the age of eighty-six. He had combined profound loyalty to religious heritage and tradition with unbounded love and devotion to the Jewish people and its national resurgence in its Homeland. From 1935 he was a member of the Zionist Executive and a member of the first elected Government. He founded the Rav Kook Institute, a publishing house specializing in studies in Judaism, Jewish history, and the future of Israel, and enriched Hebrew literature with important memoirs, and studies in Halakha and political problems, and was revered by all parties and trends, both religious and secular.

Debates at the Close of the First Knesset Session ★ Export of Army Uniforms to Germany ★ Israel's Nuclear Reactor ★ The Hula Ranch

The debate on the 1962–1963 budget began on February 27, 1962, and did not end until August 1, when it was adopted at third reading by a vote of forty-two to twenty-seven. In most sections the difference between the majority and minority proposals was only IL 1 million. The three days before adjournment of the first session of the Fifth Knesset on August 8 were crowded with questions and motions for the agenda. On August 6 alone twenty-nine questions were raised, taking up eleven pages in the *Divrai Haknesset*, and motions for the agenda filled twenty-one pages in the official record.

Avraham Drori (Herut) revived a subject debated thoroughly and at length on June 30 and July 1, 1959, when the Knesset by a vote of fifty-seven to forty-five approved the sale of arms to West Germany. Drori now demanded that "for the sake of the nation's moral stature, for the salvation of its sons, and to reduce hostility to the State, the Knesset firmly declares that this shameful deal must be rescinded." The "deal" involved was the manufacture by an Israeli factory of military uniforms for Germany. Drori charged that the Foreign Minister "has tried to deny the truth—the simple truth—that the degree of enmity if not the enmity itself of certain Eastern European nations is determined by among other things   the degree of friendship we demonstrate for Germany."

Yacov Riftin (Mapam) recalled a question that Rabbi Nurock had asked the Minister of Commerce and Industry, Pinhas Sapir, a week earlier: "Is the Minister aware that at the Ata plant seamstresses who have been through Nazi concentration camps are being compelled to sew uniforms for the German Army and for this reason have gone on strike?" Sapir replied that "the information on which the question is based has been denied by the factory and hence the question is not in place." David Hacohen (Mapai) asked Riftin why it was permissible to pick oranges and ship them to Germany and not to sew uniforms. Hacohen, Riftin retorted, seemed unable to distinguish between giving a murderer a gun and any other kind of giving, and was thus comparing the sewing of uniforms with shipment of medicine.

"During the 1959 debate on selling arms to Germany," said Sapir, "everyone had had a chance to speak and the Knesset made its decision. "I also recall," he said, "that in the debate on accepting reparations from Germany those who have now spoken maintained that this would enslave us forever to the German economy. Let me quote our export figures. In 1954 Germany bought $1.5 million of goods from us, and in 1961, $24 million. That is a sixteen-fold increase. Now the list of products we export to Germany includes citrus fruit. Though David Hacohen has already replied to Riftin, the question is really addressed to me. What applies to uniforms applies equally to citrus fruit. We send Germany fruit juice and concentrated fruit juice. Knesset member Riftin knows that a considerable part of the canning industry is controlled by the kibbutzim he represents. I have never heard anyone from these kibbutzim complain about shipping fruit juice to Germany. On the contrary, I have heard that these producers fight among themselves each year for the biggest orders."

The Minister then requested that the proposals for cancelling the uniform deal be dropped. Though Esther Wilenska (Communists) supported the proposals, it was decided by a large majority, fifty to twenty-eight, to drop the matter without referral to committee.

Shlomo Lorentz (Agudat Israel) complained about missionary activities in Israel, especially the building of a Christian village named Nes Amim in western Galilee. He was not saying it was forbidden for Christians to come and live in Israel; moreover, he had read in the papers that the heads of the village had undertaken not to engage in missionary activities. Nevertheless, he asked, was there any guarantee? He proposed that the Knesset or one of its committees consider this problem in order to find a fundamental solution and put an end to missionary activities once and for all.

The Minister of Religious Affairs, Warhaftig, replied: The Government is not indifferent to the problem of missionary work in Israel; the problem is serious. While we believe in freedom of religion, it is highly doubtful whether missionary activities properly belong under this heading. Yet he did not feel that a Knesset debate was likely to contribute to a solution and suggested referring the question to committee.

Yacov Hazan spoke of the nuclear arms race. "A balance of terror can be maintained only as long as nuclear weapons are restricted to the four Great Powers," he said. "The fact that they alone are responsible for their own fate and that of the entire human race is what restrains them and gives humanity hope that a disarmament treaty will be achieved before it is too late. This hope will be reduced to a desperate degree if nuclear arms fall into the hands of numerous other nations, large and small." Therefore, he maintained, "the only way out of this dilemma is indefatigable initiative on our part to secure the exclusion from our region of aggressive arms in general and nuclear weapons in particular. Obviously this can be done only if the Great Powers undertake not to provide our region with these weapons or the know-how for their construction and if international supervision is maintained over nuclear development in all the countries in the region."

His proposal was supported by Tewfik Toubi (Communists), who declared: "The Communist faction in the Knesset calls for a debate in which the Knesset will commit the Government to work for a Middle East free of atomic weapons and remove the danger of these arms being obtained by any government in this part of the world. We may differ on the problem of Palestine and that of relations between Israel and the Arab states. We feel that the Government of Israel is depriving the Palestine Arab nation of its rights and thus placing obstacles in the way of peace. There is no reason why there should not be unanimity in cases where our lives are concerned. The danger of nuclear arms must not be allowed to hang over our heads. We must not permit nuclear weapons to sit in judgment between our two peoples. This would be disastrous."

Ben-Gurion spoke on the problem at some length:

> Knesset member Hazan apparently does not realize that he contradicts himself. He said—and there is a certain amount of truth in it—that the use of atomic weapons anywhere in the world, even by a small country, is liable to lead to a worldwide conflagration. It follows logically that everything should be done to deny access to such arms to any country, large, medium, or small. This does not apply to our region alone. For instance, if an atomic bomb is detonated in Patagonia, it will be equally disastrous; the danger will exist even if there is not one atomic bomb in our entire region.
>
> Speaking of our region, we could go even farther than Mr. Hazan. Back when his party was in the Government—as it was on two occasions, during the Third and Fourth Knessets— the Government adopted a basic policy, confirmed by the Knesset on December 17, 1959, which said that "until such time as there is general worldwide disarmament, the Government of Israel proposes to all its Arab neighbors—Egypt, Saudi Arabia, Iraq, Jordan, Syria, Lebanon—a treaty for complete disarmament and demobilization of forces in Israel and the abovementioned Arab states on condition that constant and free mutual inspection is guaranteed and the sovereign frontiers of each and every one of these states are not infringed."
>
> Unfortunately, our proposal did not receive support from the peace-loving world. I was amazed that even at the Peace Movement convention held recently, if I am not mistaken in the Soviet Union, not one participant spoke in favor of our proposal, although that alone can guarantee that war will not break out at least in our region which even without nuclear weapons could set off a world war.

When several African states came up with a proposal in the UN Assembly calling for direct negotiations between the Arab states and Israel to settle their disputes, it was supported by a number of Latin American and European states but not by the United States. In this the United States was unfortunately not alone. Soviet Russia, which has no equal in professing world peace, also voted against it, as did the entire Communist bloc.

On December 21, 1960, when Hazan's colleagues were in the Government, I made an announcement in reply to a question by a Knesset member regarding the nuclear reactor. Here is what I said, word for word: "With the help of the American government we have set up a reactor for study purposes in Nahal Rubin with an output of a thousand thermal kilowatts."

The development of the Negev, which we consider a prime objective for the next decade, necessitates scientific research in many fields. For this purpose we have set up a scientific institute for the study of desert fauna and flora in Beersheba. Also, we are now building a reactor with an output of twenty-four thousand thermal kilowatts for research purposes which will serve the needs of industry, agriculture, medicine, and science and prepare Israeli scientific and technical personnel for the construction of a nuclear power station in the future, which we assume will be in ten to fifteen years' time. Like the American reactor, this one too is designed solely for peaceful purposes and has been built under the direction of Israeli experts. It resembles the reactor that the Canadian government helped install in India, though ours has a smaller output.

A week ago the Foreign Affairs and Security Committee convened to consider the situation created, or likely to come about, as a result of Nasser's demonstration of long-range missiles and the renewed threats against Israel that he made on that occasion. Were it not already being considered by the committee, I would propose that the matter be referred to it. Since the committee is already meeting for that purpose, and Knesset member Hazan knows it, there is no need to refer it again.

Knesset member Josef Sapir (Liberal Party) spoke on what he called "the failure of the Hula Ranch." "My generation was raised on the epic of the Hula," he said. "The Hula was both a source of the dread malaria and a source of wealth for the national economy. By dint of great effort we converted the Hula from a swamp to a fertile area of greenery and source food crops. The results of this source of wealth, after five years of work, are an investment of IL6 million and a deficit of IL2 million. Now the question is, what happened? Why, in the most fertile area in the State of Israel, the area richest in water and cheap water at that, are we on the brink of failure? For the first time in the history of agricultural settlement in Israel we have a piece of territory with conditions not known since the days of Petah Tikva, Gedera, Zikhron Yacov, and Nahalal, and still we end up with a deficit of IL2 million and failure."

A debate on the issue was proposed by Rimalt, and the Minister of Agriculture, Moshe Dayan, agreed.

The Hula development plan was drawn up in 1956. The deficit mentioned was cumulative. IL12 million had been invested in the development and IL7 million more for equipment for the Hula Authority. Actually the losses totaled over IL2.5 million, Dayan pointed out. He could not say for certain, but he did not think there would be losses this year. There might even be a profit. But one could not be sure. The Hula Authority had failed and he proposed that it be liquidated and the land transferred to non-governmental bodies. There had already been four committees and it was good, said Dayan, that the question had been brought out into the open in the Knesset.

The decision was to hold a debate but it could not take place during that session of the Knesset. On the last day, August 8, the Knesset briefly considered the state of the nation's libraries, institutions for retarded children, care for incurable patients, transportation of workers to their jobs, and public transportation systems. The preceding day had been devoted to discussions of laws of kashrut, custodianship, and the Tenants Protection Law, which were given second and third readings. On the last day second and third readings were given to the Development Loan Law, Compulsory Savings Law, and Income Tax Amendment Law.

In a closing address the Speaker, Kadish Luz, summarized the work of the initial session: "The outcome of our year's work is 57 laws given third reading, 19 bills in committee, and 2 bills on the agenda for second and third reading. Members of the Knesset submitted some 100 private bills this year compared to 90 such bills during the four years of the Third Knesset, and 51 in the Fourth Knesset. Of these, 30 bills were withdrawn, 24 were referred to committee for preliminary discussion, five were given third readings by the Knesset, and four are ready for the first reading. Nine hundred questions were asked and 136 motions for the agenda given preliminary consideration, of which 73 were referred to committees and 13 debated in the Knesset. Fifty motions were withdrawn from the agenda."

At the start of the winter session, he announced, the Knesset will choose the President of the State. The session will open on October 29, 1962, and the Presidential election will take place the following day. The first session of the Fifth Knesset was thereupon adjourned.

Section 2. The Economy; Arab Refugees; a Spy Sensation

Yitzhak Ben-Zvi Starts His Third Term as President ★ He Visits African Countries ★ The Knesset Honors "First Pioneers"

THE second session of the Fifth Knesset opened on Sunday, October 29, 1962, with eulogies for three patriots who had died recently: Minister Giora Josephthal, Knesset member Herzl Berger, and Deputy Speaker Hanan Rubin. Eulogizing the Minister of Development and Housing, the Prime Minister said:

> Dr. Giora Josephthal who has been taken from us prematurely, was one of the outstanding pioneers of German Jewry and in his short lifetime combined loyalty to the ideal of Jewish and human redemption and practical and resourceful executive ability. He was large in physical stature, and refined and noble of spirit. He demanded of himself more than of others and always tried to set a personal example. Everything he undertook he carried out with zeal and with reverence.
>
> He began as a worker, a settler, and a member of the kibbutz movement. He devoted his full energy and the love of Israel that burned within him to the absorption, welfare, and advancement of immigrants, and strove relentlessly to bridge the cultural and economic gap between the different communities. When appointed a member of the Government he continued with unflagging energy in the work of integrating the exiles and helping immigrants find their place in our society. All his life he regretted the dissension in the labor

camp and the fragmentation of the nation. He was convinced that all sections of the pioneer movement shared basic common principles and that differences of opinion in ephemeral matters should not be allowed to erect barriers between the parties.

He also believed that the main objectives of the State security, absorption of immigrants and ingathering of the exiles, the fructification of the desert, and the uplifting of man should be elevated above any interparty differences. Anyone who had the privilege of working with him esteemed him as a pioneer par excellence, a valued friend, a man of scruples devoted to the vision and the work of upbuilding Israel and of human brotherhood. His untimely demise is a heavy loss to the kibbutz movement, to the Histadrut, the Israel Labor Party, the State, and the Government. Great is our pain and sorrow on this irreplacable loss.

Meir Argov eulogized Herzl Berger and Yacov Hazan paid tribute to the memory of Hannan Rubin.

A delegation from the United Jewish Appeal was now visiting Israel, the Speaker announced. This fund-raising organization was celebrating its twenty-fifth anniversary. Financial contributions of American Jewry had reached a very high level and were a powerful factor in the rescue, immigration, settlement, and housing of large numbers of Jews from the Diaspora. During that quarter of a century the United Jewish Appeal had collected a total of $1.4 billion, a phenomenon unmatched by any other people or country. Thousands of active volunteers in the central office and in twenty-three hundred Jewish communities had devoted themselves unsparingly. "More power to them in their fine work!" the Speaker exclaimed.

The next day, October 30, 1962, the Speaker called for the election of a President. The sole candidate was the incumbent, Yitzhak Ben-Zvi. As their names were read in alphabetical order, the members cast their ballots. The three-man committee that tallied the vote announced that sixty-two ballots were in favor of Ben-Zvi and forty-two had been left blank. The Speaker declared that Ben-Zvi had been chosen as President of the State for a third term.

The following day the President-elect came to the Knesset to take his oath of allegiance to the State of Israel and its laws. After being sworn in he said:

> During the fifteen years of our young State's existence we have taken in more than one million immigrants from East and West and the eyes of millions are turned toward their historic Homeland. Our generation has had the privilege of witnessing a miracle of renewal in the Homeland such as has not been seen since the exodus from Egypt. We have had the privilege of witnessing and taking part in our redemption and liberation in the Homeland through the sweat and blood of its sons. We have had the privilege of being recognized by the family of nations as an equal, a sovereign nation free of foreign yoke in command of its own fate in its historic land, the Land of Israel.
>
> In the past ten years—during which I have had the honor of holding this responsible post after the first and unforgettable President of the State of Israel, Dr. Chaim Weizmann, to whose blessed memory we will pay tribute on the tenth anniversary of his demise in a few days—I witnessed and took part in the continued building and consolidation of the State's foundations, foundations laid by the fathers of the Hibat Zion [Lovers of Zion] and Zionist movements and the pioneers of all the Aliyot that preceded and accompanied the creation of the State.
>
> We must guide our sons in the path of the Homeland's first builders, who raised it up

from the dust, and at the same time cultivate the national awareness of the younger generations—not only our own sons and daughters, who have had the privilege of growing up in the atmosphere of a free Homeland, but also among our brothers in exile.

Our profound faith in our historic destiny, in the Eternal of Israel who will not be false, and our powerful desire to attain justice on earth—on these we have relied and these are our support and our foundation. And it is my prayer to the Rock of Israel that we may be privileged to see with our own eyes in the coming five years true peace in our country and between all nations, that we may see the flourishing of our country, the integration of our scattered sons and the enhancement of Israel's name in the world.

"Mr. President," Speaker Kadish Luz responded, "for the third time the Knesset has entrusted you with the exalted position of President of the State. Your public work, scientific contributions, personal qualities, and exemplary life have elevated you to the stature of the nation's elect. Your mode of life as President of the State has gained you the nation's love and esteem. We wish you good health and long life and may peace prevail in Israel and through the entire world."

On the tenth anniversary of the death of Dr. Weizmann, the first President, on November 5, 1962, the Speaker paid tribute to his memory and his work. The members of the Knesset stood in silent tribute.

In the middle of 1962, Professor Martin Buber, president of the Israel National Academy of Sciences, announced his desire to resign from the Academy for reasons of health. On the Academy's recommendation President Ben-Zvi appointed Professor Aharon Katzir to succeed Buber.

The heads of State of many African countries had visited Israel in 1961–1962: The President of the Republic of Dahomey, Hubert Maga, was in Israel from September 21–29, 1961; the President of Costa Rica, Dr. Francisco Orlich, visited from March 4–9, 1962; the President of Gabon, Leon Mboya, from May 6–16, 1962; the President of the Central African Republic, David Dacko, from June 6–11, 1962; the President of Liberia, D. William Tubman, from June 21–July 1; and the President of the Ivory Coast, Felix Houphouet-Boigny, from July 19–25. The Prime Minister and the Minister for Foreign Affairs conferred with the visitors on mutual relations and the Middle East situation, especially the violations of the Armistice Agreements and United Nations Charter by several Arab states and the discrimination against Israel in the United Nations General Assembly and the Security Council.

At the invitation of the heads of several of these African states President and Mrs. Ben-Zvi paid a series of official visits to that continent. The Presidential entourage left Israel on July 29, 1962, and the next day arrived in the Congo (Brazzaville), where they remained until August 3. From there they proceeded to the Central African Republic, where they remained until August 8. On August 9 they arrived in Liberia and remained until August 15. In every place they visited they received an enthusiastic welcome from both the heads of state and the population, who demonstrated their warm friendship for Israel and its people. The President signed treaties of friendship with the countries he visited. The tour was a great success and strengthened the ties of friendship between Israel and nations of Africa.

The Knesset on December 4, 1962, paid tribute to the "First Pioneers," who in their renewal of agricultural settlement in the country had laid the foundations of the State.

Representatives of the first fourteen agricultural settlements were invited to take part: Mikve Israel, the first agrarian school founded in 1870; Petah Tikva, the "Mother of Settlements" founded in 1878; Rishon LeZion, Rosh Pina, and Zikhron Yacov, all founded in 1882; representatives of the Yemenite immigration as well as representatives from Nes Ziona, Ekron, Yesod Hama'ala, Gedera, Hadera, Motza, Bat Sholomo, Rehovot, and Mishmar Hayarden, all of which were established in the last quarter of the nineteenth century.

The "First Pioneer" celebrations marked the eightieth anniversary of Rishon LeZion in Judea, Rosh Pina in Galilee, and Zikhron Yacov in Sharon. Actually these settlements were not really the first, for immigrants had never stopped coming to Israel nor had the desire to settle there ever ceased since the defeat of Bar Kochba in the year 135 of the Christian Era. The State of Israel was proclaimed on May 14, 1948, but this would never have come about had it not been for scores of years of heroic pioneering work and creative effort in building Jewish settlements and towns; reviving the Hebrew language and culture; developing a ramified national economy in agriculture, trade and industry, and transport on land, sea, and air; the organization of armed Jewish self-defense, and the manifestations of the will and the resourceful action which led to national independence.

Since the beginning of the Lovers of Zion movement and the Zionist movement that followed, we had been accustomed to speak disparagingly of the "Old Yishuv." This attitude disregarded the nation's sense of history. The Old Yishuv was the product of immigration of Yemenite, Sephardi, and Ashkenazi Jews scores and hundreds of years before the terms "Hibat Zion" and "Zionism" were invented. The immigration of these groups and individuals, with their ideals and messianic longings, involved perils and hardships much greater than those undergone by the later immigrants. In the Middle Ages and up to the last quarter of the nineteenth century travel to Israel posed difficulties that our generation cannot imagine, and life here meant constant dangers and exposure to endless pressures. To come and live here called for courage and devotion in a very high degree. Though we are far removed from their outlook and way of life, the generations that built and sustained the Old Yishuv, with all its faults, are worthy of the greatest admiration. It was they who maintained contact between the people and the land, body and soul, and it is in large measure thanks to them that we now have the State. Let us not deprecate or forget the significance of their accomplishment.

The tribute to the First Pioneers was thus most appropriate and Kadish Luz did well to note in his address that "throughout the entire period of our dispersion, despite the tremendous difficulties and hazards, Jews did not cease coming to Israel." He was also right in stressing that "The first Aliya (that is, starting with Mikve Israel) was unique in being the result of profound impulses among the Jews in Eastern Europe and Yemen to renew our national life by settlement, especially agricultural settlement, in the Land of Israel."

The Economy After the Currency Devaluation of 1961

On November 6, 1962, the Minister of Finance, Levi Eshkol, reviewed the economic situation since the announcement of the new exchange rate of 3 Israeli pounds to the dollar on February 9, 1961.

Consumer prices had risen by 6.7 percent. Not all of this rise, however, could be attributed to the devaluation. Even in 1960–1961, before the devaluation, the price index had risen 3 percent in the corresponding nine-month period. Prices in 1962 had thus risen only by 3.7 percent more than in the same period in the preceding two years. On imported equipment, in which investments play an important part, the rise in prices was greater than expected. The boom in the building industry due to increased immigration also resulted in a considerable rise in building costs. The devaluation naturally increased our foreign currency reserves—by $100 million—not only because of income from the sale of oranges and from exports in general, but income from other sources as well, that is, not derived from the sale of locally produced goods or services. The devaluation did not cause any slowdown in the growth of production—real production increased by 10–12 percent— and the level of employment was not affected.

A considerable increase was evident in the income of self-employed workers, and wages had also risen in construction, ports and transport work, as well as for many professionals such as doctors, engineers, and teachers. In the first months of 1962, as a result of a new system of grading as well as seniority and family allowances, the basic wage of industrial and agricultural workers also rose. An increase was also noted in individual incomes from German reparations and private receipt of funds from abroad.

The focal point of the boom was in the building trade, where a 20 percent expansion over 1961 could be expected by the end of the year, with a marked rise in the price of apartments and building lots. The construction boom, as we said, was in part a result of the growing immigration. In 1960, 23,644 persons arrived; in 1961, 46,650; and in 1962, 59,600. Owing to the great growth in local demand a slowdown had occurred in the growth of exports. The building boom had used up our total local cement output and we even had to import some. There had also been an increase in income from tourism, aviation, and shipping. In 1960 there was a total of 117,662 tourists; in 1961, 159,624; in 1962, 183,701. But imports had increased as well.

In the first nine months of 1962 imports rose about 50 percent over the same period the previous year. This increase represented mainly raw materials and equipment rather than processed consumer goods. In the field of services exports had increased considerably but at the same time there was a large increase in imports for defense purposes. The expansion of defense imports was chiefly responsible for the growing deficit in the balance of trade during the first half of 1962. This would be likely to affect the balance of trade for the year as a whole, and the blame could not be placed on devaluation or on economic policy. We made it a rule not to accept foreign currency loans unless they were for a period of twelve to fifteen years with an interest rate of not more than 6 percent. Private investments had increased and in this connection the devaluation had a desirable effect.

Binyamin Avniel (Herut) noted that in 1961 we had exported goods for $68 million to the European Common Market and imported a total of $174 million. To the free-trade areas we had exported goods for $61 million, so that our exports to both these blocs came to $129 million, or 52 percent of our total, whereas the United States and Canada accounted for only 15 percent of our exports, Asia 8 percent, and Africa 5 percent. Despite our total export of $229 million, we had imported from the West European countries a total of $301 million. From 1959 to the present the balance-of-trade deficit had increased from $317 million in 1950–1959 to $403 million in 1961. The Governor of the Bank of Israel had said that in the last nine months the increase in the deficit had been 5 percent more than the big increase in 1959–1961. Thus, he emphasized, while the situation had not been worsened by the establishment of a single rate of exchange for the dollar, signs of improvement were not in evidence.

Another member, Israel Guri, listed the difficulties facing the Israeli economy: the lack of land suitable for cultivation, shortage of water and other natural resources, the extremely long borders in relation to the country's width and area, and the burden of defense expenditure that consume a substantial part of the national budget and would continue to do so as long as peace with our neighbors was not achieved. In addition, the cultural gap between the two sectors of the population [Oriental and European] would prove dangerous if it were not rapidly reduced. Israel had taken in a million immigrants, had tripled its population since its foundation, and aspired to double its present population in the next twenty years by immigration and natural increase. Any observer of economic affairs had to take these realities into account—here we had a unique and unprecedented colonization operation. Guri went on to say, in substance:

> The objective observer rightly assessed israel's outstanding achievements in science, productivity and production, security, growth of its stature among the nations, expansion of friendly ties with many countries, improved services, audacious feats of engineering, and good reputation and credit rating in the international money market. He could not, however, ignore the fact that owing to a lack of experience our production and service facilities were not always able to cope with demands and challenges. We still lacked experience and know-how, so that today, as in the past, serious errors and failures were being made.
>
> It was thanks to the fine qualities of the Israeli—whether laborer, engineer, scientist, man of education and culture, owner of productive capital, the man of planning and administration, or the man of leadership in the State—thanks to qualities that nourished the pioneering ardor of at least the first three waves of Aliyot, that we had gotten where we were. But these qualities alone would not have sufficed were it not for the aid of the Jewish people—aid unprecedented in scope in any other nation—as well as the various forms of material assistance provided by the United States and the powerful stream of reparations and personal restitution payments.
>
> One of the weak points of the Israeli economy was that since the birth of the State part of the assistance had not been used as intended, for development projects and the creation of work and means of livelihood for the masses of new immigrants. Instead it had been applied to raise the standard of living continually, at a rate disproportionate to the country's present creative capacity. Indirect benefits from the foreign funds flowing into the Israeli economy by various channels were unavoidable, and even permissible, provided that public funds did not serve as a source of inordinate profits and wages in the areas of services and brokerage. The trouble was that part of this public money had been used directly to raise living standards and this had to be stopped.
>
> Since the publication on August 15 of the Bank of Israel's report, which noted an increase in payments in the first half of the year, the situation had deteriorated further. If we did not succeed in putting a stop to it, severe upheavals were in store for the economy because of the inflationary effects of such an increase, out of all proportion to the growth in production.
>
> To sum up, developments in the Israeli economy in the first year after devaluation were more positive than could have been expected after such an extreme measure. The economy has not been undermined, but it appears that the effect of some of the measures adopted by the Government could be only temporary and that longer-range measures would be necessary

if we wished to avoid another devaluation in a short time. These measures must of necessity be harsh and painful, the more so because in many respects the population had grown accustomed to living in the atmosphere of a hothouse. In a democratic regime a healthy economy could be achieved only through joint effort by all sectors of the public.

Guri's speech marked the end of the debate and the meeting was adjourned. Two weeks later, on November 20, the debate was renewed. Following a response by the Minister of Finance the following resolution was adopted by a vote of thirty-four to nineteen: "The Knesset has heard the review of the economic situation by the Minister of Finance and after a debate has taken note of it." All the resolutions submitted by the opposition parties were rejected.

Golda Meir Addresses the Knesset on the Arab Refugee Problem

Late in 1962 the world was alarmed by the Cuban Missile Crisis: the attempt by Soviet Russia to erect missile bases on the Caribbean island capable of delivering nuclear warheads of appalling destructive magnitude upon vital centers of the United States. President John F. Kennedy warned Soviet Premier Nikita Khrushchev that America could not tolerate such a threat at its doorstep, and there seemed a serious prospect of a conflict endangering the survival of the two Great Powers, and not only of them. In the end a sense of responsibility won out, and Khrushchev agreed to remove the missiles from Cuba.

Meanwhile peace between the world's two most populous nations, China and India, was broken by Chinese aggression. Prime Minister Nehru of India wrote to heads of government all over the world, Israel included, to explain his country's position in the grave and perilous situation in which the Chinese had placed it.

In his reply Prime Minister Ben-Gurion expressed the hope that the tension and fighting between India and China would quickly be ended by direct negotiations, enabling both countries to apply their resources to the work of progress and development both sorely needed. In conclusion he emphasized that every effort to prevent aggression and adjust differences by peaceful means, especially between neighboring states, would always enjoy Israel's complete understanding and sympathy. In this connection he mentioned our own efforts to resolve the differences between ourselves and our neighbors in this way and said: "All our efforts have been and are directed toward the preservation of peace in our area and throughout the world. . . . It is for this reason that we also proposed a general disarmament in Israel and in the Arab states to our Arab neighbors under mutual supervision, even in advance of global disarmament, since in this we see the most effective way of preventing wars. Moreover, we have expressed our readiness to sign non-aggression treaties with our neighbors. I am in total agreement with the view expressed by Your Excellency that it is incumbent upon all of us to do everything in our power to eliminate the use of force in international relations."

On November 12, 1962, the Foreign Minister, Golda Meir, stated that a month earlier, during the general debate in the UN General Assembly, she had tried to explain that it was a mistake to think that the tension in the Middle East was a result solely of Arab-Israel relations. "Anyone who follows affairs in the Middle East," she had said, "knows that in this last year the focus of trouble in the area has again been the bitter struggle within the Arab world, which has made the Arab League no longer a façade of unity, even superficially."

Within a few days concrete proof of the truth of her words had been produced. In the Arabian peninsula, within Yemen and on its borders, powerful detachments of the Egyptian Army were operating against Yemenite tribes that resisted the revolution engineered in the capital of the country a few weeks earlier. Egyptian warplanes were bombing tribal villages and encampments, and Egyptian warships were shelling them from the sea.

The Egyptian Foreign Minister on October 2, 1962, indignantly disclaimed any thought of foreign intervention in the events in Yemen. Only a few days after that, however, Egypt's role from the very start in all the stages of the struggle in Yemen had become public knowledge. Egypt's spokesmen had distinguished themselves on every occasion and in every place by spurious outcries against aggression, by professed support of the principle of self-determination in theory—and by armed intervention in practice. In the past Israel had refrained, and would now refrain, from meddling in inter-Arab quarrels, Mrs. Meir declared. That was how we behaved more than a year ago when the union between Syria and Egypt was so dramatically ended, and, of course, the same line of policy guided us on other occasions of this kind. In its programs the Government of Israel had in a number of instances made clear that it seeks friendly relations with all states, irrespective of their internal regimes. However, as inter-Arab quarrels grew more serious and acute, and perhaps just for that reason, the Arab leaders of these countries of blind and unbridled hatred against Israel were continuing to preach without respite that we must be destroyed, and were devoting all means and the best part of their resources to preparations threatening our existence.

At the tenth anniversary celebrations of the Egyptian Revolution on July 23, 1962, in Cairo, Nasser had declared: "We have to prepare our civil and military industry, we have to put force against force, and we must stand against Israel and those who back it. There is no escape from the obligation to restore the rights of the Palestine people and hence there is no escape from the duty of preparing and sacrificing ourselves."

At the UN General Assembly on October 12, the Iraqi Foreign Minister said: "The rights of the Arab inhabitants of Palestine are not negotiable—justice and self-determination are not negotiable. One's own country and existence are not negotiable. The Arab people of Palestine will never surrender their rights. They are determined to regain their lost homeland."

At the UN General Assembly on October 2, Mahmoud Fawzi, Egyptian Foreign Minister, said: "The position of my government relating to Palestine is firmly based on the inalienable rights of the Arab nation of Palestine. My country, which has borne the brunt and by far the main sacrifices of supporting the Palestinian Arabs in the struggle for the restoration of these rights, will unflinchingly continue to give unstinting support to our Arab brothers and sisters in Palestine."

Mrs. Meir went on to say, among other things:

> The Arab leaders exploit the Arab refugees in their countries for the purposes of their political war against us. In their eyes, it is not a human problem. We have accepted hundreds of thousands of Jewish refugees from Arab lands. Without waiting for compensation from the Arab governments for their abandoned property, we have done everything in our power

to absorb these Jewish refugees who immediately became citizens of Israel. The Arab leaders, however, do not look upon the refugees as human beings for whose lot they should be solicitous, but as one of the instruments in their war against Israel, one of the weapons in planning their military operations against us.

That, and only that, is the truth of the matter. They hope to ruin or undermine Israel from within through a mass return of refugees, and thereby make an invasion from outside easier. As long as the question of Arab belligerency in all its forms is unsolved, there can be no practical solution of the refugee problem, whereas the ending of Arab belligerency and the willingness of the Arab governments to pursue normal relations of neighborliness will of themselves bring about a solution of the problem of the refugees.

I must say a word or two about the Annual Report of Dr. John Davis, Director of the United Nations Relief and Works Agency, published a few weeks ago. Dr. Davis exceeded his authority in the widest way. Not only did he take it upon himself to be the spokesman and the judge of what the refugees want, but he set himself up as the spokesman of all the Arab nations. Even when he states an ostensibly personal opinion, after all he is still an official of the United Nations. While, after supposed inquiry, he reaches political conclusions on matters that are outside his jurisdiction, he has failed to persuade the Arab leaders to do what is certainly his responsibility—to examine the lists of those enjoying relief from the United Nations, ascertain the numbers of the refugees, and determine their genuine identity, that is to say, define who is a refugee and who is not, who has long since established himself yet still holds a ration card, who has died, and so on and so on.

Dr. Davis evaded a further duty laid upon him: the examination of opportunities of self-rehabilitation. Here, too, he professed to be the judge as to economic opportunities of development in the Arab countries—and all this to prove that there is no room in those countries to absorb refugees. Two years ago, the then Secretary-General of the United Nations, Dag Hammarskjöld, proposed a far-reaching program for the development of all the countries in the Middle East. It was wrecked by the Arabs. Was it in the light of that sabotage that Dr. Davis reached his conclusion?

We observe socioeconomic processes within the refugee community which have been and are conducive to the absorption of many of them in the Arab countries, even in present conditions and in spite of the political opposition of the Arab leaders to this positive and progressive trend. This process of absorption of Arab refugees among their own race in the lands where they live will tend to provide a natural solution of the problem of the Arab refugees, whatever the circumstances may be. It will go forward much more rapidly if and as the attitude of the Arab rulers changes, and they decide that the refugee problem, too, must be solved, and give up their immoral and perverse policy of exploiting the refugees for the purposes of their struggle against Israel.

In a debate that took place in this House a year ago, our basic position was summarized by the Prime Minister and myself, and the House displayed a wide unanimity with us on the principles of the matter. The Prime Minister said on October 11, 1961: "If an Arab refugee problem still exists, this is entirely the result of the violation of the UN Charter by the Arab rulers and their callous treatment of members of their own people. They have treated the Arab refugees not as human beings and members of their own people but as a weapon with which to strike at Israel, treating them as nothing more than a political and military weapon with which to undermine and destroy Israel."

And I said on November 6, 1961: "We are ready to enter into negotiations with the Arab states on the refugee issue, we are ready to discuss things with them, to negotiate on compensation—and we have always said: mutual compensation, and this was recalled by the Prime Minister in his statement—even if there is no peace, but on condition that what will be discussed is a solution of the problem of the refugees in the Arab States. That is to say, it must be with the agreement of the Arab leaders. Then we will sit down and negotiate with them. We will draw up the balance sheet of compensation, and if they want us to, we shall gladly help them also to settle the refugees in their country. We have had experience in settling refugees."

And this too I said then: "We took in tens of thousands of refugees. The declared stand of the State of Israel is not 'No, not a single refugee,' but a solution of the refugee problem in the Arab States."

The Knesset at that time, at the end of 1961, adopted the following resolution: "The Knesset takes note of the attitude of the Government on the Arab refugee issue, as expressed in the declaration of the Prime Minister to the Knesset on October 11, 1961, and in the speech of the Foreign Minister in the Knesset debate on November 6, 1961, which will serve as the fundamental guiding line for the Israel delegation to the UN in the debate on the Arab refugee problem. The Knesset decides: there can be no returning the Arab refugees to Israel territory, and the only solution to the problem is their settlement in the Arab states."

Since that debate, I am sorry to say, there has been no change on basic issues. Rather the opposite: threats to destroy us are intensified, accompanied now by a flow of aggressive armament, and Nasser arrogantly declares that his missiles can reach any place south of Beirut. All these menaces and phrases, all this preparation, do not bring peace in our region any nearer, and obviously do not prepare the ground for the only practical solution of the problem of the refugees.

We were happy, last year, when thanks to the initiative of a number of African and Latin American countries that have no selfish interest whatever in our region, the UN General Assembly showed itself inclined to solve Arab-Israel problems, including the problem of the refugees, through direct negotiations. A number of countries went along with that welcome initiative, and I hope that it will find stronger expression in the continuation of the present Assembly. Despite the speeches that we have heard from Arab representatives, we are convinced that for us and for our neighbors the day must come when we shall live in amity and cooperation. Then the entire Middle East will become a region where the tens of millions of people will dwell in peace, and only then will its economic potentialities and rich cultural heritage find fulfillment. This Israel believes, and toward this end we shall devote all our efforts.

At the end of a two-day debate the Knesset, by a vote of sixty-three to eleven, adopted a resolution on behalf of Mapai, the National Religious Party, Ahdut Haavodah-Poalei Zion, Poalei Agudat Israel, Shituf V'Ahvah, Kidmah u'Fituah, and the Liberal Party, as follows: "After hearing and debating the survey by the Foreign Minister, the Knesset reiterates its resolution of November 6, 1961, in the matter of the refugees which says, 'There can be no returning of the Arab refugees to Israel territory, and the only solution to the problem is their settlement in the Arab states.' " Dissident proposals by Herut, Mapam, and the Communists were rejected by votes, respectively, of forty-three to thirteen, fifty-five to six, and sixty-six to five.

The Israel Ber Spy Case

The day after the "First Pioneers" celebration, the Knesset considered the infirmities of a latter-day character—one Israel Ber, a former Hagana and Israel Defense Forces officer, who was sentenced to eighteen years in prison for passing security secrets to the agent of a foreign state. A parliamentary inquiry commission into the unhappy affair was called by Menahem Begin, the leader of the Herut movement.

"In order to clarify the importance of the question," Mr. Begin said in the Knesset on December 5, 1962, "let me bring to the attention of the members certain passages from the verdict of the Supreme Court. The Court found that Israel Ber had the trust and confidence of all those in possession of Army and security secrets and had transmitted information of a most secret and confidential nature. The apellant (Israel Ber) was explicitly warned by the security services that the person with whom he was maintaining contact was a foreign agent, and in full awareness of his acts continued to maintain the contact and to pass on information.

"The basic question is: in warning Ber, did the security services also warn his superiors in possession of the army and security secrets, whose trust and confidence Ber had? Are we to assume that the warning mentioned by the court was given to Israel Ber and/or his superiors only in March, a few weeks before he was arrested and charged? If that is the case, so be it. However, there is also the possibility that the warning was given a long or a short time before the month of March, and his superiors knew or should have known that he was maintaining contact with a foreign agent, and still permitted him access to secret documents. Can there be any greater or graver omission than that from the standpoint of national security?"

Therefore Begin called for the parliamentary committee of inquiry. The Speaker immediately gave the floor to the Prime Minister and Minister of Defense, who said that he had asked for authoritative information about Ber on which he could rely.

Ber had come to Israel in the fall of 1938. He joined the Hagana in Jerusalem and was sent to the Field Companies in Gan Yavne and to a course at the Kadoorie School. From the spring of 1939 until the autumn of that year he served with units performing guard duties in British Army camps. From the end of 1939 until the summer of 1940 he was a watchman in Jerusalem. In the summer of 1940 he was taken into the training section of Hagana and instructed in courses in the Hagana German Department. In 1944 he was a member of the Hagana Planning Bureau, and in 1945 became Planning Officer.

At the outbreak of the War of Independence he headed the Planning Department in the Operations Branch. At the start of 1949 he headed the Staff Duties Department and the Operations Branch. In 1949 his appointment was canceled and he went on leave. On July 24, 1950, he was discharged from the regular army. From March 1 until July 1953 he was the commander of a course for instructors in military history. On September 28, 1956, he was invited for a talk with the Chief of the Security Services, in the course of which Ber admitted having met a certain person and spoken to him, adding that the late Col. Nehemia Argov had told him not to maintain any contact with that man. The Chief of the Security Services concurred and stressed that no contact should be had with him or others like him. In the trial it was proved that the man was indeed a foreign agent.

Ben-Gurion continued:

> Even the Minister of Defense could not know what was going on at every point in the country and be personally acquainted with everyone, and that was why he had asked for authoritative information. He also wanted to know what went on before he was Minister of Defense. Lest what I said be misinterpreted, as it very well may be, so long as I am Minister of Defense, I assume full and exclusive responsibility for everything which goes on in the Ministry of Defense—everything: contraventions, felonies, treason, everything else. But

there was a time when there was no Ministry of Defense in Israel, when there was no State of Israel, when all there was was the Hagana. I also took part in Hagana affairs but never during that time did I meet Ber, though as chairman of the Jewish Agency Executive I was responsible for all Hagana activities and was in contact with people like Eliyahu Golomb, who did not have an official function, with Israel Galilee, and with a certain General Zionist whose name I will not mention. I met the General Staff only on rare occasions, for I usually worked through Golomb.

In 1946 the Executive assigned to me the Portfolio of Defense and as military advisor I appointed Prof. Yohanan Ratner, with whom I consulted on many occasions, including throughout the War of Liberation. I am unable to say if I did or did not meet Ber or make his acquaintance during the War of Liberation. Maybe yes, maybe no. Before the war, it seems to me, I was not acquainted with him. But I must say that I met him after the war in connection with one thing only—the history of the war he was writing and I met him without distrust.

I did not know then what the preceding speaker knows now, and many other people did not know it either. He was a veteran Hagana man and had also been active in the War of Liberation. He was thought well versed in military history and we held conferences in this connection and I assigned him to set the record straight with regard to the Battle of Latrun about which many incorrect things have been written. While ostensibly it was a defeat, since the 7th Brigade suffered heavy casualties, it was in my opinion a victory, in that it was this battle which saved Jerusalem. Sometimes a battle in one place serves to rescue a difficult situation in another place. I do not wish, at this point, to go into details but since many incorrect things were published at the time by people who were not aware of what really happened, I gave him this assignment.

At that time I was not one of those who knew ahead of time exactly what would happen in the distant future. I did not suspect him of espionage until I learned that he had been arrested, and on what grounds. But never was he let in on any military or security secrets—not because of any suspicion on my part but because I make it a rule to reveal such secrets only to the people who are required to know them in connection with their duties, people in whom I have complete faith. I have many friends and acquaintances in whose honesty I have perfect faith. Yet even to them I do not reveal these things, nor even to my closest friends in the party—and I have close friends not only in the party. This is a rule with me, and one to which I commit everyone in possession of secrets: that they are to reveal them only to persons required to know them in connection with their duties.

As you already heard from what I read to you, Ber was completely discharged from the regular service, since his appointment had been canceled in 1949. Hence he did not receive secrets from me nor from the few people in possession of them, and they are very few indeed. In general they are the Chief of Staff, the Deputy Chief of Staff, the Head of the Intelligence Branch, and the Chief of the Security Services. I am certain that they did not reveal secrets to him, not because they suspected him but because such secrets are not revealed to persons not required to know them. And when it was necessary to maintain secrecy until a certain time about something which hundreds of people had of necessity to know about, I found a method that worked and I say this to the credit of the persons whom I took into confidence: I called together the newspaper editors and let them in on it, emphasizing that though hundreds of people knew it, still it was a secret. To their credit I must say that they have known how to keep a secret, not only in this case but in many others as well.

To those who wish to know the truth and to speak only the truth I will repeat: I am the one who appoints the people who are in possession of secrets and they pass them on only to those who are required to know them. No secret has ever been transmitted to Ber, not because he was suspect but because he did not belong to the group of people required to know secrets in connection with their duties.

The Prime Minister and Minister of Defense then moved that Mr. Begin's motion be rejected. Yacov Riftin (Mapam) moved that Mr. Begin's proposal be referred to the Foreign Affairs and Security Committee. A vote was taken and Riftin's motion, as well as Mr. Begin's, was rejected.

Section 3. A New President and a New Prime Minister

Educational Television, Pro and Con

K NESSET member Menahem Porush (Agudat Israel) in a motion for the agenda on November 21, 1962, objected to the fact that the Cabinet had debated the subject of educational television without bringing it to the Knesset. A ministerial committee had been set up, he claimed, that had decided in favor of the plan, and obviously this was the beginning of general television with all that it entailed.

There was no country possessing television, he said, which did not regret it and whose educators were not decrying its corruption of the youth. Television led to an increase in juvenile delinquency because in trying to attract mass audiences it had no choice but to provide cheap programs that poisoned the souls of the youth. Proponents of television claimed that its introduction would prevent local viewers from tuning in Cairo, Beirut, or Damascus, but this was not so, Porush argued. How could local television ensure that viewers would still not spend many hours daily gazing at Arab programs dispensing hatred and poison? Accordingly he proposed that the matter be opened for debate.

Moshe Kol (Liberal Party), Emma Talmi (Mapam), and Esther Raziel-Naor (Herut) also asked for the debate. Kol maintained that educational TV would to a large extent supplant books. Emma Talmi was opposed to receiving TV from the Rothschilds. Esther Raziel-Naor claimed that from what she had seen, television was not a medium for education but merely for communication. She feared it would provide neither education nor learning but mechanical indoctrination.

Ami Assaf, Deputy Minister of Education, told of the development of the plans for educational television. In April 1962 Lord Rothschild of London had proposed that the Prime Minister and Minister of Education appoint a delegation to study what had been done in educational television in other countries, especially the United States. If it then recommended its introduction and the Government concurred, the Rothschild family would be prepared to finance telecasts to twenty schools over a period of two to three years. They would finance the equipment, the receivers, and the production costs for that period, after which the Government would judge and decide whether or not it wished to continue.

The delegation which went to examine the matter consisted of two persons: Mr. Roe, representing the Rothschild family in Israel, and Dr. Meir Shapira, principal of Beit Hakerem High School. They spent several weeks in the United States and other countries and their recommendations were favorable, though with certain reservations. When there were cases of both success and failure, it was better to learn from the successes and the failures.

Israel, as was well known, had a shortage of teachers, especially qualified teachers, and this obligated us to try educational television. Though it could not replace the teachers or make up the shortage, it could be of great assistance to teachers if it succeeded. We had experience with school radio broadcasts and the results had proved satisfactory. The number of schools listening to them was steadily increasing and now stood at 340.

Under the terms of the agreement with the Rothschild family, the Minister of Education and Culture would be responsible for the form, content, style, scheduling, grades, and age groups of the programs. In everything connected with the curriculum the financial sponsors were not asking for any right to interfere. All they requested was that the production or translation of the programs be done by the experts they recommended. The Government had not yet decided on the proposal. If it was accepted, the program would be operated on a trial basis for a two or three-year period starting in 1964–1965. Ami Assaf proposed that the matter be referred to the Education and Culture Committee.

The proponents of a debate in the Knesset did not agree and it was decided to hold a debate in the plenum. It was opened on January 1, 1963, by the Minister of Education and Culture, Abba Eban. He apprised the Knesset that two days earlier the Government had voted in favor of a television experiment in cooperation with the Rothschild Memorial Group. Under this plan televised lessons on selected subjects would be transmitted to a limited number of elementary and secondary schools and teachers' seminaries both in the National and National Religious System. It would thus be possible to train educators in new pedagogical methods developed in the many countries in which the new medium had been harnessed for the advancement of education. The Rothschild Memorial Group would underwrite all the expenses while the Minister of Education and Culture would have exclusive responsibility for the content and form of the programs. In planning programs the Ministry would consult and cooperate with the nation's teachers and with the Knesset Education and Culture Committee.

The experiment would continue for two or three years, Eban said. In the light of the results the Government would decide if and how it should be expanded to be available to the educational system as a whole. The Knesset was not being asked at present to decide on general television. As an experiment the project did not require any such decision and only around 1966–1967 would the Knesset be called on to decide. The only question now under discussion was whether there were any prospects that this technology could help raise the standards of instruction in those subjects in which it would be introduced.

The Government believed that it was something we should take advantage of. Experience in other countries showed that the benefits of educational TV were immense and under the present circumstances no detrimental effect need be feared. The effectiveness of television had already been proved. Its use was expanding in every educational system that could afford it. It was in use in many of the states in the United States; France had pioneered in introducing it on a large scale; five years ago it was being used in England by eighty schools, today by six thousand. Teachers in villages and settlements far from the large centers of population attached more importance to it than urban teachers. The great advantage of television was that through visual demonstration it made things concrete for the pupil. That was the most effective form of teaching, especially in the natural sciences and in language instruction. It would also help in teaching Hebrew. All the leaders of educational systems that had introduced TV were confident of its effectiveness and working toward its expansion.

Esther Raziel-Naor commented that what Israeli education needed was better teachers and a better image of the teacher. If the teachers were unqualified, even the most complicated equipment wouldn't help. Moshe Kol stressed that though the report by Dr. Shapira and Mr. Roe stressed that in other countries too the method was still in the experimental stage, this was no reason not to try it in Israel. In the trial stages it would not cost the country anything and if it succeeded we would then decide about the cost.

There was no reason, Ishar Smilansky said, why the experiment should not be tried in a small group of schools for several years to enable us to learn its advantages and disadvantages. There was no good reason why we should not give it a try ourselves since other countries that had tried it were favorably impressed. Television should not be considered the be-all and the end-all, but merely an additional audio-visual teaching aid that would transmit culture from areas of high concentration to areas of low concentration.

Emma Talmi saw the greatest danger to the classroom teacher. The live teacher was at a disadvantage compared to the one on the screen. The TV teacher would seem more patient and more tolerant; he would not discriminate between one pupil and another; nor would he make demands on the pupil. Yet the live teacher was the mainstay of our educational system. And Ruth Hetkin said essentially the same thing. The teacher on the screen would most likely be very talented but what about his classroom counterpart, who would still have to explain to his pupils what it was that they had seen on the screen? Mikunis complained that the Government had made a decision before the Knesset had a chance to consider the matter, and Porush raised the same objection.

The debate, resumed on January 8, 1963, wound up on March 6. In replying to the strictures, Abba Eban proposed that his Ministry be responsible for all televised lessons, the ministerial committee appointed a few months back would decide on the location of the transmitters, and the Knesset Education and Culture Committee would keep track of the experiment's progress. His proposal was adopted by a vote of fifty-five to forty-three.

National Parks and Nature Preserves ★ Restoration of Historic Sites

The Prime Minister on December 3, 1962, submitted to the Knesset a National Parks and National Preserves Bill. It called for the establishment of a ten-member National Parks Council to advise the Minister of the Interior to designate as national parks areas distinguished by natural beauty, suitability for recreation, the study of nature, and the country's history, or because of natural preserves they contained. The bill also called for a twenty-member Parks Authority to manage these areas, with the right to delegate its powers to local authorities on parks located within their geographical jurisdiction. Licenses for businesses, crafts, or industry within the area of a national park would be issued only with the consent of the Parks Authority and in accordance with the conditions it would stipulate.

Under the projected legislation the Minister of the Interior with the advice of the Minister of Agriculture was entitled to announce in *Reshunot* that a particular area was designated as a Nature Preserve. The provisions applying to the designations of national parks would also apply to Nature Preserves. The law was intended to protect and preserve the countryside and sites of historical importance for present and future generations. In our time the countryside had been placed in greater jeopardy because of intensive development programs and unplanned urban expansion. Modern countries recognized the importance of these rural areas for health and recreation and spared no effort and expense to bestow these benefits on their inhabitants. This was not a luxury but an educational and cultural necessity—something, moreover, that strengthened a people's ties with the land. In the course of a debate on the budget for the Prime Minister's Office on June 12, 1962, Knesset member Yizhar had made some points that it would be appropriate to quote at this point.

"It is impossible to live where everything is completely planned and organized to the extent of eliminating every vestige of the country's original natural organic visage," he said. "A man must have a place to go where he can gain refreshment and shake off the dust of the city, what is manmade, hemmed-in, and routine, and restore his spirit through contact with what is primeval, open, natural, and unspoiled by man. No utilitarian new building can take the place of a seventy-year-old tree that has been cut down. A stout eucalyptus, an old sycamore, a glade of oaks—these are a man's roots."

"Allow me to add," the Prime Minister now said, "that the fact that the northern half of the State of Israel is densely populated requires that great attention be devoted to planning. We must ensure suitable areas for what this bill terms national parks. There are areas in the north where the population density is 650 persons per square kilometer. Such a density makes it necessary to provide unbuilt, free areas where the masses can go to escape the din of the city and get some fresh air. It is also necessary to preserve natural features, flora and fauna of scientific interest. Rare plants and animals are in danger of extinction because of the ease with which every place is accessible these days, especially in a small country. To avoid these undesirable results it is customary to allocate areas for Nature Preserves in which rare animals and plants are protected from harm. National parks can encompass not only forests but any natural landscape of unusual character, and even historic monuments.

"These parks are generally open to the public and the appropriate authorities prepare access roads and other facilities to encourage people to visit them. They also play a role in the country's economy, as they are an important factor in the development of the tourist industry.

"Back in 1949 the Planning Department of the Ministry of the Interior began to work on preliminary proposals for national parks. In 1950 I appointed a special committee to submit recommendations with regard to the location, establishment, and management of national parks. Even back then the committee recommended that a special Authority be established for this purpose. The Planning Department spent several years working on plans for this. Work was also carried out by the Department for Landscape Improvement and Development of Historic Sites in the Prime Minister's Office which was set up six years ago. This department has already created a number of national parks and restored ten historical sites, and work is now in progress on a dozen additional sites and parks which will be opened to the public in the very near future. There is also a unit in the Ministry of Agriculture that deals with Nature Preserves containing rare fauna and flora. In recent years various public bodies have been organized to foster an interest in nature and archaeology.

"Welcome as they are, all these activities are not sufficiently covered by law. The purpose of this bill, therefore, is to unite under one body—the Parks Authority—all the functions now being exercised by the several different authorities, and to provide it with the local means to protect treasures of nature from irreparable damage or destruction."

Under the proposed law the members of the Parks Authority, numbering not more than fourteen, would be appointed by the Prime Minister with Government approval. This would be the executive body. In addition the Ministry of the Interior would set up a National Parks Council, whose task would be to designate park areas.

The Prime Minister moved that the bill be adopted on first reading and referred to either the Education and Culture Committee or the Public Services Committee.

Debate on the law began on December 11, 1962. *Rahel Zabari* (Mapai), the first speaker, criticized the division of authority among the Prime Minister's Office, the Ministry of the Interior, and the Ministry of Agriculture. What purpose was served by this fragmentation? There was also fragmentation in the selection of sites, she pointed out. The bill provided that parks be designated by the Council and Nature Preserves by the Ministry of Agriculture. Why not a single body? Individuals and public bodies should also be encouraged to protect the landscape and foster a love for it. At Ein Gedi, she said, there was a small group enthralled by the beauty of the place and developing a special way of making people aware of it. There were also ways in which natural beauty was corrupted. Eucalyptus trees that had been planted on the shores of Lake Kinneret concealed the lake's beauty from people passing by.

Avraham Drori (Herut) complained about anarchy on the seashore. Anyone who wanted to could come and destroy a piece of it. Our country's magnificent shoreline had been serrated by boulders and dangerous pits. The seashore promenade of our largest city had become a hotbed of crime and a source of ugliness and the water itself a sewage outlet. The law ought to be expanded to cover not only national parks and nature preserves but the contours of the landscape and historical sites. On the slopes of Mount Carmel and along the nation's main transportation arteries quarries had set their teeth in full view of the citizen, the immigrant, and the tourist. Could quarries not be located on the inside slopes?

Ruth Hektin (Ahdut Haavodah-Poalei Zion) noted that a rare flower, the Gilboa Iris, was found in only one place in the world and that was the slopes of Mount Gilboa. Scientists told us that 150 species of flora were unique to Israel. The Hula was also the home of rare species some of which could also be found in Siberia while others were distinctly tropical. The fact that Israel was located on an ecological crossroads no doubt contributed to this meeting of flora from three continents. We also had some 400 kinds of birds which lived in or passed through Israel, some of which like the honeysucker, a delightful little bird, was unique to our country. Nor did we lack wild animals such as the gazelle and other mammals. But due to lack of protection they were being destroyed.

Israel Yeshayahu (Mapai): Improving the landscape was not only a matter of beautification but an inextricable part of the country's redemption and fructification. Our country had been desolate as long as its sons were dispersed in the four corners of the world. Various conquerors also devastated it. Noteworthy in this respect were the nomadic tribes, which systematically destroyed all the vegetation in their path. To our good fortune the land was now settled and being worked by its rightful owners, but its desolation was not yet at an end or its days of mourning over. It was not yet "beautiful of vista, the joy of the whole earth," as the Psalmist described it. A deterioration could even be noted. The buildings we were putting up so hastily were ugly and parks were scarce in the vicinity of houses. In residential areas there were no trees or even greenery.

Moshe Sneh (Communists): The Hebrew language had special terms of respect and affection for the land. One of these was Eretz Hatzvi (the Land of Beauty) and if there was any sense or purpose to the proposed law it would be to restore the country's crown of beauty. For that reason it should be welcomed. While ostensibly it dealt merely with a marginal problem of the Torah, actually it dealt with one of the basic elements of our national revival, for "homeland" was not only a geographic or even historical or political concept, it was an emotional one—the love for one's homeland was most natural, like the love of a child for its mother. In the First Knesset the Prime Minister had spoken of the country's afforestation. While something had been accomplished through the years it was nothing compared to what was needed.

Gideon Ben-Israel (Mapai): Considerable work had been done by the Landscape Improvement Department, which had dealt with scores of places like Ein Gedi, Shivta, Avdat, and the wonderful park in Ashkelon which was a successful combination of a park and unspoiled nature. The law should apply not only to historical sites of ancient times but also those of more recent vintage. The Landscape Improvement Department had done a nice piece of work in reconstructing the scenes of battle at Yad Mordekhai. This program should be continued, for this sort of thing, too, inculcated a love of the country.

In summing up the discussion on December 17, 1962, the Prime Minister indicated his great satisfaction with the style and content of the speeches. Not only did he agree with many of the objections expressed in the debate, he intended to add some of his own. He had presented the bill as approved by the Ministerial Legislation Committee without adding to or detracting from it. Yet he took issue with its main provisions. Just as most of the members had spoken on a personal basis rather than for their parties, he too would speak in his own name. Only one complaint was not completely justified, he felt, namely, that the bill had come too late. Then he went on to say:

> Many things were done in this field of landscape preservation and improvement by one of the Government ministries long before the submission of this law. Though it happened to be the Prime Minister's Office, this work must not be credited to the Prime Minister but rather to the Directors of his office and especially the Director of the Landscape Improvement Department, Yacov Yannai. Much important work has also been done already in restoring historical sites as well as in improving the landscape in the Galilee, the Central Region, the South, and the Negev.
>
> The Landscape Improvement Department has been in existence for six years and here are some of its accomplishments: In Hatzor, in the Galilee, roads have been built and landscape gardening carried out. Several sites have been restored and a museum will soon be built.
>
> In Bar'am in upper Galilee there is a synagogue dating back to the time of the Mishnah [second century of the Christian Era]. An access road has been built and ruined buildings around the synagogue removed. The façade and gate of the synagogue have been partially reconstructed as have some of the walls and the majority of the inside pillars, and extensive landscaping has been carried out.
> it.
>
> Yehiam—a medieval fortress is being unearthed and a park is being planned to go around Beit Sh'arim—is well known for its tombs of the first and second centuries of the Christian Era. Access roads and pathways have been built, the hillside has been landscaped, the gates and façades restored, and the inside of the caves illuminated so that it is possible to read the inscriptions, which are partly in Hebrew and partly in Greek. A museum for local finds has also been built.

Beit Alfa—the synagogue dating back to the sixth century has been reconstructed. A suitable structure has been built over the wonderful mosaic floor, lighting has been installed, and flowerbeds have been planted all around.

Megiddo—as a result of the excavations by the University of Chicago's Oriental Institute in 1935, the site was in a state of great disorder. Now at long last it has been given proper treatment, and after three years' work has become the biggest attraction in the area. A museum has been built and the entire area cleaned up. Access roads and lookout points have been built. The main attraction is the tunnel that carried water into the city from a spring located outside the walls. This too has been cleaned up and illuminated.

Beit Shaan—the ancient Roman theater in the center of the city has been unearthed. It dates to the second century and compares favorably with other Roman theaters throughout the world. The entrances are intact and the seats have been restored and are usable. A 120-dunam park is now being planted around it. After completion of this work next spring the site will be opened to visitors.

Caesarea—this large city of the Second Temple period with its walls and towers has been reconstructed and considerable attention has also been devoted to the buildings from the Herodian and Byzantine periods which came to light in the course of the excavations. Reconstructions include the original eastern gateway to the city and the bridge. A road has been paved around the entire site. Landscaping has also been carried out.

Ma'ayan Harod—this spring, known to us from the days of Gideon, was found to be blocked up. It has since been reopened and now flows into a pond that has been created at the site. A park is also being created to include Gideon's cave and part of Hankin Forest.

Gan Hashlosha—the natural pond here was accessible only to very few. A park has been planted and is now the chief attraction of the area. The site is bustling with people. The pond has been enlarged and improved, trees have been planted around it, and access roads built to the park.

Meron—the tomb of Rabbi Shimon Bar-Yohai is visited by tens of thousands of people each year. In recent years improvements have been made by the Landscape Improvement Department. The same is true of Safad. The ancient synagogues have been renovated and better lighting has been installed. An access road and steps leading to the ancient cemetery have been built. In the past year archaeological excavations have been carried out in the citadel with the Department's help. The tomb of Maimonides in Tiberias has been made accessible to visitors through landscape work just completed. The roads have also been improved.

Mount Zion in Judea—a place visited by great numbers of people, it has received special attention. The ascent has been made easier thanks to a road and a stair. Extensive landscaping work has been carried out, as well as work on the important buildings. This year a road will probably be built to the summit, which will save visitors the effort of climbing stairs.

Shivta in the south—the streets of the old city have been cleaned up and access roads and a parking lot built. Two Byzantine churches have been partially restored as have several ancient wine presses. Explanatory signs have been erected throughout the city.

Avdat—as you have heard from the previous speaker who hails from the area, the hill has been excavated, revealing two Byzantine churches. The Roman citadel and the acropolis have been cleaned up and the Byzantine-Nabatean caves made accessible to visitors. The Byzantine bathhouse on the hillside has been reconstructed. Access roads have been built, parking facilities provided and explanatory signs posted on all parts of the site. Rest rooms have also been built and a museum for local finds will be erected in the near future.

Ashkelon—a previous speaker mentioned the park of several hundred dunams which has been planted there. The site is a wonderful combination of parkland, seashore, and antiquities. Roads and pathways have been built and public facilities installed.

Ein Gedi—much work was done here by volunteers and credit should be given where due, but the chief contribution has been made by the Landscape Improvement Department. A road has been built to the Spring of David, and the entire area cleared, so that the ascent to the spring is now easier. The paths and bridges have been improved. Additional facilities are to be built in the near future.

I need hardly mention what has been done at Ramat Rahel, in Emek Hefer, and the signs erected in many places explaining in Hebrew and in a European language the historic and archaeological sites as well as those connected with the War of Independence. While not enough has yet been done in this respect, lookout points giving an unobstructed view of the surroundings have been built at twelve places throughout the country, and the Department plans to continue with this work.

At this point I must mention the work of afforestation which was rightly mentioned by Mr. Sneh. This great undertaking must in the main be credited to the Keren Kayemet. From the creation of the State until the close of the 1961–1962 planting season over 70 million forest trees were planted at 160 different sites—an area of 300,000 dunams in all. Everyone who comes to Jerusalem knows that a large part of the Jerusalem hills which were once bare are now covered by young forests. Planting sites are to be found all over the country: in Kfar Szold, Rammim (Manara), and Hanita in the north, along the eastern border at Ein Gev, Mount Gilboa, Ma'anit and the Modiin area, the Jerusalem hills and Adulam to Dimona, Shivta, and Sde Boker in the south.

These forests consist of coniferous species (pines, cypresses, etc.), eucalyptus, and other trees. Plantings have included rows of trees along the nation's highways, though unfortunately not on all of them. Rows of grass to act as windbreaks have been planted in the Negev to protect agricultural crops. In these forest areas the Keren Kayemet creates parks and recreation areas that provide diversion and relaxation for young and old. Such sites are located in the Hanita forest on Mount Meron, the Birya Forest, the Balfour Forest, the Rangers Forest on Mount Carmel, the Menashe Forest, the Ben-Shemen Forest, the Presidents' Forest in the Jerusalem corridor, and the Jerusalem Forest.

The Government has placed large tracts of land for tree planting at the disposal of the Tel Aviv and Ramat Gan Municipalities. The Government should have applied pressure to see that these areas were used for their intended purpose. I must note with regret that instead of planting trees the Tel-Aviv Municipality has earmarked many of these areas for buildings that could easily have been erected elsewhere.

Ben-Gurion agreed with Knesset member Rahel Zabari and other members who felt that the question of entrance fees to national parks should be looked into carefully. The bill, he believed, was deficient in its designation of the bodies in charge of landscape improvement, nature preservation, and the restoration of historical sites. Speaking in his own name, he went farther than any of the speakers who had advanced objections to the proposed legislation. The Council and the Parks Authority, which would be completely under the jurisdiction of the Prime Minister's Office, did not answer the real need. What was needed was an advisory council composed entirely of writers, artists, scientists, zoologists, botanists, historians, and architects—people who understood history, nature, and natural architecture; and there should be a commissioner to serve as the liaison between this Council and the Government.

"Our country has not been blessed with many natural resources," he remarked, "but one thing we do have is the seacoast, the first thing encountered by people coming here, whether as tourists, allies or non-allies, or immigrants. This encounter should not be disappointing. There have been many justified complaints about the destruction and defoliation of our seacoast. Improvement of the coast will without doubt meet opposition by private interests, but if we wish to restore to our country its 'crown of beauty,' as Sneh put it, the first thing we should turn our attention to is the seashore—the Mediterranean shore from north to south and the small section of coast in Eilat.

"The same holds true of the Carmel. This is the most beautiful area in the country. It is a unique combination of mountain and sea, and more than any other region it has preserved its forests. Here too there is liable to be a clash with some private interests and the Knesset will have to intervene.

"This year I visited the Scandinavian countries. I saw their abundant wealth, high standards of living, social progress, but did not envy them for this, for we are a young State and will be able to catch up in these respects. What I did envy was their abundant forests and lakes. Finland, for example, which is ten times as large as Israel, has forests over 60 percent of its territory and has more than sixty thousand lakes.

"While we cannot import lakes to Israel, I believe that technology, which many for some reason disparage, will be capable of things that now seem impossible and will give us even lakes in the Negev and in areas unsuitable for agriculture and settlement. That is a long way off, of course. Though we will never be able to compete with the Scandinavian countries in lakes, there is no reason why our country should not be covered with forests and woods wherever possible, especially, with the help of special legislation, on the seashore and on the Carmel."

On behalf of the Ministry of the Interior he proposed that the National Parks and Nature Preserves Bill be referred to a committee. The House Committee, it was decided, would determine to which committee it should be turned over.

Moslem and Christian Minorities in Israel

A national census in Israel was taken twice. The first, on November 8, 1948, showed a population of 785,678—including 716,678 Jews and 69,000 non-Jews. Because the country was at war, not all the Arabs could be counted. By the beginning of 1950 the population was estimated at 1.19 million—1,029,000 Jews (86.4 percent) and 161,000 non-Jews (13.5 percent). On May 22, 1961, a complete and accurate census could be taken because by that time the population was stable. Of a total of 2,179,500 counted, 1,932,400 (89.04 percent) were Jews and 247,079 (10.93 percent) non-Jews. Of the non-Jews 170,800 (69 percent) were Moslems, 50,500 (20.5 percent) Christians, 24,000 (10 percent) Druze, and 1479 (0.5 percent) others.

The majority of the non-Jewish population is concentrated in some hundred villages located mainly in the Galilee and the Triangle area. The urban Arab population is centered in two Arab cities, Nazareth and Shfaram, and six mixed cities: Tel Aviv/Jaffa, Haifa, Akko, Ramla, Lod, and Jerusalem. The Arab increase resulted from refugees who returned under the family reunification plan; about 35,000 returned to Israel and 3000 departed. The Arab birth rate is among the highest in the world: 42.8 per thousand in 1960 compared to 18.6 per thousand for the Jewish population. From the birth of the State to the end of

1963, 139,379 persons emigrated from Israel, only 5000 of them non-Jews. Of these, 88,373, including 4457 non-Jews, were declared emigrants.

More than two-thirds of the non-Jewish population are Moslems. In May 1961 the Knesset enacted the Kadis Law designed to regulate the appointment of Kadis [Moslem religious judges] and the administration of the Shari'a [religious] courts. At present in Israel there are four Moslem courts, as well as a Moslem court of appeals in Jerusalem. The Government allocates the funds from the income from Waqf [Moslem religious] properties for the Moslems' religious needs, such as renovation of mosques and erection of new ones, repairs to cemeteries, religious needs, and charities. These allocations are disbursed through Moslem committees for religious affairs in Jaffa, Haifa, Acre, Lod, and Ramla. A Moslem Religious Council has been set up under the chairmanship of Sheikh Musa Ambari, president of the Shari'a court of appeals. The other members of the court are the secretaries of the Moslem councils and Moslem dignitaries through-out the country. Its functions include recommending the welfare uses to which the Waqf funds will be put and to supervise religious education in the home for orphans in Acre.

In 1962–1963, IL350,000 were allocated to these institutions compared to IL250,000 in the previous year. In 1962 a regional center for vocational training, also erected from these funds, was opened at Tamara in western Galilee; and in the same year a fund for constructive loans for the needy was set up. The 1962–1963 budget included the erection of a vocational high school in Nazareth, a second Moslem orphans' home in Acre, a work-shop in the orphans' home, and other Moslem needs.

The Israeli Government is prepared to enable Israeli Moslems to fulfill the injunction of the Koran regarding the pilgrimage to Mecca. This has not yet been implemented be-cause of the refusal of Arab states to allow pilgrims from Israel to pass through their ter-ritory.

Christians, about 20 percent of the non-Jewish population, make up various religious communities, the most important of which are the Catholics, about 20,000, headed by Archbishop George Hakim; and the Greek Orthodox, over 15,000, headed by the Metro-politan Isidoros. In addition there are smaller communities, such as the Latin Church, about 7000; the Maronites, about 2500; and the Protestants, about 1700.

The jurisdiction of the Christian courts is not as broad as that of the Shari'a courts. Their competence extends only to matters of marriage, divorce, alimony, and the exe-cution of wills; in other matters of personal status they have jurisdiction only if both sides consent. On the other hand, the Christian communities enjoy extensive autonomy in the organization of their religious courts. These courts and the appointment of religious judges are not regulated by the Knesset laws as in the case of the Moslem, Druze, and Rabbinical courts, but by the churches themselves, whose centers are not in Israel. This is the main difference between the Moslem and Druze organizations and those of the Christians. The regulation of the Christian courts, management of church property, schools, and other communal affairs, especially in the Old City of Jerusalem, are to a large extent controlled by the church centers which are located outside Israel.

Up to 1957 the Druze did not have the status of a religious community and in all matters of personal status and religious property were subject to the Moslem courts. But on April 15, 1957, with their consent the Druze were declared an independent religious community and since that time they have enjoyed autonomy in matters of religious juris-diction. On October 30, 1961, the spiritual leadership of the Druze community was recognized as a Religious Council, the community's supreme religious institution, and on November 1, 1961, the Council adopted the 1948 personal status law of the Lebanese Druze community as the religious law of the Druze community in Israel.

In 1962 and 1963 the Government began to carry out the first stages of the master plan for development of Arab and Druze villages. The object of this plan was to complete the development of basic services in all such villages, including the expansion of the road network, piped-in water supply, hookup to the national power grid, housing, education, expansion of municipal and health services, and development of farming, trade, and industry. The plan calls for an overall investment of more than IL55 million, with over IL31 million of it provided by the Government. In the 1962–1963 budget IL6 million were allocated, double the amount in 1961–1962. The plan for 1962–1963 (to be covered by Government funds) included housing—IL1.6 million; education—IL1 million; roads—IL300,000; drinking water—IL500,000; agricultural development—IL500,000; electricity—IL850,000; municipal services—IL400,000; health—IL35,000; and the development of handicraft and industry—IL625,000. The Government will seek to encourage industry in Arab villages through joint Jewish-Arab investments, to creat jobs for inhabitants who are now compelled to commute long distances.

As of July 1, 1962, more than IL12 million had been paid in compensation for 137,000 dunams of land acquired from 8558 persons. This meant that more than half of all potential claimants received compensation for approximately 40 percent of all land for which such compensation had to be paid. An additional 3000 claimants were negotiating for payments for 30,000 dunams of land, by direct negotiations with the Development Authority, or in court. The courts are authorized to propose compensation on the basis of the value of the property in 1950. The compensation proposed by the Development Authority is 100 percent higher. In 1959 the Minister of Finance appointed a public committee consisting mainly of Arabs to recommend the amount of compensation to be paid. The Development Authority generally pays 10 to 15 percent more than the amount recommended.

Nevertheless, the claimants are not always satisfied with the settlement. Frequently the payment of compensation is hampered by internal arrangements stemming from elements of the traditional social structure in the villages such as joint ownership of land. The greater obstacle to settling claims was the absence of a final date for their submission. April 1, 1963, was set in Yalkut ha Pirsumim as the deadline for agreements on the basis of recommendations by the public committees; after that date claimants would not be entitled to compensation on this basis but would have to appeal to the courts.

Over two thousand Arab and Druze intellectuals are employed by the Government ministries and various public institutions, the great majority as teachers in the national school system. The office of the Advisor on Arab Affairs in the Prime Minister's Office is seeking ways to provide suitable employment for non-Jewish intellectuals. In 1962 eighty such persons were working in the Arab-Israel Bank, forty-five in other banks, and fifteen (who had taken a special course) in the Ministry of Finance.

In 1961–1962 approximately a hundred Arab and Druze students were enrolled in institutes of higher education. Of this number seventy-seven, some of them Bedouins, were attending the Hebrew University of Jerusalem. The training and professional advancement of Arab workers is handled by the Bureau of the Advisor on Arab Affairs in the Prime Minister's Office. Study days and courses are held and studies and surveys are published on Arab social and cultural affairs, the Arab language, folklore, and so on. Special attention is devoted to the development of Oriental studies in high schools in order to bring students closer to the Arab cultural tradition and enhance mutual understanding among all citizens of the State.

On November 1, 1961, the Government decided to set up a Ministry of Housing to be headed by Joseph Almogi, until then Minister without portfolio. From the outset, housing had constituted a major lever in implementing the policy of population dispersal announced by the first elected Government. Despite mass immigration and the natural increase, housing construction had not lagged behind population growth. From 1949 to 1960, 413,000 new housing units were erected, including 354,000 permanent dwellings. Housing was a central element in the creation and development of new agricultural and urban settlements and in the peopling of undeveloped areas. From 1949 to 1960 8600 apartments were built by the Government in Beersheba, 3145 in Kiryat Shmona in upper Galilee. In 1961–1962 19,000 housing units were built; in 1962–1963—21,500; in 1963–1964—23,000. These figures do not include building by private enterprise.

The housing budget for 1962–1963 was IL330,700,000. The breakdown was as follows: immigrant housing and public institutions—IL249,075,000; housing in agricultural settlements—IL16.25 million; housing under the Savings for Housing Plan—IL26.5 million; liquidation of ma'abarot—IL11.4 million; housing for slum evacuees—IL5,625,000; housing in development areas—IL17,850,000; and housing for members of the minority communities—IL4 million.

From 1955 to the end of 1962 41,883 persons joined the Savings for Housing Plan and had saved a total of IL138 million; 15,000 persons had joined the plan from 1955 to 1958 and had saved IL41.6 million; in 1959 4068 joined and saved IL14.9 million; in 1960 6385 joined, saving IL18.8 million; in 1961 7727 with IL27.1 million, and in 1962 8673 with IL35.6 million. In 1963 10,569 joined the plan and saved IL25,326,600.

The Passing of Yitzhak Ben-Zvi, Israel's Second President

Yitzhak Ben-Zvi, second President of Israel, died on April 23, 1963, during the second session of the Fifth Knesset. He had been elected on December 12, 1952, re-elected for a second five-year term on October 28, 1957, and again on October 30, 1962. He was laid to rest on April 24, 1963, in the family plot in Har Hamenuhot Cemetery, Jerusalem.

Heavy grief descended over the State and the Jewish people in the Diaspora. Tens of thousands of Israeli citizens joined in the State funeral procession that passed through the streets of the capital. Representatives of myriad countries, communities, and religions took part. Cables and letters of participation in the nation's sorrow were received from heads of state and Jewish organizations and communities throughout the Diaspora. The Government of Israel declared a period of national mourning.

Yitzhak Ben-Zvi was born in Poltava in the Ukraine, on November 24, 1884, the son of Zvi Shimshelevitz, a member of B'nai Moshe, the secret order founded by Ahad Ha'am. When he came to the Land of Israel, the father changed his name to Shimshi, and his eldest son was called after him, Yitzhak Ben-Zvi. In 1904, when he was twenty and still a student in Poltava, Ben-Zvi visited Israel. Those were the days when the Russian revolutionary movement was in its infancy, and many of the Jewish youth believed that redemption was in sight for the Jewish people, oppressed in the Pale of Settlement of the Russian Czarist empire. Although the young man's heart was with the revolution against Czarist tyranny, he felt with a profound Jewish instinct that even if it brought about the liberation of the Russian people, it would not basically change the unsound and diseased situation of the Jewish people, for the source of our troubles lay not in any particular regime, but in the fact that we lived in exile, among a strange people, dependent on it for good or ill; and that only by returning to the land of our fathers and becoming an independent nation would we cast off the burden of exile.

After organizing self-defense in Poltava, for which his father and brother were exiled to Siberia, Yitzhak came to settle in the Homeland in 1907—for good. Immediately upon arriving, during the Feast of Passover, he set out for Petah Tikva to meet a young friend who was a disciple and one of the closest colleagues of Ber Borochov, who tried to establish the theory of the Return to Zion on a Marxist foundation. Despite his respect and esteem for Borochov, Ben-Zvi was not enthusiastic for his theory. He followed his independent point of view in laboring for the redemption of Israel, becoming one of the leaders of the Poalei Zion movement in this country and the creator of the Hebrew literature of labor. For a short time he lived in Jaffa, where a group of Poalei Zion members cherished the dream of a military organization to be called Bar Giora, which took the practical form of the establishment of Hashomer in 1908. Ben-Zvi was its political and spiritual head. After Jaffa, Ben-Zvi settled in Jerusalem. In his eyes, Jerusalem was the heart of the Homeland, and he rarely stirred from it in all his days.

He and his wife, Rahel, were among the first teachers in the first Hebrew High School in Jerusalem. Ben-Zvi headed the Poalei Zion movement in Israel, which did not in all respects follow the lead of Poalei Zion abroad. It struck out on its own new path toward the realization of the vision of redemption—the path of labor, settlement, defense, revival of the Hebrew language, development of a ramified rural and urban economy, and independent Jewish organization. In the prewar days he was one of the few who appreciated the merits of what is known as the Old Yishuv, though he did not ignore its faults, and he was already familiar with all the tribes of Israel—Bukharans, Persians, Yemenites, Kurds, and the rest. Even in his youth he understood that practical work in the Homeland— immigration, settlement, the revival of Hebrew, and the accumulation of Jewish strength— was the reliable road to resurgence, and he always regarded the goal of resurgence as sovereign independence, namely, a Jewish State.

Ben-Zvi saw that the Jewish community in this country relied mostly on the protection of foreign consuls who had extensive rights under the Ottoman Empire, and that it did not constitute an independent political factor. He realized the need to activate Ottoman Jewry as a political force, especially after the Young Turk Revolution in 1908; and he decided to go to Constantinople to study the Turkish language and Ottoman Law with a view to political activity in that city. When his studies were interrupted in 1914 by the outbreak of the First World War, he returned to Jerusalem.

When he realized that most of the Jews in the country were foreign nationals, especially Russians, and subject to deportation if Turkey entered the war on Germany's side, he founded, together with several veteran public figures in Jerusalem, an Ottomanization Committee in the home of the Haham Bashi (the Sephardi Chief Rabbi). Together with a young friend who had studied law with him at the Turkish University in Constantinople, he worked for the naturalization of Jews who were foreign citizens, so that they would not be deported. With this colleague, he approached the Turkish Commander of Jerusalem, Zakki Bey, and proposed the establishment of a Jewish militia to defend Jerusalem in case of war. His proposal was accepted, and scores of young Jews in Jerusalem, including that great writer, the late Joseph Chaim Brenner, joined his force and began military training.

This effort did not last long. Jamal Pasha, Commander of the Ottoman forces on the southern front, ordered the dissolution of the militia, and started a campaign of oppression and punitive measures against national movements among both Jews and Arabs in this area. He had a number of Arab leaders in Beirut hanged, and the same fate might have befallen Jewish leaders had it not been for the intervention of the American Ambassador, Henry Morgenthau, in Constantinople, who took all the Jews of Palestine under his protection by order of President Woodrow Wilson. Thus the lives, but not liberty, of the Jewish leaders were saved. Ben-Zvi and his friend were arrested, interrogated, and imprisoned in Jerusalem.

As former students of a Turkish university, they enjoyed easy conditions. During the day they could move about freely in the courtyard of the government buildings, which included the prison, and were allowed to receive visitors. Of the older leaders of the community, there was only one brave man who was not afraid to come and visit the two young prisoners. This was Albert Entebi, a Sephardi Jew, representative of the Alliance Israelite Universelle in Jerusalem, and one of the proudest and most stalwart Jewish leaders in Jerusalem at the time. At meetings in prison with the Executive of the Poalei Zion party, the two prisoners decided that if they were sentenced to deportation they would go to the United States and organize a pioneering movement, and if that country joined the Allies against Germany and Turkey, they would establish a Jewish Legion in the American Army to fight for the conquest and liberation of the Homeland. An order for perpetual exile was indeed issued against Ben-Zvi and his colleague, and they were placed on board a ship bound for Egypt. When they arrived in Alexandria, they were arrested by the British authorities as enemy nationals, and again it was only thanks to the intervention of the American Consul that they were set free and allowed to depart for the United States.

The plan that Ben-Zvi and his younger colleague worked out in prison was carried out. They organized a pioneering movement, called Hehalutz, all over the US and Canada. After America entered the war they established, together with Pinhas Rutenberg, Jewish battalions, though not in the American Army as they had intended—for America had declared war on Germany, not on Turkey—but in the British Army.

Ben-Zvi remained in the United States for three years. Besides useful work in organizing Hehalutz, the Jewish Congress, and the Jewish Legion, he devoted most of his time, together with his young colleague, to writing a basic book on the Land of Israel, past and present. The book was to be in ten volumes, but after the appearance of the first the two authors volunteered for the Jewish Legion and were sent to Canada for basic training, afterward to Britain, and finally to Egypt. In the Tel-el-Kabir Desert they met the Palestinian volunteers, headed by the late Berl Katznelson, Shmuel Yavne'eli, Eliyahu Golomb, and Dov Hos.

At this meeting the idea of a general and comprehensive unity of the workers in the

Land of Israel took shape, and at the beginning of 1919 the Zionist Socialist Association of Workers in the Land of Israel—Ahdut Haavodah—was founded in Petah Tikva. Since most of the members of the Hapoel Hatzair Party refused to join this association, there was founded a year later, in December 1921, the General Federation of Labor, known as the Histadrut. Ben-Zvi, one of the principal founders of the Histadrut, did not regard the working-class organization as separate from the nation as a whole—in this he differed from his teacher and colleague, Borochov. He saw it as one of the principal factors in the organization of the entire people and its activation as a pioneering force. Immediately after his discharge he took his place at the head of those who organized the Jewish community, and later was elected chairman of the Jewish National Council.

When the first British High Commissioner, Sir Herbert Samuel, arrived, Ben-Zvi was appointed, together with the late David Yellin, Chaim Margalit, and Kalvariski, to the Palestinian Council, which had ten Palestinian members—four Moslems, three Jews, and three Christians. In May 1921, after the disturbances in Jaffa and the stoppage of Jewish immigration by the High Commissioner, Ben-Zvi resigned from the Council in protest against the Mandatory Government's inaccurate statements about the disturbances, the behavior of the government forces, and the temporary stoppage of immigration as a reward to the rioters. In the first elected assembly of the Jewish community, Ben-Zvi, together with Yellin and Dr. Jacob Thon, were appointed as the Presidium of Three that headed the Jewish National Council. Later he became sole chairman.

Upon the establishment of the State, Ben-Zvi was one of the active members of the Knesset. But along with his variegated public work, he did not abandon the pursuit of learning. While continuing to study the Bible and the Talmud, he devoted himself to historical research, centered on two subjects closer to his heart than any others: 1. The eternal bond that was preserved, not only in emotion and instinct, but in practice between the Jewish people and its land. By constant effort he succeeded in revealing the uninterrupted continuity of Jewish settlement in the Land of Israel and the existence of Jewish agriculture in the Homeland in all ages. Many are aware of his special interest and deep affection for the ancient Jewish community in Peki'in. 2. The second object of his researches, in which he had no rival in Israel, and especially characteristic of his sentiments, was the history and customs of the tribes of Israel—in particular the far-off and forgotten tribes, even if they had become separated from the mass of the people, either in the Diaspora or as far back as the days of the First and Second Temples, like the Karaites and the Samaritans.

His love and devotion to all sections of the Jewish people, despite their dispersion, differences of opinion, and varied customs, was displayed in these studies, and it was this devotion that won for Ben-Zvi such love from the entire Jewish people as, I believe, was vouchsafed to no other man in our own and past generations. It was this that made him the President of Israel, not only as one elected to the post, but as the man who was chosen, beloved, and trusted by the nation, a privilege to which there is no parallel among our people, rent and divided as it is by a multitude of parties, communities, and tribes.

I had the privilege of working with Yitzhak Ben-Zvi ever since I arrived in this country in the spring of 1906. I have never known a man so great in achievement and spirit, and at the same time so humble, modest, and simple in all his ways with the great and the small. More than any other man of his era he symbolized the love and unity of Israel, and the entire people felt this. I do not know of another person in our generation who enjoyed the pure and sincere love of all the tribes and communities of the people as did Yitzhak Ben-Zvi. For his ways, his words, his customs, and his attitudes were the essence of simplicity, nobility, true sincerity, and purity of heart. Ben-Zvi was the most esteemed and beloved Jew in Israel and in departing from us entered into the eternal shrine of Jewish history.

One week after the President's death the Knesset convened for a special session. He was eulogized with deep emotion by the Speaker and by representatives of every party.

Anti-Israeli Federation of Egypt, Syria, and Iraq ★ Visit of Former German Defense Minister ★ Shazar Becomes the Third President of Israel

In his review of the security and political picture on the fifteenth anniversary of the State of Israel (May 6, 1963), the Prime Minister also touched on the problem of primacy:

"It would be vain to seek for the beginning of our enterprise of resurgence. Something that has lived in the hearts of our people for millennia, a tradition going back to the fathers of the nation, four thousand years ago, has no beginning. Jewish history, which is unique in the annals of mankind, was not created in a vacuum and has not been exempt from the influence of international conditions and the influence of the peoples among whom the Jews lived. The national and social struggles of the nineteenth century in Europe, when the Jews were mainly a European people, left a deep impression on the first pioneers."

In the 70 years between the founding of Petah Tikva and the proclamation of the State of Israel, Ben-Gurion pointed out, 333 rural and urban settlements were built and the Jewish population grew from 20,000 to 650,000. In the 15 years of independence, 543 settlements were built and over a million immigrants arrived.

After reviewing the political policy adopted by Israel in the First and all subsequent Knessets, which centered on efforts to achieve economic, social, and political cooperation with all the neighboring countries, the Prime Minister spoke of the treaty of federation concluded a few weeks earlier, on April 17, 1963, by Egypt, Syria, and Iraq. It stated that "This unity is a revolution, especially because it is strongly connected with the question of Palestine and the national duty to liberate it." So that there should be no mistake about the meaning of "liberation of Palestine" and how it is to be carried out, the treaty declared that the aim of the union was "the establishment of a military unity [of the three states] capable of liberating the Arab homelands from the dangers of Zionism."

"In the past week, on May 1," Ben-Gurion said, "a member of the British Cabinet, the Lord Privy Seal, Mr. Heath, was asked by a member of Parliament what joint policy had been agreed upon by Britain and America if there should be an attack on Israel by the Arab countries. Mr. Heath replied in the name of the government: 'We are in close touch with the United States Government concerning events in the area. However, we have no reason to believe that the Arab states are contemplating an attack on Israel.' The Lord Privy Seal chose his words carefully. He did not say that they had reason to believe that the Arab states were *not* contemplating an attack on Israel, but that they had no reason to believe that the Arab states were contemplating an attack on Israel. Did he not believe the political declaration by the leaders of the three Arab countries? Or perhaps his Ambassador in Egypt, Syria, or Iraq had received an undertaking that the promise 'to liberate Palestine' had been given only to deceive public opinion in these countries, and that in fact the Arab countries had no intention whatever of attacking Israel?

"The armaments that the Soviet Union and Czechoslovakia were supplying to Egypt were continuing to flow. Russian instructors were improving the training of the Egyptian Army. We had grounds to believe that the Arab countries *were* contemplating an attack on Israel and that this danger could be prevented in two ways and in two ways only: by strengthening the deterrent power of the Israel Defense Forces and by securing the moral and political support of all those world forces which were as concerned as we are for the maintenance of peace in this area and the world."

After a two-day debate and the Prime Minister's reply on May 15, Akiva Govrin's motion on behalf of the Coalition parties was adopted. It read:

1. The Knesset takes cognizance of the Prime Minister's statement to the Knesset on May 6, 1963.
2. The Knesset draws the attention of the Great Powers and world public opinion to the threat to Israel's existence contained in the plan of action of the Federation of Egypt, Syria, and Iraq, headed by Nasser.
3. The Knesset instructs the Government to increase and strengthen the deterrent power and state of preparedness of the Israel Defense Forces and to continue to reinforce the border settlements.

On May 20, 1963, Begin called into question the invitation of the former German Defense Minister Strauss to visit Israel. "I believe," he stated, "that the Government's decision in this matter—if the Government has so decided—is politically speaking a step devoid of wisdom, and morally speaking devoid of all responsibility. For this reason we request that while there is still time the Knesset hold a debate on this grave, unfortunate, and revolting Government decision, in order to bring about its cancellation." Mikunis and Barzilai seconded Begin's proposal.

Minister of Finance Eshkol replied that since we began maintaining certain practical relations and ties with Germany several elections had taken place and though one could not say that the matter was not controversial, the citizens had made their opinion clear. On May 15 the Moscow *Pravda* had featured on page one a reception given by the Prime Minister in the Kremlin for the Director of the Board of the Krupp Works, and we all know the relationship between Krupp and the Nazi regime. Krupp was even tried for Nazi crimes. Nothing like this is known of Strauss. Our feeling is that in this situation we should take Germany's position among the European states into account. He proposed that the motion by Begin, Mikunis, and Barzilai be dropped, and it was rejected, forty-seven to thirty.

On May 13, 1963, Knesset Speaker Luz announced that there were two candidates for the office of President of the State: Shneur Zalman Shazar and Peretz Bernstein. Balloting by the Knesset took place on May 21, 1963. Shazar received sixty-seven votes and Bernstein forty-four; seven ballots were left blank, twelve Knesset members were absent, and Knesset member Ami Assaf had died and not yet been replaced. The Speaker announced that Shazar had been elected President of the State and would take his oath of office the following day.

Next morning a delegation on behalf of the Knesset set out for the home of the President-elect to congratulate him and invite him to take his oath of office in the Knesset. Just before 11 A.M. he arrived at the Knesset, in the company of an Adjutant and the Chief of Protocol and escorted by a guard of mounted and motorcycle policemen. Mr. Shazar entered the chamber to the sound of blasts on the traditional shofars [rams' horns]. All members and guests arose and sat down only after the President had taken his seat on the rostrum. The Speaker asked Mr. Shazar to rise, and then read for him the declaration of allegiance. The President, his head covered, placed his left hand on the Bible, raised his right, and said, "I, Shneur Zalman, son of Sarah and Yehuda Leib Shazar, pledge allegiance to the State of Israel and its laws, and pledge faithfully to carry out my functions as President of the State of Israel." He signed the declaration. The Speaker invited him to deliver his inaugural address. The President said:

The thirty days of mourning have not yet passed for the second President of the State of Israel, beloved by the nation, illustrious pioneer and the dearest of friends to me, Yitzhak Ben-Zvi of blessed memory. We still breathe the atmosphere of noble simplicity with which he surrounded the office of President as long as he filled that position.

Moreover, we still remember with gratitude and deep emotion the miracle of our beginnings, when this place was occupied by the first President of the State, who restored our ancient glories, the man who was for decades the president of the World Zionist Organization, the late Chaim Weizmann. And now you, the nation's elect, have come forward and decided that I must this day ascend and occupy this office. In all humility and with profound misgivings I accept your verdict.

Our State is a State of redemption. Only twenty years ago we were clearly shown what could lie in store for our people when it was devoid of sovereign independence. The lesson of those days is eternally graven in our hearts; and therefore no sacrifice is too heavy for our people to safeguard the peace, freedom, and future of the State of Israel.

Like the best of states, Israel guarantees liberty and equality for all its citizens, without distinction of nationality, race, community, or origin. It is the State of all its people, and it is concerned for the welfare of them all. Whenever clouds of blood, race hatred, and hostility between nations overcast the world's skies, we are among those that love peace, sow the seeds of international fraternity, and are devoted to the freedom of man. This was the message of Israel's genius, through the prophets of righteousness and truth at the beginning of our springtime, and our sons have fought in all the world's struggles, together with the best of all nations, for the advancement of man to the fullness of this ideal.

Our country is open to all the Jews of the world, who are coming here and will yet come here from all the lands to which they have been dispersed. We shall always remember that we still have a people all over the world, a people that is of our bone and our flesh, a people subject to incitements in one corner of the world, and spiritual self-abasement in another, and nevertheless remains devoted to Israel's heritage and its hope for resurgence, and strives to preserve its individuality. We are with it in its trials and tribulations; and we long with all our hearts to see its sons share in our struggle and our constructive endeavors. Let us not rest until all the younger generation of Jewry are devoted partners with us in bearing the burden of responsibility for the rebirth of our people. Long is the road ahead, and strewn with many trials, but the light of the Divine Presence of our redemption shines upon it.

After congratulations by the Speaker, all the members rose, cried "Long Live the President!" and sang the national anthem.

A New Criminal Code ★ The Knesset Memorializes Ami Assaf and Dr. Chaim Boger

On June 4, 1963, the Minister of Justice, Dr. Dov Joseph, placed before the Knesset a revised Code of Criminal Procedure.

On several occasions I have mentioned the preparation under way for presentation of a comprehensive bill to codify criminal procedure. I am happy now to submit this bill for first reading. The need to update the laws of criminal procedure has been felt more and more in recent years. The existing code consists of many different layers, including Ottoman legislation, remnants of which are still in force; extensive Mandatory legislation likewise was enacted in bits and pieces at various times with provisions of English Common Law added to it; and a considerable body of Israeli legislation and rulings. Apart from these superimposed layers, amendments have also been numerous in every period. The result is a legal system of substantial complexity in which it is hard for a citizen charged with an offense to know just which procedures are applicable in his case. This complexity dates back to the early period of the Mandate Government when the legislator first attempted to complement the Ottoman procedural law and then to replace it with a more modern system and to reorganize the judicial institutions.

An important factor in the development of the criminal procedure was the structure of jurisdiction of the criminal courts. At first there were four kinds of judges who sat in criminal cases of first instance: Local Magistrates, who generally were empowered to try contraventions and misdemeanors and could impose sentences of up to one year of imprisonment and a fine of 100 pounds; British Magistrates, who could impose up to two years of imprisonment and a fine of 200 pounds; judges of the District Courts, who could try all noncapital offenses and impose any penalty prescribed by law; and finally the Supreme Court and the District Courts, which tried capital cases.

To this hierarchy of judicial authorities was added the right of an accused, when brought before a Local Magistrate, to demand a trial by a British Magistrate or when brought before a Magistrate's Court to be tried by a District Court; likewise the Magistrate's Court had the authority to refer cases to the District Court. In certain cases this also applied to the Attorney General. If we also remember that with regard to felonies the Mandatory legislator adopted the method of preliminary investigation, we will understand the reasons for the differences of procedure among the various Palestinian courts—especially since the Mandatory authorities did not see fit to enact a single piece of legislation to cover all judicial instances but merely enacted various laws from time to time.

From the first days of the Mandatory Government to the present things have changed considerably. At the end of the Mandate the difference in judicial authority between Local and British Magistrates was abolished and instead a differentiation was made between Magistrates and Chief Magistrates. This was maintained for some time in Israel as well. The court for serious offenses was likewise abolished. The Courts Law of 1957 divided them in a simple way by authorizing Magistrate's Courts to try all contraventions and misdemeanors and the District Courts to try felonies. The Magistrates Courts were likewise in every case authorized to impose the maximum penalties provided by law. Preliminary investigations were limited to a relatively few cases in comparison to previous practice. Instead of being mandatory in all felony cases, preliminary investigation is now optional and applies only to felonies carrying a sentence of ten years or more.

Let me indicate an important way in which this bill differs from the present law. The first point relates to the question of who does the prosecuting. The existing procedure considers the prosecutor to be the Attorney General, who is customarily cited as the plaintiff. Recently it was decided that if the indictment is submitted by the Police, the State shall be cited as plaintiff. It appears that owing to the special status of the Mandatory Government and the lack of clarity regarding its sovereignty over the Mandate area, the legislator at the time preferred the practical arrangement of making the Attorney General be the plaintiff. Today, however, the State is considered to be demanding public satisfaction in a criminal case. We therefore propose that in a criminal case the plaintiff be the State and that it be represented by the prosecution.

The bill has a number of other noteworthy elements but because of its scope and extent I am unable to list all of them at this time. I am confident that the Law Committee will produce a better draft after studying the bill. I wish to express the hope that in view of the scope of this legislation the Committee will do its best to conclude its hearings as early as possible.

At the conclusion of a debate on June 10 and 11 the proposed Code of Criminal Procedure was referred to the Law Committee.

Ami Assaf, the son of S. Wilkomitz, one of the first and best teachers in the Yishuv, died of a heart attack on July 5, 1963.

Ami Assaf was born in Rosh Pina on July 22, 1903. He was a member of Kibbutz Kfar Yehoshua. For five years he served as Deputy Minister of Education and Culture and invested much energy and talent in the development of education in Israel. On July 27, 1963, he was eulogized in the Knesset by the Speaker, Kadish Luz, by the Minister of Education and Culture, Abba Eban, and by Shmuel Shoresh, a leader of the kibbutz movement.

The Speaker said in part:

After a typical long day's work in which he participated in a meeting of his party's central committee, delivered a speech summing up an extensive debate on the problems of education in Israel, and read far into the night, Ami Assaf's heart suddenly stopped beating. His father, the distinguished teacher Wilkomitz, came to Israel at the end of the First Aliya but his way of life and outlook were closer to that of the new immigrants of the Second Aliya. It was in the atmosphere and ideology of that Aliya that Assaf grew up.

His mother tongue was Hebrew. His style of speech was Hebrew from the start. The landscape of Israel was the natural setting in which he developed a thorough feeling for independence and national integrity. The public affairs of the Second Aliya endowed him with an unreserved readiness for pioneering effort and strength for creative and revolutionary action, like the revolution of growth and creation wrought on desolate land by the first rain. Ami Assaf absorbed the atmosphere and ideals of the Second Aliya—Zionism, labor, agriculture, national independence, equality among men, nonexploitation and mutual aid. Like many others he ventured, together with his friends, to lay the foundations for a new settlement in the Homeland, to build and mould an ideal which he followed from youth to his last day.

Assaf used to say that Kfar Yehoshua was his agricultural college, as well as a university for social life, proper personal relations, and the consolidation of a group which carried out the ideals of this movement. He was the author of numerous articles and published a book devoted to clarification of the ideological foundations of the moshav movement and description of the situation in its settlements. A member of the Knesset from the outset to his last day, and one of its active participants, his speeches always attracted attention. He was for many years Deputy Minister of Education and Culture and his important work in the Ministry and speeches in the Knesset are well known.

"Great and many were the achievements of Ami Assaf as a pioneer and settler," the Minister of Education and Culture added. "But the crowning glory of his life undoubtedly was his accomplishments in Israeli education at the time of its great expansion. To this work he devoted his entire strength of spirit and ardent diligence. He knew full well that the fate of his nation would be decided in the lists of knowledge and intellect. When Ami was brought to his final resting place in Kfar Yehoshua, many wreaths were laid on his grave. Most of them came from the children of Israel in their hundreds of schools who had lost a teacher and educator, a loyal friend who looked after their interests and fought their battles."

After Shmuel Shoresh, a member of the secretariat of the Moshav Movement, had described Assaf's life work, the Knesset rose in tribute to his memory.

Some weeks earlier Israel suffered another sad loss with the death of Dr. Chaim Boger [Bograshov] on June 8. Dr. Boger was born in the Crimea on September 25, 1876, received his Ph.D. at the University of Bern in Switzerland, and came to Israel in 1906, where he was hired as a teacher in the Hebrew High School founded by Dr. Matmon-Cohen. His entry marked the beginning of the school's expansion from a small institution with five teachers and thirty-five students to a modern high school with a student body of hundreds. After Turkey's entry into World War One he was forced to leave the country and he opened a Hebrew school in Egypt, attended by six hundred refugee children from Israel. Returning in 1919, he became the principal of the high school together with Dr. B. Z. Mosinson. He was a diligent worker in the Zionist movement and a member of the Zionist Executive.

Dr. Boger was eulogized in the Knesset by Speaker Luz, and the members rose in tribute to his memory.

David Ben-Gurion Resigns ★ Levi Eshkol Presents the New Government

At the end of the Cabinet meeting of June 16, 1963, Prime Minister Ben-Gurion announced that he was resigning from the Government for personal reasons. He had planned to make the announcement on the morrow of the Independence Day celebrations, but because of new complications in the Middle East—the tripartite federation of Egypt, Syria, and Iraq and the appeal he had sent to the heads of governments of nations with which Israel had diplomatic relations—he deferred it until now. The first reply from a foreign statesman regarding the menace of the Arab federation came from French President Charles De Gaulle. The reply, which was friendly, was submitted to the Cabinet on June 16.

Though the Prime Minister's resignation necessitated the resignation of the entire Government, it had to remain in office until the Knesset had expressed confidence in a new government. Ben-Gurion therefore requested a leave of absence until such a new government had been formed. The request was granted. Several members of the Government tried to persuade him to remain on at least as Minister of Defense. Ben-Gurion, however, declared that he had spent fifteen years at his post and that his decision was final. The Cabinet was invited to lunch at the home of the new President, Zalman Shazar, where Ben-Gurion proposed that the President immediately summon all the parties and name Levi Eshkol to form a new government.

The following day the Minister of Finance informed the Knesset that the Prime Minister had resigned for personal reasons and that in accordance with the Law of Transition the present Government would remain in office until its successor was formed. On June 24 the Speaker announced that he had received the following message from the President: "I hereby inform you that I have this day entrusted Knesset member Levi Eshkol with the task of forming a new Government." The same day Eshkol presented the new Government to the Knesset, as follows:

Levi Eshkol, Prime Minister and Minister of Defense; Abba Eban, Deputy Prime Minister; Yigal Allon, Minister of Labor; Joseph Almogi, Minister of Housing and Development; Zalman Aranne, Minister of Education and Culture; Joseph Burg, Minister of Welfare; Israel Bar-Yehuda, Minister of Transport; Moshe Dayan, Minister of Agriculture; Zerah Warhaftig, Minister of Religious Affairs; Dov Joseph, Minister of Justice; Golda Meir, Minister of Foreign Affairs; Pinhas Sapir, Minister of Finance, Commerce, and Industry; Behor Shalom Shitreet, Minister of Police; Moshe Shapira, Minister of the Interior and Health; Eliyahu Sasson, Minister of Posts.

In his address to the Knesset, Eshkol said:

> I have the honor to present to the Knesset a Government supported by all the parties of the previous coalition: Mapai, the National Religious Party, Ahdut Haavodah-Poalei Zion, Poalei Agudat Israel, Shituf v'Ahvah, and Kidmah u'Fituah. This is a continuity government. Its plan of action for the coming years will be guided by the principles embodied in the statement of Basic Policy submitted to the Fourth Knesset on December 16, 1959, which subsequently served as the Basic Policy of the Government presented on November 2, 1961, apart from changes that have taken place through legislation enacted by the Fourth and Fifth Knessets. For the convenience of members this statement of basic principles has been tabled in the House.
>
> We shall also be bound by the existing coalition agreements. In spite of its continuity in party composition and in platform, the Government differs from its predecessor. David Ben-Gurion, to my profound regret, will not be its head.
>
> For decades before we achieved independence and after the establishment of the State, almost without interruption, David Ben-Gurion stood at the head of our national struggle. With his soaring vision, penetrating insights, his boldness in decision and his capacity for action, he led our people in the momentous struggles which brought about the establishment of the State and the ingathering of the exiles, and determined its status in the world and its character at home. More than any other man in our generation he deserves the title of "The Maker of the State." He has won the love and the profound gratitude of the entire nation.
>
> Ben-Gurion has succeeded in harnessing the spiritual and physical energies of the resurgent Israeli nation and directed them to the execution of the tremendous tasks imposed on our generation by the fiat of Jewish history. In his ardent faith in the mission of our eternal

people he has been able to overcome all obstacles—provocation and hostility all around us and indifference abroad—and he has succeeded in preventing weakness at home.

On the foundations of the pioneering achievements of the first builders of the new Jewry in this country, and the yearning of the generation, he has forged with boldness and determination the instruments for our national resurgence: the State and its army, the Israel Defense Forces, which crushed the enemies who rose to destroy us, and established the boundaries of Israel. He has struggled for the realization of the vision of the generations, the vision of the return to Zion—he has struggled and prevailed. It is his identification of our people's noblest aspirations for revival, which have inspired us throughout two thousand years of exile and suffering, that will establish David Ben-Gurion's place in history as one of our people's greatest visionaries and men of action in all generations. He is assured of this title in his own right, irrespective of any official position or title.

Members of the Knesset, this Government, which I have the honor to present to you and the heavy responsibility of heading, will persevere in the path that has been followed by the previous Governments, in line with changes in circumstances. The Government's policies as a whole are given in detail in a statement of basic principles and will certainly find expression in debates in the future.

On June 26, 1963, after a three-day debate, the Knesset expressed confidence in the new Government by a vote of sixty-four to forty-three, and the members of the Cabinet signed declarations of allegiance.

Section 4. Again the "Lavon Affair"

Ben-Gurion in 1964 Seeks Judicial Inquiry into Ministerial Findings of 1960–1961 on the "Security Mishap" of 1954

THE "security mishap" of 1954, popularly known as the "Lavon Affair," flared up again more than a decade later, after this writer had retired to private life. To refresh the reader's memory, we must revert briefly to earlier events.

On November 2, 1961, after the elections to the Fifth Knesset, Ben-Gurion presented his new Cabinet, in which he remained as Prime Minister. On that occasion, in a clear reference to the "affair," he declared that neither the Knesset nor the Government exercised judicial functions; that the Knesset's authority did not extend to revising past events, and that the Government had no right to adjudicate a dispute between individuals. No member of either the Coalition or the Opposition disputed this view, and the Knesset voted confidence in the new Government.

What he considered a miscarriage of justice by the ministerial Committee of Seven in 1960–1961, however, would give the Prime Minister no peace, since he considered the moral integrity of the supreme organs of the State indispensable to its existence. In order to bring about a judicial inquiry to rectify the wrong, he felt it necessary that as thorough an examination as possible be made of all the data available on the deliberations of the ministerial committee. Accordingly he ordered all State bodies possessing material directly or indirectly connected with the affair to place them at the disposal of Hagai

Eshed, a trusted journalist. The study by Eshed continued for more than a year. For security reasons it could not be published—military censorship had deleted more than half of it—but his report was turned over to the Prime Minister.

The sole basis, and a doubtful one at best, for the findings of the Committee of Seven, in effect exonerating Lavon, was the testimony a secretary gave to Gideon Hausner, Attorney General at the time, when he questioned her in Paris, at the committee's request. She recalled, though vaguely, that in 1954 she had changed a sentence in one of the letters that figured in the case. But a police investigation in 1961 (when the woman was back in Israel) and the material now compiled by Eshed made it clear beyond doubt that if she made a change it was not in the crucial letter by the Senior Officer dated July 19, 1954, but in one dated November 1, 1954.

The Senior Officer, of course, was one of the principals in the case. He had written to the Chief of Staff, Moshe Dayan, not one letter but two. The first was so prolix and vague that Dayan requested another, clearer and more concise. The second letter contained the expression "the Minister of Defense directed me," and it was not a forgery, as claimed by some, but a condensed version of what he had written in the original letter. It was on the basis of this revised letter that the Chief of Staff informed the General Staff that the "security mishap" had been implemented on the order of Minister of Defense Lavon.

The police investigation established, with reference to this all-important letter, that (1) its date had not been altered; (2) no changes had been made and the words "according to Lavon's orders" were in the original letter; (3) it had not been typed by the secretary who many years later gave the testimony but by another typist.

Two private attorneys, A. Hoter-Yishai and M. Tunik, volunteered to examine all the documents in Ben-Gurion's possession from the legal standpoint. When their judgment supported the likelihood that the Committee of Seven had perverted justice, the former Prime Minister proposed to his successor, Levi Eshkol, who had been an active member of that ministerial committee, that he ask the Supreme Court to examine its findings.

If the court determined that the committee had acted properly, he explained, its conduct would be cleared and vindicated, while if it were found that the committee had acted improperly, it would amount to an honest error that the Prime Minister himself wanted to set straight. On the other hand, should he, Ben-Gurion, bring the issue to the court and it determined that the committee had perverted justice, it would seriously hurt the prestige of the Prime Minister. "Let me think it over," Eshkol replied. Ben-Gurion agreed and a week later returned to receive his decision. The Prime Minister rejected the suggestion. "In that case," Ben-Gurion said, "I will ask the Minister of Justice for a judicial hearing."

On October 22, 1964, Ben-Gurion therefore submitted the issue to the Minister of Justice, Dr. Dov Joseph, and the Attorney General, Ben-Zev. He turned over to them the compilation of data made by Hagai Eshed, the legal analysis of the two private attorneys, and documents from his own contacts with the Committee of Seven, when he was Prime Minister. He urged "the creation of a committee of inquiry consisting of Justices of the Supreme Court (1) to investigate the Government's refusal in 1960 to set up a judicial inquiry, as requested by the accused Senior Officer, and its appointment instead of a ministerial committee; and (2) to determine whether the procedures and findings of this committee were in accord with truth, justice, and the laws of the land."

Two weeks later, on November 6, 1964, the opinion of the Attorney General as submitted to the Minister of Justice was published in the press. The Attorney General dealt with each of the three sets of documents delivered to him: the personal memorandum by David Ben-Gurion, the survey by Mr. Eshed, and the legal opinion by the lawyers Hoter-Ishai and Tunik.

First he discussed the Eshed survey, which was in the nature of historical research on the events of the years 1954–1960. "To Mr. Eshed's credit," he declared "let it be said that he does not present his conclusions as the final word but states that a number of investigations have to be made before the case can be considered closed. Eshed's aim is to show that there is plenty of evidence, including some found after the Committee of Seven finished its work, that would undermine its conclusions absolving Lavon of giving the order to the officer on July 16, 1954. It is therefore on this aspect alone that Eshed's work should be reviewed—his contribution to the clarification of the matter assessed. It is my opinion that Eshed succeeded in achieving this aim."

With respect to the opinion submitted by the lawyers, the Attorney General had this to say:

> The opinion of Hoter-Yishai and Tunik is mainly a critique of the committee's procedures. It is impossible to disregard the fact that the criticism is sharp. The committee is accused of no less than exceeding its authority, bias, and preventing important witnesses and testimony, which would have completely changed the picture, from being heard.
>
> The major principle in our system of justice is that flawed legal procedure does not have the effect of nullifying proceedings and findings, unless injustice is caused thereby. If injustice is caused—if, moreover, any proceedings, whether judicial or quasi-judicial, are impaired, according to the principles of natural justice—the proceedings are considered null and void.
>
> From the conclusions submitted by the ministerial Committee [of Seven] for the Cabinet's approval we learn that the committee did not hear witnesses and that the majority of its members were of the opinion that it was not authorized to do so. The committee thus admits that it declined to operate properly in inquiring into a dispute that is essentially a question of facts. Had the committee limited itself to procedural conclusions, this flaw in its work would perhaps not have been crucial. But since it drew conclusions on factual questions—such as the finding in Paragraph 8 to its conclusions that "There is good reason to believe that this testimony (that which the 'secretary' gave in Paris) is accurate, and that the Senior Officer submitted a forged letter to the Olshan-Dori Committee [1954] as proof that he received the order from Lavon," or the decisive finding further on that "We establish therefore that Lavon did not give the order upon which the Senior Officer based himself, and that the security mishap was implemented without his knowledge"—the committee's decision not to hear witnesses is grave. It must be added that the committee also declined to hear the Senior Officer and refused to permit his lawyer to appear and present his claims. In this way the committee infringed on the right of a man to appear and defend himself against accusations directed against him, and artificially limited the field of its inquiry.

The Attorney General then quoted a considerable amount of judicial material to prove that an accused is entitled to be present and to cross-examine the prosecution's witnesses, and he stated:

> The Committee of Seven appears to have ignored the above principles and conducted its work without observing the principles of natural justice and the rules for conducting

proceedings of this kind. To this it should be added that even in gathering its material the committee showed impatience both in that it refused to hear witnesses and in that it accepted the evidence of the secretary as something proved and beyond dispute, although it was aware that the matter was still the subject of a police inquiry.

Of course, in this matter the committee showed a certain amount of restraint by noting that "police inquiry is now in progress in this connection, but it is sufficient for the purposes of this inquiry to say that there is a reasonable assumption that this statement is correct." The question remained, however, whether this inquiry was something special, different from the need to investigate the truth of the case itself. No court of law would pass judgment before an investigation is completed. In view of this and without going into all the other arguments of Messrs. Hoter-Yishai and Tunik, I feel that the *factual findings of the Committee of Seven would not have stood the test of an Israel court.* (Emphasis is mine—D.B-G.)

The Attorney General then referred to the personal memorandum in which Ben-Gurion outlined his connection with the "Lavon Affair" and its aftermath through the years, particularly, in his own words: "My reactions to the actions of the members of the Government who dealt with it through the Committee of Seven that ended with my resignation on January 31, 1961." Ben-Gurion, Ben-Zev stated, had concluded with a request to appoint an "inquiry committee made up of Supreme Court judges," as already quoted above. In parentheses Ben-Zev noted that "The Attorney General has no authority to appoint an inquiry committee, hence such a request is superfluous."

The Attorney General's opinion went on to note that the Committee of Seven had undertaken to determine the facts in a controversial matter without having any judicial or quasi-judicial standing recognized by law. Its mistake was that it took upon itself to rule upon extremely complicated questions of fact, thus playing a quasi-judicial role. Its factual conclusions were in the nature of personal opinions and had no judicial value: "No investigator making a scientific study of this matter would feel himself bound by the findings of the committee, and could, moreover, easily discover its defects."

He listed various arguments for and against a new investigation and concluded: "There are cases in which the truth refuses to come to light, when it appears only after many hard trials, or accidentally, or at an unexpected time. But whatever the Cabinet decides, whether to reopen the affair or not, it must take into consideration that it still possibly will not have had the final word."

The Minister of Justice on his part declared that "A committee of inquiry should be appointed under the Inquiry Committee Ordinance to carry out a complete, thorough, and comprehensive investigation of the entire matter of the 'security mishap' to determine who was responsible for it, whether or not the Minister of Defense or anyone else gave the order for it, and whether or not the Senior Officer acted on his own without the Minister's knowledge."

Three days after publication of the opinions of the Attorney General and the Minister of Justice, on November 9, 1964, Prime Minister Eshkol informed the Knesset that Moshe Dayan had resigned as Minister of Agriculture and the Cabinet had decided to co-opt Chaim Gavati to take his place. Yehuda Sha'ari (Liberal Party) claimed that Dayan had not resigned for reasons of health or because of a crisis in his Ministry but because of differences of opinion between himself and the Prime Minister. The present Cabinet, he charged, was demoralized and paralyzed by internal contradictions: "We feel, in addition, that this Government should resign because it has brought us an economic disaster de luxe." The proposal to co-opt G'vati was approved by a vote of forty to twenty-nine with nine abstaining.

Mapai Central Committee Debates the Conduct of the Ministerial Committee ★ Ben-Gurion Disputes Eshkol on Its Origin

The grave criticism leveled by the Attorney General against the procedures and conclusions of the Committee of Seven made a powerful impression on public opinion, as well as on the ruling Mapai Party. Many demanded that the party's governing bodies convene to consider the problem, but the Prime Minister and the top leadership sought to prevent this. At the meeting of the Mapai Secretariat on December 12, 1964, Prime Minister Eshkol, having considered the matter and consulted other Cabinet members, announced his conclusion that they could not accept the proposal of the Minister of Justice and still maintain a Government. Dayan asked that the subject be discussed before the next Cabinet meeting by the party Central Committee, which accordingly was convened next day.

Eshkol opened that party discussion. "They want us," he said, "to set up an inquiry committee, after the Committee of Seven, to investigate things that happened ten years ago. I told the members and I will say this publicly: we are opening a Pandora's Box of disasters. It won't end with this matter alone. In the next fifteen years we may find ourselves investigating the glorious fifteen years that have just passed." He ended with these words: "I want to say to you, my friends, and I have purposely left this to the end, that there won't be a Government if we allow ourselves to vote for an inquiry committee."

Ben-Gurion came to the meeting late but read the stenographic record of what Eshkol had said. He thereupon reiterated what he had told the Secretariat gathering, namely, that the Prime Minister had failed in a matter of inordinate gravity, in which the nation's honor was at stake, and that he ought to resign. Even a jurist with no party affiliations like the Attorney General, he pointed out, found that the Committee of Seven had "conducted its work without observing the principles of natural justice and the rules for conducting proceedings of this kind," and asked whether "the needs of this inquiry were special needs different from the need to investigate the facts of the case itself."

He had resigned as Prime Minister in 1961, Ben-Gurion recalled, because his colleagues had committed an injustice. Now that the Attorney General had denounced the conduct of the Committee of Seven, one of whose most active members was the present Prime Minister, Eshkol should have resigned as soon as he read the Attorney General's report, lest anyone suspect him of personal or party machinations. When the findings of the Committee of Seven were submitted to the Government on December 25, 1960, Ben-Gurion said, he had announced that he could no longer be a member of that Government. On being urged by his colleagues to reconsider, he had replied that "The state does not depend on one man and it will get by without me." Neither did the State depend on Levi Eshkol, he contended, and in light of the Attorney General's opinion he ought to resign.

"Aspersions," he went on "were cast on scores of officers, lieutenant-colonels, and majors and the person responsible refused to mention names when asked to do so by members of the Foreign Affairs and Security Committee. Is not this alone sufficient cause for investigation and clarification? It is said that there were other mishaps as well. Eshkol has been Prime Minister and Minister of Defense for only one year; I assume there have been no mishaps in his time. But I was Prime Minister and Minister of Defense for fifteen years and I want every such affair, if there were any, investigated. Why this fear of a Pandora's Box? If it appears that in our country there is no moral integrity, no justice, and that for fear that someone might resign, injustices committed by Cabinet Ministers are tolerated, this is a dangerous stain on the escutcheon of the State of Israel and one that must be wiped off and cleaned away. The moral integrity of the State is more important than anything else. And the moral integrity of the State is first of all the moral integrity of its Government."

The Minister of Justice, Dov Joseph, then spoke. "Although I was a member of the Cabinet when the 'security mishap' occured in 1954," he said, "I did not know about it, nor did the other Cabinet members. I have been asked why I have suddenly felt the need to order an investigation. Because only now, when I am in receipt of the material on the case, am I in a position to decide whether or not an investigation should be held. It has been provided by the man who used to be Prime Minister and I have studied it from A to Z.

"By law I am entitled to appoint an inquiry committee without consulting the Cabinet, but I thought that this would not be right because of the political significance of the case. The Committee of Seven admits that it did not hear witnesses and this alone is sufficient. It should be borne in mind that this concerns not merely two people but the entire Government. As the Attorney General has said, the legal and public significance of the 'security mishap' and all its ramifications required from the beginning a comprehensive and thorough investigation with the full authority of the law."

Prime Minister Eshkol immediately took the floor and declared: "When we set up a ministerial committee rather than an inquiry committee, we did so with the approval of the Cabinet, of the party, the Knesset, and God."

A little background: The question of a committee of inquiry was first considered by the Cabinet on October 23, 1960, when the accused Senior Officer wrote to the Chief of Staff demanding such an inquiry. The Chief of Staff transmitted the letter to the Minister of Defense (Ben-Gurion) who, at the Cabinet meeting of October 23, 1960, referred it to the Minister of Justice, Pinhas Rosen. The then Minister of Finance, Levi Eshkol, asked, "will the Minister of Justice be the one to decide the issue?" Ben-Gurion, who as Prime Minister was chairing the meeting, replied:

"He can appoint an inquiry committee but not if the Cabinet should rule otherwise. I have consulted the Attorney General and he has informed me that he advised the Minister of Justice to do so. It is a matter of common decency. A person is entitled to defend his honor. Though Lavon may be a very important man, everyone is equal before the law. I understand that there are members who would like the issue to be decided by the Cabinet. I am completely opposed to this. The Government cannot take it upon itself to do the deciding. I am firmly opposed to the Cabinet's assuming something not within its capacity. This is something only an inquiry committee or jurists can do—jurists who have no preconceived opinion or prejudice in favor of one side or another and know how a judicial inquiry should be conducted."

"Perhaps the Cabinet will not investigate but simply decide to put an end to the affair once and for all," Eshkol interjected at that time. To which Ben-Gurion replied. "There will be no end to this business until a committee rules according to law. Nor will there be an end to it if the Senior Officer's request is rejected."

Since there was other urgent business on the agenda of that session, the matter was deferred to the next Cabinet meeting, on October 30, 1960. There the Prime Minister again gave his view: "There is a question about the past: Was an order given or not? If it was, who gave it? This is a question that can be resolved only through judicial procedure by disinterested persons who have the legal authority to interrogate witnesses under oath and to put on trial anyone who lies."

At the same meeting the Minister of Justice, Pinhas Rosen, repeated what he had said early in 1955 on first hearing about the "security mishap," namely, that it was inconceivable that a man like Lavon could do something as crazy as that. (Rosen did not ask himself how the Senior Officer, who was not crazy either, could do it.) He proposed the creation of a ministerial committee. It would examine also whether a judicial inquiry was necessary, "and in a ministerial committee the Prime Minister's opinion in this matter will certainly carry a lot of weight."

"A ministerial committee?" the Prime Minister interjected. "I did not say a ministerial committee. I said an inquiry committee." Rosen thereupon asked: "And if the Government recommends a ministerial committee?" Ben-Gurion replied, "I will not appear before a ministerial committee."

Following a debate—we are still in October 1960—the Prime Minister put Rosen's proposal to a vote. It was approved by twelve to nothing with two abstentions (Bentov and Barzilai). Ben-Gurion indicated in advance that he would not participate in the voting.

At neither this meeting nor the previous one did anyone propose that the Knesset decide between an inquiry committee and a ministerial committee. When it was determined that the committee would have five members, one of the Ministers who had approved a ministerial committee and had been elected to it made an insulting remark to his colleagues (because he wanted a large group), withdrew from the committee, and left the meeting. The Cabinet met again the next day to elect a member to replace him.

The Minister of Justice, in opening the meeting, announced that Prime Minister Ben-Gurion was unable to participate and had requested him (Rosen) to preside. The member who had made the insulting remark apologized. Eshkol reported that in preliminary talks with those present they had affirmed their desire to localize the issue as far as possible and that earlier he had also persuaded Hazan, Barzilai, Bentov, and Riftin to the same effect. In the end a Committee of Seven was decided upon. Again, no one proposed to bring the matter to the Knesset or its Foreign Affairs and Security Committee.

Thus the ministerial committee was elected on the sole initiative and by the decision of the Cabinet, and Eshkol had no right, four years later, to tell the Mapai Central Committee that "with the approval of the Knesset a ministerial committee rather than an inquiry committee had been elected." The Knesset had had no role in the decision.

The party's Central Committee meeting on December 13, 1964, was attended by practically all the Mapai members of the Knesset. They knew that Eshkol's statement that the ministerial committee had had Knesset approval was incorrect. Ben-Gurion asked, "Was there a Knesset decision in the matter?" "Yes," Eshkol replied. "When was this decision taken?" Ben-Gurion asked. Eshkol answered, "There was a Knesset decision in miniature. The Knesset dealt with the matter through the Foreign Affairs and Security Committee, which with respect to security matters is a Knesset in miniature."

But this too was erroneous. No one in the Foreign Affairs and Security Committee had proposed a ministerial committee rather than a committee of inquiry. And in the three Cabinet meetings in which the Senior Officer's request for a committee of inquiry was discussed, no one, not even Eshkol, had proposed that the Foreign Affairs and Security Committee be consulted on the mechanism for investigation. Throughout October 1960 that Knesset committee had been dealing with Lavon's testimony and the conflicting testimony of Moshe Sharett and Shimon Peres. Only after the ministerial committee had issued the conclusions that resulted in the resignation of Ben-Gurion—that is, after December 25, 1960—did the Minister of Justice ask the Foreign Affairs and Security Committee to suspend its hearings on the "security mishap."

The Knesset Discusses Eshkol's Resignation ★ Ben-Gurion Charges that Rosen Distorts the Facts

At the end of the Central Committee session at midnight on December 13, 1964, twenty-five members were still waiting to be heard and it was agreed to resume the next day. The meeting was called off, however, because the Prime Minister had decided to resign.

On December 15 Eshkol tabled in the Knesset a letter of resignation addressed to the President. In it he argued that "The Committee of Seven was not bound by any rules of procedure but decided on its own methods of work." This was apparently his response to the serious criticism of the committee made in the Attorney General's report of November 6, 1964. As for the statement by the Minister of Justice that "new evidence has been discovered," Eshkol wrote: "After an examination was conducted, on my instructions, into the sources of this contention, I have reasonable grounds for saying that the material that, on the face of it, was new in the Minister of Justice's opinion, either is not new at all or is not sufficient prima facie to serve as decisive proof that it would have compelled the committee to alter its conclusions had it been submitted to it."

The letter of resignation was delivered to President Shazar on December 14, the day after the meeting of the Mapai Central Committee. The Prime Minister spoke twice at that meeting but made no mention of any examination that had been conducted "on the sources of this contention." With respect to the reasons for his resignation, Eshkol wrote: "It is my conviction that the great majority of the members of the Government are not prepared to accept the proposal of the Minister of Justice. Meanwhile this matter has become the subject of discussions among the parties. In my view this is a matter of State and the Government should be free to decide it. In the situation that has been created I cannot continue to bear the responsibility. I have, therefore, found it necessary to inform the Government this evening of my resignation." A strange reason indeed for resigning!

On being invited to a meeting of the Central Committee on December 17, Ben-Gurion wrote to the Party Secretary as follows:

Levi Eshkol's resignation has achieved its main purpose—the prevention, for the time being, of free discussion in the matter of an inquiry committee. In view of this I see no need or purpose of wasting the evening hours speaking to deaf ears, but will continue firmly with my efforts to reveal the whole truth, something that has been impaired by the Committee of Seven. Neither manifestos nor demonstrations by the newspapers, nor even sincere entreaties by upright people who do not grasp the full significance of our obligation to uphold the moral integrity of the governing bodies of the State, will deter me so much as a hair's breadth from fulfilling my duty to the nation and to the State. I am confident that the truth will out and that justice will be done.

In the Knesset debate on the resignation of the Prime Minister (tantamount to the resignation of the entire Government), Pinhas Rosen, former Minister of Justice and chairman of the Committee of Seven, maintained that in view of its failures in most of its fields of endeavor, the Eshkol Cabinet should have resigned much earlier. Yet he concentrated on one point, in which he considered the resignation belated: "The last moment at which the Government should have resigned was when the Attorney General's report was released for publication by the Minister of Justice with the Prime Minister's approval." He looked upon this report as a slap in the face of the Prime Minister, the Minister of Police, the Minister of the Interior, the Minister of Justice, and everyone who had served on the Committee of Seven.

"What has happened here, gentlemen?" Rosen exclaimed. "On November 1 the Minister of Justice asked the Attorney General for an opinion on the material submitted by Mr. Ben-Gurion. Five days later, on November 6, the Attorney General provided it. What kind of a thorough job could he do in five days? And if those two lawyers had really wanted to be objective, as colleagues in the legal profession, they could have requested explanations from me and from other people."

Rosen did not think that the Knesset was the proper place to investigate the matter. On the other hand, it would be easy enough to investigate even though it was obvious to him that "The Attorney General did not verify the facts but according to this report merely accepted them as presented." The report, he said, "maliciously misinterprets things that were said behind closed doors. It should be obvious to anyone who read the minutes of that meeting [of the Committee of Seven] that I did not intend that my statements be taken as a verdict. I could not possibly have referred to that letter [of the Senior Officer on July 19, 1954] because, as I said at that meeting, the substance of the letter required additional clarification. What I was referring to was the reliability of the two officers, the Senior Officer and the Reserve Officer. Nonetheless, Ben-Gurion holds me to that statement word for word, as if it were a legal verdict. Now I ask you: Where is it written that a judge, an arbitrator, or an investigator is not allowed to change his mind?

"The Attorney General does not say that such things were done but that prima facie he has reason to think so. And I say that even prima facie findings are invalid when the other side is not heard. It would seem that according to the Attorney General the rule that the other side must be heard is valid only in a court of law when the accused is standing before his judge. Yet even a common thief is given the opportunity to state his case before being brought to trial. But I have no quarrel with the Attorney General, who is certainly a good jurist and according to all opinions honest, even if inexperienced in the ways of democratic parliamentary life, but I am very astonished by the Minister of Justice."

Though he was being referred to by most of the speakers, Ben-Gurion was unable to attend the Knesset during those days. But as Prime Minister when the Committee of Seven was appointed, and no less familiar than any other member of the Cabinet or of the Committee of Seven with the deliberations in the Cabinet at that time, he considers it his duty to point out here a number of errors made by Pinhas Rosen. First, he will note one fact that Mr. Rosen did not mention, nor was he obliged to, though it was highly relevant.

This one fact is that on the day when Ben-Gurion submitted the material to the Minister of Justice and the Attorney General (October 22, 1964), he met with Rosen, with whom he had worked in the Government for thirteen years and whose honesty, despite differences on some political questions, he highly esteemed. He not only told Rosen that he had submitted the data to officials that morning, but informed him of the contents of the material and of his proposal that three Supreme Court Justices examine whether the Government's refusal to grant the Senior Officer's request for a judicial board of inquiry was in order; whether the Government was authorized to judge in a dispute between two individuals as the Committee of Seven had done; and whether the committee's findings accorded with the principles of truth, justice, and the laws of the land.

Ben-Gurion advised Rosen that the material contained an analysis of the deliberations of the ministerial committee by two lawyers on the basis of an examination of its minutes, and that he, Ben-Gurion, had told the lawyers that he considered their analysis correct and just. He also told them that he knew of things that had taken place behind the scenes and were not in the minutes but in party documents—facts that reached him only in 1964, though in effect they pertained to the years 1954–1955 and 1960–1961; that it was clear to him that the responsibility for the Committee of Seven rested not on Rosen but on Eshkol, since it was he who had misled the Committee of Seven with regard to Ben-Gurion's opinion of the committee and in other matters and it was mainly he who had prevented the hearing of witnesses, though Rosen had demanded it several times.

A second fact that Mr. Rosen disregarded: as the committee's chairman he defined its authority at its first meeting as follows: "To study the material and to tell the Government what future action should in our opinion be taken." He said essentially the same thing at the Cabinet meeting at which it was decided to appoint a ministerial committee: "I (that is, Pinhas Rosen) am not at all certain if we will be able to bring this affair to a conclusion without an additional inquiry committee. I have said this several times." Then, at the committee's meeting on December 5, 1960, he again referred to its limited authority: "The Cabinet spoke explicitly of procedural conclusions." The secretary of the committee, Katriel Katz, who was also the Cabinet Secretary at the time, said, "I can confirm that." And Rosen added, "That is, not material conclusions." Mr. Eshkol thereupon asked, "What are we now?" Rosen replied, "A study committee."

Moreover, in a letter to Prime Minister Ben-Gurion on November 20, 1960, Rosen had written:

> The conclusions of the committee will be purely procedural. We have been assigned to study the material relating to the affair and to advise the Cabinet how to proceed in clarifying the issues and whether additional measures should be taken to further that clarification. Our proposal can be one of the following: (1) to authorize the committee to draw factual conclusions on the basis of the material before it; (2) to authorize the committee to act on a clarification committee; (3) to authorize the committee to act as an inquiry committee; (4) to appoint a different inquiry committee in which the Opposition will not participate.

The committee never requested the Cabinet to authorize it to serve in any of the capacities that Mr. Rosen listed. In violation of the definition of the committee's authority, which he had given at its first meeting, he brought to the Cabinet meeting findings that, in Mr. Rosen's own words, were "material" rather than procedural and that concluded with the statement: "We are, therefore, of the opinion that the clarification of this affair should be considered complete and final." Mr. Rosen told the Knesset that a man has the right to change his mind. This is correct, but he has no right, of his own accord, to change the authority given to him by a different body.

No less strange was Rosen's claim in the Knesset that the committee had not heard witnesses: "The majority of the committee was of the opinion that the hearing of witnesses was not within its authority." Actually he had himself questioned a number of people and submitted a résumé of this testimony to the committee. And at its meeting on December 5, 1960, as chairman, he had told the committee, "I think we should invite Sharett, Lavon, and the Senior Officer." Eshkol opposed this and also objected to asking the Cabinet whether witnesses should be heard.

At the committee's meeting of December 13, 1960, Rosen supported Moshe Dayan (the Chief of Staff in 1954 and a member of the Cabinet when it set up the Committee of Seven), who wished to appear before the committee. Shapira asked that Dayan be heard because he was a Cabinet member; Ben-Aharon was opposed. Rosen, however, declared that he would like to hear both Dayan and Sharett (then Prime Minister). Shitreet wanted to hear the three or four witnesses suggested by Rosen. Eshkol was opposed because "We are not an inquiry committee." Shitreet countered, "We are an examination committee." At the end of the meeting a test vote was taken. Three members were in favor of hearing a few witnesses, two were opposed, and one abstained. At no time was any vote taken not to hear witnesses, nor is there any evidence in the shorthand record that a majority was against it.

Rosen also ignored the fact that he had sent Attorney General Hausner to question witnesses in Paris and then brought him before the committee to testify, and that this evidence influenced the committee perhaps more than anything else because a secretary had admitted in effect that she had altered a letter on the instructions of the Senior Officer. Yet on December 15, 1960, Mr. Hausner informed the committee that "What the secretary told me in Paris constitutes grounds of the first order *for additional investigation*." And indeed, on his orders, an investigation was carried out after the secretary's return to Israel, in which several others were questioned as well. That examination was made by the officer in charge of the Police Laboratory for Criminal Investigation, Avraham Hagag. In his signed report Hagag summarized his education and training, gave details of the investigation, and the following "conclusions":

> 1. I have not found that the two-page document was tampered with in any way to make it appear either more or less recent than it really is.
> 2. In my opinion, the two pages of the document are of the same age and were subjected together to the same office treatment.
> 3. The dates appearing on the first page of the document are as originally written and have not been altered. No attempt has been made to alter the typewritten portion, and it is an integral part of the document as a whole. The portion written by ballpoint pen is likewise original and the impression of the writing is evident on the reverse side of page 1 and page 2 as well.

On reading these findings, the then Prime Minister (Ben-Gurion) asked the police how the expert had been able to determine that the copy of the Senior Officer's letter to the Chief of Staff was typed on July 19, 1954, and that nothing had been altered or "corrected" on the second page. It was explained that the expert had located the typewriter that had been in use that month in the Senior Officer's office. In every typewriter the impression of one or more of the letters varies in the course of time, and he found in the letter of July 19, 1954, the same peculiarities as in all other letters written at that time on the same typewriter; therefore the date must be correct. A chemical examination of the second page likewise revealed that no changes had been made. Nevertheless, the Prime Minister was still uncertain about the secretary's testimony. She had told the Attorney General that she altered a letter, and when shown a copy of the letter of July 19, 1954, hesitantly identified it as the one in question. Yet the examination by the police expert as well as the interrogation later carried out at the Attorney General's request showed that this letter had not even been handled by this particular secretary.

The mystery was solved three years later, in the second half of 1963, on the basis of the material examined by Hagai Eshed. It appeared that on his return from the United States the Chief of Staff, General Dayan, who had been out of the country from July 11 to August 19, 1954, asked the Senior Officer for a written report on the "security mishap." On November 1, 1954, the officer sent him a long letter that included the sentence, "At the end of the meeting the Minister of Defense asked me to remain and in a conversation between us there again arose the question of the activation. . . . After that the Minister of Defense instructed me to order . . . to act . . . . The ellipses indicate military security censorship.] On receipt of this letter Dayan asked for a report that would be more concise and clear, and on the same day the Senior Officer sent him a shorter letter.

The first letter contained thirty lines, the second nineteen. The second said, "Following a discussion in the matter of. . . the Minister of Defense ordered me to activate. . . " Ben-Gurion saw photostats of both these letters and realized that this was the "change" mentioned by the secretary. What had been altered was not a single sentence but the entire letter. This letter, however, bore the date November 1, 1954. In the letter of July 19, 1954, no change had been made, nor had the letter even been typed by the secretary whom Mr. Hausner questioned in Paris. More cautious than Rosen, Hausner had felt it necessary to question the secretary again after her return to Israel. In the light of additional material from the Senior Officer's office, Hagag then once more examined the letter of July 19, arriving at the same conclusion as previously, namely, that no alteration or forgery had been made either in the date or the contents. Subsequently he twice received more material and on January 27, 1961, wrote: "The additional findings support the conclusions in my original report."

At the Mapai Central Committee discussion, after publication of the Attorney General's opinion, as to whether an inquiry committee ought to be set up, Prime Minister Eshkol stated, "I have reviewed the matter with objective lawyers; even the unhappy question of whether the letter of July 19, 1954, was forged. In this matter we have three or four reports by the police. It seems that the man who examined the letter was not a typewriter expert but a handwriting expert. The handwriting expert said that this was the first time he had tried out the method of a certain professor in the United States."

Either Mr. Eshkol had not read the expert's report, to which a résumé of his training and professional experience had been duly appended as required by law, and had been misled by some official, or he deliberately said things contrary to the truth.

In the Knesset debate on December 15, 1964, touched off by the resignation of Prime Minister Eshkol, Yacov Hazan said, "A dense and suffocating fog has descended on our political life, something that distorts its image and camouflages the true nature of the naked power struggle now going on in Israel. This fog is called 'the affair.' There is no justification for Ben-Gurion's demand to reopen the investigation, for if anyone could have brought the inquiry to a conclusion it was he, and he did not do so."

Even people who differ with Hazan's political views will admit that, like his colleague and leader Meir Ya'ari, he is one of the most honest and decent personalities in the Knesset and in public life. In this debate, alas, he got himself lost in the fog to which he alluded, by confounding two "affairs" that, though related, were quite different in nature.

Until October 1960 there was the controversy known as "the Lavon Affair," or simply "the affair." But from then until the end of the year there was a second affair that, though growing out of the four-year-old "security gap," was a second issue. It was the question of a miscarriage of justice by the ministerial Committee of Seven set up in 1960 in consequence of the Senior Officer's application for a judicial inquiry.

The majority of the Cabinet, bypassing the judicial processes, decided in 1960 to form the ministerial committee. According to the terms of reference set at the time by Minister of Justice Rosen, who served as committee chairman, the seven Ministers were to "study the material and tell the Government what in their opinion should be done in the future"—that is, as he explained at a committee meeting, its conclusions were to be procedural rather than material. Nevertheless, the committee went ahead to make material conclusions in a "complete and final" manner.

Four members of the Cabinet—Giora Josephthal, Abba Eban, Moshe Dayan, and Joseph Burg—refused to confirm these conclusions. Ben-Gurion, then Prime Minister, did not take part in the voting at all, because, as he put it, "While the Committee of Seven had no authority to pass judgment and did not do so in the manner of judges or investigators, the Cabinet has a rule of collective responsibility and I cannot share responsibility for a miscarriage of justice. I am not a partner to the committee's appointment, to its conclusions, nor to the Government's decision. Therefore I am not your partner in the Government and it is up to me to resign."

This was a new "affair," not a repetition of the "Lavon Affair." It involved a miscarriage of justice by seven Ministers and a Government decision to sustain the miscarriage.

Further on in his speech Hazan repeated the same mistake: "During his term of office the then Prime Minister and Minister of Defense, David Ben-Gurion," he said, "could have set up a committee of inquiry at will. He could have refrained from consenting to the Committee of Seven. Yet he consented to it." In fact Ben-Gurion was not only *able to* refrain from consenting but refused to consent, objecting to it strongly both at the Cabinet meeting on October 23, 1960, when the issue was first raised, and at the meeting of October 30, 1960, when it was debated again. He was overruled by the majority. Hazan was doubly in error in saying that the then Prime Minister consented to the ministerial committee. The Government of which he was head had decided by majority according to its own wishes, against those of the Prime Minister.

Hazan was similarly mistaken in saying that "all the committees with the exception of the first, which reached an impasse, decided that he (*i.e.*, Lavon) was innocent." No committee had investigated the question of Lavon's guilt or innocence, whether he had given the order or the Senior Officer had acted on his own, except the Olshan-Dori Committee, which arrived at an impasse. Only the ministerial committee announced the material conclusion—and this without questioning the parties concerned—that Lavon did not give the order: a conclusion about which the Attorney General, having examined all the material not available either to Hazan or the ministerial committee, said: "The Committee of Seven conducted itself without observing the principles of natural justice and the rules of conducting proceedings of this kind."

This and this alone was the affair that occupied Ben-Gurion and disturbed his rest. It was because of this that he resigned from the Government in 1961, not because of the Lavon Affair, which did not concern him at all, since he was not in the Government when it occurred. If any Prime Minister or Minister of Justice or Minister of Defense should have investigated who was responsible for the "security mishap," it was the Prime Minister or Minister of Justice or Minister of Defense at the time, namely, Moshe Sharett and Pinhas Rosen. It is surprising that an intelligent man like Hazan was unable to distinguish between the Lavon Affair of 1954 and the Ministerial Committee Affair of 1960.★

On December 22, 1964, a week after the debate over his resignation, Eshkol announced that the President had entrusted him with the formation of a new Government. The Cabinet he would present would be identical in its party and personal makeup with that which had resigned a week earlier, and would operate on the basis of the same policy outlines and coalition agreements.

The Government was confirmed the same day by a vote of fifty-nine to thirty-six, with nine abstaining. The following day the Prime Minister announced that in accordance with the Transition Law he was appointing the following Deputy Ministers: Shimon Peres, Deputy Minister of Defense; Israel Shlomo Ben-Meir, Deputy Minister of the Interior; Aharon Yadlin, Deputy Minister of Education and Culture; Kalman Kahana, Deputy Minister of Education and Culture; Yitzhak Raphael, Deputy Minister of Health. These appointments did not require Knesset approval.

★ Although outvoted at that time, Ben-Gurion has consistently maintained that the Cabinet did not have the constitutional authority to arrogate any judicial rights to themselves. — EDITORS

X

CHALLENGES AND
ACHIEVEMENTS: 1962–1966

Oriental Immigrants; Revised Land
Policy; Sixth Knesset Elected;
Three-Year Economic Plan

Section 1. Fifth Knesset Completes Its Full Term

Knesset Praises Efforts To Integrate All Communities

ON September 12, 1964, Prime Minister Eshkol addressed the Knesset on the integration of the many communities. The number of immigrants absorbed since the advent of the State was double the population of the State on the day it was proclaimed. Immigrants had come from all countries, spoke scores of languages, and were the products of cultures at differing levels of development. The cultural range extended from illiterates to scientists and intellectual leaders of the first rank. A considerable part of what had been accomplished in the sixteen years of statehood was the work of new immigrants. The new urban and rural settlements as well as the expansion of existing towns had for the most part been achieved by new settlers.

A large proportion of the immigrants had gone to build up new cities. Beersheba, formerly a small Bedouin town, now had a population of more than seventy thousand. Dimona, Kiryat Gat, Beit Sha'an, the Jewish city of Safad, the Jewish city of Jaffa, Kiryat Shmona, and other urban communities had been created. Half of the fifty thousand members of the country's labor councils were new immigrants, a substantial number among them from Asia and Africa. In some of the North African countries that had sent large numbers of immigrants the Jewish intelligentsia remained behind. In the past two years efforts had been made, with some success, to bring them over; also, a considerable number of young Moroccans studying in France had come to settle in Israel.

The new farming settlements constituted the crowning glory of the new immigration. One can attest this without deprecating the accomplishments of the older kibbutzim and moshavim. The great majority of settlers in the hundreds of new villages arrived after the establishment of the State and set up these enterprises without prior training. The Lahish region, created ten years ago, consisted in a very great measure of new immigrants from Asia, Africa, and Eastern Europe. Within a year or two, denizens of transit camps became builders of new villages and towns.

Young people who came to Israel illiterate acquired a basic education in the Army, absorbed its spirit of valor, and proved their capability in the Sinai Campaign. About one-quarter of all secondary-school students are the children of immigrants from Asia and Africa. We have introduced a system of graduated school fees, but are still far from the record of many American and European countries where all education, from kindergarten through university, is free. For several years now work has been going on to eradicate illiteracy outside the Army as well. To a large extent this is done by volunteers. Especially noteworthy in this respect in the work of Joseph Maimon of Jerusalem who pioneered this undertaking and set an example for the scores and hundreds of people who followed. Yet much work still remains to be done, since we still have some 200,000 illiterates in Israel.

To meet the influx, about three hundred thousand apartments for immigrants have been built by the Government. This does not include dwellings built by immigrants on their own or those built for sale or rent by private contractors. The full housing needs, of course, have not yet been met and much work lies ahead. Crowded living conditions are still common among large families, particularly immigrants from Asia and Africa, and numerous slums remain from before the creation of the State. To ensure decent housing for all remains a challenging task.

The rate of intermarriage between members of the various communities, less than 10 percent in 1952, rose to approximately 15 percent in 1962—slow but encouraging. In the majority of the cases the husband is of European origin, the wife of Asian or African origin. The most important single factor reducing intercommunal differences is the IDF. In the military services all communal barriers are removed, there is more equality among members of the differing communities than anywhere else, and the possibilities of cultural advance and promotion depend only on the individual soldier's qualities. Even if he enters as a total illiterate, no soldier leaves the Army without a minimum basic education. The percentage of officers of Asian and African origin is increasing from year to year, and they have no feeling of inferiority in the services. Understandably, this creates some problems. After acquiring education and self-awareness in the Army, it is not easy for a soldier to return to his culturally impoverished family and previous mode of existence. In recent years the Ministry of Education has taken measures to eradicate illiteracy among elderly people as well.

Much work yet remains to be done, the Prime Minister made clear, in absorption and integration of the exiles—in bridging the educational and economic gaps between immigrants from radically different backgrounds. It is not merely a question of Sephardim and Ashkenazim; immigrants from Bulgaria are overwhelmingly Sephardim, yet there is little difference between them and their Russian counterparts, who are all Ashkenazim.

In the debate on Mr. Eshkol's survey, complaints of discrimination and injustice were heard.

Baruch Uziel of the Liberal Party, for instance, charged that there were cases of communal discrimination. Though this was done by individuals rather than by national or Zionist institutions, it created bad feeling, disappointment, and bitterness. He quoted from a study published in 1962 by the Sociology Department of the Hebrew University showing that new immigrants of East European origin became economically established more quickly than those from North Africa. In income and profession the East European Jews approached the status of longtime residents, assisted in this by their kinship and affinity with the European oldtimers. Thus country of origin was a factor in dividing immigrants into social classes. The Oriental communities were handicapped by large families. The political parties, he claimed, exploited feelings of communal discrimination in their competition for votes. Some of the Ashkenazim feared the danger to their hegemony posed, as it were, by the high rate of natural increase in the Sephardi Oriental communities. He quoted what a Hebrew poet had written in *Davar* shortly before the creation of the State: "If a miracle does not occur within one or two generations, the entire heritage of traditional Israel will be in the hands of Oriental Jewry, a prospect that ought to give us much cause for concern: our age-old traditions will be polluted and go to the dogs."

Uziel added that "there was a time when the torch was carried by Sephardi Jewry and was then handed over to the Ashkenazim. This is merely an historic pledge that is now being returned to us, now that the once rich and glorious Jewry of Europe has been reduced. In restoring the torch to its original bearers, it is incumbent upon this Jewry to behave with the modesty of great inheritors. We must fight mutual manifestations of disrespect. What is required is mutual love. And this cannot be legislated in the Knesset. A different spirit is needed. Opportunities for children of the poorer classes to get ahead must be created. More must be done for large families, especially with respect to housing. Skills must be taught to young and old. For a poor country this will be a heavy additional burden, but everything undertaken in this generation by the people of Israel has been difficult. Just as we direct tremendous efforts toward defense, we must do the same in the cardinal problems of integration. Incidentally, in striving for integration, we must be careful not to impose the culture of one community on another; it should not be imposed from above. On the contrary, the good qualities of every community should be fostered, and free from any stigma of inferiority, so that people may compete freely, even as Jacob struggled with the angel until morning.

"Above all," he concluded, "the Sephardim and members of the Oriental communities should be given an appropriate part—not necessarily in proportion to their numbers—in the legislature and other elected and administrative institutions."

Israel Yesha'yahu asked: What is the source of this problem? According to our sages, "God did Israel a favor in scattering them among the nations." Every other nation that experienced a like "favor" ended up in disintegration and assimilation, whereas our dispersion has served us as a defense and a hope that we would survive until redemption. If one community was destroyed, others remained to carry on Jewish life. The wonder of it is that despite the great dispersion and protracted separation all parts of the nation have preserved, above all else, the awareness, the feeling and way of life of one people.

But when the ingathering of the exiles began, it appeared that what was good for the Diaspora was a sore trial for the ingathered communities. The two thousand years during which the Jews did not live together in one place have marked them with endless differences in customs, culture, education, and even in facial features and skin color. Before we came to Israel the distinguishing mark of each of us was that he was Jewish, but now we are marked by our regions of origin. This is a problem with which we must come to grips, no less than with any other problem of an ingathering of the exiles and building up the country. This problem is acute—partly material, partly psychological and emotional, though the two are inseparable. Seventeen years have passed since the creation of the State and more than eighty years since the beginning of the ingathering. Clearly time is pressing. The process of integration will not be concluded in one generation. Yet the process will continue only if we pave the way for it at present.

The Government's declared policy, its plans and its accomplishments in the laws passed by the Knesset, Yesha'yahu said, are all on the right track toward the goal of an ingathering of the exiles and integration of their communities without diversion or retreat. This is especially true of the educational system, the Army, and the agricultural settlements which are the highroad leading to an integrated nation of Israel. What is being done is praiseworthy and should be encouraged.

Despite all this progress, does discrimination, whether intentional or unintentional, still exist? I have devoted considerable effort to studying this problem and have come to the conclusion that though there may be individual contrary cases here and there, generally great care and caution is taken to preclude such occurrences. I have always felt and still feel that the Asian and African immigrants will achieve complete redemption only by their own efforts, by revolutionary educational leadership from within. They generally conduct themselves with a quiet nobility, a sense of rational responsibility, love of the Homeland and the nation of Israel, and it may be assumed they will continue to do so in the future. But it is also true that they need assistance if they are to become equal partners with the advantaged segment of the nation that comes from Europe and America.

Mordekhai Bibi (Ahdut Haavodah) noted: While the ingathering of the exiles is one of the most glorious phenomena of our national resurgence, it involves problems, and progress is slow and often very painful. It is hard to rejoice in the glories and not see the dark shadows. If we consider the Israeli social structure from the point of view of specific gravity, rather than class structure, we are likely to find the following elements: (1) a small upper class of persons engaged in science, politics, literature, the Army, economics, etc., which consists largely of people of Western origin, with a small number of Orientals; (2) a lower class, materially and spiritually impoverished, with a large preponderance of Orientals and a small segment of Westerners; (3) a middle category, encompassing the great majority of the nation, in which there is a vast potential of Oriental talent and ability in no way inferior to that found among Westerners.

The polarization of the first two categories has overshadowed the third and even denied it the chance to compete on the basis of its actual strength and ability. While the Western middle class has the powerful backing of the elite, the Oriental middle class has no such support. Since the elite is the guiding and controlling force in society and its contact with the masses is generally through those from the same country of origin, obstructions have developed in the lines of communication between the elite and the Oriental strata of society. Thus the gap increases between the communities.

The existence of discrimination, Mr. Bibi said, is determined by the feeling of the persons who claim they are being discriminated against. And since the majority of the Oriental community has such a feeling, the other side ought to listen to what they have to say and to act accordingly. The absorption of immigration is, everybody agrees, a magnificent undertaking that imparts new values to every immigrant. But even in magnificent collective achievements, the share of the Oriental communities is hidden. For example, the illegal immigration (ha'apala) medals and commemorative stamps have completely disregarded the illegal immigration by land—that is to say, from the Arab countries. The Oriental Jews were the most creative and progressive elements and the vanguard of pioneers of progress, science, and culture in the nations in which they lived.

Let me make the following proposals for the advancement of intercommunal relations, he concluded: (1) allocation of funds for public opinion research to detect and specify the weak points; (2) the creation of a positive social atmosphere and the molding of public opinion in such a way as to eliminate prejudice and foster understanding and closer relations; (3) provision of equal opportunities in actual practice and the punishment of those who violate this principle; (4) adoption of a social welfare policy that will improve the living conditions of the laboring classes and especially will provide suitably large allowances to improve the housing conditions of large families; (5) provision of legal sanctions against anyone who casts a slur on another person's communal background; (6) laws providing compulsory education, better enforcement of the ban on the employment of school-age children, and high-school and university education for children of underprivileged families; (7) allocation of funds for the collection and dissemination of the values of Oriental culture among the public at large, and above all the maintenance of a close watch on the development of intercommunal relations with an eye to encouraging what is positive and eliminating barriers. These are things that must be done with the advice and cooperation of the nation as a whole.

Mordekhai Zer (born in Persia): "Were it not for the immigrants from Europe, and I say this in full awareness and responsibility, were it not for the Jewry of Europe, the State of Israel would never have come into existence. Without this influx of pioneers possessing know-how, education, political experience, and international connections the State of Israel would never have been established. At the same time I think it would be a disaster if European Jews considered it their right also to carry over—as they have done— the negative characteristics acquired in their countries of origin.

"Every one of us has absorbed the culture and way of life of the Gentiles among whom we lived—that is unavoidable. There is a certain arrogance in Christianity and it influenced the Jews in Europe. This is a fact, though it does not apply to all of them. I do not mean to make generalizations, but it is something we cannot ignore. Each side has also brought with it a number of good qualities and we need not suppose that the eventual integrated culture will be that of Europe. Not everything in European culture is the acme of perfection. The problem is how to combine the good in both sectors. From this rostrum I wish to issue a call to the entire nation, a call for greater tolerance between our two sectors who share the same fate."

It proved to be one of the most enlightening debates ever held in the Knesset. It ended on January 18, 1965, with the adoption, thirty-nine to two, of the following resolution:

(a) The Knesset takes note of the Prime Minister's survey in the Knesset on Tuesday, December 8, 1964, as well as his response to the debate on January 18, 1965.

(b) The Knesset expresses its esteem for the efforts being made by the Government and public institutions to absorb, acclimatize, and integrate all the immigrants from various countries. These efforts are reflected in the field of education in all its stages, as well as in agricultural settlements, employment, housing, and development, and every aspect of life. The Knesset expresses its hope and desire that these efforts will be continued and expanded.

(c) The Knesset feels that full partnership among persons from all countries of origin is an indispensable condition for the survival and welfare of the society and the State. This partnership must be expanded and amplified in every area of national, public, and private life, including representation and participation in the Diplomatic Corps and the Civil Service and in the public and private sectors of the economy.

(d) The Knesset calls upon the nation of Israel in all walks of life to conduct themselves, in private and in public, in keeping with the injunctions of ingathering of the exiles and integration of the communities in order to deepen the awareness of unity among the people of Israel and the equal rights the State accords to every individual and every group.

Diplomatic Relations with West Germany ★ The Plight of Soviet Jewry ★ A New Land Policy

A special meeting of the Knesset on January 25, 1965, paid tribute to the memory of Winston Churchill, who had been buried the previous day. President Zalman Shazar and David Ben-Gurion had represented Israel at the funeral in London. Churchill was eulogized by the Speaker, Beba Idelson, and by the Prime Minister, who said:

> In his undaunted resistance and struggle against the Nazi kingdom of hell, Churchill was the perfect combination of a great man at a great hour. He joined battle and he prevailed. The longed-for decision was not the result of one man's war or the victory of a single nation. It was not through him alone that the sons of light prevailed against the sons of darkness. Nevertheless, this one man was a symbol and a catalyst, a focal point of hope and a kingpin of forces in this struggle of giants. As far back as the beginning of the century, Sir Winston Churchill supported the cause of Zionism. Thirteen years later he spoke on Mount Scopus of a free and sovereign state, one that would be unconquerable. Churchill belonged to the entire world. His memory will light the way for generations to come in every corner of the globe.

All Knesset members and guests rose in tribute to the departed leader.

The debate on the budget was held on January 26. The 1964–1965 budget had been IL 3.7 billion, including an Ordinary Budget of IL 2,402,000,000 and a Development Budget of IL 1,298,000,000. For 1965–1966 the budget proposed amounted to IL 4 billion, of which the Ordinary Budget would be IL 2,665,000,000 and the Development Budget IL 3,335,000,000.

The chairman of the Finance Committee, Israel Guri, who brought the budget proposal for second reading, announced that income for 1965–1966 was estimated at IL 4 billion for a balanced budget. A number of amendments were made to the budget as proposed by the Government; all were rejected.

On February 10, 1965, Deputy Speaker Aryieh Ben-Eliezer announced that a petition signed by a hundred thousand Israeli citizens, concerning the status of Jews in the Soviet Union had been submitted to the Speaker. While Soviet Jewry had not been destroyed, it could hardly be said to be living. It had in fact been erased from the map of Jewish communities in the world, as a direct result of a policy aiming at its complete assimilation. Though this policy had not achieved its aim, it led to the denial to Jews of the national and cultural rights accorded to every other national group in the Soviet Union.

The Soviet Jewish community was completely cut off from its sister communities throughout the world. Synagogues all over Russia had been closed, and only a very few remained. Jews were forbidden to teach their language or the history of their people to their children. They could not sing songs of love or lament their fate in their own tongue. Three million Jews were without Hebrew or Yiddish newspapers, books, prayer-books, and religious articles, and in many parts of the Soviet Union a Jew could not even obtain a religious burial. The enlightened nations of the world—and first and foremost the Jewish State—could not let this attempt to liquidate a people go on without protest.

The problem, moreover, affected the life of Israel. The Soviet leaders had to be made aware that the fate of our brethren in their country concerned us directly. Above all, we could not accept a denial of their right to return to their Homeland and we would demand unceasingly that this policy be rescinded and that justice be done.

"With regard to the question raised in the petition and the statement by Knesset member Ben-Eliezer," Foreign Minister Golda Meir declared, "the entire nation, both in Israel and the Diaspora, is united in its profound concern and sense of pain. The Government proposes that the problem be referred to the Foreign Affairs and Security Committee."

Shmuel Mikunis for the Communists moved that the proposal be dropped, as it was based on a distortion of the facts, was a stinging affront to the proud and creative Jewry of the Soviet Union, and served the purposes of the Cold War against the Soviet Union. But Mrs. Meir's proposal was adopted, forty-six to two.

On March 8, 1965, Knesset member Moshe Unna, as chairman of the Joint Education and Constitution Committee, brought the Broadcasting Authority Law of 1965 for second and third reading. The purpose of this legislation was to transfer all broadcasting services to a public corporation, independent of the Government and its ministers. During the first reading many objections had been raised, alleging continuance of some dependence on the Government. The Knesset committee had taken these into account, and after a brief debate the revised law was adopted on third reading.

Esther Raziel-Naor protested the fact that this year again the Independence Day military parade would not be held in Jerusalem. A year earlier Knesset member Chaim Landau had pressed a similar complaint, charging that political pressure or "friendly advice" had been brought to bear by "friendly nations." She hoped that this was not the case, Esther Raziel-Naor said, and that it was a national disgrace if true.

Eliezer Rimalt claimed that in 1964 preparations had been made for the parade in Jerusalem but that it was moved to Beersheba as a result of pressure by the latter city. This year, too, the Government had stated that the parade would be held in Jerusalem, preparations had been made, and suddenly the country was told that it would take place in Tel Aviv. Why had it originally been scheduled for Jerusalem and what had led to the change of plans? Moshe Kol proposed that the matter be referred to committee. By a vote of thirty-nine to twenty-six his proposal was defeated, and by an even larger majority it was decided not to debate the subject in the Knesset.

The Prime Minister announced on March 16, 1965, that on March 7 the Federal German Republic had declared its desire for full diplomatic relations with Israel. The Government approved acceptance of the proposal and signaled its readiness to establish diplomatic relations immediately. The balance sheet of our relationship with Germany in recent years included both the horrors of the past and the hope for a future that would be completely and utterly different. Following a debate that day and a reply by Deputy Prime Minister Abba Eban, Knesset members asked that the voting be by roll-call. It was resolved that "The Knesset takes note of the Prime Minister's announcement of the establishment of diplomatic relations with the Federal German Republic in accordance with the request of its Government." Herut, Mapam, and the Communists were opposed, Ahdut Haavodah abstained, and all the other parties voted in favor of the resolution. Accordingly, the Cabinet decision was sustained.

On March 22, 1965, the Knesset was informed that Yitzhak Raphael had ceased to serve as Deputy Minister of Health. Three days later the Prime Minister announced that Joseph Almogi, Minister of Housing and Development, had resigned from the Government; that Shimon Peres had ceased to function as Deputy Minister of Defense; and that the Government had decided to co-opt Knesset member Chaim Zadok as Minister of Commerce and Industry.

On March 18, 1965, the Minister of Agriculture, Chaim Gavati, announced the Government's new land policy.

On September 11, 1963, the Prime Minister had appointed a committee to examine real estate policy in Israel. The committee had been assigned to investigate: (1) the sale of state land in urban areas; (2) the terms under which Keren Kayemet and state lands were leased in urban and rural areas; (3) the restraint of speculation in privately owned land; (4) the use for other purposes of agricultural land in urban areas and on the borders of public land in urban areas; (5) the methods of land taxation and registration practiced by public authorities. The members of the committee were Joseph Weitz, chairman, Yacov Arnon (Director of the Ministry of Finance), Shmuel Ben-Shabbat of the Keren Kayemet, David Kohav, Meir Silverstone (Director of the Ministry of the Interior), Moshe Ben-Zev (Attorney General), David Tenne (Director of the Ministry of Housing).

The committee concluded its work at the start of July, 1964. Most of its decisions were unanimous, though differences had arisen on a number of fundamental questions, especially whether urban land should be sold or leased and the methods of assessing lands that were sold or leased. The Government considered both the committee's majority and minority proposals. The goals of its policy were: (1) to preserve agricultural land and ensure its use for its designated purpose; (2) to ensure the implementation of building plans for housing, industry, and services for an evergrowing population; (3) to promote the population dispersal program; (4) to ensure that the entire public would benefit from the country's development and the rise in land values.

The area suitable for agriculture in Israel is very limited, not exceeding 4 million dunams, *i.e.*, less than 4 percent of the country's entire area. This required careful preservation of the land that in the future would have to provide food for a population of millions. The Government had therefore decided that, without a decision to that effect by the Cabinet or ministerial committee appointed for that purpose, the Government's representatives in the authorized bodies would not consent to the use of agricultural land for other purposes. One section specified: "Agricultural land shall not be sold but only leased for the purpose of producing agricultural produce and the erection of buildings and installations required for the housing and other needs of the settlers and for the purpose of agricultural production."

The Government's decisions were as follows:

Agricultural land shall be leased for a period not exceeding forty-nine years. If the lessee uses the land for the purposes for which it was leased, the lease shall, at his request, be extended for an additional period of forty-nine years and the land shall be used for the same purposes. Agricultural land shall be leased in the form of "estates" (an estate is the amount of land required for the support of an agricultural settler under the conditions prevailing in the area). Rental fees for agricultural land shall be 2 percent of the net income. New agricultural settlements shall be granted a reduction in rental fees during their first years.

The settler, *i.e.*, the person who receives an estate, and the dependent members of his family, shall not be permitted to hold more than one estate owned by the Lands Administration. The lessee of agricultural land shall live on his estate and work it consecutively and regularly for the purposes for which it was leased.

The lessee of agricultural land shall not be permitted to sublet it unless compelled to stop working it temporarily, for a period not to exceed three years in a period of ten consecutive years and provided the Lands Administration has given its consent. The lessee shall be permitted, with prior approval from the Director [of the Lands Administration], to transfer his lease to another person provided the land is used for the same purpose.

On the death of the lessee the property shall not be divided among his heirs and the estate shall revert to the Lands Administration. The heirs shall be entitled to compensation for investments made in the estate to an amount equal to the property's real value. The foregoing notwithstanding, the estate shall not revert to the Lands Administration if the heirs come to an arrangement whereby one of them shall receive it for the period of lease after it has been proved to the satisfaction of the Director of the Lands Administration that the said heir possesses the means and the capacity to continue working the estate effectively. In a moshav ovdim [a cooperative society] the land will be made over to the heirs only with the consent of the society.

Contracts for lease of agricultural lands shall stipulate that use of the land for any other purpose will result in termination of the lease and repossession by the Lands Administration. Upon repossession of the land, the lessor shall be entitled to compensation for his investments therein and for termination of his rights thereto, in an amount to be determined by the council and under conditions which it shall prescribe.

With regard to urban land, it was decided that with the exception of abandoned built-up urban properties, such land shall not be sold but only leased; however, sale shall be permitted of urban lands and such Government lands as the Government shall decide upon, subject to the provisions of Section 2 (7) of the Lands Administration Law, 1960.

Other land would be leased or sold only after its planning has been completed and only for the purposes provided in the plan. In the initial phase the land shall be let under license only, and leasing shall be permitted only after development and construction has been completed in accordance with its designated purpose. The value of urban land would be its real market value, that is, the price it would fetch in sale to a voluntary buyer by a voluntary seller as assessed by the Government appraiser.

Urban land would be leased for a period not exceeding forty-nine years. At the end of that time the right of lease shall, at the request of the lessor, be extended for another forty-nine years in which event it shall be reassessed. In return for the right of lease the lessor shall pay the following leasing fee: at the time of signing the licensing agreement an amount equal to 40–80 percent of the value of the land (hereinafter called the initial leasing fee); in addition an annual leasing fee equal to 5 percent of the remainder. This applies to buildings for purposes of industry, commerce and crafts, tourism, and housing.

The sale or lease of urban lands, with the exception of land designated for public purposes or public buildings, shall be by published tender. At the recommendation of the Lands Administration the council can waive the need for a tender.

The foregoing notwithstanding, urban lands that the Government is especially interested in developing and settling may be made over under conditions different from those described above. Such conditions shall be stipulated by the council according to directives by the Government or by anyone the Government has authorized. Transfer or taking over of rights to urban land by the holder thereof shall require prior consent by the Lands Administration.

The Knesset after a three-day debate adopted by a vote of thirty-three to seven a Coalition proposal that said: "The Knesset has taken note of the Ministry of Agriculture's announcement of the Government's land policy." Dissenting proposals by Herut, the Liberal Party, Mapam, the Independent Liberals, and the Communist Party were rejected.

Fate of Israeli Prisoners in Syria ★ Crime in Israel ★ Survey of the Police and Prisons Services

At the Knesset meeting of June 9, 1965, Yacov Meridor (Herut) called attention to the tragic plight of Israelis imprisoned in Syria and urged action on their behalf:

> Eighteen months ago, in December 1963, eight Israeli citizens were released who had been held captive in various Syrian prisons and subjected to hellish tortures. Their liberation and return took a long time. Some of the men had gone through eleven years of confinement and almost inconceivable tortures. Only one of the eight retained his senses, while the other seven had to be placed in mental hospitals. We remember the day of their return to our northern border, the joy and happiness of the families and of the entire Israeli nation, and their grief on learning the horrible facts of their incarceration in the Syrian prisons.
>
> A few days ago I received first-hand information that confirms that not all the Syrian captives had been returned and that at least four are still being held. Among them are soldiers who succumbed to the blandishment of Radio Damascus and crossed the border. One of them was taken off a Finnish ship in Ladakiah harbor and sent straight to El Maza prison. The four are Yosef Shemesh, Shlomo Yifrahi, Yitzhak Reznik, and Avraham Deskal. The Syrians, of course, deny any knowledge of these names or that these men are under their jurisdiction or are being held captive by them.
>
> A few months ago a documentary book, *The Captives of Syria*, was published by Yehezkel Hameiri, the Kol Yisrael correspondent in the north of Israel. Reading it

makes your hair stand on end. You ask yourself: Where are we? In a sovereign State of Israel with an Army, a budget, a Knesset? The question is, Have we done all that we could? Are there no means to put an end to such tidings in this day and age?

For eleven years the Israeli prisoners were tormented to the point of insanity in El Maza prison and especially in the desert prison of Tadmor. Why did the Syrians do it? Why did they deprive them of their basic human rights and human dignity? In my opinion there are two reasons. One is the Syrian leaders' innate sadism—sadism of Nazi proportions. The second is political. In exchange for our eight prisoners they received seventeen Syrian saboteurs and spies who in our prisons enjoyed humane treatment based on the Geneva Convention. In contrast, what the Syrians returned to us were broken human beings. In view of the fact that Israeli citizens are still rotting in Syrian prisons, I requested that the Knesset consider the matter.

With Meridor's consent the Foreign Minister proposed that the question be referred to the Foreign Affairs and Security Committee.

On June 14, 1965, Minister of Police Behor Shitreet reported on the activities of the Police and the Prisons Service during 1964. The personnel of the Israel Police hailed from 47 different countries; native-born policemen numbered 1204 or 19 percent of the total. At the end of the year the force included 6254 regular policemen, among them 431 policewomen and 473 members of the minority communities. There were 2.5 policemen per 1000 inhabitants. The force had continued to provide general and professional training for personnel of all the ranks at training bases in Shfar'am and Jerusalem. The level of schooling of policemen was as follows: elementary education, 53 percent; partial elementary education, 12.5 percent; partial secondary education, 14.4 percent; high-school education 17 percent; post-high-school education, 0.8 percent; higher education, 1.6 percent.

One of the compulsory courses was Hebrew, and the level of training was adjusted to the trainees' level of education and intelligence. Nineteen courses were given in the Seminar of Social and Political Problems; the faculty included university lecturers, Army officers, senior police officers, and other experts in various fields of police work.

The main problem confronting the police was manpower. The large turnover of personnel limited its operative capacity. From the founding of the State until the time of the report a total of 16,558 persons had been recruited. Of the 10,304 who had been struck from the force during that period, 7388 (71.7 percent) had resigned. The high dropout rate was detrimental to the service because it took considerable time, effort, and expense to produce a good policeman. Potential recruits were carefully screened. Of 5087 applicants in 1964 only 863 were selected. At the end of that year the total force numbered 7445, compared to 7059 the previous year. It was an inescapable fact that the country's population was increasing (2,523,000 in 1964 as against 2,429,000 in 1963) and this naturally had its effect on the work of the police.

During the year approximately a million complaints, offenses, and other kinds of cases were dealt with. Among these were 85,917 felonies and misdemeanors, 380,150 traffic violations, 18,059 traffic accidents, 187,000 incidents of various kinds, and so on. These figures gave some idea of the workload. Besides safeguarding lives and property, ensuring public order, and bringing offenders to justice, the police had marginal tasks such as implementation of court orders, border controls, and the like. A few examples:

in 1964 the police dealt with 72,233 arrest warrants for unpaid debts (of which 70,505 were carried out); 198,286 court summonses; 30,598 notifications of lost property and 32,405 notifications of recovered property, all of which consumed time and manpower. Every public gathering meant that forces had to be removed from regular service because of the lack of sufficient manpower reserves.

The crime rate in 1964 reached a new high: 58,312 persons, including 17,910 minors (16,593 boys and 1317 girls), were charged with a total of 38,700 felonies and misdemeanors. Though the figures for juvenile offenders refer to the number of indictments rather than the number of offenders, the actual number of juvenile offenders was 5558, which was in itself disquieting. At the request of Interpol a study on juvenile gangs was made. It was found that according to the usual definition, Israel had no such gangs. Most of the groups known to the police existed not for the purpose of committing crimes but merely for having a "good time," in the course of which the young people committed various offenses such as vehicle theft and burglary from kiosks. While not a weighty aspect of the crime situation, these groups were a nuisance to the public and to the police and should be regarded as the first stage in the development of genuine juvenile gangs and given proper attention. As the Talmud says, "One transgression leads to another," and some juvenile offenders already had long records.

The Nazi Crimes Investigation Section carried out 55 new investigations, 40 on the basis of requests from abroad and the rest on its own initiative. A total of 2448 witnesses were questioned, 22 reports were sent to authoritative bodies abroad, 96 witnesses were sent to testify before German and Austrian courts, and 202 witnesses were invited to give evidence in Israeli courts, 47 of them in the presence of investigating judges from West Germany.

The crime rate was increasing throughout the world and Israel was no exception. Offenders everywhere were making use of new technological devices to commit their offenses. As a result the police would have to acquire greater quantities of the appropriate equipment and communication and transport means in order to keep pace with the criminals.

Police patrols were an independent factor in preventing crime. In 1964 patrol personnel dealt with 157,000 incidents, made 96,000 arrests on court orders, prepared 14,000 reports on offenses of the contravention category, and issued 345,000 traffic citations. This was in addition to the tens of thousands of operations not requiring written reports, such as services to the public or intervention to restore order and keep the peace. Regular airborne patrols were carried out to detect infiltrators and to locate missing children and adults, fugitive offenders, and the like. The struggle of the Border Police against infiltrators bent on espionage and sabotage was difficult and complex and required stamina, courage, and perseverance. During the war they succeeded in liquidating several espionage gangs in armed conflicts after tracking them down for a considerable time.

Represented in the Border Police were the majority of the various national and religious communities in Israel. Relations of comradeship and mutual understanding prevailed as well as a fine esprit de corps. Excellent relations also existed between the Border Police units and the local authorities. When necessary, Border Police personnel also performed the duties of regular police and took part in extensive operations requiring considerable manpower.

A growing problem was that of traffic and traffic accidents. At the end of 1964 there were 172,048 registered motor vehicles (apart from Army and police vehicles), an increase of 28,076 over the previous year. During the year 11,862 accidents occured that took the lives of 325 persons, including 56 children. A total of 15,664 persons including 2676 children were injured, and 316,402 persons were convicted of traffic violations.

National Police Headquarters received 753 complaints against members of the force, of which 57 proved to be well founded and resulted in disciplinary action; 434 were found to be groundless; the rest were still being investigated. But not only complaints were received. Praise and thanks for services and acts of assistance rendered by policemen were also common.

There were six prisons, Mr. Shitreet reported:

1. *Ma'asiyahu* (named after an officer of the law in the days of King Usiahu (II Chronicles 26:11), for prisoners who did not constitute a public menace or had already served part of their terms elsewhere. The capacity of Ma'asiyahu was 300 persons and it took in about a third of all convicted persons, especially first offenders sentenced to two years or less. It included an infirmary, a workshop, and a large farming area.

2. *Ramla Central Prison*, adjoining Ma'asiyahu, contained the largest number and the most dangerous kind of prisoners—those convicted of murder, espionage, and other serious felonies. The prison had a psychiatric department to provide treatment for those needing it. Capacity, 400 prisoners.

3. *Shata Prison*, with a security rating second only to Ramla Prison, held prisoners sentenced to up to five years. The prison contained various workshops.

4. *Damon Prison*, with a capacity of 250, for persons sentenced to up to three years. Young offenders of the minority communities were held in a special section where they received treatment, instruction, and vocational training along the lines of Tel Mond Prison (see below). It had a variety of workshops, including a well-equipped printing shop and a bookbinding shop which turned out files and ledgers for all the Government Ministries.

5. *Tel Mond Prison* for young offenders. Its capacity had been increased to 180. Three classrooms were added to the fine elementary school on the premises. The nature study room was augmented by a large number of interesting exhibits. Here, too, there were various shops for vocational training in such trades as mechanics, metalworking, woodworking, sewing.

6. *Neveh Tirtsa Prison for Women*, capacity 100. At any given time the number of prisoners ranged between 30 and 50. They were taught sewing, hairdressing, flower raising, and various handicrafts.

In prisons for men the subjects taught included woodworking, metalworking, autobody repairs, auto mechanics, shoe repairing, bookbinding, translation of books into Braille, farming, and many handicrafts. Much attention was being devoted to culture and education in the prisons, especially to the eradication of illiteracy. All the prisons provided courses in languages, especially Hebrew and Arabic, general studies, citizenship, the Bible, Talmud, drama, and music. Physical training and sports were also encouraged. All the prisons had libraries with books in Hebrew, Arabic, and foreign languages. During the year a total of 2650 books were added, including 900 textbooks. The prisons also had synagogues and chapels but not in separate structures.

Voluntary associations for the rehabilitation of offenders and prisoners were active in Jerusalem, Tel Aviv, Haifa, Natanya, and Gedera. Each was headed by a judge or lawyer, and the central organization was headed by a Justice of the Supreme Court.

This survey by the Minister of Police was received with great interest and prompted many questions.

The Knesset Refuses To Investigate Eshkol's Criticism of Ben-Gurion ★ A New Libel Law Is Adopted

Vague criticism of the first Prime Minister, Ben-Gurion, by the current Prime Minister, Levi Eshkol, had appeared in the press. On June 23, 1965, Menahem Begin, speaking on behalf of Gahal—a bloc consisting of Herut and the Liberal Party—demanded formation of a parliamentary committee of inquiry (under the Knesset Basic Law, Section 22) to examine the strictures.

What Mr. Begin wanted probed, specifically, were statements by Eshkol at a Mapai Central Committee meeting on May 13, 1965. He had not mentioned the name or the function of the person he stigmatized, referring to him as "that man" or "that member." After venting his spleen on the unnamed culprit with regard to party matters, Eshkol had said, "There were things that were not in order with that man with whom I worked in the Government for twelve years; he has not revealed all. For several reasons, especially out of respect for ourselves and the fifty years and more, I will not enter into details."

Histadrut Secretary Aharon Becker rose to deplore Eshkol's allusions, and Golda Meir immediately countered with a sharp and agitated rebuke to the Prime Minister.

The following day Eshkol's words were published in full in *Davar*. Preferring not to rely on the press report, Ben-Gurion requested that the Party Secretary, Reuven Barkatt, give him the stenographic record. *Davar*, he found, had indeed printed the statement word for word. Ben Gurion then published the following:

> I demand that Eshkol reveal to the nation, either on the floor of the Knesset or in a signed letter to the press, everything that was "not in order" with me as Prime Minister or Minister of Defense. Let him not invoke "respect for ourselves" while slandering to thousands of people the man who stood at the helm of the State of Israel for fifteen years. I carried out my task as the representative of the nation, not of Eshkol's associates, and the nation is entitled to know what is not in order. Eshkol, too, in working together with me in the Government, did so not as an emissary or hireling of mine but as one of the representatives, and a loyal one, of the people. He must tell the nation all the things he is covering up "out of respect for ourselves." Let him not settle for a vague slander in the Mapai Secretariat but reveal to the whole nation of Israel the crimes I committed as Prime Minister and Minister of Defense and let them do the deciding.

Instead of replying, Eshkol sent a Mapai spokesman to express his regret that he "did not proofread the stenographic record before it was released to the press." If he was misquoted, why did he not write to the paper to ask for a correction? If statements by the present Prime Minister concerning a former Prime Minister are misrepresented by a newspaper, is it not his duty to rectify the error immediately? Mr. Begin was right when he said in the Knesset, "What has proofreading to do with this?" To stress the seriousness of the episode, Begin also said:

> The Mapai people are in the habit of referring to the British Parliament as a model. Just imagine Sir Alec Douglas-Home claiming that things were not always in order under Mr. Macmillan, and that Macmillan was not revealing everything! Would the British Parliament let it go at that or would it—without party distinction—demand to know what was not in order? The present Prime Minister is not new to governmental practice. During the twelve years he mentioned he was a member of the Government, one who held the key portfolio of Minister of Finance. Now he comes to tell us things were not in order and that his predecessor is not revealing all. I assume that in his central position he could and in fact did know during those twelve years just what it was that was not in order. But only now does he tell us these things. The question, Mr. Eshkol, is why were you silent all this time? Why did you not tell the Mapai Secretariat and the public at the time that things in the Government were not in order, instead of waiting until 1965?

> The reason the Prime Minister gives for not revealing that things were not in order was "out of respect for ourselves," and since he was speaking at a meeting of his party this can only be interpreted as meaning "out of respect for the party's honor." Now in a matter of such gravity to the nation is the party's honor to be the deciding factor?

> Since the Prime Minister, despite the dramatic outcry of his predecessor, has declined to this day to be more specific, all we can do is ask: What did you mean, Mr. Eshkol, in saying that in your predecessor's time there were things that were not in order? I cannot recall, Mr. Chairman, a case in which a demand for the committee of inquiry was ever more justified than this. We must know just what it was that was not in order so it won't recur.

Mr. Eshkol took the floor. He said: "Mr. Speaker, honorable Knesset, I did not make any statements anywhere, Mr. Begin. The quotation in question was taken without my permission from a stenographic record that I had not proofread, and for which I am therefore not responsible. I have not searched for flaws in the deeds of my predecessors during their terms of office. Incidentally, what I said did not refer to the time when my colleagues were in office. I therefore request and propose that the motion be dropped."

Speaker Kadish Luz immediately put the Prime Minister's proposal to a vote and it was sustained, forty-three to thirteen, with eleven abstaining. Among those who voted in favor of dropping the matter were a considerable number of Mapai members present at the Secretariat meeting at which Mr. Eshkol made the statements quoted by Mr. Begin. Ben-Gurion was not present when Begin tabled his motion. On July 19, 1965, however, he made the following declaration in the Knesset:

> Honorable Speaker, members of the Knesset: On June 23 Knesset member Menahem Begin proposed a parliamentary inquiry to investigate "the things that were not always in order" during my premiership, as claimed by the present Prime Minister, Mr. Levi Eshkol. The honorable member said that the Mapai spokesman was trying on behalf of Mr. Eshkol to hide behind the pencil of the secretary who took down Mr. Eshkol's statement in shorthand. Now I do not suspect Mr. Begin of being concerned with the honor of the previous Prime Minister and his motives are not my affair. The Prime Minister's reply to Mr. Begin was, "I did not make any statements anywhere" and in the same speech he said explicitly, "I do not wish to say that I assume, etc." But what was in this "etc." Mr. Eshkol

did not reveal. Afterward he added, "What I said did not relate to the time when my colleagues were in office," that is, not to my term of office as Prime Minister and Minister of Defense, which lasted only fifteen years.

Unfortunately I must note that the statements by the present Prime Minister in the Knesset do not correspond with what he said at the meeting of the Mapai Secretariat, as a result of which a parliamentary inquiry committee was proposed. At that meeting, on April 13, 1965, Mr. Eshkol referred to my term of office in the Government and this is what he said in the presence of scores of persons: "I do not even wish to say that I assume—and you will agree with me—that there were things that were not in order with this man with whom I worked in the Government for twelve years, but he has not revealed all; for several reasons, especially out of respect for ourselves and the fifty years and more, I will not enter into details." This was printed word for word the next day, May 14, 1965, in *Davar*, which is read by thousands of people. Incidentally, let me state that I did not know Eshkol fifty years ago and certainly not before then, even though I have been in the country for nearly sixty years.

When I received the stenographic minutes of that Secretariat meeting, I published the following statement in *Davar*: "These are very grave assertions indeed and if there is any truth in them at all I demand that Eshkol reveal to the entire nation either on the floor of the Knesset or in a signed letter to the press, all the things that were not in order with the previous Prime Minister and Minister of Defense. Let him not pretend he is keeping silent 'out of respect for ourselves' while slandering to thousands of people the man who stood at the helm of the State of Israel for fifteen years."

Mr. Eshkol did not reply. He also evaded the same demand when it was made in the Knesset on June 25, 1965. It is not correct that "he did not make any statements anywhere," as he then claimed, nor that his statements "did not refer to the time his predecessor was in office." And here in the Knesset, too, I say that the nation will judge.

Eshkol did not respond to this declaration.

On July 20, 1965, the Chairman of the Law Committee, Moshe Unna, presented the Libel Law of 1965 for second reading. The original Libel bill was first tabled in the Knesset in February 1962 but evoked widespread criticism. Following consultations between the Minister of Justice and representatives of the Journalists Association, the Government drew up a revised version, which was submitted for first reading in July–August 1963. This time, too, there was widespread criticism, some claiming it was too lenient and others too harsh.

What was involved was a clash between two fundamental concepts of a well-ordered society, which on the one hand safeguards the dignity of man and individual freedom without which no democratic society can survive, and on the other safeguards the freedom of the press, that vitally important instrument of a free society. The legislators had to keep both values in mind and find a balance between them, in the interests of the individual and of the public as a whole. The committee devoted special attention to a more precise definition of libel and defamation. After a lengthy debate the draft bill was largely accepted and most of the objections were overruled. The main clauses of the bill were the following:

> Libel includes statements that, if published, could defame a man in the eyes of his fellows or make him a target of hatred, scorn, or ridicule; that defame a man because of acts, behavior, or qualities attributed to him; that could damage a man in his official capacity, whether public or otherwise, in his business, profession, or trade; or that defame a man for

his ethnic origin or religion. For the purposes of this section, a "man" is taken to be either an individual or a corporate group.

For the purpose of this bill "publication" shall constitute dissemination by word of mouth or writing or print or by way of drawings, images, movement, or any other medium. Libelous publication shall be taken to include (without excluding other means of publication): (1) if it was intended for a person other than the injured party and reached that person or any person other than the injured party; (2) if it was in writing and the writing under the circumstances was liable to reach a person other than the injured party.

The bill was adopted on third reading on July 21, 1965.

At the request of thirty-six members the Knesset convened on September 1, 1965, to discuss amendments to this law. By a vote of fifty-one to forty-four it was decided not to discuss the matter in the Knesset and by a vote of fifty-three to forty-four not to refer the matter to committee.

"The proposers of the various amendments have given the impression that these deliberations were not thorough and resolute," the Chairman of the Law Committee said in a personal comment. "As the person responsible for the committee's work I wish to bring the following facts to the Knesset's attention: The committee began its deliberations on May 11, 1964, and held forty meetings in which the bill was discussed. Journalists, lawyers, and other interested parties were given the opportunity to appear before it. A meeting was held in which the committee went over the bill, paragraph by paragraph, then in a second meeting it was reviewed as a whole, and some sections were even reviewed a third time. No bill has ever been given such thorough consideration by the committee. Committee members and various interested parties were given an unusual opportunity to explain their positions. There is a considerable discrepancy between the moderate statements of the journalists' representatives who proposed certain amendments and the unparalleled furor that the press has raised in hopes of influencing the Knesset to adopt amendments."

This marked the close of the fourth and last session of the Fifth Knesset.

Election to the Sixth Knesset ★ As Its Oldest Member, Ben-Gurion Addresses the Opening Session

The elections to the Sixth Knesset were held on Tuesday, November 2, 1965. A total of 1,244,706 persons exercised the right to vote. The number of valid votes was 1,206,728 compared to 1,006,964 in the Fifth Knesset. This time Mapai and Ahdut Haavodah, running as the Alignment, received 443,379 votes, for 45 seats—in the elections to the Fifth Knesset these two parties had received 415,500 votes out of a total of 1,006,964, and 50 seats; the Herut-Liberal bloc (Gahal) drew 356,957 votes, 26 seats—in the elections to the previous Knesset these two parties had received 275,854 votes, 34 seats; the National Religious Front obtained 107,966 votes, 11 seats—compared with 98,786 votes, 12 seats, in the Fifth Knesset; the Israel Workers List (Rafi—a new party that split off from Mapai) got 95,328 votes, 10 seats; Mapam, 79,985 votes, 8 seats—in the Fifth Knesset 75,564 votes, 9 seats; Independent Liberals, 45,299 votes, 5 seats—in the Fifth Knesset they had been in a single bloc with the Liberals; Agudat Israel; 39,795 votes, 4 seats (Fifth Knesset:

37,178 votes, 4 seats); New Communist List (which split off from the Israel Communist Party), 27,413 votes, 3 seats; Kidmah u'Fituah 23,430 votes, 2 seats; Poalei Agudat Israel, 22,066 votes, 2 seats—in the previous Knesset 19,428 votes, 2 seats; Shituf v' Ahvah, 16,464 votes, 2 seats; Haolam Hazeh Koah Hadash 14,124 votes, 1 seat; Communist Party, 13,617 votes, 1 seat (42,111 votes, 5 seats in the Fifth Knesset). Four other lists failed to win even a single seat.

The first session of the Sixth Knesset was opened on Monday, November 22, 1965, with an address by President Shazar. He used the occasion to eulogize elected representatives of the nation who had died during the four years of the Fifth Knesset, a larger loss than during any previous Knesset. Among them were outstanding personalities renowned for their rich accomplishments, some old in years and some who had been cut down in the prime of life, breaking the cord of their splendid service: the second President of the State, Yitzhak Ben-Zvi, and Knesset members in the order of their demise: Giora Yoseftal, Herzl Berger, Hanan Rubin, Mordekhai Nurock, Aharon Yacov Grinberg, Ami Assaf, Meir Argov, Avraham Drori, Israel Bar-Yehuda, Moshe Sharett, Israel Guri, of blessed memory for all eternity. Everyone rose for a minute of silence.

As required by law, the President invited the oldest member of the Knesset, David Ben-Gurion, to conduct the opening session. The former Prime Minister extended his heartfelt good wishes to all the Knesset, old and new, that they might accomplish their mission loyally, responsibly, and in sober awareness of our situation, our needs, and our destiny. In making his declaration of allegience as a Knesset member he said:

> We are a people like all other peoples, but our resurgence, our continued existence, and our historic tasks are unique in the annals of mankind.
>
> The background to every act of national resurgence has always been the reality of a people living in its land, even if subordinate to foreign rule. The national liberation movement in every country has been nourished by this reality, and all that was required for the realization of its aspirations was to throw off the yoke of foreign rule. We had been severed and sundered from our Homeland for centuries, and dispersed among the nations in all parts of the globe. Three unique factors were operative in the renewal of the State of Israel: (1) the messanic vision, which lived in our people's hearts in all generations and accompanied us in all our wanderings; (2) the pioneering efforts of those who returned to Zion in recent generations, who, with the labor of their hands and the creative achievements of their spirit, established a ramified independent economy, a glorious defense force, a resuscitated Hebrew culture rooted in our ancient tradition and heritage and patterns of self-rule even under foreign domination; (3) the devoted aid of Jewry throughout the world. We were also supported by the conscience of humanity, after the terrible Holocaust in the time of Nazi rule, as was revealed at the United Nations General Assembly in November 1947.
>
> With the rise of the State the vision of redemption has not yet been realized. We are still far from being able to rest on our laurels. Since the renewal of our independence, our numbers have been multiplied three and a half times, but Israel contains only 18 percent of the Jewish people, and no more than 40 percent of our area is populated.
>
> Until the establishment of the State there were two factors providing for immigration: the messianic vision and distress. Most of the Jews from the lands of distress have already arrived in Israel, apart from the great Jewish center in Eastern Europe which has been cut off from Jewry and the Homeland these fifty years. The gates of departure are still barred and bolted; but we have not lost hope that all those Soviet Jews who wish to join us will be allowed to do so. In the meantime, however, immigration is diminishing and in all the other lands of distress there are only some half million Jews.

But with the rise of the State a new factor has been created which we have not yet adequately utilized, bound as we are to the tradition of the Zionist Organization, whose vitality has declined and which has almost lost its meaning. This new factor is the power of attraction of the State, of Israel's independence and its pioneering, revolutionary, and redemptive work. Our tasks in the lands of distress are not yet at an end, but the center of gravity, both for quantity and for quality, of the Jewish people, which until the First World War dwelt in Europe, has since passed to the North American continent, to some extent to South America as well, and there are considerable concentrations of Jews in the West European countries, especially in Britain and France.

If the State of Israel consolidates its strength and stability, and raises its standards, material and economic, moral and spiritual—which is not beyond our power—there is no doubt that even in lands where there is no distress and pressure, many will be attracted to the ancient Homeland of our people, for they will find here values and assets not enjoyed by Jews in any other country: Jewish independence, integrity, and originality expressed in every sphere, in economy and statesmanship, society and culture, science and learning. With four things Israel will attract immigrants from the prosperous lands: the radiance and integrity of her democratic and progressive institutions; the cultural and moral standards of the people; the opportunity for creative, pioneering initiative; and suitable economic conditions.

We must not forget for a moment that most of our territory is neither peopled nor cultivated. Israel has been blessed with two seas. The Biblical promise, 'And I shall set thy border even from the Red Sea into the Sea of the Philistines' (Exodus 23:31), has been fulfilled only in our own times. During the First Temple period, Eilat on the Red Sea was Israel's only port, and even that only occasionally, while in the days of the Second Temple, from Hasmonean times until the Destruction, Jaffa, on the Mediterranean, which the Bible called the Sea of the Philistines, was the only Jewish port.

Seventeen years ago we liberated Eilat, after liberating Jaffa and Haifa, and our territory extends from the Mediterranean to the Red Sea, so that we have direct maritime contact with Europe, America, and West Africa through the Mediterranean, and with Asia, Australia, and East Africa through the Red Sea. But unless the Negev is populated and transformed into Israel's industrial center—for almost all our country's natural resources are concentrated in the Negev—Eilat will not fulfill its great economic and political functions in our relations with the peoples of Asia and East Africa, for which it is qualified by its position at the crossroads of three continents. Nor can we ignore the dangers to our security of our concentration in the narrow strip of the Mediterranean coast, especially in the neighborhood of Jaffa, and there can be no dispersal of the population without dispersal of industry. We have not done enough, until now, to develop industry even in the existing development towns.

Moreover, although for geographical, historical, political, and economic reasons our international relations are now concentrated in the West, we must pay heed to the changes that are taking place on the political map of the world, especially in Asia and Africa. We shall betray our own future if we ignore the crucial fact that the majority of the human race lives on the continent of Asia, where all the world's dominant religions were born, where human culture was nurtured in days of yore, and where the largest nations in the world live. The way to them is through Eilat and the Negev.

We were the only nation in the Middle East and the entire world in ancient times that struck out a special and independent path of its own in its religious and moral concepts. We faced a constant struggle, political and ideological, and sometimes military as well, with our neighbors until the destruction of the Second Temple. Later, we were the only people that did not submit to Christianity and Islam, when these two creeds, that derived from Jewish sources, conquered the great and powerful nations amongst whom we lived.

We are alone among the peoples in tradition, language, and faith. All the neighboring nations were vanquished and wiped off the face of the earth; no trace of them is left except in ruins and remains, pyramids and buried inscriptions. In our day, even the name of Egypt— which of all the nations has the longest history, stretching over six thousand years and more, and which, in the Nile Valley, was one of the most ancient civilized states—has been obliterated. But the people of Israel still survives, preserving its historical continuity; after two thousand years it has returned from dispersion to the land of its origins, revived its State, and resuscitated its ancient language—the only Biblical people that still continues to speak the tongue that was spoken by its ancestors since the days of our Father Abraham four thousand years ago.

Yet although we are members, with equal rights, in the United Nations, many of the other member states do not recognize Israel; and, what is worse, our neighbors are not reconciled to the very fact of our existence, and we are still beleaguered on all our land frontiers. Not only do our neighbors plan a war of extermination, but we are subjected to guerrilla warfare by bands of murderers and saboteurs dispatched across the borders from time to time, and the Arab League's economic boycott against us still continues. The problem of our security is as grave as ever it was. We must maintain constant and ever growing readiness, and increase the deterrent power of the Israel Defense Forces.

At the same time, we should not ignore the isolated voices that emerge here and there, from those who adopt a sober and realistic view of Israel-Arab relations and call for the recognition of Israel's existence and the establishment of normal relations between the two Semitic peoples. We must, of course, encourage every possible contact with those Arabs who aspire for peace, since a covenant of peace and cooperation with all our neighbors has always been our hearts' desire, ever since we proclaimed the revival of our independence almost eighteen years ago. At the same time this is a necessity for the world at large.

The peace for which we long will surely come, but until it comes we must dedicate ourselves to the maintenance of our security. Our peace and security depend on two things: the deterrent strength of the Israel Defense Forces and our status on the international scene. Both of these depend, among other things, on the moral integrity of our sovereign institutions. This is the great responsibility that rests upon members of the Knesset as representatives of the nation—and not only on them, for it is the responsibility of each and every citizen.

The secret of our survival among foreign and hostile peoples, the secret of our endurance as few against the many, in days of old and in our own time, the secret of our victory in the War of Independence, which gave us life, freedom, and independence is our qualitative superiority, moral and cultural. Only by preserving and constantly enhancing this dual superiority can we consolidate and increase the strength of our forces, preserve and improve our international standing, intensify the attraction of our country, and deepen the attachment of Diaspora Jewry to the State of Israel.

Israel must find paths to the Asian peoples, carriers of ancient and original cultures, including China, the largest of the world's nations. We must strengthen our cultural, economic, and political ties with the peoples of Europe and America, among whom Diaspora Jewry lives, and from which we have inherited the achievements of science and technology. We must continue to offer sincere and fraternal assistance, as far as our modest capacity allows, to the nations of Africa, whether liberated or achieving their liberation, and maintain relations of friendship, as well as economic and political cooperation, with them.

At the same time, Israel's fate, future, and status will be determined above all on the home fronts, and decisively in these four spheres:

1. The capacity of the State and the will of the people to attract immigrants from all the dispersions, especially from the prosperous lands where most of the Jewish people is now concentrated, and their speedy and adequate absorption.

2. Our capacity and pioneering will to develop the land, including the extensive wastes of the Negev and the south, and the empty areas in the north, and to build a ramified economy in agriculture and industry, shipping and communications, which can stand on its own feet and guarantee the people of Israel economic independence and an adequate standard of living.

3. A constantly growing effort to foster education—general and vocational—in primary, secondary, and higher institutions, and to transform the people of Israel, without distinction of community, creed, or race, into an important creative center in all areas of science and research, literature and learning, art and spiritual achievement.

4. The molding of a new, free, and progressive society, based on mutual aid and love of our fellow men, justice, and peace, without deprivation or discrimination—a society that will be the pride of every Jew wherever he may dwell and a light unto the Gentiles.

Israel's tasks will not be carried out only by the power of government, law, and administration, but by the voluntary effort of the majority of our people. The security of the State, the absorption and integration of the immigrants, the fructification of the desert, a high standard of culture for the whole of the younger generation and the transformation of Israel into a center of literature and science, research and learning, cannot be accomplished without voluntary pioneering by young and old. Our educators must endeavor to raise the standards of our people, foster its latent pioneering capacity, its moral integrity, practical ability, and intellectual qualities. To this end special effort must be invested in raising the status of teachers, training them to be true educators who set an example to their pupils. Moreover, it is not only the youth that must be educated. Every person in Israel, professionals included, must not only make demands of others, of the State, the municipality, the management of the plant where he works; but must make demands of himself as well. In this lies the true measure of a person's greatness and social responsibility, the essence of the pioneering effort without which our historical objectives will remain unfulfilled.

After all the members of the Knesset present had made their declarations of allegiance, Kadish Luz was again nominated as Speaker and elected with a majority of 102 votes with 9 abstaining. Eight Deputy Speakers were elected: Israel Yesha'yahu, Dvora Netzer, and Ruth Hektin from the Alignment; Aryeh Ben-Eliezer and Joseph Serlin from Gahal; Tova Sanhedrai from the National Religious Party, Yitzhak Navo from Rafi, and Emma Talmi from Mapam.

Section 2. Plans To Meet Economic Recession

A New Coalition Government Is Formed ★ Eshkol Outlines the Tasks and Policies for the Period Ahead

AFTER consulting with the parties in the Sixth Knesset, President Shazar once more entrusted Eshkol with the task of forming the Government, and on January 12, 1966, Eshkol presented to the Knesset a Cabinet consisting of members from the Alignment, the National Religious Front, Mapam, the Independent Liberals, and Poalei Agudat Israel. Three members of the previous Government—Dov Joseph, Minister of Justice; Golda Meir, Minister of Foreign Affairs; and Akiva Govrin, Minister of Tourism—were not included. The eighteen members of the proposed Government were: Levi Eshkol, Prime Minister and Minister of Defense; Abba Eban, Minister for Foreign Affairs; Yigal Allon, Minister of Labor; Zalman Aranne, Minister of Education; Yosef Burg, Minister of Social Welfare; Mordekhai Bentov, Minister of Housing; Israel Barzilai, Minister of Health; Chaim Gavati, Minister of Agriculture; Israel Galili, Minister without portfolio; Zerah Warhaftig, Minister of Religious Affairs, Moshe Carmel, Minister of Transport; Pinhas Sapir, Minister of Finance; Chaim Zadok, Minister of Commerce and Industry; Moshe Kol, Minister of Development and Tourism; Bekhor Shalom Shitreet, Minister of Police; Moshe Shapira, Minister of the Interior; Yacov Shimshon Shapira, Minister of Justice; Eliyahu Sasson, Minister of Posts.

In presenting the Cabinet, Eshkol declared:

The work of the new Government will be founded on the Basic Policy, which is mainly that followed by the previous governments and partial revisions decided upon in the negotiations with the parties composing the Coalition. These Basic Principles have been placed before you.

Israel's aspirations and efforts on the international scene will continue to be directed toward the extirpation of aggression and belligerency; the eradication of racial and religious discrimination; the completion of the liberation of peoples from colonial regimes and the speeding up of their development. We shall do our utmost for international and regional agreements for the limitation and abolition of armaments, including nuclear arms, with agreed mutual supervision.

It is only natural that the attention of the Government in the spheres of security and foreign affairs during the coming years should be directed chiefly toward the situation in the Near East. Israel's central aim in the Near East is the advancement of peace. We aspire toward relations founded on respect for the independence and integrity of all the states in the area. The time has come for Arab statesmen to show a wise sense of reality and abandon their declared purpose of changing the map of the Middle East under the delusion that Israel's existence in the area may be ignored. Israel and her people constitute an inseparable part of this area. This is not a nation that has intruded all of a sudden into the life of the Middle East. It is one of the nations that molded the character of the region and determined its place in human history. It is both capable and ready to make its contribution in the future as well, and—while developing itself—to promote the progress and prosperity of the Middle East.

Insofar as there exist in the Arab world tendencies, however weak and hesitant, toward moderate and positive thinking about Israel-Arab relations, we shall try to encourage and foster them to the best of our ability. Unfortunately, however, we know that the tendency being proclaimed in the Arab world today is opposed to peace and coexistence. It finds expression in the accumulation of strength with a view to a conflict at the appropriate time. The heads of the Arab states are fostering in the Arab world the idea of preparation for war. They are intensifying the arms race in the Middle East. They are maintaining and stimulating to further activity the "Palestine Liberation," and "El Fatah" organizations.

We shall therefore continue to consolidate Israel's military strength. A strong State of Israel is a guarantee of the first order for the maintenance of peace in our area. Our aim is the prevention of war. This aim, supported by every peace-loving nation in the world, dictates the enhancement of Israel's strength in all spheres: manpower, the economy, culture, technology, and science.

I expressed the hope two years ago that parallel with the improvement of our ties with the United States, France, and Britain, there should also be more understanding between the Soviet Union and Israel. True, there has not been much progress in this direction but we should not despair of the aim itself. Israel plays no part in what is called the Cold War. Israel supports the principle of abstention from the use of force for the solution of territorial disputes, as defined by the Soviet Union at the beginning of 1964. Representatives of the Soviet Union stated then that this principle is of universal application.

Mr. Eshkol then addressed himself to the problems of the economy of Israel:

The aim of our economic policy is to build and maintain a healthy and progressive economy in agriculture, industry, transportation—land, sea, and air—tourism, commerce, science, and technology, while maintaining a suitable standard of living for the people in nutrition, housing, education, health, culture, and so forth. We have not yet attained a balance between these two aspirations. The rate of progress in the welfare of the population is partly at the expense of the development and consolidation of the economy. This is the result of our special position as a country absorbing mass immigration from lands of distress. The days ahead call for an effort to climb still higher on the ladder of economic independence. Everyone admits that in what we have done up to now we have laid the foundations for economic independence, but what was good for the State's first eighteen years is not sufficient for the years to come.

Our main problem today is to obtain a maximum output for the existing factors of production. We must thoroughly investigate the profitability of our enterprises and ways to enhance their productivity and output. We must make progress in minimizing the deficit in our trade balance. We must slow down the increase of consumption per capita from its present rate of 6 percent—a rate almost unexampled anywhere else in the world. The growth in consumption should be smaller than the rise in output. More of our domestic resources should be invested in the economy, in order to increase exports. The output of every employee in production, services, and administration should be raised by increasing productivity. The public, Histadrut, and Government economy—like the private economy—must face the test of competition, efficiency, and higher productivity. They must become more profitable. Our enterprises must operate on standards customary abroad, at least in the West European countries, so that we may be able to face competition in international markets.

Something has gone wrong in labor morale and labor relations in this young State. We are witnessing strange and harmful phenomena, a peculiar and anarchic class struggle, in which no labor movement that respects itself and the nation as a whole can acquiesce. These phenomena take the form of pressures that are unlawful and unrecognized by the Histadrut or other labor unions, by means of sudden, and what are known as "wildcat" strikes and work stoppages. There are slowdown strikes, speedup strikes, sitdown strikes, and hunger strikes. An outstanding feature of this behavior is the failure to observe written agreements, and exorbitant demands by both lower-paid workers and those who enjoy good wages and conditions.

The Government must erect barriers against the creation of unjustified wage pressures in its own domain, in the public service. We must realize that there is a limit to wage benefits and social improvements in all income scales, just as there must be a limit to excessive profits and wasteful spending of luxuries and show.

Mr. Eshkol stressed the urgency of population dispersal and peopling the country's desolate areas; solution of the problem of housing for dwellers in slums and unsafe buildings in the cities; and the expansion of kindergarten and high-school education. He then read the names of the members of the new Cabinet and proposed that the Knesset approve the Government and its basic policy. After a debate that ended the same day, the Knesset expressed confidence in the Government by a vote of seventy-one to forty-one. A few days later, on January 17, 1966, the Minister of Finance announced the appointment of the Deputy Ministers: Dr. Zvi Dinstein as Deputy Minister of Defense; Dr. Kalman Kahana and Aharon Yadlin as Deputy Ministers of Education and Culture; Aharon Ozen as Deputy Minister of Agriculture; Dr. Israel Shlomo Ben-Meir as Deputy Minister of the Interior; and Yehuda Sha'ari as Deputy Minister of Development.

An Examination of Economic Policy Prompted by the 1966–1967 Budget

A budget for 1966–1967 was laid before the Knesset on February 14, 1966, by the Minister of Finance, Pinhas Sapir. Economic policy, he said, was no different from the previous year. He presented the following survey of that area of national life:

. The absorption of immigration that in the past eighteen years arrived here completely destitute, to an overwhelming extent, has guided our policy all these years. The provision of housing and sources of livelihood for immigrants, the expansion of the educational system and other social services, the creation of hundreds of settlements in all parts of the country and the development of agriculture and industry have all demanded large investments. It is this absorption and development—almost unparalleled in the world—that has enabled Israel to increase her population almost fourfold since the establishment of the State. This drive led to an increase of three and a half times in the nation's Gross National Product since 1952—the first year for which we have exact figures—to a total of IL 11 billion in 1965; a growth in the number of workers from 544,000 to approximately 900,000; a rise in exports from $86 million to $750 million last year. We have passed from austerity and rationing to abundance and prosperity.

Concomitantly, and as a result of this growth and the constant security burden, the trade deficit has increased from $307 million in 1952 to approximately $500 million in 1965. Reparations and personal indemnification payments from Germany, the United Jewish Appeal, bonds, private investments, and other forms of imported capital have enabled us not only to cover the growing deficit but even to increase our foreign currency surplus. In 1965 alone our surplus rose from $600 million to approximately $700 million.

It must be understood, however, that this imported capital is in large part in the form of loans; long-term loans on easy terms, but when the time comes they must be repaid and we have already reached that stage. In 1966 the Government and other economic factors will be repaying loans to the amount of $250 million or IL750 million. This is an enormous sum that also is reflected in the State budget. But a country in a situation like ours can ill afford to live without a foreign currency surplus. What this boils down to is that we can ill afford a deficit to the tune of a half billion dollars a year. If the deficit does not shrink—and the tendency in recent years has unfortunately been in the opposite direction—foreign currency reserves will be exhausted and we shall have to face a condition when we shall not possess enough dollars to buy the vital necessities for defense and industrial production.

We are now in a phase in which we are able to undertake a gradual transition from an increasing deficit to its reduction without any grave crisis in production and employment, while we still have extensive reserves of foreign currency. We are not compelled to continue developing at the accelerated pace we have known so far because with the final abolition of the Ma'abarot [temporary housing for new immigrants] this year, we have actually made good all arrears in the physical absorption of new immigrants; and unless the miracle we all hope for should come to pass, we shall unfortunately not absorb any major immigration in the near future.

These factors have determined our policy during the last year, as reflected in the decisions of the Cabinet Economic Committee and the Knesset Finance Committee. Their significance was evident in a certain slowing down in the rate of growth and development, and in the consolidation of our holdings.

We have decided on decelerated building enterprises, more selectivity in investments, and a more rigid policy on foreign loans. Not all of this can be done within one year and not all decisions, for various reasons, have been implemented in their entirety. But what has been done has brought positive results. Exports grew by 13 percent and reached approximately $750 million, of which $320 million went directly to industrial exports, apart from invisible exports of tourist purchases. On the other hand, direct and invisible imports rose at a very slow rate to $1,235,000,000. As a result the deficit dropped in comparison with the preceding year, and is now less than a half billion dollars. I do not consider this drop an essential improvement in our current balance but only a return to the normal trend from which we deviated in 1964. In 1966 we shall reach an export of $330 per capita, which nobody needs to be ashamed of. The fact that this year it is possible not to increase imports without detriment to investments, security, and the standard of living points to the fact that with joint efforts we can reduce imports by at least $100 million.

But I should warn you: we are one of the only countries in the world with a net import of $500 per capita. It is doubtful whether a country such as ours can keep this up for long. Imports at such a rate constitute a burden that a population of two and a half million is unlikely to be able to carry. We must make sure that we don't find ourselves one day in an unbearable situation. Incomplete statistical returns for 1965 show that a certain slowing down took place in our race for higher living standards. While in recent years there was an annual increase of 6 to 7 percent per capita, in 1965 we reached only about 5 percent. We have come to a state of abundance in the production and consumption of basic food products and even such durable products as radios, gas stoves, and refrigerators will soon be found in practically every home in Israel.

A slowdown has taken place mainly in the building industry. New construction, which is what will determine the building rate in coming years as well, declined from 5.5 million square meters in 1964 to 4.5 million square meters in 1965, though this is still considerably larger than the figure for 1963. The slowdown in building, which had grown out of all proportion in 1964, was mainly the result of the Government policy designed to cut back construction of public buildings and impose certain limitations on private building. Excessive building was a negative economic phenomenon. And I can note with satisfaction that this industry has now returned to normal.

Positive development can also be noted in other branches of the economy, though the rise in production was less than in previous years because of the policy of economic restraint. There has been a 10-percent increase in industrial output, which totaled almost IL 7 billion, although manpower grew by only 1.5 percent and hours of work by .4 percent, thus indicating a considerable increase in output per worker. This is due to the increasing introduction in recent years of advanced methods of automation in industry. Agriculture showed only a small increase in output this year despite a growth of approximately 4 percent in the labor force. Unemployment continued to decline to a point hitherto unknown in this country, and the daily unemployment figures were even lower than in 1964.

To this I should add the continued development of the economic infrastructure. A few examples will indicate the economy's expansion in 1965. During the year the deep-water harbor at Ashdod was completed, as was the new harbor at Eilat with its installations for the bulk loading of minerals. Also completed at Eilat was the first stage of the oil jetty capable of accommodating supertankers. In overland communications, the railroad from Beersheba to Dimona has been completed and the work is continuing on the line to Oron. A regular rail link to Ashdod port has been provided and lines have been laid inside the harbor itself. Considerable progress has been made in the construction of the highway from Sodom to Eilat; and a large part of the road to Beersheba has been repaved and widened. The widening of the Natanya-Hadera highway has been completed. The entrances to Tel Aviv and Jerusalem have been widened and improved.

In electric power, a new generating plant in Haifa is nearing completion. It will have a capacity of 280,000 kilowatts, increasing the present generating capacity by 40 percent; a call for tenders has been issued for an additional plant. The high-tension line to Paran has been completed, in the near future the line to Timna will be completed as well, and Eilat will be hooked up to the national power grid.

With regard to the development of natural resources, the phosphate-processing plant at Oron has been put into operation and the clay-processing plant at Mahtesh Ramon is being run in. The investment in these two plants is IL 50 million. Drilling for oil and gas has also been increased and has produced results, such as the new gas field at Barbour. With the discovery of additional wells oil production has risen. The output of 150,000 barrels reached in January 1965 may meet only a tenth of our needs but it is nothing to be scoffed at. We have begun to use the gas that has been discovered as a substitute for other forms of fuel. The National Water Carrier was completed and put into operation and work is continuing on the consolidation of the new settlements. The refineries have been expanded to the point where they can produce five million tons a year, compared to a million tons at the time when we took them over from the British seven years ago.

Improvements in services such as aid to education, health, employment, and housing are continuing. The work of the social welfare services has been directed mainly at helping raise the standard of living and living conditions of the poorer classes. We have completed construction of over nineteen thousand housing units, eleven thousand of them alloted to new immigrants while the remainder have gone to liquidate the Ma'abarot, to evacuees from slums, to young marrieds living in slums in development areas, and so on. In the past four years fifty thousand dwelling units have been built by the public housing scheme to improve the living conditions of the poorer classes. This does not include the new immigrants who received apartments immediately upon their arrival. In 1965 a start was made on seventeen thousand housing units that will be completed in 1966.

We have continued to improve the standards of general education. The number of pupils and students is now approximately seven hundred thousand. We have done all we could to expand and improve educational facilities from the children of underprivileged families by waiving high-school fees for 40 percent of all pupils, by expanding the kindergarten system to include children below the compulsory education age, by enlarging the network of long day classes. We have improved the earning capacity of people without a calling by giving vocational courses to tens of thousands of youths and adults in development areas and other parts of the country, and have increased the welfare and national insurance grants. We have expanded the category of children benefiting from support by the National Insurance, raised the family grants to the children of salary earners, and increased the childbirth grant.

These activities this year have strengthened the economy and raised the standard of living of the poorer classes. I will not mention what has been done to augment our security and the deterrent power of the Army. All these positive developments, however, are overclouded by one grave negative phenomenon, in the area of wages. Here all the barriers were broken, bringing to a climax a process that began a number of years ago. Actually it has been going on for ten years, ever since the strikes of the professionals in 1956.

This process is one of considerable rise in wages accompanied by a steep decline in labor relations and labor morale. The wage increases have been completely divorced from increase in productivity and the economy's possibilities. Consequently there have been repercussions in various spheres, economic and budgetary. Wages per employee have risen an average of 17–18 percent during the past year alone, and the average income per employee has risen to IL470 a month in comparison with IL406 in 1964. This figure, moreover, is misleading because it includes working youths and others whose salaries are lower than the average.

Thus the past year showed a continuation and even a speedup of the trend that has prevailed in the economy for some years now. Since 1961 average real wages per employee have risen by 28 percent. If we break this down by branches of the economy the following picture emerges: In agriculture the average real wage rose by 28 percent, in industry by 23 percent, in construction by 38 percent, in commerce and finance by 23 percent, in transport by 29 percent, in public and business services by 32 percent, and in personal services by 19 percent.

These increases far exceeded the rise in labor productivity and were therefore a decisive factor in the rise of prices, both because of the increased demand and the growth in production costs. It has been the cause of an increase in imports and in the trade deficit. Because of the larger consumption stemming from increased wages we have not been able to expand sufficiently the investments required for increased production and, on the other hand, we have increased imports. We have lived at the expense of the future. We have eaten and consumed more than we have produced, as if someone else footed the bill. I have no doubt that many will ask: If so, why did you permit it? The Government has been fighting this process for the past ten years, but this is part of the price we pay for a free democratic regime. There are so-called "socialist" states where there are no strikes, no wage demands or workers' committees, where the government sets the wages and that is that. In a democratic nation what happens is up to the citizens. Today we have arrived at a point at which the Government must use the means at its disposal to prevent the large increases in earnings from causing economic shocks.

When we prepared the budget for 1966–1967, we found ourselves in a situation in which income was far behind even the minimal expenditures. During the year direct wage increases in the budget reached IL 260 million as a result of higher wages to employees. We faced a substantial rise in the security budget. The debts we have to meet rose considerably and our participation in the rehabilitation budget of the Jewish Agency went up as well. All these factors add up to a total of at least IL600 million.

The first possibility we had was to curtail the services the State provides for its citizens. This could mean a retreat from all the economic and social principles that have guided us for years. In effect it would mean a cutback in education and health, housing and welfare, and perhaps in defense as well. This would certainly have a deleterious effect on the absorption and integration of new immigrants. In theory it was possible to submit a deficit budget—to print the money we lacked. This would have greatly increased the existing inflationary pressures, and the weak would have been the first to suffer, as always happens in inflation. Economically speaking, it would have meant a reduction in our competitive capacity and a dangerous blow to the stability of our currency.

The third possibility was to submit a balanced budget that would safeguard the currency and social services by increased income from taxes. State income from direct and indirect taxes and fees will go up by IL 566 million this year, of which IL 306 million are derived from the natural growth in income resulting from economic expansion and efficient collection. The remainder, IL 260 million, constituting only 8.5 percent of all taxes to be collected in 1966–1967, will be obtained by raising the rate of direct and indirect taxes and fees. The additional taxes are merely a direct consequence of the wage increases to which the Government has committed itself in this year's budget. Increased taxes will not be limited to the Government only. The local authorities whose taxes were frozen for the past four years will also have to balance their budget by this means.

The budget for 1966–1967 totaled IL4,633,000,000, or IL633 million more than for the preceding year. The largest item of expenditure was for defense, but it had to be kept secret. The second largest item of expenditure was for education, which since the creation of the State had grown more than any other. Whereas the national budget increased fifty times, the education budget grew two hundred times, and the budget for higher education seven hundred times. In 1948–1949 the number of pupils and students from kindergarten through university was 140,817, and in 1965–1966 it was 733,034. In 1948–1949 there were 25,406 Jewish children in kindergarten, 91,133 in elementary school, 10,218 in high school, 757 in teachers' and kindergarten teachers' seminaries, and 1935 in institutes of higher learning. In 1966–1967 the figures were: kindergarten—96,000, elementary school—414,100, high school—137,987, institutes of higher learning–26,714.

Debate on the budget began only on February 22, 1966. Moshe Dayan (Rafi) spoke not of the budget itself but of the fiscal policy outlined by the Minister of Finance:

> The negative developments in our economy mentioned by the Minister of Finance are not the result of objective difficulties but are our own doing. The expenditures increased as a result of wage rises in excess of what the Government itself was responsible for. Our difficulty in competing in export markets is not due to the fact that the Common Market discriminates against us but only because our production costs are high or, as the Minister of Finance puts it, because we have a hundred thousand workers who are redundant in their present jobs. And when we speak of economic difficulties, we should realize that these are not objective stumbling blocks but the result of an incorrect economic policy. The problem and solution depend on ourselves alone.
>
> The Minister of Finance suggests we study his speech of last year, and the question we must ask ourselves is, What was done during the past year, 1965, to achieve the economic aims posed by the Minister in that speech, and in what way does this year's budget ensure the achievement of the present objectives? Last year the Minister of Finance said that the

central aim of our economic policy is to approach economic independence and means to this end are the exposure of local production to competition from imports, increased labor efficiency, economic moderation, and restraint of wage increases. These are the main measures he mentioned last year and referred to again this year. The question is, What was done last year and what is it proposed to do in these fields this year?

A year ago the Minister of Finance spoke of redundant workers from which our economy suffers. This year he gave a figure of a hundred thousand redundant workers. The question is, what has the Government, and not only the Government, done? The problem cannot be solved only within a governmental framework. This Government, formerly known as Mapai, now the Alignment, has a majority in the Histadrut and in all the major labor councils. And the representatives of this party cannot claim that there is any foreign body preventing them from carrying out any policy they consider essential. What was done a year ago and what is now being proposed to free ourselves from excess workers? The Government itself has redundant workers. There is duplication of functions between the Government and the Jewish Agency, between Amidar and the Jewish Agency, the Jewish Agency and the Immigrant Absorption Department. What has the Government done and what does it intend to do in this matter?

The most serious point, however, is the third one, which the Minister called restraint or moderation of the cost-of-living allowance. Last year he said in his budget speech, "There is a continuous process of increase in real wages. The cost-of-living allowance today results in increased production costs and hence increased prices. The effect of this is likely to be quite serious in a country such as Israel which is a large importer of raw materials and finished products. The result is nothing but an unjustified increase in production costs and a decline in the competitive ability of Israeli products of foreign markets. I see no alternative but to change this system. I am certain that in 1965 we will consider this once again." This was in December 1964. Did we reconsider it in 1965? And if we did, what were the results?

I believe in preserving the value of the workers' wage. The question is how to do it. The answer must come within the framework of an overall economic policy. The Minister of Finance is afraid that if a cost-of-living allowance is paid in June or July of this year, it will be disastrous for the country, but he must tell us what the economic policy is.

Last year the Minister of Finance, the Government, and the Histadrut decided that the cost-of-living allowance would be on the order of 3 percent. The Governor of the Bank of Israel said the same thing. On January 25, 1966, the Governor said, "The Government has confirmed the Horowitz Committee's recommendations unanimously, but what happened subsequently exceeded the recommendations. Wages were raised by 25 percent rather than 3 percent as we recommended, and most of the distortions that the committee recommended be eliminated have remained in effect."

As to why the wage rise was given, the Minister of Finance has two answers. One is that they have him by the throat, that is, they threatened to go on strike. The second is the "will of the people." What the people want, the Government has to give. But these two answers are good at election time only. Now the Minister of Finance maintains, as his speech at the Mapai Central Committee was quoted in *Davar*: "Even if there is a month-long school strike, we must not give in." Now the question is, What happened to the "will of the people"? What happened to his throat? Why before the elections a few months back did he have to give in because it was the will of the people and there was no choice and why does he not give in now?

I have before me a list of strikes between the time of the publication of the conclusions of the Horowitz Committee regarding a maximum salary raise of 3 percent and the elections. The longest strike of all was that of the postal workers. It lasted three weeks and perhaps more (they struck two or three times). The doctors' strike lasted two days. The strike of the Accountant General's workers one day. The Government hospital workers struck for two hours, the Government Ministries' Archives two days, and then an additional period of six days. The railroad engineers struck for twenty-four hours. The civil servants with university degrees struck for one day. The radio technicians for one day, the telephone and postal workers for two days, pharmacists five days, and when they gave in to these unjustified strikes and demands after a day or two, it only brought on further strikes. Every day we read in the newspapers of new strikes, and two days later the Minister of Finance has sat down and come to an arrangement with them. Others read about these arrangements also and this brings on additional strikes.

With all his ideological reasoning as to the will of the people, the Minister has for some reason not mentioned another reason why these wage hikes were given before the elections to the Histadrut and the Knesset. A short while back the secretary of Mapai, Golda Meir, said that the nation had to be told the truth about the economic situation. Let me ask the Alignment people: Do you not think that there is something cynical and perhaps worse in increasing wages before the elections and in so doing destroying the economy and after the elections telling the public about the shaky economic situation?

These wage hikes, which according to the Governor of the Bank amounted to 25 percent, have had serious repercussions in the economy, and according to the Minister of Finance if we don't overcome them we are liable to end up with an out-and-out crisis and he won't be the man to dig the grave of the Israeli economy. Allow me, as a member of the public, to say that a Minister of Finance or a Government that agrees to wage increases in election years that they feel are disastrous to the national economy, in order to attract voters—that is to say, that they are prepared to undermine the national economy for partisan interests—in my opinion are betraying their national trust.

Private investments this year declined considerably, in contrast to a marked increase in each of the past few years. Should the Government now, in addition to this, reduce and cut back its development projects? For example, let me take the water program in the development budget. In order to create an additional 300 million cubic meters of water by 1970, we will have to invest IL 350 million a year. Even though this was proposed by the water planners, the amount was set at IL 50 million only, which means that there will be no additional water before, during, or after 1970. Without this additional water we will not have a single cubic meter to spare for the development of agriculture, as I read in the five-year plan for agricultural development. And I am speaking not of the settlement of the Galilee but of the modest plan to create two or three new settlements a year, a plan that requires an additional 10 million cubic meters of water yearly. This will not be available nor will there be sufficient water for industry. So what is the sense of this budgetary cutback?

In the budget speech I have found no signs of a beginning toward the implementation of the Minister of Finance's declared policy, or any start at overcoming what he termed the central shortcomings in our economy. The present economic policy—not that conducted on election platforms but that under which we live—is in effect abandoning the two main objectives of the State of Israel: to make the country capable of absorbing additional immigration in order to increase the population, and to create a nation that lives off the labor of its own hands, or what is known as economic independence.

Zev Tsur (Alignment) also complained of the steep increase in the national budget due to a 38 percent increase in salaries. He laid the blame for this mainly on the clerical and professional workers but also complained of a lack of understanding of the importance of increasing production and exports and of the slowdown in the rate of growth of agriculture and industrial production.

Zev Sharef (Alignment, who was later appointed Minister of Commerce and Industry in this Government) sharply criticized those members of the Coalition parties who had attacked the budget. The main tests of a coalition were in votes of confidence and the budget. Regarding the Minister of Finance's assertion that a democratic government does what the citizens want and can only show the way—advise and guide—Sharef said that this was not completely correct:

> The Government cannot limit itself to this function, which is less than that of a traffic policeman. The Government is one of the country's leading employers and must and can intervene in negotiations over wages, prices, profits, and profitability. This is what is done in countries such as the United States. It happens in countries where the socialists rule intermittently, such as England, France, and Holland, and it must be done in Israel as well. The Government of Israel must be a strict and tight-fisted employer for several reasons—because it serves as an example for the rest of the employers; and because it spends the taxpayer's money. It does not waive its profits because it doesn't have any. It gives what it receives because it has no other funds. When there is a feeling that the Government is being overgenerous, it has a harmful effect on the taxpayer and on the public at large.

> No one objects to the fact that defense expenditures have increased. We all welcome the increased outlays on education and health. But when the Minister of Finance tells us that without the steep rise in wages there would have been no need of new taxes, this tends to be confusing, for the Government is supposed to be a master in its own house, not only in the matter of wages but the hiring, promotion, and transfer of workers. It must set an example in matters of efficiency. We have heard here that a certain percentage of workers is redundant; we may assume that this applies also to the public sector of the economy and to the Government ministries and in this connection, too, the Government must set an example. I would like to add that cutting expenditures is impossible without laying off workers. It would be better to reduce the number of workers and give the rest more work to do. Efficiency will follow of itself. And what is true of the Government is equally true of the municipalities.

Debate on the budget was postponed for several days.

Review of Education in Israel

On March 28, 1966, the Minister of Education and Culture, Zalman Aranne, reviewed the activities of his Ministry. The budget of the Ministry in the first year of the State, he said, was approximately IL1 million. Eighteen years later, in the budget year 1966–1967, it is almost half a billion pounds, or more exactly IL471.5 million. This is 10.4 percent of the overall national budget. The Ministry's ordinary budget is IL384,580,000; the budget for development of primary and secondary school buildings, IL15.5 million; and for higher education, IL71,420,000.

During the past year, 1965–1966, a total of IL401,418,000 was paid out. This year the budget has grown by IL70,082,000, or 17.5 percent. Of the regular budget, IL19,982,000 (5.2 percent) is earmarked for kindergartens, IL238,631,500 (62 percent) for elementary education, IL1,276,800 (18.5 percent) for secondary education, IL4,690,600 (1.2 percent) for supplementary education, IL21,884,200 (5.7 percent) for teacher training, IL15,361,000 (4 percent) for scientific projects, cultural, and artistic programs, IL3 million (0.8 percent) for the sports authority, and IL9,753,500 (2.6 percent) for miscellaneous expenditures.

In 1964–1965 a survey was taken of classroom density in elementary schools. Approximately 48 percent of the classrooms had up to thirty pupils; 22 percent had thirty to thirty-five pupils; 17 percent had thirty-five to forty; and only 10 percent had forty to forty-four. Only 3 percent of the total number of classrooms had more than forty-five pupils. Classroom density is decreasing from year to year. Large amounts of money are being invested for this purpose. In the past two years alone, 1965 to 1967, IL 65,795,000 has been spent for the erection of elementary-school buildings and IL 37,484,000 for high-school buildings.

Two years ago complaints were heard of discrimination against the national religious system. At the request of the Ministry of Religious Affairs, the Central Bureau of Statistics conducted a survey of elementary and special schools in 1964–1965. It covered 1411 elementary schools with a total of 449,334 pupils: 386,376 in the Hebrew school system, 52,579 in the Arab school system, and 10,466 in special schools. The survey showed that the allegation of discrimination against religious education is unfounded.

The average area per classroom was found to be 41.3 square meters and the average area per pupil 1.4 square meters. In elementary schools of the Hebrew system the average area per classroom was 42.9 square meters. In the national system it was 44.6 square meters, in the national religious system 42.1 square meters, and in the independent system (Agudat Israel) 32.9 square meters. But in the national religious system the average number of pupils per class was lower (twenty-nine to thirty-one). Consequently the average area per pupil in the national system was 1.45 square meters and in the national religious system 1.44 square meters, so that the fears of discrimination appeared unfounded.

The aggregate number of pupils and students at all levels increased in 1955–1956 by 28,000 (24,000 in the Hebrew school system and 4000 in the Arab school system). In its eighteenth year the educational system therefore encompassed a total of 729,000 pupils and students at all levels—657,000 in the Hebrew school system and 72,000 in the Arab school system. Of these, 97,000 are in preschools (86,000 Jews, 11,000 Arabs); 475,000 in elementary schools (417,000 Jews, 58,000 Arabs); 8000 in post-secondary schools; 7000 in seminaries for teachers and kindergarten teachers; 22,000 in institutions of higher education; 8300 in agricultural schools; 9700 in continuation classes; and 34,000 in vocational schools.

The total number of pupils and students (733,000, including 72,000 non-Jews) can be broken down as follows: kindergarten, 93,000; elementary schools, 461,000; post-elementary schools, 108,000; teachers' seminaries, 6500; institutes of higher education, 22,000; other institutions, 41,500. If we compare the number of students taking matriculation exams in Israel with the countries of Western Europe, we find that in 1964–1965, 9343 pupils or 18.4 percent of their age group took the exams. Comparative figures for the year 1963 in other countries are Norway, 18 percent; France, 17 percent; Austria, 16 percent; Sweden, 14 percent; Belgium, 12 percent; England, 10 percent; Denmark, 9 percent; Germany, 8 percent; and Holland, 7 percent.

The year 1965–1966 will go down in the history of Israeli education as the year in which a large step forward was taken in bridging the educational gap between children of Western (European and American) origin and those of Eastern (Asian and African) origin. Along with the increase in the number of eighth-grade (elementary-school) pupils of Oriental families there has been an increase in secondary education as well. Of the additional 8000 pupils who graduated from grade 8 to grade 9 (high school) in 1964–1965 approximately half, or 4000 were of Oriental origin. Children of Oriental immigrants accounted for 23.5 percent of all pupils in morning high schools, 57 percent in evening high schools; 17.8 percent in continuation classes; 46.6 percent in agricultural schools; 43.5 percent in vocational schools; 76.6 percent in partial post-elementary education, and 32.2 percent in seminaries for teachers and kindergarten teachers.

Arab and Druze elementary education has not yet attained the level of its Hebrew counterpart either in quality of instruction or in physical conditions such as buildings and equipment. The main reason for this is that the local population and authorities do not show the same interest and initiative in fostering education and taking on the required social and financial burdens.

The Ministry of Education, however, has done much to advance Arab and Druze elementary education in recent years. Two years ago a seminary for Arab and Druze teachers was opened in Haifa. The seminary has a high academic level as well as good physical conditions and is designed to provide qualified teachers of a satisfactory level for Arab and Druze elementary schools, obviating the need for using unqualified teachers. The Ministry has prepared texts for nearly all subjects studied in elementary schools, the shortage of which in recent years has placed considerable obstacles in the way of education and teaching.

Recently Arab and Druze post-elementary education has expanded and diversified as well. Qualitative progress has been expressed in the growing percentage of students who pass their matriculation exams. The main financial burden of post-elementary education in Arab and Druze villages is borne by the Ministry of Education. In recent years the Ministry has provided large grants and loans from its development budgets to improve the accommodations of educational institutions, in most cases through the erection of suitable new buildings. Unfortunately some local Arab authorities have declined the loans on easy terms that have been placed at their disposal.

The marked progress in education in the past eighteen years is the result of the nation's abiding alertness to the problem; the growing response to its needs by the Knesset and the Government; the accumulating experience of the younger generation of teachers and educators; the devotion of teachers, young and old; the rising standard of living of education workers; the stabilization of the way of life and rising standard of living of large portions of the new immigrants and their increasing concern with their children's education; and last but not least, the work of the Ministry of Education and Culture.

For several years now the programs of activity of the Ministry have not been planned on a one-year basis but designed to cover periods of three to five years. The following are the activities in which the Ministry was engaged in 1964–1965, the current year, and will also be engaged in 1967: kindergarten for three to four year-old children of poor families; special enrichment programs that already cover 120,000 children in kindergartens and schools in development areas and immigrant settlements; improvement of elementary schools in order to reduce the number of dropouts; reduction of classroom density; the provision of new teaching aids; assistance in the operation of educational television; increased pedagogical activities especially within the existing curriculum; increasing the number of students attending seminaries for teachers and kindergarten teachers; the gradual phasing out of unqualified teachers from the elementary schools; improving the system of supplementary courses for qualified and non-qualified teachers; improving the educational system for Arab and Druze children; increasing the percentage of fourteen-to-seventeen-year-olds attending school; opening high schools to even more members of the poorer classes by partial and full exemptions from school fees; additional high schools in development areas; reduction of the gaps among the various ethnic communities; the improvement and expansion of agricultural schools; the preparation of a sufficient number of students for the universities; increasing the inculcation of the Jewish consciousness and social values in high schools; continued activity to stamp out adult illiteracy; and increased cultural activities in the development areas.

At the same time agricultural education in Israel is increasing and adapting itself to new developments in agriculture. Vocational education continues to expand to meet the needs of our growing industries; the vocational schools already constitute a valuable asset in our educational system, one not possessed by every other country. The dropout rate in vocational schools in recent years has declined and is now the smallest of any post-elementary-education framework. In the next few years thousands of technicians will be needed and the vocational schools will be able to play their part in training technicians of certain levels. Because we are few we must extract all the latent value in our manpower resources.

The major challenges facing our education system are to reduce the existing gap between the quality and quantity in the manpower required for the development of the country and the society; to prevent dropouts, which at the elementary level are relatively small, at the secondary level very high, and at the level of higher education considerable; to reduce as rapidly as possible the still large educational gaps among the various communities; and to place greater stress on national and social values in the education of the younger generation. The Israeli education system has to its credit important accomplishments but is not yet fully prepared to come to grips with the great challenges ahead.

A dispute has developed, Mr. Aranne said, between the Ministry of Education and the Teachers Union concerning the eight-year elementary school. The Ministry feels that the present system does not derive the maximum advantage from the eight years of elementary study. The present grades 7 and 8 do not sufficiently prepare and direct elementary-school graduates to education in a secondary school, and as a result the dropout rate in secondary schools is very high.

In 1965–1966 students attending institutes of higher education totaled 22,300. Of this number, 11,000 were at the Hebrew University in Jerusalem (including the branch in Tel Aviv), 4400 at the Technion in Haifa, 260 at the Weizmann Institute at Rehovot, 3800 at Tel Aviv University, 1900 at Bar-Ilan University, 900 at the University Institute of Haifa, and 182 at the Institute of Higher Education at Beersheba. The breakdown by subjects was as follows: 13,700 were in liberal and social sciences and law; 3800 in technological subjects; 3660 in natural sciences; 800 in medicine, and 400 in agriculture.

In 1964–1965 a total of 9343 high-school students took matriculation exams. Of these 6886, or 73.7 percent, passed all the exams. An additional 1200, or 12.8 percent, passed in every subject but one. Accordingly, if we include those who required supplementary exams, 8086 students, or 86.5 percent, were entitled to matriculation certificates. In 1965, 750 foreign students also passed the exams and will receive matriculation certificates.

The IL 14,173,000 earmarked for expansion will, among other things, make possible the addition of 2500 three- and four-year-olds to the kindergartens, bringing the total kindergarten population to 22,500; 150 more long day classes, bringing the total to 2200; additional grouping-method classes, making a total of 2050; group coaching in Hebrew and arithmetic for 20,000 pupils; and an additional 100 special education classes.

In 1966–1967 an additional 5000 pupils will be exempted from school fees, which will mean that 45 percent of all high-school students will make no payments. All secondary-school pupils in development towns, immigrant settlements, and border kibbutzim will pay no tuitions.

The teaching staff in the elementary schools in 1955–1956 included 3900 unqualified teachers (including kindergarten teachers). However, two-thirds of these are very near the qualified level and each year about 500 unqualified teachers receive qualification after passing the required tests. The student body in teacher training institutes is rising annually according to plan: in 1965–1966 the number rose by 29 percent and now totals about 3000.

Between 1948–1949 and 1966–1967 the number of pupils and students increased from 140,817 to 757,200. Jewish students increased from 129,688 to 679,743; non-Jewish students from 11,129 to 77,477.

Growth of Unemployment Disquiets the Government ★ The Knesset in Its New Home in Jerusalem

On May 9, 1966, the Knesset also heard an assessment of the employment situation by Yigal Allon, Minister of Labor. Some disturbing predictions he had made earlier were unfortunately coming true. The substance of his report was as follows:

In January 34,054 persons applied for work at the offices of the Employment Service. Of these, 26,891 were directed to normal employment and 3891 to relief work. In February the number seeking jobs declined to 31,933, of whom 25,970 were directed to normal employment and 4030 to relief work. In March the number declined further to 27,668, of whom 21,781 were directed to normal employment and 3750 to relief work. In April there was a seasonal rise in work applicants to 29,504, of whom 23,360 were directed to normal employment. The average daily unemployment figures for these months were: January—4096, February—4214, March—3405, April—4432. (In April of the previous year—2493.) It is doubtful that the employment bureaus have a record of all the unemployed. According to manpower surveys by the Central Bureau of Statistics, only slightly more than half of all the unemployed seek work through the employment bureaus. The actual unemployment figure is certainly higher than in the official reports.

The nationwide figure does not show the true seriousness of the situation. In several development towns the unemployment rate amounted to 16 to 20% of all breadwinners. The result was considerable suffering for the families of the unemployed and a serious blow to efforts to populate the development areas. The causes of increased unemployment are many. Completion of projects that employed large numbers of people—such as the National Water Carrier, the ports of Ashdod and Eilat, the Dead Sea Works, the Ashdod B power station, the Beersheba-Dimona rail line, and the nuclear reactor at Dimona, besides many small development projects—left many jobless. The main reason for the decline in employment, however, is in the cutback in construction of housing and public buildings throughout the country, especially in development towns.

Until recently building and public works provided employment for ninety thousand workers or 10 percent of the entire labor force. In 1953 buildings with a total floor area of 6 million square meters were erected compared to only 5 million in 1963. We estimate that this year the figure will be 3.5 million square meters. This sharp decline is due to reduced immigration. Even today there are thousands of vacant apartments in the development towns and large cities. Another cause of rising unemployment is the growing mechanization and introduction of automated processes in industrial plants, which expands production while reducing the work force. The limited export possibilities for locally produced goods are also a leading factor in the unemployment situation. We are still far from maximum utilization of existing means of production, and no new plants for export purposes are required.

Construction is an important element in the employment picture. Economically speaking, however, it does not improve the trade balance, but just the opposite. If it exceeds reasonable limits, it also tends to make for inflation. Manpower will have to be directed to more productive industries, both to save on imports and to increase exports. The basic solutions to the employment problem lie in greater utilization of the existing means of production by raising productivity, providing additional industries suited to the country's resources, expanding the tourist industry, and further development of agriculture, especially produce for export.

Despite constant progress in productivity and production, most of our goods are still far from being competitive. Unit production costs are higher than in the countries with which we must compete. There are markets awaiting us in the developing and the advanced countries. The developing countries lack means of production, and their level of consumption is increasing. These markets provide a serious challenge to Israeli producers and exporters. Advanced countries, on the other hand, suffer from a shortage of labor and are concentrating more and more on giant production enterprises. There we can find markets for products that for them are marginal but for Israel are of considerable importance. Our exports to the world's affluent markets can and must be increased.

Israel is endowed with qualities connected with its history, as well as its natural beauties and social innovations, that make the country an outstanding tourist attraction. Services for tourists should be improved in quality, reduced in price, and imbued with hospitality, so that the tourist industry can play an economic role such as it plays in France, Italy, and Spain.

Our varied combinations of soil and climate and the solutions of the water problem will make possible an expansion and improvement of agricultural output for export, both by enlarging our present settlements and creating new ones. Similarly we must stimulate our shipping industry, an enterprise that is now limited by territorial factors. Norway, with a population not much larger than ours, is one of the world's greatest maritime powers.

Greater economic activity should be channeled to the development towns at the expense of the large centers of population. Industry should be concentrated in the developing areas to deter migration from there to the densely crowded centers of population. Eilat, for instance, is capable of absorbing many scores of families. Our merchant marine is manned by seventeen hundred Israelis and forty-seven hundred non-Israelis. The diamond industry can absorb hundreds of workers, requiring only a short period of training. Hundreds of farms in cooperative settlements are waiting for people to move in.

The kibbutzim can take in hundreds of additional families. We should do everything we can to divert state-owned industries, especially those connected with the defense establishment, to the development areas.

In the debate that followed the Minister's report several members claimed that the true unemployment picture was more alarming than he had indicated. Aryeh Ben-Eliezer (Gahal) declared that in the development towns there were ten thousand unemployed breadwinners who had to support between fifty and seventy thousand persons. The old-timers among us could remember when they were out of work and it didn't bother them because they were young and generally unmarried. Today a person returning home after looking for work in vain finds a family of ten waiting for him—children who need food, clothing, education, and minimal housing. We should not console ourselves with memories of the past.

Moshe Dayan spoke of the main causes for concern. One was that the population hardest hit by unemployment had the greatest number of children and problems, and was the least capable of weathering economic shock. Had the recession been felt in the agricultural sector, the situation would not be so serious; the farmers are better able to bear financial hardship than inhabitants of the development areas. The problem, he pointed out, cannot be measured by statistics on the national average. Our economic substructure is unstable—this is the basic cause of the present difficulties. When a disturbance hits a country with a shaky financial foundation, it is doubly and triply disturbing.

The nation's present leadership has been unable and unwilling to follow a consistent policy in line with our economic situation, he charged. The Minister of Finance himself emphasized a disproportionate rise in our standard of living. In estimating what we can allow ourselves in higher living standards on the basis of increased productivity, he mentioned a 3-percent rise in basic pay. Then the leadership comes along and proposes a 10-percent increase, not including a cost-of-living allowance. It is obviously a fiscal policy divorced from the country's financial capacity and followed intentionally, although not happily. The increase we are getting this year is double what the economy can bear, this despite the fact that for a year now we have been saying that improvement in our standard of living must be linked to the country's economic capacity. Why was there a wage rise of 25 percent rather than the 3 percent recommended by the Horowitz Committee? We all know that it was due to pressure by the labor union representatives.

On the challenge of unemployment there can be no differences: The unemployed worker must be provided with a job and the means for a decent standard of living, at the expense of the public as a whole. The solution depends, Dayan said, on two imperatives: (1) confidence in the economy and a leadership capable of drawing in investment capital again to create more jobs; (2) a consistent and radical, even if unpopular, policy of reduction of expenditures and in the administrative costs in industry; we must live within the means of the economy, raising living standards only as the economy's capacity increases.

The Knesset adopted the following Coalition motions. (1) In accordance with its basic policy the Government will act to ensure employment for all who seek it, and to this end will provide relief employment and public works as needed. (2) The Knesset notes the Government's declaration that top priority in employment will be given to development areas, for which purpose development and building works will be implemented through a system of economic incentives and intensified planning. (3) A policy of full employment and strengthening of the economy requires increased efficiency on the part of industry and services and the harnessing of all factors for increased productivity and output to enhance the competitive capacity for our products and to augment exports.

On Wednesday, August 31, 1966, the Knesset convened for the first time in its newly erected building in the Kirya in Jerusalem. In opening the meeting, Speaker Luz said:

> Honorable members, it is a great privilege for me to open the first meeting of the Knesset in its new home. We are now in the middle of the Jewish month of Elul. In this same month many years ago two great events occurred which have a historical bearing on this present occasion.
>
> It was in the month of Elul, on the initiative of the Prophets Hagai and Zechariah, that the construction of the Second Temple was recommenced after the initial work had been stopped about a dozen years earlier by the Persian authorities as a result of pressure of the local inhabitants. Chapter One of the Book of Hagai says: "And the Lord stirred up the spirit of Zerubavel, the son of Shealtiel, Governor of Judah, and the spirit of Yehoshua, the son of Yehozadok the high priest, and the spirit of all the remnant of the people. And they came and did work in the house of the Lord of Hosts, their God. In the four and twentieth day of the sixth month in the second year of Darius." Hence, the construction of the Second Temple began this month, the month of Elul, 2488 years ago.
>
> The second event was the completion of the wall of Jerusalem by Nehemiah, as related in Chapter 4 of the Book of Nehemiah: "They which builded on the wall, and they that bare burdens, with those that loaded, everyone with one of his hands wrought in the work, and with the other hand held a weapon." And in Chapter 6 it says, "So the wall was finished in the twenty and fifth day of the month of Elul in fifty and two days." It was in this month 2411 years ago. From the political and defense standpoints it was a great achievement and the work succeeded. "For the people had a mind to work" and "the joy of Jerusalem was heard even far off."
>
> Today we have completed the work of the Knesset building, the home of the supreme sovereign institution of the State, and our joy will be heard from far off. In order to strengthen the wall of Israeli parliamentarianism, this ceremonial meeting will consider the Basic Law of the Cabinet that will be added to the Basic Law of the Knesset and the Basic Law of the Presidency, in order to carry out the words of the prophet: "I have set watchmen upon thy walls, O Jerusalem." I now give the floor to the Prime Minister.

Prime Minister Eshkol then said, among other things:

> This festive day in which the Knesset inaugurates its new home should rightly be marked by a distinguished act of legislation concerned with the forms to be taken by the Government and the law in Israel. The purpose of this bill is to assemble and concentrate in one basic law the Cabinet's rules of operation, and thus in a single constitutional law to regulate in a thorough and comprehensive manner the work methods of the Israeli Government, the executive arm of the State of Israel.
>
> The seat of the Cabinet shall be in Jerusalem. In this we make no innovation; we merely give constitutional sanction to a fact any deviation from which would be inconceivable. The Cabinet will continue to derive its power from the confidence of the Knesset. The function of the President of the State in forming new Cabinets will remain as it was. The President will continue to bear responsibility for the selection of a member of the Knesset whom he charges with the task of forming a government. The Prime Minister must be a

member of the Knesset. The President shall, immediately after the elections and no later than the inauguration of the new Knesset, begin negotiations on the formation of a new government with the representatives of the parties so that it will be possible to present the new Cabinet to the Knesset soon after its inauguration and thus reduce the interim period.

An innovation is the requirement of Knesset confirmation for an exchange of functions within a Cabinet or the creation, cancellation, or unification of Ministries. Though the meetings of the Cabinet and ministerial committees are secret, this practice has not been embodied in the law until now. The Government proposes Section 24, which stipulates this and forbids publication of Cabinet deliberations.

Mr. Eshkol proposed that the draft of the bill be referred to the Law Committee, and it was so decided by a vote of fifty-one to twenty-three. Those opposed thought this legislation should be returned to the Cabinet for further study.

A Three-Year Economic Plan 1967–1969 Is Presented to the Knesset

Thirty-three members requested that a special session of the Knesset be called to discuss the Government's fiscal plans and the deteriorating economic situation. On reviewing the request, the Government announced that it would present a Three-Year Plan for the economy at a special Knesset session on October 11, 1966.

At the opening of this meeting the Speaker paid tribute to the memories of Border Policemen Joseph Amar, Yacov Gigi, Avraham Levi, and Nissim Cohen who were killed by a mine planted by Syrian murderers. All members rose in solemn tribute to their memory. The Speaker then asked that they rise again in remembrance of Mrs. Vera Weizmann, the wife and helpmate of our first President, Dr. Chaim Weizmann. "In his book," the Speaker recalled, "Weizmann wrote that his wife was gifted with an ability to penetrate straight to the heart of the problems of our movement. She often warned him of pitfalls before he himself was aware of them. She organized his social and political life, through all its stormy vicissitudes, yet managed to have a life and a career of her own. She was the Municipal Doctor in Manchester, was active in women's organizations, and was one of the founders of WIZO. After her husband's death she continued to be active in the Weizmann Memorial Foundation, in assembling material by and about her late husband and in Israeli social and public life. Blessed be her memory."

On behalf of the entire Knesset the Speaker then congratulated David Ben-Gurion on his eightieth birthday: "In his sixty years in this country," he said, "Mr. Ben-Gurion has left his mark on the labor movement, the Jewish community, and the Zionist movement. He was one of the founders of the Poalei Zion Party and among the initiators of its newspaper; a soldier in the Jewish Legion in World War 1; a torchbearer of the idea of unity in the labor movement; a founder of the Ahdut Haavodah Party and the Histadrut; a promoter of unification of Ahdut and Hapoel Hatzair in the Israel Labor Party (Mapai); and a member and chairman of the Zionist Executive and the Jewish Agency Executive. Beginning with the publication of the notorious White Paper, and during and after World War Two, he played a central and decisive role in the campaigns on the public, political, and defense levels which led to the creation of the State of Israel. He was to a large extent the Commander-in-Chief in the War of Independence and the initiator of the Sinai Campaign. During his fifteen years as Prime Minister and Minister of Defense, assisted by his colleagues in the Government, he conducted national affairs that included the creation of the Israel Defense Forces, the absorption of the mass immigration, the intensification of the country's development and the enhancement of its security. In your name, members of the Knesset, I congratulate David Ben-Gurion and wish him many more years of good health, fruitful work, and satisfaction."

The Knesset then addressed itself to the Government's announcement of its economic program for the years 1967–1969. Without diverting its attention from the increasingly serious border situation, the Prime Minister announced, the Cabinet at its meeting on September 11, 1966, had approved an economic plan for the coming three years. It read as follows:

The two fundamental economic problems confronting the State of Israel today are the import-export gap and unemployment. The solution of the one depends on the solution of the other. In order to increase exports and replace imports by home production, productivity must be raised and competitive capacity enhanced. This is also the way to ensure full and productive employment for Israel's citizens, veterans and newcomers. The main principles of the economic policy that will be put into operation during the three years 1967–1969 are:

1. A change in the composition of employment by the direction of additional manpower to production for export in order to increase the numbers employed in industry, agriculture, shipping, and tourism.

2. A change in the composition of investment by directing a higher proportion to export branches—i.e., increasing productive investments and reducing investments for consumption.

3. Reduction of unit production costs by raising efficiency and productivity on the one hand, and a policy of restraint on incomes and taxes on the other, in order to bring down the cost of production and improve the competitive capacity of our produce in world markets. This will be achieved by utilization of existing equipment as well as by mechanization and automation.

I. Encouragement of Exports and Investments

1. In order to determine the composition of productive investment and increase such investments, the Government will endeavor to secure appropriate profitability in export undertakings—in industry, agriculture, transportation, tourism, and other branches capable of increasing their exports.

2. Additional concessions under the Law for the Encouragement of Capital Investments will be given to undertaking manufacturing for export or replacing vital imports, and also for enterprises in development areas. Steps will be taken to ensure that they meet their obligations.

3. Suitable financing will be ensured in the development budget for investments in industry and agriculture geared to export and also in transport, tourism, and telecommunications.

4. Export incentives will be granted in the form of exemption from compulsory payments, tax rebates, etc., for enterprises producing for export. The incentives will be uniform and allocated, by objective criteria, in accordance with the contribution made by the export enterprises to the national economy.

5. Where a cost-of-living allowance has to be paid, the Government will consider reimbursing to exporters for the cost-of-living allowance, in order to prevent damage to exports.

6. Special incentives will be given for the development of new export branches and the conquest of markets.

7. All the above shall be done, provided the exporting is carried out under conditions of reasonable competition.

II. Employment

1. The Government will encourage the full utilization of existing productive capacity and will increase investments in existing and new enterprises—whether private or owned by the State, the Histadrut, or the kibbutzim—with special attention to development areas, immigrants' villages, and Arab villages in order to find productive employment in industry, agriculture, shipping, and tourism for immigrants, youth, and workers (Jewish and Arab) laid off in branches where activity has declined, such as construction and public services.

2. The Government will immediately set up a special headquarters to work constantly on the formulation and implementation of plans for urgent employment. The Histadrut, the Industrialists' Association, and other economic bodies will be invited to take part.

3. Whenever workers, in accordance with the needs of the economy, move to other branches and trades, the Government will take steps, in coordination with the Histadrut, to safeguard the social benefits to which they are entitled through their previous employment. The Government will also provide the vocational training required for their employment in new undertakings and help provide housing for workers moving to development areas.

III. Greater Efficiency in Production and Services

1. All necessary steps will be taken for the efficient and full utilization of manpower in production and services by increasing output and improving organization and management.

2. To lower the cost of public services, measures will be taken for economy in branches, efficiency, and staff reductions.

3. To improve quality and reduce production costs, the Government will encourage the amalgamation of enterprises for large-quantity production, and the rationalization and reduction of middlemen's and marketing costs.

4. Employers and workers will be asked to increase the number of enterprises working according to norms. Output above the norms will entitle the workers to premium payments. Norms and the operation of incentive-pay arrangements will be constantly tested and adapted to changes taking place in equipment, materials, and workers' skills. The norms in a particular undertaking will be measured anew on the initiative of employer or workers if, in the opinion of either party, there have been changes in working conditions, equipment, technology, materials, or methods. In case of differences of opinion, the issue shall be submitted to the Central Productivity Council. The Productivity Institute will decide in cases in which the Council does not arrive at a decision.

5. Planned removal of protection for local production shall continue by a gradual and systematic reduction in tariffs in order to improve the efficiency and productivity of the enterprises and the quality of their products, and enhance their competitive capacity.

6. The Government will assist applied industrial research and market research.

IV. Wages and Labor Policy

1. In 1967 basic pay in productive branches will rise, in accordance with labor contracts, by up to 5 percent.

2. In accordance with decisions adopted by the Histadrut, wage increases in 1968 and 1969 will follow the rise in the net national product, taking into account the position in the various branches and the prospects of increasing output, productivity, employment,

and exports. Wage rises for workers in services in 1968 and 1969 will not exceed the average increase in the net national product in industry, taking into account the position in the economy and the need to encourage exports.

3. To preserve the real value of the workers' wages, the cost-of-living allowance system will be maintained. However, in view of the position of the economy and the effort required to overcome the danger of unemployment and to increase production, the following proposals are made to the Histadrut: In 1967 and 1968 only half the increase in the cost-of-living allowance will be paid, while heads of families earning up to IL 400 a month will be fully compensated for price increases in accordance with the arrangement arrived at as from July 1966. Measures will be taken to ensure that seniority increments, family allowances, and rises in grade in accordance with progress in work shall not serve as excuses for concealed increases in basic pay.

4. During the three years social benefits will be maintained at their present level.

5. All those concerned will endeavor to improve labor relations and morale, to put an end to unjustified absenteeism, and augment the responsibility of workers and employers for the economy.

V. Prices

1. The Government will work for price stability in the economy by a comprehensive economic policy to prevent surplus demand, including: fiscal and monetary policy; control of monopolies and cartels; removal of the protection of local production from competitive imports; and the maintenance of the Price Headquarters. In the case of vital commodities and services, in which there is no real competition, prior notification of intention to raise prices will be required.

2. In order to prevent price increases, the Government will refrain from raising direct and indirect taxes, imposing compulsory loans, and permitting increases in local rates, except in case of emergency.

3. The Government will continue to use subsidies as a means of stabilizing prices. Subsidies for keeping down the price of commodities will be held to their present level and no changes will be made which are liable to increase prices.

VI. Fiscal Policy and Credit

1. The State Budget will be balanced and will serve as an instrument for the advancement of the aims of economic policy: expansion of imports, provision of employment, and the implementation of social policy.

2. The Ordinary Budget will be maintained at its present level, taking into account the growth of the population and the provision of suitable reserves. The Government will take measures for efficiency economies in administrative expenditure.

3. Credit policy will be coordinated with overall economic policy in order to ensure the growth of production and prevent inflationary pressures.

4. The cheapest possible credits will be assured for branches of export and industry which vitally require it to finance their production.

5. The Government will work to encourage the various types of saving plans.

VII. Social Policy

1. Government policy will be directed, by suitable means, to averting the easy amassing of riches at the public's expense.

2. Special efforts will be made to ensure full production and stable employment in development areas and to increase their population.

3. The Government will establish a committee to examine recommendations for legislation designed to maintain employment and for unemployment insurance.

4. Action will be taken to raise National Insurance payments. If necessary, the possibility of raising payment for low-income groups will be examined.

5. Income tax rebates will be granted to new immigrants during their first three years in Israel.

6. The Government will continue to implement its plans for housing new immigrants, newlyweds, and farmers, and for liquidating slums.

7. The Government will continue to expand and improve the educational network, and to narrow the educational gap, with special attention to development areas and poor urban areas.

8. Institutions for expanding education, culture, and art, as well as religious facilities, will be built in development areas.

9. To raise the birth rate, the Government will endeavor to improve housing and schooling conditions for newlyweds.

10. The Government will continue improving health and social welfare services.

VIII. Distributing the Burden

In addition to steps already taken to ensure the cooperation of the affluent in carrying the burden, the Government will work for:

1. Improving assessment and collection of taxes.

2. Reduction of deductible business expenses recognized by the Income Tax authorities.

3. Increase of capital gains tax from 25 to 30 percent.

4. Examination of bank and insurance company commissions with a view to reducing them by 10 percent, while streamlining their work and cutting their expenses.

5. Reduction of the foreign currency allocation for travelers abroad from $500 to $300.

6. Consideration of an increase from 25 to 30 percent in income tax deducted at source for discounting of bills.

In explaining the three-year economic plan, Prime Minister Eshkol said:

In 1962–1965 the economy enjoyed a boom and overemployment as a result of the large amounts of capital that flowed in following devaluation [on February 9, 1962, the rate of exchange was set at IL 3 to the dollar; previously various rates were in force], and also because of public and private investments in the economy, and large-scale immigration. This prosperity resulted in a growth in investments and in production. Exports increased as well. This year, 1966, exports will reach a total of $850 million. Our foreign currency reserves have also reached a record high of more than $700 million. Imports, however, have also increased rapidly.

Wage increases at the end of 1965 and the beginning of 1966 were excessive. The rise in basic pay in addition to the cost-of-living allowance and creeping increases in pay far exceeded the economy's capacity and reduced the competitiveness of our products on foreign markets. I have no doubt that had the wage rise at the beginning of 1966 been smaller, our exports this year would have been greater and the unemployment figure lower. Moreover, it is clear that had salaries been raised an additional 5 percent (the cost-of-living allowance) over and above the 17 to 20 percent at the beginning of the year, it would have further impaired the competitiveness and profitability of our industries, cut back investments and exports, and resulted in lower production and employment levels. Nevertheless we decided to compensate breadwinners with low incomes for the general rise in prices.

Consultations on the economic policies for the next three years began approximately three months ago. There was criticism to the effect that these consultations went on for a long time. This disregarded the fact of life that in a democratic society with a coalition government different groups have to be persuaded of the need for any proposed change in policy.

The experience of the first months of our policy of economic moderation shows that industrialists have adjusted or are beginning to adjust to the new situation and to operate more efficiently. The recession is having the effect of a blast of fresh air in sobering people up and making them see things with open eyes. The number of unemployed is less than thirty thousand. The Government will do everything in its power to provide a constructive long-range solution for this problem. The plan before you details the measures the Government is committed to taking. A special effort will be made to distribute the burden justly over all parts of the population, especially on those better able to bear it. I will request that the Knesset consider this plan.

At the end of the debate Moshe Bar-Am (Alignment) for the Coalition parties proposed that "The Knesset takes note of the Prime Minister's announcement." The proposal was adopted by fifty votes to nineteen.

XI

THE SIX–DAY WAR, 1967

The Months That Led to the "Days"; Arabs Mass for Invasion; Israeli Victory

Section 1. A Government of National Unity

Soviets Spread the Lie of an Israeli Buildup Against Syria ★ Egypt Masses Its Forces in Gaza ★ UN Emergency Units Are Withdrawn ★ Nasser Closes the Gulf of Eilat

THE political situation, which had almost never been satisfactory, deteriorated sharply at the end of 1966. The last four months of that year were marked by the attempted Egyptian takeover in Yemen, as a first step toward domination of Saudi Arabia and other oil-rich Arab countries. Nasser's adventure in Yemen did not succeed. The local tribes resisted the invaders and Egyptian losses kept increasing. The heavy costs of maintaining an army far from home, aggravating internal economic difficulties, compelled Nasser to recall most of his forces. He left reduced contingents, however, in the hope that after the departure of the British from Aden he would manage to dominate the Arabian Peninsula.

The tripartite Federation of Egypt, Syria, and Iraq, formed on April 17, 1963, "with the object of liberating the Arab homeland from the Zionist peril," did not long survive. What they failed to achieve by political organization they tried to do by organized sabotage and murder. At the beginning the marauding gangs were headed by Shukeiry, who had the support of several of the Arab states. But his intrigues did not go over well with some of these countries and a rival force arose—an organization centered in Syria that called itself Al Fatah. Of all the Arab states, Syria is the most unstable. Struggles among various parties as well as among leaders of the principal Ba'ath Party had caused frequent revolutions and counter-revolutions ever since the departure of the French. Until the Sinai Campaign in 1956 most of the wrecking and murder attacks had come from Egypt, but when the Gaza Strip was pacified under supervision of the UN Emergency Force, headquarters for these forays moved to Syria.

Attacks on Jewish settlements in the Hula and Jordan Valleys from the Golan Heights practically never ceased, and became especially intense in the final months of 1966. Acts of sabotage, mining of roads, shooting-up of civilian settlements were almost daily events. Most of the saboteurs came directly from Syria, others crossed over from Lebanon and Jordan. With the approval of the Syrian Government an Al Fatah newspaper was published in Damascus and Al Fatah units trained with the Syrian Army. On October 11, 1966, the Syrian Prime Minister declared that "Syria has not been appointed to safeguard Israel's security and to curb the revolution of the Palestinian nation. My government will never withdraw from the war of popular liberation and the restoration of Palestine." And a day later the Chief of Staff, while inspecting military maneuvers in the presence of an Egyptian delegation, said, "The activities that are being denounced are lawful, and it is our duty not to stop but rather to encourage and strengthen them." On October 13 he announced that "the war for the liberation of Palestine has begun."

The Syrian Government, of course, said different things to different people. When speaking to its nation, Army, and Arab neighbors it took an aggressive tone, accompanied by acts of terror on Israeli territory. But in the international arena things were different. On October 13, 1966, the Syrian delegate to the UN presented a letter to the President of the Security Council contending that Israel's accusations of Syrian responsibility for the acts of sabotage were groundless. Syria not only denied all responsibility for the saboteurs but dared proclaim that it was threatened by an attack by Israel, a lie that found its way into the Soviet press. The delegations of the United States, Britain, France, and New Zealand showed in the Security Council debate on October 14 that they knew very well who was responsible for the violence and for planning aggression, but the sabotage gangs could be certain that one of the Great Powers would veto any condemnation of Syria.

Not every member of the Israeli Government was prepared to see the unpleasant reality as it was. The Minister of Information, Israel Galili, asserted in an article in an Alignment newspaper that "conditions have been created for improved relations with the Soviet Union, something which is an object of vital interest for Israel."

No one could take issue with the second half of that sentence. Israel had always been anxious for friendly relations with the Soviet Union, as with all other nations. We had not forgotten the position taken by that country in the UN Assembly in May 1947, when the first delegate to demand the creation of a Jewish State in the Land of Israel as the Jewish people's right was Andrei Gromyko. Moreover, after the General Assembly by more than a two-thirds majority had decided on the creation of a Jewish State and for the first time since World War Two the two leading powers found themselves in agreement on something, the Soviet Union was virtually the only country that resisted all attempts by the US State Department to revoke that decision. For a full year, until the War of Independence was over, the Soviet Union consistently opposed any move by Bernadotte or others to detract from the image and rights of the young Jewish State.

Only after the complete elimination of British rule from the area did the Soviets change their tack and become the protector to all the Arab states that openly declared their intention to destroy Israel. This Soviet hostility was revealed in all its blatancy in the first months of 1967, when the Egyptian leader concentrated his forces on the Israel border in order to implement his avowed purpose of many years' standing—Israel's destruction.

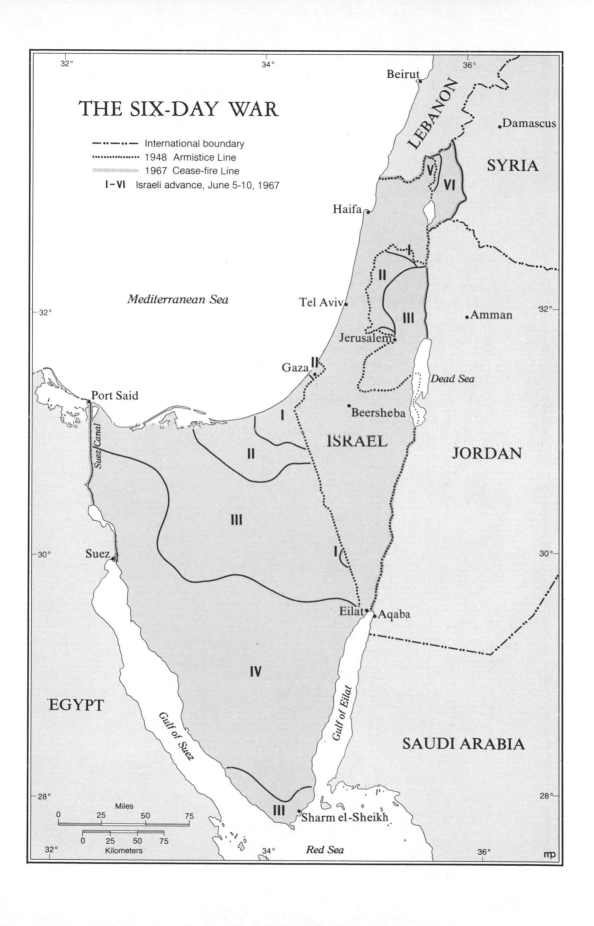

THE SIX-DAY WAR

- — ·· — · — · — International boundary
- ················· 1948 Armistice Line
- ▬▬▬▬▬ 1967 Cease-fire Line
- **I – VI** Israeli advance, June 5-10, 1967

Beirut

LEBANON

Damascus

SYRIA

V

VI

Haifa

I

II

Mediterranean Sea

Tel Aviv

III

Amman

Jerusalem

Gaza II

II

Dead Sea

I

Beersheba

ISRAEL

JORDAN

Port Said

Suez Canal

II

III

Suez

I

Gulf of Suez

Eilat Aqaba

IV

Gulf of Eilat

EGYPT

SAUDI ARABIA

III

Sharm el-Sheikh

Red Sea

Miles

0   25   50   75

0   25   50   75

Kilometers

mp

In a Knesset debate on October 18, 1966, Gen. Moshe Dayan rightly declared that "Israel's response cannot be limited to the Security Council." Even Yacov Hazan of Mapam recognized that "The Soviet Union bears grave responsibility for the dangerous deterioration of the situation on the Syrian border," adding, "As a believer in the Soviet Union's mission of socialism and peace, I must raise my voice in protest against its betrayal of this mission in our region. This is a serious blow at the faith of peace-loving persons throughout the world."

After the debate the Knesset adopted the following resolution by a vote of sixty-one to two, with two abstaining:

> The Knesset denounces the acts of sabotage and murder committed on Israeli territory by organized marauders infiltrating across the border. The Knesset calls on the Security Council to uphold its obligation to maintain the peace, to require the Syrian government to comply with its commitments under the UN Charter and the Armistice Agreements and desist from all acts of aggression against Israel. The State of Israel, like any independent peace-loving state, will maintain its sovereign right to self-defense, recognized by international law, and to preserve its territorial integrity and the welfare of its citizens.

The feeling grew that even the quasi-peace that had prevailed for ten years was being undermined. It led the Minister of Labor, Yigal Allon, on October 24, 1966, to propose an Emergency Labor Law permitting the mobilization of manpower for work in vital industries even during a callup of the reserves, in order to ensure the maintenance of a minimum level of supplies and vital services and contribute to the nation's overall war effort.

On November 8, 1966, Levi Eshkol, Prime Minister and Minister of Defense, announced that the Government had canceled its decision of December 1963 to reduce the tour of military duty by four months. In accordance with the Defense Service Law, 1959, men would now serve thirty months while women would continue to serve twenty months as formerly. The Foreign Affairs and Security Committee had heard the Governments's explanation for this move and agreed to the decision.

After the Soviet veto of the Security Council's condemnation of the Syrian acts of sabotage, Knesset member Joseph Serlin (Gahal) called for a debate to let our neighbors know that Israeli blood was not free for the taking and that our borders were not open on one side only. The Soviet veto, he said, served to encourage criminals by assuring that their crimes would go unpunished. The purpose of the debate would be to convince our neighbors that we would never be reconciled to innocent bloodshed on our borders by gangs organized under the auspices of the governments that officially outfitted them. We were not eager for battle—we wanted peace, but that peace must be defended with all our strength. The Prime Minister proposed, and Serlin agreed, that the debate be referred to the Foreign Affairs and Security Committee.

Meanwhile, conditions on the Syrian border continued to worsen. Since the last military coup in Syria at the beginning of 1966, forty attacks and acts of sabotage had occurred. The President of Syria announced, "Our watchword is a people's war. What we want is total and unlimited war, one that will put an end to the Zionist entity." In August 1966 Radio Damascus declared, "The Syrian revolutionary government will no longer complain to the UN. Israel will be the one to do the complaining and the defending. Syria's strategy from now on is to take the offensive." On October 10 the Syrian Prime Minister said, "We will not stop the revolution of the Palestinian people. We will set the whole region on fire and any move on the part of the Israelis will mean a final grave for them." Syria's Chief of Staff, General Sweidani, said, "These operations by Al Fatah are legal and it is not our duty to stop them but rather to encourage and strengthen them."

And aggressive activities were indeed intensified. On April 7, 1967, the settlements of Haon, Ein Gev, and Gadot were bombarded by fifty pieces of artillery. The attack began at 9:45 A.M. when the Syrians opened fire on an Israeli tractor working the fields of Haon. These fields had never been under dispute and had been cultivated by the Kibbutz for years with no Syrian interference. The first time the Syrians ever opened fire on Jewish workers in this area was in November 1966. On UN initiative the Mixed Armistice Commission reconvened at that time and at the start of April work was resumed, then was suspended because of the rains. On April 7, the weather having improved, work was undertaken again by an unshielded tractor. Within a quarter of an hour the Syrians opened artillery fire on the tractor from the position of Amrat Az ad-Din. An Israeli security force returned fire with heavy machine guns and silenced the Syrians.

But at 10:20 A.M. the Syrians attacked with tanks from Hirbet Batin. They also lobbed a number of shells at Kibbutz Tel Katzir and went on to use mortars against the Jewish workers. The UN representatives proposed a cease-fire to which Israel agreed at 11:30. A quarter of an hour later the firing in the Haon area stopped. The quiet, however, did not last long. At 11:50 the Syrians struck again, bringing heavy mortars (122 mm.) and other weapons into action. The Israeli force succeeded in silencing their weapons and work in the kibbutz was resumed. Bombardment from the Golan Heights continued, however, and buildings at Kibbutz Tel Katzir were damaged by tank fire.

After several hours of tank and heavy mortar fire in the Haon and Tel Katzir sectors, the Israel Air Force was called into action against emplacements at the Tawafik pillbox and Amrat Az ad-Din. The Syrians opened antiaircraft fire but no Israeli plane was hit, while the Syrian artillery was silenced and five tanks were destroyed. At first the Syrian Air Force made no attempt to intervene, but after their artillery had been canceled out Syrian fighter planes appeared. The Israeli aircraft had gone into action at 1:30 P.M. and at 2 P.M. Syrian MIGs at Damascus took off, headed for the Israeli border. Israeli Mirages covering the Air Force operations against Syrian artillery went to meet the MIGs.

Contact was established between two Mirages and four MIGs. Two MIGs were immediately shot down. At 3:30 P.M. the two surviving MIGs approached Kibbutz Shamir. More dogfighting followed and a third MIG was downed. The Syrians called in additional MIGs and as soon as contact was established three more were destroyed. The Israel Air Force had been ordered to attack only military targets and avoid injury to civilian settlements on the other side of the border. Later four Syrian MIG-17s tried to strafe Kibbutz Ein Gev but Israeli planes drove them off. After the failure of their air assault the Syrians opened artillery fire against Ein Gev and Gadot and a number of buildings were destroyed. The Israel Air Force again went into action and the Syrian artillery was silenced completely. Ein Gev, Tel Katzir, and Gadot, which had suffered severe damage, began rebuilding immediately.

Early in May the Soviet Government surprised the world with an imaginary story (whether on its own behalf, Syria's, or Egypt's it is hard to tell) of a tremendous Israeli buildup along the Syrian frontier. Eshkol invited the Soviet Ambassador to tour the northern border with him and see for himself that this was not true. The Ambassador declined: no doubt he knew well enough that the story had been made up. The truth was that after the Syrian attacks on the Galilee kibbutzim, a few score border policemen were posted to the north to keep an eye on Syrian saboteurs. But according to false information received in Cairo from Soviet sources, eleven Israeli brigades were concentrated in the north. On May 19 the UN Secretary-General informed the Security Council that reports by UN observers indicated no sign of the alleged Israeli buildup on the Syrian border. Evidently Nasser needed such false reports for his aggressive designs against Israel.

The action that touched off the events of June was the withdrawal of the UN peace-keeping forces from the Gaza Strip and the Gulf of Sharm el-Sheikh. More that ten years earlier, on November 5, 1956, the General Assembly had voted to post UN contingents in the Gaza Strip and Sharm el-Sheikh. The detachment in the Gaza Strip was intended to ensure the cessation of acts of sabotage and murder by the fedayeen, and that in Sharm el-Sheikh was to guarantee freedom of Israeli navigation in the Straits of Eilat. These had been two conditions for Israel's withdrawal from the Gaza Strip and Sharm el-Sheikh after the defeat of the Egyptian Army in Sinai. The UN Emergency Force comprised 978 Indian troops, 795 Canadians, 579 Yugoslavs, 530 Swedes, 430 Brazilians, 61 Norwegians, and 2 Danes.

On August 5, 1957, Dag Hammarskjöld wrote that he had reached an agreement with Nasser that "The UN forces will not move from where they are until they complete their mission. In the event that Egypt requires the evacuation of the UN forces, the matter will be brought for the consideration of the UN General Assembly. If the Assembly finds that the function of the UN force has been fulfilled, it will depart. If the Assembly finds that its function has not yet been fulfilled, but Egypt notwithstanding requires evacuation, this shall constitute violation of the agreement with the United Nations."

In March 1960 the Israeli Prime Minister had met Hammarskjöld in New York. At the time there were rumors that the UN Emergency Force was about to evacuate Sharm el-Sheikh. The Prime Minister told Hammarskjöld that these rumors had aroused concern in the Israeli Government, because there was a danger that the Straits of Eilat would again be closed to Israeli shipping in violation of the undertakings by the maritime nations in the General Assembly in February and March 1957; and that under Article 51 of the UN Charter Israel had the right to use force to defend its freedom of navigation in international waters. Hammarskjöld at that time assured the Prime Minister that the rumors were groundless and that the Emergency Force would not be evacuated from either Sharm el-Sheikh or the Gaza Strip without the Assembly's consent. For some reason, however, Hammarskjöld's successor, U Thant, did not comply with these undertakings for the Emergency Force.

The situation on the Syrian border deteriorated further. Murder detachments continued operations against Jewish settlements in the Galilee, and the Egyptian dictator began to concentrate his forces in the Sinai desert. This thrust into Sinai began in the middle of May 1967 on the excuse that Syria was in danger of an Israeli attack. The Israel Government, as already noted, assured the UN that the stories of Israeli troop buildups along the Syrian border were inventions, and U Thant himself in his May 19 report to the Security Council stated the UN observers had confirmed the absence of Israeli military concentrations or troop movements along the northern border. Nevertheless, the influx of Egyptian forces into Sinai continued at an increasing rate.

Before May 14 there were less than two infantry divisions and a small amount of armor in Sinai, by May 21 there were four divisions. Egyptian artillery and Air Force in particular had been augmented and now numbered eighteen thousand men. On May 16 Egypt's Chief of Staff notified Gen. I. G. Rikhye, the Indian commander of the UN Emergency Force in Sinai and the Gaza Strip: "I have instructed the armed forces of the United Arab Republic to be prepared for action against Israel the moment the latter carries out an act of aggression against any Arab state. In the light of these orders, our forces have been concentrated in Sinai on our eastern frontier. To ensure the complete safety of all UN forces in observation points along our borders, we request that these forces be removed at once."

Thus the problem of the Emergency Force was handed to the Secretary-General. For some reason U Thant saw fit to inform Nasser that any request for a temporary shift of the force would be treated as a demand for its complete removal from Gaza and Sinai, and Nasser readily accepted this interpretation. U Thant thereupon ordered the commander of the UN forces in Sinai and Gaza to evacuate the troops.

The Indian general had originally been ordered to concentrate the Gaza forces in the interior of the Strip and nothing was now said about removing the UN force from Sharm el-Sheikh. But after receiving a copy of the Egyptian Chief of Staff's cable to Rikhye of May 16, U Thant notified the Egyptian delegate at the UN that a partial removal of the UN forces was unacceptable; that Nasser had to choose between having them remain where they were or removing them completely. Nasser chose the second alternative; on May 19 General Rikhye informed the Israeli authorities that as of 4 P.M. that day the Emergency Force had ceased to fulfill its mission.

That day, it happened, President Shazar arrived in Canada to take part in celebrations marking the hundredth anniversary of its confederation. On his arrival he said, among other things, "The very fact that my trip to represent Israel at the Centennial celebration of Canada has proceeded as it was planned should serve as proof that Israel is not overcome by nervousness, though it is deeply concerned by the hostile concentration of Egyptian troops." He added, "It is not our intention to provoke or attack any of our neighbors. But if it is Egypt's intention to provoke us or Syria's policy to continue aggressive action against our territory, there can be no doubt that we will defend our territory as we should."

On May 19 U Thant informed the General Assembly that the Emergency Force had been withdrawn from Sinai and the Gaza Strip. The Canadian delegates, who had had a substantial part in mobilizing the UN Force and had supplied a considerable portion of its troops, were dissatisfied with the Secretary-General's hasty action. But Nasser had achieved the freedom of action he wanted. After the Egyptian forces occupied positions at Sharm el-Sheikh he announced that he would under no circumstances permit ships flying the Israel flag to pass through the Gulf of Aqaba and would prevent access to foreign ships carrying strategic materials to and from Israel. He went even further, proclaiming, "These Jews have threatened war, and we say to them: Come and get it, Egypt is ready!" Nasser knew very well that closing the Straits was tantamount to declaring war against Israel and this was his intention.

On Monday, May 22, the Prime Minister addressed the Knesset on the political situation. Enemy Egyptian forces had moved into Sinai on May 15, he announced. Cairo explained that this was in response to an Israeli military buildup for an attack on Syria. Israel refuted this misinformation and UN observers supported the denial. He went on to say:

Egyptian military forces in Sinai have increased. From thirty-five thousand they are now eighty thousand. Artillery forces have grown, as have the number of aircraft. In view of the increasing tension the Great Powers should exert all their influence to forestall the danger of a conflagration in the Middle East. A special responsibility devolves on the Soviet Union, which has influence in Damascus and Cairo but has not yet openly taken exception to the Damascus government's policy toward Israel. I would say the opposite: Moscow looks for excuses and pretexts. The Soviet Union should put into effect its avowed policy of seeking peaceful, nonviolent solutions without discrimination which would help maintain the peace.

The concentration of Egyptian forces in Sinai has reached such proportions as to intensify the tension in this region and arouse anxiety in the world. The situation on both sides of the border must be restored to its former state. In view of the announcement by the UN Secretary-General, all members of the United Nations and especially the Great Powers should denounce acts of sabotage committed against a fellow member state and demand their cessation, because they violate international agreements and the UN Charter. The full weight of international influence should be brought to bear to ensure the preservation of the tranquillity that has prevailed on the Egyptian-Israeli border since 1957 by respect for the vital international rights of all nations, including Israel.

Honorable Knesset: At the outset the movement of Egyptian forces into Sinai was interpreted in world capitals as a mere show of strength without any military significance. We whose borders were threatened felt that we had to take all necessary measures to meet any eventuality. From this rostrum I wish to say once again to the Arab states, including Egypt and Syria, that we do not intend aggression. We have no interest in attacking their security, their territory, or their legal rights. In view of the Egyptian concentrations on the border and the evacuation of the UN Emergency Force, I have ordered a limited callup of the reserves which has taken place according to plan.

In conclusion I call upon the nations of the region to respect mutually the sovereignty, integrity, and international rights of each and every state. The State of Israel, confident in its ability to defend itself and steadfast in its strength and spirit, expresses at this time readiness to join in the effort to strengthen the tranquillity and advance the cause of peace in our region.

Ben-Gurion (Rafi) proposed that discussion on the Prime Minister's report be referred to the Foreign Affairs and Security Committee, since some things requiring clarification could not be made public without harm to the State. The Prime Minister interrupted the meeting for a short time to enable the parties to confer on whether the debate should be held in the Knesset or in the Foreign Affairs and Security Committee. The consultation brought a decision to debate the crisis at once in the Knesset.

Menahem Begin (Gahal) was the first speaker: In the present situation there are things which ought not to be said in public, he agreed; but there are also things that must be said from the rostrum of the Knesset so that they may be heard by all the nations of the world, the enemy included. In recent days our security situation has deteriorated, nor will this quickly pass. Our nation, which has withstood many tests, should know this. Our country does not want bloodshed. It will not acquiesce under any circumstances to the shedding of Jewish blood in the land of its fathers, with impairment of its national sovereignty, acts of hostility, infiltration, minings. Against this aggression it will exercise in full its right of national self-defense recognized under international law.

A week ago Egypt issued two statements: one that it was sending its forces toward Israel; the other that if Israel attacked Syria, Egypt would go to war against us. I wish to say, in full respect, that what the Prime Minister told the Knesset today about the interpretation of a show of strength coming from abroad was not correct. That idea came from us, from Government sources. I will not go into whether this resulted from advice from abroad or the interpretations abroad came as a result of the Israeli idea. The fact remains that Government sources tried to explain the enemy's intention as merely a show of strength, and in this way exonerated it of grave offenses. The well-known reality is that Egypt is maintaining a state of war with Israel. If such a country sends its armies, tanks, planes, and guns toward our borders, it is an open and explicit threat of aggression. Yet the Israeli Government talks of demonstrations and a show of strength.

Egypt, Mr. Begin continued, has said that if Israel attacks Syria she will make war on us. This is an explicit threat of aggression, since Israel has not attacked Syria but on the contrary, Syria is directly and indirectly perpetrating acts of aggression against Israel. For that reason plain words must be used today in speaking to the world and to the enemy, in order to avoid further deterioration of the situation and acts of aggression that may develop into total conflict. You should have been more explicit today, Mr. Prime Minister. The political campaign conducted by this Government must be more persistent and urgent, and must include the demand that forces concentrated on the borders of Israel return to their former bases. The UN Emergency Force in Egypt and the Gaza Strip has been disbanded and no longer exists. Freedom of navigation to and from Eilat is a sine qua non and nothing more need be said. Finally, the enemy in the south threatens war if we exercise our right of national self-defense against aggression from the enemy in the north. It must therefore be clearly stated that no threat of aggression from the south will make Israel acquiesce to aggression from the north.

Yacov Hazan (Mapam): Enemies must be made aware of our position, which is absolutely clear and decisive: We do not want war. We want peace, but peace will not be bought by capitulation, or yielding on a just cause. The enemy must be made aware that we consider this array of forces a battle array and that we are ready. He must be made clearly aware that we are prepared to repulse any attack with all the determined resolve of a nation that loves peace but knows how to defend itself and will do so consolidated and united. Our friends throughout the world and the peace-loving powers must be made aware that we are on the brink of war, with no conscience-stilling illusions to absolve them from responsibility. Let us not lull ourselves or the world. The concentration of tens of thousands of troops and hundreds of tanks near our borders is a direct threat of war. We are ready for it. We want peace but we will fight till victory if war is imposed upon us.

Jaber Mu'addi (Druze faction): In these crucial hours in the history of the Israeli nation I wish first of all in the name of the Druze bloc and the Druze community in Israel to send heartfelt greetings to the soldiers of the IDF standing guard on the borders. The Druze community will place all its resources and capacity at the disposal of this great army. The UAR decision to close the Straits of Tiran is tantamount to declaring war on the State of Israel, a war that must necessarily end in the enemy's defeat.

Many others spoke, and the debate did not end until the following day. The Prime Minister informed the Knesset that this morning the President of Egypt announced his intention to block the international waterway connecting the Gulf of Eilat with the Red Sea to ships flying the Israeli flag and to ships of other flags carrying materials of a strategic nature. Any interference with freedom of shipping in the Gulf and the Straits is a gross violation of international freedom of navigation, an attack on the sovereign rights of other nations, and an act of aggression against Israel. The hour ahead of us is therefore fateful, not only for Israel but for the world. The Government of Israel will uphold the policy adopted by the UN General Assembly on March 1, 1957. "I will provide further information on the situation in the Foreign Affairs and Security Committee, where the discussion will continue," the Prime Minister said. By a vote of eighty-nine to four, continuation and summation of the debate were referred to the Foreign Affairs and Security Committee.

After the announcement that the Straits of Eilat had been closed to Israeli shipping our Government received a request from the President of the United States, Lyndon B. Johnson, to refrain from any action for forty-eight hours. A ministerial committee decided to accede to the request. It was proposed that Foreign Minister Abba Eban go to Washington to meet with the President. The Prime Minister opposed the suggestion and was supported by Golda Meir. However, when information was received from Israel's Ambassador in Paris that President Charles de Gaulle was also prepared to meet with an Israeli spokesman, it was decided that Eban would make the trip.

The meeting with de Gaulle lasted half an hour. Present were the French Foreign Minister, Maurice Couve de Murville, and Israel's Ambassador, Walter Eytan. Abba Eban's report was rather optimistic. Eytan was also optimistic. Meanwhile the Israeli Ambassador to Great Britain reported that the British Prime Minister, Harold Wilson, was prepared to meet with Eban, who immediately flew to London. Wilson told him that Britain would support Israel on the issue of freedom of navigation if it was raised through the UN or in the framework of an international operation with the United States participating.

On the day Eban arrived in Washington (May 24) President Johnson left for Canada. Eban met with him only on May 26. The President showed sympathy and friendship for Israel but pointed out that any action by the United States to ensure freedom of navigation in the Straits of Eilat would require Senate approval.

In Israel, a lack of confidence in the Government grew and anxiety was rising even in the armed forces. Many people called for changes in the Government, especially in the Defense Ministry and the Premiership. Even some key members of the largest party (Mapai) had lost faith in the Prime Minister and demanded his removal. But the top leadership—Golda Meir, Zalman Arrane, Shaul Avigor, and others—supported Eshkol and opposed any change in his status.

Public Pressure Helps Obtain a National Unity Government ★ Moshe Dayan Becomes Minister of Defense

On May 23, members of the National Religious Party proposed to Mapai that the Government be broadened to include Rafi and Gahal. Next day Rafi and Gahal representatives met in the office of the Minister of the Interior, Moshe Shapira, with the aim of bringing about changes in the national leadership. Menahem Begin remarked: "For years Eshkol was a Minister in Ben-Gurion's Government. Maybe he will agree to it this time as well." The National Religious Party people were doubtful. Shapira proposed that Ben-Gurion be appointed Minister of Defense, but Shimon Peres reminded him that when Ben-Gurion resigned in 1963, it was for good. If Ben-Gurion were prepared to resume the Premiership, Begin said, he would be willing to nominate him. Peres inquired and returned with a negative reply from Ben-Gurion.

Yitzhak Raphael (National Religious Party) was doubtful whether the Alignment would agree to forego the Premiership. Aryeh Ben-Eliezer (Gahal) proposed that Begin persuade Eshkol to invite Ben-Gurion to join the Government. Eshkol declined to do this. Begin then proposed that Eshkol nominate Ben-Gurion as Minister of Defense in a Government headed by Eshkol. This too Eshkol rejected. "The Army people," he said, "feel that Ben-Gurion was not successful as Minister of Defense. He made many mistakes that were covered up." The National Religious Party pressure on Mapai did not let up, and several Mapai leaders announced they would agree to co-opt four additional members into the Cabinet: two from Gahal, one from Rafi, and the secretary-general of the party, Golda Meir. Rafi spokesmen declared that they would agree only if their member, Moshe Dayan, were Minister of Defense.

Davar reported on May 25 that "No talks are being held in connection with any expansion of the Coalition, nor are any planned." A spokesman for the Prime Minister's office also issued an official denial of any such talks—"groundless and even harmful," he termed the rumors.

The Mapai secretariat convened that day, and the meeting was opened by Golda Meir. "On Tuesday, two days ago," she said, "the Prime Minister at his own initiative met with the representatives of the two largest opposition parties, Gahal and Rafi. He wished to have these members participate in deliberations on current affairs. But a whispering campaign has been started to the effect that there will be additions and changes in the country's leadership, and I wish to make the following proposal: the party considers the Government in its present form authorized to conduct national affairs at this time too. The party opposes participation of Opposition members on a permanent basis. This means no changes in the Government in any form, neither replacements nor additions, but only participation of Opposition personnel in deliberations on problems presently confronting the State and the nation."

The next speaker was Arrane, Minister of Education: "For several days now attempts have been made to undermine the Government's standing in the eyes of the nation. There is a campaign to discredit it. Public morale in this country, and first of all that of the Army, is being undermined. I cannot say that there have been any shortcomings in civilian, military, or foreign policy matters. So what has happened? What has happened is that there is Nasser, there is U Thant, and there is Syria. Why should the Government be the one to pay for it?"

Pinhas Sapir, the Minister of Finance, spoke even more sharply. He concluded by saying: "Anyone who thinks that it is merely a matter of co-option and strengthening is mistaken. It is a scheme to undermine the Government, something that should be resisted by every citizen, and not only by members of the party."

The Ahdut Haavodah secretariat was also meeting at the same time. Minister of Transport Moshe Carmel was in favor of a National Unity Government, but found himself in the minority. The next morning, May 26, a delegation of the Haifa section of Mapai headed by Mayor Abba Houshy appeared before the Cabinet. Houshy told the Prime Minister that the Haifa branch was in favor of a National Unity Government and proposed the co-option of Dayan and Begin. Eshkol replied that Gahal and Rafi representatives were already participating in security consultations and there was no need to enlarge the Government—everything was going fine. Houshy and his friends did not agree on this score, and even some members of the Cabinet came out in favor of a National Unity Government. Some of them suggested that Yigal Allon be appointed Minister of Defense. Eshkol rejected this proposal as well.

The unrest intensified in the nation, even within Mapai. At the Cabinet meeting on May 26 the Minister of Religious Affairs, Dr. Zerah Warhaftig, proposed that Gahal, Rafi, and Agudat Israel be co-opted into the Government. Several Mapai members argued that proposing to expand the Government was tantamount to an expression of no-confidence. The National Religious Party people replied that, on the contrary, their proposal was intended to strengthen the Government. The Prime Minister suggested that Gahal and Rafi representatives participate in the Foreign Affairs and Security Committee, but the Minister of Justice explained that only Ministers could participate in ministerial committees. He proposed instead that members of Rafi and Gahal be named Ministers without portfolio.

On Saturday night (May 27) Gahal people met with representatives of the Alignment. This was two days after the Mapai secretariat meeting that had voted against the co-option of Gahal and Rafi. Meanwhile there had been a change in the Alignment's position. Its spokesmen, after it was explained to them that legal considerations precluded their participation in the ministerial committee, now agreed to the co-option of Gahal and Rafi. Golda Meir asked the Gahal representatives why they made their entry into the Government conditional on co-option of Rafi. "There is no agreement between Rafi and ourselves on joint co-option," they replied. "On the contrary, Shimon Peres told us we are free to join without Rafi. However, the main question confronting us is that of a National Unity Government. Failure to include Rafi will impair this objective. And we know that if Dayan is not Minister of Defense, Rafi won't join the Government." The Alignment people replied that to designate Dayan as Minister of Defense would detract from Eshkol's prestige, and there would therefore be no National Unity Government.

Dayan, who had just returned from a tour of the front lines, was summoned on Sunday, May 28, to the Prime Minister's office. Eshkol offered to make him Minister without portofolio or Deputy Prime Minister, but Dayan declined. He said he would accept only a post of practical value, and the Prime Minister replied that he would look into it. At 8:30 that evening Eshkol discussed the political situation in a nationwide broadcast. The speech was hesitant and unclear and had a depressing effect on the public. Afterward Eshkol met with the Army's generals. They complained of the Government's indecision and lack of policy, and did not come away encouraged. The newspapers next day published articles critical of the Prime Minister's radio address. The independent daily *Haaretz* ran an editorial titled, "Needed: National Leadership," which said in part:

> During the war of Independence we had a Provisional Government that extended from Mapai on the left to the General Zionists on the right. This coalition, in which Mapai was a minority (four members out of thirteen), centered in effect around one man who by virtue of his personality was able to serve in the double capacity of Prime Minister and

Minister of Defense, and act as a clearinghouse for political and military thinking. Ben-Gurion frequently encountered powerful opposition within the Government, and often had to give in, but even those who opposed him from time to time admitted that he radiated inspiration that imparted strength to the Government, the military command, the Provisional Council of State, and the entire nation.

What Mr. Ben-Gurion provided to the coalitions of the War of Independence and the Sinai Campaign—farsighted thinking, resourcefulness, clarity of vision in evaluating rapidly changing situations, decisiveness in both advance and retreat and in rejecting ill-considered advice—all this we sorely lack. This does not mean that Ben-Gurion never erred, but even those who criticized some of the measures he took in past security crises know that in the final account he did not fail us.

What we need now, first and foremost, is not an expanded Government as such (though it would be very desirable that the ban against Rafi and Gahal be rescinded). Twenty Ministers instead of sixteen will not mean our salvation. As long as Mr. Eshkol continues as Prime Minister and Minister of Defense, what good are traditional advisors? If we had confidence in Mr. Eshkol's ability to steer the ship of state in these troubled times we would willingly follow him; but this certainty is lacking, and more and more people feel this. Mr. Eshkol's address last night over Kol Israel has served to enlarge their number. He is not cut out to be Prime Minister and Minister of Defense in the present situation. True, it is hard to switch horses in midstream, but there are sufficient historical precedents when leadership was changed in situations similar to that in which we now find ourselves.

Our decisions now should not be influenced by the dispute between Mapai and Rafi, nor should the decision on Eshkol be taken in the light of past events. People who fought vigorously for Eshkol against Ben-Gurion now declare openly that Ben-Gurion is again indispensable. The proposal that Ben-Gurion be Prime Minister and Moshe Dayan Minister of Defense, while Mr. Eshkol handles "civilian" affairs, seems to us well taken. Likewise Gahal should be co-opted into the Cabinet. The Government in its present composition is failing to provide leadership in a time of peril and must make way for new leadership. Time is pressing.

On Monday evening, May 29, the Prime Minister in the Knesset again reviewed the events of the past few weeks: the Egyptian military buildup in Sinai, the hasty withdrawal of the United Nations Emergency Force from the Gaza Strip and Sharm el-Sheikh, and Nasser's announcement of the closing of the Straits of Eilat to Israeli shipping. He could not describe the situation in greater detail, he said, but members of the Foreign Affairs and Security Committee were being kept up to date.

David Ben-Gurion was slated to speak on behalf of Rafi, but the Speaker announced that the Government would not propose a debate; by the rules a debate would be held if at least one-third (forty) of the members demanded one within twenty-four hours of the Government's announcement. Ben-Gurion, however, addressed a news conference in the Knesset building. He would not take up much of the listeners' time, he said, because there was no sense in speaking about what had or had not been done hitherto:

I am not one of those who feel they can change the past. The only question we must consider is that of the immediate future. Several of the Arab leaders, headed by the Egyptian President, are declaiming day and night that Israel must be destroyed—not the entire nation of Israel throughout the world, but that part of it which is living in its own land. The gravity of these threats must not be disregarded, and therefore I have a few things I wish to say about the conduct of the war.

Every child knows that one cannot fight a war without an army. To our good fortune we have an army that can be relied on, an army which with all its quantitative limitations is not inferior in devotion and valor to any other in the world. Nevertheless we must keep in mind two things of vital importance: (1) in a democracy an army does not act on its own behalf or on behalf of its military commanders but on behalf and at the behest of the civilian government; (2) and no less important, a war is conducted not by military operations alone. Israel's defense establishment has never been involved in any campaign that was not one of defense. Now the closing of the Straits of Tiran, which is an international waterway, to Israeli shipping is an act of aggression and something against which we must defend ourselves by force. Even a defensive campaign is not carried out solely by military force; it requires political action as well. And the conduct of the war, if forced upon us, will require responsibility and perspicacity, both military and political.

Not all the problems now facing us can be spoken about here. At this time I wish only to stress the seriousness of the situation. Our conduct and our leadership in these days or weeks may well determine our fate, and the only considerations that should guide us at this time are those of security and survival. If anyone has considerations that are more important, there is nothing I can say to him.

Let me conclude with a prayer that we may be worthy of the devotion our soldiers are showing and will continue to show in this time of trial, and the concern for our fate being manifested by the Jewish people throughout the world.

Popular dissatisfaction was mounting. The parents, brothers and sisters, relatives, and acquaintances of soldiers were learning of the Army's growing lack of confidence in the Minister of Defense, who was also Prime Minister. On May 30 *Davar* published a manifesto by the author Chaim Hazaz:

> The nation calls upon its leaders to abandon their disputes and unite in a broad emergency government, one worthy of the Army of Israel and the moral force of the nation. Men of accomplishment, men who command support, men of experience and wise counsel must forego their prerogatives and contentions and work together in the Government in the cause of defense. No one is unfit for the cause of defense! It is a matter of life and death for the nation!

Yitzhak Ziv-Av, who was a loyal employee of the Ministry of Defense during the War of Independence, published in *Haaretz* a bitter indictment of the Mapai secretary-general, Golda Meir—"a one-woman stumbling block"—for her destructive political fanaticism in obstructing national unity. "The nation's marvelous mobilization," he declared, "entitles it, in my opinion, to a Government that expresses this unparalleled unity."

Only the Mapam organ, *Al Hamishmar*, maintained that "the hour is not ripe for the addition of Opposition representatives to the Government. A Government in which Herut participates will not be the same Government that the United Workers Party [Mapam] supported in the Sixth Knesset." The top leadership of the Alignment realized, however, that public pressure for a National Unity Government was mounting. The Prime Minister declared that he intended to set up "advisory committees" or "a war council"—to include such persons as Yadin, Laskov, Dayan, Allon—which would solve the problem of "unity." When asked if he would accept appointment to this council, Dayan replied in the negative.

A number of the top leaders advised the Prime Minister to name Yigal Allon Assistant and Representative of the Prime Minister and Minister of Defense. Eshkol was inclined to agree. In a meeting between Golda Meir, Knesset member Barkatt, and Rafi representatives Peres and Almogi, she proposed that Dayan be made Minister without portfolio. The Rafi spokesman rejected this offer. General Yadin met with the Prime Minister and advised him to appoint Dayan Minister of Defense. Eshkol proposed other forms of integration but remained unwilling to relinquish his Defense portfolio.

Even members of Mapai began to demand that the Defense portfolio be taken out of Eshkol's hands and given to Dayan. The lack of confidence in the Government continued to grow. *Haaretz* ran an article titled "Inept Government Should Resign." Several Mapai Ministers informed Eshkol of the growing exasperation among the people and even among the members of the Alignment. On the evening of May 30 the chairman of the Alignment bloc, Moshe Bar-Am, convened its members in the Knesset building and demanded that the Prime Minister be present. At first Eshkol announced that he would be unable to attend, but when Bar-Am warned him that if he did not show up the faction would mutiny, he came.

The discussion was opened by one of the veteran members, Akiva Govrin. He demanded that Rafi and Gahal be co-opted into a National Unity Government and that Dayan be appointed Minister of Defense as a condition for unity. The Minister of Posts, Israel Yisha'yahu, proposed that Allon be made Minister of Defense. "I have not proposed that anyone be Minister of Defense," Eshkol interrupted. "When Begin and Moshe Shapira proposed that I make Dayan Minister of Defense, I told them I agreed to Gahal and Rafi joining the Government and to having two Gahal representatives and one from Rafi join the Foreign Affairs and Security Committee."

But Speaker Luz also favored the appointment of Dayan as Minister of Defense. Knesset member Zev Tsur, of Ahdut Haavodah, was opposed but former Commerce and Industry Minister Chaim Zadok was in favor. If Rafi was willing to join, and this depended on Dayan's being Minister of Defense, then it should be done, he said. Golda Meir was not present. David Hacohen, chairman of the Foreign Affairs and Security Committee, and Minister of Transport Carmel also demanded Dayan's appointment. The meeting ended without a decision because the Prime Minister had to leave.

The following day, May 31, Golda Meir met with the Prime Minister. They were both dejected because of the growing opposition to Eshkol's remaining Minister of Defense and agreed to join the minority favoring Yigal Allon for that portfolio. In the afternoon Eshkol met with Dayan in the Prime Minister's office in Tel Aviv and proposed that he become Deputy Premier. Dayan refused. If not appointed Minister of Defense, he said, he would prefer to serve in the Army in any capacity the Chief of Staff saw fit. When Eshkol asked, What, for instance? Dayan replied, Commander of the Southern Front, as he was well acquainted with Sinai. Eshkol felt this would solve the problem and summoned the Chief of Staff, Gen. Yitzhak Rabin, to discuss the assignment of the Southern Front to Dayan. Toward evening he informed the Alignment's Political Committee that Dayan had been taken care of—he would command the Southern Front.

On the same day, unaware of Eshkol's new arrangement, the Mapai Secretariat met in Jerusalem. After a sharp debate a large majority voted in favor of recommending that Dayan be co-opted as Minister of Defense. Meanwhile the Prime Minister had telephoned Shapira to tell him of the new arrangement: Allon would be Defense Minister and Dayan Commander of the Southern Front. Shapira angrily replied that this was out of the question, since it meant that Gahal and Rafi would not join the Government, and demanded that the Prime Minister convene the Government that evening. The meeting was called.

Meanwhile the Mapam Political Committee was also in session. Riftin proposed that the party leave the Government if Dayan were appointed Minister of Defense, but he was supported by only two members, R. Mahler and E. Peri. The majority decided that changes of personnel in the Government were a matter for the parties concerned, and if Mapai chose to give Dayan the Defense portfolio, Mapam would go along.

The Cabinet convened at 9:45 P.M. at the Kirya in Tel Aviv. Eshkol announced that the Mapai Political Committee had decided to separate the Defense portfolio from the Premiership in order to lighten his burden in the present emergency. The Defense portfolio would be given to Allon; as for Dayan, he had been given the choice between the Deputy Premiership and command of the Southern Front and had chosen the latter.

The National Religious Party Ministers were furious. They insisted that Dayan be Minister of Defense because otherwise there would be no National Unity Government. Shapira threatened that the National Religious Party would leave the Government. Even Minister Moshe Kol (of the Independent Liberals) demanded that Dayan be Minister of Defense. At 11 that evening one of the Prime Minister's functionaries told Rafi secretary Peres that in a conversation with the Prime Minister, Dayan had agreed to accept a command post in the Army.

The next day, Thursday, June 1, Peres phoned Dayan to ask if it was true that he had declined the Defense portfolio in the National Unity Government. Dayan said it was not, and that what he had told Eshkol the previous day was that if he could not have the Defense portfolio, he would be prepared to serve in the Army on one of the fronts.

On June 1 *Davar* reported that it had been agreed that Allon would be Minister of Defense and Dayan given an Army post. *Haaretz* at the same time wrote:

> Yesterday, upon the urging of the top leadership of Ahdut Haavodah and Golda Meir, the Prime Minister offered the Defense portfolio to Yigal Allon, thus putting an end to the possibility of forming a broad emergency Government. The decision in favor of Allon was taken at a brief meeting of the Alignment's Executive Committee, after which the Mapai Secretariat was convened. The members of the Secretariat were presented with the fact that a final decision had been taken before they had had a chance to consider the matter, though it, rather than the committee, was the authorized body.
>
> And yesterday it was felt in Mapai circles that a large majority in favor of Dayan was developing in its governing bodies. However, the Prime Minister and the Mapai Secretariat together with the heads of Ahdut Haavodah tried to prevent Dayan's appointment at any price. Mr. Eshkol was firmly opposed to being divested of the Defense portfolio but as a result of the pressure in the last few days in favor of giving it to Gen. Dayan, the veteran leadership of Mapai has decided to forestall additional pressure by giving it to Yigal Allon, something to which the National Religious Party is opposed. To create the impression of a broad national government, the Alignment decided to co-opt Rafi and Gahal into the Government by offering Dayan the Foreign Affairs portfolio and making Abba Eban the Deputy Prime Minister.
>
> It seems that Dayan is not prepared to accept this offer, for he stressed in his reply that he was not interested in just any portfolio but wanted to contribute his abilities to defense matters by being given direct responsibility for the Defense portfolio.

But on the same day, June 1, the problem was settled. Allon announced that he would not accept the Defense portfolio, and it was given to Dayan. Thus a National Unity Government came into being despite the opposition of the top Mapai leadership. But the decision was preceded by meetings and discussions among various party leaders.

At a meeting of the Mapai people that morning Eshkol gave his own version of the negotiations of the preceding few weeks. He concluded by saying that during his term of office as Prime Minister and Minister of Defense he had succeeded where his predecessor had failed—in finding a way to the United States. Shaul Avigor expressed satisfaction with Allon's presumed assumption of the Defense portfolio, as he would be a loyal partner to the Prime Minister.

At noon Eshkol announced that he had to go to a meeting with the representatives of the National Religious Party, Gahal, and Rafi at the Prime Minister's office. Five ministers were present at the meeting: Barzilai (Mapam), Galili (Ahdut Haavodah), Moshe Kol (Independent Liberals), Moshe Shapira (National Religious Party), and Yacov Shimshon Shapiro (Mapai). Eshkol extended an official invitation to the heads of Gahal to join the Government. They replied that it depended on whether Dayan would be Minister of Defense. Eshkol countered that Dayan preferred to be Commander of the Southern Front. Ben-Eliezer asked, "Then who will be Defense Minister?" Eshkol replied, "You'll find out." But Ben-Eliezer insisted, "Why don't you tell us who the Minister of Defense will be?" "You'll know tomorrow," Eshkol told him. The Gahal leaders went away disappointed.

And the debate at the Mapai secretariat continued. David Hacohen called for Dayan as Minister of Defense and he was seconded by Baruh Azania, Dvorah Netzer, Aliza Shidlovsky from Kinneret, Moshe Wartman from Haifa, Ephraim Reisner, Asher Yadlin, Akiva Govrin, Reuven Barkatt, Senta Yoseftal, Chaim Zadok, and Rahel Tzabri. Only Aranne was in favor of Allon. Golda Meir claimed that the Secretariat had never voted for the co-option of additional members to the Government and that this prevented a vote being taken. Immediately afterward she adjourned to her office, where she phoned Galili to tell him, in a tone of bitter disappointment, that most of the speakers favored Dayan over Allon. She informed the Prime Minister of this as well.

In the streets women were demonstrating: "For national security—Dayan is the man!"

At 3 P.M. Minister Kol called on the Prime Minister and demanded that Dayan be accepted as Minister of Defense. General Yadin made the same demand. Eshkol's apartment was flooded with people clamoring for Dayan to assume the Defense Ministry. Toward evening, after consultations with Hazan and Mayor Houshy of Haifa, Eshkol invited Dayan to his office and asked him to become Defense Minister.

Unaware of this development, the members of Rafi met at Ben-Gurion's home in Tel Aviv at 8:30 that evening. Peres said, "Ben-Gurion has proposed Dayan as the most suitable candidate. He has recommended him as a man of outstanding qualities. In our system of government Moshe is the man best suited to conduct the war. His appointment is a source of encouragement to the troops and to the nation. I move that Rafi confirm the appointment and give Moshe its blessing." Ben-Gurion requested the floor. "After thinking it over," he said, "I am in favor of Rafi's consenting to the appointment of Moshe Dayan as Minister of Defense."

Only Almogi still maintained that we should not join Eshkol's Government.

"In my opinion," he said, "Dayan's entering the Government is like nailing a mezuzzah on the church door." Ben-Gurion asked for the floor again: "I understand Almogi, but for my part I have changed my mind. It has been explained to me that Dayan's co-option is necessary in order to restore the Army's confidence in the national leadership. The Army must have confidence and it will if Moshe is Minister of Defense. The same is true of the nation. Eshkol will still be Prime Minister but at least he won't be Minister of Defense."

The Cabinet met at 9:30 P.M. to approve the formation of the National Unity Government, with Dayan as Minister of Defense. Eshkol congratulated the new members on their assumption of the burden of national responsibility. The National Unity Government went into operation immediately, even before being approved by the Knesset.

Prime Minister Eshkol made the prescribed declarations:

> Mr. Speaker, honorable Knesset: I shall now make announcements in accordance with certain articles of the Transition Law:
>
> a. In accordance with Section 11-e of the Transition Law of 1945 I have the honor of announcing that the Government has decided to accede to my request to be released from the post of Minister of Defense, as soon as the Knesset confirms the appointment of Knesset member Moshe Dayan as Minister of Defense.
>
> b. In accordance with Section 11-d of the Transition Law of 1945, I have the honor to announce that the Government has decided on the co-option of three Knesset members, namely Menahem Begin and Joseph Sapir as Ministers without portfolio, and Moshe Dayan as Minister of Defense.
>
> c. In accordance with Section 11-a(b) of the Transition Law of 1949 I hereby announce that Knesset member Zvi Dinstein has ceased to serve in the capacity of Deputy Minister of Defense.
>
> I request the Knesset to confirm my announcement of the co-option of additional members into the Government.

The majority, with three opposed, voted in favor of the Government proposals. This approval came on Sunday, June 4. The war began on Monday, June 5, 1967.

Begin and Sapir immediately submitted declarations of allegiance. The Speaker announced that Dayan would sign his declaration at the first opportunity, but according to the Transition Law he assumed his post immediately, now that his appointment had been confirmed by the Knesset. Minister Dayan did not attend the Knesset meeting because he was occupied with the war that had begun that morning. He appointed Gen. Zvi Zur as his deputy.

Section 2. Conflict and Victory

Preparations and Proclamations by Arab Leaders ★ Israel's "Natural Right" to Self-Defense

WHAT would go down in history as the Six-Day War began early in the morning on Monday, June 5, 1967, though the decision had been made earlier by the Egyptian dictator, Nasser, without doubt the most talented statesman of all the Arab leaders.

He had been making open preparations for the war for at least three weeks, if not for several weeks or months before the outbreak. It is useful to summarize the background.

After the Sinai Campaign of 1956 Nasser repeated many times that war with Israel was inevitable, but that he would make it when he was certain of victory. The more the Soviet Union came to support the Arabs, the more confident Nasser grew of victory. He had more confidence in the new bosses of the Soviet Union than he had had in Khrushchev, because he felt or imagined that Khrushchev was anxious for a détente with the United States and was not so implacably hostile to Israel. Moreover, as long as Israel had friends such as the US, France, and recently Britain as well, there was no certainty that it could be defeated. Krushchev's successors, however, returned a considerable distance back down the road to Stalinism, and relations between Russia and the United States had cooled. The new Soviet leaders made no secret of their enmity to Israel and from year to year bolstered their relations with Syria, Egypt, and most of the other Arab countries.

Another addition to the Arabs' circle of friends was Red China, which, despite its exclusion from the United Nations, was growing in international importance. The abundant arms Nasser received from Russia and the large number of Egyptian students and officers studying in communist universities gave him reason to believe he could defeat Israel—and there was no more certain way of provoking a war than by closing the Straits of Eilat. He knew that the majority of the maritime nations had promised Israel to declare in the United Nations that innocent navigation in the Straits of Eilat was an international right, and that under Article 51 of the UN Charter this right could be defended by force if interfered with by force; but he also knew what value to attach to declarations and promises in matters that did not affect the vital interests of those who made them.

Being certain of support by the Soviet Union and the other communist states, he was not overly perturbed by the friendly statements of the European nations and the United States to the effect that Israel's rights were safeguarded by international law and the Western countries. He had ample reason to make light of such assurances: though Israel's freedom of navigation had twice been assured by the Security Council, no one had lifted a finger to make Egypt open the Suez Canal to Israeli shipping. He had sufficient grounds to believe that if he succeeded in expelling from Sharm el-Sheikh the UN Emergency Force protecting Israel's freedom of navigation, and Israel then exercised its right to defend itself by force, he would at long last destroy Israel, the one achievement that might enable him to dominate the Arab nations. The huge amounts of arms and military training provided by Russia and other communist countries made him confident of finally defeating the Jewish State.

The measures he took in the three weeks preceding the Six-Day War show how convinced he was of victory. On May 16 Egypt declared a state of emergency. Its military forces were ordered to be in a "state of full preparedness for war." All the armed forces were arrayed for action and started moving toward the Israeli frontiers. On May 17 Cairo and Damascus announced that Egypt and Syria were "ready for battle." Large Egyptian forces in Sinai headed east. In Amman it was announced that Jordanian forces were being mobilized. On May 18 Radio Cairo continued to report that Egyptian and Syrian forces were on maximum alert, while Iraq and Kuwait declared general mobilizations. On May 19 the United Nations Forces officially withdrew from the Gaza Strip and Sharm el-Sheikh. The United Nations flag was lowered in Gaza. On the same day Egyptian military preparedness was intensified.

Following consultations at the headquarters of the Commander of the Egyptian Navy, two submarines, one destroyer, and four missile boats set out from their Mediterranean base in order to blockade Israeli shipping in the Red Sea. On May 20 an Egyptian force consisting of a paratroop battalion and an infantry brigade reached Sharm el-Sheikh, and long-range Soviet-made 130-mm. guns were emplaced there. A number of Egyptian brigades were withdrawn from Yemen and moved to the Sinai. Total Egyptian troops in Sinai reached eighty thousand, organized in two armored divisions and five infantry and armored-infantry divisions. Artillery divisions were also posted there. Marshal Amer, who later either committed suicide or was murdered after the Arab defeat, told the newspaper *Al Ahram*:

> Our armed forces have taken up positions enabling them to react and to act as a deterrent. The time has come to put an end to the policy of arrogance and boastfulness adopted by the Israeli foe, a policy based on collaboration between Western reactionary forces and imperialism, growing American support for Israel, and the misguided belief that the tying down of forces in Yemen limits the President's (Nasser's) scope for maneuver. Lately the enemy has exceeded all bounds in his threats and preparations to commit armed aggression against Syria. Our armed forces are now prepared to inflict crushing blows on the Zionist enemy. The forces now arrayed against the Israeli foe will strike down any hostile aggression, on any battlefield, in any direction, and will strike valiantly.

On May 21 Ahmed Shukeiry announced that eight thousand Palestinian warriors had been placed under the command of Egypt, Syria, and Iraq. In Egypt even the reserves were called up. On May 22 Cairo announced that the President had accepted an offer by the Iraqi Army and Air Force to assist him in the war. On May 23 King Feisal of Saudi Arabia announced in London that he had ordered Saudi forces to cooperate in the war against Israeli aggression. On May 24 Jordan announced that the general mobilization was complete and that the government had given the Iraqi and Saudi armies permission to enter Jordan. Twenty thousand Saudi troops took up positions along the Jordanian-Saudi border. On May 26 Nasser proclaimed in Cairo that if war broke out, Israel would be totally annihilated. The Arabs, he said, were prepared and were capable of victory. On May 28 general mobilization was announced in the Sudan. On May 29 Algeria announced that army units were being sent to the Middle East to aid Egypt. On May 30 Egypt and Jordan signed a military pact. On May 31 the Iraqi Air Force moved from its base at Habaniya to its westernmost base not far from Israel.

On June 3 the Egyptian Commander, General Mortaji, issued the following Order of the Day to the troops in Sinai:

> Our forces are arrayed in accordance with a clearly defined plan. We are completely ready to carry the war beyond Egypt's borders. The outcome of his great hour will be of historic importance to our Arab nation and to the Holy War. This is the day we have been waiting for—to restore the plundered land to its rightful owners. I have been asked, When will the time come for the Jihad (Holy War)? The time is now!

On June 4 a military treaty was concluded between Egypt and Iraq. At 10:15 that evening Radio Cairo explained the significance of this pact: "The Arab armies now surround Israel in every sense of the word. Add to this the joint defense treaty between Egypt and Syria, and you will see just how encircled Israel is."

The American government, which in 1957 undertook to safeguard freedom of navigation in the Straits of Eilat, sent a special envoy, Charles Yost, to Egypt. He was not received by Nasser and conferred only with Egyptian Foreign Minister Mahmoud Riad, with no results. The attempt to mobilize the maritime nations that had underwritten freedom of navigation in 1957 did not succeed. France even announced that it did not consider itself committed to either party to the dispute and Britain was not willing that the joint declaration include a provision that "the signatories are prepared to safeguard the right of passage."

Israel had no choice but to invoke Article 51 of the United Nations Charter which recognizes "the natural right of a member of the United Nations to self-defense."

First and Second Days, June 5 and 6

In the early morning hours of June 5, 1967, Israeli radar stations throughout the country showed enemy jets over Egypt heading for Israel. Egyptian armored vehicles rolling toward the Israeli border in Sinai were also detected. Shells from artillery and mortars stationed in the Gaza Strip landed in the fields of Nahal Oz, an Israeli kibbutz near the city of Gaza. The kibbutzim of Kissuffim and Ein Hashlosha near the Strip were also hit.

The Israel Defense Forces were ordered to strike.

At 7:45 A.M. the Israeli Air Force went into action. The target was ten Egyptian airfields. The plan was to reach all the fields, near and far, simultaneously. Nine were hit right on schedule: El Arish, Jebel Libni, Bir Gafgafa, Bir Tamada, Abu Suweir, Kabritt, Inshas, Beni Suef. The tenth base, Faid, was reached a few minutes late.

Most of the Egyptian Air Force was caught on the ground. The Israeli planes flew as low as possible so that enemy radar would not spot them. In eighty minutes the majority of Egypt's fighter, bomber, and transport planes were demolished. Four airfields in Sinai— El Arish, Jebel Libni, Bir Gafgafa, and Bir Tamada—and most of the airfields beyond the Suez Canal were put out of action. The Israeli Air Force showed absolute supremacy in the skies on almost every front and the war was therefore decided to a large extent in the first three hours. Egyptian aircraft of various makes were destroyed on all ten airfields, some of them blasted together with their pilots while preparing for takeoff. Within eighty minutes Gen. Mordecai Hod, Commander of the Air Force, reported to the Chief of Staff, "Sinai is empty." Eighty minutes later he reported, "There is no longer anything to fear. We have achieved most of our objectives."

After two hours and fifty minutes the largest part of the Egyptian Air Force was wiped out. In less than three hours, three hundred war planes were annihilated, including thirty Tupolev-16 heavy bombers, twenty-seven Ilysushin medium bombers, seventy MIG-19 fighters, seventy-five MIG-17 fighters, twelve Sukhoi-7 fighter bombers, ninety MIG-21 fighters, as well as thirty-two transport planes and helicopters, including the large MI-6s. At 10:40 A.M. Minister of Defense Dayan broadcast a message to the soldiers of the Israel Defense Forces:

> At this time we do not have precise situation reports of the battles on the southern front. Our planes are locked in bitter combat with enemy aircraft and our ground forces have set out to silence the Egyptian artillery now shelling our settlements opposite the

Gaza Strip and to stop the Egyptian armored forces trying to cut off the southern part of the Negev in the initial stage of the campaign. The Egyptians have mobilized under their command, and gained the support of, the Syrian, Jordanian, and Iraqi Armies. They are also supported by units from Kuwait and Algeria. They are greater in numbers but we will overcome them. The people on the home front will have to endure suffering. But the supreme effort is demanded of you, the troops, the fighters on land, sea, and air, serving in the defense trenches of the border settlements or advancing with the armored columns. Soldiers of the Israel Defense Forces, you are our hope and security this day.

The Air Force at that hour was contending mainly with the Egyptian Air Force. After planes from Jordan, Syria, and Iraq began attacking towns and settlements inside Israeli territory, the Air Force went into action against these aircraft as well. At the same time the Israel Defense Forces, spearheaded by armor, engaged the enemy within the Gaza Strip and Sinai. Savage battles ensued between armor and infantry. The Israeli settlements on the border of the Gaza Strip were under continual enemy bombardment; those hardest hit were Kissuffim, Ein Hashlosha, Nirim, Nahal Oz, Kfar Aza, Be'erotayim, Miflassim, and Sa'ad.

At 1 A.M. on June 6 the Chief of Staff, Gen. Yitzhak Rabin, addressed the soldiers of the Israel Defense Forces as follows:

> In the northern Sinai sector our forces have taken Rafiah, Sheikh Zuwaid, and, toward evening, El Arish. One column is advancing along the road from El Arish to Abu Agheila. Other forces have taken Khan Yunis and Dir el-Balah and are now fighting on the outskirts of Gaza. In the central sector we have captured the strongholds of Auja el-Hafir and Tarat Um Basis and have penetrated the enemy stronghold of Um Katef where they are now fighting. In the southern sector we have captured a number of advanced posts in the Kuntilla area. Our forces have taken a large number of prisoners and booty, including artillery and tanks. The enemy has suffered heavy losses while our casualties have been relatively light. The victory of our Air Force in today's battles is an unprecedented achievement. I will now ask the Commander of the Air Force to provide information on the aerial campaign.

General Hod then spoke:

> We have come to grips with the Air Forces of Egypt, Jordan, and Iraq. In this campaign we have destroyed 374 aircraft with certainty, and another 24 have probably been destroyed. We have lost 19 pilots, of whom 8 were killed and 11 are missing. Some of them have been taken prisoner by the enemy. Our losses in aircraft are 4 Ouragans, 4 Mystères, 4 Super-Mystères, 2 Mirages, 1 Vautour, and 4 Fouga-Magisters. Men of the Air Force, our job is not yet over! The Air Force remains fresh and strong and is prepared to carry on its work to ensure victory for the Israel Defense Forces.

Until after midnight of the first day the IDF had maintained battle secrecy, while Egypt was broadcasting descriptions of "victories." At 8:50 A.M. the Egyptian broadcasting service announced, "Citizens, we stand as one man heart and soul behind our heroic commander, Gamal Abdel Nasser. We shall repulse with iron determination the traitorous aggression begun against us this morning by Israel. Victory is ours, the Arab nations! Victory is that of our brave soldiers, our free heroes. Onward to Tel Aviv!"

At 9:24 A.M. Radio Cairo cried, "Brothers and soldiers in Gaza, in Sinai, and in Sharm el-Sheikh, heroic brothers in Jordan and Syria! Forward to Tel Aviv! Every Arab must take revenge for 1948 and advance across the Armistice lines to destroy the nest of the Zionist gangs in Tel Aviv." One minute later Radio Damascus chimed in, "We are with you, comrades in arms in Cairo. We are with you comrades in arms in Gaza, in Sinai, and in Sharm el-Sheikh. We are with you, masses of our Arab nation in Jordan, in your honorable advance to Tel Aviv. Strike! Have no mercy! We are with you!" Radio Damascus then addressed the Syrian nation:

> Brothers, citizens! The fire of battle has been struck and will no longer be extinguished. The hour of revenge is at hand. The campaign of liberation has begun. Set fire, burn and destroy the Zionist invaders. The powder keg has exploded and the flames of the war of liberation are rising high. To arms, Arabs! Forward to the heart of Palestine! We shall meet in Tel Aviv! We shall crush the invaders and aggressors. Hurry to battle, Arabs! The bells of victory are pealing, for the hope of liberation has been realized.

Nor was Jordan silent. At 9:40 A.M. Radio Amman broadcast the following:

> Arabs everywhere! The hours of liberation and restoration of our plundered rights is at hand. In the fateful battle we are now waging against the forces of evil and of Zionist aggression we will destroy the artificial boundaries and restore our plundered rights. Forward to the Holy War, to victory!

Following these choral responses by Syria and Jordan, Radio Cairo proclaimed the first victories: the "downing" of twenty-three Israeli planes. At 10:10 the number jumped to forty-two, and by 12:40 Egypt announced that seventy Israeli aircraft had been "destroyed." Other Arab stations reported the bombing of Tel Aviv, Haifa, and other cities in the north of Israel. Until 1 A.M. (June 6), however, Israel did not lift the mantle of secrecy or deny the Arabs their bogus "victories." Toward evening Radio Cairo addressed Israel in Hebrew:

> Our forces are attacking you on all possible fronts, on every front and in every village. At this moment our bombs are destroying all your towns and cities. We have declared total war on Israel. We do not wish your death, but there is no way out, so die you must, We will have no mercy. Who is to blame for your plight, you miserable wretches? Your leaders are to blame. Our forces are encircling everywhere and striking with fortitude and honor. Your leaders are tools of the imperialists, and it is they who have brought you to this bitter end. They have made Israel a black stain on the heart of our beloved Arab homeland.

In another broadcast, Radio Cairo said, "Where are you, Moshe Dayan? In 1956 they called you Minister of Victory. Today you are Minister of Defeat. Our valiant Syrian nation took out one of your eyes, today we will take out the other!"

These broadcasts and proclamations made it clear that our war was not only with Egypt, but with Jordan, Syria, and Iraq. On the first day of the fighting the Air Force had to go into action against Nasser's allies as well. On that day twenty Jordanian Hunter fighters and seven transport planes and helicopters were demolished; in Syria thirty MIG-21s, twenty MIG-17s, and two Ilyushin-28s were destroyed. Two-thirds of the Syrian Air Force was eliminated in one hour. On the airfields of Iraq six MIG-21s and three Hunters were finished off.

Without doubt the false confidence of victory in the four Arab states stemmed from the position taken by the Soviet Union in the preceding twelve years, ever since the first Soviet-Egyptian arms deal (through Czechoslovakia) in October 1955. Moscow had supplied Egypt, Syria, and Iraq with 2000 tanks, 700 fighter and bomber aircraft, and thousands of field guns. In that period Egypt alone spent $4 billion on augmenting its armed forces. It had acquired from the Soviet Union over 500 planes, 1300 tanks, 540 field guns, 130 medium-range guns, 200 120-mm. mortars, 600 antiaircraft guns, 650 antitank guns, 12 submarines, and more. Before the Six-Day War there were over 500 Soviet officers and instructors in Egypt.

Ever since the Syrian attack on Israeli settlements in northern Galilee on April 7, 1967, when the Israeli Air Force had been compelled to go into action and had shot down six Syrian MIGs, Soviet propaganda had been stepped up. Israel, it shouted, was "working on behalf of American imperialism and the Western oil companies." Incessantly the Russians repeated that large Israeli forces were concentrating on the Syrian border. By focusing their propaganda on alleged military buildups in the north, the Soviets may well have intended to divert the attention of the Israeli Government and the world from the Egyptian preparations in the south, in the Sinai peninsula.

This time the "evil" did indeed break out from the south rather than the north. Following his defeat in Sinai in the seven days at the end of October and beginning of November 1956, Nasser devoted great efforts to transforming northwestern Sinai into a fortified military base for large-scale attack on Israel. The roads existing before the Sinai Campaign were improved and repaved, and new roads were built. Near the Israeli border along the line running from Gaza through Rafiah to El Arish and from El Arish to Abu Ageila to Kuseima, large systems of fortifications were erected; behind them a network of defenses, fortified camps, and airfields extended into the heart of Sinai.

During this decade the Gaza Strip was turned into an armed camp, dug in and equipped with armor, artillery, and other types of weapons. When Egyptian forces began to enter Sinai on a large scale on May 15, 1967, they thus found already prepared logistical systems of ammunition, fuel, and supplies. At the start of the war on June 5 the forces arrayed in Sinai and the Gaza Strip totaled seven divisions, some hundred thousand men. At their disposal were a thousand tanks and hundreds of field guns; interceptors and fighter-bombers had been posted on the Sinai airfields.

The infantry divisions were deployed across the axes in eastern Sinai, with the armored forces concentrated in depth in the central and southern parts of the peninsula. "Palestinian" Infantry Division 20 was bivouacked in the Gaza Strip and Division 7 between Rafiah and El Arish; Division 2 took up a position on the central axis in Abu Ageila and Kuseima; Division 31 was posted to the west and south of El Arish and Abu Ageila, in Jebel Libni, and Bir Hasneh; Division 6 was posted in the southern flank between Nahal and Kuntilla. Every infantry division included large numbers of tanks. Two armored divisions were posted in central Sinai: Armored Division 4, the crack Egyptian formation, was stationed between Bir Gafgafa and Bir Tamada; and Armored Division 1 to the south of Kuntilla, not far from Eilat, was prepared to break through into the Israeli Negev to sever Eilat and the Gulf from Israel.

Opposing this Egyptian force was an Israeli infantry and armored force with a strength of more than three divisions, commanded respectively by Generals Israel ("Talik") Tal, Ariel ("Arik") Sharon, and Avraham Yoffe, under the overall authority of the Commander of the Southern Front, Yesha'yahu Gavish. Each division consisted of armored infantry and paratroop brigades, artillery and engineer battalions, and signal and medical units.

At 8:15 A.M. on Monday, June 5, General Gavish ordered his three divisional commanders to move out to meet the enemy: Tal along the Khan Yunis-Rafiah axis in the direction of El Arish; Sharon toward the Ktziot-Abu Ageila axis, and Yoffe toward the center of the Jebel Libni-Bir Gafgafa-Bir Lahfan triangle. The Egyptian array of battle in the Rafiah sector was twelve kilometers deep in every direction and included four brigades, a hundred tanks, and a large quantity of artillery. Two infantry brigades held the Rafiah crossroads. A Palestinian division consisting of two brigades was bivouacked in the Gaza Strip to the north. The Egyptians planned this deployment to drive through to El Arish, capital of Sinai, from which they could cut off the entire Gaza Strip. This array was studded with fortifications, mines, tanks, antitank guns, and large concentrations of artillery.

General Tal's division attacked Rafiah with two spearheads: an armored force under the command of Colonel Shmuel and a paratroop force under the command of Colonel Raful, transported on halftracks and reinforced by Patton tanks under the command of Colonel Uri. Operating along with them was an additional armored force commanded by Colonel Man. General Sharon's division was assigned to break through and conquer the large system of fortifications the Egyptians had set up to block the Nitzana-Ismailia axis, the central axis of Sinai. This area had been of great importance in the Sinai campaign of 1956, and since then the Egyptians had reinforced it.

At 1 A.M., after the first day of the conflict, General Rabin was able to announce that in the northern Sinai sector our forces had taken Rafiah, Sheikh Zuweid, and El Arish; and that one column had started down the El Arish-Abu Agheila road. Other forces had taken Khan Yunis and Dir el-Balah and were now fighting on the outskirts of Gaza. In the central sector we had taken the outposts of Auja el-Hafir and Tarat Um Basis, and had penetrated the enemy stronghold of Um Katef. In the southern sector a number of advance outposts in the Kuntilla area had been overcome. Our forces gathered up a large number of prisoners and booty, including artillery and tanks. The enemy had suffered heavy losses, while Israeli casualties were relatively light.

General Tal's division broke through the northern axis to a depth of sixty kilometers and destroyed four infantry brigades, about a hundred tanks, and a large quantity of artillery and mortars. General Sharon's division cracked the fortified stronghold of Abu Ageila, thus commanding the only passage from Nitzana and Ismailia that was passable for armor and vehicles. This was one of the most complex battles fought by our forces in the Six-Day War: a combined operation of armor, infantry, paratroops, and artillery.

General Yoffe's division was assigned to make its way through the Sinai sand dunes to the rear of the Bir Lahfan area. This was completed mainly on the second day. On captured Egyptian maps this area was marked as impassable to armor. The armored brigade commanded by Colonel Issachar traversed fifty kilometers of sand dune to get around to the rear of Bir Lahfan, sixty kilometers south of El Arish, and there the clash with the enemy began. At approximately 11 P.M. a large Egyptian armored force was spotted moving out from Jebel Libni. A tank battle began that lasted thirteen hours, until 10 A.M. the next day. Issachar's brigade defeated a numerically superior enemy force.

On the second day General Tal's division divided in two. In the morning one force set out toward the airfield at El Arish in the south while the second proceeded along the road leading to Kantara on the northern axis.

The fighting continued all night Monday and into Tuesday, June 6. Gaza City fell into our hands and the entire Strip was mopped up. Along the coastal axis our forces advanced westward from El Arish. On the El Arish-Bir Lahfan-Jebel Libni axis tank battles took place. Abu Agheila was captured and our forces continued their victorious drive toward Kusseima and Bir Hasneh. On June 7 Israelis advancing on the northern axis reached a point just west of Romani. On the central axis our army reached the Bir Gafgafa area. To the south the enemy stronghold of Bir Hasneh was captured and our forces reached Bir Tamada and the Mitleh Pass. The entire Kuntilla area was taken. In a combined naval and paratroop operation Sharm el-Sheikh was captured and the Israeli flag was raised. At 6 P.M. on June 7 the Chief of Staff was able to make the following radio announcement to foreign and local correspondents and the entire nation:

> Today we are in a position where the main Egyptian Army in Sinai has been defeated. There are still delaying actions here and there. The enemy is directing all his efforts to getting back across the Suez Canal and our forces are taking care of him. We are now in Romani, near the Mitleh, and in Bir Gafgafa, with the entire area under our forces' control, and the Egyptians are directing their main efforts to reaching the other side of the Suez Canal.

On the night of June 7 and the following day heavy tank battles were still raging west of Bir Gafgafa in the Mitleh area. The enemy also threw the remainder of his aircraft against our armored forces. The backbone of the Egyptian armor had been broken. Six to seven hundred armored vehicles lay in ruins in Sinai. Hundreds of tanks had fallen into our hands, some burned out and others in operating condition. After only four days of fighting the entire Sinai Peninsula, including the Gaza Strip and Sharm el-Sheikh, was in the hands of the Israel Defense Forces. The Egyptian air and land forces had been crushed. On June 8 Nasser agreed to a cease-fire, after having arrogantly announced the previous day that he would reject the UN Security Council's call for a cessation of hostilities.

The fate of Jordan and Syria, which had come to Nasser's aid, was no better. On May 30 King Hussein of Jordan flew to Egypt to sign a military pact placing the Jordanian Army under Egyptian command. The aggressive purpose of their agreement was publicly expressed by Nasser after the signing: "This is the stage of serious action rather than declarations. From now on we work hand in hand with Jordan. This agreement will unite the armed forces of Jordan and Egypt, and thus we will all be on the front lines."

At 11:45 A.M. on June 5 the Jordanian Army began an artillery bombardment of Mount Scopus in the north of Jerusalem and Ramat Rahel in the south, while flat-trajectory weapons of all sorts opened fire from Jordanian positions along the municipal armistice line in Jerusalem. At the same time the Jordanians began bombarding many Israeli settlements along the border. Artillery fire was aimed at Ramat Hakovesh, Mei Ami, Tirat Zvi, and Kibbutz Bohan near the city of Tulkarem. At 12:15 P.M. Jordanian Hunter planes attacked Kfar Yavetz in the central part of the country and at 12:25 the city Netanya was attacked by Jordanian fighters. Kibbutz Eyal was shelled by artillery at the same time. At 12:30 Jordanian planes attacked Kfar Sirkin near Petah Tikva. During this stage the Israelis did not return fire for two hours. Nevertheless the Jordanians continued their artillery barrage and expanded operations along the entire border from Givat Oz in the north to Kibbutz Lahav in the Lahish area. Fire from weapons of all types was also directed at every part of Jerusalem. At 1 P.M. a Jordanian force assaulted what had been the High Commissioner's Palace (Government House) in Jerusalem, located in a no-man's land

and serving as headquarters for the United Nations Truce Supervision Observers. The Israel Defense Forces counterattacked and expelled the Jordanian force.

In the evening (June 5) the Jordanian Army opened fire on many settlements with long-range artillery. This time the targets included Lod Airport, Tel Baruh on the northern outskirts of Tel Aviv, and the city of Netanya. Later Tel Aviv itself was shelled, as was Kibbutz Nir Eliyahu. Finally, an hour and a half after midnight, Kibbutz Tirat Zvi in the Beit Sha'an Valley was bombarded for the second time. Throughout the day and night Jerusalem and Mount Scopus were subjected to bombardment. Among the targets hit by Jordanian artillery fire were hospitals.

As mentioned, there was bitter fighting on June 5 in the Sinai Peninsula and the Gaza Strip, and the Israeli Air Force was compelled to go into action against the Jordanian Air Force as well as against Iraqi planes that had also attacked Israeli targets. On the night of June 5–6 the Air Force Commander, General Hod, was able to report the destruction of twenty Jordanian Hunter jets, seven transport planes and helicopters, as well as an attack on the Iraqi airfield in which six MIG-21s and three Hunters were demolished. Israel's armor and infantry forces captured Kafr Bidu in the south. Meanwhile an Iraqi task force had entered Jordan and was advancing toward the Jericho Valley. Though Israeli planes bombed the Iraqi brigade on Tuesday, June 6, Iraq's newspapers came out with giant headlines: "We have entered Israel. Target Tel Aviv. Our forces have won the day with honor. The enemy flies in panic. Arab armored forces breaking into enemy positions and advancing inside conquered Palestine. Tel Aviv bombarded by mortar fire and razed to the ground. The Egyptian Air Force has liquidated the Zionist strongholds. Eshkol admits defeat."

At the beginning of the Jordanian provocation it was still conceivable that Jordan did not intend to put up a serious fight but was merely trying to demonstrate to Egypt that it was upholding the military pact. But when Jordanian attacks increased, it proved necessary to capture the entire west bank and to liberate the Old City of Jerusalem and the surrounding area. An armored brigade commanded by Col. Uri Ben-Ari on the coastal plain was ordered to advance to the northern part of the Jerusalem corridor, break through in the area of Ma'aleh Hahaimsha, and occupy the mountain ridge between Jerusalem and Ramallah. The terrain through which the brigade advanced was extremely rugged. The Jordanian Legion was dug in on heights which it was difficult for tanks to attack. All Jordanian positions were fortified and equipped with concrete bunkers and all the axis ways to them were mined.

Coming up from the coastal plain, Ben-Ari's armored brigade turned to the left and began an open assault. The tanks fired at point-blank range to silence the bunkers and the brigade's armored infantry proceeded to clear the mined routes of advance. These operations began in the afternoon of June 5 and continued the entire night. At midnight the tanks got past the Jordanian positions. The armor advanced eastward, and Nebi Samuel fell to the brigade. When the Israelis regrouped beside the mountain at dawn, they controlled the crossroads leading to the Old City of Jerusalem, Ramallah, and Jericho.

On the same night a paratroop brigade under Col. Mordekhai Gur burst into the built-up area north of the Old City, which was fortified to an extraordinary degree. This area, the Sheikh Jarah Quarter, the police school, and the American Quarter, lay between the new city of Jerusalem and Mount Scopus, which had remained in our hands even after the War of Independence, and also between Ramallah and the Old City controlled by the Jordanians. During the nineteen years in which they occupied this area the Jordanians had fortified it with exceeding thoroughness by means of concrete-reinforced bunkers hewed out of solid rock, deep communication trenches, and concealed firing positions. As the Israeli paratroop brigade began to enter the area, the Jordanians increased their fire. At 2:20 A.M. on June 6, with the help of tanks, artillery fire, and reconnaissance units, the brigade broke through. Two battalions charged forward, one in the police school sector, the other in the Sheikh Jarah sector to the south.

The breakthrough operation continued until 7 A.M. and was especially fierce. The paratroopers first had to pass through the field of fire of the Jordanian Legion's advanced positions, which were densely packed and kept firing continuously. The capture of the advance posts was followed by four unbroken hours of fighting in trenches and bunkers, from rooftops and cellars. At dawn the tanks were started up again and the third battalion went into action in the southern sector. The mopping-up operations continued until approximately 10 A.M., especially in the area of the American Quarter and the Rockefeller Museum next to the northern wall of the Old City containing the Damascus Gate and Herod's Gate. The paratroop brigade secured a land connection with Mount Scopus.

Parallel with the breakthrough of Ben-Ari's armor, an infantry brigade supported by tanks, a paratroop unit, and a reconnaissance unit captured the enclave of Latrun. This force later participated with the armored brigade in the capture of Ramallah.

On the second day of the fighting—Tuesday, June 6—Mordekhai Gur's paratroopers stood north of the Old City and at the foot of Mount Scopus; Ben-Ari's armored brigade was on the side of the hill facing Givat Shaul (Tel el Ful). At the same time the Israel Defense Forces in northern Israel were proceeding with the conquest of the West Bank of the Jordan.

The battle of the Shomron Hills was conducted by a division of the Northern Command under Gen. Elad Peled, including two armored brigades that broke through in the area of Jenin and continued in the direction of Nablus, and infantry forces advancing toward Nablus from Tulkarem and Kalkiliya.

At the outbreak of the fighting the Northern Command was arrayed for defense on two fronts—the Syrian and the Jordanian. On the opening day of the war it was surprised by the fact that there was practically no enemy activity on the Syrian front, while the Jordanians began a heavy bombardment. At noon the division was ordered to attack on the Jordanian front, with the object of encircling Jenin for an advance toward Nablus, to occupy the Jordanian section of the Um el-Fahem hills within artillery range of the airfield at Ramat David.

The forces went into action and at approximately 5 P.M. (June 5) crossed the Armistice line. An infantry force from the Beit Sha'an Valley headed south in order to make the Jordanians think that an attack was planned on Damya (Adam) Bridge, which would have put the entire northern half of the West Bank in danger of encirclement. This was what prevented the Jordanians from concentrating all their forces against Israel's main thrust in the Jenin sector. Meanwhile the main force of the brigade, commanded by Colonel Moshe, moved in and on its first thrust overran the Jordanian border defense system opposite Moshav Ram-On.

The plan for the conquest of Jenin depended on a deep flanking operation to capture the outposts commanding the city on the west side. The Israeli armored force on the ridge west of Jenin advanced and by 7:30 P.M. had taken the villages of Kfar Dan and El Yimoun on the hills and, continuing to the southeast, captured the village of Bourkin at night and entered the Valley of Dotan. The assault on Jenin from this direction began at 3 A.M. Tuesday. Meanwhile the second armored force advanced and occupied the western end of the Valley of Dotan, opening a second route of advance toward Nablus.

On June 6 we expanded control over key areas of the West Bank. Having completed the destruction of the Egyptian airfields, the Israeli Air Force made itself felt in the battles on the Jordanian front. Our planes attacked the Jordanian artillery positions at Ma'aleh Haadumin which were raining fire on the Jewish part of Jerusalem. Thirty Jordanian Patton tanks that managed to reach the Jerusalem hills from the Jordan Valley engaged Ben-Ari's brigade. Our planes also took part in the battle and, together with the tanks of our brigade, destroyed a number of the enemy tanks. The remainder, fleeing to the east, again fell to our aircraft.

In the morning our armored brigade captured Givat Shaul. Part of this contingent headed south and took Sha'afat, and after an additional battle it captured French Hill. The entire area from the wall of the Old City to Atarot (Kalandia) was in our hands. During the day the regional brigade attacked the Abu Tor neighborhood and took it in house-to-house combat. The fighting was especially fierce, with the enemy putting up a stubborn defense. During the night the paratroopers assaulted the ridge to the east of Jerusalem where two peaks, A-Tor and Augusta Victoria, still remained in enemy hands. With tank support the paratroopers, advancing under the cover of night, waged a fierce shooting battle with the enemy in the Old City and captured part of the built-up area in A-Tor.

Third, Fourth, and Fifth Days, June 7–9

Wednesday, June 7, 1967, will be remembered as one of the great days in Jewish history: the day when the Old City of Jerusalem was liberated and the Temple Mount and Western Wall restored to Jewish hands.

Paratroopers in A-Tor under Mordekhai Gur that day carried out a decisive assault on the eastern ridge in order to complete the encirclement of the Old City. At 8:30 A.M. the Air Force, accompanied by a heavy artillery barrage, attacked Augusta Victoria and at the same time two paratroop battalions charged up the hill, one in the north in the direction of Mount Scopus and another in a frontal attack up the steep western slope. The third battalion advanced south along the wall from the area of the Rockefeller Museum.

In this concentrated assault, carried out with the support of tanks and infantry units equipped with recoilless guns, the entire Augusta Victoria ridge commanding the Old City was captured. The three battalions, the tanks, and the reconnaissance units were immediately diverted to the Lions Gate and the east wall of the Old City. An artillery barrage was leveled at the Moslem Quarter of the Old City near this gate and tanks kept the enemy's firing positions on the wall pinned down. One of the tanks knocked open the door of the Lions Gate with a shell.

The brigade commander quickly burst through the gate on his half-track and, hurrying through the city, turned left and reached the Temple Mount. He was followed by the three brigades that deployed from the Temple Square to mop up the entire Old City.

The first paratroopers reached the Western Wall at 10 A.M. A short time after the brigade commander reached the Temple Square, the leader of the Arab City came up and declared there would be no violent resistance to the Israeli forces. Snipers continued firing for a few more hours but the paratroopers took good care of them. At the same time the Jerusalem Regional Brigade was operating in the southern part of the city. One of the Brigade's forces, attacking from Mount Zion eastward outside the southern wall, mopped up the entire area to the Pool of Shiloah and the Dung Gate. In the afternoon the brigade advanced southward, capturing the Legion positions at Mar Elias and continuing on southward.

The enemy collapsed. Advancing quickly against relatively light resistance, the Brigade conquered Bethlehem, liberated the Gush Etzion area and the city of Hebron, and from there sent out two armored units—one in the direction of Dahariyeh and the other to the area of Samua (Eshtamoah), where on Thursday, June 8, they joined up with the Southern Command forces from Beersheba. On Wednesday, June 7, Ben–Ari's armored brigade completed the conquest of the area between Jerusalem and Nablus. Two battalions, descending to Jericho, reached the Jordan Valley by two different routes. Jericho was taken in a rapid thrust of armored forces that passed back and forth through the city several times, breaking down the enemy's resistance. Following the conquest of the city, the Brigade forces set out to blow up the bridges on the Jordan and to link up with the forces of the Northern Command in the upper part of the Jordan Valley. The third battalion headed north from Ramallah to Nablus through a series of valleys and ravines. At its destination it made contact with Northern Command forces that had taken Nablus.

The northern section of Jordan had been opened on the second day of the fighting, Tuesday, with an assault on Jenin by an armored brigade of Peled's division. Jordanian tank reinforcements arrived, but Peled's Shermans succeeded in knocking out their Pattons. The force gained control of the hills southeast of Jenin. After the capture of the outposts resistance within Jenin itself, first by tanks and artillery and then by the local police, had to be overcome. When the police had been defeated, white flags appeared. Meanwhile, however, a Jordanian Patton battalion had reached the Kabatiyeh crossroads and was advancing on Jenin. The Israeli Air Force was called in and knocked out the enemy tanks.

While the fighting in Jenin and its environs was going on, Peled's division sent an additional armored brigade under Uri to the north of the Shomron Hills. On Wednesday this brigade began a night attack on the Jordanian armored force. It took Toubas without any resistance and continued to the junction of the road leading from Damya Bridge to Nablus. A surprising sight met the eyes of our armored troops. Peace and quiet prevailed in the city. Inhabitants on both sides of the main road were waving gaily at our tank crews. Later it was learned that the Nablunites had been expecting Iraqi troops from the Damya Bridge direction. After a few minutes they realized their mistake, dispersed, and locked themselves in their houses. Sniping began. A force from the Golani Brigade helped nail down control of the city.

Continuing its advance, the armored brigade met a Jordanian armored force assigned to defend Nablus. The encounter occurred at 11:30 A.M. and a tank battle at very close quarters ensued. The Israel Air Force joined in and the Jordanian tanks were reduced. The battle was at an end. The conquest of the West Bank was complete.

The bitter struggle for the Golan Heights began on Friday, June 9, after fighting on the Egyptian and Jordanian fronts had ended. Within one day the Heights were conquered and the ceasefire went into effect on the Syrian front as well

Next to the conquest of the Old City and surrounding areas, this operation was perhaps the most difficult. The terrain presented enormous obstacles. Our forces in the lowlands had to scale a mountain on which the Syrian Army was entrenched in a series of trenches and bunkers. The length of the Heights from the Banyas in the north to Tawafik in the south was sixty kilometers. From a width of fifteen kilometers at the foot of Mount Hermon the Heights widened to a breadth of twenty-five to thirty kilometers in the Boutmiyeh area, and farther south narrowed again, ending in a sharp point where the Yarmuk emptied into the Jordan River. On three sides—east, north, and south—the Golan Heights were practically impregnable. Only from the lowlands of the Galilee in the west, bounded by the Yarmuk in the south and Mount Hermon in the north, was the area at all accessible. This gave the Syrians an inestimable strategic advantage and they had spent the nineteen years since the War of Independence fortifying the Heights.

Though the border with Israel constituted less than 4 percent of Syria's land frontier, all of Syria's military efforts for nearly twenty years had been concentrated on this small sector. Here they had numerous military strongholds occupied permanently, summer and winter. Concrete bunkers were provided for housing, equipment, and ammunition. The bunkers and operational positions were connected by deep narrow trenches and every outpost was surrounded by broad barbed-wire fences and minefields. Three Syrian infantry brigades, each provided with an armored battalion, were permanently maintained here. At the start of the war three more infantry brigades were added. The Syrians also had a "shock force" consisting of two motorized and two armored brigades.

Documents found in Syrian Army headquarters after the victory attested to a plan to invade and conquer the northern part of Israel. They spoke of an invasion force of two divisions, each with an armored spearhead. One division was to have crossed the border in the Jordan Valley and advanced toward Tiberias; the second was to erect a bridgehead on the West Bank in the vicinity of Mishmar Hayarden and overrun the entire eastern Galilee up to the Gush Halav-Safad line on the first day with Haifa as the final objective. Practical preparations for the invasion included the equipment of units in the Mishmar Hayarden area with rubber boats.

When the war actually started, the Syrians had preferred to await the results in the southern and central zones. In the meantime they engaged in warlike activities that, in their view, involved little danger to themselves. Their artillery was directed at Israeli settlements on the border, and especially against Rosh Pina, on the assumption that it was situated on an important strategic crossroads. The Israelis in those settlements were forced to live in bunkers. There were places where settlers had to remain in bunkers for five straight days.

In the first stage of the war, before the Syrian airfields were attacked, Syrian planes struck at several Israeli settlements and airfields in the north. The IDF returned fire with aircraft and artillery. The Israeli artillery was in an inferior position, exposed to the Syrian fire. The exchange of fire continued during the second day of the war as well. Syrian infantry and an armored force of company strength made three attempts to advance in the direction of Tel Dan, and once in the direction of Sh'ar Yashuv. The attackers sustained heavy losses when Israeli tanks and planes went into action against them. An additional attack on Ashmura was also repulsed. Syrian artillery fire and Israeli artillery and aircraft fire continued from Monday, June 5, until Friday, June 9. As it finished its work on other fronts the Israeli Air Force daily stepped up its attacks on airfields in southern Syria.

On Friday morning ground forces of Gen. David Elazar's Northern Command began the assault on the Golan Heights. Starting at 9:40 A.M., the Air Force increased its operations on this front—the only one that remained after Egypt and Jordan had agreed to the cease-fire ordered by the United Nations.

The spearhead of the breakthrough was an armored brigade commanded by Colonel Albert which set out at 11:30 A.M. on June 9 from Giv'at Haem, north of Kfar Szold in upper Galilee. It was preceded by men of the Engineering Corps who cleared mines, and by bulldozers that opened a way for the armored vehicles on the rocky slopes. On reaching its marshaling area at the foot of the Heights, Albert's brigade was subjected to a heavy artillery barrage. The path that had been cleared was very narrow and if any vehicle got stuck it would have obstructed the advance of the entire force. From time to time the Syrian fire was silenced by Israeli warplanes. But despite the bombardment, the forces pressed forward. The tank battalion had crossed the border and attacked the Syrian outpost of Na'amoush. At this position, as at those positions taken later in the breakthrough, no delays were encountered because after the Israeli tank unit had passed, the remaining Syrians stopped fighting, and if they had not managed to escape unarmed, they were taken prisoner.

From Na'amoush, despite heavy losses, the armored force continued to fight its way forward toward the village of Kala. On reaching the outskirts of the village, which was a military garrison, the force was met by and engaged a Syrian armored battalion. Again the Air Force moved in to support the tanks. Meanwhile the Brigade's main force advanced northeast along a parallel axis toward the village of Za'oura, which was taken without particular difficulty. From there it headed for the outposts above Za'oura, the conquest of which took several hours. The topmost positions were captured at 4:30 P.M. From there the force headed south and at nightfall joined the force fighting at Kala. This linkup meant that at the end of the first day's fighting a powerful Israeli armored force was entrenched on the Golan Heights.

While Albert's brigade was pushing ahead, additional IDF forces had broken through in the sectors to the north and south of its route of advance, capturing a series of Syrian outposts. Operating to the north of the armored brigade's route was a force of Golani infantry under the command of Colonel Yonah, assigned to take the Syrian posts in the Za'oura-Kfar Szold-Banias triangle. The post that loomed most menacingly over the northeastern part of the Hula Valley was Tel Aziziat, accessible only from the rear, that is, from the east. The approach was commanded by two other Syrian positions, Burj Banil and over it Tel el-Faher. The offensive therefore began with a battle for Tel el-Faher.

Around 5 P.M. on Friday, June 9, the force set out on half-tracks and then, at the base of the ridge, began the assault on foot. The first attacking force crashed into the southern part of the outpost, after soldiers threw themselves on the mined barbed-wire fences to enable their comrades to get through. The second force entered the northern part of the outpost. In both parts fierce hand-to-hand fighting followed as the Syrians attempted to counterattack and charge out of bunkers. Only after a tough battle was the enemy vanquished and the outpost taken. In the wake of Tel el-Faher all the other Syrian outposts in the sector, including Burj Babil and Tel Aziziat, also fell. The armored brigades now had a strong rear, free of enemy nests of resistance.

Other Israeli forces operated south of Kfar Szold on Friday afternoon. Additional Nahal and Golani units captured the Syrian positions of Ourfiyeh and Mamoun to the north. Here too the Engineering Corps quickly opened a route, which was traversed toward evening by an additional armored brigade under the command of Colonel Uri (the brigade had been transferred north after the conquest of Nablus). The armored force pushed eastward, ascended the terrace at the foot of the Heights, and that evening captured the village of Ravyeh above Kibbutz Gonen.

That day all the Syrian front-line outposts north of Bnot Yacov Bridge were overcome. Paratroopers captured the positions north and south of Darbashiyeh, Jalabina, and the area south of it. Infantry forces mopped up the a-Doufil'yeh area above Kibbutz Shamir and captured the positions of Dardarah and Tel Hilal. At nightfall the armored forces marshaled for another day of fighting. The routes had been cleared of natural obstacles and wrecked vehicles; ammunition, fuel, and supplies came through and all the wounded were evacuated. Serious casualties had been evacuated previously in the thick of battle by helicopters that landed right on the firing lines.

Sixth Day, June 10 ★ The Cessation of Hostilities

On the morning of Saturday, June 10, the Israeli forces began the second phase of the attack on the Golan Heights, again with aerial support. After a few hours of fighting the Syrian defense collapsed completely. That morning another armored force under the command of Colonel Moshe went into action on the northern front. It attacked the positions of El Hamra and helped Golani capture the Banias, then headed west along the border. Together with a reconnaissance unit the armor captured Nuhcileh and Abasiyeh in the north, returned to the Banias, ascended to Ein Fouh and Za'ourah and pushed on to capture Masadeh. Other armored contingents set out for less difficult terrain, with gentler slopes and a network of roads, in which Syrian resistance was already subsiding.

The conflict in this area quickly turned into a rout. Before abandoning their gun emplacements, the Syrian troops blew up ammunition dumps. They fled eastward by vehicle and on foot. In most places they did not even take the trouble to destroy their weapons, ammunition, and secret documents. Albert's armored brigade set out from Kala, and a short time later captured Mansour, in the east, on the way to Kuneitra. It was hardly able to engage the fleeing enemy: tanks fired upon proved to be empty, having been deserted by their crews without a fight. The brigade reached the entrance to Kuneitra practically without interference. In Kuneitra itself there was a tremendous amount of booty. Tanks had been abandoned with engines still running and their radios on.

Kuneitra was taken at 2 P.M. without a fight. A short while later a Golani unit arrived and took charge of the town. Part of the force sent on to take control of the northern sector of the front ascended Mount Hermon by helicopter and unfurled the Israeli flag on its southern peak. Uri's armor began its second day of fighting on the Golan Heights in the Ravyeh-Kanaba area, where it had to overcome a Syrian force that put up a hard fight. From there it proceeded south to Kfar Nafeh on the Bnot Yacov Bridge-Kuneitra road.

The leading unit reached Kfar Nafeh at 2:30 P.M. and continued on to Kuneitra, which the brigade's reconnaissance unit reached at 4 P.M.

From Kuneitra the armed forces headed south in the direction of the Boutmiyeh crossroads. At the same time an additional armored force crossed the border in the Darbashiyeh area, hitting the Oil Road (from Iraq). This force headed south, crossing the Bnot Yacov Bridge-Kuneitra road to the south of Kfar Nafeh; continuing along the Oil Road, it also arrived at the Boutmiyeh crossroads. At the same time paratroop and infantry forces, setting out from Jalabina in the south, took control of the Customs House area above the Bnot Yacov Bridge. The infantry gained control of the area extending from the upper Customs House to the vicinity of Kfar Nafeh.

When the breakthrough had begun in the northern part of the Syrian front on Friday the division under General Peled, which included paratroop, infantry, and armored forces, was arrayed in the southern section. This division attacked on the northern front on Saturday at noon, when the Syrian Army was already in flight. When the division opened its attack, it was not yet clear whether the Syrian collapse included the northern sector as well. There the Syrians had been entrenched on a fortified ridge stretching from Tawafik through Kfar Hareb to El Al and further to the north. The ridge commanded the entire surrounding area and access to it was especially difficult.

Peled's attack opened with air support, followed by artillery support. The air strike, which began at 12:45 P.M. and continued for one hour, concentrated mainly on the Syrian positions at Tawafik. The paratroop and tank forces moved in for the attack at 2 P.M. Despite the steep slope the tanks managed to negotiate a path and the paratroopers scrambled after them. At 3:30 the paratroop and tank force took control of upper Tawafik, which was found to be devoid of enemy forces. It became clear that the headlong flight had encompassed the southern sector as well. Still it was not yet known whether the villages and positions in the interior had been abandoned, and a rapid advance was called for. The commander of the helicopter unit who went ahead to examine the situation gained the impression that the Syrians had given up the entire Golan Heights and so a paratroop force was immediately transported by helicopter to the area of Hareb, above Ein Gev, and took it at 4 P.M. An additional helicopter jump brought them to the village of El Al, farther to the east, which was taken as well.

While the division's main force was advancing along the Tawafik-Boutmiyeh axis infantry forces mopped up the area northeast of Lake Kinneret. Another infantry group headed east from the Almagor area, crossed the Jordan, the position at the estuary, the position of Beit Habak, and the area of Hill 62 above the valley of Batiheh. A second force headed north from Ein Gev and mopped up all the Syrian positions along the shores of the Kinneret. Meanwile the division completed its advance to the Boutmiyeh crossroads, and the circle was complete.

When the cease-fire on the Syrian Front went into effect at 6 P.M. the Israel Defense Forces controlled the entire Golan Heights up to the line extending from the western peak of Mount Hermon south through Masadeh, Kuneitra, and the Boutmiyeh crossroads, then descending to the Yarmuk River. It was along this line that the cease-fire was established.

With the agreement for a cease-fire by Israel and Syria on Saturday, the Six-Day War came to an end. Israel's losses in this war were 803 killed (777 soldiers and 26 civilians);

3006 injured (2811 soldiers and 195 civilians), or a total of 3809 casualties. Enemy losses were: Egypt, 11,500 dead (10,000 enlisted men, 1500 officers) and another 5000 taken prisoner; Syria, 2950 (450 dead and 7500 injured, all of them soldiers); Jordan, 6094 dead and missing, according to the Jordanian Prime Minister on July 5, 1967.

Losses in material: Egypt, 338 aircraft and about 700 tanks; Syria, 61 aircraft and 130 tanks; Jordan, 29 aircraft and 170 tanks; Iraq, 23 aircraft.

On the day the war ended the Soviet Union broke diplomatic relations with Israel, duly followed within a few days by Czechoslovakia, Poland, Bulgaria, Yugoslavia, and Hungary.

Section 3. After the War

Nasser's Reaction to Defeat ★ *The Fate of Jerusalem and the Surrounding Area*

As long as the fighting continued in Sinai the Egyptian radio and newspapers proclaimed impressive victories: Tel Aviv in flames, the Israeli Air Force destroyed, Haifa and the cities of the Galilee in ruins, and so on. It was impossible to maintain these fairy tales after the Egyptian Army had been crushed and the entire Sinai Peninsula, the Gaza Strip, and Sharm el-Sheikh were in the hands of the Israel Defense Forces. On June 7 Nasser was still declaring that he would reject the UN demand for cessation of hostilities. On June 8 he agreed to the cease-fire.

Nasser was one of those rare artists who can change history by word of mouth. The day after the cease-fire he addressed his nation on radio, extolling the valor of the Egyptian Army and people. If they had suffered a grave defeat in the past few days, it was only because American and British airplanes had assisted the enemy's war effort. It was just a case of villainous imperialist collusion—the brave Arab forces had been confronted by an enemy three times as large as those of Israel alone. The same thing, he explained, had happened to the forces of the Jordanian Arab Legion, which waged a valiant struggle under the leadership of King Hussein. He went on to say:

> My heart was bleeding as I followed the battles of the heroic Arab Army in Jerusalem and other parts of the West Bank on the night when the enemy and his plotting allies massed no less than four hundred aircraft over the Jordanian front. The Algerian people, under their great leader, Boumédienne, gave without reservation and without stinting for the battle. The people of Iraq and their faithful leader, Abad ar-Rahman Aref, gave without reservation or stinting for the conflict. The Syrian Army fought heroically, consolidated by the forces of the great Syrian people under the leadership of their national government. The peoples and governments of Sudan, Kuwait, Yemen, Lebanon, Tunisia, and Morocco adopted honorable stands. All the peoples of the Arab nation without exception throughout the Arab homeland adopted a stand of manhood and dignity, a stand of resolution and determination.
>
> There were also great nations outside the Arab homeland who gave us invaluable

moral support, but the plot, and we must say this with the courage of men, was bigger and fiercer. The enemy's main concentration was on the Egyptian front, which he attacked with all his main force of armored vehicles and infantry, supported by air supremacy the dimensions of which I have outlined for you. Our armed forces in Sinai were obliged to evacuate the first line of defense. They fought fearful tank and air battles on the second line of the defense. We then responded to the cease-fire resolution, in view of assurances contained in the latest Soviet draft resolutions of the Security Council, as well as French statements to the effect that no one must reap any territorial expansion from the recent aggression, and in view of world public opinion, especially in Asia and Africa, which appreciates our position and feels the ugliness of the forces of international domination which pounced on us.

We must learn the lesson of this setback. In this connection there are three vital facts. (1) The elimination of imperialism in the Arab world will leave Israel with its own intrinsic power; but whatever the circumstances, however long it may take, the intrinsic Arab power is greater and more effective. (2) Redirecting Arab interests in the service of Arab rights is an essential safeguard—the American Sixth Fleet moved with Arab oil, and there are Arab bases, placed forcibly and against the will of the peoples, in the service of aggression. (3) The situation now demands a united word from the entire Arab nation; this, in the present circumstances, is an irreplaceable guarantee.

Now we come to an important point in this heart-searching by asking ourselves: Does this mean that we do not bear responsibility for the consequences of the setback? I tell you truthfully and despite any factors on which I might have based my attitude during the crisis, that I am ready to bear the whole responsibility. I have taken a decision in which I want you all to help me. I have decided to give up completely and finally every official post and every political role and return to the ranks of the masses and do my duty with them like every other citizen.

The forces of imperialism imagine that their enemy is Gamal Abdel Nasser. I want it to be clear to them that their enemy is the entire Arab nation, not just Gamal Abdel Nasser. The forces hostile to the Arab national movement try to portray this movement as an empire of Nasser. This is not true, because the aspiration for Arab unity began before Nasser and will remain after Nasser. I always used to tell you that the nation remains, and that the individual—whatever his role and however great his contribution to the cause of his homeland—is only a tool of the popular will, not its creator.

In accordance with Article 110 of the Provisional Constitution promulgated in March 1964 I have entrusted my colleague, friend, and brother, Zakariya Mohieddin, with taking over the post of President and carrying out the constitutional provisions on this point. After this decision, I place all I have at his disposal in dealing with the grave time through which our people are passing. In doing this, I am not liquidating the revolution—indeed, the revolution is not the monopoly of one generation of revolutionaries. I take pride in the brothers of this generation of revolutionaries.

The sacrifices made by our people and their flaming spirit during the crisis and the glorious pages of heroism written by the officers and soldiers of our armed forces with their blood will remain an unquenchable torch in our history and a great inspiration for the future and its great hopes. The people were splendid as usual, noble as their nature, believing, sincere, and loyal. The members of our armed forces were an honorable example of Arab man in every age and every place. They defended the grains of sand in the desert to the last drop of their blood. In the air they provided, despite enemy supremacy, legends of dedication and sacrifice, of courage and willingness to perform the duty in the best way.

All my heart is with you, and I want all your hearts to be with me. May God be with us all, a hope in our hearts. Peace and the blessing of God be with you.

The last words were uttered in a choked voice.

Before offering to resign, on June 9 and 10, Nasser took care to organize mass demonstrations demanding that he remain in office. After feeding his nation the fairy tale of a "military umbrella of imperialist states," the fairy tale that the United States and Britain had supported Israel, he could undertake full responsibility for the defeat. Every Egyptian would understand that their Army was no match against such mighty empires. The demonstrations came off as planned and Nasser, of course, remained in the saddle, notwithstanding the "finality" of his resignation.

At the end of the Six-Day War, Israel controlled all of the western part of the Land of Israel, including the Gaza Strip, the West Bank (Shomron and Yehuda), the Golan Heights east of the Jordan, and the Sinai Peninsula. In the Government differences of opinion developed with regard to the conquered areas. Some Ministers demanded annexation of all the occupied territories. Others opposed any annexation. A few proposed the creation of an independant state on the West Bank and the maintenance of a Jewish garrison on the west side of the Jordan River. The Government as a whole refrained from taking a stand on the issue, except with respect to East Jerusalem. At a meeting on June 15 the Cabinet decided to annex East Jerusalem and the surrounding area—Mount Scopus, the Mount of Olives, Sheikh Jarah, Sur Baher, Sha'afat, and the airport at Atarot (Kalandia). The Knesset confirmed this decision on June 27.

At the United Nations Security Council the Soviet Government proposed that Israel be branded an "aggressor" and that an immediate and unconditional withdrawal from all the territories occupied in the war, East Jerusalem and the surrounding area included, be ordered. On June 14, 1967, the Security Council rejected this proposal and adopted a resolution calling on Israel to ensure the safety and well-being of the inhabitants of the areas in which military operations took place and to help to return to their homes the people who had fled during the fighting. It also called on the governments concerned to respect scrupulously the humane principles governing treatment of prisoners of war and the protection of the civil population in time of war. Not satisfied with this resolution, the Soviet Union initiated an emergency session of the United Nations General Assembly.

The Assembly convened on June 17. Again the Soviet delegation offered a resolution denouncing the "aggressive acts of Israel," and demanding immediate and unconditional withdrawal of its forces from all the occupied territories and compensation to all the Arab states. The resolution was defeated. The Assembly also rejected a milder version by India'and Yugoslavia calling for evacuation of the occupied territories. However, by a vote of ninety-nine to zero with eighteen abstentions the Assembly passed a resolution calling on Israel to abstain from making any change in the status of Jerusalem. We had reason to expect that this resolution would suffer the same fate as that which had called for the internationalization of Jerusalem nineteen years earlier, provided the Israeli Government and people quickly ensured a large Jewish population not only in the Old City but in the surrounding areas as well.

At the end of July, the Government having failed to take any step in this direction—though the Prime Minister had been assigned to deal with the problem of the Old City of Jerusalem and the surrounding areas—David Ben-Gurion made this statement in the Knesset:

Seven weeks have passed since the wonderful victory of the IDF, a victory without equal in Jewish history and perhaps in world history. There is no doubt that the most important and dearest of all the territories which the valor of the IDF has restored to our control is the Old City of Jerusalem and its surrounding area, to which the eyes of the entire world and especially world Jewry are turned. The Knesset member addressing you esteems the valor and victory of the IDF in this area no less than any Jew in Israel or throughout the world; but as a Jew who believes in the world tradition of his people, he cannot feel that mere military control deriving from a justified victory that was longed for through the centuries can alone change the face of reality.

When after the renewal of the State of Israel twenty years ago the IDF took control of cities in our land whose inhabitants were non-Jews—Moslems, Druze, and Christians— in no place were the inhabitants harmed. Not one of the inhabitants of these towns and villages was expelled, evicted, or taken captive. The Arab refugees who take up so much world attention left the country during the Mandate period on the instructions of the Arab High Command in those days which promised them that as soon as the Arab armies invaded the projected State of Israel, they would regain not only their homes and property but that of the Jews as well and that the Jews themselves would be thrown into the sea.

Since the creation of the State of Israel not one person, Arab or Druze, Moslem or Christian, has been expelled. Yet when the Arab Legion overcame the small Jewish community in the Old City, not a single Jew was allowed to remain, the synagogues were destroyed and razed, all the men were taken captive and those women and children who remained alive were driven out to the western side of the city. Even the promise embodied in the Armistice Agreement with Jordan—to permit every Jew free access to the Holy Places in Jerusalem and the surrounding area—has been violated all this time. The Jewish community was permitted no access to its Holy Places, which preceded in time all the places holy to Christians and Moslems and even these religions themselves. No Jew was allowed to approach the Western Wall or any other place in the Old City until the IDF redeemed it and opened wide its gates to all Jews or non-Jews who thirsted to set eyes on the Eternal City of King David.

The IDF redeemed the Old City and opened its gates but did not alter its reality and human environment, nor was that the function or duty of the IDF. *Military victory alone does not change a living reality.* There is only one way to ensure for all eternity the Jewishness and Israeliness of Jerusalem and the surrounding area to the foot of Mount Scopus in the east, to beyond the airfield at Atarot in the north, and to Rahel's Tomb in the south—and not by the removal of non-Jews from this area, not a single one. On the contrary, all that is and will be required of us is to improve the economic and social conditions of the present inhabitants. But as soon as possible we must also settle, rebuild, and populate the Jewish Quarter in the Old City that was destroyed by the Arabs twenty years ago and all the empty and unpopulated areas to the east, north, and south of the city, with thousands and tens of thousands of Jewish families from the New City and from other parts of Israel and with Jewish volunteers from the Diaspora.

Only such an irrevocable fact of renewal and completion will provide final and unquestionable permanence to the redeeming work of our glorious Army in the Six-Day War and put a stop to the debate going on in the UN since November 29, 1947, on the character, image, and regime of Jerusalem, capital of the Eternal People from the time of King David and to the end of time, if there will be such an end. The beginning of this work, to which we must devote all our capacity and efforts, should be the renewal of the university opened on Mount Scopus forty-two years ago in the presence of Dr. Weizmann and the author of the Balfour Declaration. I do not propose moving the entire university from west to east Jerusalem, but in the very near future at least half of its faculties should be transferred to Mount Scopus. Not only must the teachers, students, and facilities be transferred, but housing quarters for students and professors must be erected in order to obviate the necessity of daily commuting from west to east. In the vicinity of Mount Scopus there are empty areas, both State and privately owned.

We must not content ourselves merely with renewal of the university on Mount Scopus. We must enlarge the airport at Atarot to enable it to handle the largest, fastest, and most modern aircraft, so that pilgrims, immigrants, and tourists will be able to come from all parts of the world straight to the Eternal Capital of Israel. Nor is that all. We must plan, design, and erect Jewish settlements to the north, east, and south of Jerusalem—naturally only on empty land without prejudicing present inhabitants one iota.

Outside the Jewish Quarter of the Old City, Jewish settlements will be created which will live by industry and crafts, transportation and commerce, and as far as possible, agriculture as well. Not only many of the present inhabitants of Israel but large numbers of Jews from the lands of prosperity—people with capital, initiative, vision, resourcefulness, wisdom, and know-how—will come to settle in the environs of east Jerusalem without displacing the present inhabitants, Arabs or others. On the contrary, nothing will so raise the economic and cultural level of the local Arab and other inhabitants as a modern Jewish community with a high level of culture and creative enterprise.

Only such settlement work within and around the Old City will restore Jerusalem for all eternity to the nation that created eternal value in it and made the city the joy of the world, even its ruins and poverty. We can enhance its reputation and honor by making it blossom as one of the greatest and most important spiritual and scientific centers in a world that is renewing and uplifting itself. Maybe in our day the prophecy will come true that "out of Zion shall go forth the law and the word of the Lord from Jerusalem."

Since then more than a year passed but the Prime Minister, entrusted by the Cabinet with the building of Jerusalem and the surrounding areas, did nothing to secure and buttress the redeeming work of the Israel Defense Forces, the best of whose soldiers and commanders had laid down their lives in the Six-Day War. This has been the most unfortunate failing of the year that followed the Six-Day War.

Arab Violations of the Cease-Fire ★ The Prime Minister Visits the United States and Confers with President Johnson

On the third day of the Six-Day War, June 7, 1967, the UN Security Council voted unanimously to order a cease-fire between the Israeli and Arab forces. The cease-fire with Jordan went into effect at 10 P.M. that day. Only on the evening of July 8 did Egypt agree to a cessation of hostilities, and in Syria the cease-fire went into effect at 6 P.M. on June 10, the last day of the struggle. None of these states, alas, observed its commitment.

The first to violate the cease-fire—not counting the Al Fatah marauders who practically never stopped attacking Israel—was Syria. On June 18 Syrian troops in armored personnel carriers tried to approach Israeli positions at points north of Kuneitra which had been agreed upon with the UN and opened fire. Israeli forces put them to flight.

Egyptian violations of the cease-fire began on July 1. An Egyptian force of company strength penetrated at a point fifteen kilometers south of Port Said and opened fire with mortars on the Israeli forces. Five Jewish soldiers were wounded. The Egyptian force was expelled. The next day the Egyptian Army opened fire with mortars from their side of the Suez Canal. This fire was also silenced. From then on there was hardly a day when the Egyptians did not attack us. On July 4, 1967, they opened fire with artillery and continued to do so daily. On July 8 they also called aircraft into play. A MIG-21 was shot down by the Israeli forces south of Port Said. On July 11, 1967, two Egyptian Sukhoi jets penetrated Sinai airspace. An Israeli antiaircraft unit responded: one Sukhoi was shot down and the other fled back across the canal.

On July 14 and 15 the Egyptians initiated heavy exchanges of fire along the entire canal. Eight Israeli soldiers were killed and forty injured. On July 15 Israel's planes attacked the Egyptian positions and shot down six of their planes. One Israeli plane was hit but the pilot bailed out safely and was rescued by our forces. A mass exodus ensued from the Egyptian settlements on their side of the canal. At the end of July the UN representative in charge of cease-fire affairs, Gen. Odd Bull, proposed that both Israel and Egypt agree to refrain from navigation in the Suez Canal for one month. Two weeks earlier, on July 14, the Minister of Defense, Gen. Moshe Dayan, had advised him that Israel insisted on mutuality in this matter: either both sides would refrain from navigation in the canal or both would sail at will. Egypt agreed to Odd Bull's proposal on August 3, and on August 27 the agreement to refrain from navigation was extended indefinitely. The other forms of Egyptian aggression, however, did not cease.

On October 21, 1967, the Israeli destroyer *Eilat* was on a routine patrol along the Sinai coast opposite the area under IDF control. In the afternoon it reported that it was under attack by Egyptian forces and had been hit. At 5:30 a green rocket was fired at Port Said and immediately thereafter a heavy missile was spotted homing on the ship. An attempt was made to shoot it down but without success. The missile hit the ship in the vicinity of the boilers. A minute or two later a second missile hit the engine room. Fire broke out. The crew calmly got the destroyer under control, but as it was no longer able to sail, the ship cast anchor. Two hours later it was hit by an additional missile and began sinking. The Israel Air Force and Navy carried out extensive rescue operations throughout the night. The crew numbered 199 officers and men. Losses were 47 killed and missing and 46 injured.

On October 25 Israeli artillery hit the two large refineries in the city of Suez that supplied 80 percent of Egypt's fuel. The fuel dump and petrochemical complex there were also hit. Two days later, following a debate on complaints lodged by both Israel and Egypt, the UN Security Council passed a resolution condemning all violations of the cease-fire in the Middle East and demanding that the member states concerned cooperate fully and promptly with the UN. Nevertheless Egypt, Syria, and Jordan persisted in their violations of the cease-fire, and the sabotage gangs stepped up their activities.

From June 10, 1967, to June 10, 1968 (apart from the *Eilat* casualties) Israel suffered 663 casualties, of whom 137 were killed and 526 injured. In Israel itself there were 33 casualties: 21 in Yehuda and Shomron; 18 in Syria; 85 in the Beit Sha'an Valley; 223 in the Jordan Valley; 50 in the Arava; 48 in the Gaza Strip and northern Sinai; and 85 in Egypt. During the same year the Arab saboteurs suffered 447 casualties: 399 killed and 48 injured; 7 in Israel; 46 in Yehuda and Shomron; 6 in Syria; 15 in the Beit Sha'an Valley; 296 in the Jordan Valley; 72 in the Arava; 5 in Gaza and northern Sinai. A total of

1643 saboteurs were arrested; by the end of the year 750 had been released. In an operation in the Karameh on March 21, 1968, over 200 saboteurs were killed; 40 Jordan Legionaires perished and 30 Jordanian tanks were destroyed; 120 saboteurs were arrested, and at this writing are still being detained. The IDF casualties in that battle were 28 killed and 69 injured.

Gen Chaim Barlev was appointed Chief of Staff on January 21, 1968, in place of General Rabin, who became Israel's Ambassador in Washington.

At the beginning of January 1968 Prime Minister Eshkol visited President Lyndon B. Johnson at the LBJ Ranch in Texas. In a joint communiqué they expressed mutual esteem, friendship, and a desire to increase cooperation. It stressed that the President of the United States would "keep Israel's military defense capability under active and sympathetic examination and review in the light of all relevant factors, including the shipment of military equipment by others to the area." From the United States the Prime Minister flew to Canada, then to Britain, where he met and conferred with the governments of these countries.

By the end of January the exchange of prisoners with Egypt had been completed. Within three weeks Israel returned 4481 prisoners (including 493 officers) in exchange for 8 Israelis: 6 Navy men and 2 pilots.

Immediately after that Egypt began work at the southern part of the canal on the extrication of fifteen foreign ships that had been trapped when Egypt blocked up the canal on June 6, 1967. This work was suspended on January 30 after an artillery duel that resulted from an Egyptian attempt to sail ships north of Ismailia in open violation of the agreement arrived at between Israel and Egypt through U Thant's representative in matters of the cease-fire.

President de Gaulle Blames Israel for the War ★ Ben-Gurion Responds in a Private Letter

At a press conference on November 27, 1967, President Charles de Gaulle spoke at some length about the Jewish people, Israel, and the Six-Day War, making accusations that agitated and distressed world Jewry. This is what he said:

> The establishment between the two World Wars—for we must go back that far—of a Zionist Home in Palestine and subsequently, after World War Two, the establishment of the State of Israel aroused many fears at the time. And many people, among them even many Jews, wondered whether the implantation of this community on land obtained on more or less justifiable conditions and in the midst of fundamentally hostile Arab nations would not arouse incessant and endless frictions and conflicts. Some even feared that the Jews, hitherto dispersed, who had remained what they always were—that is, an elite people, self-assured and domineering—would after assembling in the place of their ancient greatness transform into burning and conquering ambition the moving hopes that they had expressed for nineteen centuries: "Next year in Jerusalem."
>
> Despite the ebb and flow of misunderstandings that they gave rise to in various countries

at different times, the Israelis were the object of a considerable amount of interest and even of sympathy, especially in the Christian world. This sympathy derived from the splendid memorial of the Scriptures and from all the founts of a wonderful liturgy and even more from the compassion aroused by their ancient tragedies that achieved poetic expression amongst us in the legend of the Wandering Jew—a sympathy that was further increased as a result of the criminal persecutions that were their lot during the Second World War and subsequently, since their return to Palestine, by their constructive accomplishments and the valor of their soldiers.

For this reason, and unrelated to the vast help in money, influence, and propaganda that Israel has received from Jewish circles in America and Europe, many countries, France among them, viewed with satisfaction the establishment of their State in the area permitted them by the Great Powers, and also hoped that by showing a little modesty the Israelis would arrive at a modus vivendi with their neighbors. It must be noted that since 1956 these psychological facts have changed. The Franco-British operation at Suez revealed to the world a warlike Israel bent on expansion, and the action taken by it thereafter to double its population by the absorption of new elements gave reason to believe that the territory it had acquired would not suffice for long, that it would be bent on enlarging it and using any opportunity that arose. That is why the Fifth Republic disengaged itself from the special and very close bonds that the previous regime had forged.

On the other hand, the Fifth Republic endeavored to encourage the easing of tension in the Middle East. We maintained friendly relations with the Israeli Government and even provided it for possible defense needs with the arms it wished to buy. At the same time we counseled moderation, especially with reference to the disputes over the waters of the Jordan and the incidents that occurred from time to time between the armed forces of the two sides. Similarly, we did not give our consent to Israel's permanent settlement in one of the quarters of Jerusalem over which it had gained control, and we kept our Embassy in Tel Aviv. After putting an end to the Algerian affair, we restored the same policy of friendship and cooperation with the Arab peoples of the Orient that France has pursued for centuries in that part of the world and that today, for logical and emotional reasons, must be one of the cornerstones of our foreign policy. It goes without saying that we did not conceal from the Arabs that we considered the State of Israel an established fact and would not agree to its destruction. On this basis we expected that the day would come when our country would be able to assist directly in the achievement of a lasting peace in the Middle East, providing no new drama erupted to tear it to shreds.

But alas this drama occurred. It was prepared by the very grave and constant tension resulting from the scandalous fate of the refugees in Jordan, as well as threats of destruction directed against Israel. On May 22 the [Gulf of Aqaba] affair annoyingly created by Egypt offered a pretext to those who were eager for a fight. In order to preclude hostilities, France as early as May 24 [1967] proposed to the other three Great Powers jointly to enjoin both sides from opening fire. On June 2 the French Government announced officially that it would place the blame on whoever began armed action, and repeated this with the utmost clarity to all the Arab states.

I myself stated this to the Israeli Foreign Minister, Mr. Abba Eban, when I met him in Paris on May 24. "If Israel is attacked," I told him, "we will not permit her to be destroyed; but if you attack, we will denounce your initiative. Despite the numerical inferiority of your population I have no doubt that in the event of war you will gain military achievements, as you are much better organized, more united, and better armed that the Arabs. Afterward, however, you will be stuck in one place, and in ever increasing difficulty, since war in the Middle East will necessarily result in a regrettable increase of tension the world over and result in unfortunate consequences for many countries. In the final account all these un-pleasantnesses will be attributed to you, who will have become conquerors."

Yet the voice of France went unheeded, Israel attacked, and in six days of fighting achieved its intended objectives. In the areas it seized it is presently organizing a regime of conquest that is bound to be accompanied by oppression, repression, and expulsion; and a resistance movement is being organized that Israel, on its part, terms terrorism. It is true that the belligerent parties are at the moment observing in a more or less regular fashion the cease-fire ordered by the United Nations. However, it is obvious that the conflict has been suspended only temporarily and that the only solution can be through international action.

Unless the United Nations buries its own Charter, such a settlement must be based on evacuation of territory seized by force, the end of belligerence, and recognition of all states involved by all others. Afterward it will almost certainly be possible by United Nations decision and by means of its troops to establish the exact demarcation of the borders and the conditions of life and security on both sides, the future of the refugees and minorities, and a system of freedom of navigation of shipping to all flags in the Gulf of Aqaba and the Suez Canal. For any settlement, especially that mentioned above, to be brought about—and to it, in France's opinion, should be added the internationalization of Jerusalem—for such a settlement to be achieved requires the agreement of the Great Powers; this will have the effect of strengthening the settlement of the United Nations.

If such a settlement is put into effect, France is prepared to provide political, military, and economic aid to ensure that it is effectively enforced. But one cannot see how any agreement could emerge until one of the biggest of the "Big Four" has disengaged from an odious war that it wages elsewhere, for everything is today part of a whole. Without the Vietnam drama, the conflict between Israel and the Arabs would not have become what it is. And if peace were restored to Southeast Asia, the Middle East would soon regain it as well, thanks to the general relaxation that would follow.

From his home in Sde Boker, on December 6, 1967, David Ben-Gurion wrote to the French President:

My dear General:

This is the third time I have taken the initiative in writing to you and I am doing so because at the conclusion of our conversation on June 17, 1960, you said you would be happy if we maintained direct contact and urged me to write to you directly whenever I wished. I would not have dared to bother you now if not for our meeting during the funeral of Dr. Adenauer in Bonn, when we held a warm and friendly conversation at your behest, although you were aware that I was only a private citizen. What has caused me deep concern is the speech in which you devoted much space to the State of Israel, Zionism, and the Jewish people. This speech contained a number of regrettable and worrisome statements.

As one of your admirers even before we met in person, my respect for you arose not only because of your friendship and help for Israel over many years but because of your great historic acts during and after World War Two to save the honor and standing of France, to which, I feel, all nations owe thanks for its contribution to the social and cultural progress of humanity from the time of the French Revolution at the end of the eighteenth century to the present. I take exception to the unjust criticism of you by many people in France, Israel, and other countries. I believe they did not study your words closely enough.

I do not consider that I have the right to argue with your views on French policies toward other peoples, including Israel, if you do not ask me to do so. But I am aware that there are many people in the Christian world who know and understand but little of the Jewish experience, because of its uniqueness in human history in the days of antiquity, in the Middle Ages, and in modern times. Because of my honor and respect for you I find myself morally obliged to you, to my people, and to the French nation that helped us so much in recent times, both before and after the renewal of the Jewish State, to explain the true intentions and practical actions of the Jewish State, as one who was its Prime Minister and Minister of Defense for fifteen years, since the day of its creation, and had no small part in shaping its foreign and defense policies; and who for fifteen years before that, as the head of the Zionist Federation Executive in Jerusalem, played an active and often decisive role in shaping Zionist policy that led up to its creation.

In ancient times we were the first people in the world to hold to the faith of one God, something that to other nations (with the exception of a few individuals) was inconceivable and undesirable, and we suffered thereby. The Greeks said we were a "godless people" because they did not find statues of gods in our towns. The Romans accused us of being idle, because we did not work on one day of the week. I do not need to tell you what many Christians said of us after Christianity became the dominant faith in the Roman Empire, and the Jews refused to adhere to this religion that derived from the Jewish people in the Land of Israel.

Twice our independence was destroyed in our Homeland. Jerusalem was razed by the triumphant Romans, and its name was wiped out for some time. But our forefathers who were exiled to Babylon twenty-five hundred years ago sat beside the Rivers of Babylon and mourned the Memory of Zion (Psalms, 137) and took an oath: "If I forget thee, O Jerusalem, may my right hand forget its cunning. If I do not remember thee, let my tongue cleave to the roof of my mouth, if I do not set Jerusalem above my highest joy!" And they have been faithful to this oath until the present day. This took place before Paris, London, or Moscow even existed.

You know no less than I that many nations adopted the Christian (and later the Moslem) faith under compulsion. Attempts were made to compel us as well, and there were Jews who could not or dared not withstand the threat of death. Yet our nation as a whole chose to suffer martyrdom for its faith, and you doubtless know what happened to us in the fifteenth century in Spain, and not there alone.

I know of no other people that was exiled from its land, dispersed among the nations of the world, so hated, persecuted, expelled, and slaughtered (in your days and mine alone 6 million Jews were destroyed by the Nazis), yet did not vanish from history, did not despair nor assimilate (although many did), but yearned incessantly to return to its land, and believed in its messianic deliverance for two thousand years; and indeed did return to its land in our day and renewed its independence. And I know that there never was a people in this land— called always in Hebrew the Land of Israel—that was so entirely identified all of its life with this land. Although there were many conquerors (Egyptians, Assyrians, Babylonians, Persians, Greeks, Romans, Arabs, Seljuks, Crusaders, Mamelukes, Ottomans, and British) this country was never the one and only homeland to any people other than the Jews.

I am aware that there is no other case in human history of a people returning to its land after eighteen hundred years. This is a unique fact, but one that operated in every generation, for there was no generation when the Jews did not try (although not all of them succeeded) to return to their Homeland. A second fact is that the Christian world and the League of Nations, which was composed almost entirely of Christian peoples, recognized the historic link between the People of Israel and the Land of Israel and endorsed the Balfour Declaration.

We have the records of the British Royal Commission headed by Lord Peel that in

1936 was assigned to study what had been done and remained to be done in Palestine. After examining the relevant records, the Commission wrote: "It is clear to us that by the words 'Establishment of a National Home in Palestine' H.M.G. recognized that in the course of time a Jewish State was likely to be established, but it was not in their power to say when it would happen." And Palestine included all the western part of the Land of Israel and all the east of the Jordan, for this was the Jewish Land during the time of Joshua Bin-Nun. It was only in 1922 that Winston Churchill, then Colonial Secretary, removed Trans-Jordan from the Land of Israel that was to become a "National Home" for the Jewish people.

There is a widespread belief that the calamity wrought by the Nazis in World War Two—the murder of 6 million Jews in Europe—brought the civilized world (including Russia, for in the UN General Assembly debate in May 1947 the first to demand the creation of a Jewish State in Palestine was Soviet Representative Gromyko) to vote for the establishment of a Jewish State. There can be no greater mistake. The destruction of 6 million Jews in Europe was the most dreadful blow to the Jewish State, the creation of which was begun by European Jews in 1870, for it was they who most needed the State and were most qualified to found it. The creation of the State of Israel in our times began with the foundation of the first Jewish agricultural school, Mikve Israel, by French Jews of the Alliance Israelite Universelle under the leadership of Cremieux, who was Minister of Justice in the government of Gambetta after the abdication of Napoleon III.

Jewish immigration and settlement with the aim of renewing Jewish independence in the Land of Israel started with the formation of this school in 1870. Then the country's established Jewish inhabitants, together with immigrants from Russia, Rumania, and other European countries (and some from Africa and Asia as well) began building agricultural settlements with the goal of reviving the country from its desolation and establishing a Jewish State. This was a long time before the existence of any "Zionist" government and several years before the foundation of the World Zionist Organization by Dr. Theodor Herzl, who published his book, *The Jewish State*, in 1896.

The depth of connection between the Jewish people and the Land of Israel is shown by the fact that when Herzl despaired of receiving a charter for large-scale Jewish settlement (with the aim of creating a Jewish State) from the Turkish government and Joseph Chamberlain in England proposed Uganda in Africa as an alternative, it was precisely the Russian Jews, whose rights in their native country were limited and where pogroms were organized by the government itself, who at the 1904 Zionist Congress opposed any substitute for the Land of Israel, so that the Uganda proposal was dropped.

I myself, who was born in the Russian part of Poland, and came here in 1906 when the country was part of the Ottoman Empire, never had the slightest doubt that we could settle millions of Jews on both sides of the Jordan without dislodging one Arab, because less than 10 percent of the country was settled; and I myself worked in new Jewish villages, formerly empty wasteland.

In 1920, after the Balfour Declaration had been confirmed by the League of Nations, I drew up a memorandum concerning the boundaries of the Jewish National Home in which the areas both east and west of the Jordan River were included. This memorandum was sent on behalf of the World Poalei Zion Union (a Zionist Socialist Party) to the British Labour Party. It said in essence that according to the League of Nations declaration the problem of the boundaries of the Land of Israel could be solved in only one way—by treating the Land of Israel as a single economic and political unit for the purpose of establishing a Jewish commonwealth. This view was accepted by the Labour Party and until 1922 the entire country was included in the mandate for a national home.

But as one living in this country I knew that there was such a thing as an Arab problem and that we must strictly observe Arab rights; and at the beginning of 1934, immediately after being elected to the Zionist Executive, I held talks with Arab leaders, both Moslem and Christian, in Palestine, Lebanon, and Syria. My premises in these talks were: the Arab nations have a whole series of countries in North Africa from Egypt to Morocco, and in the Middle East from Iraq, Syria, and Lebanon to Saudi Arabia and Yemen. The area of these countries in North Africa is 8,195,964 square kilometers and in the Middle East 3,607,929 square kilometers, making a total of 11,803,893 kilometers. The population of these countries (including Christian, Kurdish, and Berber minorities) is 94,587,000 (in 1963). The area of the Land of Israel (Palestine) on both sides of the Jordan is 60,000 square kilometers, and the population (1963) is 4,181,000 (2,356,000 in Israel and 1,825,000 in Hussein's kingdom).

In talking with the Arab leaders, I had basic premises, which after thorough consideration were accepted by the other side: They had vast stretches of land in East Asia and North Africa, most of it still under foreign domination, with a population of tens of millions. The area of the Land of Israel was no more than one half of one percent of this area and the Arab population on both sides of the Jordan was only 1.5 percent of the population of Arab East Asia and North Africa. According to Jewish tradition, deeply rooted in Jewish history and the Book of Books, the Land of Israel (on both sides of the Jordan) is the land of the Jewish people. However, it is not empty. Arabs have been living there since the Arab conquest in the seventh century, and now number over a million, or slightly less than 1.5 percent of the Arab population in all Arab countries. Obviously the Arabs living in the Land of Israel have all the rights of the inhabitants of any democratic country, and an undemocratic Jewish State is inconceivable.

This was the subject of the negotiations. The first Arab leader with whom I talked was Auni Abdul Hadi, the leader of the Istiklal (Independence) Party in the Land of Israel. I told him that we would help all the Arab states gain independence and unite in an Arab Federation if he would agree to permit us to make the Land of Israel on both sides of the Jordan into a Jewish State that would then join this federation. After thorough consideration he asked me, "How many Jews do you want to bring over?" I told him that I believed that in twenty years (this was in 1934) we could bring 4 million.

He jumped up excitedly, saying, "I'm going to Baghdad and Damascus to tell my Arab friends—we will give them 6 million, not 4, if they help us gain independence and unite." But then he calmed down and regained his seat, saying, "But you Jews are quicker and more talented than we are. You'll bring in as many Jews as you want in a short time, even less than twenty years. What guarantee can you give us that the Arab countries will gain freedom from foreign rule and be able to unite?"

Before holding my talks with the Arab leaders, I conferred with the British High Commissioner, General Wauchope, a very honest man. I told him that I was going to conduct negotiations with Arab leaders and asked whether the British government would consent to a Jewish-Arab agreement. He replied: "I have never discussed this with the members of the Cabinet and cannot speak in their name but I know their mind and am certain that they will support such an agreement." On the basis of this I told Auni Abdul Hadi that I would bring a guarantee from the League of Nations. He thought for a while and said that all the members of the League of Nations were Christians and could not be trusted. "My dear Mr. Auni," I replied, "I cannot bring you guarantees from Allah." That was the end of the conversation.

My chief talks, however, were conducted with Musa Alami, a confidant of the Mufti, who was the top leader of the Arabs of the Land of Israel. At the time Alami was Chief Prosecutor of the Mandate Government and was known as a decent, honest, and loyal man. Our talks continued for several months because he would bring my statements to the Mufti, return with questions and comments, and return to the Mufti with questions and answers from me. The basis of these talks was the proposal I had made to Auni Abdul Hadi: the liberation of all the Arab peoples from foreign domination, unification of all the Arab peoples, and the transformation of the entire Land of Israel on both sides of the Jordan into a Jewish State in which Arab citizens would enjoy equal rights and which would join the Arab Federation.

After several months of secret negotiations an agreement on the basis of my proposal was finally arrived at, but the Mufti required that I meet with the Syrian-Palestinian Arab Committee in Geneva, affiliated with the League of Nations. If they were in accord, the kings of all the Arab countries—Saudi Arabia, Yemen, and Iraq (at the time Egypt was not considered an Arab country)—would be convened to sign an agreement with the Zionist Executive (that is, the Jewish Agency) that would then be submitted to the Mandatory Government.

Talks on the same basis, to which they agreed, were also held with George Antonious, a Syrian Christian Arab living in the Land of Israel, who was considered the theoretician of the Arab nationalist movement, and with Riad a-Soula, the Prime Minister of Lebanon (later assassinated by an Arab zealot). In the same year I went to Europe to meet with the Arab Committee in Geneva affiliated with the League of Nations. The Mufti wrote them of my coming and about the nature of our talks. The committee consisted of two men: Saki Arsalan, an elderly Druze who had abandoned his people and became an extreme Arab nationalist, and a Syrian named Ikhan Bey al-Jabri, the father-in-law of Musa Alami. Being the chairman of the committee, Saki Arsalan did all the speaking. After I had explained the terms of the agreement he said to me, "You want a Jewish majority and a Jewish State in the Land of Israel. The British will never allow you to become a majority, so how can you expect it of us Arabs?" After further discussion I saw that there was no budging him from his position and we parted.

His younger colleague, Ikhan Bey al-Jabri, accompanied me to the train. When we left Arsalan's home Ikhan Bey said to me, "This is not the final word; we will still discuss the matter." Once again he stipulated that the entire conversation remain secret.

I had to remain in Europe for a few weeks. On my return to Jerusalem I found a French quarterly, *La Nation Arabe*, published by the committee in Geneva, which reported our entire talk in slightly distorted form. Musa Alami who was (and still is) a thoroughly modest man, was ashamed to see me, though I explained to him that I realized that his father-in-law had had no hand in this publication.

Meanwhile, as World War Two approached, the British Government changed its policy and after a meeting with Arabs and Jews in London in 1939 issued a White Paper that in effect revoked the undertakings of the Mandatory Government, put a stop to Jewish immigration, and promised the creation of an independent State in Palestine within ten years. Before this period had passed the war broke out in which the Nazis exterminated 6 million Jews, who more than anyone else needed and were capable of and eager to build a Jewish State.

Despite the publication in 1922, when he was Colonial Secretary, of the White Paper that cut off Trans-Jordan from the Land of Israel and gave it to Abdullah, Winston Churchill remained a loyal friend and supporter of the Jewish people and the Balfour Declaration. After the war he was not reelected, and having received an absolute majority for the first time, the British Labour Party formed a government.

It was well known that the Labour Party favored the establishment of a Jewish State. At the end of 1944 it adopted a resolution calling for the creation immediately after the war of a Jewish State on both sides of the Jordan, with its Arab inhabitants transferred to other Arab lands, which would also be granted full independence. Such a proposal for the transfer of the Arab inhabitants of the Land of Israel had never been made by the Zionist Organization.

What happened after World War Two is well known: Bevin and Attlee refused to uphold the resolution and referred the Palestine question to the UN. During the debate in the UN General Assembly in May 1947 the Soviet delegate, Gromyko, demanded the creation of a Jewish State in Palestine because the Jewish people had the right to a State of its own in its historic land. A committee appointed to study the problem produced two resolutions. While all the members agreed that the British Mandate should be quickly liquidated, they were divided on the remaining questions. The minority proposed a federated Jewish-Arab state, whereas the majority favored partitioning western Palestine and the creation of two separate states, a Jewish state to include the Negev and an Arab state, on the West Bank of the Jordan, to be linked to it economically. As for Jerusalem, it was decided that it should be a *corpus separatum* under international control, the Jewish inhabitants of which would be citizens of the Jewish State and the Arab inhabitants—citizens of the Arab state.

We decided by a large majority to accept the majority proposal, although the removal of Jerusalem from the State hurt us deeply. If the Arabs would then have agreed to the UN decision—which was adopted by a two-thirds majority led by Soviet Russia, the United States, and France, with Britain abstaining—the problem would have been solved and peace would have reigned in the Middle East. But the Arabs rejected the resolution and announced that they would use force to fight it; when the partition resolution was adopted by a large majority the next day, November 29, 1947, the Arabs began to attack the Jews. The attacks quickly increased both in number and ferocity as the Palestinian guerilla gangs were joined by Syrians, Iraqis, and also a number of Egyptians (from the Moslem Brotherhood).

The British Army, which then had a hundred thousand troops in the country, could have kept the peace but the Labour government under Clement Attlee as Prime Minister and Ernest Bevin as Foreign Secretary implacably opposed a Jewish State and did not maintain peace and order or prevent the Arab riots. The Jewish population was defended by the Hagana, an underground organization that generally had the upper hand until the Arab Legion (that is, the Jordanian Army) openly joined in on the side of the gangs, destroying four Jewish villages near Hebron and killing most of their inhabitants. Everywhere else the Hagana was on top. When the Hagana defeated Arab gangs in Haifa, Tiberias, Safad, and the New City of Jerusalem, the Arabs were informed that if they handed in their arms, they could stay put and enjoy equal rights.

While the majority of the Arab committees agreed, a few proposed consulting the Arab High Committee, which was no longer in the country, having fled after its men assassinated a high British official. In effect the decision was in the hands of the Mufti, who had also fled. The Arab High Committee told them not to turn in their arms but to leave the country, because in two or three weeks, after the British left, five Arab armies from Egypt, Syria, Jordan, Lebanon, and Iraq would invade and within ten to fourteen days would wipe out the Jews and they would all return—not only to their homes but to those of the Jews as well. Thus all the Arabs left Beit Sha'an, Tiberias, and Safad while only four thousand remained in Haifa and in Jaffa.

Now we come to what is known as the refugee problem. After the State of Israel came into being on May 14, 1948, not one Arab was expelled and only a few left for America. All those called refugees left during the Mandate. The Arabs began to leave two days after the UN partition resolution on November 29, 1947. Many Arabs went over to the territory the UN had designated as an Arab state; the rich immediately went to Lebanon, and some to Syria. When the partisan warfare intensified in the towns—in all these places the attacking Arabs mostly were not local residents but groups organized in the neigboring countries of Syria, Lebanon, Egypt, and Iraq, and in the last few days of the British Mandatory rule by the Arab Legion as well, though it still belonged to the British Army—the Arabs were requested on all occasions by their Jewish neighbors and by the Hagana to stay put, but by the orders of the Mufti in Egypt almost all of them departed.

When the Jewish State came into being, the gates were opened to Jewish immigrants, and during four years seven hundred thousand Jews came here, including five hundred thousand from Arab countries: Iraq, Yemen, Morocco, Libya, Egypt, Tunisia, Syria, and Lebanon. Many of them settled in the abandoned towns and quarters—Jaffa, Haifa, Tiberias, Beit Sha'an, Safad, and in abandoned villages. Despite the Arab attacks that began on the morrow of the UN partition decision, when hundreds of Jews were murdered, not one Jew fled the country. Only four hundred thousand Arabs left. The Jewish refugees from Arab countries lost all their belongings, which are still today in the hands of the Arabs.

The State of Israel that came into being on May 14, 1948, bears no responsibility for the Arab mass flight, and even took in forty thousand who had fled as part of a family reunification plan. We took in a much larger number of Jewish refugees who were forced to leave their property and capital in Arab lands. And we did not have homes for them, nor food, nor work, and we made superhuman efforts to integrate them—and we managed to do this within ten years, and to do so we organized an austerity regime. But the Arab states never wished to lift a finger to help the refugees who fled to their lands, when the English were still ruling Palestine. Arab leaders have learned to exploit the refugees as a weapon against the people of Israel.

And now, my dear General, I come to the amazing expressions in your speech—harsh, hurtful, and insulting expressions, based on incorrect or inexact information in your hands.

You spoke of the creation of the "Zionist" homeland between the two World Wars: "elite people, self-assured and domineering," replacing a heartfelt desire ("Next year in Jerusalem!") by a burning and conquering ambition, lack of humility, a warlike Israel desirous of expansion, the dream of those wishing to exploit the Eilat Straits blockade, and so forth. Before I discuss actual facts and trends, I will note something that is still not accepted because of many historic and religious reasons throughout the world: *the consciousness that dominated all we have done and will do.*

We are a people like all others, with the rights and obligations pertaining to every other nation. We are a small people, most of which does not live in its land, and who knows whether most of it will ever return? But those who do live in their land do not do so because they conquered, plundered, or pillaged something from others but because we found our land when it was abandoned, not entirely empty but on the whole desolate, and we made this wilderness flourish by the sweat of our brow, by our stubborn and pioneering labor. We did not rob or take away one inch of land from those who worked it, but we made this desert blossom. The place on which now stands the largest city in Israel, Tel Aviv, was during my first years here a wilderness of sand dunes, without a tree, without any greenery, without any living things, although nearby ran a small river, which today irrigates even the kibbutz I live in, fifty kilometers south of Beersheba. I worked as a hired laborer fifty-nine years ago in a place that was then empty and desolate, where a few dozen Bedouin survived by hunting—and today it has a kibbutz of five hundred adults and hundreds of children and it is one of the more magnificent farm villages in the Jordan Valley, and it is called Kinneret. Not by force, not only by money, we converted a poor and arid land into a fertile land, and we built settlements, villages, and towns in the desolate abandoned areas where no living thing was to be found.

I am not ashamed of the name "Zionist," but we were promised by England (with French consent) a national, not a "Zionist" homeland. "Zion" is one of our holiest and most precious places in Jerusalem, the City of David, but "Zionist" is the name of members of the movement that sought to return to "Zion," so that we should once again become a normal, independent people, rooted in its Homeland, like most peoples, if not all of them.

And in the declaration that was given by Balfour and later endorsed by the French government, we were promised reconstitution of our national Homeland, which had remained our Homeland.

Although we were forcibly separated from it by cruel foreign conquerors, we never ceased for one day during two thousand years to pray and yearn for our return to this land. And in no country in which we lived, until the French Revolution, did we or the native people ceased existing two thousand years ago, and I am also aware that there are Jews who were accorded equal rights. That is one of the great episodes of the French people that will never be forgotten. But the man who seventy years ago envisioned the Jewish State, and entranced most of his people with that vision, Dr. Theodor Herzl, came to this great illuminating vision through the Dreyfus Affair and the terrible revelations of anti-Semitism that ensued therefrom.

Once again I say: we will never forget the moral heroism of men like Colonel Piccard, men of statehood and conscience like Clemenceau, Zola, Jaurès, and others who stubbornly and heroically fought for justice, year after year, until they won through. But the hatred that emerged at the end of the nineteenth century appears again and again in one or another country. We Jews see ourselves as a people with all the rights accruing to a free and independent people, and we dare to believe it is our due, and this is not by charity.

I am fully aware that for centuries the Christian world considered that the Jewish people ceased existing two thousand years ago, and I am also aware that there are Jews who think so too. We pity such Jews, but we are not angry at them. If they wish to cease being Jews, that is their business. But they do not speak on our behalf, just as Pétain did not speak in the name of the French people in its great sorrow, but rather Charles de Gaulle, although he was almost alone and ostracized. I have heard slanderous things against my people from a great Jew whom I value for his greatness, his penetrating historical insight, and vision of a more just, healthier society, though I do not accept his doctrines—Karl Marx.

We are not a "domineering" people. I realize there are exceptions among us whose slogans and clichés are alien to the overwhelming majority of the Jewish people and its sacred tradition. But for fifteen years I held responsible positions in the Zionist movement and the Eretz Israel [Land of Israel] Community, and for fifteen years I was Premier and Defense Minister in the State of Israel, and I know how profound is our ambition and intense desire for peace—peace with our neighbors and peace among the nations. I was not our sole arbiter in all these years, neither in the Zionist movement nor the State of Israel. I had to persuade the majority of my colleagues and countrymen to follow the course which I felt to be best, most honest, and most just, and succeeded. Allow me to mention a few examples pertaining to points raised in your speech, my dear General.

A few days before our Declaration of Independence, there arose the question whether we should define the State's borders. Two lawyers in the Provisional Government claimed that the law made it obligatory. I was opposed to this. I claimed that no such law existed, that the American people when it declared its independence did not define its borders, and this was the main thing in my view. I told my colleagues: if the Arabs had accepted the borders set out by the UN General Assembly on November 29, 1947, not one of us would have complained and cast doubts, although to my mind most of the lines were not just, especially the removal of Jerusalem from the State boundaries and the putting of it under an international entity, which was not done anywhere else in the world.

And you, my dear General, noted in your words with charm and emotion the heartfelt wish the Jews expressed for two thousand years: "Next year in Jerusalem!" We never exchanged this wish for "a burning and conquering ambition." We said, and I would say most of us support this: if the Arabs had, like us, accepted the UN resolution, there would not, for us, have arisen any question of borders. We accepted them joyfully, though mixed with sorrow. But the Arabs announced that they would fight this resolution and destroy the State we were to bring into being in three more days, and then opened war on us even before the declaration of statehood—and the UN did not protest, and did not oblige them to accept the resolution. Under such conditions we were not obliged to accept a UN decision that, as it were, applied to one side only. If we could expand our borders and liberate Jerusalem in the war that the Arab peoples were launching against us, we would liberate Jerusalem and western Galilee and they would become part of the State.

There was no one in our midst who proposed to conquer additional territories before the outbreak of war—which in fact began two days after the UN General Assembly decision, with an attack on our commercial center in Jerusalem—and the British did not even allow us to defend ourselves. We were not duty-bound to accept discrimination—one form of treatment for the Arabs and another for ourselves. If the UN did not exist, and the Arabs could act as they pleased, we were free as well. And our ties with Jerusalem preceded those of any other people in the world or any other faith or religion.

On May 14, 1948, I proclaimed the establishment of a Jewish State to be known as Israel, on the basis of a declaration I had drawn up the night before, and which was approved by the Provisional Council of State that morning, six hours before the official proclamation. The Declaration says: "We appeal—in the very midst of the bloody onslaught launched against us now for months—to the Arab inhabitants of the State of Israel to preserve peace and participate in the upbuilding of the State on the basis of full and equal citizenship and due representation in all its provisional and permanent institutions." In it I added another appeal: "We extend our hand to all neighboring states and their peoples in an offer of peace and good-neighborliness, and appeal to them to establish bonds of cooperation and mutual help with the sovereign Jewish People settled in its own land. The State of Israel is prepared to do its share in common effort for the advancement of the entire Middle East."

My dear General, every word in this appeal came from the heart, the hearts of all of us, and was signed by every party, from the Communists on the left to the fanatically religious Agudat Israel on the right, from Socialists on the left to the Revisionists on the right. And if our call had been heeded, and the Arab states had acted in compliance with the UN General Assembly resolution and the UN Charter, *there would have been no war or dispute between us and the Arabs to this day*, and none of us would have conceived of such a "conquering" idea as occupying land beyond the borders laid down by the UN, though we did not accept these boundaries wholeheartedly. For peace is dearer to us than anything else, but it is either a two-way affair or fraudulent.

We would not have had to lose six thousand of the cream of our youth in a War of Independence that was forced upon us, eight hours after we declared our independence, by five Arab states—Egypt, Jordan, Syria, Lebanon, and Iraq—whose armies outnumbered ours forty to one. There would not have been the Sinai Campaign nor the Six-Day War if the Arabs had accepted the UN decision instead of setting out to nullify it by force. Not one of us would have conceived of attacking our neighbors for the purpose of improving our borders or increasing our territory. We declared many times, with the concurrence of the entire nation, that we were prepared to conclude a peace treaty for the next hundred years on the basis of the status quo. Though we had a rightist group propounding "territorial integrity," it never proposed—and if it had no one would have listened to it—that we go to war to increase the areas of the State, though the entire world, at least the Christian world and the entire Jewish world, considered the Land of Israel on both sides of the Jordan one country and hoped it would be restored as promised by the Torah and the Prophets.

The Book of Genesis says: "And the Lord appeared unto Abraham, and said, Unto thy seed will I give this land" (Genesis 12:7), and the Book of Deuteronomy says: "Then the Lord thy God will turn the captivity. . . and gather thee from all the nations, whither the Lord thy God hath scattered thee. And the Lord thy God will bring thee into the land which thy fathers possessed, and thou shalt possess it" (Deuteronomy 30:3–5). This was reiterated by the Prophets—Isaiah 56:8, Jeremiah 28:14, Ezekiel 11:17, Nehemiah 7:9— and this was the intention of the Balfour Declaration, confirmed by France and by the League of Nations. Yet when the UN General Assembly decided differently, we consented, and had the Arabs accepted it and maintained the peace, we would have remained loyal to this resolution.

While it is true that for two thousand years we have believed in the vision of our Prophets and many among us still believe in the coming of the Messiah who will bring all Jews, dead and living, to the Holy Land from all corners of the world, we have never had a "burning conquering ambition" but a burning faith in the vision of peace of our Prophets: for "nation will not bear sword against nation, and neither shall they learn war any more" (Isaiah 2:4, Micah 4:3). For the foundation of our existence after two destructions brought upon us by the Babylonians and the Romans and the hatred with which the Christian peoples engulfed us for sixteen hundred years was our spiritual link with the Book of Books. When I appeared in Jerusalem in 1936 before the Royal Commission, I said, "The Bible is our mandate." It was from the Bible that we drew the power to survive in a hostile world and to retain our faith that we would return to our Homeland and that peace would reign on earth.

And now I would like to remind you, dear General, of our conversation during my visit in June 1960 in the garden of the Elysée Palace. Also present were Premier Debré and my friend Shimon Peres. You asked me: "What are your dreams for the real borders of Israel? Tell me, I will not repeat it to anyone else." I told you that if you had asked me that question twenty-five years ago, I would have said that the northern border is the Litani River and the eastern is Trans-Jordan, and I conducted negotiations on this with Arab leaders. But you ask me today, I said. I'll tell you. We have two main aims: peace with our neighbors and a great Jewish immigration. *The area of the land of Israel in our hands can absorb many more Jews than the number of those likely to come*, and therefore the borders we have are sufficient, and, please God, the Arabs should sign a peace treaty with us on the basis of the status quo. And then you asked: "What is the relationship between the State of Israel and American Jewry?" I replied: The economic, political, and cultural situation of American Jews is good, but all the same they have a profound relationship with the State of Israel.

And even after the Sinai Campaign thirteen years ago and the Six-Day War, I can assure you that it was not because of our wish to expand Israeli territory that the two wars took place. If only Egypt had kept its undertaking of the cease-fire agreements, and the Security Council resolutions on freedom of shipping in the Suez Canal and especially the Straits of Eilat (or Aqaba), and the rulers of Egypt and Syria had not declared day after day that their purpose was the annihilation of Israel, it would never have occurred to us to deviate from the borders set out by the cease-fire agreements.

This was my determined opinion all through the years, and I am happy to state that it was supported by the overwhelming majority of my nation, and even those who pro-pounded "territorial integrity" never suggested we go to war to that end.

I know that the government of the Fifth Republic and you, my dear General, like other European countries, as well as the US and Russia, have kept the French Embassy in Tel Aviv. But all the meetings with Ambassadors have taken place in Jerusalem, and I am unaware of a single protest from the United Nations or one of its members when the govern-ment of Jordan in 1948 conquered the Old City of Jerusalem and expelled the Jews therefrom and destroyed its synagogues and blocked our access to the Holy Places, all in contravention of the cease-fire agreements.

We have never harmed any Christian or Moslem places of worship in our area, and we demand no special credit for that; it was out of a human obligation and a sense of respect for others' beliefs.

As you know, I am now an ordinary citizen in my country. After serving for fifteen years as Prime Minister and Minister of Defense, I felt it best to transfer the reins of government to younger people, and am now engaged in writing a history of Israel since the year 1870,* when French Jews established an agricultural school named Mikve Israel (which in Hebrew means both "the hope of Israel" and "Israel's ingathering") as the first foundation for the State of Israel's renewal.

But I know the mind of my people, both in Israel and the Diaspora, and I know that my people, no less than others, is devoutly loyal to the vision of world peace, the coming of which the Prophets of Israel were the first in human history to witness. And if the Great Powers would influence the Arab peoples—and they can do so, because the Arab nations require arms from the Great Powers and much time will elapse before they can produce these weapons on their own—to keep the peace in the Middle East, I am concinced that Israel will never break the peace.

As a man who was Prime Minister during the Fourth Republic, I know that the friendly relations that obtained between us, ever since the renaissance of Israel, also held during the days of the Fifth Republic, and I did not expect a friendship more faithful or sincere than that I found with you. You wish for good and friendly relations with the Arab states. I do not see in this a contradiction to continued friendship with Israel. Although the Arab rulers continue to threaten us with destruction, as in the past, I would not advise any nation to break off ties with the Arab states. Insofar as we will be obliged to defend ourselves, I do not want the soldiers of other nations to die in our defense, but that our sons should defend our people. What I would ask of our friends is that they should not withhold from us the help necessary to keep our deterrent force capable of stopping our neighbors from attacking us.

I must apologize for having been so lengthy. I felt it my duty—if only out of gratitude for your friendship and help for Israel, and for the personal friendship you showed me even this year in our recent meeting—to explain to you *our true position on international issues.* We believe that the Jew deserves what is the due of every man, and the Jewish people deserves what is due to every nation, small or large. We consider ourselves equal in everything, and duty-bound in all, no less and no more. And as to the "elite people" you mentioned in your speech, our Torah says, "Thou has avouched the Lord this day to be thy God. . . and the Lord hath avouched thee this day to be his chosen people" (Deuteronomy 26:17–18). The Jewish People was the first people in the world that recognized the one and only God, and thereby it became a peculiar people, a chosen people.

And the Book of Joshua (Chapter 24) says, "And Joshua said unto the people, Ye are witnesses against yourselves that *ye have chosen the Lord, to serve him.* And they said, we are witnesses. . . . So Joshua made a covenant with the people that day, and set them a statute and an ordinance in Shechem." And in later generations the Sages of Israel said, "God went to all the nations and asked them to accept his Law. When they refused, he asked Israel, and they said, 'We shall do and we shall obey!'" Hence it is clear that according to our faith it was not the Almighty who chose Israel, but Israel who chose the Almighty, and this is an historic fact known to every Christian and Moslem in the world. Just as a Greek need not be ashamed that twenty-four to twenty-six centuries ago his nation preceded all others in discovering certain scientific truths, neither are we.

---

* The reference is to this book.—EDITORS

But our people does not consider itself superior to others. Naturally we are proud that it was our Law that was the first to say, "Thou shalt love thy neighbor as thyself," as well as what it says further in the same chapter: "And if a stranger sojourn with thee in your land, ye shall not vex him. But the stranger that dwelleth with you shall be unto you as one born among you, and thou shalt love him as thyself; for ye were strangers in the land of Egypt: I am the Lord your God" (Leviticus 19:18, 33–34). There was no such law even in the Athens of Pericles, Socrates, and Plato.

And with our powerful desire to enable every Jew who so wishes to live in our land as a Jew and as a human being with rights and obligations equal to those of any other person and nation, all our lives we have been and will be devoted to the ideals of peace, human brotherhood, justice, and truth, as commanded by our Prophets.

Please accept my profound esteem and gratitude for all that your great people has done in the past two hundred years to promote human values and national liberty, and permit me to express to you, dear General, my esteem for what you have done to augment the name, honor, and standing of your country, and for the loyal help and true friendship that you have shown all these years to the Jewish People in its land; and I hope that the friendly relations between Israel and France—as part of the friendly relations between all peoples— will continue with your assistance and the help of every people and person faithful to the ideals of the Book of Books.

Please accept, Mr. President, my best wishes for your success in your high mission.

Pronouncement by de Gaulle at a Meeting with the Syrian Prime Minister ★ The French President Writes to Ben-Gurion

In the middle of December, after this letter had been sent to General de Gaulle, the press reported a meeting between the General and the Syrian Prime Minister, and statements that de Gaulle made at that meeting on his own behalf and in a joint communiqué. These statements showed that some of the accusations made by the Israeli press against the French President were exaggerated and unfounded. Ben-Gurion published the following letter in *Haaretz* from Sde Boker, under date of December 18, 1967:

Jewish and world public opinion was startled by a number of offensive and distressing statements about Israel in a speech by the President of France a few weeks ago. Many people in France and even those closest to General de Gaulle had difficulty in understanding the sudden change in relations between France and Israel. Only one Israeli "intellectual," Meir Reudensky, understood this strange mystery. According to him, "the former [Israeli] Prime Minister had a hand in spoiling the relations," a process that had its origin in the Sinai Campaign of 1956.

Though it is now more than eleven years since the Sinai campaign, until the publication of de Gaulle's speech a few weeks ago no one in Israel knew that relations between France and Israel had been spoiled. In fact everyone understood exactly the opposite.

The President of the French Republic made no secret of his continued friendship for Israel and at a banquet in honor of the Israeli Prime Minister in 1960 he surprised everyone present by announcing that "Israel is France's friend and ally." The friendship of de Gaulle was expressed not only in words but in deeds. French friendship for and trust in Israel, as manifested in matters of the most vital security, was equaled by practically no other friendly country. Just as we must not forget the help we received from previous governments, we must not deprecate or disparage the assistance proffered to us during the Fifth Republic, which played no small part in our military victory in the Six-Day War.

No less than anyone else, the writer of these lines was astonished and disturbed by the General's speech a few weeks ago. It contained a number of distressing and inaccurate points, and even some of de Gaulle's friends and associates were surprised and grieved by some of the statements made by their esteemed President. And were the "previous Prime Minister" certain that the "relations with France" were the only thing he had "spoiled" since the creation of the State, he would be quite happy and would pray that many more things be "spoiled" in this way.

Nevertheless, the deep regret caused by General de Gaulle's statement should not be allowed to becloud the non-inimical character of his later announcements, especially that which he made at the conclusion of the Syrian Prime Minister's visit to Paris at the end of the year. While we may not be completely happy with everything de Gaulle said on this occasion, we ought not to disregard some honest and straightforward points he made to the Syrian Premier, who is known through the world for his fervent hatred of Israel and his openly expressed aspiration to destroy it by any means at hand or not at hand.

At a banquet at the Elysée Palace before the Syrian Prime Minister's departure, President de Gaulle said that France would extend active assistance to international efforts to normalize relations in the Middle East and that peace would be obtained "only by prevention of conquests by military force, cessation of hostilities de jure and de facto, and by safeguarding the rights of all the nations concerned, for instance in the matter of navigation—those rights enjoyed by all other nations." And a joint Syrian-French communiqué issued the same day said that the only permanent peace possible in the Middle East would be one based on justice. Prior to this meeting the Syrian leader had known of only one basis for peace in the Middle East—the destruction of Israel.

No one need delude himself that the Syrian leader will henceforth profess international justice. Though it is doubtful whether the Arab leaders will accede to the conditions of de Gaulle spelled out to his Syrian guest—cessation of hosilities de jure and de facto and freedom of navigation for all nations—the significance of two such demands pronounced publicly by the French President in the presence of the Syrian Prime Minister should not be underrated. Less than for any other nation is it good policy, for us to allow relations with another people to deteriorate, nor should we disregard the fact that General de Gaulle is the spokesman of France in these years, and every year can be decisive for our security and well-being.

On Saturday, January 6, 1968, the French Ambassador brought President de Gaulle's reply, dated December 30, to Ben-Gurion at Sde Boker and on the President's behalf requested that both letters be published simultaneously in Paris and in Israel. Ben-Gurion agreed and proposed that they be released for publication at 3 P.M. on January 9 (in Paris, at 2 P.M.). De Gaulle's letter read as follows:

Mr. Prime Minister:

I studied your letter of December 6 with deep interest. As you know, the wider issue of the renaissance and fate of the State of Israel truly fascinates me, and causes profound emotion. This is especially the case because the conflict that flared up once again in the Middle East has brought in its wake important results of intimate concern to France because of the political, economic, moral, religious, and historic reasons of which you are aware. And finally, it is surely apparent to you that I have the highest regard for you, and that I remember well our personal relations during the past decade.

Accordingly, I was not surprised by the significance of your reasoning. I know that the revival of Israel in the Land of Israel—as you described it after your active participation therein—encompassed much faith and daring and many difficulties, and that the development of semidesolate areas by the new State, thanks to the immigration of so many Jews, and the help of so many communities throughout the world, are truly praiseworthy. You also mention and justly so, that my country and I myself extended our support to the establishment of this national venture, and you need not doubt the fact that in the hour of need, we would oppose its destruction, as was promised in our various conversations. I have publicly declared that Israel is "a friendly state and an ally."

But these are precisely the reasons, as I always said—and first of all to you personally— why Israel must act with moderation and restraint in her relations with her neighbors and with regard to her territorial ambitions. And particularly so since the land initially recognized by the Great Powers as making up your State is considered by the Arabs as their territory; because the Arabs—in whose midst Israel has settled—are a proud people and one deserving respect, to whom France is bound by an old and natural friendship; and because they are entitled to develop despite all their natural obstacles and the grave and humiliating setbacks they experienced during centuries of occupation and, finally, their own dispersion.

Naturally, I do not deny that the regrettable closure of the Strait of Aqaba injured only your country, and that your country was justified in feeling threatened, considering the tension that prevailed in the region after the abundant vituperation and diatribes against Israel on the one hand, and the lamentable fate of the refugees in Jordan and Gaza on the other hand. But I remain convinced that Israel went beyond the limits of necessary moderation when she ignored the warnings given to her government by the French government, unleashed hostilities, conquered Jerusalem and considerable Jordanian, Egyptian, and Syrian territories, pursuing there the repressions and expulsions that are inevitably the results of an occupation and that, as everything indicates, aim at annexation—and has announced to the world at large that the solution to the dispute can come only on the basis of those conquests and not on the condition of a withdrawal from these areas.

I regret this the more since with the withdrawal of its forces, there could emerge a solution containing recognition of your State by your neighbors, guarantees for security on both sides of the frontiers to be determined by international arbitration, a just and honorable future assured for the refugees and minorities, and free navigation for all through the Gulf of Aqaba and the Suez Canal. This could become possible in the context of the United Nations, a solution that France is prepared to aid if necessary, not only in the political field but on the spot as well.

This solution, which would bring peace to the Middle East, could facilitate peace throughout the world and, to my mind, serve the interests of the nations concerned, including you own, but would not, I realize, satisfy all of Israel's wishes.

If I had any doubts about this, my perusal of your letter and all that you write on the importance of Canaan on both sides of the Jordan in the eyes of the Jews—in the past and the present—would have provided me with proof. This was also the case as regards the profound emotion aroused among many Jews when I said that the Jewish people is "an elite, self-assured and domineering." I did not say that in denigration, and no insult is implied in my words. It was just because of these characteristics that the Jewish people could survive and remain as it is after two thousand years of unheard-of conditions.

But what has happened? Instead of continuing in its shocking dispersal, Israel has become a state like any other whose existence and survival depend on its political policies. And many people have learned that no policies are worthy of consideration unless they are adapted to realities.

With my fondest regards for the New Year.

A Drive to Merge Mapai, Rafi, and Ahdut Haavodah ★ Ben-Gurion Refuses to Join the Unified Labor Party

After the creation of the National Unity Government there was a movement in the Rafi Party to reunite with Mapai. The secretary of the Rafi, Shimon Peres, held unofficial talks with Mapai leaders. In the Alignment, that is, Mapai and Ahdut Haavodah, the inclination to unity also increased. On September 24, 1967, the Rafi Central Committee met to consider the subject. The discussion focused on two points: (1) whether Dayan's entry into the Cabinet as a Rafi representative meant that the party, under the principle of collective responsibility, was obliged to support every Government decision; (2) whether there was any prospect of change in the leadership, something being sought by Rafi and many members of Mapai. The continuation of the debate was postponed for several days; and on September 26 David Ben-Gurion, being unable to attend the meeting, sent the following letter to Peres:

Please inform the members of the Central Committee as follows:

(1) It was with great interest that I listened at yesterday's meeting to members who took issue with me and my appraisal of the situation in the country and in the movement.

(2) To the member who asked me (doubtless in all sincerity and with good intentions) to let bygones be bygones, I wish to say: There is no need to forget the past, neither the good nor the bad, for a knowledge of the past both near and remote is of great value. Nevertheless, one's attitude toward people (and to movements as well) should be based not on their past but on their present conduct. This I learn from the Prophet Ezekiel who said (18: 21–22): "But if the wicked will turn from all the sins that he hath committed, and do that which is lawful and right, he shall surely live, he shall not die. All his transgressions that he hath committed, they shall not be mentioned unto him; in his righteousness that he hath done, he shall live." He also said (verse 24): "But when the righteous turn away from his righteousness, and committed iniquities, all his righteousness that he hath done shall not be mentioned; in his trespass that he hath trespassed and in his sin that he hath sinned, in them shall he die."

(3) To the member who invited me, as a member of the rank and file, to return with him to Mapai, it is my right and duty to say that I consider myself a rank-and-file man, and always have, when I was a laborer in the agricultural settlements in Yehuda, the Galilee, and Shomron, when I was secretary of the Histadrut, and when I served as emissary of the Zionist movement and the State of Israel. No matter who they are, colleagues are bound to have differences of opinion and I have had such differences with members dearest and closest to me. (To my deep regret the majority of them are no longer alive.) Yet none of us ever required his colleagues to accept his opinion rather than to follow the dictates of his own conscience.

(4) As I said at last night's meeting, majority rule applies only to parliaments and courts of law. In a parliament it is the majority that enacts legislation that every citizen is bound to abide by, even if he sides with the minority that opposed this legislation. The same holds true for majority opinions in courts of law. But membership in a political party (where the country is not a dictatorship) is a matter of free individual choice, and no one is compelled to remain in a party against his conscience and moral scruples merely because the majority of its members have so decided. Our Torah rightly says, "Thou shalt not follow a multitude to do evil" (Exodus 23:2).

(5) After being a member from the day it was founded in 1930 until the middle of 1965, I left Mapai when it became obvious to me that its leadership was acting in violation

of truth, justice, and democratic principles, something it has not desisted from to this day. In my opinion this process had its beginning at the meeting of December 13, 1964.

(6) You may wonder why I am quoting such a recent date, for many believe that I left the party because of the miscarriage of justice committed by the ministerial Committee of Seven on December 25, 1960. True, that miscarriage of justice was the cause of my resignation from the Government, because the Government is bound by a rule of collective responsibility, a principle I consider vital and essential, and I could not be partner to such a miscarriage of justice. Therefore, though many members urged against it, I tendered my resignation. Yet at that time I still believed that the miscarriage of justice had resulted from an innocent error, as I said in my letter of resignation to the President of January 31, 1961.

(7) To do what I could to rectify the wrong, I assembled and submitted material pertaining to the miscarriage of justice to the Minister of Justice and the Attorney General, with the proposal that a panel of judges be appointed to examine whether the procedures and conclusions of the Committee of Seven were in accordance with truth, justice, and the laws of the land. This was on October 22, 1964. Two weeks later the Attorney General published his opinion that "the Committee of Seven appears to have conducted its work without observing the principles of natural justice and the rules for conducting proceedings of this kind." He went on to ask whether "the needs at this inquiry were special needs different from the need to investigate the facts of the case itself," and added, "I feel that the factual findings of the Committee of Seven would not have stood the test of an Israeli court."

(8) Until then I had faith and confidence in the members of the Committee of Seven, feeling that they had been guided by erroneous considerations, and that to err is human.

(9) It was only at the Mapai Central Committee of December 13, 1964, which dealt with the demand for the appointment of a judicial inquiry committee, that I was shocked to learn, from what Eshkol said, that he had purposely acted in complete violation of the injuction of the Prophet Zephaniah, who said of the remnant of Israel, "they shall not do iniquity, nor speak lies, nor shall a deceitful tongue be found in their mouth" (3:13). Moreover, Eshkol repeated his statements several times, not only to members of his party but to the Knesset, and the party leadership, in full awareness, consented to such a violation of truth and justice on the part of the Prime Minister of Israel.

(10) Not long before the outbreak of the Six-Day War, tension and apprehension increased among the tens of thousands of persons mobilized in the Israel Defense Forces as a result of the strange behavior of the Minister of Defense and Prime Minister. This apprehension encompassed practically the entire nation, for there was not a family in Israel which did not have a son, grandson, relative, or acquaintance in the mobilized forces, and the members of the Coalition, especially the National Religious Party headed by Moshe Shapira, Rafi headed by Shimon Peres, and Gahal headed by Menahem Begin and Yosef Sapir, came to the conclusion that Levi Eshkol must be replaced. Some demanded his replacement both as Prime Minister and Minister of Defense, others merely as Minister of Defense. The Mapai leadership, headed of course by Eshkol himself, opposed this with all its strength. The question of Dayan replacing Eshkol as Minister of Defense was discussed by the top leadership. Although Eshkol, Golda Meir, Shaul Avigor, Zalman Aranne, and one other person were opposed, the majority decided that Eshkol should be replaced as Minister of Defense by Dayan. Nevertheless, when the matter was duly brought to the Knesset for approval on June 5, 1967, the day the Six-Day War broke out, Eshkol said, "When I felt the hour of trial on the battlefield approaching, I took the initiative of setting up an emergency Government in which I proposed that Gahal and Rafi participate. As you all know by now, the negotiations have borne fruit and I welcome the expansion of the Government." Eshkol could not possibly have been ignorant of the fact that most, if not all, of the members of the Knesset knew where the initiative had really come from, and that

despite his strong opposition he had been compelled to relinquish the Defense portfolio by the majority of the members of his party.

At the start of World War Two, when Chamberlain was compelled by his colleagues to resign in favor of Churchill, he did not dare to or conceive of fabricating any story that it was done on his own initiative. After the elections to the Sixth Knesset, however, its members were accustomed to hearing such fabrications by the Prime Minister without doing anything about it—though I, your servant, was compelled as far back as July 19, 1965, in the first session of the Fifth Knesset, to make a personal declaration to the effect that Eshkol's statements on June 23, 1965, in reply to Mr. Begin's demand for a parliamentary inquiry committee to investigate Eshkol's accusations that things were "not in order" under his predecessor were not true, something no one denied. (*Divrai Haknesset*, Vol 43, p. 2655.)

(11) Immediately after my remarks at last night's meeting of the Central Committee, Moshe Dayan raised a very serious question: In the Government that he had entered as the representative of Rafi, there was a rule of collective responsibility. Since Rafi rejected the Prime Minister, how could he continue to serve in such a Government?

I must admit that after resigning from Mapai and organizing Rafi, I was completely opposed to any member of Rafi serving in the Government. However, the special situation, without parallel since the State of Israel's renewal, a situation created as a result of the expulsion of the United Nation Forces from Sharm el-Sheikh, Nasser's threats and the mobilization of his armies in Sinai for war against Israel, an emergency of a gravity unequaled since the War of Independence twenty years ago, caused the demand by the National Religious Party, Gahal, and Rafi for Dayan to replace Eshkol as Minister of Defense. Though I was always opposed to Rafi's participation in Levi Eshkol's Government, I concluded that in this hour of emergency the enhancement of the Army's morale had priority over everything else, and agreed to Dayan's being appointed as Minister of Defense even if Eshkol remained as Prime Minister.

I felt that victory in the impending war (this was a week before its outbreak) and the needs of the Israel Defense Force had priority over all other considerations. This answers Dayan's question. The war is over but even today, in view of Nasser's behavior week after week at the Suez Canal and what is likely to happen in the other occupied territories, I am not certain that the emergency has passed and therefore I feel that Dayan is needed now as well, not as a political representative of Rafi but as a Minister of Defense whose political perspicacity, military assertiveness, and humane approach to our neighbors and Arab citizens can be relied upon. If the situation returns to normal—at least to what it was before the expulsion of the UN from Sharm el-Sheikh—only then will the question arise and have to be dealt with. For the time being Dayan must remain in the Government as representative of the Nation's security, not merely as a representative of Rafi.

(12) Finally, the main question facing Rafi and its Central Committee is whether to join the so-called three-way merger under the conditions laid down by the Mapai Central Committee as stated in Golda Meir's letter of September 24, 1967, to Shimon Peres. Here I must note something that is perhaps incidental and that does not determine the final answer. The three-way merger in my opinion is in the nature of a fraud. Ahdut Haavodah has no intention of merging in the three-way party but rather of enjoying the best of both worlds: to participate in the "United" Party while continuing to exist as an independent party with its own newspaper and apparatus under the name of Hakibbutz Hameuhad, as if there was an Ahdut Haavodah Party apart from Hakibbutz Hameuhad, even though a few members of that movement, such as Mr. Dorman, are not now members of Ahdut Haavodah and there are several members of Ahdut Haavodah who do not belong to Hakibbutz Hameuhad. Both these bodies in effect are one. But this is not the main point— the main point is the merger with Mapai.

(13) At last night's meeting of the Central Committee, I stated that I had not taken part in the negotiations with Mapai and neither opposed nor favored them. Those in favor, especially Peres and Almogi, feel that the three-way merger will result in *improved leadership* both in the country and in the movement within one year, and no later than the *agreed* or *elected* conventions—and the difference between the two is not at all clear to me. Some members are almost certain of an improvement in leadership, some are slightly more doubtful, but both consider that in addition to its importance per se, the merger had serious prospects of improving the situation. I do not share even the qualified optimism of some of the members; on the other hand, I have no grounds for denying the possibility of improved leadership for the country and the movement. Any member who believes in these prospects is completely justified in joining the three-way merger. Unfortunately, I cannot fully share even the mildest optimism these members profess. I view with great seriousness the moral decay in the past two or three years, both in the Mapai leadership and the newspaper *Davar*, which serves its purposes, though officially it is the paper of the Workers of the Land of Israel and brandishes the name of Berl Katznelson on its masthead. It is with great revulsion that I read in *Davar* articles and editorials that rightly belong in the wastebasket. After participating in this paper from the day it first appeared forty-two years ago, I have been compelled by moral, personal, and social considerations to stop doing so.

(14) I think all my colleagues know that from the day I arrived in Israel sixty-one years ago, I have been calling for unification of the labor movement and have taken part in every merger in Israel and the Diaspora up to the present, not only for "Zionist Socialist" reasons (terms that have lost all meaning in the last generation) but because of the needs of the nation in Israel and the Diaspora and our national requirements.

(15) For many years before my resignation from Mapai (actually since the creation of the State) I have given considerations of State priority over all other considerations and the supreme consideration of State, in my opinion, is "*the national security and the integrity of its leaders.*" This is quoted from a letter I sent to the Mapai secretary on December 30, 1960, one day before resigning from the Government on account of the miscarriage of justice by the Committee of Seven, in reply to a multitude of letters received from members who felt my resignation would be a national disaster, and so on. In that letter I added that "I have not ignored and will not ignore the needs of the party and the movement and will continue to serve them to the best of my ability." At that time I did not even conceive of seceding from Mapai, as I explained above.

Yet four and a half years later, when the first signs of moral decay appeared, I could not remain in a party whose leaders were alienating themselves from truth, justice, and democratic principles, and transforming the party into a herd. And I would not be true to my conscience if I lent my support to a party whose leaders' moral integrity is not a condition for their election. Therefore, though I understand the viewpoint of Shimon and Almogi and their right to act according to their lights, as long as the moral integrity of the country's leadership is not ensured, I cannot join them.

(16) Like Peres and Almogi, I know that Mapai has thousands of members loyal to the movement's moral and social principles but, being absorbed in their pioneering work in the kibbutzim and moshavim, they are unable to devote sufficient attention to problems of state.

(17) I do not wish to say that Peres and Almogi do not stand a chance, nor do I see any moral blemish in their joining the merger, or doubt that Mapai's thousands of loyal members are capable of correcting things that are wrong and ensuring a leadership that will bring honor to the State and the movement, if only they would devote to the needs of the nation the same measure of concern and strict loyalty as they do to their blessed agricultural work. Though I am compelled to remain on the outside, and perhaps in complete

isolation until, if ever, the situation is rectified, I extend to those members who plan to join the three-way merger my heartfelt wishes for success in the difficult task they are undertaking.

The deteriorating external situation, despite the glorious victory in the Six-Day War and the National Unity Government formed about a week before the fighting began, encouraged the drive in Rafi and in Ahdut Haavodah for a unified labor movement. The Rafi secretariat decided to call a second session of the Rafi convention to deal with this issue. It met on December 12, 1967, and lasted two days. About forty members spoke— some in favor of the merger, some opposed, some doubtful. Ben-Gurion said:

> The main reason this meeting has been called is to decide whether or not to merge with Mapai or, as it is called, the three-way merger. I will not vote on this question. I did not take part in the negotiations with Mapai, I did not approve or disapprove of them, and I see no objection to members deciding to return to Mapai. But I will not vote for a simple reason: every vote binds the person who casts it as well as every other member. If the ballots are divided fifty-fifty, a single vote can decide the issue. Therefore a member who is unwilling to accept majority rule on this question is not entitled to vote and thus to commit others. As I am not prepared under any circumstances to return to Mapai as long as it is under the present leadership, I do not feel I have the right to cast my vote and thus commit other members.

> Facing the danger of Egyptian aggression in May 1967, multitudes of soldiers and officers realized something that only a few had known previously: Levi Eshkol is unfit for the post of Prime Minister and Minister of Defense. It is well known that the leaders of Gahal and the NRP together with Rafi wanted Eshkol replaced by a different member who was not prepared to return to the Government under any circumstances, and especially insisted that Eshkol be replaced as Minister of Defense by Moshe Dayan. This the Mapai leadership opposed with all its strength. The Army's apprehensions, however, got through even to the members of Mapai and the party secretariat began to demand that Dayan replace Eshkol as Minister of Defense. Eshkol, Golda Meir, Avigor, Arrane, and perhaps someone else in the top leadership resisted it to the limit, but the majority in the Mapai secretariat voted in favor of Dayan. It was decided to form a National Unity Government in which Menahem Begin and Josef Sapir would participate as representatives of Gahal.

> The co-option of Dayan and formation of the National Unity Government raised the Army's confidence in the Government. There is no need to dwell on the greatness of the Six-Day War and its effect on Diaspora Jewry throughout the world. But only a few imagined that the military victory settled things once and for all. Who could say what serious tests lay in store for us? We had to settle East Jerusalem with all possible dispatch. We had to move at least half the Hebrew University to East Jerusalem, rebuild the Jewish Quarter destroyed by the Arab Legion twenty years ago, reopen the airfield at Atarot, and settle the areas to the north and south of the capital. More than six months had passed but those whose duty and responsibility it was to devote themselves to these historic acts were busy with "more important" matters.

> It was clear to anyone with eyes in his head that our marvelous victory would stand us in good stead only if we could increase the Jewish population by encouraging people to have more children, which meant reversing the present trend, and by attracting more and more immigrants from the only remaining sources—the lands of prosperity. If every young Jew in Canada, the United States, Latin America, South Africa, and Western Europe were called upon to put in a year of service and study in Israel; if every Jewish family were

required to send at least one of its sons or daughters to settle in Israel; if every Jewish capitalist were invited to invest at least part of his money in profitable undertakings in Israel and every Cabinet Minister mobilized the cream of his workers and an appropriate part of his budget to *absorb* this immigration; and if the Government of Israel were headed by a man of vision, foresight, and wisdom who would devote all his energy and time to the attraction and absorption of immigrants, just as the Minister of Defense was required to invest all his time and energy to defense needs, only then would immigrants come and be absorbed on a large scale. Immigration is essentially a defense problem, because nothing is as important for the nation's security and future as the fostering and proper absorption of increased immigration, something in which every citizen of Israel can lend a hand with advice, assistance, and guidance. The secret of Aliya lies in the ability to absorb it, and its absorption depends on the desire and capability of the nation and its Government in full awareness of the objective.

Is there no way of ensuring the people of Israel at this fateful time capable leadership worthy of this task and this objective? This is why I have no right to return to Mapai as long as the present leadership is in the saddle.

In closing, let me say to my colleagues who favor the merger, believing that they will succeed in correcting the faults that led them to leave Mapai: would that together with many honest and loyal members of Mapai and Ahdut Haavodah you succeed in rectifying the errors and assuring Israel of the leadership it needs and deserves. Then will I proclaim aloud: you were right, dear friends, and more power to you.

Moshe Dayan said in part:

There are newspapers that depict us as mindless disciples of Ben-Gurion, and if he wants to torpedo the merger we will all be his loyal servants. There are newspapers that depict us as chasers after seats, which is why we are not going along with Ben-Gurion. And there are newspapers which accuse us of both.

This convention was called to decide whether or not to join the merger; to let people express their opinions on whether to return to Mapai or continue as an independent party. If the convention decides to merge with Mapai, I will do so. If it decides to follow an independent course, I will do so, and happily. Nevertheless, I will vote for the merger. I will not do so happily because I will be going there not to lend support but to propose that Eshkol cease to be Prime Minister and to fight for a different economic policy and a Minister of Finance other than Pinhas Sapir; to fight for a different election system and to change many things in the Histadrut. Naturally it is much easier to go along with the group in which I am partner than to go where I will come into conflict daily with the leadership.

I have to explain at greater length why I am voting for a merger. The question is not only *if* we will fight but *for what*. David Ben-Gurion says that the Mapai top leadership has to be changed and that if we succeed in doing so, he will admit that merger was a correct course. Now the Mapai leadership can be changed from within Mapai. And if you want to set up a different party it is not in order to replace a leadership but to replace Mapai altogether—to constitute an alternative.

I do not consider changing the Mapai leadership the only question, nor is the question one of bringing about a change in our political life, or in the election system or the economic or immigration policy. The question is whether we are capable of providing an alternative to a united party consisting of Mapai and Ahdut Haavodah. And before that comes the question of whether or not we have any partners. I have spent much time trying to persuade Menahem Begin to get Gahal to support a change in the election system, and I do not think that an interparty list will succeed. In the elections two years ago we received ten seats and I feel that ideologically and morally Rafi has lost none of its stature.

We are now at a crossroads—whether to continue as an alternative party—and I wish to say what I believe. I believe in a struggle even in an unpleasant context. We must struggle unflinchingly and uncompromisingly and seek in each and every issue the proper associates and positive achievement. I will vote in favor of a merger but if the majority decides against it, not only will I remain in Rafi as an independent party, but I will be happier than if it had joined the merger.

Barukh Ber said:

Moshe Dayan tried to justify favoring a merger by saying that he wants to be a partner in the practical day-to-day work of bringing about the necessary changes in our political life. If we could only be confident that this would be possible and we would have the opportunity to change what we feel needs changing in this country, I would vote in favor of a merger. But I remember that Dayan himself once learned that participation in a government is no guarantee of participation in good works, and when he found that he had to be a partner in bad works he chose to resign. The question is not whether we will participate but in what will we participate.

And I am not speaking of the next few years. Today we have a National Unity Government. The country's main problem now is that of security. Dayan is a member of the National Unity Government and I have not heard that he is satisfied with what is being done in the area of security. We are not, however, speaking of the next two years but of a longer period in which perhaps other problems will be at the center of our political life. The question is, Will we be able even then to expect good things from the merged party?

Dayan spoke of Aliya. He feels that the present Minister of Finance is not attracting Aliya. Have we reason to feel that by joining the party we will enhance the prospects of Aliya in the next few years? Will we hold both the Defense and Finance portfolios in that united party? I fear that our influence in the united party will be negligible. We and Ahdut Haavodah will each be given only 22 percent. Dayan has tried to show how small our chances are outside the united party. I have not heard him say that the chances inside the party are any greater.

For two years now Rafi has been fighting for matters of principle. The nation has hung its hopes on us. Many who did not support us have regretted it to this day. Many of those who set up the Eshkol Supporters Organization and besmirched Rafi are now sorry. Can we ignore this public? We do not represent merely thirty thousand members of Rafi. We represent a hundred thousand people who voted for us in the last election and perhaps two hundred thousand who would vote for us in the coming elections. We must be careful. If you decide on a merger there will be no way back.

Two alternate proposals were put to a vote on the evening of December 14: (1) the Rafi convention decides on the creation of a united labor party in which it will participate; (2) the Rafi convention decides to continue its independent existence. The number of eligible voters was 1169; 904 ballots were cast. The first proposal received 523 votes, approximately 58 percent; the second received 364 votes, approximately 42 percent. There were 16 abstentions. (One envelope was empty.) Thus Rafi approved the union.

Following several months of negotiations among Mapai, Ahdut Haavodah, and Rafi, the three-way merger called the Israel Labor Party came into being on January 21, 1968.

Nine of the ten Rafi members in the Knesset joined the merger. The one who did not join was Ben-Gurion.

Twentieth Anniversary Parade in Jerusalem ★ Ben-Gurion in the Knesset Urges Increased Immigration and Dedication As a "Chosen People"

Israel's twentieth Independence Day fell on a Friday. The celebrations were therefore advanced one day so that the Army would not have to put in several hours of marching on the Sabbath Eve.

On April 27, 1968, one week before the celebrations, the UN Security Council unanimously adopted a resolution calling on Israel to abstain from holding a military parade in Jerusalem, though it was obvious to all members of the Council that on this, the twentieth anniversary of the State, it was inconceivable for the parade not to be held in the nation's capital, reunited for the first time since the destruction of the Second Temple two thousand years earlier. The Jordanian government demanded that if the parade were held in Jerusalem, Israel be subjected to sanctions. Yet even the Soviet Union announced that it would not vote in favor of sanctions unless the United States did so as well.

Arab terrorists threatened to sabotage a Jerusalem parade, but the Government of Israel knew it could rely on its police and security forces to prevent any disruption and interference. And in fact the parade came off in perfect order with no interference whatsoever, and the enormous gap between the vainglorious boasts of the terrorists and their actual power was evident for all to see.

It was the largest and most impressive military parade in the State's twenty-year history. It began at 9:40 A.M., when the Presidential Guard and the Israel Defense Forces band entered the reviewing area opposite the President's platform. From the early-morning hours people had been streaming into the grandstand area and along the parade route that was bedecked with the national colors. The grandstand area was festooned with flags in the colors of the decorations awarded by the Israel Defense Forces to those who had participated in the three historic campaigns—the War of Independence twenty years ago, the Sinai Campaign eleven years ago, and the Six-Day War a year ago.

The parade began with an aerial show. Three hundred planes filled the sky. The first to appear were aircraft completely manufactured in Israel led by five Fouga Magister jets emitting trails of smoke in blue and white, the national colors. These were followed by two additional formations of Fougas, one in the form of a Star of David and the other the number 20. In the recent war these planes, armed with cannon, bombs, and rockets, had successfully carried out combat missions and destroyed scores of enemy tanks and vehicles. While the Fougas were flying overhead, forty-eight Mirage fighters streaked by underneath. These planes had shot down eleven enemy aircraft in aerial combat in the year preceding the Six-Day War and forty-six planes in the war itself.

Next came the debut of the Skyhawk jets acquired from the United States; eight such planes took part. These were followed by fourteen Vautour bombers, and thirty-six Ouragans—veteran craft that had fought in the Sinai Campaign, and had shot down MIG-21s;

then came twenty-four Mystères and nineteen Super-Mystères—our first supersonic fighters—which in the Six-Day War shot down MIGs and Ilyushin bombers; six large four-engine transport planes capable of paradropping supplies; nine Dakota transports, in service ever since the War of Independence, which in 1956 had dropped paratroopers into Sinai; eighteen Nord transport and paratroop planes; seven Super Frelon helicopters capable of carrying thirty fully armed troops; thirteen Sikorski helicopters, the kind that carry the war against terrorism into enemy territory, and nineteen Zell-205 helicopters recently acquired from the United States. The aerial exhibit concluded with a low-altitude flight by a MIG-21 that had been brought to Israel by an Iraqi Christian pilot two years earlier. It aroused great excitement among the spectators.

Then came the parade of land forces, opened by a group of military police on motorcycles and jeeps, followed by columns of armor—light tanks, Shermans, Pattons, and Centurions—and an artillery formation with guns of all types. The people were especially thrilled by the "booty" that had fallen to the Israeli forces in the Six-Day War. Largely Soviet-made tanks and guns, they were still in their original colors: Egypt, desert yellow; Syria, green; Jordan, yellow with green camouflage stripes. Finally came the massive infantry formations—paratroopers, women soldiers, combat engineers, Gadna cadets, troops of the Minorities Unit, the Nahal, the Israel police, and many others.

The parade came off in perfect order and few noticed the absence of the foreign military attachés who had chosen not to attend.

President Shazar received cables of congratulation on the anniversary from thirty-one Heads of State: the Presidents of Austria, Iceland, the United States of America, Bolivia, and Burma; the Queen of England, the Presidents of Gabon and South Africa; the Queen of Holland, the Presidents of India, Upper Volta, South Vietnam, and Turkey, the Emperor of Japan, the King of Laos, the Crown Prince of Luxembourg, the Governor-General of Malta, the President of Mexico, the King of Nepal, the Presidents of the Philippines, Peru, Finland, Chad, and Cuba; the Prince of Cambodia, the Governor-General of Canada, the President of Switzerland, the King of Sweden, and the King of Thailand.

The anniversary observations concluded with a special meeting of the Knesset on Monday, June 5. On behalf of his colleagues from all the parties on the Knesset Presidium, the Speaker, Kadish Luz, invited the first Prime Minister of Israel to be the sole speaker at this ceremonial meeting. Ben-Gurion said:

> The fifth day of Iyar in the year 5708 (May 14, 1948), when our natural and historic right to create the State of Israel was proclaimed, was undoubtedly one of the greatest and most glorious days in our nation's history. But the work of creating a Jewish State did not begin, nor did it end, on that day. The State of Israel came into being by virtue of three things: the vision of redemption bequeathed to us by the Prophets of Israel, the creative enterprise of the pioneers of the last century, and the heroism of our present-day warriors. Our State will survive and will fulfill its historic vision if the Jewish people and its government will succeed in attracting and absorbing immigration on an ever increasing scale and strive to be a select people. It is on these elements that our security, our survival, and our historic destiny depend.
>
> For hundreds of years Jews have prayed three times a day, "Sound the great trumpet for our freedom and raise the standard for the ingathering of our exiles and assemble us in our land from the four corners of the earth. . . and return in mercy to Jerusalem thy city. . . and quickly establish the throne of David therein." For hundreds of years this prayer remained unanswered because no practical action was taken to fulfill it.

Then, in the nineteenth century, a change came about. The Jewish emancipation in Western Europe in the wake of the French Revolution gave rise on the one hand to assimilation and on the other to a deepened Jewish awareness and a new appreciation of the vision of redemption. The new Hebrew literature, especially *The Love of Zion* by Abraham Mapu, with its invocation of the spirit of the Bible in its ancient glory, and a fresh conception of religion on the part of leading rabbis such as Alkalai, Kalisher, Mohliver, and their disciples. All blazed a trail to a new concept of messianic redemption and gave the Jew faith in his capacity to change and to mold his own fate and that of his nation, to rebuild his country and bring about his redemption by natural means—by Aliya, by settlement, and by fructification of the desert wastes of his ancient Homeland; and from the depths of the nation there sprang forth a latent pioneering desire and a creative ability which harnessed all one's forces to the realization of the vision without flinching from any difficulty, obstacle, or danger.

Though this creative faith was initially held by only a few, the living example of the first pioneers soon inspired tens, hundreds, and eventually thousands and tens of thousands. The first step was taken by Moses Montefiore, a Sephardi Jew born in Italy, and an honorary British subject. In 1856 he bought the first orange grove near Jaffa in order to teach the people of Israel agriculture. The French-Jewish Alliance Israelite Universelle went even further: in 1870 it built Mikve Israel, the first agricultural school in the land of Israel. Heading the Alliance was Adolphe Cremieux, the Minister of Justice in Gambetta's government. In the sixties of the nineteenth century he foresaw the Jewish return to their Homeland and the renewal of the Jewish State and sent Karl Netter here to see how it could be accomplished: "Here is the plan of the new institution in which you will be able to educate and accustom the coming generation to working the land; through it you will prepare a shelter for our brothers who today or tomorrow will be refugees from Gentile hatred; through it you will gradually regain the Holy Land to which the eyes of all Israel, the old generations and the new, are always turned. And you, gentlemen, do not be afraid and ask, How can we do this great thing? For if you will only sound the great trumpet to our brothers dispersed in the countries of the world, you will find that tomorrow will make today's dreams come true."

And an appeal for contributions issued by the Alliance said: "The Holy Land is the land of our fathers, the cradle of our faith, of our Prophets, and of our sages. The Holy Land is also fertile. Its ample resources have not yet been exhausted. All that is needed is to develop its resources, to remove the stones weighing it down, and to cultivate it diligently, and the land that formerly was very bountiful will once again become our Promised Land."

It was Jerusalem's privilege that one of its sons, Yoel Moshe Salomon, was one of the three initiators who in 1878 built the country's first Jewish village in modern times, Petah Tikva. His two associates in this pioneering effort were Yehoshua Stamfer and David Meir Guttman, both from Hungary. Yehiel Michel Pines said of them: "Petah Tikva was built by three things, the ideas of Yoel Moshe Salomon, the money of David Guttman, and the energy of Yehoshua Stamfer. This was the proverbial triple-stranded cord."

With regard to the nationalist vision the Bilu people brought with them we have a letter written by a Biluist sixty years before the creation of the State. One may look through all classical Zionist literature without finding a more succinct, pungent, and apt description of the way in which the State of Israel was created than in this letter written in Jaffa on November 7, 1882. The writer was A. Dubnov, the brother of the Jewish-Russian historian Shimon Dubnov. The letter makes it obvious that the ideas it expresses were not those of the writer alone but those of all his comrades who together with him had come to work at Mikve Israel. Even then they saw the need not only for agriculture and industry but for arms which would make it possible for the Jewish people to be master in its ancient land.

The same need was felt by the men of the Second Aliya who founded Hashomer, the beginning of the Israel Defense Forces—forty years before the promulgation of the IDF Ordinance on May 26, 1948, twelve days after the signing of the Declaration of Independence.

The State of Israel and everything in it is the work of people who returned to Zion, immigrants who came to rebuild the wasteland. It was they who laid the foundations for the State, though one should not disregard the considerable moral, economic, and political assistance rendered by Jews in the Diaspora, among whom we might mention three: Edmond de Rothschild, who was justly known as the Father of the Yishuv; Dr. Theodor Herzl, the father of the Zionist Organization; and Dr. Chaim Weizmann, the father of the Balfour Declaration.

It is one of the wonders of our nation's history in recent generations that the initiators of agricultural settlement with the avowed purpose of renewing Israel's independence in its ancient homeland—Cremieux, Netter, and Rothschild—arose among French Jewry, the most assimilated Jewish community in the nineteenth century. Dr. Herzl aroused the enthusiasm of the Jewish people and brought them here with the two words "The Jewish State" that led the League of Nations to recognize "the historical connection between the Jewish people and the Land of Israel and its right to renew its national home therein."

In the few years of his Zionist activity, 1897–1904, Dr. Herzl did not accomplish anything of importance in the Land of Israel but he created the Zionist Organization and transformed the Jewish people into a political factor of international importance. Dr. Weizmann invested much effort in the work of settlement and was the first Zionist leader who came to settle here without any external compulsion. Yet until the rise of Hitler in 1933 and the danger it portended for world Jewry, he did not properly appreciate the value of mass immigration. At the Zionist Congress of 1931 he was not elected president because in an interview with a journalist he had said there was no need for a Jewish majority in the Land of Israel.

At the Zionist Congress of 1933 the Labor delegation was the largest group and the Executive that was elected consisted mainly of representatives of the Labor movement: Eliezer Kaplan, Moshe Sharett, and this speaker. At the Histadrut convention that followed this congress I explained why I considered Aliya to be the main objective of the Zionist movement. I said in part:

"The disaster that has befallen German Jewry is not limited to that country. The Hitler regime constitutes a danger to the entire Jewish people and not to it alone. It is a regime which will not long survive without war, a war of revenge against France, Poland, Czechoslovakia, and the other neighboring countries that contain German minorities, or against the spacious Soviet Union. Germany will not go to war today because it is not prepared, but it is making ready for tomorrow. I don't want to make predictions but insofar as we must look to the future there is no doubt that we now face the danger of war no less than we did before 1914, and that such a war will exceed the last one in destruction and in horror.

"The Jewish people is not a world force that can prevent or forestall this danger, or even reduce or limit it, but there is one corner of the world in which we are a major, albeit not overwhelming, force and it is on this that our entire future as a nation depends. What will our strength and our significance here be on the day of judgment when this calamity comes about? Who knows, perhaps only four or five years, if not less, stand between us and this terrible day. And in this time we must double our numbers because on the day of decision our fate may well depend on the size of the Yishuv. This is one of the reasons why we must consider Aliya our chief aim."

I went to London to hold talks with Colonial Secretary Cunliffe-Lister and other political figures on the question of Aliya and in these talks was assisted considerably by Dr. Weizmann, though at the time he was merely a private person; the president of the Zionist Organization was Nahum Sokolov. In the three years 1933–1935 nearly 140,000

Jews came to Israel and at a meeting in London that year High Commissioner Wauchope told me that this was not the limit. Mussolini's war in Abyssinia, however, resulted in rioting in Palestine in 1936, which continued until 1939, when the Chamberlain-MacDonald White Paper in effect revoked the Balfour Declaration, disavowed the Mandate commitments, and promised within ten years' time to create a Palestinian state in which the Jews would forever remain a minority. A few months later Germany's attack on Poland marked the outbreak of World War Two, and on September 3, 1939, Britain declared war on Germany. On September 8, as chairman of the Zionist Executive, I summoned the leaders of the Hagana and told them:

"The declaration of war against Hitler has altered the situation. The Arabs' capacity for harm has not stopped but now under the new circumstances it carries less weight. Our positive strength, on the other hand, is likely to increase and comprises two elements: (1) the local Jewish community—half a million Jews with a high level of culture and creative and fighting capacity are a not insignificant factor in this part of the world; (2) world Jewry, especially the Jews of the United States; England knows that in this Gog-and-Magog encounter America may hold the key to victory. While the Jews are only 3 percent of the American population, their power and influence in political life is several times greater than their numbers. And now, on the brink of war, we must make clear what are our goals. They are two: (1) we must strive for the establishment of a fact, that of a Jewish State; (2) The war makes it incumbent on us to create a Jewish Army."

And American Jewry did not fail us. In the first two years of the war I spent much time in that country. In May 1942 all the Zionist parties and organizations came together for the first time and adopted the Biltmore Resolution, named after the New York hotel in which the convention took place. This resolution called for three things: (1) the opening of the gates of Palestine to Jewish immigration; (2) the placing of Aliya in the hands of the Jewish Agency; (3) the establishment of Palestine as a Jewish commonwealth integrated in the world's democratic structure. The resolution was adopted unanimously and only the Hashomer Hatzair delegate abstained. On my return I presented this plan to the Zionist Executive in Jerusalem which ratified it unanimously. On October 16, 1942, I presented it to the Zionist Steering Committee, which confirmed it by a vote of twenty-two to three. (The opposing votes were cast by two members of Hashomer Hatzair and one immigrant from Germany.) And thus the plan became the official program of the World Zionist movement.

Though the Churchill government was in sympathy with the Zionist cause, during the war it refused to make any change in the White Paper, since it considered the major objective to be the overthrow of the Nazi regime. Nevertheless it favored the creation of a Jewish State as soon as the war ended. In the postwar elections in England the Labour Party received an absolute majority and a government was formed by Attlee with Ernest Bevin as Foreign Secretary. At a convention in 1944 the Labour Party had decided on the creation, after the war, of a Jewish State in all of Palestine with the Arabs being transferred to the Arab countries, something the Zionist movement had never proposed. Attlee and Bevin, however, proceeded to disavow their party's stand and on February 19, 1947, after holding talks with the Jews and the Arabs and being unable to arrive at an agreement with either side, Bevin announced that his government had decided to refer the Palestine question to the United Nations, which had been founded in 1945.

In a debate on the Palestine question in May 1947 in the UN General Assembly the Soviet delegate, Andrei Gromyko, surprised the entire world by demanding the establishment of a Jewish State in part of Palestine. For me it was no surprise, because I had been informed previously by someone close to President Roosevelt that in a meeting with Stalin the latter had spoken in favor of creating a Jewish State in Palestine. What happened after that is well known. The majority of a UN commission sent to Palestine proposed the partition of the country and the creation of a Jewish State in the western part. And on November 29, 1947, more than two-thirds of the Assembly, including Russia and America, voted in favor or it. On the fifth day of Iyar 5708 the Jewish State was proclaimed at the Tel Aviv Museum because the road to Jerusalem had been closed off by the Arabs. On the same day President Truman extended the new State de facto recognition, and two days later the Soviet Union recognized it de jure.

The State of Israel is unique in its development and its place in the world. No other nation in history was deprived of its state, dispersed throughout the world, and after many, many centuries returned to renew its statehood in its ancient homeland. No other modern state was invaded on the day on its creation, outnumbered forty to one, and drove back all its enemies. The danger of destruction by its neighbors has not disappeared in all these years nor will it disappear in the near future, despite the fact that three times in the past twenty years Israel has defeated enemies who vastly outnumbered it. The most brilliant and glorious IDF victory of all, the Six-Day War eleven months ago, proved once more that quantity alone is not decisive.

Nevertheless, no one can say with certainty if this was the last battle, and only in the last battle can final victory be achieved. The bitter truth is that if, God forbid, the Arab armies defeat us only once, say in the fifth war, or the tenth, it may well be final because the Arab leaders' aspiration, like Hitler's, is to wipe us off the face of the earth. This then is our fate, and it enjoins upon us two things: to attract and absorb immigration at an ever-growing rate, and to be a select people. Only in these ways can our security be assured and our State fulfill its historic mission.

During the British Mandate, which lasted thirty years, some 452,000 Jews came here. The Jewish Agency (the official name of the Zionist Executive) had a recognized international status and was in charge of Jewish immigration. Only on rare occasions did the Mandatory Government take a favorable attitude toward such immigration, most of the time being either indifferent or hostile, and it was only the Zionist Executive that could handle immigration and care for the new immigrants. Yet when the State of Israel came into existence there was an historic obligation to transfer the problem of immigration to the Israeli Nation and the Jewish Government, because absorption of immigration is something that depends on the nation, on the people, and their Government.

However, it remained in the hands of the Jewish Agency because the majority of the members of the Government continued to live in the past. Some even feared that putting immigration into Government hands would weaken the World Zionist movement, failing to realize that after the creation of the State practically the entire Jewish people, with the exception of small minorities on the Left and on the Right, had become loyal friends of the Jewish State and, since they did not consider it their duty to come and settle here, even the Zionists were no more than friends. Most of the immigrants in fact were not Zionists at all. It was not by virtue of the UN decision of November 29, 1947, that the State of Israel came into existence, since the leaders of the neighboring states announced that they rejected it and would nullify it by force of arms and throw the Jews into the sea. This was one occasion on which they kept their word, because with the departure of the British High Commissioner, eight hours after the Jewish State's renewal, the Arab armies moved in to destroy it. Not one country raised a finger in our defense and it was only thanks to the valor of the IDF that Israel was transformed into a Jewish State.

Now, after the Six-Day War, Israel needs Aliya more than ever because our wondrous victory, which has aroused tremendous enthusiasm among Diaspora Jewry and amazement the world over, has intensified hatred and the urge for revenge on the part of the Arab leaders. We have heard what the Egyptian President, Gamal Abdel Nasser, said on June 9,

1967, after the defeat of the Egyptian Army: "No matter what the circumstances, and no matter how long it takes, the intrinsic forces of the Arabs are greater and more capable of action," and when imperialism has been liquidated in the Arab world and Israel stands alone, the day of revenge will come.

We need Aliya, which will augment our strength and capacity. And there will be such Aliya, in ever growing numbers if the intelligentsia of Israel will bring to its Jewish counterpart in America and Western Europe the news of our work here, of its great significance for Jews and for all humankind. There is a Jewish elite in the United States and other countries which will appreciate this significance and will be attracted to participate in our labors. The people and the Government of Israel will have to help in their absorption and incorporation in projects that will provide them satisfaction, both spiritually and practically. Israeli industrialists can help the leading industrialists in the lands of prosperity join in the creative economic undertakings now being developed here. Israel's pioneering youth can bring word to the cream of Jewish youth in the prosperous countries of our pioneering social projects, which are unparalleled anywhere in the world. And the finest of the Jewish youth will be attracted here just as the men of the First, Second, and Third Aliyot were attracted—not by a higher standard of living but because of a vision. There are Jews in America and Western Europe who hunger for a vision, and since the creation of the State an additional attractive force has been created—that of Jewish national independence.

Obviously not all the Jews in the prosperous countries will come here but if even a minority come and find spiritual satisfaction, they will provide an additional attractive force for their friends and relatives. This, however, will not come about unless the Government as a whole and the Prime Minister in particular look upon the attraction and absorption of immigration as the chief and most vital task of the State of Israel and the Israeli nation. Immigration ends not with entry into the Promised Land but with its proper integration, and this will not be assured without full attention on the part of the Government.

Yet we must realize that even if augmented and intensified, immigration alone will not solve all our problems, not even that of security. We have no prospects of matching our neighbors numerically. There is not even the possibility of preventing the quantitative gap from widening. At the time of the War of Independence twenty years ago Egypt's population was 15 to 16 million; now it is 30 million. The population of all the Arab nations combined is 100 million.

No one knows what these 100 millions are thinking because, with the possible exception of Lebanon, there is in the Arab states no freedom of thought and speech. We hear only what the leaders and their lackeys have to say, and these leaders are growing more and more venomous each year. Nor is it a question of mere words. After the Sinai Campaign of 1956 had secured for us more than ten years of freedom of navigation in the Straits of Eilat, the Egyptian leader came and, not without assistance by the UN Secretary-General, tried to close them again, realizing full well the consequences of this provocation. While the Six-Day War proved to the entire world our military superiority, a sober view of international relations tells us that our supremacy in the military sphere is a whole lot greater than in the international-political arena—an arena in which weakness can detract seriously, and sometimes dangerously, from military superiority.

Never since the creation of the Jewish State has our international weakness been so much in evidence as in recent years. Twenty years ago, in the War of Independence, the Soviet Union stood by our side aggressively and stubbornly and as a result we were able to acquire Czechoslovak war materials that assured us of victory. In 1956, before the Sinai Campaign, I revealed in the Knesset the extent of the aid we had received from France, and the part French arms played in the Six-Day War as well is also well known.

Even our bitterest enemies know that our Army is superior to all the Arab armies, but even the finest army—and it is doubtful whether any army in the world surpasses the IDF in quality, capability, and devotion—cannot fight empty-handed, and we are still far from producing all the equipment we need for our defense. Perhaps even more than others, we need loyal friends. We know full well how our neighbors acquire friends, East and West. They have fifteen votes in the UN and there is practically always at least one Arab on the Security Council. Their markets are several times larger than those of Israel; their oil resources are perhaps the greatest in the world. In none of these things will we be able to compete. If, nonetheless, we have managed to gain friends—and perhaps on almost every continent—it is solely because of a spiritual superiority.

It is a wonderful fact that this profound truth was mentioned in the days of antiquity by the greatest of our Prophets. And it is only because we received the Torah that we have maintained a separate existence under conditions in which no other nation has survived. Moses our Teacher said two things that are no less true today than they were three thousand and three hundred years ago. He, the greatest of our Prophets, said: "Ye shall be a peculiar treasure unto me above all people" (Exodus 19:5). And he repeated this in saying, "The Lord thy God hath chosen thee to be an official people unto himself above all people that are upon the face of the earth" (Deuteronomy 7:6).

Even among a special people there may be those who are empty; there may be money-grubbers, honor-seekers, swindlers, and deceitful persons. But this does not detract from the fact of being a nation that is chosen and elite, such as we have been in practically every generation. The State of Israel would not have come into being were it not for this fact, for there is no other example in human history of a nation cut off from its homeland for centuries and dispersed among hostile peoples, which preserved its uniqueness, character, and destiny and returned to its homeland after two thousand years of exile. And if our Army has been victorious three times it is only because it too is elite, and it is only an elite nation that can produce an elite army and enjoy the respect of nations that differ from it in race, tradition, and creed.

When the first Prime Minister of Israel submitted the Defense Service Bill to the Knesset on August 15, 1949, he said: "Our defense needs will not be satisfied unless our Army becomes a foundry for a fighting pioneering youth; since we are but few, we need spiritual supremacy more than any other army in the world. Only by developing our moral and intellectual advantage to the maximum will our Army fulfill its objective of maintaining national security."

Eight months after the creation of the State, one week after the end of the War of Independence, the Prime Minister of the Provisional Government, who was also Minister of Defense, convened intellectuals, authors, teachers, and scientists for a discussion in which he told them: "For many years to come the major part of our efforts and means will have to be devoted to defense. Defense, however, is only a means for our survival and independence. The State of Israel has another element that is unique—the redemption of the People of Israel and the ingathering of the exiles. We are few, a unique people, dispersed through all parts of the world, speaking many languages, influenced by many cultures, divided into various communities and tribes. This motley assortment must be melted down and recast in the image of the nation renewed. Within a short time we must do something that has never been done before, neither by us nor by any other nation. And this can be done only on one condition: that we succeed in mobilizing completely our one advantage—the moral and intellectual advantage of the Jewish people—because the State of Israel must be a model and an example."

Even if we succeed in bringing here a few million more Jews—and I am certain that it can be done, if the nation and its Government devote themselves to it heart and soul—we will not equal our neighbors in numbers. Yet this quantitative inferiority will be canceled out by a qualitative preponderance; and just as an army's quality depends on that of its commanders and trainers, so the quality of the nation will be dependent on the example set by its leaders. And as long as they will, in life and deed, "walk uprightly and work righteousness and speak the truth in their heart," as it says in the Book of Psalms, we can be certain that our nation will be an elite people in the future as well, and by virtue of it will attract the best of its compatriots from every place of exile, the lands of prosperity no less than those of hardship, and will acquire the friendship of nations the world over. Our future, I repeat, depends on two things—on increased immigration and on remaining an elite people.

Following this address by Ben-Gurion, the special session of the Knesset celebrating the twentieth anniversary of Israel's independence was adjourned.

XII

TWENTY YEARS—AND THE YEARS TO COME

Summing Up Two Decades of Growth; Looking to the Future

Section 1. Evolution of Defense and Key Legislation

From Hashomer through Hagana to Israel Defense Forces ★ Four Laws Setting a Nation's Course

O F all the objectives that confronted the State of Israel in its first twenty years the most difficult and the one marked by the most success was the creation of the Israel Defense Forces. Just as the State was not created on May 14, 1948, the day independence was proclaimed, so the IDF was not organized on May 26, 1948, the day the organization order was promulgated.

The first builders of the State, in the last thirty years of the nineteenth century, were compelled to take the defense of their lives and property into their own hands. The Ottoman regime was unstable, corrupt, and impotent, and in most parts of the empire anarchy reigned. No settlement in the land of Israel, Jewish or Arab, could be certain of survival, nor expect any help from the Ottoman authorities. During the Second Aliya at the beginning of the twentieth century Israel Shohat and his friends organized the first armed Jewish defense force, known as Hashomer. This, fifty years before the establishment of the State of Israel, was the original nucleus of the IDF. Hashomer had a twofold objective: to safeguard the Jewish settlements and individuals, and to foster friendly relations with their Arab neighbors; it succeeded in both.

Though the men of the First Aliya—from the founders of Mikve Israel (1870) and Petah Tikva (1878) to the founders of Metulla (1896)—had already given an example of self-defense on an individual basis, Yitzhak Ben-Zvi noted in 1957 in the preface to his book, *Hashomer:*

They did not arrive at any permanent and lasting public organization; Hashomer, on the other hand, was from the very outset intended to be a lasting and permanent union. Its function, which it inherited from its first nucleus (Bar-Giora) was to protect the lives and property of the Jewish population everywhere and at all times—not merely a single neighborhood or village but the entire population; and every member undertook to devote all his strength and his entire life to this. Enlistment for life—this was the object and function of Hashomer. Though few in numbers and lasting merely thirteen years—from the winter of 1907 to the spring of 1920—Hashomer left its mark both on its own generation and the following one, on the defenders of Tel Hai, the defense operations of the Third Aliya, and the young generation that participated in World War Two and in the war for Israel's independence.

The transition from Hashomer to the Hagana was not easy, nor was that from the Hagana to the IDF. Although the Hagana produced units that outdid Hashomer in fitness, training, and esprit de corps, many Hashomer veterans felt that nothing could be better than the former group. Similarly, many veterans and supporters of the Hagana felt that nothing could be more important or excellent than the crack Hagana units, of which the most distinguished was undoubtedly the Palmah.

The difficulties of organizing the IDF, which had to be subordinate to one authority and one only—the Government of Israel—were greater and far more numerous than those encountered in the organization of Hagana. All political parties in Israel, from the extreme right to the extreme left, had willingly signed the Declaration of Independence. The Israel Defense Forces Organization Ordinance said explicitly: "The Israel Defense Army, consisting of land, sea, and air forces, is hereby created. No armed force shall be created apart from the Israel Defense Army. The Minister of Defense is responsible for the implementation of this order." It was adopted unanimously by the Provisional Government. However, not only did the dissident organizations, which prior to independence had announced that they would cease to exist as soon as the State was proclaimed, refuse for a considerable time to accept the Government's authority, but even a party with two members in the Cabinet (Mapam) complained about Army matters to the Executive of the Histadrut (Labor Federation). And one of the commanders of the Palmah issued a directive to all units not to obey any order that did not come from Palmah headquarters. Naturally, he was obliged to rescind it.

In the end the IDF overcame the unfortunate legacy of a nation deprived of independence and national responsibility for nearly two thousand years. The entire world now knows that there is no military force more disciplined, united, valiant, and peace-loving than the IDF. The Israel Defense Forces was organized and trained along these lines from the very beginning under the experienced and talented direction of Chiefs of Staff Yacov Dori, Yigael Yadin, Mordekhai Makleff, Moshe Dayan, Chaim Laskov, Zvi Tsur, Yitzhak Rabin, Chaim Bar-Lev, and their gifted and loyal associates on all levels—the cream of Israel's youth.

The major objective of Israel—the ingathering of the exiles, that thousands-of-years-old legacy of faith and hope bequeathed by our Prophets and teachers—is still far from fulfillment. The "four-year development and absorption plan to double the country's population by mass immigration," put forward by the first elected Cabinet on being presented to the Knesset on March 8, 1949, two months after the end of the War of Independence, was achieved fully and even beyond expectations. In the first four years a total of

683,458 persons arrived, which with a natural increase of 88,400 made a total of 771,858. On the day the State was proclaimed the Jewish population was 650,000; four years later it was 1,404,000, an increase of more than 100 percent. Even with an absorptive capacity many times greater than Israel's, the United States of America did not double its population in the first twenty years after gaining its independence.

The demand by a few members of the Provisional Government that only selective immigration be permitted, because they feared that unlimited Aliya would destroy the young State, did not deter the majority. Although during the four years of mass immigration and several years thereafter an austerity regime was necessary and the immigrants were integrated only with great difficulty, in none of the subsequent twelve years was the immigration anywhere near as large as in the first four. The best year thereafter was 1957, the year after the Sinai Campaign, when 69,733 immigrants arrived. The worst was 1953, when only 10,347 arrived.

Not all the immigrants remained. During the twenty years even some oldtimers left the country. Not all who left declared that they were departing permanently, but the number of declared emigrants from 1949 to 1967 was 99,130. The Central Bureau of Statistics sets the actual number at nearly double that figure—183,728. The following official table shows the number of immigrants, of declared and actual emigrants, and the natural population increase among Jews for the twenty-year period:

YEAR	IMMIGRANTS	NATURAL INCREASE	DECLARED EMIGRANTS	ESTIMATED EMIGRANTS
1948	101,076	———	———	1145
1949	239,076	———	3259	7407
1950	169,405	———	4313	9466
1951	173,901	34,762	7647	10,476
1952	23,375	35,345	11,128	13,500
1953	10,347	35,085	8644	13,000
1954	17,471	31,411	5774	7500
1955	36,303	33,370	3922	6400
1956	54,929	33,135	6245	11,400
1957	69,733	34,137	6411	11,400
1958	25,919	32,854	7724	11,700
1959	22,983	33,993	7095	9750
1960	23,487	34,577	7206	8860
1961	46,571	32,697	4090	7330
1962	59,473	33,195	3698	7644
1963	62,156	33,647	2678	10,866
1964	52,456	35,435	2151	9121
1965	28,456	36,840	1878	7941
1966	13,451	37,280	2195	7793
1967	16,454	35,280	2772	10,529

The principal laws enacted during the first years of the State were the Defense Service Law, on September 8, 1949; the Law of the Return, July 5, 1950; the Compulsory Education Law, September 12, 1949, supplemented on August 12, 1953, by the National Education

Law; and the Equal Rights for Women Law of June 18, 1951. This legislation to a large extent fixed the country's character and direction.

The Defense Service Law established the character and spirit of the IDF. The Law of the Return identified the historical destiny of the State of Israel as the ingathering of the exiles. It stipulated that it was not the State that gave the Diaspora Jew the right to settle in Israel, but that the right was inherently his by virtue of his being Jewish. This right had existed prior to the establishment of the State and is the foundation on which the State was built and renewed. The Education Law guaranteed free compulsory education for every boy and girl from the age of six to fourteen without distinction of sex, religion, or nationality; and later it was fortified by establishing the purpose of education in Israel, and thus molding the nation's image. Section II says:

> The purpose of national education is to base elementary education in the State on the culture of Israel, the achievements of science, love for the Homeland, and loyalty to the State and people of Israel, training for agricultural and manual labor, pioneering achievements, and the aspiration for a society built on freedom and equality, tolerance, mutual aid, and love of one's fellowman.

The Equal Rights for Women Law gave legal sanction to the Basic Policy of the first elected Government, which stated that "there shall be full and complete equality for women, equality of rights and obligations in political, social and economic life and in the entire system of laws." The Ottoman legal system, part of which is still in force in Israel, discriminates against women. Even certain laws and regulations of religious communities, including Judaism, discriminate against women. The first article of the Equal Rights Law, 1951, states:

> Women shall be treated as men with regard to every legal action. No provision in the law discriminating against women per se shall be implemented. Married women shall have the same right of possession as single women. The right of possession of goods acquired before marriage shall not be impaired by the bond of marriage. The father and the mother are jointly the natural guardians of their children. If one of the parents is deceased, the remaining one shall be the natural guardian. This law shall not be taken to impair any legal enactment protecting women per se.

Vital Statistics: Education, Population, Settlements, Budgets, Economy

In the year the State was founded, 1948, Jewish pupils and students totaled 97,668: 15,695 in kindergartens; 67,464 in elementary schools; 11,470 in high schools; 1255 in vocational schools; and 1255 in seminaries for teachers and kindergarten teachers, and miscellaneous. In that year education had not as yet been brought under Government control; but after the formation of the first elected Government (March 1949) control of education was transferred from the National Committee (which had existed during the Mandatory regime) to the Israeli Government.

THE EDUCATIONAL SYSTEM IN ISRAEL

	1948/49	1967/68
Total students	140,817	774,399
Educational system	134,887	698,612
Academic institutions	1,635	28,520
Other institutions	4,295	47,267

	Hebrew School System	Arab School System	Hebrew School System	Arab School System
Total	129,688	11,129	691,490	82,909
Kindergartens	25,406	636	93,395	9,243
Elementary schools	91,133	6766	385,589	56,946
Special schools	—	—	12,570	52
Schools for working youths	—	—	6,691	239
Post-elementary schools (total)	10,218	14	123,160	2,909
High schools	6411	14	58,114	2,357
Evening high schools	—	—	2,117	—
Continuation classes	1048	—	9,654	—
Vocational schools	2002	—	41,044	267
Agricultural schools	—	—	7,865	285
Other post-elementary schools	—	—	—	—
Preparatory post-teachers and kindergarten teachers' seminaries	713	—	7,502	316
Academic institutes	1,635	—	28,520	—
Other institutes	583	3712	34,063	13,204

Since the creation of the State only two censuses have been held. The first, on November 8, 1948, showed a population of 782,000—713,000 Jews, 69,000 Arabs and others. However, at that time only the Jews were completely counted, because due to the war a considerable number of non-Jewish inhabitants in western Galilee, in the vicinity of Nazareth and Acre, the Midgal (Ashkelon) area, Beersheba, and the Arab villages in the Sharon could not be canvassed. At the close of 1948 (a few days before the war ended) the entire population within the borders of the State of Israel was estimated at 867,000—759,000 Jews and 108,000 non-Jews.

The second census, held on May 21, 1961, showed a population of 2,179,491—1,932,357 Jews and 247,134 non-Jews (11.3 percent). Of the Jews, 730,466 had been born in Israel and 1,201,911 abroad. The non-Jews included 170,830 Moslems, 50,543 Christians, 24,282 Druze, and 1479 others. Of the 1,201,911 Jews born abroad, 123,426 came from Iraq, 78,932 from Turkey and Persia; 61,869 from Yemen and Aden; 475,123 from Russia, Poland, and Rumania; 56,304 from Czechoslovakia and Hungary; 48,804 from Bulgaria and Greece; and 357,453 from other countries. By 1967 the population of Israel was 2,773,900 (2,383,660 Jews and 390,300 others); at the end of 1968 it was 2,807,000 (2406,500 Jews and 400,500 others).

From 1919 to May 14, 1948, a total of 452,158 immigrants arrived: 44,809 from Asia and Africa, 385,066 from Europe and America, and 22,283 unknown. From May 15, 1948, until 1961 arriving immigrants totaled 981,589; 512,034 from Asia and Africa, 450,127 from Europe and America, and 19,428 unknown. From May 15, 1948, until the end of 1951 the immigrants arriving totaled 684,201: 330,456 from Asia and Africa, 334,971 from Europe and America, and 18,774 unknown. From 1952 to 1954 the total immigration was 51,193: 39,978 from Asia and Africa, 11,187 from Europe and America, and 28 unknown. From 1955 until May 22, 1961: 246,195 — 141,600 from Asia and Africa, 103,969 from Europe and America, 626 unknown.

MARRIAGES, DIVORCES, BIRTHS AND DEATHS, 1951–1957

| YEAR | MARRIAGES | | DIVORCES | | BIRTHS | | DEATHS | |
	JEWS	ARABS	JEWS	ARABS	JEWS	ARABS	JEWS	ARABS
1951	15,556	1293	2373	144	43,249	7293	8487	1339
1952	16,154	1444	2399	180	45,131	7425	9786	1880
1953	14,037	1292	2299	142	44,364	8188	9277	1639
1954	13,257	1258	2142	126	41,046	7905	9635	1693
1955	13,530	1212	2050	106	42,339	8347	8969	1563
1956	13,724	1374	1944	126	43,411	8876	10,276	1749
1957	14,522	1461	2076	127	44,817	9123	10,644	1843
1958	14,711	1851	2136	131	42,872	9777	10,018	1597
1959	14,486	1617	2000	137	44,599	10,005	10,606	1450
1960	14,467	2065	2091	119	44,981	11,021	10,404	1649
1961	14,094	1774	1919	104	43,719	11,150	11,022	1641
1962	14,738	2100	2029	87	44,255	12,101	12,060	1641
1963	16,035	2283	2118	135	26,384	13,107	12,737	1688
1964	17,222	2016	2105	108	49,143	14,401	13,708	1783
1965	18,097	2186	2197	106	51,311	14,835	14,471	1790
1966	18,599	2063	2126	111	51,989	15,159	14,709	1873
1967	18,217	1808	1963	126	50,681	14,299	15,656	1987

The breakdown of the Jewish population by age groups in the 1961 census was as follows: Age 4 and under, 215,655 (11 percent); age 5–9, 231,276 (12 percent); age 10–14, 224,144 (11.6 percent); age 15–19, 152,488 (7.9 percent); age 20–24, 128,092 (6.6 percent); age 25–29, 128,862 (6.7 percent); 30–34, 124,501 (6.5 percent); 35–44, 17,930 (12.3 percent); 45–54 [figures not given]; 55–64, 151,748 (12.1 percent); 65–74, 73,235 (3.8 percent); 75 and over, 29,699 (1.5 percent).

In the same census the distribution of the Jewish population, native-born and immigrant, by type of settlement and residence, was as follows:

	BORN IN ISRAEL	BORN ABROAD	TOTAL
All types of settlements	730,446	1,201,911	1,932,357
Total urban settlements	606,942	1,027,524	1,634,466
Cities	514,943	832,033	1,346,976
Urban settlements	91,999	195,491	287,490
Rural settlements	123,504	174,387	297,891
Villages	28,048	57,975	86,023
Moshavim	52,540	71,592	124,132
Kibbutzim	39,516	37,445	76,961
Temporary settlements	241	1741	1982
Farms and institutions	2428	4104	6532
Others	703	1530	2333

In the 78 years from the foundation of Mikve Israel in 1870 to the creation of the State 302 agricultural settlements were established; in the first 4 years after the birth of the State 263 new agricultural settlements were founded and by the end of 1967 the new agricultural settlements came to 669. At the end of 1967 the Jewish agricultural population was 494,652 in 804 rural settlements, of whom 234,826 were in 158 villages, 121,613 in 345 moshavim, 4970 in 22 moshavim shitufim, 883,310 in 233 kibbutzim, and 12,083 in 46 institutions and farms.

In 1948–1949 Jews were cultivating a total of 1,310,000 dunams of land, including 292,000 dunams under irrigation. Non-Jews were cultivating 340,000 dunams, including 8000 dunams under irrigation. In 1967–1968 Jews were cultivating 3,320,000 dunams, including 1,599,000 dunams under irrigation, and non-Jews cultivated 870,000 dunams, including 41,000 dunams under irrigation. In 1948–1949 there was a total of 355,000 dunams of plantations, broken down as follows: Citrus fruit, 125,000 dunams; grapes, 48,000 dunams; seed fruits, 25,000 dunams; olives, 137,000 dunams; bananas, 5000 dunams; subtropical crops, 15,000 dunams.

In 1966–67 there were 883,000 dunams of plantations, 756,000 cultivated by Jews and 127,000 by non-Jews. The distribution was as follow: Citrus fruit, 458,000 dunams (Jews 453,000 dunams, non-Jews 5000 dunams); grapes, 111,000 dunams (Jews 96,000, non-Jews 15,000); seed fruits, 55,000 dunams (Jews 54,000, non-Jews 1000); drupe fruits, 62,000 dunams (Jews 48,000, non-Jews 14,000); olives, 110,000 dunams (Jews 28,000, non-Jews 82,000); bananas, 23,000 dunams (all by Jews); subtropical fruits, 16,000 dunams (all by Jews); other crops, 48,000 dunams (Jews 38,000, non-Jews 10,000).

In 1948–1949 Israel had a total of 53,000 dunams of forest, of which 13,000 were owned by the Government, 25,000 by the Keren Kayemet, and 15,000 by others. In 1955–1956 the forested area reached 440,000 dunams, of which the Government owned 109,000 dunams, the Keren Kayemet 317,000, and others 14,000. In 1966–1967 forests totaled 462,000 dunams, of which the Government owned 108,000, the Keren Kayemet 340,000, and others 14,000.

We have no industrial census of the labor force for the first years of the State. The only survey we have was made in 1955, when the number of persons employed was 585,700: 162,200 in agriculture, afforestation, and fishing; 127,000 in industry, crafts, mining and minerals; 54,300 in building; 11,900 in electricity, water, and sanitary services; 78,600 in commerce, banking, and insurance; 36,000 in haulage and storage; 171,400 in services (including government, public, and personal services).

The total number of Jews employed in 1967 was 830,700: 104,200 in agriculture, afforestation, and fishing; 203,800 in industry, crafts, mining, and minerals; 63,000 in building and public works; 18,500 in electricity, water, and sanitary services; 111,600 in commerce, banking, and insurance; 51,100 in haulage and storage; 266,800 in services; 62,700 in government, public, and administrative services; 137,300 in health, education, welfare, religious, and legal services; 66,800 in personal services; 1700 unknown.

FOREIGN TRADE BALANCE IN THOUSANDS OF DOLLARS

Year	Net Imports	Net Exports	Imports Surplus	Export/ Import Ratio (%)	Foreign Trade Per Person (in dollars)		
					Imports	Exports	Deficit
1949	251,906	28,495	223,411	11.3	241	27	214
1950	300,325	35,147	265,178	11.7	237	28	209
1951	381,682	44,254	336,928	11.7	255	30	225
1952	322,261	43,489	278,772	13.5	201	27	174
1953	279,929	57,636	222,293	20.6	170	35	135
1954	287,248	86,301	200,948	31.0	170	51	119
1955	334,453	89,056	245,397	26.6	192	51	141
1956	375,593	106,501	269,092	28.4	205	58	147
1957	432,829	140,127	292,707	32.4	224	72	152
1958	420,930	139,102	281,828	33.0	211	70	141
1959	427,291	176,383	250,908	41.3	207	85	122
1960	495,646	211,276	284,370	42.6	234	100	134
1961	583,912	239,082	344,830	40.9	267	109	158
1962	626,222	271,403	354,819	43.3	273	118	155
1963	661,987	338,285	323,752	51.3	278	142	136
1964	815,500	351,801	463,699	43.1	329	142	187
1965	810,956	406,095	404,699	50.1	316	158	158
1966	813,807	476,926	336,881	58.6	310	181	129
1967	747,456	518,046	229,410	69.3	275	191	84
★1967	749,456	533,046	216,410	71.1	276	196	80

★(Includes Occupied Territories)

The national budget for 1948–1949 was: income—IL 28.9 million, expenditures— IL 27.5 million (not including the full defense budget). In 1968–1969: both income and expenditures that year came to IL 7,009,700,000: the regular budget was IL 4,120,700,000; the development budget, IL 1,776,800,000; and for repayment of debts and business enterprises, IL 1,112,200,000.

The number of telephones in the country, 18,400 in 1948–1949, reached 358,500 by 1967–1968.

From 1949 to the end of 1967 a total of 44,641,000 square meters of buildings were erected for housing, businesses, offices, factories, public buildings, and farm buildings. The housing problem, of course, has not yet been fully solved.

Economic independence has not been achieved, though the foreign trade balance has been considerably reduced. In 1949 net imports totaled $251,906,000 and net exports $28,495,000. The surplus of imports over exports was $223,411,000, and the export-to-import ratio was 11.3 percent. In 1966 net imports totaled $811,453,000, net exports, $476,771,000; the import-over-export surplus was $334,682,000, and the export-to-import ratio, 58.8 percent. In 1967 net imports were $746,456,000, net exports, $518,046,000; the import-over-export surplus was $229,410,000 and the export-to-import ratio, 69.3 percent.

The population dispersal policy that the first elected Government set as one of the prime defense and economic objectives has also progressed, if slowly. In the Negev, containing 60 percent of the area of the State (before the Six-Day War), the following cities were created in the past twenty years: Beersheba (before the creation of the State a village of 3000 Arabs, now a Jewish city of over 70,000), Eilat, Dimona, Arad, and Yeruham; and in upper Galilee: Kiryat-Shmoneh, Nahariya, and Carmiel. A number of agricultural settlements have also been established in the Negev: Ein Gedi, Ein Yahav, Hatzeva, Sde Boker, Yotvata, Grofit, Tsofar, and others. Yet more than 95 percent of the Negev still remains desolate and unpopulated.

In June 1967, after the Six-Day War, there were 599,377 non-Jewish inhabitants on the West Bank, 356,261 in the Gaza Strip, 6396 on the Golan Heights (practically all Druze); 23,675 in the Old City of Jerusalem and another 42,182 in the vicinity of East Jerusalem. Of the inhabitants of the Old City in Jerusalem 82.4 percent were Moslem, 16.8 percent Christians, and 0.8 percent Druze and others.

During the two decades the Jewish Agency spent $167.1 million on Aliya. In these years many changes occurred in the "geography" of the Diaspora. Several Jewish centers were liquidated and their inhabitants practically all came to Israel. This was especially true of Bulgaria, Yugoslavia, Yemen, Libya, and Iraq. Considerable parts of the Jewish communities of Turkey and Iran also moved to Israel. In Egypt and Algeria only a few Jews remained. Most of the immigrants from Algeria went to France, but recently some of them have come to settle in Israel.

The amount spent on absorbing these immigrants in these years was $245 million. This included caring for their immediate needs on arrival, moving them to their place of settlement, and meeting other needs during their first period after arrival. Of these immigrants 95,000 learned Hebrew in Ulpanim [Intensive Language Institute] after their arrival.

The burden of providing housing for the 1.3 million immigrants who came in the last twenty years was beyond the capacity of the Jewish Agency and was borne mainly by the Israeli Government. The expenditure for housing was $240.5 million. During the first period of mass immigration the Jewish Agency had to lodge immigrants temporarily in ma'abarot (transit camps). With the help of the Jewish Agency and the Government 230,000 permanent housing units have been built. The Jewish Agency also spent $173.7 million on education for new immigrants. This outlay made it possible to bring over youngsters aged thirteen to seventeen. On the initiative of the first Prime Minister, the United Jewish Appeal set up an educational fund that ensured high-school education for immigrants by constructing youth centers.

The largest single item of expenditure by the Jewish Agency during these twenty years was agricultural settlement; $771.1 million was spent in the creation of 480 settlements (compared to 291 before the creation of the State) with a population of 35,000 families or more than 100,000 persons. The area under cultivation by these new settlements is half a million dunams, or 45.5% of all land cultivated by Jews.

With the help of the commercial banks, the Agency provided 75,000 loans totaling

$81.6 million to middle-class immigrants during the years 1956–1966 and $9.8 million in 1967–1968. At this writing [1969] 90 percent of these loans have been repaid.

Despite the generous contribution of Diaspora Jewry the Agency was only partially able to carry out its function in immigration and was compelled more and more to rely on Government assistance. As of March 1967 the total income of the Jewish Agency from the United Jewish Appeal was $944.8 million. Only 53.5 percent of the amount spent by the Agency during the first twenty years was received from abroad. The remainder was provided by the Israeli Government out of German reparations and other sources.

Despite the improved economic situation and the reduction of unemployment, part of the population has remained incapable of working or limited in its capacity to work. Assistance has had to be provided to 15,000 persons including 6800 elderly and disabled persons. The Jewish Agency has spent $52.4 million for this purpose.

Section 2. What of the Future?

The Legacy of a Unique Nation

THE annals of the Jewish people are unique in human history. For four thousand years it has stood alone among the nations and has had to fight for its survival and historic destiny. The struggle continued while it lived in its own land and was intensified after its independence was twice destroyed, when only few of its members remained in the Homeland, and the overwhelming majority were dispersed among the nations. For nearly two thousand years it carried on a never-ending struggle of the spirit.

Even after the nations of the world, first in the Council of the League of Nations on July 24, 1922, and then in the UN Assembly on November 29, 1947, recognized the Jewish people's right to renewed independence in its historic Homeland, and after the proclamation of the State of Israel on May 14, 1948, its neighbors did not desist from assailing Judaism and the Jews. In the first twenty years of the State its builders had to go to war three times to defend their lives, independence, and historic mission: the War of Independence of 1948, the Sinai Campaign of 1956, the Six-Day War of June 1967. Despite brilliant victories in all three—not without heavy losses—peace is still far away, and behind the Arab leaders who have not ceased threatening to destroy Israel stand two mighty powers, the Soviet Union and Red China, and their satellites in Europe and Asia.

In ancient times Israel was isolated because unlike the other nations its people believed in one God rather than a multitude. The Prophet Yesha'yahu (Isaiah) says (45:6,7) "I am the Lord and there is none else. I form the light and create darkness; I make peace and create evil: I, the Lord, do all these things." The Jews believed that man was created in the image of God—that is to say, without distinction as to race, nationality, or religion. This is why our Torah says: "If a stranger sojourn with thee in your land he shall be unto you as one born among you and thou shalt love him as thyself." This was not said in any other country—not in Greece nor in Rome, in India, China, Egypt, or Bablyon. The Prophets of Israel believed in the equality of all peoples and peace among them.

The Prophet Amos said (9:7): "Are ye not as children of the Ethiopians unto me,

O Children of Israel? saith the Lord." And Isaiah said (2:2–4): "And it shall come to pass in the last days that nation shall not lift up sword against nation, neither shall they learn war anymore." Unlike all other nations, Christians and Moslems included, the people of Israel did not consider the Golden Age to be in the past but in the future—in the end of days. According to the faith of the Jewish people, redemption occurred not in the distant past but would come in the future at the end of days.

Who is the ideal man? The Psalmist answers (15:2): "He that walketh uprightly and worketh righteousness, and speaketh the truth in his heart." And the Prophet Micah summed up the entire Torah as follows (6:8): "He hath showed thee, O man, what is good; and what doth the good Lord require of thee, but to do justly and to love mercy, and to walk humbly with thy God?" And the Prophet Yirmi'yahu (Jeremiah) says (9:22–23): "Thus saith the Lord, let not the wise man glory in his wisdom, neither let the mighty man glory in his might, let not the rich man glory in his riches: but let him that glorieth glory in this, that he understandeth and knoweth me, that I am the Lord which exercised loving kindness, judgment and righteousness in the earth for in these things I delight, saith the Lord."

And there is an entire book in the Bible, the Book of Jonah, that is not a historical document but whose purpose is to show that in the eyes of the Lord all nations are equal. The book tells how the Prophet Jonah was sent by the Lord to Nineveh, the great city, to bring them to desist from their evil. Jonah did not want to go, and en route from Jaffa to Tarshish by ship a mighty tempest arose. Jonah knew that it was on his account that the storm had arisen and proposed that the sailors throw him into the sea. This they did, albeit reluctantly, and he was saved by a great fish. Again the Lord told him to go to Nineveh. When Jonah saw that one could not flee from the Lord, he proceeded to Nineveh and preached to them to desist from their evil ways and they heeded him and all the evil with which he threatened them did not come about and Jonah was exceedingly vexed. Jonah went to the east of the city and sat in the shade and the Lord appointed a plant to provide shade over his head. However, the next morning the Lord made the plant wither and the sun beat on Jonah's head so that he fainted. And the Lord said to him: Do you do well to be angry with the plant which has withered and is no more? And Jonah said, I do well to be angry, angry enough to die. Then the Lord said to him—and this is the moral of the entire story: "You pity the plant for which you did not labor and nor did you make it grow, which came into being in the night and perished in the night. And should I not pity Nineveh, that great city in which there are more than 120,000 persons who do not know their right hand from their left and also much cattle?"

In other words, every nation is precious unto the Lord and He wishes them to do good so they may live, they and their cattle. And when the angels of the Lord told Abraham that the Lord saw that the sin of Sodom was great and He was about to destroy it, he said to the Lord, "Wilt thou also destroy the righteous with the wicked? Shall not the judge of the earth do right?"

In ancient times the Children of Israel had neighbors: Edom, Moab, Amon, Sidon, Tyre, Aram—names familiar to every Bible reader. What has remained of them apart from a few archaeological relics? It is hard to accept the fact that these nations have been utterly destroyed. Of their language, culture, and faith, nothing remains, not a single living remnant. The Jewish people in its own land is the only Mediterranean nation that continues to speak the language spoken by the ancestors three and four thousand years ago and to profess the faith of the Patriarch Abraham and our great teacher Moses. Twice the

Jewish people were uprooted from their land. For two thousand years they have been dispersed over the entire globe. They have wandered from country to country and speak the seventy languages of the nations among whom they lodged. Yet never did our nation sever ties with the land from which it was exiled. Three times a day it prays: "Sound the great trumpet of our freedom and raise the standard to rally our exiles and gather us in from the four corners of the earth and return to Thy city Jerusalem with compassion and build it speedily soon in our day to last for all eternity and the throne of David quickly establish therein."

Ninety years ago this prayer inspired the Jews to an act of unparalleled daring. On the desolate, malaria-infested land on the banks of the Yarkon River they built the first Jewish village in modern times, Petah Tikva. After that other villages were established: slowly at first and then by the scores and hundreds, all over our country. The Hebrew language, which was considered by the nations of the world to be holy but dead, returned to life. A hundred years ago the language of Abraham our Father and Moses our Teacher was the mother tongue of not a single Jewish child in the entire world; today it is spoken by hundreds of thousands of boys and girls, youths and old men. And five years after the most terrible holocaust the world has ever known—the murder by the Nazis and their allies of six million European Jews, who for the previous two hundred years had constituted the spiritual, moral and cultural center of world Jewry and paved the way for the return and upbuilding of Zion—the State of Israel was renewed.

In the twentieth century dozens of new countries have come into being in Africa, Europe, and Asia. There is, however, a fundamental difference between the State of Israel and all these other countries. At about the same time as the State of Israel was renewed, four other Asian states—India, Pakistan, Burma, and Ceylon—also came into being. The Indians, Burmese, Ceylonese, and Pakistanis had been living in these countries and had spoken the same language both before and after the creation of their states. The only basic change brought by independence was the elimination of foreign rule. The same was true in all the other new states—except the State of Israel. While our people lived in the land of Israel three and four thousand years ago, it was not the elimination of foreign rule that brought about the creation of the State but the return to Zion. Even after the defeat of Bar Kochba in the year 135 of the Christian Era, Jews have always lived in Israel and immigration has continued without interruption from that time to this day.

The Jewish population in Israel was very small. In 1850 there were 10,000; in 1880, 20,000; in 1900, 50,000; in 1914, 85,000; and in 1919, 56,000. (Jews of Russian nationality had to leave the country when Turkey entered World War One on the side of Germany in 1915.) In 1931 the Jewish population was 174,600; in 1940, 467,500; in 1948 (on the day the State was proclaimed), 650,000 (5.7 percent of the world's Jewish population); and at the end of 1967, 2,383,600 (17.5 percent of the world's Jewish population). In its twentieth year the State created by the return to Zion thus did not have even twenty percent of the Jewish people.

In the year of Israel's twentieth anniversary its military forces won one of the greatest and most brilliant victories not only in Jewish history but in world history. Yet no military victory alone can solve Israel's problems. Like the victories in the War of Independence in 1948 and the Sinai Campaign in 1956, the victory in the Six-Day War of 1967 did not even solve Israel's problem of defense and security. Nor has the settlement, education, and economic work with so much accomplishment to its credit during these two decades yet solved all the problems in these areas. The cultural and economic gap between the various communities has not been completely eliminated, economic independence has not yet been assured, tens of thousands of immigrants still remain illiterate, and a considerable number of them still do not have decent housing. Moreover, our victory in the Six-Day War has resulted in new problems and intensified others that had not been conspicuous previously.

The Six-Day War gave rise to two factions professing slogans that seem diametrically opposed—territorial integrity and peace with the Arabs. Yet there have been people who professed both; one of them was Dr. Chaim Weizmann, who on February 3, 1919, came to an agreement with Feisal, the son of Sherif Hussein of Mecca, who at the time was considered the representative of the entire Arab world, containing these provisions:

> Article II. Immediately following completion of the Peace Conference, definite boundaries between the Arab state and Palestine shall be determined by a commission to be agreed upon by the parties thereto.
> Article III. In the establishment of the Constitution and Administration of Palestine all such measures shall be adopted as will afford the fullest guarantee for carrying into effect the British Government's Declaration of November 2, 1917 (the Balfour Declaration).
> Article IV. All necessary measures shall be taken to encourage and stimulate immigration of Jews into Palestine on a large scale, and as quickly as possible to settle Jewish immigrants on the land.

Even before that, on December 12, 1918, the London *Times* published a declaration made by Feisal to a Reuters correspondent:

> The two principal branches of the Semitic family, the Arabs and the Jews, understand one another, and I hope that after the exchange of opinion at the Peace Conference, which will be guided by the principle of national self-determination, each of the two peoples will successfully advance towards the fulfillment of its aspirations. The Arabs are not jealous of the Zionist Jews, and will treat them fairly. The Jews, in turn, have promised nationalist Arabs that they also will be treated fairly."

While in exile in America, I wrote in *Der Yiddische Kempfer*, the Poalei Zion organ is the United States, on the 6th of Shevet 5678 (1918):

> Even if proclaimed and recognized by the Council of Nations, the Jewish State will not come into being overnight. The Land of Israel is not unpopulated. Within what must be considered the bounds of the Land of Israel, a territory of fifty-five to sixty thousand square kilometers on both sides of the Jordan, live slightly more than a million people. On the west side of the Jordan alone there are approximately three-quarters of a million (including fifty-eight thousand Jews). On no account must the rights of these people be prejudiced, yet according to the calculations of Professor Karl Blad the country's plains under irrigation can support a population of 6 million

When I was appointed a representative of the World Union of Poalei Zion in 1920, I sent to the British Labour Party a memorandum concerning the meaning of the Balfour Declaration:

> Immediately after the Peace Conference discussions, the borders shall be set between the Arab State and Palestine. In the establishment of the Constitution and Administration of Palestine, all such measures shall be adopted as will afford the fullest guarantees for carrying into effect the British Government's (Balfour) Declaration of November 2, 1917. All neces-

sary measures shall be taken to encourage and stimulate the immigration of Jews into Palestine on a large scale, and as quickly as possible to settle Jewish immigrants upon the land.

After my election to the Zionist Executive in 1933 I conducted negotiations with Arab leaders on the basis of a proposal I made to Musa Alami, one of the leading Arabs in the Land of Israel, and a confidant of the Mufti of Jerusalem. It envisaged the creation of a Jewish State to include both sides of the Jordan, in return for our support for the establishment of an Arab Federation in the neighboring states and an alliance of the Jewish State with it. Musa Alami replied immediately that this was something we could talk about. Negotiations went on for several months between myself and the Mufti, with Musa Alami acting as go-between, and an agreement was finally reached, though Musa Alami and the Mufti stated that it required ratification by the Syrian-Palestinian Committee affiliated with the League of Nations in Geneva.

I also carried on negotiations with Auni Abdul Hadi, leader of the Istiklal (Independence Party) who accepted the proposal in principle but demanded guarantees that the Jewish State would not be granted independence before the creation of the Arab Federation. When I suggested that guarantees be provided by the British government, he declined on the grounds that the British were swindlers and as for the League of Nations, they were Christians and could not be trusted. We also held talks with representatives of Lebanon, Syria, and Egypt but there were no results because none of them was able to commit itself to anything concrete.

But now we have behind us twenty years of a Jewish State and three attempts on the part of the Arab countries to destroy it. The great problem raised by the Six-Day War is how we will survive in the future. At this writing, not one Arab leader in the Middle East is prepared to discuss peace with us. The main question is how we can safeguard our security and avoid ending up as a minority.

Imperatives for Survival: a Higher Birthrate, More Immigration, Bigger and Better Labor Forces

One of the most vital elements in the equation of survival is the fact that the Jewish birthrate is much lower than that of our neighbors and is decreasing annually. In 1951 the birthrate among Jews was 26.3 per thousand and among non-Jews 37.6 (there are no figures for earlier years). In 1966 the Jewish birthrate in Israel was 16.1 per thousand as against 43.4 among non-Jews. In 1949 the non-Jewish population in Israel was 160,000 and at the end of 1967 390,300; in nineteen years it had increased two and a half times by natural increase alone. But in these nineteen years the natural rate of increase among Jews declined sharply, from 23.1 to 14.9 per thousand.

After the Six-Day War the population of the West Bank was 599,377, all of them non-Jews; in the Gaza Strip, 356,261; the Golan Heights, 6346 (practically all of them Druze); the Old City of Jerusalem, 23,675 and in the surrounding area 42,182—a total of 1,027,891. If its natural rate of increase continues as previously, the non-Jewish population in these areas in another twenty years will be 2.5 million, and in Israel itself 1 million.

Hence the "complete Land of Israel," not including Trans-Jordan, will contain 3.5 million non-Jews. And if the Jewish birthrate continues to decline as in previous years, the outcome for the State of Israel is not hard to imagine.

During the British Mandate three censuses were taken. In 1922 the population of the western part of Palestine was 757,182 (83,794 Jews and 673,388 non-Jews). In 1931 the population was 1,035,821 (174,610 Jews and 861,211 non-Jews). The Jewish population had grown by 90,816. A total of 89,791 immigrants had arrived in a nine-year period, and though some of them did not stay (we have no statistics) there is no doubt that the major part of the increase was due to immigration. In 1944 the population was 1,697,970—553,600 Jews and 1,144,370 non-Jews. In eleven years the Jewish population had increased by 378,990 persons. In that period (1932–1943, inclusive) immigration came to 341,189. Again the population growth was mainly due to immigration.

In 1967 the Jewish birthrate in Israel touched a new low: 14.9 per thousand (the high point was 26.5 per thousand in 1950). These figures show that for survival and security of the State of Israel a higher birthrate and increased immigration are essential.

When Eshkol presented his Government on January 21, 1966, after the Knesset elections of November 2, 1965, he also presented the Government's basic policy for the next four years. A long chapter was devoted to the Government's economic policy for the coming period. Yet scarcely ten months later, on October 11, 1966, the Prime Minister presented a new economic plan for the three-year period January 1, 1967, to December 31, 1969. This was because of the deteriorating economic situation resulting from the fact that during the elections the Coalition parties, especially the "Alignment for Unity of the Workers of the Land of Israel," had promised wage increases of 25 to 35 percent. In explaining the new plan, Eshkol said, "Several changes have come about in the economic situation and not all of them positive. I refer first of all to the *excessive increase in wages at the end of 1965 and the beginning of 1966*." The wage increases resulting from regrading were sharply excessive. It was in this plan that Eshkol first introduced a clause "to encourage childbirth by improving living conditions, alleviating the cost of education," and so on. However, at this writing practically nothing had been done in this connection. But since practically nothing had been done to implement the other aspects of the policy, either before or after the Six-Day War, we cannot complain that the birthrate problem is an exception.

The very fact that the subject of birthrate was introduced into the economic plan showed that the Government had no understanding of the problem. Since the problem of the birthrate does not affect all the inhabitants but only the Jewish community, it cannot be solved by the Government. Israel provides equal rights for all its citizens, without distinction of race and nationality. Although, as proclaimed in the Declaration of Independence, it is a Jewish State, it is only in the matter of immigration that the law, specifically the Law of the Return, distinguished between Jews and non-Jews. Since the supreme objective of the State is the ingathering of the exiles, the Law of the Return applies only to Jews. In every other respect there is complete equality. Consequently, if the Government plans to increase the birthrate by providing special assistance to large families, the main beneficiaries will be Arab families, which are generally larger than Jewish families.

Since it is only the Jews who need such incentives, the Government is unable to deal with the problem, and the matter should be transferred to the Jewish Agency or some special Jewish organization. If the Jewish birthrate is not increased, it is doubtful that the Jewish State will survive. As we have seen, from 1951 to 1966 the Jewish birthrate declined from 26.1 to 16.1 per thousand, whereas among the Arabs it rose from 37.6 to 43.4. The bodies that must deal with this problem are Jewish men's and women's organizations in Israel and the Jewish Agency. And this must be done in two ways: (a) to bring home to the Jewish woman and the Jewish family that the future of their nation depends on their producing a sufficient number of healthy children; (b) to provide large Jewish families with more economic, social, and educational assistance, including better housing, sufficient income, and the possibility of providing elementary, secondary, and higher education.

Jewish women's organizations, such as WIZO and the Working Mothers Organization, are doing good work. There are also organizations of Jewish intellectuals. It is incumbent upon them to explain to women of European origin as well as to those born in Israel and to every Jewish woman capable of understanding the unique needs of a nation such as Israel that their prime obligation to their people is to have at least four children, and, as far as possible, within eight to ten years after getting married.

When I was Secretary of the Histadrut, I raised the problem of the birthrate in its Executive. A woman member of Hashomer Hatzair attacked me for having "imperialistic" ideas. I am almost certain that this member—I am happy to say she is still alive and saw her husband return safely to Israel after being tortured in a prison in Prague to make him confess to spying for the imperialists—will no longer denounce me for urging a higher birthrate. It is not an imperialist idea but a vital need for the people of Israel. Any Jewish woman who, as far as it depends on her, does not bring into the world at least four healthy children is shirking her duty to the nation, like a soldier who evades military service. And it is the duty of the Jewish people as a whole to provide women with the economic, cultural, and social conditions to enable them to give these children a proper upbringing and education.

Every Jewish mother can and must understand that the unique situation of the Jewish people, not only in Israel but throughout the world (for the fate of Diaspora Jewry depends to a large, if not an overwhelming, extent on the security and well-being of the nation in Israel), imposes on her a sacred duty to do her utmost for the nation's rapid growth. One of the conditions for growth is that every family have at least four sons and daughters, and the more the better.

Information alone will not increase the birthrate. Families of limited means require generous financial assistance that must increase with each additional child. Though the particulars of this assistance must be carefully worked out, it must be provided solely by a general Jewish organization rather than by the Government or any State institution. Enlightened information, particularly by intellectuals and Jewish mothers who understand the vital importance of a high birthrate, and general financial aid to families of limited means from a Jewish economic institution concerned with the nation's future—these are the two essentials for the survival and strengthening of the Jewish State.

We noted earlier that the State of Israel resulted from the return to Zion, but that in the first twenty years not even one-fifth of the nation has returned to its Homeland. The greatest and most terrible disaster that struck the State was that which occurred before its renewal: the murder of 6 million European Jews by the Nazis in Germany and elsewhere. These were the Jews who in the preceding century laid the first foundations for the State, who needed and aspired to it with all their hearts, and who were qualified and prepared to build it. It is a very grave mistake to think that the Nazi holocaust resulted in the creation of the State in 1948. Had the martyred 6 million remained alive after World War Two, the Jewish population of Israel would have been not less than 4 million in its first ten years and not less than 6 million at the end of twenty. But the evil cannot be undone. Many of the victims of the holocaust marched to their deaths singing "Hatikva," yet before the coming of the Messiah they cannot be restored to life.

Before the creation of the State two factors made for Aliya. One was the vision of national resurgence which had lived in the hearts of the Hebrew nation for thousands of years. The Book of Deuteronomy says (30:3–5): "The Lord thy God will turn thy captivity and have compassion upon thee and will return and gather thee from all the nations, whither the Lord thy God has scattered thee. If any of thine be driven out to the outmost parts of heaven, from thence will the Lord thy God gather thee, and from thence will He fetch thee: And the Lord thy God will bring thee into the land which thy fathers possessed and thou shalt possess it; and He will do thee good and multiply thee above thy fathers." This was repeated in the visions of all Prophets and took root deep in the hearts of the Jewish nation through all its generations. The second factor for Aliya was the political and economic hardship of the Jews in Eastern Europe, Asia, and Africa. But with the creation of the State a third factor came into being: *the attractive force of the Jewish State.*

Jewish immigration for the purpose of building up the country and renewing Jewish independence in its ancient Homeland preceded the Zionist movement by many score years. The French Revolution at the end of the eighteenth and beginning of the nineteenth centuries, in laying the foundations of Jewish equality in Western Europe, gave rise to an assimilationist movement among West European Jewry on the one hand, and on the other nourished nationalist yearnings and freed the Jews from dependence solely on a miracle from heaven and the coming of the Messiah.

Another important element in this transformation was the Damascus blood libel of February 1848, in which a French monk disappeared and his colleagues accused the Jews of killing him to use his blood for the Passover festival. The Turkish Governor had the Jewish leaders of Damascus arrested, and they and their children were cruelly tortured to make them confess to a crime they did not commit. The top leaders of West European Jewry, Moses Montefiore in England and Adolphe Cremieux in France, joined the campaign to rescue Damascus Jewry. They succeeded: the Turkish government outlawed blood libels of this nature. The sages of Israel, headed by the Sephardi Rabbi of Serbia, Yehuda Shlomo Alkalai, concluded that the return to Zion could not be put off until the coming of the Messiah but that we must return to the country in order to build and develop it, for "it depends only on us and if we are not for ourselves, who will be?"

This was some twenty years before publication of Moses Hess's book, *Rome and Jerusalem*, more than forty years before Pinsker's *Self-Emancipation*, and more than fifty years before Herzl's *Jewish State*. Little by little a movement grew and gained strength, first under the name of Hovevei Zion (Lovers of Zion) and afterward under the name of Zionism. Adolphe Cremieux and his colleague, Karl Netter, established the first agricultural high school at Mikve Israel, in 1870, based on the idea of a return to Zion in order to establish a Jewish State. Most of the immigration prior to World War Two came from Europe, which in the nineteenth century contained the great majority of world

Jewry. But with the creation of the Jewish State in 1948 the gates of the country were opened wide to every Jew who wished to come. By that time, alas, 6 million of the Jews of Europe who had laid the State's foundations and most needed it had been destroyed; so that after the foundation of the State the majority of the immigration came from Asia and Africa. There, though their number was not large, most Jews chose to come to Israel. A large community remained in Russia, but after the Bolshevik takeover and the death of Lenin their contact with world Jewry and the Land of Israel was severed.

In Israel's twentieth year the world population of Jewry was nearly 13.5 million, including 120,000 in Asia (apart from Israel, Asiatic Russia, and Asiatic Turkey), 240,000 in Africa (including 160,000 in South Africa), 6.8 million in North and South America, over 1.2 million in Western Europe (including Asiatic Turkey), 3 million in "communist" Europe—nearly 2.75 million of them in Russia and a quarter of a million in the other European communist countries. As long as the gates of Russia remain closed to a Jewish exodus, there are objective prospects of large-scale Aliya in the coming years only from the lands of prosperity—Western Europe, North and South America, and South Africa—which together contain more than 8.1 million Jews. In these countries there is no impelling force of poverty, though there are anti-Semitic movements here and there. But in the past twenty years the attracting force of the State of Israel has been added and this is not something to be disregarded.

While it is not likely that all or most of the Jews of the countries of prosperity will come to Israel in the foreseeable future, the Israel Government and the Zionist Federation are to blame for the meager Aliya from these countries. From the day the State was founded to the Six-Day War the majority of the members of the Government demanded of American Jewry—since World War One the largest Jewish community in the world— as well as from the Jews of the other lands of prosperity only financial and political assistance, something that was provided generously. As in the days of the British Mandate, Aliya was left in the hands of the Zionist Executive, though the electors of this Executive (outside of Israel) were very far from considering Aliya as a personal duty. Herzl defines Zionism as "the Jewish people in the making," yet with few exceptions the Zionists of the United States, England, and other affluent lands did not consider themselves "in the making." They used their financial and political influence to help Jews in the lands of distress and aided in the settlement of Israel, but without being requested or volunteering (except for a small minority) to come and settle here.

A small minority in the Government (including the first Prime Minister) considered that the essence of Zionism lay in Aliya—in work within and not merely on behalf of Israel—but this idea was rejected by a majority of the Government and by the leaders of the Zionist organization, which in effect lost its true Zionist character after the creation of the State. Prior to the establishment of the State, the gates of the country were not yet open to every Jew who wanted to come, and Aliya, to the extent that it was permitted by the Mandatory Government, was very limited. Until the creation of the State there were Zionists who did not even believe in a State, and many of the non-Zionists were opposed to it for various assimilationist or ghettoish reasons.

With the establishment of the State the proportion was reversed: apart from minorities on the Left and on the Right (Communists and the very wealthy—though here there were exceptions) who did not accept the State enthusiastically, the Jewish people accepted it with joy and eagerness. Aside from the few who actually came to live here, those who called themselves Zionists were in fact little more than "fans" of the Jewish State, like any other Jew who did not consider himself duty-bound to settle in Israel. The fact is that the majority of the immigrants both before and after the creation of the State were not Zionists, or at least did not call themselves Zionists.

In ancient times Yehoshua Bin Nun (Joshua) and the Jews he brought to Israel did not call themselves Zionists, nor did those who returned from Babylonian exile in the days of Zerubavel, Ezra, and Nehemiah. Even the Jews who established the first agricultural settlements in the second half of the nineteenth century with the aim of laying the foundations for a Jewish State were not known as Zionists. The term did not exist until the nineties of that century, a few years before the advent of Herzl. *The vision of redemption* and that alone was what brought them here. Those who emigrated from their countries of origin because of hardship (mass hardship emigration began in the 1880's) did not come to Israel but made their way to North and South America and South Africa, many of them to England and France. Many among them who wished to come to Israel found its gates closed against them.

When the State came into being, a minority in the Government maintained that Aliya should henceforth be the concern of the independent Jewish people and its Government. But the Zionist parties and their representatives in the Government were bound by tradition and habitual ways of thinking, and immigration remained the affair of the Zionist Organization, though its members did not recognize the importance of and need for Aliya —this even after Zionist congresses began convening in Jerusalem and adopting resolutions on the importance of immigration.

The Six-Day War to a large extent altered the situation and raised public awareness alike in Israel and in the Diaspora of the importance of Aliya. The wonderful victory aroused great enthusiasm both in Israel and the Diaspora, perhaps even more than the creation of the State itself in 1948. A volunteer movement came into being in the lands of prosperity, but the volunteers had no address in Israel to which to turn. Immigration does not end with the immigrant's arrival. In fact, it only begins then. Immigrants must be absorbed and integrated, because it is their integration that determines whether or not they will stay. And integration can be done properly only by the people living in the country that desire it and by their government, for it is the government that has the legal authority to ensure integration.

Conventions have been held on the subject of Aliya and are likely to be held in the future as well. The largest of them was the 27th Zionist Congress, the polemics of which centered around immigration. But even a "Zionist Congress" is no more qualified to handle Aliya than the Zionist Executive. Though the chairman of the Zionist Executive, the president of the Zionist Organization, and the Israel Prime Minister favored having the Zionist Executive continue to handle Aliya, in the end pressure increased as a result of the new outlook that followed the Six-Day War. A compromise was reached: the Zionist Executive would handle immigration and the Government would handle integration, as if the two things were separate and distinct.

Regarding the possibility of large-scale immigration from the lands of prosperity, many people in Israel hold the "Marxist" view that it will not come because the decisive factor is the economic situation, which in these countries is no worse and is generally better than in Israel. These "Marxists" do not know that even the father of Marxism was not an exploited and hungry worker. The main point is that they ignore the lessons of Jewish history: those who laid the foundations of the State from 1870 to 1948 came here not because under the Turks and the British the economic situation was more flourishing or the lives of Jews any safer than in the countries of their birth, but solely because of a vision of redemption which they wished to implement by pioneering zeal.

The fact is that the first "mass" immigration after the Balfour Declaration came from the United States and Canada. These were the Jewish battalions in the First World War that had been organized with the help of two men who had been exiled from Israel "for all time" by the Turkish Government at the beginning of the war. Even the founders of Petah Tikva, Rishon LeZion, Rosh Pina, Zikhron Yacov, Yesod Hamaalah and all the other settlements founded in Israel before the Zionist Organization went into action did not come because of better economic conditions than in their countries of origin but because of a vision of redemption through pioneering.

After all, living conditions in the State of Israel are not all that much worse than in the lands of prosperity and there are young people, and not only young people, in those countries who feel a profound need for a life that involves more than movies, cars, and fancy apartments. What they are looking for is the satisfaction of moral and social needs and an historic vision. There are also Jews in the lands of prosperity who are deeply apprehensive about the growing assimilation and the fragmentation of the Jewish soul in the Diaspora, who are increasingly aware that only in Israel can a Jew live a full life, both as a Jew and as a human being. If the people in Israel and its Government will consider the integration of immigrants one of their main national duties and apply their full pioneering capacity and strength to this objective, there are very good chances that immigration will grow. Nor can we know beforehand what dimensions it will reach if only the integration is done properly and those who are settled here bring their relatives and friends, especially if Israel is loyal to the supreme injunction given by the greatest of its Prophets—to be a unique people.

What has been done in Israel in the seventy years before and the twenty years after the birth of the State proves that the Jewish people do indeed have the makings of a unique people. Without this character it would not have maintained its national existence in the centuries of dispersion; and in its own land it would not have overcome, three times in succession, enemies surrounding it who outnumbered it ten, twenty, and forty to one. The secret of the Jewish nation's survival in the Diaspora in conditions that no other people would have withstood, and the survival of the State during its first twenty years despite neighbors dedicated to its destruction, is nothing but the *superior quality of the Hebrew nation*. More than anything else the future of the State of Israel depends on the preservation and enhancement of this superiority.

The Six-Day War and the consequent demographic changes have again raised a basic question that is as yet hardly felt or recognized by the general public but that must be viewed in all its severity by anyone who does not live only in the past twenty years. This is the problem of Jewish labor. We face a danger, perhaps the most serious of all, that in the next twenty years work will be taken out of the hands of the Jewish laborer and the Israeli nation will be transformed, as Ahad Ha'am foresaw sixty years ago, into a "culturally advanced minority."

In 1911 this profound philosopher of the Hibat Zion movement arrived in Israel for the last time. In those days the question of Hebrew labor was a very pressing one. At the time of the Second Aliya (1904–1914) there were only a few score Jewish agricultural settlements (then known as colonies) and practically all the work was done by non-Jews. The Second Aliya people had come to work the land because they considered Jewish agricultural independence the prime and essential means of renewing our independence in the Homeland. Though a considerable part of the land of these settlements had been acquired by national means (thanks mainly to Edmond de Rothschild) hardly any of the labor was being done by Jewish workers. Few of the men of the Second Aliya who had come here to cultivate the land had ever done such work, and the great majority had never done manual work at all.

By contrast the Arab has been an agricultural laborer from time immemorial. An economic factor also favored the Arab worker: his needs were much fewer than those of his Jewish counterpart. This and his docility made him preferable to the Jew; thus in most of the settlements practically all the work was done by Arabs and it was not easy for a Jew to find work. Only in winemaking were the farmers compelled to use Jewish labor, because according to Jewish law, wine touched by non-Jews is not kosher.

The pioneers of the First Aliya had recognized the importance of Jewish labor. The founders of Petah Tikva, Rishon LeZion, Zikhron Yacov and Rosh Pina and the Bilu immigrants saw the prime importance of labor, and in 1891 a society named Haaretz v'Haavodah was founded by Meir Dizengoff (later Mayor of Tel Aviv), and Aharon Rosenberg, one of the founders of Rehovot, emphasized the importance of labor. The preamble to the society's regulations said: "Manual labor and honest sweat bind the work to its maker with bonds of flesh and blood that are not easily severed. Even the bond between money and goods is a tie that is easily undone. Without Hebrew laborers the settlements will not survive, and not only that, there is a danger of creating a Frankenstein's monster. . . . Hebrew labor is to the Yishuv what blood is to the body of a healthy person: it is they who will give it life and they who will preserve it from decadence and extinction." The society's founders stressed the need "to develop a clan of settlers loyal to the land who will achieve their aim, not by the disbursement of money but by the sweat of their brows."

These ideals, however, did not long survive and in the summer of 1892 the society was disbanded. Thousands of Arab workers were employed by the settlements, and only a few score or a few hundred Jews at most. When Ahad Ha'am came to Israel in 1911, this was the burning question. He devoted much of his time to it and on his return to Odessa published an article, "Inventory," in which he said, "Even if Jewish resettlement in Palestine eventually expands to maximum, we must be reconciled to the fact that there will exist an elite segment, a cultivated cultural minority, whose strength is in its brainpower and capital, but that the rural majority whose strength is in the labor of its hands will not be ours even then." Ahad Ha'am went on to conclude that there is no hope of a Jewish State because "the foundation of the life of any state is its workers and farmers—the rural majority that we do not now have—and it is hard to imagine that we ever will have this, even if we establish settlements in all parts of the country."* His reasoning was that "the Jew is too clever and too cultured, and is incapable of limiting his life and aspirations to a small plot of land that provides him with a meager living by the sweat of his brow."

---

* *Collected Writings of Ahad Ha'am*, p. 424.

Ahad Ha'am was mistaken. Hebrew labor won out, and were it not for this victory, the Jewish State would not have come into being. However, the Six-Day War and the addition of over a million Arabs to the territory under the control of the Jewish State has once again evoked the specter of mass non-Jewish labor, unless there is large-scale immigration and suitable measures are taken to safeguard Jewish labor. Ahad Ha'am was acquainted with the Russian peasantry (the local Arab peasantry was no more advanced) and he was unaware that Jewish agriculture could be any more advanced. At the time of the Second Aliya the minimum subsistence area per family was 250 dunams, whereas today with the use of modern implements and chemistry unknown at the time, farmers with only 25 dunams of land produce more income than 250 did then.

All the same, the addition of a million Arabs to the work force holds a danger that within the next twenty years or less most of the work will revert to non-Jewish hands, bearing out Ahad Ha'am's view that we would become "an elite class whose strength is in brainpower and capital" rather than in labor. The reason Hebrew labor won out during the Second Aliya and the Mandate period is that every loyal Zionist understood that without Jewish labor there would be no Jewish State, and so proceeded to develop Jewish agriculture and industry based on more advanced means of production and on settlers who were more diligent and highly educated. While "Communist" Russia has 60 million peasants and "capitalist" America only 6 million, Russia from time to time has to buy food from America, because with his advanced means of production the American farmer produces crops ten times greater than his Soviet counterpart.

In the first period of Jewish settlement, from the time of the Biluim during the Ottoman period until midway through the Mandatory regime, agriculture was the leading branch of the economy. Now, of course, we will not be able to live without industry, advanced forms of transportation on land, sea, and air, and expanded agricultural settlement. Only if we make an effort through education and technology to raise our standards of work to those of the most advanced countries, such as Japan and the United States, by introducing the most modern tools and machinery, and providing the young generation with high-quality technological training—education whereby one highly trained person can do the work of ten ordinary workers—will we be able to safeguard for Jewish labor that self-sufficiency without which no political or economic independence is viable.

Fortunately the Jewish people is gifted with the same qualities possessed by the most highly developed and scientifically advanced nations. There is no reason why we should not raise our technological ability to the maximum. By combining technological superiority with productive labor we will succeed in being a nation of both labor and learning, and only in this way will we obviate the danger of labor being taken out of Jewish hands. We will continue to be a working nation as long as we provide our youth with the best technological education in all areas of labor—field, factory, aviation, seafaring, and mining—just as we have provided our Army with the best military training and an awareness of its value as the guarantor of the survival of the nation and the Homeland.

Little Israel is faced with all the problems of any new and underdeveloped state, problems that have not yet been completely solved. But gradual progress is being made, thanks to the high (though not as high as it could be) level of Israeli knowhow and the pioneering spirit of the best of its youth—carrying out missions in Asia, Africa, and Latin America with the same enthusiasm, devotion, and modesty that they show in building the defense forces, creating communal settlements, establishing kibbutzim, founding border settlements. Their purpose is to create a new modern society based on freedom, cooperation, and brotherly love.

In days of old the Prophets of Israel required their nation to be a unique people and a light unto the Gentiles. To this day this prophecy lives in the hearts of the best of the Jewish people and it is this that guides them. In Israel patterns of social living found nowhere else in the world are being expanded and can serve as an example for other nations. Even the IDF is different from all other armies, serving as it does not only for defense but for building and settlement, and for the elevation of man. It has a special unit, the Nahal (from the initials of the Hebrew words for Fighting, Pioneering Youth), that educates Israeli youth for agricultural settlement and builds border settlements—generally kibbutzim—that serve as defensive strongholds and as guideposts for the new society.

The essence and the significance of Jewish history lies in the preference of quality over quantity. For our security, survival, and status in the world and the preservation of the legacy of our Prophets to the end of time, Israel must strive incessantly for moral, cultural, technological and social improvement and to be a unique people.

INDEX